S0-ATV-261

E Volume 6

The World Book Encyclopedia

a Scott Fetzer company
Chicago
www.worldbook.com

The World Book Encyclopedia

For information on other World Book publications, visit our website at **www.worldbook.com** or call **1-800-WORLDBK (967-5325).** For information about sales to schools and libraries, call **1-800-975-3250 (United States); 1-800-837-5365 (Canada).**

World Book, Inc.
233 North Michigan Avenue
Chicago, IL 60601
U.S.A.

Beyond the Page
Use your smartphone or tablet to scan this QR code and see a chronology of events, activities, and other special material prepared by World Book editors. (You will need to download a QR code reader to your device if you have not already done so.) If you do not have a mobile device, simply type this URL into your browser: http://www.worldbook.com/current

About the SPINESCAPE®
The SPINESCAPE design for the 2014 edition—*Vibrant World of Facts*—represents, through the image of layers of colorful fabric, the beauty of discovery of the rich tapestry that is the world of knowledge. An important part of learning is the recognition that individual facts acquire relevance and meaning when they are understood to be part of a larger whole. *The World Book Encyclopedia,* as a comprehensive, general reference work, presents and places in context information that spans all areas of knowledge, enabling users to explore a broad spectrum of facts and uncover the nature of their relationships.

Photo credit:
© SIME/eStock Photo; © Bruno Morandi, Hemis/Corbis Images; © Bruno Morandi, Getty Images

Library of Congress Cataloging-in-Publication Data

The World Book encyclopedia.
volumes cm
Includes index.
Summary: "A 22-volume, highly illustrated, A-Z general encyclopedia for all ages, featuring sections on how to use World Book, other research aids, pronunciation key, a student guide to better writing, speaking, and research skills, and comprehensive index"--Provided by publisher.
ISBN 978-0-7166-0114-2
1. Encyclopedias and dictionaries. I. World Book, Inc.
AE5.W55 2014
030--dc23

2013023368

Printed in the United States of America by RR Donnelley, Willard, Ohio
1st printing November 2013

Logo applies to text stock

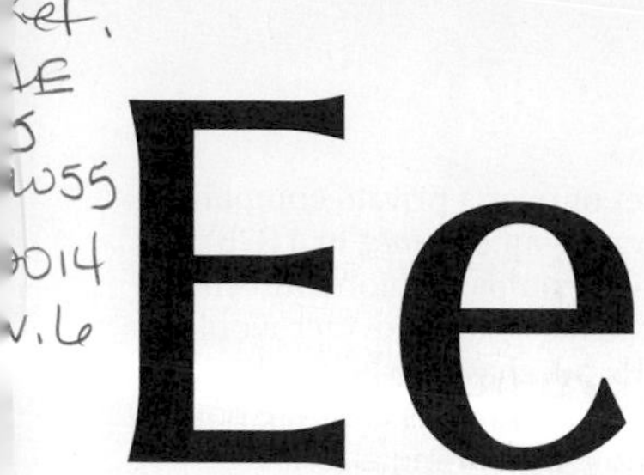

E is the fifth letter of the alphabet used for the modern English language. The letter *E* is also used in a number of other languages, including French, German, and Spanish.

The letter *E* is the second of the English vowel letters (see **Vowel**). The *E* sound can be heard in such words as *beet* (long *E*) or *bet* (short *E*).

Scholars believe that *E* evolved from an Egyptian *hieroglyph* (pictorial symbol) that represented a man with his arms upraised, shouting for joy. Hieroglyphs were adapted to be used for a Semitic language by around 1500 B.C. The alphabet for this Semitic language—the earliest known alphabet—is called Proto-Sinaitic. By 1100 B.C., an alphabet for another Semitic language, Phoenician, had evolved from Proto-Sinaitic. See **Semitic languages.**

The Phoenician letter that can be traced to the Egyptian joy hieroglyph is the fifth letter of the Phoenician alphabet, *he,* which was the Phoenician word for "Lo!" (an exclamation of wonder or surprise). The Phoenicians used the letter to represent the beginning *H* sound of *he*. The ancient Greeks did not use this sound. However, when the Greeks adopted the Phoenician alphabet about 800 B.C., they changed *he* to *epsilon* and used the letter for the long *E* sound. The letter kept that sound when it was adopted by the Etruscans around 700 B.C. and by the Romans by about 650 B.C. Peter T. Daniels

See also **Alphabet.**

WORLD BOOK map and illustrations

Development of the letter *E*

Seafarers and traders aided the transmission of letters along the coast of the Mediterranean Sea.

The Latin alphabet was adopted by the Romans from the Etruscans around 650 B.C. The Romans wrote from left to right, so the letter reversed direction again.

The Etruscan alphabet was adopted from the Greek about 700 B.C. Etruscan was written from right to left, so the letter that evolved from *epsilon* faced the opposite direction again.

Faster ways of writing letters developed during Roman times. Curved, connected lines were faster to write than imitations of the *inscriptional* (carved) Roman letters. The inscriptional forms of the letters developed into capital letters. The curved forms developed into small letters. The form of most small letters, including *e,* was set by around A.D. 800.

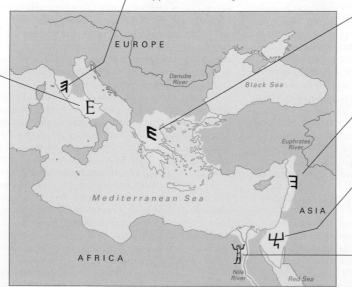

The Greek alphabet evolved from the Phoenician by around 800 B.C. The Greek letter *epsilon,* which was adapted from *he,* faced the opposite direction from the Phoenician letter because Phoenician was written from right to left, and Greek, by around 500 B.C., was written from left to right.

The Phoenician alphabet had evolved from the Proto-Sinaitic by around 1100 B.C. The Phoenician letter *he* was much the same as the Proto-Sinaitic letter, but it was rotated on its side.

A Proto-Sinaitic alphabet for a Semitic language evolved from Egyptian hieroglyphs by around 1500 B.C. The Proto-Sinaitic letter that came from the joy hieroglyph was more abstract.

The Egyptians, about 3000 B.C., drew a hieroglyph that represented a man shouting for joy.

E-book, or *electronic book,* is a collection of *digital* (numerically encoded) files containing the text, and sometimes the illustrations, of a book. E-books are viewed on a computer, a cell phone, or on a special handheld device called a *reader.* There are many formats and programs for storing e-books and various readers or apps (applications) on which to read them. Some formats are *incompatible* with one another—that is, an e-book in one format will not work with a reader in another format.

E-books are available for purchase on the websites of publishers and online bookstores. Some libraries offer e-books over the Internet at no cost.

E-books first appeared in 1998, but were not initially popular. The online retailer Amazon.com, Inc., introduced its e-book reader, Kindle, in 2007. Kindle became the first such device to have general appeal. In addition to displaying digital books, Kindle had wireless capabilities that allowed customers to purchase and download products from the Amazon store onto the device. Kindle spurred the company's sales of e-books. By 2011, e-book sales surpassed printed book sales on Amazon. Another maker of readers, Sony, sold e-books in a format that was open and could be read on other readers in addition to its Sony Reader. The bookseller Barnes & Noble also offered a reader, Nook. Keith Ferrell

E. coli, *EE KOH ly,* is among the most extensively studied bacteria in the history of science. There are hundreds of different strains of this microbe, whose full name is *Escherichia (EHSH uh RIHK ee uh) coli.* Since the mid-1900's, scientists worldwide have used *E. coli* to study basic biological processes, especially the behavior of *genes* (units of heredity).

Outside the laboratory, most strains of *E. coli* live harmlessly in the intestines of people, cattle, and other animals. But *E. coli* can produce serious illness if it causes blood or urinary infections. One strain, called *E. coli* O157:H7, causes severe intestinal illness. A typical infection with *E. coli* O157:H7 begins with intense abdominal cramps and watery diarrhea that often turns bloody in a few days. Most patients recover in about a week. But the infection can cause damage to the kidneys and *anemia* (low red blood cell count), and a few patients die.

E. coli O157:H7 lives in a small percentage of cattle but does not make them sick. Most infections with *E. coli* O157:H7 are caused by eating undercooked ground beef contaminated with the bacteria. Infections have also been traced to contaminated vegetables and unpasteurized milk and apple cider. Infected people can also pass the illness to others. The best ways to prevent infection are to cook ground meat completely, clean fruits and vegetables thoroughly, and wash hands often.

Anyone with severe or bloody diarrhea should see a doctor promptly to identify the cause and get proper treatment. If tests of several people detect an outbreak of *E. coli* O157:H7, public health officials will take steps to find the source of the illness to prevent infection of other people. David L. Swerdlow

E-commerce, also called *electronic commerce* or *e-business,* is the electronic exchange of money or other valuables for goods and services. The Internet enables businesses to participate in e-commerce with other businesses and with consumers.

Business-to-business transactions, also called *B2B transactions,* involve the coordination of purchases and deliveries over the Internet or over a private company-to-company network known as an *extranet.* In a B2B transaction, a manufacturing company might transmit an order for raw materials. The materials provider would, in turn, transmit a bill to the purchaser, who might pay the bill electronically. Only the materials are transported physically. Computers handle everything else.

An e-commerce *trading exchange* is a central Internet site where many buyers and sellers gather electronically. There, suppliers can bid on a company's request. The company can select the bid that best suits its needs and budget, and then arrange for purchase and delivery.

Business-to-consumer transactions involve direct sales to individuals. Many businesses operate online stores on the Internet. Internet-based merchants can present far more products than would be possible in a walk-in store. Online merchants deliver some products, such as computer software or data files, to a customer's computer over the Internet. Sellers generally deliver physical products to the purchaser or ship them to a local store, where the purchaser may pick them up.

Most consumers make e-commerce purchases with credit cards or *debit cards,* which deduct purchase costs directly from a bank account. Others use special accounts created solely for electronic purchases. Most e-commerce sales are *secure transactions,* which encode card and purchase information as it leaves the consumer's computer and then decode it for the retailer.

Another popular form of consumer e-commerce is the *online auction,* at which sellers present items for examination by Internet shoppers who bid against one another for the right to purchase them. The largest and most popular online auction site is eBay. Online auction sites earn money by charging the seller a small fee or by collecting a portion of the purchase price of items sold.

Banks and government institutions offer many e-commerce services to consumers over the Internet. Consumers can use the Internet to access their accounts, pay bills, and even pay taxes. Keith Ferrell

E-mail, or *electronic mail,* is a message sent from one computer to another over a computer network. E-mail (also spelled *email)* messages can be sent and received over a private network, such as one operated within a company, or over a public network, such as the Internet. A message can consist of text only, or it may include one or more attached files containing text, illustrations, sound clips, or moving pictures.

To send and receive e-mail, an individual must have an *e-mail address.* Such an address serves the same function as a street address in traditional mail delivery. Companies called *Internet service providers* (ISP's) generally offer their customers e-mail addresses along with Internet connections. Some other companies offer free Web-based e-mail addresses supported by advertising.

Files called *electronic mailboxes* store delivered e-mail on a networked computer. To read a message, a user opens the file attached to his or her address. The user can generally respond to the message by hitting a "reply" button. Users can send e-mails to one individual at a time or to many, depending upon how many e-mail addresses they type into message headings.

As e-mail became more widely used, many companies began to send unsolicited e-mail messages to long lists of users. These messages are often called *spam.*

Most spam consists of advertisements that direct users to an Internet site where they may purchase a product or service. Processing a large volume of messages sent by "spammers" slows the *servers* (computers that distribute information) at ISP's and other companies. An increase in spam can thus result in slower service for subscribers as well as in a need to delete the unwanted "junk mail." Several countries have enacted laws designed to reduce spam by placing strict controls on the use of e-mail to send unsolicited advertisements. *Filters* on e-mail systems can automatically detect and delete some spam. Jarice Hanson

See also **Cyberbullying; Instant messaging.**

E = mc² is an equation developed by the German-born American physicist Albert Einstein that relates *mass* (amount of matter) and energy. In the equation, *E* stands for energy, *m* stands for mass, and c^2 is the speed of light *squared* (multiplied by itself). The equation shows that mass is a form of energy and that a tiny amount of mass can be changed into large quantities of other kinds of energy. For example, a mass of 1 gram could produce about 25 million kilowatt-hours of energy for use as electric power. This energy could power a home for several thousand years.

The equation laid the basis for the application of nuclear energy. When Einstein announced it in 1905, scientists knew of no way to change mass into energy. But scientists now know of two ways to release this energy. *Fission* involves splitting certain heavy atoms into lighter ones. This process powers nuclear reactors and simple nuclear weapons. *Fusion* involves combining certain light atoms into heavier ones. This process keeps the sun and stars hot and bright and powers advanced nuclear weapons. In both fission and fusion, the atoms at the end of each process have less total mass than did the atoms at the beginning of each process. This missing mass, or *mass defect,* is converted to energy according to Einstein's equation. Matthew Stanley

See also **Einstein, Albert; Nuclear energy** (Artificial fission).

E Pluribus Unum, *ee PLUR uh buhs YOO nuhm,* is the Latin motto on the face of the Great Seal of the United States (see **Great Seal of the United States**). This phrase means *out of many, one.* It refers to the creation of one nation, the United States, out of 13 colonies. It also applies to today's federal system. Benjamin Franklin, John Adams, and Thomas Jefferson, members of the first committee for the selection of the seal, suggested the motto in 1776. It can be traced to the *Epistles* of the ancient Roman poet Horace. Since 1873, the law requires that this motto appear on one side of every U.S. coin that is minted. Critically reviewed by the Department of the Treasury

See also **United States, Government of the** (picture: Symbols of the United States).

Eagle is the name of some of the largest and most powerful birds in the world. Among birds of prey, only condors and some species of vultures grow larger than eagles. Eagles look fierce and proud, and they can soar gracefully high in the air. People often picture them as courageous hunters and as symbols of freedom and power. But eagles are not always as bold and fierce as they look. Most will eat whatever flesh is easiest to get, including *carrion* (dead animals).

Eagles carefully avoid danger. They usually stay away from human beings and rarely attack except when cornered. A few *species* (kinds) of eagles also may attack when defending their nests and young. An eagle's chief weapons are its powerful legs, feet, and *talons* (claws). Some eagles also bite in self-defense. Eagles seldom attack newborn lambs or other livestock.

A bald eagle, its powerful wings spread wide, lands on a tree branch. A bald eagle kills prey with its long, curved *talons* (claws). It then tears up the prey with its strong beak.

Roman warriors used a golden figure of an eagle as a sign of strength and bravery. Russian and Austrian emperors also used eagles as symbols. The United States chose the bald eagle as its national bird in 1782.

The body of an eagle

Eagles vary in size, depending on the species and the individual. Females generally grow larger than males. Wingspreads of different species range from about 3 to 8 feet (0.9 to 2.4 meters). Most eagles weigh about 7 to 12 pounds (3.2 to 5.4 kilograms), but some weigh as little as 1 pound (0.45 kilogram) and others weigh as much as 20 pounds (9.1 kilograms).

If the wind and other flying conditions prove favorable, some species of eagles can carry prey weighing nearly as much as themselves. Normally, however, eagles carry only smaller prey.

The head of an eagle is large and covered with feathers. An eagle also has large eyes. Most birds have keener sight than do people and other animals, but eagles and hawks are said to have the keenest sight of all. Eagles can probably sight their prey while soaring high in the air. But they usually watch from perches or fly close to the ground while hunting. Eagles have large, strong, hooked beaks, which they use to tear up prey. The golden eagle's beak measures about 2 inches (5 centimeters) long. The bald eagle's beak grows even larger.

Facts in brief

Names: Adult, eagle; young, eaglet or eyass.
Incubation period: 28-45 days or more.
Length of life: 10-50 years or more.
Where found: Throughout the world, except in Antarctica and where people have killed them off or destroyed their habitat.
Scientific classification: Eagles are in the family Accipitridae. Within the family, the larger species are generally called *eagles* and the smaller species *hawks, kites,* or *buzzards,* but there is no rigid distinction.

The golden eagle is a feared hunter. Its prey includes rabbits, squirrels, and even young deer and lambs. The golden eagle can carry prey weighing as much as it does.

WORLD BOOK illustration by Stanley W. Galli

Feet and legs. Eagles have strong legs and feet. Most eagles have scaly, bright yellow skin on their feet. Eagles seize and kill prey with their long, curved talons. They also use their talons to carry prey to a feeding place. When eagles fight, they dive at each other and try to strike with their talons. The legs of golden eagles and several other species have a covering of feathers. The lower part of the bald eagle's legs is bare.

Feathers and wings. Eagles have such long, broad wings and tails that they look clumsy when they walk on the ground. But their wings easily support their heavy bodies when they fly. Eagles can glide great distances without flapping their wings. The long feathers in their wings are strong and stiff, and the feathers are shaped so the air flows smoothly over the surface of the wing. When the eagle soars, the feathers spread out like fingers and bend up at the tips.

Adult eagles of most species are dark brown or black, but many have light-colored areas. Young eagles typically develop an adult color pattern at 4 or 5 years of age.

The life of an eagle

Wild eagles that survive to adulthood may live from 10 to 30 years. In captivity, some eagle species can live 50 years or more. Most eagles first breed when they reach about 5 years old. Mated eagles often stay together. If one member of a pair dies, the other may find another mate. Sometimes, the male and female choose new mates even when both remain alive.

In winter, bald eagles may gather in areas with plentiful food. But during the breeding season, each pair claims a territory around its nest and keeps other eagles away. The golden eagle may defend a territory of about 20 to 60 square miles (50 to 160 square kilometers). The bald eagle holds a smaller territory.

Nests of eagles sometimes are called *aeries* or *eyries* (both pronounced *AIR eez* or *IHR eez*). Bald eagles usually nest in the tops of tall trees that stand near water. Some build nests on cliffs. Golden eagles often nest on high cliffs in the mountains. Some eagles in Asia nest on the ground. Eagles tend to use the same nest every year. However, some eagles have two or more nests. They use one nest for a year and another the next year.

Eagles build nests mainly with sticks, often adding fresh leaves. The birds usually add new material each year they use a nest, so many old nests are huge. A new nest may measure 3 feet (0.9 meter) across and 18 inches (46 centimeters) deep. But an old one may reach 10 feet (3 meters) across and 15 feet (4.5 meters) deep.

Eggs grow about 3 inches (7.6 centimeters) long and 2 inches (5 centimeters) across. Females lay one, two, or—rarely—three eggs each year. Eagle eggs vary slightly in color. The eggs of golden eagles, for example, are white or spotted with reddish-brown or gray. Eggs of bald eagles are mostly white. Eagles lay their eggs at different times of the year. Birds from colder climates lay eggs in early spring, while those from warmer regions often do so during the late fall and winter.

The eggs hatch in five to six weeks or more, depending on the species. In that time, the female *incubates* the eggs—that is, she sits on them to keep them warm. The male incubates them occasionally and brings food to the female while she sits. After the eggs hatch, both parents guard the nest and take food to the young.

Young eagles are called *eaglets* or *eyasses.* Eaglets hatch with their eyes open and their bodies covered with grayish-white *down* (soft, fluffy feathers). Regular feathers begin to grow at 2 to 3 weeks of age. Eaglets cannot tear up their own food until they reach 5 to 7 weeks old. They leave the nest at 10 to 12 weeks but cannot fly well at first. They must stay near the nest and receive food from the parents for a few more months, until they can hunt well enough to get their own food.

Many kinds of eagles hatch two eggs. But in tropical species, only one eaglet usually survives. One eaglet often hatches two or three days before the other. The older one is larger and takes more than its share of food. It also might attack the other eaglet and even kill it.

Food. Eagles hunt only during the day. They spend the night in their nests or on a safe perch. Often, two eagles hunt together. Some eagles eat only certain types of prey. But most hunt a wide variety of prey and occasionally eat carrion or steal prey from other animals.

The golden eagle eats rabbits, hares, ground squirrels, and birds. Sometimes, it consumes young deer and lambs, and it may also eat carrion. The golden eagle usually flies low over open hillsides, dropping down quickly to seize its startled prey.

The bald eagle eats mainly fish. It hunts primarily by watching for prey from a perch. It snatches fish from the water while flying. If pulled into the water by its catch, a bald eagle can swim to shore with the catch by floating and using a rowing motion with its wings. It sometimes takes fish away from other birds, such as gulls and ospreys. Occasionally, bald eagles catch coots and other water birds by hovering over them and forcing them to dive repeatedly until they are exhausted. In addition, the eagles sometimes catch birds in the air with spectacular aerial maneuvering. Bald eagles also capture mammals and sometimes eat carrion.

Kinds of eagles

About 60 species of eagles live worldwide. Most are native to tropical regions, particularly in Africa and Asia. Only two species, the bald eagle and golden eagle, are native to the continental United States and Canada.

The bald eagle is not really bald. Its head has a covering of white feathers, as does its tail. A young bald eagle is dark brown and has scattered light markings. The bald eagle lives only in North America.

Until the mid-1900's, hunters and trappers killed large numbers of bald eagles. United States federal law has protected the species since 1940 in the lower 48 states and since 1959 in Alaska. But the continued shooting and trapping of the birds, as well as accidental collisions with vehicles, caused further population declines. The number of bald eagles also dropped because of the pollution of lakes and rivers with pesticides, especially DDT, and industrial wastes. Some of these pollutants built up in the bodies of fish that the eagles ate. In most cases, the pollutants did not kill the birds, but they interfered with the birds' ability to reproduce. By the mid-1970's, there were only about 2,000 to 3,000 bald eagles making nests in the lower 48 states.

Since then, however, the bald eagle has made a remarkable comeback. The U.S. government has implemented strict regulations to protect eagles from harmful chemical wastes and from illegal hunting or trapping. Conservation groups have restocked former nesting areas with young eagles. Bald eagles also have become more accustomed to people and now often nest in nonwilderness areas close to human activity. Today, more than 30,000 bald eagles live in the lower 48 states. An estimated 100,000 or more inhabit Canada and Alaska.

The golden eagle is dark brown with a patch of golden brown feathers on the back of its neck. A young golden eagle has dark plumage with white patches on its wings and tail. Golden eagles live in Europe, Asia, northern Africa, and much of North America. Plains Indians once used golden eagle feathers in their bonnets, and the golden eagle became known as the "war eagle." Some golden eagles migrate south to spend the winter in the southwestern United States and Mexico. Many golden eagles were killed in California, Colorado, Wyoming, and Texas by sheep ranchers who feared the birds would kill young lambs. In Texas, hired hunters shot thousands of these birds from airplanes. Federal law has protected the golden eagle since 1962. But some birds probably still fall victim to illegal shootings.

Other kinds of eagles include the *white-tailed eagle* and *Steller's sea-eagle.* Both are closely related to the bald eagle and have similar habits. The white-tailed eagle breeds in many parts of Asia and mainland Europe, and in Iceland and Greenland. It has a white tail like the bald eagle, but its head is dark. Steller's sea-eagle is dark, except for a white tail and white shoulders. It ranks as one of the largest and most powerful of all eagles. It breeds on the Pacific coast of Siberia and in North and South Korea, and sometimes visits the Aleutian Islands near Alaska.

The *harpy eagle* of tropical South America is another of the world's largest and strongest eagles. It lives in the dense rain forests. The harpy eagle preys on capuchin monkeys, sloths, and other mammals. It is black and white with a gray head and a long, black crest. The harpy eagle raises one eaglet at a time and feeds it for nearly a year after it hatches. The parents probably breed only once every two years. See **Harpy eagle**.

The *great Philippine eagle,* found only in the Philippines, looks much like the harpy eagle and lives in much the same way. It eats monkeys and other mammals, as well as large birds and reptiles. It builds its nest in giant trees in the rain forests. These eagles are becoming scarce because hunters shoot many of them, and people cut down the birds' rain forest habitats. The *crowned eagle* of Africa also inhabits rain forests and eats monkeys.

The *martial eagle,* another of the largest eagles, lives in the grassy plains of Africa. It eats *hyraxes* (small animals related to elephants) and a variety of other animals. The *African fish-eagle,* a relative of the bald eagle, lives beside lakes and rivers. It makes a wild, screaming call with its head turned far back over its shoulders.

The *white-bellied fish-eagle* of southern Asia and Australia is a gray-and-white bird that lives on tropical coasts. It eats fish and sea snakes, snatching them from the sea with its talons. The *serpent-eagles* and *snake-eagles* from Africa, Asia, and Europe reside in the tops of tall trees. They eat snakes and lizards. The *steppe eagle* of central Asia lives on treeless plains. It sometimes nests on the ground. Many types of eagles from Europe and western Asia, including some steppe eagles, migrate to Africa each winter. Great flocks of them fly over Egyptian deserts every spring and fall. James W. Grier

See also **Bird** (pictures: Birds of the desert).

Eagle was the popular name for a $10 gold coin minted in the United States between 1795 and 1933. It was not minted from 1805 to 1837. It was one of three coins named in 1792 in the first act of Congress to authorize coinage. For many years, it was the highest denomination of any U.S. coin. In 1933, a law was passed to take all gold coins, including eagles, out of circulation. In 1986, however, the U.S. Mint began selling gold and silver *bullion coins* called American Eagles. Investors buy these coins for their value as metals rather than as money. The mint began selling platinum American Eagles in 1997. The *face value*—that is, the value printed on the coin—is $20 for gold eagles, $1 for silver eagles, and $100 for platinum eagles. Burton H. Hobson

Eagles, Fraternal Order of, also known as the F.O.E. or the Eagles, is a fraternal organization. It has chapters called *aeries* throughout the United States and Canada. Women in auxiliary chapters are also active in national, state, and local programs. The F.O.E. sponsors programs for youth and senior citizens. It also supports medical research on a variety of diseases. The order promotes state old-age pensions, social security legislation, Mother's Day observances, health research, civic activities, and legislation banning job bias against older workers. The F.O.E. was founded in Seattle in 1898. Its motto is *People Helping People.* Its international headquarters are in Grove City, Ohio.

Critically reviewed by the Fraternal Order of Eagles

Eagleton, Thomas Francis (1929-2007), became the only person ever nominated by a national convention for vice president of the United States who resigned his candidacy. In 1972, the Democratic National Convention chose Eagleton, a U.S. senator from Missouri, as the running mate of Senator George S. McGovern of South Dakota. Twelve days later, Eagleton revealed that he had been hospitalized three times between 1960 and 1966 for treatment of emotional exhaustion and depression. The revelation touched off a nationwide controversy over his qualifications for the vice presidency. McGovern said he feared the dispute was distracting the public from the election's key issues. Eagleton resigned at McGovern's request and was replaced by Sargent Shriver.

Eagleton was born on Sept. 4, 1929, in St. Louis. He was elected circuit attorney of St. Louis in 1956, attorney general of Missouri in 1960, and lieutenant governor in 1964. He served in the U.S. Senate from 1969 to 1987. Eagleton died on March 4, 2007. David S. Broder

Eakins, *AY kihnz,* **Thomas** (1844-1916), was one of the greatest American Realist painters of the 1800's. He painted portraits and scenes of outdoor life and sporting events, such as swimming, sculling, hunting, and prize fighting. Eakins brought great vitality and insight to his art. He tried to achieve scientific accuracy and careful detail without losing feeling. The colors are dark in his indoor paintings and portraits, but he captured subtle effects of light and atmosphere in his outdoor scenes.

Eakins's most famous portraits include *Walt Whitman* (1888); *The Thinker* (1900); and two group portraits, *The Clinic of Dr. Gross* (1875) and *The Clinic of Dr. Agnew* (1889). Among his famous outdoor paintings is *Max Schmitt in a Single Scull* (1871).

Eakins was born on July 25, 1844, in Philadelphia. He began his art training at the Pennsylvania Academy of Fine Arts and studied anatomy at Jefferson Medical College in Philadelphia. In 1866, he went to Paris to study at the École des Beaux-Arts. When he returned to the United States in 1870, he established himself as a portrait painter in Philadelphia. But he did not gain widespread public or critical acceptance. He taught at the Philadelphia Academy and lectured on anatomy at other art schools. Eakins helped develop photographic techniques for studying the human body in motion. He was also a sculptor. He died on June 25, 1916. Sarah Burns

See also **Whitman, Walt** (picture).

Eames, *eemz,* **Charles** (1907-1978), was an American designer who became internationally famous for creating some of the most imaginative furniture of the 1900's. Eames was noted for his skillful use of plywood and plastic to create comfortable, practical, and inexpensive chairs of high quality. Some of his most influential designs are still used in homes and offices worldwide.

In 1946, Eames introduced the most famous of his *Eames chair* designs. It consisted of a molded plywood seat and back that seemed to float on a thin metal frame (see **Furniture** [The 1900's and 2000's; picture: Classics of modern furniture design]). His *stacking chairs* have molded fiberglass bodies and aluminum legs. They can be stacked one on top of another for storage. His other designs include a lounge chair made of molded plywood on a metal pivot base and a chair with four wire legs supporting a molded plastic shell. Eames was also an architect noted for his house designs, such as the steel-frame Eames House (1949) in Pacific Palisades, California. He also designed toys and museum exhibitions.

Charles Ormond Eames, Jr., was born on June 17, 1907, in St. Louis. He married Ray Kaiser, an American architect and designer, in 1941. They worked as partners until his death on Aug. 21, 1978. Nancy E. Richards

Philadelphia Museum of Art

Thomas Eakins became noted for his pictures of sports events, such as this work, *Between Rounds,* painted in 1899.

Ear

Ear is the sense organ that makes it possible for us to hear. Hearing is one of our most important senses. It enables us to communicate with one another through speech. The development of speech itself depends mostly on hearing. Children learn to talk by listening to and imitating the speech of other people. Hearing can also alert us to danger. We hear the warning honk of an automobile horn or the whistle of an approaching train. Even while asleep, we may hear a fire alarm or the barking of a watchdog. In addition, hearing provides pleasure. For example, it enables us to enjoy music, the singing of birds, and the sound of the surf.

Hearing is a complicated process. Everything that moves makes a sound. Sound consists of vibrations that travel in waves. Sound waves enter the ear and are changed into nerve signals that are sent to the brain. The brain interprets the signals as sounds.

Besides enabling us to hear, our ears help us keep our balance. The ears have certain organs that respond to movements of the head. These organs inform the brain about any changes in the position of the head. The brain then sends messages to various muscles that keep our head and body steady as we stand, sit, walk, or move in any way.

Many kinds of animals have ears similar to those of human beings, and some have an extremely keen sense of hearing. Hearing is vital to the safety and survival of numerous animals. Sounds may warn them of approaching enemies or other dangers. In addition, many animals sing, growl, hiss, or make other sounds and depend partly on their sense of hearing to communicate with one another.

This article deals mainly with the human ear. It describes the parts of the ear, the sense of hearing, and the sense of balance. It also discusses disorders of the ear. The last section of the article describes some of the differences in the ears of various kinds of animals.

Parts of the ear

Human beings have an ear on each side of the head. The ears extend deep into the skull. Each ear has three main parts: (1) the outer ear, (2) the middle ear, and (3) the inner ear.

The outer ear consists of three parts. They are: (1) the auricle, (2) the external auditory canal, and (3) the eardrum.

The auricle is the fleshy, curved part of the ear on the outside of the head. The auricle has no bone. It consists mainly of tough, elastic tissue called *cartilage,* which is covered by a thin layer of skin. The loosely hanging lower part of the auricle is called the *earlobe.* It is made up of fat.

Three small muscles attach the auricle to the head. In human beings, these muscles have no practical use. However, some people can move them and so wiggle their ears. In many animals, these muscles are well developed and highly movable. Cats, dogs, foxes, horses, rabbits, and many other animals can turn their ears in the direction from which a sound is coming and so improve their hearing.

The external auditory canal is the opening you see if you look directly into the ear. This passageway leads to the eardrum.

The external auditory canal is about 1 inch (2.5 centimeters) long. It curves somewhat in the shape of a *C.* The canal is lined with skin. The skin on the outer third of the canal has hairs, sweat glands, and glands that produce earwax. Earwax helps protect the eardrum by trapping dirt that would otherwise lodge against the membrane. Sometimes, earwax builds up in the canal and must be removed by a doctor. Never try to remove earwax yourself, especially by sticking small objects into the ear. You could easily puncture the eardrum.

The inner two-thirds of the auditory canal is surrounded by the *temporal bone,* which is the hardest bone in the body. The temporal bone also surrounds the middle ear and the inner ear. The bone protects the delicate structures of these parts of the ear.

The eardrum, also called the *tympanic membrane,* separates the outer ear from the middle ear. It is a thin, round, tightly stretched membrane about ⅜ inch (10 millimeters) in diameter.

The middle ear is a small chamber behind the eardrum. Three bones called the *auditory ossicles* extend across the chamber. The bones are linked together and connect the eardrum to the inner ear. The three bones have the Latin names *malleus,* which means *hammer; incus,* which means *anvil;* and *stapes,* which means *stirrup.* The bones look somewhat like the objects for which they are named. The malleus is the largest auditory ossicle. One end of the bone is attached to the eardrum, and

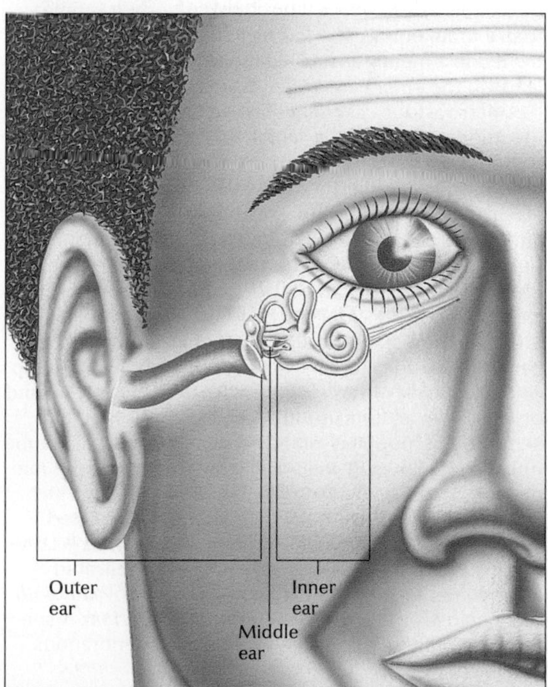

WORLD BOOK illustration by Colin Bidgood

The human ear extends deep into the skull. Its main parts are (1) the outer ear, (2) the middle ear, and (3) the inner ear.

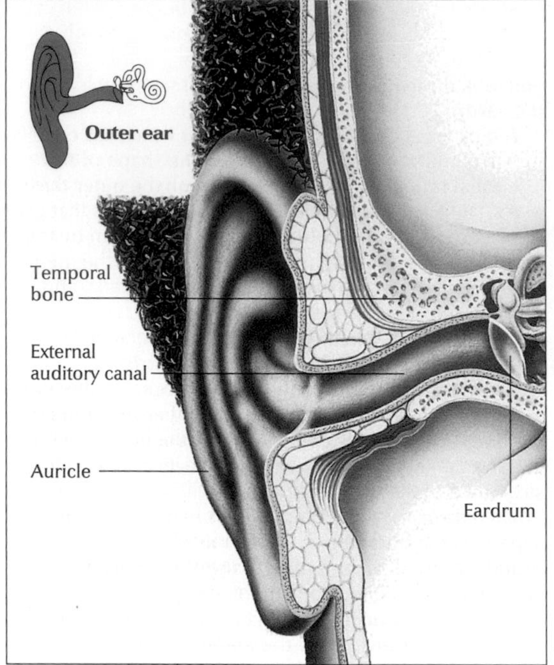

The outer ear consists of the *auricle,* which is the fleshy part of the ear on the side of the head; a passageway called the *external auditory canal;* and the *eardrum.* The inner two-thirds of the auditory canal is surrounded by the *temporal bone.*

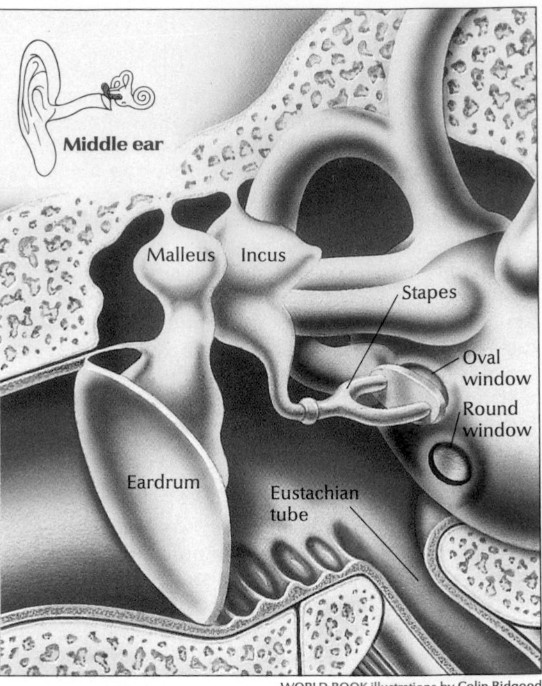

WORLD BOOK illustrations by Colin Bidgood

The middle ear has three bones—the *malleus, incus,* and *stapes.* They link the eardrum to the *oval window,* a membrane of the inner ear. The *Eustachian tube* leads from the middle ear to the back of the throat.

the other end is joined to the incus. The incus, the second largest ossicle, connects the malleus to the stapes. The stapes is the smallest bone in the body. It is tinier than a grain of rice. The footplate of the stapes is attached to a membrane called the *oval window,* which leads to the inner ear.

A narrow tube called the *Eustachian tube* connects the middle ear to the back of the throat. The tube is collapsed most of the time. It opens when you open your mouth, yawn, swallow, or blow your nose. When the Eustachian tube opens, air passes between the middle ear and the throat and so makes the air pressure on the inner side of the eardrum equal that on the outer side. If the Eustachian tube did not open, the eardrum would rupture when the air pressure, which varies with altitude, changes suddenly. The air pressure outside the eardrum changes rapidly, for example, when you go up or down quickly in an elevator, dive underwater, or land or take off in an airplane. In such cases, you have the sensation of "popping" of the ears as the Eustachian tube opens and allows air to escape from or to enter the middle ear.

The inner ear has many delicate, interconnected structures and is sometimes called the *labyrinth.* A labyrinth is a group of passageways with a complicated arrangement. The inner ear consists of a *bony labyrinth* that encloses a narrower *membranous labyrinth.* A special kind of fluid is contained within the membranous labyrinth.

The inner ear has three basic parts, which are connected. They are (1) the vestibule, (2) the semicircular canals, and (3) the cochlea.

The vestibule is a small, round chamber about ⅕ inch (5 millimeters) long. It forms the central part of the inner ear. Its bony walls connect the semicircular canals and the cochlea. Two *sacs* (baglike structures) lie within the vestibule. These sacs are called the *utricle* and the *saccule.* The inner wall of each sac has a swelling lined with *hair cells.* Hair cells are specialized sense cells with tiny, hairlike projections. The hair cells are attached to nerve fibers. A delicate membrane lies above the hair cells. Small mineral grains called *otoliths* are embedded in the membrane.

The vestibule has two small membranes that face the middle ear. One is the *oval window,* which is attached to the footplate of the stapes. The other is the *round window,* which lies just below the oval window.

The semicircular canals are behind the vestibule. They consist of three canals set at right angles to one another. They are called the *lateral, superior,* and *posterior* canals. The lateral canal is horizontal. The two other canals are vertical. The superior canal lies in front of the posterior canal. Each canal forms two-thirds of a circle.

Each semicircular canal contains a fluid-filled *duct* (tube). One end of each duct widens and forms a pouch. This pouch, called the *ampulla,* has hair cells that are attached to nerve fibers.

The ducts of the semicircular canals are joined to the utricle. The utricle, in turn, is connected by a duct to the saccule. The semicircular canals and the utricle and saccule make up the inner ear's organs of balance. They are sometimes called the *vestibular organs* or the *labyrinthine organs.*

The cochlea is in front of the vestibule. It resembles a snail shell and forms a spiral that coils 2 ¼ times around its tip. Three fluid-filled ducts wind through the cochlea. One begins at the oval window, and another at the round window. These two ducts join at the tip of the spiral. The third duct, called the *cochlear duct,* lies between the first two. One wall of the cochlear duct consists of the *basilar membrane.* This membrane supports the *organ of Corti,* which has over 15,000 hair cells and is the actual organ of hearing. A membrane called the *tectorial membrane* lies above the hair cells.

The nerve of the inner ear is known as the *auditory nerve* or the *vestibulocochlear nerve.* It has two branches—the *cochlear nerve* and the *vestibular nerve.* Fibers of the cochlear nerve extend to each hair cell of the organ of Corti. Some fibers of the vestibular nerve lead to the hair cells of the utricle and the saccule, and others extend to the hair cells of the ampulla of each semicircular canal.

The sense of hearing

Sound consists of vibrations that travel in waves through the air, the ground, or some other substance or surface. Sounds vary in *frequency* and *intensity.* Frequency is the number of vibrations produced per second and is measured in *hertz.* One vibration per second equals 1 hertz. A high-frequency sound has a high pitch, and a low-frequency sound has a low pitch. The full range of normal human hearing extends from 20 to 20,000 hertz. As a person grows older, however, the ability to hear high-frequency sounds decreases. Intensity is the amount of energy in a sound wave. It is measured in *decibels.* A person can barely hear a sound of zero decibels. Sounds above 140 decibels can be painful to the ears. In some cases, they may seriously damage the ears.

This section describes (1) how sounds travel to the inner ear and (2) how sounds reach the brain.

How sounds travel to the inner ear. Sound waves enter the external auditory canal of the outer ear and strike the eardrum, causing it to vibrate. The vibrations from the eardrum then travel across the three auditory ossicles of the middle ear—from the malleus, which is attached to the eardrum, to the incus and then to the stapes. The footplate of the stapes vibrates within the oval window, which creates waves in the fluid that fills the ducts of the cochlea of the inner ear.

Besides transmitting sound waves to the oval window, the auditory ossicles of the middle ear *amplify*

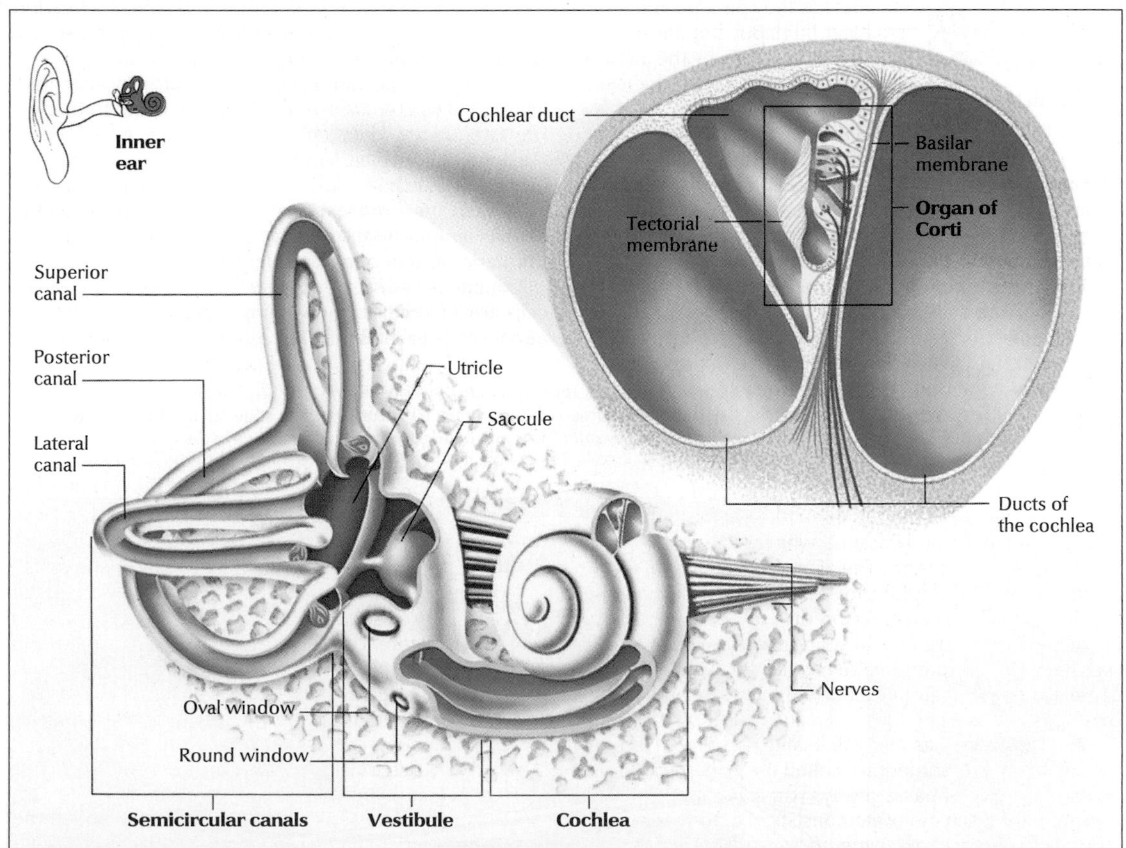

WORLD BOOK illustrations by Colin Bidgood

The inner ear consists of the *vestibule, semicircular canals,* and *cochlea.* The vestibule includes the *utricle* and *saccule,* which with the semicircular canals form the ear's organs of balance. The cochlea has three fluid-filled ducts, shown enlarged at the right above. One wall of the central *cochlear duct* consists of the *basilar membrane.* This membrane supports the *organ of Corti,* which has over 15,000 hair cells and is the actual organ of hearing. The *tectorial membrane* lies above the hair cells.

How sounds travel to the inner ear

Sound waves enter the ear through the external auditory canal. They strike the eardrum, causing it to vibrate. The vibrations travel across the malleus, incus, and stapes. The footplate of the stapes vibrates within the oval window, creating waves in the fluid that fills the ducts of the cochlea.

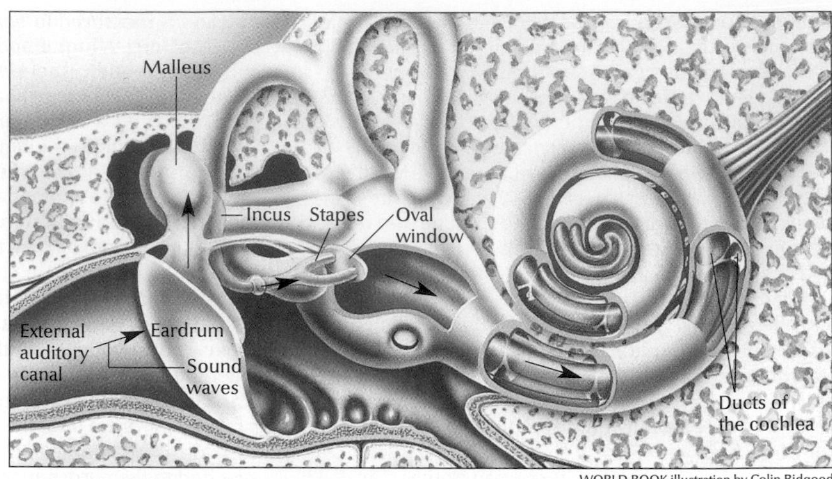

WORLD BOOK illustration by Colin Bidgood

http://bit.ly/11IYIrU

(strengthen) the waves. Sound waves do not travel as easily through the cochlear fluid of the inner ear as they do through the air. They diminish by about 30 decibels as they pass through the cochlear fluid. But amplification of the sound waves by the auditory ossicles makes up for the loss in intensity.

Sound waves can also be conducted to the inner ear through the bones of the skull. This process is called *bone conduction.* Some of the sound produced by your voice travels to your inner ears in this way. This fact explains why your own voice sounds different to you in a recording.

How sounds reach the brain. The movements of the footplate of the stapes in the oval window produce waves in the cochlear fluid. The cochlear fluid pushes against the basilar membrane, causing it to move. The hair cells of the organ of Corti on the basilar membrane slide against the overhanging tectorial membrane. The hairs bend and so create impulses in the cochlear nerve fibers attached to the hair cells. The cochlear nerve transmits the impulses to the *temporal lobe,* the hearing center of the brain. The brain interprets the impulses as sounds. See **Brain** (Sensing the environment).

Sounds of high, middle, and low frequency affect hair cells at different locations along the basilar membrane. High-frequency sounds move hair cells near the base of the spiraling cochlea. Middle-frequency sounds move hair cells near the middle of the spiral, and low-frequency sounds affect those near the top. The nerve fibers of the basilar membrane also send impulses of the same frequency as that of a particular sound.

The intensity of a sound determines how many hair cells are affected and how many impulses the cochlear nerve sends to the brain. For example, loud sounds

How the ear changes sounds into nerve impulses

The waves in the fluid that fills the ducts of the cochlea, *below left,* push against the basilar membrane. The hair cells of the organ of Corti on the basilar membrane slide against the overhanging tectorial membrane, *below right.* The hairs bend and so create impulses in the cochlear nerve fibers attached to the hair cells. The cochlear nerve transmits the impulses to the brain.

WORLD BOOK illustrations by Colin Bidgood

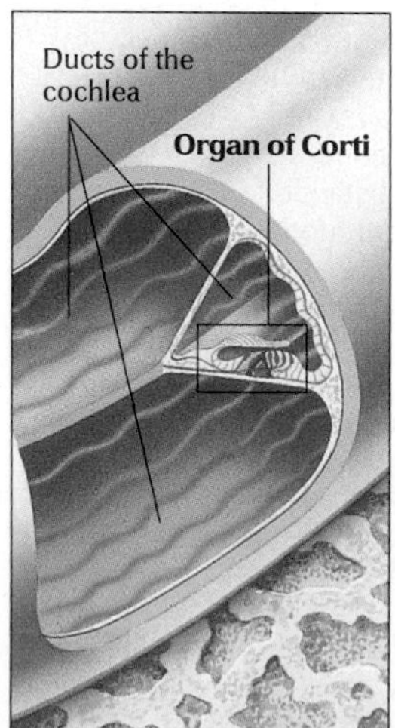

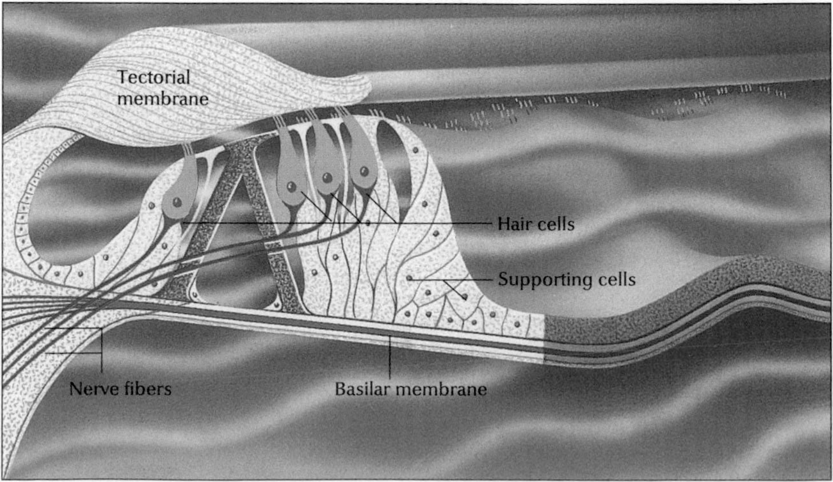

move a large number of hair cells, and the cochlear nerve transmits many impulses.

A person's ability to tell the direction from which a sound comes depends on *binaural hearing*—that is, hearing with both ears. For example, a sound coming from the right side of a person reaches the right ear a fraction of a second sooner than it reaches the left ear. The sound is also slightly louder in the right ear. The brain recognizes this tiny difference in time and loudness and so determines the direction from which the sound came.

The sense of balance

Most people are less aware of the sense of balance than they are of hearing, vision, and other senses. But without a sense of balance, we could not hold our body steady, and we would stagger and fall when we tried to move.

The brain's response to information from various sense organs keeps the body balanced. The vestibular organs—that is, the semicircular canals, utricle, and saccule—inform the brain about changes in the position of the head. The eyes and certain pressure-sensitive cells in the limbs and other parts of the body also inform the brain about changes in the position of the body. The brain then coordinates movements of various muscles that keep the head and body steady. These muscle movements occur automatically and are therefore called *reflex actions.*

This section describes (1) how the semicircular canals respond to movement, (2) how the utricle and saccule respond to gravity, and (3) disturbances of the organs of balance.

The response to movement. The semicircular canals respond to changes in the angle of the head, as by turning, tilting, or bending. Such movements cause the fluid in the ducts of the canals to flow in a certain direction.

Different types of movements affect different canals. Turning the head, for example, affects the lateral, or horizontal, canal in each ear. The fluid moves in opposite directions in the ducts of the two canals. In one ear, the movement of the fluid stimulates the hair cells in the ampulla, the pouch at the end of the duct. The nerve fibers attached to the hair cells then send an increased number of impulses to the brain by way of the vestibular nerve. In the other ear, the movement of fluid has the opposite effect, and the vestibular nerve sends fewer impulses to the brain. If you turn your head to the left, for example, the impulses to the brain from the left ear increase, and those from the right ear decrease. The brain determines which way the head has turned by the difference in the number of impulses from the two ears.

When the head is stationary, the canals in both ears send the same number of nerve impulses to the brain. The brain then recognizes that the head is stationary.

The response to gravity. The utricle and saccule react to the pull of gravity. They work by means of the otoliths, the small mineral grains embedded in a membrane above the hair cells within the organs. The vestibular nerve fibers attached to the hair cells are stimulated when the otoliths press against the hair cells. The force with which the otoliths press against the hair cells depends on the strength of the pull of gravity. The vestibular nerve sends this information to the brain. The brain's response maintains the body's posture.

The utricle and saccule do not work under conditions of zero gravity, which occur in outer space. But the semicircular canals do function under zero gravity.

Disturbances of the organs of balance may make it difficult for a person to hold the head and body erect. If the vestibular organs are damaged or diseased, they send too many or too few impulses to the brain. The brain interprets these abnormal messages as an imbalance of the body. The person then has a false feeling of motion, or dizziness. This condition is also called *vertigo.* A person whose vestibular organs have been destroyed may gradually learn to depend entirely on eyesight and other senses to maintain balance.

Some people suffer from *motion sickness* when they travel by boat, automobile, train, or airplane or when they whirl about rapidly. The symptoms of motion sickness include vertigo, nausea, and vomiting. Motion sickness is caused by excessive stimulation of the vestibular organs. But researchers do not know why some people develop motion sickness more easily than others do. See **Motion sickness.**

Disorders of the ear

Disorders of the ear may result in hearing loss. Some disorders may also affect the sense of balance. The causes of ear disorders are (1) birth defects, (2) injuries, and (3) diseases.

Birth defects. Some children are born without outer ears or with deformed outer ears. The eardrum and auditory ossicles may also be absent or deformed. In certain cases, such defects can be corrected by surgery. Surgeons may construct outer ears with tissues from other parts of the child's body. They may insert artificial ossicles made of plastic or wire or transplant healthy ossicles from a person who has died. Some children are born without inner ears or with poorly developed inner ears. Defects of the inner ears cannot be repaired. In many cases, a child born with defects of the ears also has defects in other parts of the body.

About 30 to 40 percent of all cases of birth defects of the ears are inherited. In some other cases, a disease that a woman contracts during pregnancy may damage the ears of her child. For example, a woman who has rubella during the first three months of pregnancy may give birth to a child with defective inner ears. A condition called *erythroblastosis fetalis* can also damage a baby's auditory system. In this condition, the blood of the unborn child contains a substance called the *Rh factor,* which is not in the expectant mother's blood. The mother's body produces substances that attack the Rh factor. The reaction may damage the child's inner ear and auditory nerve. However, most cases of erythroblastosis fetalis can be prevented. See **Rh factor.**

Certain drugs that a woman might take during pregnancy can prevent the normal development of the baby's cochlea or auditory nerve. A baby's ears may also be damaged if the child experiences head injuries, a lack of oxygen, or some other shock during or immediately after birth.

Newborn babies suspected of having a severe hearing loss should have their hearing tested within a few days after birth. Many deaf children can learn to speak and to read lips. But to do so, they need training at an early age. Children with a mild hearing loss can be fitted with hearing aids.

Injuries. Blows to the head, severe burns about the head, and other head injuries can damage the outer, middle, or inner ear. In some cases, the injuries may cause temporary hearing loss. In other cases, the loss may be permanent.

Sudden pressure changes can damage the ears and cause hearing loss. Scuba divers, for example, are exposed to changes in water pressure as they dive to great depths underwater and return to the surface. They must descend and ascend slowly to avoid injury.

Extremely loud noises, such as explosions or gun blasts, can rupture the eardrum and fracture or dislocate the auditory ossicles. Loud noises may also damage the delicate tissues of the inner ear. Many cases of blast injuries of the middle ear can be surgically repaired, but those of the inner ear cannot.

Exposure to loud noises over a long period can also damage a person's hearing ability. People who work in noisy places or who often listen to loud music may suffer a gradual hearing loss. People should avoid loud noises as much as possible and wear ear protectors while in noisy places.

Certain drugs, including aspirin and some antibiotics, can damage the cochlear hair cells or the auditory nerve. A person who regularly takes such a drug may suffer from loss of hearing. In some cases, hearing is restored after the person stops taking the drug.

Diseases. The human ear is subject to a number of diseases. The most common ones include (1) otitis media, (2) otosclerosis, (3) acoustic neuroma, (4) Ménière's disease, and (5) presbycusis.

Otitis media is an infection of the middle ear. It most commonly strikes children and can cause severe hearing loss if not treated promptly. There are three main types of otitis media—*acute, chronic,* and *serous.*

Acute otitis media results when an infection of the nose or throat spreads to the middle ear. Pus accumulates in the middle ear, causing pain and some hearing loss. Most cases of acute otitis media can be treated with antibiotics.

Chronic otitis media is a middle ear infection that is especially severe or that occurs repeatedly. It may cause the eardrum to rupture. Pus then frequently oozes from the middle ear. In most cases, a ruptured eardrum heals naturally. In other cases, it must be surgically repaired. Surgeons repair a ruptured eardrum with connective tissue from a person's veins or muscles. In some cases of chronic otitis media, pus continuously drains from the ear. The infection gradually destroys the auditory ossicles. Skin from the external auditory canal may grow into the middle ear, forming a small sac called a *cyst.* If the skin cyst continues to grow, it may damage parts of the inner ear, the facial nerve, and the brain. Most skin cysts can be surgically removed, and the damaged auditory ossicles can be replaced with artificial or transplanted ones.

Serous otitis media results if the Eustachian tube, which connects the middle ear to the back of the throat, becomes blocked. The blockage may be due to a respiratory infection, adenoid infection, allergic reaction, or certain birth defects. The blockage causes fluid to build up in the middle ear. The fluid interferes with the transmission of sound vibrations across the eardrum and auditory ossicles. Ear pain and drainage, which are symptoms of acute and chronic otitis media, do not occur in serous otitis media. Physicians often treat serous otitis media by slitting the eardrum and inserting a tube to allow the fluid to drain. They then treat the condition that caused the Eustachian tube to become blocked.

Otosclerosis is a disease of the auditory ossicles. In most cases, it begins during early adulthood, and it may slowly progress. In otosclerosis, a spongy bonelike material grows around the stapes. As this material grows, it interferes with the movement of the stapes within the oval window. The person suffers a gradual hearing loss. Doctors do not know the causes of the disease. They treat it by replacing the stapes with an artificial one. In most cases, the surgery improves hearing ability.

Acoustic neuroma is a tumor of the auditory nerve. The victim suffers a gradual decline in hearing ability, *tinnitus* (ringing or other noises in the ears), and dizziness. The tumor can be surgically removed. If the tumor is not removed, it may grow into the base of the brain and seriously damage vital brain functions.

Ménière's disease is a disorder of the inner ear marked by periodic attacks of hearing loss, tinnitus, and vertigo. After repeated attacks, the victim may suffer severe hearing loss. The exact cause of the disease is not known. However, researchers have found that the condition involves an increase in the volume and pressure of the inner ear fluid. The pressure of the fluid damages the hair cells of the cochlea and the vestibular organs.

Physicians may prescribe certain drugs to relieve the vertigo caused by Ménière's disease. But the drugs cannot prevent hearing loss. In severe cases of the disease, surgery is performed to drain the excess fluid and so help reduce the pressure inside the inner ear. Doctors may also cut the vestibular nerve to prevent vertigo, but this surgery is performed only if the patient's hearing is poor.

Presbycusis is a gradual loss of hearing that occurs with aging. It commonly develops among people who are more than 60 years old. Some ear specialists believe that the disease occurs because the cochlear nerve, like other tissues of the body, simply wears out as a person grows older. Others believe that the number of hair cells in the inner ear decreases with age, resulting in hearing loss. Victims of presbycusis have difficulty especially in hearing high-pitched sounds. They also find it hard to hear in noisy environments. In addition, they may have tinnitus.

No cure has been found for presbycusis. Most people who have the disease can hear and understand speech fairly well. However, severely disabled people may benefit from hearing aids and lip-reading lessons. Family members can help relatives who have presbycusis by pronouncing words slowly and distinctly, and by using visual signs along with speech to communicate.

The ears of animals

Many animals have ears that serve as organs of hearing and balance. But the structure of the ears varies greatly among different kinds of animals. Animals also differ in their ability to respond to sounds of exceptionally high or low frequency. For example, bats, cats,

Interesting features of the ears of various animals

WORLD BOOK illustrations by Patricia J. Wynne

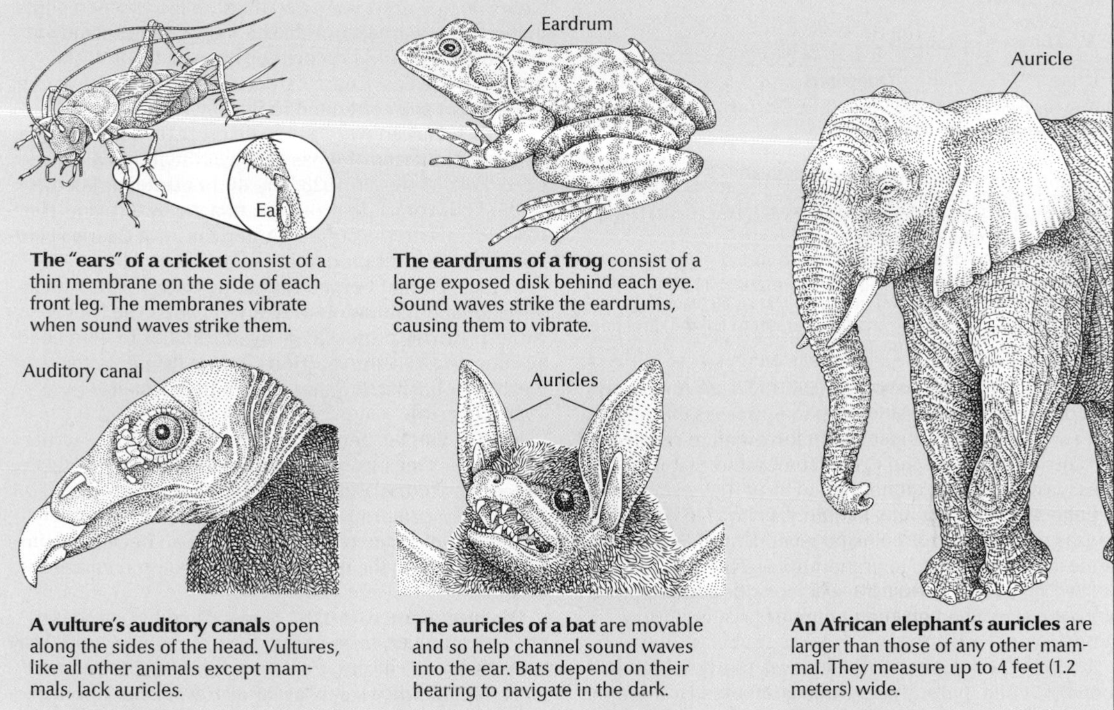

The "ears" of a cricket consist of a thin membrane on the side of each front leg. The membranes vibrate when sound waves strike them.

The eardrums of a frog consist of a large exposed disk behind each eye. Sound waves strike the eardrums, causing them to vibrate.

A vulture's auditory canals open along the sides of the head. Vultures, like all other animals except mammals, lack auricles.

The auricles of a bat are movable and so help channel sound waves into the ear. Bats depend on their hearing to navigate in the dark.

An African elephant's auricles are larger than those of any other mammal. They measure up to 4 feet (1.2 meters) wide.

dogs, some insects, and certain other animals can hear sounds of far higher frequency than human beings can hear.

Only a few kinds of insects have true hearing organs. Their "ears" consist simply of thin membranes that vibrate when sound waves strike them. Among different insects, the "ears" are on the legs, sides, or other parts of the body. See **Insect** (Hearing).

Fish do not have outer ears or eardrums. But some have a simple type of inner ear on each side of the head. These fish can hear sound waves that travel through the water. Sound vibrations are carried to the inner ear by a gas-filled sac called the *air bladder.* Some types of fish have a chain of ossicles that connect the air bladder to the inner ear. See **Fish** (Hearing; Other senses).

Frogs, toads, and other amphibians have middle ears and inner ears. The middle ear of a frog consists of an eardrum and a small chamber with one bony ossicle. The eardrum of a frog is a large exposed disk behind the eye on each side of the head. See **Frog** (Senses).

Like amphibians, most reptiles have eardrums, middle ears, and inner ears. In some reptiles, the inner ears are highly developed. Most snakes lack eardrums, but they are not deaf, as many people think. Sounds are transmitted to the inner ears of snakes chiefly by the bones of the skull. See **Reptile** (Sense organs); **Snake** (Sense organs).

Birds have external auditory canals, middle ears, and inner ears. The cochlea of the bird inner ear is slightly curved but not coiled. The hearing ability of birds is similar to that of human beings. See **Bird** (Senses).

All mammals have coiled cochleas. In addition, mammals are the only animals that have auricles. In many mammals, these outer ear parts are movable and help channel sound waves into the auditory canal. African elephants have the largest auricles of any animal. Their auricles measure up to 4 feet (1.2 meters) wide. The auricles help the animals cool off in hot weather. Heat escapes from the elephant's body partly through the skin of the auricles. Other animals, including certain kinds of rabbits and foxes, have unusually large auricles that serve the same purpose. See **Mammal** (Senses).

A few animals, including dolphins, some bats, and some whales, depend on hearing to navigate in the dark. They find their way about by a process called *echolocation.* The animals make sounds and listen for the echoes that are produced when objects reflect the sounds. From the echoes, they determine the distance to an object and the direction in which it lies. See **Bat** (Echolocation); **Dolphin** (The bodies of dolphins); **Whale** (Senses). Peter A. Santi

Related articles in *World Book* include:

Audiology	Hearing aid	Otoscope	Tinnitus
Deafness	Mastoid	Sound	

Outline

I. Parts of the ear
- A. The outer ear
- B. The middle ear
- C. The inner ear

II. The sense of hearing
- A. How sounds travel to the inner ear
- B. How sounds reach the brain

III. The sense of balance
- A. The response to movement
- B. The response to gravity
- C. Disturbances of the organs of balance

IV. Disorders of the ear
- A. Birth defects
- B. Injuries
- C. Diseases

V. The ears of animals

Questions

What is *presbycusis?*
How do sounds reach the brain?
What is the *organ of Corti?*
What are the only animals that have auricles?
How do the semicircular canals work?
What are some kinds of injuries that can result in hearing loss?
What causes motion sickness?
How does earwax help protect the eardrum?
What causes the sensation of "popping" of the ears when you rapidly ascend or descend in an elevator or airplane?
How does *binaural hearing* enable a person to tell the direction from which a sound comes?

Earhart, *AIR hahrt,* **Amelia** (1897-1937), an American aviator, became the first woman to fly across the Atlantic Ocean alone. She was also the first woman to receive the Distinguished Flying Cross. The United States Congress awarded her that honor.

Early life. Amelia Mary Earhart was born in Atchison, Kansas, on July 24, 1897. She received a modest inheritance from her maternal grandmother. The money helped give her a secure life with considerable opportunity for travel. She became a volunteer nurse during World War I (1914-1918).

In 1920, Earhart moved to California to live with her mother. While there, she became fascinated by aviation.

© Holmes-Lebel from FPG

Amelia Earhart was an American pilot who became one of the world's most famous aviators. In 1937, Earhart disappeared without a trace while attempting to fly around the world. Since that time, her fate has been the source of much speculation.

Flying was a new and dangerous sport at that time. Earhart took flying lessons from an instructor named Neta Snook. Snook was one of only a few women pilots in the 1920's. Earhart purchased her own plane and set an unofficial altitude record for women. In 1924, she moved to the East Coast. Earhart became a social worker in 1926, but she continued to fly.

Flights. Earhart rode as an observer on a transatlantic airplane flight from Trepassey Bay, Newfoundland, to Burry Port, Wales, in 1928. The flight made her famous as the first woman to cross the Atlantic by airplane. Her resemblance to the famous American pilot Charles Lindbergh also contributed to her fame.

In 1929, Earhart helped found the Ninety-Nines, an international organization of women pilots. The Ninety-Nines provides professional opportunities to women in aviation. In 1931, she married George Palmer Putnam, a wealthy publisher. Putnam had helped organize her 1928 flight.

In 1932, Earhart became the first woman to fly across the Atlantic Ocean alone. She took off from Harbour Grace, Newfoundland, and landed in a pasture near Londonderry, Northern Ireland. She went on to set other speed and distance records. Earhart also became an important figure in the movement to develop commercial aviation.

Disappearance. In 1937, Earhart and her navigator, Frederick J. Noonan, set off to fly around the world. They took off from Oakland, California, on May 20, flying west. They made it safely as far as Hawaii. But upon takeoff from Hawaii, the plane became damaged. After repairing and adjusting the plane, Earhart and Noonan started the journey over—this time flying east. They took off from Oakland again on June 1 and flew to Miami, Florida. They then flew from Miami to Puerto Rico. On June 30, they landed in New Guinea. They had traveled about 20,000 miles (32,000 kilometers), more than three-fourths of their planned flight.

On July 1, Earhart and Noonan left New Guinea and began the longest leg of their journey. They tried to fly 2,600 miles (4,200 kilometers) over open water to Howland Island in the central Pacific Ocean. The next day, a U.S. Navy vessel picked up radio messages from Earhart. She reported empty fuel tanks. But efforts to make radio contact failed. An extensive search found no trace of the plane or crew. Earhart and Noonan probably crashed into the ocean and died. Their plane likely ran out of fuel after navigation errors took them off course.

Janet R. Bednarek

See also **Airplane** (Fliers of the golden age).

Earle, Sylvia Alice (1935-), is an American oceanographer and environmentalist. In 1979, she was the first person to dive solo to 1,250 feet (381 meters) beneath the surface without being connected to a support vessel. During that dive, she reached the floor of the Pacific Ocean near Hawaii.

In 1981, Earle and her then-husband, engineer Graham Hawkes, founded a company called Deep Ocean Engineering. The company designs and builds underwater research vehicles known as *submersibles.* From 1990 to 1992, Earle served as chief scientist of the National Oceanic and Atmospheric Administration (NOAA), a branch of the Department of Commerce. For NOAA, Earle helped determine environmental damage caused by Iraq's destruction of Kuwaiti oil wells during the Persian Gulf War of 1991.

Earle was born on Aug. 30, 1935, in Gibbstown, New Jersey. After graduating from Florida State University, she earned a Ph.D. degree in botany from Duke University. She is the author of *Sea Change: A Message from the Oceans* (1995). Charles Pellegrino

See also **Exploration** (picture).

Early, Jubal Anderson (1816-1894), was a Confederate general in the American Civil War (1861-1865). He opposed *secession* (withdrawal) from the United States. However, after Virginia seceded in 1861, he joined the Confederate Army and became a lieutenant general. Early commanded a brigade and division in the Army of Northern Virginia.

Confederate General Robert E. Lee sent Early's corps in June 1864 to threaten Washington, D.C. Early led this campaign with boldness and skill. He bombarded the outskirts of the Union capital but was not strong enough to take the city. Later in 1864, he participated in the burning of Chambersburg, Pennsylvania. Early then retreated to the Shenandoah Valley and tried to delay the advance of the Union cavalry under General Philip H. Sheridan. Sheridan defeated Early decisively in March 1865.

Early was born on Nov. 3, 1816, in Franklin County, Virginia, and graduated from the U.S. Military Academy in 1837. He then studied law. Early served in the Second Seminole War (1835-1842) and the Mexican War (1846-1848). After the Civil War, he helped found the Southern Historical Socicty, an organization that worked to preserve the Confederate view of the war. Early died on March 2, 1894. John F. Marszalek

Early childhood education provides planned learning experiences for children from birth through age 8. All early childhood education programs work to promote a child's emotional, intellectual, physical, and social development. Good programs strengthen children's feelings of self-worth and expand their ability to learn and organize information.

Young children learn from everyone and everything around them. But planned learning takes place chiefly in (1) activities planned by families, (2) formal education programs, and (3) child-care programs.

Activities planned by families give children a foundation for a lifetime of learning. Some activities occur at home as part of daily routines. For example, many families set aside a time each day to read to their youngest members. Other family activities may involve concerts, plays, or trips to museums or zoos. Adults can obtain help in planning activities by attending parent education classes or participating in family support programs. These programs help families promote the development of their children and gain access to community resources and services. A number of books, Web sites, and other resources also provide suggestions for family learning.

Formal education programs include (1) programs for infants and toddlers; (2) preelementary programs, such as those offered by nursery schools and kindergartens; and (3) elementary programs. The best such programs are staffed by people with special training in educating young children. Early childhood educators believe that children's intellectual, social, emotional, and physical abilities are closely connected and should be developed at the same time. Skilled early childhood teachers create learning experiences that are appropriate for each child's stage of development and individual needs.

Child-care programs exist chiefly to provide care for the children of working families. Superior programs provide a safe environment, skilled adult supervision, and a wide range of activities, including educational experiences. Lawrence O. Picus

Related articles in *World Book* include:

Child
Day care
Education (Early childhood education)
Head Start
Kindergarten
Montessori method
Parent education
Preschool

Earnhardt, Dale (1951-2001), an American stock car driver, won the Winston Cup (now Sprint Cup) Championship seven times, tying the record set by Richard Petty. Earnhardt won the championship in 1980, 1986, 1987, 1990, 1991, 1993, and 1994. The Sprint Cup Series is the national racing championship for stock cars—American sedans with many modifications to increase speed and power. Earnhardt was noted for his aggressive driving style and his consistently high finishes in stock car races.

In 1979, he was named Winston Cup Rookie of the Year by the National Association for Stock Car Auto Racing (NASCAR). In 1980, Earnhardt became the only driver to win the Winston Cup as a second-year competitor.

Ralph Dale Earnhardt was born on April 29, 1951, in Kannapolis, North Carolina. Earnhardt began his racing career when he was 19 years old. He was the son of stock car pioneer Ralph Earnhardt. Dale Earnhardt was killed in a crash during the final lap of the Daytona 500 race on Feb. 18, 2001. His son, Dale Earnhardt, Jr., is also a leading stock car driver. Sylvia Wilkinson

Earp, Wyatt (1848-1929), was a peace officer in the American West. He became best known for his role in the famous gunfight at the O.K. Corral in Tombstone, Arizona. Earp moved to Tombstone in 1879. He worked there as a stagecoach guard, card dealer, and deputy United States marshal. In 1881, a feud developed between Ike Clanton's gang and three of the Earp brothers—Wyatt, Virgil, and Morgan. Virgil Earp was Tombstone's marshal. The feud peaked in October when the Earps and their friend Doc Holliday shot to death three of Clanton's gang at the O.K. Corral. The Earps said they were trying to make an arrest. Others said it was murder. Later, Wyatt worked as a saloonkeeper and prospector.

Montgomery Foto Service

Wyatt Earp

Wyatt Berry Stapp Earp was born March 19, 1848, in Monmouth, Illinois. As a young man, Earp worked as a buffalo hunter. During the 1870's, he was a police officer in Wichita and Dodge City in Kansas. He died on Jan. 13, 1929. Roger D. McGrath

Earphones. See **Headphones.**

NASA/Goddard Space Flight Center

Earth, our home planet, has oceans of liquid water and continents that rise above sea level. NASA scientists combined satellite photographs with surface data to create this detailed image of Earth's land masses and oceans. The swirling mass of clouds west of Mexico is a large hurricane.

Earth

Earth is a small planet in the vastness of space. It is one of several planets that travel through space around the sun. The sun is a star—one of hundreds of billions of stars that make up a galaxy called the Milky Way. The Milky Way and trillions of other galaxies make up the universe.

The planet Earth is only a tiny part of the universe, but it is the home of human beings and, in fact, all known life in the universe. Animals, plants, and other organisms live almost everywhere on Earth's surface. They can live on Earth because it is just the right distance from the sun. Most living things need the sun's warmth and light for life. If Earth were too close to the sun, it would be too hot for living things. If Earth were too far from the sun, it would be too cold for anything to live. Living things also must have water to live. Earth has plenty. Water covers most of Earth's surface.

The study of Earth is called *geology,* and scientists who study Earth are *geologists.* Geologists study different physical features of Earth to understand how they were formed and how they have changed over time. Much of Earth, such as the deep interior, cannot be studied directly. Geologists must often study samples of rock and use indirect methods to learn about the planet. Today, geologists can also view and study the entire Earth from space.

This article deals with the planet Earth as it is studied in geology. For information on Earth as the home of human beings, see the article on **World** in *World Book.*

Earth as a planet

Earth ranks fifth in size among the sun's planets. It has a diameter of about 8,000 miles (13,000 kilometers). Jupiter, the largest planet, is about 11 times larger in di-

Steven I. Dutch, the contributor of this article, is Professor of Earth Science at the University of Wisconsin, Green Bay.

Earth at a glance

Age: At least 4 ½ billion years.
Mass: 6,600,000,000,000,000,000,000 (6.6 sextillion) tons (6.0 sextillion metric tons).
Motion: *Rotation* (spinning motion around an imaginary line connecting the North and South poles)—once every 23 hours 56 minutes 4.09 seconds. *Revolution* (motion around the sun)—once every 365 days 6 hours 9 minutes 9.54 seconds.
Size: *Polar diameter* (distance through Earth from the North Pole to the South Pole)—7,899.83 miles (12,713.54 kilometers). *Equatorial diameter* (distance through Earth at the equator)—7,926.41 miles (12,756.32 kilometers). *Polar circumference* (distance around Earth through the poles)—24,859.82 miles (40,008.00 kilometers). *Equatorial circumference* (distance around Earth along the equator)—24,901.55 miles (40,075.16 kilometers).
Area: *Total surface area*—196,900,000 square miles (510,000,000 square kilometers). *Land area*—approximately 57,100,000 square miles (148,000,000 square kilometers), 29 percent of total surface area. *Water area*—approximately 139,800,000 square miles (362,000,000 square kilometers), 71 percent of total surface area.
Surface features: *Highest land*—Mount Everest, 29,035 feet (8,850 meters) above sea level. *Lowest land*—shore of Dead Sea, about 1,391 feet (424 meters) below sea level.
Ocean depths: *Deepest part of ocean*—area of the Mariana Trench in Pacific Ocean southwest of Guam, 35,840 feet (10,924 meters) below surface. *Average ocean depth*—12,200 feet (3,730 meters).
Temperature: *Highest,* 134 °F (57 °C) in Death Valley, California. *Lowest,* -128.6 °F (-89.6 °C) at Vostok Station in Antarctica. *Average surface temperature,* 59 °F (15 °C).
Atmosphere: *Height*—More than 99 percent of the atmosphere is less than 50 miles (80 kilometers) above Earth's surface. The atmosphere fades into space about 600 miles (1,000 kilometers) above the surface. *Chemical makeup of atmosphere*—about 78 percent nitrogen, 21 percent oxygen, 1 percent argon with small amounts of other gases.
Chemical makeup of Earth's crust (in percent of the crust's weight): oxygen 46.6, silicon 27.7, aluminum 8.1, iron 5.0, calcium 3.6, sodium 2.8, potassium 2.6, magnesium 2.0, and other elements totaling 1.6.

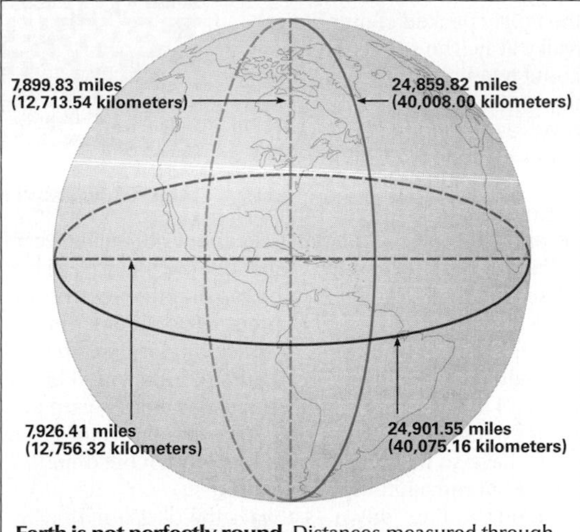

Earth is not perfectly round. Distances measured through the poles are shorter than those at the equator.

WORLD BOOK map

ameter than Earth. Mercury, on the other hand, has a diameter of about two-fifths that of Earth.

Earth, like all the planets in our solar system, travels around the sun in a path called an *orbit.* Earth is about 93 million miles (150 million kilometers) from the sun. It takes one year for Earth to complete one orbit around the sun. The innermost planet, Mercury, is only about one-third as far from the sun as Earth and circles the sun in only 88 days. Neptune, the outermost planet, is 30 times as far from the sun as Earth and takes 165 Earth years to circle the sun.

How Earth moves. Earth has three motions: (1) It spins like a top around an imaginary line called an *axis* that runs from the North Pole to the South Pole, (2) it travels around the sun, and (3) it moves through the Milky Way along with the sun and the rest of the solar system.

Earth takes 24 hours to spin completely around on its axis so that the sun is in the same place in the sky. This period is called a *solar day.* During a solar day, Earth moves a little around its orbit so that it faces the stars a bit differently each night. Thus, it takes only 23 hours 56 minutes 4.09 seconds for Earth to spin once so that the stars appear to be in the same place in the sky. This period is called a *sidereal day.* A sidereal day is shorter than a solar day, so the stars appear to rise about 4 minutes earlier each day.

Earth takes 365 days 6 hours 9 minutes 9.54 seconds to circle the sun. This length of time is called a *sidereal year.* Because Earth does not spin a whole number of times as it goes around the sun, the calendar gets out of step with the seasons by about 6 hours each year. Every four years, a day is added to bring the calendar back into line with the seasons. These years, called *leap years,* have 366 days. The extra day is added to the end of February and occurs as February 29.

The distance around Earth's orbit is 584 million miles (940 million kilometers). Earth travels in its orbit at 66,700 miles (107,000 kilometers) an hour, or 18.5 miles (30 kilometers) a second. Earth's orbit lies on an imaginary flat surface around the sun called the *orbital plane.*

Earth's axis is not straight up and down, but is tilted by about 23 ½ degrees compared to the orbital plane. This tilt and Earth's motion around the sun causes the change of the seasons. In January, the northern half of Earth tilts away from the sun. Sunlight is spread thinly over the northern half of Earth, and the north experiences winter. At the same time, the sunlight falls intensely on the southern half of Earth, which has summer. By July, Earth has moved to the opposite side of the sun. Now the northern half of Earth tilts toward the sun. Sunlight falls intensely over the northern half of Earth, and the north experiences summer. At the same time, the sunlight falls less intensely on the southern half of Earth, which has winter.

Earth's orbit is not a perfect circle. Earth is slightly closer to the sun in early January (winter in the Northern Hemisphere) and farther away in July. In January, Earth is 91.4 million miles (147.1 million kilometers) from the sun. In July, it is 94.5 million miles (152.1 million kilometers) from the sun. This variation has a far smaller effect than the heating and cooling caused by the tilt of Earth's axis.

Earth and the solar system are part of a vast disk of stars called the Milky Way Galaxy. Just as the moon orbits Earth and planets orbit the sun, the sun and other stars orbit the tightly packed center of the Milky Way. The solar system is about two-fifths of the way from the center of the Milky Way and revolves around the center at about 137 miles (220 kilometers) per second. The solar system makes one complete revolution around the center of the galaxy in about 240 million years.

http://bit.ly/11KBVLP

Earth's size and shape. Most people picture Earth as a ball with the North Pole at the top and the South Pole at the bottom. Earth, other planets, large moons, and stars—in fact, most objects in space bigger than about 200 miles (320 kilometers) in diameter—are round because of their gravity. Gravity pulls matter in toward the center of objects. Tiny moons, such as the two moons of Mars, have so little gravity that they do not become round but remain lumpy instead.

To our bodies, "down" is always the direction gravity is pulling. People everywhere on Earth feel "down" is toward the center of Earth and "up" is toward the sky. People in Spain and in New Zealand are on exactly opposite sides of Earth from each other, but both sense their surroundings as "right side up." Gravity works the same way on other planets and moons.

Earth, however, is not perfectly round. Its spin causes it to bulge slightly at its middle, the *equator.* The diameter of Earth from North Pole to South Pole is 7,899.83 miles (12,713.54 kilometers), but through the equator it is 7,926.41 miles (12,756.32 kilometers). This difference, 26.58 miles (42.78 kilometers), is only 1/298 the diameter of Earth. The difference is too tiny to be easily seen in pictures of Earth from space, so the planet appears round.

Earth's bulge also makes Earth's circumference larger around the equator than around the poles. The circumference around the equator is 24,901.55 miles (40,075.16 kilometers). Around the poles, however, it is only 24,859.82 miles (40,008.00 kilometers). The circumference is actually greatest just south of the equator, so Earth is slightly pear-shaped. Earth also has mountains and valleys, but these features are tiny compared with the total size of Earth, so the planet appears smooth from space.

Earth and its moon. Earth has one moon. Earth's moon has a diameter of about 2,159 miles (3,474 kilometers)—about one-fourth of Earth's diameter.

The sun's gravity acts on Earth and the moon as if they were a single body with its center about 1,000 miles (1,600 kilometers) below Earth's surface. This spot is the Earth-moon *barycenter.* The barycenter is the point of balance between the heavy Earth and the lighter moon. The path of the barycenter around the sun is a smooth curve. Earth and the moon circle the barycenter as they orbit the sun. The motion of Earth and moon around the barycenter makes each "wobble" in their path around the sun.

Earth's spheres

Earth is composed of several layers, or *spheres,* somewhat like the layers of an onion. The solid Earth consists of a thin outer layer called the *crust.* A thick rocky layer called the *mantle* lies beneath the crust. The crust and the upper portion of the mantle are called the *lithosphere.* At the center of Earth is the *core.* The outer part of the core is liquid, while the inner part is solid. Much of Earth is covered by a layer of water or ice called the *hydrosphere.* Earth is surrounded by a thin layer of air, the *atmosphere.* The portion of the hydrosphere, atmosphere, and solid land where life exists is called the *biosphere.*

The atmosphere. Air surrounds Earth and becomes progressively thinner farther from the surface. Most people find it difficult to breathe more than 2 miles (3 kilometers) above sea level. About 100 miles (160 kilometers) above the surface, the air is so thin that satellites can travel without much resistance. Detectable traces of atmosphere, however, can be found as high as 370 miles (600 kilometers) above Earth's surface. The atmosphere has no definite outer edge but fades gradually into space.

Nitrogen makes up 78 percent of the atmosphere, while oxygen makes up 21 percent. The remaining 1 percent consists of argon and small amounts of other gases. The atmosphere also contains water vapor, carbon dioxide, water droplets, dust particles, and small amounts of many other chemicals released by volcanoes, fires, living things, and human activities.

The lowest layer of the atmosphere is called the *troposphere.* This layer is in constant motion. The sun heats

WORLD BOOK illustration by Amie Zorn, Artisan-Chicago

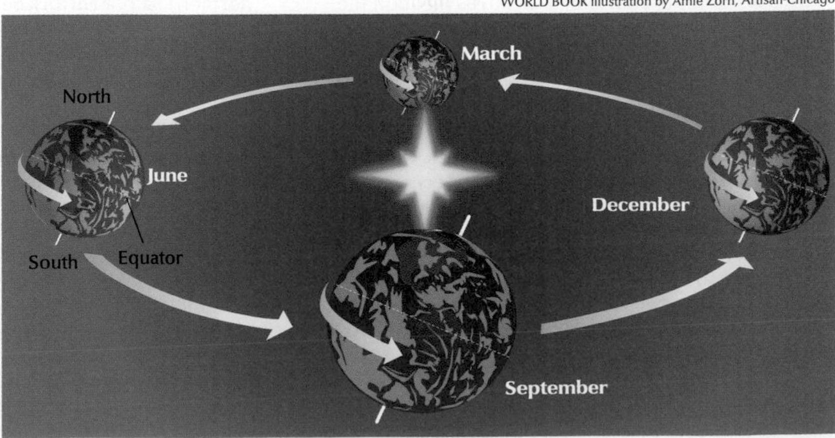

The motions of Earth

Earth spins around its axis once every 24 hours. This motion creates day and night. Earth also travels around the sun once every 365 days. This motion creates the year. The entire solar system revolves around the center of the Milky Way Galaxy.

Earth's spheres Earth's layers, or *spheres*—the atmosphere, hydrosphere, lithosphere, and biosphere—form a complex system that interacts and functions as a whole. Matter and energy flow constantly back and forth between the spheres in cycles. A change in one can produce unexpected changes in another.

NASA; WORLD BOOK illustrations by Amie Zorn, Artisan-Chicago

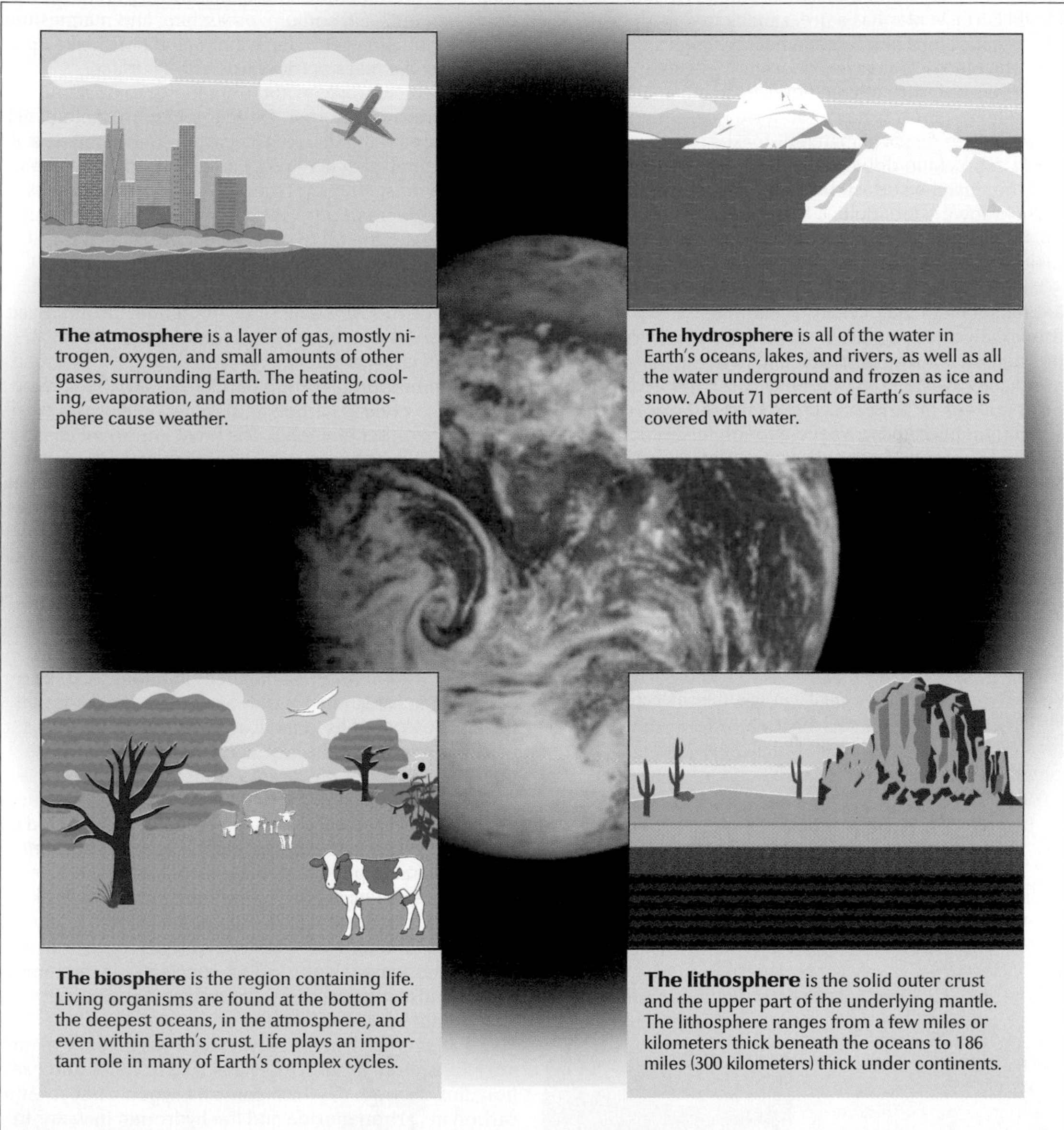

The atmosphere is a layer of gas, mostly nitrogen, oxygen, and small amounts of other gases, surrounding Earth. The heating, cooling, evaporation, and motion of the atmosphere cause weather.

The hydrosphere is all of the water in Earth's oceans, lakes, and rivers, as well as all the water underground and frozen as ice and snow. About 71 percent of Earth's surface is covered with water.

The biosphere is the region containing life. Living organisms are found at the bottom of the deepest oceans, in the atmosphere, and even within Earth's crust. Life plays an important role in many of Earth's complex cycles.

The lithosphere is the solid outer crust and the upper part of the underlying mantle. The lithosphere ranges from a few miles or kilometers thick beneath the oceans to 186 miles (300 kilometers) thick under continents.

Earth's surface and the air above it, causing warm air to rise. As the warm air rises, air pressure decreases and the air expands and cools. The cool air is denser than the surrounding air, so it sinks and the cycle starts again. This constant cycle of the air causes the weather.

High above the troposphere, about 30 miles (48 kilometers) above Earth's surface, is a layer of still air called the *stratosphere.* The stratosphere contains a layer where ultraviolet light from the sun strikes oxygen molecules to create a gas called *ozone.* Ozone blocks most of the harmful ultraviolet rays from reaching Earth's surface. Some ultraviolet rays get through, however. They are responsible for sunburn and can cause skin cancer in people. Tiny amounts of human-made chemicals have caused some of the natural ozone to break down. Many people are concerned that the ozone layer may become too thin, allowing ultraviolet rays to reach the surface and harm people and other living things.

Water vapor, carbon dioxide, methane, and other gases in the atmosphere trap heat from the sun, warming Earth. The heat-trapping quality of these gases causes the *greenhouse effect.* Without the greenhouse effect of the atmosphere, Earth would probably be too cold for life to exist.

The hydrosphere. Earth is the only planet in the solar system with abundant liquid water on its surface. Water has chemical and physical properties not matched by any other substance, and it is essential for life on Earth. Water has a great ability to absorb heat. The oceans store much of the heat Earth gets from the sun. The electrical charges on water molecules give water a great ability to attract atoms from other substances. This quality allows water to dissolve many things. Water's ability to dissolve materials makes it a powerful agent in breaking down rocks. Liquid water on Earth affects not just the surface but the interior as well. Water in rocks lowers the melting temperature of rock. Water dramatically weakens rocks and makes them easier to melt beneath Earth's surface.

About 71 percent of Earth's surface is covered by water, most of it in the oceans. Ocean water is too salty to drink. Only about 3 percent of Earth's water is fresh water, suitable for drinking. Much of Earth's fresh water is not readily available to people because it is frozen in the polar icecaps or beneath Earth's surface. Polar regions and high mountains stay cold enough for water to remain permanently frozen. The region of permanent ice on Earth is sometimes called the *cryosphere.*

The lithosphere. The crust and upper mantle of Earth from the surface to about 60 miles (100 kilometers) down make up the lithosphere. The thin crust is made up of natural chemicals called *minerals* composed of different combinations of elements. Oxygen is the most abundant chemical element in rocks in Earth's crust, making up about 47 percent of the mass of all rock. The second most abundant element is silicon, 27 percent, followed by aluminum (8 percent), iron (5 percent), calcium (4 percent), and sodium, potassium, and magnesium (about 2 percent each). These eight elements make up 99 percent of the mass of rocks on Earth's surface.

Two elements, silicon and oxygen, make up almost three-fourths of the crust. This combination of elements is so important that geologists have a special term for it: *silica.* Minerals that contain silica are called *silicate minerals.* The most abundant mineral on Earth's surface is quartz, made up of pure silica. Another plentiful group of silicates are the *feldspars,* which consist of silica, aluminum, calcium, sodium, and potassium. Other common silicate minerals on Earth's surface are pyroxene (pronounced *PY rahk seen)* and amphibole (pronounced *AM fuh bohl),* which consist of combinations of silica, iron, and magnesium.

Another important group of minerals are the *carbonates,* which contain carbon and oxygen along with small amounts of other elements. The most important carbonate mineral is *calcite,* made up of calcium, carbon, and oxygen. *Limestone,* a common rock used for building, is mostly calcite. Another important carbonate is *dolomite,* composed of carbon, oxygen, calcium, and magnesium.

Earth has two kinds of crust. The dry land of the continents is made up mostly of granite and other light silicate minerals, while the ocean floors are composed mostly of a dark, dense volcanic rock called *basalt.* Continental crust averages about 25 miles (40 kilometers) thick, but it is thicker in some areas and thinner in others. Most oceanic crust is only about 5 miles (8 kilometers) thick. Water fills in the low areas over the thin basalt crust to form the world's oceans. There is more than enough water on Earth to completely fill the oceanic basins, and some of it spreads onto the edges of the continents. This portion of the continents surrounded by a band of shallow ocean is called the *continental shelf.*

The biosphere. Earth is the only planet in the universe known to have life. The region containing life extends from the bottom of the deepest ocean to a few miles or kilometers into the atmosphere. There are several million known kinds, called *species,* of living things, and scientists believe that there are far many more species not yet discovered.

Life affects Earth in many ways. Life has actually made the atmosphere around us. Plants take in water and carbon dioxide, both of which contain oxygen. They use the carbon in carbon dioxide and the hydrogen in water to make chemicals of many kinds and give off oxygen as a waste product. Animals eat plants to get energy and return water and carbon dioxide back into the environment. Living things affect the surface of Earth in other ways as well. Plants create chemicals that speed the breakdown of rock. Grasslands and forests slow the erosion of soil.

Inside Earth

Beneath Earth's solid crust are the mantle, the outer core, and the inner core. Scientists learn about the inside of Earth by studying how waves from earthquakes travel through the planet.

WORLD BOOK illustration by Raymond Perlman and Steven Brayfield, Artisan-Chicago

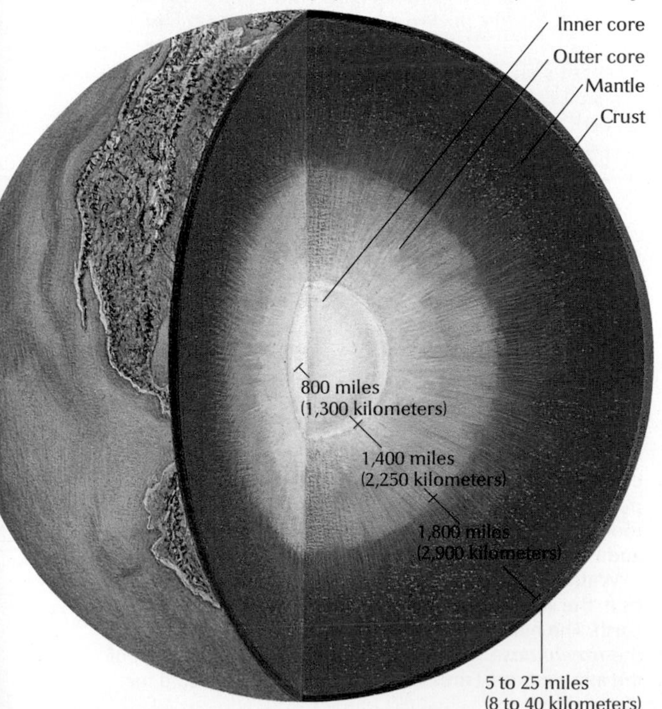

Earth's rocks

The solid part of Earth consists of rocks, which are sometimes made up of a single mineral, but more often consist of mixtures of minerals. Geologists classify rocks according to their origin. *Igneous rocks* form when molten rock cools and solidifies. *Sedimentary rocks*

Earth's three kinds of rocks

Geologists classify rocks into three main kinds, according to their origin: (1) igneous, (2) sedimentary, and (3) metamorphic. Each type of rock is formed through a different process.

© Joyce Photographics from Photo Researchers

Granite, an igneous rock, is formed mainly by the slow cooling of molten rock from deep inside the crust.

© Joe McDonald, Bruce Coleman Inc.

Limestone, a sedimentary rock, forms when the mineral calcite from the shells of marine organisms solidifies into rock.

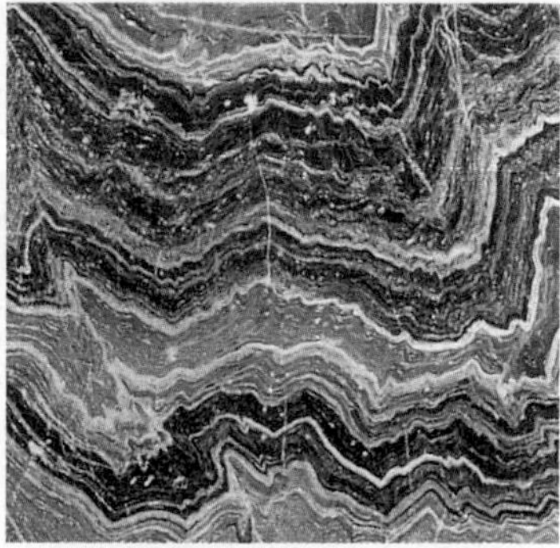

© Lee Boltin

Schist and other metamorphic rocks result when igneous and sedimentary rocks are changed by heat and pressure.

form when grains of rock or dissolved chemicals are deposited in layers by wind, water, or glaciers. Over time, the layers harden into solid rock. *Metamorphic rocks* develop deep in Earth's crust when heat or pressure transform other types of rock.

Igneous rocks form from molten material called *magma.* Most of Earth's interior is solid, not molten, but it is extremely hot. At the base of Earth's crust, the temperature is about 1800 °F (1000 °C). In some portions of the crust, conditions are right for rocks to melt. Rocks can melt more easily near the crust if they contain water, which lowers their melting point.

Where conditions are right, small pockets of magma form beneath and within the crust. Some of this magma reaches the surface, where it erupts from volcanoes as lava. Igneous rocks formed this way are called *volcanic* or *extrusive.* Vast quantities of magma, however, never reach the surface. They cool slowly within the crust and may only be exposed long afterward by erosion. Such igneous rocks are called *plutonic* or *intrusive.* Plutonic rocks cool slowly. During this slow cooling, their minerals form large crystals. Plutonic rocks tend to be much coarser than volcanic rocks.

Igneous rocks that are rich in silica tend to be poor in iron and magnesium, and the opposite is also true. Volcanic rocks that are iron-rich and silica-poor are basalt. Plutonic rocks of the same makeup are called *gabbro.* Silica-rich volcanic rocks are called *rhyolite (RY uh lyt),* and plutonic rocks of the same composition are granite. Granite lies under most of the continents, while basalt lies under most of the ocean floors.

Sedimentary rocks. Rocks on Earth's surface are under constant attack by chemicals and mechanical forces. The processes that break down rocks are called *weathering.* Water is effective at dissolving minerals. When water freezes, it expands, so expanding ice helps pry apart mineral grains in rocks. In addition, living things produce chemicals that help dissolve rocks.

Once rocks break apart, the loose material is often carried away by erosion. Running water erodes rocks. Wind and glaciers also contribute to erosion. Erosion is usually a relatively slow process, but over millions of years, erosion can uncover even rocks many miles or kilometers below the surface.

Materials derived from weathering and erosion of rocks are eventually deposited to form sedimentary rocks. Rocks that are made up of small pieces of other rocks are called *clastic rocks.* Rocks containing larger pebbles are called *conglomerate.* The particles in these conglomerate rocks are cemented together when minerals dissolved in the water crystallize between the grains. The most abundant sedimentary rocks, called *mudrocks,* consist of tiny particles. Some of these rocks, called *shale,* split into thin sheets when broken. Sandstone is a sedimentary rock made up of sand cemented together.

Other sedimentary rocks form when dissolved materials undergo chemical reactions and settle out as tiny solid particles. These rocks are called *chemical sedimentary rocks.* Common chemical sedimentary rocks include some types of limestone and dolomite. Some chemical sedimentary rocks form when water evaporates, leaving dissolved materials behind. Rock salt and a mineral called *gypsum* form this way.

Some sedimentary rocks, called *biogenic,* are formed by the action of living things. Coal is the remains of woody plants that have been transformed into rock by heat and pressure over time. Most limestone is formed by microscopic marine organisms that secrete protective shells of calcium carbonate. After the animals die, the shells remain and solidify into limestone.

Metamorphic rocks. When rocks are buried deeply, they become hot. Earth's crust grows hotter by about 70 °F per mile (25 °C per kilometer) of depth. Pressure also increases with depth. At a depth of 1 mile (1.6 kilometers) beneath the surface, the pressure is about 6,000 pounds per square inch (41,360 kilopascals). As rocks are heated and subjected to pressure, minerals react and the rocks become metamorphic. Shale is transformed to slate, limestone, and eventually into marble under pressure. Many metamorphic rocks contain recognizable features that tell of their origin, but others change so much that only the chemical makeup provides evidence of what they originally were.

Cycles on and in Earth

Earth can be thought of as a huge system of interacting cycles. In each cycle, matter and energy move from place to place and may change form. Eventually, matter and energy return to their original condition and the cycle begins again. The cycles affect everything on the planet, from the weather to the shape of the landscape. There are many cycles on and within Earth. A few of the most important are (1) atmospheric circulation, (2) ocean currents, (3) the global heat conveyor, (4) the hydrologic cycle, and (5) the rock cycle.

Atmospheric circulation. Air warmed by the sun near the equator rises and flows toward Earth's poles, returning to the surface and flowing back to the equator. This motion, combined with the rotation of Earth, moves heat and moisture around the planet creating winds and weather patterns.

In some areas, the winds change directions with the seasons. These patterns are often called *monsoons.* In summer, air over Asia is heated by the sun, rises, and draws moist air from the Indian Ocean, causing daily rains over most of southern Asia. In winter, the air over Asia cools, sinks, and flows out, pushing the moist air away and creating dry weather. A similar pattern occurs in the Pacific Ocean near Mexico and brings moist air and afternoon thunderstorms to the southwestern United States in the summer.

Ocean currents are driven by the winds and follow the same general pattern. The continents block the flow of water around the globe, so ocean currents flow west near the equator, then turn toward the poles when they strike a continent, turn east, then flow back to the equator on the other side. In all the oceans, the currents form great loops called *gyres.* The gyres flow clockwise north of the equator and counterclockwise south of it.

The global heat conveyor is an enormous cycle of ocean water that distributes the oceans' heat around Earth. Water in the polar regions is very cold, salty, and dense. It sinks and flows along the sea floor toward the equator. Eventually, the water rises along the margins of the continents and merges with the surface water flow. When it reaches the polar regions, it sinks again. This three-dimensional movement of water mixes heat throughout the oceans, warming polar waters. It also brings nutrients up from the deep ocean to the surface, where they are available for marine plants and animals.

The hydrologic cycle. Water from the oceans evaporates and is carried by the atmosphere, eventually falling as rain or snow. Water that falls on the land helps break rocks down chemically, nourishes plants, and wears down the landscape. Eventually, the water returns to the sea to start the cycle over again.

The rock cycle. Earth has many more kinds of rocks compared to other planets because there are so many processes acting to form and break down rocks. Geologists sometimes speak of the *rock cycle* to explain how different rock types are related. The cycle may begin with a flow of lava from a volcano cooling to form new igneous rocks on Earth's surface. As the rock is exposed to water, it breaks down and the resulting materials may be carried away to be deposited as sedimentary rocks. These rocks may eventually be so deeply buried that they change in form to become metamorphic rocks. They may even melt, creating the raw material for the next generation of igneous rocks.

Rocks rarely go through the entire rock cycle. Instead, some steps may be skipped or repeated. For example, igneous rocks can be subjected to heat and pressure and transformed directly to metamorphic rocks. Sedimentary rocks can be broken down by weathering and then reassembled into a new generation of sedimentary rocks. Metamorphic rocks can also be weathered to form the raw material for a new generation of sedimentary rocks. Any rock type, igneous, metamorphic, or sedimentary, can be transformed into any other type.

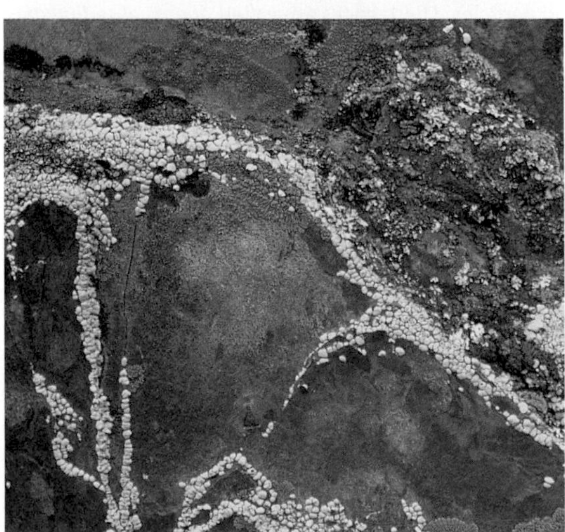

Lichens help to form soil. These rootless, plantlike organisms produce an acid that dissolves parts of rocks. Bits of rock then mix with decaying matter to form soil.

Flowing water erodes rocks, dissolving minerals and depositing them elsewhere. Over millions of years, water can carve deep channels into solid rock, such as this sandstone in Arizona.

Earth's interior

Geologists cannot study the interior of Earth directly. The deepest wells drilled reach less than 8 miles (13 kilometers) below the surface. Geologists know that the whole Earth differs in composition from its thin outer crust. Deep in Earth, pressures are so great that minerals can be compressed into dense forms not found on the surface.

One way geologists determine the overall composition of Earth is from chemical analysis of meteorites. Certain types of meteorites, called *chondrites,* are remains of the early solar system that persisted unchanged in space until they fell to Earth. Geologists can use chondrites to estimate the original chemical composition of the entire Earth.

Unlike chondrites, Earth is made up of layers that contain different amounts of various chemical elements. Geologists learn about Earth's interior by studying vibrations generated by earthquakes, using instruments called *seismographs.* The speed and motion of vibrations traveling through Earth depends on the composition and density of the material they travel through. Geologists can determine many properties of Earth's interior by analyzing such vibrations.

The mantle. Beneath the crust, extending down about 1,800 miles (2,900 kilometers), is a thick layer called the mantle. The mantle is not perfectly stiff but can flow slowly. Earth's crust floats on the mantle much as a board floats in water. Just as a thick board would rise above the water higher than a thin one, the thick continental crust rises higher than the thin oceanic crust. The slow motion of rock in the mantle moves the continents around and causes earthquakes, volcanoes, and the formation of mountain ranges.

The core. At the center of Earth is the core. The core is made mostly of iron and nickel and possibly smaller amounts of lighter elements, including sulfur and oxygen. The core is about 4,400 miles (7,100 kilometers) in diameter, slightly larger than half the diameter of Earth and about the size of Mars. The outermost 1,400 miles (2,250 kilometers) of the core are liquid. Currents flowing in the core are thought to generate Earth's magnetic field. Geologists believe the innermost part of the core, about 1,600 miles (2,600 kilometers) in diameter, is made of a similar material as the outer core, but it is solid. The inner core is about four-fifths as big as Earth's moon.

Earth gets hotter toward the center. At the bottom of the continental crust, the temperature is about 1800 °F (1000 °C). The temperature increases about 3 °F per mile (1 °C per kilometer) below the crust. Geologists believe the temperature of Earth's outer core is about 6700 to 7800 °F (3700 to 4300 °C). The inner core may be as hot as 12,600 °F (7000 °C)—hotter than the surface of the sun. But, because it is under great pressures, the rock in the center of Earth remains solid.

Earth's crust

The hot rock deep in Earth's mantle flows upward slowly, while cooler rock near the surface sinks because hot materials are lighter than cool materials. The rising and sinking of materials due to differences in temperature is called *convection.* As Earth's mantle flows, it breaks the crust into a number of large slabs called *tectonic plates,* much as slabs of ice break apart on a pond. The slow flow of Earth's mantle drags the crust along, causing the continents to move, mountains to form, and volcanoes and earthquakes to occur. This constant motion of Earth's crust is called *plate tectonics.*

In some places, usually under the oceans, Earth's plates are spreading apart. New magma from the mantle rises to fill the cracks between the plates. Places where plates spread apart are called *spreading centers.* Many

© Danilo G. Donadoni, Bruce Coleman Inc.

Glaciers scour valleys and flatten landscapes. The heavy mass of ice grinds away rock, which it carries away in dark ribbons and leaves behind as a ridge called a *moraine* when it melts.

© David Muench

Wind erosion sculpted Delicate Arch in Utah from a wall of ancient sandstone. Wind-driven sand wore away soft parts of the rock to reveal the unusual shape.

volcanoes occur where plates pull apart and magma wells up from within the mantle to fill the gap. The material from the mantle is made of iron and magnesium-rich silicate rocks. It hardens to form rocks and creates oceanic crust made of basalt.

Subduction. Earth's crust cannot spread apart everywhere. Somewhere, an equal amount of crust must be removed. When two plates push together, one of the plates sinks back into Earth's mantle, a process called *subduction.* The sinking plate eventually melts into magma in Earth's interior. Much of the magma created in subduction zones does not reach the surface and cools within the crust, forming plutonic rocks. The heat from the magma also helps create metamorphic rocks.

Continental crust is too thick and light to sink into Earth's interior, so only plates of dense oceanic crust are subducted. The boundary where the two plates meet is marked by a deep trench on the ocean floor. The trenches are the deepest places in the oceans, up to 36,000 feet (11,000 meters) deep.

The upper plate that remains on the surface when two plates collide may be continental crust or oceanic crust. This plate is also changed by subduction. As the two plates move together, the edge of the upper plate is compressed. The crust becomes thicker and higher, creating a mountain range. When the rocks of the sinking plate reach a depth of about 60 to 90 miles (100 to 150 kilometers), they begin to melt and form magma. Some of the magma reaches the surface to form volcanoes. Regions with many volcanoes, such as Peru, Japan, and the northwestern United States, lie near areas where subduction is happening.

Mountain building. Occasionally, as a plate sinks into Earth's mantle, it drags along a continent or a smaller land mass. Continental crust is too thick and light to sink. Instead, it collides with the opposing plate. If the opposing plate is also a continent, neither plate will sink. This type of collision often forms a vast mountain chain in the middle of a continent. The Himalaya were formed in such a way from the collision of two plates of continental crust.

The series of events that happen during formation of a mountain range is called *orogeny.* Orogeny includes the elevation of mountains, folding and crumpling of the rocks, volcanic activity, and formation of plutonic and metamorphic rocks that occur when plates collide. Long after mountains have vanished from erosion, geologists can still see the changes orogeny produces in the rocks.

Terrane collisions. Smaller pieces of continental crust that collide with another plate are often added to the edge of the larger plate. These added pieces of crust are called *terranes.* Most of the land in the United States west of Salt Lake City has been added to North America by terrane collisions in the last 500 million years.

Earthquakes. Earthquakes occur when rocks on opposite sides of a break in the crust, called a *fault,* slide past each other. The boundaries between plates are faults, but there are faults within plates as well. Occasionally, forces within the plates cause rocks to fracture and slip even though the rocks are not at a plate boundary. The boundaries between two plates sliding past each other are called *transform faults.* The San Andreas Fault in California is a transform fault, where a portion of crust called the Pacific Plate is carrying a small piece of California northwest past the rest of North America.

The shaping of the continents. Several times in Earth's history, collisions between continents have created a huge *supercontinent.* Although the crust of the continents is thick, it breaks more easily than oceanic crust, and supercontinents broke quickly into smaller pieces. Material from Earth's mantle filled the gaps, creating new oceanic crust. As the continents moved apart, new ocean basins formed between them. About one-third of Earth's surface is covered by continental crust, so the pieces cannot move far before colliding. As two continents collide, an old ocean basin is destroyed. The process of continents breaking apart and rejoining is called the *Wilson cycle,* after the Canadian geologist John Tuzo Wilson, who first described it.

The continents have probably been in motion for at least the past 3.8 billion years. Geologists, however, only have evidence from rocks to understand and reconstruct the motion over the past 800 million years. Most of the oceanic crust older than that has been subducted into the mantle long ago.

Geologists have determined that, about 800 million years ago, the continents were assembled into a large supercontinent called Rodinia. What is now North America lay at the center of Rodinia. The flow of material in Earth's mantle caused Rodinia to break apart into many pieces, which collided again between 500 million and 250 million years ago. Collision between what is now North America, Europe, and Africa caused the uplift of the Appalachian Mountains in North America. Collisions between part of present-day Siberia and Europe created the Ural Mountains.

By 250 million years ago, the continents reassembled to form another supercontinent called Pangaea. A single, worldwide ocean, called Panthalassa, surrounded Pangaea. About 200 million years ago, Pangaea began to break apart. It split into two large land masses called Gondwanaland and Laurasia. Gondwanaland then broke apart, forming the continents of Africa, Antarctica, Australia, and South America, and the Indian subcontinent. Laurasia eventually split apart into Eurasia and North America. As the continental plates split and drifted apart, new oceanic crust formed between them. The movement of the continents to their present positions took place over millions of years.

Earth's changing climate

The ice ages. Throughout the history of Earth, the climate has changed many times. Between 800 million and 600 million years ago, during a time called the Precambrian, Earth experienced several extreme climate changes called *ice ages* or *glacial epochs,* separated by warm periods. The climate may have grown so cold that some scientists believe Earth nearly or completely froze several times. The theory that the entire Earth froze is sometimes called the *snowball Earth.* Other scientists think that the changes from a cold to a warm climate occurred too quickly for Earth to completely freeze.

Most of the time, Earth has been largely ice free. Brief ice ages occurred about 450 million years ago and again about 250 million years ago. In the last few million years, however, Earth's climate began to cool. Glaciers began forming in Antarctica about 35 million years ago, but the climate there was warm enough for trees to grow until

Earth's plates

Earth's crust is broken into many large slabs called *tectonic plates.* The slow flow of the hot, soft rock in the mantle drags the plates along, causing the continents to move in the directions shown by the arrows. Places where plates spread apart, called *spreading centers,* are shown with arrows pointing in opposite directions. Most of Earth's spreading centers are found beneath oceans.

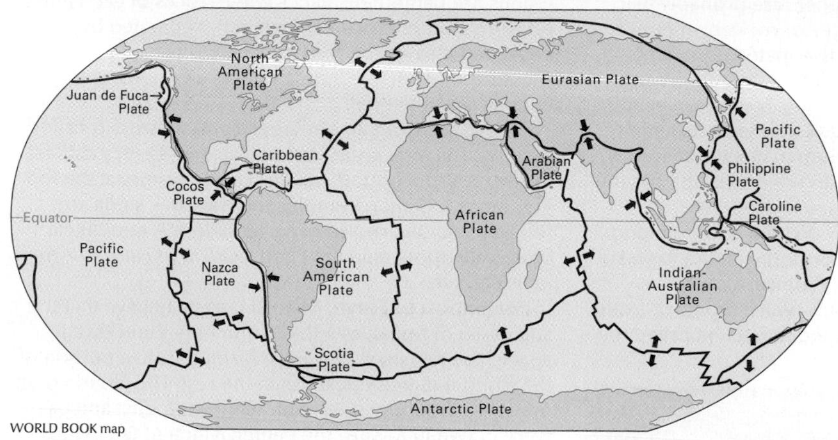

WORLD BOOK map

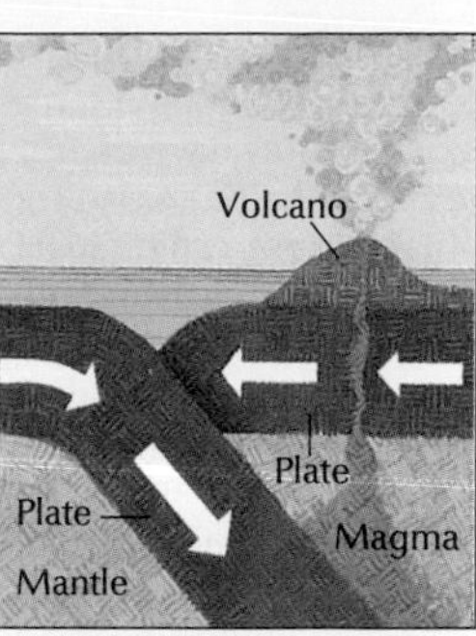

WORLD BOOK illustration by John F. Eggert

When two plates collide, one plate may slide under the other. Some of the plate material melts and then rises as magma. When it reaches the surface, it produces a volcano.

about 5 million years ago. By about 2.6 million years ago, at the beginning of a time called the Pleistocene Epoch, ice had accumulated on other continents as well.

Numerous separate ice advances, periods when ice sheets covered vast areas, occurred during the Pleistocene Ice Age. The advances alternated with periods when the climate was warmer and the ice melted. Geologists analyzing sediment deposits from the North Atlantic Ocean determined that there were at least 20 advances and retreats of ice sheets in the past 2 million years. At least four ice advances were big enough to extend over much of Europe, cover most of Canada, and reach deep into the United States.

The most recent advance of ice began about 70,000 years ago and reached its farthest extent about 18,000 years ago. The vast glaciers and sheets of ice scoured out the basins of the Great Lakes and blocked rivers. So much water was trapped in the form of ice that sea level around Earth dropped as much as 390 feet (120 meters), exposing parts of the present ocean floor.

The most recent ice advance ended about 11,500 years ago. Most scientists believe that Earth is currently in an *interglacial period,* and another ice advance will follow.

Why ice ages occur. Scientists do not fully understand why Earth has ice ages. Most believe that tiny changes in Earth's orbit and axis due to the gravitational pull of other planets play a part. These changes alter the amount of energy received from the sun.

Many scientists also believe that variations in the amount of carbon dioxide in the atmosphere are responsible for long-term changes in the climate. Carbon dioxide, a "greenhouse gas," traps heat from the sun and warms Earth's atmosphere. Most of Earth's carbon dioxide is locked in carbonate rocks, such as limestone and dolomite. Earth's climate today would be much warmer if the carbon dioxide trapped in limestone were released into the atmosphere.

When mountains rich in silicate minerals wear down through weathering and erosion, calcium and magnesium erode from the rocks. These elements are carried to the sea by water. There, living organisms absorb the chemicals and use them to make protective carbonate shells. The organisms eventually die and sink to the bottom to form limestone deposits. This process, called the *carbonate-silicate cycle,* removes carbon dioxide from the atmosphere. With less carbon dioxide in the atmosphere to trap heat from the sun, Earth's climate may cool enough to cause an ice age.

Limestone and dolomite deposits exposed to weathering and erosion return carbon dioxide to the atmosphere and contribute to global warming. In addition, some limestone on the ocean floor can be carried down into Earth's mantle by subduction. Beneath the crust, the limestone breaks down into magma under heat and pressure. The carbon dioxide in the limestone can then return to the atmosphere during volcanic eruptions.

Scientists theorize that volcanoes continued to emit carbon dioxide into the atmosphere during the Precambrian ice ages. Eventually, the carbon dioxide warmed Earth through the greenhouse effect, causing the ice to melt rapidly.

History of Earth

The history of Earth is recorded in the rocks of Earth's crust. Rocks have been forming, wearing away, and reforming ever since Earth took shape. The products of weathering and erosion are called *sediment.* Sediment accumulates in layers known as *strata.* Strata contain clues that tell geologists about Earth's past. These clues include the composition of the sediment, the way the strata are deposited, and the kinds of fossils that may occur in the rock.

Space exploration has expanded our understanding of Earth's origin. The Hubble Space Telescope has observed what appear to be stars in the process of forming planets. Since the mid-1990's, scientists have found other stars that have planets surrounding them. These discoveries have helped scientists develop theories about the formation of Earth.

Age of Earth. Scientists think that Earth probably formed at about the same time as the rest of the solar system. They have determined that some chondrite meteorites, the unaltered remains from the formation of the solar system, are up to 4.6 billion years old. Scientists believe that Earth and other planets are probably that old. They can determine the ages of rocks by measuring the amounts of natural radioactive materials, such as uranium, in them. Radioactive elements *decay* (change into other elements) at a known rate. For example, uranium gives off radiation and decays into lead. Scientists know the time it takes for uranium to change to lead. They can determine the age of a rock by comparing the amount of uranium to the amount of lead.

The known history of Earth is divided into four long stretches of time called *eons.* Starting with the earliest, the eons are Hadean, Archean, Proterozoic, and Phanerozoic. The first three eons, which together lasted nearly 4 billion years, are grouped into a unit called the Precambrian. The Phanerozoic Eon, when life became abundant, is divided into three *eras.* They are, from the oldest to the youngest, the Paleozoic, Mesozoic, and Cenozoic eras. Eras are divided into *periods,* and periods are divided into *epochs.* These divisions and subdivisions are named for places where rocks of each period were studied. Periods are mostly separated by important changes in the types of fossils found in the rocks. As a result, the lengths of eras, periods, and epochs are not equal.

A chart showing an outline of Earth's history is called a *geological time scale.* On such a chart, Earth's earliest history is at the bottom, and its recent history at the top. This arrangement resembles the way rock strata are formed, with the recent over the oldest. A geological time scale appears in the chart *Outline of Earth's history* in this article.

Formation of Earth. Most scientists believe that the solar system began as a thin cloud of gas and dust in space. The sun itself may have formed from a portion of the cloud that was thicker than the rest. The cloud's own gravity caused it to start contracting, and dust and gas were drawn in toward the center. Much of the cloud collapsed to the center to form a star, the sun, but a great ring of material remained orbiting around the star. Particles in the ring collided to make larger objects, which in turn collided to build up the planets of the solar system in a process called *accretion.* Scientists believe that many small planets formed and then collided to make larger planets.

Earth's early development. Scientists theorize that Earth began as a waterless mass of rock surrounded by a cloud of gas. Radioactive materials in the rock and increasing pressure in Earth's interior produced enough heat to melt the interior of Earth. The heavy materials, such as iron, sank. The light silicate rocks rose to Earth's surface and formed the earliest crust. The heat of the interior caused other chemicals inside Earth to rise to the surface. Some of these chemicals formed water, and others became the gases of the atmosphere.

In 2001, an international team of scientists announced the discovery of a crystal of the mineral *zircon* that they determined to be 4.4 billion years old. Zircon, made up of the elements zirconium, silicon, and oxygen, is a hard, long-lasting mineral that resists erosion and weathering. Through chemical analysis of the zircon, the scientists determined that liquid water probably existed on Earth's surface when the crystal was formed. They concluded that Earth's crust and oceans may have formed within about 200 million years after the planet had taken shape.

Astronomers believe that the sun was about 30 percent fainter when Earth first formed than it is today. The oldest rocks on Earth, however, provide evidence that Earth was warm enough for liquid water to exist on the surface. Scientists believe that the atmosphere must have trapped more heat from the sun than it does today. Over millions of years, the water slowly collected in low places of the crust and formed oceans.

After the main period of planet formation, most of the remaining debris in the solar system was swept up by the newly formed planets. The collisions of the newly formed planets and debris material were explosive. The impacts created the cratered surfaces of the moon, Mars, Venus, and Mercury. Earth was also struck, but

Layers of sedimentary rock called *strata* provide clues to Earth's history. The dark layers here contain iron oxide, evidence that Earth's atmosphere contained oxygen 2 billion years ago.

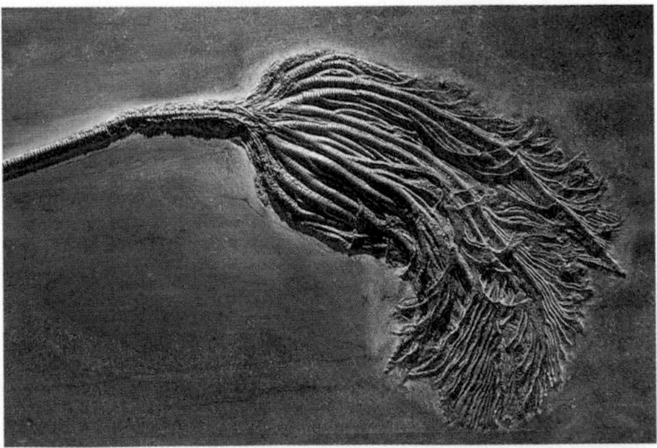

Fossils provide clues about the history of life on Earth. This fossil *crinoid* (sea lily) is preserved in limestone that formed during the Jurassic Period, about 145 million years ago.

the craters produced by the impacts have all been destroyed by erosion and plate tectonics. There is evidence that plate tectonics has been active for at least 3.8 billion years.

Some scientists believe that Earth's early atmosphere contained hydrogen, helium, methane, and ammonia, much like the present atmosphere of Jupiter. Others believe it may have contained a large amount of carbon dioxide, as does the atmosphere of Venus. Scientists agree that Earth's earliest atmosphere probably had little oxygen.

Geologists have determined that, about 2 billion years ago, a change in Earth's atmosphere occurred. They know that because certain kinds of iron ores created in oxygen-poor environments stopped forming at that time. Instead, large deposits of red sandstone formed. The red color results from iron reacting with oxygen to form *iron oxide,* or rust. The sandstone deposits are evidence that Earth's atmosphere contained some oxygen. The air was not breathable at that time, but the atmosphere may have had about 1 percent oxygen.

The oxygen in the atmosphere today comes mainly from plants and microorganisms such as algae. These organisms use carbon dioxide and give off oxygen through the process of photosynthesis. The amount of oxygen increased in the atmosphere of the early Earth as oxygen-producing organisms developed and became more plentiful.

Life on Earth. Many rocks contain fossils that reveal the history of life on Earth. A fossil may be an animal's body, a tooth, or a piece of bone. It may simply be an impression of a plant or an animal made in a rock when the rock was soft sediment. Fossils help scientists learn which kinds of plants and animals lived at different times in Earth's history. Scientists who study prehistoric life are called *paleontologists.*

Many scientists believe that life appeared on Earth almost as soon as conditions allowed. There is evidence for chemicals created by living things in rocks from the Archean age, 3.8 billion years old. Fossil remains of microscopic living things about 3.5 billion years old have also been found at sites in Australia and Canada.

For most of Earth's history, life consisted mainly of microscopic, single-celled creatures. The earliest fossils of larger creatures with many cells are found in Precambrian rocks that are about 650 million years old. Many of these creatures differed from any living things today.

The Paleozoic Era. Fossils become abundant in Cambrian rocks that are about 542 million to 488 million years old. This apparently sudden expansion in the number of life forms in the fossil record is called the Cambrian Explosion, and it marks the beginning of the Paleozoic Era. The Cambrian Explosion actually occurred over tens of millions of years, but it appears sudden in the fossil record. The earliest abundant fossils consist of only a few kinds of organisms. Over the course of hundreds of millions of years, the number of species increases gradually in the fossil record.

Most fossil organisms found in Paleozoic rocks are *invertebrates* (animals without a backbone), such as corals, *mollusks* (clams and snails), and *trilobites* (flat-shelled sea animals). Fish, the earliest *vertebrates* (animals with a backbone), are first found in Ordovician rocks about 450 million years old. Ordovician rocks about 470 million years old contain the oldest known fossil evidence of land plants. The first *tetrapods* (four-legged animals) to live on land appear as fossils in Devonian rocks about 380 million years old.

Fossil remains preserved in rocks show that by 300 million years ago, large forests and swamps covered the land. The carbon-rich remains of some of these forests are preserved as coal deposits in the United States, Canada, the United Kingdom, and other parts of the world. The Carboniferous Period is named for these enormous deposits of coal.

The earliest fossil remains of *amniotes* are found in rocks of the Carboniferous Period. Amniotes lay eggs with leathery shells that can develop away from the water. These eggs gave amniotes an advantage over amphibianlike tetrapods that had to return to water to lay their eggs. Toward the end of the Paleozoic Era, in rocks from the Permian Period, some fossil amniotes begin to show some characteristics of mammals.

Several times in Earth's history, there have been great *extinctions,* periods when many of Earth's living things die out. The greatest of these events, called the Permian extinction, happened about 251 million years ago. As much as 95 percent of the species on Earth during the Permian became extinct in a relatively short time. The cause of this event is a mystery, though many scientists suspect that huge volcanic eruptions in what is now Siberia may have disturbed the climate, causing many organisms to die out.

The Mesozoic Era. Following the Permian extinction, the fossil record shows that reptiles became the dominant animals on land. The most spectacular of these reptiles were the dinosaurs. The Mesozoic is often called the Age of the Reptiles, but mammals and birds also appear in the fossil record in rocks from 200 million to 140 million years old.

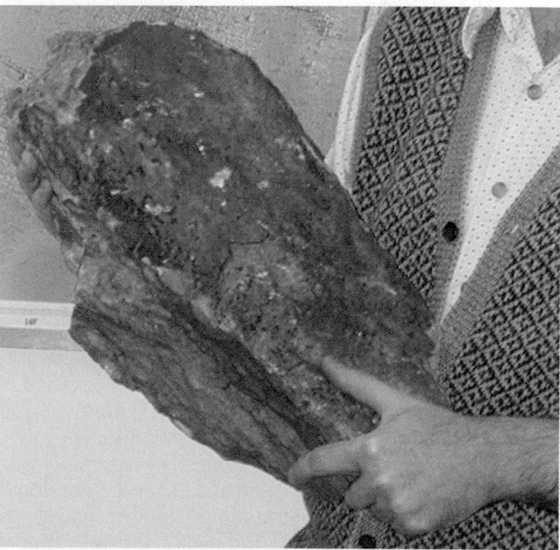

The oldest materials on Earth are crystals of *zircon,* a hard, durable mineral. In 2001, geologists announced that a single crystal of zircon, found in this piece of sandstone from Australia, was formed about 4.4 billion years ago. Scientists believe that Earth itself formed about 4.6 billion years ago.

WORLD BOOK illustration by Ian Jackson, WILDlife Art

Precambrian time included roughly Earth's first 4 billion years. The crust, the atmosphere, and the oceans were formed, and the simplest kinds of life appeared.

© Darwin Wiggett, First Light

Precambrian rocks exposed on Earth's surface are often highly weathered. This portion of the Canadian Shield, a region of ancient crust near Lake Superior, is about 2.5 billion years old.

WORLD BOOK illustration by Ian Jackson, WILDlife Art

The Paleozoic Era saw the development of many kinds of animals and plants in the seas and on land. Fossil evidence of the earliest known land plants is about 470 million years old.

© Michael T. Sedam, Corbis

Paleozoic sandstones make up part of the rock formations in Monument Valley, Utah. The rocks that once surrounded these formations have been worn away by weathering and erosion.

Fossil plants of the Mesozoic Era represent two main groups, *gymnosperms* and *angiosperms*. Gymnosperms have naked seeds, and most are cone-bearing. They include conifers, cycads, and ginkgoes. These gymnosperms evolved in the late Paleozoic Era and were dominant into the Cretaceous Period. Angiosperms have covered seeds and are flowering plants. They became the dominant plant group after the Cretaceous Period and continue to be so today.

The dinosaurs died out in another great extinction about 65 million years ago. Most scientists believe that the extinction was caused by the impact of an asteroid with Earth. The impact would have thrown so much dust into the atmosphere that the surface would have been dark and cold for months, killing off plants and the animals that fed on them. Scientists believe a large, buried crater in the Yucatan region of Mexico, called Chicxulub *(CHEEK shoo loob)*, is the place the asteroid struck. Debris from the collision has been found all over the world, and deposits created by large sea waves caused by the impact have been found in several places around the Gulf of Mexico.

The Cenozoic Era. The wide variety of plants and animals that we know today came into existence during

WORLD BOOK illustration by Ian Jackson, WILDlife Art

The Mesozoic Era was the Age of Reptiles. Plant-eating dinosaurs, such as this *Stegosaurus,* fed on cycads and conifers, early trees that thrived before modern flowering trees appeared.

© Ric Ergenbright Photography

Mesozoic chalk cliffs in Dover, England, formed under warm shallow seas during the Cretaceous Period, late in the Mesozoic. Movement of Earth's crust later pushed the rock above sea level.

WORLD BOOK illustration by Ian Jackson, WILDlife Art

The Cenozoic Era included the Pleistocene Ice Age, when glaciers swept slowly across large areas before melting. The moving ice created a variety of landscapes in northern lands.

© Douglas Faulkner, Photo Researchers

Cenozoic glaciers often carried huge rocks far from their place of origin. Melting ice left these boulders, called *erratics,* on the ground when the Pleistocene age ended thousands of years ago.

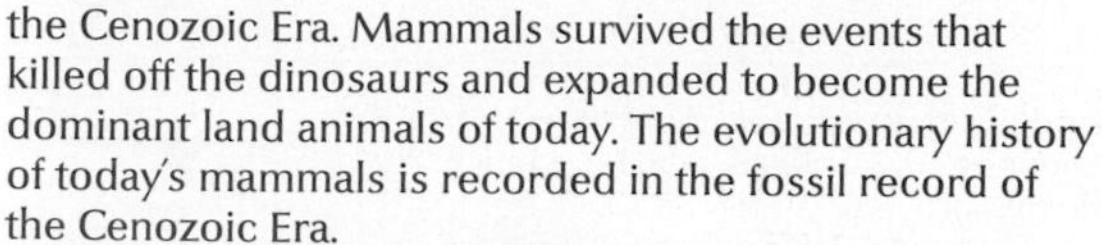

the Cenozoic Era. Mammals survived the events that killed off the dinosaurs and expanded to become the dominant land animals of today. The evolutionary history of today's mammals is recorded in the fossil record of the Cenozoic Era.

During the Eocene Epoch, ancestors of the horse, rhinoceros, and camel roamed Europe and North America. By the Oligocene Epoch, dogs and cats had appeared, along with three-toed horses about as large as sheep. The mammals grew larger and developed in greater variety as prairies spread over the land during the Miocene Epoch.

By the Pliocene Epoch, many kinds of mammals had grown to gigantic size. Elephantlike mammoths and mastodons and giant ground sloths roamed the prairies and forests. These animals died out at the end of the Pleistocene Epoch.

Fossils of the first human beings appeared on Earth approximately 2 million years ago. The first modern human beings appeared later, perhaps less than 200,000 years ago. Humanity's years on Earth are only a brief moment among the billions of years during which Earth has developed.

Steven I. Dutch

Outline of Earth's history

This geological time scale outlines the development of Earth and of life on Earth. Earth's earliest history appears at the bottom of the chart, and its most recent history is at the top. This chart is based on information from the International Commission on Stratigraphy.

Era	Period	Period or epoch	Range (years ago)	Development of life on Earth	
Cenozoic Era	Quaternary Period	Holocene Epoch	11,500 to present	Human beings hunted and tamed animals; developed agriculture; learned to use metals, coal, oil, gas, and other resources; and put the power of wind and rivers to work.	Cultivated plants
		Pleistocene Epoch	2.6 million to 11,500	Modern human beings developed. Mammoths, woolly rhinos, and other animals flourished but died out near the end of the epoch.	Human beings
	Neogene Period	Pliocene Epoch	5.3 million to 2.6 million	Sea life became much like today's. Birds and mammals continued to develop into more modern forms and spread around the world.	Horses
		Miocene Epoch	23 million to 5.3 million	A greater variety of apes appeared in Asia and Africa. There were bats, monkeys, and whales, and primitive bears and raccoons. Flowering plants and trees resembled modern kinds.	Apes
	Paleogene Period	Oligocene Epoch	34 million to 23 million	Primitive apes appeared. Camels, cats, dogs, elephants, horses, rhinos, and rodents developed. Huge rhinoceroslike animals disappeared near the end of the epoch.	Early horses
		Eocene Epoch	56 million to 34 million	Birds, amphibians, small reptiles, and fish were plentiful. Primitive bats, camels, cats, horses, monkeys, rhinoceroses, and whales appeared.	Grasses
		Paleocene Epoch	65 million to 56 million	Flowering plants became plentiful. Invertebrates, fish, amphibians, reptiles, and mammals were common.	Small mammals
Mesozoic Era		Cretaceous Period	145 million to 65 million	Flowering plants appeared. Invertebrates and amphibians were plentiful. Many fish resembled modern kinds. Dinosaurs with horns and armor became common. Dinosaurs died out.	Flowering plants
		Jurassic Period	200 million to 145 million	Cone-bearing trees were plentiful. Sea life included shelled squid. Dinosaurs reached their largest size. The first birds appeared. Mammals were small and primitive.	Birds
		Triassic Period	251 million to 200 million	Cone-bearing trees were plentiful, as were fish and insects. The first turtles, crocodiles, and dinosaurs appeared, as did the first mammals.	Dinosaurs
Paleozoic Era		Permian Period	299 million to 251 million	The first seed plants—cone-bearing trees—appeared. Fish, amphibians, and reptiles were plentiful.	Se pla
	Carboniferous Period	Pennsylvanian Epoch	318 million to 299 million	Scale trees, ferns, and giant scouring rushes were abundant. Fish and amphibians were plentiful. The first reptiles appeared. Giant insects lived in forests where coal later formed.	Reptiles
		Mississippian Epoch	359 million to 318 million	Trilobites had nearly died out. Crustaceans, fish, and amphibians were plentiful. Many coral reefs were formed.	Amphibians
		Devonian Period	416 million to 359 million	The first forests grew in swamps. Many kinds of fish, including sharks, armored fish, and lungfish, swam in the sea and in fresh waters. The first amphibians and insects appeared.	Fish
		Silurian Period	444 million to 416 million	Trilobites and mollusks were common. Coral reefs formed.	Corals
		Ordovician Period	488 million to 444 million	Spore-bearing land plants appeared. Trilobites, corals, and mollusks were common. Tiny animals called graptolites lived in branching *colonies* (groups).	Graptolites
		Cambrian Period	542 million to 488 million	Fossils were plentiful for the first time. Shelled animals called trilobites, and some mollusks, were common in the sea. Jawless fish appeared.	Trilobites
Precambrian time			4 ½ billion (?) to 542 million	Coral, jellyfish, and worms lived in the sea about 1,100 million years ago. Bacteria lived as long ago as 3 ½ billion years. Before that, no living things are known.	Bacteria

60 million years ago
Paleocene Epoch
Earth's crust consists of rigid plates that shift continually, carrying the world's land masses with them. The map at the right shows the locations of the continents about 60 million years ago. At that time, the continents were approaching their present positions, which are shown in black outline.

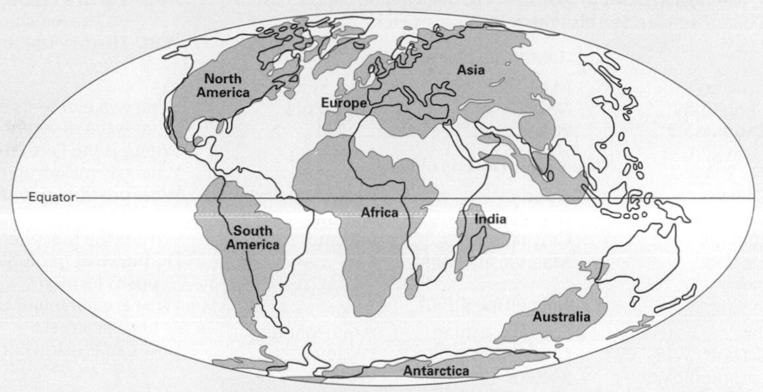

120 million years ago
Cretaceous Period
Scientists theorize that the continents formed from the breakup of two great land masses: (1) Laurasia to the north, and (2) Gondwanaland to the south. The map at the right shows these two land masses as they were breaking apart about 120 million years ago. Laurasia broke up to form Eurasia and North America. Gondwanaland separated into Africa, Antarctica, Australia, India, and South America.

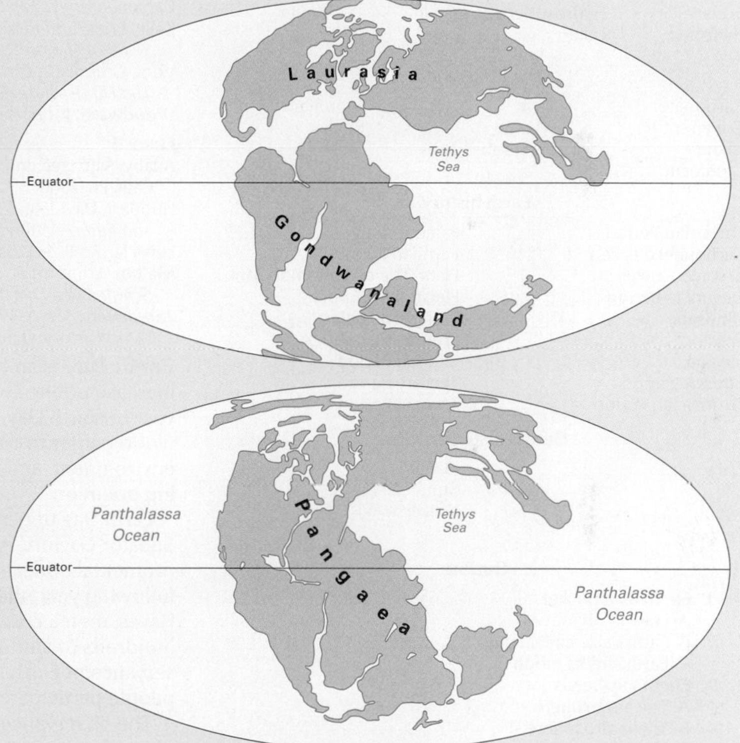

200 million years ago
Triassic/Jurassic Period
Scientists believe that Laurasia and Gondwanaland formed in the breakup of a single giant land mass call Pangaea, *right.* A vast ocean called Panthalassa surrounded Pangaea. Scientists theorize that Pangaea started splitting apart to form Laurasia and Gondwanaland about 200 million years ago.

290 million years ago
Permian Period
Scientists know less about the positions of Earth's land masses before 200 million years ago. They think a number of smaller continents collided to form Pangaea. By 290 million years ago, most of the land had probably joined together, *right.* The developing continent of Pangaea lay largely in the Southern Hemisphere.

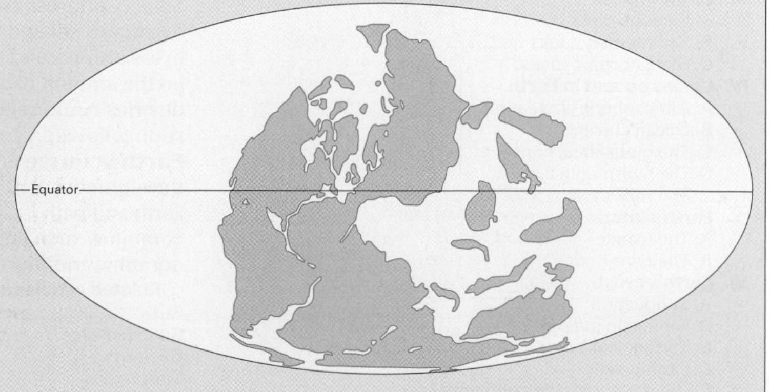

WORLD BOOK maps. Based on University of Chicago Paleographic Atlas Project.

Related articles in *World Book*. See **Geology** and its list of *Related articles*. See also the following articles:

Earth as a planet

Equator
Geography
Geophysics
Map
North Pole
Pole
Solar system
South Pole

Motions and forces of Earth

Climate
Earthquake
Equinox
Erosion
Flood
Glacier
Gravitation
Magnetism (Earth)
Plate tectonics
Season
Volcano

The atmosphere

Air
Carbon cycle
Carbon dioxide
Global warming
Greenhouse effect
Meteor
Stratosphere
Weather
Wind

The hydrosphere

Estuary
Hydrology
Hydrosphere
Lake
Ocean
River
Water

The lithosphere

Carbonate
Continent
Island
Landform
Lava
Mantle
Mineral
Mountain
Rock
Soil

Earth history

Cambrian Period
Carboniferous Period
Cretaceous Period
Devonian Period
Dinosaur
Fossil
Ice age
Jurassic Period
Ordovician Period
Paleontology
Permian Period
Plant (The evolution of plants)
Pleistocene Epoch
Prehistoric animal
Prehistoric people
Silurian Period
Tertiary Period
Triassic Period

Other related articles

Gaia
Life
Moon
Pangaea
Planet
Sun
Universe

Outline

I. Earth as a planet
A. How Earth moves
B. Earth's size and shape
C. Earth and its moon

II. Earth's spheres
A. The atmosphere
B. The hydrosphere
C. The lithosphere
D. The biosphere

III. Earth's rocks
A. Igneous rocks
B. Sedimentary rocks
C. Metamorphic rocks

IV. Cycles on and in Earth
A. Atmospheric circulation
B. Ocean currents
C. The global heat conveyor
D. The hydrologic cycle
E. The rock cycle

V. Earth's interior
A. The mantle
B. The core

VI. Earth's crust
A. Subduction
B. Mountain building
C. Terrane collisions
D. Earthquakes
E. The shaping of the continents

VII. Earth's changing climate
A. The ice ages
B. Why ice ages occur

VIII. History of Earth

Questions

What two elements make up most of the rocks in Earth's crust?
What is the difference between a solar day and a sidereal day?
Where is the Earth-moon barycenter located?
What gas makes up most of Earth's atmosphere?
What possible outcomes can occur when two of Earth's plates collide?
What is the biosphere?
During what geological period were most of Earth's coal deposits formed?
What are the major differences between continental crust and oceanic crust?
How can erosion contribute to global warming?

Additional resources

Level I

Carson, Mary K. *Far-Out Guide to Earth.* Bailey Bks., 2011.
Kelly, Erica, and Kissel, Richard. *Evolving Planet: Four Billion Years of Life on Earth.* Abrams Bks. for Young Readers, 2008.
Vogt, Gregory L. *Earth's Core and Mantle.* 21st Century Bks., 2007. *The Lithosphere: Earth's Crust.* 2007.
Woodward, John. *Planet Earth.* DK Pub., 2009.

Level II

Allaby, Michael, and others. *The Encyclopedia of Earth.* Univ. of Calif. Pr., 2008.
Huddart, David, and Stott, Tim. *Earth Environments: Past, Present and Future.* Wiley, 2010.
Luhr, James F., ed. *Earth.* DK Pub., 2003.
Mathez, Edmond A., and Webster, J. D. *The Earth Machine: The Science of a Dynamic Planet.* Columbia Univ. Pr., 2004
Zalasiewicz, Jan A. T*he Planet in a Pebble: A Journey into Earth's Deep History.* Oxford, 2010.

Earth Day is an annual observance, held on April 22, to increase public awareness of environmental issues. Each year on Earth Day, millions of people throughout the world gather to clean up litter, to protest threats to the environment, and to celebrate progress made in reducing pollution.

Earth Day began in the United States. In 1969, U.S. Senator Gaylord A. Nelson suggested that a day of environmental education be held on college campuses. The following year, the lawyer and environmentalist Denis Hayes, then a recent graduate of Stanford University, led hundreds of students in planning and organizing the observance of Earth Day on April 22, 1970. About 20 million people participated in this celebration.

The observance of Earth Day in 1970 helped alert people to the dangers of pollution and stimulated a new environmental movement. That same year, the United States Congress created the Environmental Protection Agency to set and enforce pollution standards. Congress also passed the Clean Air Act of 1970, which limited the amount of air pollution that cars, utilities, and industries could release. Other new environmental laws soon followed. Denis Hayes

Earth science is the study of Earth and its origin and development. It deals with the makeup and structure of Earth and with its atmosphere and waters. Earth science combines such fields as geology, meteorology, oceanography, and physical geography. Maria Luisa Crawford

Related articles in *World Book* include:

Earth
Geochemistry
Geology
Geophysics
Hydrology
Meteorology
Ocean
Oceanography
Paleontology
Plate tectonics

A massive earthquake can cause incredible damage and great loss of life. This photograph shows damage caused by a magnitude 7.0 earthquake that struck Haiti on Jan. 12, 2010. The quake largely destroyed the Haitian capital, Port-au-Prince, and is estimated to have caused over 200,000 deaths.

Earthquake

Earthquake is a shaking of the ground caused by a sudden shift in Earth's rocky outer shell. Earthquakes rank among the most powerful events on Earth. A severe earthquake may release 10,000 times as much energy as did the first atomic bomb. The results can be terrifying. The shaking can damage buildings, bridges, and other structures so badly that they fall down. Earthquakes can also cause avalanches and landslides on land. In the ocean, quakes can cause a series of huge, destructive waves called a *tsunami (tsoo NAH mee).* After a quake, broken gas or power lines may cause fires. All of these effects can cause the loss of human life.

The force of an earthquake depends on how much the ground shifts. Powerful earthquakes can jolt firm ground violently for great distances. During minor earthquakes, the shaking may be no greater than that caused by a passing truck. Earthquakes can occur just below Earth's surface or at depths down to about 435 miles (700 kilometers) underground.

Scientists think that several million earthquakes occur every year. On average, only about 150,000 of them are strong enough to be felt by humans. Of those, about 15,000 quakes are strong enough to cause significant property damage, and about 150 are strong enough to cause major loss of life.

Scientists monitor quakes using instruments called *seismometers.* These instruments record the *displacement* (change in position) of the ground or a structure. Scientists cannot predict the exact time, place, and *magnitude* (strength) of an earthquake. However, they can often make forecasts about the likelihood of a strong quake for regions with well-known earthquake histories.

Quakes also occur beyond Earth. Scientists have recorded quakes on the moon. They think that quakes have also taken place on other moons and planets, including Mars.

Dangers from earthquakes

Earthquakes almost never kill people directly. Instead, they cause death or injury through falling objects and the collapse of buildings, bridges, and other structures.

Earthquake damage results from the shaking and cracking of ground. Shaking can damage or destroy structures. It can also cause landslides and avalanches. The cracking of ground can break gas and water lines. If the quake displaces the ocean floor up or down, it can produce a tsunami. Hazardous chemical spills may also occur during a quake.

Collapsing buildings cause a large proportion of quake injuries and deaths. Even the most powerful earthquake poses little threat on open ground. However, the shaking can make buildings so unstable that they collapse. The collapsing structures injure, kill, or trap the people inside.

Earthquakes can also cause soft soil to act temporarily like a liquid, rather than a solid. This effect is called *liquefaction.* Anything on top of liquefied soil may sink into the soft ground. This soil may also flow toward lower ground, burying anything in its path. If liquefaction occurs under a building, the building can topple over.

Outline

I. **Dangers from earthquakes**
   A. Collapsing buildings
   B. The cracking of ground
   C. Tsunamis
   D. Landslides or avalanches
   E. Fire
II. **Reducing earthquake damage**
   A. Building design
   B. Building location
III. **How an earthquake begins**
   A. Where a quake begins
   B. Why a quake begins
IV. **How an earthquake spreads**
   A. Body waves
   B. Surface waves
V. **Where earthquakes occur**
   A. Interplate quakes
   B. Intraplate quakes
VI. **Measuring earthquakes**
   A. The Richter scale
   B. The moment magnitude scale
   C. The Modified Mercalli Intensity (MMI) scale
VII. **Predicting earthquakes**
   A. Short-term forecasts
   B. Long-term forecasts
VIII. **Using earthquakes to study Earth's interior**
IX. **Quakes elsewhere in the solar system**

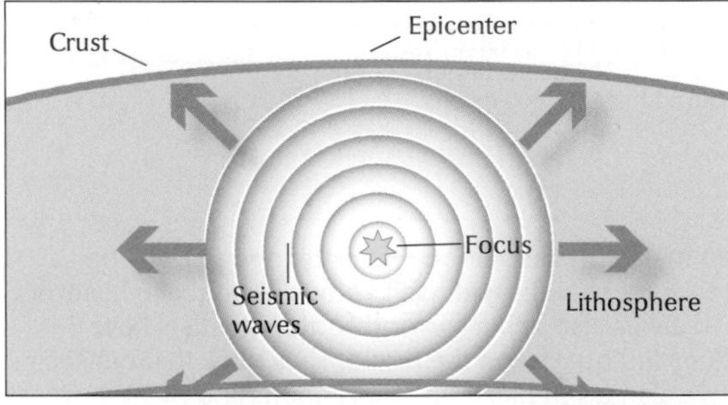

WORLD BOOK illustration

An earthquake occurs when Earth's rock suddenly breaks and shifts, releasing energy in vibrations called *seismic waves.* The point on Earth where the rock first breaks is called the *focus.* The point on the surface above is known as the *epicenter.*

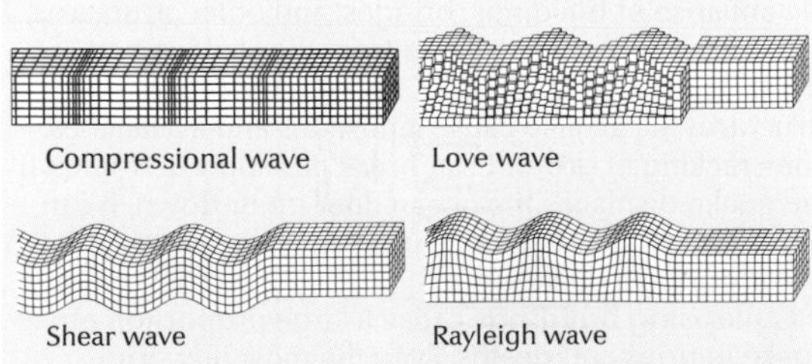

Reprinted with permission of Bruce A. Bolt, from *Nuclear Explosions and Earthquakes: The Parted Veil* (San Francisco: W. H. Freeman and Company. Copyright © 1976).

Different seismic waves travel through rock in different ways. A *compressional wave* travels through Earth, compressing and expanding the rock. When a compressional wave hits the surface, it can cause houses and other structures to contract and expand. A *shear wave* also travels through Earth, moving rock back and forth. At Earth's surface, it can shake structures violently. A *Love wave* travels along Earth's surface and moves the ground from side to side. A *Rayleigh wave* also travels through the rock at the surface, making the surface roll like waves on the ocean.

The cracking of ground in an earthquake can range from minor cracks to large, deep gashes several feet or meters wide. Most earthquakes occur along a *fault.* A fault is a fracture in Earth's rocky outer shell where sections of rock slide past each other. In some cases, one side of the fault can move many feet or meters relative to the other side. Any structures that cross the cracked region—such as bridges, pipelines, power lines, houses, or fences—may be wrenched apart. Cracks in the ground may occur near the fault or in regions of soft sediment farther away.

Tsunamis often occur when an underwater earthquake ruptures a *normal fault* or a *reverse fault,* displacing the sea floor up or down. In a normal or reverse fault, the break in the rocks is more or less vertical. The rocks move up or down along it.

In another type of fault called a *strike-slip fault,* the fracture also extends straight down. However, the blocks of rock slide past each other horizontally. Strike-slip faults on the sea floor seldom cause tsunamis because the sideways motion does not displace the water.

Tsunamis seem small in the open ocean. But they gain height and strength as they enter shallower waters near land. Tsunamis can travel long distances. In 1700, an earthquake in the Pacific Northwest caused a tsunami that was measured in Japan. In 1868, an earthquake off the coast of Arica, Chile, caused a tsunami that reached 2 miles (3.2 kilometers) inland. A 2004 earthquake near the Indonesian island of Sumatra caused a tsunami that spread throughout the Indian Ocean. The tsunami caused death and destruction in coastal areas of Southeast Asia, South Asia, and East Africa.

Landslides or avalanches can be triggered by earthquakes in regions of unstable ground. The 1970 Ancash earthquake in Peru occurred offshore. But it caused a large landslide of ice, mud, and rocks in the nearby Andes Mountains. The landslide buried many thousands of people in the surrounding area. An earthquake in 1958 caused a landslide on Lituya Bay, in Alaska. The landslide entered the water, producing a local tsunami that rushed 1,700 feet (520 meters) up a nearby mountain.

Fire is another consequence of earthquakes in populated regions. Ruptured gas lines are a major fire threat. In addition, the shaking or cracking of the ground can break water pipelines, making it difficult to put out any resulting fires. Fires burning out of control can cause more damage than the original earthquake. For example, fires caused most of the destruction and death associated with the San Francisco earthquake of 1906.

Reducing earthquake damage

Engineers, architects, and city planners can reduce the damage caused by earthquakes through proper planning and building design. Government agencies can regulate land use near faults and enforce strict building codes in regions of hazard. Fixing or removing older structures whose design is not quake resistant can also reduce damage. People can make their homes safer by anchoring large objects, such as appliances and furniture, to the floor or wall. Installing automatic shutoff valves for gas lines is another precaution.

There are two key factors to consider when building in earthquake-prone regions: the design of the structure and its location. Concerns related to location include the

How a tsunami occurs

A tsunami can occur when an underwater earthquake displaces a large part of the sea floor. In this illustration, a tsunami wave spreads from a fast-rising section of ocean floor. The rising plate lifts the water above it, raising a hump of water that quickly ripples outward. As the ripple enters shallow water, it slows and grows in height.

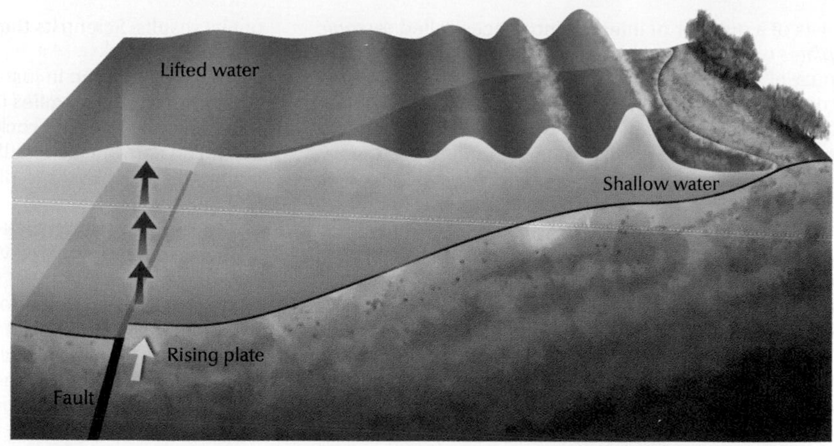

WORLD BOOK illustration by Matt Carrington

type of soil or rock beneath and whether the structure will span a fault. Safe design takes into account the types and frequencies of earthquakes that might occur.

Building design is a key factor in determining how well a structure will withstand earthquakes. Stone or brick buildings with no metal frame, such as adobe houses, can collapse even in small quakes. Single-story wood-frame houses are more flexible. They generally remain standing even during strong shaking. Taller buildings with relatively open first stories—such as those with lower-level parking areas—can collapse more readily. In such buildings, all the energy from the shaking may concentrate at the base, causing the building to fall.

Certain structural elements can make steel-frame buildings more earthquake resistant. For example, *shear walls* might connect the columns. They are strong walls designed to resist the sideways force called *shear,* which causes much earthquake damage. Shear walls in the center of a building, such as those that surround stairwells and elevators, form what is called a *shear core.* Walls may also be reinforced with diagonal beams in a process called *cross-bracing.*

Tall buildings in regions with strong quakes are sometimes built on rollers or shock absorbers. This technique, called *base isolation,* enables the building to move independent of the ground, reducing the violence of shaking. Some modern base isolation systems include electronic motion sensors that adjust the strength of the shock absorbers. These adjustments allow the building to move only as much as the power of the earthquake demands.

Building location affects earthquake safety. The type of ground that is being built upon can influence the choice of building methods. In addition, engineers and architects may avoid building on dirt or soil basins and landfills. Basins and landfills trap and intensify the shaking, making it go on for longer. In addition, soft sediments, such as former lake beds and landfills, can liquefy during strong earthquakes.

It is best to avoid building structures across faults. Movement along a fault can crack the building foundation and possibly cause the building to collapse. In some areas, regulations forbid the construction of large buildings, such as schools, hospitals, or office buildings, close to an active fault. However, pipelines, roads, railroads, and water lines still must cross faults. In these cases, damage due to an earthquake can be reduced several ways. Pipelines can have flexible sections built along the pipe, so that the pipeline can adjust without breaking. Water lines can include an open basin or pond at the fault to catch the water in case of a break.

How an earthquake begins

Where a quake begins. Earthquakes occur in Earth's *crust* (outer layer) and upper *mantle,* the layer directly below the crust. In those two layers, the rocks are brittle enough to crack rapidly. Together, the crust and upper mantle make up the *lithosphere.* The lithosphere con-

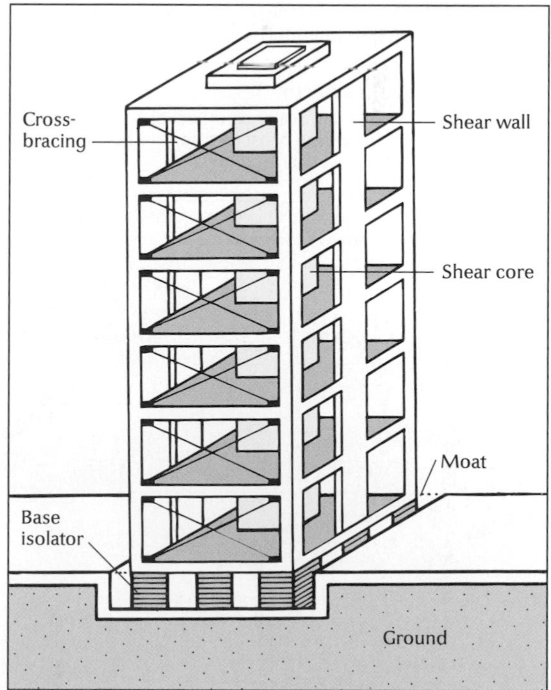

WORLD BOOK illustration by Doug DeWitt

An earthquake-resistant building includes such structures as *shear walls,* a *shear core,* and *cross-bracing. Base isolators* act as shock absorbers. A moat allows the building to sway.

sists of a number of interlocking pieces called *tectonic plates* or *lithospheric plates,* similar to pieces in a jigsaw puzzle. The plates move slowly on an underlying layer of rock. The underlying layer is so hot it flows, even though it remains solid. The plates may move several inches or centimeters per year relative to each other. The theory of how these plates behave is called *plate tectonics.*

Most earthquakes occur at the boundaries where plates meet, also called *faults.* Many plate boundaries are vertical. Earthquakes happen along these faults down to about 20 to 25 miles (30 or 40 kilometers) in depth. Other boundaries lie at an angle, where the edge of one plate sinks and thrusts under the edge of another. This process is called *subduction.* Subduction zone faults start at the surface and may slope downward as deep as about 435 miles (700 kilometers).

The point deep within Earth where an earthquake originates is called the *hypocenter* or *focus.* Scientists identify the hypocenter by giving its latitude, longitude, and depth below the surface. The point on Earth's surface directly above the hypocenter is the *epicenter.* The earthquake may take place entirely underground, or it may reach the surface.

Why a quake begins. The inside of Earth is under enormous *stress* (pressure). The stress comes from the weight of the overlying rocks and the force of the tectonic plates moving. Even though plate motions are slow and constant, the plates do not always slide past one another easily. Instead, strain can build up along a fault, often for decades or centuries. When the stress becomes stronger than the rocks along the fault, the fault *slips*—that is, the rocks on either side suddenly snap into a new position. The snapping releases energy, much as a stretched rubber band releases energy when you let go of one end. When the energy is released, an earthquake results. Scientists then say that the fault has *failed* or *slipped.*

A slip can happen in just seconds. It can move along a fault at speeds of 1.8 miles (3 kilometers) per second.

The surface at which rocks grind against each other during an earthquake is called the *fault plane.* The grinding breaks many rocks to pieces. Stronger rocks in the fault plane, however, can resist more stress without breaking. Such strong rocks may stop the slipping.

The size of the slip area varies. In a small earthquake, the sides of the fault might slip less than ½ inch (1 centimeter) over an area of about 120 square yards (100 square meters). Only seismometers would notice such a slip. During a stronger earthquake, the sides of the fault might slip as much as 33 feet (10 meters). The fault plane might extend hundreds of miles or kilometers long and tens of miles or kilometers deep.

Not all fault motion produces large earthquakes. Some faults slip slower or more often. The movements may last for weeks and can occur as frequently as every six months. They also involve less shifting of the rocks than major earthquakes do. Scientists describe such patterns as *episodic tremor and slip* or *slow earthquakes.*

Other processes outside of plate boundaries can occasionally cause earthquakes. If an area is volcanically active, excess pressure from *magma* (molten rock underground) can suddenly crack the lithosphere, causing an earthquake. The high pressure and temperature of underground volcanic activity may also cause a quake.

Scientists suspect human activities of triggering some earthquakes. The activities that may cause quakes include filling reservoirs, pumping water into drilled holes, and extracting fluids, such as petroleum or *groundwater* (water beneath the surface), from wells. Underground bomb explosions can trigger earthquakes

Where earthquakes occur

This map shows where many major earthquakes have occurred. Each dot on the map represents a major earthquake. Most earthquakes occur near and along the boundaries of the rocky plates that cover Earth's surface.

WORLD BOOK map

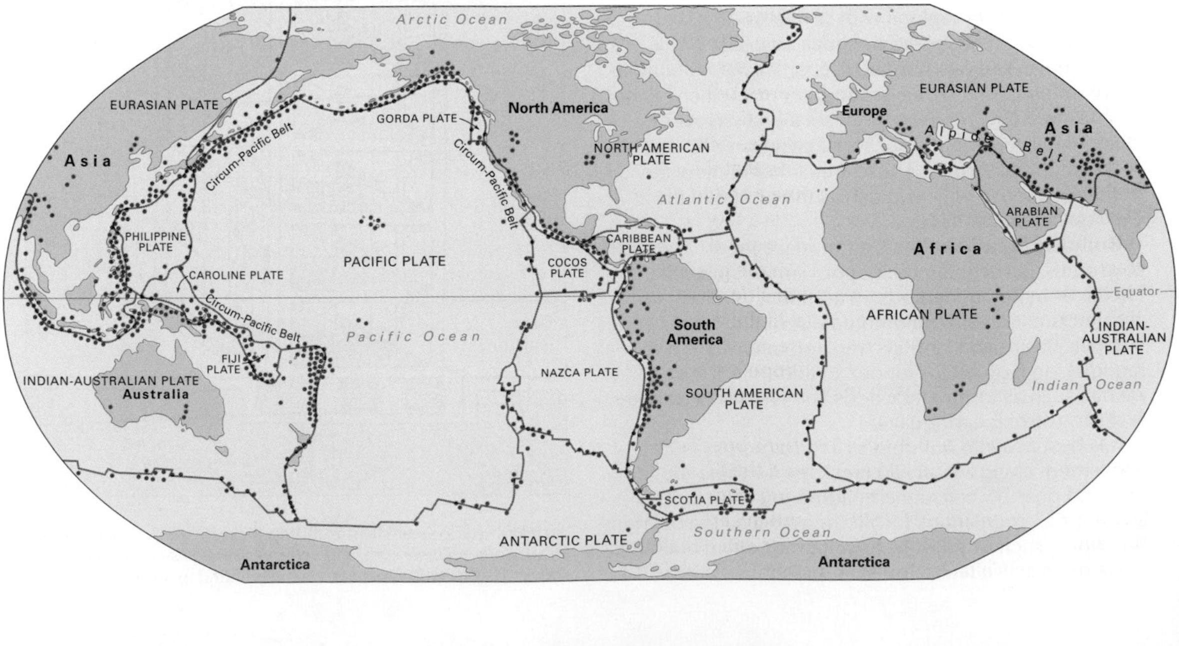

Types of faulting

Movement of the ground called *faulting* causes most earthquakes. In *normal faulting,* two tectonic plates move apart and one drops down. In *reverse faulting,* two plates collide and one is pushed under the other. In *strike-slip faulting,* the plates slide past each other. *Oblique faulting* is a combination of strike-slip faulting and reverse faulting. In oblique faulting, two plates slide past each other as one plate slides under the other.

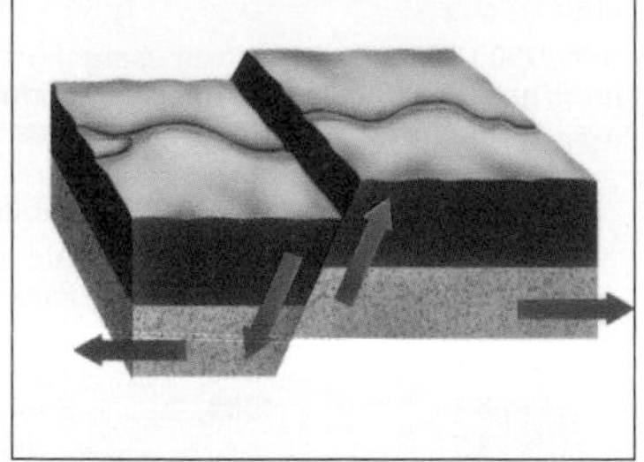

Normal faulting

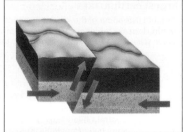

Reverse faulting

Strike-slip faulting

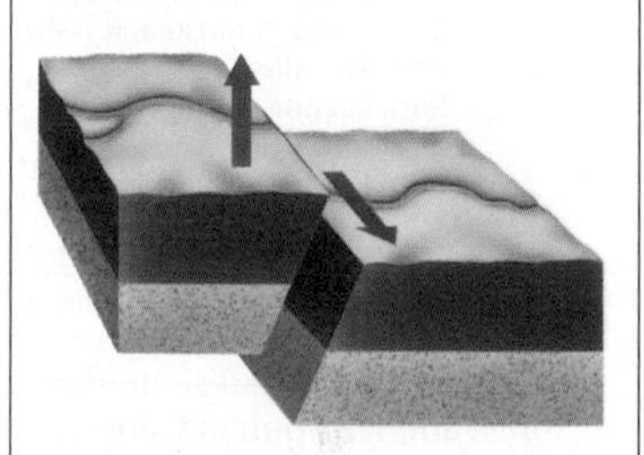

Oblique faulting

WORLD BOOK illustrations

in the area. Even collapses of underground mines can resemble small earthquakes.

How an earthquake spreads

When an earthquake strikes, the energy travels through Earth's crust in waves of vibration called *seismic waves.* Seismic waves move out from the hypocenter in all directions. As the waves travel, they gradually weaken. For this reason, there is generally less shaking farther from the hypocenter.

There are two chief kinds of seismic waves, *body waves* and *surface waves.* Body waves, the fastest seismic waves, travel through the ground. Surface waves, which are slower, travel only on the surface of Earth.

Body waves can cause significant earthquake damage. There are two types of body waves, *pressure waves*—also called *compressional waves, primary waves* or *P waves*—and *shear waves*—also called *secondary waves* or *S waves.* P waves cause particles in the ground to move back and forth in the direction that the wave is traveling. To picture a P wave, imagine a coiled metal spring. If you squeeze and then release a few coils at one end of the spring, the spring will expand and contract much as a P wave moves through the ground. S waves move the particles from side to side, in a direction perpendicular to the direction that the wave is traveling. To picture an S wave, imagine a rope lying on the ground. If you shake one end of the rope left and right, the rope will move in an S shape that travels along its length, much like an S wave.

P waves are also called primary waves because they are the fastest-moving body waves and the first to be detected. P waves travel at speeds ranging from about 1 to 5 miles (1.6 to 8 kilometers) per second in Earth's crust. They move faster in the mantle. P waves can travel through both solid material and fluids.

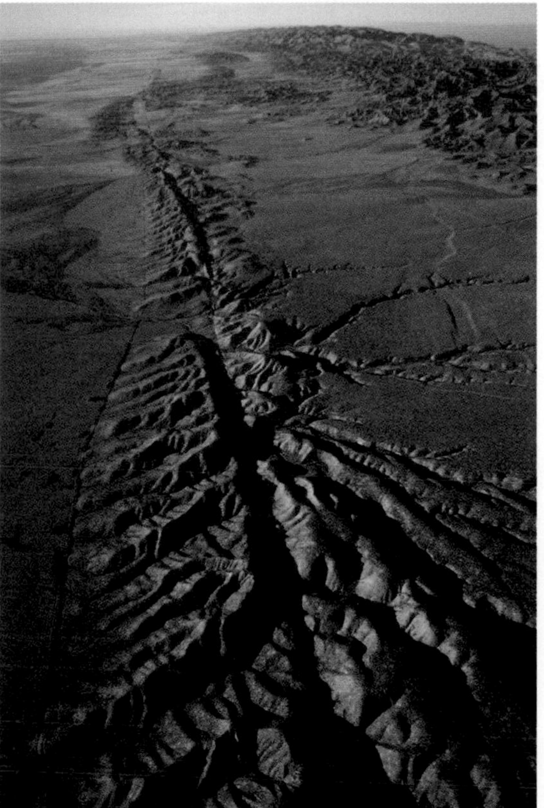

© Kevin Schafer, Alamy Images

A fault is a fracture in Earth's crust, along which earthquakes can occur. The San Andreas Fault, *shown here,* runs about 600 miles (970 kilometers) through California and into the Pacific Ocean.

Largest earthquakes

This table lists some of the largest earthquakes since 1900. Magnitude is given using the moment magnitude scale, which measures large earthquakes more accurately than the conventional Richter scale. For a list of the earthquakes that have caused the most deaths, see **Disaster** (table).

Year	Location	Magnitude	Year	Location	Magnitude
1905	Northern Mongolia	8.4	**1965**	Aleutian Islands	8.7
	Northwestern Mongolia	8.4	**1968**	Pacific Ocean floor, near Japan	8.2
1906	Pacific Ocean floor, near Ecuador	8.8	**1977**	Sumbawa Island, Indonesia	8.3
1917	Western Samoa	8.4	**1979**	Northwestern Ecuador	8.1
1922	Central Chile	8.5	**1989**	South Pacific Ocean floor, near Macquarie Island, Australia	8.1
1923	Kamchatka Peninsula, Russia	8.5	**1994**	Kuril Islands	8.3
1924	Southeastern Philippines	8.3		Northwestern Bolivia	8.2
1933	Pacific Ocean floor, near Japan	8.4	**2001**	Western Peru	8.4
1938	Banda Sea floor, near Indonesia	8.5	**2003**	Hokkaido, Japan	8.3
1950	Arunachal Pradesh, India	8.6	**2004**	Indian Ocean floor, near Sumatra	9.1*
1952	Kamchatka Peninsula, Russia	9.0	**2005**	Indian Ocean floor, near Sumatra	8.6
1957	Aleutian Islands	8.6	**2007**	Indian Ocean floor, near Sumatra	8.4
1958	Kuril Islands	8.3	**2010**	Central Chile	8.8
1960	Southern Chile	9.5	**2011**	Pacific Ocean floor, near Japan	9.0
1963	Kuril Islands	8.5	**2012**	Indian Ocean floor, near Sumatra	8.6
1964	Southern Alaska	9.2			

*Estimate from the U.S. Geological Survey. Other sources place the magnitude as high as 9.3.

Source: U.S. Geological Survey.

S waves are also called secondary waves because they move about 65 percent slower than P waves and are thus detected after P waves. S waves can travel only through solids, not through fluids. If seismic waves encounter Earth's liquid outer core or a magma chamber beneath a volcano, for example, only the P waves will pass through.

The time between arrivals of the P and S waves increases with distance from the hypocenter. Because P and S waves travel through the interior of Earth, they lose energy rapidly. P and S waves are *refracted* (bent) and reflected at boundaries between layers inside Earth. These boundaries include those between the crust and the mantle, between the mantle and the outer core, and between the outer core and the inner core. Boundaries between loose soil and dense rock in the crust may also affect a wave's speed and movement.

Surface waves are long, slow waves. They produce what people feel as slow rocking sensations and can cause significant damage to buildings.

There are two types of surface waves, *Love waves* and *Rayleigh waves.* Love waves move the ground from side to side. They generally travel about 2.8 miles (4.5 kilometers) per second. Rayleigh waves move the ground up, backward, down, then forward in a rolling motion. Rayleigh waves move slower, at about 2.3 miles (3.7 kilometers) per second. The types were named for two British physicists, Augustus E. H. Love and Lord Rayleigh. Using mathematics, Love and Rayleigh predicted the existence of the waves in 1911 and 1885, respectively.

Because surface waves travel only at the surface, their energy does not weaken as fast as that of body waves. As a result, surface waves remain strong farther from the epicenter than body waves do. Surface waves from strong earthquakes can travel around Earth many times.

Where earthquakes occur

Most earthquakes occur along faults at the boundaries between Earth's tectonic plates. Such earthquakes are called *interplate quakes.* Some earthquakes, called *intraplate quakes,* happen in the interiors of plates, away from plate boundaries.

Interplate quakes are the most common earthquakes and generally have the largest magnitudes. The bigger a fault, the more powerful the earthquake that can strike there. There are three types of plate boundaries where earthquakes occur: (1) divergent boundaries, (2) convergent boundaries, and (3) transform boundaries.

Divergent boundaries, also known as *extensional boundaries,* occur where the plates are spreading apart. Most faults that occur at these boundaries are called *extensional faults.* Examples of these faults are common at the underwater mountains called *mid-ocean ridges.* Earthquakes at these faults are generally weaker than other earthquakes. Most extensional faults are normal faults.

Convergent boundaries, also called *compressional boundaries,* are areas where plates move toward each other. Most faults that occur at these boundaries are *reverse faults,* in which one plate slides up and over another plate. Convergent boundaries feature a less steep reverse fault called a *thrust fault.* Two examples of thrust faults are subduction zones and the zones where plates carrying continents collide. Because subduction zones are long and sloping, they can produce some of the biggest earthquakes. In addition, earthquakes due to subduction can affect broad regions. The largest earthquakes of the past century were subduction zone quakes, including that which caused the Asian tsunami of 2004 and that which struck Chile in 2010.

Transform boundaries, or *transcurrent boundaries,* occur where two plates are sliding horizontally past each other. Most faults that occur at these boundaries are called *strike-slip faults,* where two blocks slide by each other without compression or stretching. The main strike-slip fault at a plate boundary is a *transform fault.* The San Andreas Fault in California is a strike-slip fault.

Earthquakes along transform faults usually affect smaller regions than convergent boundaries. But such earthquakes can still be destructive, particularly if the fault runs through a populated area. The Haiti earthquake of 2010 involved a transform fault near Haiti's capital, Port-au-Prince.

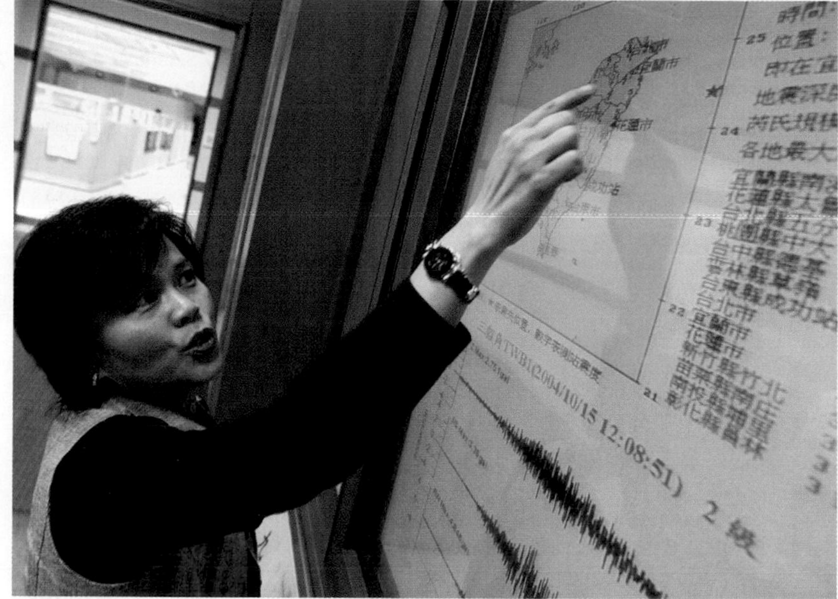

AP Photo

A seismologist uses a map and other data to pinpoint the origin of an earthquake. The wavy lines are vibrations recorded by an instrument called a *seismograph.*

http://bit.ly/1actUGm

Undersea transform faults are less dangerous. They seldom cause tsunamis. In addition, because nothing is built directly on top of undersea faults, they generally cause little damage.

Intraplate quakes are caused by stress that builds up within plates over long periods. The quakes often occur along zones of weakness inside the plates, such as old fault lines. Quakes can also be caused by volcanic activity. Although intraplate quakes happen less frequently than interplate quakes, they can affect a wider region. The area is often larger because such earthquakes occur in the older, stronger rock in the middle of plates. The strength of the rock enables the seismic waves to travel long distances. Among the largest intraplate quakes were three quakes centered in New Madrid, Missouri, in 1811 and 1812. These earthquakes were so powerful that they changed the course of the Mississippi River.

Measuring earthquakes

Seismometers measure ground displacement over time at places called *seismic stations.* A seismometer includes a weight suspended in a frame. When the frame moves due to an earthquake, the weight does not move with it. The seismometer electronically measures the difference in motion between the weight and the frame to determine the movement of the ground. A record of ground motion plotted over time is called a *seismogram.* In the past, seismograms were plotted by a recording device called a *seismograph* attached to the seismometer. Today, computers plot seismograms.

Many seismic stations include a *broadband* seismometer, which can detect shaking over a wide range of frequencies. If several seismic stations record an earthquake, scientists can determine the quake's hypocenter, magnitude, and starting time. These calculations are based on the arrival times of P and S waves at each of the stations.

The Modified Mercalli Intensity (MMI) scale

The chart below shows the Modified Mercalli Intensity (MMI) scale of earthquake intensity. In Roman numerals from I to XII, the scale describes the damage and effects of the shaking caused by a quake.

I. Not felt except by a few people under favorable conditions.
II. Felt only by a few people at rest, especially on the upper floors of buildings.
III. Felt by people indoors, especially on the upper floors of buildings. The vibrations resemble those of a passing truck. Many people do not recognize it as an earthquake. Standing automobiles may rock slightly.
IV. Felt indoors by many people, outdoors by a few during the day. At night, some people awaken. The sensation feels like a heavy truck striking a building. Dishes, windows, and doors rattle. Standing automobiles rock noticeably.
V. Felt by nearly everyone. Sleepers awaken. Some dishes and windows break. Unstable objects overturn. Liquids spill.
VI. Felt by all. Many people frightened. Dishes and windows break. Furniture moves, and plaster falls. Damage is slight.
VII. Difficult to stand. Minor damage in buildings of good design and construction; considerable damage in poorly built or badly designed structures.
VIII. Slight damage in specially designed structures; considerable damage in ordinary buildings with partial building collapse. Great damage in poorly built structures. Chimneys, columns, monuments, and walls fall over. Heavy furniture overturns. Branches break from trees.
IX. Considerable damage in specially designed structures. Great damage in substantial buildings, with partial collapse. Buildings shifted off foundations. Underground pipes break. Cracks appear in the ground.
X. Most stone and brick structures destroyed with their foundations. Some well-built wooden structures and bridges destroyed. Serious damage to dams. Large landslides. Rails bent slightly.
XI. Few, if any structures remain standing. Bridges and underground pipelines destroyed. Rails bent greatly.
XII. Damage nearly total. Lines of sight and level are distorted. Objects thrown into the air.

Source: Adapted from U.S. Geological Survey (http://earthquake.usgs.gov/learn/topics/mercalli.php).

The Richter scale is perhaps the best-known measurement of an earthquake's intensity. It is also called the *local magnitude* (ML) scale. The American seismologist Charles F. Richter originally defined earthquake magnitude in the 1930's. He defined it according to the maximum ground displacement, measured in *microns* (millionths of a meter), recorded at 100 kilometers (62 miles) distance from the quake. On the Richter scale, a one-point increase in magnitude equals a tenfold difference in displacement. For example, magnitude 3 quakes have 1,000 microns of displacement. Magnitude 4 quakes have 10,000 microns of displacement. An increase of one point indicates about 32 times greater energy.

The moment magnitude scale is the preferred method to measure large earthquakes. Scientists determine a *moment magnitude* by studying the earthquake's entire *waveform*—that is, all the wave types, frequencies, and durations—at numerous seismic stations. They thus can determine how much energy was released by the quake and how the energy was distributed on the fault plane. The largest earthquake ever recorded on the moment magnitude scale measured 9.5. It took place along the Pacific coast of Chile in 1960.

The Modified Mercalli Intensity (MMI) scale measures the intensity of the shaking caused by an earthquake. Giuseppe Mercalli, an Italian *volcanologist* (scientist who studies volcanoes), devised the scale in 1902. Two American seismologists, Harry O. Wood and Frank Neumann, refined it in 1931. The scale describes the damage and effects of the shaking using Roman numerals ranging from I to XII. The same earthquake will have different MMI values from place to place, with the largest values near the epicenter. MMI values of VI or higher indicate that the shaking was strong enough for everyone to notice it without using a seismometer.

Predicting earthquakes

A successful earthquake prediction would specify the time, location, and magnitude of the earthquake. Scientists cannot yet predict earthquakes at this level of detail. However, the history of quakes in an area can be used to calculate the probability that a large earthquake will strike within a given time. History can also suggest if one quake will be followed by a larger or smaller one within a certain period. Scientists make two types of forecasts, short-term and long-term.

Short-term forecasts tell the likelihood of future earthquakes, just as weather forecasts give the likelihood of rain. The state of California has probability forecasts extending 24 hours into the future that are updated every hour. The forecasts are based on the pattern of recent earthquakes. The forecasts give the chance of shaking of VI or more on the MMI scale for various areas.

Long-term forecasts use the history of large earthquakes along major faults. For example, in 1997, scientists calculated that there was a 12 percent probability of a major quake in the next 30 years near the Turkish city of İzmit. A major earthquake struck there two years later, in 1999. The statewide forecast for California in 2008 indicated a 46 percent chance of a magnitude 7.5 or greater earthquake in the next 30 years.

New technology can allow a few seconds up to a minute of warning at distant locations after a quake has started. Alarms can send warnings over the Internet faster than earthquake waves can travel. Many countries, including Japan, Mexico, Taiwan, and Turkey, either have or are developing such alarms. Scientists and engineers are working to have earthquake warnings trigger automated responses. The responses might include slowing trains and stopping traffic at traffic lights to avoid accidents. They might also close valves on pipelines to minimize fire hazards.

Using earthquakes to study Earth's interior

As body waves from an earthquake travel through different layers of Earth, including the mantle and core, their paths bend and their speeds change. These changes affect the time it takes for the waves to arrive at distant seismic stations. Using the global pattern of the arrival times of the seismic waves from big earthquakes, scientists have learned much about Earth's interior. Early seismologists discovered that the most important changes to seismic waves occur at the boundaries between the crust and mantle, the mantle and outer core, and the outer core and inner core. This discovery led to the earliest descriptions of the layers of Earth's interior.

Modern seismic networks and computer systems can detect smaller changes in seismic wave speeds within Earth's interior layers. Over time, earthquakes occur in many different places on Earth and send seismic waves in different directions. Scientists can analyze the seismic waves passing in different directions through the same region to map the wave speed variations in three dimensions. This technique of mapping is called *seismic tomography*. Faster wave speeds indicate regions of material that are colder or denser than their surroundings. Regions of slower wave speeds may be material that is hotter or less dense than its surroundings.

Quakes elsewhere in the solar system

Scientists have observed or predicted seismic activity on several bodies in the solar system. From 1969 to 1972, Apollo astronauts set up seismometers on the moon. The instruments recorded tiny moonquakes up to magnitude 5.5. These quakes may result from Earth's gravitational pull on the moon and from meteorite impacts. The sun's heat might also cause moonquakes, as the lunar surface expands and contracts due to heating and cooling. Shaking from a moonquake lasts longer than it would on Earth. Scientists think the longer duration results from the moon rocks being drier and more broken up than Earth's.

Mars is another rocky planet that may have quakes. The Viking 2 space probe launched in 1975 landed a partially functional seismometer on Mars. The device recorded wind noise and, possibly, a magnitude 3 quake. Images taken from Mars's orbit show boulders that have rolled downhill and avalanches of rocky debris that have fallen off cliffs. Quakes may have triggered such land surface changes. The length, relative ages, and number of faults on Mars indicate that the planet has more seismic activity than Earth's moon. If spacecraft can put more seismometers on Mars, recordings of quakes will help scientists to compare the planet's crust, mantle, and core with those of Earth.

Venus has some tectonic features similar to Earth's, such as thrust faults. As a result, astronomers think Venus may also have quakes. Joann Stock

Related articles in *World Book* include:

Earth (Earthquakes)
Geophysics
Haiti earthquake of 2010
Japan earthquake and tsunami of 2011
Landslide
Mantle
Mediterranean Sea (The seabed)
Moment magnitude
Plate tectonics
Richter magnitude
Ring of fire
San Andreas Fault
San Francisco earthquake of 1906
Seismograph
Seismology
Tsunami
Tsunami of 2004

Additional resources

Bolt, Bruce A. *Earthquakes.* Rev. ed. W. H. Freeman, 2006.
Brumbaugh, David S. *Earthquakes.* 2nd ed. Prentice Hall, 2010.
Fradin, Judith B. and D. B. *Earthquakes.* National Geographic Children's Bks., 2008. Younger readers.
Gates, Alexander E., and Ritchie, David. *Encyclopedia of Earthquakes and Volcanoes.* 3rd ed. Facts on File, 2007.

Earthworm, also called *night crawler,* is a name used for many kinds of common worms found in moist, warm soil throughout the world. The earthworm is a well-known fishing bait, so it is sometimes called a *fishworm* or *angleworm.*

Earthworms contribute to the growth of plants. The worms help break down decaying matter in the soil. The soil is loosened and mixed as the earthworm burrows through the ground. In addition, worms are important food for birds and other animals.

Earthworms range in size from only $\frac{1}{25}$ inch (1 millimeter) long to up to 11 feet (3 meters) long. They have a smooth, reddish-brown body made up of rings called *annuli.* The worm's body is built like two tubes, one inside the other. The inner one is the digestive tube. The outer one is the body wall. Earthworms have no eyes or ears. However, they have a mouth and can sense heat, light, and touch.

An earthworm crawls by lengthening its front part and pushing through the soil, then pulling the hind part forward. The animal's body wall has two kinds of muscles that it uses to crawl. Circular muscles surround the body and can make it shrink or spread out. Longitudinal muscles run the length of the body and can shorten or lengthen the worm. Numerous pairs of *setae* (bristles) along its underside prevent the worm from slipping.

The earthworm has no lungs or gills. It breathes through its thin skin, which is in contact with the air between the particles of soil. If the weather becomes too dry and warm, a worm will die. Earthworms feed on dead plant material found in the soil. This is why some people say an earthworm eats its way through the soil.

An earthworm is a *hermaphrodite*—that is, an animal with both male and female reproductive organs. But each worm must mate with another worm to form eggs. After mating, eggs are laid in a cufflike structure that surrounds the earthworm's body. The *clitellum,* a few large annuli of the body, produces this cuff for the eggs. As the earthworm moves, the cuff slides along the body and over the head. It closes completely around the eggs to make a sacklike *cocoon.* After several weeks in the cocoon, the young earthworms hatch. David F. Oetinger

Scientific classification. Earthworms are in the class Clitellata of the segmented worm phylum, Annelida. The common earthworm is *Lumbricus terrestris.*

Earwig is an insect that has a large pair of pincers at the rear of its body. Earwigs may be found under stones, in decayed bark of trees, and in moist places. They come out and are most active at night. Most earwigs measure from ¼ to 1 inch (0.6 to 2.5 centimeters) in length. There are hundreds of *species* (kinds).

Earthworm The earthworm's body is made up of segments. On each segment, except the first and last, are four pairs of tiny bristles called *setae* that help the worm move through the earth.

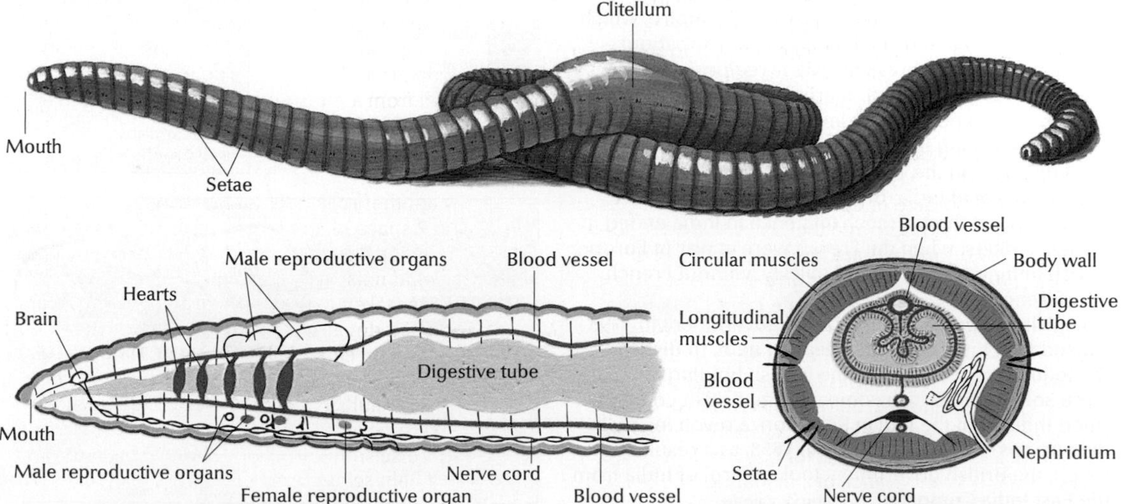

WORLD BOOK diagrams by Margaret Estey

An earthworm has five pairs of "hearts" in the front part of its body. The "hearts" help circulate the worm's blood.

A worm's waste matter is given off by organs called *nephridia,* which function like human kidneys.

Earwigs have a hard, shiny body covering. Their upper wings are short and leathery, while the lower ones appear gauzelike. Their heads carry long, delicate feelers, called *antennae.* These insects live worldwide but are most common in tropical and subtropical regions.

Earwigs may destroy fruit and flowers, but they aid farmers by eating thrips, snails, and caterpillars. Most native American species are harmless. The *European earwig* damages crops. This species has spread to North America. Earwigs received their name from the false belief that they enter a sleeping person's ear to lay their eggs. Sandra J. Glover

Scientific classification. Earwigs make up the order Dermaptera. The European earwig's scientific name is *Forficula auricularia.*

See also **Insect** (picture: Familiar kinds of insects).

East, in international relations. See **Cold War.**

East Germany. See **Germany** (History).

East India Company was the name of several European companies that opened trade with India and the Far East in the 1600's. East India companies were private enterprises given charters by the governments of England, the Netherlands, Denmark, and France. The companies received special trading rights from their governments. The English (later British) East India Company had the longest life—nearly 260 years—and the greatest influence. It opened India and the Far East to English trade and eventually brought India into the British Empire.

Before 1600, Portugal controlled most European trade with India and the Far East. The English company was formed in 1600 and soon began competing with the Portuguese. The Dutch company was formed in 1602, the Danish company in 1616, and the French company in 1664. During the 1600's, the Dutch and English companies seized most of the Portuguese holdings and drove most of the Portuguese traders out of India. The Dutch gained control of the islands that became the Dutch East Indies (now part of Indonesia).

To protect itself, the English company made agreements with the rulers of India during the 1600's. The company carried on trade without trying to acquire territory. But in the early 1700's, the Mughal Empire, which had ruled India and given it political unity for about 200 years, began to break up. Many regional states emerged, and fighting often broke out among them. The English and French tried to improve their positions in India by intervening in Indian politics and taking sides in local disputes. In the 1740's and 1750's, the French tried to win control of India, but the British, under Robert Clive, stopped them. French influence in India ended in the early 1800's, when the French were at war in Europe. British influence then spread quickly, without French interference.

Legislation passed by the Dutch government in 1798 caused the Dutch company, deep in debt, to disband the following year. In 1845, the Danish holdings in India were sold to the British company. The British company ruled India until the Indian Rebellion, a revolt led by Indian troops from 1857 to 1859. In 1858, as a result of the revolt, the British government took control of India from the East India Company. Alan W. Cafruny

See also **Clive, Robert; Dutch East India Company; India** (History); **Indian Rebellion; Raffles, Sir Thomas Stamford.**

East Indies, in its widest sense, refers to southeastern Asia, including India, Myanmar (formerly Burma), Thailand, Laos, Cambodia, and Vietnam; the islands around the Malay Archipelago; and the Philippines. In a narrower sense, the term *East Indies* refers to only the islands of the Malay Archipelago. Indonesia, formerly the *Netherlands Indies,* forms part of this island group.

The term *Indies,* or *Ind,* was first used in the 1400's. Christopher Columbus thought he was finding a short route to the rich Indies when he landed in America. He therefore called the islands the *Caribbean Indies.* Later, these islands were named the *West Indies* and the Pacific islands were called the *East Indies,* to distinguish the two groups. Harold Crouch

See also **Southeast Asia.**

East Pakistan. See **Bangladesh.**

East Roman Empire. See **Byzantine Empire; Rome, Ancient** (The decline of the empire; map; Division of the Roman Empire).

East Sea. See **Japan, Sea of.**

East Timor, *TEE mawr* or *tee MAWR,* also called Timor-Leste, is a small country in Southeast Asia. It occupies the eastern side of the island of Timor. This island lies in the Timor Sea, about 300 miles (480 kilometers) north of Australia. Dili is East Timor's capital and largest city. The country's official name is the Democratic Republic of East Timor.

Portugal began trading in East Timor during the 1500's and gradually established control of the region. After the Portuguese withdrew in 1975, Indonesia invaded and occupied East Timor. In 1999, the East Timorese voted overwhelmingly for independence. That same year, the United Nations (UN) began administering East Timor and helping it prepare for full independence. East Timor became independent on May 20, 2002.

Government. East Timor is a republic with a multiparty political system. The president is head of state and supreme commander of the armed forces, and is elect-

East Timor

International boundary
Road
National capital
Other city or town
Elevation above sea level

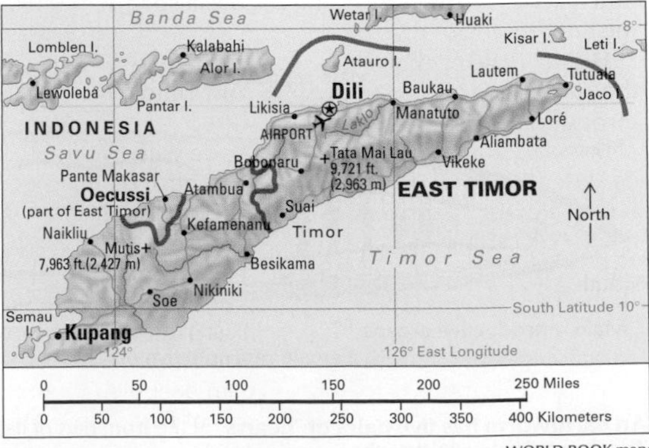

WORLD BOOK maps

East Timorese fishermen haul in their nets on a beach near Dili, the country's capital. Fishing and agriculture are important economic activities in East Timor.

© Julio Etchar, The Image Works

ed by the people to a five-year term. The prime minister is chosen by members of the National Parliament, the nation's legislature, to head the government. Like the president, members of the National Parliament are elected to five-year terms. East Timor is divided into 13 districts for purposes of local government. The Supreme Court of Justice is the nation's highest court.

People. East Timor's two official languages are Tetum and Portuguese. But more than a dozen local languages are spoken, as well as Bahasa Indonesia and English. Although the East Timorese belong to a number of separate ethnic groups, most of the people are of Malay or Melanesian ancestry. Some East Timorese are descendants of Portuguese settlers.

Most of the people are Roman Catholics, and the Catholic Church plays a central role in cultural and political life. Some East Timorese practice variations of traditional religions along with Catholicism.

Land. East Timor consists of the eastern side of the island of Timor, the region of Oecussi in western Timor, and the two small islands of Atauro and Jaco. The rest of the island of Timor belongs to Indonesia. Much of East Timor's land is rugged and mountainous. But the coastal plains in the south and parts of the north are fertile.

Daytime temperatures average about 75 °F (24 °C) throughout the year, with cooler temperatures at higher altitudes. Monsoon winds produce distinct wet and dry seasons. In the north, the wet season normally lasts from December to April. Rainfall is typically higher, and the wet season longer, in the south.

Economy. East Timor is a developing country. It has a high unemployment rate, and many of its people live in poverty. Agriculture accounts for much of East Timor's economic production. Corn and rice are the leading food crops. Coffee is the leading cash crop. Oil and natural gas reserves in the Timor Sea are also important to the country's economy.

History. People have lived on the island of Timor for thousands of years. Sandalwood from Timor was traded throughout Asia in ancient times.

In the 1500's, Portugal began to trade with the people of Timor. Portugal gradually gained control of the eastern part of the island in the 1600's and 1700's. Meanwhile, the Netherlands gained control of the western part of the island and most of what is now Indonesia. In 1859, Portugal and the Netherlands agreed to divide the island under the Treaty of Lisbon. East Timor became a colony of Portugal, called Portuguese Timor, in 1896.

In 1942, during World War II, Japan occupied Timor. In 1945, at the end of the war, control of East Timor returned to Portugal.

In 1975, Portugal withdrew from East Timor, and a brief civil war erupted. One of the parties in the conflict, the Revolutionary Front for an Independent East Timor (FRETILIN), declared East Timor's independence in November 1975. In December, Indonesia, which already possessed the western part of the island, sent military troops to take control of the eastern section. In July 1976, Indonesia annexed East Timor as its 27th province, but its authority there was never accepted by the UN.

Many in East Timor resisted Indonesian rule. During this period, as many as 200,000 East Timorese died, many from starvation and disease. In the 1990's, the United States and other nations joined nongovernmental organizations in accusing Indonesia of human rights violations in East Timor. In 1996, Carlos Ximenes Belo, the Roman Catholic bishop of Dili, and José Ramos-Horta, the international spokesman for the independence movement, won the Nobel Peace Prize for their efforts to secure a just settlement of the conflict.

In 1999, Indonesia proposed that the East Timorese should vote on whether they favored independence or a form of *autonomy* (self-government) under Indonesian rule. Almost 80 percent of East Timor's people voted for independence in the referendum, which took place In August 1999. After the vote, opponents of independence, assisted by the Indonesian armed forces, launched a campaign of terror against the East Timorese. The violence left at least 1,000 people dead and destroyed much of East Timor's *infrastructure* (public buildings, roads, and utilities). At least 250,000 residents were forced into refugee camps in Indonesia.

In September 1999, the UN sent an Australian-led multinational military force to East Timor to stop the violence. In October, Indonesia's legislature voted to end

Facts in brief

Capital: Dili.
Official languages: Portuguese and Tetum.
Area: 5,774 mi² (14,954 km²). *Greatest distances*—north-south, 96 mi (154 km); east-west, 228 mi (367 km).
Elevation: *Highest*—Tata Mai Lau, 9,721 ft (2,963 m). *Lowest*—sea level.
Population: *Estimated 2014 population*—1,232,000; density, 213 per mi² (82 per km²); distribution, 72 percent rural, 28 percent urban. *2010 census*—1,066,409.
Chief products: coffee, corn, natural gas, oil, rice.
Flag: The flag has a small black triangle within a larger yellow triangle at the staff. A white star is in the middle of the black triangle. The rest of the flag is red. See **Flag** (picture: Flags of Asia and the Pacific).
Money: *Basic unit*—United States dollar. One hundred cents equal one dollar.

Indonesia's claim to the territory. The UN, together with East Timorese leaders, began administering the region.

In 2001, 16 political parties competed in elections for an 88-member Constituent Assembly. The former resistance group FRETILIN won a majority of Assembly seats. The Assembly passed a new constitution in early 2002. In April 2002, the long-time resistance leader José Alexandre Gusmão, known as Xanana Gusmão, was elected president by the people of East Timor. Full political power was transferred to the new government on May 20.

In 2006, violence broke out in the capital, Dili, after the government fired more than a third of the army. The fired soldiers had been on strike protesting discrimination within the army. Several nations sent peacekeeping forces to East Timor to help control the violence. Prime Minister Mari Alkatiri resigned after he was blamed for the crisis. In 2007, Ramos-Horta was elected president. Xanana Gusmão, the former president, became prime minister after no party won a majority of seats in legislative elections. In 2008, rebels attacked President Ramos-Horta and Prime Minister Gusmão in their homes in a failed coup attempt. Gusmão was not injured, but Ramos-Horta was wounded. The government imposed emergency rule for two months to prevent further violence. In 2012, voters elected former guerrilla fighter Taur Matan Ruak to the presidency. International peacekeepers, satisfied with the progress made in East Timor, withdrew by the end of 2012. Geoffrey Robinson

See also **Dili.**

Easter is the most important Christian festival of the year. Easter celebrates the return to life of Jesus Christ, the founder of Christianity, after his Crucifixion. Jesus's return to life is called the Resurrection. The Gospels tell that on the morning two days after Jesus's death, his tomb was found empty. Soon, Jesus's followers began to see him and talk with him. Christians believe Jesus's Resurrection means that they, too, can receive new life after death. The Easter festival celebrates this belief.

Most Christians observe Easter on the first Sunday after the first full moon following the first day of spring in the Northern Hemisphere. Thus, the festival can occur on any Sunday between March 22 and April 25. In the Eastern Orthodox Churches, the celebration of Easter may take place later because these churches use additional factors in calculating the date of the festival.

The Easter festival is closely associated with spring. The new plant life that appears in spring symbolizes the new life Christians gain because of Jesus's Crucifixion and Resurrection. The word *Easter* may have come from an early English word, *Eastre.* Some scholars say Eastre was the name of a pagan goddess of spring, the name of a spring festival, or the name of the season itself. Other scholars believe the word *Easter* comes from the early German word *eostarun,* which means *dawn.* This word may be an incorrect translation of the Latin word *albae,* meaning both *dawn* and *white.* Easter was considered a day of "white" because newly baptized church members wore white clothes at Easter observances.

Many European Christians call Easter *Pascha.* This word comes from the Hebrew word *pesah,* meaning *passover.* Jesus was celebrating the Jewish festival of Passover shortly before he was arrested and sentenced to be crucified. Passover recalls how God rescued the Jews from slavery in ancient Egypt (see **Passover**). Christians believe that Easter is also a time of rescue. They say that by his death and Resurrection, Jesus rescued them from eternal death and punishment for their sins.

Religious observances of Easter

Easter is the center of an entire season of the Christian year. The first part of the season is Lent, a period of about 40 days before Easter Sunday. Some churches exclude Sundays, and others exclude Saturdays and Sundays, from this period. During Lent, Christians prepare for Easter. They consider it a time for *penance*—that is, a time to show sorrow for sins and to seek forgiveness. One common form of Lenten penance for Christians is fasting, which limits the kinds or the amounts of food that are eaten. Christians patterned Lent after the 40 days Jesus prayed and fasted in the wilderness to prepare for teaching and leading his people. Easter Sunday is followed by a 50-day period ending on Pentecost, the seventh Sunday after Easter. Pentecost is a festival in memory of the descent of the Holy Spirit upon the apostles.

The beginning of Lent. In Western churches, Lent begins on Ash Wednesday. Many churches, especially Roman Catholic, Anglican, and Lutheran, hold services on this day. This service often includes the blessing of ashes on the foreheads of worshipers, and words based on Genesis 3:19, "you are dust, and to dust you shall return." The ceremony reminds participants to begin their Lenten penance in a humble spirit.

In the Eastern Orthodox Churches, members attend an evening service on the Sunday before Ash Wednesday. This Sunday is sometimes called Forgiveness Sunday because at the end of the service worshipers ask the priest and one another for forgiveness for their sins. Lent officially begins in the Eastern Orthodox Churches on the next day, called Pure Monday.

Holy Week is the final week of Lent. Some churches hold special services every day of the week. Holy Week recalls the events leading to Jesus's death and Resurrection. For more information about these events, see **Jesus Christ** (The Passion).

Palm Sunday is the first day of Holy Week. It celebrates the story of Jesus's triumphal entry into Jerusalem, where people spread palm branches before him. During Palm Sunday services, many churches distribute cut palm leaves, sometimes woven into the shape of a cross. Greek Orthodox Christians receive branches of fragrant bay leaves. The leaves are used in cooking.

Maundy Thursday, also called Holy Thursday, recalls

Palm Sunday processions commemorate Jesus's triumphal entry into Jerusalem. These children are taking part in a procession in Algeciras, Spain.

© tipograffias/Shutterstock

Good Friday marks the death of Jesus. This parade held in Mexico reenacts how Jesus carried his cross through the streets of Jerusalem to the hill where he was crucified.

Jesus's last meal and his arrest and imprisonment. Many Protestant churches hold Communion services on this day. During Maundy Thursday Mass, Roman Catholic priests often wash the feet of 12 church members or poor people in remembrance of how Jesus washed the feet of his 12 disciples at the time of the final meal. A priest takes the *Host* (the wafer of bread regarded as Jesus's body) from the main altar to a shrine on the side. The shrine symbolizes the place where Jesus was held prisoner after his arrest. All decorations are removed from the main altar as a symbol of the stripping of Jesus's garments before the Crucifixion.

Good Friday observes the death of Jesus on the cross. Most churches hold mourning services. Some services last from noon until 3 p.m. to symbolize the last three hours of darkness while Jesus suffered on the cross. The Eastern Orthodox Churches follow services with ceremonies recalling how Jesus was taken from the cross and placed inside a tomb. In many Spanish-speaking countries, Christians hold processions in which people carry statues of the dying Jesus and his mother, Mary. Many Christians eat little or no food on Good Friday.

Holy Saturday is chiefly a day of solemn *vigil* (watch). The major activity of the day comes at nightfall as observance of the Resurrection approaches. Roman Catholic and Eastern Orthodox churches hold vigil services that often include the baptism of new members. The vigil service leads up to a dramatic moment. The lights in each church are put out, leaving everyone in darkness. Then, the priest lights one tall candle, representing the risen Jesus. The flame from this candle is used to light other candles held by worshipers, which symbolizes the spreading of Jesus's light throughout the world. In Eastern Orthodox Churches, the ceremony is timed so that the priest lights his candle exactly at midnight. After all the candles have been lit, the service becomes an Easter celebration, with joyous music and the reading of the Easter story from the Bible. Traditionally, newly converted Christians were baptized on this day, after having received religious instruction during Lent.

Easter Sunday celebrates the Resurrection of Jesus. Roman Catholic and Eastern Orthodox churches hold Saturday evening services, but most Protestant churches wait until Sunday morning to hold their main Easter services. Many churches and communities, particularly in the United States, have additional outdoor Easter services at sunrise. At that time, the light of the rising sun recalls the light that comes back to the world with the newly risen Jesus. Catholic and Orthodox churches also hold additional services on Easter Sunday, especially for those who missed the long services of the preceding night. For many Christians, Easter Sunday is set aside for feasting and celebration.

The end of the Easter season. During the 40-day period beginning with Easter Sunday, Christians celebrate the time when Jesus reappeared to some of his followers. This period ends on Ascension Day, or Ascension Thursday. On this day, the story of Jesus's rise to heaven is read in churches. In Catholic churches, the Easter paschal candle is put out on Ascension Day. The Easter season concludes 10 days later with the feast of Pentecost, when the apostles reported that the Holy Spirit had entered into them. Christians believe that the church began at that time.

Easter symbols

Many symbols remind Christians of the original Easter events and their meaning. Most of these symbols are used only during the Easter season. The rest are part of Christian life and worship throughout the year.

The crucifix and the cross are present in churches and many homes throughout the year. A crucifix is a cross with an image of Jesus's body hanging from it. It symbolizes the sacrifice Jesus made by allowing himself to be killed. An empty cross—that is, without Christ crucified—reminds Christians of Jesus's victory over death and the new life and hope this brings to believers.

Sunday is an Easter symbol that is also observed the year around. Christians traditionally worship on Sunday because that day is associated with the Resurrection.

Fresco (early 1460's) by Piero della Francesca; SCALA/Art Resource

The Resurrection is the central event in the celebration of the Christian festival of Easter. This Italian Renaissance painting shows the risen Jesus with one foot on his tomb. He holds a flag that symbolizes his authority over humanity.

Candles are burned during many Easter celebrations, especially the vigil and midnight services before Easter Sunday. Christians associate Jesus with the light from candles, calling him "the Light of the World." Many churches extinguish candles on their altars on Good Friday to show that Jesus's light has gone out. In Roman Catholic churches, the special paschal candle is lit on Easter Sunday next to the main altar. The candle represents Jesus's return to life. The candle is often lit during the next 40 days, until it is put out on Ascension Day.

Easter lilies are used to decorate churches and homes. The large, pure white blossoms remind Christians of the pure new life that comes to them through the Resurrection of Jesus.

Eggs and rabbits are the only familiar symbols unrelated to the Easter story. Eggs, which represent new life, have been a symbol of spring since ancient times. Christians adopted the egg as an Easter symbol because of the relationship between Easter and the renewal of life. Rabbits are associated with the fertility of spring because of their ability to produce many young. Some parents tell their children that the Easter Rabbit, or Easter Bunny, brings Easter eggs.

The lamb is a particularly important Easter symbol in central and eastern European countries. It represents Jesus and relates his death to that of the lamb sacrificed on the first Passover. Christians traditionally refer to Jesus as "the Lamb of God." Many people serve lamb as part of the Easter feast. In many homes, a lamb-shaped cake decorates the table. Many Eastern Orthodox Christians hang pictures of the Easter lamb in their homes.

Other foods. Besides lamb and eggs, certain other foods are associated with the Easter season. Pretzels, for example, were originally a Lenten food. Their twisted shape suggested arms crossed in prayer. Hot cross buns, now eaten throughout the Easter season, were first baked in England to be served on Good Friday. The buns have a cross made of icing on the top.

Easter customs

A number of popular customs are observed during the Easter season. Some are followed by most Christians. Others are observed in a particular area or by a particular group.

Carnivals provide opportunities for feasting and merrymaking before the solemn fast days of Lent. The word *carnival* comes from the Latin word *carnelevarium,* which means *removal of meat.* The most famous carnival is the Mardi Gras, celebrated on Shrove Tuesday, the day before Lent begins. *Mardi Gras* is a French term that means *Fat Tuesday.* It refers to the practice of feasting on foods made with fat before fasting during Lent. Carnivals often feature parades in which people wear elaborate costumes. The best-known Mardi Gras parade in North America takes place in New Orleans.

Easter eggs. Exchanging and eating Easter eggs is a popular custom in many countries. In most cases, chicken eggs are used. The eggs are hard-boiled and dyed in various colors and patterns. Many countries have their own traditional patterns. Probably the most famous Easter eggs are those designed in Ukraine and Poland, where Christians decorate the eggs with complicated red, black, and white patterns.

In many countries, children hunt for Easter eggs hidden about the home. Children in the United Kingdom, Germany, and some other countries play a game in which eggs are rolled against one another or down a hill. The egg that stays uncracked the longest wins. Since 1878, children in Washington, D.C., have been invited to roll eggs on the White House lawn.

Passion Plays, which dramatize Jesus's *passion* (suffering), tell the Easter story. Such plays have been performed during the Easter season since the Middle Ages, which began about A.D. 400. The most famous one is usually presented every 10 years in Oberammergau, in southern Germany. It dates from 1634. In the United States, Passion Plays are staged annually in several cities.

Feasting. Easter Sunday is a feast day. Many Christians in eastern Europe and those of eastern European ancestry in North America have their Easter feast blessed by a priest. The priest may go to the home, or families may take their food to church for the blessing.

Wearing new clothes for Easter is a custom common among many Christians. It may have originated from the old practice of having newly baptized Christians wear new white clothes for the Easter celebration. Like many other Easter symbols, the new clothes represent the new life offered through the death and Resurrection of Jesus.

Easter promenades of people in new clothes are a tradition in many European towns and villages. Some of these promenades are led by a person holding a cross or an Easter candle. In New York City, thousands of people stroll in the Easter Parade down Fifth Avenue to show off their new clothes following Easter services.

Other customs. Many communities follow customs of the Easter season that are special to them. In Bethlehem, Pennsylvania, for example, a trombone choir of the Moravian Church plays hymns throughout the city before dawn on Easter Sunday to call church members to a sunrise service in the old Moravian cemetery. At the cemetery, the trombones play a joyful chorus as the sun appears on the horizon. Peter W. Williams

Related articles in *World Book* include:

Ash Wednesday	Lent	Passion Play
Easter lily	Mardi Gras	Pentecost
Good Friday	Maundy Thursday	Resurrection
Holy Week	Palm Sunday	Shrove Tuesday
Jesus Christ		

Easter Island, in the South Pacific Ocean, is famous as the site of enormous statues of people that were carved hundreds of years ago. The island lies about 2,300 miles (3,700 kilometers) west of Chile. For location, see **Pacific Islands** (map). Easter Island has been governed by Chile since 1888.

Easter Island covers 63 square miles (164 square kilometers). Its soil is stony. The only fresh water comes from wells, *tanks* (pools), and crater lakes in the island's three extinct volcanoes. About 6,000 people live on the island. Most of the people are Polynesians. The rest are Chileans. Spanish—the language of Chile—is the official language. But both Spanish and a Polynesian language called Rapanui (pronounced *RAH puh NOO ee)* are spoken. Easter Island's Spanish name is Isla de Pascua. Its Polynesian name is Rapanui. Tourism and the production of wool for export are the main industries.

Scientists believe that Easter Island was settled between about A.D. 900 and 1200. The settlers were Poly-

© Shutterstock

Huge stone statues on Easter Island were carved hundreds of years ago. More than 600 of them are scattered on the island. Some of the statues rise as high as 40 feet (12 meters).

nesians who sailed to the remote island from islands to the west.

The early islanders created the statues, which are called *moai (MOH eye).* The statues were possibly intended to honor ancestors. Today, more than 600 statues are scattered on the island. Most are from 11 to 20 feet (3.4 to 6 meters) tall. Some rise as high as 40 feet (12 meters) and weigh as much as 90 tons (82 metric tons). The islanders used stone hand picks to carve the statues from the rock of an extinct volcano. They set up the statues on raised temple platforms called *ahu.* Huge red stone cylinders were balanced on the heads of some statues, like hats. Even today, erecting such large statues and balancing the cylinders on them would be difficult.

A bloody war between two groups of Easter Islanders broke out about 1680. During the following period of about 150 years, the victors in the war and their descendants toppled the moai from their platforms, in most cases breaking the necks of the statues. About 15 moai have been restored to their original positions.

Jacob Roggeveen, a Dutch explorer, was the first European to see Easter Island. He discovered it on Easter Sunday, 1722, and gave the island its name. In 1862, slave ships from Peru arrived. Their crews kidnapped about 1,400 Easter Islanders and brought them to Peru to work on plantations. All but 100 of these islanders died in Peru. The survivors were taken back to Easter Island in 1863. During the voyage home, 85 islanders died. The 15 survivors carried home the germs of smallpox and other diseases, which spread to remaining islanders. Many of the islanders died from the diseases.

During the early 1870's, many Easter Islanders left their homeland. In 1877, only 110 people remained there. Since then, the native population has grown, and Chileans have moved to the island. Robert Langdon

Easter lily is a flower that has become a sign of Easter. It is a tall plant with long, pointed leaves. The large, fragrant, trumpet-shaped flowers are a waxy white color.

Easter lilies grow worldwide. American florists formerly grew the Madonna lily of southern Europe. But its blooming periods are not regular. New kinds of Easter lilies have been brought to America from China, Japan, and Bermuda. The Bermuda Easter lily blooms early. The Chinese and Japanese lilies are the hardiest flowers. These lilies bloom outdoors in June or July. Florists can force Chinese and Japanese lilies to bloom just before Easter by growing them in greenhouses. James S. Miller

Scientific classification. The most commonly grown Easter lily is *Lilium longiflorum,* variety *eximium.*

See also **Lily.**

Eastern Catholic Churches are a group of independent but related Christian churches in eastern Europe, the Middle East, Africa, and Asia that are *in communion* (in spiritual fellowship) with the Roman Catholic Church. Eastern Catholic Churches accept the same doctrine and celebrate the same sacraments as does the Roman Catholic Church. But unlike the Catholic Church in the West, Eastern Catholic Churches allow married men to become priests. In addition, each of the Eastern Catholic Churches uses its own *liturgy* (acts of worship) and maintains its own structure, law, and customs.

Eastern Catholic Churches include the Maronite Church in Lebanon, the Chaldean Church in Iran and Iraq, the Catholic Coptic Church in Egypt, and the Syro-Malabar Church in India. The Melkite, Ukrainian, Ruthenian, and Russian Catholic churches are Eastern Catholic Churches of the Byzantine Rite. About 12 million people belong to Eastern Catholic Churches.

Eastern Catholic Churches are also referred to as Eastern Rite Churches because they have retained the liturgies that developed in the East Roman Empire. They also are sometimes called Uniat or Uniate Churches because many were separated from, and later were united with, the Roman Catholic Church. Peter E. Fink

See also **Copts.**

Eastern Hemisphere. See Hemisphere.

Eastern Orthodox Churches are the major Christian churches in Greece, Russia, eastern Europe, and the Middle East. As a federation of churches, they are united by common beliefs and traditions. Individually, they are usually called by their national names, such as the Orthodox Church of Greece or the Russian Orthodox Church. About 250 million people belong to the Eastern Orthodox Churches.

Eastern Orthodox beliefs are based on the Bible and on *holy tradition* (doctrines worked out mostly during early centuries of Christianity). The decrees of church councils and the writings of early church leaders reflect the authority of church beliefs.

History. For the first 300 years following Jesus Christ, Christianity struggled for survival in the pagan Roman Empire. Today's distinction between the Eastern Orthodox and *Western* (Roman Catholic and Protestant) churches did not exist.

A turning point in church history came in 313 when Roman Emperor Constantine the Great granted Christians freedom to practice their religion. He called the First Ecumenical Council, also known as the first Nicene Council, in Nicaea (now Iznik, Turkey) in 325. This was the first of seven ecumenical councils held between 325 and 787. These councils established church organization and doctrine (see **Nicene Councils**). In 330, Constantine established a new imperial capital, which he named in his honor, Constantinople (now Istanbul, Turkey). The city became the center of eastern Christendom.

The year 1054 is generally considered the date of the *schism* (split) between the Eastern and Western churches. The two churches had been drifting apart for hundreds of years before the final schism. Many political, cultural, and geographical factors contributed to the final split. Two religious issues are generally considered the chief causes of the break. One issue concerned a phrase called the *filioque* that the Western church added to the Nicene-Constantinopolitan Creed. Another issue was the Roman papal claims to authority over the entire church. Both issues led to a historic dispute in the 800's between Patriarch Photius of Constantinople and Pope Nicholas I (see **Photius**). Disputes continued until, in 1054, delegates of Pope Leo IX issued an *anathema* (solemn curse of excommunication) against the patriarch of Constantinople. The patriarch then summoned a council that excommunicated the papal delegates.

In 1204, Western Christians on the Fourth Crusade increased the bitterness between Eastern and Western churches when they sacked Constantinople on their way to the Holy Land (Palestine). In 1453, the Ottoman Empire captured the city. The conquerors, who were Muslims, ruled most Orthodox Christians until the 1800's. Only in Russia, then under the rule of the czars, did the Orthodox church remain free of Muslim control. Under the Muslims, the patriarch of Constantinople was considered the senior bishop of all Orthodox believers. Muslim power declined in the 1800's, and several Orthodox churches gained self-government as subject peoples won their independence.

Ecumenical Patriarch Athenagoras I held a historic meeting with Pope Paul VI in 1964 in Jerusalem. The meeting was the first between a patriarch of Constantinople and a pope since 1439. In 1965, the two religious leaders lifted the mutual anathemas of 1054.

Organization. The Eastern Orthodox Churches consist of a number of independent and self-governing churches and some churches that are not completely self-governing. Four of the self-governing churches hold places of special honor for historical reasons. They are, in order of seniority, the churches of Constantinople (in Turkey), Alexandria (in Egypt), Antioch (Damascus, Syria), and Jerusalem. Other major self-governing churches, by rank, are those of Russia, Georgia, Serbia, Romania, Bulgaria, Cyprus, Greece, Albania, Poland, the Czech Republic and Slovakia, and America. Eastern Orthodox Churches give the greatest honor to the *ecumenical patriarch,* the leader of the Church of Constantinople.

Eastern Orthodox Churches in Canada, Finland and other western European countries, central Africa, Japan, and Sinai (Egypt) are not yet fully self-governing. They were founded by missionaries and settlers from Orthodox churches in other countries and continue to be supervised by their mother churches. Nearly all people in Bulgaria, Cyprus, Greece, Romania, and Serbia belong to an Eastern Orthodox church. The church cooperates closely with the government in many of these countries.

Clergy. There are three *major orders* of Orthodox clergy—bishops, priests, and deacons. There are also two chief *minor orders*—subdeacons and readers. The priesthood includes *married* and *monastic* clergy. Most married priests head parishes. Monastic clergy usually live in monasteries. Parochial clergy can marry only before ordination. Once ordained, priests and deacons cannot marry. Bishops must be unmarried.

Deacons, subdeacons, and readers assist the priest during religious services. The spiritual life and administration are governed by the principle of shared responsibility between the clergy and *laity* (nonclergy). The laity often take part in the administration of their church and in the election of their clergy.

Doctrines. Eastern Orthodox Churches teach that their church is faithful to the teachings of the apostles and free from errors in matters of doctrine. But they do not believe that any one person in the church is infallible. The Bible and holy tradition are the most important sources of Eastern Orthodox teachings. Daily church services are based on the Bible, especially on the Psalms. The services also include many hymns and prayers that reflect the Biblical teachings.

The Nicene-Constantinopolitan Creed expresses the beliefs of Eastern Orthodoxy. The creed probably dates from the First Council of Constantinople in A.D. 381. It is the only creed used in church services.

Eastern Orthodox Christians disagree with Roman Catholics and other Western Christians over the Nicene Creed and the doctrine of the Holy Trinity implied in the filioque addition. Orthodox Christians use the creed's original text, which states that the Holy Spirit proceeds from the Father. They base their belief on a passage in the Gospel of John (John 15:26). Roman Catholics and other Western Christians use a later form of text, which states that the Holy Spirit proceeds from the Father *and from the Son.* This additional phrase is the filioque. The filioque and the papal claims to primacy and infallibility are the major doctrinal disagreements between the Eastern Orthodox Churches and the Roman Catholic Church.

Services in the Orthodox churches consist of the Divine Liturgy, the Divine Office, and Occasional Offices. The Divine Liturgy is the celebration of the *Eucharist.* The Divine Office consists of prayers and readings called Matins and Vespers and several lesser offices. Occasional Offices include services for baptisms, marriages, and funerals. All services are sung or chanted, usually in the language of the congregation.

The Eucharist is celebrated according to one of four rites. The two most common are the Liturgy of St. John Chrysostom and the Liturgy of St. Basil. The clergy and the congregation perform the Eucharist together. The Eucharist consists of the Liturgy of the Word and the Liturgy of the Eucharist. The Liturgy of the Word includes the singing of psalms, the reading of Scriptures, and a sermon. The Liturgy of the Eucharist includes the Eucharistic prayer, called the *anaphora,* and the distribution of Holy Communion.

Church buildings. Orthodox churches are richly decorated with religious art. *Icons* (holy images) form an essential part of Orthodox worship. They stimulate the faith and piety of the worshipers. See **Icon.**

In each church an altar stands in the center of the sanctuary. A solid screen or partition, called an *iconostasis,* divides the sanctuary from the rest of the church. The congregation looks into the sanctuary through doorways in the iconostasis.

Sacraments. Eastern Orthodox Churches have seven major sacraments and several minor ones.

The Eucharist, a sacramental remembrance of the death and resurrection of Christ and his victory over death, is a mystical sharing in the life and being of Christ by all believers. In the Eucharist, the faithful receive bread and wine that has been transformed into the body and blood of Christ by the Holy Spirit.

Baptism admits people into the church. A priest immerses the candidate for baptism into water three times, saying "The servant of God is baptized in the name of the Father and of the Son and of the Holy Spirit." The Eastern Orthodox Churches practice infant baptism.

Chrismation is administered immediately after baptism. It is understood as the bestowal of the Holy Spirit, granting the newly baptized person full membership in the church and the right to participate in the Eucharist.

Confession (or Penance) is a sacrament in which a person confesses sins to God in the presence of a priest. The priest forgives the sins in the name of God and offers the person spiritual advice.

Marriage joins husband and wife and forms a family. Eastern Orthodox Churches teach that one marriage is the ideal. However, they tolerate divorce and allow divorced persons to remarry. But the Eastern Orthodox Churches believe the first marriage is the greatest in the eyes of God. Most Orthodox churches permit only three marriages. When a divorced person remarries, several of the joyful ceremonies of the original marriage sacrament are replaced by prayers asking forgiveness.

Holy orders admits men to the major and minor orders of the clergy. Only a bishop can ordain. A congregation gives its consent to those taking holy orders by saying *axios,* meaning *he is worthy,* during the service.

Anointing of the sick, also called *holy unction,* is a sacrament in which a priest anoints a sick person and prays for forgiveness of the person's sins and for his or her recovery. Paul Meyendorff

Related articles in *World Book* include:

Byzantine art
Byzantine Empire
Eastern Catholic Churches
Greece (Religion)
Greek Orthodox Archdiocese of America
Liturgy
Patriarch
Religious life (The Eastern Orthodox Churches)
Russia (Religion)

Eastern Star is an international organization for women and men associated with the men's fraternal society of Masons. Its official name is the Order of the Eastern Star. Members belong to several groups, including the General Grand Chapter, grand chapters for various states of the United States, and the Supreme Grand Chapter of Scotland. All Eastern Star groups support charitable projects and sponsor social activities for their members. The General Grand Chapter is by far the largest Eastern Star group. Its members are chiefly wives, daughters, mothers, widows, sisters, half sisters, granddaughters, stepmothers, stepdaughters, and stepsisters of Masons who have earned at least the degree of Master Mason. Master Masons and Masons of higher degrees also may join the General Grand Chapter. The executive officer of the General Grand Chapter is a woman whose title is Most Worthy Grand Matron. Headquarters of Eastern Star are in Washington, D.C.

Critically reviewed by the Order of the Eastern Star

See also **Masonry**.

Eastman, George (1854-1932), was an American businessman and inventor. He made photography accessible to amateurs by introducing the low-cost, easy-to-operate Kodak camera and the roll of film.

Eastman was born on July 12, 1854, in Waterville, New York. His family moved to Rochester, New York, in 1860. There, he developed a dry photographic plate, which he began manufacturing in 1880. In 1888, Eastman introduced the Kodak. This lightweight, box-shaped camera contained film wound on rollers, eliminating the need for glass photographic plates. By the early 1900's, the Eastman Kodak Company had become the largest photographic film and camera producer in the world. Eastman died on March 14, 1932. Reese V. Jenkins

See also **Photography** (Technical improvements).

Eastman Kodak Company is one of the world's largest manufacturers of photographic equipment. It develops, manufactures, and markets photographic products for both traditional and digital photography, including cameras, film, photographic chemicals, processing equipment, and digital storage media. The company's other products include X-ray equipment and film, and computer scanners.

The American businessman George Eastman founded the company in 1880 as a result of his interest in making amateur picture-taking easier and less expensive. He revolutionized photography in 1885 when he introduced roll film, which used a paper base instead of glass. The company marketed its first camera in 1888, and in 1889 it introduced the first flexible, transparent roll film for commercial purposes. The company struggled to adapt as digital photography became widespread in the 2000's. It filed for bankruptcy in 2012. The company's headquarters are in Rochester, New York.

Critically reviewed by the Eastman Kodak Company

Eastman School of Music, a division of the University of Rochester, is one of the most noted comprehensive music schools in the United States. Its resources include professional recording studios; practice and rehearsal rooms; several performance spaces; and North America's largest academic music library, the Sibley Music Library. The American camera manufacturer George Eastman founded the school in 1921. Eastman provided a new building for the school and later established an endowment and gave funds for additional facilities. Critically reviewed by the Eastman School of Music

Eastwood, Clint (1930-), is an American motion-picture actor and director. He is best known for his roles in violent action films, especially Westerns and urban police dramas. Eastwood usually plays tough, alienated loners. Many of his films take a pessimistic view of human nature, emphasizing greed, cruelty, and violence. His films often include one strong female character who helps the hero to some kind of redemption. Eastwood won Academy Awards as best director for *Unforgiven* (1992) and *Million Dollar Baby* (2004). Both films also won Academy Awards as best picture, and Eastwood also earned best actor nominations for both films.

Eastwood first attracted international fame for his performance as a gunman in three European-made Westerns that were directed by Sergio Leone of Italy. They were *A Fistful of Dollars* (1964), *For a Few Dollars More* (1965), and *The Good, the Bad, and the Ugly* (1966). Eastwood played police detective Harry Callahan in five action movies: *Dirty Harry* (1971); *Magnum Force* (1973); *The Enforcer* (1976); *Sudden Impact* (1983), which he also directed; and *The Dead Pool* (1988). Eastwood's other important films as an actor include *Coogan's Bluff* (1968), *Escape from Alcatraz* (1979), and *In the Line of Fire* (1993).

Clinton Eastwood, Jr., was born on May 31, 1930, in San Francisco. He made his film debut in *Revenge of the Creature* (1955). He made his debut as a director with *Play Misty for Me* (1971), a film in which he also starred. He also directed and starred in *High Plains Drifter* (1973), *The Outlaw Josey Wales* (1976), *The Gauntlet* (1977), *Bronco Billy* (1980), *Pale Rider* (1985), *The Bridges of Madison County* (1995), *Absolute Power* (1997), *Space Cowboys* (2000), *Blood Work* (2002), and *Gran Torino* (2008). Eastwood directed, but did not appear in, *Bird* (1988); *Midnight in the Garden of Good and Evil* (1997); *Mystic River* (2003); a pair of films about World War II, *Flags of Our Fathers* and *Letters from Iwo Jima* (both 2006); and *Changeling* (2008). From 1986 to 1988, he served as the elected mayor of Carmel, California. Louis Giannetti

Eating disorder is a term used to describe illnesses characterized by a disturbance in attitudes and behaviors relating to eating, body weight, and body image. Eating disorders include *anorexia nervosa, bulimia nervosa* (commonly referred to as *bulimia), binge-eating disorder* (BED), and *eating disorder not otherwise specified* (EDNOS).

People with anorexia nervosa are underweight and usually restrict their eating. Many have severe weight loss. Individuals with bulimia nervosa and BED experience periods of overeating called *binges.* But bulimia nervosa is always associated with attempts to neutralize excessive caloric intake, usually by vomiting. EDNOS refers to any eating disorder that has prominent eating or body image symptoms that are different from the usual symptoms of anorexia nervosa or bulimia or that has most, but not all, of their defining symptoms. Another pattern of disordered eating is *night eating syndrome* (NES), characterized by abnormal overeating at night.

Eating disorders can cause serious medical complications, including osteoporosis and irregular heartbeat. They can even cause death. Eating disorders are far more common in women than in men. They typically begin in the teenage years or early 20's, but they can also occur in childhood and at older ages. They are more common in industrialized nations and in urban areas. But eating disorders occur across all ethnic and socioeconomic groups. Researchers suggest that social pressure to be thin contributes to the development of eating disorders. But most agree that psychological, social, cultural, and genetic factors all contribute to a person's risk.

Health professionals consider eating disorders to be mental illnesses. People with the disorders are often unwilling to seek or accept treatment, and signs of the illnesses can be hard to detect. Physicians and others who treat eating disorders attend to the medical, nutritional, and psychological dimensions of the disorder. Treatment focuses on addressing the psychological aspects through psychotherapy. Drug therapy is also effective, especially for treating bulimia and BED. Anne E. Becker

See also **Adolescent** (Eating disorders); **Anorexia nervosa; Binge eating; Bulimia.**

Eaton, Peggy. See **O'Neale, Peggy.**

Eaton, Theophilus (1590-1658), a Puritan founder of New Haven colony, sailed from England for Boston in 1637 with 250 colonists. The group was invited to settle in Massachusetts, but the controversy over Anne Hutchinson was raging there, and news from England suggested that the colony might lose its charter (see **Hutchinson, Anne M.**). Most important, Eaton, a wealthy merchant, wanted a good harbor for trade.

Eaton and his friends left Boston, and in 1638, they settled New Haven. They purchased land from the Indians and organized a church and court. Eaton was elected governor in 1639 and ruled almost as a dictator until his death on Jan. 8, 1658. He helped found the New England Confederation (see **New England Confederation**). Eaton was born in Stony Stratford, England. John W. Ifkovic

Eaton, Timothy (1834-1907), was a noted Canadian merchant. He established T. Eaton & Company (later Eaton's of Canada, Ltd.), which became Canada's first large department store chain. The chain eventually became one of the greatest retailing empires in North America. Eaton helped pioneer a number of retailing strategies, including fixed prices on cash sales, money-back guarantees, and, in 1884, mail-order catalog sales.

Eaton was born near what is now Ballymena, Northern Ireland. He came to Canada in 1854. Eaton worked in a variety of establishments before purchasing a store in Toronto in 1869. The store became a success, and Eaton expanded the scope and scale of his operations rapidly. Eaton established branches that eventually developed into a chain of department stores. Eaton died on Jan. 31, 1907, but his company prospered under his heirs' ownership for most of the 1900's. Sears Canada, Inc., acquired control of the company in 1999 and dropped the Eaton name in 2002. Peter A. Coclanis

Eberhart, Richard (1904-2005), was an American poet. His *Selected Poems (1930-1965)* won a 1966 Pulitzer Prize. Eberhart won the 1977 National Book Award for *Collected Poems, 1930-1976.* Meditating on birth, war, disease, and death, he wrote poems that are, to use a phrase from one of them, "true originals of imagination." As he confronted these mysteries of human experience, the force of his feeling erupted into a series of surprise effects in his poems. These effects include mixtures of abstraction and outcry, rough meters, inverted word orders, and sudden strikingly brilliant and lyrical lines.

Eberhart was born on April 5, 1904, in Austin, Minnesota. He published his *Collected Verse Plays* in 1962. His prose was collected in *Of Poetry and Poets* (1979). His *Collected Poems, 1930-1986* was published in 1988. He died on June 9, 2005, at age 101. Bonnie Costello

Ebla was a city-state that flourished during the 2000's B.C. in what is now northern Syria. A large ruin mound called Tell Mardikh, near the city of Aleppo, marks the former site of Ebla's capital. The exact dates of Ebla's existence are not known, but archaeologists have uncovered substantial remains from the late 2000's B.C. and the early 1000's B.C. At its height, Ebla was one of Syria's dominant powers. It stretched 80 miles (200 kilometers) from north to south and 40 miles (100 kilometers) from east to west. The city-state of Mari was Ebla's main rival.

Ebla's economy was based on agriculture. The people also manufactured textiles and metal products for trade. Ebla received large payments called *tributes* from less powerful city-states. A king, advised by ministers and the heads of family groups, ruled Ebla. The royal palace, with thousands of officials and servants, was the center of government.

In the 1970's, archaeologists found the ruins of a royal palace dating from around 2400 to 2350 B.C. The ruins contained thousands of clay tablets, written in an early Semitic language, that contained information about Ebla's culture. Remains from about 1800 B.C. to 1600 B.C. include fortifications, palaces, and temples. This phase of Ebla's history probably ended when the Hittites attacked northern Syria about 1600 B.C. Richard Zettler

Ebola virus, *eh BOH luh,* is a virus that has led to several outbreaks of deadly disease in Africa. It is named for the Ebola River in northern Democratic Republic of the Congo (DRC). The first known outbreaks occurred in this region and in western Sudan in 1976, killing hundreds of people. Outbreaks also happened in Sudan in 1979; in western DRC, then called Zaire, in 1995; and in Uganda in 2000. Since 2000, Ebola has also broken out among populations of gorillas in Africa, killing many animals.

In human beings and monkeys, the virus causes Ebola hemorrhagic fever, an illness characterized by fever, headache, diarrhea, vomiting, and massive internal bleeding. Most hemorrhagic viruses have a *host,* often a rodent or insect, which carries the virus but does not become ill. Scientists have not yet identified the host for Ebola virus. The virus is spread by contact with the blood or other bodily fluids of an infected person, body tissue, or unsterilized needles or other equipment. Symptoms appear within 5 to 10 days of infection. About 80 to 90 percent of all people who become infected die.

There is no known cure or vaccine for Ebola virus. Prevention efforts involve educating people about how the virus is transmitted and isolating individuals who become infected. Jennifer A. Rupp

Ebony, *EHB uh nee,* is a hard, black wood. It can be polished to an almost metallic luster. Ebony trees grow in Australia, Asia, Africa, and tropical regions of North and South America. Only the *heartwood* (inner wood) is dark-colored. The *sapwood* (outer wood) has a lighter color. In some species, the heartwood is light-colored. A hard gum in the heartwood is probably responsible for ebony's brittleness, which makes it easy to carve.

Ebony is used mainly for black piano keys, flutes, knife and brush handles, wood inlays on furniture, and other ornamental objects. The persimmon trees of the United States and Asia are species of ebony. But these trees have little commercial value. Christopher W. Dick

Scientific classification. Ebony and persimmon trees are in the genus *Diospyros.*

See also **Persimmon.**

Ecclesiastes, *ih KLEE zee AS teez,* is a book of the Hebrew Bible and the Christian Old Testament. The meaning of its name in Hebrew, *Qohelet,* is unclear. It may be related to a Hebrew word for *assembly,* which was translated into *Ekklesiastes,* or *assembly man,* in Greek. In some English Bibles, the title is translated as *Preacher.*

The book is a collection of proverbs set within the narrator's life story. Many of its ideas are unique in Biblical thought. For example, Ecclesiastes expresses pessimism about the value of human existence. The narrator is troubled by injustice and that the meaning of life is hidden from people. The book urges people to enjoy life's pleasures but not make pleasure their goal. In the end, life is empty, the "vanity of vanities." A moving last chapter speaks about the narrator's approaching death.

Ecclesiastes is one of the Bible's *wisdom books,* or books that give instruction for living. According to tradition, the author is Solomon, the Israelite king famous for his wisdom (see **Solomon**). However, the style and language indicate that the book was written in the 400's or 300's B.C., long after Solomon's reign. Carol L. Meyers

Echidna, *ih KIHD nuh,* is a type of mammal that lays eggs. Along with the platypus, echidnas are the only surviving *monotremes.* Monotremes are a group of mammals that lay eggs. All other mammals give birth to live young. Echidnas are also called *spiny anteaters.* They have coarse, brown hair. Many sharp spines jut from their back and sides. They eat chiefly ants and termites. Echidnas live in a wide range of habitats in Australia and New Guinea. There are several *species* (kinds).

Echidnas measure over 12 inches (30 centimeters) long. They weigh from 7 to 22 pounds (3.2 to 10 kilograms). Their nostrils and mouth are at the end of a long, thin snout. Echidnas have a long tongue and sticky saliva to lick up insects. An echidna has no teeth. It crushes its food with horny plates at the base of the tongue and on the roof of the mouth. Echidnas have strong claws. They sometimes use their claws to dig burrows. An echidna also digs rapidly straight into the ground and partly buries itself for protection against enemies.

Female echidnas lay one egg a year. The egg has a tough, leathery shell. It hatches in a pouch that forms on the female's belly each mating season. The young echidna remains in the pouch for several weeks. During that time, it feeds on the mother's milk. Michael L. Augee

Scientific classification. Echidnas make up the family Tachyglossidae.

See also **Animal** (picture: Animals of the temperate forests).

Echinacea, *EHK uh NAY shee uh* or *EHK uh NAY see uh,* is a plant that grows purplish flowers on slender stems. The narrow-leaved purple coneflower, pale purple coneflower, and common purple coneflower are the most common *species* (kinds) of echinacea. They develop pinkish-white to purple flowers, and the leaves range from oval-shaped to lance-shaped. People have commonly used these three species in medicines.

Traditionally, Native Americans used echinacea roots and root extracts to treat such ailments as colds, headaches, snakebites, stomachaches, and toothaches. Today, people may take preparations of echinacea to help treat colds, influenza, and various infections. People also take echinacea extracts to help boost their immune systems. Research suggests that such extracts increase the activity of *phagocytes* in the body. Phagocytes are white blood cells capable of destroying disease-producing bacteria and other harmful material.

Gardeners commonly plant echinacea as ornamental flowers. Because of overcollection, some wild species of the plant are in danger of disappearing. Lyle E. Craker

Scientific classification. Echinacea makes up the genus *Echinacea.* The narrow-leaved purple coneflower is *Echinacea angustifolia.* The pale purple coneflower is *E. palida.* The common purple coneflower is *E. purpurea.*

Echinoderm, *ih KY nuh durm,* is the general name of certain spiny-skinned sea animals. There are thousands of kinds of echinoderms. Starfish, brittle stars, sand dollars, sea urchins, and sea cucumbers are among the most common kinds. All echinoderms have an internal bony skeleton. Their spines are part of the skeleton. The echinoderm *phylum* (large animal group) is the only major phylum made up entirely of sea animals.

An adult echinoderm has *radial symmetry.* Its body parts are arranged around its center like the spokes of a wheel around the hub. Echinoderm bodies are usually divided into five sections, with the mouth in the center.

Echinoderms are the only animals that have many tiny tubelike structures called *tube feet.* The tube feet project from the body in rows. Echinoderms use the tube feet for moving, feeding, breathing, and sensing. The outer tip of each tube often forms a suction disk for gripping hard surfaces. Within the echinoderm's body, a tiny bulb attached to the tube foot forces water into it to make it lengthen. An internal system of water-filled canals connects the tube feet to each other and to a sievelike plate that usually opens to the sea water. The entire system of tube feet and canals is called the *water vascular system.*

Echinoderms reproduce by laying eggs that develop into larvae and swim freely. The larvae have *bilateral symmetry* (two similar halves). The larvae sink to the ocean bottom and change into the adult, radial form.

John C. Ferguson

Scientific classification. Echinoderms make up the echinoderm phylum, Echinodermata.

Related articles in *World Book* include:

Brittle star	Sea lily
Sand dollar	Sea urchin
Sea cucumber	Starfish

Echo is a sound heard when it is reflected back to its source after striking some object. When we shout or clap our hands, we produce sound waves that travel through the air in all directions. We first hear the sound when the waves reach our ears by the most direct path (see **Sound** [The nature of sound]). If the waves also hit a large object, such as the side of a building, they bounce back and may reach our ears a second time. The second sound is an echo. It is probably named for the nymph Echo in Greek mythology (see **Narcissus**).

A single sound may produce more than one echo. Such repeated echoing usually occurs in valleys and canyons where there are many sound-reflecting surfaces. The sound waves bounce from wall to wall and may often produce several echoes. Such repeated echoes are called *reverberation.*

Echoes can help us find out how far we are from echo-producing objects. Sound waves travel about 1,115 feet (340 meters) per second. It takes 10 seconds for sound to reach an object a mile away and return.

Echoes are useful in many practical applications. *Fathometers* use underwater echoes reflected from the bottom of a body of water to determine the water's depth. Ships at sea use *sonar* to detect and locate underwater objects from their echoes. Similarly, *radar* and *laser range finders* measure the distance to far away objects by detecting echoes from bursts of electromagnetic energy that reflect off these objects.

Edward J. Tucholski

See also **Bat** (Echolocation); **Radar** (Pulse radar; diagram); **Sonar.**

Echolocation. See **Bat** (Echolocation); **Dolphin** (The bodies of dolphins); **Mammal** (Senses); **Whale** (Senses).

Eck, Johann (1486-1543), was a Roman Catholic theologian who debated Martin Luther at Leipzig, Germany, in 1519. He made Luther admit to holding some of the same opinions as did John Hus, a reformer who was executed in 1415 as a *heretic*—that is, a person with ideas opposed to church teachings. During the debate, Luther attacked the Council of Constance for condemning Hus. Eck claimed that to deny the authority of the council was heresy.

Eck, a brilliant, aggressive man, helped engineer Luther's excommunication in 1521 and fought Protestantism the rest of his life. Eck's writings vigorously defended the office of the pope, purgatory, oral confession, and other Catholic teachings rejected by Luther and his followers. Eck also attacked Swiss reformer Huldreich Zwingli and the Reformation in Switzerland. Eck was born in Swabia, now in southwestern Germany, on Nov. 13, 1486. In 1510, he became a professor of theology at the University of Ingolstadt in southern Germany. Eck died on Feb. 10, 1543. M. U. Edwards

See also **Hus, John; Luther, Martin; Reformation.**

Eckert, J. Presper, Jr. (1919-1995), was a pioneer in the development of the modern electronic digital computer. He was the chief engineer on the project that built ENIAC (Electronic Numerical Integrator And Computer), one of the world's first general-purpose electronic digital computers. He also helped develop UNIVAC (UNIVersal Automatic Computer), the first computer to achieve commercial success.

John Presper Eckert, Jr., was born on April 9, 1919, in Philadelphia. He graduated from the Moore School of Electrical Engineering at the University of Pennsylvania in 1941. During World War II (1939-1945), the United States Department of War desperately needed to calculate quickly the firing tables used by gunners to aim artillery. In 1943, the department accepted a proposal to build an electronic computer for this purpose. The proposal's authors were Eckert, then a graduate student at the University of Pennsylvania, and engineering professor John Mauchly. Eckert, Mauchly, and their team completed the machine, ENIAC, in late 1945 and first demonstrated it publicly in 1946. Later in 1946, Eckert and Mauchly founded the Electronic Control Company (later renamed the Eckert-Mauchly Computer Corporation). Remington Rand, Inc. (now part of Unisys Corporation) bought the company in 1950. Eckert and Mauchly completed UNIVAC while working at Remington Rand. Eckert died on June 3, 1995. Paul N. Edwards

See also **Computer** (The first electronic computers; picture: ENIAC); **Mauchly, John William.**

Eckhart, Johannes (1260?-1328), was a German theologian. He is usually called *Meister* (Master) *Eckhart.* Eckhart was an influential preacher, and his sermons helped shape Christian mysticism in the late Middle Ages (see **Mysticism**). His sermons also played a role in the development of German as a literary language.

Eckhart taught that the goal of a Christian was union with God. A person achieved this union through total detachment from worldly matters. Eckhart believed every person's soul contained a divine spark. Through this spark, the soul might unite with God. To create the state of mind required for the mystical union with God, a person had to withdraw from sin. The person also had to conquer time and human nature.

Eckhart was born in Hochheim, near Erfurt, and studied in Erfurt and at the University of Paris. He entered the Dominican Order as a young man and held several positions of authority in the order. Eckhart taught in Cologne, Germany, from 1320 to 1326, when the church questioned the orthodoxy of some of his ideas. He admitted he might be in error but refused to acknowledge that he taught *heresy* (false doctrine). He died while awaiting the pope's decision on his case. In 1329, Pope John XXII condemned as heresy 28 ideas from Eckhart's writings. Timothy B. Noone

Eclampsia. See **Preeclampsia.**

Eclipse is the darkening of a heavenly body. It occurs when the shadow of one object in space falls on another object or when one object moves in front of another to block its light. A *solar eclipse* takes place when the sun appears to become dark as the moon passes between the sun and Earth. A *lunar eclipse* occurs when the moon darkens as it passes through Earth's shadow.

Heavenly bodies other than Earth and the moon also can eclipse each other. The planet Jupiter sometimes blocks sunlight from its moons. Likewise, Jupiter's moons sometimes cast shadows on the planet. Sometimes the moon or some other heavenly body blocks light from a planet or a distant star. Astronomers use the term *occultation* for this blocking action. Astronomers also refer to a certain kind of *variable star* as an *eclipsing binary* (see **Star** [Binary stars]). An eclipsing binary consists of two stars that revolve around each other so that each periodically blocks the light from the other. This article discusses chiefly lunar and solar eclipses.

When eclipses occur. Earth and the moon always cast shadows into space, and the moon orbits Earth about once every month. But an eclipse—either solar or lunar—does not occur every month. The moon's orbit is tilted about 5° to Earth's orbit around the sun. For this reason, the moon's shadow generally misses Earth, and so a solar eclipse does not occur. Likewise, the moon most often escapes being eclipsed by passing above or below the shadow of Earth. Thus, a solar or a lunar eclipse can occur only when Earth, the sun, and the moon are in nearly a straight line.

Astronomers can predict eclipses with great accuracy. At least two solar eclipses and as many as three lunar eclipses may be seen each year from various places on Earth.

Solar eclipses occur when the moon's shadow sweeps across the face of Earth. The shadow usually moves from west to east across Earth at a speed of about 2,000 miles (3,200 kilometers) per hour. People in the path of the shadow may see one of three kinds of eclipses. A *total eclipse* occurs if the moon completely blots out the sun. If the moon is at its farthest point from Earth when a total eclipse occurs, the eclipse may be only an *annular eclipse.* In such an eclipse, the moon darkens only the middle of the sun, leaving a bright ring around the edges. A *partial eclipse* occurs if the moon covers only part of the sun.

A total solar eclipse is one of nature's most impressive sights. The dark moon appears on the western edge of the sun and moves slowly across the sun. At the moment of total eclipse, a brilliant halo flashes into view around the darkened sun. This halo is the sun's outer atmosphere, the *corona.* The sky remains blue but darkens. Some bright stars and planets may become visible from Earth. After a few minutes, the sun reappears as the moon moves off to the east. The period when the sun is totally darkened may be as long as 7 minutes 40 seconds, but it averages about 2 ½ minutes.

A total solar eclipse can be seen only in certain parts of the world. These areas lie in the *path of totality,* the path along which the moon's shadow passes across Earth. The path of totality is never wider than about 170 miles (274 kilometers).

A partial solar eclipse or a partial phase of a total eclipse should be viewed only with special filters that cut the solar light to a safe level. Sunglasses and smoked glasses do not provide enough protection.

You can also view the sun indirectly with a *pinhole projector*—two pieces of cardboard, one with a small hole punched through it. Hold this piece so that sunlight passes through the hole and casts an image on the other piece. Spaces between tree leaves can also serve as pinholes, casting images on the ground.

A total solar eclipse can be viewed safely without protection only when the disk of the sun is completely hidden and only the corona is visible. The corona is no brighter than a full moon.

Lunar eclipses take place when the moon passes through the shadow of Earth. A *total eclipse* occurs if the entire moon passes through Earth's shadow. A *partial eclipse* occurs if only part of the moon passes through the shadow. A total lunar eclipse may last up to 1 hour 40 minutes. A lunar eclipse may be seen by most of the people on the night side of Earth. There is no danger in viewing a lunar eclipse.

The moon does not become completely dark during most lunar eclipses. In many cases, the moon becomes reddish. Earth's atmosphere bends part of the sun's light

A total eclipse of the sun, as shown here, starts at the left. The moon gradually covers the sun, shown photographed through a filter. At the time of total eclipse, photographed without a filter, the sun's *corona* (outer atmosphere) flashes into view. The sun reappears as the moon moves on.

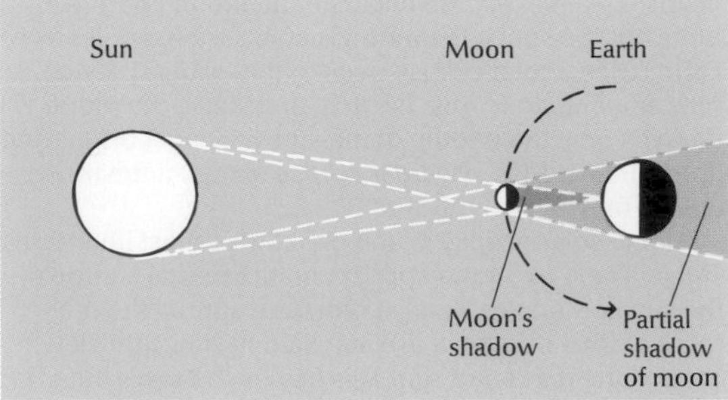

A solar eclipse occurs when the moon passes between the sun and Earth. In areas on Earth that lie in the moon's shadow, the sun cannot be seen at all or is visible as only a bright ring. In areas in the partial shadow of the moon, only a portion of the moon blocks the sun.

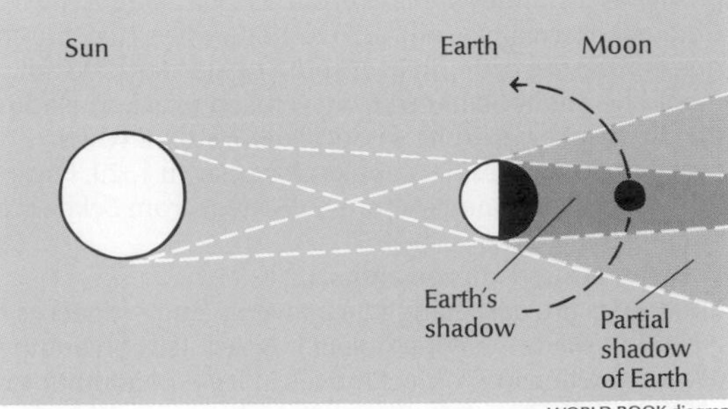

A lunar eclipse takes place when Earth is directly between the sun and the moon. The moon gradually becomes darker as it moves into the shadow of Earth, but it does not become completely dark. With the sun, Earth, and the moon positioned as shown, the moon is totally eclipsed.

around Earth and toward the moon during a lunar eclipse. This light is red because Earth's atmosphere scatters the other colors present in sunlight in greater amounts than it does red.

The study of eclipses. Eclipses have fascinated people for thousands of years. The people of ancient China thought solar eclipses occurred when a dragon in the sky tried to swallow the sun. Modern astronomers have learned much by studying eclipses. They have observed solar eclipses to determine the exact relative positions of Earth, the sun, and the moon. In 1939, astronomers observed that the moon's surface cooled rapidly during a lunar eclipse. They thus theorized that a layer of fine dust covers the moon. The theory was proved correct by space probes on the moon in the 1960's. Astronomers have also observed eclipses to study possible changes in the strength of gravity and the size of the sun.

Measurements of the sun's corona and certain other studies can be made best during a total solar eclipse. The physicist Albert Einstein claimed in his theory of general relativity that light from stars beyond the sun bends slightly from a straight path as it passes the sun. Normally, the glare of the sun drowns out starlight passing near the sun. But this light can be photographed during a total solar eclipse. Photographs taken during an eclipse in 1919 strongly supported Einstein's theory.

Astronomers study eclipses by heavenly bodies other than Earth and the moon. They have determined the size of distant stars by observing eclipsing binaries.

In 1675, the Danish astronomer Olaus Roemer used observations of eclipses of Jupiter's moons to show that light travels at a *finite* (limited) speed and to measure this speed. Jupiter eclipses its moons when the moons pass behind that planet as seen from Earth. Roemer noted that the time at which an eclipse becomes visible depends on how close Earth is to Jupiter. The eclipse becomes visible later when Earth is relatively far from Jupiter than it does when Earth is relatively close to Jupiter. However, the actual eclipse is not "late." The light merely takes more time to reach Earth. Roemer's measurement was within 25 percent of the actual speed of light. Lee J. Rickard

Total solar eclipses, 1985-2015

Date	Path of total eclipse
Nov. 12, 1985	South Pacific Ocean
March 18, 1988	Indonesia, Philippines, Pacific Ocean
July 22, 1990	Northern Siberia, Aleutian Islands
July 11, 1991	Hawaii, Mexico, Central America, Colombia, Brazil
June 30, 1992	South Atlantic Ocean
Nov. 3, 1994	South America, South Atlantic Ocean
Oct. 24, 1995	Southern and southeast Asia, Indonesia
March 9, 1997	Mongolia, eastern Siberia
Feb. 26, 1998	Pacific Ocean, Central America, Colombia, Venezuela, Caribbean Sea
Aug. 11, 1999	North Atlantic Ocean, Europe, Middle East, southern Asia
June 21, 2001	Atlantic Ocean, central Africa
Dec. 4, 2002	Antarctica, south Indian Ocean
Nov. 23, 2003	Antarctica, south Indian Ocean, Australia
March 29, 2006	West Africa, southwestern Europe
Aug. 1, 2008	Siberia
July 22, 2009	Western Pacific Ocean
July 11, 2010	Central Pacific Ocean
Nov. 13, 2012	South Pacific Ocean
March 20, 2015	Scandinavia, northern Siberia, Arctic Ocean

École des Beaux-Arts, *ay KAWL day boh ZAHR,* is a national school of fine arts in Paris. The École des Beaux-Arts is one of the oldest and most prestigious fine arts schools in the world. It dates from a school founded by Cardinal Jules Mazarin in 1648. Some of the great French artists who trained at the school include Degas, Monet, Moreau, Renoir, and Sisley. The École des Beaux-Arts became famous during the 1800's and early 1900's for its architectural teaching. It promoted the design of buildings according to ancient Greek and Roman architectural models. It influenced the teaching of architecture and the design of civic buildings in many countries, including the United States. However, after the late 1960's, the school no longer offered architectural instruction.

Today, the École des Beaux-Arts offers a wide range of visual arts courses, including drawing, engraving, lithography, mosaic, painting, photography, printmaking, sculpture, stained-glass windows, and tapestry. The school is known for emphasizing traditional design. The full name of the École des Beaux-Arts is École Nationale Supérieure des Beaux-Arts. P. A. McGinley

© Shutterstock

© Jane Shaw, Bruce Coleman Inc.

Ecology is the study of living things and how they interact with one another and with the nonliving elements of their environment. Ecologists study these relationships wherever life is found—from the savannas of Africa, *above left,* to the coral reefs of the tropical oceans, *above right.*

Ecology

Ecology, *EE KAHL uh jee,* is the branch of science that deals with the relationships living things have to each other and to their environment. Scientists who study these relationships are called *ecologists.*

The world includes a tremendous variety of living things, from complex plants and animals to simpler organisms, such as fungi, amebas, and bacteria. But whether large or small, simple or complex, no organism lives alone. Each depends in some way upon other living and nonliving things in its surroundings. For example, a moose must have certain plants for food. If the plants in its environment were destroyed, the moose would have to move to another area or starve to death. In turn, plants depend upon such animals as moose for the *nutrients* (nourishing substances) they need to live. Animal wastes and the decay of dead animals and plants provide many of the nutrients plants need.

The study of ecology is important because our survival and well-being depend on ecological relationships around the world. Even changes in distant parts of the world and its atmosphere affect us and our own environment.

Although ecology usually is considered a branch of biology, ecologists must employ such disciplines as chemistry, physics, and computer science. They also rely on such fields as geology, meteorology, and ocean- ography to study air, land, and water environments and their interactions. This *multidisciplinary* approach helps ecologists understand how physical environments affect living things. It also helps them assess the impact of environmental problems, such as acid rain or the greenhouse effect (see **Acid rain; Greenhouse effect**).

Ecologists study the organization of the natural world on three main levels: (1) populations, (2) communities, and (3) ecosystems. They analyze the structures, activities, and changes that take place within and among these levels. Ecologists normally work out of doors, studying the operations of the natural world. They often conduct field work in isolated areas, such as islands, where the relationships among the plants and animals may be simpler and easier to understand. For example, the ecology of Isle Royale, an island in Lake Superior, has been studied extensively. Many ecological studies focus on solving practical problems. For example, ecologists search for ways to curb the harmful effects of air and water pollution on living things.

Populations

A population is a group of the same species that lives in an area at the same time. For example, all the moose on Isle Royale make up a population, as do all the spruce trees. Ecologists determine and analyze the number and growth of populations and the relationships between each species and the environmental conditions.

Factors that control populations. The size of any population depends upon the interaction of two basic forces. One is the rate at which the population would grow under ideal conditions. The second is the combined effect of all the less-than-ideal environmental factors that limit growth. Such limiting factors may include low food supply, predators, competition with organisms of the same or different species, climate, and disease.

The largest size of a particular population that can be supported by a particular environment has been called the environment's *carrying capacity* for that species. Real populations normally are much smaller than their environment's carrying capacity for them because of the effects of adverse weather, a poor breeding season, hunting by predators, or other factors.

Factors that change populations. Population levels of a species can change considerably over time. Sometimes these changes result from natural events. For example, a change in rainfall may cause some populations to increase and others to decrease. Or the introduction of a new disease can severely decrease the population of a plant or animal species. In other cases, changes may result from human activities. For example, power plants and automobiles release acidic gases into the atmosphere, where they may mix with clouds and fall to earth as acid rain. In some regions that receive large amounts of acid rain, fish populations have declined dramatically.

Communities

A community is a group of animal and plant populations living together in the same environment. Wolves, moose, beavers, and spruce and birch trees are some of the populations that make up the forest community of Isle Royale. Ecologists study the roles different species play in their communities. They also study the different types of communities, and how they change. Some communities, such as an isolated forest or meadow, can be identified easily. Others are more difficult to define.

A community of plants and animals that covers a large geographical area is called a *biome.* The boundaries of different biomes are determined mainly by climate. The major biomes include deserts, forests, grasslands, tundra, and several types of aquatic biomes. See **Biome**.

The role of a species in its community is called its *ecological niche.* A niche consists of all the ways that a species interacts with its environment. It includes such factors as what the species eats or uses for energy; what predators it has; the amounts of heat, light, or moisture it needs; and the conditions under which it reproduces. Ecologists have long noted that many species occupy a highly specialized niche in a given community. Various explanations have been proposed for this. Some ecologists feel that it results from competition—that if two species try to "fill" the same "niche," then competition for limited resources will force one of the species out. Other ecologists maintain that a species that occupies a highly specialized niche does so because of the rigid physiological demands of that particular role in the community. In other words, only one species occupies the niche not because it has out-competed other species, but because it is the only member of the community physiologically capable of playing that role.

Changes in communities occur over time in a process called *ecological succession.* This process occurs as a series of slow, generally predictable changes in the number and kinds of organisms in an area take place. Differences in the intensity of sunlight, protection from wind, and changes in the soil may alter the kinds of organisms that live in an area. These changes may also alter the number of populations that make up the community. Then, as the number and kinds of species change, the physical and chemical characteristics of the area undergo further changes. The area may reach a relatively stable condition called the *climax community,* which may last hundreds or even thousands of years.

Ecologists distinguish two types of succession—primary and secondary. In *primary succession,* organisms begin to inhabit an area that had no life, such as a new island formed by a volcanic eruption. *Secondary succession* takes place after an existing community suffers a major disruption—for example, after a climax forest community is destroyed by fire. In this example, a meadow community of wildflowers and grasses will grow first, followed by a community of shrubs. Finally trees will reappear, and the area will eventually become a forest once more, until it is disturbed again. Thus the forces of nature ultimately cause even climax communities to change. Increasingly, ecologists view fires and other large natural disturbances as acceptable and even desirable. See **Forest** (Forest succession).

Ecosystems

An ecosystem is the most complex level of organization in nature. It is made up of a community and its *abiotic* (nonliving or physical) environment, including climate, soil, water, air, nutrients, and energy. Ecologists who try to link together the many different physical and biological activities in an environment are called *systems ecologists.* Their studies often focus on the flow of energy and the cycling of materials through an ecosystem. They generally use powerful computers to help understand the data obtained from field research and to predict future developments.

Energy flow. Ecologists categorize the elements that make up or affect an ecosystem into six main parts, based on the flow of energy and nutrients through the system: (1) the sun, (2) abiotic substances, (3) primary producers, (4) primary consumers, (5) secondary consumers, and (6) decomposers. A simplified ecosystem is illustrated in this article.

The sun provides the energy that nearly all *primary producers* need to make food. Primary producers consist mainly of green plants, such as grass and trees, which make food by the process of photosynthesis (see **Photosynthesis**). Plants also need *abiotic substances,* such as phosphorus and water, to grow. *Primary consumers* include mice, rabbits, grasshoppers, and other plant-eating animals. Foxes, skunks, and other *secondary consumers*—or predators—eat animals. *Decomposers,* such as bacteria and fungi, break down dead plants and animals into simple nutrients. The nutrients go back into the soil and are used again by plants.

The series of stages energy goes through in the form of food is called a *food chain.* In one simple food chain, grass is the primary producer. A primary consumer, such as a rabbit, eats the grass. The rabbit, in turn, may be eaten by a secondary consumer, such as a fox or a hawk. Decomposing bacteria break down the uneaten remains of dead grass, rabbits, foxes, and hawks, as well as animal body wastes. One of the food chains on Isle Royale has trees as primary producers, moose as primary consumers, and wolves as secondary consumers.

Most ecosystems have a variety of producers, consumers, and decomposers, which form an overlapping network of food chains called a *food web.* Food webs seem especially complex in many tropical and oceanic ecosystems.

Some species eat many things, but others have very specific food requirements. Such primary consumers as koalas and pandas eat chiefly one type of plant. Koalas eat primarily eucalyptus and pandas eat primarily bamboo. If these plants died off, so would the animals.

Energy moves through an ecosystem in a series of transformations. First, primary producers change the light energy of the sun into chemical energy that is stored in plant *cytoplasm* (cell material). Next, primary consumers eat the plants, changing the energy to a different kind of chemical energy that is stored in body cells. This energy changes again when the secondary consumer eats the primary consumer.

Most organisms have a low *ecological efficiency.* This means they are able to convert only a small fraction of the energy available to them into stored chemical energy. For example, green plants can change only about 0.1 to 1 percent of the solar energy that reaches them into plant material. Most of the energy captured by the plants is burned up during plant growth and escapes into the environment as heat. Similarly, *herbivores* (plant-eating animals) and *carnivores* (meat-eating animals) convert into their own body cells only about 10 to 20 percent of the energy produced by their food.

Because so much energy escapes as heat at each step of the food chain, all ecosystems develop a *pyramid of energy.* Plants (primary producers) form the base of this pyramid. Herbivores (primary consumers) make up the next step, and carnivores (secondary consumers) form the top. The pyramid reflects the fact that more energy passes through the plants than through the herbivores, and more through the herbivores than through the carnivores. In many land ecosystems, the pyramid of energy results in a *pyramid of biomass.* This means that the total *biomass* (weight) of the plants is greater than the total weight of the herbivores, which in turn exceeds the total weight of the carnivores. In the oceans, however, the biomass of primary producers and animals is about the same. Photosynthetic organisms grow so rapidly in the oceans that they can support proportionately more animals than can the plants on land.

Ecologists have collected information on a pyramid of biomass on Isle Royale. They studied the relationship in the pyramid among plants, moose, and wolves. In one study, ecologists found that it takes 762 pounds (346 kilograms) of plant food to support 59 pounds (27 kilograms) of moose. This is the amount of moose needed to support 1 pound (0.45 kilogram) of wolf.

Cycling of materials. All living things are composed of certain chemical elements and compounds. Chief among these are water, carbon, hydrogen, nitrogen, oxygen, phosphorus, and sulfur. All of these materials cycle through ecosystems again and again.

The cycling of phosphorus provides an example of this process. All organisms require phosphorus. Plants take up phosphorus compounds from the soil, and animals get phosphorus from the plants or other animals they eat. Decomposers return phosphorus to the soil after plants and animals die.

In natural, undisturbed ecosystems, the amount of phosphorus remains fairly constant. But when an ecosystem is disturbed, especially by human activity, the

WORLD BOOK diagram by George Suyeoka

An ecosystem This diagram shows a highly simplified ecosystem. *Ecosystem* is a scientific term for all the living and nonliving things in a given area and the relationships among them. In any ecosystem, the most important relationships involve the movement of food and energy through the system, starting with the sun and involving the other main parts of the ecosystem. In the diagram, each of the six main parts of the ecosystem is color-coded as indicated by the key, *below.*

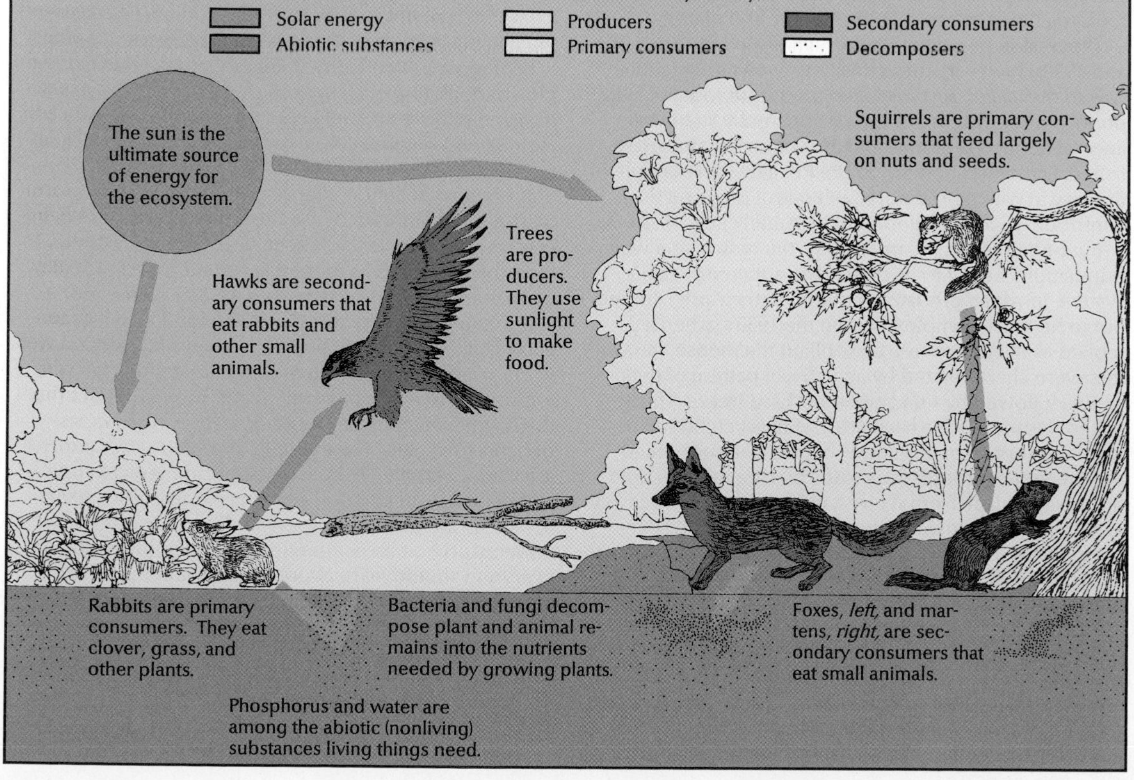

Solar energy
Abiotic substances
Producers
Primary consumers
Secondary consumers
Decomposers

The sun is the ultimate source of energy for the ecosystem.

Squirrels are primary consumers that feed largely on nuts and seeds.

Trees are producers. They use sunlight to make food.

Hawks are secondary consumers that eat rabbits and other small animals.

Rabbits are primary consumers. They eat clover, grass, and other plants.

Bacteria and fungi decompose plant and animal remains into the nutrients needed by growing plants.

Foxes, *left,* and martens, *right,* are secondary consumers that eat small animals.

Phosphorus and water are among the abiotic (nonliving) substances living things need.

phosphorus often "leaks out." This reduces the ability of the ecosystem to support plants. One way people alter the phosphorus cycle is by replacing forests with farmland. Without the protection of the forests, phosphorus is eroded with the soil and swept away into rivers and lakes. There, it often causes undesirable excess growth of algae. Eventually, the phosphorus becomes locked in sediments at the bottom of lakes or the sea. Because of this loss of phosphorus, farmers must use costly fertilizers to put the element back into the soil.

Changes in ecosystems occur daily, seasonally, and, as in the case of ecological succession, over periods of many years. Sometimes changes take place severely and abruptly, as when a fire sweeps through a forest or a hurricane batters a seashore. But most of the day-to-day changes, especially in the nutrient cycles, are so subtle that ecosystems tend to appear stable. This apparent stability among plants and animals and their environment has been called the "balance of nature." In the past, this concept of balanced, largely unchanging ecosystems was thought to be especially descriptive of climax communities. But these earlier views were based on short-term studies. Now that ecologists have had an opportunity to study ecosystems over longer periods, they have had to alter some of their ideas.

Conclusions based on population studies from Isle Royale point out some of this change in thinking. For a long time, Isle Royale had neither moose nor wolf. Then, the first moose swam to the island in about 1900. By 1930, ecologists estimated that the moose population had reached about 3,000. There was evidence that the moose were eating many of the plants on the island. In 1933, the moose began to die of starvation. Ecologists had predicted this decline because they understood the food relationship between the moose and plants.

The moose population increased again between 1948 and 1950. However, about this time, wolves made their way to the island. As they killed moose for food, the wolf population grew. Eventually, an apparently stable balance of about 600 moose and 20 wolves became established. Ecologists pointed to Isle Royale as an example of the way in which predators can control prey and thus contribute to the development of stability in ecosystems.

But beginning in the mid-1960's, the moose and wolf populations began to fluctuate. The apparently stable system, in which predators controlled their prey, turned out to be more complex. During the 1950's, when it looked as if wolves were controlling the moose, the winters were characterized by an unusual pattern of deep snows followed by rain and then a hard freeze. This resulted in snow with a hard crust. Wolves could run easily on the surface of this snow, but the heavier-bodied moose broke through the crust. Thus the moose could not easily escape from wolves, nor could they effectively use their sharp, powerful hooves for defense. Under these conditions, the wolves could easily kill moose.

Around 1965, winters on Isle Royale returned to normal, and the wolves caught fewer moose. By the early 1980's, the moose population had again become extremely large, even though the wolf population had also grown. Then the wolf population began to decline, despite the abundance of moose. By the late 1980's, ecologists feared that wolves might disappear from Isle Royale. All of these population changes forced ecologists to reevaluate their thinking about how predators and prey control one another's populations. Ecologists recognized that although wolves and moose certainly can influence the size of each other's populations, these animal groups can completely determine one another's population size only under unusual circumstances.

In the 1990's, Isle Royale's moose population declined again. Ecological studies indicated that changes in the availability of food plants and nutrients were important factors in this decline. For example, the moose would eat the leaves of aspen trees, but not the unpleasant-tasting needles from spruce and fir trees. And since spruce and fir needles also did not taste good to the island's decomposers, the needles piled up on the forest floor, trapping nitrogen and other nutrients from entering the soil. Thus the quality of the soil declined, and the growth of trees was stunted. This has meant less food for the moose and a decline in moose population.

As for the wolves of Isle Royale, it appears that inbreeding and diseases—not lack of moose—are behind the die-off of the population. Thus, predator-prey models of population control probably are oversimplifications, and what looks like a stable, balanced situation may in fact derive from the interaction of various changeable forces. Natural systems are filled with compensating mechanisms that help stabilize nature. Hence populations often need to be understood from the perspective of the entire ecosystem.

Applied ecology

Applied ecology is the use of ecological studies to achieve practical goals. These studies help us to preserve and manage natural resources and to protect the environment. Applied ecologists work with scientists from different fields to try to solve problems concerning the health and well-being of people, plants, and animals.

Ecologists are concerned about the rate at which people are depleting such nonrenewable resources as coal, gas, and petroleum, and about the pollution caused by their extensive use. Ecologists believe that if the human population continues to grow, such problems as depletion of fuels, pollution, deforestation, congestion, poverty, and the disruption of climate will also worsen. An increasing concern is the loss of natural ecosystems and their many species as more forests and grasslands are converted to farmland, urban areas, and wasteland.

Some people think that the studies and activities of ecologists conflict with people's economic interests. But ecologists believe that ecological knowledge is essential for long-term economic well-being. They point out that the maintenance of natural ecosystems provides many benefits to society. For example, if air and water supplies are clean, people will be healthier, and medical costs will decrease. In addition, many ecologists think we can use the principles of ecology, such as energy flow, to understand human economies better. Ecologists believe everyone should learn about ecology and the environment, so that people can live in greater harmony with the rest of the world. Charles A. S. Hall

Related articles in *World Book* include:

Adaptation	Biodiversity
Air pollution	Conservation
Animal	Environment
Balance of nature	Environmental pollution

Gaia	National park	Recycling	Wildlife conservation
Habitat	Phenology	Water pollution	
Limnology	Plant		

Outline

I. **Populations**
 A. Factors that control populations
 B. Factors that change populations
II. **Communities**
 A. The role of a species
 B. Changes in communities
III. **Ecosystems**
 A. Energy flow
 B. Cycling of materials
 C. Changes in ecosystems
IV. **Applied ecology**

Questions

What role do *decomposers* play in a food chain?
What is primary succession and secondary succession?
How does phosphorus "leak out" of an ecosystem?
What are some of the factors that may limit a population's size?
Why do many ecologists feel it is important to limit human population growth?
What is the difference between a community and an ecosystem?
What is an *ecological niche?*
Why do ecological pyramids develop?
What makes up the abiotic environment?

Additional resources

Bailey, Jill, ed. *The Facts on File Dictionary of Ecology and the Environment.* Facts on File, 2004.
Begon, Michael, and others. *Ecology.* 4th ed. Blackwell, 2006.
Slobodkin, Lawrence B. *A Citizen's Guide to Ecology.* Oxford, 2003.
Weigel, Marlene. *UXL Encyclopedia of Biomes.* 3 vols. UXL, 1999. Younger readers.

Econometrics, *ih KAHN uh MEHT rihks,* is the branch of economics that applies mathematics and statistics to economic theory. Businesses and governments use econometrics to analyze and predict economic activity.

Econometrics puts economic relationships into mathematical form and uses statistical data to study those relationships. Econometricians often develop a set of formulas, called a *model,* establishing relationships among economic factors. Models may describe the economy of a city, a nation, or the world. Econometricians use computers to store data and make calculations.

As early as the 1600's, the English economist Sir William Petty stressed the use of mathematics and statistics in economics. In the late 1800's, the French economist Léon Walras laid the foundation for econometrics with his mathematical description of the market economy. In 1969, the econometricians Ragnar Frisch of Norway and Jan Tinbergen of the Netherlands won the first Nobel Prize awarded for economics. Another econometrician, Lawrence R. Klein of the United States, won the 1980 Nobel Prize for economics. Thomas F. Dernburg

Economic Advisers, Council of, is a three-member group that advises the president of the United States on economic policies. The council reports to the president on current economic conditions, and it predicts future economic activity. It also helps the president prepare economic reports to Congress. In addition, the council works to increase cooperation among various government agencies by advising them on economic policies.

Congress established the council in 1946 in an effort to promote the nation's economic growth and stability. The council studies problems concerning the national economy and suggests ways for the president to deal with them. Such problems include unemployment and any decrease in the purchasing power of the nation's money. The president appoints the members of the Council of Economic Advisers, subject to Senate approval. Louis W. Stern

Economic determinism is a theory for interpreting history which states that a society's economic system shapes its social, political, and religious institutions. The German social philosopher Karl Marx first fully developed the theory in the mid-1800's, though other thinkers had introduced the idea earlier. It became one of the essential principles of his political philosophy, generally known as *Marxism.*

Marx rejected the idea that individuals, religion, or other factors cause political changes in society. Instead, he attempted to show that political changes result only from alterations in how a society produces and distributes goods and services. For example, he believed the political systems of capitalistic countries resulted from the growth of factories and other economic developments. Capitalistic countries include the United States, Canada, and many European nations.

Economic determinism also is related to Marx's theory of *class struggle,* which regards conflict between classes as inevitable. According to Marx, a society's economic system shapes its class structure. The class with the greatest economic power also possesses the greatest political power. Therefore, classes with little political strength can gain power only by changing the economic system. Richard C. Wiles

See also **Communism** (The ideas of Marx); **Marx, Karl.**

Economic indicator is a number that shows how well an economy is performing. Such numbers measure a variety of factors, including the production of goods and services, employment conditions, and consumer needs, beliefs, and behaviors. Economic indicators help governments, businesses, and the public understand economic conditions and make informed decisions.

The most widely used economic indicator is *gross domestic product* (GDP). GDP is the market value of all goods and services produced within a country during a given period. GDP excludes production by facilities that are owned by a nation's citizens but operate in other countries, and it includes production by foreign-owned facilities within the country. Some economists use a similar measure, called *gross national product* (GNP), instead of GDP. GNP includes all production by a nation's firms, regardless of the firms' locations, and excludes production by foreign-owned facilities.

Other economic indicators include *unemployment rates, consumer confidence measures,* and *price indexes.* An unemployment rate represents the percentage of jobless individuals in a community's total *labor force*—that is, in the segment of the population that is willing and able to be employed. Consumer confidence represents consumers' beliefs and expectations concerning the economy. Measures of consumer confidence are based on information gathered in surveys. Price indexes represent the prices of various items. Some price indexes track changes in the *cost of living*—that is, the amount of money needed to buy a standard amount of consumer goods and services. Roberto Serrano

See also **Cost of living; Gross domestic product; National income; Unemployment.**

Economic sanctions. See **Sanctions, Economic.**

© Tim Boyle, Getty Images

Economics is a branch of knowledge that studies how people choose to use their scarce resources to meet competing desires. Many capitalist economies have exchanges where stocks, currencies, or commodities are traded. This photo shows traders from the CME Group, an exchange in Chicago.

Economics

Economics is the study of how people choose to use their scarce resources to meet their competing desires. *Resources* include money, property, and time. A resource is considered *scarce* when people cannot obtain as much of it as they would choose if the resource were free. Scarcity forces people to make choices about how best to use their resources. A consumer chooses whether to use his or her income to buy food or a book. A parent chooses how to *allocate* (distribute) his or her time between working for income and caring for children. A factory owner chooses whether to expand production by hiring more workers or purchasing more machinery. A government may collect trillions of dollars in tax revenue, but it still has to choose whether to devote these funds to improving highways or building new schools. All of these are examples of the kinds of choices that might be made concerning the allocation of resources.

Scarcity also implies that people have to compete for resources and for the goods and services that they desire. In economics, *goods* are items that people value—for example, food, clothes, and books. *Services* are activities performed that have value, such as a haircut, legal advice, or police protection. The form that the competition might take is determined by the nature of the economy. An *economy* is made up of a broad mix of participants—buyers and sellers; workers and employers; and businesses, governments, and other organizations—all involved in the production and exchange of goods and services.

The rules of the economy determine the nature of competition. In a *market economy,* people compete for goods and services by offering and setting prices. In nonmarket settings, the forms of the competition might include lobbying government officials or waiting in line to obtain goods. Within the rules of the economy, people determine how many and what types of goods and services they want, how to go about producing these goods and services, and how to distribute them among all the people who are competing to obtain them. The choices made also determine what jobs are available, how much people earn, and how people live. *Economists* seek to examine these choices, to observe their causes and effects, and to understand how the various forces of an economy interact.

The organization of economies

Typically, the organization of an economy lies between two extreme models—*capitalism* and *central planning.* Under the capitalist model, households and privately owned businesses trade goods and services in markets. *Households* may be made up of individuals living alone, families, or unrelated groups of people living together. Businesses are made up of (1) individuals who own their business, (2) owners working together in a business partnership, or (3) corporations in which owners hold stock in a business.

Under a capitalist model, households and businesses own their own property. This property can include goods—such as factories, land, houses, and televisions and other consumer goods—as well as ideas, such as inventions and brand names. Businesses in capitalist economies choose what goods to produce and at what price to sell those goods. Consumers in these economies choose whether or not to purchase goods at the prices they find. By the late 1800's, the United States and Canada were considered to be mostly capitalist nations, although their governments still played important roles in their economies.

At the other extreme, under the model of central planning, the government controls the economy, and it has a much larger role in choosing which goods and services to produce and how they will be distributed. For much of the 1900's, both the Union of Soviet Socialist Republics, or Soviet Union, and the People's Republic of China centrally planned their economies.

The economies of all nations combine elements of capitalism and central planning. The economic mixture within a nation may change over time. For example, the governments of the United States and Canada have expanded economic regulation, spending, and welfare programs since 1900. Further, in response to World War I (1914-1918) and World War II (1939-1945), the central government in both nations practiced extensive central planning. There are also examples of nations moving in the opposite direction. In the late 1980's, the Soviet Union began increasing the role of markets in its economy. That trend continued as the country broke up into independent states in 1991. China also began moving toward a less centrally planned economy in the 1980's.

The free market. Capitalist economies rely on *free markets,* which permit people to engage in economic activities largely free from government control. The Scottish economist Adam Smith, in his classic work *The Wealth of Nations* (1776), set forth the principles of a free-market system. According to Smith, society benefits if individuals are allowed to pursue their own self-interest in markets where competition sets the prices that allocate goods among buyers and sellers. Smith believed that competition would, without control or direction, act "as if by an invisible hand" to determine market prices.

A number of factors go into making the "invisible hand" work in a free market. Sellers prefer to sell their goods for higher prices to make more profit. Buyers prefer to pay lower prices so that they can buy more items with their income. If the sellers of a good ask too high a price, the quantity demanded of that good will be less than the quantity supplied. Sellers with lower costs who are having trouble finding buyers will compete by asking a lower price. Buyers will then be willing to buy more of the good. On the other hand, when sellers ask too low a price, quantity demanded exceeds quantity supplied. Buyers who want the item but are having trouble buying it will then compete by raising the prices they offer. Sellers will then be willing to sell more of the good. The competition on both sides of the market ultimately leads to a set of market prices where the quantity supplied is equal to the quantity demanded. When this occurs, the market is said to be in *equilibrium.*

In a capitalist economy, there are numerous types of markets. The wages employers pay to workers are set in labor markets. Real estate markets determine the rents and selling prices for houses and factories. Interest rates, which in loans represent the price of obtaining goods sooner rather than later, are set in capital markets for lending and investing.

Government intervention. The role played by governments in an economy depends on the degree to which the system favors capitalism or central planning. Even in capitalist systems, however, governments play an important role. Governments are different from households and businesses, because governments can force people to pay taxes or to take actions. As a result, governments provide a number of services that businesses and households typically do not.

Governments establish the property-rights structure for the economy. To enforce property rights, governments establish police forces and provide for courts of law. The courts settle disputes between buyers and sellers and order people who harm others or damage the property of others to pay *compensation* (payment to make up for a loss). Governments also provide national defense against attempts by other countries to take or damage the nation's resources.

In many economies, governments play more expanded roles. Many governments seek to reduce unemployment and keep prices low using fiscal and monetary policies. *Fiscal policy* is devoted to managing the amounts of tax revenue and government spending. *Monetary policy* involves managing the money supply and the value of a nation's currency. Monetary policy is typically conducted by the nation's central bank, which is a government agency in many countries. In the United States, the central bank is the Federal Reserve System. Although established by the federal government, the Federal Reserve is mostly an independent agency. It adjusts the money supply by buying and selling bonds, setting requirements that banks hold money in reserve, and setting the interest rate at which the Federal Reserve makes loans to national banks. Currently, the Federal Reserve uses monetary policy to influence the *federal funds rate,* the interest rate at which national banks make loans to each other. The Federal Reserve does not, however, have direct control over this rate.

Governments in many countries regulate or own public utilities that provide electric power, natural gas, sewers, and water treatment. They provide schools and build roads. Many governments regulate economic activity. For example, they may use antitrust laws to promote competition. Governments may also set standards

Article outline

I. The organization of economies
- A. The free market
- B. Government intervention
- C. The world economy

II. Economics and society
- A. The standard of living
- B. Economic growth
- C. Distribution of income

III. History of economic thought
- A. Early theories
- B. The classical economists
- C. Karl Marx and Communism
- D. Modern economics

IV. Careers in economics

Price V. Fishback, the contributor of this article, is Professor of Economics at the University of Arizona.

Important terms in economics

Antitrust laws are regulations that seek to promote competition in markets.
Asset is a resource that retains value.
Balance of payments is a statement of all the goods, services, investments, and money into and out of a country during a given period.
Bond is a certificate issued by a government or business that promises to make a series of interest payments and then pay the listed value of the bond on a specific date.
Boom is a period of rapid economic growth.
Business cycle describes the fluctuation of business activity in a nation's economy.
Capital is a resource—such as factories and equipment—that can be used to produce other goods. It also refers to the money that is available for investment.
Capitalism is an economic system in which markets *allocate* (distribute) goods and services, and wherein much of the property is owned by private individuals.
Central planning is an economic system that calls for government control of most of the important economic activities.
Communism is a political, social, and economic system in which most or all property is owned by the state and is supposed to be shared by all.
Competition is a process in which people seek to outperform others to achieve their goals.
Corporation is a business organization in which ownership shares are sold to the owners, called *stockholders*. If the corporation fails, stockholders are not required to put more money into the corporation to cover its losses or debts.
Cost of living is the cost of obtaining a standard of living.
Depression is an extended slump in business activity.
Distribution is the process by which goods and services are divided among consumers.
Economic globalization is the trend toward greater ease in exchanging goods and services across national boundaries.
Economic indicator is a measure of economic activity, including production, employment, and consumer attitudes.
Entrepreneur is a person who develops, manages, and receives the profits or bears the losses from a business.
Exchange rate is the price of one nation's currency in terms of the currency of another nation.
Expansion is a period of economic growth.
Export is a good or service sold in another country.
Fiscal policy is government policy that manages the amount of tax revenue and government spending.
Game theory is used to develop models of the strategies people follow when they interact with others.
Goods are broadly defined as anything that has value, including food, haircuts, health, and free time. In the measures of economic activity (such as exports, imports, or GDP), goods have a more narrow definition as objects that people value. They include such things as food, clothing, televisions, and books.
Gross domestic product (GDP) is the market value of all final goods and services produced within a country's boundaries during a given period, regardless of who owns the production facilities. For example, production by a Japanese-owned firm inside France would be included in France's GDP, but production by a French-owned firm inside Japan would not be included in France's GDP.
Gross national product (GNP) is the value of all goods and services produced by the people from a country during a given period, even if production facilities are in another country. For example, production by a Japanese-owned firm inside France would not be included in France's GNP but would be included in Japan's GNP.
Import is a good or service bought from another country.
Income is money, goods, or services earned from resources. It includes earnings from labor, rent from real estate, interest from bank accounts, stocks, and other capital, and profits from owning a business.
Inflation is a reduction in the value of money. It is often associated with a general rise in monetary prices.
Inputs are the elements used in production. They include natural resources, capital, labor, and technology.
Interest, in loans and borrowing, is the price of obtaining something sooner rather than later. A loan's *interest rate* is usually stated as the amount of yearly interest owed as a percentage of the value of the loan or asset. The money paid out to an investor on savings and investments is also called interest.
International trade is the exchange of goods and services across national boundaries.
Investment is the use of resources to create capital that can be used to expand future production. The term also often refers to putting money into monetary assets with the goal of increasing the income from the asset to be received in the future.
Labor force includes all the people who have jobs and all the people who are seeking work but do not have jobs.
Laissez faire means *allow to do* in French. It refers to government policy that allows markets to operate without government restrictions.
Macroeconomics is a branch of economics concerned with the economy as a whole, including total production, overall employment, and general price levels.
Market is a setting in which people trade goods and services.
Microeconomics is a branch of economics concerned with the choices of individuals and organizations.
Monetary policy is the area of government policy that uses changes in the money supply to influence the economy.
Money is a means of more easily making exchanges of goods and services. It also can be used as a measure of value and serves as an asset that can hold its value.
Monopoly exists when there is only one seller of a product in a market.
Output is the amount produced or the end result of a production process.
Poverty is the lack of enough income and resources for people to live adequately by community standards.
Price is the value of a good or service. A market price is the value at which a good is exchanged in a market.
Production is the process by which goods and services are made or prepared for use.
Productivity is the ability to produce goods and services. Productivity increases when a larger amount of goods or services can be produced using the same amount of resources.
Profit, or net income, is the value left after all costs of production have been subtracted from revenue.
Quantity demanded refers to a specific quantity desired by a buyer at a given price. For example, at a price of $50, buyers might have a quantity demanded of 100 objects.
Quantity supplied refers to a specific quantity that sellers are willing to sell at a given price. For instance, at a price of $40, sellers might be willing to provide a quantity supplied of 80 objects.
Recession is a period of decreased business activity. Such periods are also called *contractions*.
Services are activities performed that have value to someone. They include education from teachers, medical care from doctors, haircuts from hairstylists, and protection from police.
Standard of living is a level of material comfort for an individual or a group.
Stock is a right of ownership in a corporation. Ownership of stock often is divided into a certain number of *shares*.
Subsidy is a government payment designed to encourage an economic action.
Tariff is a tax on imports or exports.
Tax is a payment to the government, which is often used to finance government services and activities.
Unemployment is the condition of a person who is out of work and actively looking for a job.

The pattern of the economy

The distribution of money, goods, and services makes up the pattern of a typical economy. The circle at the left illustrates how money flows from people to industry, and then back to the people. The circle at the right shows how people use their skills to produce goods and services. The finished goods and services then move from industry back to the people.

WORLD BOOK diagrams by Bill and Judie Anderson

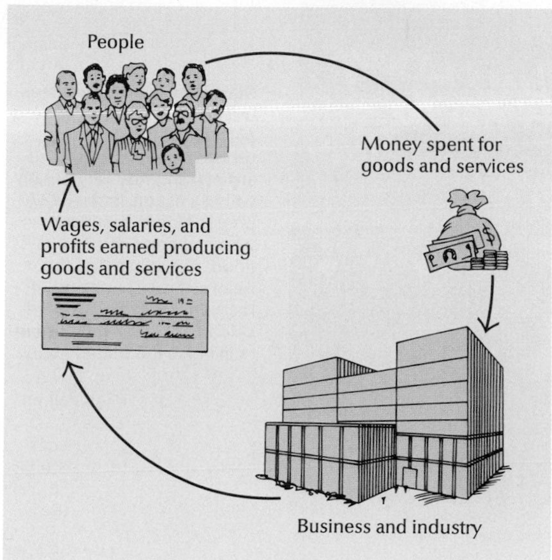

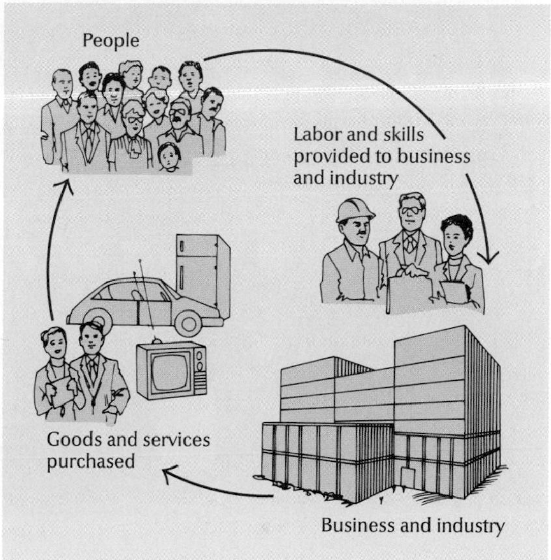

for working conditions and wages; ban harmful or misleading marketing practices; require certain goods to be inspected before they can be sold; set policies to limit pollution; and prohibit businesses from discriminating against people on the basis of race, sex, or age.

Nearly all government decisions affect the distribution of income and wealth. Many governments collect taxes and redistribute them to the poor, unemployed, retired, and disabled. Many nations regulate or provide health care. Government policies also influence the distribution of income indirectly. For example, regulations that limit the number of sellers can raise the sellers' income at the expense of consumers. In some nations, leaders set policies that favor the few and leave many of the nation's people in poverty.

The world economy. Throughout history, people and organizations from different nations have exchanged goods and services in the world economy. During the late 1800's, national economies became more *integrated,* meaning that increasing numbers of goods were exchanged across national boundaries, the number of people migrating to new countries rose, and there was increased investment in foreign countries. As a result, differences across countries in prices, wages, and interest rates narrowed. This process of integration was halted by World War I; the Great Depression, a worldwide economic slump that occurred during the 1930's; and World War II. Since the end of World War II, national economies have again become more integrated with one another. The process, renamed *globalization* in the modern era, has been encouraged by many factors, including developments in transportation, communications, and computer technology.

When people voluntarily choose to trade with each other, both sides gain from the trade. The potential for gains from trade across national boundaries has led governments and international organizations to become more interested in promoting *free trade*—trade without limits or restrictions. The United States has worked to develop freer trade with Canada and Mexico under the North American Free Trade Agreement (NAFTA). Similarly, the European Union (EU) has reduced many trade barriers between its member countries. In addition, many nations have joined the World Trade Organization (WTO) to work toward increasing free trade worldwide.

Nearly all countries, however, adopt some policies that restrict international trade to protect domestic businesses from foreign competition. The restrictions often force consumers to pay higher prices for goods from the protected businesses. Such restrictions include import tariffs and import quotas. Import *tariffs* are taxes on goods purchased from other countries. Import *quotas* limit the quantity of goods that people can import from foreign countries. Some nations also pay *subsidies* to aid their own nation's businesses. The practice of establishing trade barriers to help certain national businesses is commonly called *protectionism.*

International trade involves the exchange of goods and services across national boundaries. Since countries often have different types of money, known as *currencies,* markets have developed to trade them. The price of one currency in terms of another is the *exchange rate.* The value of a nation's currency rises when there is greater demand for products sold by people of that nation. For example, if Americans want to buy more Japanese products, Americans demand more *yen,* Japan's currency. The yen therefore increases in value because it takes more dollars to get each yen. Exchange rates that are allowed to rise and fall on world currency markets are called *floating exchange rates.* Many governments intervene in currency markets if the exchange rate for their currency rises or falls too much.

© Margaret Bourke-White, Time Life Pictures/Getty Images

Standard of living is a measure of the general well-being of an individual, family, or group of people. The standard of living may vary greatly within a nation. In this 1937 photo, African Americans who had been victims of a flood line up at a Red Cross relief station. They stand directly in front of a billboard celebrating the high standard of living in the United States.

Economics and society

The standard of living. The economic activities of households, businesses, governments, and organizations have a powerful impact on the lifestyles and living conditions of the general population. The *standard of living* is a measure of the general well-being of an individual, family, or group of people.

Economists use *gross domestic product per person* as the most common measure of the average standard of living in a nation's economy. The gross domestic product (GDP) is the market value of all final goods and services produced within an economy during a particular time. To obtain the GDP per person, the value of a nation's goods and services is divided by the nation's population. When making comparisons over time, economists focus on *real* GDP per person, which adjusts GDP for general changes in prices. When making comparisons between countries, GDP per person is adjusted for differences in currency values in each country. The adjustments are made to make sure that the differences reflect differences in actual goods and services and not differences in prices.

The countries with the highest GDP per person include Australia, Canada, many of the European Union countries, Japan, and the United States. People in these countries typically have more food, more consumer goods, better housing, greater educational opportunities, and better medical care than the rest of the world's people.

GDP per person does not measure all of the dimensions of economic welfare. For example, it does not give a full picture of the income distribution in a nation. People are thought to have a higher standard of living if they spend a smaller share of their income on basic food, they live longer and healthier lives, their environment is less polluted, they have more freedom, they are better educated, or they have more *leisure* (time spent not working). Therefore, economists use a variety of measures to compare standards of living.

Economic growth. Improvement in the standard of living typically occurs when an economy increases its output of goods and services during an *expansion,* a period of economic growth. A period of decreased economic activity is called a *recession, contraction,* or, in severe cases, a *depression.* The pattern of fluctuations between expansions and recessions is known as the *business cycle.*

At the most basic level, the output in a nation's economy is determined by the amount of labor, capital, and natural resources a nation has. *Labor* is the amount of effort people devote to an activity. *Capital* refers to goods, such as buildings and machinery, which can be used to produce other goods. *Natural resources* include such things as land, minerals, water, and petroleum.

To achieve economic growth, a nation's economy must add to its *inputs* (items required for production) of labor, capital, or natural resources, or improve the way that it uses them. Advances in technology, knowledge, and organization allow people to get more out of each input and to combine inputs more effectively. Such advances increase *productivity,* which is the amount of goods or services produced using a given set of inputs in production.

Savings and investments play an important role in economic growth. People *save* when they use less than the full amount of the income they have earned. Many people in developed countries put their savings in banks, where the money can earn *interest.* The banks, in turn, lend the money to others in the economy. Some people *invest* their savings in stocks and bonds sold by corporations, which in turn use the funds to expand production. Many people also invest their time and money in obtaining education and job training that improves their skills, also known as *human capital.* As people save and invest more, economies tend to grow faster.

The economic organization of the country also plays an important role in economic growth. Many studies show that countries with governments that protect the freedoms of individuals and property rights, and that offer impartial courts, tend to lead the list of countries with the highest GDP per person. Countries with unstable governments that are troubled by such problems as civil wars or high levels of corruption tend to grow more slowly.

Distribution of income. People receive income in a variety of ways. Most people earn wages or salaries in exchange for their work. Business owners receive income in the form of *profits,* which is the revenue left over after subtracting the costs of all the inputs. People who own shares of stock in a corporation may receive income in the form of payments called *dividends.* Owners of land and buildings receive payment called *rent.* Many people receive *transfer payments* from government programs, such as unemployment insurance or social security. People who sell land or stocks at prices higher than the original prices they paid receive income in the form of *capital gains.*

The distribution of income varies by country. In a country with highly unequal distribution of income, the highest-earning 10 percent of the households might receive nearly 50 percent of the nation's income. In many of the countries with the highest GDP per person, the share of income held by the top 10 percent in the early 2000's was between 20 and 31 percent.

Income distributions are determined in part by the mixture of markets and central planning in an economy. In market economies, people tend to rank higher in the income distribution when they are older, have more education, work more hours, or have more inherited wealth. Sometimes, people become wealthy because they are lucky. A household's position in the income distribution often changes from year to year. College students rank low in the distribution while in school and move much higher after they graduate. People employed in industries that experience booms and busts also move up in the distribution when they are employed and down when they are unemployed. Some people remain low in the income distribution because they are discriminated against. In many economies, particularly centrally planned economies, people gain more income as they gain more influence over government policies.

One of the world's major economic problems is *poverty*—that is, when people lack the income and resources to live adequately by the standards of their community. The percentage of a population that lives in poverty is called the *poverty rate.* In the early 2000's, roughly 30 percent of the population in less developed countries was living on less than $1 per day, the amount per person that the World Bank has set as the international poverty line. The factors that determine economic growth and the income distribution strongly influence the poverty rate. Some nations and many charities and individuals offer aid to people in less developed countries to help relieve the suffering from poverty.

© Andy Sacks, Stone/Getty Images

Agricultural economics studies the production and distribution of goods in an economy's farm sector. Farms, such as this hog farm, form an important part of many national economies.

History of economic thought

Early theories. The ancient Greek historian and author Xenophon wrote about how best to organize households and public affairs in *Oeconomicus.* The title, made up of the Greek words for *house* and *management,* is the source for the English word *economics.* The Greek philosopher Aristotle discussed exchanges between individuals and the role of money and interest in society. Philosophers in the Middle Ages, from about the A.D. 400's through the 1400's, wrote a great deal about how to define economic value.

Between the 1500's and the 1700's, the economic policies of nations were strongly influenced by *mercantilism.* Leaders of mercantilist nations sought to maintain their political and military power and to increase their share of the world's wealth. To achieve these goals, they increased their supplies of gold and silver by exporting more goods than they imported. In addition, mercantilist leaders often strictly regulated agriculture, industry, and trade within their own nations.

During the mid-1700's, a group of French economists known as the *physiocrats* argued that the key to creating additional wealth was through increases in agricultural productivity. To stimulate such production, they argued that governments should reduce taxation and allow freer trade. The physiocrats described their recommended policy as *laissez faire,* pronounced *LEHS say FAIR,* a French term that means *allow to do.* The term is still in use in economics today.

Fields of economics

Because of the broad scope of economic activity, the study of economics consists of a number of branches and fields. Two major branches are *microeconomics* and *macroeconomics.* Microeconomics deals with the activities and choices of individual households, businesses, governments, and organizations. Macroeconomics deals with features of the economy as a whole, including total production, overall employment, and the general price level. There are a number of specialized fields within economics, each of which studies a specific type of activity or a certain part of an economy.

Agricultural economics focuses on the production and distribution of goods in the farm sector.

Comparative systems compares and contrasts the operations of economies that range from central planning to market economies and the mixed economies in between.

Development economics examines the conditions of less developed countries and the impact of policies designed to promote their development.

Econometrics uses statistical methods to measure the relationships between economic factors.

Economic history examines the organization and success of economies over time.

Economic theory develops models that predict how decision makers respond to changes in the world around them.

Experimental economics involves the use of controlled experiments to observe economic behavior and to understand the roles of specific economic factors.

Game theory is a branch of economic theory that examines the strategies that decision makers follow when they interact with others.

Growth theory develops models that attempt to show how various factors influence economic growth.

History of economic thought studies how economists' views of society have changed over time.

Industrial organization, or **industrial economics,** examines how firms are organized, how they choose prices and quantities, and how they decide upon other business strategies. The strategies often differ under alternative market structures and different degrees of government regulation.

International economics is devoted to the interactions of individuals, businesses, and governments in the world economy.

Labor economics focuses on the interactions of workers and employers. The topics studied include how people allocate their time between work and leisure, the factors influencing wages and working conditions, the importance of human capital, and the roles played by unions.

Natural resource and environmental economics examines the use of natural resources and the impact of economic activities on the environment.

Public choice economists study how people inside and outside the government influence policy decisions.

Public economics examines the impact of government policies, such as taxation, social welfare programs, and business regulations.

Urban economics focuses on the economies of cities.

The classical economists. Most economists today consider Adam Smith to be the father of modern economics. Smith greatly expanded on the laissez faire ideas of the physiocrats. He believed that the government could best promote the general well-being by protecting individual freedoms, providing a "regular administration of justice," and promoting competition and free trade. Smith also warned against allowing sellers to make agreements that reduced competition. Smith's ideas have become central features of the policies toward markets followed by many developed economies.

© Hulton Archive/Getty Images

Adam Smith, a Scottish economist, is widely regarded as the founder of modern economics. He set forth the principles of a free-market system in his book *The Wealth of Nations* (1776).

Three British economists of the late 1700's and the 1800's were particularly influential in expanding on Smith's theories and challenging them. David Ricardo developed the concept of comparative advantage and demonstrated the benefits of free trade among nations. Thomas Robert Malthus warned that rapid population growth would surpass the world's resources and lead to food shortages, disease, and wars. John Stuart Mill made popular the notion of an economic equilibrium and described how the equilibrium changed when factors in the economy changed. Although Mill supported the idea of a free-market economy, he favored some government interventions to promote a more even distribution of wealth.

Karl Marx and Communism. Some writers disagreed with the classical economists' belief that competition under a capitalist system would lead to economic progress. Karl Marx, a German philosopher of the 1800's, viewed human history as a struggle between classes over ownership of the means of production. Marx argued that technological change under capitalism would lead to a series of depressions. The depressions—each more severe than the last—would leave workers in a worse condition and put more resources into the hands of a small ruling class. Eventually workers would revolt and gain control of economic resources and the government. Marx's theories influenced the development of a number of socialist and Communist governments during the 1900's.

Modern economics. During the late 1800's and the early 1900's, economists began to use scientific methods to study economic problems. Alfred Marshall of England developed the theory of how prices and quantities traded are affected by changes in supply and demand. The French economist Leon Walras applied mathematical analysis to show how changes in one market lead to changes in all other markets until the economy reaches a general equilibrium. Wesley Clair Mitchell of the United States studied increases and decreases in economic activity during the course of a business cycle.

The Great Depression of the 1930's caused a number of economists to seek new explanations for economic

Snark/Art Resource

A poster from the Communist Soviet Union promoted the role of women workers in the country's economy. Communists believe workers should control society's economic resources.

depressions. John Maynard Keynes, a British economist, argued that wages and prices did not always adjust in the ways that the classical economists had predicted. The economy could, therefore, reach a stable position with high unemployment. Keynes suggested that governments could help end depressions by creating budget *deficits,* in which government spending exceeded tax revenues. Extra spending and lower taxes would create employment and provide people with more income that they would then use to buy goods and services or invest in new projects.

Joseph A. Schumpeter of Austria emphasized the role of *entrepreneurs* (people who organize and manage a business or industrial undertaking) in developing innovations that drive economic growth. His theories of the business cycle described how waves of *innovation,* or new ways of doing things, stimulated growth but could eventually lead to overexpansion by businesses and then the next recession. Schumpeter predicted that the growth of big business would ultimately cause expansions in government regulation that would work against big business. Friedrich von Hayek, another Austrian economist, argued that markets promoted economic welfare because prices provided large amounts of information at low cost. He thought that protecting the economic freedom of individuals was central to the success of economies.

During the last half of the 1900's, many economists made significant contributions. The American economist Simon Kuznets developed new methods for measuring output, income, and productivity. Milton Friedman, another American economist, argued that changes in the money supply led to business-cycle fluctuations. He recommended that central banks increase the money supply at a constant rate to stabilize prices and promote economic growth. Economists who support these ideas are known as *monetarists,* and Friedman was a leading spokesman of this school of thought.

The American economist Robert E. Lucas, Jr., is a leader among *rational expectations theorists.* Economists in this school argue that when people correctly predict changes in government fiscal and monetary policies, the policies become less effective at stimulating production. For example, a government could try to stimulate demand for goods by increasing the money supply. Suppliers with rational expectations, however, might recognize that the rise in demand for their products is due only to a rise in the amount of money available in the economy and not to an increase in the amount of products that consumers want to buy. In such an instance, suppliers would raise their prices but would not increase the amount of goods produced. Then the result of the government policy would be *inflation* (a decline in the value of money), and no change in real GDP. The insights from rational expectations theory have led economists and policymakers to pay closer attention to the availability of information in determining the effectiveness of monetary and fiscal policies.

The American economists Paul A. Samuelson and Kenneth Arrow and the French-born American economist Gérard Debreu were among the leaders in using mathematics to describe and extend economic theories. The Hungarian-born American mathematician John von Neumann and the Austrian economist Oskar Morgenstern paved the way for the widespread use of *game theory,* a method based upon formal logic used for studying strategies when people interact with others. The American mathematician John Forbes Nash, Jr., contributed to the development of game theory with important insights on how to predict behavior in settings where people might get more benefit by not cooperating with one another.

Research today generally seeks to understand the relationships between various parts of the economy. Many economists—such as Daniel L. McFadden and James J. Heckman of the United States—have greatly expanded the use of statistical methods to identify the relationship between economic variables. In addition, the methods of economic analysis have increasingly been applied to areas outside the field's traditional boundaries. The American economist Gary Becker, for instance, established that economic methods could be used to study such issues as discrimination, crime, marriage, families, and addiction.

Careers in economics

Many economists find career opportunities in the business world as market analysts, consultants, and business managers. They help businesses understand production costs, markets, investment options, and other issues. Economists also help governments evaluate economic conditions and develop economic policies. Many economists teach and conduct research at colleges and universities. In addition to professional economists, thousands of other workers carry out statistical and clerical duties that are associated with economics.

A college degree in economics, business administration, or mathematics is essential for a person considering a career in economics. College students who major in economics are expected to take courses in calculus and statistics. The courses for someone pursuing a degree in economics frequently include basic and advanced classes in microeconomics and macroeconomics, as well as courses in some of the individual fields of economics.

People who wish to teach economics at a college or university usually must have a doctor's degree in economics. However, some schools, especially two-year institutions, may hire instructors with master's degrees. Many companies and government agencies require economic analysts to have graduate training.

Price V. Fishback

Related articles in *World Book* include:

Biographies

Arrow, Kenneth Joseph
Boulding, Kenneth Ewart
Friedman, Milton
Frisch, Ragnar
Galbraith, John Kenneth
Keynes, John Maynard
Klein, Lawrence Robert
Kreps, Juanita Morris
Kuznets, Simon
Lewis, Sir Arthur
Malthus, Thomas Robert
Marshall, Alfred
Marx, Karl
Mill, John Stuart
Monnet, Jean
Myrdal, Gunnar
Nash, John Forbes, Jr.
Quesnay, François
Ricardo, David
Robinson, Joan Violet
Samuelson, Paul Anthony
Schumpeter, Joseph Alois
Smith, Adam
Tinbergen, Jan
Veblen, Thorstein Bunde
Ward, Barbara
Weber, Max

Economic systems and theories

Capitalism
Collectivism
Communism
Economic determinism
Fascism
Gresham's law
Laissez faire
Manorialism
Mercantilism
Socialism
Syndicalism

Government and economics

Antitrust laws
Commerce, Department of
Federal Reserve System
Five-year plan
Government regulation
Gross domestic product
Minimum wage
National debt
National income
Price control
Public utility
Rationing
Social security
Subsidy
Taxation
Treasury, Department of the
Welfare

International economics

Andean Community
Asia-Pacific Economic Cooperation
Balance of payments
Common market
Devaluation
Developing country
European Economic and Monetary Union
European Union
Exchange rate
Exports and imports
Foreign aid
Free trade
Gold standard
International Monetary Fund
International trade
Mercosur
North American Free Trade Agreement
Reciprocal trade agreement
Sanctions, Economic
Tariff
Third World
Trade
World (Economic systems)
World Bank

Other related articles

American Enterprise Institute for Public Policy Research
Bank
Business
Business cycle
Capital
Cartel
Conglomerate
Consumer Price Index
Consumption
Corporation
Cost-benefit analysis
Cost of living
Deflation
Depreciation
Depression
Econometrics
Economic indicator
Freedom (Economic freedom)
Income
Industry
Inflation
Input-output analysis
Investment
Labor force
Labor movement
Labor union
Manufacturing
Marketing
Money
Monopoly and competition
National Bureau of Economic Research
Physiocrats
Price
Production
Productivity
Profit
Property
Recession
Standard of living
Supply and demand
Unemployment
Value
Value-added tax
Wages and hours

Additional resources

Backhouse, Roger E. *The Ordinary Business of Life: A History of Economics from the Ancient World to the Twenty-First Century.* 2002. Reprint. Princeton, 2004.
Boyer, Robert. *The Future of Economic Growth.* Edward Elgar, 2004.
Carson, Robert B., and others. *Economic Issues Today.* 8th ed. M. E. Sharpe, 2005.
Harford, Tim. *The Undercover Economist: Exposing Why the Rich Are Rich, the Poor Are Poor, and Why You Can Never Buy a Decent Used Car.* Oxford, 2005.
Mokyr, Joel, ed. *The Oxford Encyclopedia of Economic History.* 5 vols. Oxford, 2003.
Tucker, Irvin B. *Survey of Economics.* 5th ed. Thomson Learning, 2006.

Ecosystem. See Ecology.

Ecstasy is the common name for a synthetic drug that has stimulant and hallucinogenic properties. Taken in pill form, it is commonly used at large, all-night dance parties called *raves.* The drug produces feelings of relaxation, decreased anxiety, and heightened senses. Ecstasy also causes muscle tension, increased heart rate and blood pressure, and sweating. These symptoms, when combined with the vigorous physical activity of dancing, can lead to severe dehydration, heart or kidney failure, and even death. Ecstasy is also known as MDMA, for its chemical name, 3-4 *m*ethylene*d*ioxy*m*eth*a*mphetamine.

Short-term use of Ecstasy may cause confusion, depression, sleep problems, anxiety, and paranoia. These symptoms can last for weeks after taking the drug. Scientists have found that Ecstasy damages neurons in the brain that produce *serotonin,* one of the brain's most important messenger chemicals. Serotonin helps regulate mood, aggression, sleep, and sexual activity. Long-term use of Ecstasy can cause damage to the brain in areas that control thought, memory, and learning.

The production, possession, distribution, and sale of Ecstasy is prohibited in the United States and most other countries. The drug is often produced in illegal, makeshift laboratories and can contain impurities, including dangerous chemicals. Paula DeGraffenreid Riggs

See also **Drug abuse.**

Ectoplasm. See **Cell** (The cytoplasm).

© awl-images/Masterfile Corporation

Quito is Ecuador's capital and second largest city. It lies on a plateau almost 2 miles (3 kilometers) above sea level. Spaniards, who conquered what is now Ecuador in the 1500's, built many beautiful churches and public buildings in Quito. The Virgin of Quito, a winged statue of the Virgin Mary, overlooks the city from the top of El Panecillo hill.

Ecuador

Ecuador, *EHK wuh dawr,* is one of South America's smallest countries in land area. It lies on the west coast of the continent between Colombia and Peru. The equator crosses Ecuador and gives the country its name. *Ecuador* is the Spanish word for *equator.*

The Andes Mountains rise through much of central Ecuador. About half of Ecuador's people live in the valleys and on the plateaus of the Andes. Quito, Ecuador's capital, lies more than 9,000 feet (2,700 meters) above sea level on an Andean plateau.

A flat, tropical plain extends west of the Andes along the Pacific Ocean. This coastal plain is developing faster than any other part of the country. Since the mid-1900's, many people have moved to the coastal plain to farm its rich soil. Others have moved to the coastal city of Guayaquil to find jobs. Guayaquil is Ecuador's largest city. It is also the country's leading commercial center and chief seaport. East of the Andes Mountains is a large tropical rain forest called the Oriente.

Ecuador has important petroleum deposits, and oil ranks as the country's leading export. However, the work of oil companies has caused environmental problems, particularly in the Oriente. Service industries and agriculture are also important to the country's economy.

The Galapagos Islands, a group of islands about 600 miles (970 kilometers) off the coast, belong to Ecuador. These islands are known for their unique animals and plants. The British biologist Charles R. Darwin studied the varieties of plant and animal life on the islands before writing *The Origin of Species* (1859). This book presented Darwin's theory of *evolution* (gradual change).

Much of what is now Ecuador once made up part of the Inca Empire. Spanish conquerors overthrew the empire in 1534 and ruled the country for almost 300 years. Ecuador gained independence in 1830.

Facts in brief

Capital: Quito.
Official language: Spanish.
Official name: República del Ecuador (Republic of Ecuador).
Area: 102,460 mi² (265,369 km²). *Greatest distances*—north-south, 450 mi (724 km); east-west, 395 mi (636 km). *Coastline*—1,278 mi (2,057 km), including the Galapagos Islands.
Elevation: *Highest*—Chimborazo Volcano, in the Andes Mountains, 20,702 ft (6,310 m) above sea level. *Lowest*—sea level, along the coast.
Population: *Estimated 2014 population*—15,300,000; density, 149 per mi² (58 per km²); distribution, 67 percent urban, 33 percent rural. *2010 census*—14,483,499.
Chief products: *Agriculture*—bananas, barley, beef, cacao, coffee, corn, milk, oranges, potatoes, rice, sugar cane, wheat. *Fishing*—anchovies, mackerel, shrimp, tuna. *Forestry*—balsa wood. *Manufacturing*—chemicals, processed foods, straw hats, textiles, wood products. *Mining*—petroleum.
National holiday: Independence Day, August 10.
National anthem: "Salve, O Patria" ("Hail, O Fatherland").
Money: *Basic unit*—United States dollar. One hundred cents equal one dollar.

Outline

I. **Government**

II. **People**
- A. Way of life
- B. Education

III. **The land**
- A. The Coastal Lowland
- B. The Andes Highland
- C. The Eastern Lowland
- D. The Galapagos Islands

IV. **Climate**

V. **Economy**
- A. Service industries
- B. Agriculture and fishing
- C. Manufacturing and mining
- D. International trade
- E. Transportation
- F. Communication

VI. **History**

The state flag, used by the government, bears the coat of arms. The civil flag, flown by the people, has no coat of arms.

The coat of arms shows a condor, Chimborazo Mountain, and the first steamboat built in Ecuador.

Government

Ecuador is a republic. Since 1979, Ecuadoreans have elected their government. The people elect a president to a four-year term. The president appoints a Cabinet to help carry out the functions of government. The Asamblea Nacional, or National Assembly, is the country's lawmaking body. The people elect Assembly members to four-year terms. However, the president may dissolve the Assembly and call new elections within the first three years of its term.

Ecuador has 24 provinces. The president appoints a governor to each province except Pichincha Province, which does not have a governor. The Supreme Court is Ecuador's highest court.

Ecuador has had 20 constitutions since it gained independence from Spain. Most of these constitutions have provided for an elected legislature. However, until 1979, people who were *illiterate* (unable to read and write) were barred by law from voting. Leaders of the Ecuadorean government have at times suspended or replaced the country's constitution to stay in office or to increase their power. Many of Ecuador's rulers have been military leaders or have had the support of the armed forces.

Ecuador has had many political parties. The parties generally have been based on individual personalities rather than on specific sets of ideas.

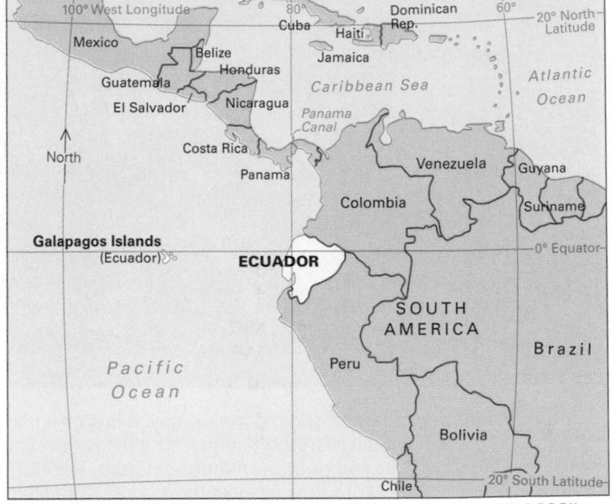

WORLD BOOK map

Ecuador lies in western South America along the Pacific Ocean. It is bordered by Colombia and Peru.

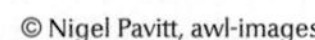

© Nigel Pavitt, awl-images

Plaza de la Independencia, also called Plaza Grande, lies in Quito's historic center. The Palacio Municipal, or city hall, *shown here,* stands on the east side of the plaza. The Palacio de Gobierno, the presidential residence, faces the city hall from across the plaza. A statue atop a tall pillar commemorates an 1809 declaration of independence from Spain.

Cuenca's New Cathedral has beautiful sky-blue *cupolas* (domes) on its towers. The church, officially named the Catedral Metropolitana de la Inmaculada Concepción de María, was constructed from the 1880's to the 1970's. Most Ecuadoreans belong to the Roman Catholic Church.

People

About 75 percent of the people of Ecuador identify themselves as *mestizo*—that is, of mixed European and *indigenous* (native) ancestry. Ten percent identify themselves as white; 7 percent as indigenous; and 5 percent as Afro-Ecuadorean. Afro-Ecuadoreans include blacks of African descent; people of mixed African and indigenous ancestry; and people of mixed African and European ancestry, called *mulattoes*. Whites of European ancestry make up the wealthiest and most powerful group in Ecuador. Indigenous people and people with African ancestry are the poorest and suffer the effects of racial discrimination.

Spanish is Ecuador's official language. In predominantly indigenous areas, indigenous languages may be used as the official language. Most Ecuadoreans belong to the Roman Catholic Church, but evangelical and Pentecostal churches have gained followers.

Way of life. Most Ecuadoreans live in cities, which have people of different backgrounds and cultures. Social inequalities are striking. In general, social class corresponds with ethnicity. A few wealthy people, mostly whites and light-skinned mestizos, enjoy a standard of living like that of upper middle-class North Americans. Most white people work in business, government, or trade, or as professionals in specialized fields. Some whites in Quito and other Andean cities own *haciendas* (large estates or farms) that produce crops for the domestic market and for export. Many whites who live on the Pacific coast own plantations that produce such export crops as bananas; cacao, which is used to make chocolate; and coffee. Others own fish farms.

Mestizos generally make more money and have better educational opportunities than Afro-Ecuadoreans and indigenous people. Some mestizos own small businesses or work in cities as civil servants. Others work as laborers on plantations.

Most Afro-Ecuadoreans live in urban areas and hold relatively low-paying jobs. Many work as maids or security guards or sell goods on the street. A small number of Afro-Ecuadoreans work as teachers, lawyers, and government employees. Rural blacks generally own plots of land that are small or of poor quality, and they often move to the cities in search of a better living. The Afro-Ecuadorean population is largest in the Chota Valley of the northern highlands, the coastal province of Esmeraldas, and the cities of Guayaquil and Quito.

Most indigenous Ecuadoreans are poor. In the past, they lived mainly in the Andean countryside and worked on haciendas. Since the 1950's, however, many have moved to urban areas. In the countryside, indigenous Ecuadoreans farm small plots of their own land or work on haciendas. In the cities, they mainly perform low-paying jobs. A small number of indigenous people belong to the middle class, working as artisans, merchants, and government employees. Some indigenous people travel between Ecuador, Europe, and the United States as merchants or musicians.

Since the 1960's, a number of organizations have worked to promote the rights of Ecuador's indigenous people and people with African ancestry. These groups have had some success. For example, they have worked with the government on development projects and have helped indigenous people acquire land.

Education. The Ecuadorean government requires all children from ages 6 to 14 to go to school. However, rural schools have limited resources, and many rural children do not attend school. Ecuador has a number of public and private universities and technical schools.

Most Ecuadorean adults can read and write. However, a higher percentage of whites and mestizos are literate than indigenous people and Afro-Ecuadoreans. In general, whites and mestizos also get more years of formal schooling than indigenous and Afro-Ecuadorean people. Among the indigenous population, men are more likely to receive formal schooling than women are.

The land

The mainland of Ecuador has three regions: (1) the Coastal Lowland, (2) the Andes Highland, and (3) the Eastern Lowland. The Galapagos Islands also belong to Ecuador.

The Coastal Lowland is a flat plain along Ecuador's Pacific coast. It was formed by mud and sand that were carried down the mountains by rivers and deposited along the shore. The plain ranges from 12 to 100 miles (19 to 160 kilometers) wide and covers about a fourth of the country. In the north, the plain is wet and swampy. In the south, near Peru, it is a desert. In between, tropical forests cover much of the Coastal Lowland. The trees have been cleared in some places, and the people farm the land. The Coastal Lowland has several rivers, including the Esmeraldas and the Guayas.

© Hemis.fr/SuperStock

Cotopaxi is one of the highest active volcanoes in the world. It rises 19,347 feet (5,897 meters) in Cotopaxi National Park in northern Ecuador. The volcano's cone is covered with glaciers and snow fields. Lava and hot ash rapidly melt snow on the flanks of the cone, sending big flows of mud down the mountainside.

The Andes Highland, often called the Sierra, also makes up about a fourth of Ecuador. Two parallel ridges of the Andes Mountains extend the length of the country from north to south. A series of high plateaus lies between them. The mountain peaks rise over 20,000 feet (6,100 meters). Cotopaxi, a volcano in northern Ecuador, is one of the highest active volcanoes in the world. It rises to a height of 19,347 feet (5,897 meters).

The Eastern Lowland, or the Oriente, covers almost half the country. The Eastern Lowland is a region of thick tropical forests in the eastern foothills of the Andes and in part of the Amazon River Basin. Many rivers, including the Napo and the Pastaza, flow through the Eastern Lowland. They make up part of the Amazon River system. Little of the region has been developed, and its people travel mostly by boat on the rivers.

The Galapagos Islands cover about 3,000 square miles (7,800 square kilometers) in the Pacific Ocean. Most of the islands are the peaks of volcanoes. Some of them rise 5,000 feet (1,500 meters) high.

Climate

Ecuador's climate varies according to the altitude. The Coastal Lowland and the Eastern Lowland are hot and humid. The Peru Current cools the Coastal Lowland slightly. The temperature in the lowlands averages about 75 °F (24 °C). The Peru Current also cools the tropical climate of the Galapagos Islands.

In the Andes Highland, the plateaus have springlike weather all year and an average temperature of 57 °F (14 °C). The climate is colder at higher altitudes. Snow covers the Andes from an altitude of about 16,000 feet (4,880 meters) up.

An average of 55 inches (140 centimeters) of rain falls in Ecuador every year. Heavy rainfall occurs in the Eastern Lowland and in the northern part of the Coastal Lowland. The southern part of the Coastal Lowland and the Galapagos Islands receive light rainfall.

© age fotostock/SuperStock

The Galapagos Islands are known for their variety of animals and plants. Giant tortoises like this one weigh more than 500 pounds (230 kilograms) and grow up to 4 feet (1.2 meters) long.

Economy

Service industries make up the largest part of Ecuador's *gross domestic product* (GDP)—that is, the total value of goods and services produced in the country each year. Leading service industries include communication, education, finance, government services, real estate,

Land regions of Ecuador

The map below shows the mainland regions of Ecuador—the Coastal Lowland, the Andes Highland, and the Eastern Lowland.

WORLD BOOK map

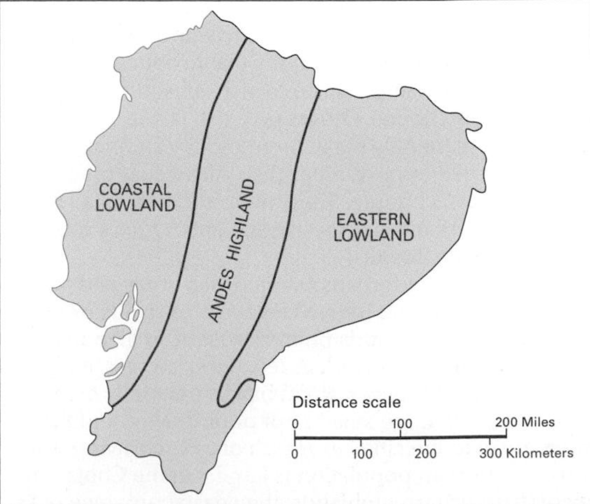

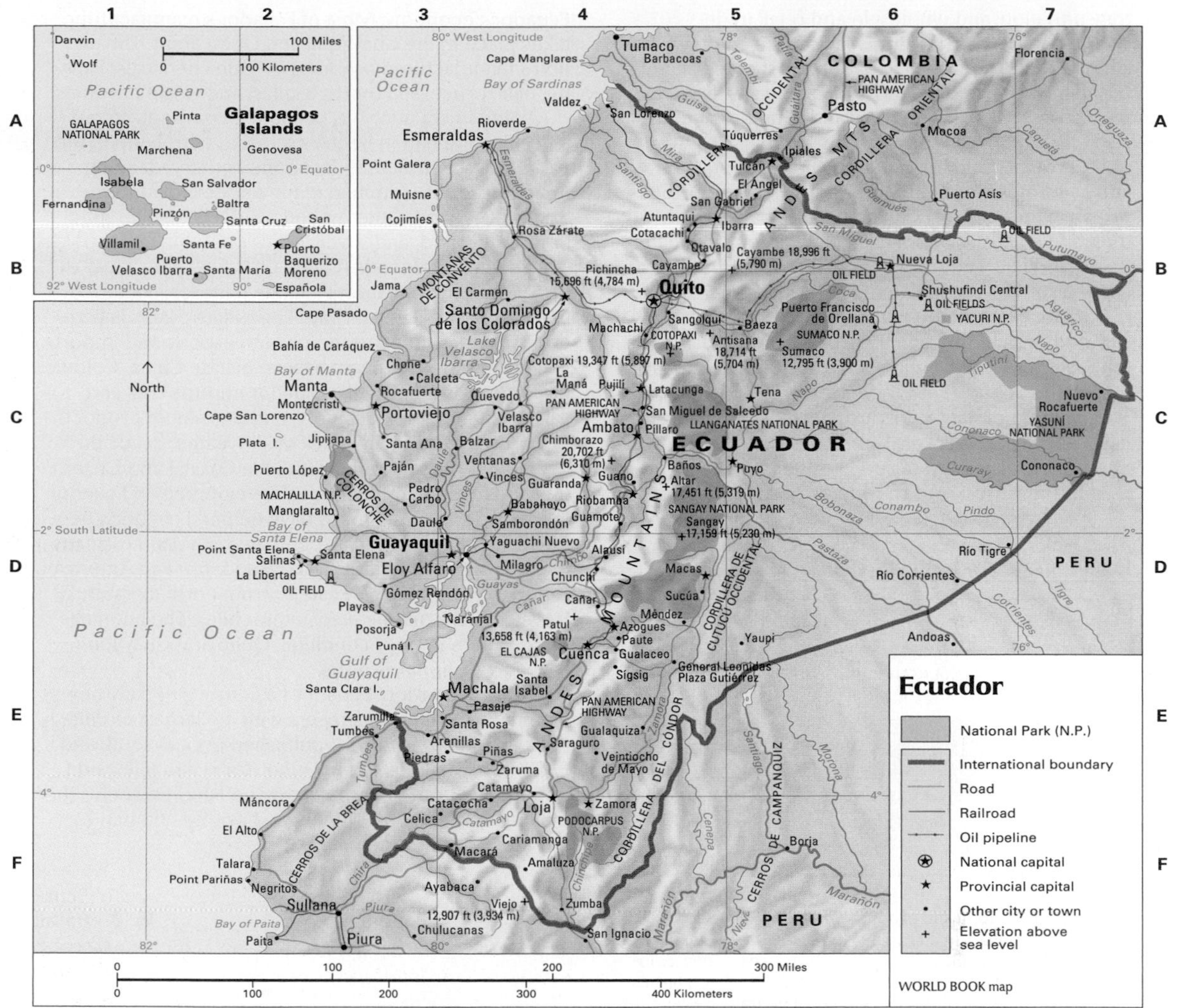

Provinces*

Azway ....712,127 ..E 4
Bolivar ....183,641 ..C 4
Cañar ....225,184 ..D 4
Carchi ....164,524 ..A 5
Chimborazo ...458,581 ..D 4
Colón (Galapagos Islands) ....25,124 ..B 1
Cotopaxi ....409,205 ..C 4
El Oro ....600,659 ..E 3
Esmeraldas ....534,092 ..A 3
Guayas ....3,645,483 ..D 3
Imbabura ......398,244 ..B 5
Loja ....448,966 ..F 4
Los Ríos ....778,115 ..D 4
Manabí ......1,369,780 ..C 3
Morona-Santiago ....147,940 ..D 5
Napo ....103,697 ..C 5
Orellana ....136,396 ..C 7
Pastaza ....83,933 ..C 5
Pichincha ....2,576,287 ..B 4
Santa Elena ....308,693 ..D 2
Santo Domingo de los Tsáchilas ....368,013 ..B 4
Sucumbíos ....176,472 ..B 6
Tungurahua ...504,583 ..C 4
Zamora-Chinchipe ....91,376 ..F 4

Cities†

Ambato ....165,185 ..C 4
Arenillas ....17,346 ..E 3
Atuntaqui ....21,286 ..B 5
Azogues ....33,848 ..D 4
Babahoyo ....90,191 ..D 4
Bahía de Caráquez .....20,921 ..C 3
Balzar ....28,794 ..C 3
Baños ....12,995 ..C 5
Buena Fe* ....38,263 ..C 3
Calceta ....17,632 ..C 3
Cañar ....13,407 ..D 4
Cariamanga .....13,311 ..F 4
Catacocha ....6,617 ..F 3
Catamayo ....22,697 ..F 4
Cayambe ....39,028 ..B 5
Chone ....52,810 ..C 3
Cotacachi ....8,848 ..B 5
Cuenca ....329,928 ..E 4
Daule ....65,145 ..D 3
El Carmen ......46,358 ..B 3
El Guabo* ....22,172 ..E 3
Eloy Alfaro .....230,839 ..D 3
El Triunfo* ......34,863 ..D 3
Esmeraldas ....154,035 ..A 3
Flavio Alvaro* ....6,197 ..B 3
Gualaceo ....13,981 ..E 4
Guano ....7,758 ..C 4
Guaranda ....23,874 ..C 4
Guayaquil ....2,278,691 ..D 3
Huaquillas* ......47,706 ..E 3
Ibarra ....131,856 ..B 5
Jipijapa ....40,232 ..C 2
La Libertad ......95,942 ..D 2
La Maná ....23,775 ..C 4
Latacunga ....63,842 ..C 4
La Troncal* .....32,259 ..D 3
Loja ....170,280 ..F 4
Macará ....12,587 ..F 3
Macas ....18,984 ..D 5
Machachi ....16,515 ..B 4
Machala ....231,260 ..E 3
Manta ....217,553 ..C 2
Milagro ....133,508 ..D 4
Montecristi .....46,312 ..C 2
Naranjal ....28,487 ..D 3
Naranjito* ....28,546 ..D 3
Nueva Loja ......48,562 ..B 6
Otavalo ....39,354 ..B 5
Pasaje ....52,673 ..E 3
Paján ....6,977 ..C 3
Pedro Carbo ....20,220 ..D 3
Piñas ....15,517 ..E 3
Playas (General Villamil) ......34,409 ..D 3
Portoviejo .....206,682 ..C 3
Puerto Baquerizo Moreno ....6,672 ..B 2
Puerto Francisco de Orellana ..40,730 ..B 6
Pujili ....10,064 ..C 4
Puyo ....33,557 ..C 5
Quevedo ......150,827 ..C 4
Quito ....1,607,734 ..B 4
Riobamba .....146,324 ..D 4
Rocafuerte ....9,204 ..C 3
Rosa Zárate .....28,928 ..B 4
Salinas ....34,719 ..D 2
Salitre* ....10,840 ..D 3
Samborondón ..42,637 ..D 3
San Gabriel .....14,487 ..B 5
San Lorenzo ....23,265 ..A 4
Sangolquí ....75,080 ..B 5
Santa Ana ....9,681 ..C 3
Santa Elena .....39,681 ..D 2
Santa Rosa ......48,929 ..E 3
Santo Domingo de los Colorados ...270,875 ..B 4
Sucúa ....7,805 ..C 5
Tena ....23,307 ..C 5
Tulcán ....53,558 ..A 5
Velasco Ibarra ..35,686 ..C 3
Ventanas ....38,168 ..C 3
Vinces ....30,248 ..C 3
Yaguachi Nuevo ....17,806 ..D 3
Zamora ....12,386 ..F 4
Zaruma ....9,677 ..E 4

Physical features

Aquarico River ....B 7
Altar (mountain) ....C 5
Antisana (volcano) ....B 5
Baltra (island) ....B 2
Bay of Manta ....C 2
Bay of Santa Elena ....D 2
Bay of Sardinas ....C 3
Bobonaza River ....D 6
Cape Pasado ....B 3
Cape San Lorenzo ....C 2
Catamayo River ....F 3
Cayambe (volcano) ......B 5
Cerros de Colonche (mountains) ....D 3
Chimborazo (volcano) ....C 4
Chinchipa River ....F 4
Coca River ....B 6
Cononaco River ....C 6
Cordillera Cutucu Occidental (mountains) ....D 3
Cordillera Occidental (mountains) ....A 5
Cotopaxi (volcano) ....C 4
Curaray River ....C 6
Daule River ....C 3
Esmeraldas River ....A 4
Española (island) ....B 2
Fernandina (island) ......B 1
Galapagos Islands ....B 1
Genovesa (island) ....A 2
Guayas River ....D 3
Gulf of Guayaquil ....E 3
Isabela (island) ....B 1
Lake Velasco Ibarra .....C 3
Marchena (island) ....A 1
Mira River ....A 5
Napo River ....C 7
Pastaza River ....D 6
Patul (mountain) ....D 4
Pichincha (volcano) ......B 4
Pindo River ....D 6
Pinta (island) ....A 7
Pinzón (island) ....A 7
Point Saint Elena ....D 2
Puná (island) ....E 3
San Cristóbal (island) ....B 2
San Miguel River ....B 6
San Salvador (island) ....A 1
Sangay (volcano) ....D 5
Santa Clara (island) ......E 3
Santa Cruz (island) ....B 2
Santa Fe (island) ....B 2
Santa Maria (island) .....B 2
Santiago River ....A 4
Sumaco (volcano) ....C 5
Tiputini River ....C 7
Vinces River ....C 3
Zamora River ....E 4

*Does not appear on map; key shows general location.
†Population of municipalities, which may include rural areas as well as the urban center.

Source: 2010 census.

transportation, and wholesale and retail trade.

Agriculture and fishing. Agriculture employs about a fourth of the people in Ecuador. Most of the nation's bananas, cacao, coffee, and sugar cane are raised on plantations in the Coastal Lowland. Oranges and rice are also grown in many coastal areas.

Most of the food for Ecuador's urban population comes from haciendas in the Andes Highland. Crops grown in the Andes Highland include barley, corn, potatoes, and wheat. Farmers raise cattle for meat and for dairy products. The Andes Highland also produces such export crops as broccoli and flowers.

Ecuador ranks as the world's leading producer of balsa wood, which grows in the Coastal Lowland. Forests in the Eastern Lowland yield such tropical hardwoods as mahogany.

Ecuador's coastal waters are rich in fish. Ecuadoreans catch anchovies, mackerel, and tuna along the coast. Shrimp and tilapia are raised in ponds.

Manufacturing and mining are also important to Ecuador's economy. Most of Ecuador's manufacturing takes place in the Guayaquil and Quito areas. The nation's manufactured products include chemicals, Panama hats, processed foods, textiles, and wood products.

Mining in Ecuador has become increasingly important since the nation began exporting petroleum in the early 1970's. Petroleum—by far the country's leading mined product—is mined in the northern part of the Eastern Lowland. Other mined products include gold, limestone, sand, and silver.

International trade. Crude oil is Ecuador's chief export. Other major exports include bananas, cocoa, coffee, cut flowers, and shrimp. The United States is Ecuador's main trading partner for both exports and imports. Ecuador's other trading partners include China, Colombia, Peru, and Venezuela. Ecuador imports cars and trucks, chemicals, machinery, and petroleum products.

Transportation. The lack of all-weather roads between the Andes Highland and the Coastal and Eastern lowlands held back economic development in Ecuador for many years. New roads have helped Ecuador's people move from the thickly populated highland plateaus to the less crowded Coastal Lowland. The Pan American Highway runs through Ecuador from north to south. However, few people own automobiles. The country's railroads are in poor condition. Quito and Guayaquil have international airports.

Communication. Ecuador has dozens of daily newspapers. The daily newspapers with the largest circulations include *El Universo,* published in Guayaquil, and *El Comercio,* published in Quito. Radio and television stations are both government-owned and privately owned. Both the government and private companies provide telephone services.

Ecuador's gross domestic product

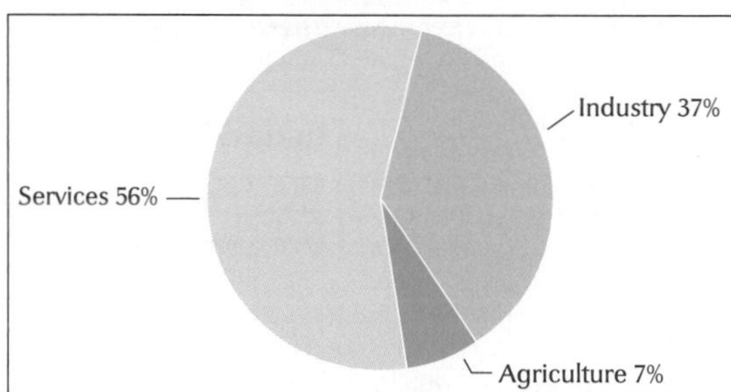

Ecuador's gross domestic product (GDP) was $41,402,000,000 in United States dollars in 2006. The GDP is the total value of goods and services produced within a country in a year. *Services* include community, government, and personal services; finance, insurance, real estate, and business services; trade, restaurants, and hotels; and transportation and communication. *Industry* includes construction, manufacturing and mining, and utilities. *Agriculture* includes agriculture, forestry, and fishing.

Production and workers by economic activities

Economic activities	Percent of GDP produced	Employed workers: Number of people	Employed workers: Percent of total
Manufacturing & mining	26	571,300	12
Community, government, & personal services	17	897,900	18
Finance, insurance, real estate, & business services	15	248,600	5
Trade, restaurants, & hotels	14	1,377,200	28
Transportation & communication	11	292,300	6
Construction	10	290,100	6
Agriculture, forestry, & fishing	7	1,177,000	24
Utilities	1	19,400	*
Total†	100	4,873,800	100

*Less than one-half of 1 percent.
†Figures do not add up to 100 percent due to rounding.
Figures are for 2006. Employment figures, except for agriculture, are for urban areas only.
Sources: Ecuador National Institute of Statistics; International Labour Organization; International Monetary Fund; Food and Agriculture Organization of the United Nations.

© A. Upitis, FPG

Bananas, one of Ecuador's most important crops, are grown on plantations in the Coastal Lowland. They are packed in boxes and loaded on ships at Guayaquil, the country's chief port. Ecuador is a leading exporter of bananas.

History

Indigenous period. During the late 1400's, Inca Indians from Peru conquered much of what is now Ecuador. At that time, many different American Indian tribes lived in Ecuador. In less than 50 years, the Inca united many of these tribes under a single government and taught the people the Inca language, Quechua.

Spanish rule. In 1534, Spanish conquerors defeated the local rulers and took control of Ecuador. Some indigenous groups that had resented the Inca joined the Spaniards in the conquest. Most of the Spaniards settled in the Andes Highland. They made Quito their capital and built many beautiful churches and public buildings there. The Spaniards set up large haciendas and forced the Indians to work on them. Some Spaniards established plantations in the Coastal Lowland and brought black Africans to work as slaves. Many Spanish men married indigenous women, and their children became Ecuador's first mestizos.

The French emperor Napoleon I invaded and conquered Spain in the early 1800's. The rulers of the Spanish colonies in Latin America took advantage of Spain's weakness to demand independence. In 1822, General Antonio José de Sucre defeated the Spaniards at the Battle of Pichincha, near Quito, and ended Spanish rule in Ecuador. Ecuador then joined in a confederation called Gran Colombia, which included what are now Colombia, Panama, and Venezuela. In 1830, Ecuador left the confederation and became an independent country.

Independence. Rival leaders fought for power in the early years of the new nation. Presidents, dictators, and *juntas* rose and fell. A junta is a small group, usually of military officers, that takes over a government and rules by decree. Most of Ecuador's early rulers ignored the rights and needs of the people.

In 1861, Gabriel García Moreno became president. García, a member of the Conservative Party, ruled with the support of the Roman Catholic Church and the landowners of the Andes Highland. During his rule, the government planned roads and railroads, developed agriculture and industry, and encouraged international trade. García was assassinated in 1875. Other Conservatives followed him in office, but none had enough power to continue his plans and policies.

In 1896, General Eloy Alfaro, a member of the Liberal Party, seized control of the government. The Liberals drew support from business executives in Guayaquil and from military leaders. They ended the power of the church over the government, finished the railroad connecting Quito and Guayaquil, and tried to modernize the government. But they did little to solve basic social problems, such as the poverty of the Indians. In addition, the Liberals used electoral fraud to stay in power.

The 1900's. By 1925, the government's failure to solve Ecuador's economic and social problems had led to widespread dissatisfaction. New political parties, workers' and peasants' unions, and state employees' federations formed as a result. Ecuador had 22 presidents or chiefs of state from 1925 to 1948. None of these leaders served a complete term.

In the 1930's, José María Velasco Ibarra emerged as a leading political figure. He criticized traditional political parties and sought to appeal to the poor and oppressed.

Antonio José de Sucre commanded the armies that liberated Ecuador, Peru, and Bolivia from Spanish rule. In 1822, Sucre freed Ecuador by winning the Battle of Pichincha near Quito.

His followers regarded him as a symbol for honest and free elections. Although Velasco was elected president five times from the 1930's to the 1960's, he had difficulty holding on to power. He finished just one of his terms.

A border dispute between Ecuador and Peru led to war in 1941. That year, Peru seized territory that Ecuador had claimed in the Amazon River Basin. Latin American leaders met in Rio de Janeiro, Brazil, and worked out a settlement that gave most of the disputed territory to Peru. However, Ecuador still claimed the land, and fighting broke out between the two countries several times. It was not until 1998 that Ecuador and Peru signed a treaty that set the border and ended the dispute.

Ecuador experienced political calm and progress from 1948 to 1960. More and more people were permitted to vote, and they elected presidents who served full terms. Galo Plaza Lasso, a Liberal Party candidate, won election to the presidency in 1948 and served until 1952. Former President Velasco, a political independent, followed him. Velasco, who claimed a special interest in helping the poor, enjoyed widespread popularity. Camilo Ponce Enríquez, a conservative politician, became president in 1956 and served until 1960.

In 1960, Velasco won another term as president. However, he was forced out of office after trying to levy new taxes. Vice President Carlos Julio Arosemena Monroy replaced him. In 1963, the armed forces overthrew Arosemena and suspended the Constitution. The armed forces leaders, who said they had acted to prevent a Communist take-over, had the support of the U.S. Central Intelligence Agency (CIA). A military junta began to make land and tax reforms, but the people soon demanded an end to military rule.

In 1966, military leaders named Clemente Yerovi Indaburu as temporary civilian president. Yerovi called a constitutional convention. The convention wrote a new constitution and chose Otto Arosemena Gómez to serve as president until an election could be held. Velasco was elected president once again in 1968. In 1970, he suspended Ecuador's Constitution and began to govern as a dictator. Military leaders overthrew Velasco in 1972, and General Guillermo Rodríguez Lara took power. In 1976, Ecuadorean military commanders removed Rodríguez from office and took over the government.

In 1979, Ecuador adopted a new constitution, and elections were held to establish a new civilian government. In the decades that followed, the country held elections regularly.

León Febres Cordero became president in 1984. He emphasized *free enterprise,* the idea that economic activities should be free from most government control. But his economic policies became unpopular, and his government was accused of corruption. In 1987, members of the military kidnapped Febres Cordero and beat him. He returned to office and completed his term.

In 1996, Abdalá Bucaram Ortiz, a former Olympic runner, became president. He was a *populist* (supporter of the common people) who viewed the upper classes as the source of many ills. Bucaram's policies raised the price of basic services. He became known for his odd behavior. For example, he shaved off his mustache on live TV and released a CD of his music called "A Crazy Man Who Loves." Six months after his election, the National Congress (now the National Assembly) forced him from office, claiming he was mentally unfit to serve.

In 1998, voters elected Jamil Mahuad president. During Mahuad's presidency, Ecuador suffered an economic crisis. Many banks closed, and numerous people lost their savings and their jobs. In January 2000, an alliance of young military officers and indigenous activists forced Mahuad out of office. Colonel Lucio Gutiérrez, a leader of the revolt, became president in 2003.

Indigenous groups and *leftists* (people with strongly liberal political beliefs) supported Gutiérrez at first. To secure his hold on power, Gutiérrez formed an alliance with populist parties in the National Congress and reorganized the Supreme Court. However, his government soon became linked with corruption. Public protests erupted in Quito. The legislature, with the backing of the military, removed Gutiérrez from office in 2005.

Recent developments. In 2006, Ecuadoreans elected leftist candidate Rafael Correa, of the political organization Alianza País, president. Under Correa's leadership, Ecuador's political system began a transformation. Political parties that had dominated politics in the late 1900's declined, and the Alianza País became the dominant organization. Correa's government emphasized state planning, nationalism, government intervention in the economy, and a new commitment to social justice.

In 2008, Ecuadoreans approved a new constitution by a *referendum* (direct vote). The Constitution expanded civil and social rights and included measures to protect the natural environment. Correa was reelected easily in 2009 and 2013. In 2011, voters approved, by referendum, reform of the judicial system and regulation of the media. Critics who opposed the reforms argued that Correa sought to increase his power and limit unfavorable media coverage. Carlos De La Torre

Related articles in *World Book* include:

Andes Mountains
Balsa
Chimborazo
Cotopaxi
Galapagos Islands
Guayaquil
Inca
Jívaro Indians
Latin America
Pichincha
Quito
Sucre, Antonio

Additional resources

Becker, Marc. *Indians and Leftists in the Making of Ecuador's Modern Indigenous Movements.* Duke Univ. Pr., 2008.
Clark, A. Kim, and Becker, Marc, eds. *Highland Indians and the State in Modern Ecuador.* Univ. of Pittsburgh Pr., 2007.
Lyons, Barry J. *Remembering the Hacienda: Religion, Authority, and Social Change in Highland Ecuador.* Univ. of Tex. Pr., 2006.
Pineo, Ronn F. *Ecuador and the United States.* Univ. of Ga. Pr., 2007.

Ecumenical council. See Vatican Council I; Vatican Council II.

Eczema, *EHK suh muh* or *ehg ZEE muh,* is a skin disorder characterized by itching and inflammation. The inflamed skin may be dry, swollen, and crusty, or it may ooze fluids. There are several forms of eczema, none of which is contagious. Common types include *atopic eczema, neurodermatitis,* and *contact dermatitis.*

Atopic eczema, also called *atopic dermatitis,* tends to run in families. Most cases begin during infancy and are outgrown by 3 or 4 years of age. Some continue through adulthood, flaring up occasionally—especially when the victim is upset, angry, or worried. Treatment includes the use of lotions or ointments, some of which may contain drugs called *corticosteroids.*

Neurodermatitis forms thickened patches on the skin, particularly on the back of the neck or on an ankle. In most cases, people develop the condition by scratching an area repeatedly when they are nervous. Scratching damages the skin and makes it itch even more, which leads to more scratching. Treatment involves eliminating the habit of nervous scratching.

Contact dermatitis is an allergic reaction to certain substances a person touches. Poison ivy or poison oak, for example, causes this type of eczema wherever the plant touches the skin. Treatment of contact dermatitis includes avoiding further contact with the substances that cause the reaction. Yelva Liptzin Lynfield

Edda, *EHD uh,* is a term that refers to two separate works of medieval Icelandic literature. The *Poetic,* or *Elder, Edda* is a collection of anonymous poems composed in the 1000's and 1100's. The *Prose,* or *Younger, Edda* is a textbook for poets written during the 1200's by the Icelandic poet and historian Snorri Sturluson. Snorri's work was the first to be called *Edda,* a name that may be related to an Icelandic word meaning *song* or *poem.* Later, the term was applied to the *Elder Edda,* too.

Twenty-four of the 38 poems in the *Poetic Edda* are heroic tales, many of them concerned with the exploits of the hero Sigurd (Siegfried in German). The remaining 14 poems contain mythological material, including accounts of the creation and end of the universe. The longest of these poems is *The Sayings of the High One.* It contains practical wisdom and reveals the moral attitudes of the people of medieval Scandinavia.

Snorri's *Prose Edda* consists of a preface and three sections. The first narrates myths about Scandinavian deities. The second explores features of poetic diction. The final section is a poem of 102 verses, each illustrating a type of meter or stanza form. Richard N. Ringler

See also **Mythology** (Teutonic mythology); **Sigurd; Snorri Sturluson.**

Eddington, Sir Arthur Stanley (1882-1944), was a British astronomer who pioneered in the investigation of the internal structure of stars. Eddington wondered what prevents a star from collapsing inward under its own gravitational pressure. In 1926, he showed that enough outward pressure is produced by the light and other electromagnetic radiation inside the star, and by the gas of which the star is composed.

Eddington led the campaign in the United Kingdom for acceptance of the *theory of general relativity,* a set of ideas proposed by German-born physicist Albert Einstein. The theory deals with the physical laws that govern time, space, mass, motion, and gravitation. During a solar eclipse in 1919, Eddington's observation team detected the bending aside of starlight by the sun's gravitational field. Their observation supported Einstein's theory, which had predicted that effect. In 1924, Eddington showed a fundamental relationship between the mass and brightness of a star. In most cases, the more mass a star has, the brighter it is.

Eddington was born on Dec. 28, 1882, at Kendal, England. He studied at Manchester and Cambridge universities, and directed the Cambridge University Observatory from 1914 to 1944. He died on Nov. 22, 1944.

Karl Hufbauer

See also **Sun** (Core).

Eddy, Mary Baker (1821-1910), was an American religious thinker and leader. She founded the Christian Science denomination—the Church of Christ, Scientist—in 1879. She developed a theology of spiritual healing, which remains controversial but continues to influence Christianity. See **Christian Scientists.**

Eddy, whose maiden name was Mary Morse Baker, was born on July 16, 1821, on a farm in Bow, New Hampshire. In her youth, she rebelled against the New England Puritan idea of a harsh and unforgiving God. But her religious upbringing also gave her a deep love of the Bible.

The Christian Science Publishing Society

Mary Baker Eddy

Eddy's personal misfortunes increased her religious questioning. In 1844, her first husband died after less than a year of marriage. She married Daniel Patterson in 1853. During much of this time, she was in poor health, and she began to investigate methods of healing. In 1862, she met Phineas Quimby, who claimed to relieve people of their ailments through what today would be called the power of suggestion. Her contact with Quimby reinforced her own growing conviction that disease had a mental, rather than a physical, cause. But Eddy eventually broke with Quimby, insisting that true healing came from God's power acting on, not through, the human mind.

Eddy gained this conviction in 1866, when she recovered from an injury while reading about one of Jesus's healings in the Gospels. For the next nine years, she studied the Bible, practiced and taught healing, and wrote. In 1875, she published the "textbook" of Christian Science, ultimately named *Science and Health with Key to the Scriptures.* In it, she stated that disease and other evils result from the human mind's ignorance of our relationship to God. She taught that through Christian discipleship, people can follow Jesus's command that his followers practice spiritual healing. Eddy saw his healing works and Resurrection as demonstrating that the true nature of reality is spiritual, not bound by material limits.

Eddy devoted the rest of her life to advancing what she saw as her discovery of the "science," or underlying spiritual laws, that explain Biblical events and show their continuing meaning. Eddy's second marriage ended in divorce in 1873, and she married Asa G. Eddy in 1877.

In 1892, she reorganized the Christian Science church into its present form. In 1908, she founded the newspaper *The Christian Science Monitor* as a crucial link between her church and the world. Eddy died on Dec. 3, 1910. Stephen Gottschalk

Edelweiss, *AY duhl vys* or *AY duhl wys,* is a flower that grows in the mountain regions of Europe and Asia. The edelweiss has long, narrow leaves and grows from 4 to 12 inches (10 to 30 centimeters) tall. White, star-shaped flowers grow from the leaves.

WORLD BOOK illustration by Christabel King

Edelweiss

The edelweiss can be cultivated in cool regions of America and Europe. In its native countries the edelweiss is considered a rare plant, because it grows wild in high regions and is difficult to obtain. James S. Miller

Scientific classification. The scientific name for the edelweiss is *Leontopodium alpinum.*

Edema, *ih DEE muh,* is swelling of body tissues caused by fluid build-up between cells. Cells are bathed and nourished by fluid that always seeps from *capillaries,* the tiniest blood vessels. Normally, the seepage is balanced by reabsorption of fluid into the capillaries and by drainage into the *lymphatic system* (see **Lymphatic system**). When this balance is upset, edema results.

Edema may be *local*—that is, limited to one part of the body—or it may be general, affecting tissues throughout the body. Local edema commonly results when injured capillaries leak their contents into nearby tissue spaces. Such local edema is corrected by treating the injury and by elevating the affected body part.

The most common cause of general edema is heart failure. When a weak heart does not circulate the blood effectively, the kidneys cannot remove enough water and salt from the bloodstream. As a result, the blood volume increases, and excess liquid seeps into the body tissues, particularly the legs and lungs. The condition is called *pulmonary edema* when excess fluid accumulates in the lungs, causing shortness of breath. Physicians treat edema due to heart failure with drugs or surgery to improve heart function. Patients also receive *diuretics,* medicines that increase the amount of water and salt that are eliminated by the patient's kidneys.

General edema also often results if poor diet, liver disease, or kidney disease causes a drop in the blood plasma's protein content. Proteins in blood plasma play a major role in the blood's ability to retain fluid. High-protein diets help correct this type of edema.

Problems with lymphatic drainage cause *lymphedema.* This condition often requires long periods of bed rest, with the affected body parts elevated and tightly wrapped to reduce swelling. The most dramatic form of lymphedema is *elephantiasis,* a disease in which parts of the body swell and the skin becomes rough and thickened like that of an elephant. Giacomo A. DeLaria

See also **Diuretic; Elephantiasis.**

Eden, *EE duhn,* was a region described in the Bible as the place where God planted a garden for Adam and Eve. The name comes from a Sumerian word that means *plain.* Chapter 2 of Genesis tells that the garden contained beautiful fruit-bearing trees, and the tree of life and the tree of the knowledge of good and evil. A stream flowed from the garden and divided into four rivers. Two of these are thought to be the Tigris and Euphrates rivers. The other two, called Pishon and Gihon, have not been identified. The four rivers may represent an ancient belief in four great streams that surrounded the world. See also **Adam and Eve.** H. Darrell Lance

Eden, Sir Anthony (1897-1977), Earl of Avon, succeeded Sir Winston Churchill as prime minister of the United Kingdom from 1955 to 1957. Eden was the leader of the British Conservative Party during that time. He was largely responsible for the United Kingdom's decision to join France in attempting to seize the Suez Canal in October 1956 after Egypt had *nationalized* (taken control of) it in July. He was criticized greatly for this action. Under United Nations pressure, a cease-fire was quickly arranged (see **Suez Canal** [History]). Eden resigned in January 1957.

Eden was born on June 12, 1897, in Durham, England. In World War I (1914-1918), he fought in France and was awarded the Military Cross for distinguished service. He graduated from Oxford University in 1922. Eden entered Parliament in 1923. He became the United Kingdom's foreign secretary in 1935 but resigned in 1938 because Prime Minister Neville Chamberlain yielded to the demands of dictators Adolf Hitler of Germany and Benito Mussolini of Italy. Eden again served as foreign secretary from 1940 to 1945 and from 1951 to 1955. He received the title Earl of Avon in 1961. Keith Robbins

Edentate, *ee DEHN tayt,* is the traditional name for a group of mammals that have incomplete sets of teeth or no teeth at all. Anteaters, armadillos, and sloths are the only living edentates. These animals are most common in South America, but they also inhabit Central America and parts of North America. The armadillo is the only edentate that lives in the United States. Edentate means *toothless,* but armadillos and sloths have back teeth. Some edentates have a hard, bony covering. Others are covered only by hair. Bruce A. Brewer

Scientific classification. Edentates traditionally made up the order Xenarthra. Scientists now classify them in other orders.

See also **Anteater; Armadillo; Ground sloth; Sloth.**

Ederle, *AY duhr lee,* **Gertrude Caroline** (1906-2003), a famous American swimmer, became the first woman to swim the English Channel. In 1926, at the age of 19, Ederle swam the channel from France to England. Her time of 14 hours 39 minutes for the 35-mile (56-kilometer) distance broke the previous record and stood as the women's record for 35 years.

From 1921 to 1925, Ederle set 29 United States and world records for races ranging from 50 yards to a half mile. In the 1924 Summer Olympic Games, she won a gold medal as a member of the championship U.S. 400-meter freestyle relay team. She also won bronze medals for finishing third in the 100-meter and 400-meter freestyle races. Ederle was born on Oct. 23, 1906, in New York City. She died on Nov. 30, 2003. William F. Reed

Edgerton, Harold Eugene (1903-1990), an American engineer and inventor, revolutionized high-speed photography with his *electronic stroboscope,* an instrument that can produce single or rapidly repeating flashes of light. Edgerton used this device to produce famous stop-action photographs of such subjects as a bullet tearing through a playing card. See **Ballistics.**

Edgerton also used the stroboscope in motion-picture photography, enabling him to show high-speed processes in slow motion. This technique was used in *Quicker 'n a Wink,* a film short that won an Academy Award in 1940. His other inventions include the first electronic flash equipment used to take aerial photographs at night, deep-sea cameras, and sonar systems. See **Sonar.**

Edgerton was born on April 6, 1903, in Fremont, Nebraska. He received a Doctor of Science degree from Massachusetts Institute of Technology (MIT) in 1931. He became an assistant professor at MIT in 1932 and remained at MIT until his death on Jan. 4, 1990.

J. Kim Vandiver

Edgeworth-Kuiper belt. See Kuiper belt.

Edict of Nantes. See Nantes, Edict of.

Edinburgh, *EH duhn buh ruh* (pop. 477,000), is the capital and second largest city of Scotland. Glasgow is the largest city. Edinburgh stands on the hills south of the Firth of Forth. The city's original name was *Din Eidyn* or *Dineidin,* which means *fortress on a hill.* For the

Edinburgh Castle stands on a huge rock overlooking the city. Bagpipers in kilts lead frequent parades past the castle gates.

location of Edinburgh, see **Scotland** (political map).

The city's main thoroughfare, Princes Street, lies at the south edge of Edinburgh's New Town area. This area, which was built during the late 1700's and the early 1800's, was laid out in a symmetrical pattern. Many of Scotland's great buildings stand along the north side of Princes Street. Railroad trains pass through a small valley along the south side. Princes Street Gardens, which are famous for their flower clock, are in the valley.

South of the valley, Edinburgh Castle stands atop Castle Rock. Within the castle walls is the Norman Chapel of Saint Margaret. This chapel was probably built during the 1000's. Along the Royal Mile, which leads from the castle to the Palace of Holyroodhouse, stand historic houses and Saint Giles's Cathedral.

Edinburgh has long been important as a cultural and educational center. The University of Edinburgh and the Royal High School were founded in the 1500's. The Advocates' Library, where the philosopher David Hume was once librarian, was founded in 1682. Major art collections are housed in the Royal Scottish Academy Building and the National Gallery of Scotland. The National Museum of Scotland has exhibits on Scottish history and culture. The annual Edinburgh International Festival attracts performing artists from many countries.

Edinburgh publishers have sponsored well-known magazines, including the *Edinburgh Review* and *Chambers's Edinburgh Journal.* Many leading Scottish authors, and John Knox—who led the Protestant Reformation in Scotland—lived in Edinburgh.

Edinburgh is a banking and insurance center. It has many electronic and medical technology companies. Its traditional industries include baking, brewing beer, distilling whisky, and papermaking. A. S. Mather

For the monthly weather in Edinburgh, see **United Kingdom** (Climate). See also **Scotland** (picture).

Edinburgh, Duke of. See **Philip, Prince.**

Edinburgh, *EH duhn buh ruh,* **University of,** is one of the oldest universities in the United Kingdom. The university was founded in Edinburgh, Scotland, in 1583. It consists of three colleges: humanities and social science, medicine and veterinary medicine, and science and engineering. Its website at http://www.ed.ac.uk offers additional information. P. A. McGinley

Edirne, *eh DIHR neh,* formerly Adrianople, *AY dree uh NOH puhl* (pop. 119,298), is an ancient Turkish city. It was the European capital of the Ottoman Empire from 1361 until the Ottomans captured Constantinople in 1453. Edirne is in northwestern Turkey, near the Bulgarian border (see **Turkey** [political map]). Edirne was once a great trading center. Today, it is still an important regional trading city in Turkey. The mosque of Selim II, built in the 1500's, stands in Edirne. It is considered the masterpiece of the great Ottoman architect known as Mimar Sinan (in Turkish, *mimar* means *the architect).*

The Roman emperor Hadrian founded the city on the ruins of an ancient Thracian city and named it Hadrianopolis. Several major battles took place near the city, among them the defeat of Roman troops by Visigoths in A.D. 378. The Ottomans took over the city in 1360. Russian troops captured it in 1829 and 1878. Bulgarians briefly occupied the city in 1913 during the Balkan Wars. Edirne became a part of the new Republic of Turkey in 1923. F. Muge Gocek

Photo of Thomas Edison in 1878; National Park Service

Edison's phonograph, perhaps his favorite invention, played sounds recorded on a cylinder covered with tinfoil.

Thomas Alva Edison

Edison, Thomas Alva (1847-1931), was one of the greatest inventors and technological innovators in history. His most famous contributions include useful electric lighting and the world's first electric power system. He invented the first practical machine that could record and play back sound. He called this device the *phonograph.* Edison also made improvements to telegraphs, telephones, and motion pictures.

Edison looked for many different solutions when attempting to solve problems. When he created new or improved devices, he made a variety of designs. Sometimes, he borrowed features from one technology and adapted them to another. Edison obtained 1,093 United States patents, the most the U.S. Patent Office (now the U.S. Patent and Trademark Office) has ever issued to one person. Altogether, he received thousands of patents from some two dozen nations.

Edison also created one of the first modern research laboratories. Some scientists and historians regard this development as Edison's greatest achievement. Edison's research laboratory grew out of the way he worked. He often worked alongside his assistants. He observed how others solved mechanical, electrical, and chemical problems. Then he tried to improve upon their ideas. By the early 1900's, many industrial corporations had seen the success of research labs and established their own.

Outline

I. Early life
- A. Early interests
- B. The young telegrapher

II. Inventor and businessman
- A. The Wizard of Menlo Park
- B. Edison in West Orange

III. Personal life
- A. Family and friends
- B. Philosophy
- C. Honors

Edison was an active businessman. He created new companies to manufacture and sell his products. Income from selling his products helped support his research laboratory and the development of more devices. As a result, Edison and other manufacturing pioneers in the late 1800's helped make the United States an industrial world power.

Armed with self-confidence and determination, Edison overcame a number of technical and commercial failures. He became world famous by his mid-30's and a millionaire by his mid-40's. His name—and the electric light bulb that he designed—became worldwide symbols of bright ideas and technical creativity.

National Park Service, Edison National Historic Site

Edison at age 14

Early life

Edison was born on Feb. 11, 1847, in Milan, Ohio. He was the seventh and youngest child of Samuel and Nancy Elliott Edison. Edison's father fled from Canada during the rebellions of 1837, in which Canadian rebels unsuccessfully revolted against British rule. Samuel Edison worked as a shingle maker and land investor. When Al—as the family called young Edison—was 7 years old, the Edisons moved to Port Huron, Michigan. There his father ran businesses in lumbering and land investing.

Early interests. Edison received limited formal education. His mother, a former teacher, guided his learning. Edison was mischievous and inquisitive. He loved to pull pranks and practical jokes. He was also eager to read, particularly science books. His reading led him to experiment with chemicals and to construct elaborate models. He built models of a working sawmill and a railroad engine, both powered by steam.

Even as a child, Edison was interested in business. He grew vegetables on his father's farm and sold them in town. At age 12, Edison began to sell newspapers, candy, and sandwiches on passenger trains between Port Huron and Detroit. When he was 15, he published and sold a newspaper called the *Weekly Herald.*

Edison Birthplace Museum

Edison's birthplace was this red brick house in Milan, Ohio. Edison lived in Milan until he moved with his family to Port Huron, Michigan, when he was 7 years old.

By this time, Edison had developed hearing problems. His hearing worsened as he grew older. Late in life, he could only hear people shouting directly into his ear.

The young telegrapher. At age 15, Edison rescued the son of a telegraph operator from the path of a railroad car. As a reward, the operator gave Edison telegraph lessons. In 1863, Edison began work as a telegraph operator for the Western Union Telegraph Company. During the following four years, he worked as a telegrapher in a number of Midwestern cities. Edison learned much about the scientific aspects of telegraphic communication. He experimented with telegraph equipment. He also read newspapers, scientific journals, and books.

Inventor and businessman

In 1868, Edison moved to Boston as a telegraph operator. He soon made improvements to the process used to print telegraphs and to a device that transmitted images over telegraph lines. Edison also applied for his first patent. But the invention—an electric vote-recorder for legislatures—was never used.

In 1869, Edison moved to New York City. There he met leaders in the business community, who appreciated his work as an inventor. At the time, Edison's inventions included improved *stock tickers,* telegraph devices used to report the purchase and sale of stocks. In 1870, Edison moved to Newark, New Jersey, and started a stock ticker manufacturing company.

Edison hired associates with mechanical talent to help develop a steady stream of inventions. He continually tried to improve the devices he sold. He also kept systematic notes of his activities. He used these notes to organize research and to defend his patents.

In 1874, Edison completed the design of the *quadruplex,* a device that made telegraphs faster and more efficient. Edison called it the *quadruplex* because it could send four messages at the same time over a single wire. In 1875, Edison and his staff developed an electric pen that cut stencils out of paper for copying documents.

The Wizard of Menlo Park. In the spring of 1876, Edison built his first research laboratory in the rural community of Menlo Park, New Jersey. The work done by Edison and his assistants at Menlo Park would make him famous throughout the world. Three of his greatest inventions originated there: (1) an improved telephone transmitter, (2) the phonograph, and (3) the electric light. Menlo Park is now part of a township known as Edison.

Telephone transmitter. Edison was one of many inventors who improved the "speaking telegraph," as the telephone was then called. Alexander Graham Bell, a Scottish-born inventor, patented the telephone in 1876. In 1877, Edison designed a carbon-based transmitter. It made the voice of a speaker louder and clearer over the telephone. Before his invention, people had difficulty hearing anything said over the telephone. Until the 1980's, most phones used transmitters based on Edison's improvement.

The phonograph. In 1876 and 1877, Edison experimented with ways to record and replay messages. These experiments led to the invention of his phono-

Brent Groth

Edison's baggage-car laboratory, shown in this restoration, was part of the train on which he worked when he was 12. Young Edison conducted chemical experiments in this car.

graph. To record messages, Edison attached a needle to a *diaphragm*, a metal disk that vibrated in response to sound waves. The needle rested against a rotating cylinder wrapped with tinfoil. When the disk vibrated, the needle made varying impressions in the foil. To reproduce the sound, another needle was attached to a diaphragm and funnellike horn. This needle retraced the impressions or grooves in the foil. It vibrated the diaphragm and thus the air in the horn, re-creating the original sound waves.

In December 1877, Edison had a machinist build the phonograph. When it was done, he recorded the nursery rhyme "Mary Had A Little Lamb." Then Edison showed his phonograph to the editors of *Scientific American* magazine. The next spring, he demonstrated it for scientists, members of Congress, and President Rutherford B. Hayes. Newspapers and magazines helped spread enthusiasm for the invention and its inventor. Edison became one of the most famous Americans alive. Stories of his childhood, pictures of his "invention factory," and interviews with the inventor went out to the whole world. As a result, Edison became known around the world as the "Wizard of Menlo Park."

The electric light. In 1878, Edison began his most ambitious project. He developed a system of electric lighting to be used in homes, stores, offices, and factories. He found support for this project from J. P. Morgan, a powerful banker. Many inventors at the time were investigating electric lighting. They thought electric lighting would be cheaper, safer, and more reliable than the gas lighting that was popular in cities and suburbs.

Edison threw himself and his assistants into the complex work of developing a variety of electric light and power devices. This work required a system of generators, wires and cables, switches, motors, meters, and *lamps* (light bulbs). The lamps were probably the most famous component of the system.

An *incandescent lamp* produces light by passing an electric current through a *filament* (fine thread or wire). The electric current heats the filament so that it glows. Edison had to figure out how to make practical, long-lasting incandescent lamps.

Edison and his associates placed the filament inside a glass vacuum bulb. They spent months searching for an affordable filament material that would produce the best light. In October 1879, they tested a carbon filament made from burned sewing thread, resulting in their first practical incandescent light bulb. In 1880, they began using bamboo filaments, which lasted longer.

Electric utilities and manufacturing. In 1881, Edison moved back to New York City. He personally supervised the construction of his first central power station in the United States. It opened in 1882 on Pearl Street and served the business community in lower Manhattan. By 1884, this station delivered electric lighting to more than 500 customers and more than 10,000 lamps.

Edison's agents introduced his lighting system in other countries. They established companies to install Edison's system abroad. In 1882, small central stations opened in London and in Santiago, Chile. In 1883, an Edison central station began operating in Milan, Italy. In 1885, a major station opened in Berlin, Germany. By the 1890's, hundreds of communities throughout the world had Edison power stations. Edison also developed and sold small generating plants. They could be used in individual houses, businesses, or ships.

National Park Service, Edison National Historic Site

A printing telegraph for stockbrokers was one of Edison's first inventions and one of many he made in telegraphy.

From the collections of the Henry Ford Museum and Greenfield Village

A telephone from the late 1800's was one of many that used Edison's transmitter, which made the speaker's voice louder.

Edison started companies that manufactured his inventions. The products of these companies included power stations, light bulbs, and underground conductors. In 1892, the American businesses that manufactured Edison's electric lighting components became part of the General Electric Company.

Edison in West Orange. In 1886, Edison moved to Llewellyn Park, a residential area of West Orange, New Jersey, near New York City. Just blocks away, he built a laboratory 10 times the size of the one in Menlo Park. Edison envisioned the lab as a large-scale research facility for the industrial development of inventions.

The West Orange laboratory carried out chemical, mechanical, and electrical experiments. Edison added a staff of more than 50 experimenters, machinists, and draftsmen. In addition, the new lab included a library with thousands of journals and books. Eventually, Edison's research and development center included manufacturing plants.

Motion pictures. Edison helped found the motion-picture industry. His interest seemed to take shape after he met Eadweard Muybridge, an English photographer. Like many people at the time, Muybridge was experimenting with photographing motion. In 1888, Edison envisioned a motion-picture device that "does for the Eye what the phonograph does for the Ear." His assistant, W. K. L. Dickson, began to record a series of images on celluloid film. Showing the images in rapid succession made them look like continuous action.

Edison's staff developed a camera and built the first film studio. In 1894, Edison's company introduced a commercial device for viewing motion pictures, called the *kinetoscope*. It consisted of a cabinet with a peephole or eyepiece on top. A customer put a coin in the machine to watch a short motion picture through the hole. In 1896, Edison's company introduced projectors designed by other inventors. *The Great Train Robbery* (1903), directed by Edwin S. Porter, ranks among the most notable films in the Edison catalog.

In the late 1800's, Edison also began working on motion pictures that included sound. Dickson had experimented in this area, and other inventors were working on it. One problem was that the sound was not loud enough for large audiences to hear. In addition, getting the sound to match the images was difficult. Edison's new version of the *kinetophone*—a combination kinetoscope and phonograph—debuted in 1913. It solved the problem of *synchronizing* (matching) the sound and images. The device used a pulley to attach a phonograph to a projector.

Edison and other inventors tried to control the motion-picture industry. In 1908, they formed the Motion Picture Patents Company. The company largely controlled the production, distribution, and exhibition of motion pictures in the United States. But in 1915, a federal court declared the company to be an illegal *monopoly*—that is, a business that unfairly controls the market for a product. Afterward, Edison and most other members of the Motion Picture Patents Company lost much of their influence in filmmaking.

Phonograph developments. Edison exercised more direct control over his phonograph business than over his motion-picture business. He kept a close interest in the commercial and technical development of phonographs and recordings, especially when new competition emerged. Edison also set the general policies and strategies for his phonograph business. His guidelines determined which artists and tunes his company should record and release. The phonograph remained Edison's favorite invention.

In the early 1900's, the preferred format for sound recordings shifted from cylinders to flat discs. Discs were easier to mass produce and store than cylinders.

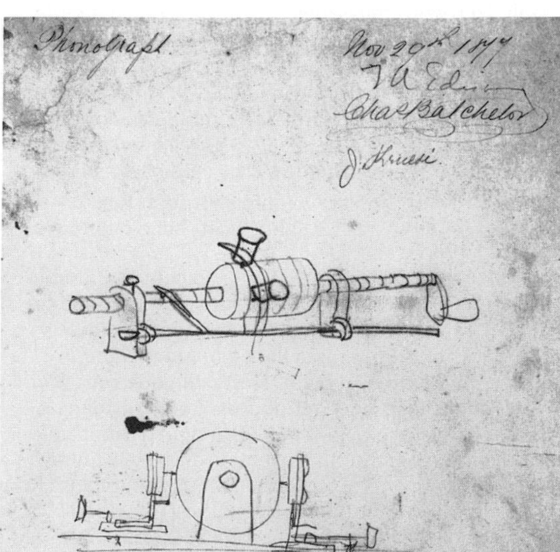

National Park Service, Edison National Historic Site

A page from Edison's sketchbooks shows a front and a side view of his cylinder phonograph. The sketchbooks include drawings and notes on his inventions and experiments.

Henry Ford Museum

Edison's first incandescent electric light, *below,* was perhaps his most important invention. Edison, *far left,* President Herbert Hoover, and Henry Ford inspected the device in 1929 in a reconstruction of Edison's Menlo Park laboratory at Greenfield Village in Dearborn, Michigan.

Museum of Science and Industry, Chicago (WORLD BOOK photo by Chris Stanley)

Edison adopted the disc format in 1913. However, he continued to offer cylinder machines and recordings until 1929. The Ediphone, Edison's dictating machine, was based on his cylinder phonograph.

Ore milling and cement. In the late 1800's, Edison planned a complete system for mining and refining iron ores. Steel mills in the eastern United States needed high-grade ore. Edison would crush low-grade ore and use electromagnets to separate the iron, thus making a concentrated ore for the mills. For this enterprise, Edison designed huge equipment and built a plant in New Jersey. At the plant, raw ore moved continuously on conveyor belts. The system resembled the assembly line later perfected by the American automaker Henry Ford.

Edison invested more than $1 million in ore milling. But the project ended in failure. Rich iron ore discovered in Minnesota proved cheaper to mine and process.

During the early 1900's, Edison manufactured *portland cement,* a gray powder used to make concrete. The manufacturing plant made use of his iron ore project's crushing and grinding technology and its large-scale mass-production techniques. Edison's portland cement went into new bridges, highways, and buildings. More than 45,000 barrels of the cement were used to build the original Yankee Stadium in New York City. Edison also devised a way to build concrete houses quickly.

Batteries. Edison had worked with batteries since his earliest days as a telegrapher. During the 1880's and 1890's, he experimented with lighter, more durable, and more powerful batteries. In the early 1900's, Edison began to manufacture rechargeable storage batteries of a nickel-iron-alkaline design. He also set up a chemical plant to provide the materials. Edison batteries were used in electric trucks and automobiles and for electric starters in gasoline-powered cars. They were also used in railway cars, submarines, and mining lamps.

Final work. During World War I (1914-1918), Edison headed the Naval Consulting Board, a group of inventors and business people who aided the war effort. He also faced manufacturing problems. They were caused by shortages of *phenol,* a chemical used in the production of phonograph records. During the 1920's, Edison turned most of his businesses over to his son Charles. Edison continued to work and experiment while suffering from several illnesses in his later years. From the late 1920's until the end of his life, Edison sought a natural substitute for rubber plants as a source of latex. He died at his home in Llewellyn Park on Oct. 18, 1931.

Personal life

Edison valued long, hard work. He believed that inventors should focus on practical projects that businesses or consumers would buy. "Genius is 1 percent inspiration and 99 percent perspiration" is a quotation often associated with Edison—although Edison once wrote that he could not remember ever saying it.

Edison tried to learn from mistakes, but he was selective in admitting his errors. It was easy for him to learn something from a series of failed chemical tests. But he had difficulty admitting more serious mistakes. For example, Edison failed to appreciate the advantages of the Serbian engineer Nikola Tesla's *alternating current* (AC) electric power system over his own *direct current* (DC) system. Direct current is an electric current that flows in only one direction. Alternating current, on the other hand, changes direction many times each second (see **Electricity** [Alternating and direct current]).

Family and friends. On Dec. 25, 1871, Edison married Mary Stilwell, who had worked in one of his companies. The couple had three children—Marion; Thomas Alva, Jr.; and William. Edison nicknamed Marion and Tom "Dot" and "Dash" after the telegraph code. Mary died in 1884.

In 1885, Edison met Mina Miller, the daughter of a wealthy Ohio industrialist. They married in 1886 and had three children—Madeleine, Charles, and Theodore. Of Edison's six children, Charles became the most famous. He served as secretary of the United States Navy in 1940

© Photos 12/Alamy Images

The West Orange laboratory in New Jersey was Edison's workplace and true home for the last 44 years of his life. The laboratory's many rooms and buildings are now a national historic site. They feature exhibits of original inventions and working models developed by Edison.

and as governor of New Jersey from 1941 to 1944.

One of Edison's most famous friends was Henry Ford. The industrial leaders became friends after Edison encouraged Ford to use gasoline engines in automobiles. The two friends later took automobile camping trips with the industrialist Harvey Firestone and the naturalist John Burroughs. The Edisons and the Fords also kept adjoining winter homes in Fort Myers, Florida.

Philosophy. Always a man of many ideas, Edison stayed informed about technology, business, and current affairs. He had a down-to-earth manner and a frank opinion on most matters. Edison often expressed faith in progress and industry. He believed that mass production would bring a higher standard of living. He also believed that technology could solve social problems.

Honors. Edison received honors from throughout the world. France appointed him to the Legion of Honor, its highest civilian award, in 1878. The U.S. Congress presented him with the Congressional Gold Medal, the highest honor it can give, in 1928. Henry Ford brought Edison much attention with an international celebration called "Light's Golden Jubilee" in 1929. It honored Edison and the 50th anniversary of his incandescent lamp.

A number of major historical sites and museums in the United States honor Edison. They include his birthplace in Milan, Ohio, and his winter home in Fort Myers, Florida. The restored Menlo Park laboratory is part of Greenfield Village, a collection of historic buildings in Dearborn, Michigan. The Thomas Edison National Historical Park at West Orange, New Jersey, includes Edison's laboratory and home. Theresa M. Collins

Related articles in *World Book* include:

Electric light (History)
General Electric Company
Invention (The late 1800's)
Light bulb
Motion picture (The invention of motion pictures)
Phonograph (History)
Telephone (History)
Tesla, Nikola
Vacuum tube (History)

Additional resources

Carlson, Laurie M. *Thomas Edison for Kids.* Chicago Review Pr., 2006. Younger readers.
Collins, Theresa M., and others. *Thomas Edison and Modern America.* Bedford/St. Martin's, 2002.
Delano, Marfe F. *Inventing the Future: A Photobiography of Thomas Alva Edison.* National Geographic Soc., 2002. Younger readers.
Edison, Thomas A. *The Papers of Thomas A. Edison.* Johns Hopkins, 1989-. Multivolume work.
Stross, Randall E. *The Wizard of Menlo Park: How Thomas Alva Edison Invented the Modern World.* Crown, 2007.

EdisonLearning, Inc. is a profit-seeking organization that manages public schools under contract with local school districts or charter school authorities. The organization's goal is to offer superior education for about the same amount of money per student that districts spend in their other schools. EdisonLearning's role has stirred debate about whether nonpublic authorities should be allowed to run schools funded with public tax dollars.

EdisonLearning hires its own administrators, teachers, and staff and offers its own learning program. At EdisonLearning schools, both the school day and the school year are significantly longer than the United States average. Students in EdisonLearning schools generally have the same mix of abilities, ethnic backgrounds, and family income levels as do students in the rest of a district.

EdisonLearning offers a comprehensive curriculum for kindergarten through grade 12. This curriculum stresses fundamentals of reading and mathematics in kindergarten through second grade. Emphasis on problem-solving, thinking, and writing increases as students mature. EdisonLearning also focuses on technology as a learning resource and a communication tool. The project uses narrative report cards, cumulative portfolios, and other nontraditional measures of student progress.

Chris Whittle, an American publishing executive, founded the organization, originally called the Edison Project, in 1992. It was named for the American inventor Thomas Edison to highlight the organization's commitment to inventiveness and technical creativity. A team of experts in education, social science, and technology developed the curriculum. The project opened its first schools in 1995. It changed its name to Edison Schools in 1999. In 2002, Edison Schools took over the management of 20 public schools in Philadelphia. That same year, it established a new branch, called Edison Schools UK (now EdisonLearning Ltd.), to manage schools in the United Kingdom. The U.S. organization changed its name to EdisonLearning, Inc. in 2008. Lawrence O. Picus

See also **Charter school; Edison, Thomas Alva.**

Editor. See **Journalism; Magazine; Motion picture** (Post-production); **Newspaper; Publishing.**

Editorial is usually a brief newspaper or magazine article that gives the publication's position on current events. It may also be a radio or television broadcast. An editorial may criticize, praise, or merely discuss the actions of some public official or group. Newspaper editorials often encourage actions that the editor of the paper thinks will benefit the community. For instance, an editorial may back a campaign for more police officers. Editorials are also used to express strong political views. Editorials are usually unsigned, so that they appear as the official opinion of the news organization.

An editorial usually begins by stating an issue. It may end with a conclusion in the form of advice, a plea, or a command. In style, it is much like an essay (see **Essay**). Editorials usually are in some clearly marked form when they appear in print. They often appear on a special editorial page. Magazine editorials usually discuss problems of national interest and scope. William McKeen

See also **Pulitzer Prizes** (Prizes in journalism; table: Editorial writing).

Edmonds, Sarah Emma Evelyn (1841-1898), became the most famous woman soldier of the American Civil War (1861-1865). Edmonds, a Canadian, served in the Union Army disguised as a man. She used the name Frank Thompson.

Edmonds was born in December 1841 in New Brunswick, probably in Magaguadavic. She came to the United States in the 1850's. In 1861, she enlisted in a unit organized by a friend. She served mainly as a nurse and messenger. She also went on several spying missions to learn the size and location of Confederate troops. At times while spying, she pretended to be a black male laborer, a white female peddler, and a black female cook.

Edmonds gained fame when she wrote about her disguise and spying missions. In 1897, the Grand Army of the Republic, a group of Union Army veterans, made Edmonds its only woman member. She died on Sept. 5, 1898. Gabor S. Boritt

Edmonds, Walter Dumaux (1903-1998), an American author, became known for his novel *Drums Along the Mohawk* (1936) and other books on the history of upstate New York. He won the Newbery Medal in 1942 for a story for young people, *The Matchlock Gun* (1941). His *Bert Breen's Barn* (1975) won the 1976 National Book Award for children's literature.

Edmonds was born on a farm near Boonville, New York, on July 15, 1903. His first novel was *Rome Haul* (1929). Marc Connelly and Frank Elser adapted it into a play, *The Farmer Takes a Wife* (1934). Edmonds died on Jan. 24, 1998. Nancy Lyman Huse

Edmonton is the capital of the Canadian province of Alberta. The city and its surrounding communities form one of Canada's most populous metropolitan areas. Edmonton lies along the North Saskatchewan River in central Alberta. Its industries service a large farming region and aid in the development of natural resources in northern Canada. The city is a major refining, manufacturing, and distribution center for Alberta's petroleum and petrochemical industries. Edmonton is often called the *Gateway to the North.*

The metropolitan area. Though Edmonton has a downtown core of high-rise office and residential buildings, the metropolitan area is largely a region of spread-out suburban-style residential and shopping areas. Within the City of Edmonton, West Edmonton Mall is one of the world's largest shopping centers. It includes hundreds of shops, an indoor water park, an amuse-

City of Edmonton

Edmonton is the capital of Alberta. The map shows important points of interest in the city.

City boundary
Expressway
Other road
Railroad
Point of interest
Park

ALBERTA
Edmonton

WORLD BOOK maps

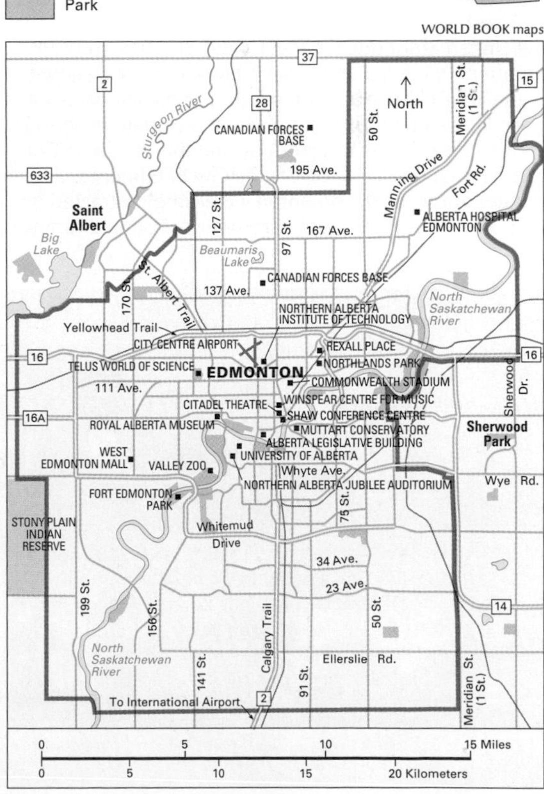

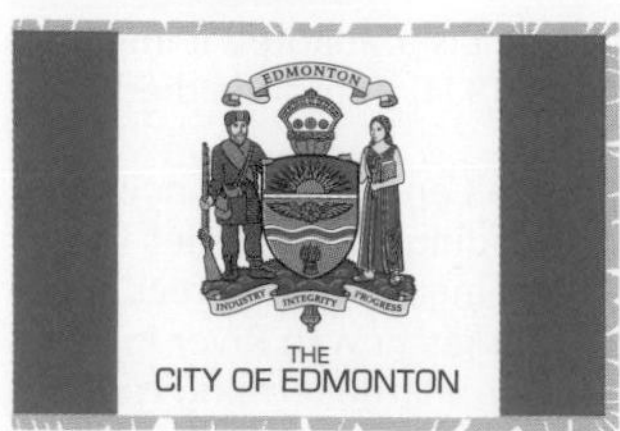

Symbols of Edmonton. The flag's blue bars represent the North Saskatchewan River and strength. The white background of the crest signifies peace. The winged wheel stands for industry and aviation, the wavy ribbon for the river, and the sheaf for farming.

Facts in brief

Population: 812,201. *Metropolitan area population*—1,159,869.
Area: 264 mi^2 (684 km^2). *Area of metropolitan area*—3,640 mi^2 (9,427 km^2).
Altitude: 2,200 ft (671 m) above sea level.
Climate: *Average temperature*—January, 7 °F (−14 °C); July, 61 °F (16 °C). *Average annual precipitation* (rainfall, melted snow, and other forms of moisture)—19 in (48 cm). For the monthly weather in Edmonton, see **Alberta** (Climate).
Government: Council-manager. *Terms*—3 years for the mayor and the 12 councilors.
Founded: 1795. Incorporated as a town in 1892. Incorporated as a city in 1904.

ment park, movie theaters, a casino, and an ice rink. Another popular attraction is Whyte Avenue in the Old Strathcona district of the city, with its many bars, boutiques, and cafes.

Major landmarks in downtown Edmonton include the Alberta Legislature Building; the City Hall, featuring a glass pyramid roof; Sir Winston Churchill Square; and the High Level Bridge. The massive steel bridge, completed in 1913, crosses the North Saskatchewan River valley, which winds through the city. Edmonton has abundant parkland, including many natural habitat areas, especially in the river valley.

The City of Edmonton has several industrial districts. "Refinery Row," a large complex of petroleum industries, lies just east of Edmonton in the hamlet of Sherwood Park. Fort Saskatchewan is another industrial city in the region. Other settlements in the metropolitan area include Leduc, St. Albert, Spruce Grove, and Stony Plain.

People. Edmonton's early white settlers were mostly of British origin. They came mainly from eastern Canada, the United Kingdom, and the United States. Significant numbers of central and eastern Europeans also settled in the area. Ukrainian immigrants in particular have influenced local culture. Their influence is evident in church architecture, folk dance troupes, and the Ukrainian Cultural Heritage Village, east of the City of Edmonton.

After about 1970, Edmonton increasingly attracted immigrants from many parts of the world. Today, a variety of community groups and activities provide evidence of this ethnic diversity. The annual Heritage Festival features dozens of cultures.

Today, many people in Edmonton have some British, Irish, or German ancestry. Other large ethnic groups include people of Chinese, French, Polish, and Ukrainian backgrounds. Many people are of mixed descent.

Education. A majority of schools in Edmonton are public or Roman Catholic schools. Edmonton also has independent private schools, as well as *charter schools* that operate according to special contracts called *charters.* Some of Edmonton's schools are *francophone* schools, in which French is spoken.

Edmonton is an important center for post-secondary education. The University of Alberta, one of Canada's major universities, has its main campus in Edmonton. Grant MacEwan University, Concordia University College, King's University College, NorQuest College, and the Northern Alberta Institute of Technology are also in Edmonton. The Edmonton Public Library has branches throughout the city. The city and provincial governments each maintain public archives in Edmonton.

Culture and recreation. Venues for the performing arts in Edmonton include the Northern Alberta Jubilee Auditorium, the Winspear Centre, and the Citadel Theatre. The Edmonton Symphony Orchestra, the Edmonton Opera, and the Alberta Ballet perform in the city. Festivals devoted to art, music, and theater take place

Edmonton is the capital of Alberta and one of the largest cities in the province. This photograph shows Edmonton's downtown skyline, *background,* and some private homes, *foreground.* The glass pyramids rising through the trees on the left side of the picture are part of the Muttart Conservatory, which houses a variety of plants.

every summer. The Edmonton International Fringe Theatre Festival, held every August in Old Strathcona, is one of the largest festivals of its kind.

Museums in Edmonton include the Royal Alberta Museum, which features exhibits on the history and wildlife of Alberta; the Art Gallery of Alberta; the Alberta Aviation Museum; and TELUS World of Science. Fort Edmonton Park includes a replica of the trading post from which the city developed. Northlands Park, a large exhibition area, hosts fairs and sporting events. The city is also home to Edmonton Valley Zoo. Elk Island National Park, located east of the city, is known for its bison herd.

People in Edmonton play and watch a wide variety of sports. Ice hockey is probably the most popular. Edmonton has two professional sports teams: the Edmonton Eskimos of the Canadian Football League and the Edmonton Oilers of the National Hockey League.

Economy. Petroleum is especially important to the local economy. Edmonton has numerous companies related to petroleum exploration, drilling, and distribution, as well as the refining and manufacturing of petroleum products. Many of the fuels, fertilizers, and chemicals produced in Edmonton are sold throughout western Canada. Edmonton exports oil and natural gas to eastern Canada, the Pacific coast, and parts of the United States. Edmonton also provides work crews and supplies for petroleum and pipeline projects throughout Alberta.

Other industries in Edmonton service a major agricultural area in central Alberta. The region raises large amounts of cereal grains, hay, and livestock. The city and provincial governments and local educational institutions also employ many people.

Edmonton City Centre Airport, near downtown, provides service to various locations in western Canada. Edmonton International Airport is in nearby Leduc. The Yellowhead Highway, the northern branch of the Trans-Canada Highway system, runs through Edmonton. Two railroads serve the city. Daily newspapers in Edmonton include the *Edmonton Journal* and *Edmonton Sun.*

Government. A city council, consisting of a mayor and 12 councilors, governs the City of Edmonton. The councilors represent 12 *wards* (districts). The people elect all members of the council for three-year terms. The council sets government policy. A city manager appointed by the council handles daily government operations. Other cities and towns in the Edmonton metropolitan area have separate local governments.

History. Cree and Blackfoot Indians lived in the Edmonton area before Europeans arrived there. In 1795, the North West Company and the Hudson's Bay Company each built a fur-trading post near the present-day city of Fort Saskatchewan. Both companies moved their posts several times. The Hudson's Bay Company posts were called Edmonton House and, later, Fort Edmonton. The name Edmonton comes from an English city. In 1830, Fort Edmonton was rebuilt near the present site of the Alberta Legislature Building. It became a major supply center for smaller posts across a wide area.

In 1870, the government of Canada acquired the vast fur-trading region known as Rupert's Land from the Hudson's Bay Company. Rupert's Land included what is now Alberta. Canada's government wanted to promote agricultural settlement in the region. However, settlement progressed slowly. In 1891, a railway line connected Calgary, to the south, with a *terminus* (ending point) near the North Saskatchewan River. The town of South Edmonton (later called Strathcona) was established at the site of the rail terminus. Coal mining in the region grew to supply train locomotives.

From about 1900, settlers poured into central Alberta. New railways arrived, and Edmonton emerged as a boom town that supplied small agricultural communities throughout the region. Edmonton was incorporated as a town in 1892 and as a city in 1904. In 1905, it became the capital of the newly established province of Alberta. In 1912, Strathcona, which had been a rival town, became part of Edmonton.

Edmonton's growth slowed after the start of World War I in 1914. It slowed again during an economic downturn in the early 1920's, and when the Great Depression struck in the 1930's. During the early 1900's, bush pilots began flying small planes into northern Canada. Edmonton became a major supply center for northern construction projects during World War II (1939-1945).

In 1947, the "Leduc strike" near the town of Devon became the first in a series of major oil discoveries in central Alberta. Edmonton became a supplier for oil drilling camps. The city soon developed a number of industries based on petroleum. These industries, along with the steady expansion of education and government, led to rapid urban growth in the mid-1900's.

A great oil boom in the 1970's led to urban renewal and the construction of many high-rise buildings. Major building projects included the construction of a light rail rapid transit system, Northlands Coliseum (now called Rexall Place), and Commonwealth Stadium. A collapse of oil prices in the 1980's led to a temporary economic slowdown. But the development of *bituminous sands* in the Athabasca region revived Edmonton's fortunes. Bituminous sands are deposits of sand that contain bitumen, a substance used to produce oil and other fuels.

A tornado struck Edmonton in 1987, killing 27 people and causing considerable property damage. In 2001, Edmonton became the first North American city to host the World Championships in Athletics, a major track and field meet. David Jay Bercuson

See also **Alberta** (pictures).

Edom was an ancient kingdom that is mentioned often in the Old Testament. It stood southeast of the Dead Sea in what is now southern Jordan. Edom enjoyed its greatest prosperity between 1200 and the 700's B.C. The Old Testament describes the Edomites as descendants of Esau, the brother of Jacob (Genesis 36:1). Moses was not allowed to enter Edom on his journey to the promised land (Numbers 20:18-21). The Edomites spoke a language similar to Hebrew and probably worshiped many gods.

The country's rich copper and iron mines contributed to the splendor of the Kingdom of Israel, which had conquered Edom under David. Edom's prosperity began to decline in the 700's B.C. In the next 200 years, Judah, Assyria, and Babylonia ruled Edom. An Arab people called the Nabataeans invaded Edom during the Persian period of the 500's and 400's B.C. At the same time, many Edomites invaded southern Judah. They helped establish a territory there called Idumea. The Hasmonean dynasty conquered the Idumeans in the 100's B.C., and converted them to Judaism. H. Darrell Lance

Education is the process of gaining knowledge and abilities. Although much learning occurs outside school, classrooms like this one are the main source of formal, organized education.

Education

Education is the process by which people acquire knowledge, skills, habits, values, or attitudes. The word *education* is also used to describe the results of the educational process. Ideally, education should help people develop an appreciation of their cultural heritage and live more satisfying lives. It should also enable people to become productive members of society, both as citizens sharing in democratic processes and as workers in the economy. The most common way to get an education is to attend school. But much education takes place outside the classroom.

Education involves both learning and teaching. Sometimes, people learn by teaching themselves. But they also learn with the help of other people, such as parents or teachers. Parents are a child's first and perhaps most important teachers. But few parents have either the time or the ability to teach their children everything they need to know. Instead, parents turn over many educational responsibilities to professional educators.

Teachers and administrators have the chief responsibility for education in schools. The organized instruction they provide is called *formal education.* Learning that results from less-organized instruction is called *informal education.*

This article deals mainly with formal education, especially the kind given in schools. But many other institutions and agencies also provide education. Churches, for instance, educate their members through church teachings. Such organizations as the Boy Scouts, Girl Scouts, and 4-H provide educational activities in many communities. In addition, television, radio, newspapers, and magazines may offer educational programs and articles. Since the late 1900's, computers have become increasingly important in education. The ability to quickly search for information on the Internet has greatly influenced the way education is provided.

Nations vary greatly in the kind of schooling they provide and in their manner of regulating and supporting education. Most developed nations, including most of Europe, have long-established educational systems. Such nations usually have high *literacy rates* (percentages of citizens who can read and write). Less developed countries, on the other hand, generally have low literacy rates. Many less developed countries have a severe shortage of teachers and classrooms.

A modern society cannot survive without education. Education helps people acquire the skills they need for everyday activities, such as reading a newspaper and managing their money. It also gives individuals the specialized training they may need to prepare for a job or career. For example, people must meet certain educational requirements and obtain a license or certificate before they can practice accounting, law, medicine, or other professions.

Education also helps people acquire skills that make their lives more interesting and enjoyable. Such skills include those needed to participate in a sport, paint a picture, or play a musical instrument.

Some educators study the *objectives* (goals) of education. This has led to the classification of educational objectives into three areas: (1) the *cognitive area,* (2) the *affective area,* and (3) the *psychomotor,* or *locomotor, area.* The cognitive area aims at increasing a person's knowledge and intellectual skills. It deals with the ability to think and reason effectively. The affective area deals with feelings, values, and appreciations. It promotes the development of moral and spiritual values and healthy attitudes and emotions. Education in this area is often called *character education* or *citizenship training.* The psychomotor area involves the development of a person's muscular or mechanical skills. These skills often in-

The contributor of this article, Lawrence O. Picus, is Professor of Education at the University of Southern California.

© Lindsay Hebberd, Corbis

Elementary education provides students with basic skills, such as reading and writing, that they will use throughout life. This teacher in India is helping her students learn the alphabet used to write the Hindi language.

© Barbara Filet, Stone

Informal education takes place in a variety of settings outside school, including libraries and museums. This family is learning about racing cars from an interactive display at an automotive museum in Los Angeles.

clude handwriting, speech, physical education, and technical abilities.

Countries throughout the world invest large amounts of time, money, and other resources to provide education for their citizens. Millions of people throughout the world are directly involved in education as students or teachers. Millions more hold nonteaching jobs related to education. Such jobs include school cafeteria workers, nurses, and secretaries; school bus drivers; textbook publishers; and producers of educational materials and equipment.

Kinds of education

The school systems of all modern nations provide both *general education* and *vocational education.* Most countries also provide *special education* programs for children with disabilities or other special needs. *Adult education* programs are offered for people who wish to complete or improve their education after they no longer attend regular elementary schools or high schools. Colleges and universities also provide a wide range of programs for people who want to continue their education during adulthood.

General education aims at producing intelligent, responsible, well-informed citizens who take an active interest in the world around them. Its primary goal is to transmit a common cultural heritage rather than to develop trained specialists.

Almost all elementary education is general education. Elementary schools teach skills that people use throughout life, such as reading, writing, and mathematics. Students learn moral values and the rights and duties of citizenship. They also receive instruction in a variety of subjects, including geography, history, and science. In industrialized countries, almost all young people continue their general education in high school. Most college students are also required to take some general education courses.

In Western nations, advanced general education is frequently called *liberal education.* Liberal education aims at broad mental development. Students are taught to investigate all possible solutions to a problem before reaching a conclusion or planning a course of action. The branches of learning that aid in this development are called the *liberal arts.* These include the humanities, mathematics, and the biological, physical, and social sciences. Liberal education is important to democracies because democratic governments depend on the ability of citizens to judge ideas and events intelligently.

Vocational education aims primarily at preparing individuals for a job. Some high schools, called *vocational high schools,* specialize in vocational programs. Vocational high school students are also required to take some general education courses. Community colleges and specialized schools offer advanced vocational and technical training in a variety of areas. In addition, universities and separate professional schools prepare students for careers in such fields as architecture, business, engineering, law, medicine, nursing, teaching, and theology.

Many businesses and industries conduct vocational programs to help their employees develop new skills and improve the quality of products and services. One type of education, known as *human resource development* (HRD), helps employees learn precisely what to do in their jobs and how to work as part of a team. HRD is usually referred to as *training.* Instructors in HRD are generally called *trainers* rather than teachers.

Vocational education is important in countries striving to develop an economy based on modern technology. It is especially important in developing countries in Africa, Asia, and Latin America. See **Vocational education.**

Special education provides educational opportunities for people with disabilities or special talents. Most countries support special education programs for people who have difficulty hearing, seeing, or speaking; have other physical or mental disabilities; or are emotionally disturbed.

For children with disabilities, special education usually involves modified instructional techniques and the use of different materials, such as recorded books instead of printed ones. It may also involve simplifying the

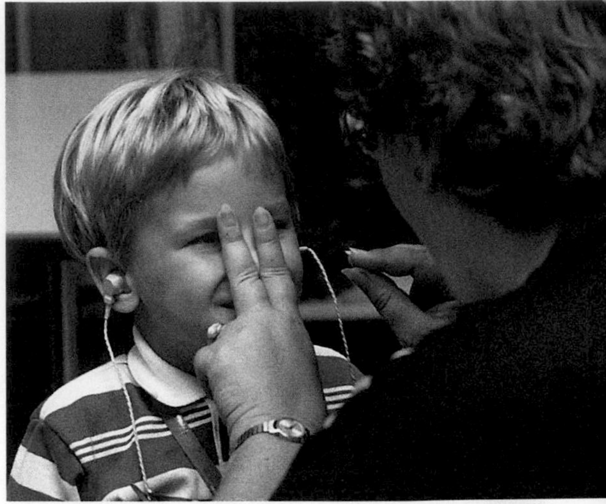

Jeffrey Silvester, FPG

Special education programs provide instruction for disabled or gifted students. This teacher is helping a hearing-impaired child learn how to recognize and pronounce words.

language of instruction or allowing students more time to take a test. Special education services can also include the use of aides, tutors, and special therapies.

Special education also involves programs for *gifted* children—that is, children who may be unusually intelligent or have exceptional ability in art, mathematics, or some other area. Special education helps such children develop their talents while they receive a well-rounded education.

Adult education. Most countries support general and vocational education programs for adults. Such *continuing education* programs enable men and women to continue their formal education or develop a particular skill or hobby. Courses range from elementary reading, arithmetic, and foreign languages to advanced commercial, technical, and professional training. In the United

© Lawrence Migdale

Continuing education programs enable adults to continue to learn. Some adults, such as these senior citizens who are studying painting, want to learn new skills to use in their leisure time.

Chicago Botanic Garden

Learning by doing is an important educational method. These children are learning how plants grow by caring for flowers at a botanical garden.

States, many adults take a series of tests called the General Educational Development Tests (GED) to earn a certificate equal to a high school diploma.

Millions of adults participate in some kind of adult education. Many colleges and universities provide *extension courses,* which allow adults to take college-level courses. Many extension courses are scheduled for evening hours so that people who work during the day can attend. Governments sponsor many adult education programs, including programs for people in the armed forces. Businesses, community agencies, hospitals, industries, labor unions, libraries, museums, prisons, and television stations also provide organized educational opportunities for adults. See **Adult education.**

The study of learning and teaching

Education requires the dual activities of learning and teaching. Ideally, teaching should result in increased opportunities for learning. This section discusses how the two activities take place.

How people learn. There is no complete agreement among scientists and educators on the nature of human learning. But certain ideas are generally accepted. Learning theories are based largely on findings of modern psychology.

Types of learning. Psychologists have traditionally focused on four main types of learning: (1) *classical conditioning,* (2) *instrumental conditioning,* (3) *multiple-response learning,* and (4) *insight learning.*

Classical conditioning is based on *stimulus-response relationships.* A stimulus is an object or a situation that excites one or more sense organs, thus leading to a response. In classical conditioning, learning occurs when a new stimulus begins to produce a response similar to a response originally produced by a different stimulus. Studies of classical conditioning are based on experiments performed in the early 1900's by the Russian physiologist Ivan P. Pavlov. Pavlov trained dogs to salivate to such signals as lights, tones, or buzzers by presenting these signals when he gave them food. Classical conditioning occurred when the new stimulus (the lights, tones, or buzzers) began to elicit the response of salivation in much the same way that the original stimulus (the food) did. Pavlov called the learned response a *conditioned response* because it depended on the conditions of the stimulus. Classical conditioning is often called *respondent learning.*

In instrumental conditioning, a person learns to perform an action as a result of what happens after the action is made. For example, a child may learn to beg for candy. There is no one stimulus that elicits the response of begging. Instead, the child begs because such behavior occasionally results in receiving candy. Every time the child receives candy, the tendency to beg becomes greater. Receiving candy, therefore, reinforces the child's behavior. The American psychologist B. F. Skinner performed important experiments with instrumental conditioning in the 1930's. Skinner's experiments were based on those performed earlier in the 1900's by the American psychologist E. L. Thorndike. Instrumental conditioning is also called *operant conditioning.*

Multiple-response learning involves the combination of many learned actions to form a more complicated pattern of behavior. In most cases, various stimuli guide the process. For instance, in memorizing a poem or learning a new language, a student first learns sequences of words. The student then combines these sequences into a complex organization. Learning that involves the combination of many parts requires much practice. To examine this kind of learning, psychologists have observed animals learning to run through a maze. After wandering the maze numerous times, the animal eventually learns the correct sequence of turns.

Insight learning involves learning to solve a problem by understanding the relationships of various parts of the problem. The Estonian-born American psychologist Wolfgang Köhler performed important insight experiments involving chimpanzees in the early 1900's. He found, for instance, that when a banana was placed high out of reach, the animals discovered that they could stack boxes on top of one another to reach it.

Theories of learning. Scientists have developed numerous theories to further explain the processes of learning. Most such theories fall into one of four main categories: (1) theories that emphasize the forming of habits, (2) theories that emphasize cognition, (3) humanistic theories, and (4) physiological theories.

Many psychologists believe that people learn new things by forming habits. These psychologists believe that when we experience a new problem, we use responses learned from past experiences to solve it. If this procedure does not lead to the solution, we use a *trial-and-error approach*—that is, we try many possible solutions until we find the right one. This process, in turn, leads to the formation of new habits. Many people learn to modify their habits through *behavior modification* techniques. These techniques often involve systems of rewards to encourage and reinforce new habits, such as improvements in classroom behavior.

A second group of psychologists stresses *cognition* (the act of knowing) above the importance of forming habits. These experts feel that the development of habits cannot explain the complex processes involved in the understanding of concepts and ideas. Instead, the cognitive approach emphasizes the importance of the learner's discovering and perceiving new relationships and achieving insight and understanding.

A third group of psychologists focuses on *humanistic theories.* According to these theories, much human learning results from each individual's need to express creativity. Almost any activity—including athletics, business dealings, and homemaking—can serve as a creative outlet. The psychologists in the humanistic group believe that people gain a sense of control, growth, and knowledge from engaging in challenging activities. For learning to occur, people must feel independent, confident, worthy, and respected by others.

Some scientists examine the changes in the nervous system that take place during learning. They practice a *physiological* approach to the study of learning. This approach emphasizes bodily processes, such as specific changes in the nervous system, that take place to produce learning.

How teachers guide learning. The teacher's main task is to create conditions that will encourage and stimulate learning. Teachers must help students develop their own initiative and ability to think critically. Good teachers guide students in seeking important knowledge and analyzing possible solutions to problems. They also help students understand important values involved in dealing with various problems. Teachers use a variety of methods to achieve the desired learning goals. They also use such teaching aids as books, audio-visual materials, computers, and field trips.

Good teachers are well educated, know their subject, and understand their students. They are familiar with the principles of education, the psychology of human development, and the theories of learning.

Theories of teaching have not been as fully developed as have theories of learning. Many educators feel that theories of learning provide sufficient guidelines for teaching. Teachers generally combine behavior modification, cognitive, and humanistic principles. A large number of teachers do not consciously follow any theory but rather depend on experience and intuition to guide them. See **Teaching.**

Education in the United States

Unlike most countries, the United States does not have a national educational system. Instead, each U.S. state is responsible for organizing and regulating its own system of education. The systems organized by the various states have much in common. This section discusses how the state systems are organized, controlled, and supported. It also discusses the role of the federal government in education.

The organization of U.S. education. Formal education in the United States is divided into various levels that are arranged somewhat like the rungs of a ladder. Early childhood education is the first rung of the educational ladder. It is followed by elementary education, intermediate education, secondary education, and higher education. Ordinarily, students complete one stage before they continue to the next.

School attendance is *compulsory* (required) in every state. The age through which attendance is required

School enrollment in the United States

The graph below shows the changes in U.S. public and private school enrollment since 1890. The table gives the number of students enrolled during selected years.

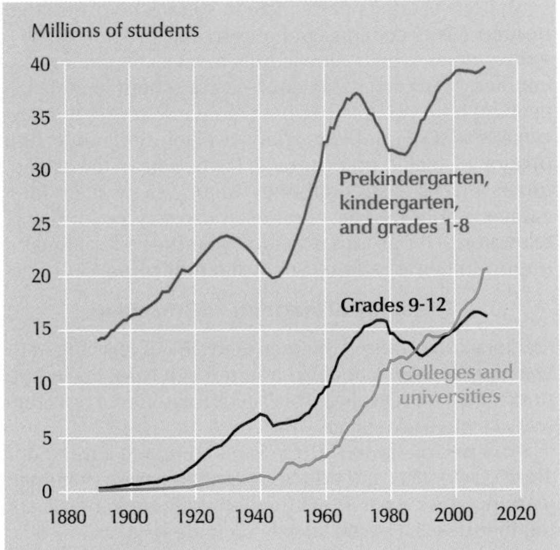

Year	Prekindergarten, kindergarten, and grades 1-8	Grades 9-12	Colleges and universities
1890	14,036,000	298,000	157,000
1900	16,262,000	669,000	238,000
1910	18,529,000	1,115,000	355,000
1920	20,964,000	2,500,000	598,000
1930	23,740,000	4,812,000	1,101,000
1940	21,127,000	7,130,000	1,494,000
1950	22,207,000	6,453,000	2,659,000
1960	32,412,000	9,600,000	3,216,000
1970	37,011,000	14,418,000	7,136,000
1980	31,639,000	14,570,000	12,097,000
1990	34,392,000	12,472,000	13,819,000
2000	38,594,000	14,779,000	15,312,000
2010	39,312,000	16,038,000	20,550,000

Source: U.S. Department of Education.

Years of schooling completed

Since 1910, the percentage of Americans age 25 and over with four years of high school or college has risen sharply. The percentage with under five years of grade school has fallen.

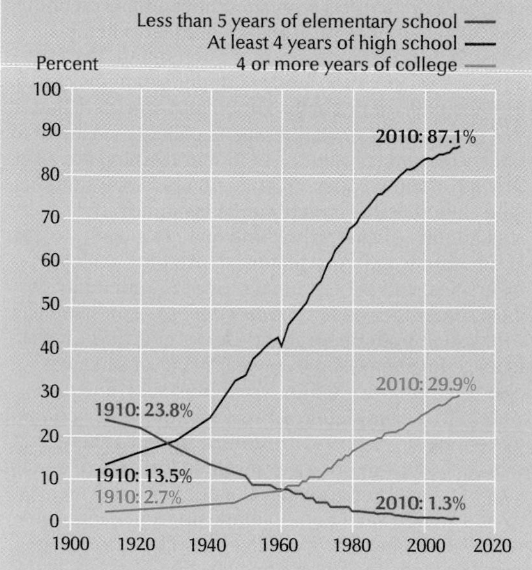

Sources: U.S. Census Bureau; U.S. Department of Education.

varies among the 50 states, ranging from 15 to 18 years. Many states make certain exceptions to the age requirements. In most states, for example, students fulfill the attendance requirements when they graduate from high school, even if they have not reached the required age.

Early childhood education is generally designed for children 5 years of age and younger. Its chief aim is to develop the habits, attitudes, and skills that provide readiness for school. Children who develop an interest in learning before they enter elementary school will likely do better in school than children who have not developed such an interest. In the United States, more than half of all children from age 3 through age 5 attend some kind of early childhood education program. The programs are of two main types: (1) *preschools,* also called *nursery schools,* and (2) *kindergartens.*

Individuals, private organizations, and some school systems operate preschools. Most preschools are designed for children 3 or 4 years old. The children learn to get along in a group supervised by a teacher. They are encouraged to express feelings and ideas through building, dancing, drawing, playing, singing, and speaking. Some preschools use a teaching method developed by the Italian educator Maria Montessori. The *Montessori method* recommends the use of special teaching materials and learning tasks to help children develop awareness, confidence, and independence. See **Montessori method.**

The U.S. federal government sponsors a special preschool program called Head Start. The program has helped set up thousands of schools, called Head Start centers, for young children from low-income families. The centers provide the children with learning experiences they may not receive at home. See **Head Start.**

Various public and private organizations sponsor *day-care,* or *child-care,* centers for children. Some of these centers resemble preschools, but others simply provide care for young children and do not offer planned education. See **Day care.**

Most school systems and many private organizations operate kindergartens, intended mainly for 5- and 6-year-olds. Kindergartens offer more advanced activities than do most preschools. They help prepare children for the learning experiences that follow in elementary school. See **Kindergarten; Preschool.**

Elementary education. Children generally attend elementary school from about age 6 or 7 to about 11 or 12. Most elementary schools provide kindergartens for 5- and 6-year-old children, though elementary education itself usually begins in first grade. Most U.S. communities have at least one elementary school. Elementary schools are also called *grade schools* or *grammar schools.*

A traditional elementary school offers educational programs for children in kindergarten through fifth grade (called K-5 programs), or kindergarten through sixth grade (K-6). Some schools provide programs for grades K-8. Children of similar age are usually in the same grade. They meet in the same classroom with the same teacher for most or all of the day. This traditional arrangement is sometimes called a *self-contained classroom.* Some self-contained classrooms may include students from more than one grade level. The pupils are expected to meet the standards for their age group before being promoted to the next grade. But promotion practices differ from school to school.

Some communities have *nongraded,* or *ungraded,* schools. In nongraded schools, the pupils are not grouped according to age. Instead, pupils of different ages meet together for certain subjects or activities. Each student is encouraged to advance at his or her own rate. Frequently, the groups are composed of children with similar abilities or interests. In most nongraded schools, pupils receive general evaluations rather than specific grades. Achievement tests indicate a child's progress. Nongraded plans of organization are also called *continuous progress plans.*

Some elementary schools use a teaching method called *team teaching.* In these schools, teachers are organized into groups called *teams.* Each team is responsible for a large group of students. Each teacher on a team may teach a certain subject or a certain part of a unit of study to the entire group. In some cases, the pupils may be divided into smaller groups to allow more time for individual instruction and group discussion. See **Elementary school.**

Intermediate education. Since the 1960's, there has been an increased emphasis on the intermediate or middle grades. As a result, most school systems today offer special programs for the middle grades. These middle school or junior high school programs are designed to help students make the transition from elementary schools to the more demanding secondary schools. The grade structures of these schools vary widely. Most offer grades 6-8, but such combinations as grades 6-7, 7-8, and 7-9 are also common. Some intermediate schools include grade 5 as well.

In some schools, children in the middle grades receive instruction in self-contained classrooms. In others, students attend different classes with different teachers for each subject. This arrangement is known as *departmentalized instruction.* Many intermediate schools today offer a combination of the two, with students spending part of their day in a self-contained classroom and the rest of the day moving among departmentalized classes. See **Junior high school; Middle school.**

Secondary education in the United States is the responsibility of senior high schools. It is designed to help students become responsible members of the community and to prepare them for a job or for advanced studies. High school graduates receive a diploma to show that they have completed their secondary education. Almost all the young people in the United States enroll in high school, and most remain through graduation.

Many communities have four-year high schools with grades 9-12. Others offer high school programs for grades 10-12. High schools enroll students who have completed middle or junior high school, or an eight-year elementary school program. Some high schools are nongraded and operate much as nongraded elementary schools do.

Most high schools offer both general and vocational courses of study. These schools are called *comprehensive high schools.* Students who plan to continue their education after high school usually take a general, or *college preparatory,* course of study. Many high schools offer *advanced placement* classes for college-bound students. Students who pass these courses, and meet certain minimum scores on nationally administered examinations, can earn college credit.

Students who intend to get a job immediately after graduation may choose a vocational course of study. Some large school systems operate separate vocational high schools. However, many states have changed high school graduation requirements to include more college preparatory coursework. As a result, many vocational programs have experienced drops in enrollment. See **High school.**

Higher education is education beyond high school. More than half of all high school graduates in the United States get some advanced schooling. The United States has several thousand institutions of higher learning. Over half are privately owned and operated, and most of these are small liberal arts colleges. Many of the publicly owned institutions of higher learning are large state universities. Most college and university students in the United States attend public institutions.

Institutions of higher learning include a wide variety of community colleges, technical institutes, colleges, universities, and professional schools. Community colleges, sometimes called *junior colleges,* offer two-year programs in both general and career education. Most technical institutes offer two-year programs in such fields as automotive engineering, business, and electronics. After completing a two-year course at a community college or technical institute, a student receives an *associate's degree*—or a certificate in the case of certain types of specialized training. Colleges and universities provide a wide selection of liberal arts and career programs. Most offer a four- or five-year liberal arts program that leads to a *bachelor's degree.*

Many colleges and most universities offer advanced courses leading to a *master's* or *doctor's degree.* Most universities also have professional schools, which provide training and award degrees in such fields as business, dentistry, education, engineering, law, and medicine. Students ordinarily must complete a certain amount of college work before gaining admission.

Expenditures for education in the United States*

These graphs show the yearly expenditures for U.S. education since 1950 and these expenditures as a percentage of U.S. *gross domestic product* (GDP). GDP is the total value of goods and services produced within a country annually. Larger enrollments and rising prices have contributed to a rapid increase in school expenditures since 1950.

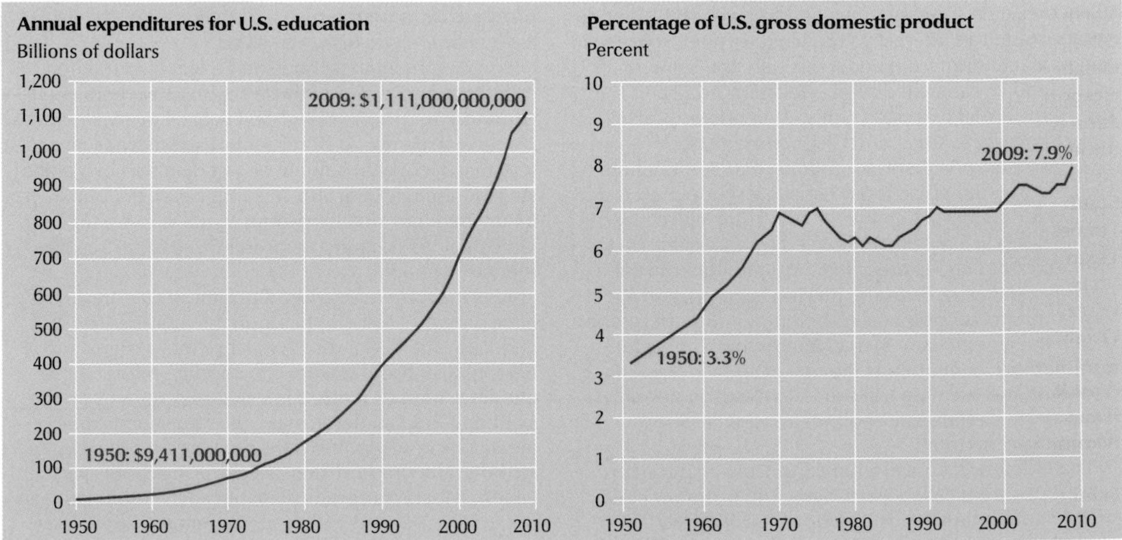

*Includes operating costs, capital outlays, and interest for all public and private schools from kindergarten through graduate school.
Source: *World Book* estimates based on data from the U.S. Department of Education.

Students, teachers, and school expenditures

United States	Number in private schools*		Number in public schools*		Public school expenditures†	
	Students	Teachers	Students	Teachers	Per student	Total
Alabama	95,600	8,800	748,900	47,500	$ 9,400	$ 6,684,000,000
Alaska	7,500	500	131,700	8,100	16,800	2,006,000,000
Arizona	55,400	3,900	1,077,800	51,900	8,600	8,625,000,000
Arkansas	28,900	2,400	480,600	37,200	9,700	4,241,000,000
California	623,200	45,700	6,263,400	313,800	9,400	60,081,000,000
Colorado	63,700	4,800	832,400	49,100	9,600	7,187,000,000
Connecticut	72,500	7,400	564,000	43,600	15,800	8,708,000,000
Delaware	26,600	2,100	126,800	8,600	12,800	1,519,000,000
District of Columbia	17,800	1,900	69,400	6,400	19,800	1,353,000,000
Florida	344,000	26,600	2,634,500	183,800	9,500	23,328,000,000
Georgia	150,300	13,300	1,667,700	115,900	10,200	15,977,000,000
Hawaii	37,100	3,000	180,200	11,400	13,400	2,225,000,000
Idaho	18,700	1,400	276,300	15,200	7,600	1,958,000,000
Illinois	289,700	20,300	2,104,200	138,500	12,500	23,495,000,000
Indiana	120,800	8,400	1,046,700	62,300	9,900	9,681,000,000
Iowa	45,200	3,200	491,800	35,800	9,600	4,731,000,000
Kansas	44,700	3,400	474,500	34,700	11,500	4,805,000,000
Kentucky	70,600	5,300	680,100	44,400	10,100	5,887,000,000
Louisiana	147,000	10,100	690,900	49,600	11,400	7,277,000,000
Maine	18,300	1,900	189,200	16,300	13,600	2,350,000,000
Maryland	145,700	13,200	848,400	58,200	14,600	11,592,000,000
Massachusetts	137,100	14,900	957,100	69,900	15,300	13,943,000,000
Michigan	153,200	10,900	1,649,100	92,700	11,500	17,218,000,000
Minnesota	89,500	6,400	837,100	52,800	11,700	9,270,000,000
Mississippi	54,700	4,500	492,500	33,100	8,600	3,967,000,000
Missouri	118,000	9,000	918,000	67,800	10,300	8,827,000,000
Montana	10,400	900	141,800	10,500	10,900	1,436,000,000
Nebraska	39,000	2,700	295,400	22,300	11,500	3,054,000,000
Nevada	25,100	1,600	428,900	22,100	8,900	3,606,000,000
New Hampshire	26,500	2,600	197,100	15,500	12,900	2,491,000,000
New Jersey	232,000	19,000	1,396,000	115,200	17,600	23,589,000,000
New Mexico	23,700	2,000	334,400	22,700	9,700	3,186,000,000
New York	486,300	42,000	2,766,100	214,800	19,400	48,635,000,000
North Carolina	110,700	10,000	1,483,400	105,000	9,100	12,470,000,000
North Dakota	7,800	600	95,100	8,400	10,100	929,000,000
Ohio	246,300	16,800	1,764,300	111,400	11,900	19,398,000,000
Oklahoma	34,000	2,900	654,800	42,700	8,400	5,082,000,000
Oregon	56,800	4,400	582,800	28,800	10,700	5,530,000,000
Pennsylvania	301,600	23,700	1,786,100	131,000	13,000	21,832,000,000
Rhode Island	24,900	2,300	145,200	11,400	16,200	2,139,000,000
South Carolina	62,300	5,100	723,100	47,000	10,000	6,627,000,000
South Dakota	11,500	900	123,700	9,300	9,500	1,080,000,000
Tennessee	98,300	8,600	972,500	65,400	8,700	7,768,000,000
Texas	313,400	25,700	4,850,200	333,200	9,300	40,688,000,000
Utah	22,000	1,900	582,800	25,500	7,100	3,639,000,000
Vermont	10,400	1,300	92,400	8,700	16,100	1,413,000,000
Virginia	128,100	11,400	1,245,300	70,800	11,700	13,505,000,000
Washington	94,300	7,000	1,035,300	53,400	10,400	9,940,000,000
West Virginia	13,900	1,300	282,700	20,300	11,300	3,059,000,000
Wisconsin	130,500	9,600	872,400	58,400	11,800	9,696,000,000
Wyoming	2,900	300	88,200	7,200	15,700	1,268,000,000
Total	5,488,500	437,400	49,373,300	3,209,600	11,200‡	518,997,000,000

*Figures are for fall 2009.
‡National average.
Figures for individual categories may not add up to totals due to rounding. Source: U.S. Department of Education.

†Figures are for the 2008–2009 school year.

Some professional schools are not connected with a university but award the same kinds of degrees that professional schools of universities do. See **Community college; Universities and colleges.**

Control and support of U.S. education. The Constitution of the United States makes no mention of education. However, the 10th Amendment gives the states any powers the Constitution does not prohibit or specifically grant to the federal government. Because the Constitution does not give the federal government control over education, the states have this power. But the Constitution does give Congress the power to provide for the "general welfare of the United States." Congress has used this power to deal with educational matters that affect many Americans.

Control. Every state has passed laws governing education and has set up a system of public schools. A state school system provides facilities for every level of education, from early childhood education through higher education. Parents may send their children to public schools, or they may enroll them in private schools that are independent of state control. Private schools controlled by religious groups are generally called *parochial schools.* The Roman Catholic Church maintains most of the parochial schools in the United States.

Various court decisions have held that parents may even educate their children at home. But children who receive home schooling must receive an education equal to that of public school pupils. A state may test children educated outside the public school system to ensure that they meet standards set for students who attend public schools.

Every state except Hawaii has transferred some of its control over public education to local *school districts.* Under rules set by the state, a school district is responsible for running the local public schools, from hiring teachers and constructing buildings to planning courses of study. Each state government determines the number and composition of school districts in the state. Some large districts include all or part of a city or county. Other districts are much smaller and may include only a rural township or community. In some states, all districts include grades K-12, while in other states there are elementary (K-6 or K-8) districts and high school (7-12 or 9-12) districts instead of, or in addition to, K-12 districts.

Since the early 1990's, many states have allowed the establishment of *charter schools.* Charter schools typically are independent of government regulations. They receive a charter for their operation either from the local school district, from another public institution such as a state university, or from the state board of education. The organization of charter schools varies because of differences in charter school legislation from state to state, and the preferences of those who establish the schools. See **Charter school.**

Financial support for U.S. public education comes almost entirely from local, state, and federal tax money. Private schools are supported mainly by tuition fees and by contributions from churches, private organizations, wealthy donors, and former students.

In the past, almost all the money needed to support the public schools came from local *property taxes.* Citizens pay property taxes based on the value of buildings, land, and certain other items they own. Over time, as the cost of education increased, and as taxpayers began to resist increases in property taxes, states began to provide more support for the cost of education.

State funds are used both to increase available resources for schools, and to help equalize differences in the ability of local school districts to raise property taxes. Many legal experts and educators consider property taxes an unfair method of supporting public schools. For more information about property taxes and school financing, see the section *How should education be financed?* later in this article.

The federal government and education. Various agencies and branches of the federal government deal with educational matters. Congress decides how much money the government will spend on education and what types of programs federal funds will support. Many federal departments and agencies are responsible for distributing the funds and managing the programs approved by Congress. In addition, the Supreme Court of the United States and other federal courts decide constitutional questions relating to education.

The chief educational agency of the federal government is the United States Department of Education. The department finances and administers programs to improve education. It also conducts educational research. The National Center for Education Statistics, a division of the department, collects and publishes information on educational activities in the United States.

The federal government aids and encourages education in two main ways: (1) It tries to ensure that all children have equal educational opportunities, and (2) it provides funds for certain types of education when such aid is considered beneficial to the nation as a whole.

Ensuring equal opportunity. The federal government cannot directly control education in the states. But it can insist that every state provide equal educational opportunities for all its citizens. For example, in the historic 1954 case of *Brown v. Board of Education of Topeka,* the Supreme Court ruled that compulsory segregation of the races in public schools was unconstitutional. Other rulings have helped promote equal opportunity for such groups as women, people with disabilities, and people who do not speak English. The section in this article titled *Education for whom?* gives further information about equal opportunity.

Providing financial assistance. The federal government spends billions of dollars a year on education. Some of this money supports educational institutions owned and operated by the federal government. These schools include the air force, military, and naval academies; schools for American Indian children; and schools for the children of military personnel and government employees overseas.

The federal government grants large sums to state departments of education. Some of the money is used to support state educational programs. But most of the funds are distributed among local school districts, which may use them for purposes specified by Congress. For instance, Congress provides money for special services for children from low-income families. Local districts also receive federal funds to purchase textbooks, pay for school health services, and finance experimental education programs. A district must make these programs and services available to all children, including those who attend private schools.

The federal government also grants loans and scholarships to college and university students to help pay their tuition and other school expenses. In addition, the government grants funds to public and private institutions of higher learning. Without federal aid, many colleges and universities would be forced to close.

Education in the United Kingdom

The four divisions that make up the United Kingdom—England, Northern Ireland, Scotland, and Wales—have separate educational systems. Each system is run by its own government department, which works closely with local school authorities.

Children in the United Kingdom are required by law to begin school at the age of 5, except for children in Northern Ireland, who must begin school at age 4. The children are required to continue in school until they are 16. Generally, students attend *primary* (elementary) school until they are 11 or 12 years old. After that point, they attend *secondary* (high) school. There are several types of high schools in the United Kingdom. Some high schools provide a college preparatory education. Others stress a more technical or vocational education. However, most students attend comprehensive schools, which provide all types of high school education.

The majority of British schoolchildren attend free primary schools and high schools that are supported by public funds. The rest go to private institutions called *independent schools* that are supported by fees paid by parents and by private gifts of money. There are several types of independent schools. The best known are the English *public schools,* which provide high school education. Although these schools are actually private institutions, they are called *public schools* because the earliest of these schools were established for the children of the middle classes. Some of these schools—such as Eton, Harrow, and Winchester—traditionally have trained students for the practice of law and for high-ranking positions in the government, the Church of England, and the British armed forces.

Institutions of higher education in the United Kingdom include two of the oldest and most famous universities in the world: the University of Oxford, founded in the 1100's, and the University of Cambridge, probably established in 1209. The University of London is the United Kingdom's largest traditional university. The Open University has more students, but it has no regular classrooms. Instead, the Open University provides instruction by radio, television, correspondence, the Internet, and other methods. Other universities in the United Kingdom include the University of Wales and the University of Glamorgan, in Wales; the universities of Aberdeen, Edinburgh, Glasgow, and St. Andrews, in Scotland; and Queen's University Belfast and the University of Ulster, in Northern Ireland.

Although they are mainly supported by public funds, universities in the United Kingdom are not part of the government-run system of education. Instead, they are independent, self-governing bodies. The universities themselves decide what subjects they teach, what degrees they award, and what staff they appoint. The Quality Assurance Agency for Higher Education (QAA) reviews the standards of the schools.

Cost of education in selected countries

This graph shows the average amount of money each country spends per student for elementary, secondary, and higher education.

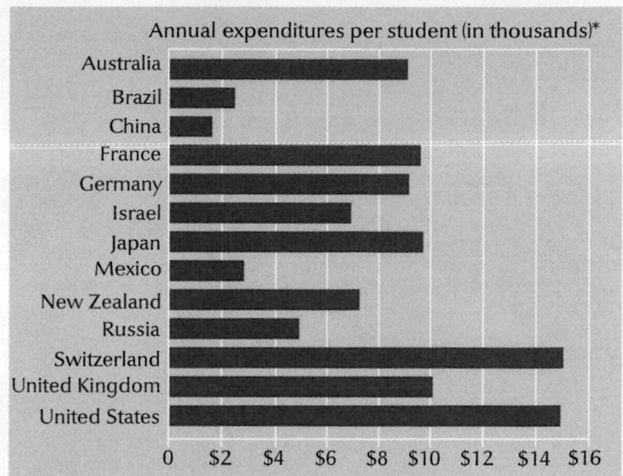

*In U.S. dollars.
Figures are for 2008.
Source: Organisation for Economic Co-operation and Development.

Education in Canada

Canada, like the United States, does not have a national educational system. Each province and territory organizes and regulates its own system of education. The national government controls schools for Indians, Inuit, and children of Canadian military personnel overseas.

Public education is free throughout Canada. Most private schools charge tuition fees. Children are required to attend school for 10 years in most provinces. Most communities offer education to students from kindergarten through 12th grade. Students who plan to seek employment after completing their required education can take a two-year vocational course during high school. Students who plan to continue their education take a four- or five-year general or vocational course.

Canada has dozens of degree-granting institutions that are members of the Association of Universities and Colleges of Canada. Other institutions of higher learning include technical institutes and community colleges. In Canada, a community college combines the last one or two years of high school and the first one or two years of college.

Each Canadian province has a department of education headed by a minister of education. The department sets educational policies and standards for the entire province. But local authorities also have considerable control over their schools. Each province is divided into local school districts, each of which has a school board and a superintendent.

Canada's provincial governments share the cost of education with local school districts. In six provinces—Alberta, British Columbia, Manitoba, Ontario, Quebec, and Saskatchewan—public funds are used to support religious schools. The other provinces provide little or no funding for religious schools. Many Roman Catholic schools, especially in Quebec, teach in French. Most Protestant and nonreligious schools in Canada teach in English.

© Natalie Forbes, Corbis

Education in Vietnam, *shown here,* and in some other countries is entirely controlled by the government. The majority of countries, however, have both public and private schools.

Education in other countries

This section provides a general discussion of education throughout the world. See the individual country articles for discussions of education in each country.

Organization. In many countries, early childhood education begins at schools similar to nursery schools and kindergartens. In other countries, elementary school is the earliest level of formal education. Elementary schools in every country teach children to read and write and to work with numbers. The pupils also learn their country's customs and their duties as citizens. In most countries, the pupils also study such subjects as geography, history, and science.

In most nations, elementary education is compulsory and free. But countries vary in the amount of schooling they require and are able to provide. In many less developed countries, most children receive only an elementary education. In such countries, secondary and higher education are available only to outstanding students or to those who can afford to attend private schools. But in highly developed countries, young people are usually required to complete from 9 to 11 years of school, or sometimes more. The requirement typically includes 3 to 6 years of secondary school. Many countries have junior secondary schools similar to the junior high schools and middle schools in the United States. In some school systems, students take an examination to determine what kind of secondary school they will attend. Some students are admitted to academic schools, and others attend vocational or specialized schools. In many European countries, secondary school students hold jobs and complete their education by taking part-time courses.

Throughout the world, students typically must complete their secondary education before they can be admitted to an institution of higher learning. They may also have to take a standardized test or an entrance examination. In many countries, the test results determine what kind of higher education a student will receive. The developed countries of Europe have many colleges and universities, and a wide variety of advanced technical and professional schools.

The educational system of almost every nation includes some form of schooling for students with disabilities. Most countries also provide for adult education at various levels. Many developing countries support schools that teach adults to read and write.

In many countries, especially in Europe, *boarding schools* are an important source of education. Boarding school students live at school instead of at home. Some educators believe that social values can be taught more effectively if students live at school. Israel has collective communities called *kibbutzim,* in which children spend most of their time together.

Control. Most countries have both public and private schools. In these countries, the majority of elementary-

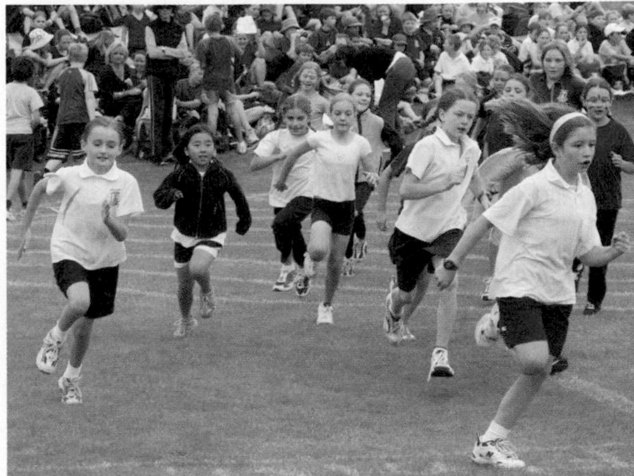

© Rob Walls, Alamy Images

Physical activity is an important feature of elementary and secondary education in many parts of the world. These students are participating in a school athletic event in Hobart, Australia.

© Cumes Julia, Gamma

Elementary schools in every country emphasize reading, writing, and working with numbers. In many countries, the schools also teach history, science, and other subjects. These students are participating in a reading exercise in a classroom in the Johannesburg area of South Africa.

and secondary-school children attend public schools. The Netherlands is one of the few nations in which more children are enrolled in private schools at all levels than in public schools..

In most nations, the central government has at least some control over the public school system. In France, the national government has complete control over the public schools. The French government's *ministry* (department) of education decides all questions of educational policy and manages the public schools. In many other countries, including most European nations, the central government exercises control over certain aspects of the school system. These countries have ministries of education, which decide educational policy. But the ministries transfer some responsibilities to local authorities.

Financial support. In every nation, public funds are used to support education. Most countries that permit private schools also provide some financial support for such schools. In the Netherlands, public funds pay all the expenses of private schools. Other countries provide only partial support. Tuition fees and individual contributions pay the rest of the expenses of private schools.

Nations provide public funds for education in various ways. In some countries, the national government pays all public education costs. But in other countries, the national government shares the cost of education with other levels of government, such as states, provinces, or cities. In some of these countries, the national government supplies most of the funds. In others, the funds come mainly from lower levels of government.

Many countries obtain additional funds for public education from tuition fees, voluntary contributions, and other private sources. Some developing nations receive foreign aid for education.

History

The first major milestone in the history of education occurred in prehistoric times with the development of language. Language enabled people to communicate more precisely than they could by signs and gestures. But early people had only a spoken language. They had no system of writing or numbering and no schools.

Young people in prehistoric societies were educated through *apprenticeship, imitation,* and *rituals.* Through apprenticeship, a young person learned, for example, how to build a shelter by working with an older, experienced master builder. Through imitation, young people acquired the language and customs of their parents and other adults in their society. Through the performance of rituals, they learned about various aspects of life and the ties that bound them to their group. The rituals usually involved myths, which dealt with such things as the group's history and its gods and heroes.

Today, young people in all societies still learn through apprenticeship, imitation, and rituals. But as society has grown increasingly complicated, teachers and schools have taken on more and more responsibility for educating the young.

The beginning of formal education. A second major milestone in the history of education was the invention of writing. The Sumerians, who lived in the Tigris-Euphrates Valley, invented a writing system about 3500 B.C. The Egyptians devised a writing system about 3000 B.C. Both systems used a method of writing numbers as well as words. The development of writing made possible the beginning of schools as we know them.

Before people developed writing, teachers had to repeat orally what was to be learned until the student memorized it. A child could thus learn only what the teacher had memorized. But by using writing systems and teaching children to read, teachers could make available the knowledge of many people, not only their own. However, the first writing systems, which were a kind of picture writing, were awkward and difficult to master. As a result, special schools arose in which teachers taught reading, writing, and calculation.

About 3000 B.C., both the Sumerians and the Egyptians established schools to teach reading and writing. Many of the schools were taught by priests. Most students came from upper-class families. Only a small number of boys, and even fewer girls, received schooling.

A student's training, which lasted from about the age of 5 to 17, was strict and monotonous. Students learned to write by copying the same literary selections again and again. They learned arithmetic by copying business accounts. Those who completed their education formed a separate social class called *scribes.* Scribes were hired for any task that required a knowledge of reading, writing, or arithmetic.

Civilization spread from Sumer and Egypt to the eastern shores of the Mediterranean Sea. About 1500 B.C., tribes in this region, who each spoke one of the closely related Semitic languages, developed the world's first alphabet. The alphabet gave education another valuable tool. Alphabetic systems make writing easier than picture systems because they require far fewer symbols.

Certain Hebrew Semitic tribes developed a more democratic educational system. Other educational systems had been designed mainly for the sons of upper-class families. But the Hebrews required boys of every social class to attend school. The Hebrew schools were religious institutions conducted by priests called *scribes.* They taught boys to read the sacred writings of the Hebrew people, which were collected in a volume called the Torah. Hebrew girls did not attend school but were taught at home by their mothers.

Ancient Greek education. The Greeks made the greatest educational advances of ancient times. In fact, Western education today is based largely on the ancient Greek model. Greek civilization flourished from about 700 B.C. to about 330 B.C. During this period, Greek arts, philosophy, and science became the foundations of Western thought and culture. Homer and other Greek writers created new forms of expression, including lyric and epic poetry.

Ancient Greece was divided into *city-states,* independent states that consisted of a city and the region surrounding it. The educational system of each city-state aimed to produce good citizens. Athens and Sparta, two of the most powerful city-states, had different ideals of citizenship. In Sparta, citizens were judged largely by their political and military service. The government controlled education. Boys received physical and military training, but few learned to read or write. In Athens, unlike Sparta, citizens were judged more by the quality of their minds. Athenian citizens were also expected to develop their bodies and serve the state.

Athens made the greatest educational advances of any Greek city-state. But Athenian education was far from democratic. Education was limited to the sons of Athenian citizens. Less than half of all Athenians were citizens. Slaves made up a large part of the population and were not considered worthy of an education.

Athenian boys started their education at about age 6. But they did not go to schools as we think of schools today. A trusted family slave took them from teacher to teacher, each of whom specialized in a certain subject or certain related subjects. Boys studied reading, writing, arithmetic, music, dancing, and gymnastics. As the boys advanced, they memorized the works of Homer and other Greek poets. Boys continued their elementary education until they were about 15 years old. From about ages 16 to 20, they attended a government-sponsored *gymnasium.* Gymnasiums trained young men to become citizen-soldiers. They emphasized such sports as running and wrestling and taught civic duty and the art of war. Students held discussions to improve their reasoning and speaking ability.

Some Athenian gymnasiums became centers of advanced learning. By the 400's B.C., advanced learning in Athens consisted of *philosophy* and *rhetoric.* Philosophy included the study of logic, mathematics, morals, and science. Rhetoric included the study of government, history, and public speaking.

During the 400's and 300's B.C., Athens produced such great philosophers and teachers as Aristotle, Plato, and Socrates. About 387 B.C., Plato founded a school of philosophy that became known as the Academy. Some scholars believe the Academy was the world's first university. Aristotle founded a similar school called the Lyceum in 335 B.C.

Most young Athenian women received no formal education. They mainly learned domestic skills—such as how to prepare food, make clothing, and care for infants—from their mothers. However, some women belonged to religious organizations through which they developed skills in music, poetry, and dancing.

Greece, like other countries in ancient times, had many somewhat secret religious groups that carried on educational activities. Even Plato's Academy and Aristotle's Lyceum resembled religious brotherhoods united by sacred oaths and ceremonies. Some occupational organizations also had religious and educational functions. For example, early medical science developed among families who joined together in a secret religious society to educate their children in the study of medicine.

In these religious and occupational groups—as in all areas of Greek life—young males associated closely with adult men. The Greeks believed that a boy could best learn what he is and should try to become by imitating an older, ideal model. For this reason, every young Greek male became the companion of an older citizen. In most cases, this person was a friend of the boy's father or a relative. It was hoped that a strong love would develop between the two. As a result, the younger male would want to imitate his companion and in so doing take on his virtues.

Ancient Roman education. After about 600 B.C., an advanced civilization began to develop in Rome. By about 100 B.C., the Romans had built the most extensive educational system to that time. Their system was patterned after that of ancient Athens. But unlike the Athenians, the Romans provided schooling for girls as well as boys. The children of wealthy citizens were taught by a *ludus* (introductory teacher) from about the age of 7 to 10. These children learned to read and write both Greek and their native language, Latin. Girls received only an elementary education. Boys from about 10 to 14 years old attended a secondary school run by a *grammaticus* (teacher of grammar). In secondary school, the boys continued their study of Greek and Latin grammar and literature. The Romans also established institutions of higher learning. These institutions were schools of rhetoric, which prepared young men for careers in law and government.

Between 100 B.C. and A.D. 100, Roman poets, historians, and orators created a written literature that included the sacred myths and beliefs of the Roman people. The greatest poet was Virgil. Other important writers included the poet Ovid, the historian Cornelius Tacitus, the general and statesman Julius Caesar, and the orator and statesman Marcus Tullius Cicero. The Latin writings of these men, along with the works of Greek scholars and poets, became the basic curriculum for formal education throughout the Western world.

Although the Romans adopted many Greek educational traditions, they surpassed the Greeks in some fields. In agriculture, engineering, and law, for example, the Romans not only developed greater knowledge and experience, but they also put this knowledge into writing. As a result, written information and formal instruction played an increasingly vital role in the apprenticeships in these fields.

By about A.D. 200, Roman culture had spread over much of the Western world, and most educated people thought of themselves as Roman citizens. Indeed, the basic issue of teachers and philosophers had become "What does it mean to be a good Roman?"

Religion and early Western education. The religion of the Hebrew people, Judaism, became the parent

Miniature from a French manuscript by an unknown artist, Bibliothèque Nationale, Paris

The University of Paris became known throughout Europe in the Middle Ages for its faculty of famous scholars and teachers.

religion of two other religions—Christianity and Islam. Much of the Hebrews' holy writing became the Old Testament in the Christian Bible. The New Testament, which deals with Jesus Christ and His followers, was added as further revelation of God's truth. The Muslims, whose religion is Islam, incorporated much of the Bible in their holy book, the Qur'ān. All three religions thus have a common origin as well as sacred books and other things in common. These common elements had important effects on early Western education.

The followers of each of the three religions believed (1) that one God created and rules the universe; (2) that He permits no competition; (3) that He has revealed Himself to people; (4) that from the sacred, written record of this revelation, people find their ultimate meaning and basic duty; and (5) that God's chosen people have a sacred mission. Hebrews, Christians, and Muslims each developed educational systems in which the young were taught these beliefs. They were also taught that their particular religious group was spiritually superior to other groups.

Hebrews, Christians, and Muslims each developed a class of scholars who interpreted their group's sacred writings and explored how those writings could be applied in different conditions, times, and places. Each group tended to view itself as a chosen people. As a result, the groups' educational systems tended to emphasize a sharp line between "believers" and "nonbelievers." Christians and Muslims felt an especially strong need to convert nonbelievers, usually through missionary work but sometimes through warfare. This missionary impulse led Christians to spread their educational system to many cultures.

Early Chinese and Indian education. Christian missionaries worked to establish their educational systems in India and China. But the Indians and Chinese already had sacred books, written traditions, and formal schooling that they had used for centuries. Many Chinese and Indians felt that the Christian missionaries represented cultures that were spiritually and intellectually shallow.

Education in India was influenced by the religious traditions of Buddhism, Hinduism, and Islam. Much education involved the passing of sacred knowledge from one generation to another. The most important Hindu sacred writings, called the Upanishads, appeared between 800 and 600 B.C. In China, the ideas of the philosopher Confucius were the strongest influence on education. These ideas, called Confucianism, emphasized the need to develop moral character and responsibility. The Confucians believed that people could perfect themselves through study. They made no sharp distinction between academic education and moral education.

Christian education in the Middle Ages. The Christian church played an important part in shaping European formal education during the Middle Ages, which lasted from about the A.D. 400's through the 1400's. Before the collapse of the West Roman Empire in the 400's, peoples in western and southern Europe had already begun to shift their loyalty from the Roman state to the Christian church. In fact, the basic issue of teachers and philosophers had now become "What does it mean to be a good Christian?" rather than "What does it mean to be a good Roman?"

Christian parents were expected to know the laws and beliefs of Christianity and to teach them to their children. Religious authorities controlled most formal education. But for many centuries, only those people who were being prepared for a religious vocation received such schooling. Some youngsters were educated by their local priests or in the bishop's household. Others were taught in monastery or cathedral schools.

In the monastery and cathedral schools, students studied such subjects as church music, theology, and Latin, the official language of the Western church. They also studied subjects similar to those studied in ancient Greece and Rome. These subjects were divided into two groups, which together were known as the *seven liberal arts.* The first group, called the *trivium,* consisted of grammar, rhetoric, and logic. The second group, called the *quadrivium,* consisted of arithmetic, geometry, astronomy, and harmonics.

Many young people who did not receive formal schooling became apprentices to skilled masters and learned a trade. Young men learned the arts and values of *chivalry* (the qualities of an ideal knight), which prepared them for military or government careers. Business people, craftworkers, merchants, and other groups formed professional societies called *guilds.* The guilds ranked among the leading educational institutions of the Middle Ages. They provided informal education in technical and social matters for guild members, as well as some formal education for members' children.

The rise of the universities. The first modern universities developed in Europe during the 1100's. The universities did not originate as places or as groups of buildings. They began instead as collections of scholars organized into corporations with certain privileges and responsibilities. In fact, the word *university* comes from a Latin term for *corporation* or *guild.*

Most European universities were patterned after one of two models. The model for the majority of universities in the north was the University of Paris. The University of Paris developed in the 1100's from a teacher's guild at a cathedral school. The school taught several subjects and granted degrees. The universities that followed this model typically specialized in liberal arts and theology and were run by corporations of teachers. These universities received certain privileges from religious and governmental authorities. For instance, the universities could, within limits, try their own members for *heresy*—that is, for holding or teaching ideas that conflicted with those of the church.

Most southern European universities were modeled after the University of Bologna in Italy, which came into existence about 1100. These universities began as students' guilds, and most of their students were mature and successful professional people. The guilds hired the professors and set the working conditions. Most southern European universities were nonreligious in origin and specialized in law or medicine.

By 1500, nearly 80 universities had been founded in Europe. Some survived only a short time, but others still exist. Those still in existence include Cambridge and Oxford universities in England; the universities of Montpellier, Paris, and Toulouse in France; Heidelberg in Germany; Bologna, Florence, Naples, Padua, Rome, and Siena in Italy; and Salamanca in Spain.

The Renaissance was a period in European history when many people showed a renewed interest in the world and a growing spirit of individuality and independence. It began in Italy during the 1300's and spread across Europe during the 1400's and 1500's.

During the Renaissance, *classical humanist* scholars stressed the human experience of the ancient Greeks and Romans, rather than the religious experience of the Middle Ages. The classical humanists were deeply interested in the Greek and Roman classics. Scholars of the Middle Ages had valued the writings of a few Greek and Roman authors because their logic and rhetoric could be used to support Christian teachings. The humanists, on the other hand, valued the Greek and Roman classics for what they said about civilized life as well as for their logic and rhetoric.

The humanists, like the ancient Athenians, believed that the main purpose of education was to train well-rounded, cultured citizens. They considered the ancient Greek gymnasium the ideal type of school. During the 1300's and 1400's, schools patterned after the Greek gymnasiums arose in many parts of Europe. They admitted mostly the sons of upper-class families, who studied Greek and Latin and the works of the ancient writers. Because there were few textbooks, students had to memorize texts read to them in class. They also learned how to behave like gentlemen and took part in body-building sports.

In time, these schools developed into the European *secondary school,* which was designed for upper-class boys and offered a liberal arts program based on Greek and Latin sources. These schools had different names in different countries. They were called *gymnasia* in Germany, *lycées* and *collèges* in France, and *grammar schools* in England. Boys entered secondary school between the ages of 6 and 9. Until the 1800's, secondary schools provided the only formal education for most upper-class European boys, except for those who attended the universities.

Children of the lower classes attended *primary school,* where they learned reading and writing in the *vernacular* (native language), arithmetic, history, literature, and geography. In Europe, the primary school was an alternative to the secondary school. Usually, primary school graduates could not enter a secondary school or a university. Primary schools began to appear in Europe in the 1500's, but universal education did not begin in Europe until the 1800's.

During the Renaissance, many classical humanists produced literary works in the vernacular as well as in Greek and Latin. In the 1300's, for example, the great Italian poet Petrarch wrote more than 400 poems in Italian. Geoffrey Chaucer of England wrote his masterpiece, *The Canterbury Tales,* in English. Some scholars translated the Latin Bible into vernacular tongues.

The vernacular writings had only a small audience, however, because relatively few people could read. In addition, books were scarce and expensive because they had to be laboriously written by hand. Only a few people could arrange to borrow one or hire a scribe to copy it. Even university students had to memorize a book from hearing it read by the professor.

The invention of printing as we know it became yet another milestone in the history of education. About 1440, a German metalworker named Johannes Gutenberg invented movable type in Europe. He also devised a special press to print from his movable type. Almost immediately, large numbers of low-cost books and pamphlets became available. As a result, thousands of people wanted to learn to read and write. In addition, the great quantity and variety of printed matter enabled people not only to learn without an instructor but also to acquire the knowledge to become teachers themselves. Moreover, printing spread knowledge faster than ever before. People could thus quickly learn about new theories, experiments, and discoveries.

The Reformation. The invention of printing occurred at a time when the Roman Catholic Church was torn by conflict. This conflict led to the Reformation, the religious movement of the 1500's that gave birth to Protestantism. In the 1300's and 1400's, certain reformers had begun to question some teachings of the church and to press for changes. One of their main beliefs was that all Christians should be able to read the Bible in their own language. But until the invention of printing, most Europeans knew little about the reformers' arguments. By the 1500's, pamphlets criticizing the church had become widespread throughout the Christian world. In addition, relatively inexpensive Bibles in vernacular translations became widely available. The argument that every Christian should learn to read the Bible thus became practical for the first time.

During the 1500's, Protestant sections of Europe, including parts of Germany and Switzerland, established elementary schools to teach the children of common citizens to read the Bible in their native language. These vernacular schools also taught Christian morality and beliefs.

Meanwhile, the Roman Catholic Church expanded its educational activities as part of the movement called the Counter Reformation. Several Catholic religious orders established vernacular schools for Catholic children. The number of secondary schools also expanded rapidly during the Reformation in both Protestant and Catholic regions of Europe.

The Enlightenment, also called the Age of Reason, was a period of great intellectual activity that began in the 1600's and lasted until the late 1700's. During this period, scientists came to believe that, through reasoning and experimentation, they could discover the laws by which nature operates. This idea led to the development of the modern scientific method and created a scientific revolution.

To carry out experiments, scientists needed new tools. Inventors met these needs with such instruments as the microscope, sextant, and slide rule. Aided by the new instruments, scientists advanced rapidly. Discoveries by the English scientist Isaac Newton revolutionized astronomy. Robert Boyle of Ireland, Antoine Lavoisier of France, and Joseph Priestley of England founded modern chemistry. France's René Descartes invented analytic geometry. The English physician William Harvey discovered how blood circulates in the human body.

The advance of science affected education. Science began to be taught in the schools, though it did not become a major subject of elementary and secondary education until the mid-1800's. By the late 1700's, however, the demand for an extensive scientific curriculum in universities had become overwhelming.

As knowledge of natural science expanded, such philosophers as Descartes and England's Thomas Hobbes and John Locke began to urge the development of a social science. They suggested that human societies could be viewed as "universes" that were understandable through scientific investigations. These philosophers also believed that the reasons people behaved as they did could be understood through science.

The scientific revolution also affected education by changing the nature of *technology.* Technology refers to all the ways people use their inventions and discoveries to satisfy their needs and desires. A technology that is not based on science can be mastered through apprenticeship. But a technology based on science requires formal schooling. By assisting their parents, for example, children could learn to plow, sow, and reap in a traditional manner. But with the development of complicated farm machinery and scientific farming methods, agriculture came to depend on people trained in science.

By the late 1700's, the technologies of textile manufacturing, transportation, and many other fields had become increasingly dependent on highly educated engineers and scientists. Trade and technical schools arose in many parts of Europe. In the United States, such leaders as Benjamin Franklin and Thomas Jefferson called for the addition of "useful" subjects to the school curriculum. By "useful," they meant science courses that could be applied to technology.

The rise of universal public schools. By the late 1700's, the nation, rather than the church, had become the chief symbol that united the people of several European countries, as well as the people of the United States. As people shifted their greater loyalty to their nation, the church's control over formal schooling declined while the government's control increased.

Modern *nationalism*—the idea that a person owes primary allegiance to the nation—first reached its fullest expression in France during and after the French Revolution (1789-1799). By 1833, the French government had taken control of all the nation's schools. The Kingdom of Prussia, a German-speaking state, also developed a national school system in the early 1800's. Through its schools, Prussia made nationalism the highest ideal of German-speaking peoples. When its king became the first emperor of a united Germany in 1871, many people believed the system of nationalistic schools had contributed to Prussia's rise to power. As a result, other nations began to follow Prussia's lead.

By the early 1900's, public elementary education was free and compulsory in most European countries. Some countries also provided free secondary schooling. Vocational and technical education also made great strides in Europe during the 1900's. Many nations added *infant schools* (nursery schools) to their systems in the mid-1900's.

Since the early 1900's, the ideal of free, compulsory education has taken root in almost every country. Most countries have adopted the plan of educational organization used in the West—that is, division into early childhood, elementary, secondary, and higher education.

Development of British education. In the early 1800's, the United Kingdom took steps toward a national system of education. British educators Andrew Bell and Joseph Lancaster developed methods for providing elementary education cheaply by using pupils as teachers. In their systems, teachers taught older students, called *monitors,* who in turn taught younger students. Schools that used these systems were called *monitorial schools.* In 1833, Parliament voted to provide government money for schools. In 1839, the government claimed the right to inspect the schools to which it gave money.

In 1870, Parliament passed England's Elementary Education Act. The act established local school boards and provided tax-funded elementary schools in areas where no schools existed. Parliament passed a similar act for Scotland in 1872. England, Wales, and Scotland made rapid progress in setting up a national system of education. In Northern Ireland, the system developed later. The Parliament of Northern Ireland passed an Education Act in 1923.

During the 1920's and 1930's, several official reports influenced British primary and secondary education. They included *The Education of the Adolescent* (1926) and *The Primary School* (1931). The first report proposed that primary education should end at about age 11, after which all children should go on to secondary education. The second report recommended the more informal and active methods of teaching used in British primary schools today. The 1944 Education Act created a ministry of education and reorganized and expanded the British educational system.

For many years, the central government in London and local authorities worked in partnership to provide and control education. However, in the 1990's, the responsibility for education shifted from the central gov-

The Country School (1871), an oil painting on canvas by Winslow Homer; the St. Louis Art Museum

One-room country schools were common in the United States in the 1800's. One teacher taught all the grades, *shown here.* Teaching methods of the 1800's stressed memorization and discipline.

ernment to regional government bodies. Today, separate government departments for England, Wales, Scotland, and Northern Ireland work closely with school authorities to administer the individual educational systems of the four divisions.

Development of Canadian education. From the early 1600's to the mid-1700's, the Catholic Church controlled most formal education in Canada. Most colonists of this period were French Catholics who lived in the St. Lawrence River Valley. They set up French-language elementary schools where parish priests and members of religious orders were the main teachers. The Jesuits established a few classical secondary schools for boys. One of these, the Seminary of Quebec, was founded in 1663. It was named Laval University in 1852.

In 1763, Britain (later the United Kingdom) gained control of all Canada. After that date, English settlers established many English-language schools. These included Protestant elementary and secondary schools for upper-class boys. After about 1800, the British tried to set up a common school system for French Catholics and English Protestants in Quebec. But Catholic opposition killed the effort. In 1846, a law established separate Protestant and Catholic school systems for Quebec. During the 1850's and 1860's, Ontario, which was largely Protestant, developed an educational system in which taxes supported both public and religious schools.

The British North America Act, passed in 1867, brought about the federation of the Canadian provinces. The act left education under provincial control. It also guaranteed public support for religious schools in the provinces—including Ontario and Quebec—that had provided such support before 1867. During the late 1800's, elementary education became free and compulsory throughout Canada.

Development of U.S. education. Most of the colonists who came to America set up schools like those they had known in Europe. Protestants and Roman Catholics established and supported their own schools. Most were elementary schools designed to teach reading, writing, and religion. School attendance was not compulsory in the American Colonies. Only about 1 child out of 10 went to school. Many children learned a trade by becoming apprentices. The children of wealthier colonists studied under tutors or were sent to private schools supported by tuition fees or to schools in England.

In 1642, the Massachusetts Bay Colony, the largest New England colony, passed a law requiring parents to teach their children to read. In 1647, Massachusetts passed the first law in America requiring communities to establish public schools. The law required every town with at least 50 families to start an elementary school, and every town of 100 families or more to have a Latin grammar school. Like other colonial schools, these town schools taught religion. But unlike other schools in the colonies, they were partially supported by public funds. The elementary schools were open to all children. The grammar schools were attended mainly by boys preparing for college. The Boston Latin School, which opened in 1635, was the first Latin grammar school—and the first secondary school of any kind—in the American Colonies. In 1636, Massachusetts founded Harvard College, the first institution of higher learning in the colonies. By the early 1800's, it had become Harvard University.

The 1700's. Secondary schools called *academies* arose in many of the colonies during the 1700's. Academies offered more practical courses than did Latin grammar schools. A student could take such subjects as bookkeeping and navigation in addition to religion and liberal arts courses. Most academies were private schools supported by tuition fees. Some admitted girls, and some were established for girls only.

When the Revolutionary War in America ended in 1783, the United States had 18 institutions of higher learning. Several were partially state supported and controlled. In 1785, Georgia chartered the first state university, but it did not open until 1801. In 1795, North Carolina University (now the University of North Carolina at Chapel Hill) became the first state university to hold classes.

Unification through education. After the Revolutionary War, many Americans were concerned with unifying their new nation. Attempts to promote unity had two important effects on education: (1) the development of standardized textbooks and (2) the building of state public school systems.

During the 1700's and early 1800's, a number of educators produced books designed specifically for Americans. Noah Webster's famous "Blue-Backed Speller" helped standardize spelling and pronunciation in the United States. Millions of elementary school students used illustrated reading books published by William H. McGuffey. These "McGuffey Readers" taught patriotism and helped form literary tastes in the United States.

Early American educators also emphasized that good Americans were honest, hard-working, courageous, and deeply religious. In trying to develop an idealized view of Americans, early educators often described other people as lacking in these traits. This tendency was reflected in the textbooks, where people whose way of life differed from the American way were described unfavorably. For instance, authors sometimes described Spaniards as unusually cruel and lazy. Similarly, some authors wrote that the American Indians were savages who needed to be civilized.

During the 1800's, increasing numbers of Americans looked to education to provide common goals and a sense of national unity. To achieve this goal, they proposed that each state set up a system of free, compulsory, tax-supported schools. They wanted the schools to be free of religious control but devoted to building character and teaching patriotism. The school systems were soon established throughout the country.

Certain religious groups, especially Roman Catholics and Lutherans, disliked some of the principles taught in public schools. As a result, they maintained and controlled alternate schools. In addition, some people, particularly the wealthy, disliked the fact that public schools tended to equalize everyone. They continued to send their children to private schools. But for generations, immigrants from many countries and of many religions found public schools an entry into the mainstream of American life.

Advances in public education. In 1837, Massachusetts established a state board of education to coordinate its public school system. This board became a model for boards in other states. The first secretary of the Massachusetts board, the educator Horace Mann, did much to strengthen education in the state. Under his leadership, Massachusetts began the nation's first public *normal school* (teacher-training school) in 1839. In 1852, the Massachusetts legislature passed the first compulsory school-attendance law in the United States. By the end of the 1800's, 31 of the 45 states had school-attendance laws. By 1918, every state had one.

Boston opened the nation's first public high school in 1821. Some people believed that the use of public funds to support secondary schools was illegal. However, in 1874, the Michigan Supreme Court ruled that local governments could use tax money to support secondary schools as well as elementary schools. Public high schools soon opened in other states.

Advances in higher education. Churches and other private organizations founded several hundred small liberal arts colleges in the 1800's. In 1833, Oberlin Collegiate Institute (now Oberlin College) in Ohio became the first coeducational college in the United States. In 1862, Congress passed the Morrill, or Land-Grant, Act, which gave vast areas of federal land to the states. The act re-

Important dates in education

c. 2500 B.C. The Sumerians and Egyptians established schools to teach the skills of reading and writing.

387 B.C. Plato founded the Academy, a school of philosophy and science, in Athens. Many scholars consider the Academy the world's first university.

335 B.C. Aristotle founded a school called the Lyceum in Athens. Students and teachers at the Lyceum pursued higher learning through lectures, discussions, and research.

c. A.D. 970 Al-Azhar University, a center of Islamic learning, was founded in Cairo, Egypt.

1100's The first modern universities developed in Europe. Early European universities included the University of Paris, the University of Bologna, and Oxford University.

c. 1440 Johannes Gutenberg invented movable type in Europe. The development of printing made books and pamphlets widely available.

1538 The first university in the Western Hemisphere, the University of Santo Domingo, was founded in the Dominican Republic.

1600's The Enlightenment, also called the Age of Reason, began in Europe, leading to major advances in such fields as astronomy, chemistry, mathematics, and physics.

1635 The Boston Latin School, the first secondary school in the American Colonies, began classes.

1636 Massachusetts chartered Harvard College, the first college in the American Colonies.

1663 The Seminary of Quebec was founded. It became Laval University, one of Canada's leading universities, in 1852.

1829 The University of Cape Town, the oldest university in South Africa, was founded as South African College.

1837 Friedrich Fröbel, a German educator, started the first kindergarten, in Blankenburg, Germany.

1850 The University of Sydney, the first university in Australia, was established.

1852 Massachusetts passed the first compulsory school-attendance law in the United States.

1870 The British Parliament passed England's Elementary Education Act. The act set up local school boards and provided new tax-funded elementary schools in areas where no schools existed.

1954 The Supreme Court of the United States ruled in *Brown v. Board of Education of Topeka* that public schools segregated by race are unequal and thus unconstitutional.

1991 Tim Berners-Lee, a British computer scientist, developed the World Wide Web, which gave teachers and students access to a huge body of educational materials on their computers.

Brown Bros.

Higher education for women became available during the 1830's in coeducational colleges. These students attended Vassar College in the early 1900's, when it was a women's college.

Photograph from *Community Schools* by Elsie Ripley Clapp. © The Viking Press, Inc. (Morris Library, Southern Illinois University)

Progressive education rejected the formal teaching methods of the 1800's. Pupils at this progressive school of the 1930's learned about community life by building a miniature town.

quired each state to sell the land and use the proceeds to start agricultural and technical colleges. In 1890, Congress passed the Second Morrill Act. This act withheld grants from states that denied admission to land-grant schools on the basis of race. A state could receive grants, however, if it provided separate schools for African Americans. As a result, many Southern States established black land-grant colleges and universities.

New theories of education. The late 1800's and early 1900's brought far-reaching changes in U.S. education. Margaretha Schurz opened the nation's first private kindergarten in 1856 in Watertown, Wisconsin. William T. Harris helped establish the nation's first public kindergarten in St. Louis, Missouri, in 1873. The kindergartens used play and creative activities as teaching methods. Francis W. Parker, an Illinois educator, adopted these methods for use in elementary schools. Parker believed that a wider variety of teaching methods could better encourage the complete development of each child. In addition, Parker and other educators broadened elementary school courses by adding such subjects as geography, history, and science.

The new child-centered theories of education influenced many educators who felt that the schools had not kept up with changes in society. These educators proposed that teachers adopt such methods as field trips, group discussions, and creative activities to help prepare children for life in a democracy. John Dewey and William H. Kilpatrick were two of the principal supporters of such ideas, which became known as *progressive education.* See **Progressive education.**

Joliet Junior College, the nation's oldest junior college, opened in Joliet, Illinois, in 1901. About 1910, several U.S. cities began building junior high schools.

Increased government support. Vocational education developed rapidly after Congress passed the Smith-Hughes Act in 1917. The act granted the states federal funds for vocational education in the fields of agriculture, home economics (now called *family and consumer sciences*), and industrial arts.

The federal government greatly increased its financial aid to education during the mid-1900's. After World War II (1939-1945), Congress began granting federal funds to armed forces veterans to attend colleges and other schools.

School desegregation. In 1954, the Supreme Court of the United States ruled in *Brown v. Board of Education of Topeka* that racially segregated public schools were unconstitutional. The court based its decision on the constitutional guarantee of equal protection under the law. Seventeen states and some school districts in other states had school segregation laws in 1954. By the early 1960's, a few states affected by the Supreme Court ruling had integrated their school districts. By 1970, every U.S. state had at least some integrated schools, though integration remained far from complete.

In the late 1900's, the U.S. educational system experienced a number of changes. Larger school enrollments after World War II created a need for more school buildings, and inflation increased the cost of constructing and operating schools. Teachers' organizations became more aggressive as they bargained for improved benefits for their members. Partly as a result of these efforts, the average annual salary of U.S. schoolteachers increased by more than 70 percent during the 1960's.

The federal government's role in education continued to grow. The Elementary and Secondary Education Act (ESEA), passed by Congress in 1965, provided local school districts with funds to help educate children from low-income families. In 1981, the Educational Consolidation and Improvement Act updated and expanded ESEA services. Large sums of money for higher education were also provided by the National Defense Education Act of 1958, the Higher Education Facilities Act of

1963, the Higher Education Act of 1965, and the Education Amendments Act of 1972.

In the late 1980's and early 1990's, reformers began experimenting with a number of new educational models. In 1991, American business leaders established New American Schools, a nonprofit organization that helps public schools carry out reforms. Numerous school-reform efforts, several of which were supported by New American Schools, produced dramatic improvements in student performance. Some of the better-known of these reform programs were Accelerated Schools, Success for All, Roots and Wings, the Audrey Cohen College System of Education, and the Modern Red Schoolhouse.

Recent developments. By the beginning of the 2000's, public elementary and secondary schools in the United States enrolled more pupils than at any time in the nation's history. School districts struggled to build enough schools to handle the high enrollment while keeping class sizes small. Some districts shifted to year-round school calendars where schools are open every month of the year. In year-round systems, students are enrolled in different tracks, and one track is on vacation at any given time. If the school uses three tracks, it can increase its student capacity by 50 percent.

In 2001, Congress passed a law that increased the role of the federal government in public education. The law, called the No Child Left Behind Act, introduced new requirements for student testing and measures for holding schools accountable for student progress.

Current issues in education

Educators, policymakers, and parents throughout the world debate many issues relating to education. Major issues include what should be taught, how can student performance be improved, who should choose a child's school, who should teach, who should be educated, and how should schools be organized and financed.

What should be taught? Through the years, the chief purposes of education have included acquisition of knowledge, intellectual discipline, preparation for citizenship, individual development, vocational training, and character education. Most educators believe education should serve all these purposes. But some experts feel education should serve some purposes more than others. These people often favor either *curriculum-based education* or *needs-based education.*

Curriculum-based education emphasizes the acquisition of knowledge and skills. It focuses on the study of such subjects as language, science, and mathematics. Its supporters believe it provides all students with the knowledge they need to function in society. Many countries have national curriculums that provide standard guidelines for learning in all public schools. Such curriculums seek to unite the country's people through a common body of knowledge. They seek to promote *cultural literacy*—that is, knowledge of the basic information an individual needs to succeed in modern society. Standard curriculums also help students who transfer from one school to another.

In the United States, curriculum-based education gained widespread support during the late 1950's, after the Soviet Union launched Sputnik 1, the world's first artificial satellite. Many U.S. citizens became fearful that the Soviets had surpassed the United States in science and technology. In response to these concerns, many schools adopted a more rigorous curriculum that emphasized mathematics and the physical sciences. In 1983, a federal group known as the National Commission on Excellence in Education recommended a core curriculum for high school students. The curriculum included courses in English, mathematics, science, social studies, and computer science.

Needs-based education stresses the total development of the individual. Students are encouraged to express their feelings and ideas and to study subjects that interest them. Needs-based education is intended to help children develop emotionally, physically, and socially as well as intellectually. It became popular during the 1960's, when educators began to focus on the special educational needs of minority students, students with disabilities, and others.

Supporters of needs-based education have started hundreds of schools outside the established school systems. In the United States and other countries, a number of individuals and groups introduced nontraditional schools, sometimes called *alternative schools* or *free schools.*

How can student performance be improved? Over the years, educators have tried to create a system that both supports individual development and teaches the knowledge and skills required by society. However, studies have shown that many students lack a basic understanding of language, science, mathematics, geography, history, and other subjects.

Educators have explored numerous methods for measuring and improving student performance. Such methods include standardized testing programs, literacy programs, and accountability testing. Many parents and educators have called for additional measures, such as longer school hours, more homework, increased teacher salaries, and stricter discipline in the classroom.

Standardized testing programs. Many countries have national standardized testing programs that seek to measure the performance of students. Standardized testing can identify what information students know, what information students have difficulty learning, and which students experience the greatest difficulty. The findings of such programs can help educators recognize and address shortcomings in the school system. In the United States, for example, a federally funded program called the National Assessment of Educational Progress (NAEP) has collected information about the skill and knowledge levels of U.S. students since 1969.

Despite the widespread use of standardized tests, many educators criticize the programs. Some critics argue that the tests are unfair to students from lower social and economic groups or different cultural backgrounds. Such students may be unfamiliar with words, terms, and concepts used in the tests. To give these students an equal chance, many educators have tried to prepare *culture-fair* or *culture-free* tests. Such tests might consist of pictures, symbols, and nonsense syllables that are equally unfamiliar to everyone. Some critics also argue that testing programs do not measure true understanding of information and fail to encourage educational progress. Nevertheless, most educators believe that testing is a useful and necessary tool in education.

Literacy programs. Experts throughout the world have identified illiteracy as one of the greatest problems facing education. Many developed countries—including the United States, the United Kingdom, and Canada—have large numbers of adults who are *functionally illiterate*—that is, unable to read and write well enough to meet the demands of society. Many countries have implemented literacy programs that rely on volunteer teachers. In the 1960's, for instance, the Chinese government recruited about 30 million volunteer teachers with the slogan "You Who Can Read, Teach an Illiterate."

During the 1980's, many schools began to experiment with different teaching methods and increased free time for reading in an effort to stimulate young students' interest in reading. Some schools established adult reading centers to teach illiterate parents how to read and how to help their children develop good reading skills.

Accountability testing. Many schools have experimented with more aggressive efforts to improve education. One of the most popular means of upgrading education is the use of *accountability systems.* Under an accountability system, teachers and schools are held responsible for students' progress. In the United States and other countries, governments have launched comprehensive testing programs to track the performance of students throughout their school careers. The programs help identify schools that consistently produce poor test scores. Once identified, failing schools receive intense scrutiny and help. If a school continues to perform poorly, it may be reorganized or closed.

In the United States, the federal No Child Left Behind Act of 2001 established annual state tests for children in grades 3 through 8. The legislation also included measures for identifying low-performing schools and for assisting students in those schools. Under the law, if a school consistently performs poorly, its students may receive funds for tutoring or for transportation to other public schools.

People who favor accountability systems believe such systems promote the effective teaching of basic skills. Many educators claim, however, that these systems fail to promote analytical or creative thinking.

Who should choose a child's school? In many countries, including the United States, children have traditionally attended schools assigned to them through a government system. However, growing numbers of people believe that all parents should be able to choose their child's school. Many parents prefer to send their children to private schools or to public schools that offer special programs. Other parents choose to educate their children at home.

Some school systems have established *magnet schools* as a way of enabling families to send their children to specific schools beyond their normal school boundaries. These schools are called *magnets* because they are designed to attract students from many different social and cultural groups. A magnet school is a public school that offers special training in a particular field, such as engineering or the visual and performing arts. Students generally must apply for admission.

In magnet schools, parents work closely with educators and may help establish the schools' curriculum, admission requirements, performance standards, and other policies. As a result, a magnet school's curriculum tends to reflect the educational priorities of the community it serves. For example, in many parts of the United States, magnet schools specializing in bilingual education serve Hispanic American students.

Other forms of school choice include *open enrollment* and *voucher systems.* Open enrollment allows parents to send their children to a public school in or outside their local district, provided that their choice does not interfere with desegregation plans. In the United States, some states allow open enrollment statewide. Other states offer open enrollment within districts.

Under voucher systems, a government provides families with *vouchers* (coupons) worth a fixed amount of money to be spent on education for each child. Families may then use the vouchers at a public school of their choice. In some instances, families may also use the vouchers at private schools.

Voucher systems have been the subject of much debate. Supporters of vouchers claim that having options enables parents to send their children to better schools. They also argue that voucher systems increase competition among schools, which leads to improved instruction. Opponents of voucher systems argue that the plans unfairly benefit wealthy families who have the resources to learn about school options and to send their children greater distances. They also argue that voucher programs may weaken public education and increase segregation. In addition, many people feel that public funds should not be used to fund education offered by religious groups, which operate many private schools.

Because of the disagreements surrounding voucher systems, their use in the United States has been limited. Some cities, including Milwaukee and Cleveland, and some states, including Florida and Indiana, have issued publicly funded vouchers for low-income children to attend private schools. A number of private foundations have also provided vouchers for poor children in large U.S. cities. In 2004, the United States Congress passed a law to create a federally funded voucher system for students in Washington, D.C. The law allows the vouchers to be used at private schools. Several states, including Arizona and Georgia, use voucher systems that permit children with disabilities to attend private schools at state expense.

Who should teach? Some people have argued that poor student performance is largely the result of ineffective teaching. These claims were supported by studies that found that some teachers lack basic knowledge of the subjects they teach. The studies led to an intense review of the teacher-training programs at many universities and colleges. In many cases, these programs did not require people who majored in education to master the subject that they wished to teach. To improve their teacher-training programs, some universities and colleges raised the standards for admission to the programs. Many also began requiring students to select a major other than education.

Many teachers and educators have argued that poor student performance is not necessarily the result of poor teaching. Many teachers feel that they have little control over how their schools are operated or over what textbooks and teaching methods are used. In addition, many teachers feel that they are overloaded with other responsibilities at their schools besides teaching.

Various plans have been suggested for improving teacher performance. These plans include *in-service training, master-teacher programs, merit-pay programs,* and *national certification.* In-service training helps working teachers improve their performance. In master-teacher programs, successful, experienced teachers work closely with beginning teachers to provide support and advice. Merit-pay programs reward teachers with additional pay if their students regularly achieve at high levels. National certification is a movement to improve teaching by creating high standards of training and performance for teachers throughout a country. Many governments have standards that people must meet before they can work as teachers. These standards may involve passing a test or achieving a certain level of education.

School systems in many countries have difficulty finding a sufficient number of qualified teachers. In some cases, teacher shortages have forced school systems to relax their standards so that people from other fields could become teachers. In addition, many school systems have had to raise salaries to make teaching a more attractive career choice.

Education for whom? During the mid-1900's, several groups began to win educational opportunities that had previously been denied to them. Such groups included minority groups, people with disabilities, and women.

Desegregation and busing. Racial segregation in public schools became illegal in the United States following the Supreme Court's 1954 decision in *Brown v. Board of Education of Topeka.* The court renewed its support for integration in 1971, when it ruled in *Swann v. Charlotte-Mecklenburg Board of Education* that students could be bused to different schools to achieve desegregation. Many school districts then adopted extensive busing programs to promote integration. Despite these efforts, however, studies continued to show that most minority students still attended schools with predominantly minority enrollment. This failure to achieve racial balance led to growing opposition to busing among both white and minority families.

In the 1990's, several Supreme Court decisions limited schools' obligation to use busing plans and other measures to encourage desegregation. School districts then phased out most such plans. Today, many African American students still attend segregated schools.

Other countries have experienced segregation in their educational systems. In South Africa, for instance, most students attended racially separate public schools until 1991. Since then, many black children have begun to attend previously all-white public schools.

Bilingual education. Students may face a disadvantage in school if their native language is different from the majority language. To address this concern, many school systems offer *bilingual education*—that is, instruction in two languages. Countries with large immigrant populations rely on bilingual programs to help provide full educational opportunities for all students. However, some people oppose bilingual education because they feel it threatens national identity.

In the United States, bilingual education is especially important in areas with large Asian and Hispanic populations. The U.S. government first provided funds for bilingual education in public schools in 1968. In 1974, the U.S. Supreme Court ruled in *Lau v. Nichols* that schools must provide special programs for students who do not speak English.

Canadian school systems have used bilingual education to help students become fluent in both French and English. Although English is Canada's majority language, both English and French are officially recognized. As a result, many parents want their children to learn both languages. See **Bilingual education.**

Multicultural education is emphasized in countries where the population consists of groups from different ethnic or cultural backgrounds. It encourages students to appreciate cultural diversity and to develop positive images of themselves and of people from other cultures. It seeks to reduce social conflict and ethnic or racial tension.

In the early 1900's, the United States and its schools functioned as a "melting pot." That is, schools brought together people from many cultural backgrounds and taught them to think of themselves primarily as Americans. During the 1960's, however, the civil rights movement drew attention to particular groups in the nation's schools and communities. In the following years, educators developed a broader curriculum designed to help individuals from all backgrounds value their ethnic heritage. The program later expanded to examine the distinct histories, contributions, and aspirations of various cultural groups.

Education for children with disabilities. For many years, children with disabilities lacked many of the basic educational opportunities that were afforded to other students. But since the late 1900's, civil rights laws in various countries have improved the access to public education for people with disabilities. In the United States, for example, the Americans with Disabilities Act of 1990 orders that people with disabilities must have equal opportunities to benefit from all government-run programs, services, and activities, including public schools. In the United Kingdom, the Education Act of 1996 requires school systems to provide appropriate arrangements for children with special needs. Despite these advances, however, community attitudes and poor facilities can still lead to inadequate education for people with disabilities.

People often disagree over where the education of students with disabilities should take place. Many parents, people with disabilities, and advocates believe that students with disabilities should be included in regular classes, with any necessary services and aides provided there. Others believe that appropriate education for students with disabilities can best be provided in separate special education classes.

Nonsexist education. Since the 1800's, women's movements have challenged long-standing ideas about the proper roles and educational needs of women. As a result, girls and women have won a wide range of new educational opportunities.

In the United States, Title IX of the Education Amendments Act of 1972 prohibited discrimination on the basis of sex by universities and other schools receiving federal funds. In 1975, the government issued detailed regulations outlawing such discrimination in admissions, athletics, course offerings, hiring, and other school activities. As a result, home economics, shop, and other

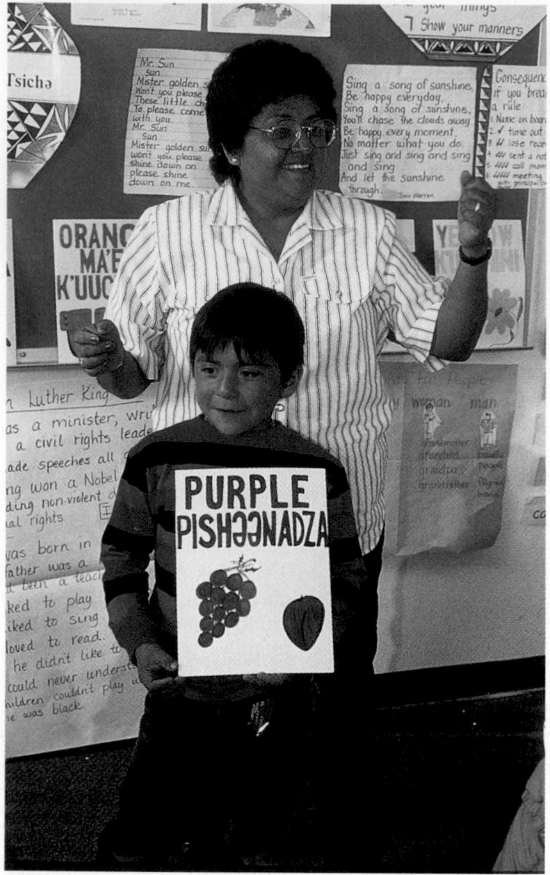

© Robert Daemmrich, Stone

Bilingual education teaches in two languages, a new language and one that a student already speaks. This Native American teacher and student are working on the names of colors.

classes became coeducational. Schools also began to admit girls to boys' sports teams or to provide separate girls' teams.

Since the late 1900's, the number of women enrolled in colleges and universities has increased dramatically. The number of women serving on school faculties has also increased. In addition, many high schools and colleges now offer *women's studies* courses. Such courses examine issues affecting women, women's history, and the contributions of women in various fields.

How should schools be run? Many proposals for improving education involve sweeping changes in how schools are organized and operated. Such changes are often called *school restructuring* or *school reform.* Restructuring generally seeks a more flexible approach to schooling that encourages new ideas and creativity. It usually transfers decision-making authority from central-office administrators to principals and teachers.

Restructuring is difficult to put into practice. Many school systems, however, have adopted a procedure called *school-site management* or *school-based management.* In this procedure, a team that typically consists of community leaders, parents, and teachers may help set school policies, select textbooks, manage the school budget, and participate in hiring teachers. Thus, decision making occurs at the local school level, close to the students who are served by the school.

Some people believe that public school systems should be *privatized*—that is, managed by private organizations rather than by the government. In the United States, a private organization called EdisonLearning, Inc. manages some public schools under contracts with local districts and charter school authorities. The popularity of EdisonLearning has stirred debate about what role—if any—nonpublic organizations should play in running schools funded with tax dollars. Supporters claim that private organizations can provide superior instruction for approximately the same amount of money. Opponents, however, argue that public education should not be entrusted to private organizations seeking to make a profit.

How should education be financed? Many people disagree over how education should be financed. In most countries, the national government shares the cost of education with other levels of government, such as states, provinces, or cities.

Schools in the United States have traditionally received money through property taxes. However, many critics argue that the property tax is an unfair method of financing public education. Poor school districts raise far less money from property taxes than rich districts do because the total property value in poor districts is much lower. As a result, critics argue, rich districts can provide better schools and educational programs than poor districts.

In 1973, the Supreme Court of the United States ruled that using property taxes to finance public schools did not violate the Constitution. However, the court acknowledged the need for reform in school financing. Since the 1970's, many U.S. states have sought to reduce the dependence on property taxes. In 1994, Michigan sharply reduced the use of property taxes in financing its public schools. Other states—including California and Oregon—have limited the use of property taxes and increased their reliance on other sources of funding. But other sources—such as income taxes and sales taxes—may be less stable than property taxes because they can be greatly affected by changes in economic conditions.

At the beginning of the 2000's, many concerns about financing education involved the amount of money spent per student. One concern focused on whether the amount spent is enough to meet the educational needs of each child. Many people want governments to spend more money on education. The problem with determining adequate spending levels has been in deciding what constitutes an adequate education and then estimating what such an education should cost.

Many people also wonder how much student performance will improve if more money is spent on education. Research on this issue has failed to provide clear answers. Those who argue that more money will lead to better student performance do not know how much money it takes to make significant improvements. Others question whether there is a direct relationship between learning and the amount of money spent. These issues are made even more difficult by the growing recognition that children from diverse backgrounds may need different educational programs to succeed.

Lawrence O. Picus

Related articles in *World Book.* See the *Education* section of articles on various countries, and the *People* section of the articles on states and provinces. See also:

American educators

Aycock, Charles Brantley
Bancroft, George
Barnard, Frederick Augustus Porter
Barzun, Jacques
Beecher, Catharine Esther
Berry, Martha M.
Bethune, Mary McLeod
Cary, Mary Ann Shad
Clark, Kenneth Bancroft
Crandall, Prudence
Dewey, John
Eliot, Charles William
Flexner, Abraham
Franklin, John Hope
Frazier, E. Franklin
Gallaudet (family)
Hall, G. Stanley
Hearst, Phoebe Apperson
Hesburgh, Theodore Martin
Hobby, Oveta Culp
Hope, John
Johnson, Charles Spurgeon
Locke, Alain LeRoy
Lyon, Mary
Mann, Horace
Mays, Benjamin
McAfee, Mildred Helen
McAuliffe, Christa
McGuffey, William Holmes
Moton, Robert Russa
Nabrit, James Madison, Jr.
Quarles, Benjamin Arthur
Sánchez, George Isidore
Sanford, Maria L.
Skinner, B. F.
Thomas, Martha Carey
Thorndike, Edward Lee
Washington, Booker T.
Webster, Noah
Wiggin, Kate Douglas
Willard, Emma Hart
Willard, Frances Elizabeth Caroline
Wilson, Woodrow
Witherspoon, John
Woodson, Carter Goodwin
Woolley, Mary Emma

British educators

Blackstone, Sir William
Kelvin, Lord
Newton, Sir Isaac
Owen, Robert
Raikes, Robert
Russell, Bertrand
Smith, Adam
Tyndall, John
Whitehead, Alfred North

Other educators

Akiva ben Joseph
Braille, Louis
Fröbel, Friedrich W. A.
Grant, George Monro
Herbart, Johann F.
Loyola, Saint Ignatius
Maritain, Jacques
Melanchthon, Philipp
Mistral, Gabriela
Montessori, Maria
Pestalozzi, Johann H.
Piaget, Jean
Plato
Socrates

Educational institutions

See the list of *Related articles* for the **School** article. ***World Book*** also has articles on various universities and colleges in the United States, Canada, and other countries.

Educational programs

Adult education
Agricultural education
Alternative school
Bilingual education
Career education
Character education
Chautauqua
Competency-based education
Cooperative education
Cuisenaire method
Curriculum
Day care
Degree, College
Differentiated instruction
Distance learning
Early childhood education
EdisonLearning, Inc.
Fellowship
Gifted children
Head Start
Home schooling
Job Corps
Language arts
Liberal arts
Montessori method
Moral education
Multiculturalism
National Assessment of Educational Progress
New mathematics
No Child Left Behind Act
Outward Bound
Parent education
Religious education
Scholarship
Sex education
Social studies
Special education
Suzuki method
Vocational education

History

Aztec (Family life)
Baby boom generation (Effects of the baby boom)
Colonial life in America (Education)
Egypt, Ancient (Education)
Enlightenment
Greece, Ancient (Education)
Humanism
Inca (Communication and learning)
Indian, American (Family life)
Maya (Communication and learning)
Middle Ages (Learning and the arts)
Pioneer life in America (Education)
Renaissance
Rome, Ancient (Education)
Scholasticism

Organizations and agencies

American Council on Education
American Federation of Teachers
Canadian Education Association
Childhood Education International, Association for
Education, Department of
National Catholic Educational Association
National Congress of Parents and Teachers
National Education Association
National Honor Society
Parent-teacher organizations
UNESCO
UNICEF
United Nations University

Other related articles

Academic freedom
African Americans (Beyond the civil rights movement)
Audio-visual materials
Brown v. Board of Education of Topeka
Careers
Coeducation
Counseling
Creationism (The 1900's)
Developmental psychology
Educational psychology
Elementary and Secondary Education Act
Grading
Guidance
Information science
Learning
Learning disabilities
Library
Literacy
National Defense Education Act
Reading
School prayer
Sex discrimination
Student government
Study
Teaching
Television (Public television; Closed-circuit television; Effects on learning)
Testing
Voucher

Outline

I. Kinds of education
A. General education
B. Vocational education
C. Special education
D. Adult education
II. The study of learning and teaching
A. How people learn
B. How teachers guide learning
III. Education in the United States
A. The organization of U.S. education
B. Control and support of U.S. education
C. The federal government and education
IV. Education in the United Kingdom
V. Education in Canada
VI. Education in other countries
A. Organization
B. Control
C. Financial support
VII. History
VIII. Current issues in education
A. What should be taught?
B. How can student performance be improved?
C. Who should choose a child's school?
D. Who should teach?
E. Education for whom?
F. How should schools be run?
G. How should education be financed?

Questions

What are the three areas into which educational objectives are divided?
How did people in prehistoric times provide education for their children?
What are some of the differences between public schools and private schools?
What is the aim of general education? What is the aim of vocational education?
What were some of the main educational advancements of the ancient Greeks?
What unit of government in the United States has general authority over public education?
What are humanistic theories of learning?
What are the main arguments for and against the use of voucher systems in education?
Where did the first modern universities develop? When did they develop?
What are segregated schools? Why did the United States Supreme Court declare these schools unconstitutional?

Additional resources

Al-Bataineh, Adel T., and Nur-Awaleh, M. A., eds. *International Education Systems and Contemporary Education Reforms.* Univ. Pr. of Am., 2005.
Bartlett, Steve, and Burton, Diana, eds. *Education Studies: Essential Issues.* Sage, 2003.
Collins, John W., III, and O'Brien, N. P., eds. *The Greenwood Dictionary of Education.* Greenwood, 2003.
Dudley, William, ed. *Education and College.* Greenhaven, 2003.
Guthrie, James W., ed. *Encyclopedia of Education.* 8 vols. 2nd ed. Macmillan Reference, 2003.
Lawton, Denis, and Gordon, Peter. *A History of Western Educational Ideas.* Woburn Pr., 2002.
Marlow-Ferguson, Rebecca, ed. *World Education Encyclopedia.* 3 vols. 2nd ed. Gale Group, 2002.
Medina, Loreta, ed. *Bilingual Education.* Greenhaven, 2003.
Pulliam, John D., and Van Patten, J. J. *History of Education in America.* 8th ed. Merrill, 2003.
Reynolds, Cecil R., and Fletcher-Janzen, Elaine, eds. *Concise Encyclopedia of Special Education.* 2nd ed. Wiley, 2002.

Education, Adult. See Adult education.
Education, Agricultural. See Agricultural education.
Education, American Council on. See American Council on Education.
Education, Board of. See School (Public schools; The growth of the public school system); **Teaching** (Preparing to teach classes; Employment practices).

Education, Department of, is an executive department of the United States government that seeks to promote educational excellence throughout the nation. It also works to ensure that all U.S. citizens have equal access to education. The secretary of education, a member of the president's Cabinet, heads the department. The president appoints the secretary of education with the approval of the U.S. Senate. The department's official Web site at http://www.ed.gov presents information on its activities.

The seal of the United States Department of Education

Functions. In the United States, the primary responsibility for public education lies with state governments and local school districts. As a result, the Department of Education does not establish schools or govern educational institutions. Instead, its responsibilities fall into six main categories: (1) providing leadership in addressing critical issues in education; (2) collecting data, overseeing research, and distributing research findings involving the nation's schools; (3) helping students pay for their education beyond high school; (4) helping communities and schools meet the needs of students; (5) preparing students for employment; and (6) working to ensure equal educational opportunities for all Americans.

The department is concerned with schools at all levels, including preschools, elementary schools, high schools, and colleges and universities. It also focuses on technical training, adult education, and education and training for people with disabilities. In addition, the department administers programs to improve the skills of students whose native language is not English.

Secretaries of education

Name	Took office	Under President
*Shirley M. Hufstedler	1979	Carter
Terrel H. Bell	1981	Reagan
William J. Bennett	1985	Reagan
*Lauro F. Cavazos	1988	Reagan, G. H. W. Bush
Lamar Alexander	1991	G. H. W. Bush
Richard W. Riley	1993	Clinton
Roderick R. Paige	2001	G. W. Bush
Margaret Spellings	2005	G. W. Bush
Arne Duncan	2009	Obama

*Has a separate biography in *World Book.*

© B. Christopher, Alamy Images

Headquarters of the United States Department of Education, *shown here,* are in Washington, D.C. The Department of Education promotes educational opportunities for all U.S. citizens.

History. Congress set up a federal agency called the Department of Education in 1867. It was not a Cabinet-level agency. Congress later renamed the agency the Bureau of Education and made it part of the Department of the Interior. Still later, Congress changed the name of the bureau to the Office of Education and moved it to the Federal Security Agency. In 1953, the Office of Education became part of the newly created Department of Health, Education, and Welfare (HEW). In 1972, Congress established the Education Division within HEW. The Education Division included the Office of Education, the National Institute of Education, the Fund for the Improvement of Post-Secondary Education, and the National Center for Education Statistics.

Congress created the Department of Education as a Cabinet-level agency in 1979. The department began operating in 1980. It absorbed the Education Division of HEW, and HEW became the Department of Health and Human Services.

Critically reviewed by the Department of Education

Related articles in *World Book* include:

Education
Elementary and Secondary Education Act
FFA
Flag (picture: Flags of the United States government)
National Assessment of Educational Progress
National Defense Education Act
No Child Left Behind Act

Education, Early childhood. See Early childhood education.

Education, Vocational. See Vocational education.

Education Association, National. See National Education Association.

Education Week, American, acquaints the public with the work of education, and with its problems, achievements, and needs. The chief sponsors of American Education Week include the American Legion, the National Education Association, the National Congress of Parents and Teachers (more commonly known as the National Parent Teacher Association or National PTA), and the United States Department of Education. Education Week, first observed in 1921, is now held each year in the fall.

A typical American Education Week program opens with proclamations from state governors and mayors. These proclamations stress the importance of education. The rest of the week includes such activities as open house programs, special television programs, and exhibits in businesses, schools, and libraries.

Each year, the sponsoring organizations select a theme for American Education Week. Themes have included *Better Education—Your Job; America Has a Good Thing Going—Its Schools;* and *Invest in Learning.*

Critically reviewed by the National Education Association

Educational guidance. See Guidance.

Educational psychology is a branch of psychology that involves the scientific study of teaching and learning. Educational psychologists have traditionally worked to help teachers improve learning in schools. But where and how people learn has changed, due to the spread of powerful multimedia computers and the Internet into schools, homes, and the workplace. Today, educational psychologists increasingly study how people learn outside school from television, electronic games, and the Internet. As knowledge and technology change more quickly, educational psychologists also study how people continue to learn throughout life.

What educational psychologists study. Educational psychologists study how people develop physically and mentally from infancy to old age. Teachers use this information to design learning environments that match the developmental needs and abilities of learners. Educational psychologists also examine how students learn and what motivates them to learn. They develop tests and other methods to measure what students learn, such as cumulative portfolios of a student's work. These assessment tools play an important role in efforts to improve schools and graduation rates.

Educational psychologists also study how learning is affected by individual differences in ability, learning style, cultural background, gender, and home environment. Such studies can help teachers more effectively teach a diversity of students.

Careers in educational psychology. Many educational psychologists work as professors at colleges and universities. There, they instruct future teachers to apply principles of learning in the classroom. Schools employ educational psychologists to work with teachers to improve learning. As lifelong learning grows in importance, more educational psychologists are working outside of schools. Many companies hire educational psychologists to help employees keep up with rapid changes in information. Educational psychologists also work in the fields of online learning and educational technology.

Most educational psychologists employed by universities, laboratories, and corporations have a Ph.D degree. Those who work in public schools must have an M.A. or M.Ed. degree, and some of them have a Ph.D. or Ed.D degree. W. Patrick Dickson

Related articles in *World Book* include:

Developmental psychology
Education (The study of learning and teaching)
Learning
Psychology
Teaching
Testing

Edward (1330-1376), known as the Black Prince, is one of the most famous English warriors in history. He was the oldest son of King Edward III and the father of King Richard II.

According to later tradition, Edward wore black armor at the Battle of Crécy in France in 1346. Although he was only 16 years old, Edward commanded a wing of his father's army in this first great battle of the Hundred Years' War (1337-1453). In 1356 at Poitiers, France, Edward defeated a French army and captured the French king.

Edward was born on June 15, 1330. He died on June 8, 1376.

John Gillingham

Detail of bronze statue from the tomb of Edward by an unknown artist; by the kind permission of the Dean and Chapter of Canterbury, Canterbury Cathedral, Canterbury

Edward, the Black Prince

Edward I (1239-1307) became king of England in 1272. As king, he conquered Wales and tried to gain control of Scotland. Edward belonged to the Plantagenet family of English rulers.

Detail from a manuscript by an unknown artist, The British Library, London
Edward I

Edward I was born on June 17, 1239, in Westminster (now part of London). He succeeded his father, Henry III, as king. Edward fought wars against the Welsh in 1277 and in 1282 and 1283. He conquered Wales in the second war. In 1301, Edward gave the title Prince of Wales to his son, who later became Edward II. Since then, it has become customary for English monarchs to give the title to their oldest son.

In 1292, Edward chose John Balliol as ruler of Scotland from among several men who claimed the Scottish throne. Edward treated Balliol as a vassal and demanded that Scotland supply troops to fight the French. When Scotland instead allied with France, Edward invaded Scotland and forced Balliol to give up the throne. Edward then seized the Stone of Scone, the stone upon which Scottish kings were given royal power for hundreds of years. He placed the stone in London's Westminster Abbey, where English kings were crowned.

But the Scots continued to fight England. They were led first by William Wallace and then by Robert Bruce. Bruce had himself crowned king of Scotland in 1306. Edward died while on his way to subdue the new king.

Edward's Scottish policy resulted in hostile relations between the English and the Scots for the next 250 years. It also led to an alliance between Scotland and France. As a result, England had to fight both countries at the same time. Edward's need for money to supply his army and government led him to call Parliaments more often than had any previous king. These Parliaments consisted of representatives of the nobility, the church, and common people. In return for grants of money from Parliament, Edward agreed that taxes could be levied only with Parliament's consent. He also sponsored laws on more topics than any previous king.

Edward I was not the first English king named Edward. People in England give numbers to their kings and queens with the same name only if the monarchs ruled after the Norman Conquest of 1066. There were three Anglo-Saxon kings named Edward who ruled England before 1066: Edward the Elder (870?-924), Edward the Martyr (963?-978?), and Edward the Confessor (1002?-1066). See **Edward the Confessor.** John Gillingham

See also **Bruce, Robert; Model Parliament; Wallace, Sir William.**

Edward II (1284-1327) was one of the most unsuccessful kings in English history. He was a poor general and was disliked by nearly all his barons and even by his wife, Queen Isabella.

Edward, a member of the Plantagenet royal family, was born on April 25, 1284, in Caernarfon, Wales. He was the first heir to the English throne to get the title Prince of Wales. He succeeded his father, Edward I, in 1307. Many political trials and executions troubled the young king's reign. In 1314, he lost a key battle to the Scottish leader Robert Bruce at Bannockburn, Scotland.

In 1325, Queen Isabella visited France. From there, she and her lover, Roger Mortimer, organized an invasion of England. They and their supporters forced Edward to give up the throne to his son Edward III in 1327. Edward II was murdered that year. John Gillingham

See also **Bannockburn, Battle of; Prince of Wales.**

Edward III (1312-1377) became king of England in 1327. He succeeded his father, Edward II, and belonged to the Plantagenet family of English rulers. During the 1330's, Edward invaded Scotland. He won victories there, but he could not crush the Scottish spirit of independence.

Edward's forces won the Battle of Crécy in what is now the Normandy region of France. This conflict was the first major battle between France and England in the Hundred Years' War (1337-1453). Edward claimed to be the rightful king of France and conquered much of that country. He paid for the war by introducing an efficient system of taxing imports. In the last few years of his reign, Edward failed to provide vigorous leadership. The French recovered some of their land, and Edward's popularity fell. Even so, he was long remembered as an ideal king and a fine soldier. Edward was born on Nov. 13, 1312, in Windsor, near London. John Gillingham

See also **Edward** (the Black Prince); **Hundred Years' War; Salic Law.**

Edward IV (1442-1483) became king of England in 1461. He was the son of Richard, Duke of York, and was the first king of England from the House of York. Before Edward's reign, the Houses of York and Lancaster—two branches of the royal Plantagenet family—had begun fighting each other in the Wars of the Roses (see **Wars of the Roses**).

As leader of the Yorkists, Edward was proclaimed king in 1461 by supporters in London and then won a major victory at Towton against the forces of Henry VI of the House of Lancaster. But in 1470, the powerful Earl of Warwick shifted his support to the House of Lancaster. Edward then fled to Holland (see **Warwick, Earl of**). The next year, Edward returned with an army and regained the throne. He then ruled England until his death in 1483. As king, Edward strengthened the royal power and paved the way for the absolute monarchy of the Tudors. Edward IV was born on April 28, 1442, in Rouen, France. Ralph A. Griffiths

Detail of an oil portrait by an unknown artist; National Portrait Gallery, London
Edward IV

Edward V (1470-1483?) succeeded his father, Edward IV, as king of England in April 1483 at the age of 12. But before he was crowned, his father's brother, Richard, Duke of Gloucester, imprisoned Edward and Edward's younger brother, also named Richard, in the Tower of London. In June, Gloucester took the throne as Richard III. Edward and his brother were probably murdered soon afterward on an order from Richard III. However, there is no proof of murder, and no one knows for certain what happened to the boys. The remains of two children were discovered in the Tower of London in 1674, and some people believe that they may have been those of Edward and his brother.

Edward was born Nov. 2, 1470, at Westminster (now part of London). He lived most of his short life in the borderlands between England and Wales. Ralph A. Griffiths

Edward VI (1537-1553) was king of England and Ireland from 1547 until his death on July 6, 1553. He was the son of King Henry VIII, whom he succeeded. Edward's mother was Jane Seymour, Henry's third wife. Edward belonged to the English ruling family known as the House of Tudor.

Edward was only 9 years old when he became king, so his uncle Edward Seymour, who soon became the Duke of Somerset, governed for him. In 1549, the Earl of Warwick, later called the Duke of Northumberland, took Somerset's place. Edward, Somerset, and Northumberland all wished England to remain Protestant.

When Edward was 15 years old, he became fatally ill with tuberculosis. Before dying, he named his Protestant cousin Lady Jane Grey, who was also Northumberland's daughter-in-law, as his successor. Edward's half sister Mary, a devout Roman Catholic, had been next in line for the throne. Lady Jane reigned for only nine days before losing the throne to Mary. Edward VI was born on Oct. 12, 1537, in what is now London. Richard L. Greaves

Edward VII (1841-1910) became king of the United Kingdom of Great Britain and Ireland in 1901. He was the first son of Queen Victoria and Prince Albert and belonged to the royal family of Saxe-Coburg and Gotha.

Edward was born Albert Edward on Nov. 9, 1841, in London. He became Prince of Wales when he was an infant. He studied at Edinburgh, Oxford, and Cambridge universities. In 1863, he married Princess Alexandra, whose father later became King Christian IX of Denmark.

Visual Educ. Serv.

Edward VII

During Queen Victoria's widowhood, Edward represented her at public gatherings (see **Victoria**). He was a patron of the arts and sciences and helped found the Royal College of Music. He was also one of England's leading sportsmen. His horses won the English Derby three times.

Edward was greatly interested in foreign affairs. On a visit to India in 1875 and 1876, he improved relations between the United Kingdom and the princes of India. His official visit to France in 1903 helped to renew friendship between the British and French governments. He became the first reigning British monarch to visit Russia. Edward died on May 6, 1910. His son, George Frederick, succeeded him as King George V. James J. Sack

Edward VIII (1894-1972) became king of the United Kingdom on Jan. 20, 1936, and gave up the throne on December 11 that same year. He was the oldest son of King George V and Queen Mary of the British ruling family known as the House of Windsor. Edward succeeded his father as king.

Foulsham & Bansfield, United Press Int.

Edward VIII

Edward was born June 23, 1894, in London. He was made Prince of Wales in 1911 at Caernarfon Castle, Wales. He was the first Prince of Wales to deliver his address in Welsh. Edward attended the Royal Naval College and Oxford University. He served in World War I (1914-1918) as aide-de-camp to Sir John French, who during part of the war was commander of the British Expeditionary Force in France.

Edward became a great traveler, and was often called *the empire's salesman.* After the war, he visited Canada, the United States, South America, Africa, India, Australia, and New Zealand, promoting world peace, British trade, and the unity of the British Empire. Edward's democratic spirit, charm, and diplomacy made him popular. In the United Kingdom, he took an interest in the living conditions of the underprivileged and working classes.

Edward fell in love with Wallis Warfield Simpson, an American divorcée. Because his government and many of his subjects did not want her as queen, Edward gave up his throne. He then left England in self-imposed exile. His brother, George VI, who succeeded him, gave him the title Duke of Windsor. Edward married Simpson in June 1937. After World War II began in 1939, Edward volunteered for a position in the British armed forces. In September of that year, he visited England briefly for the first time since leaving and was assigned as a liaison officer in France. Shortly before France fell to the Germans in 1940, Edward and his wife escaped to Spain. Later that year, George VI made him governor of the Bahamas, then a British colony. He served there until 1945. After the war, Edward lived mostly in France. He died on May 28, 1972. Keith Robbins

Edward, Lake. See Lake Edward.

Edward the Confessor (1002?-1066), an Anglo-Saxon king descended from Alfred the Great, was crowned in 1042. As king, Edward lacked influence among England's Anglo-Saxon nobles because he had lived in the Normandy region of northwestern France before becoming king. Edward's Anglo-Saxon father-in-law, Godwine, Earl of Wessex, tried to dominate Edward's reign. Edward resisted Godwine's efforts by relying on Norman advisers and administrators. Godwine died in 1053.

Edward was a pious man. In the mid-1000's, he built a church that became Westminster Abbey. In 1161, Pope Alexander III *canonized* him (declared him a saint) and gave him the title of Confessor. Edward's feast day is October 13.

Edward was childless, and a dispute arose over who should succeed him. His cousin William, Duke of Normandy, claimed Edward had promised him the throne. But when Edward died on Jan. 5, 1066, the English nobles chose Harold, Godwine's son, as king. Harold took the throne as Harold II. William then invaded England, defeated Harold, and was crowned king (see **William I, the Conqueror**). Joel T. Rosenthal

See also **Westminster Abbey.**

Edwards, John (1953-), was the Democratic nominee for vice president of the United States in 2004. Edwards and U.S. Senator John F. Kerry, the presidential nominee, lost to their Republican opponents, President George W. Bush and Vice President Richard B. Cheney. At the time of the election, Edwards was a member of the U.S. Senate, representing North Carolina.

Johnny Reid Edwards was born in Seneca, South Carolina, on June 10, 1953, and grew up in Robbins, North Carolina. He earned a bachelor's degree from North Carolina State University in 1974 and a law degree from the University of North Carolina in 1977. After graduation, Edwards married Elizabeth Anania, whom he had met in a law class. The couple legally separated in 2010, and Elizabeth died later that year. They had four children—Wade, Catharine, Emma Claire, and John Atticus, who is called Jack. In 1996, Wade died at the age of 16 in a Jeep accident. In 2008, Edwards became the father of another daughter, Frances Quinn—the product of an extramarital affair with videographer Rielle Hunter. Hunter worked on his campaign for the 2008 Democratic presidential nomination.

U.S. Senate
John Edwards

Edwards worked as a law clerk to a federal judge from 1977 until 1978, when he joined a law firm in Nashville. In 1981, he moved to a law firm in Raleigh, North Carolina. In 1993, he and a partner started their own firm, Edwards and Kirby. Edwards specialized in personal injury cases in which ordinary people sued huge corporations. He won large settlements for the injured person in several such cases.

Edwards was elected to the Senate in 1998. In 1999, his fellow senators chose him to question key witnesses in the Senate impeachment trial of President Bill Clinton. Edwards also delivered the closing argument for the defense. The Senate found Clinton not guilty. In 2001, Edwards co-sponsored a Patients' Bill of Rights with Democratic Senator Edward M. Kennedy and Republican Senator John McCain. The Senate approved the bill, but the U.S. House of Representatives did not pass it.

In 2003, Edwards declared his candidacy for the presidency. He did not seek reelection to the Senate. In 2004, Edwards dropped out of the presidential race, and Kerry asked him to be his running mate. Edwards's Senate term ended in January 2005. His campaign for the 2008 Democratic presidential nomination was unsuccessful.

In June 2011, federal prosecutors charged Edwards with using illegal campaign contributions to cover up his extramarital affair with Hunter. The indictment also included charges of conspiracy and making false statements. A trial began in April 2012. In May, a jury found Edwards not guilty of one of six charges but remained deadlocked on the rest. Federal prosecutors dropped the remaining charges against Edwards in June.

John Kenneth White

Edwards, Jonathan (1703-1758), was a famous minister of Puritan New England. As a philosopher, preacher, revivalist, and theologian, he became the leading intellectual figure in colonial America.

Edwards was born on Oct. 5, 1703, in East Windsor, Connecticut. Many of his forefathers had been Congregational pastors. He entered Yale University at age 13 and graduated at 17. In 1726, he became assistant pastor of a congregation in Northampton, Massachusetts. The chief pastor was his grandfather, Solomon Stoddard, a famous Congregational clergyman. After Stoddard died in 1729, Edwards became chief pastor.

During the 1730's and 1740's, Edwards's sermons contributed to a series of religious revival movements that spread through New England. These movements became known as the Great Awakening. They led to a new, more spiritual understanding of the church. At the same time, Edwards defended many traditional church doctrines. He was attacked and praised by both radicals and conservatives. His aim was to reconcile traditional Calvinist teachings with the notions of religious experience in the 1700's. See **Calvin, John; Great Awakening.**

During the Great Awakening, Edwards wrote a number of works on the psychology of religion. Edwards based these writings on his observations of how people behaved during intense religious experiences.

In the 1740's, Edwards tried to exclude from the sacrament of the Lord's Supper any parishioner who had not had a distinct conversion experience. Some members of his congregation opposed this change, and Edwards was dismissed in 1750. From 1751 to 1757, Edwards was a missionary to an Indian settlement in Stockbridge, Massachusetts. There, he wrote his major work, *Freedom of Will* (1754). In it, he defended the Christian doctrine of predestination (see **Predestination**). He argued that people's choices in life depended on their character, "inclined" either by God or by sinful human nature. Edwards died on March 22, 1758. Mark A. Noll

Edwards Air Force Base, California, is the site of the United States Air Force Flight Test Center. It also houses the Dryden Flight Research Center of the National Aeronautics and Space Administration (NASA). The base covers about 301,000 acres (121,800 hectares) in the Mojave Desert, northeast of Los Angeles. Test pilots fly experimental aircraft nearby. Edwards also served as a landing site for U.S. space shuttles from 1981 to 2011.

The base was established as a bombing and gunnery range in 1933. It became Muroc Army Air Base in 1942. In 1949, the base was renamed for Captain Glen Walter Edwards, a test pilot killed in an aircraft crash nearby.

Wayne Thompson

EEG. See **Electroencephalograph.**

Eel is the name for numerous long, slimy fish that look like snakes. There are hundreds of *species* (kinds) of eels. Most live in the ocean. Such *saltwater eels* include morays, congers, snake eels, and snipe eels. Scientists know little about these eels. The most studied eels belong to a group often referred to as *freshwater eels.* These eels can live in both salt water and fresh water. Other kinds of long, slender fish are called "eels," including electric eels. But scientists do not consider such animals true eels. This article will discuss freshwater eels.

Freshwater eels include the American eel and the European eel. American eels live along the Atlantic coast of North America. European eels are found along the Atlantic coast of Europe and in the Mediterranean Sea.

WORLD BOOK illustration by Colin Newman, Linden Artists Ltd.

The European eel is a long, thin fish that resembles a snake.

Life cycle. American eels and European eels begin life in the Sargasso Sea, an area of the Atlantic Ocean northeast of the Caribbean Islands. The female eel lays eggs there in spring before she dies. Each egg hatches into a tiny, narrow *larva,* the next stage in a true eel's development. The larva, known as a *leptocephalus,* resembles a clear willow leaf. As ocean currents carry it northward, it undergoes a *metamorphosis* (change in body form) and develops into a transparent miniature eel, or *glass eel.*

By the time this miniature eel reaches the coast of North America or Europe, it has developed some coloration and is known as an *elver.* Scientists believe that male elvers stay in salt water along the coast. Most female elvers swim into rivers and other bodies of fresh water. Elvers are strong swimmers, and the female may climb waterfalls or dams to reach inland waters.

The elver gradually increases in size and turns a dull, yellowish-green. It is then called a *yellow eel.* During this stage, which usually lasts 7 to 10 years, the eel reaches its full size. Most females grow 3 to 4 feet (91 to 122 centimeters) long and most males about 1 ½ feet (46 centimeters) in length. Eventually, the eel undergoes a second metamorphosis and becomes an adult. The skin color on its sides changes to silver, its eyes get larger, and it becomes sexually mature and able to breed. In its adult stage, the eel is called a *silver eel.*

Migration. Each fall, large numbers of silver eels group together and begin to migrate back to the Sargasso Sea for breeding. Scientists do not know how the eels find their breeding places. They believe that eels use their sense of smell to find their way back, and that the animals rely on ocean currents for direction. Studies have shown that eels can detect weak electric currents generated by movements of water. These electric currents may serve as navigational guideposts for the eels.

Eel fishing. Many people enjoy eating freshwater eels, and fishing crews harvest great numbers of eels each year. Eels are caught in large nets or in specially built cages. Some freshwater eels have become endangered because of overfishing. John E. McCosker

Scientific classification. True eels belong to the order Anguilliformes. Freshwater eels make up the genus *Anguilla.* The American eel is *Anguilla rostrata.* The European eel is *A. anguilla.*

See also **Electric eel; Fish** (pictures).

Eelgrass is the name of two types of underwater plants. One type grows in salt water and the other in fresh water.

Marine eelgrass grows in bays and other shallow coastal waters. It roots on the ocean bottom and bears slender, floating stems. Its tapelike leaves may be 6 feet (1.8 meters) long. A variety of animals live in eelgrass or feed on it.

Freshwater eelgrass is also known as *tape grass* and *wild celery.* It grows in the mud of shallow ponds, sending ribbonlike leaves from the root. James D. Mauseth

Scientific classification. Marine eelgrass makes up the genus *Zostera.* Freshwater eelgrass makes up the genus *Vallisneria.*

Eelworm is a tiny, threadlike worm that lives as a parasite in plants. Eelworms are also called *plant nemas.* They may do great damage to crops. Certain eelworms attack plant leaves, stems, or roots and produce hard swellings called *galls.* Other destructive eelworms can puncture plant tissue and suck cell sap out through their hollow, spearlike *stylets.* The eggs and *larvae* (young) of many eelworms can withstand cold and dryness for relatively long periods. Warmth and moisture make them active again. Female eelworms can become so swollen with eggs that they look like tiny lemons. They soon die and the body wall forms a tough *cyst* (sac). The eggs are released when the cyst breaks. David F. Oetinger

Scientific classification. Eelworms belong to the roundworm phylum, Nematoda.

Efficiency, in science and technology, is the ratio of the work we get *out* of a machine to the amount of energy put *into* it. Efficiency may also be defined as the ratio of power output to the total power input. The difference between the energy put in and the work delivered often appears in the form of heat due to friction. For example, most electrical energy going into an electric motor is put out as mechanical energy by turning a shaft that does useful work, such as pumping water or drilling. But part of the energy given to the motor is wasted as heat in the bearings and wires.

Scientists express efficiency in percentage. If a motor returns three-fourths of the energy put into it, the motor has an efficiency of 75 percent. Human beings have an efficiency of about 24 percent in converting the energy in the food we eat into mechanical energy, such as walking. An electrical transformer can be over 98 percent efficient. Robert B. Prigo

See also **Energy; Machine.**

Effigy Mounds National Monument, *EHF uh jee,* is in northeastern Iowa, 3 miles (5 kilometers) north of Marquette. It contains more than 200 prehistoric mounds built by early Indian peoples known today as *mound builders.* Some of the mounds are hundreds of feet long and were built in the form of animals. The monument was established in 1949. For the monument's area, see **National Park System** (table: National monuments). Critically reviewed by the National Park Service

Eft. See **Newt.**

EFTA. See **European Free Trade Association.**

Egbert (? -839) was king of Wessex in England from 802 until his death. His name is also spelled *Ecgberht.* Egbert may have tried to claim the throne after the death of the Wessex king in 786. However, the new king, along with the king of Mercia, drove him into exile. Egbert lived for several years in the kingdom of the Franks, at the court of Charlemagne. Egbert returned to England in 802 and became king of Wessex. He fought for control of the other Anglo-Saxon kingdoms. Egbert eventually gained the submission of Kent, Sussex, Surrey, Essex, Mercia, East Anglia, and Northumbria, as well as the Celts in Cornwall. Egbert's reign laid the basis for the unification of England under his heirs, beginning with his grandson Alfred the Great. See also **Anglo-Saxons; England** (The Anglo-Saxon period). Mary Frances Smith

Egg is a special structure made by female animals. An egg can develop into a new individual. Birds reproduce by laying eggs, as do many reptiles, fish, insects, and other animals.

An egg develops from a female sex cell, called an *egg cell* or *ovum.* In most living things, an egg cell will only develop into a new individual after joining with a male cell, called *sperm.* The sperm and the egg cell join in a process called *fertilization.* In some animals, such as ants and termites, the egg cell can develop into a new organism without being fertilized by a sperm.

A fertilized egg cell develops into an *embryo.* In humans and most other mammals, the embryo grows inside the female. In most other animals, the fertilized egg cell develops outside the parent's body, in a structure called an egg. The egg may have a special covering that encases and protects the developing embryo. The egg also carries a supply of food for the developing embryo.

Animal eggs vary widely in size. They range from a cell that cannot be seen without a microscope to a hard-shelled container larger than a fist. Larger animals tend to produce bigger eggs, but this is not always the case.

Animals also differ in the number of eggs they produce. Oysters, for example, lay eggs that are eaten by many forms of aquatic life. Few of these eggs survive to become adults, but an oyster produces as many as 500 million eggs in a year. Animals whose young have a good chance of survival generally lay fewer, larger eggs. They often protect the eggs carefully. For example, the great spotted kiwi of New Zealand lays just one egg each year. The egg weighs about one third as much as the mother. Both parents guard the egg until it hatches.

Some kinds of eggs

All higher animals produce eggs. This illustration shows eggs laid by birds, an insect, a fish, an amphibian, and a reptile. They are not shown in their actual size relationships.

WORLD BOOK illustration by Jean Helmer

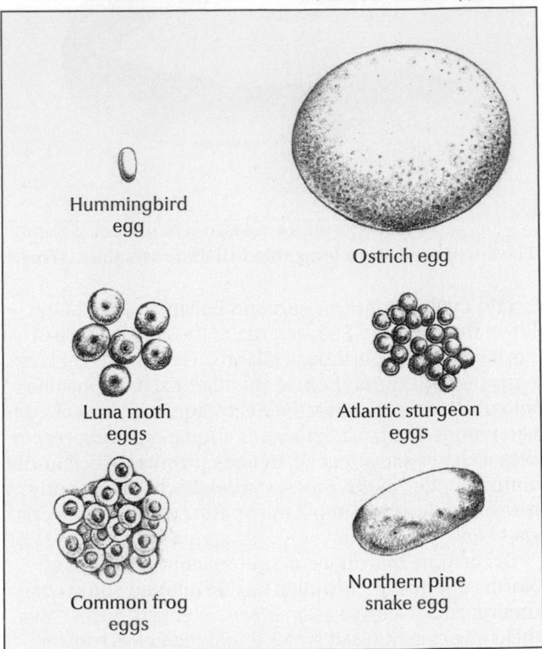

Kinds of eggs

The features of eggs have evolved over time so that the eggs of each animal are suited to its lifestyle and environment. Earthworms lay eggs enclosed in capsules filled with a nourishing, milky fluid. A female water-flea produces *summer eggs,* which she carries in a special pouch on her back. She also produces *winter eggs,* which are enclosed in protective capsules. Moths, butterflies, and other insects usually lay their eggs in clusters. They may lay them on the ground, on the leaves or stalks of plants, or in water.

Fish eggs. Fishes may lay large numbers of eggs. A sturgeon, for example, lays about 7 million eggs in a year. Some fish eggs are heavy and sink to the bottom of the stream, lake, or ocean. Other kinds of fish eggs are light and transparent and float together in a mass on the water. Sharks and skates lay eggs in leathery cases that can often be found on an ocean beach.

Amphibian eggs. Amphibians also lay their eggs in water, even though the adults often live on land. The American toad produces as many as 6,000 eggs at a time in two long strings of jelly. Frogs and salamanders also produce large, jellylike masses of eggs.

Reptile eggs. Unlike fish and amphibians, reptiles can lay eggs with shells that will not dry out on land. As a result, reptiles can live away from water. Most reptiles lay eggs with a white, leathery protective shell. They often bury the eggs in the ground for protection.

Mammal eggs. Some kinds of mammals, called *monotremes,* also lay eggs. They are the duck-billed platypus and the echidna. In all other mammals, including humans, the young develop inside the mother.

Bird eggs are the best known kind. Bird eggs have hard shells for protection.

Birds provide significant care for their eggs. One of the most important ways is through *incubation*—that is, sitting on the eggs to warm them. Incubation helps a chick develop quickly and safely inside the egg.

Most birds build a nest for their eggs. A nest may be a shallow scrape on the ground or a well-woven basket hanging from a tree branch. Other birds lay their eggs in holes in trees, on rock ledges, or on sandy beaches.

The eggs a bird lays at one time are called a *clutch.* Small songbirds generally lay 5 or 6 eggs in a clutch, whereas a mallard duck can lay up to 15. Birds in tropical regions tend to have smaller clutches than birds living in cooler climates. However, a warmer climate enables tropical birds to have more clutches per year.

Bird eggs can have a wide range of shell colors. The eggs are naturally white unless they contain some *pigment* (coloring substance). Among birds whose eggs lie well hidden within the nest, the eggs are usually not pigmented. Such birds include those that are *nocturnal* (active only at night), such as owls and nightjars, and birds such as woodpeckers that lay their eggs in holes.

Some birds lay their eggs on the ground, where the

Parts of a chicken egg

WORLD BOOK illustration by Zorica Dabich

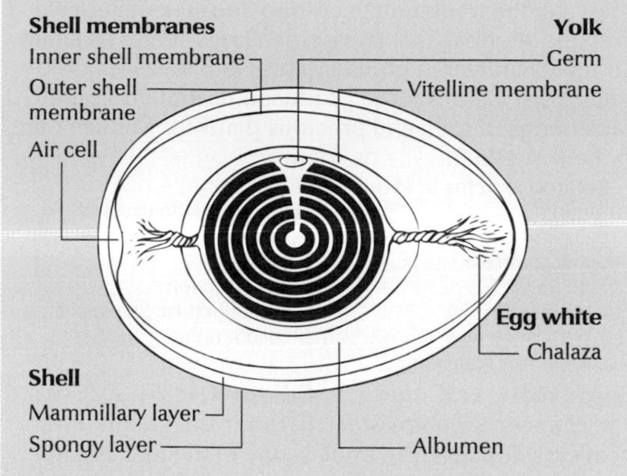

eggs might be seen by predators. These birds generally lay eggs colored to match the nest or the ground. Patterns of spots, lines, or blotches on the egg can also help it blend in with its background. The eggs of the piping plover, for example, blend into the sand well in which they are laid. A person walking on a beach could walk right over a clutch without seeing them.

Ostriches, on the other hand, lay light-colored eggs that are easily visible on the sandy soil. Many gulls also lay eggs that are much lighter than the surrounding rocks or sand. Scientists do not fully know why these eggs lack protective coloration. Some scientists think that darker eggs might get too hot in the sun, killing the chick growing inside. Light-colored eggs, by contrast, reflect more sunlight. They do not retain as much heat.

Some other birds' eggs also do not blend in with their surroundings. American robins and many other songbirds lay bright blue or blue-green eggs. Many of these birds nest in shrubs or trees, where protective coloring might not be as necessary. A group of birds called *tinamous,* native to Central and South America, lay bright glossy eggs that resemble glazed pottery. Scientists do not fully know what purpose such appearances serve.

Dinosaur eggs. Most scientists regard birds as the living descendants of dinosaurs, and dinosaur eggs resemble bird eggs in many ways. Like bird eggs, for example, dinosaur eggs have hard shells. The largest dinosaur eggs yet found are about 2 feet (60 centimeters) long. Scientists believe that large size and hard shells provided protection when animals began laying their eggs on the ground, instead of burying them. Scientists also have evidence that at least some dinosaurs cared for their eggs in nests, as do modern birds.

Parts of a bird egg

A bird's egg has five principal parts. They are (1) the germ, (2) the shell, (3) the shell membranes, (4) the albumen, and (5) the yolk.

The germ is the most important part of an egg. It is the fertilized ovum that develops into a young bird. Usually, the ovum must be fertilized before the rest of the egg develops. However, some birds, including chickens, will lay eggs that are not fertilized. The other parts of the egg provide food and protection for the growing bird.

The shell consists mostly of the mineral calcium carbonate. This substance is interwoven with a network of proteins called the *protein matrix* that gives the shell strength. The shell consists of two main layers—an inner *mammillary layer* and an outer *spongy layer.* Eggshells have tiny pores that permit gases to pass back and forth. An eggshell also allows water to pass, but not enough to cause the egg to dry out.

Shell membranes are two thin skins just inside the shell. Water and gases can pass through these skins. The membranes stabilize the egg's contents and separate them from the shell. A space called an *air cell* forms between the shell membranes after the egg is laid. The air cell is usually found on the wider end of the egg.

The albumen makes up most of the volume of a bird egg. It is semi-liquid and clear to somewhat cloudy. The albumen is often called the "egg white" because it turns white when cooked. The albumen protects the embryo and provides nutrition for the young bird.

The yolk serves as the main source of food for the embryo in later stages of development. The yolk is a yellow substance enclosed in a sac called the *vitelline membrane.* The yolk is lighter than the albumen and so usually floats above the center of the egg. Within the albumen is a white, twisted, ropelike structure called the *chalaza.* It helps keep the yolk in the middle of the egg and prevents the yolk from breaking apart against the eggshell if the egg is moved. The germ is attached to the yolk. The chalaza also protects the embryo by holding it so that it is surrounded by soft albumen.

Development of a bird egg

A bird egg takes 21 to 25 hours to develop inside the female, regardless of its size. No bird can normally lay more than one egg in a day.

The egg begins development as an ovum in the female ovary (see **Ovary**). Each ovum is nestled in a sac called a *follicle.* Several *ova* (the plural of ovum) are present in the ovary. As laying time approaches, an ovum grows in size attached to a yolk. When the yolk reaches full size, the ovum breaks out of the follicle and is fertilized if sperm are present. The egg then travels down a tube called the *oviduct.* During this time, the albumen surrounds the yolk and shell membranes are added. After the egg enters the uterus, the shell is produced around the egg and then pigmented. Shell production takes about 12 hours, after which the egg is laid through an opening called the *vagina.* By this time, a fertilized ovum has already begun to develop into an embryo.

Once laid, the egg is incubated. Small songbirds often incubate their eggs for 12 to 14 days. The incubation period for chickens is 21 to 22 days. Large birds, such as eagles and swans, can require up to 36 days to incubate their eggs. A fully developed chick hatches from the egg having consumed all of the albumen and yolk. The chick pecks at the shell until the egg breaks open. A chick often has a specialized *egg tooth* on its bill. This sharp tooth helps break the eggshell from the inside. The egg tooth disappears soon after the chick has hatched.

Eggs as food

People eat the eggs of many birds, reptiles, amphibians, and fish and of some *invertebrates* (animals without backbones). The eggs of fish, sea urchins, and shellfish are called *roe.* People eat many kinds of roe, especially shad, salmon, and sturgeon roe. People traditionally reserve the term *caviar* for sturgeon roe from the Caspian and Black seas. Caviar is a prized and expensive delicacy.

Chicken and duck eggs are an important part of the diet in many countries. In certain regions, the eggs of other birds are commonly eaten, including the eggs of emu, goose, guineafowl, ostrich, quail, and turkey.

Chicken eggs provide an excellent source of protein, iron, and phosphorus. Eggs are a rich source of vitamins A and D and of B vitamins. The yolks of chicken eggs also contain a fatty substance called *cholesterol.* Too much cholesterol in the diet can be harmful to those who are at risk of cardiovascular disease.

In addition to being eaten without accompaniment, eggs have many important culinary uses. They are used to prepare omelets, quiches, custard, salads, and baked goods. Egg yolks are used in cooking to produce an *emulsion*—that is, a mixture of liquids that do not ordinarily mix well. Common emulsions made with egg yolk include mayonnaise and some salad dressings. Cooks use egg whites to make a foam in certain recipes, especially when stirred rapidly or whipped.

White and brown eggs have the same food value. The United States Department of Agriculture classifies consumer eggs as Grade AA, A, or B. These standards are based on the condition of the shell, yolk, and white and on the size of the air cell.

People in Japan, China, and Mexico are among the world leaders in egg consumption. According to the American Egg Board, the average person in the United States eats about 250 eggs per year. About 75 of these come from manufactured egg products, rather than being whole eggs from the shell.

Chicken egg production

A farm chicken can lay up to 350 eggs in a year. China ranks as the world's leading egg producer. Other top egg-producing nations include India, Japan, Russia, and the United States. More than 79 billion chicken eggs are produced in the United States each year. For a list of the leading egg-producing states in the United States, see **Chicken** (graph: Leading egg-producing states).

In Europe and North America, people concerned with the welfare of animals have raised awareness of the ethics of modern egg production. They debate the ethical implications of raising millions of chickens in huge "factory farms." In such facilities, birds are confined to cramped indoor cages for their entire lives. More people are choosing to buy eggs from producers that keep their chickens in cage-free enclosures. Eggs from chickens fed an organic or other special diet are also popular (see **Organic food**).

Other uses for eggs

Chicken eggs are also used to produce *vaccines* and for other uses in the biological laboratory. Vaccines are produced by growing disease-causing germs inside eggs. These germs stimulate the body's immune system to fight a particular infectious disease.

Some animal feeds contain eggs. Eggs are also used in the production of some adhesives, cosmetics, shampoos, and specialty inks and paints.

Eggs are a common symbol in religious traditions and in art. In many cultures, an egg can symbolize Earth, fertility, rebirth, and the cycle of life. Such symbolism is shown in the tradition of coloring eggs for Easter celebrations. A goose that lays golden eggs serves as an important character in popular fables and folktales. Goldsmith Peter Carl Fabergé produced beautifully crafted Easter eggs of gold and precious gems for Russian czars in the early 1900's. David C. Lahti

Related articles in *World Book* include:

Albumin
Bird (Laying and hatching eggs; pictures)
Caviar
Easter (Easter eggs)
Embryo
Fish (How fish reproduce)
Insect (The life cycle of insects)
Poultry
Reproduction
Snake (picture: Snakes hatch from eggs)

Eggleston, *EHG uhl stuhn,* **Edward** (1837-1902), wrote *The Hoosier Schoolmaster* (1871), a fresh, delightful story of early Indiana. The book is one of the first attempts to write a story about American regional life in the West. *The End of the World* (1872) deals with the Millerites, a religious group that expected Christ's second coming in 1843. *The Graysons* (1887) shows Abraham Lincoln as a young lawyer. Eggleston was born on Dec. 10, 1837, in Vevay, Indiana. Besides being a writer, he was also a Methodist circuit rider and a historian. He died on Sept. 4, 1902. Bert Hitchcock

Eggplant is a plant that bears large egg-shaped fruit. The fruit also is called *eggplant* and sometimes *garden egg.* The purple variety of fruit has been a popular vegetable in the United States since about 1860, even though it has moderately low levels of vitamins and calories. Eggplants with white, brown, yellow, or striped fruits are used chiefly as ornaments. It is believed the first eggplant grew in northern India and later spread to China, Europe, and South America. Now eggplant grows in many tropical lands. The fruit grows on a bush that stands from 2 to 6 feet (61 to 180 centimeters) high. The fruit hangs among the grayish-green hairy leaves and sometimes grows nearly as large as a football. It grows only in warm weather, and takes 115 to 120 days to

WORLD BOOK illustration by Kate Lloyd-Jones, Linden Artists Ltd.

The eggplant is a plant that produces large fruit shaped somewhat like an egg. The fruit is often served as a vegetable.

ripen. Where the warm season is too short, the seeds must be planted in a greenhouse. Then the seedlings are transplanted after warm weather begins. Little black flea beetles often attack eggplants and eat holes in the leaves. These beetles must be controlled to grow eggplants successfully. Albert Liptay

Scientific classification. The eggplant's scientific name is *Solanum melongena.*

Eglantine, *EHG luhn tyn,* is a wild rose, commonly called *sweetbrier.* The plant grows as a shrub and sometimes reaches a height of 6 feet (1.8 meters). It has curving brown stems covered with sharp, hooked prickles. Its small leaves grow close together. They are dark green on top and pale green underneath.

The flowers are a soft pink color. Both the leaves and blossoms have a sweet, spicy scent. The plant bears bright red or orange fruits. These fruits appear after the flowers have fallen. The eglantine originated in Europe. It grows in parts of the eastern United States. Eglantine is used in general landscaping for hedges or screen plantings. Walter S. Judd

Scientific classification. The eglantine's scientific name is *Rosa rubiginosa.* Some scientists classify it as *Rosa eglanteria.*

Ego, *EE goh,* is a term used in psychoanalysis to describe one of the three parts of the mind. The two other parts are the *id,* or instincts, and the *superego,* or conscience. The ego resolves conflicts among the individual's instinctual impulses, his or her sense of guilt, and the demands of external reality. For example, the ego regulates emotions and impulses that might not be acceptable to other people. The ego also governs such areas as memory, thought and decision making, walking and other voluntary movements, and perceptions, such as hearing, feeling, and sight.

Psychoanalysts sometimes use the word *ego* to mean a person's self. In popular usage, the word has come to mean selfishness, self-love, or self-esteem.

Allen Frances

See also **Psychoanalysis.**

Egret, *EE greht,* is any of eight *species* (kinds) of birds that belong to the heron family. The name *egret* comes from the French word *aigrette,* which means *heron.* Like other herons, egrets have long legs, a long neck, and a long, thin bill. Most egrets have white feathers. During the mating season, egrets grow long plumes on the back, neck, and head. These plumes are sometimes called *aigrettes.*

Egrets live throughout much of the world, except for the Arctic and Antarctica. Adults range from 17 to 40 inches (43 to 102 centimeters) long and have a wingspread of up to 67 inches (170 centimeters).

In the late 1800's and early 1900's, egret plumes were prized as decorations for women's hats. Hunters killed great numbers of egrets for the plumes, and several species were threatened with extinction. Finally, countries passed laws to protect egrets from hunters, and fashions changed. As a result, the egret population has gradually increased.

Kinds. In North America, the most commonly seen egret is the *great egret,* also called the *common egret.* The bird ranks as the largest egret. It is also found in South America and the Eastern Hemisphere. The *snowy egret,* a smaller species, lives mainly in the southern United States. It grows especially beautiful plumes. The *cattle egret* is one of the most widespread kinds. Until the mid-1800's, this bird lived chiefly in Africa. The cattle egret now inhabits every continent except Antarctica. The *reddish egret* lives mainly along the Gulf Coast of the United States and in Mexico and the Caribbean region. It has two color forms. In one form, the bird is white. In the other, it has a reddish head and neck and a gray body. The *slaty egret* of Africa ranks as the smallest species of egret.

Habits. Most egrets live near water. They feed on fishes, frogs, and other animals found in or around water. To catch a prey, most egrets stand motionless in shallow water until the animal comes close to them. Then they quickly seize the animal with their bill. They also may slowly stalk a prey or try to chase it down. The cattle egret usually feeds on insects in upland areas. It often follows cattle, horses, or other grazing animals, preying on the insects those animals disturb.

Egrets often nest with other herons in large colonies that may include hundreds of members. Egrets build their nests in bushes or trees. The female usually lays three to five light-blue or light-green eggs. The young are covered with down when they hatch. Both parents care for the babies and bring them food. After the mating season, egrets often wander widely and may be seen in areas where they do not nest. James J. Dinsmore

Scientific classification. Egrets belong to the heron family, Ardeidae. The scientific name of the great egret is *Ardea alba;* the snowy egret is *Egretta thula;* the cattle egret is *Bubulcus ibis;* the reddish egret is *Egretta rufescens;* and the slaty egret is *Egretta vinaceigula.*

See also **Heron.**

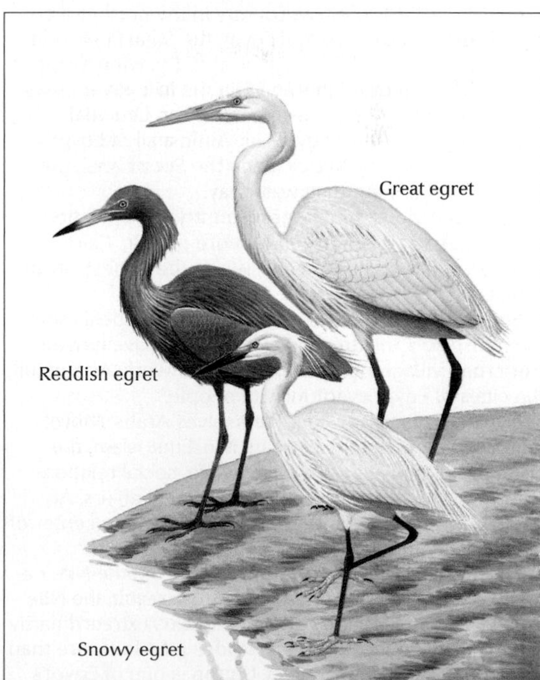

WORLD BOOK illustration by Trevor Boyer, Linden Artists Ltd.

Egrets belong to the heron family. They have long legs, a long neck, and a long, thin bill. There are eight species. Three species found in the United States are shown here.

© Corbis

Cairo, Egypt's capital and largest city, is also the largest city in Africa and the largest city in the Middle East. The Nile River, the longest river in the world, flows northward through the Cairo metropolitan area. The river provides precious water for agriculture and industry.

Egypt

Egypt is a Middle Eastern country in the northeast corner of Africa. A small part of Egypt, the Sinai Peninsula, is in Asia. Little rain falls in Egypt, and dry, windswept desert covers most of the land. But the Nile River flows northward through the desert and serves as a vital source of life for most Egyptians. Almost all of Egypt's people live near the Nile or along the Suez Canal, the country's other important waterway.

Egypt is Africa's third largest country in population. Only Nigeria and Ethiopia have more people. Cairo, Egypt's capital and largest city, is also the largest city in Africa.

Egypt's population has increased tremendously since the mid-1900's. In addition, many people have moved from rural villages to cities in search of work. As a result, the cities of Egypt overflow with people.

Most Egyptians consider themselves Arabs. More than 90 percent of Egyptians are Muslims. Islam, the Muslim religion, influences family life, social relationships, business activities, and government affairs. Al-Azhar University in Cairo is the world's leading center of Islamic teaching.

For thousands of years, floodwaters from the Nile deposited rich soil on the riverbanks. As a result, the Nile Valley and Delta region of Egypt contains extraordinarily fertile farmland. Agriculture provides jobs for more than one-fourth of Egypt's workers. Cotton is one of Egypt's most valuable crops. Other crops grown in Egypt include corn, fruits, rice, sugar cane, and wheat.

Egypt has expanded a variety of manufacturing industries since the mid-1900's. Cement, cotton textiles, and processed foods are among the chief manufactured products. Petroleum provides much energy, as does hydroelectric power from the Aswan High Dam on the Nile River.

Egypt is a birthplace of civilization. The ancient Egyptians developed a great culture about 5,000 years ago. They created the first national government, as well as early forms of mathematics and writing. For the story of this civilization, see **Egypt, Ancient.**

Egypt's hot, dry climate has helped preserve many

Facts in brief

Capital: Cairo.
Official language: Arabic.
Official name: Arab Republic of Egypt.
Area: 386,662 mi² (1,001,450 km²). *Greatest distances*—east-west, 770 mi (1,240 km); north-south, 675 mi (1,086 km). *Coastline*—Mediterranean Sea, 565 mi (909 km); Red Sea, 850 mi (1,370 km).
Elevation: *Highest*—Jabal Katrinah, 8,651 ft (2,637 m) above sea level. *Lowest*—Qattara Depression, 436 ft (133 m) below sea level.
Population: *Estimated 2014 population*—86,022,000; density, 222 per mi² (86 per km²); distribution, 57 percent rural, 43 percent urban. *2006 census*—72,798,031.
Chief products: *Agriculture*—corn, cotton, grapes, milk, oranges, potatoes, rice, sugar cane, tomatoes, wheat. *Manufacturing*—cement, chemicals, cotton textiles, motor vehicles, processed foods, steel. *Mining*—petroleum.
National anthem: "Beladi, Beladi" ("My Country, My Country").
Money: *Basic unit*—Egyptian pound. One hundred piasters equal one pound.

products of ancient Egyptian culture. Tourists from all over the world travel to Egypt to see such wonders as the Great Sphinx. The Great Sphinx is an enormous stone sculpture with the head of a human being and the body of a lion. Tourists can also marvel at the huge pyramids that the ancient Egyptians built as tombs for their *pharaohs* (rulers).

After ancient times, Egypt was ruled by a series of foreign invaders. In 1953, Egypt became an independent republic. Since then, it has played a leading role in the Middle East, especially in Arab affairs.

Government

Egypt is a republic with a strong national government. A constitution adopted in 1971 declared Egypt a democratic and socialist society. A military government took control of Egypt in 2011 after widespread protests forced President Hosni Mubarak to relinquish power. The military replaced the 1971 constitution with a temporary charter. The charter was in effect until a new constitution was approved by a *referendum* (direct vote of the people) in late 2012. The Egyptian army, however, suspended that constitution in July 2013 and installed a new government. The constitution was to be amended ahead of 2014 elections.

National government. Egypt's national government has three branches. They are (1) an executive branch headed by a president, (2) a legislative branch to pass laws, and (3) a judicial branch, or court system.

Egyptian voters elect the president. The president appoints the vice president. The president also appoints a prime minister and Council of Ministers (cabinet). In turn, the national government selects all local administrators. Thus, the president has great influence and authority at all levels of government. The president also commands Egypt's armed forces.

Egypt's legislative body is called the People's Assembly. The Egyptian people elect a majority of the assembly members. Traditionally, the president appoints 10 members.

The legislative branch also includes a smaller body called the Shura Council. The council's role is mainly advisory.

Local government. Egypt is divided into political units called *governorates.* A governor appointed by the president heads each governorate. The governorates are divided into districts and villages. The districts and villages also are run by appointed officials. Elected councils at each level of local government assist the appointed leaders.

Politics. Egypt's political environment changed in 2011. The National Democratic Party, which had ruled the country for decades, was dissolved, and opposition parties were allowed to participate in general elections. All Egyptian citizens aged 18 or older are required to vote.

Courts. The Supreme Constitutional Court is the highest court in Egypt. Lower courts include appeals courts, *tribunals of first instance* (regional courts), and district courts.

Egypt's president appoints judges on the recommendation of the minister of justice. The courts are otherwise independent. There are no juries in Egypt's court system.

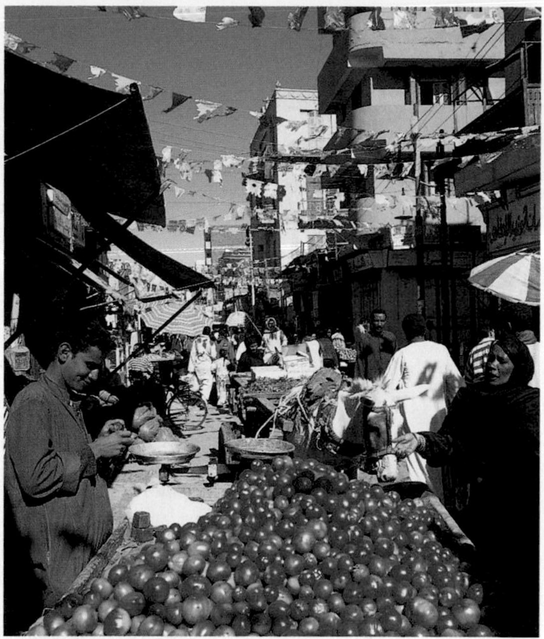

© SuperStock

Outdoor marketplaces called *suqs* are found in many Egyptian cities and towns. Many people enjoy going to suqs to make purchases, visit with friends, and relax.

Symbols of Egypt include the flag, *above left,* and the coat of arms, *above right.* The eagle is a symbol of Saladin, a Muslim leader who lived during the 1100's. The eagle's claws hold a panel bearing the country's name.

WORLD BOOK map

Egypt lies mainly in the northeast corner of Africa, bordered by the Mediterranean Sea, Israel, the Red Sea, Sudan, and Libya.

Egypt map index

Cities and towns

Name	Population	Key	
Abnub	67,479	C	4
Abu Qurqas	57,613	C	4
Abu Tij	70,860	D	4
Abu Zanimah		B	5
Abu Kabir*	102,603	B	4
Ad Dabah		B	3
Akhmim	101,243	D	4
Al Arish	138,195	A	5
Al Badari	42,802	D	4
Al Balyana	46,981	D	4
Al Bawiti		C	3
Alexandria (Al Iskandariyah)	4,110,015	A	3
Al Fashn	65,645	C	4
Al Fayyum	316,722	B	4
Al Ghanayim*	48,151	D	4
Al Ghurdaqah	160,746	C	5
Al Hawamidiyah*	109,468	B	4
Al Iskandariyah, see Alexandria			
Al Jamaliyah	63,635	A	4
Al Jizah, see Giza			
Al Kharijah	61,020	D	4
Al Mahallah al Kubra	442,884	A	4
Al Manshah	66,408	D	4
Al Mansurah	437,311	A	4
Al Manzilah*	75,210	A	4
Al Matariyah	100,502	A	4
Al Minya	239,804	C	4
Al Qahirah, see Cairo			
Al Qasr		D	3
Al Qusaymah		B	6
Al Qusayr	35,903	D	6
Al Qusiyah	69,489	C	4
An Nakhl		B	5
Armant	76,698	D	5
Ashmun*	84,871	B	4
Ash Shabb		F	3
As Sallum		A	1
As Sinbillawayn*	86,729	B	4
Aswan	265,004	E	5
Asyut	386,006	D	4
At Tur		C	5
Ayn Dallah		C	2
Ayn Sukhnah		B	5
Az Zaqaziq	302,611	B	4
Baltim		A	4
Banha	158,389	B	4
Bani Mazar	79,553	C	4
Bani Suwayf	193,535	B	4
Baris		E	4
Biba	57,620	B	4
Bilbays	136,499	B	4
Bilqas Qism Awwal*	95,001	A	4
Bir Abu al Husayn		F	3
Bir Jifjafah		B	5
Bir Misahah		F	2
Bur Safajah		D	5
Bur Said, see Port Said			
Cairo (Al Qahirah)	7,786,640	B	4
Damanhur	241,895	A	4
Damietta (Dumyat)	203,187	A	4
Daraw	38,178	E	5
Dayrut	72,987	C	4
Dhahab		C	6
Dikirnis*	67,770	A	4
Dishna	52,674	D	5
Disuq*	108,868	A	4
Diyarb Najm*	53,457	A	4
El Alamein		A	3
Faqus*	78,877	B	4
Giza (Al Jizah)	2,681,863	B	4
Hawsh Isa*	47,373	B	3
Hihya*	44,479	B	4
Idfu	115,946	E	5
Idku*	97,419	A	3
Ismailia	300,449	B	5
Isna	67,217	E	5
Jamsah		C	5
Jirja	102,701	D	4
Kafr ad Dawwar	113,506	A	3
Kafr ash Shaykh*	147,380	A	4
Kafr az Zayyat*	74,854	B	4
Kawm Umbu	71,623	E	5
Luxor	197,594	D	5
Maghaghah	75,538	C	4
Mallawi	140,215	C	4
Manfalut	82,522	C	4
Marsa al Alam		E	6
Matruh	120,888	A	2
Minuf*	87,842	B	4
Mit Ghamr*	116,180	B	4
Mut	20,293	D	3
Naj Hammadi	45,118	D	5
Nasr*	85,266	B	3
Port Said (Bur Said)	570,768	A	5
Qalyub	106,804	B	4
Qasr al Farafirah		D	2
Qina	206,831	D	5
Qus	60,237	D	5
Ras Gharib	31,414	C	5
Rosetta (Rashid)	69,827	A	3
Samalut	90,671	C	4
Sharm ash Shaykh		C	6
Shibin al Kawm	177,060	B	4
Shubra al Khaymah	1,016,722	B	4
Sidi Barrani		A	1
Sinnuris	82,134	B	4
Siwah		B	1
Suez	510,935	B	5
Suhaj	189,695	D	4
Tahta	85,331	D	4
Tanta	421,076	A	4
Tima	67,357	D	4
Zafaranah		B	5
Zifta*	95,320	B	4

*Does not appear on map; key shows general location.
Source: 2006 census.

Armed forces. Egypt maintains a large military, consisting of an army, a navy, an air force, and an air defense command. About 470,000 people serve in Egypt's armed forces. In addition, the country's military reserves have about 480,000 members. Men between the ages of 18 and 30 may be drafted for three years of military service.

People

About 99 percent of all Egyptians live along the Nile River and the Suez Canal, in an area that covers only about 4 percent of Egypt's total land. The rest of the country's people live in the deserts and mountains east and west of the Nile.

Most Egyptians consider themselves Arabs (see **Arabs**). Bedouins make up a distinct cultural minority among the Arab population. Bedouins are *nomads*—that is, herders who move about to find pastures for their flock. Most former Bedouins have settled and become farmers, but some nomadic tribes remain in the deserts.

The Nubians make up the largest non-Arab minority in Egypt. These people originally lived in villages along the Nile in northern Sudan and the extreme south of Egypt, in a region called the Nubian Valley. Construction of the Aswan High Dam in the 1960's forced the Nubians to move north along the Nile.

Ancestry. Since ancient times, numerous groups of people have invaded Egypt and have intermarried with native Egyptians. As a result, present-day Egyptians can trace their ancestry not only to ancient Egyptians, but also to such groups as Arabs, Ethiopians, Persians, and Turks, as well as Greeks, Romans, and other Europeans.

Language. Arabic is Egypt's official language. Regional Arabic dialects have different sounds and words. The dialect of Cairo is the most widely spoken dialect throughout Egypt. The Bedouin dialects differ from those spoken by the settled residents of the Nile Valley. People in some desert villages speak Berber rather than Arabic. Many educated Egyptians speak English or French as a second language. See **Arabic language.**

Population density

The population distribution of Egypt is extremely uneven. The vast majority of the people live along the Nile River and its delta. Egypt's deserts are thinly populated.

WORLD BOOK map

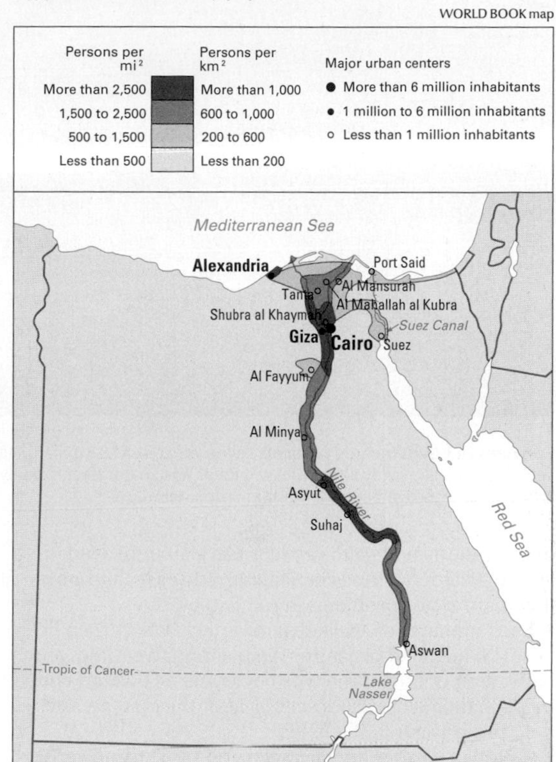

Way of life

Lifestyles in Egypt's cities differ greatly from those in its villages. Egyptian city dwellers cope with such typical urban problems as housing shortages and traffic congestion. Although many live in poverty, others enjoy modern conveniences and government services that the cities offer.

Rural life changed greatly during the 1900's. Many jobs in rural areas are now done with the help of machines. But much work is still done by hand, and donkeys, water buffaloes, and camels continue to be used for some heavy tasks. For people throughout Egypt, the beliefs and traditions of Islam form a unifying bond.

City life. Cairo is Egypt's largest city and the largest city in Africa. The port city of Alexandria is Egypt's second largest city. Cities in Egypt are overcrowded. Traffic moves slowly, and public transportation is inadequate. Riders crowd onto streetcars and trains.

Great extremes of wealth and poverty characterize Egyptian cities. Attractive residential areas exist beside vast slums. Lack of sufficient housing is a serious problem. Many people crowd into small apartments. Many more build makeshift huts on land that belongs to other people, or on the roofs of apartment buildings. Some of the poorest people in Cairo take refuge in historic tombs on the outskirts of the city, in an area known as the City of the Dead.

The cities provide a variety of jobs. Educated Egyptians work in such professions as business and government. Workers with little or no education find jobs at factories or as unskilled laborers.

Rural life. Until the 1900's, the vast majority of Egyptians lived in the countryside. Today, more than half of Egypt's people still live in rural areas. Almost all of them are peasants called *fellahin.* They live in villages along the Nile River or the Suez Canal. Most fellahin farm small plots of land or tend animals. Many fellahin do not own land. They rent land or work as laborers in the fields of more prosperous landowners. A small minority of Egypt's rural people are Bedouins who move about the deserts with their herds of camels, goats, and sheep.

The traditional village home used to be a simple hut built of mud bricks with a straw roof. Most huts consisted of one to three rooms, with few furnishings, and a courtyard. Today, many village homes are made of fired bricks or concrete, and they are larger and more comfortable than in the past. Electric power is commonly available, as are televisions, radios, and cassette recorders. Many villages have gained wealth from the earnings of fellahin who have worked outside Egypt, especially in the rich Arab countries of the Persian Gulf. The spread

© Norman Owen Tomalin, Bruce Coleman Collection

Farmers in Egypt include peasants called *fellahin.* Many fellahin farm small plots of land in the fertile valley along the Nile River and in the river's low-lying delta. The farmworkers shown here are tending crops near Luxor.

© Thomas Nebbia, Woodfin Camp, Inc.

Some parts of Cairo house many poor people. Egypt's crowded cities lack enough housing for the growing population.

of education and health services has also improved the lives of villagers. However, illiteracy, disease, and poverty remain major problems in rural areas.

Each member of a village family performs certain duties. The husband organizes the planting, weeding, and harvesting of crops. The wife cooks, carries water, and helps in the fields. Children look after the animals and help bring water to the fields.

Egyptian villages are characterized by a strong sense of community. People come together to celebrate feasts, festivals, marriages, and births. Islam, the religion of most Egyptians, provides a strong unifying bond. *Mosques* (Islamic houses of worship) serve as centers of both religious and social life.

Clothing. Styles of clothing in Egypt reflect the different ways of life. Many well-to-do city dwellers wear clothing similar to that worn in the United States and Europe. Rural villagers and many poor city dwellers wear traditional clothing. Fellahin men wear pants and a long, full shirtlike garment called a *galabiyah.* Women wear long, flowing gowns in dark or bright colors.

Some Egyptians follow Islamic customs in their appearance. Men grow beards and wear long, light-colored gowns and skullcaps. Women wear robes and cover their hair, ears, and arms with a veil.

Food and drink. Most villagers and poor city dwellers in Egypt eat a simple diet based on bread and *ful* or *fool* (broad beans). At a typical evening meal, each person dips bread into a large bowl of hot vegetable stew.

Government-run stores in the cities distribute such food as meat, cheese, and eggs at controlled prices. However, supplies at these stores often run out. The well-to-do city people have more varied diets. They can afford to buy large quantities of meat and imported fruits and vegetables.

Sweetened coffee and tea are favorite beverages throughout Egypt. People also drink the milk of goats, sheep, and water buffaloes.

Recreation. Soccer is popular in Egypt. Many people attend matches or watch their favorite teams on television. But the main form of recreation in both cities and villages is socializing. People enjoy going to the *suq* (outdoor marketplace) to make purchases and to visit with friends. They like to sit and talk while drinking cups of coffee or tea, or relax by smoking a kind of water pipe known as a *shisha.*

Religion. Islam is the official religion of Egypt. More than 90 percent of the Egyptian people are Muslims—followers of Islam. Almost all of them follow the Sunni branch of Islam. Coptic Christians make up the largest religious minority group in Egypt.

Islam influences many aspects of life in Egypt. Religious duties include praying five times a day, *almsgiving* (giving money or goods to the poor), fasting, and, if possible, making a pilgrimage to Mecca, Saudi Arabia, the sacred city of Islam. Muslim traditions also affect government and law. For example, the government collects contributions from the wealthy and gives the money to the poor to fulfill the almsgiving requirement of Islam.

The government officially controls Islam in Egypt, and it appoints major Muslim religious leaders. In villages and city neighborhoods, some Muslims form brotherhoods and hold festivals and ceremonies outside of official control. Some of these groups use force in opposing the government and its religious leaders, whom they view as corrupted by non-Islamic values.

By law, Coptic Christians and other religious minorities may worship freely. But some radical Muslim groups have committed acts of violence against the Coptic community in Cairo and in parts of southern Egypt. See **Copts; Islam; Mosque; Muslims.**

Education. About half of Egypt's adult population can read and write. Illiteracy is highest in rural areas. The government is working to improve the quality and availability of education. For the country's literacy rate, see **Literacy** (table: Literacy rates for selected countries).

According to law, all children from ages 6 up to 14 must go to school. But in some places, schools are so crowded that students go for only part of each day to make room for other students. Many teachers provide tutoring services outside school. Education at public elementary and high schools and public colleges is free. Egypt also has many private schools and a few private universities.

Cairo University is the largest institution of higher learning in Egypt. Al-Azhar University, one of the world's oldest universities, was founded around A.D. 970. It is a center of Islamic scholarship.

Egypt's educational system has problems from the elementary through the university level because of overcrowding and lack of funds. There is a shortage of teachers and school buildings, especially in rural areas. Despite these problems, Egypt's university graduates are among the best trained in the Arab world.

The arts. Egypt has a rich artistic tradition. Ancient Egyptians created many fine paintings and statues. They also produced and enjoyed music and stories. For more information about the arts of ancient Egypt, see **Egypt, Ancient** (Painting and sculpture; Music and literature).

Today, Egypt ranks as a center of the Arab publishing and motion-picture industries. The celebrated works of Egyptian writers and filmmakers have spread Egypt's culture throughout the Arab world. During the mid-1900's, the works of such writers as Tawfiq al-Hakim and Taha Hussein realistically described Egyptian and Arab society. In 1988, the Egyptian author Naguib Mahfouz became the first Arabic-language writer to win the Nobel Prize in literature.

Egyptians enjoy traditional and classical music, as well as modern Egyptian and Western music. Egypt's most

© Josef Polleross, The Image Works

Muslims pray at a *mosque* (Islamic house of worship) in Cairo. Islam, the Muslim religion, is the official religion of Egypt. Most Egyptians follow the Sunni branch of Islam.

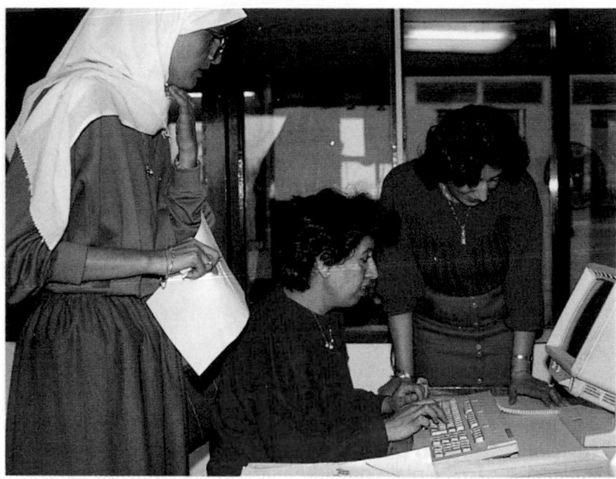

© Catherine Osborne, Photo Researchers

Styles of clothing in Egypt vary. Many Egyptians wear clothing similar to that worn in North America and Europe. Others, such as the woman wearing a headscarf, follow Islamic custom.

popular singer of the 1900's, Um Kulthum, blended Eastern and Western themes in her songs.

The land

Egypt consists mostly of sparsely settled deserts. But the inhabited areas—along the Nile River and the Suez Canal—are densely populated.

Egypt has four major land regions: (1) the Nile Valley and Delta, (2) the Western Desert, (3) the Eastern Desert, and (4) the Sinai Peninsula.

The Nile Valley and Delta region extends along the course of the Nile River, which measures about 1,000 miles (1,600 kilometers) in Egypt. The Nile flows northward into Egypt from Sudan to Cairo. Just north of Cairo, the river splits into two main branches and forms a delta. The Nile River delta measures about 150 miles (240 kilometers) at its base along the Mediterranean Sea, and about 100 miles (160 kilometers) from north to south. See **Nile River; Delta.**

The valley and delta region contains most of Egypt's farmland. Without the precious waters of the Nile, Egypt would be little more than a desert wasteland. For thousands of years, annual floods of the Nile deposited valuable soils upon the narrow plain on either side of the river and upon the low-lying delta. Almost all of Egypt's people live in the valley and delta region. Many of them farm its fertile soil.

In the southern part of the valley, the Aswan High Dam provides water for irrigation of the lands along the Nile. It also prevents severe damage from the Nile's annual flooding. Lake Nasser, a huge lake created behind the dam, catches and stores the floodwaters. The Aswan High Dam allows Egyptians to cultivate usable farmland more thoroughly. But the dam also collects a great deal of valuable soil. As a result, this soil is no longer deposited on the farmland that borders the Nile. See **Aswan High Dam; Lake Nasser.**

The Western Desert, also called the *Libyan Desert,* is part of the huge Sahara that stretches across northern Africa. It covers about two-thirds of Egypt's total area. The Western Desert consists almost entirely of a large, sandy plateau with some ridges and basins, and pit-shaped areas called *depressions.* The Qattara Depres-

my. But Mubarak was much less outspoken on many controversial issues and worked to repair Egypt's ties with other Arab countries. Egypt was readmitted to the Arab League in 1989.

Egypt's strategic importance enabled it to gain economic and military aid from the United States and the Soviet Union. But these alliances did not benefit the people greatly. Egypt's problems remain much the same as throughout the 1900's. The population is too large for Egypt's resources and continues to grow rapidly.

In 1990, Iraq invaded Kuwait. Egypt took a leading role in Arab opposition to the invasion. In early 1991, war broke out between Iraq and a coalition that was formed by the United States, Egypt, and other nations. Egyptian troops participated in the efforts to liberate Kuwait (see **Persian Gulf War of 1991**).

In October 1992, an earthquake struck Cairo and neighboring suburbs. The disaster caused more than 560 deaths and about $1 billion in property damage.

Violence by radical Islamist organizations, particularly the Islamic Group, increased in the early 1990's. These groups attacked Egyptian Christians and foreigners, especially foreign tourists. In a crackdown on the violence, Egyptian authorities raided extremist strongholds. They made mass arrests and imprisoned thousands of suspects. A number were executed. The Egyptian government also used the state-controlled media to discredit armed Islamist groups. As a result, extremist violence became less of a threat by the end of the 1990's. But restrictive emergency regulations remained in place.

In the early 2000's, Egypt saw a resumption of violence against tourist areas. Bombings in 2004 and 2005 killed a number of people at resorts on the Red Sea. Egyptian officials blamed Islamist extremists for the attacks.

Egypt held its first multicandidate presidential election in September 2005, and President Mubarak was reelected to a fifth term. Egyptians also elected a new parliament in 2005. Mubarak's party kept a majority, but the Muslim Brotherhood gained 20 percent of the seats. The Muslim Brotherhood party was banned at the time, but candidates ran as independents.

In January 2011, antigovernment protests erupted across Egypt. Government forces killed hundreds of people while trying to contain the protests. The unrest was fueled in part by poor economic conditions and accusations of government corruption. Protesters called for an end to Mubarak's presidency. Mubarak stepped down on February 11. He handed power to the Egyptian military and left Cairo. The popular uprising in Egypt followed similar events in Tunisia and helped spark unrest elsewhere in the region. Mubarak was sentenced to life in prison for ordering the killing of protesters, but he was released in August 2013.

Amidst steady demonstrations against military rule, Egyptians voted in parliamentary elections in late 2011. Islamist parties won a vast majority of the seats. In June 2012, voters elected Mohamed Morsi of the Freedom and Justice Party (FJP) as Egypt's new president. The FJP is the political arm of the Muslim Brotherhood.

In November, Morsi sparked large protests by attempting to give himself what some Egyptians considered dictatorial powers. In December, Egyptian voters approved a new constitution. In July 2013, however, after mass protests and antigovernment demonstrations, the Egyptian army suspended the constitution and forced President Morsi from office. More than 1,000 people died as protests led to violence between Morsi supporters and security forces. Adly Mansour, head of the Supreme Constitutional Court, was named interim president. Mansour's government was to amend the constitution and plan elections for 2014. Michael J. Reimer

Related articles in *World Book* include:

Biographies

Boutros-Ghali, Boutros
Faruk I
Mahfouz, Naguib
Mubarak, Hosni
Muhammad Ali
Nasser, Gamal Abdel
Qutb, Sayyid
Sadat, Anwar el-

Cities

Alexandria
Aswan
Cairo
El Alamein
Giza
Port Said
Suez

History

Arab-Israeli conflict
Arab League
Egypt, Ancient
Fātimid dynasty
Israel
Mamluks
Middle East
Muslim Brotherhood
Sudan
Suez Canal
Suez crisis
Syria
United Arab Republic
Valley of the Kings

Physical features

Gaza Strip
Lake Nasser
Mount Sinai
Nile River
Red Sea
Sahara
Sinai Peninsula

Other related articles

Abu Simbel, Temples of
Al-Azhar University
Asp
Aswan High Dam
Copts
Cotton
Irrigation
Islam
Lotus
Muslims
Papyrus
Pyramids
Sphinx

Outline

I. Government
- A. National government
- B. Local government
- C. Politics
- D. Courts
- E. Armed forces

II. People
- A. Ancestry
- B. Language

III. Way of life
- A. City life
- B. Rural life
- C. Clothing
- D. Food and drink
- E. Recreation
- F. Religion
- G. Education
- H. The arts

IV. The land
- A. The Nile Valley and Delta
- B. The Western Desert
- C. The Eastern Desert
- D. The Sinai Peninsula

V. Climate

VI. Economy
- A. Service industries
- B. Manufacturing
- C. Agriculture
- D. Mining
- E. Tourism
- F. Energy sources
- G. International trade
- H. Transportation and communication

VII. History

Additional resources

Bradley, John R. *Inside Egypt: The Land of the Pharaohs on the Brink of a Revolution.* Palgrave Macmillan, 2008.
Gutner, Howard. *Egypt.* Children's Pr., 2009. Younger readers.
Humphreys, Andrew. *The National Geographic Traveler: Egypt.* 3rd ed. National Geographic Soc., 2009.
Moscovitch, Arlene. *Egypt: The Culture.* Crabtree Pub. Co., 2008. *Egypt: The Land.* 2008. *Egypt: The People.* 2008. All revised editions. All for younger readers.

WORLD BOOK illustration by Linden Artists Ltd.

The Nile River was the lifeblood of ancient Egypt. Its floodwaters deposited rich, black soil on the land year after year, enabling farmers to grow huge supplies of food. The Nile also provided water for irrigation and served as ancient Egypt's main transportation route.

Ancient Egypt

Egypt, Ancient, was the birthplace of one of the world's first civilizations. This advanced culture arose about 5,000 years ago in the Nile River Valley in northeastern Africa. The ancient Egyptian civilization thrived for over 2,000 years and so became one of the longest lasting civilizations in history.

The mighty Nile River was the lifeblood of ancient Egypt. Every year, the river overflowed and deposited a strip of rich, black soil along each bank. The fertile soil enabled farmers to raise a huge supply of food. The ancient Egyptians called their country *Kemet,* meaning *Black Land,* after the dark soil. The Nile also provided water for irrigation and was Egypt's main transportation route. For all these reasons, the ancient Greek historian Herodotus called Egypt "the gift of the Nile."

The ancient Egyptians made outstanding contributions to the development of civilization. They created the world's first national government, basic forms of arithmetic, and a 365-day calendar. They invented a form of picture writing called *hieroglyphics.* They also invented *papyrus,* a paperlike writing material made from the stems of papyrus plants. The Egyptians developed one of the first religions to emphasize life after death. They built great cities in which many skilled architects, doctors, engineers, painters, and sculptors worked.

The best-known achievements of the ancient Egyptians, however, are the pyramids they built as tombs for their rulers. The most famous pyramids stand at Giza. These gigantic stone structures—marvels of architectural and engineering skills—have been preserved by the dry climate for about 4,500 years. They serve as spectacular reminders of the glory of ancient Egypt.

The Egyptian world

The land. Ancient Egypt was a long, narrow country through which the Nile River flowed. Deserts bordered the country on the east, south, and west. The Mediterranean Sea lay to the north. The Nile River flowed north out of central Africa through the Egyptian desert to the Mediterranean. The Egyptians called the desert *Deshret,* meaning *Red Land.* The Nile's course through Egypt was about 600 miles (1,000 kilometers). The river split into several channels north of what is now Cairo, forming the Nile Delta. Rolling desert land lay west of the Nile Valley, and mountains rose to the east.

The Nile River flooded its banks each year. The flooding started in June, with the rainy season in central Africa. The rains raised the level of the river as the

Ancient Egypt

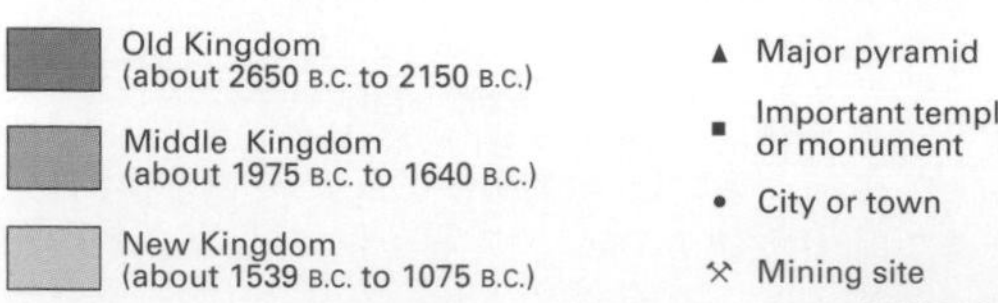

This map shows ancient Egypt during three periods, known as the Old Kingdom, Middle Kingdom, and New Kingdom.

Nile flowed northward. The floodwaters usually went down in September, leaving a strip of fertile land about 6 miles (10 kilometers) wide on each riverbank. Farmers then plowed and seeded the rich soil. The Egyptians also depended on the Nile as their chief transportation route. Memphis and Thebes—two capitals of ancient Egypt—and many other cities developed along the river because of its importance to farming and transportation.

The people. Most people of ancient Egypt lived in the Nile River Valley. Scholars believe the valley had from about 1 million to 4 million people, and possibly more, at various times during ancient Egypt's history. The rest of the population lived in the delta and in oases west of the river, in the Libyan Desert.

The ancient Egyptians had dark skin and dark hair. They spoke a language that was related both to the Semitic languages of southwestern Asia and to certain languages of northern Africa. The Egyptian language was written in hieroglyphics, a system of picture symbols that stood for ideas and sounds. The Egyptians began to use this system about 3000 B.C. It consisted of over 700 picture symbols. The Egyptians used hieroglyphics to inscribe monuments and temples and to record official texts. For everyday use, they developed simpler hieroglyphic forms called *hieratic* and *demotic*.

During the New Kingdom (about 1539-1075 B.C.), ancient Egypt had three main social classes—upper, middle, and lower. The upper class consisted of the royal family, rich landowners, government officials, high-ranking priests and army officers, and doctors. The middle class was made up chiefly of merchants, manufacturers, and craftworkers. The lower class, the largest class by far, consisted of unskilled laborers. Most of them worked on farms. Prisoners captured in foreign wars became slaves and formed a separate class.

Ancient Egypt's class system was not rigid. People in the lower or middle class, as well as slaves, could move to a higher position. They improved their status mainly through marriage or success in their jobs. Even slaves had rights. They could own personal items, get married, and inherit land. They could also be given their freedom.

Life of the people

Family life. The father headed the family in ancient Egypt. Upon his death, his oldest son became the head. Women had almost as many rights as men. They could own and inherit property, buy and sell goods, and make a will. A wife could obtain a divorce. Few other ancient civilizations gave women all these rights.

Children played with dolls, tops, and stuffed leather balls. They had board games with moves determined by the throw of dice. They also had several kinds of pets, including cats, dogs, monkeys, baboons, and birds.

Kings commonly had several wives at once. In many cases, a king's chief wife belonged to the royal family.

Education. Only a small percentage of boys and girls went to school in ancient Egypt, and most of them came from upper-class families. These students attended schools for scribes. Scribes made written records for government offices, temples, and other institutions. They also read and wrote letters for the large numbers of Egyptians who could not read and write.

The king's palace, government departments, and temples operated the scribal schools. All the schools prepared the students to become scribes or to follow other careers. The main subjects were reading, literature, geography, mathematics, and writing. The students learned writing by copying literature, letters, and business accounts. They used papyrus, the world's first paperlike material, and wrote with brushes made of reeds whose ends were softened and shaped. The Egyptians made ink by mixing water and *soot*, a black powder formed in the burning of wood or other substances.

Most Egyptian boys followed their fathers' occupations and were taught by their fathers. Some boys thus learned a trade, but the majority became farmers. Many parents placed their sons with master craftsmen, who taught carpentry, pottery making, or other skills. Boys who wanted to become doctors probably went to work with a doctor after finishing their basic schooling. Most girls were trained for the roles of wife and mother. Their mothers taught them cooking, sewing, and other skills.

Ancient Egypt had many libraries. A famous library in Alexandria had about 500,000 papyrus scrolls, which dealt with astronomy, geography, and many other subjects. Alexandria also had an outstanding museum.

Food, clothing, and shelter. Bread was the chief food in the diet of most ancient Egyptians, and beer was the favorite beverage. The bread was made from wheat, and the beer from barley. Many Egyptians also enjoyed a variety of vegetables and fruits, fish, milk, cheese, butter, and meat from ducks and geese. Wealthy Egyptians regularly ate beef, antelope and gazelle meat, and fancy cakes and other baked goods. They drank grape, date, and palm wine. The people ate with their fingers.

The Egyptians generally dressed in white linen garments. Women wore robes or tight dresses with shoulder straps. Men wore skirts or robes. The Egyptians often wore colored, shoulder-length headdresses. Rich Egyptians wore wigs, partly for protection against the sun. Wealthy Egyptians also wore sandals made of papyrus or palm leaves. The common people usually went barefoot. Young children rarely wore any clothes.

The ancient Egyptians liked to use cosmetics and wear jewelry. Women wore red lip powder, dyed their hair, and painted their fingernails. They outlined their eyes and colored their eyebrows with gray, black, or green paint. Men also outlined their eyes and often wore as much makeup as women. Both sexes used perfume and wore necklaces, rings, and bracelets. Combs, mirrors, and razors were common grooming aids.

The Egyptians built their houses with bricks of dried mud. They used trunks of palm trees to support the flat roofs. Many city houses were narrow buildings with three or more floors. Most poor Egyptians lived in one- to three-room huts. The typical middle-class Egyptian lived in a one- or two-story house with several rooms. Many rich Egyptians had houses with as many as 70 rooms. Some of these homes were country estates with orchards, pools, and large gardens. Egyptian houses had small windows placed high in the walls to help keep out the sun. The people spread wet mats on the floors and hung them on the walls and porches to help cool the air inside their houses. On hot nights, they often slept on the roof, where it was cooler.

Ancient Egyptian furniture included wooden stools, chairs, beds, and chests. People used pottery to store, cook, and serve food. They cooked food in clay ovens or over fires and used charcoal and wood for fuel. Oil lamps provided lighting. The lamps had flax wicks and burned oil in shallow bowls or hollowed-out stones.

Recreation. The ancient Egyptians enjoyed numerous leisure activities. They fished and swam in the Nile River. Sailing on the Nile was a popular family activity. Adventurous Egyptians hunted crocodiles, lions, hippopotamuses, and wild cattle with bows and arrows or spears. Many Egyptians liked to watch wrestling matches. At home, the Egyptians played *senet*, a board game similar to backgammon.

Religion

Gods and goddesses. The ancient Egyptians believed that various *deities* (gods and goddesses) influenced every aspect of nature and every human activity. They therefore worshiped many deities. The main god was the sun god Re. The Egyptians relied on Re and the goddess Rennutet for good harvests. The most important goddess was Isis. She represented the devoted mother and wife. Her husband and brother, Osiris, ruled over vegetation and the dead. Horus, son of Isis and Osiris, was god of the sky. He was called the lord of heaven and was often pictured with the head of a falcon.

In each city and town, the people worshiped their own special deity as well as the major ones. The people of Thebes worshiped Amun. Amun was later identified with Re and called Amun-Re. In time, Amun-Re became the chief deity. Other local deities and their main centers of worship included Ptah, the creator god of Memphis; Thoth, the god of wisdom and writing in Hermopolis; and Khnum, the creator god of Elephantine. Many deities were pictured with human bodies and animals' heads. Such a head suggested a real or imagined quality of the animal and made identification of the deity easy.

Most ancient Egyptians prayed at home because the temples did not offer regular services for people. Each temple was either regarded as the home of a certain deity or dedicated to a dead king. A temple built in honor of Amun-Re at Karnak was the country's largest temple. It had more than 130 columns that rose about 80 feet (24 meters). Brilliantly colored paintings decorated the columns and walls in the temple's Great Hall, which still ranks as the largest columned hall ever built.

The priests' main job was to serve the deity or king, who was represented by a statue in the temple. The king reigning at the time was considered the chief priest of Egypt. Each day, he or other local priests washed and dressed the statue and brought it food. Priests also offered prayers requested by individuals.

The afterlife. The ancient Egyptians believed that they could enjoy life after death. This belief in an *afterlife* sometimes led to much preparation for death and burial. It resulted, for example, in the construction of the pyramids and other great tombs for kings and queens. Other Egyptians had smaller tombs.

The Egyptians believed that the bodies of the dead had to be preserved for the next life, and so they *mummified* (embalmed and dried) corpses to prevent them from decaying. After a body was mummified, it was wrapped in layers of linen strips and placed in a coffin. The mummy was then put in a tomb. Some Egyptians mummified pets, including cats and monkeys. A number of Egyptian mummies have lasted to the present day.

WORLD BOOK illustration by Linden Artists Ltd.

A typical country estate in ancient Egypt had a shallow pool enclosed in a courtyard. The pool served as a decoration but also was stocked with fish. Wealthy families had a number of servants and owned at least one dog and several cats. Girls played with dolls and often wore their hair in pigtails. Boys had their heads shaved, except for a braided lock on one side.

The Egyptians filled their tombs with items for use in the afterlife. These items included clothing, wigs, food, cosmetics, and jewelry. The tombs of rich Egyptians also had statues representing servants who would care for them in the next world. Scenes of daily life were painted on walls inside the tombs. The Egyptians believed that certain prayers said by priests would bring the scenes, as well as the dead, to life.

Many Egyptians bought texts containing prayers, hymns, spells, and other information to guide souls through the afterlife, protect them from evil, and provide for their needs. Egyptians had passages from such texts carved or written on walls inside their tombs or had a copy of a text placed in their tombs. Collections of these texts are known as the Book of the Dead.

Work of the people

Most of the workers in the fertile Nile Valley were farm laborers. Great harvests year after year helped make Egypt rich. Many other people made their living in manufacturing, mining, transportation, or trade.

The Egyptians did not use money. Instead, they traded goods or services directly for other goods or services. Under this *barter* system, workers were often paid in wheat and barley. They used any extra quantities they got to trade for needed goods.

Agriculture. Most farm laborers worked on the large estates of the royal family, the temples, or other wealthy landowners. They received small amounts of crops as pay, partly because landowners had to turn over a large percentage of all farm production in taxes. Some farmers were able to rent fields from rich landowners.

Ancient Egypt was a hot country in which almost no rain fell. But farmers grew crops most of the year by irrigating their land. They built canals that carried water from the Nile to their fields. Farmers used wooden plows pulled by oxen to prepare the fields for planting.

Wheat and barley were ancient Egypt's main crops. Other crops included lettuce, beans, onions, figs, dates, grapes, melons, and cucumbers. Parts of the date and grape crops were crushed to make wine. Many farmers grew flax, which was used to make linen. The Egyptians raised dairy and beef cattle, goats, ducks, sheep, geese, and donkeys. Some people kept bees for honey.

Manufacturing and mining. Craftsmen who operated small shops made most of the manufactured goods in ancient Egypt. The production of linen clothing and linen textiles ranked among the chief industries. Other important products included pottery, bricks, tools, glass, weapons, furniture, jewelry, and perfume. The Egyptians also made many products from plants, including rope, baskets, mats, and sheets of writing material.

Ancient Egypt had rich supplies of minerals. Miners produced large quantities of limestone, sandstone, and granite for the construction of pyramids and monuments. They also mined copper, gold, and such semiprecious gems as turquoise, amethyst, and malachite. Much of Egypt's gold came from the hills east of the Nile and from Nubia, a country south of Egypt.

Trade and transportation. Ancient Egyptian traders sailed to lands bordering the Aegean, Mediterranean, and Red seas. They acquired silver, horses, and cedar logs from Syria, Lebanon, and other areas of southwestern Asia. They got ivory, leopard skins, gold, cattle, and spices from Nubia. For these goods, the Egyptians bartered gold, other minerals, wheat, barley, papyrus sheets, and wine.

Transportation within ancient Egypt was chiefly by boats and barges on the Nile River. The earliest Egyptian boats were made of papyrus reeds. Moved by poles at first, they later were powered by rowers with oars. By about 3200 B.C., the Egyptians had invented sails and begun to rely on the wind for power. About 3000 B.C., they started to use wooden planks to build ships.

During ancient Egypt's early history, most people walked or rode donkeys when they traveled by land. Wealthy Egyptians were carried in special chairs. During the 1600's B.C., the Egyptians began to ride in horse-drawn chariots.

Crafts and professions. The royal family and the temples of ancient Egypt employed many skilled architects, engineers, carpenters, artists, and sculptors. They also hired bakers, butchers, teachers, scribes, accountants, musicians, butlers, and shoemakers. The Egyptians' belief that their bodies had to be preserved for the afterlife made embalming a highly skilled profession. Many Egyptians served in the army and navy. Others worked on cargo ships or fishing boats.

Arts and sciences

Architecture. Ancient Egypt's pyramids are the oldest and largest stone structures in the world. The ruins of about 90 pyramids still stand along the Nile. Three huge pyramids at Giza rank as one of the Seven Wonders of the Ancient World, a list of sights compiled by ancient travelers. The first Egyptian pyramids were built about 4,500 years ago. The largest one, the Great Pyramid at Giza, stands about 450 feet (140 meters) high. Its base covers about 13 acres (5 hectares). This pyramid was built with more than 2 million limestone blocks, each weighing an average of 2 ½ tons (2.3 metric tons).

The ancient Egyptians also built temples of limestone. They designed parts of the temples to resemble plants. For example, some temples had columns carved to look like palm trees or papyrus reeds. The temples had three main sections—a small shrine, a large hall with many columns, and an open courtyard.

Painting and sculpture. Many of ancient Egypt's finest paintings and other works of art were produced for tombs and temples. Artists covered the walls of tombs with bright, imaginative scenes of daily life and pictorial guides to the afterlife. The tomb paintings were not simply decorations. They reflected the Egyptians' belief that the scenes could come to life in the next world. The tomb owners therefore had themselves pictured not only as young and attractive but also in highly pleasant settings that they wished to enjoy in the afterlife.

Ancient Egyptian sculptors decorated temples with carvings showing festivals, military victories, and other important events. Sculptors also carved large stone sphinxes. These statues were supposed to represent Egyptian kings or gods and were used to guard temples and tombs. The Great Sphinx, for example, is believed to represent either King Khafre or the god Re-Harakhte. This magnificent statue has a human head and the body of a lion. It is 240 feet (73 meters) long and about 66 feet (20 meters) high. The Great Sphinx, which is near the Great Pyramid at Giza, was carved about 4,500 years ago. Sculptors also created small figures from wood, ivory, alabaster, bronze, gold, and turquoise. Favorite subjects for small sculptures included cats, which the Egyptians considered sacred and valued for protecting their grain supplies from mice.

Music and literature. The ancient Egyptians enjoyed music and singing. They used harps, lutes, and other string instruments to accompany their singing. Egyptian love songs were poetic and passionate.

Writers created many stories that featured imaginary characters, settings, or events and were clearly meant to entertain. Other writings included essays on good living called "Instructions."

Sciences. The ancient Egyptians made observations in the fields of astronomy and geography that helped them develop a calendar of 365 days a year. The calendar was based on the annual flooding of the Nile. The flooding began soon after the star Sirius reappeared on the eastern horizon after months of being hidden. This reappearance occurred about June 20 each year. The calendar enabled the Egyptians to date much of their history. Dated materials from ancient Egypt have helped scholars date events in other parts of the ancient world.

The ancient Egyptians could measure areas, volumes, distances, lengths, and weights. They used geometry to determine farm borders. Mathematics was based on a system of counting by tens, but the system had no zeros.

Ancient Egyptian doctors were the first physicians to study the human body scientifically. They studied human anatomy and knew that the pulse was in some way connected with the heart. They could set broken bones, care for wounds, and treat many illnesses. Some doctors specialized in a particular field of medicine, such as eye defects or stomach disorders.

Government

Kings ruled ancient Egypt throughout most of its history. Sometime between 1554 and 1304 B.C., the people began to call the king *pharaoh*. The word *pharaoh* comes from words that meant *great house* in Egyptian. The Egyptians believed that each of their kings was the god Horus in human form. This belief helped strengthen the authority of the kings.

The position of king was inherited. It passed to the eldest son of the king's chief wife. Many Egyptian kings had several other wives, called *lesser wives*, at the same time. Some chief wives gave birth to daughters but no sons, and several of those daughters claimed the right to the throne. At least four women became rulers.

Officials called *viziers* helped the king govern ancient Egypt. By the 1400's B.C., the king appointed two of them. One vizier administered the Nile Delta area, and

Religion of ancient Egypt

The ancient Egyptians worshiped many *deities* (gods and goddesses) and built huge temples to honor the major ones. The Egyptians also believed they would experience life after death in an *afterlife* and sometimes made elaborate preparations for death and burial. For example, the Egyptians *mummified* (embalmed and dried) corpses to prevent the bodies from decaying and to preserve them for the afterlife. The mummy was then wrapped in linen bandages, placed in a coffin, and put in a tomb.

WORLD BOOK illustration by Linden Artists Ltd.

Gigantic pyramids, built as tombs for Egyptian rulers, were used to hide the rulers' mummies and protect their souls. Some pyramids are about 4,500 years old.

Paintings inside tombs of many ancient Egyptians show the tomb owner as young and attractive in pleasant settings, *left.* The Egyptians believed certain prayers said by priests would bring the scenes, as well as the dead, to life in the next world.

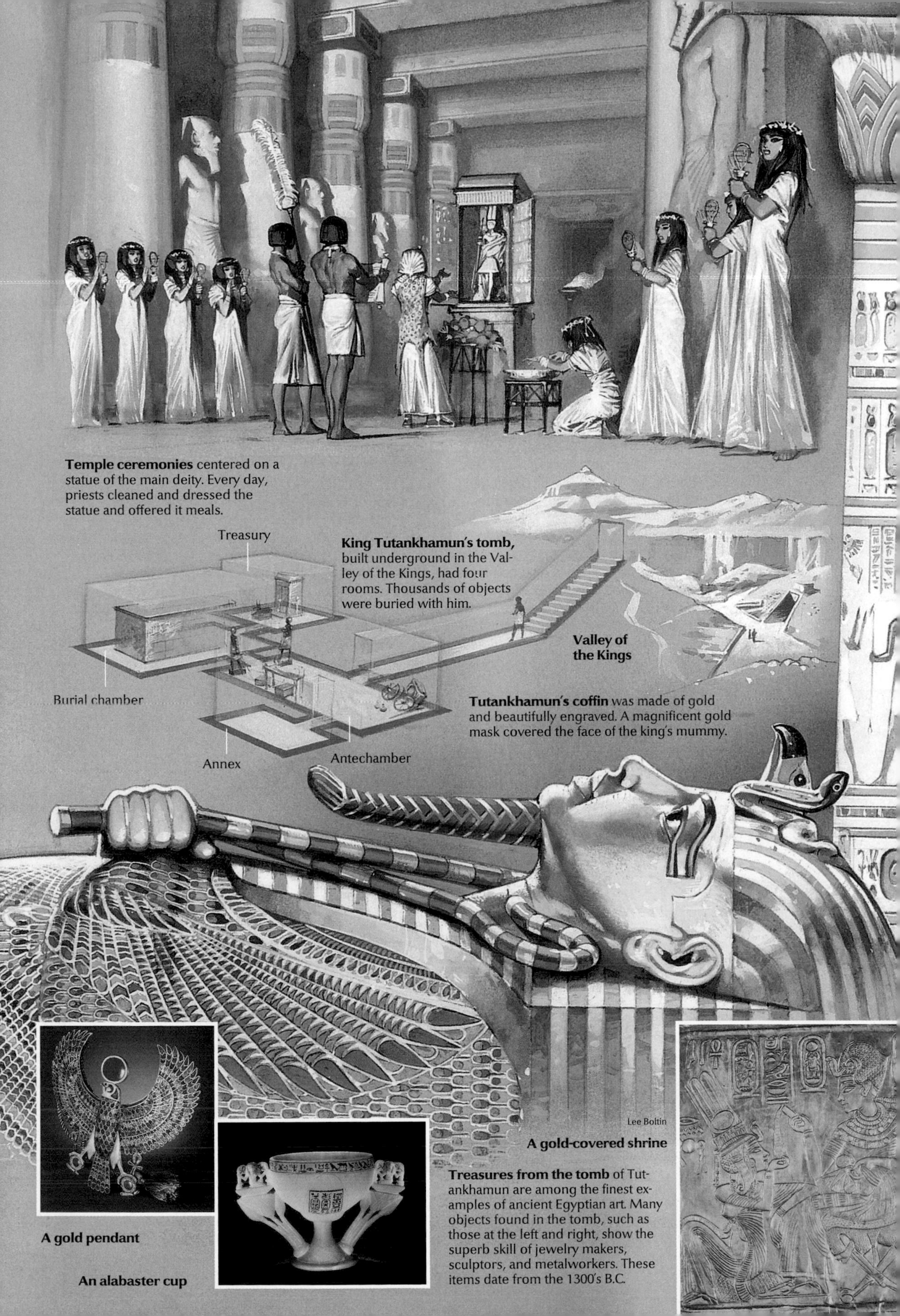

Temple ceremonies centered on a statue of the main deity. Every day, priests cleaned and dressed the statue and offered it meals.

King Tutankhamun's tomb, built underground in the Valley of the Kings, had four rooms. Thousands of objects were buried with him.

Tutankhamun's coffin was made of gold and beautifully engraved. A magnificent gold mask covered the face of the king's mummy.

A gold-covered shrine

Treasures from the tomb of Tutankhamun are among the finest examples of ancient Egyptian art. Many objects found in the tomb, such as those at the left and right, show the superb skill of jewelry makers, sculptors, and metalworkers. These items date from the 1300's B.C.

A gold pendant

An alabaster cup

the other one managed the region to the south. The viziers acted as mayors, tax collectors, and judges, and some even controlled temple treasuries. Other high officials included a treasurer and army commander. The government collected taxes from farmers in the form of crops. Skilled workers paid taxes in the goods or services they produced. The treasuries of kings and temples were thus actually warehouses consisting largely of crops and various manufactured goods. The government also levied a *corvée* (tax paid in the form of labor) to obtain troops and government workers.

For purposes of local government, ancient Egypt was divided into 42 provinces called *nomes*. The king appointed an official known as a *nomarch* to govern each province. There were courts in each nome and a high court in the capital. Viziers judged most cases. Kings decided cases involving crimes punishable by death.

In its early days, ancient Egypt had a small army of foot soldiers equipped with spears. During the 1500's B.C., Egypt built up a large army. The army included archers who were trained to shoot accurately while riding in fast-moving, horse-drawn chariots. Egypt had a large navy of long ships. These ships were powered chiefly by oarsmen, though most vessels also had sails.

History

Beginnings. The earliest known communities in ancient Egypt were villages established over 5,000 years ago. In time, the villages became part of two kingdoms. One of these kingdoms controlled the villages that lay on the Nile Delta, and the other controlled the villages south of the delta. The delta area was known as Lower Egypt. The southern region was called Upper Egypt.

Egyptian civilization began about 3100 B.C. According to tradition, King Menes of Upper Egypt conquered Lower Egypt around that time. He then united the country and formed the world's first national government. Menes founded Memphis as his capital near the site of present-day Cairo. He also established the first of 30 Egyptian *dynasties* (series of rulers in the same family).

The early dynastic period of ancient Egyptian history covered Dynasties I and II, which ruled for about 300 years. During this period, the kings built a temple to Ptah, the chief god of Memphis, and erected several palaces near the temple. The Egyptians also developed irrigation systems, invented ox-drawn plows, and started to develop a bureaucracy during the first two dynasties.

The Old Kingdom, which lasted from about 2650 to 2150 B.C., included Dynasties III through VIII. By the time Dynasty III began, Egypt had a strong central government. The Old Kingdom became known for the construction of Egypt's giant pyramids. This period is sometimes called the Pyramid Age.

The first known Egyptian pyramid was built for King Zoser at Saqqarah about 2650 B.C. The tomb rises about 200 feet (60 meters) in six giant steps and is called the Step Pyramid. During Dynasty IV, workers built the Great Pyramid and other pyramids at Giza. The Great Pyramid was built for King Khufu. Huge pyramids were built nearby for his son, King Khafre, and for King Menkaure. Farm laborers worked on the pyramids when floodwaters of the Nile covered their fields.

By Dynasty VI, the king's authority had begun to weaken as high priests and government officials fought for

Important dates in ancient Egypt's history

c. 3100 B.C. Egyptian civilization began with the union of Lower and Upper Egypt.

c. 2650-2150 B.C. The Old Kingdom was a period known for the construction of great pyramids.

c. 1938 B.C. King Amenemhet founded Dynasty XII, which greatly increased Egypt's power.

c. 1630 B.C. Hyksos rulers formed a dynasty that ruled Egypt for about 100 years.

1479-1425 B.C. The Egyptian empire reached its height during the reign of King Thutmose III.

Egyptian Museum, Cairo (Giraudon/Art Resource)

King Menes, *center,* was a legendary ruler who united Lower and Upper Egypt and set up the world's first national government.

© M. Timothy O'Keefe, Bruce Coleman Inc.

The first pyramid in ancient Egypt was built for King Zoser about 2650 B.C. It rises about 200 feet (60 meters) and is called the Step Pyramid.

© Shutterstock

King Thutmose III led military campaigns into southwestern Asia almost yearly for 20 years and brought Palestine and Syria into the Egyptian empire.

power. Dynasties VII through XI had weak rulers. Dynasties IX and X and the first half of Dynasty XI ruled during what is known as the *first intermediate period*. The capital was finally moved to Thebes.

The Middle Kingdom was the period that began in the last half of Dynasty XI and continued through Dynasty XIII or XIV. The Middle Kingdom began in the early 1900's B.C., when Mentuhotep II unified Egypt. Amenemhet I, a vizier in southern Egypt, began Dynasty XII around 1938 B.C., when he seized the throne and moved the capital to Itjtawy, near Memphis. Amenemhet and his strong successors, including Senusret I, Senusret III, and Amenemhet III, helped restore Egypt's wealth and power. During Dynasty XII, Egypt conquered Nubia and promoted trade with Palestine and Syria in southwestern Asia. The arts flourished under this dynasty.

Weak kings ruled Egypt toward the end of Dynasty XII. Settlers from Asia gradually invaded the Nile Delta, using horse-drawn chariots, improved bows, and other tools of war unknown to the native Egyptians. The invaders, called the Hyksos, seized control of Egypt about 1630 B.C., and their leaders founded Dynasty XV. The Middle Kingdom ended in the mid-1600's, but the Hyksos continued to dominate Egypt until 1520 B.C.

The New Kingdom was a period of nearly 500 years in which ancient Egypt became the world's strongest power. It began around 1539 B.C., with Dynasty XVIII. During this dynasty, native Egyptians drove the Hyksos forces out of Egypt, and Thebes regained its importance. Amun, a god worshiped mainly in Thebes, was increasingly identified with the god Re and called Amun-Re.

Egypt developed a permanent army that used horse-drawn chariots and other advanced military techniques introduced during the Hyksos period. The dynasty's early rulers led military forces into southwestern Asia. Thutmose I apparently reached the Euphrates River. Queen Hatshepsut, his daughter, also led armies in battle. Egypt developed a great empire and reached the height of its power in the 1400's B.C., under King Thutmose III. He led military campaigns into Asia almost yearly for 20 years and brought the eastern coast of the Mediterranean Sea into the Egyptian empire. Thutmose also reestablished Egyptian control over Kush and surrounding Nubia, which were valuable sources of slaves, copper, gold, ivory, and ebony. As a result of these victories, Egypt became the strongest and wealthiest nation in the world.

The course of Egyptian history changed unexpectedly after Amenhotep IV came to the throne in 1353 B.C. He devoted himself to a sun god called the Aten, represented as the disk of the sun. Amenhotep changed his own name to Akhenaten and declared that the Aten had replaced Amun and all other gods except Re. He believed that Re was part of the sunlight that came from the Aten. The king also moved the capital to a new city, Akhetaten, about 175 miles (280 kilometers) north of Thebes. Ruins of the city lie near what is now Tell el Amarna. Akhenaten's religious reforms, known as the Amarna Revolution, led to an outpouring of art and sculpture that glorified the Aten. But the changes angered many Egyptians.

Akhenaten's immediate successors ended the unrest. King Tutankhaten removed *-aten* from his name and became Tutankhamun. He restored the old state religion, allowing the worship of the old deities as well as the Aten. Horemheb, the last Dynasty XVIII king, completely

Akhenaten became king of Egypt and introduced major religious reforms.

Alexander the Great added Egypt to his empire.

Muslims from Arabia seized Alexandria and completed their conquest of Egypt.

1353 B.C. — c. 1075 B.C. — 332 B.C. — 31 B.C. — A.D. 642

Dynasty XX ended, and Egypt began to decline rapidly as a strong nation.

A Roman fleet crushed an Egyptian force in the Battle of Actium, leading to Rome's take-over of Egypt in 30 B.C.

© Erich Lessing, Magnum

King Akhenaten, *left,* started the Amarna Revolution during the 1300's B.C. He urged the Egyptians to worship a sun god called the Aten.

Detail of a mosaic *Alexander the Great at the Battle of Isso* (150 B.C.); National Archaeological Museum, Naples, Italy (SCALA/Art Resource)

Alexander the Great, king of Macedonia, ended Persia's control of Egypt. Ptolemy, one of Alexander's generals, later founded a dynasty in Egypt.

Portrait on a Roman coin (32 B.C.) (WORLD BOOK photo by James Simek)

Queen Cleopatra VII was the last ruler of Egypt's Ptolemaic dynasty. After she died in 30 B.C., Egypt became a province of Rome.

http://bit.ly/11TWulU

rejected Akhenaten's religious beliefs. Dynasty XIX kings built temples to many gods throughout Egypt. Two of the kings, Seti I and his son, Ramses II, regained Asian territories lost after the reign of Thutmose III.

Ancient Egypt began to decline during Dynasty XX. Bitter struggles for power by priests and nobles broke the country into small states. Egypt lost its territories abroad, and its weakness attracted a series of invaders.

The periods of foreign control. Ancient Egypt's decline accelerated rapidly after about 1075 B.C., when Dynasty XX ended. During the next 750 years, 10 dynasties ruled Egypt. Most of them were formed by Nubian, Assyrian, and Persian rulers. In 332 B.C., the Macedonian conqueror Alexander the Great added Egypt to his empire. In 331 B.C., Alexander founded the city of Alexandria in the delta.

The Ptolemies. Alexander died in 323 B.C., and his generals divided his empire. Ptolemy, one of the generals, gained control of Egypt. About 305 B.C., he took the title of king and founded a dynasty known as the Ptolemaic dynasty. The dynasty's rulers spread Greek culture in Egypt. They also built temples to Egyptian gods, developed Egypt's natural resources, and increased foreign trade. Alexandria became Egypt's capital, and its magnificent library and museum helped make the city one of the greatest cultural centers of ancient times.

Roman rule. Queen Cleopatra VII of the Ptolemies probably married Mark Antony, a co-ruler of Rome, in 37 B.C. Antony and his rival co-ruler, Octavian, each wanted to rule the vast Roman lands by himself. In 32 B.C., Antony combined his and Cleopatra's military forces to fight those of Octavian. The navy of Antony and Cleopatra lost the vital Battle of Actium to Octavian's fleet in 31 B.C. The couple committed suicide in 30 B.C., and Octavian made Egypt a Roman province. Rome's control of Egypt gradually weakened after A.D. 395, when the Roman Empire split into eastern and western parts. By A.D. 642, Arab Muslims had conquered Egypt. For the story of Egypt after 642, see **Egypt** (History).

Learning about ancient Egypt

The study of ancient Egypt is called Egyptology. Experts in the field are Egyptologists. Much of their knowledge comes from studying the architecture and other arts of ancient Egypt. Ruins of magnificent temples stand at Abydos, Kom Ombo, Edfu, Esna, Luxor, and Karnak. Excavations of pharaohs' tombs, such as those in a burial ground called the Valley of the Kings, near Luxor, have yielded superb paintings. Tutankhamun's tomb was filled with stunning examples of the ancient Egyptians' skill in woodworking and metalworking.

Information about ancient Egypt also comes from written records made by the Egyptians themselves and by such ancient Greek writers as Herodotus and Strabo. The Egyptians used hieroglyphics until sometime after they came under Roman rule. The ability of anyone to read Egyptian hieroglyphics was then quickly lost.

For over 1,000 years, scholars tried but failed to decipher the writing system of ancient Egypt. Then, in 1799, a rock slab with ancient Greek and Egyptian writing was found outside Rosetta, a city near Alexandria. A French scholar named Jean François Champollion began to compare the Greek and Egyptian words on the so-called Rosetta stone. By 1822, he had deciphered the hieroglyphics. Dictionaries developed since then have helped scholars translate the writings on many monuments and in temples and tombs. Salima Ikram

Related articles in *World Book* include:

Biographies

Akhenaten
Alexander the Great
Cleopatra
Hatshepsut
Hypatia
Imhotep
Khufu
Nefertiti
Ptolemy I
Ramses II
Seti I
Thutmose III
Tutankhamun

Contributions to civilization

Architecture (Egyptian)
Book (Early books)
Bread (History)
Calendar
Clothing (Egypt)
Furniture (Ancient Egypt)
Geometry (History)
Glass (History of glass)
Hieroglyphics
Mythology (Egyptian mythology)
Obelisk
Painting (Egyptian painting)
Papyrus
Pyramids
Science (picture: A knowledge of geometry)
Sculpture (Beginnings)
Ship (Egyptian ships)
Sphinx
Surveying
Textile (History)

Gods and goddesses

Amun
Anubis
Horus
Isis
Osiris
Re
Serapis
Seth
Thoth

Other related articles

Abu Simbel, Temples of
Agriculture (picture)
Alexandria
Animal worship
Asp
Cat (History)
Cleopatra's Needles
Copts
Hyksos
Kush
Lotus
Memphis
Mummy
Nile River
Nubia
Pharaoh
Rosetta stone
Scarab
Thebes (Egypt)
Valley of the Kings

Outline

I. The Egyptian world
A. The land
B. The people
II. Life of the people
A. Family life
B. Education
C. Food, clothing, and shelter
D. Recreation
III. Religion
A. Gods and goddesses
B. The afterlife
IV. Work of the people
A. Agriculture
B. Manufacturing and mining
C. Trade and transportation
D. Crafts and professions
V. Arts and sciences
A. Architecture
B. Painting and sculpture
C. Music and literature
D. Sciences
VI. Government
VII. History
VIII. Learning about ancient Egypt

Additional resources

Level I
Fletcher, Joann. *Exploring the Life, Myth, and Art of Ancient Egypt.* Rosen Pub., 2010.
Macdonald, Fiona. *Egyptians.* Sea-to-Sea Pubns., 2011.
Platt, Richard. *The Egyptians.* Sea-to-Sea Pubns., 2011.
Smith, Miranda. *Ancient Egypt.* Kingfisher, 2010.

Level II
Bierbrier, Morris L. *Historical Dictionary of Ancient Egypt.* 2nd ed. Scarecrow, 2008.

Wendrich, Willeke. *Egyptian Archaeology.* 5th ed. Wiley-Blackwell, 2010.
Wilkinson, Toby A. H. *Lives of the Ancient Egyptians.* Thames & Hudson, 2007. *The Rise and Fall of Ancient Egypt.* Random Hse., 2010.

Egyptology. See Egypt, **Ancient** (Learning about ancient Egypt).

Ehrlich, *AYR lihk,* **Paul** (1854-1915), a German bacteriologist, founded chemotherapy and showed that certain dye injections cure certain tropical diseases. He discovered the compound Salvarsan (arsphenamine), a remedy for syphilis, which he described in 1910. Salvarsan is also called "606" because it was the 606th compound that Ehrlich tested.

With the German physician Robert Koch, Ehrlich contributed to our knowledge of the tuberculosis germ. Ehrlich founded modern hematology by developing techniques for staining the various types of blood corpuscles. He also worked at increasing immunity to disease, including the development of diphtheria antitoxin.

Ehrlich developed methods of research on cancerous tissues. In addition, he produced strains of cancerous tumors that are still used in experiments with cancer-fighting substances. Ehrlich shared the 1908 Nobel Prize in physiology or medicine for his research on the potency of serum preparations. Ehrlich was born on March 14, 1854, in Strehlen, Silesia, near Wrocław. He died on Aug. 20, 1915. Audrey B. Davis

Ehrlich, *AYR lihk,* **Paul Ralph** (1932-), an American biologist, is a leader of the international movement for population control. In his book *The Population Bomb* (1968), Ehrlich claimed that the world's population was growing faster than its food supply. He warned that hundreds of millions of people would starve to death as a result of overpopulation.

Many scientists criticized some of Ehrlich's statements as exaggerations. Although he agrees that other factors are involved, Ehrlich continues to stress that overpopulation is the most important cause of hunger and environmental problems.

In 1968, Ehrlich helped form an organization called Zero Population Growth (now Population Connection). This group urges every family to have no more than two children. His other books include *Biology and Society* (1976), *Human Natures* (2002), and *One with Nineveh* (2004). Ehrlich was born on May 29, 1932, in Philadelphia.

Sheldon M. Novick

Eichmann, Adolf (1906-1962), was a lieutenant colonel in the Nazi secret police in Germany. He was convicted and executed for his part in killing about 6 million Jews during World War II (1939-1945). This state-sponsored campaign of murder became known as the Holocaust.

Eichmann directed the deportation to concentration camps of Jews from Germany and the occupied countries. After the war, he escaped to Argentina and lived there under an assumed name.

Israeli agents seized Eichmann in May 1960 and took him to Israel for trial on charges of war crimes, crimes against the Jewish people, and crimes against humanity. An Israeli court sentenced Eichmann to death in December 1961 after a trial that lasted several months. He was hanged on May 31, 1962. Eichmann was born on March 19, 1906, in Solingen, Germany.

Donald M. McKale

Eid. See **`Īd al-Aḍ-hā; `Īd al-Fiṭr.**

Eider duck, *EYE duhr,* is any of a group of ducks known for their soft, warm down feathers. Eider down is a light, highly efficient insulating material. People use it to make pillows, bedding, and coats. It grows under the duck's outer feathers and is collected from nests in the early summer. Eider ducks live in northern coastal areas of North America, Europe, and Asia. Adult males have spectacular colors and patterns on the head. Females are dark brown with brown and black streaks.

The *common eider* is the most abundant eider duck. In North America, it lives on coasts from New England north and across the Arctic to Alaska. The common eider can weigh up to 5 ½ pounds (2.5 kilograms). The female typically lays three or four greenish eggs.

Rodger D. Titman

Scientific classification. Eider ducks belong to the family Anatidae. The common eider is *Somateria mollissima.*

See also **Duck** (Sea ducks).

Eielson, *EYE uhl suhn,* **Carl Ben** (1897-1929), an American aviator and explorer, piloted the first airplane to cross the Arctic Ocean. Eielson made the flight in April 1928 with the Australian explorer Hubert Wilkins, who organized the expedition. The pair flew 2,200 miles (3,540 kilometers) from Point Barrow, Alaska, to Spitsbergen, an island in the Arctic Ocean. In December 1928, Eielson and Wilkins made the first air explorations of Antarctica. They charted several unknown islands.

Eielson was born on July 20, 1897, in Hatton, North Dakota. He became a pilot in the United States Army Air Service in 1918. Eielson went to Fairbanks, Alaska, to work as a high school teacher. He founded a commercial air service in Fairbanks in 1923. Eielson died in a plane crash in Siberia on Nov. 9, 1929, while on a rescue mission. Tom D. Crouch

Eiffel, *EYE fuhl,* **Gustave,** *goos TAV* (1832-1923), a French structural engineer, built the 984-foot (300-meter) Eiffel Tower in Paris for a world's fair in 1889. He was a leading bridge designer. His notable bridges include the wrought-iron bridge at Porto, Portugal, and the Garabit viaduct in southern France. Eiffel also designed many other iron structures, including the framework for the Statue of Liberty.

Eiffel was born on Dec. 15, 1832, in Dijon, France. He died on Dec. 27, 1923.

Terry S. Reynolds

Eiffel Tower, *EYE fuhl,* is the most famous landmark in Paris. It was erected as the symbol of a world's fair called the Universal Exposition of 1889. The tower was the world's tallest structure then, rising 984 feet (300 meters)

© Vinicius Tupinamba, Shutterstock
Eiffel Tower

above the fairgrounds. Gustave Eiffel, a structural engineer, built the tower to show how steel and iron could be used to erect tall structures. He was responsible for financing the tower's construction, which cost over $1 million. About 2 million people visited the tower in the first year. The fees they paid covered the building costs.

The Eiffel Tower stands in a park called the Champ de Mars, near the Seine River. The building includes observation decks and restaurants. J. William Rudd

See also **Paris** (picture: The sights of Paris).

Eighteenth Amendment. See **Constitution of the United States** (Amendment 18); **Volstead Act**.

Eikon. See **Icon**.

Eilat. See Elat.

Einstein, Albert (1879-1955), was the most important physicist of the 1900's and one of the greatest and most famous scientists of all time. He was a *theoretical physicist,* a scientist who creates and develops theories of matter and energy. Einstein's greatness arose from the fact that his theories solved fundamental problems and presented new ideas. Much of his fame came from the fact that several of those ideas were strange and hard to understand—but proved true.

Some of Einstein's most famous ideas make up parts of his *special theory of relativity* and his *general theory of relativity.* For example, the special theory describes an entity known as *space-time.* This entity is a combination of the dimension of time and the three dimensions of space—length, width, and height. Thus, space-time is four-dimensional. In the general theory, matter and energy *distort* (change the shape of) space-time; the distortion is experienced as gravity.

Einstein also became known for his support of political and social causes. Those included *pacifism,* a general opposition to warfare; *Zionism,* a movement to establish a Jewish homeland in Palestine; and *socialism,* a political system in which the means of production would be owned by society and production would be planned to match the needs of the community.

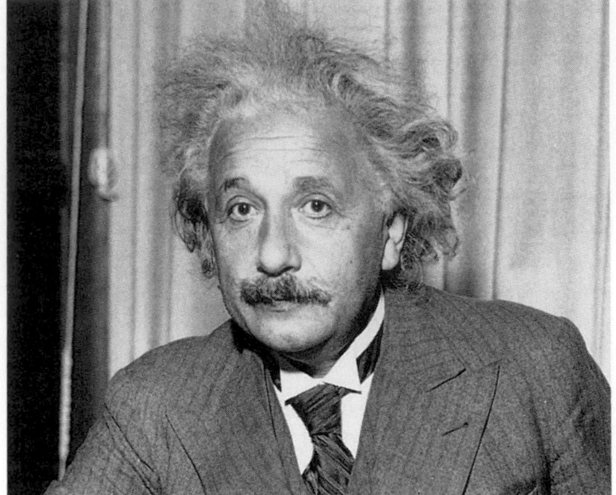

© Hulton/Archive

Albert Einstein was one of the greatest scientists of all time.

Early years

Einstein was born on March 14, 1879, in Ulm, in southern Germany, the son of Hermann Einstein and Pauline Koch Einstein. The next year, Hermann moved the family about 70 miles (110 kilometers) to Munich.

Albert Einstein's younger sister, Maria—whom he called Maja (pronounced *MAH yah*)—recalled that Einstein was slow to learn to speak. But even as a young child, he displayed the powers of concentration for which he became famous.

Einstein recalled seeing the seemingly miraculous behavior of a magnetic compass when he was about 5 years old. The fact that invisible forces acted on the compass needle made a deep impression on the boy.

A booklet on Euclidean geometry made a comparable impression on Einstein when he was about 12 years old. Euclidean geometry is based on a small number of simple, *self-evident* (obviously true) statements about geometric figures. Mathematicians use those statements to *deduce* (develop by reasoning) other statements, many of which are complex and far from self-evident. Einstein was impressed that geometric statements that are not self-evident could be proved clearly and with certainty.

Education. Einstein began to take violin lessons when he was 6 years old. He eventually became an accomplished violinist, and he played the instrument throughout his life.

At the age of 9, Einstein entered the Luitpold Gymnasium, a distinguished secondary school in Munich. He enjoyed some of his classes and performed well, but he disliked the strict discipline. As a result, he dropped out at age 15 to follow his parents to Pavia, Italy, near Milan.

Einstein finished high school in 1896, in Aarau, Switzerland. He then entered a school in Zurich, Switzerland, that ranked as one of Europe's finest institutions of higher learning in science. The school is known as the Swiss Federal Institute of Technology Zurich or the ETH Zurich, from the initials for *Federal Institute of Technology* in German. While at the ETH, Einstein met and fell in love with Mileva Maric. Mileva was a physics student from Novi Sad, in what is now Serbia.

Einstein often skipped class, relying on the notes of others. He spent his free time in the library reading the latest books and physics journals. Einstein's behavior annoyed Heinrich F. Weber, the professor who supervised his course work. Although professors customarily helped their students obtain university positions, when Einstein neared graduation, Weber did not help him get a university post. Instead, a friend helped him find a job as a clerk in the Swiss Federal Patent Office in Bern. He became a Swiss citizen in 1901.

First marriage. Meanwhile, Mileva had become pregnant. Albert and Mileva's child, a daughter they named Lieserl, was born in January 1902 at the home of Mileva's parents. In January 1903, Albert and Mileva married. They had two more children, Hans Albert in 1904 and Eduard in 1910. However, Lieserl never joined them in Bern, and her fate remains a mystery.

Famous theories. Einstein worked at the patent office from 1902 to 1909. Those years were among his most productive. His job reviewing patent applications left him with much time for physics. In 1905, he obtained a Ph.D. degree in physics by submitting a *dissertation* (a long, formal paper) to the University of Zurich. He had already completed the necessary classwork at the ETH.

The year 1905 is known as Einstein's *annus mirabilis*—Latin for *year of marvels.* In that year, the German scientific periodical the *Annalen der Physik (Annals of Physics)* published three of his papers that were among the most revolutionary in the history of science.

The photoelectric effect. The first paper, published in March 1905, deals with the *photoelectric effect.* By means of that effect, a beam of light can cause metal atoms to release subatomic particles called *electrons.* In a photoelectric device, these freed electrons flow as electric current, so the device produces a current when light shines on it.

Einstein explained that the photoelectric effect occurs because light comes in "chunks" of energy called *quanta.* The singular of *quanta* is *quantum.* A quantum of light is now known as a *photon.* An atom can absorb a photon. If the photon has enough energy, an electron will leave its atom. Einstein received the 1921 Nobel Prize in physics for his paper on the photoelectric effect.

The principle that light comes in quanta is a part of an area of physics known as *quantum mechanics.* Quantum mechanics is one of the "foundation blocks" of modern physics; Einstein's relativity theories are two others.

Brownian motion. The second paper, published in May 1905, explained *Brownian motion,* an irregular movement of microscopic particles suspended in a liquid or a gas. Such motion was named for Scottish botanist Robert Brown, who first observed it in 1827. Einstein's analysis stimulated research on Brownian motion that yielded the first experimental proof that atoms exist.

The special theory of relativity. The third paper, published in June, presented the special theory of relativity. In that paper, titled "On the Electrodynamics of Moving Bodies," Einstein made a remarkable statement about light. He said that constant motion does not affect the *velocity* (speed in a particular direction) of light.

Albert Einstein Archives from the Hebrew University of Jerusalem, Israel

Einstein and his first wife, Mileva, were photographed with their son Hans Albert Einstein in 1904. Albert and Mileva met in college, where they both studied physics. They divorced in 1919.

Albert Einstein Archives from the Hebrew University of Jerusalem, Israel

Albert Einstein and his younger sister, Maria, were especially close throughout their lives. Albert was 14 years old when this picture was taken with Maria, whom he called Maja.

Imagine, for example, that you are on a railroad car traveling on a straight track at a constant speed of one-third the speed of light. You flash a light from the back of the car to the front of the car. You precisely measure the speed of the light. You find that the speed is 186,282 miles (299,792 kilometers) per second—represented by the letter c in scientific equations. A friend standing on the ground also measures the speed of the light.

You might expect your friend's result to be $c + \frac{1}{3}c$. That would be a "common-sense" result consistent with ordinary experience with the velocities of material objects. For example, a ball thrown forward inside a railroad car would have a velocity—as measured by an observer on the ground—equal to the velocity of the car plus the velocity of the ball as measured in the car. But, strangely, in the case of the light beam, your friend's answer turns out to be the same as yours: c.

The strange fact that the velocity of light is constant has even stranger results. For example, a clock can appear to one observer to be running at a given rate, yet seem to another observer to run at a different rate. Two observers can measure the length of the same rod correctly but obtain different results.

Einstein also said that c is a universal "speed limit." No physical process can spread through space at a velocity higher than c. No material body can reach a velocity of c.

Interchangeability of mass and energy. In a fourth paper, published in September 1905, Einstein discussed a result of the special theory of relativity—that energy and *mass* are interchangeable.

Mass is a measure of an object's *inertia,* its resistance to a change in its motion. Due to inertia, an object at rest tends to remain at rest. A moving object tends to maintain its velocity. In addition, an object's weight is proportional to its mass; more massive objects weigh more.

Einstein's paper contains an equation that has become famous: $E = mc^2$. The equation says that a body's energy, *E,* equals the body's mass, *m,* times the speed of light, *c, squared* (multiplied by itself). The speed of light is so high that the conversion of a tiny quantity of mass releases a tremendous amount of energy.

The conversion of mass creates energy in the sun and other stars. It also produces the heat energy that is converted to electric energy in nuclear power plants. In addition, mass-to-energy conversion is responsible for the tremendous destructive force of nuclear weapons.

Middle years

Academic appointments. By 1909, Einstein was famous within the physics community. That year, he accepted his first regular academic appointment, as an associate professor of theoretical physics at the University of Zurich. In 1911, he became a professor at the German University in Prague, Austria-Hungary (now Charles University in the Czech Republic). In 1912, he returned to the ETH as a professor.

Einstein moved to Berlin in 1914 to become a member of the Prussian Academy of Sciences, a professor at the University of Berlin, and the director of the Kaiser Wilhelm Institute for Physics, a research center then in the planning stage. He headed the institute until 1933. After World War II (1939-1945), the institute was renamed the Max Planck Institute (MPI) for Physics. Several other MPI's for various branches of physics and for other fields of study were later founded.

Second marriage. Mileva went with Albert to Berlin in March 1914 but returned to Zurich in June. Their marriage had become unhappy; and, in 1919, Albert divorced Mileva and married his cousin Elsa Einstein Löwenthal. Einstein's sons stayed in Zurich with Mileva, and Albert adopted Elsa's daughters, Ilse and Margot.

The general theory of relativity. In 1916, the *Annalen der Physik* published Einstein's paper on the general theory of relativity. This paper soon made Einstein world-famous. He suggested that astronomers could confirm the theory by observing the sun's gravitation bending light rays. During a solar eclipse in 1919, the British astronomer Arthur S. Eddington detected the bending aside of starlight by the sun's gravitational field. His observation supported Einstein's theory.

In his theory, Einstein also showed that gravity affects time—the presence of a strong gravitational field makes clocks run more slowly than normal. In addition, equations in the general theory are the basis of descriptions of *black holes.* A black hole is a region of space whose gravitational force is so strong that nothing can escape from it. It is invisible because it traps even light.

Attacks on Einstein. Einstein's world fame came at a price. Einstein was of Jewish descent, and *anti-Semitism* (prejudice against Jews) was increasing in Germany. The physicist and his theories became targets of anti-Semitic verbal attacks. Following the 1922 murder of German foreign minister Walther Rathenau, a Jew, Einstein temporarily left Germany. He visited Palestine and a number of other Asian countries, Spain, and South America.

World travel. Threats of danger did not prevent Einstein from using his fame to promote causes dear to his heart. He took his first trip to the United States in 1921. The main purpose of the trip was not to lecture on physics but to raise money for a planned Hebrew University of Jerusalem. In July 1923, he traveled to Sweden to accept the Nobel Prize in physics that had been awarded to him in 1921.

Further scientific work. After creating the general theory of relativity, Einstein worked on a *unified field theory* that was to include all electric, magnetic, and gravitational phenomena. Such a theory would provide a single description of the physical universe, rather than separate descriptions for gravitation and other phenomena. Einstein worked on the theory for the rest of his life but never finished it; to this day, no one has developed a fully successful unified field theory.

Through the mid-1920's, Einstein was a major contributor to the development of quantum mechanics. By the late 1920's, however, he had begun to doubt the theory.

One reason for Einstein's doubt was that parts of quantum mechanics did not seem to be *deterministic.* Determinism states that strict laws involving causes and effects govern all events. As an example of apparent nondeterminism in quantum mechanics, consider an atom that absorbs a photon, thus becoming more energetic. At a later moment, the atom reduces its energy level by releasing a photon. But a physicist cannot use quantum mechanics to predict the moment of release.

In 1926, Einstein wrote a famous letter to the German physicist Max Born expressing his doubts about quantum mechanics. Einstein wrote, "The theory produces a good deal but hardly brings us closer to the secret of the Old One [by which Einstein meant God]. I am at all events convinced that *He* does not play dice."

In 1936, Einstein and the German physicists Boris Podolsky and Nathan Rosen published an article, which became known as the "EPR paper," arguing that quantum mechanics is not a complete theory. The EPR paper and a reply from the Danish physicist Neils Bohr became the basis for a scientific debate that continues to this day.

Einstein played the violin in a trio on board ship in the 1930's on his way to the United States. Einstein took his first violin lesson when he was 6 years old, and he played throughout his life.

© Hulton/Archive

Einstein did research at the Institute for Advanced Study in Princeton, New Jersey, from 1933 until his death in 1955. He is shown here reading at nearby Princeton University in 1953.

Later years

Einstein in the United States. In December 1930, Einstein traveled to the United States. His trip was the first of what were meant to be annual visits to lecture at the California Institute of Technology. But in January 1933, during Einstein's third trip, the Nazi Party seized power in Germany. The Nazis had an official policy of anti-Semitism, and so Einstein never set foot in Germany again. He returned to Europe in March 1933, staying in Belgium under the protection of that country's royal family. He then went to England.

In September 1933, Einstein sailed to the United States to work at the Institute for Advanced Study, an independent community of scholars and scientists doing advanced research and study. The institute had recently been established in Princeton, New Jersey, which would be Einstein's home for the rest of his life. Einstein became a United States citizen in October 1940.

Letter to President Roosevelt. Einstein undertook one of his most important acts in the summer of 1939, shortly before the outbreak of World War II. At the urging, and with the help, of the Hungarian refugee physicist Leo Szilard, Einstein wrote a letter to President Franklin D. Roosevelt. The letter warned that German scientists might be working on an atomic bomb. The letter led to the establishment of the Manhattan Project, which produced the first atomic bomb in 1945.

Continuing fame. After World War II, Einstein labored tirelessly for international controls on atomic energy. He had a wide circle of professional acquaintances and friends, and he was still a world figure. In 1952, he was offered the presidency of Israel—the modern state of Israel had existed only since 1948—but he declined.

Final days. By the early 1950's, Einstein's immediate family had dwindled. His son Eduard had been confined to a mental institution in Zurich for years, suffering from schizophrenia. Einstein's first and second wives, his stepdaughter Ilse, and his sister Maja, to whom he had been especially close, had died. His son Hans Albert was a professor of civil engineering at the University of California in Berkeley. Of the people emotionally close to Albert Einstein, only his stepdaughter Margot and Helen Dukas, his secretary since 1928, remained with him.

Einstein signed his last letter one week before his death. In the letter, to the British philosopher and mathematician Bertrand Russell, Einstein agreed to include his name on a document urging all nations to give up nuclear weapons. Einstein died in Princeton on April 18, 1955. Don Howard

Related articles in *World Book* include:

Dark energy
$E=mc^2$
Gravitation (Einstein's theory of gravitation)
Manhattan Project
Motion (Einstein's theories of relativity)
Nuclear weapon
Photoelectric effect
Quantum field theory
Quantum mechanics
Relativity

Additional resources

Isaacson, Walter. *Einstein: His Life and Universe.* Simon & Schuster, 2007.
Krull, Kathleen. *Albert Einstein.* Viking, 2009. Younger readers.
Neffe, Jürgen. *Einstein: A Biography.* Farrar, 2007.

Einsteinium is an artificially created radioactive element. Its chemical symbol is Es, and its *atomic number* (number of protons in its nucleus) is 99. Einsteinium has 17 known *isotopes,* forms with the same number of protons but different numbers of neutrons. The most stable isotope has an *atomic mass number* (total number of protons and neutrons) of 252. That isotope has a *half-life* of 472 days—that is, due to radioactive decay, only half the atoms in a sample of isotope 252 would still be atoms of that isotope after 472 days.

Scientists at the University of California, the Argonne National Laboratory, and the Los Alamos National Laboratory named this element for the scientist Albert Einstein. Einsteinium was discovered in 1952 in the debris from a hydrogen bomb explosion. Scientists collected the debris on filter papers carried by radio-controlled airplanes and from fallout on a nearby coral atoll.

Scientists first produced einsteinium in laboratory experiments in 1954. Today, one isotope of einsteinium, with mass number 253 and a half-life of 20 days, is produced in small amounts in nuclear reactors. Einsteinium compounds have also been prepared. Richard L. Hahn

See also **Element, Chemical; Fermium; Transuranium element.**

Einthoven, Willem (1860-1927), a Dutch physiologist, founded electrocardiography. In 1903, he invented the *string galvanometer,* which records variations of electric current. With his galvanometer, he was able to record the minute electrical impulse that travels through the heart with every beat. Modern electrocardiography is the direct outcome of papers published by Einthoven in 1907 and 1908 (see **Electrocardiograph**).

From 1908 to 1913, Einthoven studied the normal electric currents of the heart and so provided the basis for understanding abnormal electric heart currents. Einthoven received the 1924 Nobel Prize in physiology or medicine for his discovery of the way electrocardiography works. He was elected to foreign membership in the British Royal Society in 1926.

Einthoven was born on May 21, 1860, in Semarang, Java. His family moved to the Netherlands in 1870. He studied at Utrecht University and became professor of physiology at Leiden University at 25. Einthoven died on Sept. 28, 1927. Dale C. Smith

Éire. See **Ireland.**

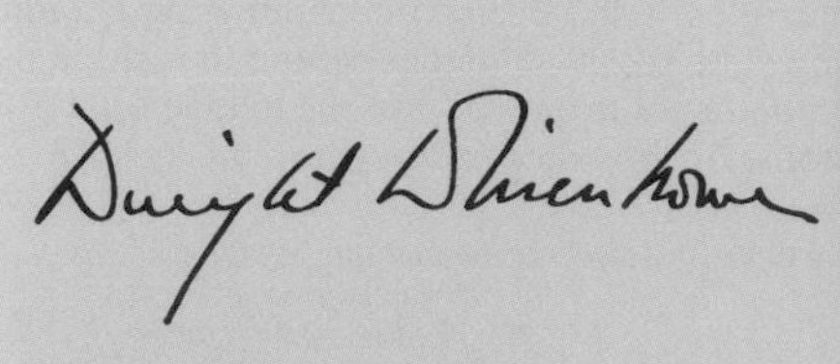

34th president of the United States 1953-1961

Truman
33rd president
1945-1953
Democrat

Eisenhower
34th president
1953-1961
Republican

Kennedy
35th president
1961-1963
Democrat

Richard M. Nixon
Vice president
1953-1961

Karsh, Ottawa

Eisenhower, Dwight David (1890-1969), leader of the victorious Allied forces in Europe in World War II, rode a wave of popularity as a war hero to become president of the United States. Eisenhower had more than 30 years of military experience when he was elected chief executive in 1952, but he was remarkably unmilitary as president. Good leadership, he believed, was not a matter of issuing orders and enforcing obedience. Instead, an effective leader inspired others to cooperate and to use their own talents to the fullest.

Eisenhower was an organized, thoughtful, and patient executive. People throughout the world loved the tall, baldheaded man they fondly called "Ike." His broad grin and friendly manner could put almost anyone at ease.

As president, Eisenhower faced many hard decisions. At home, fear of Communist influence in government led to widespread loyalty investigations. New civil rights issues aroused bitter disputes. In foreign affairs, Communist threats in Asia, Africa, and Latin America caused a series of crises. Eisenhower made little progress in reducing international tensions, yet the soldier in the White House helped keep the world at peace.

Early life

Boyhood. David Dwight Eisenhower—who was always called Dwight David—was born on Oct. 14, 1890, in Denison, Texas. His parents were David Jacob Eisenhower and Ida Stover Eisenhower, a deeply religious couple who belonged to a Protestant sect called the River Brethren. Dwight had two older brothers, Arthur (1886-1958) and Edgar (1889-1971), and three younger ones—Roy (1892-1942), Earl (1898-1968), and Milton (1899-1985). Another brother died as an infant. Dwight's parents were descended from German and Swiss immigrants who had come to Pennsylvania in the 1700's.

When Dwight was still a baby, his family moved to Abilene, Kansas. Dwight's father worked in a creamery. The sons raised and sold vegetables and found a variety of other jobs to contribute to household expenses.

Dwight was popular with his classmates, who gave him the nickname "Little Ike" to distinguish him from "Big Ike," his brother Edgar. Both Dwight and Edgar impressed their fellow students. Predictions that appeared in their high school yearbook saw Dwight becoming a history professor and Edgar, interestingly, president of the United States.

West Point cadet. After high school, Dwight worked full-time at the creamery and helped pay Edgar's first-year college expenses. Dwight had no prospects for his own higher education until a friend persuaded him to apply to the national military academies, where tuition is free. Senator Joseph Bristow of Kansas got Eisenhower an appointment to the U.S. Military Academy at West Point, New York. Although Eisenhower chose the career of a soldier, he respected his parents' opposition to war. He considered military service an opportunity for learning and discipline.

Eisenhower played on the football team at West Point. But a knee injury ended his hopes of being a star halfback and forced him to quit the team. In 1915, Eisenhower graduated 61st in a class of 164. The Army assigned the new second lieutenant to Fort Sam Houston, near San Antonio, Texas.

Eisenhower the soldier

Eisenhower's family. While off duty at Fort Sam Houston, Eisenhower coached sports teams. He also met Mamie Geneva Doud (1896-1979), a visitor from Denver, and started to take her to social gatherings at the base. On July 1, 1916, the day of his promotion to

The Space Age began on Oct. 4, 1957. That day, the Soviet Union launched the first artificial satellite, Sputnik 1, *shown here,* into orbit around Earth.

The U.S. flag grew from 48 to 50 stars, *left,* during Eisenhower's presidency. The new stars represented Alaska and Hawaii, which became the 49th and 50th states in 1959.

The world of President Eisenhower

The Korean War ended, after three years of fighting, with the signing of a truce agreement on July 27, 1953.

Controlled nuclear energy came into use. The U.S. Navy launched the first nuclear-powered vessel, the submarine *Nautilus,* in 1954. The first large-scale nuclear power plant began operations in 1956 at Calder Hall in England.

Segregated public schools were outlawed by the Supreme Court of the United States in 1954. In a landmark case, *Brown v. Board of Education of Topeka,* the court ruled that racially segregated schools were unconstitutional.

Rock 'n' roll became the leading form of popular music. A band called Bill Haley and His Comets recorded one of the first rock hits, "Rock Around the Clock," in 1954.

The merger of the American Federation of Labor (AFL) and the Congress of Industrial Organizations (CIO) in 1955 united the two leading U.S. labor federations.

The first polio vaccine, developed by the American medical researcher Jonas E. Salk, was declared safe in 1955.

The Vietnam War began in 1957, when Viet Cong guerrillas started to attack the South Vietnamese government.

The St. Lawrence Seaway, linking the Atlantic Ocean and Great Lakes, was completed by the United States and Canada in 1959.

Fidel Castro took over the government of Cuba in 1959 and soon turned the country into a Communist state.

New inventions included the *laser,* a device that produces narrow beam of intense light; and *xerography,* an inkless copying process perfected by the Xerox Corporation.

Tass from Sovfoto

first lieutenant, Dwight and Mamie were married.

The couple's first son, Doud Dwight Eisenhower, died of scarlet fever at age 3. The Eisenhowers had a second son, John Sheldon Doud Eisenhower (1922-), who became an Army officer and diplomat. In 1968, John's son, David, married Julie Nixon, the younger daughter of Eisenhower's vice president, Richard M. Nixon.

Early military career. Like most military families, the Eisenhowers continually moved from one Army post to another. Eisenhower directed tank training programs for officers and recruits at Camp Colt, in Gettysburg, Pennsylvania, during World War I (1914-1918).

After World War I ended, Eisenhower served on the staff of Brigadier General Fox Conner in the Panama Canal Zone, a strip of land surrounding the Panama Canal then governed by the United States. Conner greatly influenced Eisenhower. The young officer was especially impressed by Conner's self-discipline and attention to detail.

Conner supported Eisenhower's admission to the Army's "leadership factory," the Command and General Staff School at Fort Leavenworth, Kansas. In 1926, Eisenhower graduated first in his class of 275 top Army officers who survived the highly demanding training in tactics and other military skills.

MacArthur's aide. Eisenhower held various posts during the next few years. In 1933, he became an aide to General Douglas MacArthur, the Army chief of staff, in Washington, D.C. In 1935, MacArthur became military adviser to the Commonwealth of the Philippines, a U.S. possession since 1898. He took Eisenhower with him to the Asian country, which was being prepared for independence. Eisenhower planned the military defense of the Philippines and a military academy for the new gov-

Important dates in Eisenhower's life

1890 (Oct. 14) Born in Denison, Texas.
1915 Graduated from West Point.
1916 (July 1) Married Mamie Geneva Doud.
1942 Named commanding general of U.S. forces in the European Theater of Operations.
1943 Named supreme commander of the Allied Expeditionary Force in Europe.
1944 (June 6) Organized the Allied invasion of Europe.
1950 Named supreme commander of NATO forces in Europe.
1952 Elected president of the United States.
1956 Reelected president.
1961 Retired to his farm in Gettysburg, Pennsylvania.
1969 (March 28) Died in a hospital in Washington, D.C.

© DeeBee / Alamy Images

Eisenhower's birthplace was this two-story white frame house in Denison, Texas. The Eisenhower family moved to Abilene, Kansas, when Dwight was nearly 2 years old.

United Press Int.

Eisenhower and his wife, Mamie, were married on July 1, 1916. At the time, Ike was a first lieutenant in the United States Army, stationed at Fort Sam Houston, near San Antonio, Texas.

ernment. He took flying lessons in the Philippines and made a solo flight in 1937, when he was 47 years old.

Rise to prominence. World War II began in 1939. Germany—later joined by Italy, Japan, and other Axis powers—fought the Allies, which included Great Britain, France, and later the Soviet Union and the United States. In 1940, the United States began to build up its military forces in case it was drawn into the war. In 1941, the Army appointed Eisenhower to plan the strategy for the Third Army in war games in Louisiana. The Third Army brilliantly defeated an "enemy" force that included a tank division commanded by Eisenhower's friend George S. Patton, Jr., who also became a World War II hero. Eisenhower's performance earned him a promotion to brigadier general in September 1941. He also caught the attention of General George C. Marshall, who had replaced MacArthur as Army chief of staff.

The United States entered the war in December 1941, after Japan attacked the U.S. naval base at Pearl Harbor, Hawaii. Marshall brought Eisenhower to Washington, D.C., to serve in the Army's war plans division. Eisenhower was promoted to major general in March 1942. In June 1942, he was named commanding general of U.S. forces in the European Theater of Operations. He had been advanced over numerous eligible senior officers.

Eisenhower became a lieutenant general in July 1942. He also was named commander of Allied forces organized to invade North Africa. The invasion began in November 1942 and resulted in the recapture of the region from German and Italian forces. In February 1943, Eisenhower was promoted to the rank of four-star general, then highest in the Army. He organized the Allied invasions of Sicily in July 1943 and of Italy in September 1943. In all these campaigns, he worked to create unity among commanders from different nations. Many of these commanders were stubborn and outspoken, and Eisenhower had to be as much a diplomat as a planner.

Operation Overlord. In 1943, the United States and Great Britain set up a combined staff to plan the Allied invasion of German-occupied Europe. Marshall and Eisenhower were both highly recommended to organize the invasion. But U.S. President Franklin D. Roosevelt did not want Marshall to leave his vital work in Washington. In December 1943, Roosevelt named Eisenhower supreme commander of the Allied Expeditionary Force in Europe.

The Allies planned to cross the English Channel in early June 1944 and to invade Normandy, in northern France. The plan was called Operation Overlord, and it was the largest seaborne invasion in history.

Eisenhower set up headquarters near London and began the enormous responsibility and task of planning the invasion. He had to coordinate the armies and navies of the United States, Great Britain, and the other Allies to ensure that they worked smoothly as one force.

The success of Operation Overlord depended on low tides and calm seas for the landing boats, and clear skies for the bombers protecting them. But on June 3, the weather turned bad, with rough seas and heavy clouds. Weather experts told Eisenhower there was a slim chance that the weather would clear up on June 6. If the invasion did not begin that day, it would have to wait two weeks until the next low tide.

Eisenhower faced the anguish of decision. He could risk millions of lives on the small chance of good weather, or he could delay the landing and probably lose the vital military element of surprise. On June 5, Eisenhower made his final decision. "OK, let's go!" he ordered. The invasion began early in the morning of June 6, 1944, a day that became known as D-Day. By nightfall, the Allies had a firm hold on the beaches of Normandy. After 11 more months of bloody fighting, Germany surrendered on May 7, 1945.

Chief of staff. Eisenhower had received the newly created rank of five-star general in December 1944. A hero's welcome awaited him on his return to the United States in June 1945. He wanted to retire from the military and find a quiet civilian position. However, the nation still needed his services and, in November 1945, he replaced Marshall as Army chief of staff.

Eisenhower argued for a slow disbanding of U.S. armed forces to keep the nation strong. He also wanted to draft all 18-year-old men for one year. But this proposal attracted little support in a nation anxious to return to peacetime life.

Eisenhower also urged that the armed services be unified under a single command. But many military and political leaders opposed such a merger. In 1947, Congress passed a compromise measure unifying the U.S. armed forces under a single secretary of defense.

NATO commander. In 1948, Eisenhower retired from active military service to become president of Columbia University in New York City. He wrote a book about his wartime experiences, *Crusade in Europe* (1948), and was surprised when it became a best seller.

Dwight D. Eisenhower Library

During World War II, General Eisenhower, *right,* served as supreme commander of the Allied forces in Europe. He directed the D-Day invasion of Europe on June 6, 1944.

Eisenhower was soon back in uniform. During the late 1940's, Soviet-controlled Communist governments were established in most countries of Eastern Europe. As a result, the United States and Canada joined several Western European nations in 1949 to form a military alliance called the North Atlantic Treaty Organization (NATO). In 1950, President Harry S. Truman asked Eisenhower to become supreme commander of NATO forces in Europe, which were made up of troops from the member nations. Eisenhower eagerly accepted the job of molding this unique international army.

Road to the White House

Presidential candidate. Eisenhower became involved in politics partly as a result of deep divisions that developed in the United States over the Korean War. The war had begun in June 1950, when troops from Communist North Korea, equipped by the Soviet Union, invaded South Korea. Truman sent American troops to aid South Korea as part of a United Nations (UN) fighting force. Many Republicans supported U.S. participation. But a group of conservative Republicans led by Senator Robert A. Taft of Ohio wanted the United States to withdraw from the war, which had quickly become a bloody stalemate.

Eisenhower disagreed with Taft and the conservatives, known as the Old Guard. Eisenhower did not believe that the United States could live in peace and freedom while refusing to be involved in problems facing the rest of the world. Many Republicans urged Eisenhower to run for president in 1952, arguing that only he could unite the party's conservative and liberal wings and settle issues dividing the nation. Many Democrats also urged him to seek their party's presidential nomination. However, Eisenhower strongly believed in the two-party system and was concerned that there had been no Republican president for the past 20 years.

At first, Eisenhower refused to run for president. He had sent a letter to a New Hampshire newspaper publisher in 1948 calling it "necessary and wise" that professional soldiers "abstain from seeking high political office." He also did not want to become a candidate if it meant opposing Truman, whose defense policies he had helped design.

Truman, however, chose not to run for reelection. In addition, groups called IKE clubs sprang up throughout the country. As a result, Eisenhower decided that a soldier's duty might include service in the White House. He retired from the Army without pay or military benefits and declared himself a candidate for the Republican presidential nomination.

Election of 1952. Taft was the leading candidate for the Republican presidential nomination. At the Republican National Convention in Chicago, however, Lodge and other progressive Republicans helped Eisenhower win the nomination on the first ballot. Nixon, then a young senator from California, became the vice presidential candidate. The Democrats nominated Governor Adlai E. Stevenson of Illinois for president and Senator John J. Sparkman of Alabama for vice president.

The campaign began slowly. Eisenhower grumbled when reporters talked about his broad grin instead of his experience, "as if I didn't have a brain in my head." His campaign speeches criticized the Truman administration for "Korea, Communism, and corruption." These themes referred to Truman's conduct of the Korean War and to supposed Communist influence and corruption in the government. Shortly before the election, Eisenhower pledged: "I shall go to Korea" to help end the war.

Eisenhower had several advantages over Stevenson. For example, the new medium of television transmitted Eisenhower's kindliness and dignity far more effectively than Stevenson's intellectual wit. In addition, many Americans blamed the Democratic Party for giving the federal government far too great a role in people's lives. Other Americans believed charges that the Democrats had allowed Communists to gain high government posts. Perhaps most importantly, many people admired Eisenhower's experience and integrity. They believed that he would restore government to its proper role and raise a mighty shield against Communism.

In the election, Eisenhower received almost 34 million popular votes, 55 percent of the ballots cast. The Republicans also won control of both houses of Congress.

Eisenhower's first administration (1953-1957)

Eisenhower's methods. As president, Eisenhower delegated wide powers to aides. "This idea that all wis-

Eisenhower's first election

Place of nominating convention	Chicago
Ballot on which nominated	1st
Democratic opponent	Adlai E. Stevenson
Electoral vote*	442 (Eisenhower) to 89 (Stevenson)
Popular vote	33,936,137 (Eisenhower) to 27,314,649 (Stevenson)
Age at inauguration	62

*For vote by states, see **Electoral College** (table).

United Press Int.

In the 1952 presidential election, Eisenhower easily defeated his Democratic opponent, Adlai E. Stevenson. Standing beside him on election night was his wife, Mamie.

Vice president and Cabinet

Vice president ....*	Richard M. Nixon
Secretary of state ....*	John Foster Dulles
	Christian A. Herter (1959)
Secretary of the treasury	George M. Humphrey
	Robert B. Anderson (1957)
Secretary of defense	Charles E. Wilson
	Neil H. McElroy (1957)
	Thomas S. Gates, Jr. (1959)
Attorney general	Herbert Brownell, Jr.
	William P. Rogers (1957)
Postmaster general	Arthur E. Summerfield
Secretary of the interior	Douglas McKay
	Frederick A. Seaton (1956)
Secretary of agriculture	Ezra Taft Benson
Secretary of commerce	Sinclair Weeks
	Lewis L. Strauss (1958)
	Frederick H. Mueller (1959)
Secretary of labor	Martin P. Durkin
	James P. Mitchell (1953)
Secretary of health, *	Oveta Culp Hobby
education, and welfare	Marion B. Folsom (1955)
	Arthur S. Flemming (1958)

*Has a separate biography in *World Book.*

dom is in the president, in me, that's baloney," he said. Eisenhower made each Cabinet officer and White House assistant responsible for an area of government affairs. He chose officials for their managerial ability and strong convictions.

Shortly after Eisenhower took office, the Department of Health, Education, and Welfare (now the Department of Health and Human Services) was created. Oveta Culp Hobby became the first secretary of the department. Her appointment raised the number of Cabinet members to 10.

"Modern Republicanism" was Eisenhower's term for his legislative program. In domestic affairs, he asked for a reduction in government spending and for better federal management policies. In foreign policy, he emphasized close cooperation with the nation's allies.

In working with Congress, Eisenhower used his personal influence only for a few programs he thought essential. He was often unable to rely on the Republicans in Congress to get legislation passed because they were divided on many issues. He therefore depended on the leadership of the Democratic opposition.

By 1956, the federal government's revenues exceeded its expenses, and a small surplus appeared in the U.S. Treasury. Eisenhower's emphasis on economy also led to a reorganization of the armed forces. The "new look" involved fewer conventional forces but more nuclear weapons. Congress passed several other major fiscal reforms. It gave the nation's tax system a thorough overhaul, broadened the Social Security system, and increased the minimum wage to $1 an hour.

Despite his desire to cut costs, Eisenhower approved several multibillion-dollar public works programs that he believed would strengthen the economy. One was the St. Lawrence Seaway, a waterway that opened the Great Lakes to ocean ships. It was begun in 1954 and completed in 1959. Another was the interstate highway system, begun in 1956. A proposal to build a dam on the Colorado River drew wide criticism and was rejected.

Challenges from the Old Guard occupied much of the president's attention. One of the most troublesome of these conservative Republicans was Senator Joseph R. McCarthy of Wisconsin, who headed a subcommittee looking for Communists in the government. He had gained national attention in 1950 by charging—with no evidence—that there were Communist spies in the State Department and the Army.

McCarthy also attempted to ban books he considered to be written by Communists. He tried to keep such books out of the State Department libraries in many countries. In a June 1953 speech at Dartmouth College, Eisenhower urged his young audience, "Don't join the book burners." But Eisenhower refused to publicly criticize McCarthy, claiming it was beneath the dignity of the presidency to do so. He explained that he would not "get into the gutter with that guy." As Eisenhower expected, the Senate soon curbed McCarthy. It condemned him in December 1954 for conduct unbecoming a senator. McCarthy's influence quickly declined.

Another Old Guard member challenging the president was Senator John W. Bricker of Ohio. In January 1953, Bricker proposed a constitutional amendment that would require Senate consent for international agreements made by the president. Eisenhower opposed any measure that would reduce the president's power to conduct foreign policy, and his supporters defeated the amendment.

The Republican Party lost control of both houses of Congress in the midterm election of 1954. For the rest of his presidency, Eisenhower had to work with a Democratic-controlled Congress. This situation made it difficult to win support for his programs.

Foreign affairs. Although Secretary of State John Foster Dulles appeared to direct U.S. foreign policy, Eisenhower himself set the course. A month after his election as president, Eisenhower kept his promise to visit Korea. The trip failed to bring immediate results. A truce was finally signed on July 27, 1953.

Working behind the scenes, Eisenhower used the Central Intelligence Agency (CIA) to take action against suspected Communist-sponsored governments. The CIA helped overthrow such governments in Guatemala and Iran during the mid-1950's.

Eisenhower rejected several requests from his advisers that he use nuclear weapons during crises. But the possibility that the United States might use such weapons probably helped bring about the truce in Korea.

The president urged that the world harness nuclear power for peaceful use instead of employing nuclear weapons for war. In a major speech to the UN in December 1953, he suggested that nations contribute nuclear materials to a UN agency that would develop peaceful uses of nuclear energy. His program was called Atoms for Peace. The delegates responded with loud cheers never before heard in the UN. The International Atomic Energy Agency developed from Eisenhower's proposal.

The death of Soviet Premier Joseph Stalin in March 1953 seemed to clear the way for better Soviet-American relations. In July 1955, the leaders of France, the United Kingdom, the Soviet Union, and the United States attended a so-called *summit meeting* in Geneva, Switzerland. Eisenhower proposed an arrangement called Open Skies, under which the United States and the Soviet Union would allow air inspection of each other's military bases. But the Soviets rejected his proposal.

Illnesses. In September 1955, while on a working vacation in the Rocky Mountains of Colorado, Eisenhower suffered a heart attack. He recovered quickly, working from his hospital room by his 65th birthday in October and returning to his desk in December.

United Press Int.

Golf, Eisenhower's favorite sport, provided him with relief from the pressures of the presidency. He sometimes played with Vice President Richard M. Nixon, *right.*

The heart attack raised questions about the president's fitness to run for a second term. But Eisenhower could see no one with sufficient experience to succeed him. In February 1956, he announced that he would seek reelection. In June, just as Eisenhower was beginning to campaign, he had an attack of an intestinal disorder called *ileitis* that required surgery. Friends and foes alike wondered whether he could continue to carry the burdens of office.

Election of 1956. The Democrats again chose Stevenson as their candidate for president, with Senator Estes Kefauver of Tennessee as his running mate. A major crisis developed when three traditional U.S. allies—the United Kingdom, France, and Israel—carried out a joint air and land attack on Egypt in October 1956. The attack was designed to regain the Suez Canal, which Egyptian President Gamal Abdel Nasser had taken from its British and French owners three months earlier. The canal links the Mediterranean and Red seas and provides access to the oil-rich Middle East.

Eisenhower was shocked that the U.S. allies had secretly decided among themselves to attack. After the attack, the president moved quickly to end the crisis. He immediately ordered the suspension of planned loans to the United Kingdom. In the UN, the United States proposed a resolution for a cease-fire. Eisenhower also addressed the United States and the world on television. "There can be no law if we work to invoke one code of international conduct for those who oppose, and another for our friends," he insisted. The United Kingdom and France were outraged over what they called Eisenhower's betrayal. However, they withdrew their invasion forces when UN troops arrived to replace those forces.

Eisenhower's handling of the Suez crisis as well as his powers of recovery from illness strengthened the great confidence that American voters had in him. A few days after the speech, the voters went to the polls and awarded Eisenhower an even greater victory than in 1952.

Eisenhower's second administration (1957-1961)

Life in the White House. The Eisenhowers' eight years in the White House was the longest time they had lived in one place. In 1950, they bought a farm in Gettysburg. It was the first permanent home they owned.

Golf was the president's favorite recreation, and passers-by could sometimes see him practicing golf shots on a special green that was installed on the White House lawn. Eisenhower also liked to cook. Sometimes he invited friends to a cookout on the White House roof, where he broiled steaks on a charcoal grill.

Civil rights. The president favored a deliberate, orderly end to racial discrimination against black Ameri-

Eisenhower's second election

Place of nominating convention	San Francisco
Ballot on which nominated	1st
Democratic opponent	Adlai E. Stevenson
Electoral vote*	457 (Eisenhower) to 73 (Stevenson)
Popular vote	35,585,245 (Eisenhower) to 26,030,172 (Stevenson)
Age at inauguration	66

*For vote by states, see **Electoral College** (table).

Dwight D. Eisenhower Library

Eisenhower's family in 1958 included his four grandchildren—David, Susan, Mary Jean, and Barbara Anne, *seated, left to right.* Standing are his daughter-in-law, Barbara, and son, John.

Quotations from Eisenhower

The following quotations come from some of Dwight D. Eisenhower's speeches.

Soldiers, sailors and airmen of the Allied Expeditionary Force! You are about to embark upon the Great Crusade ... I have full confidence in your courage, devotion to duty and skill in battle. We will accept nothing less than full Victory!

Radio broadcast to Allied forces, June 5, 1944, the day before D-Day

... in the final choice, a soldier's pack is not so heavy a burden as a prisoner's chains.

First Inaugural Address, Jan. 20, 1953

We know that when censorship goes beyond the observance of common decency ... it quickly becomes, for us, a deadly danger.

Speech at Columbia University, May 31, 1954

... what counts is not necessarily the size of the dog in the fight—it's the size of the fight in the dog.

Speech to the Republican National Committee, Jan. 31, 1958

In the councils of government, we must guard against the acquisition of unwarranted influence, whether sought or unsought, by the military-industrial complex.

Farewell address, Jan. 17, 1961

cans. But in September 1957, a crisis in Little Rock, Arkansas, wrecked his hopes of proceeding slowly in a push for school integration. Governor Orval E. Faubus of Arkansas defied a federal court order to integrate Little Rock Central High School. Faubus used the Arkansas National Guard to prevent black students from entering the school. Eisenhower then placed the National Guard under federal control and sent a regular Army unit, the 101st Airborne Division, to enforce the court order and protect the black students. In a televised address, Eisenhower explained that he had acted in order to prevent further civil disorder.

The space age began on Oct. 4, 1957, when the Soviet Union launched Sputnik 1, the first artificial satellite. On Nov. 3, 1957, the Soviets launched Sputnik 2, a larger satellite that carried a dog as a passenger.

Americans were shocked that the Soviets had beaten the United States in technology, the area of its greatest pride. Many Americans also feared that the Soviet Union might have long-range missiles powerful enough to hit North America. In response, Eisenhower supported two expensive projects that went against his cost-cutting beliefs. One was an all-out effort to quickly catch up to the Soviets in space technology. The other project was to provide federal assistance to schools in support of science education.

The new space program began quickly. On Jan. 31, 1958, the first U.S. satellite, Explorer 1, went into orbit.

Crises in the Middle East and Asia troubled Eisenhower early in his second term. In 1957, he had proposed, and Congress had approved, a policy called the Eisenhower Doctrine. The policy pledged U.S. financial and military aid to any Middle East nation that asked for help against Communist aggression. In July 1958, Eisenhower used the doctrine to send troops to Lebanon to protect its pro-Western government from rebel forces. This involvement helped restore peace and protect United States oil interests in the region. The troops left in October.

In August 1958, China began shelling the Quemoy and Matsu islands, which were held by pro-Western Taiwan. Eisenhower ordered the U.S. Navy to help convoy supplies from Taiwan to the islands. This aid helped end the serious threat to Taiwan.

Midterm elections. In June 1958, congressional investigators revealed that Eisenhower's chief White House aide, Sherman Adams, had received gifts from a Boston businessman who was being investigated by the government. Adams admitted accepting the gifts but denied trying to influence officials in the businessman's favor. Eisenhower stubbornly refused to dismiss Adams. At the urging of Republicans worried about upcoming congressional elections, Adams resigned in September.

A business recession occurred in 1957 and 1958. The unemployment rate rose to 7.3 percent in July 1958. Even though the economy began to recover by the autumn of 1958, the business downturn contributed to a big Democratic victory in the midterm elections of November 1958. The Democrats increased their majority in Congress enough to override presidential vetoes.

U-2 incident. Stalin's successor, Soviet Premier Nikita Khrushchev, agreed to an exchange of visits between himself and Eisenhower and a summit meeting in Paris. Khrushchev came to the United States in September 1959. It was the first visit to the United States by a top Soviet leader.

In May 1960, just before Eisenhower left for the Paris summit, the Soviets shot down an American U-2 spy plane over their territory. In Paris, Khrushchev demanded a U.S. apology. When Eisenhower did not apologize, Khrushchev walked out and withdrew his invitation to Eisenhower to visit the Soviet Union.

A break with Cuba occurred near the end of Eisenhower's second term. Fidel Castro, who became dictator of Cuba in 1959, made the country a Communist state. In 1960, he seized all property owned by U.S. companies in Cuba. On Jan. 3, 1961, Eisenhower broke off diplomatic relations with Cuba.

Retirement. Eisenhower was the first president whose term of office was limited by the Constitution. The 22nd Amendment, which became law in 1951, limits a president to two full elected terms. In 1960, the Republicans nominated Vice President Nixon to succeed Eisenhower as president. Nixon lost the election to the Democratic candidate, John F. Kennedy.

Eisenhower left office in January 1961 and retired to his farm at Gettysburg, where he raised cattle and wrote three books of memoirs. After a series of heart attacks, Eisenhower died of heart failure on March 28, 1969. He was buried in Abilene, where a library with his papers opened to researchers soon afterward. Elmo Richardson

Related articles in *World Book* include:

Adams, Sherman
Cold War
Interstate Highway System
McCarthyism
Nixon, Richard M.
Republican Party (The Eisenhower years)
World War II (D-Day; Victory in Europe)

Outline

I. Early life
A. Boyhood
B. West Point cadet

II. Eisenhower the soldier
A. Eisenhower's family
B. Early military career
C. MacArthur's aide
D. Rise to prominence
E. Operation Overlord
F. Chief of staff
G. NATO commander

III. Road to the White House
A. Presidential candidate
B. Election of 1952

IV. Eisenhower's first administration (1953-1957)
A. Eisenhower's methods
B. "Modern Republicanism"
C. Challenges from the Old Guard
D. Foreign affairs
E. Illnesses
F. Election of 1956

V. Eisenhower's second administration (1957-1961)
A. Life in the White House
B. Civil rights
C. The space age
D. Crises in the Middle East and Asia
E. Midterm elections
F. U-2 incident
G. A break with Cuba
H. Retirement

Eisenstaedt, *EYE zehn stat,* **Alfred** (1898-1995), an American photographer, is regarded as a pioneer of informal, unposed news photography. He is known chiefly for his *Life* magazine photographs of famous people and world events. Eisenstaedt became one of the first staff photographers for *Life* in 1936. He continued to work for the magazine until 1972. The subjects of some of his memorable photographs include German dictator Adolf Hitler, United States President John F. Kennedy, American actress Marilyn Monroe, Italian dictator Benito Mussolini, and American artist Norman Rockwell.

Eisenstaedt was born on Dec. 6, 1898, in Dirschau, West Prussia (now Tczew, Poland). He first became interested in photography at the age of 14, after his uncle gave him a camera. After serving in the German army, Eisenstaedt took a job selling belts and buttons. He began selling his photographs in 1927. In 1929, he quit his sales job to work full-time as a free-lance photographer. Eisenstaedt came to the United States in 1935 and became a U.S. citizen in 1942. He died on Aug. 23, 1995.

John G. Freeman

Eisenstein, *EYE zuhn STYN,* **Sergei Mikhailovich,** *sehr GAY mih KY luh vihch* (1898-1948), was a Russian motion-picture director, theorist, and teacher. He became noted for his methods of film editing called *montage* (the arrangement of shots in sequence to suggest a symbolic meaning). For example, in *The Battleship Potemkin* (1925), a shot of an angry ship's crew, combined with soup bubbling in a kettle, implies that the sailors' resentment will soon boil over into mutiny.

Eisenstein's early films, including *Strike* (1925), *Potemkin,* and *October* (also called *Ten Days that Shook the World,* 1928), were semidocumentaries that pioneered the use of nonprofessional performers. His other films include *The General Line* (1929), *Alexander Nevsky* (1938), and *Ivan the Terrible* (two parts, 1944-1946).

Eisenstein was born on Jan. 23, 1898, in Riga, in what is now Latvia. He began making films in 1924. Because of political censorship, he completed only six feature films. His film writings have been published as *Film Form, The Film Sense, Notes of a Film Director,* and *Immortal Memories.* He died on Feb. 10, 1948.

Gene D. Phillips

Eisner, Will (1917-2005), an American cartoonist and author, was an influential figure in the history of comic strips and comic books. Eisner inspired generations of artists by advancing the appearance and storytelling power of comics. He also pioneered in creating comics for educational and vocational purposes.

Eisner created many major comics characters, notably the mysterious masked private detective known as the Spirit. "The Spirit" ran from 1940 to 1952 as a weekly multipage newspaper series. Eisner's *A Contract with God, and Other Tenement Stories* (1978) is a landmark in the development of the graphic novel. It consists of four autobiographical stories that deal seriously with such adult themes as religion and prejudice. See **Graphic novel.**

William Erwin Eisner was born in the Brooklyn sec-

Alfred Eisenstaedt, *Life* Magazine © 1945 Time Inc.

V-J Day—Times Square, a photograph taken by Alfred Eisenstaedt in 1945, captures the jubilation experienced by many Americans on learning that World War II had ended.

tion of New York City on March 6, 1917. He began drawing comics in high school. Eisner analyzed the unique relationship between text and visual images in comics in *Comics and Sequential Art* (1985). His *Life, in Pictures: Autobiographical Stories* was published in 2007, after his death on Jan. 3, 2005. Thomas Spurgeon

EKG. See **Electrocardiograph.**

El Alamein, *ehl AH lah MAYN,* is an Egyptian coastal village that lies about 65 miles (105 kilometers) west of Alexandria. For the location of El Alamein, see **Egypt** (political map). El Alamein became famous during World War II (1939-1945). In 1942, German troops led by Field Marshal Erwin Rommel advanced from Tobruk, Libya, as far east as the city in a drive toward Alexandria. Later that year, British troops led by Lieutenant General Bernard L. Montgomery defeated the Germans in two major battles at El Alamein. The battles prevented the Germans from conquering Egypt and forced them to retreat. The German retreat marked a turning point in the war. Today, an Egyptian oil field operates in the desert south of the city. See also **World War II** (The Western Desert Campaign). Robert L. Tignor

Eland, *EE luhnd,* is the largest antelope in Africa. It may stand 6 feet (1.8 meters) tall at the shoulder and weigh 1,500 pounds (680 kilograms). The eland is calm and graceful. It can run as fast as a horse and spring high into the air. All elands have long, spiraled horns and tufted, cattlelike tails. A *dewlap* (fold of skin) hangs from the neck. There are two types of elands. The common eland lives in an area from Kenya west to Angola and south to South Africa. The Derby eland lives from Sudan to Senegal and Gambia and south to the Republic of the Congo.

The eland's color varies from chestnut or bluish-gray to pale buff or fawn. Most elands have from 8 to 15 vertical white stripes on their sides, a black stripe down their backs, and black patches on the backs of the forelegs. In southern Africa, the common eland has faint markings.

Herds of up to 200 elands browse on partly forested land and open plains. During dry seasons, elands can live for weeks without water. C. Richard Taylor

Scientific classification. Elands belong to the family Bovidae. The scientific name for the common eland is *Taurotragus oryx.* The Derby eland is *T. derbianus.*

See also **Antelope** (with picture).

Elasticity is the ability of a solid to return to its original shape and size after it has been deformed by a force. All solids have some elasticity. Familiar materials that have elasticity include the steel in automobile springs and the rubber in basketballs.

Solids return to their original shape and size if the *stress* (deforming force per unit of area) does not exceed a value called the *elastic limit.* If the stress applied to a solid exceeds the solid's elastic limit, the solid will not return to its original shape after the stress has been removed. In the inch-pound system of measurement customarily used in the United States, stress is measured in pounds per square inch. In the metric system, *pascals* (newtons per square meter) are used to measure stress (see **Pascal**).

Stress is related to *strain.* Strain measures how much a given dimension of a solid changes under stress. In many solids, including metals and minerals, the stress below the elastic limit is in direct proportion to the strain. The greater the stress, the greater the strain. The ratio of stress to strain, called the *elastic modulus,* is a measure of how well a solid resists deforming forces. A solid with a high elastic modulus, such as steel, has a stronger resistance to stress than a solid with a low elastic modulus, such as rubber. Robert B. Prigo

Elat, *EE lat* (pop. 47,300), is an Israeli port on the Gulf of Aqaba, an arm of the Red Sea. It is also spelled *Eilat* (pronounced *ay LAHT*). It serves as Israel's gateway to Asia and East Africa by way of the Indian Ocean. Elat's natural beauty and seaside location make it a popular year-round resort (see **Israel** [map]).

Records indicate that a port existed at Elat's present site during Biblical times. But modern Elat was founded in 1948. Its importance increased after 1950, when Egypt banned Israeli ships from the Suez Canal. Without the canal, the Gulf of Aqaba became Israel's only outlet to the Red Sea. But Egypt also blocked the entrance to the gulf. The gulf was opened as a result of the Arab-Israeli War of 1956. Elat then grew rapidly in both size and importance. Egypt's blockade of the gulf in 1967 was a major cause of the Six-Day War. See **Israel** (History).

Elat also serves as an import center for oil. A pipeline carries oil from the city to Israel's Mediterranean coast. From there, it is either exported or sent to a refinery in Haifa. Bernard Reich

Elba, *EHL buh,* is a mountainous island in the Mediterranean Sea, 6 miles (10 kilometers) southwest of the coast of Tuscany (see **Italy** [terrain map]). The French emperor Napoleon I was exiled to Elba in 1814 (see **Napoleon I** [Exile to Elba]). Elba covers 86 square miles (224 square kilometers) and has a 40-mile (64-kilometer) coastline. It has a population of about 30,000, which increases greatly each summer as tourists arrive to enjoy the beaches and sea breezes. The chief city is Portoferraio. Products include fruits, iron, marble, and wine. Elba is part of Italy's Livorno province. David I. Kertzer

Elbe River, *EHL buh* or *ehlb,* is one of the major commercial waterways of central Europe. It rises in the western part of the Czech Republic, flows through Germany, and empties into the North Sea. The Elbe is called the Labe in the Czech Republic. It is 724 miles (1,165 kilometers) long (see **Germany** [terrain map]).

The Elbe River Basin contains some of Germany's best farmland and some important industrial centers. The river drains about 55,600 square miles (144,000 square kilometers) of land. Large oceangoing ships can travel on the Elbe from the North Sea as far as Hamburg, Germany—55 miles (89 kilometers) inland. At Hamburg, ocean vessels transfer cargo to barges that sail the Elbe. Other important cities on the Elbe include Magdeburg and Dresden in Germany, and Ústí nad Labem and Mělník in the Czech Republic. Major branches of the Elbe include the Havel and Saale rivers in Germany and the Vltava River in the Czech Republic. William H. Berentsen

Elbow is the joint that connects a person's upper arm with the forearm. The *humerus*—the bone of the upper arm—and the *radius* and *ulna*—the bones of the forearm—meet at the elbow. The three bone connections form three smaller joints within the elbow joint. These smaller joints permit certain movements. The humerus-ulna joint and the humerus-radius joint allow a person to bend the forearm up and down. The radius-ulna joint and the humerus-radius joint permit a person to rotate the forearm and turn the palm of the hand up and down.

A *capsule* (pouch) of tough connective tissue surrounds the elbow joint. This capsule and several ligaments hold the bones in place. *Synovial fluid* reduces friction at the elbow. Excessive or violent twisting of the forearm may injure the elbow ligaments, capsule, or tendons. One such injury, sometimes called *tennis elbow,* often results from playing tennis. Leslie S. Matthews

See also **Funny bone.**

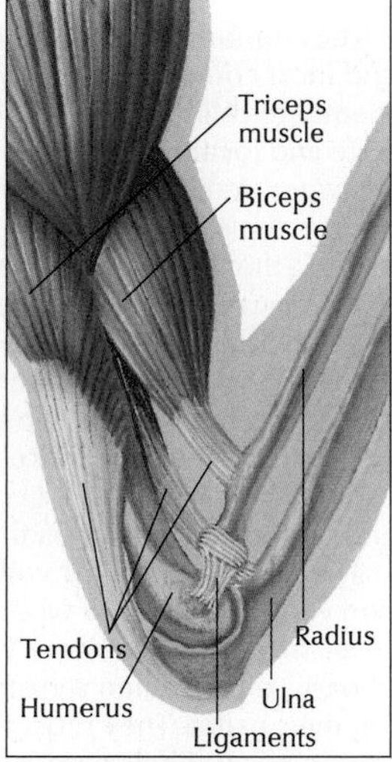

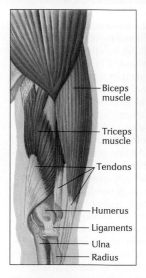

WORLD BOOK diagram by Lou Barlow

The elbow is the joint where the bone of the upper arm—the *humerus*—and the forearm bones—the *radius* and the *ulna*—meet. The elbow enables a person to "bend" his or her arm.

El Camino Real, *EHL kah MEE noh ray AHL,* was an early California highway. It is Spanish for *The Royal Highway.* It ran north from San Diego for 530 miles (853 kilometers) to Sonoma to connect the Franciscan missions. By 1823, there were 21 missions along the road. Junípero Serra founded the first mission in San Diego in 1769. The mission at San Francisco, now called Mission Dolores, was built in 1776. United States Highway 101 closely follows the old route. *El Camino Real* is also the name of the first road established by Europeans in what is now the United States. The road ran through what is now New Mexico. See **New Mexico** (Transportation).

Jerome O. Steffen

El Cid. See Cid, The.

Elder is a small tree or shrub known for its berrylike fruit. There are dozens of *species* (kinds). Elders grow in *temperate* (mild) areas of the Northern Hemisphere. The *American elder* is a shrub that grows in the eastern United States. Its leaves have five to seven leaflets with toothed edges. The plants bear clusters of small white flowers and black, purple, or red berrylike fruit. The fruit is used to make wine, pies, jelly, and jam.

Elder stems contain a soft *pith* (core) that can be removed. The pith can be hollowed to make whistles and blowguns. The ancient Greeks made a musical instrument called a *sambuke* from the elder stem. The roots, stems, leaves, and unripe fruits of elders are poisonous. Children have been poisoned from toys made from hollowed stems.

Elders thrive in moist areas. They grow quickly and often form thickets. Some other shrubs and trees are called elders, but they are not closely related to true elders. The *poison elder* is a sumac, and the *boxelder* is a maple. Michael J. Baranski

Scientific classification. Elders make up the genus *Sambucus.* The American elder is *Sambucus canadensis.*

El Dorado, *EHL duh RAH doh,* is the name of a fictitious kingdom of enormous wealth in South America. Many European explorers searched for the kingdom, including Gonzalo Jiménez de Quesada of Spain and Sir Walter Raleigh of England. But none of the explorers found it. The term has become common for any legendary place of fabulous riches.

El Dorado, which means *the gilded* in Spanish, was originally the name of a legendary South American king whose body was regularly covered with gold dust. The king would float on a raft onto a lake while emeralds and gold objects were thrown into the lake. The legend probably referred to a similar ceremony performed by a Chibcha Indian chief in what is now the South American nation of Colombia. Helen Delpar

See **Colombia** (picture: *The Raft of El Dorado*).

Eleanor of Aquitaine, *AK wih TAYN* (1122-1204), was the wife of King Louis VII of France and later of King Henry II of England. She was also the mother of two English kings, Richard the Lion-Hearted and John. Her control of Aquitaine, then a vast independent state next to France, made her a central figure in the struggle for power between France and England.

Eleanor was the daughter of William X, Duke of Aquitaine. In 1137, when Eleanor was 15 years old, she inherited Aquitaine. Her land came under French control when she married Louis VII later that year. Eleanor and Louis had two daughters. But the lack of a male heir contributed to unhappiness in their marriage. They agreed to a divorce in 1152. Within months, Eleanor married Henry Plantagenet, who became King Henry II of England in 1154. Later, they lost affection for each other, and she supported a revolt against him in 1173. The revolt failed, and Henry imprisoned Eleanor. Eleanor was freed in 1189, after Henry died and Richard became king. She greatly influenced both Richard and John during their reigns. Eleanor died on April 1, 1204. Marion Meade

See also **Henry II** (king of England).

Election is the process by which people vote for the candidate or proposal of their choice. The basis of democratic government is that citizens have the right to choose the officials who will govern and represent them. Elections thus rank as one of the most important political activities. Elections also serve as a means of peacefully transferring power from one person or group to another.

Democratic countries hold free, fair, and competitive elections to select elected representatives. Experts often analyze the nature and quality of elections as one characteristic of democratic control. However, other countries may include the words *democracy* or *republic* in their country's name without allowing free, fair, and competitive elections. The only candidates allowed on the ballot are those approved by the leaders or by a single political party. In such countries, elections are held for propaganda reasons and to demonstrate popular support for the government.

In addition to public elections, nongovernmental elections are also held to select the officials of many organizations. Labor unions, social clubs, and the student bodies of schools hold elections to select their officers.

Elections in a democracy

Election procedures differ from country to country. However, there are common principles that characterize elections in democratic nations. In the United States, Canada, and other democratic countries, nearly all adult citizens can vote. Those not permitted to vote include noncitizens, such as resident aliens who live in the United States on a permanent basis; certain criminals; and people with severe mental illness or intellectual disability. Citizens vote by secret ballot so that they can vote without fear of how others will react. The mass media—which include radio, television, magazines, and newspapers—freely discuss the candidates and issues.

In most democratic countries, political parties select candidates for public office and propose public policies. However, in some countries and in parts of the United States, local elections are *nonpartisan*—that is, candidates appear on the ballot without party identification.

Voters elect officials by either *direct* or *indirect* elections. In direct elections, the people themselves vote for public officials. In the United States, for example, citizens vote for members of Congress and for state and local officials in this way. In indirect elections, people elect representatives called *electors* to choose public officials. The president and vice president of the United States are chosen through an indirect election. The voters of each state select electors, who make up the Electoral College. The electors, in turn, choose the president and vice president based on the popular vote in the states they represent.

Under a parliamentary system of government, also called a *cabinet system,* citizens elect members of the legislature. The head of state—the king or queen of a monarchy or the president of a republic—then selects a prime minister from the members of the legislature. Australia, Canada, and certain other Commonwealth nations regard the British ruler as head of state. In such nations, the governor general makes the appointment, acting as the representative of the monarch. In most countries, the head of state can appoint only the leader of the majority party in the legislature or the head of a coalition of parties. See **Cabinet** (The cabinet system of government).

Elections in the United States

Election regulations. The Constitution of the United States requires that a congressional election be held every two years. At that time, voters elect all the members of the House of Representatives for a two-year term and about one-third of the Senate members for a six-year term. The Constitution also requires the election of a president and a vice president every four years. Federal law states that national elections are to be held on the first Tuesday after the first Monday of November.

State laws regulate all elections, including national and local ones. Such laws establish the eligibility requirements for state officials and the date on which state and local elections are to be held. They also establish the qualifications for voters. Voter registration and election laws vary among states, and local election districts have changed over time. Prior to 1900, resident aliens, for example, were allowed to vote in national elections in several states. Today, no state allows resident aliens to vote in national elections, but a few local election districts allow them to cast votes for local candidates and issues. Though states decide voter eligibility, the Constitution gives Congress the right to change state voter requirements if they violate constitutional guarantees.

Nomination of candidates. At one time, political parties nominated nearly all candidates at national, state, and local conventions or in closed meetings of party members called *caucuses.* Today, candidates for most state and local offices are nominated in *direct primary elections.* A direct primary is a contest in which voters choose the candidates who will represent each political party in the upcoming general election. Other candidates may run in the general election, where voters make their final choice. However, only the candidates who win the primaries become official party nominees. A *runoff election* may be held if no candidate in the original primary receives more than half the vote. The two candidates with the most votes run against each other, and the winner becomes the party nominee.

The qualifications for voting in a direct primary election vary according to whether the primary is closed or open. In a *closed primary,* voters must declare a choice of party, either when registering to vote or when receiving their ballot. They must then choose from among the candidates on their party's ballot. In an *open primary,* voters may cast their ballot for candidates of any party. Voters receive ballots for all parties in the election, mark one in the voting booth, and discard the rest.

Each party holds a national convention to nominate its presidential and vice presidential candidates. Many states hold special primary elections to choose delegates to those conventions. In some states, the ballot lists presidential candidates. In others, it lists proposed delegates, who may have promised to support a certain candidate. Voters can support a candidate by voting for that person's delegates. In still other states, local caucuses choose delegates to the national convention.

Election procedures. Most elections are supervised on the local level by county election officials, who divide each county or ward into voting districts called *precincts.* Election officials determine the place where votes will be cast, called the *polling place* or the *polls.* They also check voters' names against registration lists, hand out ballots, and supervise the depositing of marked ballots in ballot boxes. In most states, the officials at each polling place must represent the two major political parties. In some areas, citizens' groups station observers called *poll watchers* at the polls to ensure that election officials perform their tasks honestly.

Voters indicate their choices privately in an enclosed voting booth. Many precincts use voting machines that automatically record votes. Every state allows certain citizens to vote by absentee ballot before the election. These citizens include people in the armed services, college students, sick persons, and certain travelers.

The polls generally remain open from early morning until evening on Election Day. After the polls close, election officials count the votes for each candidate, including absentee votes. Then, all ballots and tally sheets from voting machines are sent, under seal, to city or county officials or to the board of elections. All state and national election results are filed with the chief election official, the secretary of state in most states. State and local officials then declare the winners in each race. Federal and state laws define dishonest voting practices and provide severe penalties for them. Such practices include bribing voters, impersonating another voter, stuffing a ballot box with forged votes, and tampering with voting machines. Laws also prohibit election officials from tampering with election results. Thomas S. Vontz

Related articles in *World Book* include:

Ballot
Corrupt practices
Election campaign
Election Day
Election of 2000
Electoral College
Initiative and referendum
Primary election
Recall
Term limits
Voting
Voting machine

Election campaign is a course of action designed to win votes for a certain candidate, party, or proposal. Election campaigns usually include advertisements, use of social media, public appearances, interviews, speeches, and debates. In the United States, the best-known campaign is the one for president held every four years. But thousands of other campaigns—including those for national legislative bodies, city councils, and local school boards—also take place on a regular basis. Still other campaigns involve *referendums* or *initiatives,* in which proposals are submitted to voters for approval.

Running for government office has changed dramatically as the result of technological, political, and legal developments. The campaign methods of the past—including torchlight parades, bus tours, and "whistle-stop" tours by train—are less important today. Today, air travel enables candidates to visit many places in one day, and television allows candidates to appear before national audiences on a daily basis. Most candidates have websites or use social media to provide information about their campaign positions and other topics.

Election campaign laws and procedures vary from country to country. This article focuses primarily on election campaigns in the United States. However, campaigns in other democracies share similar characteristics.

Stages of a campaign

Most election campaigns start months before the public knows the candidates are running. A candidate asks community and party leaders and possible contributors if they will give their support. In major campaigns, polls also indicate the possible support for a candidate. If the candidate and his or her advisers think they have enough backing, they begin to develop a campaign strategy.

Planning campaign strategy. Most campaign strategy is based on both research and ideology. Campaign planners study such economic and social conditions as an area's industrial production and the age, race, and income distribution of the people. They use such information, along with data from public opinion polls and the results of previous elections, to determine key issues and areas of possible strength and weakness. They attempt to craft their message and present themselves to the widest possible audience. Then the planners choose their *targets*—that is, the people and groups at whom the campaign will be aimed. The candidate and his or her advisers develop positions on issues that will likely be discussed during the campaign. They may write a series of statements called *position papers* to explain the candidate's views. They also begin to raise funds, recruit volunteers, and purchase advertising.

Announcing the candidacy marks the official start of a campaign. Most candidates hold a news conference to make their announcement. Candidates may tour their state or district and repeat their declaration several times through the media in different geographic areas.

Developing support. The pace quickens after the announcement of candidacy, and the campaign becomes more apparent to the public. The campaign organization holds meetings and fund-raising events. Signs and bumper stickers appear. The candidates and their workers strive to develop voter support through publicity, advertising, and personal appearances. They try to receive endorsements, financial support, or both from key organizations and individuals.

Candidates reach the greatest number of people through the media. Men and women who run for office receive publicity in a number of ways. For example, they issue news releases, grant interviews, hold news conferences, and appear on televised debates and talk shows. Candidates also buy advertising, including appeals on billboards, commercials on television and radio, and advertisements in newspapers. Almost all major candidates present themselves and their ideas through websites and social media. Most campaigns use a *media mix,* which is a combination of these methods.

A candidate spends much time making speeches and other personal appearances. Campaign officials encourage newspaper and television coverage of each appearance. Candidates also exchange views and debate their qualifications on short TV and radio commercials, as well as through campaign websites and social media. In addition, they may present themselves and their ideas in large blocks of program time that they have purchased on radio or TV.

Winning the nomination. A person wishing to stand as a candidate in an election at a national or local government level may first have to be nominated through an election in his or her political party. In some countries, a candidate may have to win a *primary election* before being chosen as the party's nominee. A primary election determines the candidates that will represent a political party or an alliance in the general election.

In the United States, most major presidential candidates must run against one or more other members of their party to win the nomination. The two major U.S. parties, the Democrats and the Republicans, hold national conventions to officially select their nominees for president and vice president. Most states hold primary elections to determine delegates to each party's national convention. Primary elections also determine who will represent the party in contests for most other offices. In most states, independent candidates and minor-party candidates get on the primary ballot by filing a petition signed by a specified number of voters. In some states, a state or district convention of party members selects delegates to the national convention. To get the support of national delegates from those states, a presidential candidate must first win the backing of delegates to the state or district convention. A few other states hold local party meetings called *caucuses* to select national, state, or district delegates. See **Primary election.**

Getting out the vote. As the election approaches, the pace of the campaign quickens. Candidates usually issue more frequent news releases and increase advertising. Campaign workers step up efforts to persuade voters to go to the polls and vote for their candidate.

Much of the activity during this period is devoted to getting out the vote. In a process called *canvassing,* volunteers call, e-mail, or visit voters to ask which candidates they favor. The campaign workers then try to make sure that the probable supporters of their candidate will register and vote.

On the day of the election, campaign workers may provide transportation and baby-sitting service for voters. Volunteers at the polls may keep track of supporters who have voted and contact those who have not done so. Other volunteers may observe the voting and the counting of ballots to discourage fraud.

After the election, candidates, political parties, and the media typically analyze the campaign that just ended. They review and analyze returns from a variety of perspectives. Interested parties analyze demographic factors such as age, gender, and ethnicity, along with the importance of various issues, and draw conclusions about the interests of the voters. Parties and candidates attempt to learn as much as they can from past elections in preparation for future campaigns.

Campaign organizations

Candidates and political parties assemble *campaign organizations* to carry out the many tasks and activities associated with election campaigns. A campaign organization usually consists of paid and unpaid staff members and consultants.

A presidential campaign in the United States may involve as many as 500 paid staff members and hundreds of thousands of volunteers. A campaign director heads the organization and coordinates activities. Other officials of a large campaign may include a general manager, a research director, a finance director, and a *media director,* who supervises advertising and publicity. Most candidates make frequent public appearances. Specialists called *advance people* may travel ahead to make arrangements, and professional political consultants usually help plan and conduct various operations. For example, many candidates employ a polling organization to take public opinion polls. Many hire marketing and messaging specialists to create advertisements and send messages that target likely voters. Mail, e-mail, telephone, and social media are frequently employed by campaigns. Volunteers may distribute leaflets, prepare mailings, call voters, and perform many other important tasks. The leadership, organization, and support of a campaign are critical to a candidate's success.

Campaign financing

Campaign funds are necessary to pay personnel and to finance advertising, travel, and other needs. The chief sources of funds are personal solicitations, appeals by direct mail, Internet contributions, fund-raising events, and matching funds. Bank loans are also a common source of campaign money.

Personal solicitations are individual requests by the candidate or a campaign worker. The majority of candidates raise most of their funds by soliciting donations from friends, supporters, associates, and organizations.

Appeals by direct mail involve fund-raising letters sent to party members, to people who have contributed to past campaigns, and to members of groups likely to agree with the candidate's views.

Internet contributions became an important source of campaign funding in the late 1990's and early 2000's. Internet websites allow candidates to reach large numbers of supporters at a relatively low cost. Candidates may also use e-mail lists to contact people who will likely contribute money.

Fund-raising events include parties, dinners, and concerts. Most such activities make less money than personal solicitation or direct mail, but they provide opportunities for personal appearances and help build support for a candidate.

Matching funds are available to presidential candidates in the United States if contributions to their campaign meet certain requirements. Candidates can qualify for the funds by raising at least $100,000 in individual contributions of $250 or less. The $100,000 minimum must consist of at least $5,000 in contributions from each of at least 20 states. The federal government then gives the candidate an amount of money equal to the total of each individual contribution of $250 or less.

Campaign finance laws have greatly affected campaign financing and spending in the United States. Since 1940, federal law has limited the size of campaign contributions. For years, however, the law was difficult to enforce and generally ineffective. Many people became concerned about excessive campaign spending and the candidates' dependence on large contributions from wealthy people.

The Revenue Act of 1971 encouraged small contributions by allowing an income tax credit for them. This law also enabled taxpayers to specify that $1 of their federal income tax each year be used for public financing of presidential election campaigns.

The Federal Election Campaign Act of 1971 required detailed reporting of both campaign contributions and expenses. In 1974, amendments to the act established public financing of presidential campaigns and created the Federal Election Commission to enforce the rules. The amendments limited the amount of money a candidate could raise in *hard money* contributions—that is, contributions by individuals or groups to any one candidate. The amendments also put a ceiling on presidential and congressional campaign spending in each state.

However, there were few limits on state and local party spending for candidates, and large contributions were channeled legally into general party funds. These contributions became known as *soft money.* In 1976, the Supreme Court of the United States ruled that only presidential candidates who accept public financing must stay within the spending limits. Many states enacted stricter regulation of campaign funds in the late 1900's.

In 2002, Congress passed the Bipartisan Campaign Reform Act (BCRA) to further reform the campaign finance system. The central feature of the legislation was a ban on unregulated soft money donations to national political parties. The law still allowed soft money donations to state and local party organizations in limited amounts.

In 2010, the United States Supreme Court in *Citizens United v. FEC* struck down parts of the campaign reform act, ruling that those provisions unconstitutionally limited political speech. Specifically, the federal decision allows corporations and unions to spend unlimited amounts of money on *electioneering communications*. Electioneering communications are any broadcast, cable, or satellite communications—such as public service announcements, infomercials, and commercials—that refer to a particular federal candidate and are broadcast shortly before an election in the district or state that the candidate seeks to represent. The ruling has increased the funding and prominence of *Super PACs*—political action committees that are able to raise and spend unlimited amounts of money. A political action committee is an organized group dedicated to raising money for political activity. Thomas S. Vontz

Related articles in *World Book* include:

Advertising (Political effects)
Caucus
Corrupt practices
Election
Federal Election Commission
Political action committee
Political convention
Political party
President of the United States (The presidential election; pictures)
Primary election
Public opinion poll
Television (Effects on society)

Election Day in the United States is the day on which national elections for presidential electors take place. The U.S. Congress established the first Tuesday after the first Monday in November as Election Day. It is a legal holiday in most states and in all territories. Many state elections are also held on this day. Many states forbid the retail sale of liquor while the polls are open.

Originally, Congress did not set a specific date for national elections. Each state could appoint its electors on any day within 34 days before the date in December set for the convening of electors. In 1845, Congress established Election Day to correct abuses caused by the lack of a standard election day. Robert Agranoff

Election of 2000 was one of the closest and most unusual presidential elections in United States history. The outcome—that Republican George W. Bush defeated his Democratic opponent Al Gore—remained in doubt for five weeks after the election. Bush received more electoral votes but fewer popular votes than Gore. A decision by the Supreme Court of the United States led to the final resolution of the contest (see **Bush v. Gore**).

On Election Day, November 7, over 100 million U.S. citizens went to the polls. The race was extremely close between Texas Governor Bush and Vice President Gore. In Florida, the race was particularly tight. It became obvious that the election depended on who got Florida's 25 electoral votes (see **Electoral College**).

Early in the evening, television newscasters predicted that Gore would win Florida. But official tallies from the state showed an increasing number of votes for Bush. As a result, the television networks retracted their original prediction and declared Bush the winner in Florida.

Gore called Bush to concede the election. But shortly after the call, Bush's lead in Florida began to shrink. The networks said the vote in Florida was too close to predict. Gore called Bush to retract his concession.

Recounts. On the morning of November 8, Gore led Bush in popular votes, but the winner of the electoral votes was still unknown. The count in Florida showed Bush ahead of Gore by nearly 1,800 votes out of about 6 million cast. In the case of such a close vote, Florida law called for a recount. Before the machine recount was finished, Gore requested an additional recount by hand in four Florida counties, where results were in dispute.

Court challenges. Gore sought support in the courts for the manual recounts. He argued that a recount by hand was the only way to make sure every person's vote was included in the final tally. Gore pointed out that machines did not accurately count ballots from which the *chad,* a small piece of paper that covered the punch hole, had not been completely removed. Bush fought through the courts to halt the recounts. He insisted that a manual count was less fair and less precise than a machine count because of the human judgment involved.

Some early court rulings allowed the recounts to continue. On November 13, for example, a federal judge in Miami rejected Bush's request to stop the recounts. On November 15, the Florida Supreme Court allowed more time for the recounts to be completed by changing the deadline from November 14 to November 26.

Miami-Dade County voting officials halted their recount, saying that even with the extended deadline, there would not be time to manually recount all the votes. Broward and Volusia counties met the deadline. Palm Beach County continued its recount but did not finish in time. Florida Secretary of State Katherine Harris refused to accept the tally because it was submitted about two hours after the deadline. On November 26, Harris certified a Florida win for Bush with a margin of 537 votes. Gore contested the certified vote.

When Gore's contest of the certified vote came before the Florida Supreme Court, the court ordered a manual recount of all state ballots on which no vote for president had been registered by machine. Bush appealed the ruling to the U.S. Supreme Court. On December 12, the Supreme Court justices, voting 5 to 4 in the case of *Bush v. Gore,* ruled that the Florida recounts should not continue.

The outcome. In a televised address on December 13, Gore conceded the election to Bush. Gore, with 50,996,039 votes, received 48.38 percent of the popular vote. Bush received 50,456,141 votes and 47.87 percent of the popular vote. But Bush defeated Gore 271 to 266 in electoral votes, with one elector not casting a vote. In January 2001, George W. Bush became the nation's 43rd president. Gregg Ivers

Electoral College is a group of representatives that formally elects the president and vice president of the United States. The U.S. presidential election is an *indirect election*. The voters of each state determine *electors* who represent them in the Electoral College. The electors, in turn, cast *electoral votes* on behalf of the states they represent. Electoral votes determine the outcome of the election.

All 50 states and the District of Columbia have a certain number of electoral votes. For each state, the number is equal to the number of senators and representatives the state has in the U.S. Congress. States with larger populations have more representatives, and therefore more electoral votes. The District of Columbia, which has no senators or representatives, has three electoral votes. In nearly every state, the candidate who wins the *plurality* (highest number) of the popular votes receives

Text continued on page 164.

Electoral College

The Electoral College is a group chosen by the voters of each state to elect the president of the United States. This chart shows how the college has voted since 1804, when the present system was adopted. The House of Representatives decided the 1824 election because no one won a majority. In 1872, the electoral votes of Arkansas and Louisiana were disputed and not counted.

Democratic

Republican

Year	Candidate elected	Winner's total	Total vote	Ala.	Alaska	Ariz.	Ark.	Calif.	Colo.	Conn.	Del.	D.C.	Fla.	Ga.	Hawaii	Ida.	Ill.	Ind.	Iowa	Kans.	Ky.	La.	Me.	Md.	Mass.	Mich.	Minn.	Miss.	Mo.	Mont.	Nebr.	Nev.	N.H.
1804	Jefferson	162	176							9	3			6							8			/	19								7
1808	Madison	122	175							9	3			6							7			/	19								7
1812	Madison	128	217							9	4			8							12	3		/	22								8
1816	Monroe	183	217							9	3			8				3			12	3		8	22								8
1820	Monroe	231	232	3						9	4			8			3	3			12	3	9	11	15			2	3				/
1824	J. Q. Adams	84	261							8	1						1					2	9	3	15								8
1828	Jackson	178	261	5						8	3			9			3	5			14	5	/	/	15			3	3				8
1832	Jackson	219	286	7						8	3			11			5	9			15	5	10	/	14			4	4				7
1836	Van Buren	170	294	7			3			8	3			11			5	9			15	5	10	10	14	3		4	4				7
1840	W. Harrison	234	294	7			3			8	3			11			5	9			15	5	10	10	14	3		4	4				7
1844	Polk	170	275	9			3			6	3			10			9	12			12	6	9	8	12	5		6	7				6
1848	Taylor	163	290	9			3			6	3		3	10			9	12	4		12	6	9	8	12	5		6	7				6
1852	Pierce	254	296	9			4	4		6	3		3	10			11	13	4		12	6	8	8	13	6		7	9				5
1856	Buchanan	174	296	9			4	4		6	3		3	10			11	13	4		12	6	8	8	13	6		7	9				5
1860	Lincoln	180	303	9			4	4		6	3		3	10			11	13	4		12	6	8	8	13	6	4	7	9				5
1864	Lincoln	212	233					5		6	3						16	13	8	3	11		7	7	12	8	4		11			2	5
1868	Grant	214	294	8			5	5		6	3		3	9			16	13	8	3	11	7	7	7	12	8	4		11		3	3	5
1872	Grant	286	349	10				6		6	3		4	/			21	15	11	5	/		7	8	13	11	5	8	/		3	3	5
1876	Hayes	185	369	10			6	6	3	6	3		4	11			21	15	11	5	12	8	7	8	13	11	5	8	15		3	3	5
1880	Garfield	214	369	10			6	/	3	6	3		4	11			21	15	11	5	12	8	7	8	13	11	5	8	15		3	3	5
1884	Cleveland	219	401	10			7	8	3	6	3		4	12			22	15	13	9	13	8	6	8	14	13	7	9	16		5	3	4
1888	B. Harrison	233	401	10			7	8	3	6	3		4	12			22	15	13	9	13	8	6	8	14	13	7	9	16		5	3	4
1892	Cleveland	277	444	11			8	/	4	6	3		4	13		3	24	15	13	10	13	8	6	8	15	/	9	9	17	3	8	3	4
1896	McKinley	271	447	11			8	/	4	6	3		4	13		3	24	15	13	10	/	8	6	8	15	14	9	9	17	3	8	3	4
1900	McKinley	292	447	11			8	9	4	6	3		4	13		3	24	15	13	10	13	8	6	8	15	14	9	9	17	3	8	3	4
1904	T. Roosevelt	336	476	11			9	10	5	7	3		5	13		3	27	15	13	10	13	9	6	/	16	14	11	10	18	3	8	3	4
1908	Taft	321	483	11			9	10	5	7	3		5	13		3	27	15	13	10	13	9	6	/	16	14	11	10	18	3	8	3	4
1912	Wilson	435	531	12		3	9	/	6	7	3		6	14		4	29	15	13	10	13	10	6	8	18	15	12	10	18	4	8	3	4
1916	Wilson	277	531	12		3	9	13	6	7	3		6	14		4	29	15	13	10	13	10	6	8	18	15	12	10	18	4	8	3	4
1920	Harding	404	531	12		3	9	13	6	7	3		6	14		4	29	15	13	10	13	10	6	8	18	15	12	10	18	4	8	3	4
1924	Coolidge	382	531	12		3	9	13	6	7	3		6	14		4	29	15	13	10	13	10	6	8	18	15	12	10	18	4	8	3	4
1928	Hoover	444	531	12		3	9	13	6	7	3		6	14		4	29	15	13	10	13	10	6	8	18	15	12	10	18	4	8	3	4
1932	F. Roosevelt	472	531	11		3	9	22	6	8	3		7	12		4	29	14	11	9	11	10	5	8	17	19	11	9	15	4	7	3	4
1936	F. Roosevelt	523	531	11		3	9	22	6	8	3		7	12		4	29	14	11	9	11	10	5	8	17	19	11	9	15	4	7	3	4
1940	F. Roosevelt	449	531	11		3	9	22	6	8	3		7	12		4	29	14	11	9	11	10	5	8	17	19	11	9	15	4	7	3	4
1944	F. Roosevelt	432	531	11		4	9	25	6	8	3		8	12		4	28	13	10	8	11	10	5	8	16	19	11	9	15	4	6	3	4
1948	Truman	303	531	11		4	9	25	6	8	3		8	12		4	28	13	10	8	11	10	5	8	16	19	11	9	15	4	6	3	4
1952	Eisenhower	442	531	11		4	8	32	6	8	3		10	12		4	27	13	10	8	10	10	5	9	16	20	11	8	13	4	6	3	4
1956	Eisenhower	457	531	/		4	8	32	6	8	3		10	12		4	27	13	10	8	10	10	5	9	16	20	11	8	13	4	6	3	4
1960	Kennedy	303	537	/	3	4	8	32	6	8	3		10	12	3	4	27	13	10	8	10	10	5	9	16	20	11	8	13	4	6	3	4
1964	L. Johnson	486	538	10	3	5	6	40	6	8	3	3	14	12	4	4	26	13	9	7	9	10	4	10	14	21	10	7	12	4	5	3	4
1968	Nixon	301	538	10	3	5	6	40	6	8	3	3	14	12	4	4	26	13	9	7	9	10	4	10	14	21	10	7	12	4	5	3	4
1972	Nixon	520	538	9	3	6	6	45	7	8	3	3	17	12	4	4	26	13	8	7	9	10	4	10	14	21	10	7	12	4	5	3	4
1976	Carter	297	538	9	3	6	6	45	7	8	3	3	17	12	4	4	26	13	8	7	9	10	4	10	14	21	10	7	12	4	5	3	4
1980	Reagan	489	538	9	3	6	6	45	7	8	3	3	17	12	4	4	26	13	8	7	9	10	4	10	14	21	10	7	12	4	5	3	4
1984	Reagan	525	538	9	3	7	6	47	8	8	3	3	21	12	4	4	24	12	8	7	9	10	4	10	13	20	10	7	11	4	5	4	4
1988	G. H.W. Bush	426	538	9	3	7	6	47	8	8	3	3	21	12	4	4	24	12	8	7	9	10	4	10	13	20	10	7	11	4	5	4	4
1992	Clinton	370	538	9	3	8	6	54	8	8	3	3	25	13	4	4	22	12	7	6	8	9	4	10	12	18	10	7	11	3	5	4	4
1996	Clinton	379	538	9	3	8	6	54	8	8	3	3	25	13	4	4	22	12	7	6	8	9	4	10	12	18	10	7	11	3	5	4	4
2000	G. W. Bush	271	538	9	3	8	6	54	8	8	3	/	25	13	4	4	22	12	7	6	8	9	4	10	12	18	10	7	11	3	5	4	4
2004	G. W. Bush	286	538	9	3	10	6	55	9	7	3	3	27	15	4	4	21	11	7	6	8	9	4	10	12	17	10	6	11	3	5	5	4
2008	Obama	365	538	9	3	10	6	55	9	7	3	3	27	15	4	4	21	11	7	6	8	9	4	10	12	17	10	6	11	3	/	5	4
2012	Obama	332	538	9	3	11	6	55	9	7	3	3	29	16	4	4	20	11	6	6	8	8	4	10	11	16	10	6	10	3	5	6	4

Democratic-Republican	National Republican
Progressive	Split vote (/)
Federalist	Whig
Other parties	Not voting

N.J.	N.Mex.	N.Y.	N.C.	N.Dak.	Ohio	Okla.	Ore.	Pa.	R.I.	S.C.	S.Dak.	Tenn.	Tex.	Utah	Vt.	Va.	Wash.	W.Va.	Wis.	Wyo.	Year
8		19	14		3			20	4	10		5			6	24					1804
8		/	/		3			20	4	10		5			6	24					1808
8		29	15		7			25	4	11		8			8	25					1812
8		29	15		8			25	4	11		8			8	25					1816
8		29	15		8			24	4	11		7			8	25					1820
		26							4						7						1824
8		/	15		16			28	4	11		11			7	24					1828
8		42	15		21			30	4	11		15			7	23					1832
8		42	15		21			30	4	11		15			7	23					1836
8		42	15		21			30	4	11		15			7	23					1840
7		36	11		23			26	4	9		13			6	17					1844
7		36	11		23			26	4	9		13	4		6	17			4		1848
7		35	10		23			27	4	8		12	4		5	15			5		1852
7		35	10		23			27	4	8		12	4		5	15			5		1856
/		35	10		23		3	27	4	8		12	4		5	15			5		1860
7		33			21		3	26	4						5			5	8		1864
7		33	9		21		3	26	4	6		10			5			5	8		1868
9		35	10		22		3	29	4	7		12	8		5	11		5	10		1872
9		35	10		22		3	29	4	7		12	8		5	11		5	10		1876
9		35	10		22		3	29	4	7		12	8		5	11		5	10		1880
9		36	11		23		3	30	4	9		12	13		4	12		6	11		1884
9		36	11		23		3	30	4	9		12	13		4	12		6	11		1888
10		36	11	/	/		/	32	4	9	4	12	15		4	12	4	6	12	3	1892
10		36	11	3	23		4	32	4	9	4	12	15	3	4	12	4	6	12	3	1896
10		36	11	3	23		4	32	4	9	4	12	15	3	4	12	4	6	12	3	1900
12		39	12	4	23		4	34	4	9	4	12	18	3	4	12	5	7	13	3	1904
12		39	12	4	23	7	4	34	4	9	4	12	18	3	4	12	5	7	13	3	1908
14	3	45	12	5	24	10	5	38	5	9	5	12	20	4	4	12	7	8	13	3	1912
14	3	45	12	5	24	10	5	38	5	9	5	12	20	4	4	12	7	/	13	3	1916
14	3	45	12	5	24	10	5	38	5	9	5	12	20	4	4	12	7	8	13	3	1920
14	3	45	12	5	24	10	5	38	5	9	5	12	20	4	4	12	7	8	13	3	1924
14	3	45	12	5	24	10	5	38	5	9	5	12	20	4	4	12	7	8	13	3	1928
16	3	47	13	4	26	11	5	36	4	8	4	11	23	4	3	11	8	8	12	3	1932
16	3	47	13	4	26	11	5	36	4	8	4	11	23	4	3	11	8	8	12	3	1936
16	3	47	13	4	26	11	5	36	4	8	4	11	23	4	3	11	8	8	12	3	1940
16	4	47	14	4	25	10	6	35	4	8	4	12	23	4	3	11	8	8	12	3	1944
16	4	47	14	4	25	10	6	35	4	8	4	/	23	4	3	11	8	8	12	3	1948
16	4	45	14	4	25	8	6	32	4	8	4	11	24	4	3	12	9	8	12	3	1952
16	4	45	14	4	25	8	6	32	4	8	4	11	24	4	3	12	9	8	12	3	1956
16	4	45	14	4	25	/	6	32	4	8	4	11	24	4	3	12	9	8	12	3	1960
17	4	43	13	4	26	8	6	29	4	8	4	11	25	4	3	12	9	7	12	3	1964
17	4	43	/	4	26	8	6	29	4	8	4	11	25	4	3	12	9	7	12	3	1968
17	4	41	13	3	25	8	6	27	4	8	4	10	26	4	3	/	9	6	11	3	1972
17	4	41	13	3	25	8	6	27	4	8	4	10	26	4	3	12	/	6	11	3	1976
17	4	41	13	3	25	8	6	27	4	8	4	10	26	4	3	12	9	6	11	3	1980
16	5	36	13	3	23	8	7	25	4	8	3	11	29	5	3	12	10	6	11	3	1984
16	5	36	13	3	23	8	7	25	4	8	3	11	29	5	3	12	10	/	11	3	1988
15	5	33	14	3	21	8	7	23	4	8	3	11	32	5	3	13	11	5	11	3	1992
15	5	33	14	3	21	8	7	23	4	8	3	11	32	5	3	13	11	5	11	3	1996
15	5	33	14	3	21	8	7	23	4	8	3	11	32	5	3	13	11	5	11	3	2000
15	5	31	15	3	20	7	7	21	4	8	3	11	34	5	3	13	11	5	10	3	2004
15	5	31	15	3	20	7	7	21	4	8	3	11	34	5	3	13	11	5	10	3	2008
14	5	29	15	3	18	7	7	20	4	9	3	11	38	6	3	13	12	5	10	3	2012

Splits in state electoral votes

In most elections, the candidate who wins the highest number of a state's popular votes receives all the state's electoral votes. In some elections, however, Electoral College members from the same state have voted for different candidates. This situation is shown by a slash mark (/) in the table on these two pages. Since 1804, the following splits in electoral votes have occurred:

Election	State's total vote and split
1804	Maryland 11 (Jefferson 9, Charles C. Pinckney 2).
1808	Maryland 11 (Madison 9, Pinckney 2); New York 19 (Madison 13, George Clinton 6); North Carolina 14 (Madison 11, Pinckney 3).
1812	Maryland 11 (Madison 6, Clinton 5).
1820	New Hampshire 8 (Monroe 7, J. Q. Adams 1).
1828	Maine 9 (J. Q. Adams 8, Jackson 1); Maryland 11 (J. Q. Adams 6, Jackson 5); New York 36 (Jackson 20, J. Q. Adams 16).
1832	Maryland 8 (Henry Clay 5, Jackson 3).
1860	New Jersey 7 (Lincoln 4, Stephen A. Douglas 3).
1872	Georgia 8 (Benjamin G. Brown 6, Charles J. Jenkins 2); Kentucky 12 (Thomas A. Hendricks 8, Brown 4); Missouri 15 (Brown 8, Hendricks 6, David Davis 1).
1880	California 6 (Winfield Scott Hancock 5, Garfield 1).
1892	California 9 (Cleveland 8, B. Harrison 1); Michigan 14 (B. Harrison 9, Cleveland 5); North Dakota 3 (Cleveland 1, B. Harrison 1, James B. Weaver 1); Ohio 23 (B. Harrison 22, Cleveland 1); Oregon 4 (B. Harrison 3, Weaver 1).
1896	California 9 (McKinley 8, William Jennings Bryan 1); Kentucky 13 (McKinley 12, Bryan 1).
1904	Maryland 8 (Alton B. Parker 7, T. Roosevelt 1).
1908	Maryland 8 (Bryan 6, Taft 2).
1912	California 13 (T. Roosevelt 11, Wilson 2).
1916	West Virginia 8 (Charles E. Hughes 7, Wilson 1).
1948	Tennessee 12 (Truman 11, Strom Thurmond 1).
1956	Alabama 11 (Adlai E. Stevenson 10, Walter B. Jones 1).
1960	Alabama 11 (Harry F. Byrd 6, Kennedy 5); Oklahoma 8 (Nixon 7, Byrd 1).
1968	North Carolina 13 (Nixon 12, George C. Wallace 1).
1972	Virginia 12 (Nixon 11, John Hospers 1).
1976	Washington 9 (Ford 8, Reagan 1).
1988	West Virginia 6 (Michael S. Dukakis 5, Lloyd Bentsen 1).
2000	D.C. 3 (Al Gore 2; one elector did not vote).
2008	Nebraska 5 (John McCain 4, Obama 1).

all the state's electoral votes. The exceptions to this rule are Maine and Nebraska, which use the *congressional district method.* Under this method, each of the state's congressional districts is assigned an electoral vote, which is given to the candidate who wins a plurality in the district's popular vote. But Maine and Nebraska each also have two statewide electoral votes, to represent the state's two senators.

The college in action. On Election Day, in November, voters choose among presidential and vice presidential candidates from different political parties. The votes do not directly determine which candidate will become president. Instead, they determine which party's electors will represent each state in the Electoral College. In some states, the ballots list the presidential and vice presidential candidates, not the proposed electors. For this reason, many voters do not realize they do not vote directly for the president and vice president.

In December following the election, the electors in each state assemble and cast their ballots. Either by custom or by law, the electors vote for the candidates designated by their party. In rare cases, a state's electoral votes may be split. A split occurs when an elector chooses not to vote for the party's candidates. Such an elector—sometimes called a *faithless elector*—may, in some states, be punished by law.

After the electoral votes are cast, they are sent to the vice president of the United States, acting as president of the Senate, and to the head of the General Services Administration in Washington, D.C. In January, at a joint session of Congress, the vice president opens and tallies the votes. One Democrat and one Republican from each chamber count the votes. The candidate who gets a majority of the electoral votes is declared elected. If no candidate has a majority, the state delegations in the House of Representatives choose the president from the three candidates with the highest number of electoral votes. In such an election, each state has one vote, determined by a majority vote among that state's delegation. If the vote is tied, the state is counted as abstaining.

History. The manner of electing the president was a major issue at the Constitutional Convention of 1787. The convention rejected the proposal that Congress elect the chief executive, on the grounds that the president would then be under the control of the legislature. The convention also rejected the proposal that the people elect the president directly. Eventually, the convention agreed on a method of indirect popular election, which became the Electoral College.

The Constitution established that each state legislature could decide how that state's electors are chosen. At first, most states allowed their legislatures to choose the electors. But after 1800, more and more states began choosing electors in popular elections. Today, all states and the District of Columbia use this method.

From 1789 to 1801, each elector voted for two presidential candidates on the same ballot. The person with the most votes became president, and the runner-up became vice president. But in the election of 1800, two candidates, Thomas Jefferson and Aaron Burr, received the same number of electoral votes. The election went to the House of Representatives, where each state had one vote. Jefferson was elected president, and Burr became vice president. That election led to Amendment 12 to the Constitution, ratified in 1804, providing that electors should designate their votes for president and vice president on separate ballots.

The House had to settle another presidential election in 1824. Andrew Jackson received more electoral votes than any of the other candidates, but he failed to win a majority. John Quincy Adams was the runner-up. In the House, Henry Clay, another candidate, threw his support to Adams. As a result, Adams became president, even though Jackson had a larger share of the popular vote. Clay became Adams's secretary of state in 1825.

The growth of powerful political parties has greatly influenced the role of the Electoral College. Electors today pledge to vote for the candidates from their political party, even if they do not always agree that the party's candidates are the best qualified. Because this pledge is rarely broken, the outcome of a presidential election is usually known after the electors are determined on Election Day. As a result, the Electoral College vote has become largely a ceremonial procedure.

Some people argue that the Electoral College should be replaced with direct election of the president. They point out that the college has elected four presidents whose opponents received more popular votes: John Quincy Adams in 1824, Rutherford B. Hayes in 1876, Benjamin Harrison in 1888, and George W. Bush in 2000. Some people also argue that direct election might encourage third and fourth parties, and thus increase voter choice and voter turnout. During the 2000's, several states considered a proposal that would award all of a state's electoral votes to the candidate who won the national popular vote, in effect bypassing the Electoral College. The proposal would become law only if states that totaled at least 270 electoral votes passed it.

Other people believe the Electoral College system should be preserved. They argue that the direct election of the president would reduce the importance of individual states, particularly those with smaller populations. Without the Electoral College, candidates would more likely concentrate on highly populated states and ignore other parts of the country.

Paul Gronke

Related articles. See the separate biography on each U.S. president for election information. See also:
Constitution of the United States (Article II; Amendment 12)
Electoral Commission
President of the United States
Vice president of the United States

Electoral Commission was a group created by Congress in 1877 to decide who won the presidential election of 1876. Both Republicans and Democrats claimed victory. Samuel J. Tilden, the Democratic candidate, had 184 electoral votes, or one short of a majority in the Electoral College. Rutherford B. Hayes, the Republican candidate, had 165 votes. Twenty votes were disputed.

To settle the matter, Congress created the Electoral Commission. The commission was made up of 15 members: 5 senators, 5 representatives, and 5 Supreme Court justices. Congress carefully arranged that 3 senators and 2 representatives were to be Republicans, while 2 senators and 3 representatives were to be Democrats. Of the justices, 2 Democrats and 2 Republicans were named, and these 4 had power to choose a fifth. They would probably have chosen David Davis of Illinois, an independent in politics. But his decision to accept election to the United States Senate left only Republican justices from whom to choose. Therefore, the Electoral Commission had a Republican majority of 8 to 7. By a strict party vote, the commission gave every one of the disputed votes, and the election, to Hayes. H. Wayne Morgan

See also **Electoral College; Hayes, Rutherford Birchard** (The election dispute); **Tilden, Samuel Jones.**

Electra, *ih LEHK truh,* in Greek mythology was famous for her loyalty to her father, the Greek leader Agamemnon. Clytemnestra, who was Electra's mother, and Clytemnestra's lover, Aegisthus, murdered Agamemnon. Electra sent Orestes, her younger brother, from the royal palace to protect him from Clytemnestra. Electra hated her mother, but lived with her and Aegisthus until Orestes was grown. Orestes then returned from exile to avenge the death of his father, killing Clytemnestra and Aegisthus with Electra's help. Electra is a central character in tragedies by the Greek playwrights Aeschylus, Sophocles, and Euripides.

The Swiss psychologist Carl Jung originated the term *Electra complex.* He used it to describe a girl's excessive attachment to her father and corresponding hostility toward her mother. John Hamilton

See also **Agamemnon; Clytemnestra.**

Electra complex. See **Oedipus complex.**

Electric bell is a type of bell operated by an electric current. There are two types of electric bells. One type rings continuously when the switch that controls it is on. This type of bell is commonly used in schools and factories. The other kind, the door chime, rings only once or twice when the switch is turned on—that is, when the doorbell button is pushed.

The parts of a continuously ringing bell include the switch; an electromagnet, a device that acts as a magnet when a current runs through it; and an *armature,* a movable metal part. A clapper is attached to the end of the armature. Also attached to the armature is a spring that rests against a screw. Wiring runs from the source of electric current to the switch and from the switch to the electromagnet. Another wire runs from the screw back to the source of the electric current. Together, the parts of the bell form an electric circuit.

When the switch is turned on, the current flows through the electromagnet, and the electromagnet attracts the armature. The movement of the armature causes the clapper to strike the bell and the spring to move off the screw. When the spring moves off the screw, the circuit is broken and the current stops flowing. Then, the armature falls away from the electromagnet. When the armature returns to its original position, the spring comes in contact with the screw again and reestablishes the flow of electric current. The process repeats, and the electric bell keeps ringing as long as the operating switch is on.

A door chime does not have the spring and screw. Thus, the armature and clapper move only once each time the control switch is operated, and the bell sounds only once. If a second bell is set up for the clapper to strike when it falls away from the first bell, two sounds can occur for each switch operation. Donald W. Novotny

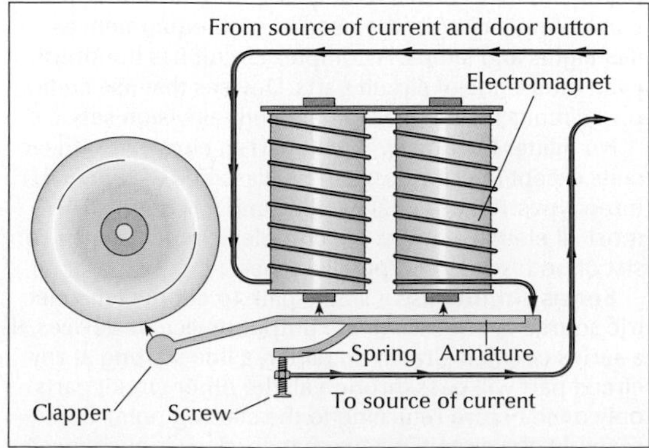

WORLD BOOK diagram by Kim Downing

An electric bell rings when a current flows through its electromagnet. The current makes the electromagnet attract the metal armature, which causes the clapper to strike the bell.

Electric car is an automobile that uses an electric motor instead of an internal combustion engine. Most electric cars are powered by rechargeable batteries and so do not consume gasoline. *Fuel cells*—batterylike devices that store energy in the form of compressed hydrogen—can also power electric vehicles.

Electric cars have several advantages over engine-powered cars. Their operation produces no exhaust, and so their widespread use could reduce air pollution. They use batteries, and so they do not necessarily consume increasingly scarce petroleum resources. Electric cars are quiet, reducing noise in congested areas.

Electric cars also have disadvantages. They often use lithium-ion batteries, which are expensive. Depending on the battery size, electric cars generally have a limited range before their batteries must be recharged. Some electric cars can travel no more than 40 miles (64 kilometers) on a single charge. Electric vehicles may have even more limited ranges in extreme weather conditions that require high use of electric power by the heating or cooling system. In contrast, many engine-powered cars can go more than 300 miles (500 kilometers) before refueling. Charging an electric vehicle battery can take several hours, but refueling an engine-powered vehicle takes a few minutes. People who park on city streets—such as apartment dwellers—may not have access to an electric outlet for recharging their electric cars.

Although electric cars do not create air pollution in their operation, many electric power plants do. Thus, charging an electric car may still add to pollution. The manufacture of batteries also causes pollution. On the other hand, electric car batteries can store excess energy created by power plants, which could help the electric power distribution system operate more efficiently.

How electric cars work. An electric car is powered by one or more electric motors. In many cases, the motors are coupled directly to the wheels. This system eliminates the need for a transmission. The driver uses an *electronic controller* to control the rate at which energy flows from the batteries to the motor or motors. When the vehicle's brakes are applied, the motor or motors become generators sending electric power back to recharge the batteries. This process, called *regenerative braking,* reduces the energy needed to drive the car.

History. The first electric cars appeared in Europe during the 1880's. They soon became popular in the United States. Americans drove more *electrics* than

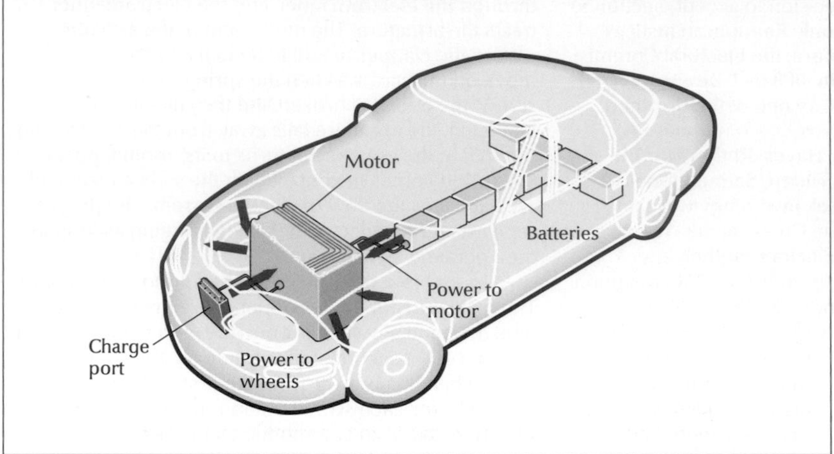

Power to operate an electric car comes from batteries that run a motor. Power to recharge the batteries (shown by red arrows) may come from the motor, wheels, or an outside charger.

WORLD BOOK diagram by Precision Graphics

gasoline cars during the late 1800's. By the early 1900's, however, gasoline-powered cars had become more powerful, performed better, needed less refueling, and were cheaper to operate than electric cars were. The electric car had almost disappeared by the late 1920's.

In the 1960's, increasing concern about air pollution and dwindling petroleum supplies renewed interest in electric cars. In the 1970's, limited production of electric cars resumed. Sales of electric cars have remained low, however, due to their high purchase price, their limited travel range, and their relatively poor performance.

Since the late 1970's, manufacturers have combined features of electric cars and gasoline-powered cars. *Hybrid cars,* for example, contain both an engine and a battery-powered electric motor. Hybrid cars benefit from regenerative breaking, which can make them much more efficient than cars powered by engines only. In 2010, General Motors released a hybrid electric car, the Chevy Volt, that contained a small gasoline engine. Unlike the engine in other hybrid cars, the Volt's engine does not directly power the car itself under most conditions. It is generally used only to recharge the car's battery and extend its range. Gregory W. Davis

See also **Battery; Fuel cell; Hybrid car.**

Electric chair. See Electrocution.

Electric charge. See Electricity.

Electric circuit is the closed path or paths followed by an *electric current.* An electric current is a flow of tiny particles called electrons. When current flows in a circuit, electric energy associated with the current can do useful work. An electric circuit has three basic parts: (1) a *source* of electric energy, such as a battery or generator; (2) an *output device,* such as a lamp; and (3) a *connection* between the source and the output device, such as a wire or cable.

The source converts some type of nonelectric energy into electric energy. For example, an electric generator changes mechanical energy into electric energy. The electric source creates an *electromotive force* (emf) that causes an electric current to flow in the circuit. Emf is measured in units called *volts,* and the current it produces is measured in units called *amperes.* Electric outlets in homes in the United States and Canada supply electric energy at voltages from 110 to 120 volts. But the electric outlet itself is not a source of electric energy. Transmission lines connect the outlet to a generator at an electric power plant, which is the source.

An output device uses the electric energy from the source to do something useful. For example, a lamp provides light and an electric motor produces mechanical motion to run a vacuum cleaner. The source and output device must be connected so that electric current can flow from the source to the device and back again. The return path prevents an electric charge from collecting in the circuit. A collected charge would oppose the flow of current and keep the circuit from functioning.

Various devices may be added to a circuit to control the current flowing in it. For example, a lamp's circuit may include a switch to turn the lamp on and off easily. When the switch is off, a gap separates the connecting wires so that the current cannot complete its path. A circuit with this kind of gap is called an *open circuit.* A *closed circuit* has no gaps in the current's path. Some circuits, including those used in homes, are equipped with a *fuse* or a *circuit breaker.* These devices act as an automatic switch that opens the circuit if too much current flows through it. Excessive current may overheat the wires and start a fire or damage output devices.

An electric circuit may be simple or complex. A simple circuit may consist of only the three basic circuit parts. Simple circuits are used in such equipment as flashlights and lamps. A complex circuit has hundreds or even thousands of circuit parts. Devices that use complex circuits include computers and television sets.

No matter how many circuit parts a circuit has, all circuits except the simplest can be classified as one of three types: (1) series, (2) parallel, and (3) complex. Almost all electric circuits are complex circuits, which consist of both series and parallel types.

Series circuits use a single path to connect the electric source or sources to the output device or devices. If a series circuit is drawn on paper, a line starting at any circuit part will pass through all the other circuit parts only once before returning to the starting point. For example, the circuit in a two-battery flashlight connects the positive terminal of the first battery to the negative terminal of the second battery. The positive terminal of the second battery touches the center terminal of the flashlight bulb. If the switch is closed, the outer terminal of the bulb touches the negative terminal of the first battery, completing the circuit and lighting the bulb.

Series circuits may be found chiefly in flashlights, some Christmas tree lights, and other simple equipment. These circuits have limited uses because any change in one circuit part affects all the circuit parts. If one light bulb in a series circuit burns out, all the other bulbs also go out because the burned-out bulb has opened the circuit.

The voltage provided by a group of electric sources connected in series is the sum of their individual voltages. But the same amount of current flows through each source and output device. For example, each battery in a two-battery flashlight supplies 1 ½ volts, and the two together supply 3 volts. The same amount of current flows through each battery and the bulb. Electric sources are connected in series to provide more voltage than one source alone can produce.

Parallel circuits provide more than one path for current. After current leaves a source, it follows two or more paths before returning to the source. If two identical flashlight bulbs are connected in parallel, current flows from a battery through each lamp individually and then back to the battery. Either bulb may be removed from the circuit without breaking the circuit for the other bulb. When both bulbs are on, each receives half the total current from the battery.

Parallel circuits provide the same voltage for every source and output device in the circuit. For example, two 1 ½-volt flashlight batteries connected in parallel provide an emf of 1 ½ volts. Electrical sources are connected in parallel to provide more current than one source can produce. But only sources with the same voltage can be connected in parallel. Otherwise, excess current would flow from one source into the other and be wasted.

All household lights and appliances are connected in parallel because a parallel circuit allows all devices to operate on the same voltage. The voltage does not change if a piece of equipment is added or removed. However, the total current passing through the fuse or circuit breaker may increase or decrease.

Circuit mathematics. Electricians and engineers use several mathematical formulas to calculate the current and voltage in each part of a circuit. The most important of these formulas are *Ohm's law* and *Kirchhoff's laws.* They were discovered by two German physicists, Georg S. Ohm and Gustav R. Kirchhoff.

Ohm's law relates the voltage and current in a circuit to the *resistance* of the circuit. Resistance opposes the flow of electricity and consumes power from the circuit by changing electric energy into heat. Electricians measure resistance in units called *ohms.* Ohm's law is expressed in the equation $E = IR$. This law states that the voltage (E) equals the current (I) multiplied by the resistance (R), through which the current flows. For example, if a current of 3 amperes passes through a resistance of 2 ohms, the voltage is 3 amperes $\times$ 2 ohms $=$ 6 volts.

In a series circuit, the total resistance equals the sum of the resistances of each device in the circuit. The addition of devices to a series circuit increases the resistance and thus decreases the total current. But in a parallel circuit, adding devices provides additional paths for the current and decreases the total resistance.

Kirchhoff's first law states that the sum of the currents entering any point in a circuit equals the sum of the currents leaving that point. This law is based on the fact that an electric charge is conserved. In other words, the amount of electric charge—electrons—entering the point per second must equal the amount of electric charge leaving the point per second. Kirchhoff's second law states that the sum of the changes in voltage around any circuit is zero. In other words, the voltage increases through the sources by the same amount that it decreases through the output devices. For example, starting at the base end of a two-battery flashlight, the emf increases through each battery. It increases by 1 ½ volts in each, for a total increase of 3 volts. The emf decreases 3 volts going through the bulb. Robert B. Prigo

Related articles in *World Book* include:

Circuit breaker
Electric current
Electric switch
Electricity
Electronics (Electronic circuits)
Fuse (electricity)
Ground

Electric current is the movement or flow of electric charges. A charge can be either positive or negative. The protons that make up part of the nucleus of every atom have a positive electric charge. The electrons that surround the nucleus have a negative charge. An elec-

Series circuits and parallel circuits

All circuits, except the simplest, are either (1) series, (2) parallel, or (3) *complex* (a combination of the two). Series circuits have their parts connected in one path. Parallel circuits have more than one path.

WORLD BOOK diagram

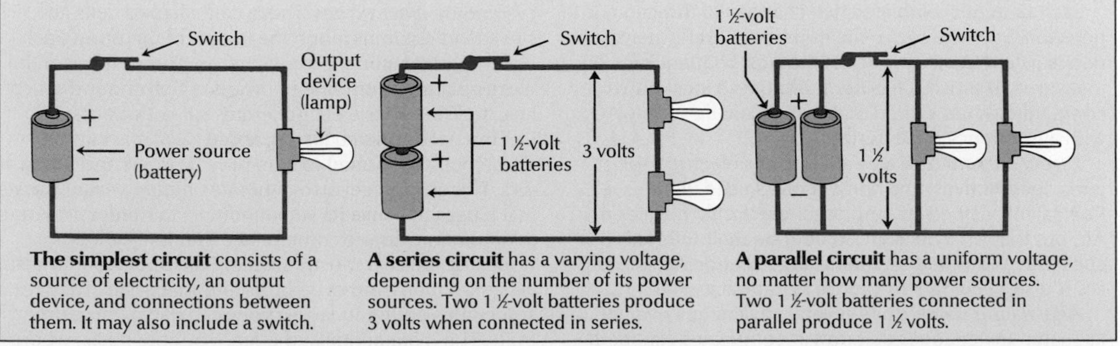

The simplest circuit consists of a source of electricity, an output device, and connections between them. It may also include a switch.

A series circuit has a varying voltage, depending on the number of its power sources. Two 1 ½-volt batteries produce 3 volts when connected in series.

A parallel circuit has a uniform voltage, no matter how many power sources. Two 1 ½-volt batteries connected in parallel produce 1 ½ volts.

tric current can consist of positive, negative, or both types of charges.

The American statesman and scientist Benjamin Franklin originated the idea that electric current flows from positive to negative. But other scientists later proved that electric current actually flows in the opposite direction—from negative to positive.

Franklin's idea also fails to describe the way electric current flows through metals. Each atom of a metal wire has at least one electron that is not held so closely by the nucleus as the others are. Such loosely held electrons can move freely through the metal. But the nucleus cannot move through the wire. Thus, current flowing through a metal wire consists of free electrons.

Conductors and insulators. Electric current flows most easily through substances called *conductors.* The number of free electrons in a substance determines how well it conducts current. Such metals as aluminum, copper, silver, and gold are good conductors because they have at least one free electron per atom. Some metals, such as lead and tin, are poorer conductors than other metals because they have less than one free electron per atom. Poor conductors resist the flow of electric current more than good conductors do. Resistance changes electric energy into heat. Engineers use units called *ohms* to measure resistance (see **Ohm**).

Substances with no free electrons, such as glass, mica, and rubber, do not normally conduct electric current. They are called *insulators.* Some substances, including germanium and silicon, are neither good conductors nor insulators. They are called *semiconductors* (see **Semiconductor**).

To produce an electric current, some type of nonelectric energy must be converted into an *electromotive force* (emf). For example, a battery creates an emf by changing chemical energy into electrical potential energy. Thus, a battery has a *potential difference* (difference in potential energy) between its ends that causes electrons to flow in a conductor. Emf is measured in units called *volts.* An emf of one volt, when connected to a conductor with a resistance of one ohm, causes 6,241,500,000,000,000,000 electrons to flow past a point in the conductor in one second. This amount of electric current is called one *ampere.* See **Volt; Ampere.**

Direct and alternating current. An electric current is either direct or alternating. Direct current (DC) always flows in the same direction. It is produced by batteries and DC generators. Alternating current (AC) regularly reverses its direction of flow. It is produced by AC generators. Nearly all homes and other buildings use AC.

Each time AC completes two changes of direction, it goes through one *cycle.* The number of cycles per second is called the *frequency* of the AC. Frequency is measured in units called *hertz.* Almost all local power companies in the United States and Canada supply AC with a frequency of 60 hertz.

Direct current operates automobile electrical systems, locomotives, and some motors used in industry. Radios, television sets, and other electronic devices use AC, but they also need DC to operate their internal circuits. Devices called *rectifiers* easily change AC into DC. DC is also necessary to charge storage batteries.

Alternating current has several advantages over DC. Its major advantage is that power companies can transmit it easily and efficiently. Electric current loses the least amount of energy when traveling at high voltages. But these high voltages are not safe to use in homes. Devices called *transformers* can easily increase or decrease AC voltage.

A conductor can carry more than one alternating current at a time. A current consisting of two or more alternating currents is a *polyphase current.* One common kind of polyphase current is *three-phase current,* which consists of three alternating currents. Phillip W. Alley

Related articles in *World Book* include:

Battery
Electric circuit
Electric generator
Electric power
Electricity
Insulator, Electric
Transformer

Electric eel is a long, narrow fish that can give off a strong electric *discharge,* or shock. Hundreds of fish *species* (kinds) can generate weak electric discharges of less than 1 volt. Electric eels can produce a discharge of up to 650 volts. This discharge can kill a fish or stun a human being, though electric eels rarely harm people.

The electric eel lives in muddy streams and small rivers of northern South America, in the Amazon and Orinoco river basins. It may reach more than 8 feet (2.4 meters) long. The fish is olive-brown with a yellow or orange belly. Its long, pointed tail makes up about four-fifths of the total body length. It has two small fins on either side of the body behind the gills, and one long fin on the underside. Unlike most fish, it has no fins on the back or tail.

The electric eel's electric current is generated by three pairs of electric organs. The largest pair runs almost the length of the fish. Each electric organ is made up of thousands of modified muscle cells called *electroplaques* or *electrocytes.* These coin-shaped cells are stacked in columns along the length of the body. Each electroplaque stores a small charge. The charges of the electroplaques combine to produce a stronger discharge. The electric eel generates powerful bursts of electric current, each lasting about $\frac{1}{500}$ of a second. These bursts are used to stun prey or to escape predators. The electric eel also generates much weaker bursts that it uses to sense its surroundings, to detect prey, and to communicate with other electric eels.

WORLD BOOK illustration by Colin Newman, Linden Artists Ltd.

The electric eel can produce an electric discharge.

Electric eels eat mostly smaller fish, but they may also eat amphibians and even birds and mammals. They sometimes gather in large groups to eat falling palm fruits. The male builds and guards bubble nests, where

Photoconductive electric eye One use for a photoconductive cell, *left,* is to count objects moving on a conveyor belt, *right.* The cell allows an electric current from a counting device to flow through it as long as the light beam from the light source shines on it. When an object on the belt cuts off the beam, the cell stops the flow of current and the counting device adds one number to its total.

WORLD BOOK photo by Ralph Brunke

WORLD BOOK diagram by Tom Morgan

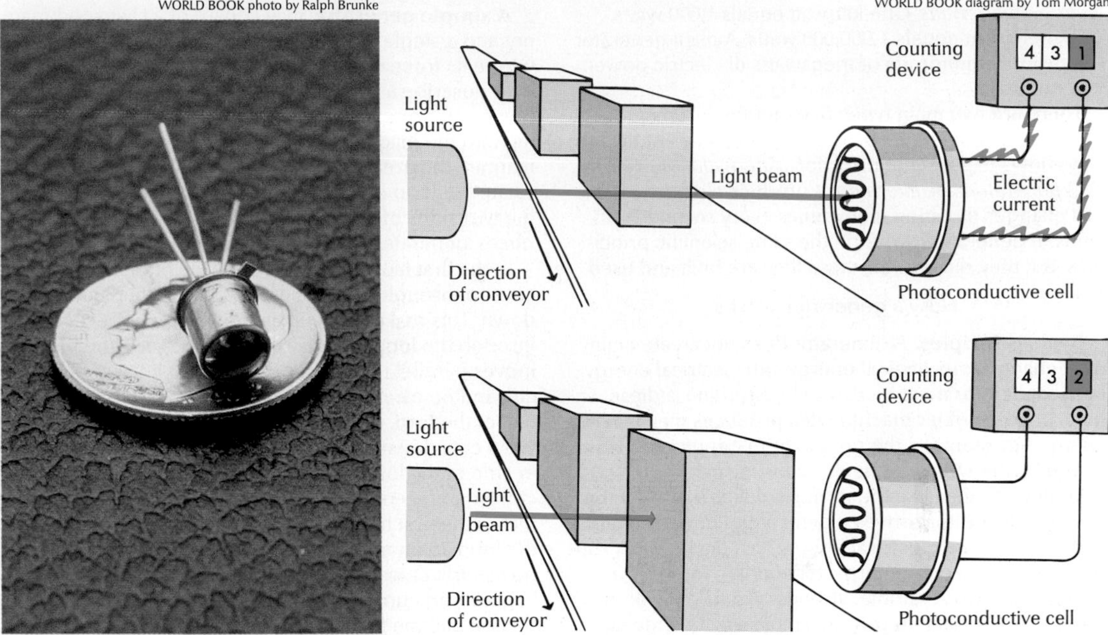

eggs and *larvae* (young) develop. The male also guards young in his mouth for several weeks after hatching, during which time he does not feed. James S. Albert

Scientific classification. The scientific name of the electric eel is *Electrophorus electricus.*

Electric eye is a device that either produces an electric current or allows a current to flow when light shines on it. The strength of the current depends upon the amount of light that falls on the electric eye. When the light stops, so does the current.

Electric eyes can be made more sensitive to light than is the human eye. They can see objects when a person would see only total darkness. Electric eyes respond not only to visible light but also to infrared and ultraviolet light. Some electric eyes react so rapidly to changes in light that they can "see" bullets in flight.

What electric eyes do. An electric eye can act as a switch to turn another device on or off. For example, an electric eye placed opposite a light across a conveyor belt can count objects on the belt. Each time an object comes between the light and the electric eye, the current flowing from the eye stops. A counting device connected to the eye then adds to the total. Electric eyes can turn on street lights or house lights by sensing when the sun goes down. They can set off burglar alarms as well.

Electric eyes also measure amounts of light. The electric eyes on some cameras measure the light and then properly adjust the shutter. Motion-picture projectors use electric eyes to produce sound from special patterns on the film. Digital cameras use an array of many electric eyes to sense light. A computer later processes and combines the electrical information gathered from the individual eyes to render a digital photograph.

How electric eyes work. Scientists call electric eyes *photoelectric cells.* There are three basic kinds of photoelectric cells—*phototubes, solar cells,* and *photoconductive cells.*

Phototubes are special vacuum or gas-filled tubes that contain *photosensitive* materials. These materials give off electrons when light strikes them. Every phototube has a *cathode* made of photosensitive material, and an *anode.* When light strikes the cathode, it causes electrons to flow to the anode and creates a current. See **Photomultiplier tube.**

Solar cells, also called *solar batteries* or *photovoltaic cells,* are made of *semiconductor* materials (see **Semiconductor**). When light shines on a solar cell, electrons are given off. They produce a current in a circuit connected to the cell.

Photoconductive cells are also made of semiconductor materials, but they do not create an electric current as solar cells do. Instead, when light shines on them, their *resistance* (opposition to the flow of current) decreases. Michael B. Radunsky

Electric fish is any of several fishes with special muscles that can generate an electric current. Electric fishes emit strong electric shocks to protect themselves from other animals and to stun or kill prey. They discharge weaker electric currents to detect animals and objects in the muddy waters where they live. The *electric eel* of South America gives the most powerful electric shock. It can produce enough current to stun a human being. An *electric catfish* lives in the rivers of tropical Africa. See also **Electric eel; Electric ray.** John J. Poluhowich

Electric generator is a machine that changes mechanical energy—the energy of motion—into electrical energy. Generators produce almost all the electric power used by people. They furnish electric power that runs machines in factories, provides lighting, and operates home appliances. Generators were once called *dynamos,* a shortened form of the term *dynamoelectric.*

The size of generators is usually measured in *kilowatts* or *megawatts.* One kilowatt equals 1,000 watts. One megawatt equals 1,000,000 watts. A giant generator can produce hundreds of megawatts of electric power. See **Kilowatt.**

There are two main types of generators. *Direct-current* (DC) *generators* produce electric current that always flows in the same direction. *Alternating-current* (AC) *generators,* or *alternators,* produce electric current that changes direction many times every second. Both kinds of generators work on the same scientific principles. But they differ in the ways they are built and used.

How a generator works

Basic principles. A generator does not create energy. It changes mechanical energy into electrical energy. Every generator must be driven by a turbine, a diesel engine, or some other machine that produces mechanical energy. For example, the generator in an automobile is driven by the same engine that runs the car.

Engineers often use the term *prime mover* for the mechanical device that drives a generator. For a generator to produce more electrical energy, this device must supply more mechanical energy. If the prime mover is a wind turbine, for example, stronger winds must flow through the turbine to produce more electric power.

Generators produce electric power by means of a principle discovered independently by two physicists in the early 1830's—Michael Faraday of England and Joseph Henry of the United States. They found they could produce electric current in a coil of copper wire by moving the coil near a magnet or by moving a magnet near the coil. This process is called *electromagnetic induction.* The *voltage,* or *electromotive force,* of the electric current produced is called an *induced* voltage or *induced* electromotive force. If the wire is part of a closed circuit of wires, the induced voltage causes an electric current to flow through the circuit.

© David R. Frazier

Electric generators at a dam furnish a tremendous amount of electric power. Water turbines drive these generators. Engineers often refer to the mechanical device that drives a generator as a *prime mover.*

A simple generator may consist of a U-shaped magnet and a single loop of wire. The area around a magnet where its force can be felt is called a *magnetic field.* To help describe a magnetic field, we think of *lines of force* going out from the north pole of a magnet and returning into the magnet at its south pole. The stronger the magnet, the greater the number of lines of force. If you rotate the loop of wire between the poles of the magnet, the two sides of the loop "cut" the lines of force. This *induces* (generates) electric current in the loop.

In the first half of the turn, one side of the loop of wire cuts up through the lines of force. The other side cuts down. This makes the current flow in one direction through the loop. Halfway through the turn, the loop moves parallel to the lines of force. No lines of force are cut, and no electric current is generated. In the second half of the turn, the side of the loop that was cutting upward cuts downward through the lines of force. The other side of the loop cuts upward. This makes the electric current induced in the loop flow in a direction opposite that of the first half of the turn. At the bottom of the turn, the loop again moves parallel to the lines of force and no electric current is generated. For every full turn, the voltage and current that are generated travel in one direction half the time and in the opposite direction the other half of the time. Twice during each turn no current flows. The voltage and current are known as an *alternating voltage* and an *alternating current.* The voltage that a generator produces can be increased by increasing (1) the strength of the magnetic field (number of lines of force), (2) the speed at which the loop rotates, or (3) the number of loops of wire that cut the magnetic field.

One complete revolution of the loop through the lines of force is called a *cycle.* The number of such cycles in a second is called the *frequency* of the voltage or current and is measured in units called *hertz.* One hertz equals one cycle per second. The electric current in North America has a frequency of 60 hertz. In most of the rest of the world, the frequency is 50 hertz.

Electromagnetism. A loop of wire rotated between the poles of a magnet produces another important electromagnetic effect in addition to generating electric current. When the loop of wire carries current, the current produces a magnetic field around the wire. This magnetic field works against the magnetic field of the magnet. It makes the loop harder to turn. The more electric current induced in the loop, the stronger its magnetic field, and the more difficult it is to turn. That is why the prime mover that turns a generator must furnish increased amounts of mechanical energy to increase the output of current by the generator. This same magnetic force in the loop causes the rotation in electric motors. Under proper circumstances, generators can act as motors, and motors as generators. See **Electric motor.**

Parts of a generator. A generator has two main parts: an *armature* and a *field structure.* The armature contains coils of wire in which the current is induced. It acts like the loop of wire in the simple generator. The field structure acts like the simple generator's magnet. It sets up magnetic lines of force. *Electromagnets* create

How electric current is generated

A simple generator may consist of a U-shaped magnet and a wire loop. Lines of force flow from the north pole of the magnet to the south pole, forming a magnetic field. Rotating the wire between the poles cuts through the lines of force and generates an electric current in the loop.

WORLD BOOK diagrams by Art Grebetz

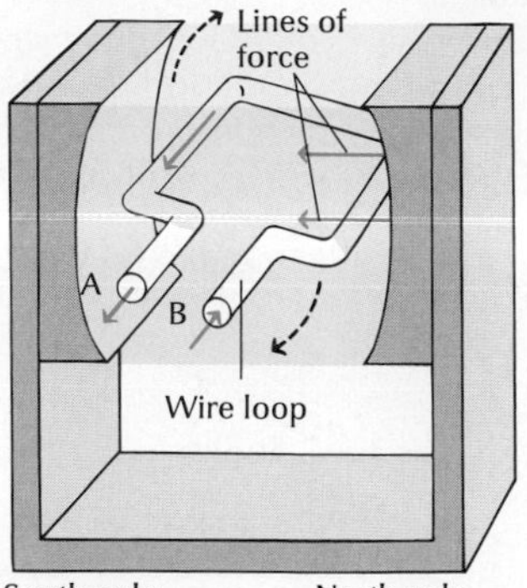

The current flows from point B to point A through the loop when the wire is rotated clockwise, as shown here.

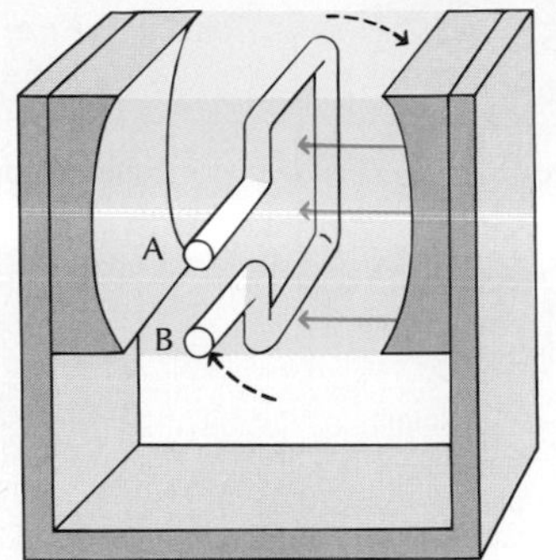

No electric current is generated in the loop in this diagram because the wire does not cut through the lines of force.

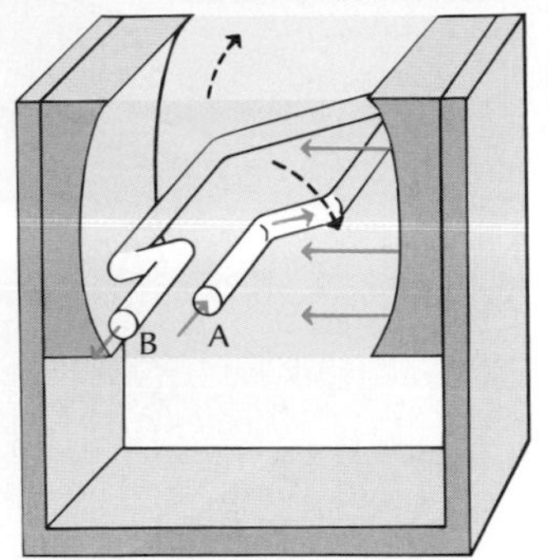

The current reverses as the wire makes the second half of the turn. The current flows from point A to point B.

lines of force in most generators (see **Electromagnet**). Some small generators have permanent magnets. These generators are called *permanent-magnet generators.* The coils for the armature and field structure are usually insulated copper wire wound around iron cores. The iron cores strengthen the magnetic fields.

Electric current can be generated either by making the armature cut the lines of force, or by making the lines of force cut past the armature. Because of this, either the armature or the field structure can be the rotating part of a generator. The rotating part is called the *rotor* and the stationary part is known as the *stator.*

Losses and efficiency of generators. Not all of the mechanical energy used to drive generators is converted to electrical energy. Some of it is converted to heat as a result of friction in the bearings supporting the generator rotor, the resistance of the copper coils to the current, and the action of the magnetic lines of force in the iron cores. Thus, generators must be cooled by blowing air through them, or by running a cooling liquid or gas past the coils, iron cores, and bearings. A generator's *efficiency* refers to its effectiveness in converting mechanical energy to electrical energy. An efficiency of 90 percent means that 90 percent of the input mechanical energy is converted to electrical energy. The remaining 10 percent is converted to heat and must be carried away by the cooling system. Large generators that use conventional electromagnets as a source of magnetic field can have efficiencies as high as 97 percent. Some generators use *superconducting* coils as their source of magnetic field. At low temperatures, superconducting coils offer no resistance to the flow of electric current. As a result, these types of generators reach efficiencies of over 99 percent.

Alternating-current generators

The simple generator we have been describing produces alternating current in a loop of wire. To be an alternating-current generator, it needs some way to send the current it produces to the device that will use it. This is done with the help of *collector rings,* or *slip rings,* and fixed pieces of carbon called *brushes.* Each end of the loop of wire is connected to a ring. The rings rotate with the loop of wire. A brush rests against each ring. Each brush is connected to a wire leading to the device that will use the electric power. The current produced in the loop of wire flows in and out of the generator through the rings and brushes to the device.

How AC generators work. Practical AC generators differ in several ways from the simple AC generator. They are usually equipped with a small auxiliary generator called an *exciter.* The exciter supplies direct current for the electromagnets used to create the magnetic field in the AC generator. The armature of an AC generator consists of copper wire wound in hundreds of coils around slots cut in an iron core. The electromagnets consist of copper bar wound around iron cores.

In most AC generators, the armature is the stator and the field structure is the rotor. This means that the electromagnets that make up the field structure rotate so the magnetic field sweeps past the armature coils. In these generators, the slip rings are used to carry the direct current from the exciter generator to the electromagnets in the field structure. Outside wires connected to the armature coils take the alternating current induced in the armature directly from the armature. Engineers have found that it is easier to conduct the relatively weak current from the exciter through the slip rings and to take the heavy current produced in the armature directly from the armature. This kind of AC generator is also called a *synchronous generator* because it generates a voltage that has a frequency proportional to, or synchronized with, the speed of the rotor.

The field structure in an AC generator may have only one electromagnet, but it often has two, three, four, or more. This means that the magnetic field produced by the field structure will have two, four, six, eight, or more poles—two for each electromagnet. The generator produces one complete cycle of current each time a pair of poles passes an armature coil, instead of one cycle for each complete revolution of the field structure. Depending on the number of electromagnets, these generators can produce one, two, three, four, or more cycles for each revolution of the field structure or of the armature.

How generators work

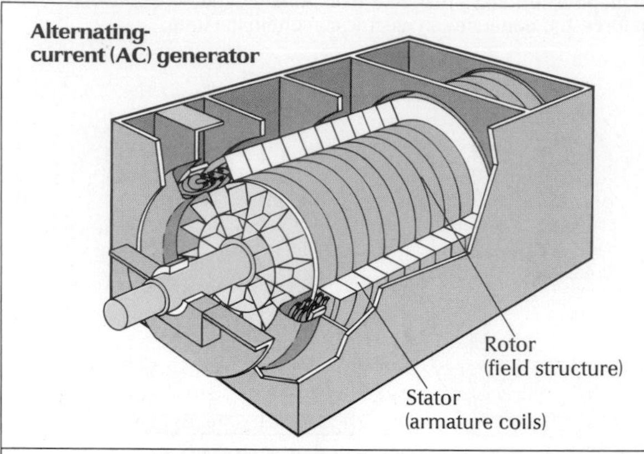

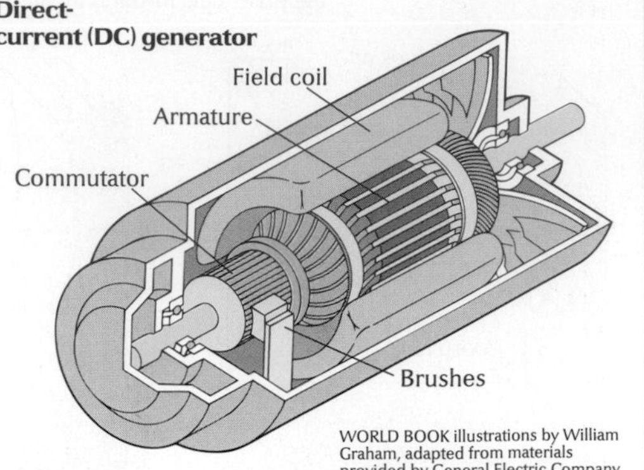

WORLD BOOK illustrations by William Graham, adapted from materials provided by General Electric Company

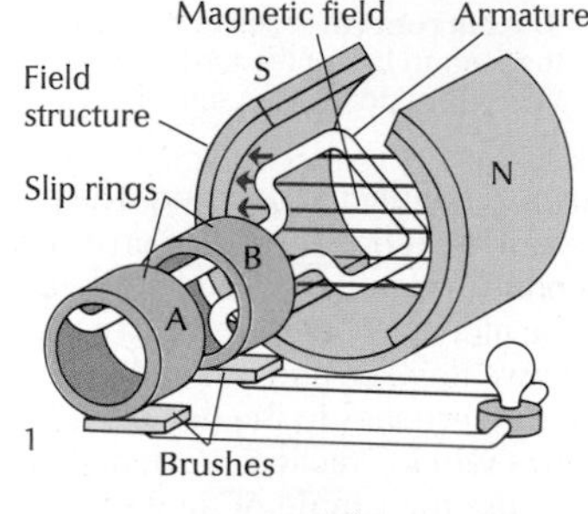

Alternating-current (AC) generator

1. A simple alternating-current generator, *left,* has each end of its wire loop, or *armature,* attached to a *slip ring.* A carbon *brush* connected to the outside circuit rests against each of the slip rings.

2. As the armature rotates, *right,* the current moves in the direction of the arrows. The brush at slip ring A conducts the current out of the armature, and the brush at slip ring B brings it back in.

3. When the armature rotates parallel to the magnetic field, *left,* no current is generated for a moment. In homes using AC current, we do not notice such stoppages because they happen so quickly.

4. When the armature rotates into the magnetic field again, *right,* the current reverses direction. It now flows out of the armature through slip ring B and back into the armature at slip ring A.

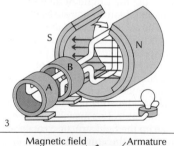

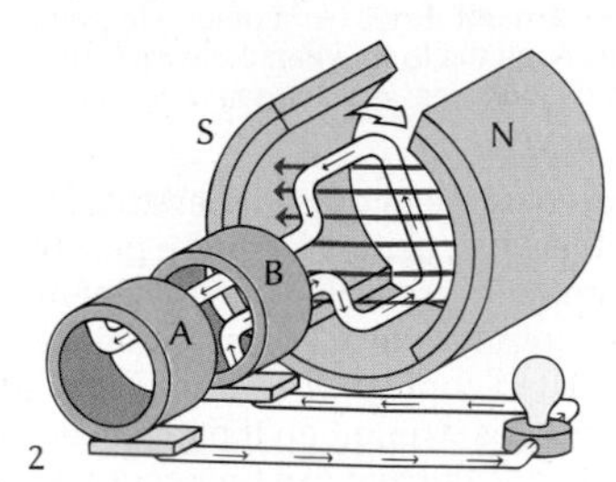

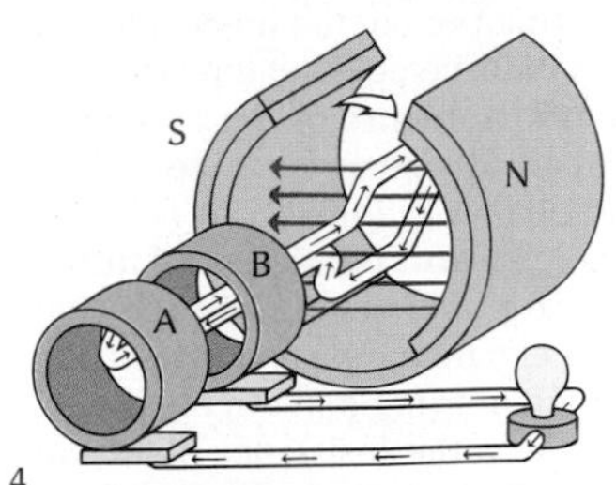

Direct-current (DC) generator

1. A simple direct-current generator, *left,* has each end of its wire loop, or *armature,* connected to a *commutator* segment. Carbon *brushes* connected to the outside circuit rest against each segment.

2. As the armature rotates, *right,* brush C rests against commutator segment A and conducts the current out of the armature. Brush D transfers the current back into the armature at segment B.

3. When the armature rotates parallel to the magnetic field, *left,* no current flows for a moment.

4. In the second half of the turn, *right,* the current in the armature reverses direction and flows out of commutator segment B. But this segment now touches brush C, so the direction of the current in the outside circuit remains the same.

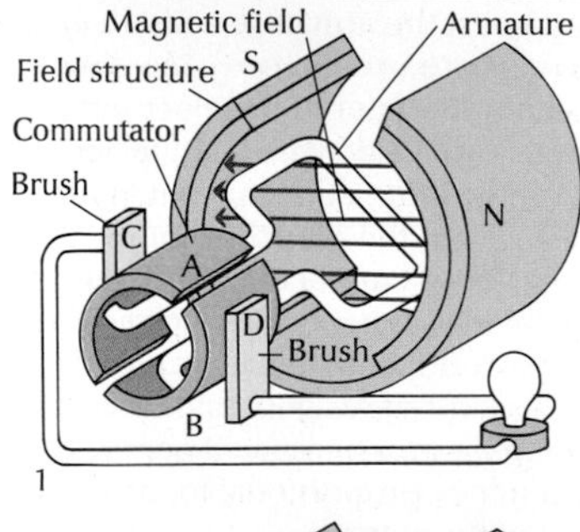

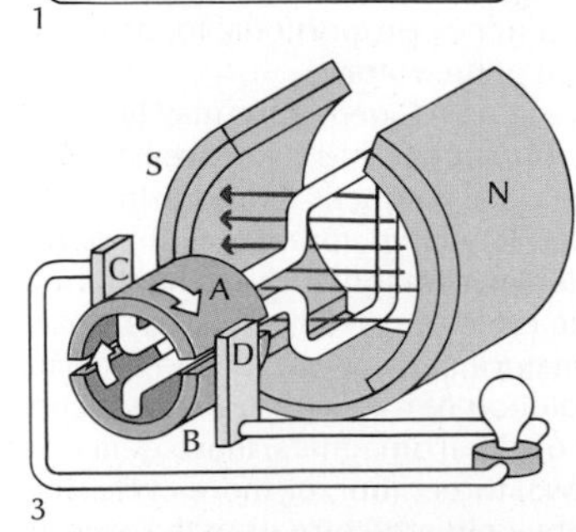

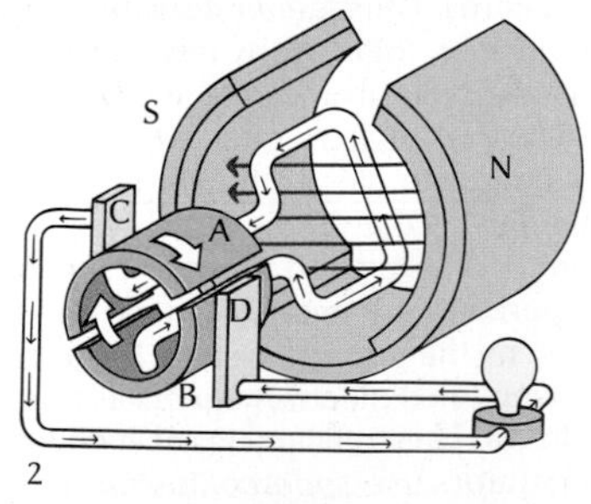

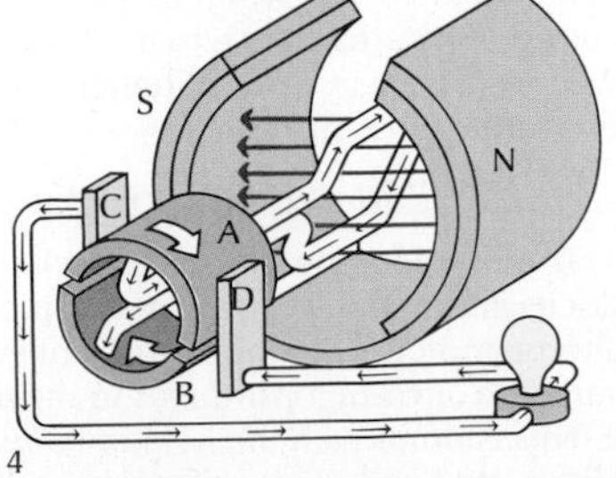

A two-pole AC generator must rotate at 3,600 revolutions per minute to generate a 60-hertz current.

Kinds of AC generators. In some AC generators, called *single-phase* generators, the armature has as many sets of coils as the field structure has poles. But most AC generators have three sets of armature coils for each pole. These generators produce three currents of electric power at one time and are called *three-phase* generators. They generate more power for the amount of materials used than do single-phase generators. Three-phase generators also lead to better transmission and use of power.

Uses of AC generators. The main generators in nearly all electric-power plants are AC generators. This is because a relatively simple electromagnetic device called a *transformer* makes it easy to increase or decrease the voltage of alternating current (see **Transformer**). Engineers build AC generators that produce current with only a certain voltage. For many large generators, this voltage is 18,000 or 22,000 volts. By means of a *step-up* transformer, the voltage can be increased as high as 500,000 or 765,000 volts to force the current over long distances. In the area where the current is finally used, a series of *step-down* transformers lowers the voltage to a usable level. Most household appliances, for example, operate on 120 volts. Some office buildings and factories use voltages ranging from 480 to over 4,000.

Nikola Tesla, a Serbian engineer who came to the United States in 1884, developed the first successful *polyphase* AC generators, or generators with more than one phase. He also developed electric motors to use alternating current and transformer systems for changing the voltage of alternating current. Tesla's inventions made it economically possible to generate current far from the places where the current is used.

Direct-current generators

To change the simple generator into a direct-current generator, two things must be done: (1) the current must be conducted from the rotating loop of wire, and (2) the current must be made to move in only one direction. A device called a *commutator* performs both tasks.

How DC generators work. The commutator rotates with the loop of wire just as the slip rings do with the rotor of an AC generator. Each half of the commutator ring is called a *commutator segment* and is insulated from the other half. Each end of the rotating loop of wire is connected to a commutator segment. Two carbon brushes connected to the outside circuit rest against the rotating commutator. One brush conducts the current out of the generator, and the other brush feeds it in. The commutator is designed so that, no matter how the current in the loop alternates, the commutator segment containing the outward-going current is always against the "out" brush at the proper time. The armature in a large DC generator has many coils of wire and commutator segments. Because of the commutator, engineers have found it necessary to have the armature serve as the rotor and the field structure as the stator.

Kinds of DC generators. In some DC generators, the direct current needed for the electromagnets that make up the field structure comes from an outside source, just as it does in most AC generators. These DC generators are called *separately excited generators.* Many other DC generators use part of the direct current they produce to operate their own electromagnets. These generators are called *self-excited generators.* A self-excited DC generator depends on *residual magnetism*—that is, a small amount of magnetism that remains in the electromagnets after the generator is shut off. Without this residual magnetism, it would be impossible to start a self-excited generator once it had stopped.

Direct current needed for a self-excited generator's electromagnets can be drawn from its armature by three connections. These are (1) *shunt,* (2) *series,* and (3) *compound,* a combination of shunt and series connections.

The type of generator used for a certain task depends on the amount of voltage control required. For example, a DC generator used to charge a battery needs only simple voltage control. It might be a shunt generator. A DC generator that supplies electric power for a passenger elevator needs more complicated voltage control. It would be a separately excited generator.

Uses of DC generators. Many DC generators are driven by AC motors in combinations called *motor-generator sets.* This is one way of changing alternating current to direct current. Factories that do electroplating and those that produce aluminum and chlorine need large amounts of direct current and use DC generators. So do locomotives and ships driven by diesel-electric motors. Because commutators are complex and costly, many DC generators are being replaced by AC generators combined with electronic *rectifiers.* Rectifiers are devices that let current flow in one direction only. They permit use of simpler, more rugged AC generators, even when DC is required. J. Eduardo Cotilla-Sanchez

Related articles in *World Book* include:

Electric circuit	Electromagnetism	Magnetism
Electric motor	Electromotive force	Magneto
Electric power	Faraday, Michael	Tesla, Nikola
Electricity	Induction, Electric	Transformer
Electromagnet	Lenz's law	Turbine

Electric guitar is a musical instrument that converts the vibrations of strings into electrical signals. These signals are strengthened and shaped by a device called an *amplifier.* A speaker then converts the signals into sound. Through the use of an amplifier and speakers, an electric guitar can produce a wide range of sounds loud enough to fill a huge concert arena.

Most electric guitars have two or three *pickups* under their strings. These electromagnetic devices convert the string's vibrations into electric signals. Pickups placed at different locations result in different tones. A switch enables guitar players to select which pickups to use. Dials on the front of the guitar also control the volume and tone from each pickup. Some electric guitars have a *tremolo arm,* also called a *whammy bar* or *vibrato arm.* This leverlike device enables the player to tighten and loosen the strings, creating richly textured sound.

Amplifiers are essential to the operation of an electric guitar. An amplifier's electronics strengthen the electrical signals from the guitar. Most amplifiers can also shape the sound from a guitar. For example, amplifiers can create the heavy, distorted guitar sounds used in many rock songs. They can also create echolike *reverberation* effects. Modern amplifiers offer an exceptionally wide range of tones and effects using *digital* (computerized) technology. Many amplifiers come with built-in speakers.

The first electric guitars were developed in the early 1930's. They had hollow wooden bodies similar to those of traditional *acoustic* (nonelectric) guitars. Solid-body electric guitars were developed soon afterward. Les Paul, an American guitarist, designed an early solid-body electric guitar in 1941. In the 1950's, Paul endorsed and helped design a popular line of electric guitars made by the Gibson company. The American inventor Leo Fender also created many well-known electric guitar designs in the 1940's and 1950's. Fender's designs include the Stratocaster and the Telecaster. Designs by Fender and models named after Les Paul remain popular with modern players. Jason Corey

See also **Guitar; Rock music.**

Electric induction. See **Induction, Electric.**

Electric light is a device that uses electric energy to produce visible light. Appliances called *fixtures* or *luminaires* hold electric light sources. These appliances are sometimes called *lamps.* But the word *lamp* may also refer to the light source itself.

This article deals with the various types of electric light. For much more information on the ways electric lights are used, see the *World Book* article **Lighting.**

There are three main types of electric lights. They are (1) incandescent lamps, (2) gaseous-discharge lamps, and (3) solid-state lights.

Incandescent lamps

The incandescent lamp is the oldest form of electric light. In an incandescent lamp, electric current passes through a wire called a *filament,* heating it. At high temperatures, the filament glows brightly, much as does a hot metal poker. This effect is called *incandescence.* The filament is usually made of tungsten, a metal that can withstand high temperatures without melting. A bulb, usually made of glass, surrounds the filament. The bulb typically holds a mixture of nonreactive gases that helps the filament to last longer. A metal base holds the parts in place and connects the light to an electric circuit.

Incandescent lamps come in many shapes and sizes. They are used in home and office lighting, as car headlights, and as flashlight bulbs. Incandescent lamps are inexpensive. But they are relatively inefficient because they turn most of the electric energy into heat, rather than light. Incandescent lamps also do not last long. The heat causes some metal in the filament to evaporate. Eventually, a gap forms, and the filament can no longer conduct current.

Halogen lamps are a particular kind of incandescent lamp. A halogen lamp typically has a quartz bulb that holds a small amount of a chemical element from the halogen family, usually bromine or iodine. During operation, the halogen in the bulb combines with evaporated tungsten and forms a gas. When this gas touches the hot filament, it breaks down, redepositing the evaporated tungsten. This process makes the filament last longer. A halogen lamp may last several times longer than a standard incandescent bulb. Halogen lamps also provide more light using less electric power.

Gaseous-discharge lamps

A gaseous-discharge lamp produces light by passing electrical current through a gas. The gas is sealed inside a bulb of glass or another ceramic material. Gaseous-discharge lamps require a strong current to start working, but then must limit the current's strength during operation. Typically, a device called a *ballast* regulates the lamp's current.

The current causes the gas to give off *electromagnetic radiation.* Visible light is a form of electromagnetic radiation. But some gaseous-discharge lamps give off invisible radiation, which must be changed into visible light. Gaseous-discharge lamps can be divided into two basic kinds: *low-pressure* lamps and *high-pressure* lamps.

Low-pressure discharge lamps hold the gas at a relatively low pressure. They include *fluorescent lamps,* a widespread form of indoor lighting. Fluorescent lamps contain a small amount of mercury gas. When current passes through the gas, the mercury atoms *ionize* (become charged) and give off electromagnetic radiation. Most of this radiation is in the form of *ultraviolet light.* Such light is beyond the violet end of the visible spectrum and thus cannot be seen by humans.

The inside of a fluorescent lamp bulb is coated with a material called a *phosphor.* The ultraviolet light strikes the phosphor, which in turn gives off visible light. Fluorescent lamps can produce different colors of light using different phosphor coatings.

Linear fluorescent lamps are long tubes designed to fit into special fixtures. Beginning in the 1940's, such lamps began replacing incandescent lamps in many buildings. The new lamps were more expensive and required new fixtures, but they cost less to operate and lasted longer. *Compact fluorescent lamps* (CFL's) are coiled into traditional light bulb shapes and can fit in the same fixtures that hold incandescent lamps.

The mercury inside a fluorescent lamp is toxic. Thus, the lamps should be handled carefully to avoid breakage. They should also be disposed of in a recycling center. Despite their mercury content, fluorescent lamps actually contribute less mercury pollution to the environment than do incandescent lamps overall. This fact is true because fluorescent lamps use far less electric power, which results in much mercury pollution when generated by coal-burning power plants.

Neon lights are another kind of low-pressure discharge lamp. They contain neon, a harmless gas that produces red-orange light when current runs through it. Neon can be combined with other gases or placed in colored tubes to produce different colors of light.

High-pressure discharge lamps hold a gas inside the bulb at a much higher pressure than do fluorescent and neon lights. The two most common high-pressure discharge lamps are *high-pressure sodium lamps* and *metal halide lamps.* These types of lamps are also called *high-intensity discharge* (HID) *lamps* because they produce a great deal of light. They are usually too bright for use inside homes and offices. Instead, they are used primarily for such outdoor applications as street lights or in large warehouses or athletic facilities.

Like fluorescent lamps, HID lamps contain mercury. But additional active chemical compounds are often added to the gas. Under high pressure, HID lamps produce a broad spectrum of light, so they usually do not require phosphors. A device called an *arc tube,* housed within an outer glass bulb, contains the gas and main-

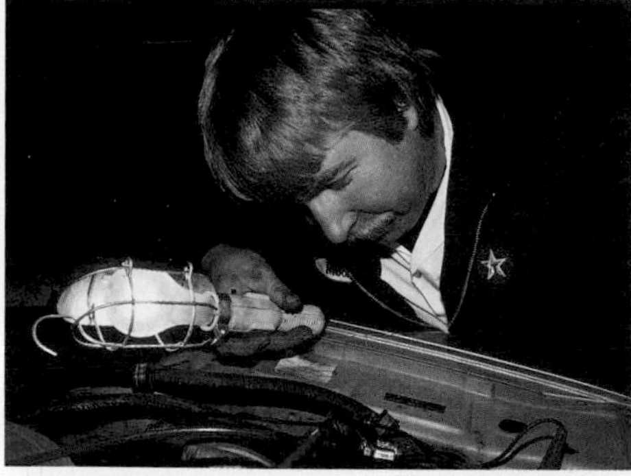

© David R. Frazier Photolibrary

An incandescent lamp

© Brooke Slezak, Getty Images

Neon lamps

WORLD BOOK photo by Ralph Brunke

Fluorescent lamps

Photographic Illustrators Corporation (Osram Sylvania)

Metal halide lamps

Sources of electric light include the incandescent and fluorescent lamps used in homes and other buildings, the metal halide lamps that light stadiums, and the neon lamps used to make signs.

tains high pressure in these lamps. Arc tubes are made of various materials that minimize corrosion by chemical compounds. With some exceptions, HID lamps usually take several minutes to build up enough pressure to achieve full brightness. After they have been turned off, HID lamps must cool down before they can restart, which can take several minutes.

High-pressure sodium (HPS) lamps are extremely efficient. They can last over 20,000 hours and are relatively inexpensive and highly reliable. They typically produce an orange-colored light, however, largely limiting their use to street lighting. They are also commonly used to supplement daylight in greenhouses.

Metal halide (MH) lamps produce white light. But MH lamps are slightly less efficient than HPS lamps. Over time, the color of an MH lamp often shifts from white to shades of pink or green. For this reason, MH lamps are often replaced before they fail completely. MH lamps are used in outdoor settings. Some are used for automobile headlights, but a special ballast is required to ensure rapid starting.

Solid-state lights

Solid-state lights, much like computer chips, make use of *semiconductors.* A semiconductor is a material that conducts electric current better than does an *insulator,* such as plastic, but not as well as does a *conductor,* such as many metals. The electrical properties of semiconductors enable manufacturers to precisely control the way current flows through them. Most solid-state lights are *light-emitting diodes.*

Light-emitting diodes (LED's) are highly efficient and last an extremely long time. LED's can be used in a variety of applications, from small colored lights on automobile dashboards to bright street lamps.

LED's use *semiconducting diodes.* In a semiconducting diode, electric current flows in one direction between two slightly different materials. The two materials share a special kind of border called a *p-n junction.* Applying a voltage causes electrons to move from the "n" side of the junction to the "p" side. The p side contains structures that have spaces, or holes, where electrons normally go. The electrons fill the holes, releasing energy in the form of light. For more information, see **Electronics.**

Different LED materials produce different colors of light. A variety of compounds have been used in LED's, but they often contain two main types of *alloys* (mixtures of metals and other materials). Aluminum-gallium-indium phosphide alloys are used for red, orange, and yellow LED's. Such alloys are abbreviated AlGaInP or AlInGaP. Indium-gallium-nitride (InGaN) alloys are used in green and blue LED's. Slight changes in the composition of these alloys changes the color of light given off.

White LED light is typically produced by one of two methods. The first method simply combines red, green, and blue LED's into a single white light source. However, each type of LED responds differently to changes in environment and temperature. Likewise, each type degrades at a different rate. Thus, special control mechanisms are required to maintain a constant white color. The second, and most common, method for producing white light involves combining a blue LED with a phosphor. Much as in a fluorescent lamp, the phosphor absorbs some of the blue light and gives off other colors. The combination of blue light from the LED and the phosphor's light results in white light.

Organic light-emitting diodes (OLED's) work in a way similar to traditional LED's. But OLED's consist of thin films containing the element carbon. OLED's are much more expensive to produce than are LED's, limiting their use to thin cell phone and television screens.

Measuring efficiency

Electric lights vary widely in *luminous efficacy*—that is, how much light they can produce using a given amount of electric power. Luminous efficacy is measured in *lumens per watt*. The *lumen* is a measure of the "amount" of light. The *watt* is a measure of electric power.

A modern incandescent bulb has a relatively low luminous efficacy, about 10 to 20 lumens per watt. CFL bulbs produce about 40 to 70 lumens per watt, and linear fluorescent bulbs produce about 50 to 100. Household LED's produce about 50 to 100 lumens per watt.

High-pressure sodium lamps can have an extremely high luminous efficacy—50 to 140 lumens per watt. Metal halide lamps have slightly lower maximum efficacies, about 50 to 110 lumens per watt.

History

Basic electric lights were invented in the early 1800's. The *carbon arc lamp* produced light from a current that leapt across a gap between two carbon *electrodes* (conductors), forming an arc of intense heat and light. It required a high voltage, lasted a short time, and was too bright for most purposes. In the middle to late 1800's, improved carbon arc lamps were used in outdoor theaters and public squares. But the lamps remained too impractical for indoor use.

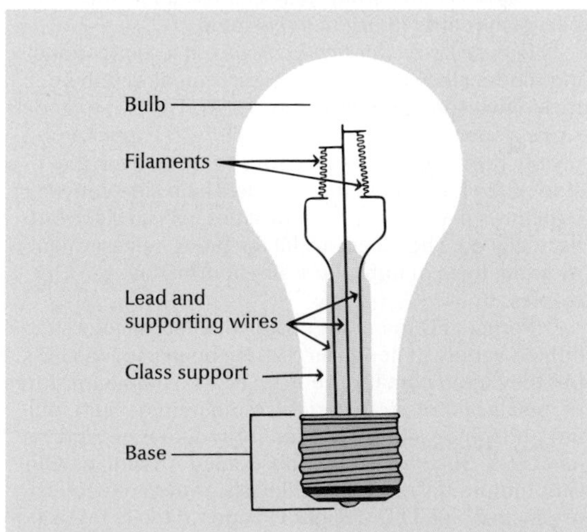

The parts of an incandescent lamp include one or more filaments, an internal support, a bulb, and a base.

Practical indoor incandescent lamps were introduced commercially in the 1880's. The basic design of incandescent lamps remains the same, but the parts have been continually refined. In the 1900's, incandescent lamps became widespread in homes, offices, schools, and other buildings.

The first mass-produced fluorescent lamp was introduced in 1938. Like incandescent lamps, fluorescent lamps have been continually improved. Today, linear fluorescent lamps serve as the main source of illumination in offices, schools, and factories. Compact fluorescent lamps, introduced commercially in the early 1980's, are often used in homes. But they have not completely replaced incandescent lamps.

HID light sources, particularly HPS and MH lamps, were developed in the 1960's and 1970's. They became the primary light sources for such outdoor public spaces as roads and parking lots.

The first practical LED's were introduced in the 1960's. They were red lights used in signals and digital displays. Over the next few decades, researchers developed LED's that produced other colors. In the 1990's, engineers developed practical versions of green and blue LED's, enabling the production of white light. In the 2010's, LED's began to widely replace other light sources. Robert B. Prigo

Related articles in *World Book* include:

Edison, Thomas A.	Light-emitting diode	Sun lamp
Flashlight	Lighting	Tesla, Nikola
Fluorescent lamp	Neon	Tungsten
Laser		Weston, Edward
Light bulb		

Electric locomotive. See Electric railroad.

Electric meter is the general name for many devices that measure quantities related to electric energy. Examples of these quantities are voltage, current, power, and *resistance* (opposition to the flow of electric current). A *voltmeter* is a meter that measures voltage. A meter that measures current is called an *ammeter*—named after the unit of current, the ampere. A *wattmeter* measures power in watts. An *ohmmeter* measures resistance in ohms. A meter that measures two or more electrical quantities is a *multimeter*. It usually has a multiple-position switch that enables the user to select the quantity to measure.

All electric meters have a device that senses either current or voltage. Various internal devices and methods of connection enable a meter to sense one quantity and display a measurement of another quantity—for example, to sense current and display power. Most meters have two input terminals connected by wires to the circuit being measured. The way in which these wires are connected depends on what quantity is being measured.

Electric meters may be either *analog* or *digital*. Analog meters, the older type, make use of a moving pointer and a scale to display measured values. Digital meters use a numerical readout panel. Digital meters also differ from analog meters in that they have no internal moving parts. In addition, digital meters have much greater sensitivity in measuring than do analog meters.

Analog meters. The main component of an analog electric meter is a coil of wire mounted inside a strong magnet. The coil rotates when an electric current passes through it, and the pointer turns with the coil. The angle to which the coil rotates is proportional to the amount of current flowing. This component can be used by itself to measure small currents. When used in this way, the component is known as a *galvanometer.*

Analog ammeters and voltmeters use a galvanometer as their main measuring element. Additional components inside the ammeter or voltmeter translate the current or voltage being measured into a current that the galvanometer can measure.

If a meter draws a large amount of current from the circuit being measured, it changes the quantity to be measured—thus producing an inaccurate result. But many people still use analog meters where extreme accuracy is not essential. In addition, workers often use an analog meter to measure a rapidly changing quantity. The meter is relatively easy to read as the pointer moves up and down the scale. It would be difficult to read the rapidly changing numbers of a digital meter.

Digital meters. The heart of a digital electric meter is an integrated circuit called an *analog-to-digital converter.* This device compares the voltage being measured with a series of voltages stored in the chip's memory. The chip quickly finds a voltage that is close to the voltage being measured. The chip then sends to the numerical readout panel a string of electric pulses that represent this voltage. Like an analog multimeter, a digital multimeter has additional components that enable it to measure a wide range of voltages and currents.

People generally prefer digital meters over analog meters of comparable cost for two reasons: (1) digital meters are more sensitive, and (2) they draw less current from the circuit being measured, and thus are mor accurate. Inexpensive digital multimeters available at retail stores are extremely sensitive. They can measure voltages and currents roughly one-thousandth as strong as those produced by a small watch battery. Meters used in research laboratories can measure quantities a million times smaller than that.

Utility meters. The most common electric utility meter found in many houses is a type of analog meter. This device measures the amount of electric energy supplied to the house. A worker for the local power company reads the meter at regular intervals, and the customer's bill is based on these readings.

The utility meter is actually an electric motor that turns whenever current is flowing through the wires connecting the house to power lines. The rate at which the motor turns increases as the current supplied to the house increases. The shaft of the motor is connected, by a system of gears, to a counter that keeps track of the number of rotations of the shaft. The total number of rotations is proportional to the total amount of electric energy used by the customer. The counter scale and the display—usually four or five dials—therefore can be labeled in units of energy. The energy unit most commonly used by power companies is the *kilowatt-hour.* A kilowatt-hour is 1,000 watt-hours. A 100-watt light bulb left on for 10 hours will use 1 kilowatt-hour of energy.

Some modern utilities use special digital meters—often called *smart meters*—to gather energy usage information from their customers. These meters can communicate electronically with the utility and report such information many times each day.

History. Hans Christian Oersted, a Danish physicist, investigated the effect of electric currents on a magnetic needle in 1820. Also in 1820, Johann Salomo Christoph Schweigger, a German physicist, built the first simple galvanometer. In 1882, Jacques Arsène d'Arsonval, a French medical researcher, greatly improved the performance of the galvanometer. The d'Arsonval galvanome-

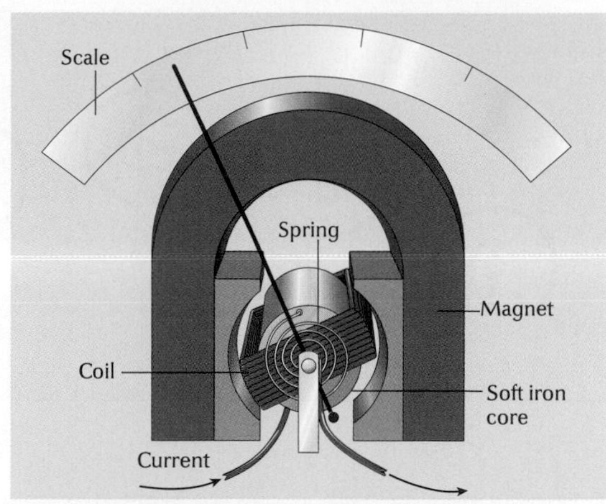

WORLD BOOK illustration by Bensen Studios

A galvanometer is the simplest analog meter. Current flows through a wire coil mounted on an iron core, creating a magnetic field in and near the core. This field interacts with the field of a magnet, causing the core and an attached pointer to pivot until they are stopped by a counterforce produced by a spring.

Keithley Instruments

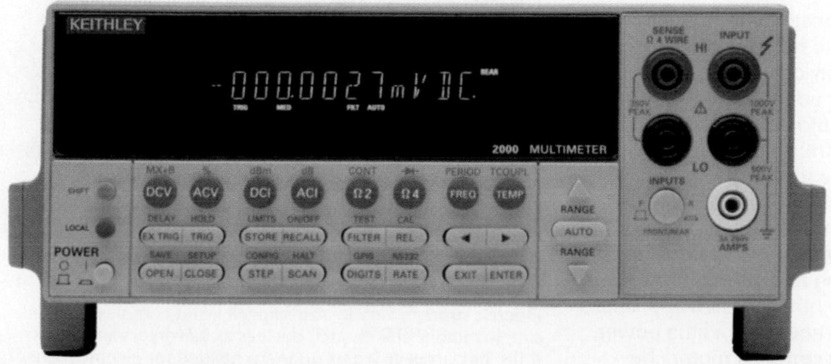

A digital multimeter can measure voltage or current in an electric circuit. The user connects two wires to the circuit. Contacts at the other ends of the wires plug into the front of the multimeter. The multimeter shown can also measure resistance.

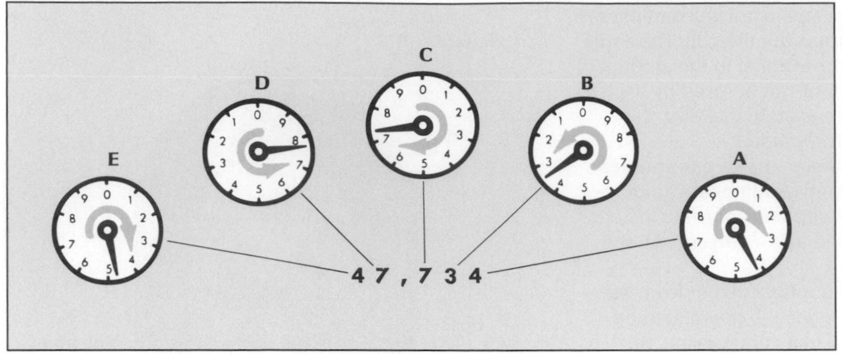

WORLD BOOK diagram

Utility-meter dials are read from right to left in units of ones, tens, hundreds, thousands, and ten thousands. The pointer of dial A must make a complete revolution for dial B's pointer to move ahead one unit, and so on. Some meters have four dials instead of five.

WORLD BOOK photo by Ralph Brunke

A utility meter measures in kilowatt-hours the amount of electric power used by customers of electric utility companies. The device is sealed tightly inside a protective glass case.

ter, the most common type of galvanometer, is named after him.

The American Oliver B. Shallenberger, then an electrical engineer with Westinghouse Electric Manufacturing Company, developed the first successful electric meter in 1888. In 1895, he patented an electric meter that became the basis for the electric utility meters used in most homes today. J. Eduardo Cotilla-Sanchez

See also **Weston, Edward.**

Electric motor is a machine that changes electric power into mechanical power to do work. Electric motors are used to operate a variety of machines and machinery. Washing machines, air conditioners, and vacuum cleaners include electric motors, as do hairdryers, sewing machines, and power drills and saws. Various kinds of motors power machine tools, robots, and other equipment to keep factories running smoothly.

The size and capacity of electric motors vary widely. An electric motor may be a tiny device that functions inside a wrist watch or a huge engine that powers a heavy locomotive. Blenders and most other kitchen appliances use small motors because they need just a little power. Trains require larger and more complex motors because the motor must accomplish a great deal of work within a short time.

There are two general types of electric motors, based on the type of electric current they use. They are (1) alternating current (AC) motors and (2) direct current (DC) motors. Alternating current usually reverses the direction of its flow 60 times per second. Alternating current is available from electrical outlets in homes, and so AC motors are commonly used in household appliances.

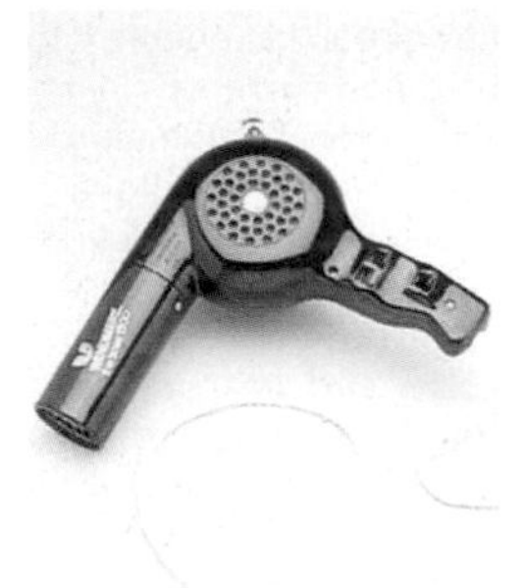

WORLD BOOK photo by Ralph Brunke

Hairdryer

WORLD BOOK photo by Ralph Brunke

Power drill

WORLD BOOK photo by Ralph Brunke

Commuter train

Electric motors vary in size, capacity, and complexity. Small, simple motors power such devices as hairdryers and power drills, but large, complex ones are needed for electric trains.

How an electric motor works An electric motor basically consists of a stationary magnet and a moving conductor. Lines of force between the poles of the magnet form a permanent magnetic field. When an electric current passes through the conductor, the conductor becomes an electromagnet and produces another magnetic field. The two magnetic fields strengthen each other and push against the conductor.

WORLD BOOK diagrams by William Graham

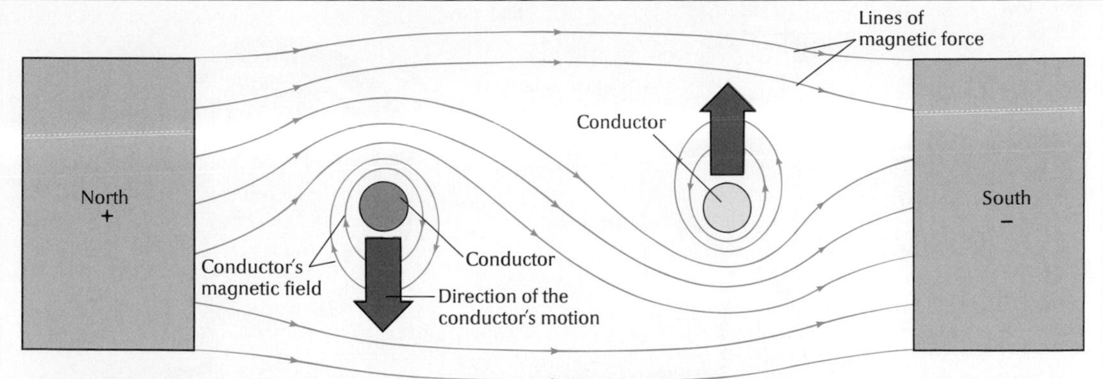

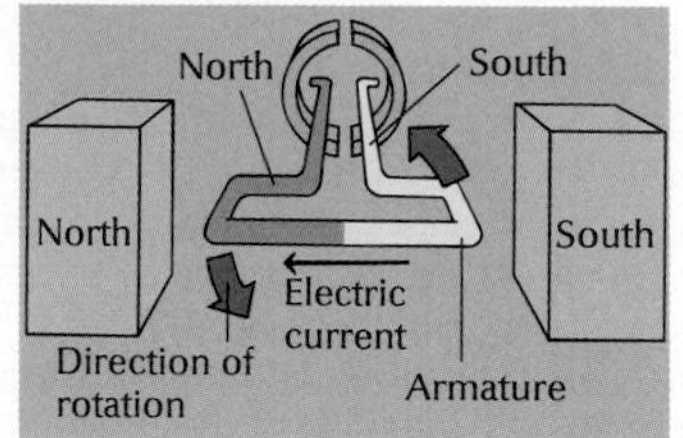

Rotation begins because the north poles of the *armature* (conductor) and the fixed magnet repel each other, as do their south poles.

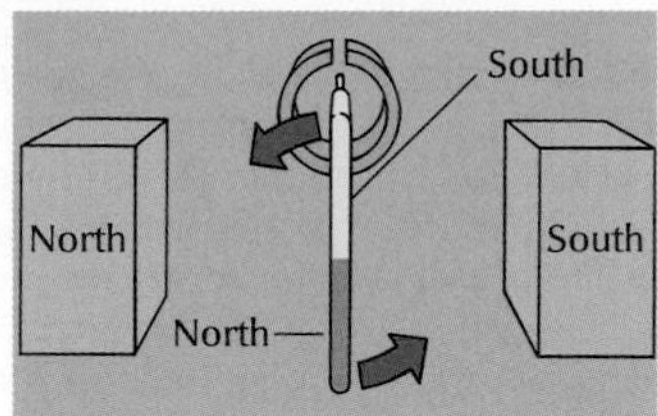

Rotation continues as the armature passes the gap in the split rings. The opposite poles of the armature and the fixed magnet attract each other.

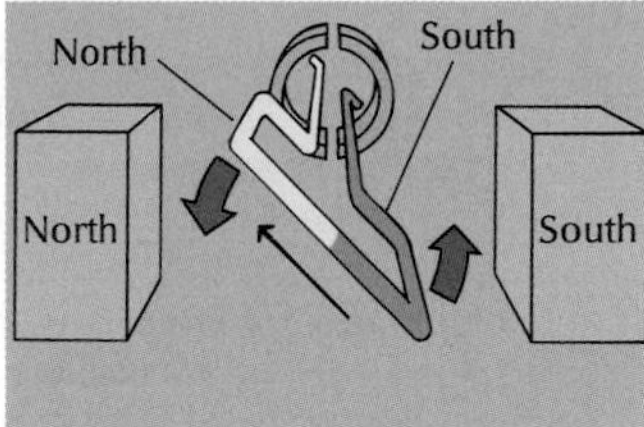

The current is reversed, as are the poles on the armature, after the armature passes the gap in the split ring. Rotation can then continue.

Direct current flows in only one direction. Its chief source is a battery. DC motors are commonly used to run machinery in factories. They are also used as starters for gasoline engines. See **Electric current.**

Electric motors depend on electromagnets to produce the force that is necessary for driving a machine or machinery. The machine or machinery driven by an electric motor is known as its *load.* A drive shaft connects the motor to the load.

Basic principles

The operation of an electric motor is based on three main principles: (1) An electric current produces a magnetic field; (2) the direction of a current in an electromagnet determines the location of the magnet's poles; and (3) magnetic poles attract or repel each other.

When an electric current passes through a wire, it produces a magnetic field around the wire. If the wire is wound in a coil around a metal rod, the magnetic field around the wire becomes strengthened and the rod becomes magnetized. This arrangement of rod and wire coil is a simple electromagnet, with its two ends serving as north and south poles. See **Electromagnet.**

The *right-hand rule* is one way of showing the relationship between the direction of the current and the magnetic poles. Hold a coil of wire in your right hand. Supposing the coil is an electromagnet, wrap your fingers around it so that they point in the direction of the current. Your thumb then points toward the electromagnet's north pole. This method works only when a current flows from a positive terminal to a negative one.

Like poles, such as two north poles, repel each other. Unlike poles attract each other. If a bar magnet is suspended between the ends of a horseshoe magnet, it will rotate until its north pole is opposite the horseshoe magnet's south pole. The bar magnet's south pole will be opposite the horseshoe magnet's north pole.

Parts of an electric motor

An electric motor consists chiefly of a rotating electrical conductor situated between the north and south poles of a stationary magnet. The conductor is known as the *armature,* and the stationary magnet is called the *field structure.* A *commutator* is also an essential part of many electric motors—especially DC motors.

The field structure establishes a constant magnetic field in the motor. The magnetic field consists of *lines of force* that exist between the poles of the stationary magnet. In a small, simple DC motor, the field structure consists of a permanent magnet called a *field magnet.* In some larger or more complex motors, the field structure is made up of one or more electromagnets that are fed electricity from an outside power source. Such electromagnets are known as *field coils.*

The armature, which is usually cylindrical in shape, becomes an electromagnet when a current passes

Parts of a direct current (DC) motor

A DC motor's most common source of power is a battery. Because direct current travels in only one direction, DC motors rely on commutators with split rings to reverse the flow of the current. The commutator also helps transmit the current between the power source and the armature.

WORLD BOOK diagrams by William Graham

Side view
Field coils
Field magnet
Brush
Commutator
Armature
Fan
To DC power source

End view
Field magnet
Brush
Commutator
Armature
Field coils
To DC power source

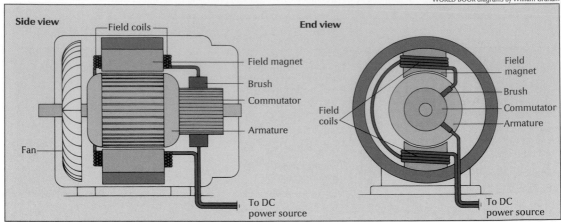

through it. It is connected to a drive shaft so that it can drive a load. In a small, simple DC motor, the armature rotates between the poles of the field magnet until its north pole is opposite the south pole of the magnet. The direction of the current is then reversed to change the north pole of the armature into a south pole. The two south poles repel each other, causing the armature to make another half turn. When the armature's two poles are next to opposite poles of the field magnet once more, the direction of the current is again changed.

Each time the direction of the current is reversed, the armature rotates a half turn. The armature would stop moving if the direction of the current were not reversed. When the armature turns, it cuts the lines of magnetic force created by the field structure. Cutting the magnetic field produces a voltage in the opposite direction of the driving force. This voltage, called a *counter-electromotive force,* reduces the speed of rotation of the armature, as well as the current it carries. If a motor drives a light load, the armature will spin rapidly and generate a large counter-electromotive force. When the load is increased, the armature rotates more slowly. It cuts fewer lines of magnetic force, thereby decreasing the counter-electromotive force. A motor that carries a heavier load thus operates more efficiently, because it uses less energy to do more work.

The commutator is used mainly in DC motors. It reverses the direction of the current in the armature and helps transmit the current between the armature and the power source. For a DC motor, the commutator consists of two or more semicircular *split rings,* which are fixed to the drive shaft, next to the armature. Each end of the armature coil is attached to a different ring.

The electric current from the external power source is conducted to the commutator by a small block called a *brush.* Another brush, located on the other side of the commutator, carries the current back to the power source. When one of the rings comes into contact with the first brush, it picks up the electric current from the brush and sends it through the armature. When the

Parts of an alternating current (AC) motor

Most AC motors receive power from electrical outlets. Alternating current reverses the direction of its flow on its own. In AC motors, the rotating conductor is often called the *rotor.* The stationary part, including the field magnet and field coils, is sometimes referred to as the *stator.*

WORLD BOOK diagrams by William Graham

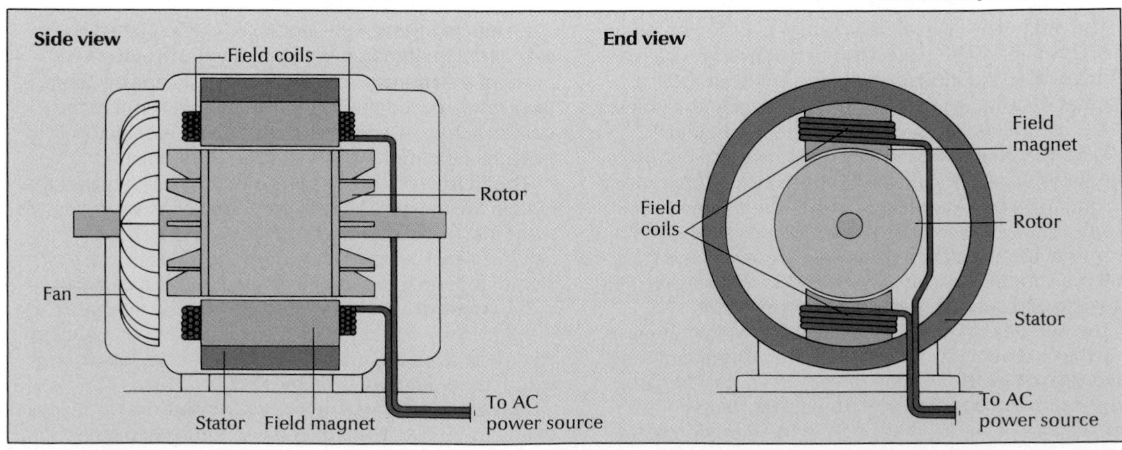

magnetic poles thereby created in the armature are next to like poles of the field magnet, the armature rotates a half turn, past one of the gaps separating the rings. The second ring of the commutator then comes into contact with the first brush and becomes the carrier of the electric current to the armature. In this way, the direction of the current has been reversed, as has the location of the poles in the armature. Like poles of the field magnet and the armature are once again opposite each other, and the armature continues to turn.

Most AC motors do not have commutators because alternating current reverses its direction independently. In AC motors that do have commutators, the commutator simply conducts the current from the external power source to the moving part of the motor and back. It consists of a round *slip ring* instead of split rings.

Kinds of electric motors

DC motors require commutators to reverse the direction of the current. There are three main kinds of DC motors—*series, shunt,* and *compound* motors. They differ from one another chiefly in the circuit arrangement between the armature and the field structure.

In a series motor, the armature and the field magnet are connected electrically *in series.* The current flows through the field magnet and then the armature. As the current flows through the structures in this order, it increases the strength of the magnets. A series motor can start quickly, even with a heavy load. However, such a load will decrease the motor's speed.

In a shunt motor, the magnet and the armature are connected *in parallel.* One part of the current goes through the magnet while the other part passes through the armature. A fine wire is wound around the field magnet many times in order to increase the magnetism. Constructing the field magnet in this way also creates further resistance to the current. The strength of the current and the level of magnetism therefore depend on the resistance of the wire rather than the load on the motor. A shunt motor will run at an even speed regardless of the load. However, if the load is too heavy, the motor will have problems starting.

A compound motor has two field magnets connected to the armature—one in series, the other in parallel. Compound motors have the benefits of both the series and the shunt motor. They can start easily with a heavy load and maintain a relatively constant speed, even if the load is suddenly increased.

AC motors are easy to build and convenient to use. They do not require commutators, and most of them operate on current provided by electrical outlets in households. In an AC motor, the moving part is often called the *rotor,* and the stationary part is frequently known as the *stator.* The most common AC motors include *induction* motors and *synchronous* motors.

The rotor of an induction motor consists of a cylindrical iron core with slots along its length. Copper bars fit into the slots and are fastened to a thick copper ring at each end. The rotor has no direct connection to the external source of electricity. The alternating current flows around the field coils in the stator and produces a rotating magnetic field. This field *induces* (creates) an electric current in the rotor, resulting in another magnetic field. The magnetic field from the rotor interacts with the magnetic field from the stator, causing the rotor to turn.

The stator in a synchronous motor also produces a rotating magnetic field. But the rotor receives current directly from the power source instead of relying on the magnetic field from the stator to induce an electric current. The rotor moves at a fixed speed in step with the rotating field of the stator. The speed is proportional to the frequency with which the alternating current supplied to the stator reverses. Because this frequency is usually fixed, synchronous motors, like shunt and compound DC motors, maintain a consistent speed, even with a changing load. They also use less energy. These motors are ideal for clocks and telescopes, which require precise timing and smooth turning.

Universal motors are built to operate on either DC or AC electricity. A universal motor uses a commutator, and its basic construction resembles the design of a DC series motor. On DC, it performs like a series motor. If AC is used, the magnetic poles of the armature and the field coils reverse with the frequency of the current. Universal motors are popular in many appliances because of their flexibility.

History

The development of electric motors began in the 1800's with the discovery of electromagnets. In 1820, a Danish physicist named Hans Christian Oersted discovered that a wire conducting an electric current produces a surrounding magnetic field. During the 1820's, a number of other scientists found ways of creating stronger and more practical electromagnets. In 1825, William Sturgeon, an English electrician, wrapped a conductor around an iron bar to produce a stronger electromagnet. In the late 1820's, the American physicist Joseph Henry showed that an even more powerful electromagnet could be made by wrapping several layers of insulated wire around a piece of iron. Also in the 1820's, the French mathematician and physicist André Marie Ampère developed mathematical theories describing the behavior of electric currents and magnets.

In 1831, the English chemist and physicist Michael Faraday demonstrated that moving a coil of wire through a magnetic field causes a current to flow through the coil. This knowledge of electromagnetic induction led to the invention of electric generators and other devices. In 1832, Ampère's instrument maker, the Frenchman Hippolyte Pixii, devised a split-ring commutator that received electric power from a DC generator.

In 1873, the first commercially successful DC motor was demonstrated in Vienna at an exhibition by Zénobe Théophile Gramme, a Belgian electrical engineer. Gramme also introduced an armature that improved the efficiency of early electric motors and generators.

In 1888, a Serbian-born engineer named Nikola Tesla invented the AC motor. Tesla designed models for induction and synchronous motors. In the early 1900's, scientists and engineers developed more advanced electric motors, including universal motors. Henry M. Louie

Related articles in ***World Book*** include:

Efficiency
Electric car
Electric circuit
Electric generator
Electricity
Electromagnetism
Electromotive force
Linear electric motor
Magnetism
Tesla, Nikola

Artstreet

Distribution substation

Artstreet

Coal-burning electric power plant

© Joe L. Pelaez, The Stock Market

Household that uses electric power

An electric power system begins with power plants, which produce large amounts of electric power. Wires carry high-voltage electric current from the power plants to substations, where the voltage is reduced. The current is then distributed to homes, offices, businesses, and factories.

Electric power

Electric power is the use of electric energy to do work. It lights, heats, and cools many homes. Electric power also runs television sets, refrigerators, vacuum cleaners, and many other home appliances. Electric power operates machinery in factories. Escalators, elevators, and computers and other business machines in stores and offices use electric power. Electric power drives many trains and subway systems. On farms, electric machinery performs such tasks as pumping water, milking cows, and drying hay.

Huge electric generators in power plants produce almost all the world's electric power. The majority of these plants burn coal, oil, or natural gas to run the generators. Most other plants drive the generators by means of nuclear energy or the force of falling water. Wires carry the electric current from power plants to the cities or other areas where it is needed. The electric power is then distributed to individual consumers.

Electric power is measured in units called *watts.* For example, it takes 100 watts of electric power to operate a 100-watt light bulb. Ten 100-watt bulbs require 1,000 watts, or 1 *kilowatt.* The amount of energy used is expressed in *kilowatt-hours.* A kilowatt-hour equals the amount of work done by 1 kilowatt in one hour. If you burn ten 100-watt bulbs for one hour or one 100-watt bulb for 10 hours, you use 1 kilowatt-hour of electric energy.

The world's electric power plants can produce nearly 4 billion kilowatts of electric power at any given time. The United States leads all other countries in generating capacity. American power plants can generate more than 900 million kilowatts. Canadian plants can produce more than 100 million kilowatts.

Sources of electric power

Large electric power plants supply nearly all the electric power that people use. The power plants first harness the energy of steam or flowing water to turn the shaft of a device called a *turbine.* The turning shaft drives an electric generator, which converts the shaft's mechanical power into electric power.

An electric generator has a stationary part called a *stator* and a rotating part called a *rotor.* In the huge electric generators that are used in power plants, the stator consists of hundreds of windings of wire. The rotor is a large electromagnet that receives electric power from a small separate generator called an *exciter.* An external source of mechanical energy, such as a turbine, turns the rotor. The turning of the rotor creates a magnetic field that turns along with the rotor. As this magnetic field rotates, it produces a voltage in the wire windings of the stator that causes a flow of electric current. See **Electric generator.**

The major types of electric power plants are (1) fossil-fueled steam electric power plants, (2) hydroelectric power plants, and (3) nuclear power plants. Various other kinds of power plants produce smaller amounts of electric power.

Fossil-fueled steam electric power plants generate about 66 percent of the world's electric power and about 71 percent of the electric power produced in the United States. Such plants burn coal, oil, or natural gas. These substances are called *fossil fuels* because they developed from the remains of prehistoric plants and animals. The fuel is burned in a *combustion chamber* to produce heat. The heat, in turn, is used to convert water in a boiler to steam. The steam then flows through a set of tubes in a device called a *superheater.* Hot combustion gases surround the steam-filled tubes in the superheater, increasing the temperature and pressure of the steam in the tubes.

The superheated, high-pressure steam is used to drive a huge steam turbine. A steam turbine has a series of wheels, each with many fanlike blades, mounted on a shaft. As the steam rushes through the turbine, it pushes against the blades, causing both the wheels and the turbine shaft to spin. The spinning shaft turns the rotor of the electric generator, thereby producing electric power. See **Turbine** (Steam turbines).

After the steam has passed through the turbine, it enters a *condenser.* In the condenser, the steam passes around pipes carrying cool water. The water in the pipes absorbs heat from the steam. As the steam cools, it *condenses* into water. This water is then pumped back to the boiler to be turned into steam again.

At many power plants, the water in the condenser pipes, which has absorbed heat from the steam, is pumped to a *spray pond* or a *cooling tower* to be cooled. At a spray pond, the water is sent through nozzles that form a spray of droplets. The spray increases the surface area of the water that is exposed to the air, quickly cooling the water. A cooling tower has a series of decks. The water spills down from one deck to another, cooling as it comes into contact with the air. The cooled water is recycled through the condenser or discharged into a lake, river, or other body of water.

Fossil-fueled steam electric power plants are efficient and reliable. But they can cause pollution. Some power plants do not use cooling towers or spray ponds. They release heated water into lakes, ponds, rivers, or streams. Such *thermal pollution* may harm plant and animal life in these bodies of water. In many areas, laws limit the discharge of heated water by power plants.

The smoke from burning fossil fuels causes air pollution and contributes to global warming if it is released into the atmosphere. Most power plants that burn these

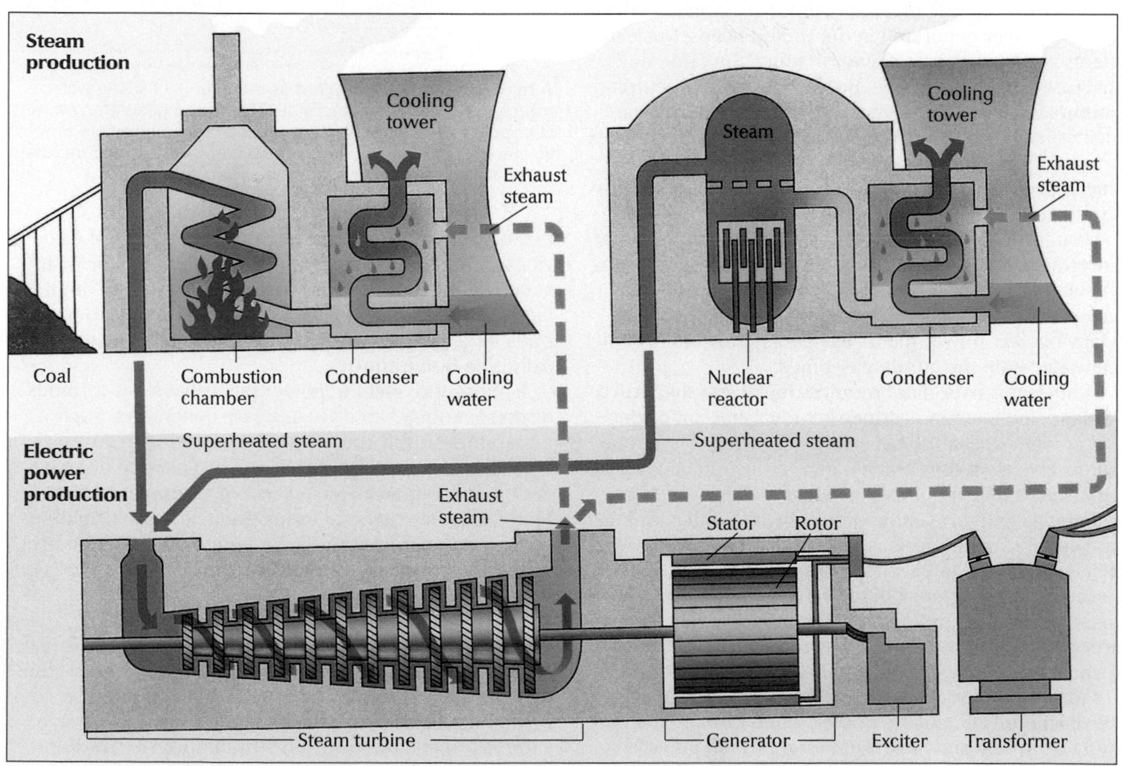

WORLD BOOK illustration by Oxford Illustrators Limited

Steam electric power plants create steam by heating water in a nuclear reactor or in a combustion chamber, where coal, oil, or gas is burned. The steam turns a turbine that runs a generator. The generator has a rotating electromagnet called a *rotor* and a stationary part called a *stator.* A separate generator called an *exciter* powers the rotor, creating a magnetic field that produces an electric charge in the stator. The charge is transmitted as electric current. A transformer boosts the voltage. Exhaust steam passes cool water pipes in a condenser and turns back to water for reheating. The water that has absorbed the steam's heat in the condenser is piped to a cooling tower.

fuels use pollution control equipment to limit the release of pollutants. However, the use of such equipment has not fully eliminated the air pollution created by plants that burn fossil fuels.

Hydroelectric power plants generate about 16 percent of the world's electric power and about 7 percent of the electric power produced in the United States. Such plants convert the energy of falling water into electric energy. A hydroelectric plant uses water that is stored in a reservoir behind a dam. The water flows through a tunnel or pipe to the plant's *water turbine,* or *hydraulic turbine.* As the water rushes through the turbine, it spins the turbine shaft, which drives the electric generator. See **Turbine** (Water turbines); **Water power.**

Hydroelectric power plants called *pumped-storage hydroelectric plants* can store energy by operating in reverse. When the demand for electric power is low, such plants can use their generators as motors to turn the turbines. The turbines then function as pumps, raising water to the reservoir. The water can be used at a later time to produce electric power.

Hydroelectric power plants cost less to operate than fossil-fueled plants and do not pollute the air. The number of hydroelectric power plants is limited, however, by the availability of water power and suitable locations for dams and reservoirs.

Nuclear power plants generate about 16 percent of the world's electric power and about 18 percent of the electric power generated in the United States. Nuclear plants produce electric power in much the same way that fossil-fueled plants do. But instead of a fuel-burning combustion chamber, a nuclear power plant has a device called a *nuclear reactor.* A nuclear reactor produces enormous amounts of heat by *fissioning* (splitting) the nuclei of atoms of a heavy element. Most nuclear plants use the element uranium as the fuel in their reactors.

Heat from the nuclear fission is used to convert water into steam. The steam drives the steam turbine that runs the electric generator. After the steam has left the turbine, it is condensed and recycled through the plant. Many nuclear power plants use cooling towers to cool the water from the condenser pipes.

A nuclear power plant requires much less fuel than a fossil-fueled plant to produce an equal amount of electric power. Nuclear plants also cause much less air pollution. However, they contain dangerous radioactive materials. As a result, the plants must install special safety systems to help prevent and quickly deal with accidents that could cause the release of radiation. Nuclear power plants cost more to build than fossil-fueled plants, partly because of the expense of the safety systems. Nuclear plants also create radioactive wastes that remain hazardous for thousands of years and therefore must be disposed of with extreme caution. See **Nuclear energy.**

Other sources of electric power produce relatively small amounts of electric power. *Wind turbines* are the most important and fastest growing of such power sources. Wind turbines use windmills to harness wind power and drive electric generators. *Geothermal power plants* use steam from the depths of the earth to run turbines that drive electric generators. Some power plants use the energy of the ocean tides to turn turbines that run generators. Others burn wood or agricultural wastes to drive generators. A few power plants convert the sun's energy into electric power by means of devices called *solar cells.* Producing electric power with solar cells is expensive. However, scientists and engineers are studying ways to improve solar cells to produce large quantities of electric power more economically. See **Solar energy.**

A number of electric power plants have gas turbines or diesel engines to drive auxiliary generators. Such generators supply the extra power needed in times of high demand. Diesel engines are also used to drive generators in isolated areas not served by power companies. Many hospitals, factories, and apartment buildings have diesel engines to drive generators in case the distribution of power from power plants is disrupted.

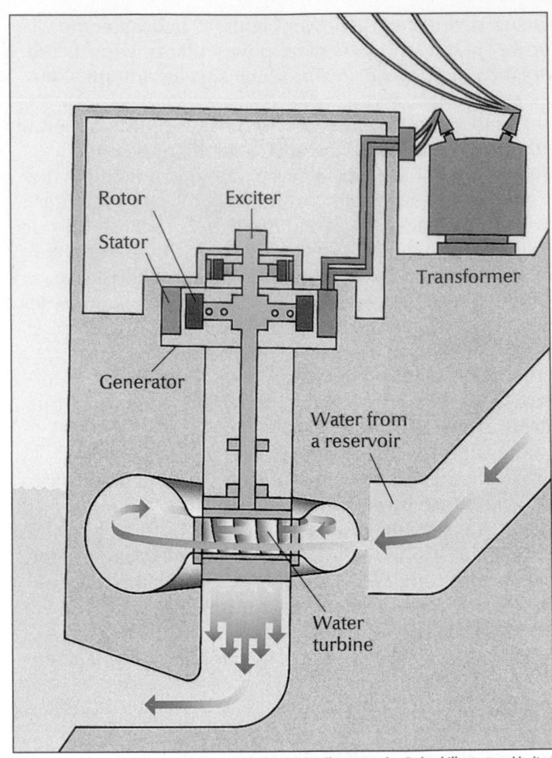

WORLD BOOK illustration by Oxford Illustrators Limited

A hydroelectric power plant uses the force of falling water from a reservoir to turn a turbine that drives a generator. An exciter powers the rotor. As the rotor and its magnetic field turn, an electric charge is created in the stator. A transformer increases the voltage of the current coming from the stator.

Transmitting and distributing electric power

The electric power generated by power plants is usually transmitted 50 miles (80 kilometers) or more to cities or other areas. From those areas, it is distributed to nearby houses, factories, farms, offices, and other consumers. An electric power distribution system is sometimes called a *power grid.*

Transmission. Most electric current travels from power plants along overhead wires called *transmission lines.* Laying underground or underwater cables generally costs more than stringing overhead wires. Cables are therefore used much less often than overhead wires.

As electric current moves along transmission lines,

the lines resist the current flow. The resistance causes the current to lose energy by heating the lines. Power plants limit energy losses by transmitting electric power at high voltages. As voltage is increased, the amount of current needed to transmit a particular amount of electric power decreases. Because less current flows through the line, less energy is lost due to resistance.

Electric current may be either *direct current* (DC) or *alternating current* (AC). Direct current flows in only one direction. Alternating current reverses direction many times each second. It is easier to boost the voltage of alternating current than that of direct current. AC is therefore easier to transmit than DC. For this reason, electric power plants generate alternating current.

The typical power plant generator can produce about 1 million kilowatts of electric power at up to 22,000 volts. Devices called *step-up transformers* then boost this voltage as high as 765,000 volts for transmission.

Distribution. Some large industries require high-voltage current and receive it directly from transmission lines. But high-voltages are unsafe in homes, offices, and most factories. The voltage must therefore be decreased before electric power is distributed to them.

High-voltage electric current is carried by the transmission lines to *subtransmission substations* near the area where the power will be used. These substations have devices called *step-down transformers* that reduce the voltage to 12,500 to 138,000 volts. The voltage is then further reduced at *distribution substations* to 2,000 to 34,500 volts. *Distribution lines* may carry this medium-voltage current directly to commercial, industrial, or institutional users. Distribution lines also carry electric power to *distribution transformers* on poles, on the ground, or in underground vaults. Distribution transformers reduce the voltage to the levels needed by most users. Wires from the transformers run to homes, stores, offices, and other users. Nearly all such consumers in the United States and Canada receive power at about 110 or 220 volts.

Providing reliable service. Equipment failures or damage caused by storms or accidents can interrupt local service of electric power. Such interruptions are known as *power blackouts.* Engineers called *load dispatchers* keep track of the flow of current through the transmission network. When a blackout occurs, the load dispatcher may restore service to the affected area by rerouting current along usable lines.

The demand for electric power often varies greatly from hour to hour. For example, sudden, dark storm clouds will increase demand because many lights will be turned on. The load dispatcher forecasts changes in demand and adjusts the generation and transmission of power accordingly. When demand exceeds the generating capacity of a power plant, the load dispatcher may reduce the voltage to prevent a blackout. Such a situation, called a *brownout,* may damage electrical equip-

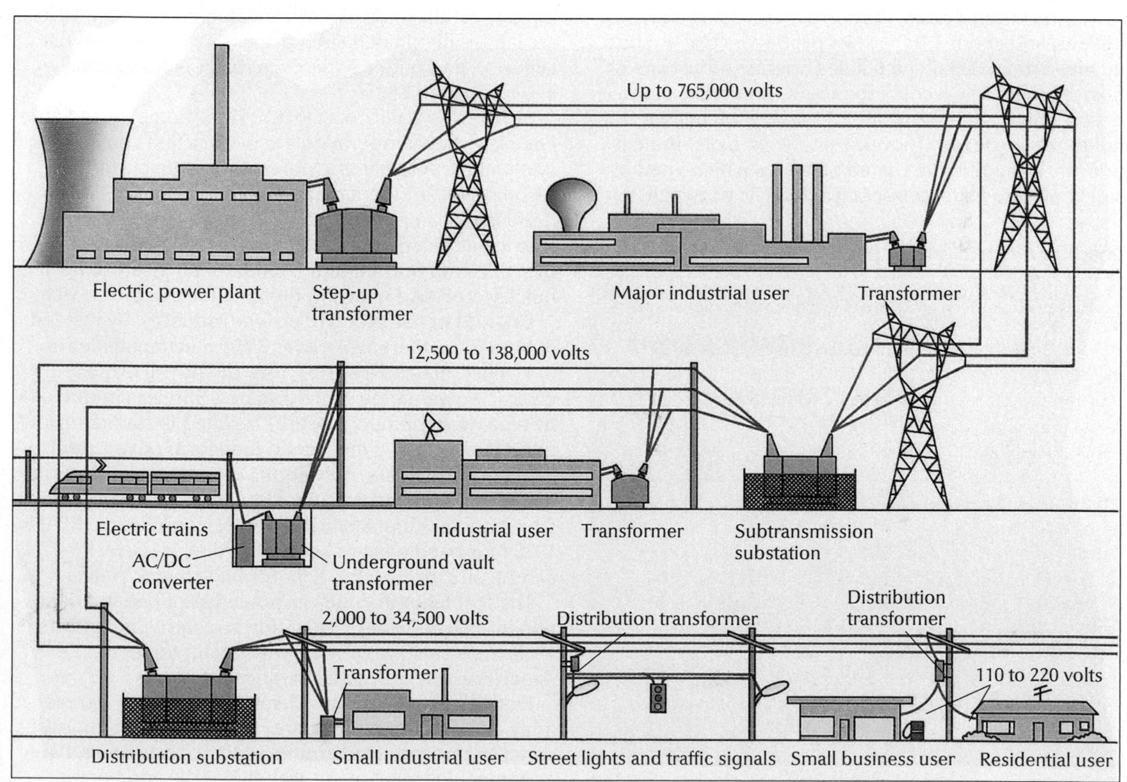

WORLD BOOK illustration by Oxford Illustrators Limited

An electric power distribution system has power lines to carry current and transformers to change its voltage. Step-up transformers boost voltages so that current can be transmitted long distances. Substations and transformers reduce voltages to levels needed by consumers. Some industrial users and transportation systems that require high voltages have their own transformers.

ment or cause it to operate less efficiently.

The transmission networks of most electric companies are interconnected, forming a power pool. Power pools enable companies to receive power from one another in an emergency. Computers control the flow of electric current through transmission networks.

The electric power industry

Organizations called *electric utilities* generate, transmit, and distribute the majority of the electric power that the public uses. Electric utilities are either owned or regulated by government agencies. In some countries, the national government owns all electric utilities. In others, stockholders or cooperatives, or local or regional governments, may own electric utilities in addition to the national government. Usually, a geographical area is served by a single electric utility. In some countries, including the United States and Canada, electric power generation has been partially deregulated. In deregulated markets, a growing number of privately owned businesses called *independent power producers* generate electric power and supply it wholesale to utilities. The United States is the world's leading generator and consumer of electric power.

Some countries can generate more electric power than they need, and they export this excess power. Canada exports electric power to the United States, France exports to the United Kingdom, and many African countries export to neighboring nations.

In the United States, there are about 3,300 electric utilities, and about 1,700 power producers that are not utilities. About 800 of the utilities operate thousands of power plants that account for about three-fifths of the nation's generating capacity. The rest of the utilities do not generate power. They only transmit it, distribute it, or both. Utilities in the United States may be owned by stockholders, cities, cooperatives, public power districts, or state or federal government agencies. Public power districts are political subdivisions that provide electric power to both incorporated cities and towns and unincorporated rural areas. Nonutilities, including independent power producers, account for about two-fifths of the nation's generating capacity.

Local and state utility commissions usually set the rates that electric utilities charge their customers. Federal agencies govern the design and licensing of power plants, regulate the interstate sale of electric power, and set and enforce pollution control standards.

In 1992, the U.S. government began to take steps to deregulate the electric power industry. Many states now have open competition among utilities and other power providers.

In Canada, the provincial governments own most major electric utilities. But stockholders own large electric utilities in Alberta and Prince Edward Island. Provincial public utility boards regulate Canada's electric utilities. The federal Canadian Nuclear Safety Commission oversees the nuclear energy industry. The National Energy Board controls the export of electric power.

Leading electric power producing countries

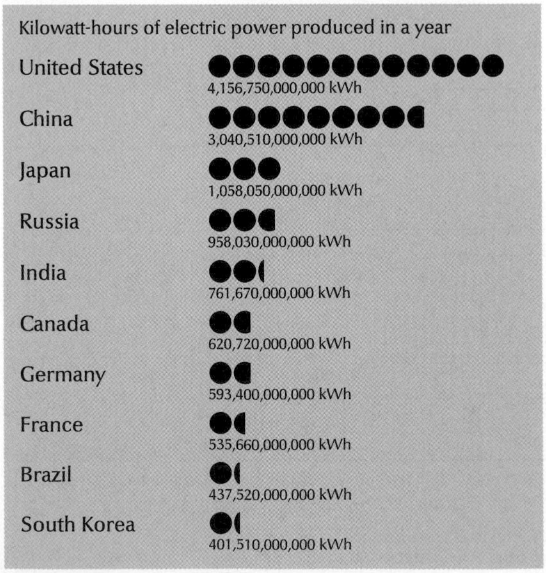

Kilowatt-hours of electric power produced in a year

United States	4,156,750,000,000 kWh
China	3,040,510,000,000 kWh
Japan	1,058,050,000,000 kWh
Russia	958,030,000,000 kWh
India	761,670,000,000 kWh
Canada	620,720,000,000 kWh
Germany	593,400,000,000 kWh
France	535,660,000,000 kWh
Brazil	437,520,000,000 kWh
South Korea	401,510,000,000 kWh

Figures are for 2007.
Source: U.S. Energy Information Administration.

History

Early developments. One of the earliest practical uses of electric power was to light the lamps of lighthouses. In 1858, South Foreland Lighthouse near Dover, England, became the first electric lighthouse. Its generator powered an *arc lamp.* An arc lamp produces bright light by means of an electric arc. Beginning in the 1870's, arc lamps illuminated such places as railroad stations, factories, and public squares in major cities in Europe and the United States.

In 1879, the California Electric Light Company in San Francisco began operating the world's first central power plant that sold electric power to private customers. Also in 1879, the American inventor Thomas A. Edison perfected a lamp that gave off light when a filament inside it was heated by an electric current. Edison's *incandescent* lamp burned much longer than an arc lamp. It quickly created a growing demand for electric service.

Growth of the electric power industry. By the end of the 1800's, there were over 3,600 electric utilities in the United States. However, they did not all provide electric power at the same voltages. Studies conducted by electrical engineers in 1891 resulted in standardization of voltages. Utilities could then form power pools.

In the early 1930's, only about 10 percent of U.S. farms had electric power. President Franklin D. Roosevelt established the Rural Electrification Administration (REA) in 1935 to expand electric service in rural areas. By the early 1990's, nearly all U.S. farms had electric power.

The first full-scale nuclear power plant began operation in 1956 at Calder Hall in northwestern England. In 1966, the world's first tidal power plant opened on the Rance River near St.-Malo, France.

Electric power today. Electric utilities rely increasingly on computerized control systems. Power lines are widely interconnected among electric companies. Power companies must plan carefully for the addition of plants and transmission lines to meet the ever-increasing demand for electric power. The construction of new plants is costly and takes several years. Many planned nuclear power plants have been canceled because of soaring construction costs as well as safety concerns.

The supply of fossil fuels will eventually run out unless economical substitutes can be developed for them. Many scientists believe that energy from Earth, the sun, wind, and oceans can be used more extensively to produce electric power in the future. Some utilities now use solar, geothermal, tidal, or wind power in addition to regular energy sources to generate electric power.

In August 2003, North America experienced its worst power outage in history. The outage affected eight U.S. states in the Northeast and Midwest and two Canadian provinces. Investigators believe that it began in Ohio after a series of routine, and brief, transmission line shutdowns. It spread as power lines overloaded and circuit breakers triggered the shutdown of several lines and coal-fired plants. After detecting power fluctuations, several nuclear power plants automatically disconnected from the grid to prevent equipment damage. Many people have criticized the instability of the nation's aging transmission system and have called for an upgrade of the transmission equipment. Henry M. Louie

Related articles in *World Book* include:

Electric current
Electric generator
Electricity
Energy supply (Sources of energy)
Rural Electrification Administration
Tennessee Valley Authority
Transformer
Turbine
Wind power

Outline

I. Sources of electric power
- A. Fossil-fueled steam electric power plants
- B. Hydroelectric power plants
- C. Nuclear power plants
- D. Other sources of electric power

II. Transmitting and distributing electric power
- A. Transmission
- B. Distribution
- C. Providing reliable service

III. The electric power industry
- A. In the United States
- B. In Canada

IV. History

Questions

What is a *brownout?*
How long must you burn one 100-watt light bulb to use 1 kilowatt-hour of electric energy?
What does a *load dispatcher* do?
Why do power plants transmit electric power at high voltages?
What is a *power pool?*
What are the three major types of electric power plants?
Why do power plants generate alternating current?
When and where did the first full-scale nuclear power plant begin operation?
What source of energy do *geothermal power plants* use?
Which type of electric power plant produces most of the world's electric power?

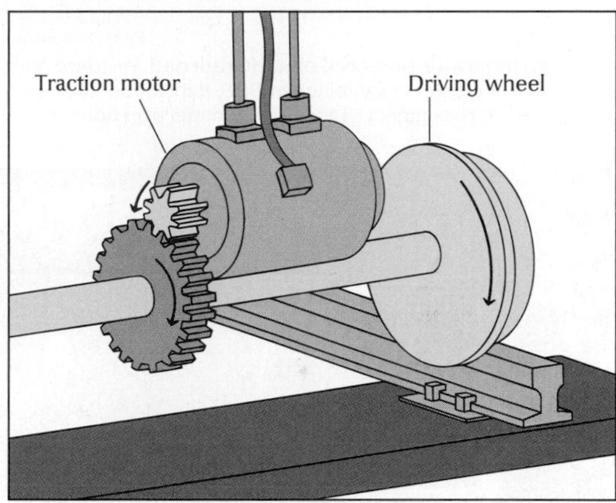

WORLD BOOK illustration by William Graham

The propulsion system of an electric train includes the traction motor and the driving wheel. The traction motor turns the driving wheel, which actually makes the train move.

Electric railroad is an electrically powered railway system. Electrically powered trains include high-speed passenger trains; some freight trains; and the subways, elevated systems, and streetcars found in certain cities. The electric power to run an electric train comes from

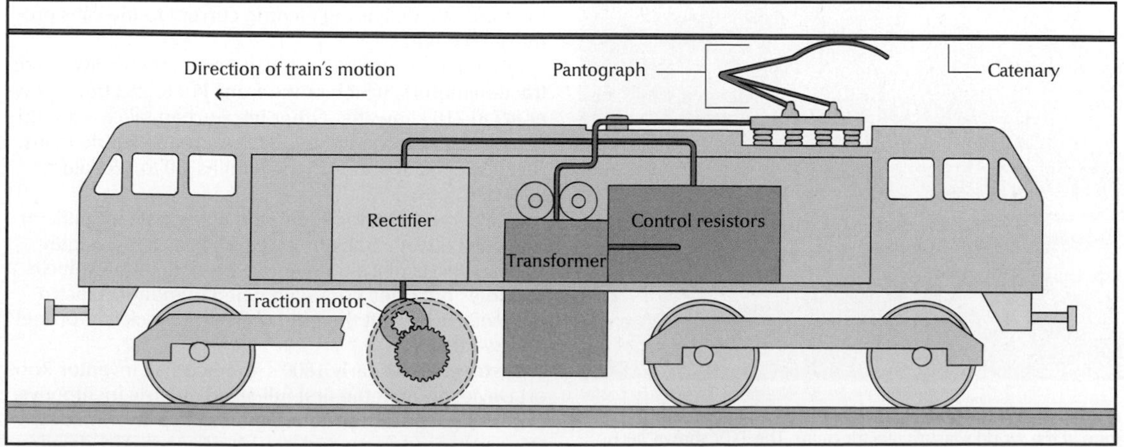

WORLD BOOK illustration by William Graham

A typical electric train receives power from a *catenary* (overhead wire) or from an electrified third rail. In the overhead wire system, *shown here,* a pantograph conducts electric current to the transformer. The current eventually arrives at the traction motors, which are part of the train's propulsion system.

Electric Railroad Assn.

The first generator-powered electric railroad, *pictured here,* was shown at the Berlin Exhibition of 1879. It included three cars that carried 20 passengers 8 miles (13 kilometers) an hour.

L Levine, Berg & Associates

A commuter train in Washington, D.C., *shown here,* receives its power through an electrified third rail. The electric power for some modern electric trains is provided by an overhead wire.

Christian Delemarre, Societé Nationale des Chemins de Fer Français

The French TGV *(train à grande vitesse,* or high-speed train) is one of the world's fastest electric trains. The TGV shown here speeds between Paris and Lyon and some Swiss cities at up to 167 miles (269 kilometers) per hour. A newer TGV reaches a top speed of 200 miles (320 kilometers) per hour. The TGV gets its power from an overhead wire.

an external source—a central power plant—rather than from an engine or generator on board the train.

Electric trains have many advantages. They are quieter than other trains and do not produce smoke or exhaust. Coal, gas, oil, nuclear power, or water power can generate electric power for an electric train. In contrast, diesel trains run only on diesel oil.

Electric trains also travel faster than any other trains. Several countries in Europe and Asia have high-speed electric trains. Some of these trains operate at 200 miles (320 kilometers) per hour. The world's fastest electric trains operate on *maglev* (magnetic levitation) systems. These trains float above their tracks. A maglev train in Tokyo exceeded 360 mph (580 kph) during an exhibition run in 2003.

Electric railroads provide *intercity service* (service between cities). These railroads also offer *intra-urban* or *commuter service,* which carries passengers within cities and between cities and their suburbs. Electric railroads are common in many European countries and in Japan. However, in the United States only about 1 percent, or 2,000 miles (3,200 kilometers), of intercity track is electrified.

Kinds of electric railroads. Most intercity electric trains receive power through an overhead wire called a *catenary.* In the overhead wire system, a steel framework connects a car to a catenary. This car is usually a *locomotive* designed to move the rest of the train. The framework, called a *pantograph,* delivers electric current from the wire to the locomotive's propulsion system. This system includes the *traction motors.* Traction motors power the *driving wheels,* which actually move the locomotive.

Intercity electric trains have one or more locomotives that pull freight or passenger cars. Most electric locomotives weigh between 100 and 200 tons (90 and 180 metric tons) and provide approximately 6,000 to 7,000 horsepower (4,500 to 5,200 kilowatts). They can reach speeds of more than 150 miles (240 kilometers) per hour.

An electrified third rail delivers electric power to most intra-urban electric trains. Trains using a third rail have metal plates called *shoes.* Two shoes attach to the bottom of a locomotive or railcar. The shoes slide along the third rail, delivering electric current to the car's propulsion system.

Some intra-urban railcars can propel themselves with traction motors, which range from 119 to 282 horsepower (89 to 210 kilowatts). Other intra-urban railcars are driven by separate locomotives. Intra-urban electric trains reach speeds of about 50 to 75 miles (80 to 120 kilometers) per hour.

Unlike most electric trains, a maglev train has little or no contact with a track or wires. The track for maglev trains consists of a single guideway, which the vehicle straddles but does not touch when in motion. Electromagnetic forces lift the train above the track and propel it forward.

History. In the early 1800's, the Scottish inventor Robert Davidson built the first full-sized electric locomotive. But the high cost of producing electric power made it too expensive for general use by railroads. The development of the *electric generator* in the mid-1800's made the modern electric railway possible. This device generated a current of high voltage at low cost.

The first commercial electric street railway began operation in Lichterfelde, Germany, in 1881. In 1887, Frank J. Sprague, an American inventor, built the Union Passenger Railway in Richmond, Virginia. This was the first large electric railway system. By the early 1900's, electric elevated trains operated in Boston, Chicago, and New York City. Europe built many electric intercity tracks in the late 1940's. The first high-speed electric train, Japan's *Shinkansen,* began running in 1964. France's TGV began service in 1981. Vernon P. Roan

Related articles in *World Book* include:

Diesel engine	Railroad
Elevated railroad	Streetcar
Locomotive	Subway
Magnetic levitation train	Transit

Electric ray is a type of fish that can give off electricity. They live on the bottom of warm seas. Most electric rays are found in shallow coastal water, but some live as deep as 1,200 feet (370 meters). There are dozens of *species* (kinds).

Electric rays have a flat, wide body and a slender, pointed tail with fins. Their colors vary, but most species are dark brown, blue, or gray with spots. Electric rays measure from 6 inches to 7 feet (15 to 215 centimeters) long. Two special organs on the upper side of the head allow the fish to give off electricity. The skin follows the honeycomb shape of the electric organs it covers.

Electric rays produce electric charges to defend themselves and to stun their prey. They eat shellfish, worms, and other small fish. The shock from a full-grown, healthy ray can stun a human being.

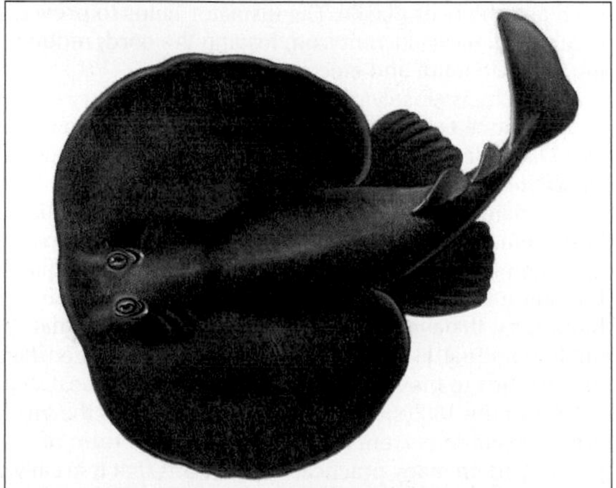

WORLD BOOK illustration by Colin Newman, Bernard Thornton Artists

An electric ray has a wide body and a pointed tail.

Electric rays are not as active as most other fish. Many cover themselves with sand or mud and remain mainly stationary or swim slowly at the sea bottom. The eggs of most fish hatch outside the female's body, but female electric rays hatch their eggs inside their bodies and so give birth to live young. John D. McEachran

Scientific classification. Electric rays make up the order Torpediniformes.

Electric shock. See **First aid** (Restoring breathing); **Shock treatment.**

Electric switch is a device that turns on or off the flow of electric current in a circuit. Light switches are common electric switches. In such switches, an insulated handle activates a hidden mechanism that completes or breaks the circuit. Turning the switch on connects two metal contacts so that current flows through the circuit. Turning it off separates the contacts and breaks the flow of current. Other electric switches operate without human control. For example, a thermostat switches on or off based on temperature. Computer chips contain many tiny switches called *transistors* (see **Transistor**).

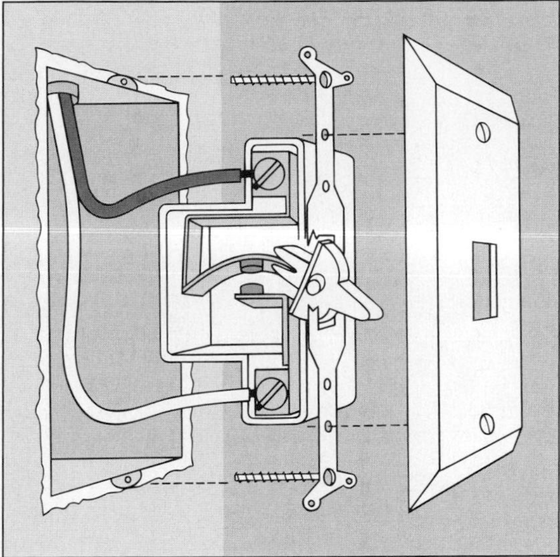

WORLD BOOK illustration by Zorica Dabich

An electric switch controls the flow of electric current in a circuit. This diagram shows a light switch in the off position. Turning the switch on connects two metal contacts—colored blue above—so that current flows through the circuit.

Electric switches may be classified according to the arrangement of their contacts. The simplest kind, a *single pole, single throw switch,* controls the flow of current along a single path. A *double pole, single throw switch* has two sets of contacts controlled by the same handle. In this way, two circuits can be controlled at the same time. A pair of *single pole, double throw switches* allows a light to be turned on and off from either of two locations. Each switch moves a contact back and forth between two wires. Electric current flows when the contacts in both switches are connected to the same wire. Flipping either of the two switches breaks the circuit by moving one contact to the other wire. Robert B. Prigo

See also **Circuit breaker; Electric circuit.**

Electric train. See **Electric railroad.**

Electrical engineering. See **Engineering** (The branches of engineering).

Electrical Workers, International Brotherhood of (IBEW), is a labor union affiliated with the American Federation of Labor and Congress of Industrial Organizations. It was organized in 1891 in St. Louis, Missouri, as the National Brotherhood of Electrical Workers. In 1899, it opened its membership to Canadians and adopted its present name.

The union's headquarters are in Washington, D.C. For membership, see **Labor movement** (table).

Critically reviewed by the International Brotherhood of Electrical Workers

© Shutterstock

A bolt of lightning is a powerful electric discharge. Lightning occurs when huge electric charges jump between clouds or between a cloud and the ground.

Electricity

Electricity is one of the most basic features of our universe. When most people hear the word *electricity,* they think of lighting, television, computers, air conditioners, and other electrically powered devices. Electricity makes possible these and many other useful things. But electricity is much more fundamental than that. The matter around us, for example, is made up of electrically charged particles. In fact, attraction among such particles holds together the atoms and molecules that make up matter. In this way, electricity is part of the structure of almost everything that exists.

Electricity includes a variety of effects related to charged particles. Perhaps the most familiar of these effects is *electric current.* An electric current is a flow of electric charges. It is electric current that flows through wires into our homes and powers our electric devices. Another familiar effect is *static electricity.* Static electricity occurs when an object or material accumulates an overall electric charge. Under the right conditions, the charge can be released in the form of a visible spark.

Electric charges come in two types: positive and negative. A positive charge will *attract* (pull on) a negative charge, and vice versa. This fact is often stated as *Opposite charges attract.* Two negative charges will *repel* (push away) each other, as will two positive charges.

Materials vary in their ability to *conduct* (carry) electric current. Current moves easily through materials called *conductors.* Metals are good conductors. Most wires used to carry electric current are made of metal, usually copper. Some liquids can also conduct electric current. For this reason, it can be dangerous to operate electrical equipment in wet conditions. Materials known as *insulators* resist the movement of current. Glass, rubber, plastic, dry wood, and dry air are good insulators. Insulators are important for electrical safety. Most electrical cords are made from a conductor covered with an insulator, such as rubber or plastic. The insulator helps to prevent heat and electric current from leaving the cord, reducing the risk of fire and electric shock.

Electricity is closely related to magnetism. Every electric influence exerts a magnetic influence, and vice versa. In fact, electricity and magnetism together make up a single force called *electromagnetism.*

Electricity is also associated with many processes in living things. In the human body, for example, electrical and chemical impulses travel along nerves, carrying information to and from the brain. Such signals tell the brain what the eyes see, what the ears hear, and what the fingers feel. Electrochemical impulses from the brain tell muscles to move and tell the heart when to beat.

During the 1800's, people learned to harness the energy of electric current to do work. This new form of power had so many practical applications that it greatly changed the way people lived. Inventors and scientists learned how to generate electric current. They found ways to use that current to produce light, heat, and motion. They developed electrically powered devices that enabled people to communicate across great distances and to process information quickly. The demand for electric power grew steadily during the 1900's. In the 2000's, most people could not imagine life without electric power.

Uses of electric power

Many aspects of our daily lives depend on electric power. People in developed nations use many electrically powered devices every day. One of the most important such devices is the computer, which uses electricity to process information. Computers are a fundamental part of the way many people live, learn, and work.

In homes. Electric appliances save hours of labor

Outline

I. Uses of electric power
- A. In homes
- B. In industry
- C. In communication
- D. In transportation
- E. In medicine and science

II. Electric circuits
- A. Simple circuits
- B. Series and parallel circuits
- C. Switches

III. Alternating and direct current

IV. Static electricity

V. Electrical safety
- A. Electric shock
- B. Outdoor dangers
- C. Electrical fire

VI. Electricity and matter
- A. Atoms
- B. Ions
- C. Molecules

VII. Conductivity
- A. Resistance
- B. Semiconductors
- C. Plasma
- D. Superconductors

VIII. Sources of electric energy

IX. Controlling current

X. Electromagnetism

XI. History

once done by hand. Such appliances include dishwashers, vacuum cleaners, and washing machines. Electric ranges, microwave ovens, and food processors help us prepare meals quickly and easily. Refrigerators and freezers preserve food. Air conditioners and electric fans cool homes. Electric heaters provide warmth and hot water. Televisions, radios, computers, video game systems, and music players furnish entertainment. Electric lights brighten dark spaces.

In industry. Modern industry would be impossible without electric power. Factories produce many items using electrically operated conveyor belts, robots, and other equipment. Manufacturers use electric instruments to ensure correct product sizes and quality. Drills, saws, and many other small tools run on electric power. Electric motors run elevators, cranes, and most other large machinery. Computers are vital to industry.

In communication. Electric energy powers almost every device people use to communicate. Telephones, TV's, radios, and computer modems all run on electric power. Communications satellites use electric energy from devices called *solar cells* to relay information around the world. Solar cells convert sunlight into electric energy. TV and radio signals are electromagnetic in nature. So are telephone and computer network signals.

In transportation. Electric energy powers subways, trolleys, and trains that carry millions of people. Most automobiles use electric sparks to ignite the gasoline that powers the engine. Increasing numbers of cars rely on electricity for part or all of their main power. Many controls in airplanes and ships are electrically powered.

In medicine and science. Health care workers use numerous electric instruments to examine patients and perform medical tests. For example, doctors look inside the body using X-ray machines and *magnetic resonance imaging* (MRI) machines, both of which use properties of electricity to operate. Machines called *electrocardiographs* (ECG's) record tiny electrical signals from the heart. ECG's help doctors to diagnose heart disease or damage. Electrically powered lasers are used for a variety of medical procedures. Their uses range from tattoo removal to vision repair to cancer treatment.

Scientists from every field use electric devices to conduct research. Microbiologists, for example, use powerful instruments called *scanning electron microscopes* to magnify and examine cells. Physicists use electrically operated *particle accelerators* to probe the interiors of atoms. Huge telescopes with electric motors and sensors help astronomers study planets, stars, and galaxies.

Electric circuits

The electric current in our homes is a flow of charged particles called *electrons.* There is energy associated with this flow. As current passes through an electric device, this electric energy may be converted to useful forms. For example, an electric range converts electric energy into heat. A light bulb converts it into light.

To make use of electric energy, an electric device

© Shutterstock

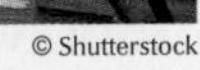

© Shutterstock

© Shutterstock

Electric energy can be harnessed and converted to other kinds of useful energy. It produces heat in this electric welder, motion in this electric car, and light in this computer monitor.

Terms used in electricity

Ampere is the unit used to measure the rate of flow of an electric current.
Conductor is a material through which electric current flows easily.
Electric charge is a basic feature of certain particles of matter that causes them to attract or repel other charged particles.
Electric circuit is the path that an electric current follows.
Electric current is the flow of electric charges.
Electric field is the influence a charged body has on the space around it that causes other charged bodies in that space to experience electric forces.
Electrode is a piece of metal or other conductor through which current enters or leaves an electric device.
Electromagnetism is a basic force in the universe that involves both electricity and magnetism.
Electron is a subatomic particle with a negative electric charge.
Insulator is a material that opposes the flow of electric current.
Ion is an atom or group of atoms that has either gained or lost electrons, and so has an electric charge.
Kilowatt-hour is the amount of electric energy a 1,000-watt device uses in one hour.
Neutron is a subatomic particle that has no electric charge.
Ohm is the unit used to measure a material's resistance to the flow of electric current.
Proton is a subatomic particle with a positive electric charge.
Resistance is a material's opposition to the flow of electric current.
Static electricity is electric charge that is not moving.
Superconductor is a material through which electric current flows without resistance.
Voltage is a type of "pressure" that drives electric charges through a circuit.
Watt is the unit used to measure the rate of energy consumption, including electric energy.

must be connected to an energy source, such as an electrical outlet or battery. A complete path must be provided for current to flow from the energy source to the device and back again. Such a path is called an *electric circuit.*

Simple circuits. Suppose a person wanted to make a battery-powered light bulb shine. Electric current will flow to the bulb only if there is a complete circuit that leads from the battery to the bulb and back. To complete the circuit, the person must connect a wire from one *terminal* (end) of the battery to the light bulb. Then, the person must connect another wire from the light bulb to the battery's other terminal. Electrons will then flow from the battery, through the light bulb, and back to the battery. The light bulb converts some of the current's energy into light, causing the bulb to glow.

Series and parallel circuits. A single battery or other power source often supplies power to more than one electric device. These instances require more complex arrangements such as *series circuits* and *parallel circuits.*

A series circuit features only one path. The same current flows from the energy source, through each of the devices on the circuit in turn, and back to the energy source. A simple series circuit might involve a battery and two light bulbs. A wire connects one terminal of the battery to one light bulb. Another wire connects that bulb to the second bulb. A third wire connects the second bulb to the battery's other terminal.

Series circuits are used in flashlights, some decorative holiday lights, and other simple devices. One weakness of a series circuit is that the failure of any part of the circuit will disrupt the entire circuit. In the example, if one light bulb burns out, the path is broken, and current cannot flow. The other light bulb will go dark as well. Also, adding more devices, such as another bulb, to the circuit lowers the current to each device.

In a parallel circuit, the current splits to follow two or more paths. One example is a circuit in which two light bulbs are attached to both terminals of a battery by separate wires. The current in such a circuit splits, with half the electrons flowing through one bulb and half flowing through the other before returning to the battery.

Unlike in a series circuit, a parallel circuit provides the same level of current to all devices, no matter the number. Also, the failure of one part of the circuit will not knock out the entire circuit. In the example, if one light burns out, the other could continue to shine. Household lights and appliances are connected in parallel circuits.

Many circuits include some parts that are series and some that are parallel. A complex circuit, like that in a computer or TV, can have millions of parts connected in various series and parallel combinations.

Switches. The simplest way to control the flow of current through a circuit is with a *switch.* A basic switch consists of two electrical conductors that can be separated to create a gap in a circuit. When the gap is open, the switch is off. No current flows. When the switch is on, the conductors are connected, and current flows.

Alternating and direct current

Current can flow through a circuit in two different ways. *Direct current* (DC) flows in only one direction. Batteries produce direct current. In a simple DC circuit, electrons flow from one battery terminal, through the circuit, to the other terminal. *Alternating current* (AC) rapidly reverses direction. In an AC circuit, individual electrons move back and forth in the wires, not traveling the entire circuit.

The current in household wiring is alternating current. In the United States and Canada, household current reverses direction 120 times per second, completing 60 full cycles. In other parts of the world, such as Australia, Europe, and South Africa, 50 cycles is the standard.

Static electricity

Electrons are part of the atoms that make up matter. Sometimes, the atoms in an object gain or lose electrons. When this happens, the entire object can take on a stationary electric charge until it is discharged. The term *static electricity* describes such situations.

Static electricity occurs, for example, when a person rubs a balloon on a shirt. The rubbing between the cloth and the balloon causes electrons to transfer from the shirt to the balloon. Electrons have a negative electric charge, so the extra electrons give the balloon an overall negative charge. The shirt, which has lost electrons, gains a positive electric charge. The opposite charges attract, enabling the two to stick together. If the conditions are right, the balloon may stick to a neutrally charged object, such as a wall.

Similarly, when a person walks across a rug on a dry day, rubbing between the shoes and the rug can transfer electrons from the rug to the person's body. The transfer gives the body a negative charge. If the person touches a doorknob or other metal object, electrons may jump from the body to the object. The person may

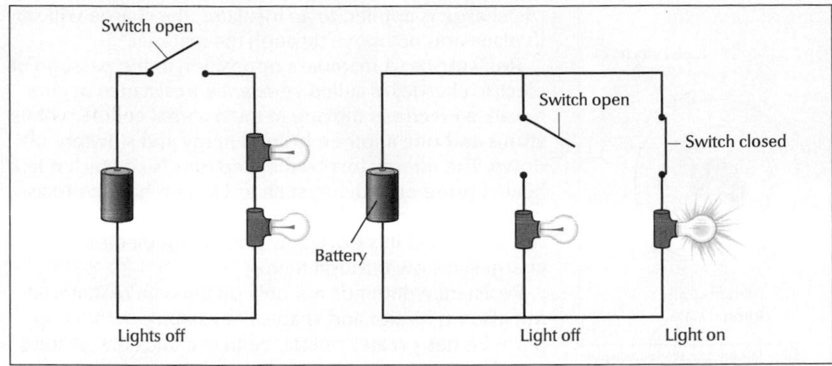

WORLD BOOK diagrams

Series and parallel circuits are used to power multiple devices. In a series circuit (far left), a single looping path connects the devices. Breaking the circuit, for example by opening a switch, cuts the flow of current to all devices. In a parallel circuit (near left), the path splits into branches. If one branch is open, devices on other branches can continue to function.

see a spark and feel a slight shock.

Static electricity also causes lightning. Most scientists think that collisions among various forms of water and ice build up areas of electric charge within a storm cloud. Parts of the cloud become positively charged. Other parts become negatively charged. Charge may eventually jump between two areas, including from cloud to cloud or from the cloud to the ground. The result is the huge electric spark we call lightning.

Static electricity has many uses in homes, businesses, and industries. For example, *electrostatic* copying machines make duplicates of printed or written material by attracting negatively charged particles of *toner* (powdered ink) to positively charged paper. Static electricity is also used in air cleaners called *electrostatic precipitators.* These devices put a charge on airborne particles, such as dust, smoke, bacteria, or pollen. Oppositely charged plates then attract the particles out of the air.

Electrical safety

Most people know that electricity can be dangerous. Understanding why can help you to avoid injury and to use electric power safely.

Electric shock occurs when an electric current passes through the body. The body relies on natural electrical and chemical signals that travel along nerves, carrying information to and from the brain. These signals regulate the beating of the heart and other vital functions. Currents flowing through the body can disrupt these signals. The currents may cause muscle contractions, heart and respiratory failure, and death. Electric current can also burn skin and other body tissues.

The danger presented by electricity depends in part on its *voltage.* Voltage measures the "push" that a source of electric energy supplies to move a charge through a circuit. For a given circuit of set resistance, the higher the voltage, the stronger the current. The voltage of a flashlight or radio battery is usually too low to generate enough current to cause serious injury. But the 120 volts available at most household outlets can create a current strong enough to severely injure or even kill a person. The danger of electric shock is much greater when a person's skin is wet. Water lowers the body's resistance to the flow of electricity. A given voltage can then pass a greater current through the body.

Most electric devices have safety features to help prevent shock. Many appliances and tools have a plug with a third prong. This prong connects the metal parts of the device to a wire leading to the ground. If the wiring in the device becomes defective, the third prong usually causes the current to flow harmlessly to the ground.

Outdoor dangers. If you climb a tree near an electric power line, you may get a shock if the tree touches the line. Storms sometimes knock down electric power lines. You could be injured or killed if you touch a fallen line when the power is still on.

Lightning discharges may involve about 100 million volts. This voltage is more than enough to kill a person. You can avoid lightning dangers by staying indoors during a storm, away from metal plumbing and fixtures, as well as corded appliances. If you get caught outdoors, stay away from open fields, open water, and high places. A forest is usually safer than open land. But do not stand under a tall or isolated tree, which is more likely to be struck. The inside of a car is generally safer than outdoors. If the vehicle is struck by lightning, its metal body will often conduct the electric charge around the outside of the car. The interior of the car will be unharmed.

Electrical fire is another danger. When an electric current passes through a conductor, it can cause the conductor to become hot. Sometimes the heat is desirable. For example, the wires in a toaster heat up to brown bread. But overheating in electrical cords or in household wiring can cause a fire. Electrical fires destroy many homes every year. To avoid fires, do not plug too many devices into the same outlet. Never use electric devices with worn or frayed cords.

Electricity and matter

The electron is the smallest free particle of negative charge. Another particle, called a *proton,* has the exact same amount of charge as the electron, but the proton's charge is positive. Along with an uncharged particle called the *neutron,* protons and electrons are the building blocks of matter.

Atoms. Protons, neutrons, and electrons combine to form atoms. Protons and neutrons join to form a core, called the *nucleus.* The nucleus is positively charged because of the protons. It is also relatively heavy, because neutrons and protons are much larger and heavier than electrons. The positively charged nucleus attracts the negatively charged electrons. The electrons are light and fast and move quickly around the nucleus.

Each type of atom has a different number of protons in its nucleus. For example, hydrogen, the simplest atom, has only 1 proton in its nucleus. An oxygen atom

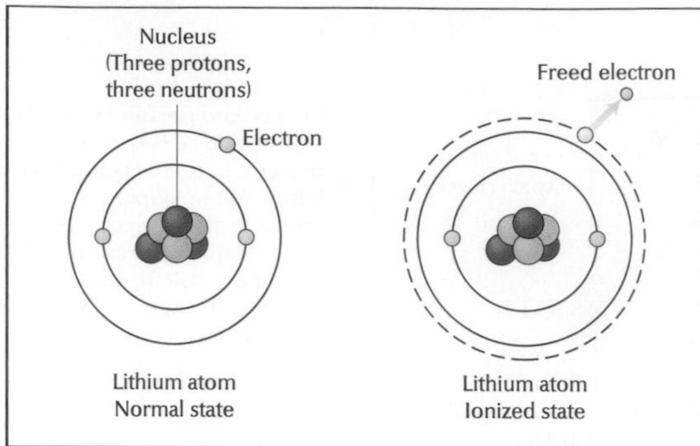

WORLD BOOK diagram by Tom Brucker, Precision Graphics

An atom becomes an ion when it gains or loses an electron and so acquires an electric charge. A normal atom, *left,* has an equal number of positive protons and negative electrons. If it loses an electron, *right,* it becomes a positively charged ion.

has 8 protons. Iron has 26. Uranium has 92. Normally, an atom has an equal number of protons and electrons. As a result, the negative charges of the electrons exactly balance the positive charges of the protons. The atom is, therefore, electrically neutral overall.

Ions. Sometimes an atom loses or gains one or more electrons. If it gains an electron, the atom takes on a negative charge. If it loses an electron, the atom takes on a positive charge. Atoms that carry an electric charge are called *ions.* Positive and negative ions attract each other and can combine to form solid materials. Ordinary table salt, for example, consists of sodium and chlorine. Each sodium atom gives up one electron to form a positive sodium ion. The chlorine takes on this electron to become a negative *chloride* ion. Strong electrical attraction between the two types of ions makes salt a solid material with a high melting point.

Molecules. Neutral atoms often come together to share electrons. If the two atoms are not identical, the electrons often spend more time near one atom than the other, making one atom slightly more positive and the other atom more negative. Electrical attraction between the positive and negative atoms causes them to join into molecules. For example, two hydrogen atoms can share electrons with one oxygen atom to make a water molecule. The electrons spend more time near the oxygen atom, giving it a slight negative charge. The two hydrogen atoms take on slight positive charges. Attraction between the atoms holds the water molecule together.

Like lone atoms, molecules can also lose or gain electrons. When this happens, the molecule itself takes on an overall charge, becoming an ion.

Conductivity

To be a conductor, a material must have charged particles that are "free" to move throughout, carrying charge with them. In most conductors, the free particles are loosely held electrons. Most metals are good conductors, because they have a large number of free electrons. In some conductors, the current is a flow of ions, rather than electrons. Salt water, for example, is a conductor because it contains sodium and chloride ions that are free to move about, forming a current.

In an insulator, on the other hand, electrons are tightly bound to atoms and are not free to move around. If electric charge is applied to an insulator, the charge will stay in place and not move through the material.

Resistance. A material's opposition to the passage of electric charges is called *resistance.* Resistance occurs because electrons moving in the material collide with atoms and one another, losing energy and slowing down. The energy lost by the electrons is converted to heat. A good conductor, such as copper, has low resistance. Insulators, such as glass or wood, have such high resistance that it is extremely difficult for electric charges to flow through them.

Resistance depends not only on the type of material but also on its size and shape. For example, a thin copper wire has greater resistance than a thick one. A long wire has greater resistance than a short one. A material's resistance may also vary with temperature. For metals, resistance typically increases with temperature.

Semiconductors are materials that conduct charges more readily than do insulators but not as well as do conductors. Silicon is the most commonly used semiconductor. By adding small amounts of other substances to a semiconductor, engineers can adjust its capacity to conduct electric charge. Semiconductors are essential to the operation of computers, television sets, electronic games, and many other devices.

Semiconductors generally have a higher resistance than conductors. For semiconductors, resistance generally decreases with temperature.

Plasma. If a gas is greatly heated, many electrons may be freed from their atomic *nuclei* (the plural of *nucleus).* When this happens, the gas becomes a *plasma.* The freed electrons make plasmas excellent conductors. The hot glowing substance inside a fluorescent light is one example of a plasma conductor. The hot materials that make up the sun and other stars are also plasma.

Superconductors. In some materials, called *superconductors,* electrons move freely, without resistance. Superconductors can thus carry current with no loss of energy. However, known superconductors function only at extremely low temperatures. For this reason, superconductors are used only in special situations. Engineers are working to develop higher temperature superconductors for use in highly efficient motors, generators, and power lines.

In superconductors, the electrons pair up in a special arrangement known as *Cooper pairs.* This arrangement is named for its discoverer, the American physicist Leon Cooper. Single electrons bump into one another while traveling through a material. But Cooper pairs can travel together in unison without colliding. This means that current in a superconducting wire never loses energy. A loop of such wire could carry a current that travels around and around forever.

As electrons move through a normal conductor, they create an invisible region of electric influence called an *electric field.* The electric field, in turn, produces a region of magnetic influence called a *magnetic field.* This magnetic field exists inside and outside the material. In a superconductor, the magnetic field is *expelled from* (pushed out of) the material.

Sources of electric energy

For current to flow, a positive charge must be applied to one end of a conductor and a negative charge to the other end. In a wire, the negative charge repels electrons, and the positive charge attracts them, causing electrons to flow from the negative end to the positive end. To maintain the difference in charges, a continuous source of energy is required. The energy may come from chemical action, motion, sunlight, or heat.

Batteries produce electric energy by means of chemical action. A simple battery has two structures called *electrodes.* Each electrode is made from a different chemically active material. Between the electrodes, the battery contains a liquid or paste called an *electrolyte.* The electrolyte conducts ions but not free electrons. The electrolyte also helps promote chemical reactions at each electrode. At one electrode, called the *anode,* the reactions separate atoms into free electrons and ions. The positively charged ions move through the electrolyte to the other side of the battery, called the *cathode.* But the freed electrons cannot follow because the electrolyte is an insulator to them. The electrons instead flow out of the battery and into a circuit connected to the anode and cathode. Having traveled the circuit, the electrons reenter the battery at the cathode. There, they reunite with ions to form neutral atoms or molecules.

Eventually, a battery runs out of chemical energy. Then it can no longer produce electric energy. Some worn-out batteries can only be discarded. Others, called *rechargeable batteries,* can be charged again by passing electric current through them in the opposite direction.

Electric generators change *mechanical energy,* the energy of motion, into electric energy. Generators basically consist of coils of wire and a magnet. A source of mechanical energy spins either the magnet or the coil. The relative motion causes the magnet to force electrons through the wire, producing a current. The mechanical energy is often supplied by the motion of steam, water, or wind turning a turbine. For a detailed discussion of the sources of electric power, see **Energy supply.**

Generators furnish most of the electric power people use. A large generator in an electric power plant can provide enough electric energy for over 1 million people. Electric current from the generator reaches homes, factories, and offices through power lines. A small generator called an *alternator* produces electric energy in an automobile. The energy is used to recharge the battery and power the electrical systems, including providing the spark that ignites the fuel in a gasoline engine. The motion of the engine turns the alternator.

Solar cells, also called *photovoltaic cells,* power most artificial satellites and other spacecraft. They also power some outdoor lighting, traffic cameras, calculators, and watches. Photovoltaic cells are made from semiconductors, usually specially treated silicon. Energy from the sun separates negative and positive charges in the semiconductor, causing current to flow through a circuit.

Some nonmetallic minerals develop electric charge along their surfaces when stretched or compressed. These materials are called *piezoelectric crystals.* Quartz is the most common piezoelectric crystal. Some microphones use piezoelectric crystals to convert sound vibrations into electrical signals for recording or radio broadcasting. Modern appliances, such as gas ranges and water heaters, have piezoelectric crystals instead of pilot lights. When compressed, the crystals produce electric sparks that ignite the gas.

Controlling current

Wires and electric devices become dangerously hot when they carry too much current. Switches called *fuses* and *circuit breakers* protect the wiring in most buildings. If too much current flows into an outlet, a fuse or circuit breaker will shut off the current. Many individual electric devices also contain fuses.

Sometimes people need to vary the strength of current. One way to adjust current strength is to vary resistance within the circuit. For example, using a light dimmer operates a device called a *variable resistor* or *rheostat.* This device adjusts the circuit's resistance, mak-

Safety with electricity

Electricity can be dangerous. But following certain precautions can help you avoid electrical injury.

WORLD BOOK illustrations by Yoshi Miyake

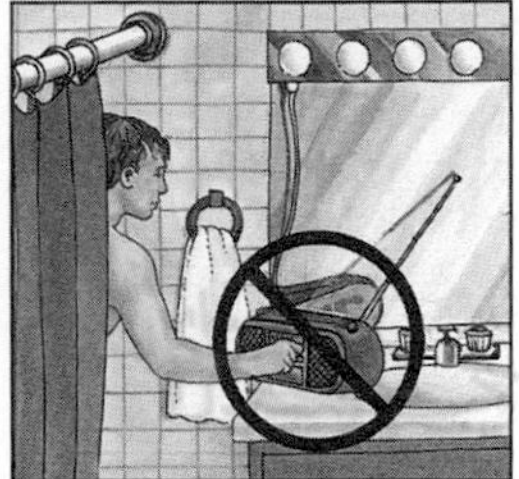

Do not touch electric devices when you are in a shower or bathtub or when you are wet.

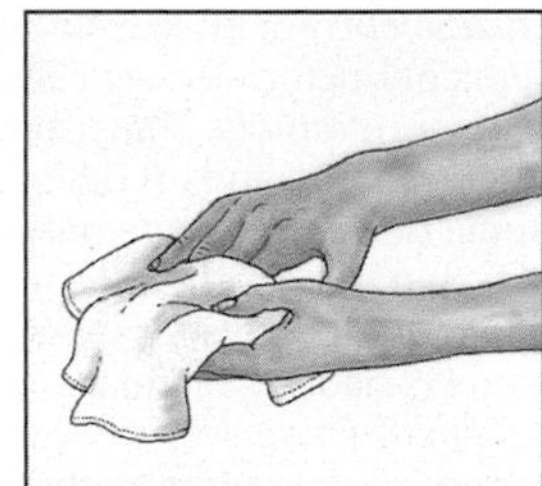

Dry your hands thoroughly before using a hairdryer, electric shaver, or other electric appliance.

Do not overload electrical outlets. Never plug in an electric device that has a damaged cord.

Insert safety plugs into unused electrical outlets within reach of children.

Do not fly kites or climb trees near power lines. Never go near fallen power lines after a storm.

Find shelter indoors during a lightning storm. Stay away from isolated trees and from metal structures.

© Shutterstock

High-tension wires carry electric current at extremely high voltages, often over 500,000 volts. Utility companies use such wires to transport electric power long distances. The high voltage combined with a low *amperage* (strength of current) reduces the loss of energy as heat.

ing the light brighter or dimmer.

Traditional switches and variable resistors cannot change current quickly enough for certain tasks. Tiny semiconductor devices called *transistors* can adjust current more rapidly. Transistors act as high-speed switches, turning on and off billions of times each second. Some devices contain millions of transistors on a single tiny chip of silicon, called an *integrated circuit* or *chip.* Integrated circuits form the heart of computers, video-game consoles, and many other devices.

Electronic devices carry electrical signals that can be varied in some way to represent information. Electronic devices include capacitors, diodes, inductors, integrated circuits, and transistors. Signals may represent sounds, pictures, numbers, letters, computer instructions, or other information. For example, transistors in a music player provide a continuous range of currents that strengthen electrical signals representing the sounds being played.

Electromagnetism

The attraction and repulsion between electric charges results from the existence of *electric fields.* An electric field surrounds each charged particle. A charged particle that enters the field of another charged particle will feel a force. If the charges are alike, the force will push them apart. But if the charges are opposite, the force will pull them together. Electric fields are how charged particles interact, even without touching. The field around a charged particle goes on almost forever, but gets weaker and weaker with distance.

Similarly, a magnet is surrounded by a magnetic field. Interaction between magnets and magnetic fields causes attraction or repulsion between magnets.

A still electric charge produces an electric field, and a still magnet produces a magnetic field. However, a moving electric field produces a magnetic field, and a moving magnetic field produces an electric field. The two fields together make up a fundamental force of the universe called electromagnetism.

Any time a charge moves, an electromagnetic field is produced. For example, passing an electric current through a coil of wire makes the coil a temporary magnet called an *electromagnet.* The electric current creates a magnetic field around the coiled wire. As long as the current flows, the coil will act as a magnet.

Magnetism can, in turn, produce electric current. For example, a coil of wire moving near a magnet causes an electric current to flow in the wire. The current flows as long as the movement continues. Generators can produce electric current in this way.

Electric and magnetic fields can change together to make *electromagnetic waves,* also called *electromagnetic radiation.* These waves carry energy known as *electromagnetic energy* at the speed of light. Visible light, radio and TV signals, and microwaves all consist of electromagnetic waves. The infrared rays that cause a person to feel heat when standing near a hot stove are also electromagnetic in nature. The ultraviolet rays that cause sunburn consist of electromagnetic waves. The X rays that doctors use to see inside the body are electromagnetic waves. The powerful gamma rays that come from nuclear reactors and from outer space are also electromagnetic waves.

History

Several thousand years ago, the ancient Greeks observed that *amber* (fossilized resin) attracts bits of lightweight material, such as feathers or straw, after being rubbed with cloth. Amber is a good electric insulator, so it easily holds a static charge. Although the Greeks did not know about electric charge, they were actually experimenting with static electricity. The Greek word for amber is *elektron.* The English words *electricity* and *electron* come from this word.

A number of peoples, including the ancient Greeks and Chinese, knew of a different substance that could attract metal. It was a black rock called *lodestone* or *magnetite.* Lodestone is a natural magnet. It attracts iron objects, which tend to be heavy. In contrast, amber attracts only light things, such as straw. In 1551, the Italian mathematician Girolamo Cardano, also known as Jerome Cardan, realized that the attracting effects of amber and of magnetite must be different. Cardano was the first to note the difference between electricity and magnetism.

In 1600, the English physician William Gilbert reported that such materials as glass, sulfur, and wax behaved like amber. When rubbed with cloth, they too attracted light objects. Gilbert called these materials *electrics.* He studied the behavior of electrics and concluded that their effects must be due to some kind of fluid. Today, we know that what Gilbert called *electrics* are actually materials that are good insulators.

Experiments with electric charge. In the 1730's, the French scientist Charles Dufay found that charged pieces of glass attracted amberlike substances but repelled other glasslike substances. Dufay decided that there must be two kinds of electricities. He called them *vitreous* (for glasslike substances) and *resinous* (for amberlike substances). Dufay had found negative and positive electric charge. However, he thought of them as two kinds of "electric fluid."

The American scientist and statesman Benjamin Franklin began to experiment with electricity in 1746. Franklin thought that there was only one kind of electric fluid. He theorized that objects with too much fluid would repel each other, but they would attract objects with too little fluid. If an object with an excess of fluid touched an object deficient in fluid, the fluid would be shared. Franklin's idea explained how opposite charges cancel each other out when they come in contact.

Franklin used the term *positive* for what he thought was an excess of electric fluid. He used the term *negative* for a deficiency of fluid. Franklin did not know that electricity is not a fluid. Rather, electricity is associated with the charges of electrons and protons. Today, we know that most positively charged objects actually have a deficiency of electrons. Negatively charged objects have an excess of electrons.

In 1752, Franklin said he performed an experiment by flying a kite in a thunderstorm. Franklin said that the kite and string became electrically charged. He therefore concluded that the storm clouds were themselves charged. He became convinced that lightning was a huge electric spark. Experiments such as the one Franklin described are dangerous. Lightning can electrocute people who fly kites in storms.

In 1767, the English scientist Joseph Priestley described a mathematical law that shows how the attraction between oppositely charged objects weakens with distance. In 1785, the French scientist Charles Augustin de Coulomb confirmed Priestley's law. Coulomb showed that the law also held true for the repulsive force between objects with the same charge. Today, the principle is known as Coulomb's law.

In 1771, Luigi Galvani, an Italian anatomy professor, found that the leg of a recently killed frog would twitch when touched with two different metals at the same time. Galvani's work attracted much attention. In the late 1790's, Alessandro Volta, an Italian physicist, offered an explanation. Volta showed that chemical action occurs in a moist material in contact with two different metals. The chemical action results in an electric current. The flow of current had made Galvani's frog twitch. Volta gathered pairs of disks, each pair consisting of one silver and one zinc disk. He separated the pairs with paper or cloth moistened with salt water. By stacking such disks in a pile, Volta built the first battery, called a *voltaic pile*.

There followed many experiments with Volta's battery and electric circuits. The German physicist Georg S. Ohm devised a mathematical law to describe the relationships among current, voltage, and resistance for certain materials. Ohm described his law in a treatise published in 1827. According to Ohm's law, a larger voltage can push a larger current through a given resistance. In addition, a given voltage can push a larger current through a smaller resistance.

Electricity and magnetism. In 1820, the Danish physicist Hans C. Oersted found that an electric current flowing near a compass needle would cause the needle to move. Oersted was the first to show a definite connection between electricity and magnetism. During the 1820's, André-Marie Ampère of France discovered the mathematical relationship between currents and magnetic fields. That relationship, called Ampere's law, is one of the basic laws of electromagnetism.

In the early 1830's, the English scientist Michael Faraday and the American physicist Joseph Henry independently discovered that moving a magnet near a coil of wire produced an electric current in the wire. Further experiments showed that electrical effects occur anytime a magnetic field changes.

The Scottish scientist James Clerk Maxwell combined all the known laws covering electricity and magnetism into a set of four equations. Maxwell's equations were published in 1865. They describe completely how elec-

A Van de Graaff generator produces static electricity, which causes this girl's hair to stand on end.

The Tesla coil is a type of transformer that can produce extremely high voltages. It was once used for electrical experimentation and, for many years, in the transmission of broadcast radio waves. It is named for its creator, the American inventor Nikola Tesla.

tric and magnetic fields arise and interact. Maxwell made a new prediction that a changing electric field would produce a magnetic field. That prediction led him to propose the existence of electromagnetic waves.

In the later 1880's, the German physicist Heinrich R. Hertz showed how to generate and detect radio waves. Hertz thus proved Maxwell correct. In 1901, the Italian inventor Guglielmo Marconi and his staff sent and received electromagnetic waves across the Atlantic Ocean. Their success set the stage for radio, TV, satellite communications, and cell phones.

The electronic age. The Irish physicist G. Johnstone Stoney believed that electric current was actually the movement of small, electrically charged particles. In 1891, he suggested that these particles be called electrons. In 1897, the English physicist Joseph John Thomson proved the existence of electrons. Thomson also showed that all atoms contain electrons. In research published in 1913, the American physicist Robert A. Millikan accurately measured the electron's charge.

In the late 1800's, scientists discovered that electrons could be dislodged from a metal surface in a *vacuum tube.* A vacuum tube is a glass tube with most of the air removed. The tube contains electrodes with wires that extend through the glass. Linking batteries to the electrodes causes a current of electrons to flow within the tube. The current can be modified by adjusting the voltage. Vacuum tubes can amplify, combine, and separate weak electric currents. This invention helped make radio, TV, and other technologies possible.

In 1947, the American physicists John Bardeen, Walter H. Brattain, and William Shockley invented the transistor. Transistors do the same jobs as vacuum tubes, but they are smaller and more durable. They also use far less energy. By the 1960's, transistors had replaced vacuum tubes in most electronic equipment. Since then, electronics companies have developed ever smaller transistors. Today, millions of interconnected transistors fit on a single chip called an integrated circuit.

Demand for power increases every year. Most of the electric energy we use comes from power plants that burn fossil fuels, such as coal, oil, or natural gas. Some electric energy comes from nuclear and *hydroelectric* (water power) plants. Smaller amounts come from solar cells, windmills, and other sources.

Many people are concerned that Earth's supply of fossil fuel is limited. Someday, it will run out. Another problem is that present methods of generating electric power may harm the environment. In response, scientists, engineers, and power companies are trying to develop alternative sources of electric energy. Such sources include solar energy, *geothermal energy* (energy from Earth's heat), wind energy, and *tidal energy* (energy from ocean waves and currents).

Many scientists hope that new electric devices will actually help curb the growing demand for electric energy. Computers, for example, can control the lighting, air conditioning, and heating in buildings to reduce energy use. Gas-based light bulbs called *compact fluorescent lamps* (CFL's) provide the same light as traditional incandescent bulbs but use only about one-fourth the energy. A newer kind of lighting based on devices called *light-emitting diodes* (LED's) is even more efficient. Many home appliances are now designed to conserve energy, and houses are being built to need less heating and cooling. Computers and communication systems enable people to work at home, often saving energy they would have used for transportation. Michelle D. Johannes

Related articles in *World Book.* See **Electronics** and **Magnetism** and their lists of *Related articles.* See also:

Biographies

Ampère, André-Marie
Bell, Alexander Graham
Coulomb, Charles Augustin de
De Forest, Lee
Edison, Thomas Alva
Faraday, Michael
Franklin, Benjamin
Galvani, Luigi
Gilbert, William
Gray, Elisha
Henry, Joseph
Hertz, Heinrich Rudolf
Latimer, Lewis Howard
Marconi, Guglielmo
Maxwell, James Clerk
Millikan, Robert Andrews
Morse, Samuel Finley Breese
Oersted, Hans Christian
Ohm, Georg Simon
Siemens, Ernst Werner von

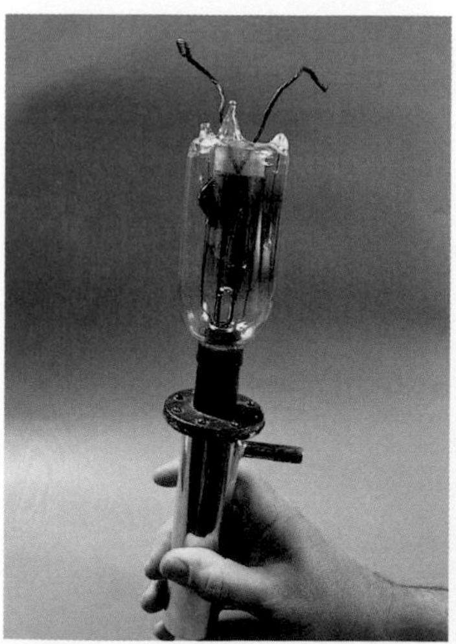

David R. Frazier

The vacuum tube led to the development of radio and television. This large early tube was made about 1922.

CERN

Huge electromagnets in devices called *particle accelerators* help scientists study the tiniest particles. In this photograph, workers adjust a magnetic detector that is part of the Large Hadron Collider, located on the border between France and Switzerland.

Thomson, Sir Joseph John	Volta, Alessandro	

Basic principles of electricity

Atom	Electromotive force	Lenz's law
Electric circuit	Electron	Matter
Electric current	Hall effect	Molecule
Electric power	Inductance	Ohm's law
Electrochemistry	Induction, Electric	Plasma (physics)
Electromagnetism	Ion	Proton

Creating and controlling electric energy

Battery	Insulator, Electric
Capacitor	Magnetic amplifier
Circuit breaker	Magneto
Electric eye	Nuclear energy
Electric generator	Piezoelectricity
Electric switch	Solar energy
Electrode	Thermocouple
Electrolysis	Transformer
Electrolyte	Turbine
Fuel cell	Water power
Fuse (electricity)	Wind power
Induction coil	

Measuring electric energy

Ampere	Joule	Volt
Coulomb	Kilowatt	Watt
Electric meter	Ohm	Wattmeter
Electroscope	Oscilloscope	Wheatstone bridge
Farad	Potentiometer	
Henry		

Uses of electric energy

Air conditioning (How air conditioning works)	Flashlight
Automobile (Providing electric power)	Heating (Electric power)
Cable	Ignition
Ceramics (Electrical equipment)	Linear electric motor
Clock (Electric clocks)	Locomotive (Electric locomotives)
Electric car	Machine tool (Nonmechanical machine tool operations)
Electric light	Microphone
Electric motor	Particle accelerator (How accelerators work)
Electric railroad	Rocket (Ion rockets)
Electrophoresis	Signaling (Electrical signals)
Electroplating	

Other related articles

Amber	Human body (The peripheral nervous system)
Electric eel	Light (Our understanding of light)
Electric fish	Lightning
Electric ray	Lightning rod
Electrocution	Lodestone
Electromotive series	Materials (Electrical properties)
Energy	Nervous system (How neurons carry impulses)
Energy supply	Safety (Safety with electricity)
Engineering (Electrical engineering)	
Fire prevention (In homes and schools)	
First aid (Restoring breathing)	

Electrocardiograph is an instrument used to diagnose heart disorders. Each time the heart beats, it produces electric currents. These currents are responsible for the rate and pattern of contraction of the heart. An electrocardiograph identifies and records these currents. The electrocardiograph may be connected to a printer, which prints a record called an *electrocardiogram,* often abbreviated either ECG or EKG. The electrocardiograph may also be connected to an *oscilloscope,* an instrument that displays the currents on a TV-type screen.

An electrocardiograph contains amplifying and recording equipment. Wires run from the machine to *electrodes*—strips of metal that conduct electric current. The electrodes are attached to the patient's skin with the use of a special jelly. Electrodes are placed on each arm and leg and at six points on the chest over the area of the heart.

The electrodes pick up the currents produced by the heartbeat and transmit them to an amplifier inside the electrocardiograph. The amplified currents then flow through a fine wire coil that hangs suspended in a magnetic field. As these currents react with the magnetic field, they move the wire. In most electrocardiographs, a sensitive lever traces the wire's motions on a moving paper chart, producing the electrocardiogram.

Each heartbeat produces a series of wavy lines on the ECG. A normal heartbeat makes a specific pattern of waves. Certain kinds of heart damage and disease change the pattern in recognizable ways.

Physicians use ECG's to diagnose heart damage from such conditions as high blood pressure, rheumatic fever, and birth defects. An ECG also helps determine the location and the amount of injury caused by a heart attack, and follow-up ECG's show how the heart is recovering. An ECG can also reveal irregularities in the heart's rhythm, known as *arrhythmias.* In addition, physicians sometimes use an ECG to determine the effects of certain drugs on the heart.

An ECG is usually taken while the patient is lying down. This procedure is called a *resting ECG.* Sometimes, an ECG is taken while the patient is exercising or after the patient has received medication to stimulate the heart. This test, called a *stress ECG,* indicates whether the heart receives enough oxygen during vigorous activity. Doctors use a stress ECG to diagnose *coronary artery disease.* See **Heart** (Coronary artery disease; Heart attack; picture: Rehabilitation); **Stress test.**

The electrocardiograph developed from the string galvanometer, invented in 1903 by the Dutch physiologist Willem Einthoven (see **Einthoven, Willem**). The electrocardiograph was first used in the United States in 1909. Julius M. Gardin

Electrochemistry is a science that deals with chemical reactions that involve electricity. Most electrochemical reactions take place in a vessel that has two *electrodes* surrounded by an *electrolyte.* Electrodes are usually solid metal. They enable electricity to enter or leave the electrolyte. An electrolyte is a substance that conducts electric current. Electrolytes often contain charged particles called *ions.* Electrochemical processes are used to produce chemicals and electric power, to refinish and plate metals, and to conduct research.

Some electrochemical processes produce electric power from chemical changes, and others use electric power to produce chemical changes. A series of reactions among the chemicals in a battery, for example, produce an electric current (see **Battery**). A similar process occurs in *fuel cells,* devices that typically use hydrogen and oxygen to produce electric power (see **Fuel cell**). In a process called *electrolysis,* an electric current passing through a chemical solution separates certain elements from the solution. For example, manufacturers make chlorine by passing electric current through salt water. Electrolysis is also used to separate aluminum, magnesium, and certain other metals from molten salts. Some metals are plated by means of electrolysis (see **Electrolysis; Electroplating**).

The corrosion of metals in the presence of moisture is a naturally occurring electrolytic process. Electrochemists study corrosion to develop ways to protect metals. Electrochemical studies also include the *electroanalysis* of solutions and other chemical systems. In electroanalysis, the composition of such systems is studied by observing their response to electrical signals.

Electrochemistry includes several special fields. Scientists in the field of *photoelectrochemistry* seek ways of using light energy to produce electric power or chemical changes. *Bioelectrochemistry* deals with electrochemical processes that occur in the body. Such electrochemical processes include the production of brain waves and nerve impulses. Marianna A. Busch

Electrocution is a means of killing a person by the use of a strong electric shock. Accidental electrocution occurs when a person accidentally comes in contact with, and is killed by, a powerful electric charge.

The electric chair is an electrocution device that has been used as a legal method of executing condemned criminals since 1890. It was supposed to be a humane alternative to hanging. However, problems associated with electrocution—including prolonged suffering and fires—led many states to adopt other methods. Electrocution is banned in most states, and it is used in other states only if the condemned person chooses it over lethal injection. For a list of the states that use electrocution to execute criminals, see **Capital punishment** (table).

Gad J. Bensinger

Electrode is a conductor through which current enters or leaves an electric or electronic device. Most electrodes are pieces of metal shaped into plates, rods, wires, or wire mesh. A battery has two electrodes—one positively charged and one negatively charged. When they are connected to an external circuit, the battery produces current. Vacuum tubes and solid-state electronic devices have two or more electrodes. Voltages are applied to the electrodes from the outside, and the electrodes establish and maintain the desired voltages and electric fields within the device. The flow of current within the device can be controlled by varying the voltages applied to the electrodes. Robert B. Prigo

See also **Battery; Electrolysis; Neon; Vacuum tube.**

Electroencephalograph, *ih LEHK troh ehn SEHF uh luh graf,* is an instrument used to measure and record the electrical voltages produced by *neurons* (nerve cells) in the brain. A recording of this electrical activity is called an *electroencephalogram.* Both electroencephalograph and electroencephalogram are abbreviated EEG. Doctors and neuroscientists use the electroencephalograph to study normal brain activity. They also use it to study abnormal brain states that are caused by injury, tumors, infection, or even death.

To record an electroencephalogram, medical personnel attach electrodes from the electroencephalograph to the patient's scalp. The electroencephalogram is usually recorded on a long, moving chart paper using ink pens that *oscillate* (move back and forth) with changes in the brain's electrical activity. When the patient is relaxed with the eyes closed, the oscillations normally form a pattern that repeats approximately 10 times a second. Such brain waves are called *alpha waves.* When the person is alert and concentrating, the alpha waves tend to disappear and are replaced by smaller and faster *beta waves.* When a person is in a deep sleep, large and slow *theta waves* and *delta waves* occur.

One of the most common medical uses of the electroencephalograph is to diagnose and study epilepsy. In epilepsy, abnormal discharges of certain neurons cause excessive electrical activity that interferes with normal brain function, resulting in a seizure. The electroencephalograph is used to detect and locate the brain regions that are responsible for seizures. Daniel S. Barth

Electrolysis, *ih LEHK TRAHL uh sihs,* is a process in which an electric current passes through a liquid, causing chemical reactions to occur. If the liquid is water, electrolysis breaks water molecules into hydrogen and oxygen. If the liquid contains metals, electrolysis removes the metals from the liquid. Electrolysis has many practical uses, especially in industry.

How electrolysis works. Electrolysis takes place in a device called an *electrolytic cell.* An electrolytic cell consists of two solid electrical conductors, called *electrodes,* placed in a liquid. Most electrodes are metal or carbon rods. The liquid may be water or another substance that conducts electric current. The liquid may contain dissolved substances called *electrolytes* that increase its ability to conduct electric current.

Wires connect the electrodes to the terminals of a battery or another source of *direct current* (current that flows in one direction). The electrode connected to the incoming current is called the *cathode.* It transfers electrons, which are negatively charged, from the battery to the electrolytic cell. The other electrode is called the *anode.* It transfers electrons out from the electrolytic cell and back to the battery. The movement of electrons produces an electric current.

The liquid in the electrolytic cell contains *ions.* Ions are atoms or molecules that have lost or gained an electron, becoming positively or negatively charged. Positive ions are attracted to the cathode of the electrolytic cell, and negative ions are attracted to the anode. The movement of ions carries electric current between the electrodes. At the cathode, electrons are transferred to atoms or molecules in the liquid. This process, called *reduction,* causes chemical reactions to take place. For example, if a water molecule near the cathode gains an electron, one of its hydrogen atoms splits off and sticks to the cathode. It soon joins another hydrogen atom, forming a molecule of hydrogen gas. The hydrogen gas bubbles out of the water. If the liquid contains ions of a metal, such as gold or silver, reduction removes the metal from the solution, causing a thin layer of the metal to form on the cathode.

At the anode, electrons are transferred from atoms or molecules in the liquid and join the current flowing back into the battery. This transfer, called *oxidation,* also causes chemical reactions. For example, when water gives up electrons at the anode, oxygen atoms split from the water molecules and join to make oxygen gas. The gas bubbles out of the water.

Uses of electrolysis. Electrolysis is used to produce many chemical substances in pure form. For example, electrolysis of ordinary salt (sodium chloride) produces pure sodium metal. Aluminum and magnesium metals can be made in a similar way. Because metal ions carry a positive electric charge, the metals collect at the negatively charged electrode. Chlorine and other chemicals are also produced by electrolysis. Because chlorine ions carry a negative charge, chlorine collects at the positively charged electrode, where it bubbles out as a gas.

Electrolysis can also purify an impure substance. For example, impure copper can serve as the anode in an electrolytic cell, and pure copper can serve as the cathode. Chemical reactions at the anode transfer positively charged copper ions to the liquid. These ions are attracted to the cathode. The copper ions stick to the copper cathode, increasing the amount of pure copper.

A kind of electrolysis called *electroplating* coats a metal object's surface with a thin layer of another metal. In electroplating, the metal that is to form the coating is dissolved in the liquid. The object to be coated is used as the cathode. This process can make an object appear more attractive or provide a surface that resists damage.

A similar process, called *anodizing,* coats a layer of protective *oxides* (oxygen compounds) on a metal used as the anode in an electrolytic cell. Manufacturers often make cookware and outdoor furniture from aluminum that has been anodized to protect it from corrosion.

Electrolysis of water produces hydrogen and oxygen gases, which can be captured as the gases bubble up at the two electrodes. This process can produce hydrogen for use in *fuel cells,* devices that convert chemical energy to electrical energy. Some scientists are experimenting with *photoelectrolysis,* in which sunlight provides the energy to produce hydrogen by electrolysis. Fuel cells powered by hydrogen produced in this manner could provide a clean, renewable energy source.

Principles of electrolysis. The English chemist Michael Faraday was the first scientist to state mathematical laws describing electrolysis. Faraday's laws state that the amount of a substance produced in electrolysis depends on the amount of electric charge that passes through the electrolytic cell. The laws also state that the amount of substance produced depends on the weight of an atom or molecule of the substance and the amount of electric charge that ions of the substance carry.

The relationship between the substance's properties and the amount of the substance produced is precise. This allows scientists to use electrolysis to identify and measure quantities of unknown substances. This technique is called *electroanalysis.* Richard Wolfson

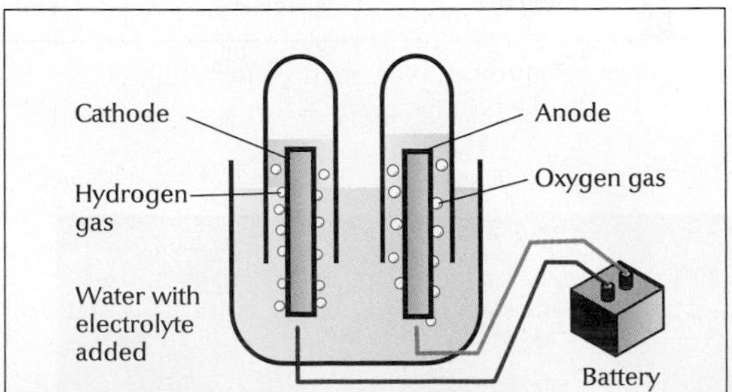

How electrolysis works. In the electrolysis of water, hydrogen gas is produced at the cathode and oxygen gas is produced at the anode. The gases are collected in tubes.

Related articles in *World Book* include:

Anodizing
Electrochemistry
Electrolyte
Electroplating
Faraday, Michael
Fuel cell
Metallurgy

Electrolyte, *ih LEHK truh lyt,* is a substance that conducts electric current. Most electrolytes must be dissolved in water or some other solvent. A battery contains an electrolyte in either a liquid or a pasty solution. Liquid electrolytes are used in electrolysis, electroplating, and other chemical processes.

When an electrolyte dissolves, it releases positive and negative *ions* (electrically charged atoms or groups of atoms). These released ions carry electric charges between two *electrodes* immersed in the solution, called the *cathode* and the *anode. Cations* carry positive electric charges toward the cathode. *Anions* carry negative electric charges toward the anode.

Strong electrolytes release many ions and conduct electric current well. These electrolytes include strong acids and bases, and most salts. *Weak* electrolytes, such as acetic acid, release few ions and conduct poorly. *Nonelectrolytes,* such as sugar, release no ions and form nonconducting solutions.

A few electrolytes conduct electric current as solids. In these *solid electrolytes,* the ions can move and carry charges without adding a solvent. Allen J. Bard

See also **Battery; Electrolysis; Electroplating; Ion.**

Electromagnet is a temporary magnet formed when electric current flows through a wire or other conductor. Most electromagnets consist of wire wound around an iron core. This core is made from magnetically soft iron. The iron loses its magnetism quickly when the electric current stops flowing through the wire. Changing the current can also vary the magnet's strength.

Electromagnets drive loudspeakers, electric doorbells, buzzers, and relays. They are used in *magnetic resonance imaging* (MRI) machines, particle accelerators, and other scientific equipment. They also produce the magnetic fields needed to make electric motors and generators work. Powerful industrial electromagnets lift heavy pieces of scrap iron.

In 1820, the Danish physicist Hans Oersted discovered that an electric current produces a magnetic field. In 1825, the English electrician William Sturgeon showed that an iron core strengthens a coil's magnetic field. The American physicist Joseph Henry built the first practical electromagnet in the late 1820's. Robert B. Prigo

See also **Electromagnetism; Henry, Joseph; Linear electric motor; Plasma; Superconductivity.**

Electromagnetic theory of light. See **Electromagnetic waves; Light** (Electromagnetic waves).

Electromagnetic waves are traveling patterns of electric and magnetic influence. They are light rays, and they travel through space at the speed of light—approximately 186,282 miles (299,792 kilometers) per second.

Electromagnetic waves are the *oscillations* (back-and-forth movements) of electric and magnetic fields. The magnetic and electric elements of a wave oscillate perpendicularly to each other. Both oscillate perpendicularly to the wave's direction of travel.

Like ocean waves, light waves have crests. The distance from one crest to the next is called the *wavelength.* The wavelength of an electromagnetic wave depends on the energy of its source. Sources with greater energy vibrate faster, resulting in shorter wavelengths.

The electromagnetic spectrum includes all the kinds of electromagnetic waves, arranged by wavelength. The chief bands of the electromagnetic spectrum are, in order of increasing wavelength: gamma rays, X rays, ultraviolet light, visible light, infrared rays, microwaves, and radio waves. Gamma rays are roughly 10-trillionths of a meter in length. Some long radio waves measure more than 6,000 miles (10,000 kilometers) in wavelength. Gamma rays carry the most energy, and radio waves carry the least energy. Objects often *emit* (give off) waves in more than one band of the electromagnetic spectrum. Scientists can better understand the nature of an object by studying all the different kinds of electromagnetic waves the object emits.

People customarily use different units to measure different bands of the electromagnetic spectrum. Radio and microwaves are usually measured in *hertz,* which count the number of waves passing a fixed point each second. Infrared, ultraviolet, and visible light are measured in *nanometers* (billionths of a meter) or *angstroms* (tenths of a nanometer) of wavelength. Gamma and X rays are described in *electronvolts,* a measure of energy.

All types of electromagnetic waves can be reflected, *diffracted* (spread), and *refracted* (bent). A wave's behavior depends on its wavelength. For example, visible light will reflect off a mirror at any angle. But X rays will reflect only at glancing angles and only off metals, such as gold or platinum.

Our atmosphere blocks some electromagnetic waves from reaching Earth, including many microwaves and all X rays and gamma rays. The atmosphere also blocks some infrared and most ultraviolet rays. This filtering by the atmosphere protects us from harmful radiation emitted by the sun and other objects in space. To study wavelengths blocked by the atmosphere, scientists must use instruments positioned above the atmosphere.

Uses. Although most electromagnetic waves are invisible to us, modern society uses all parts of the electromagnetic spectrum. Doctors use gamma rays and X rays to diagnose medical problems and to treat cancer. Airport security scanners use X rays to find concealed objects. Ultraviolet rays are used as a disinfectant, to read invisible security tags on credit cards and other documents, and in sun lamps. People use infrared rays in long-distance communication networks, night vision goggles, and TV remote controls. Microwaves are used in Global Positioning System (GPS) devices, radar systems, and wireless computer networks. They are also used to cook food. People use radio waves in cell phones, some wireless Internet devices, and radio and TV broadcasting equipment.

History. In 1864, the Scottish scientist James Clerk Maxwell predicted the existence of electromagnetic waves. In the late 1880's, the German physicist Heinrich R. Hertz verified Maxwell's prediction. In 1905, the German physicist Albert Einstein proposed that the energy of an electromagnetic wave can be represented by an individual particle later called a *photon.* In 1923, the American physicist Arthur Compton verified properties of the photon. James C. Lochner

Related articles in *World Book* include:

Electromagnetism
Gamma rays
Infrared rays
Interference
Light
Microwave
Quantum mechanics
Radiation (Electromagnetic radiation)
Redshift
Radio (How radio programs are broadcast; diagrams)
Ultraviolet rays
Waves
Wireless communication
X rays

Electromagnetism is the branch of physics that studies the relationship between electricity and magnetism. Electromagnetism is based on the fact that (1) an electric

The electromagnetic spectrum

The electromagnetic spectrum, *shown here,* has all the kinds of electromagnetic waves arranged by wavelength and frequency. It extends from short gamma rays to long radio waves. Frequencies are given in hertz and wavelengths in meters. The 10's with raised figures are a way of abbreviating numbers. For example, 10^{11} hertz is 1 followed by 11 zeroes, or 100,000,000,000 hertz. Numbers with a minus sign tell how many places the decimal point is moved in front of the number. For example, 10^{-7} meters equals 0.0000001 meter. Different wavelengths or frequencies of visible light can be seen as different colors. Frequencies are in nanometers and wavelengths in terahertz.

WORLD BOOK illustration

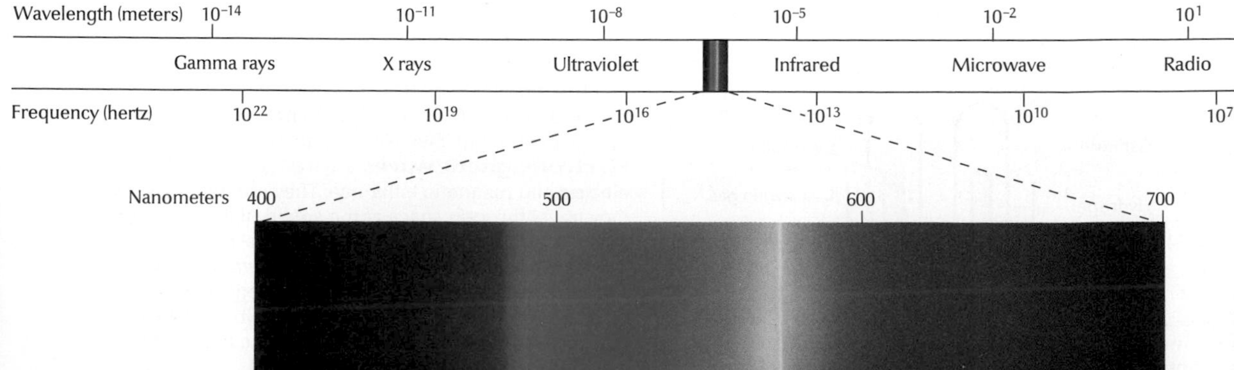

current or a changing electric field produces a magnetic field, and (2) a changing magnetic field produces an electric field.

In 1820, the Danish scientist Hans Oersted discovered that a conductor carrying an electric current is surrounded by a magnetic field. When he brought a magnetized needle near a wire in which an electric current was flowing, the needle moved. Because a magnetized needle is moved by magnetic forces, the experiment proved that an electric current produces magnetism.

During the 1820's, the French physicist André Marie Ampère declared that electric currents produce all magnetism. He concluded that a permanent bar magnet has tiny currents flowing in it. The work of Oersted and Ampère led to the development of the *electromagnet,* which is used in such devices as the telegraph and the electric bell. Most electromagnets consist of a coil of wire wound around an iron core. The electromagnet becomes temporarily magnetized when an electric current flows through the wire. If the direction of the current changes, the poles of the electromagnet switch places.

Magnetism produces an electric current by means of *electromagnetic induction.* The English scientist Michael Faraday and the American physicist Joseph Henry discovered electromagnetic induction independently in the early 1830's. In electromagnetic induction, a changing magnetic field sets up an electric field within a conductor. For example, a magnet moving through a coil of wire causes the voltage to vary along the wire. An electric current flows as long as the magnetic field passing through the wire is changing. Electromagnetic induction is the basis of the electric generator. An electric motor reverses the process. A current sent through the wire causes the wire to move in a magnetic field.

In 1864, James Clerk Maxwell, a Scottish physicist, used the earlier experiments to deduce that electric and magnetic fields act together to produce *electromagnetic waves* of *radiant energy.* The German physicist Heinrich R. Hertz proved Maxwell correct about 20 years later by discovering electromagnetic waves. Gerald Feinberg

Related articles in *World Book* include:

Electric generator
Electric motor
Electromagnet
Electromagnetic waves
Magnetism (Electromagnetism)
Magnetometer

Electromotive force is a measure of the amount of work required to carry a unit of electric charge through a circuit. It is abbreviated as emf or E. The term also refers to the amount of energy obtained from an electric source per unit of charge passing through it. Such sources of electromotive force include batteries and electric generators. If 1 joule of electric potential energy is given to each coulomb of charge passing through the source, the emf of the source is 1 joule per coulomb, called 1 *volt.* See also **Coulomb; Electric current; Joule; Volt.** Michael Dine

Electromotive series, also called the *electrochemical series* or *activity series,* is a listing of metals and hydrogen with respect to their tendency to lose electrons during chemical reactions. Metals that lose electrons more readily than hydrogen does are listed in the series before hydrogen. Those that lose electrons less readily than hydrogen follow hydrogen in the listing. The following is the order of some commonly used elements in the electromotive series: potassium, calcium, sodium, magnesium, aluminum, zinc, iron, nickel, tin, lead, hydrogen, copper, mercury, silver, platinum, gold.

Chemists use the electromotive series to predict how reactive a metal will be toward other materials. In general, the greater a metal's tendency to lose electrons, the more reactive it will be. Thus, metals that appear before others in the series tend to be more reactive than those that follow them. For example, a chemist would expect iron to react with oxygen more readily than gold does, because iron is listed before gold in the electromotive series. Iron reacts with oxygen to form rust, but gold does not. Gold maintains its luster in the presence of oxygen and is not corroded by it. Lawrence L. Garber

Electron is a negatively charged subatomic particle. A useful model of an atom portrays it as a tiny nucleus surrounded by electrons. The electrons are at various distances from the nucleus and are arranged in energy levels called *shells.* Electrons occupy almost the entire volume of an atom but account for only a small fraction of an atom's mass. An atom's chemical behavior is determined largely by the number of electrons in its outermost shell. When atoms combine and form molecules, electrons in the outermost shell are either transferred from one atom to another or shared between atoms.

Ordinarily, an atom has an equal number of electrons and *protons,* positively charged particles found in the nucleus. Each electron carries one unit of negative charge, and each proton carries one unit of positive charge. As a result, the atom is electrically neutral. If an atom gains electrons, it becomes negatively charged. If it loses electrons, it becomes positively charged. Electrically charged atoms are called *ions.*

Electrons are fundamental units of matter—that is, they are not made up of smaller units. An electron's diameter is less than 1/1,000 that of a proton (see **Proton**). An electron's mass in grams may be written as a decimal point followed by 27 zeros and a 9. An electron's antimatter equivalent or *antiparticle* is a positron. It has a mass equal to that of an electron but a positive charge. Antimatter resembles ordinary matter but with some properties reversed (see **Antimatter**). Electrons and positrons are the lightest particles with an electric charge.

The discovery of the electron is generally attributed to Sir Joseph John Thomson, a British physicist who identified it in 1897. In 1913, the American physicist Robert A. Millikan and the Russian physicist Abram F. Ioffe independently reported an accurate measurement of the electron's charge. Joel R. Primack

Related articles in *World Book* include:

Atom
Electricity
Electronics
Ion
Magnetism (In atoms)
Millikan, Robert A.
Muon
Subatomic particle
Thomson, Sir Joseph John

Electron microscope is a device that uses a beam of electrons to magnify a specimen. Electron microscopes can *resolve* (give clear pictures of) features much smaller than those visible through *optical microscopes.* Optical microscopes use visible light and lenses to magnify images. Electron microscopes can resolve much smaller images than can optical microscopes. Some electron microscopes can even resolve individual atoms. Electron microscopes serve as a major research tool in biology, chemistry, medicine, metallurgy, physics, and *nanoscience,* the study of extremely small things. Ernst Ruska and other German scientists built the first electron microscope in 1931.

In both electron and optical microscopes, the *wavelength* (distance between wave crests) of the beams that magnify the image limits the resolving power. An electron microscope can resolve smaller features because the wavelength of the electrons it uses is much shorter than that of visible light. The shortest wavelength of visible light is about 400 nanometers. One nanometer equals about 1/1,000,000 millimeter (1/25,400,000 inch). The electron beams used in most electron microscopes have wavelengths much less than 1 nanometer. There are three kinds of electron microscopes: (1) *transmission,* (2) *scanning,* and (3) *scanning transmission.*

Transmission electron microscopes pass a beam of electrons through a specimen 100 or fewer nanometers thick. The specimen scatters or absorbs part of the beam. Electromagnets called *magnetic lenses* focus electrons that pass through the specimen to a fluorescent screen, photographic plate, or digital camera. Transmission electron microscopes can magnify a specimen up to several million times.

Scanning electron microscopes focus the electron beam so that it strikes a small spot on the specimen. The beam then scans the specimen in a regular pattern. As electrons strike the specimen's surface, the surface throws off other electrons, called *secondary electrons.* A collector counts the secondary electrons point by point as the beam scans the specimen. A computer screen displays the result—a sharp image of surface features. Scanning electron microscopes are usually used to look at surfaces of thick specimens. They can magnify a specimen's surface by up to several hundred thousand times.

Scanning transmission electron microscopes pass a beam through a specimen in much the same way that transmission electron microscopes do. Instead of remaining fixed, however, the beam scans the specimen to produce an image. Albert Crewe and other American scientists used one to produce the first images of atoms in 1970. Stephen J. Pennycook

See also Microscope; Scanning probe microscope.

Electronic commerce. See E-commerce.

Kinds of electron microscopes

These diagrams show two kinds of electron microscopes: *transmission* (TEM) and *scanning* (SEM). A third kind, *scanning transmission* (STEM), is a TEM that scans the specimen as an SEM does.

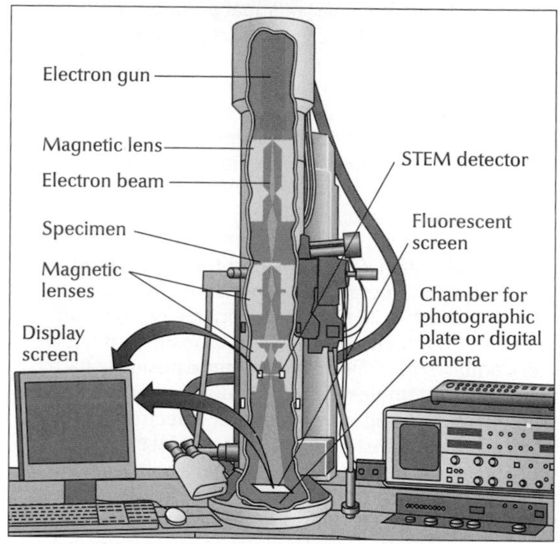

A transmission electron microscope passes electrons through the specimen to a fluorescent screen. Adding an electron detector can enable the microscope to operate as a STEM.

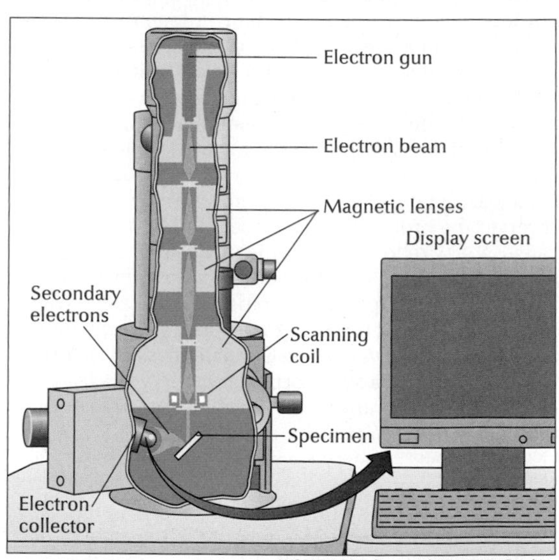

WORLD BOOK diagrams by Precision Graphics

A scanning electron microscope uses a coil to move the electron beam over the specimen. Electrons given off by the specimen enter a collector, forming an image on a display screen.

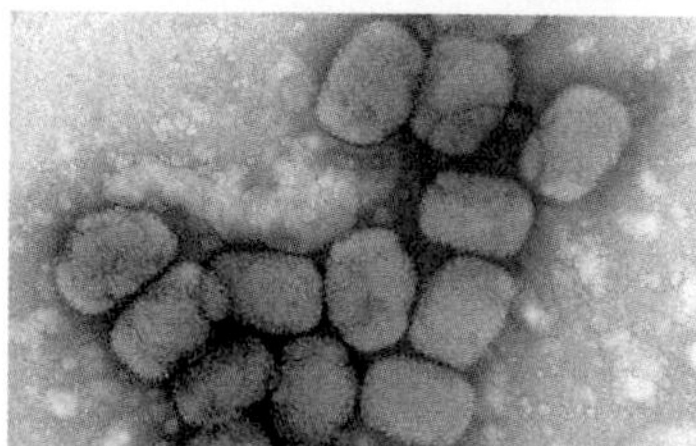

© Science Source/Photo Researchers

Smallpox viruses appear flat in this enhanced color transmission electron microscope image because the electrons pass right through them.

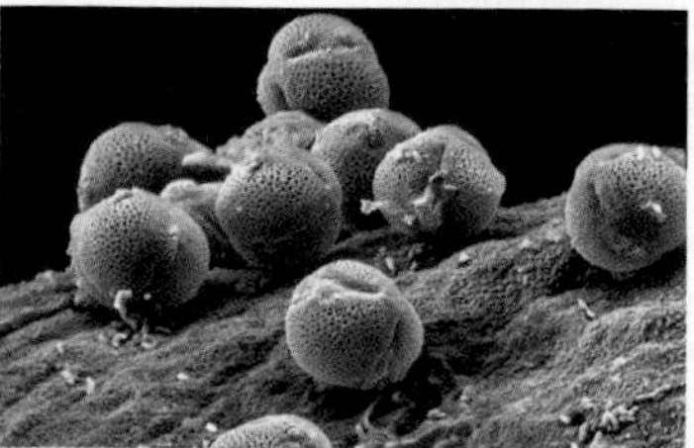

© Eye of Science/Photo Researchers

Pollen grains from a rowan tree have a hard outer coating that can be seen in this enhanced color image from a scanning electron microscope.

U.S. Department of Energy, Oak Ridge National Laboratory

Dumbbell-shaped pairs of atoms fill this image of a silicon crystal captured using a powerful scanning transmission electron microscope.

© Blizzard Entertainment, Inc.

A massively multiplayer online role-playing game (MMORPG) lets players take on the role of characters populating a virtual world. This image from the pioneering MMORPG *World of Warcraft* (2004) shows a gathering of fantasy characters, each controlled by a different player.

Electronic game

Electronic game is a game played using a computer and a video display. Such games, including *video games* and *computer games,* have become one of the most popular forms of entertainment. When electronic games were first widely introduced, most people considered them novelties or children's toys. Today, statistics indicate that the average electronic game player is an adult. As players have matured, games have grown in sophistication and diversity. Many scholars now consider electronic games to be a significant form of cultural expression, much like popular music, television, or motion pictures.

An electronic game is essentially a computer program designed to entertain. The game may run on a personal computer, a coin-operated *arcade machine,* a cellular telephone, or another computerized device. Many games are played on *video game consoles,* household computers built specifically for gaming. Most action in an electronic game takes place on the video display. Players operate the game using input devices called *controllers.*

Some of the earliest electronic games took traditional games, such as tennis, and re-created them in a computerized form. Even today, simple electronic versions of traditional card and board games remain popular. More sophisticated games simulate some extraordinary experience—such as battling monsters or flying combat aircraft—in varying levels of detail and realism. The most advanced games let the player explore and participate in vast artificial worlds. These games can be intense sensory experiences that borrow heavily from film, television, music, fashion, and even architecture.

Electronic games differ from other media in that games are highly *interactive*—that is, the player takes part in and helps guide the action. An electronic game offers players certain choices. As in a traditional game, a set of rules limits these choices and helps determine their consequences. In an electronic game, the rules are contained in lines of computer code. Rather than telling players the outcome of their choices, the computer expresses the results through the sights and sounds of the game. The players' choices and the computer's responses combine to create an experience called *gameplay.*

Article outline

I. Game design
- A. Graphics
- B. Sound
- C. Gameplay

II. Gaming platforms
- A. Video game consoles
- B. Personal computers
- C. Handheld game systems
- D. Other platforms

III. History

IV. Impact of electronic games
- A. Benefits
- B. Controversy
- C. Education

This article will discuss how game designers create electronic games, the various devices on which games can be played, and the history of electronic games. It will also discuss concerns about the effects of games on players and their use in education.

Game design

Early electronic games were created by one person or a small group of people. More complex modern games require large development teams. Such a team may consist of 20 to more than 120 people working in various roles. *Producers* manage the overall development of the game, coordinating the activities of the other team members. *Game designers* create the rules that will govern gameplay. Gameplay is so important to a game's success that some top game designers have become widely known gaming celebrities. One or more *level designers* may lay out the various areas or levels of the game. Artists and sound engineers develop the look and sound of the game. Programmers work to incorporate all these elements into the game's computer code. *Playtesters* test the game by playing it at various stages during development.

The design of an electronic game includes three major elements. They are (1) graphics, (2) sound, and (3) gameplay.

Graphics are the game's visual elements. The graphics of a simple puzzle game might consist of a few basic shapes moving over a plain backdrop. More sophisticated graphics can look nearly as realistic as photographs. Artists design some games to look as realistic as possible. Other games use stylized graphics to create a particular mood, imitating comic books, cartoons, or even fine art.

Graphics can be *two-dimensional* or *three-dimensional.* Two-dimensional graphics are flat. Three-dimensional graphics have depth.

To create two-dimensional graphics, the artist begins with a flat image that serves as a backdrop. The artist overlays the backdrop with smaller images called *sprites.* A sprite may represent a character, a weapon, or some other element in the game. Much like a paper cutout, a sprite can move around over the backdrop. Artists often animate sprites to make them appear less rigid. The artists create a series of flat images that, when flashed in rapid succession, give the illusion of motion. Carefully drawn and animated sprites can even provide the illusion of depth.

True three-dimensional graphics, by contrast, consist of computer models that resemble virtual sculptures. The models have no color, texture, or shading. Artists add these qualities by "painting" two-dimensional images onto the models. They animate the models by manipulating their parts, much as a puppeteer moves the parts of a puppet. In a completely three-dimensional game, every object is a model, and each level is like a computerized dollhouse filled with such models.

Most games combine two-dimensional and three-dimensional graphics. For example, even primarily three-dimensional games often use animated sprites to show certain effects, such as explosions.

Sound in an electronic game is generally broken into pieces, so that different sounds can accompany different events in the game. Sound designers choose prerecorded sounds from libraries or create their own sound effects.

Many games feature a musical score that plays in the background, much like the score in a motion picture. The music may change according to the action of the game. For example, the game may play a suspenseful theme when a dangerous event is about to occur.

Game developers recognize that sound can greatly enhance a game's mood and atmosphere. For this reason, modern games often feature voices recorded by popular actors and scores written and performed by professional musicians.

In some games, sound forms a critical element of gameplay. Such a game might require players to master a musical instrument or to time their actions to music.

Gameplay is the experience of playing the game. It includes the action of the game along with the interpretation of the action by the player's imagination. Games often accommodate multiple players, adding a social element to gameplay.

Sound designers develop an electronic game's music and sound effects. In this photograph, sound designers record a performer reading dialogue for use in a game.

© Pascal Guyot, AFP/Getty Images

Stylized graphics can contribute to the mood and feel of an electronic game. In this photograph, the French game designer Michel Ancel shows off the bold, colorful look of his game *Rayman: Origins.*

In many games, the player takes on the role of a character in a story. The game may provide the character with goals, or the player may be free to determine the character's wishes. The rules of the game—including limits on the character's time, energy, resources, and abilities—combine with the goals to create challenges.

In an electronic game, the display screen acts much like a video camera, following the action from a particular point of view. The way this "camera" covers the action strongly affects gameplay. In fact, people often classify games according to the relationship between the camera and the character the player controls. In a *first-person* game, the player's character acts as the camera. The player sees everything just as the character would see it. In a *third-person* game, the camera shows the player's character, typically following the character or periodically changing angle to keep the character on screen. Strategy games often show the game landscape from above, much like a map or game board. Many games give the player some control over the camera.

The use of controllers forms a critical aspect of gameplay. A computer mouse and keyboard typically serve as controllers for computer games. Video game consoles use specially designed controllers that can incorporate over a dozen buttons and multiple leverlike controls called *joysticks.* Some controllers use special sensors to detect the player's motions. This capability enables the player to interact with the game through movements and gestures. Certain games require unique controllers. Some shooting games, for example, use gunlike controllers, and some music-themed games have controllers that resemble musical instruments.

Gaming platforms

Each electronic game can only be played on a specific type of computer, called a *platform.* The most popular gaming platforms include (1) video game consoles, (2) personal computers, and (3) handheld game consoles. Developers often release multiple versions of the same game for play on different platforms.

Video game consoles often come with at least one controller but must be connected to a separate display device, usually a television. Each model of console can only play certain games, but many games come in multiple versions for different consoles. Early consoles commonly played games stored on special cartridges or cards. Later, consoles began using CD-ROM's, DVD-ROM's, and other *optical discs,* discs that are read using lasers. Some consoles can download games over specialized computer networks. Many consoles include some nongaming capabilities, such as playing movies or browsing the Internet.

Consoles are popular with gaming enthusiasts for many reasons. Unlike personal computers, which frequently require special upgrades to run games, consoles generally come with everything needed to begin playing. In addition, console games rarely *crash* (stop working) because the games are tailored to run smoothly on a specific machine. Modern consoles enable gaming enthusiasts to play together over computer networks, a capability once limited to personal computers.

Console manufacturers generally release newer, more powerful models about every five years. Game developers often continue to produce games for a console for about five years after a newer model is introduced. Thus, most consoles remain usable for about 10 years. Some hobbyists collect and play older consoles.

Personal computers also rank as popular gaming platforms. Many early computer games came on floppy disks, cartridges, and even cassette tapes. Later, computer game developers began to use CD-ROM's, DVD-ROM's, and other optical discs or to offer games for download over the Internet. To play the latest games, computer owners must regularly upgrade their machines, particularly their graphics capabilities. However, some players prefer personal computers to consoles because they can choose from a wider variety of models and accessories, enabling them to customize their gaming experience. Personal computers can also connect to the Internet and perform a much wider range of nongaming functions.

The combination of a keyboard and mouse offers players a more sophisticated range of input options than does the average video game controller. As a result, personal computers lend themselves to strategy games, which often require the player to coordinate multiple game elements. Keyboards also enable players to communicate with one another via text, making personal computers a popular choice for gaming over networks.

Personal computers also lend themselves to *casual games,* games designed to be quick and easy to learn. Casual games—many of them puzzle games or simple action games—appeal to a broader range of players than do more complex games.

Anyone with a computer and the appropriate skills can create a computer game and distribute it over the Internet. For this reason, computer game players have access to a wide range of unique, independently developed games.

Handheld game systems are essentially miniature consoles that players can carry with them. They combine a computer, video display, and controller into a single compact device. Handheld games often come on small cartridges, cards, or even optical discs.

Handheld systems have small screens and less computing power than consoles or personal computers. For this reason, they tend to feature simpler games. Some handheld games are scaled-down versions of popular console games. Other games make up for a lack of complexity with simple, innovative gameplay. Because they can be played almost anywhere, handheld systems remain fairly popular, especially among younger players.

Other platforms have varied in popularity over the years. In the late 1970's, for example, players flocked to free-standing arcade machines in public places. Arcade games eventually declined in popularity. However, players continue to enjoy arcade games, especially those that offer unique controllers. A racing arcade game, for example, might feature controls designed to mimic a race car's steering wheel, pedals, and stickshift.

As computer technology develops, new types of gaming platforms occasionally emerge. In the late 1990's and early 2000's, for example, telephone companies began offering games for play on cellular phones.

History

Historians disagree on who invented the electronic game. Many credit the American physicist William Higinbotham. In 1958, he created a game called *Tennis for Two* using electronic laboratory equipment. The game let players bounce an electronic "ball" back and forth over a "net." The German-born television engineer Ralph Baer created a similar game that was released in 1972 on the Magnavox Odyssey, the first home video game console. The game was simple, but players enjoyed the novelty of controlling the action on the TV screen.

Early computer games were created and played on large computer systems at universities and at research laboratories. The American computer programmer Steve Russell developed *Spacewar!* (1961), a game in which two spaceships fight each other. In the 1970's, the American programmer William Crowther developed the first computer game to tell a story. The game, which became known as *Colossal Cave Adventure,* was a *text-based adventure game,* a type of computer game played by reading descriptions and entering text commands.

Computer History Museum

Spacewar! (1961), an early computer game, featured two spaceships, *lower left,* that fought with each other against a field of stars.

Arcade games. The American engineer Nolan Bushnell adapted *Spacewar!* into the first commercially sold arcade game, *Computer Space* (1971). In 1972, Bushnell released *Pong,* an arcade game based on table tennis. It launched the first major video game company, Atari.

The arcade game *Pac-Man* (1980) introduced the first widely popular video game character. *Pac-Man* inspired several sequels, a popular song, a television show, and various toys and other merchandise.

The rise and fall of Atari. In 1977, Atari released the Video Computer System (VCS), later known as the Atari 2600. This early console became a huge success. Its most popular games were home versions of such arcade hits as *Space Invaders* (1978) and *Asteroids* (1979).

In 1982, Atari released two highly awaited games—*E.T. the Extra-Terrestrial* and a console version of *Pac-Man.* Critics judged both games to be of poor quality and accused the company of rushing to get them to market. Millions of copies of the games went unsold, and Atari collapsed. A widely perceived lack of quality in games convinced many people that video gaming was just a passing fad. In 1983, the industry entered a slump that lasted several years.

The Nintendo revolution. In the mid-1980's, the Japanese company Nintendo released the Family Computer (Famicom) in Japan, and later released a similar system internationally known as the Nintendo Entertainment System (NES). Nintendo revived the video game industry with the help of its feature game, *Super Mario Bros.* (1985), developed by the Japanese game designer Shigeru Miyamoto. *Super Mario Bros.* revolutionized gaming with its bright, friendly colors, original music, and imaginative characters. Unlike Atari, Nintendo became known for its strict quality control standards, and its games won the respect of critics and players.

Scholars credit much of Nintendo's success to the work of Miyamoto and his development team. His ground-breaking fantasy adventure *The Legend of Zelda* (1986) enabled players to save their progress, connecting multiple game sessions into an epic quest. *Zelda* and its sequels and the *Super Mario Bros.* games rank among the most popular video game series ever.

In the late 1980's, Nintendo released its first Game Boy handheld console. The Game Boy sold well with the help of *Tetris* (1989), a popular version of a puzzle game created by the Russian mathematician Alexey Pajitnov.

In the early 1990's, Nintendo continued to dominate the console market with its Super Nintendo Entertainment System (SNES). The SNES game *Star Fox* (1993) stood out for its innovative three-dimensional graphics. However, the SNES met vigorous competition from Sega's Genesis console. Sega's fast-moving *Sonic the Hedgehog* (1991) and many sports titles drew the attention of older audiences.

Fighting games, which feature hand-to-hand combat between virtual opponents, peaked in popularity during the early and middle 1990's. The arcade game *Street Fighter II* (1991) impressed players with its balanced characters, fine controls, and strategic complexity. *Mortal Kombat* (1992) shocked parents and politicians with its violent gameplay and gory graphics. In response, the video game industry established the Entertainment Software Rating Board (ESRB). The board rates games by recommending an appropriate age range for players.

The growth of computer gaming began in the 1980's with the spread of personal computers, such as the Commodore 64, Apple II, and IBM PC. Compared with console games, computer games generally featured inferior graphics but more mature themes that appealed to adults. Games introduced on computers during the 1980's included driving and flight simulators and the first *role-playing games,* which focus on character development and problem-solving rather than action.

From the late 1980's through the 1990's, improvements in computer technology produced an era of innovation in computer games. The introduction of the CD-ROM, for example, vastly increased the storage capacity of computer games. *Myst* (1993) used the extra capacity to add lavish graphics and rich music, creating an atmospheric, puzzle-based adventure game. This approach broadened the appeal of games and expanded the diversity of themes available to game designers.

Computers themselves became more powerful, enabling them to handle more three-dimensional graphics. Three-dimensional gameplay became standard through role-playing games, such as *Ultima Underworld: The Stygian Abyss* (1992), and first-person shooting games, such as *Wolfenstein 3D* (1992) and *Doom* (1993).

Increases in computing power led designers to develop more sophisticated strategy and simulation games. The American game designer Sidney K. Meier pioneered such games, including *Sid Meier's Pirates!* (1987) and *Sid Meier's Civilization* (1991). *Civilization* was a *turn-based* strategy game, one that let the player plan the action, which the computer carried out over a period called a *turn.* Faster paced *real-time* strategy games—such as *Dune II* (1992) and *Warcraft: Orcs & Humans* (1994)—allowed the player to issue commands to vast armies as the action unfolded. The urban planning simulator *SimCity* (1989), by the American designer Will Wright, spawned a series of popular simulation games.

The growth of computer networks enabled gaming enthusiasts to play first-person shooting games and real-time strategy games with one another over great distances. Such networks also nurtured the spread of *multi-user domains* (MUD's). These text-based adventure and role-playing games let thousands of players interact with one another in an imaginary setting.

Renewed interest in consoles. In the mid-1990's, the giant electronics manufacturer Sony Corporation entered the console business with the introduction of the PlayStation. The new console took advantage of the large storage capacity of CD-ROM's, offering games with more graphics and sound than ever before. PlayStation games, such as *Resident Evil* (1996) and *Final Fantasy VII* (1997), combined three-dimensional characters, animations, and cinematic camera techniques to produce an almost movielike experience. The PlayStation also boasted a wide range of games and quickly beat out the rival Sega Saturn console.

Despite the limited storage capacity of its cartridges, the Nintendo 64 earned a loyal following for its exceptional graphics and game design. Miyamoto's team created the Nintendo 64's controller specifically for use with three-dimensional games. In addition, the console came with Miyamoto's *Super Mario 64* (1996). Critics consider the game one of the finest ever made for the way it reimagined the classic *Super Mario Bros.* game in the context of three-dimensional play. *The Legend of Zelda: Ocarina of Time* (1998) won similar praise, combining *Super Mario 64's* three-dimensional play with an epic story line, hundreds of puzzles, and a sweeping musical score.

Competition for older players heated up during the early 2000's with the release of Microsoft Corporation's Xbox console. Rivals included Sony's PlayStation 2, Nintendo's GameCube, and Sega's Dreamcast. With such huge companies as Sony and Microsoft spending billions of dollars on development and promotion, Sega could not compete and soon shut down its console business. Nintendo continued to appeal to younger audiences, while Sony and Microsoft battled for older players.

Three series of games played central roles in the growing adult gaming market. Older sports fans were drawn into video gaming by sports titles from the developer Electronic Arts—particularly the *Madden NFL* series of professional football games. Critics credit the *Grand Theft Auto III* series of games with making the PlayStation 2 a dominant console. The games, which put players in the role of urban gangsters, sparked controversy for their violence but captured imaginations with their expansive game worlds and free-form play. Microsoft achieved great success with its *Halo* series, a first-person shooter game that let players compete in teams over a computer network.

Social gaming. In the early 2000's, a wide range of network capabilities continued to make personal computers the platform of choice for social gaming. Will Wright's *The Sims* (2000) let players build virtual neighborhoods, guiding the daily lives of their inhabitants. *The Sims* won many new players with its innovative, nonviolent gameplay. But perhaps more importantly, the

A musical video game may involve performing rock songs with controllers that mimic instruments. In this photograph, game designers test a game in the popular *Rock Band* series.

© Yoon S. Byun, The Boston Globe/Getty Images

game allowed players to create their own content and share it with others over the Internet, resulting in an online community of *Sims* enthusiasts.

The development of *massively multiplayer online role-playing games* (MMORPG's) offered even greater opportunity for social gaming. MMORPG's are essentially virtual worlds stored on remote computers known as *servers.* Thousands of subscribers can connect to a game at the same time, populating the game's world with characters. Players can meet up with one another to do battle, complete quests, and even shape the world itself. Such hugely successful MMORPG's as *Everquest* (1999) and *World of Warcraft* (2004) helped popularize this format.

Bigger games. In 2005, video game developers began introducing a generation of consoles designed to push gaming in new directions. Microsoft's Xbox 360 and Sony's PlayStation 3 both featured unprecedented graphics capabilities. Such games as *Gears of War* (2006) and *Bioshock* (2007) presented game worlds of remarkable graphic detail and depth.

Visually impressive games proved expensive to produce, and many independent game development companies struggled to survive. Many game developers turned to in-game advertisements to offset the cost of development and promotion. To reduce financial risk, established game developers increasingly relied on sequels to previous games, games based on successful movies, and other ideas with built-in appeal. Some critics worried that this trend would stifle innovation.

Broadening audiences. Some game designers, however, continued to innovate. Nintendo's Wii console, launched in 2006, stunned audiences with its unique motion-sensitive controller. Its *Wii Sports* (2006) appealed even to people who were not video game enthusiasts with its simple, social, and active gameplay. In 2010, Microsoft released Kinect, a high-tech sensor that connects to the company's Xbox 360. Kinect enabled players to control games entirely with gestures and voice commands—without using any controller.

Music games, such as *Guitar Hero* (2005) and *Rock Band* (2007), also used innovative controllers shaped like guitars and drum sets to appeal to wider audiences. The games allowed players to play along with popular rock songs on the instruments to scrolling notes on-screen.

Handheld games continued to improve as computer components grew smaller. The Nintendo DS handheld system, introduced in 2004, featured two screens, one of them doubling as a touch-sensitive controller. In 2005, Sony released the PlayStation Portable (PSP), a graphically powerful machine that could play music and movies. Both machines could also connect with the Internet. Apple Inc.'s iPhone and iPod touch devices, first released in 2007, also became popular portable gaming platforms. In 2011, Nintendo released the 3DS, featuring a screen that projected 3D visuals without the need to wear special glasses.

Impact of electronic games

Like motion pictures, TV shows, and novels, electronic games entertain audiences and provide a temporary escape from daily cares. By putting the player inside the story, games can offer a stronger sense of escape than many other forms of entertainment. Mastering a difficult game can also give a player a feeling of achievement.

Benefits. Some game enthusiasts believe that playing games sharpens their reflexes and exercises their problem-solving skills. Studies have shown that people who play games regularly perform better than nonplayers at certain surgical techniques and other complex visual tasks. Social gaming helps people meet friends with similar interests from around the world.

Controversy. Since the 1980's, many people have expressed concern that playing violent games could increase aggression, desensitize children to violence, and promote violence as a means of resolving conflict. Research on the issue has produced mixed results. Some laboratory studies show that children will reenact violence after playing violent games. But statistics indicate that overall violence has declined while electronic games have grown in popularity. Critics have blamed certain games for inspiring widely publicized incidents of youth violence. Most psychologists, however, agree that violent games and other media are not a primary cause of such outbursts.

Critics have also voiced concerns about the social values expressed in games, particularly their portrayal of women. In many games, women act as little more than "prizes" to be won by male characters. In other games, women appear overly sexualized, promoting harmful stereotypes. But some games, such as *The Sims,* appeal to female players, and many newer games include stronger female characters.

Some health experts worry that electronic games can lead to addiction or promote obesity. Games can be compelling for players, and anything compelling can become addictive. But true gaming addictions—like work or exercise addictions—are rare. Too much game play can reduce physical activity, contributing to obesity and other health problems. Some players have argued, however, that playing games generally replaces other physically inactive pursuits, such as watching television.

Education. Some education experts study the way people play electronic games because the games require intense thought, learning, decision making, and problem solving. Classroom teachers have experimented with using games, such as *Civilization,* to present educational topics in novel ways. Some game developers specialize in educational games, and such games continue to grow in importance. Kurt Squire

See also **Computer** (Dedicated computers; Games software); **Computer graphics; Game** (Electronic game; Internet games); **Nintendo; Virtual reality.**

Additional resources

DeMaria, Rusel. *Reset: Changing the Way We Look at Video Games.* Berrett-Koehler Pubs., 2007.

Kent, Steven L. *The Ultimate History of Video Games.* Prima Pub., 2001.

King, Brad, and Borland, John. *Dungeons and Dreamers: The Rise of Computer Game Culture.* McGraw-Hill/Osborne, 2003.

Electronic mail. See **E-mail.**

Electronic music is a kind of music in which sounds are produced electronically. Composers use electronic equipment to make sounds with a desired pitch, rhythm, loudness, and tone color. They assemble the sounds on magnetic tape or computer disks to create compositions and play them on a tape recorder through loudspeakers.

Many composers of electronic music use a machine called a *synthesizer* to combine, modify, and distort sounds. A synthesizer has several devices that change the pitch, tone, and amplitude of a sound. Synthesizers can imitate the sounds of traditional musical instruments but are more often used to create unique, new sounds. Synthesizers were invented because composers wanted to include a greater variety of sounds in their music than was possible with traditional instruments.

Some composers use computers to do the work of synthesizers and tape recorders. Special computer programs can manipulate sounds like a synthesizer.

In the early 1900's, several people invented equipment that could produce electronic music. These inventors included Thaddeus Cahill in the United States, Maurice Martenot in France, and Leon Theremin in Russia. But electronic music attracted little attention until the 1940's, when magnetic tape recorders came into general use.

The first notable electronic music composer was Pierre Schaeffer of France, who worked exclusively with tape recorders and recordings of everyday sounds. Other major composers included Luciano Berio (Italy), Pierre Boulez and Edgard Varèse (France), Karlheinz Stockhausen (Germany), and Mario Davidowsky (United States). In the 1960's, several Americans, including Robert A. Moog and Donald Buchla, independently developed mass-produced synthesizers.

In its early days, electronic music caused much discussion among audiences and critics. Its supporters declared that electronic techniques increased the range of musical expression. Its opponents objected to the absence of any human element in performance.

Some composers responded to objections by writing works in which performers interact with electronic instruments. Others developed computer programs that allow performers to shape computer output during a performance. These approaches permit the artist to interpret the composer's music. Mark D. Nelson

See also **Stockhausen, Karlheinz; Synthesizer; Varèse, Edgard.**

Electronic publishing is the use of computers to distribute material that traditionally would have been available in a print format. Electronically published works may be distributed on a DVD or over the Internet and can be read on a computer, cell phone, or special handheld device called a reader. Some material is available only in an electronic format. Many publishers of printed books, magazines, and newspapers also distribute electronic versions of their products.

Works published electronically offer some advantages over print. An electronic publication can provide features that print cannot, including animations, videos, audio recordings, *blogs* (personal journals of thoughts and ideas), and *podcasts* (audio or video recordings available on the Internet).

Electronic publications can be updated quickly and distributed almost instantly. In works published electronically, space is not as big a concern as it is in print publishing. Printed material must often be edited to fit the amount of space available. But a standard DVD can hold the equivalent of thousands of pages of text. With Internet distribution, text length is of little concern.

Keith Ferrell

Related articles in *World Book* include:

Desktop publishing
E-book
Encyclopedia (Today's encyclopedias)
Internet (Information and media)
Magazine (Online versions)
Newspaper (Online newspapers)
Publishing

Electronic surveillance. See **Wiretapping.**

Electronic tagging is a way of monitoring an offender's whereabouts, such as in the enforcement of house arrest. It is used as an alternative to imprisonment or for probation or parole supervision. Some types of electronic tagging include plastic anklets or bracelets, encoders that are checked via telephone or computer, and Global Positioning System devices. Each type uses signaling technology to inform authorities of an offender's location. Officials carefully select which offenders can be tagged instead of imprisoned. Criminals ineligible for tagging include those who have escape histories or who pose a threat to the community. James O. Finckenauer

© Lawrence Migdale, Photo Researchers
Scanning electron microscope with display screen

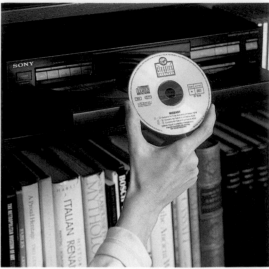

WORLD BOOK photo by Ralph Brunke
Compact disc player

© Charles Gupton, Corbis
Personal computer

© David R. Frazier, Photo Researchers
Laser scanner at checkout counter

Electronics has revolutionized such fields as communications, education, medicine, entertainment, and business and industry. The photographs above and on the next page show some of the many uses of electronics.

Electronics

Electronics is a branch of physics and engineering that involves controlling the flow of electric charges in certain devices for a useful purpose. Electronic *components* (parts) are used in a broad range of products, including computers, telephones, radios, television sets, DVD players, and medical instruments.

Electronics is part of the broad field of electricity. Electricity includes two important elements: (1) electric current and (2) electric voltage. *Electric current* is the flow of electric charges. *Electric voltage* is a type of "pressure" or force that causes the charges to move in the same direction. Familiar uses of electricity include the furnishing of energy in homes and businesses to provide light and heat, and to drive motors.

Electronics deals chiefly with the use of current and voltage to carry *electric signals.* An electric signal is an electric current or voltage modified in some way to represent information. A signal may represent sound, pictures, numbers, letters, computer instructions, or other information. Signals can also be used to count objects, to measure time or temperature, or to detect chemicals or radioactive materials.

Electronics depends on certain highly specialized components, such as *transistors* and *integrated circuits,* that serve as parts of almost all electronic equipment. The value of such devices lies in their ability to manipu-

Karl D. Stephan, the contributor of this article, is Associate Professor in the Department of Engineering and Technology at Texas State University.

NASA

Johnson Space Center's Mission Control Center in Houston

late signals extremely fast. Many components can respond to signals billions of times per second.

The field of *microelectronics* is concerned with the design and production of miniature components, chiefly integrated circuits, and of electronic equipment that uses such components. Manufacturers can create millions of microscopic electronic components on a piece of material—called a *chip*—no larger than a fingernail.

This article provides a broad overview of the basic tools and functions of electronics and the electronics industry. Separate *World Book* articles give detailed information on many of the topics. For a list of these articles, see the *Related articles* at the end of this article.

Uses of electronics

Electronics has changed the way people live. People have come to depend on electronic products in almost every part of their daily lives.

In communications. Electronic communication systems link people throughout the world. People in different countries can communicate almost instantly using telephones or the Internet. A television viewer can watch events on another continent as they are taking place. Cellular telephones, also called *mobile telephones,* enable a person to call another person while riding in a car or walking down the street. Fax machines send and receive copies of documents over telephone lines in minutes.

Processing information. Electronic computers are used in business, education, government, industry, and science. Many people also use computers in the home. People depend on computers to handle vast amounts of information with incredible speed and to solve complex mathematical problems in a fraction of a second. Online services provide computer users instant access to a wide variety of information and features through telephone lines and high-speed communications links. In the entertainment industry, electronic systems produce sophisticated special effects for motion pictures and complex graphics for computer and video games.

Medicine and research. Physicians use a variety of electronic instruments and machines to diagnose and treat disorders. For example, X-ray machines use radiation produced in a special type of electronic vacuum tube to take pictures of bones and internal organs. Physicians analyze these pictures to detect injuries and diseases. Radiation therapy, or *radiotherapy,* uses X rays and other forms of radiation as a powerful weapon against cancer. *Magnetic resonance imaging* (MRI) machines use powerful magnets and complex electronic processing devices to produce three-dimensional representations of tissues inside the body.

Computers and other electronic instruments provide scientists and other researchers with a clearer understanding of nature. For example, computers help scientists design new drug molecules, track weather systems, and test theories that describe how galaxies develop. Electron microscopes can magnify specimens by 1 million times.

Automation. Electronic controls improve the operation of many common home appliances, such as refrigerators, air conditioners, and washing machines. Microwave ovens heat food quickly by penetrating it with short radio waves produced by a vacuum tube.

Industries use computers to control other machines. Electronic robots perform a wide variety of tasks that are boring, difficult, or dangerous for people. The high level of precision that electronic control systems provide makes it possible for manufacturers to produce integrated circuits and many other advanced products.

Air, sea, and space travel depend on navigation by radar, radio, and computers. The Global Positioning System (GPS) uses electronic systems in satellites and on the ground to calculate the precise geographic locations of devices called *GPS receivers* anywhere in the world. Most automobiles have electronic controls in their engines and fuel systems. Also, electronic devices control the inflation of *air bags*—safety devices that inflate to help protect a driver or a front-seat passenger in a collision.

How an electronic system works

To provide a basis for understanding electronics, this section describes how a common product, a handheld electronic calculator, works. A calculator has a small keypad with keys for numbers and operations, and a display screen that shows results. Most calculators are powered by a small battery or by a panel of solar cells.

Beneath the keypad, tiny circuits operate the calculator. A circuit is a set of connected parts through which current flows. Pressing a key creates a pulse of electric charge representing a number or operation—in other words, a signal. The signals travel through wires to the circuits.

Each circuit has a job. Some circuits store signals temporarily, awaiting further instructions. Others change signals according to instructions. For example, a circuit might multiply two numbers together. Finally, circuits send signals that light up or darken certain areas on the display screen to show the result of a calculation.

The operations of a calculator, like most electronic systems, can be divided into three stages: (1) the input stage, in which information enters the system as signals; (2) the processing stage, in which the signals are manipulated in some way; and (3) the output stage, in which the processed signals are changed into a form that the user can understand. Systems use various types of input and output devices that produce or respond to signals. For example, radio and television broadcasting require such devices as microphones and loudspeakers. From the time signals leave the input device until they reach the output device, the signals can go through a number of changes. The electronic components working within circuits make these changes.

Electronic circuits

In any electronic device, a circuit provides a pathway for the electric current that operates the device. A calculator has a complex circuit. Many of the parts of this complex circuit are actually smaller subcircuits that perform particular jobs. Not all of the circuits necessarily work at the same time. Certain components act as electronic "switches," turning circuits "on" and "off" as needed. When a switch allows current to pass through a circuit, the circuit is on. When a switch blocks current, the circuit is off.

How a circuit works. To understand how an electronic circuit works, one must know something about atoms. Every atom has one or more *electrons*—particles that carry a negative electric charge. Atoms also contain *protons*—particles that carry a positive electric charge. Opposite charges attract each other. Like charges *repel* (push away from) each other. Circuit operation is based on the attraction between charges.

The flow of electrons in one direction at a time forms an electric current. Voltage, also known as *electromotive force,* is the "pressure" or force that drives the electrons. In circuits, voltage is the electrical attraction caused by the difference in the charges between two points in the circuit. A power source provides voltage. Batteries are a common power source. One end of a battery supplies a negative voltage, and the other end supplies a positive voltage. Electronic systems that plug into an electric outlet receive power from a commercial power plant.

Electrons flow from the negative voltage end of a circuit to the positive voltage end. This movement of elec-

Terms used in electronics

Amplification is the strengthening of a weak signal.
Amplitude is the strength of a signal. Amplitude can be measured in terms of current, voltage, or power.
Binary code is used by computers to represent information. It consists of the 0's and 1's of the binary numeration system.
Charge carrier is an electron that can flow from atom to atom and so conduct electric current.
Conductor is a material that can carry an electric current.
Digital signals represent all information using a limited number of voltage ranges, each range representing a distinct value. Under the binary code, only two voltage ranges are used.
Diode is a component that blocks current from flowing through it in one direction but allows current to flow in the other.
Doping is the process of adding impurities to a semiconductor. The impurities, known as *dopants,* add positive or negative charge carriers to the material, thereby increasing its ability to conduct current.
Free electron is an electron that can move from atom to atom and so conduct electric current. Free electrons are also called *charge carriers.*
Frequency is the number of times a second that a signal vibrates back and forth.
Hole is the absence of an electron bond in a crystal.
Insulators are materials that block electric current.
Integrated circuit is a tiny *chip* (piece) of semiconductor material, usually silicon, that contains a complete electronic circuit. One integrated circuit can do the work of thousands of individual electronic components.
Logic gates are small groups of circuits designed to imitate a logic function, such as counting or comparing information.
Microprocessor is an integrated circuit that contains memory, processing, and control circuits on one chip.
Oscillation produces an electric signal at a desired frequency.
P-n junction is the area where a p-type semiconductor meets an n-type semiconductor within a continuous crystal.
Rectification changes alternating current into direct current.
Resistor is a circuit component that decreases current flow.
Semiconductor is a material that conducts electric current better than an insulator but not as well as a conductor. Semiconductors are important because their conductivity can be altered by doping and precisely controlled by signals.
Signal is an electric current or voltage modified to represent information, such as sound, pictures, or letters.
Solid-state components control a signal flowing through a solid semiconductor material.
Switch is a component that directs the path of a current. A switch can turn a circuit on or off.
Transistor is a component that uses a small signal to control a strong current. A transistor is an arrangement of p-n junctions and other structures that can be used to amplify a signal or switch a circuit on or off.
Vacuum tube is a component that controls a signal in a container from which most of the air has been removed.
Voltage is a type of "pressure" or force that drives charges through a circuit.

Parts of an electronic system

Many parts work together in the electronic system of the calculator shown. The components are attached to a printed circuit board. Thin metal lines carry electric current between the parts. A chip called the *central processing unit* performs most calculations. It contains thousands of microscopic parts that form logic, memory, and control circuits. Other chips help process signals. Individually made components, such as capacitors and resistors, direct and control the current.

Hewlett Packard (WORLD BOOK photo by Dale DeBolt)

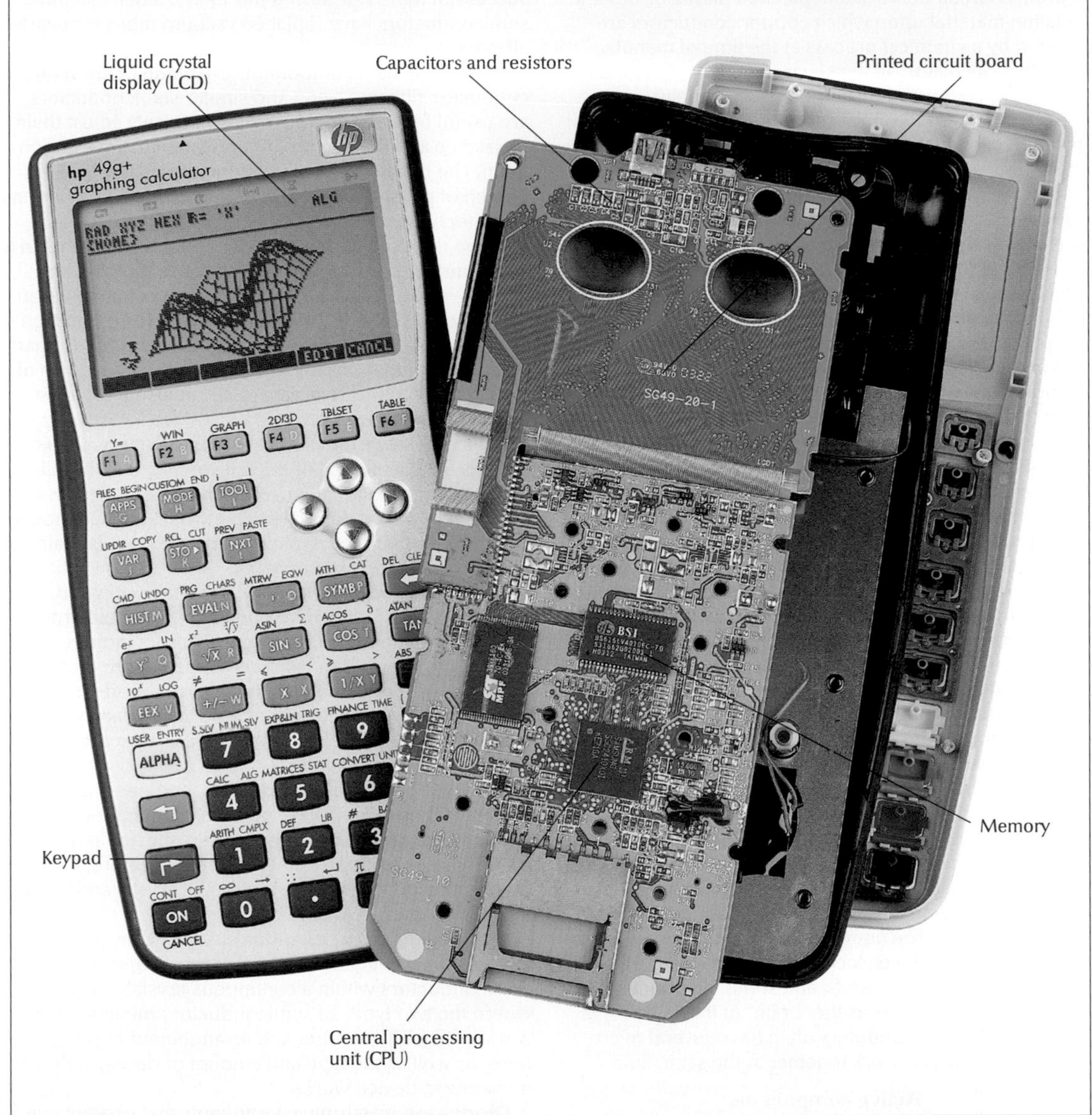

trons creates an electric current. Scientists, however, traditionally describe the direction of an electric current as flowing from positive to negative. Until the late 1800's, when the electron was discovered, scientists had mistakenly believed that charges flowed from positive to negative.

Wires and certain other parts of circuits are made of materials called *conductors,* which can carry an electric current. In conductors, which include metals, each atom has one or more electrons that can move from atom to atom. Such electrons are called *free electrons* or *charge carriers.* Circuits also contain *insulators,* materials that block current because they have no free electrons.

As electrons move through a conductor, they collide with the atoms of the material. Each collision hinders the flow of electrons and causes them to lose some energy as heat. Opposition to electric current, which changes electric energy into heat, is known as *resistance.* A build-up of heat can damage a circuit. Some electronic devices, including some computers, generate so much heat that their circuits must be continually cooled by the flow of air or liquid.

Types of electronic circuits. Manufacturers make two types of electronic circuits: (1) conventional and

(2) integrated. A calculator, like most electronic devices, has both kinds.

Conventional circuits consist of separate electronic components connected by conductors and fastened to a base. Manufacturers typically attach the components to a *printed circuit board,* a thin piece of plastic or other insulating material upon which copper conductors are printed by a chemical process at the time of manufacture. In a calculator, all the electronic parts of the main circuit are connected on a printed circuit board.

Integrated circuits have components and connectors formed on and within a chip—a tiny piece of *semiconductor* material, usually silicon. A semiconductor is a substance that conducts electric current better than an insulator, but not as well as a conductor. The chip serves not only as the base but also as an essential part of the circuit. Integrated circuits often serve as components of conventional circuits.

To make an integrated circuit, engineers prepare a large master design of the circuit with the help of a computer. A photographic process reduces the master design to microscopic size. Chip manufacturers treat silicon to alter its conductive properties by adding small amounts of impurities called *dopants,* such as boron and phosphorus. The treated regions form the chip's electronic components. One chip can contain millions of microscopic parts connected by thin "lines" of metal. Chip makers arrange the parts and connections in complex patterns in several layers. Finished circuits are mounted in casings that are connected to a printed circuit board.

The small size of an integrated circuit gives it several advantages over a conventional circuit. For example, an integrated circuit works faster because the signals have less distance to travel. Integrated circuits also use less power, generate less heat, and cost less to operate than conventional circuits. In addition, integrated circuits are more reliable because they have fewer connections that might fail. But because of the small size of their components, integrated circuits can be damaged by strong currents and high voltages.

A type of integrated circuit called a *microprocessor* performs the same types of mathematical and memory functions that a large computer does. Microprocessors control many products, including microwave ovens, video game systems, robots, and some telephones. A microprocessor serves as the "brain" of every personal computer. Larger computers often have several microprocessors that can work together at the same time.

Active components

Active components in electronics control, modify, amplify, and process electronic signals. From the early 1900's to the 1950's, vacuum tubes were an important part of most electronic equipment. Various metallic elements within an air-tight tube controlled the flow of electrons through a vacuum. Some equipment still uses special types of vacuum tubes. For example, microwave ovens use a tube called a *magnetron* to produce microwaves. Other types of vacuum tubes produce high-power radio and radar signals and X rays. For more information about the various kinds of vacuum tubes and how they work, see **Vacuum tube.**

Nearly all active components produced today are *solid-state* components. In transistors and other solid-state components, signals flow through a solid semiconductor material instead of through a vacuum. Solid-state devices use less power, last longer, and take up less space than vacuum tubes. Engineers developed the first successful transistor during the 1940's. Since that time, semiconductors have replaced vacuum tubes for nearly all uses.

Most solid-state components are made of the semiconductor silicon. Silicon and similar semiconductors are useful because engineers can precisely adjust their resistance and thus control the flow of current through them. The behavior of semiconductors relates to the branch of physics called *quantum mechanics.* See **Quantum mechanics.**

To be used for most electronic devices, the atoms of a semiconductor must form a crystal structure. In these crystals, each of an atom's outer electrons pairs with an outer electron of a neighboring atom to form a linkage known as an *electron bond* or a *covalent bond.* Ordinarily, the outer electrons are tightly bound to the atoms of the crystal, and the material acts as an insulator, resisting the flow of charges.

Engineers *dope* (treat) pure silicon crystals with extremely small amounts of dopants to increase the silicon's ability to conduct current. There are two types of doped semiconductors: (1) p-type, which contain mostly positive charge carriers; and (2) n-type, which contain mostly negative charge carriers.

To create p-type semiconductors, engineers add dopants whose atoms have one fewer outer electron than a silicon atom has. Aluminum, boron, indium, and gallium are p-type dopants. Each dopant atom creates a *hole*—that is, the absence of an electron bond—in the crystal structure. A hole acts as a positive charge, attracting electrons from neighboring atoms. Thus, a hole can move from atom to atom.

To create n-type semiconductors, engineers add dopants whose atoms have one more outer electron than a silicon atom has. Arsenic, phosphorus, and antimony are n-type dopants. At room temperature, the extra electron is free to move within the crystal and acts as a negative charge carrier.

Manufacturers make various electronic devices by forming different combinations of p-type and n-type semiconductors within a continuous crystal. The place where the two types of semiconductors meet is called a *p-n junction.* The number and arrangement of p-n junctions, as well as the type and amount of dopants, determine how a device works.

Diodes are electronic components that prevent current from flowing in one direction but not the other. A semiconductor diode consists of a piece of p-type semiconductor joined to a piece of n-type semiconductor. A diode has two *terminals* (parts for making electrical connections). The terminals connect the end of each type of semiconductor material to the circuit. A diode can be built into an integrated circuit, or can form a *discrete* (separate) component of a conventional circuit. A discrete diode is enclosed in a protective casing.

How a diode works. A diode is basically a switching device that allows current to flow in only one direction. The current is carried by the flow of holes and electrons. The *bias* (direction) of the applied voltage determines if

How semiconductor components work All semiconductor active components contain at least one *p-n junction.* The number of charge carriers near the junction determines if a current can flow through the junction. What a component does depends on how many junctions it has and how the circuit is arranged.

WORLD BOOK illustrations by Garri Budynsky, Artisan

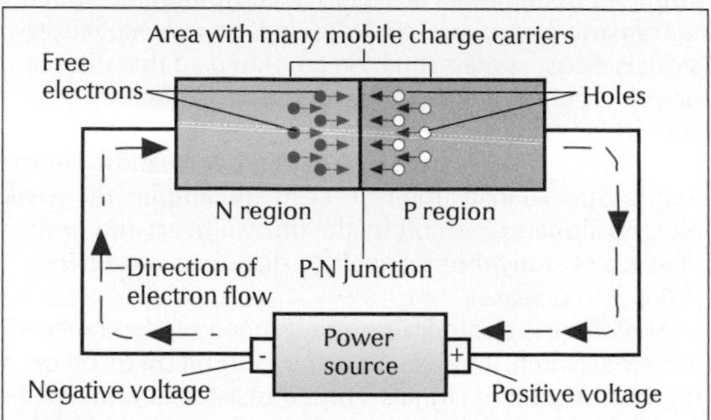

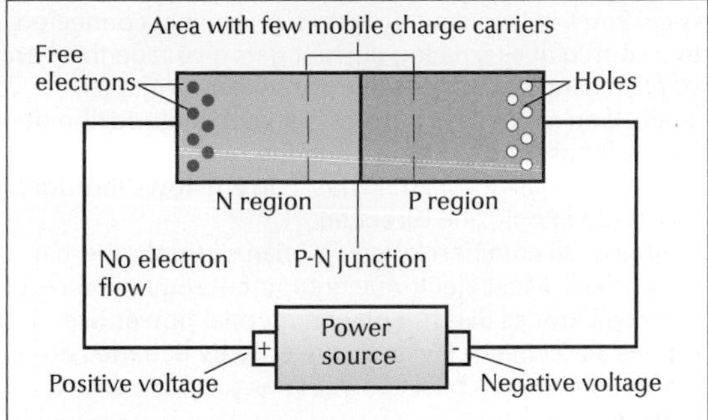

A diode has one p-n junction that can either conduct or block current, depending on the *bias* (direction) of a voltage applied to the diode's two terminals. A forward-biased diode, *left,* conducts current because charge carriers are attracted toward the junction. A reverse-biased diode, *right,* blocks current because charge carriers move away from the junction.

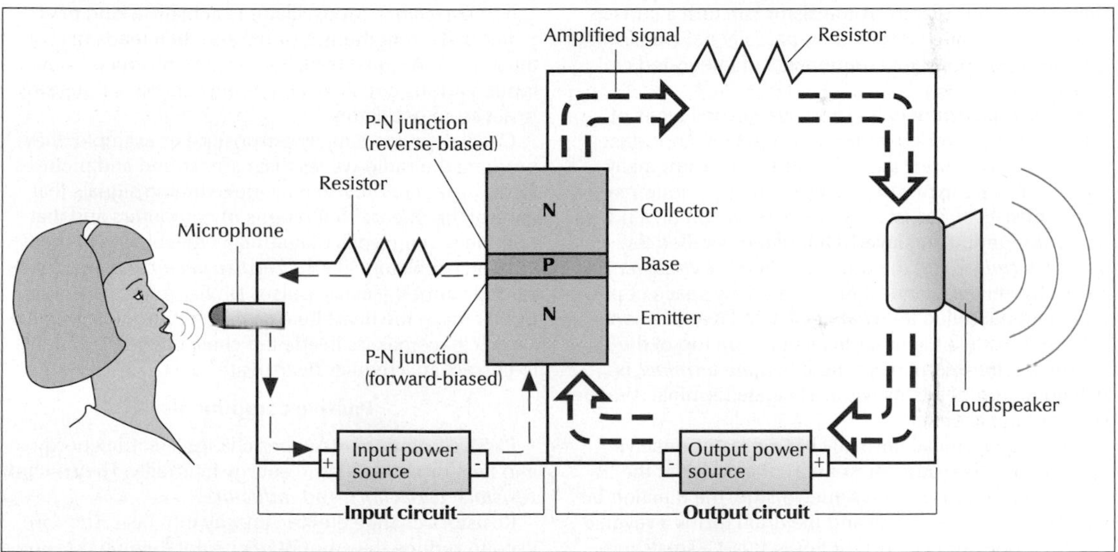

An amplifying transistor circuit can strengthen a voice signal. *Above,* a bipolar junction transistor is connected to an input circuit and an output circuit. A microphone picks up sound waves and changes each wave into a voltage signal. The voltage is applied across the transistor's forward-biased junction. As a result, free electrons from the emitter enter the base, overcoming the ability of the reverse-biased junction to block current. A strong current—fluctuating according to the pattern of the sound waves—flows through the output circuit and operates the loudspeaker.

the p-n junction blocks current or allows it to flow.

A *forward bias* allows current to flow through the junction. To create a forward bias, a battery or other voltage source applies a negative voltage to the n-type material and a positive voltage to the p-type material. In simple terms, the negative voltage repels the free electrons in the n-type material toward the p-n junction. Likewise, the positive voltage repels the holes in the p-type material toward the junction. The electrons move across the junction into the p-type semiconductor. For each electron that crosses into the p-type material, the voltage source pumps one electron into the n-type material and pulls one electron out of the p-type material. As a result, electrons flow through the circuit. A small increase in the strength of the voltage causes a large increase in the current flowing through the diode. When the voltage is removed, electron flow stops.

A *reverse bias* prevents most current from flowing through the p-n junction, though a small *leakage current* gets through. To create a reverse bias, a voltage source applies a negative voltage to the p-type semiconductor and a positive voltage to the n-type semiconductor. As a result, holes and electrons are attracted away from the junction. This creates an area on either side of the junction with no mobile charge carriers. The junction area acts as an insulator.

Uses. Diodes are used as switches and also as *rectifiers.* A rectifier circuit can change *alternating current* into *direct current.* Alternating current reverses its direction of flow many times each second. Direct current always flows in the same direction. A terminal connected to a source of alternating current gets a voltage that constantly changes from positive to negative and back again. If an alternating current is sent to a diode, the device will pass current only when the n-type semiconductor has a negative voltage. Thus, current flows through the diode in only one direction.

Almost all commercial power plants supply alternating current. Most electronic equipment requires direct current. Devices that run on commercial power use diodes as rectifiers. Devices powered by batteries do not need rectifiers because batteries produce direct current.

Transistors are arrangements of p-n junctions and other features that can be used to amplify signals or switch a circuit on and off. Just as a small movement of a mechanical switch can turn a powerful motor on and off, a transistor uses a small input signal to control the flow of a strong current. A transistor can turn a current all the way on, all the way off, or partially on. Transistors are the most important components of integrated circuits.

How a transistor works. There are several types of transistors that work in different ways. One important type is the *field-effect transistor* (FET). There are many types of FET's. A type commonly used in computer systems consists of two islands of n-type silicon on a p-type *substrate* (underlying layer). One island is called the *source terminal,* and the other is called the *drain terminal.* Between the islands there is a narrow space of p-type material called the *channel.* A thin layer of *quartz* (silicon dioxide) or another insulator is on top of the channel. A third terminal, called the *gate terminal,* is placed on top of the insulator. The gate terminal is made either of metal or silicon.

The drain terminal normally has a greater positive voltage than the source terminal. If the gate and the source terminal are at the same voltage, the junction between the p-type channel and the drain forms a reverse-biased diode, and no current flows. But if a small voltage signal is applied at the gate, the gate will then have a greater positive charge than the source. The gate's positive charge creates a region in the channel in which electrons can flow. The positively charged drain attracts electrons from the source, and a current flow is established between source and drain. In this way, a small voltage change at the gate can control a large flow of electrons from source to drain. Because the gate is insulated, no direct current flows through it. For this reason, little energy is required to switch the transistor from "off" to "on."

Another major type of transistor is the *bipolar junction transistor,* which works in a different way than the field-effect transistor. For more information on both types of transistors and how they work, see **Transistor.**

Uses. Transistors perform three main electronic functions: (1) amplification, (2) switching, and (3) oscillation.

Amplification is the strengthening of a weak, fluctuating signal. The current that flows through the transistor and the output circuit is basically a duplicate of the input signal—but much stronger. Many transistors can react to signal fluctuations billions of times per second.

Most electronic equipment would not work without amplifiers. Amplifiers are used in equipment designed to transmit or process *audio* (sound) or *video* (picture) signals. Most signals must be amplified so that they can drive an output device, such as a loudspeaker, a TV screen, or a computer display.

Amplifiers are also used to detect information. For example, special instruments record and amplify the weak electric signals given off by the human heart and brain. Physicians study these signals to diagnose certain injuries and diseases.

Switching is another important function of a transistor. As a switch, a transistor turns a circuit on or off or directs the path of signals. For a transistor to function as a switch, the strength of input signals must vary widely, so that the transistor simply turns the main supply current all the way on or off.

Oscillation converts a direct current signal to an alternating current signal of a desired *frequency* (number of vibrations per second). Transistor circuits that do this are called *oscillators.* An oscillator is actually a kind of amplifier that strengthens a signal and then feeds part of the amplified signal back into itself to produce its own input. Various circuit arrangements enable a transistor to act as an oscillator.

Oscillators serve many purposes. For example, they produce the radio waves that carry sound and pictures through space. They also produce timing signals that control the internal operations of computers and that operate certain types of automatic machinery. In medicine, an oscillator called a *cardiac pacemaker* produces carefully timed electric pulses similar to the natural pulses that make the heart beat regularly. Surgeons implant cardiac pacemakers inside the chest of certain patients to correct an irregular heartbeat.

Passive components

Passive components either change electric energy into heat or store electric energy internally. They include *resistors, capacitors,* and *inductors.*

Resistors change electric energy into heat. They are used to reduce the amount of current flowing through a circuit. The larger the resistor, the smaller the amount of current that flows through it. The current flow through a resistor is described by Ohm's Law. See **Ohm's Law.**

Capacitors and inductors store electric energy. Electronic circuits use capacitors to store information as the presence or absence of a charge. Capacitors are also used to block the flow of a direct current. Inductors, on the other hand, *impede* (obstruct) the flow of alternating current but allow direct current to flow. See **Capacitor; Inductance.**

In integrated circuits, manufacturers can treat the semiconductor chip to create areas that act as resistors and capacitors, but usually not as inductors. Inductors can be attached to integrated circuits as discrete components.

Electronics and light

Many electronic devices make use of the ability of electrons to absorb and give off energy as light. Such *optoelectronic devices* include light-sensing devices, light-emitting devices, and liquid crystal displays.

Light-sensing devices, also known as *electric eyes,* use light energy to produce or control an electric current. The heart of such devices consists of a light-sensing diode, or *photodiode,* usually made of silicon. A photodiode resembles an ordinary diode but has a window or lens that lets light fall onto the p-n junction. The light knocks some electrons out of their crystal bonds, producing pairs of free electrons and holes that can flow. Some photodiodes, such as *solar cells,* generate enough current to power other electronic and electric devices. Panels of solar cells power most artificial satellites and many smaller electronic devices, such as calculators. Other photodiodes are used to switch an external power supply on and off.

Television cameras and most video cameras use a special type of light sensor called a *charge-coupled device* (CCD). A CCD has a large array of tiny light-sensitive areas that produce an electric charge pattern that corresponds to the color and intensity of the light that strikes them. The CCD transmits "packets" of electric charge to electronic processing components that produce a digital pattern that represents the image. See **Charge-coupled device; Light** (Photoelectric effect).

Light-emitting devices use electric current to produce light. Most *light-emitting diodes* (LED's) are made from gallium arsenide or other semiconductor compounds that give off energy in the form of light instead of heat. As current flows through an LED, free electrons and holes near the p-n junction combine. When a free electron "falls" into a hole, the process releases a tiny packet of light energy called a *photon.* With a strong enough current, the junction area of the chip glows brightly. Groups of LED's are used in many flat-screen television and computer displays.

Devices called *semiconductor lasers* are special diodes that produce an extremely narrow, powerful beam of light. Lasers have many uses in communications, industry, medicine, and science. For example, with fiber-optic communication, a laser beam transforms the electric signals of a computer linked to a network, a telephone call, or a TV picture into pulses of photons. The photon signals travel at great speeds through many miles of hair-thin strands of glass or plastic called *optical fibers* without losing much strength or clarity.

Liquid crystal displays (LCD's) are commonly used in calculators, digital watches, and laptop computers. A thin layer of a special chemical called a *liquid crystal* is sandwiched between two sheets of glass. A voltage signal causes portions of the display to darken or to change the color of light transmitted from a source behind the display. These portions form the shape of a number or letter, or part of an image. See **Liquid crystal.**

How electronic circuits process information

Circuits process information by combining inputs to produce new information according to instructions. The way a circuit processes information depends on the type of signals it works with.

Electronic circuits work with two basic types of signals: (1) digital and (2) analog. Digital signals represent all information with a limited number of voltage ranges, typically two. Each voltage range has a distinct value. Analog signals vary continuously in voltage or current, corresponding to the input information. A fluctuating voltage can stand for changes in light, sound, temperature, pressure, or even the position of an object.

Digital circuits process information by counting or comparing signals. Many digital circuits can process information much faster than analog circuits. The majority of processing is done by digital circuits.

In digital processing, all input data—words, numbers, and other information—are translated into *binary* numbers, which are groups of 1's and 0's. The code is called *binary* (consisting of two) because only two digits are used. Any binary number can be represented by a combination of circuits or devices that are in one of two states. For example, a circuit can be on or off. One state corresponds to a binary 1, and the other to a 0. Each 1 or 0 is called a *bit,* a contraction of *bi*nary digi*t.* Many systems work with bits in groups called *words.* A word that consists of 8 bits is called a *byte.*

Digital processing requires three basic elements: (1) memory circuits, which store data; (2) logic circuits, which change data; and (3) control circuits, which direct the operations of the system. Conductive channels called *buses* link the elements to each other as well as to the entire system. A microprocessor combines these elements on one chip.

Memory circuits store bits permanently or temporarily. A common type of memory circuit contains millions of capacitors arranged in rows. The capacitors hold bits as an electric charge or the absence of a charge. A metal conductor connects each capacitor to the system. Transistors act as switches between the capacitors and conductors. When a signal opens a switch, bits can travel along the conductor. Other circuits then restore the bits by recharging the capacitors with the same sequence of charges.

There are two basic kinds of memory circuits—*random-access memory* (RAM) and *read-only memory* (ROM). The information in RAM can be erased or added

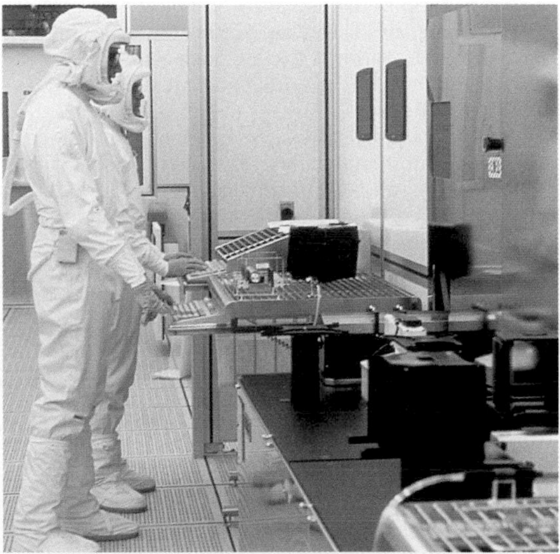

Intel Corporation

A researcher at an electronics laboratory wears special clothing designed to help protect the tiny silicon chips being tested. A single particle of dust can damage the chips.

to. *Volatile* RAM circuits store data only as long as the power is on. When the power is turned off, all the stored charges are wiped out. *Nonvolatile* RAM circuits can store data in the form of charges for long periods, even without power. RAM circuits are used in such devices as computers and certain calculators, which need to store large amounts of information for brief periods.

A ROM circuit permanently stores information installed at the time of manufacture. This information can be neither erased nor added to. ROM generally contains instructions, or *programs,* for operating the system.

Not all information is stored in circuits. For example, computers also use external storage devices, such as flash memory drives and CD-ROM's. Other types of storage devices include *compact disc drives,* also called *CD drives,* which store data on CD's, and *DVD drives,* which store information on DVD's. DVD's resemble CD's, but they can store many times more information. CD's and DVD's can store data, pictures, and sound as well as programs.

Logic circuits, also called *processors,* manipulate data according to instructions. In a processor, the bits go through a sequence of switches that change them in some way. For example, a group of switches may add two numbers together. Such a group is called an *adder.* An adder may involve hundreds of switches. During processing, bits are stored temporarily in areas called *registers,* awaiting the next instruction.

Another combination of switches can compare two bits and generate a particular output based on a set of rules established for the processor. Such circuits use binary digits to stand for such ideas as "true" or "false," instead of 1 or 0.

Designers create areas on chips that can count or compare signals by combining small groups of circuits that make simple changes in just one or two bits. These groups are often called *logic gates.* Three basic gates are (1) the NOT-gate, (2) the AND-gate, and (3) the OR-gate. If combined in large enough numbers, these gates can solve complex mathematical or logical problems.

A NOT-gate, also called an *inverter,* changes a bit from a 1 to a 0, or from a 0 to a 1. Such a function has many uses. For example, addition involves changing 0's to 1's and 1's to 0's.

Both AND- and OR-gates generate one output signal from two or more inputs. An AND-gate requires that all inputs be true—often represented by a 1—to produce a true output, or a 1. An OR-gate requires only one true input to produce a true output.

Control circuits direct and coordinate the work of all other parts of the system according to instructions stored in the memory circuits. One of the most important jobs of the control circuit is to control the movement of bits through the system. To do this, an oscillator known as the *clock* generates continuous pulses. The bits move through the circuit according to the rhythm of the clock.

Analog circuits solve problems by measuring continuously varying quantities, such as temperature, speed, and pressure. A mechanical bathroom scale is a simple example of an analog computer. Small analog circuits are parts of many electronic systems that control the operations of other machines. Analog circuits are also used in some equipment for sound recording and reproduction. For more information on analog processing, see **Analog computer**.

Digital-analog conversion. Some circuits can convert analog signals into digital signals, and digital into analog. In digital sound recording, for example, the *amplitude* (strength) of the sound wave is measured thousands of times every second and converted into a digital code signal made up of rapid bursts of current. To play the resulting digital signals, a sound system converts them back to analog signals that drive a loudspeaker. Digital signals can produce better sound quality with less background noise and distortion than analog signals can.

The electronics industry

The electronics industry is one of the largest and most important industries in the world. It involves the development, manufacture, and sales of electronic products.

Research and development. Engineers and scientists at research laboratories work to add new knowledge about electronics and to develop new electronic devices. In many countries, most basic research in electronics and related fields takes place at universities and is funded by both industry and government. The United States government sponsors electronics research through such agencies as the National Science Foundation, the National Aeronautics and Space Administration, and the Department of Energy. The government also sponsors research through its military branches.

Manufacturing and sales. The United States and Japan are two of the world's largest producers of electronic components and assembled electronic products. In the early 2010's, electronics companies in the United States employed about 800,000 workers. The sales of these companies totaled about $340 billion. During the same period, electronics companies in Japan employed about 680,000 workers. The Japanese firms had total sales valued at about $160 billion, in U.S. dollars. Other leading producers of electronic equipment include China, France, Germany, Italy, Singapore, South Korea, Taiwan, and the United Kingdom.

Careers in electronics can be divided into two main groups. These groups are (1) engineering and scientific careers and (2) technical careers.

Engineering and scientific careers range from developing new electronic devices to designing computers. Most of these careers require a college degree in engineering or physics. The *World Book* articles on **Engineering** and **Physics** discuss the requirements for becoming an electrical engineer and a physicist.

Most engineers and physicists who specialize in electronics work for electronics companies. Some of these companies do most or all of their work on military projects. Other engineers and physicists find jobs with the federal government, at colleges and universities, and in communication, medicine, or transportation.

Technical careers in electronics usually involve installing, operating, maintaining, or repairing electronic equipment. Many technical jobs require training in a trade school or community college. Such technical careers include automation control, computer networking and software maintenance, and medical technology.

Other technical jobs require only on-the-job training. Such jobs include operating certain types of electronic equipment in factories and offices. Some highly skilled technical jobs in the aerospace and communications industries require a college degree. Many people receive technical electronics training in the armed forces.

The development of electronics

Early experiments. During the mid-1800's, scientists experimented with *gas-discharge tubes*—that is, tubes from which some of the air had been removed. Most of these tubes contained a combination of such gases as oxygen and nitrogen at low pressure. Scientists discovered electric current could pass through the gas from one metal *electrode* (conductor) to another. When a battery was connected to the two electrodes, the space inside the tube glowed with bright colors. Scientists believed that one of the electrodes—called the *cathode*—gave off invisible rays that caused the colors. They named the rays *cathode rays.* As scientists removed still more air from the tubes for their experiments, the tubes became vacuum tubes.

In 1879, William Crookes, a British scientist, developed a tube to study cathode rays. The Crookes tubes were forerunners of television picture tubes.

In 1895, the German physicist Wilhelm C. Roentgen discovered X rays while studying cathode rays in a Crookes tube. By the early 1900's, many doctors were using X-ray photographs to diagnose internal diseases and injuries in their patients.

In 1897, the British physicist Joseph J. Thomson proved that cathode rays consist of negatively charged particles, later named *electrons.* Thomson's discovery led to the first practical electronic devices.

During the early 1900's, electrical engineers developed vacuum tubes that could detect, amplify, and create radio signals. In 1906, the American inventor Lee De Forest created a three-electrode, or *triode,* vacuum tube. The triode tube became a key element in radio broadcasting and reception because it could amplify signals. Commercial radio broadcasting began in 1920, and the electronics industry was born. By 1927, more than 5 million homes in the United States had radios.

The vacuum tube era lasted from the early 1900's to the 1950's. During this period, vacuum tubes made possible such electronic inventions as television, radar, and computers.

As early as 1875, the American scientist G. R. Carey had built a *photoelectric cell,* a device that produced an electric current when light shone on it. Carey's invention operated on the same principle as a TV camera, but it was not put to practical use until the early 1920's. In 1923, a Russian-born American engineer named Vladimir K. Zworykin made the first successful television camera tube. Using a cathode-ray tube as a model, Zworykin also developed a workable television picture tube during the 1920's. Experimental telecasts began in the late 1920's, but TV broadcasting did not begin on a large scale until the late 1940's.

In 1921, Albert W. Hull, an American engineer, invented the vacuum tube called the magnetron. Other engineers later discovered that the magnetron could efficiently produce microwaves—the first device to do so. Radar, which was developed gradually during the 1920's and 1930's, provided the first widespread use of microwaves.

The vacuum tube era reached its peak with the completion of one of the first general-purpose electronic digital computers in 1945. This huge machine, called ENIAC (Electronic Numerical Integrator And Computer), was built by two engineers at the University of Pennsylvania, J. Presper Eckert, Jr., and John W. Mauchly. The computer contained about 18,000 vacuum tubes and occupied about 1,800 square feet (170 square meters) of floor space. ENIAC worked 1,000 times faster than the fastest nonelectronic computers then in use.

The solid-state revolution. Three American physicists—John Bardeen, Walter H. Brattain, and William Shockley—invented the transistor in 1947. Transistors revolutionized the electronics industry, dramatically reducing the size of computers and other equipment. Transistors were used as amplifiers in hearing aids and

© DK Limited from Corbis

The Crookes tube, *shown here in a replica,* was developed in 1879 by William Crookes. The tube became a model for TV picture tubes.

Brown Bros.

The electron was discovered in 1897 by Joseph J. Thomson, *shown here.* The discovery led to the first practical electronic components.

Brown Bros.

The triode was invented in 1906 by Lee De Forest, *shown here.* This device eventually led to the development of the radio industry.

ENIAC, one of the first general-purpose electronic digital computers, was completed in 1945. John W. Mauchly, *center,* and J. Presper Eckert, Jr., *front left,* invented the huge machine.

UPI/Bettmann Newsphotos

pocket-sized radios in the early 1950's. By the 1960's, semiconductor diodes and transistors had replaced vacuum tubes in many types of equipment.

Integrated circuits developed from transistor technology as scientists sought ways to build more transistors into a circuit. The first integrated circuits were patented in 1959 by two Americans—Jack Kilby, an engineer, and Robert Noyce, a physicist—who worked independently. Integrated circuits caused as great a revolution in electronics in the 1960's as transistors had caused in the 1950's.

The first microprocessors were produced in 1971 for desktop calculators. By the mid-1970's, microprocessors were being used in handheld calculators, video games, and home appliances. Business and industry began to use microprocessors to control various types of office machines, factory equipment, and other devices.

The digital age. In the 1980's and 1990's, many products began to take advantage of digital technology. Personal computers became commonplace in the home. Digitally recorded music became available on compact discs. Manufacturers introduced the DVD, which can hold a complete video recording of a motion picture on a single disc, with significantly better picture quality than magnetic videotape.

In the 1990's, communication systems that use digital technology gained in importance. The Internet grew from a few thousand users in 1990 to many millions by the early 2000's. A digital technique called *data compression* was applied to television to remove unnecessary information from the signal. One type of digital television—*high-definition television* (HDTV)—provides a picture about four times as sharp as standard analog television does. HDTV broadcasts began in Japan in 1996 and in the United States in 1998.

Electronics today. Scientists and engineers continue to search for ways to make electronic circuits smaller, faster, and more complex. Developing technologies include *photonics* and *quantum computing.*

Photonics is the science of building circuits that use photons as signals instead of electrons. Photonic circuits use pulsed beams of photons to transmit data and commands through optical fibers. Photonic circuits can carry huge amounts of information, and they produce virtually no heat. Today, the huge information-carrying capacity of optical fibers is opening a new era in home entertain-

RCA

Vladimir K. Zworykin developed the TV camera tube and picture tube during the 1920's.

Bell Laboratories

The transistor was invented in 1947. Its inventors were William Shockley, *seated,* Walter H. Brattain, *left,* and John Bardeen, *right.* Transistors greatly reduced the size of electronic equipment.

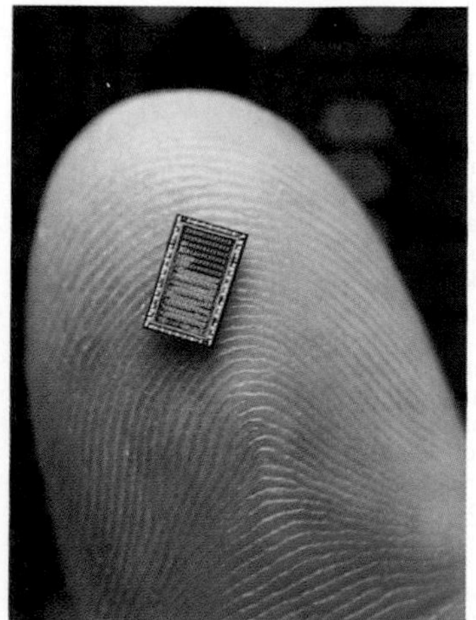

© Corbis Flirt/Alamy Images

The microprocessor was first developed in the 1970's. This tiny, powerful chip can perform most of the functions of a large computer.

© iStockphoto

The miniaturization of electronics has brought about the development of such small computing devices as this *smartphone,* which can function as both a computer and a phone. People can manipulate a smartphone by touching its screen.

ment, communications, and computer technology.

Scientists and engineers seek to develop *quantum computers,* which use the quantum-mechanical properties of photons and other particles to perform certain tasks. One such task involves making calculations related to *cryptography* (using and deciphering secret communications). Quantum computers have the potential to solve some mathematical problems millions of times faster than conventional computers.

Display techniques in electronics are also rapidly changing. Manufacturers have developed flatter display panels to replace the bulky cathode-ray tubes used in television screens and many computer screens. These displays include liquid crystal displays and *plasma displays.* A plasma display uses a layer of gas between two glass panels. An electric current passed through the gas ionizes it, producing ultraviolet light that excites red, blue, and green chemicals called *phosphors* on the surface of the glass. A display method called *digital light processing* uses a *microelectromechanical system* consisting of as many as two million tiny mirrors on a special type of integrated circuit. A powerful beam of light is directed at the mirrors, which move to reflect light onto a rear-projection display screen, producing full-color images. See **Microelectromechanical systems.**

Karl D. Stephan

Related articles in *World Book* include:

Biographies

Armstrong, Edwin
Bardeen, John
Brattain, Walter H.
De Forest, Lee
Eckert, J. Presper, Jr.
Kilby, Jack
Roentgen, Wilhelm C.
Shockley, William
Thomson, Sir Joseph J.
Zworykin, Vladimir K.

Electronic components

Capacitor
Charge-coupled device (CCD)
Computer chip
Crookes tube
Electrode
Iconoscope
Image orthicon
Photomultiplier tube
Semiconductor
Transistor
Vacuum tube

Uses of electronics

Airport (Air traffic control)
Automated teller machine
Automation
Bank (Electronic banking)
Biomedical engineering
Calculator
Camcorder
Camera
Cellular telephone
Compact disc
Computer
Computed tomography
Digital technology
Digital video recorder
DVD
Electric eye
Electrocardiograph
Electroencephalograph
Electron microscope
Electronic game
Electronic music
Global Positioning System
Handheld computer
Hearing aid
Laptop computer
Laser
Light-emitting diode
Light meter
Lock (Electronic locks)
Magnetic resonance imaging
Maser
Microelectromechanical systems
Microwave oven
Navigation (Electronic navigation)
Organ (Electronic organs)
Oscilloscope
Phonograph
Portable media player
Printer
Printing (Digital printing)
Radar
Radio
Robot
Stereophonic sound system
Synthesizer
Tape recorder
Telephone
Telescope
Television
Text messaging
Typewriter
Videotape recorder
Watch (Electronic watches)
Wiretapping
Word processing

Other related articles

Atom
Broadband communication
Communication (The development of electronics)
Data compression
Electricity
Electron
Internet
Quantum mechanics
Solid-state physics
Superconductivity
X rays (How X rays are produced)

Outline

I. Uses of electronics
A. In communications
B. Processing information
C. Medicine and research
D. Automation
II. How an electronic system works
III. Electronic circuits
A. How a circuit works
B. Types of electronic circuits
IV. Active components
A. Diodes
B. Transistors
V. Passive components
VI. Electronics and light
A. Light-sensing devices
B. Light-emitting devices
C. Liquid crystal displays
VII. How electronic circuits process information
A. Digital circuits
B. Analog circuits
C. Digital-analog conversion
VIII. The electronics industry
A. Research and development
B. Manufacturing and sales
C. Careers in electronics
IX. The development of electronics

Questions

How do electronics and the science of electricity differ in their use of electric current?
In what ways do conventional circuits differ from integrated circuits?
What advantages do semiconductor devices have over vacuum tubes?
What are the two main types of functions performed by transistors?
Why does electronic equipment that operates on a commercial power supply need a rectifier?
What is the difference between analog signals and digital signals?
What is a *p-n junction?* Why are p-n junctions important?
What are the three main elements that digital circuits need to process information?
What is a *microprocessor?*
How does a photodiode differ from an ordinary semiconductor diode?

Additional resources

Level I

Bonnet, Robert L., and Keen, Dan. *Science Fair Projects with Electricity and Electronics.* Sterling Pub., 1996.

Bridgman, Roger F. *Electronics.* 1993. Reprint. Dorling Kindersley, 2000.

Chorlton, Windsor. *The Invention of the Silicon Chip.* Heinemann Lib., 2002.

Marks, Paul. *Electricity and Electronics.* Oxford, 2002.

Level II

Gates, Earl D. *Introduction to Electronics.* 4th ed. Delmar Thomson, 2001.

Gibilisco, Stan, ed. *The Illustrated Dictionary of Electronics.* 8th ed. McGraw, 2001.

Kaplan, Daniel M., and White, Christopher. *Hands-On Electronics: A Practical Introduction to Analog and Digital Circuits.* Cambridge, 2002.

Sclater, Neil J., and Markus, John. *McGraw-Hill Electronics Dictionary.* 6th ed. McGraw, 1997.

Electrophoresis, *ih LEHK troh fuh REE sihs,* is a method of separating and purifying large biological molecules, such as proteins and deoxyribonucleic acid (DNA), through the use of an electric field. Scientists use such purified molecules for chemical and medical purposes.

In electrophoresis, a solution containing a mixture of large molecules is placed on a *conductive support,* such as wet paper or a gel. An electric current is then applied to the solution, producing an electric field that causes the positively charged molecules to move in one direction and the negatively charged ones in another. In addition, the molecules of each substance in the solution have a specific charge and therefore move in the field at different rates. Eventually, the molecules are separated at different positions on the support. The current is then turned off, and the separated molecules are removed from the support. George McLendon

Electroplating, *ih LEHK truh PLAY tihng,* is the process of putting a metallic coating on a metal or other conducting surface by using an electric current. Electroplating is used to improve the appearance of materials, for protection against corrosion, and to make plates for printing.

The article to be plated is thoroughly cleaned of grease and dirt by dipping it in acid and alkaline cleaning solutions. It is then put in a solution of the metal with which it is to be coated. The metal exists in the form of *positive ions* (atoms that have lost one or more electrons). The article is connected to the *cathode* (negative end of a source of electric energy). The *anode* (positive electric terminal) is connected to another conductor which is also dipped into the solution. The electric current acts on the metallic ions in the solution. The ions are attracted to the cathode, and the coating is deposited on the article's metal surface. If the metal in the solution and the metal of the positive terminal are the same, the electric current may remove metal from the terminal to replace metal taken from the solution.

Electroplating

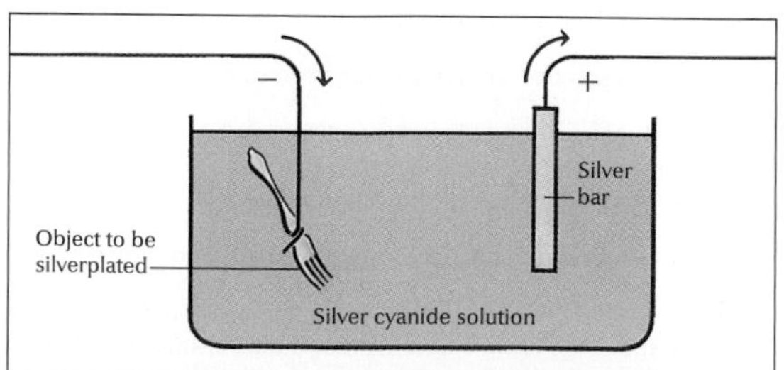

WORLD BOOK diagram by Sarah Woodward

Silverplating a fork involves applying an electric current to a silver cyanide solution. The current causes positively charged silver ions in the solution to be attracted to the fork.

The thickness of the layer deposited on the article depends on the strength of the electric current, the concentration of metallic ions, and the length of time the article has been in the solution. The terms *triple-plated* and *quadruple-plated* indicate various thicknesses of plating, not separate layers deposited on the surface.

Ornamental and protective platings are very thin, usually from $\frac{1}{1,000}$ to $\frac{2}{1,000}$ of an inch (0.03 to 0.05 millimeter) thick. For plating gold, silver, copper, zinc, and cadmium, cyanide solutions of the same metals are often used. Copper and zinc may also be plated by acid-sulfate solutions. Chromium is plated with a chromic-acid solution, and nickel is plated with nickel sulfate. Other metals plated for commercial use include platinum, lead, and tin. Alloys of two or more metals may be deposited by using a solution of salts of the metals that make up the alloy. Examples of alloys used for plating are brass, black nickel, lead-tin, and bronze.

Electroplating is also used to reproduce medals or other objects in a process called *electroforming.* This process was formerly known as *galvanoplasty.* One kind of electroforming, called *electrotyping,* is the reproduction of type forms and engravings for the printing industry. Melvin Bernstein

See also **Alloy; Electrolysis.**

Electroscope, *ih LEHK truh skohp,* is an instrument that detects the presence of an electric charge. Certain kinds of electroscopes, called *electrometers,* also measure the amount of charge present.

The simplest type of electroscope is the *gold-leaf electroscope.* This device has two slender strips of gold foil that hang straight down from a metal conductor. A nonconductor, such as cork, holds the conductor in a stand made of glass or metal. If an electrically charged object touches the conductor, the strips become charged. Both strips receive the same kind of charge and, because like charges repel each other, the strips spread apart in an upside-down V.

Gold-leaf and other simple electroscopes have been replaced by more sensitive *solid-state electrometers* for scientific research. These electronic instruments contain a *capacitor,* a device that stores an electric charge. When a charged object touches the electrometer's conductor, the charge produces a small voltage in the capacitor. The electrometer electronically amplifies this voltage so its value can be shown on a meter or on an instrument called an *oscilloscope* (see **Oscilloscope**).

Many people who work in areas where radiation may be present use an electroscope as a *dosimeter.* A dosimeter is a device that measures the amount of radiation to which a person has been exposed. An electroscope must be charged before it can be used as a dosimeter. It gradually discharges when exposed to gamma rays, X rays, or other forms of radiation. The amount of charge lost shows the level of exposure.

The first electroscope was made by William Gilbert, the physician of Queen Elizabeth I of England. He described the electroscope in a book published in 1600.

Robert B. Prigo

See also **Cosmic rays** (Cosmic ray research).

Electroshock. See **Shock treatment.**

Electrostatic attraction. See **Induction, Electric.**

Elegy. See **Gray, Thomas; Poetry** (Lyric poetry).

Element, Chemical, is any substance that contains only one kind of atom. All chemical substances are elements or *compounds* (combinations of elements). For example, hydrogen and oxygen are elements, and water is a compound of hydrogen and oxygen. Oxygen and silicon are the most plentiful elements in the crust of the Earth. Oxygen accounts for about 47 percent of the crust's *mass* (amount of matter), and silicon makes up around 28 percent of the mass.

The International Union of Pure and Applied Chemistry (IUPAC) is the recognized authority in crediting the discovery of elements and assigning names to them. For a discovery to be recognized by IUPAC, scientists must produce a sample of the element and measure certain of its properties. In addition, IUPAC prefers that another experiment confirm the discovery of the element. IUPAC recognizes the existence of 112 elements. Scientists have also claimed the discovery of elements 113 through 118.

The *Periodic table of the elements* in this article lists the recognized elements in order of increasing *atomic number.* An atom's atomic number is the number of *protons* (positively charged particles) in its nucleus. All atoms of a given element have the same number of protons.

Names and symbols of elements

The names of some elements come from Greek or Latin words. *Bromine,* for example, comes from the Greek word for *stench* (foul odor). Many elements are named for a place or an individual. Scientists at the University of California at Berkeley produced two new elements and named them berkelium and californium in honor of that city and state. Einsteinium was named for the German-born American physicist Albert Einstein. Traditionally, the scientific community has granted the discoverer of an element the right to name it, subject to acceptance by IUPAC.

Each named element has a chemical symbol consisting of one or two letters. In some cases, the symbol is the first letter of the name. For example, C is the symbol for carbon. If the first letter is already the symbol for another element, another letter of the name is used with the first. For instance, calcium has the symbol Ca. Some symbols come from an old name of the element. The symbol for lead, Pb, comes from *plumbum,* the Latin word for *lead.* Chemists use symbols to write formulas for compounds. See **Compound.**

Discovery of elements

Ancient people recognized the unique properties of a few substances that were later determined to be elements. Among the first of those were gold, copper, carbon, and sulfur. Small amounts of those elements occur naturally in pure, or nearly pure, form. As people discovered how to obtain pure metals from compounds, iron, lead, silver, tin, and other elements came to be known.

From the 1500's to the 1700's, experimenters discovered a few elements. The number of known elements began to increase rapidly in the mid-1700's. But even then, scientists had difficulty determining whether certain substances were elements or compounds. In the late 1700's, the French chemist Antoine Lavoisier created a system for classifying the known elements. But his list still included many compounds.

The Russian chemist Dmitri Mendeleev developed what scholars widely consider to be the first modern *periodic table,* published In 1869. He arranged the elements primarily in order of increasing mass but switched the order of some elements on the basis of their chemical properties. He also intentionally left gaps in his table where no known elements seemed to fit. Based on the table, Mendeleev predicted the properties of three unknown elements, which were discovered between 1875 and 1886. Around the same time that Mendeleev created his table, the German chemist Julius Lothar Meyer independently developed a similar periodic table. However, his table was not published until 1870.

Ninety-three of the elements with atomic numbers 1 through 94 occur naturally on Earth. The exception is promethium—but some scientists think it may exist on Earth in trace amounts, and astronomers have detected it in a star. Scientists produced most of the remaining recognized elements and elements 113 through 118 in machines called *particle accelerators.*

Researchers also first discovered neptunium, plutonium, and technetium as a result of accelerator experiments. Later, scientists found tiny amounts of those three elements that had been produced naturally on Earth. Elements are also created in nuclear reactors and the debris of nuclear explosions. See **Particle accelerator.**

The periodic table of the elements

The periodic table lists the elements in rows, called *periods,* in order of increasing atomic number. Elements with similar properties lie in vertical columns called *groups.* The table also lists a mass for each element and the numbers of electrons in its *electron shells,* layers at various distances from the nucleus where the positively charged nucleus holds the negatively charged electrons according to how much energy they have. In addition, the table indicates major *classes* of elements. For example, a class called the *transition metals* consists of metallic elements with some common chemical and physical properties.

Some of the mass listings are *atomic mass numbers,* while others are *relative atomic masses.* To understand those listings and the electron shell listings, you need to know about the structure of atoms and a process known as *radioactive decay.* An atom consists of a tiny, positively charged nucleus surrounded by one or more negatively charged electrons. The nucleus of the simplest kind of hydrogen atom consists of a single proton. The nucleus of every other kind of atom has one or more protons and one or more electrically neutral particles called *neutrons.*

Most elements have more than one atomic form. The different forms have the same number of protons but different numbers of neutrons. Each form of an element is known as an *isotope* of that element.

Radioactive decay is a process in which one isotope turns into another. There are several forms of this process. In each, there is a change in the isotope's number of

Periodic table of the elements

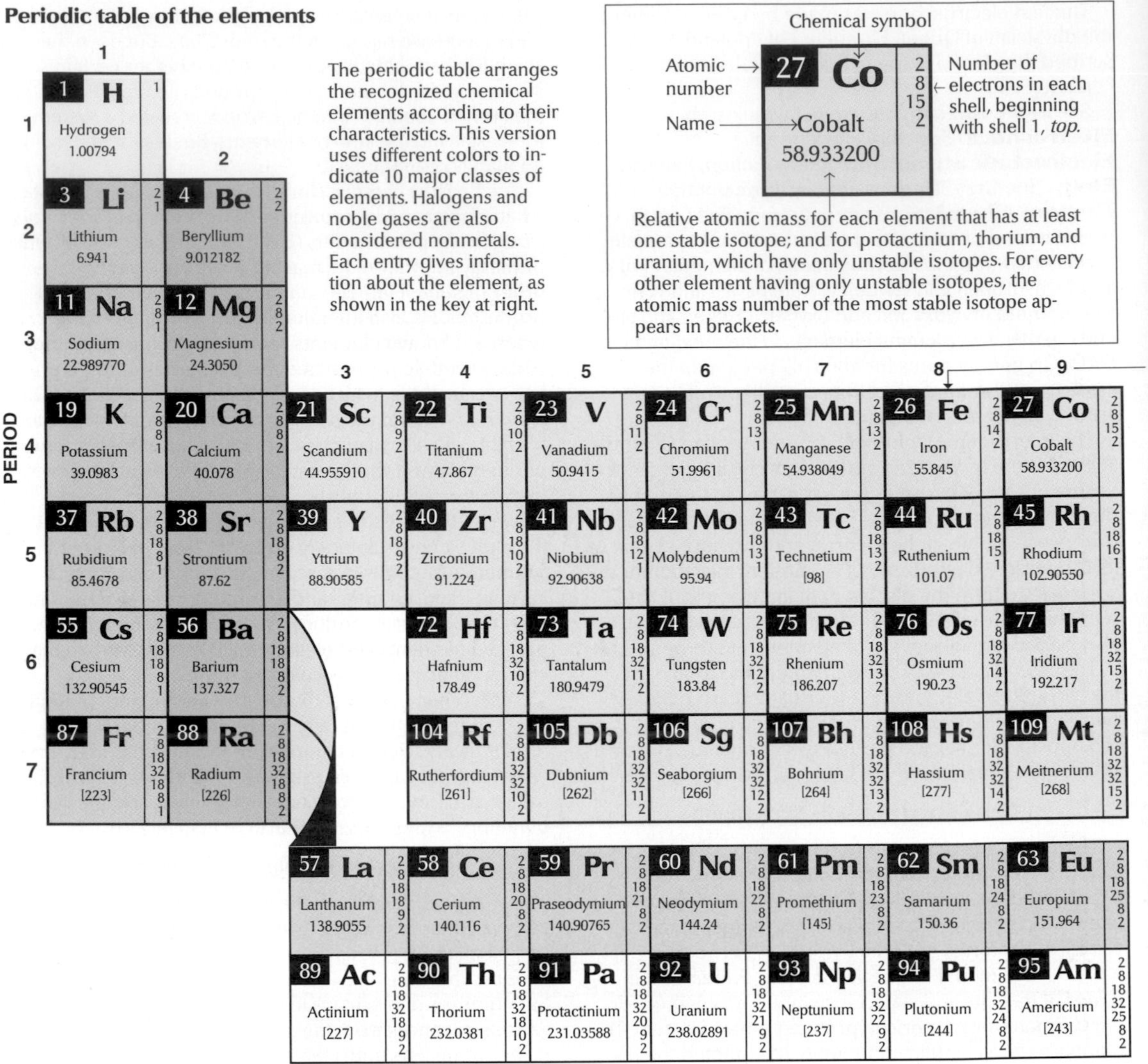

Table of the elements and their discoverers

Name	Symbol	Atomic number	Mass*	Discoverer	Country of discovery	Date of discovery
Actinium	Ac	89	[227]	André Debierne	France	1899
Aluminum	Al	13	26.981538	Hans Christian Oersted	Denmark	1825
Americium	Am	95	[243]	G. T. Seaborg; R. A. James; L. O. Morgan; A. Ghiorso	United States	1945
Antimony	Sb	51	121.760	Unknown; name applied to pure element in France in 1787		
Argon	Ar	18	39.948	Sir William Ramsay; Baron Rayleigh	United Kingdom	1894
Arsenic	As	33	74.92160	Uncertain; often credited to Albertus Magnus in Germany about		1250
Astatine	At	85	[210]	D. R. Corson; K. R. MacKenzie; E. Segrè	United States	1940
Barium	Ba	56	137.327	Sir Humphry Davy	United Kingdom	1808
Berkelium	Bk	97	[247]	G. T. Seaborg; S. G. Thompson; A. Ghiorso	United States	1949
Beryllium	Be	4	9.012182	Friedrich Wöhler; A. A. Bussy	Germany; France	1828
Bismuth	Bi	83	208.98038	Unknown; preparation described in Germany in 1556		
Bohrium	Bh	107	[264]	Heavy Ion Research Center	Germany	1981
Boron	B	5	10.811	H. Davy; J. L. Gay-Lussac; L. J. Thenard	U.K.; France	1808
Bromine	Br	35	79.904	Antoine J. Balard; Carl J. Löwig	France; Germany	1826

*A number without brackets is a relative atomic mass. A number in brackets is the atomic mass number of the most stable isotope of an element having only unstable isotopes. Data are from the International Union of Pure and Applied Chemistry and other sources.

Alkali metals	Other metals
Alkaline earth metals	Metalloids
Transition metals	Nonmetals
Lanthanide series (rare earths)	Halogens
Actinide series	Noble gases

10	11	12	13	14	15	16	17	18
								2 He Helium 4.002602 (2)
			5 B Boron 10.811 (2, 3)	6 C Carbon 12.0107 (2, 4)	7 N Nitrogen 14.0067 (2, 5)	8 O Oxygen 15.9994 (2, 6)	9 F Fluorine 18.9984032 (2, 7)	10 Ne Neon 20.1797 (2, 8)
			13 Al Aluminum 26.981538 (2, 8, 3)	14 Si Silicon 28.0855 (2, 8, 4)	15 P Phosphorus 30.973761 (2, 8, 5)	16 S Sulfur 32.065 (2, 8, 6)	17 Cl Chlorine 35.453 (2, 8, 7)	18 Ar Argon 39.948 (2, 8, 8)
28 Ni Nickel 58.6934 (2, 8, 16, 2)	29 Cu Copper 63.546 (2, 8, 18, 1)	30 Zn Zinc 65.39 (2, 8, 18, 2)	31 Ga Gallium 69.723 (2, 8, 18, 3)	32 Ge Germanium 72.64 (2, 8, 18, 4)	33 As Arsenic 74.92160 (2, 8, 18, 5)	34 Se Selenium 78.96 (2, 8, 18, 6)	35 Br Bromine 79.904 (2, 8, 18, 7)	36 Kr Krypton 83.80 (2, 8, 18, 8)
46 Pd Palladium 106.42 (2, 8, 18, 18, 0)	47 Ag Silver 107.8682 (2, 8, 18, 18, 1)	48 Cd Cadmium 112.411 (2, 8, 18, 18, 2)	49 In Indium 114.818 (2, 8, 18, 18, 3)	50 Sn Tin 118.710 (2, 8, 18, 18, 4)	51 Sb Antimony 121.760 (2, 8, 18, 18, 5)	52 Te Tellurium 127.60 (2, 8, 18, 18, 6)	53 I Iodine 126.90447 (2, 8, 18, 18, 7)	54 Xe Xenon 131.293 (2, 8, 18, 18, 8)
78 Pt Platinum 195.078 (2, 8, 18, 32, 17, 1)	79 Au Gold 196.96655 (2, 8, 18, 32, 18, 1)	80 Hg Mercury 200.59 (2, 8, 18, 32, 18, 2)	81 Tl Thallium 204.3833 (2, 8, 18, 32, 18, 3)	82 Pb Lead 207.2 (2, 8, 18, 32, 18, 4)	83 Bi Bismuth 208.98038 (2, 8, 18, 32, 18, 5)	84 Po Polonium [209] (2, 8, 18, 32, 18, 6)	85 At Astatine [210] (2, 8, 18, 32, 18, 7)	86 Rn Radon [222] (2, 8, 18, 32, 18, 8)
110 Ds Darmstadtium [281] (2, 8, 18, 32, 32, 16, 2)	111 Rg Roentgenium [280] (2, 8, 18, 32, 32, 18, 1)	112 Cn Copernicium [283] (2, 8, 18, 32, 32, 18, 2)		114 Fl Flerovium [289] (2, 8, 18, 32, 32, 18, 4)		116 Lv Livermorium [293] (2, 8, 18, 32, 32, 18, 6)		

64 Gd Gadolinium 157.25 (2, 8, 18, 25, 9, 2)	65 Tb Terbium 158.92534 (2, 8, 18, 27, 8, 2)	66 Dy Dysprosium 162.50 (2, 8, 18, 28, 8, 2)	67 Ho Holmium 164.93032 (2, 8, 18, 29, 8, 2)	68 Er Erbium 167.259 (2, 8, 18, 30, 8, 2)	69 Tm Thulium 168.93421 (2, 8, 18, 31, 8, 2)	70 Yb Ytterbium 173.04 (2, 8, 18, 32, 8, 2)	71 Lu Lutetium 174.967 (2, 8, 18, 32, 9, 2)
96 Cm Curium [247] (2, 8, 18, 32, 25, 9, 2)	97 Bk Berkelium [247] (2, 8, 18, 32, 26, 9, 2)	98 Cf Californium [251] (2, 8, 18, 32, 28, 8, 2)	99 Es Einsteinium [252] (2, 8, 18, 32, 29, 8, 2)	100 Fm Fermium [257] (2, 8, 18, 32, 30, 8, 2)	101 Md Mendelevium [258] (2, 8, 18, 32, 31, 8, 2)	102 No Nobelium [259] (2, 8, 18, 32, 32, 8, 2)	103 Lr Lawrencium [262] (2, 8, 18, 32, 32, 9, 2)

Table of the elements and their discoverers

Name	Symbol	Atomic number	Mass*	Discoverer	Country of discovery	Date of discovery
Cadmium	Cd	48	112.411	Friedrich Stromeyer	Germany	1817
Calcium	Ca	20	40.078	Sir Humphry Davy	United Kingdom	1808
Californium	Cf	98	[251]	G. T. Seaborg; S. G. Thompson; A. Ghiorso; K. Street, Jr.	United States	1950
Carbon	C	6	12.0107		Known to ancients	
Cerium	Ce	58	140.116	W. von Hisinger; J. Berzelius; M. Klaproth	Sweden; Germany	1803
Cesium	Cs	55	132.90545	Gustav Kirchhoff; Robert Bunsen	Germany	1860
Chlorine	Cl	17	35.453	Carl Wilhelm Scheele	Sweden	1774
Chromium	Cr	24	51.9961	Louis Vauquelin	France	1797
Cobalt	Co	27	58.933200	Georg Brandt	Sweden	Late 1730's
Copernicium	Cn	112	[285]	Heavy Ion Research Center	Germany	1996
Copper	Cu	29	63.546		Known to ancients	
Curium	Cm	96	[247]	G. T. Seaborg; R. A. James; A. Ghiorso	United States	1944
Darmstadtium	Ds	110	[281]	Heavy Ion Research Center	Germany	1994
Dubnium	Db	105	[262]	Joint Institute for Nuclear Research	Russia†	1971
				Lawrence Berkeley National Laboratory‡	United States	1970

*A number without brackets is a relative atomic mass. A number in brackets is the atomic mass number of the most stable isotope of an element having only unstable isotopes.
†Then part of the Soviet Union.
‡Then Lawrence Radiation Laboratory.

Table of the elements and their discoverers

Name	Sym-bol	Atomic number	Mass*	Discoverer	Country of discovery	Date of discovery
Dysprosium	Dy	66	162.50	Paul Émile Lecoq de Boisbaudran	France	1886
Einsteinium	Es	99	[252]	Argonne; Los Alamos; Berkeley	United States	1952
Erbium	Er	68	167.259	Carl Mosander	Sweden	1843
Europium	Eu	63	151.964	Eugène Demarçay	France	1901
Fermium	Fm	100	[257]	Argonne; Los Alamos; U. of Calif.	United States	1953
Fluorine	F	9	18.9984032	Henri Moissan	France	1886
Francium	Fr	87	[223]	Marguerite Perey	France	1939
Gadolinium	Gd	64	157.25	Jean de Marignac	Switzerland	1880
Gallium	Ga	31	69.723	Paul Émile Lecoq de Boisbaudran	France	1875
Germanium	Ge	32	72.64	Clemens Winkler	Germany	1886
Gold	Au	79	196.96655		Known to ancients	
Hafnium	Hf	72	178.49	Dirk Coster; Georg von Hevesy	Denmark	1923
Hassium	Hs	108	[277]	Heavy Ion Research Center	Germany	1984
Helium	He	2	4.002602	Sir William Ramsay; Nils Langlet; P. T. Cleve	United Kingdom; Sweden	1895
Holmium	Ho	67	164.93032	J. L. Soret	Switzerland	1878
Hydrogen	H	1	1.00794	Henry Cavendish	Britain	1766
Indium	In	49	114.818	Ferdinand Reich; H. Richter	Germany	1863
Iodine	I	53	126.90447	Bernard Courtois	France	1811
Iridium	Ir	77	192.217	Smithson Tennant	United Kingdom	1804
Iron	Fe	26	55.845		Known to ancients	
Krypton	Kr	36	83.80	Sir William Ramsay; M. W. Travers	United Kingdom	1898
Lanthanum	La	57	138.9055	Carl Mosander	Sweden	1839
Lawrencium	Lr	103	[262]	Joint Institute for Nuclear Research Lawrence Berkeley National Laboratory‡	Russia† United States	1961- 1971
Lead	Pb	82	207.2		Known to ancients	
Lithium	Li	3	6.941	Johann Arfvedson	Sweden	1817
Lutetium	Lu	71	174.967	Georges Urbain	France	1907
Magnesium	Mg	12	24.3050	Sir Humphry Davy	United Kingdom	1808
Manganese	Mn	25	54.938049	Johan Gahn	Sweden	1774
Meitnerium	Mt	109	[268]	Heavy Ion Research Center	Germany	1982
Mendelevium	Md	101	[258]	Lawrence Berkeley National Laboratory‡	United States	1958
Mercury	Hg	80	200.59		Known to ancients	
Molybdenum	Mo	42	95.94	Carl Wilhelm Scheele	Sweden	1778
Neodymium	Nd	60	144.24	C. F. Auer von Welsbach	Austria	1885
Neon	Ne	10	20.1797	Sir William Ramsay; M. W. Travers	United Kingdom	1898
Neptunium	Np	93	[237]	E. M. McMillan; P. H. Abelson	United States	1940
Nickel	Ni	28	58.6934	Axel Cronstedt	Sweden	1751
Niobium	Nb	41	92.90638	Charles Hatchett	United Kingdom	1801
Nitrogen	N	7	14.0067	Daniel Rutherford	Britain	1772
Nobelium	No	102	[259]	Joint Institute for Nuclear Research	Russia†	1966
Osmium	Os	76	190.23	Smithson Tennant	United Kingdom	1804
Oxygen	O	8	15.9994	Joseph Priestley; Carl Wilhelm Scheele	Britain; Sweden	1774
Palladium	Pd	46	106.42	William Wollaston	United Kingdom	1803
Phosphorus	P	15	30.973761	Hennig Brand	Germany	1669
Platinum	Pt	78	195.078	Julius Scaliger	Italy	1557
Plutonium	Pu	94	[244]	G. Seaborg; J. Kennedy; E. McMillan; A. C. Wahl	United States	1940
Polonium	Po	84	[209]	Pierre and Marie Curie	France	1898
Potassium	K	19	39.0983	Sir Humphry Davy	United Kingdom	1807
Praseodymium	Pr	59	140.90765	C. F. Auer von Welsbach	Austria	1885
Promethium	Pm	61	[145]	J. A. Marinsky; Lawrence E. Glendenin; Charles D. Coryell	United States	1945
Protactinium	Pa	91	231.03588	Otto Hahn; Lise Meitner; Frederick Soddy; John Cranston	Germany; United Kingdom	1917
Radium	Ra	88	[226]	Pierre and Marie Curie; Gustave Bémont	France	1898
Radon	Rn	86	[222]	Friedrich Ernst Dorn	Germany	1900
Rhenium	Re	75	186.207	Walter Noddack; Ida Tacke; Otto Berg	Germany	1925
Rhodium	Rh	45	102.90550	William Wollaston	1803	
Roentgenium	Rg	111	[280]	Heavy Ion Research Center	Germany	1994
Rubidium	Rb	37	85.4678	R. Bunsen; G. Kirchhoff	Germany	1861
Ruthenium	Ru	44	101.07	Karl Klaus	Russia	1844
Rutherfordium	Rf	104	[261]	Joint Institute for Nuclear Research Lawrence Berkeley National Laboratory‡	Russia† United States	1969- 1970
Samarium	Sm	62	150.36	Paul Émile Lecoq de Boisbaudran	France	1879
Scandium	Sc	21	44.955910	Lars Nilson	Sweden	1879
Seaborgium	Sg	106	[266]	Lawrence Berkeley National Laboratory§ Lawrence Livermore National Laboratory#	United States	1974
Selenium	Se	34	78.96	Jöns Berzelius	Sweden	1817
Silicon	Si	14	28.0855	Jöns Berzelius	Sweden	1823

*A number without brackets is a relative atomic mass. A number in brackets is the atomic mass number of the most stable isotope of an element having only unstable isotopes.
†Then part of the Soviet Union.
‡Then Lawrence Radiation Laboratory.
§Then Lawrence Berkeley Laboratory.
#Then Lawrence Livermore Laboratory.

Table of the elements and their discoverers

Name	Symbol	Atomic number	Mass*	Discoverer	Country of discovery	Date of discovery
Silver	Ag	47	107.8682		Known to ancients	
Sodium	Na	11	22.989770	Sir Humphry Davy	Britain	1807
Strontium	Sr	38	87.62	A. Crawford	Britain	1790
Sulfur	S	16	32.065		Known to ancients	
Tantalum	Ta	73	180.9479	Anders Ekeberg	Sweden	1802
Technetium	Tc	43	[98]	Carlo Perrier; Emilio Segrè	Italy	1937
Tellurium	Te	52	127.60	Franz Müller von Reichenstein	Romania	1782
Terbium	Tb	65	158.92534	Carl Mosander	Sweden	1843
Thallium	Tl	81	204.3833	Sir William Crookes	Britain	1861
Thorium	Th	90	232.0381	Jöns Berzelius	Sweden	1828
Thulium	Tm	69	168.93421	Per Theodor Cleve	Sweden	1879
Tin	Sn	50	118.710		Known to ancients	
Titanium	Ti	22	47.867	William Gregor	Britain	1791
Tungsten	W	74	183.84	Fausto and Juan José de Elhuyar	Spain	1783
Uranium	U	92	238.02891	Martin Klaproth	Germany	1789
Vanadium	V	23	50.9415	Nils Sefström	Sweden	1830
Xenon	Xe	54	131.293	Sir William Ramsay; M. W. Travers	Britain	1898
Ytterbium	Yb	70	173.04	Jean de Marignac	Switzerland	1878
Yttrium	Y	39	88.90585	Johann Gadolin	Finland	1794
Zinc	Zn	30	65.39	Andreas Marggraf	Germany	1746
Zirconium	Zr	40	91.224	Martin Klaproth	Germany	1789

*A number without brackets is a relative atomic mass. A number in brackets is the atomic mass number of the most stable isotope of an element having only unstable isotopes.

protons, number of neutrons, or both. Because the number of protons distinguishes one element from another, any change in the number of protons produces a different element. Such a change is called a *transmutation.*

An isotope that might decay is considered to be *unstable.* A *stable* isotope cannot decay. Of the recognized elements, 81 have one or more stable isotopes. The remaining elements have only unstable isotopes.

Different isotopes decay at different rates. The rate at which a given isotope decays is that isotope's *half-life*—the time taken for half the atoms in a sample of that isotope to decay. Half-lives vary tremendously. The half-life of meitnerium 268 is less than 1/10 of a second; the half-life of uranium 238 is almost 4 1/2 billion years.

To determine the half-life of an isotope, scientists measure the decay times of many atoms of that isotope. But when scientists have used particle accelerators to create isotopes of the heaviest elements in the periodic table—heavier than element 106, seaborgium—they have often produced only a few atoms of those isotopes. Those atoms and their decays have been detected one at a time. As a result, scientists do not express the stability of such isotopes in terms of half-life. Instead, they state the time between the creation of the isotope and its decay. They may give the value for a single atom or a range—or an average value—for all the atoms.

Atomic mass number. An isotope's atomic mass number is the total number of protons and neutrons in its nucleus. Chemists commonly designate an isotope by the name of the element followed by the isotope's atomic mass number. Thus, *copper 63* is an isotope of copper whose atomic mass number is 63. An atom of that isotope has 29 protons and 34 neutrons in its nucleus.

Relative atomic mass is the ratio of the mass of an isotope or an element to 1/12 of the mass of an atom of carbon 12, the most abundant form of carbon. Thus, carbon 12 serves as a mass standard for all other isotopes. An older term for relative atomic mass is *atomic weight.*

For an element with only one stable isotope, the relative atomic mass equals the mass of that isotope divided by $\frac{1}{12}$ of the mass of carbon 12. For an element with two or more stable isotopes, the relative atomic mass is an average value. That value depends on two factors: (1) the masses of the stable isotopes and (2) and the proportions in which those isotopes occur in nature.

For example, copper 63 and copper 65 are the only stable isotopes of that metal. Of the copper in nature, 69.17 percent is copper 63, which has a relative atomic mass of 62.93. The remaining 30.83 percent is copper 65, with a relative atomic mass of 64.93. The calculation for the relative atomic mass of copper is: $(62.93 \times 0.6917) + (64.93 \times 0.3083) = 63.55$. In this sample calculation, the values are rounded to four digits, and so the answer is approximate. The precise value listed in the table is 63.546.

The periodic table lists the relative atomic mass of each of the 81 elements that have at least one stable isotope. Of the elements with only unstable isotopes, thorium, protactinium, and uranium are most like elements with stable isotopes. Those three elements are plentiful in nature and have isotopes with long half-lives. As a result, the table also lists the average relative atomic masses of the three. The table lists atomic mass numbers for the remaining elements that have only unstable isotopes. In each case, the number listed is the atomic mass number of the isotope with the longest half-life.

Groups. Each column in the table lists a group of elements with similar chemical behavior—that is, they behave somewhat alike in forming compounds. Each group has a number from 1 to 18. The groups include the elements created only in particle accelerators. But scientists have not formed compounds with all those elements, so their chemical behavior is not always well known.

Electron shells. The similar behavior of elements in a group results from a similarity in their atoms' structure. An electrically balanced atom has the same number of electrons as there are protons in the atomic nucleus. The electrons are arranged in levels called electron shells, according to how much energy the electrons have. Generally, those closest to the nucleus have the least energy. When an electron absorbs energy, it either moves to a higher-energy shell or leaves the atom. Electrons in outer shells need to absorb the least energy to leave the atom.

Chemical reactions involve electrons' movement between atoms or a sharing of electrons by atoms. Thus, the electrons in an atom's outer shells control the atom's chemical behavior. In most groups in the table, the elements' outer shells have the same number of electrons.

Each electron shell has a number. The shell closest to the nucleus is *shell 1.* Each shell can hold only a certain quantity of electrons. Shells 1, 2, 3, 4, 5, 6, and 7 can hold, respectively, a maximum of 2, 8, 18, 32, 50, 72, and 98 electrons. However, no element has even five full shells because electrons tend to move to outer shells before the inner shells are full. The seven shells are sometimes called the K, L, M, N, O, P, and Q shells.

Classes. The periodic table uses colors to indicate classes of elements with similar properties. For example, the table in this article uses dark blue for the *noble gases,* gases that do not combine readily with other elements.

Richard L. Hahn

Related articles. Each officially recognized element has a separate article in *World Book.* See also:

Alkali metal
Lanthanide
Metal
Metalloid
Noble gas
Rare earth

Elementary and Secondary Education Act (ESEA) was the first major program of the United States government that was designed specifically to improve elementary and secondary education. The United States Congress passed the act in 1965 to support the federal government's aim of ending poverty in the nation. Under the 1964 Civil Rights Act, ESEA funds could go only to schools complying with federal desegregation orders. The U.S. Office of Education (now the Department of Education) administered ESEA.

Title I of the act established programs to help lower-income children designated as "educationally deprived." The programs included remedial reading and mathematics programs and special summer programs. Other sections of the act included benefits not limited to lower-income students. A 1966 amendment to ESEA provided funds for educational programs and facilities for children with disabilities. A 1968 amendment supplied funds for bilingual education programs.

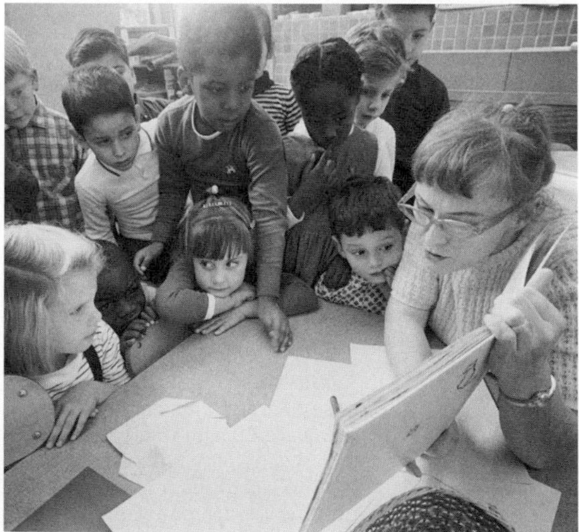

© Corbis/Bettmann

The Elementary and Secondary Education Act, passed in 1965, established such programs as remedial reading to help children learn. The teacher shown here reads to her students.

The Educational Consolidation and Improvement Act of 1981 was designed to update and improve ESEA services. It gave states more power to decide how to spend ESEA funds and reduced the need of the federal government to administer so many separate programs. Since 1981, Congress has reauthorized many ESEA programs.

In 2001, Congress passed legislation reauthorizing and revising ESEA and redefining the federal government's role in public education. The law, called the No Child Left Behind Act, introduced new federal requirements for student testing. It aimed to hold schools accountable for student progress and to assist students in schools that performed poorly. Frances Schoonmaker Bolin

See also **No Child Left Behind Act.**

Elementary school is a school for children from age 5 or 6 to age 12 or 14. Most elementary schools have six grades, though some have eight. Many include a kindergarten. Some elementary schools end with grade four, five, or six, and the students then enter a two-, three-, or four-year *middle school* or *junior high school.* Other elementary schools, called *primary schools,* cover only the first three grades. Increasingly, many schools are being reformed to focus on early childhood (pre-kindergarten to grade 1), lower elementary (grades 1-3), and upper elementary (grades 4-6). Elementary schools are sometimes called *grade schools* or *grammar schools.*

This article discusses types of elementary schools and how students are taught. For information on the history of elementary schools, see **School.**

Kinds of elementary schools. United States elementary schools may be *public, private, parochial,* or *charter.* Public schools are free and are supported by taxes. Private schools charge tuition and receive additional support from donations and gifts. Parochial schools are private schools operated by religious groups. Charter schools are public schools that operate independently of local school boards by agreement with the state.

Most elementary schools are organized as *graded* schools, where pupils of the same age study together. But some communities have *nongraded* or *ungraded* schools. Students in these schools are grouped according to ability and interest, and they advance in each subject at their own rate.

Elementary school instruction emphasizes three major areas of study: (1) communication, including reading, writing, listening, and speaking; (2) computation, which involves understanding and using numbers; and (3) character development, which deals with children's relationships with one another and their surroundings. Teachers also instruct students in such subjects as art, computers, health, music, science, and social studies.

Elementary schools seek to help children expand their knowledge of the world around them. The curriculum in many schools is based on a theme of expanding environments. In the first grade, pupils learn about the home and the family. Second-graders study the school and the neighborhood. In the third grade, teachers introduce information about one's own community in comparison with others. Fourth-graders study the state, fifth-graders

Building language skills is a major goal of elementary instruction. These students are using books, computers, and audio recordings as tools in reading, writing, and listening projects.

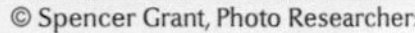
© Spencer Grant, Photo Researchers

Outdoor play at lunch or recess gives elementary school students fresh air, exercise, and a break from classroom activities. Play also provides an opportunity to see friends and develop social skills.

© Jeff I. Greenberg, Photo Researchers

study the nation, and sixth-graders, the world. In all grades, teachers help children develop social skills and help them learn to behave as members of a group.

Most elementary schools are divided into rooms in which one teacher instructs about 25 children, though many states have passed laws to reduce the student-to-teacher ratio. Such rooms are called *self-contained classrooms.* But some elementary schools have *open space classrooms,* sometimes called open classrooms. These classrooms have no walls separating them, or they have movable walls. Several classes may work together in one large area, or small groups may work separately. Both types of classrooms may have learning centers, where many kinds of instructional materials are available for students.

In lower or primary elementary grades, students may spend all or most of the day with one teacher. In the upper or intermediate grades, pupils may have special teachers for such subjects as art, music, physical education, and science. Some elementary schools use *team teaching,* in which a team of several teachers and teacher aides is responsible for 100 or more pupils.

David M. Callejo Pérez

See also **Alternative school; Early childhood education; Education** (Elementary education); **Parochial school; Private school.**

Elephants live in families of related females and their young. Adult males, called *bulls,* are more solitary, visiting family groups on occasion. This photograph shows a large bull with a family group in the background.

© Thinkstock

Elephant is the largest animal that lives on land. Among all animals, only some whales are larger than elephants. The elephant is also the second tallest member of the animal kingdom. Only the giraffe is taller. Elephants are the only animals that have a nose in the form of a long trunk, which they use as a hand. They have larger ears than any other animal, and their tusks are the largest teeth.

There are two chief kinds of elephants, *African elephants* and *Asian elephants,* also known as *Indian elephants.* African elephants live only in Africa south of the Sahara. Asian elephants live in parts of India and Southeast Asia.

Elephants are extremely strong and highly intelligent. People have tamed and trained them for thousands of years. The logging industry in some Asian countries uses elephants to carry heavy loads. People throughout the world enjoy watching elephants in circuses and zoos. Trained circus elephants stand on their heads, lie down and roll over, dance, and perform other tricks.

One of the earliest recorded uses of elephants took place in war. In 331 B.C., a Macedonian army led by Alexander the Great defeated Persian soldiers who rode elephants in battle. In 218 B.C., the famous general Hannibal of Carthage used elephants when he crossed the Alps and invaded Italy.

During the 1800's, an African elephant named Jumbo was featured by the London Zoo for more than 17 years. Visitors came from all parts of the world to see Jumbo, the largest animal in captivity at that time. He stood 11 feet (3.4 meters) tall and weighed more than 14,500 pounds (6,600 kilograms). In 1882, the American showman P. T. Barnum purchased Jumbo and made the elephant a star attraction of his circus. The word *jumbo* became a common adjective for anything extremely large.

Some people travel to Africa and parts of Asia to see wild elephants in their own environment. However, the number of wild elephants has greatly declined because people kill elephants for their ivory tusks. In addition, people have settled on much of the land where the animals lived, resulting in a loss of habitat for the elephants. Farming and industry threaten the natural resources needed by elephants to survive.

There is some uncertainty about the number of elephants that survive in the wild. In Asia, human population growth and habitat destruction have severely reduced the number of wild elephants. Scientists estimate that only about 50,000 Asian elephants survive in the wild. In Africa, the main cause of the decline in the number of elephants is illegal hunting. In 1979, an estimated 1,300,000 elephants lived in Africa. Today, there are about 500,000.

A public awareness campaign was launched in the late 1980's to save the African elephant. People throughout the world were made aware that thousands of elephants were being slaughtered every year to provide ivory jewelry and carvings. Japan was the greatest consumer of ivory. The Japanese used half the ivory that they imported for signature seals, traditional carved stamps used to print their names in ink. Wildlife experts estimated that 12,000 elephants were killed each year to obtain ivory for these seals.

The importance of elephants

Wild elephants perform several important natural functions. For example, they help turn densely wooded areas into more open areas by feeding on trees and other plants. More kinds of animals can live in these open habitats. Elephants also dig up dry riverbeds to reach the water beneath the surface of the ground. Other animals then drink this water. When elephants travel through wooded areas, they create paths used by such animals as antelope and zebras.

Kinds of elephants

African elephants are larger than Asian elephants. An African elephant is about the same height at the shoulder and the rump. Its back dips slightly in the middle. Adult African *bull* (male) elephants stand about 11 feet (3.4 meters) tall at the shoulder and weigh about 12,000 pounds (5,400 kilograms). The *cows* (females) are about 9 feet (2.8 meters) tall and weigh about 8,000 pounds (3,600 kilograms). The largest known elephant, an African bull, measured 13 feet 2 inches (4.01 meters) tall. The heaviest elephant ever weighed was over 14,500 pounds (6,600 kilograms).

Most African elephants have dark gray skin. Their forehead forms a smooth curve. Their ears measure as wide as 4 feet (1.2 meters) and cover their shoulders. Both the bulls and cows have tusks. The tusks of most African bulls grow from 6 to 8 feet (1.8 to 2.4 meters) long and weigh 50 to 100 pounds (23 to 45 kilograms) each. The tusks of most of the cows weigh from 15 to 20 pounds (7 to 9 kilograms) each. The longest tusk of an African elephant measured 11 ½ feet (3.5 meters), and the heaviest weighed 293 pounds (133 kilograms).

The trunk of an African elephant has two fleshy, fingerlike structures on the tip. The skin of the trunk has deep wrinkles. African elephants have four or five toes on each forefoot and three toes on each hind foot. A loose fold of skin joins the hind legs and the sides of the body. Asian elephants do not have this fold.

Wild African elephants live only in Africa south of the Sahara. There are two types, or subspecies, of African elephants—*forest elephants* and *bush elephants*, also known as *savanna elephants*. Bush elephants, which live in most countries south of the Sahara, are larger and have heavier tusks. Forest elephants live in Cameroon, Congo (Brazzaville), Congo (Kinshasa), Côte d'Ivoire, and other countries of central and western Africa. Both kinds of African elephants inhabit forests, grasslands, mountains, swamps, and shrubby areas. Many scientists consider the two types of African elephants to be separate species. Some scientists argue that there is a third species of African elephant, the west African elephant, that inhabits forests and savannas in western Africa.

Asian elephants live only in southern and southeastern Asia. They are found in forests and jungles of Cambodia, China, India, Indonesia, Malaysia, Myanmar, Sri Lanka, Thailand, and Vietnam.

Asian elephants have an arched back slightly higher than the shoulder and rump. An adult Asian bull stands from 9 to 10 ½ feet (2.7 to 3.2 meters) tall at the shoulder and weighs up to 8,000 pounds (3,600 kilograms). The largest known Asian bull measured 10 feet 8 inches (3.3 meters) tall. Asian cows stand about 8 feet (2.4 meters) tall and weigh about 6,600 pounds (3,000 kilograms).

Most Asian elephants have light gray skin and may have pink or white spots. An Asian elephant has two humps on its forehead just above the ears. The ears are about half as large as those of an African elephant and do not cover the shoulder. Most Asian bulls have tusks

Interesting facts about elephants

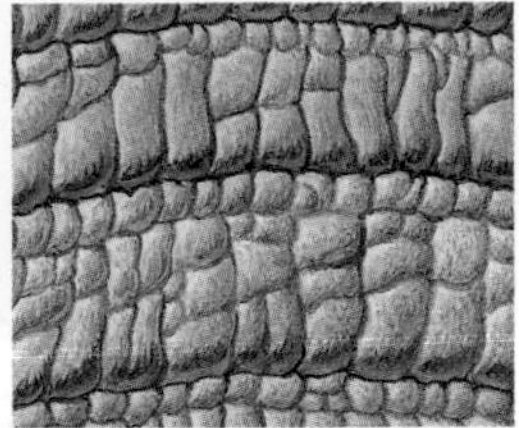

The skin of an elephant is gray and wrinkled. An adult elephant's skin measures up to 1 ½ inches (3 centimeters) thick and weighs about 1 ton (0.9 metric ton). However, it is surprisingly tender. Flies, mosquitoes, and other insects can bite into the skin.

An angry or frightened elephant can run at a speed of more than 25 miles (40 kilometers) an hour for a short distance. On a long journey, a herd of elephants travels at about 10 miles (16 kilometers) an hour.

An elephant uses its trunk as a hand. The trunk can carry a 600-pound (272-kilogram) log or an object as small as a coin. Elephants also breathe and smell with their trunks.

Elephants love water and frequently bathe in lakes and rivers. They are excellent swimmers. An elephant gives itself a shower by shooting a stream of water from its trunk.

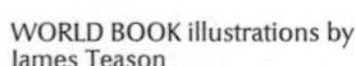

WORLD BOOK illustrations by James Teason

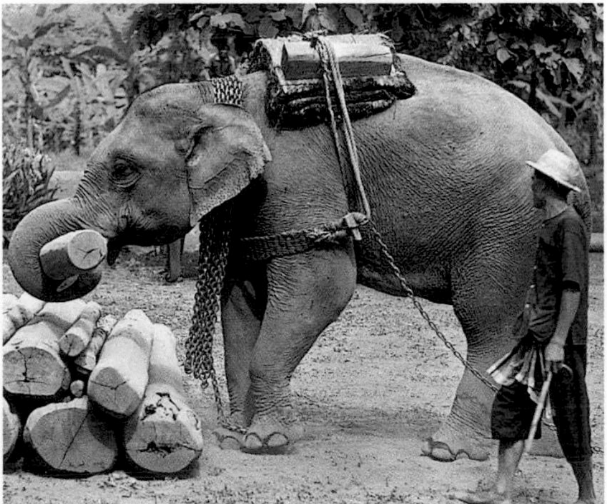

Neal Ulevich

Trained elephants, such as the Asian elephant shown here, are used in the logging industry in several Asian countries. An elephant can carry heavy loads with its trunk or on its back.

How African and Asian elephants differ

The two chief kinds of elephants, African elephants and Asian elephants, differ in size and body features. For example, African elephants are larger and have bigger tusks. These drawings show various physical differences between the two species.

WORLD BOOK illustrations by John D. Dawson

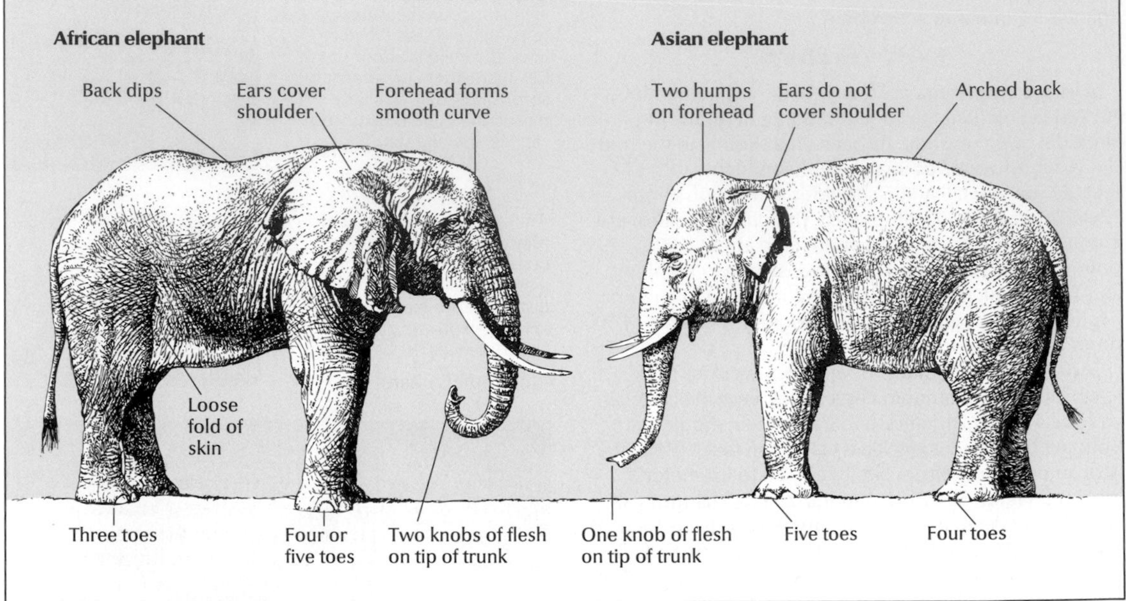

that grow from 4 to 5 feet (1.2 to 1.5 meters) long. However, some Asian males, called *makhnas,* have no tusks, and many Asian females have none. Other Asian females have extremely short tusks called *tushes.*

The trunk of an Asian elephant has smoother skin than that of an African elephant and only one fingerlike structure on the tip. Most Asian elephants have five toes on each forefoot and four on each hind foot.

The body of an elephant

The height of an adult elephant about equals the length of the back of the elephant from head to tail. Scientists may or may not include the length of the trunk as well when giving the total length. An elephant has a short, muscular neck and an enormous head with huge, triangular ears. The trunk extends from the upper jaw, and a tusk may grow from each side of the jaw at the base of the trunk. Massive legs support the body. An elephant's tail is small in relation to the rest of the animal. It measures about 3 ½ feet (1 meter) long.

Skin and hair. Elephants have gray, wrinkled skin that hangs in loose folds. The skin of an adult measures up to 1 ½ inches (3 centimeters) thick. It weighs about 2,000 pounds (900 kilograms). Elephants are called *pachyderms,* a term that comes from a Greek word meaning *thick-skinned.* However, an elephant's skin is surprisingly tender. Some insects, including flies and mosquitoes, can bite into the skin.

An elephant has no sweat glands, and so it must cool off in other ways. It may get rid of excess body heat by flapping its enormous ears or by spraying water on itself. Elephants also stay cool by rolling in mud. The mud dries on the skin and thus shields it from the sun.

At birth, elephants are often covered with sparse brown, black, or reddish-brown hair that gradually wears off as they get older. Adults appear to be nearly hairless. But there are bristles around the ears, eyes, and mouth, and sparse hair on the trunk, legs, and other parts. The end of the tail has a long bunch of thick hairs.

Trunk. An elephant's trunk is a combined nose and upper lip. It consists of a strong, flexible, boneless mass of flesh. An adult's trunk measures about 5 feet (1.5 meters) long and weighs about 300 pounds (140 kilograms).

An elephant breathes and smells with its trunk and uses it when eating and drinking. The animal sniffs the air and the ground almost constantly with its trunk. It carries food and water to its mouth with its trunk. It also gives itself a shower by sucking water into the trunk and then spraying it out again. The trunk of an adult can hold about 1 ½ gallons (6 liters) of water.

An elephant grasps objects with its trunk much as a person does with a hand. The trunk can carry a log that weighs up to 600 pounds (272 kilograms). The trunk's tip can pick up an object as small as a coin. An elephant also uses its trunk to communicate with other elephants. When two elephants greet each other, each places the tip of its trunk in the other's mouth. A mother will comfort her calf by stroking it with her trunk. Young males play-fight by wrestling with their trunks. In a true fight, the trunk is usually protected by curling it under the chin.

Tusks and teeth. An elephant's tusks are actually long, curved upper teeth called *incisors.* They are made of ivory. About two-thirds of each tusk extends from the upper jaw. The rest is in the skull. Elephants use their tusks to dig for food and water and to fight. The tusks can lift and carry a load weighing as much as 2,000 pounds (900 kilograms). Many Asian females and some Asian males have no tusks.

Elephants also have four *molars* (back teeth). The molars of an adult may measure 1 foot (30 centimeters) long and weigh about 8 $\frac{1}{2}$ pounds (4 kilograms). These teeth have jagged edges that help grind food. One molar lies on each side of both jaws, and additional molars form in the back of the mouth. The molars in front gradually wear down and drop out, and the ones in back push forward and replace them. An elephant grows six sets of molars during its lifetime. Each set consists of four teeth. The last set of molars appears when the animal is about 40 years old.

Legs and feet. The legs of an elephant are pillarlike structures. The feet are nearly round. Each foot has a thick pad of tissue that acts as a cushion. The foot expands under the elephant's weight and contracts when the animal lifts the leg. Elephants may sink deep into mud, but they can pull their legs out easily because the feet become smaller when lifted.

Senses. The trunk provides a keen sense of smell, and elephants depend on this sense more than on any other. They frequently wave their trunks high in the air to catch the scent of food or enemies. An elephant can smell a human being more than a mile (1.6 kilometers) away.

Elephants also have good hearing. They can make and hear sounds below the range of human hearing. These low sounds, called *infrasound,* travel farther than higher sounds. Elephants can communicate with each other at a distance of at least 2 $\frac{1}{2}$ miles (4 kilometers), and possibly twice that distance.

The elephant's sense of touch is most keen in its trunk, especially at the tip. An elephant can recognize the shape of an object and whether the object is rough or smooth and hot or cold.

Elephants have poor sight. Their eyes are small in relation to the enormous head. An elephant cannot turn its head completely, and so it can see only in the front and to the sides. The animal must turn around to see anything behind it.

Intelligence. Elephants have a large brain and rank high in intelligence among animals. In the wild, their social lives are complex and involve learning many behaviors and communication skills. Studies of the African elephant have shown that these animals make at least 25 different calls, each with a specific meaning. Elephants have excellent memories, which they use both in their social activities and in their travels over large areas. It seems that the *matriarch* (ruling mother) is the carrier of knowledge for the whole family. She knows the migration routes, where to find trees with fruit, how to find water during droughts, and other information for survival. This knowledge is passed on to the younger females in her family and eventually one of them will become the matriarch.

In captivity, an elephant can learn to perform a variety of tasks and tricks. Training methods differ. Some training is brutal, with trainers beating the elephant with sharp instruments and eventually breaking its will. Other trainers have tried more gentle methods and have had good results. Elephants are fast learners. A well-trained working elephant may know as many as 40 voice commands.

The life of an elephant

Elephant families. Adult males and females live separately most of the time. The cows and their babies, called *calves,* live in family units averaging about 10 members each. Families consist of three or four related adult females and their offspring, which range from newborn calves to calves up to about 12 years old. Each family is led by the oldest female, the matriarch. Males leave the family as they become adults. Adult males form loose bonds with other males and only visit the family groups occasionally.

A *population* of elephants is made up of all the family groups and independent adult males that share one area. Populations vary in size from a few hundred elephants to several thousand. Each population ranges over a particular area in search of food. In semidesert areas, elephants may have to travel over vast distances to find food. In areas with high rainfall and abundant vegetation, a population may limit itself to as little as 100 square miles (250 square kilometers).

WORLD BOOK illustration by James Teason and John D. Dawson

Internal anatomy of a female African elephant

This view of a female African elephant shows the animal's skeleton and some of its internal organs. An elephant's organs resemble those of other mammals but are much larger. For example, an elephant's heart is about 5 times as large as a human heart and more than 50 times as heavy.

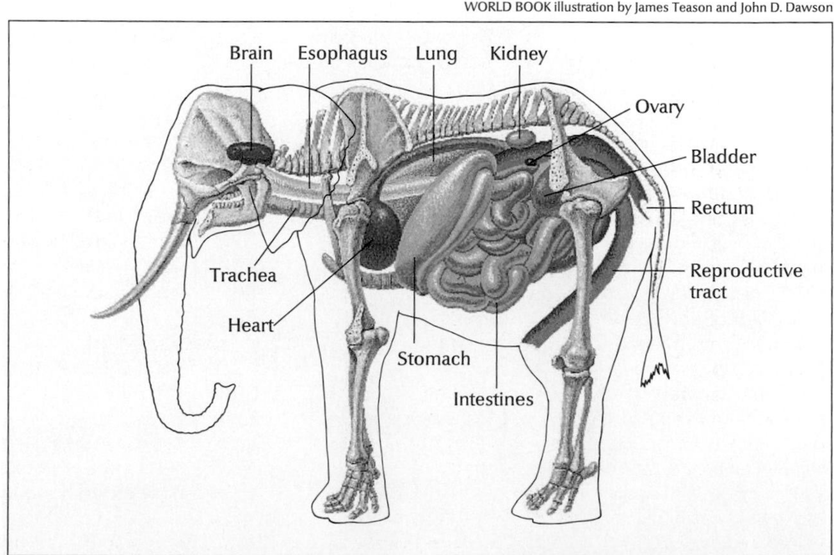

Wild elephants usually eat for about 16 hours every day. They bathe in lakes and rivers and like to roll in muddy water. After a mud bath, an elephant may cover itself with dirt. The dirt coating helps protect the animal's skin from the sun and insects. Elephants often play by tussling among themselves with their tusks and trunks.

Elephants communicate with one another in various ways, including postures, gestures, odors, and, especially, sounds. Elephants make many kinds of rumbling sounds, and each has a different meaning. For example, an elephant calf makes a hoarse, loud rumble when it is frightened, and a mother elephant uses a low, humming rumble to calm her calf. Other sounds made by elephants to communicate include screams, roars, bellows, groans, and squeaks.

Food. Elephants eat grass, water plants, and the leaves, roots, bark, branches, and fruit of trees and shrubs. Using their heads as battering rams, they sometimes knock down small trees to reach the highest leaves. An elephant can knock down a tree that measures 30 feet (9 meters) in height and has a diameter of almost 2 feet (61 centimeters).

Elephants use their tusks to rip the bark off trees. They also dig up roots and shrubs with their tusks. Elephants especially like bamboo, berries, coconuts, corn, dates, plums, and sugar cane. Elephants do not eat the flesh of other animals.

A large adult wild elephant eats about 300 pounds (140 kilograms) of vegetation a day. Wild elephants drink up to 40 gallons (150 liters) of water daily. An elephant can live without water for about three days and may travel as far as 50 miles (80 kilometers) to find it.

Travel. The padded feet of an elephant enable the animal to walk and run with surprisingly little noise. Elephants normally walk at a speed of 3 to 6 miles (5 to 10 kilometers) an hour. When making a long journey, a family walks at about 10 miles (16 kilometers) an hour. An angry or frightened elephant can run more than 25 miles (40 kilometers) an hour, but only for a short distance. An elephant walks and runs with shuffling steps. It cannot jump because of its weight and the structure of its legs.

Peter Davey, Bruce Coleman Inc.

Elephants touch trunks as a greeting. The animals also communicate among themselves by making a variety of low, rumbling noises.

Elephants usually roll in mud or swim at least once a day. They are excellent swimmers and have been known to swim to islands in lakes or off seacoasts. They hold their trunks above water when swimming.

Reproduction. Male elephants reach adulthood when they are 10 to 14 years old. But most do not mate until they are over 30 years old. The main reason for this delay is that older males prevent younger males from mating by chasing them away. In addition, females do not usually accept teen-aged males as mates. Females stay in their family and begin mating at an average age of 12. They may have their first calf at age 13 or 14 and usually produce one every four to five years until well into their 50's.

The female carries her young for 22 months. She almost always has one calf at a time, but twins occasion-

C. Haagner, Bruce Coleman Inc.

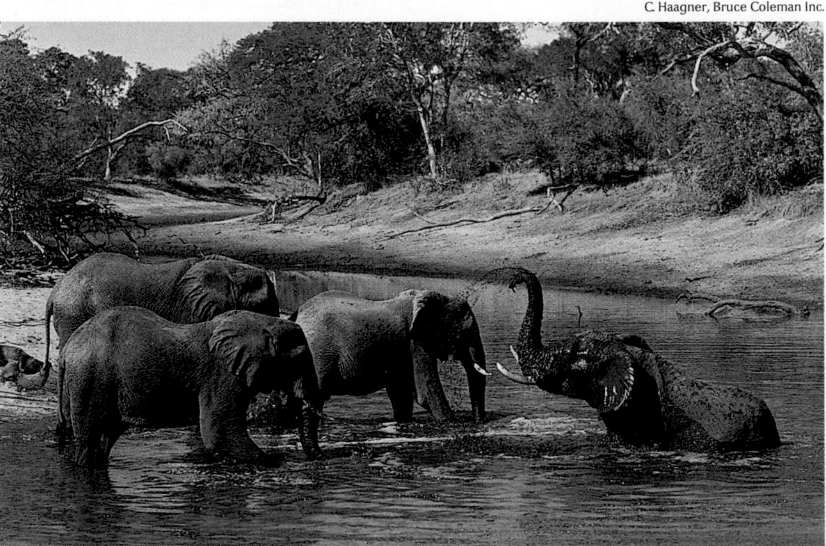

Elephants cool off by bathing. They especially like to roll in muddy water. The mud dries on the animal's skin and helps protect it from the sun. An elephant needs water and mud for cooling because its skin has no sweat glands.

Peter Davey, Bruce Coleman Inc.

A baby elephant stays with its mother until it reaches adulthood. The youngster drinks the mother's milk for three to five years. Female offspring stay with the mother until she dies.

ally are born. African elephant calves weigh from 255 to 320 pounds (116 to 145 kilograms) at birth and stand approximately 3 feet (95 centimeters) tall at the shoulder. Newborn Asian elephant calves weigh about 220 pounds (100 kilograms) and are about 2 ⅘ feet (85 centimeters) tall.

A baby elephant can walk less than an hour after birth. Its mother stays close to the youngster and protects it for several years. At first, the calf lives chiefly on the mother's milk. The young elephant drinks the milk by curling its trunk over its head so its mouth can reach the mother's breast. When the calf is 3 to 4 months old, it starts to graze on grass and other plant life. Male calves stay with the mother until they are about 14 years of age. Female offspring remain with the mother until she dies. Elephants grow throughout their lifetime. As a result, the older an elephant is, the bigger it is. Males grow more than females, and a large adult male in his 40's is almost twice the size of a female that age.

Musth. An elephant has a *temporal gland* on each side of its head, about midway between the eye and the ear. About once a year, the temporal glands of large adult males swell and discharge a dark, oily substance that has a strong odor. This substance stains the elephant's face. The temporal glands are active for two or three months yearly. During this period, an elephant is in a condition called *musth* or *must* (both pronounced *muhst*). In the wild, musth usually occurs only in adult male elephants over 25 years old.

While in musth, a captive elephant becomes dangerous if it gets excited. It may attack nearby animals, including people and other elephants. Elephants in captivity must be chained or caged during musth.

Zoologists are just beginning to understand the role of musth, which occurs periodically at a time when the elephant's body produces more than the normal amount of a hormone called *testosterone.* A male in musth has certain advantages over bulls not in musth. Although elephants also mate when not in musth, the musth male is more aggressive and thus able to fight for and guard a female. A female elephant is more likely to mate with a male in musth. Females are ready to mate during a period of sexual excitement called *estrus,* which lasts about four days at a time.

Protection against enemies. The great size of elephants protects them from almost all other animals. Lions in Africa and tigers in Asia can kill elephant calves, but such instances are rare. When under attack, the elephant family forms a circle around the calves to protect them. An elephant may scare an enemy away by sticking its ears straight out and charging. If an animal attacks, an elephant may crush it to death by stepping on it.

The greatest enemies of elephants are human beings. Until modern times, elephants could often protect themselves from hunters by a group defense. Now whole families of elephants can be gunned down by hunters.

Elephants are easily frightened in areas where they are hunted. A sudden noise, such as a gunshot, can cause a herd to panic. The animals may charge at the source of the noise or stampede away from it. When frightened or excited, elephants sometimes use their trunks to make a loud, shrill cry called *trumpeting.*

Life span. An elephant can live about 65 years. If it does not die from drought or disease or is not killed by hunters, the cause of death will usually be the wearing down of the sixth—and final—set of molars. Once the last set is worn down, the elephant dies of malnutrition.

Some people believe that old elephants go to certain places called "elephant graveyards" to die. This belief may have started because sick or aged elephants tend to go to a part of their range where there is shade and soft vegetation. In these places, people have found the bones of many elephants.

Protecting elephants

Elephants are the only survivors of a group of mammals called *proboscideans.* This group of animals once consisted of more than 350 species, all of which had long snouts or trunks. The earliest known proboscideans lived in Africa and Asia about 50 million years ago. Other proboscideans included the *mammoth* and the *mastodon.* Both animals looked much like the elephant.

Norman Myers, Bruce Coleman Inc.

A charging elephant may make itself look especially dangerous by sticking its ears straight out. Elephants sometimes crush enemies to death by stepping on them.

Today, wildlife experts agree that elephants are in great danger and need human protection to survive. People have destroyed much of the elephant's natural surroundings by clearing land for settlement and farms.

Many African and Asian nations have set aside land to protect the habitats of elephants and other wild animals. This land lies in national parks and in areas called *reserves.* But some wildlife experts fear that this amount of land is not large enough to save many wild elephants.

Illegal hunting for ivory also threatens the survival of wild elephants. Laws forbid elephant hunting in national parks and in reserves, and they limit the number that sport hunters may kill outside these areas. Sport hunting can usually be controlled, but poachers with automatic weapons can kill thousands of elephants yearly.

The number of African elephants greatly declined in the 1970's and 1980's. As a result, all trade in ivory and other elephant products was banned by the Convention on International Trade in Endangered Species of Wild Fauna and Flora (CITES) in 1989. Beginning in 1997, however, CITES members have allowed such African countries as Botswana, Namibia, and South Africa to export certain nonivory elephant products and to sell, on a limited basis, small amounts of ivory to Japan and other countries. The actions taken by CITES have helped slow the decline of African elephants. Cynthia Moss

Scientific classification. The African elephant is *Loxodonta africana.* The Asian, or Indian, elephant is *Elephas maximus.* The African bush elephant is *L. africana africana* if treated as a subspecies. The African forest elephant is *L. africana cyclotis* if treated as a subspecies.

Related articles in *World Book* include:

Animal
Circus
Ear (The ears of animals; picture)
Hannibal
Ivory
Mammoth
Mastodon
Poaching
Republican Party (picture)

Outline

I. The importance of elephants
II. Kinds of elephants
A. African elephants
B. Asian elephants
III. The body of an elephant
A. Skin and hair
B. Trunk
C. Tusks and teeth
D. Legs and feet
E. Senses
F. Intelligence
IV. The life of an elephant
A. Elephant families
B. Food
C. Travel
D. Reproduction
E. Musth
F. Protection against enemies
G. Life span
V. Protecting elephants

Additional resources

Ammann, Karl, and Peterson, Dale. *Elephant Reflections.* Univ. of Calif. Pr., 2009.
Denis-Huot, Christine and Michel. *The Art of Being an Elephant.* Barnes & Noble, 2003.
Joubert, Beverly and Dereck. *Face to Face with Elephants.* National Geographic Soc., 2008. Younger readers.
Meredith, Martin. *Elephant Destiny: Biography of an Endangered Species.* PublicAffairs, 2003.
O'Connell, Caitlin. *The Elephant's Secret Sense: The Hidden Life of the Wild Herds of Africa.* Free Pr., 2007.
Schlaepfer, Gloria G. *Elephants.* Benchmark Bks., 2003. Younger readers.

WORLD BOOK illustration by Trevor Boyer, Linden Artists Ltd.

The elephant bird, now extinct, could not fly.

Elephant bird is any of several *species* (kinds) of giant extinct birds that once lived on the island of Madagascar. These birds could not fly. The largest was about 9 feet (2.7 meters) high and weighed about 1,000 pounds (450 kilograms). Eggs that could hold 2 gallons (8 liters) were found with the birds' bones. The eggs were the largest known single cells in any animal.

Elephant birds lived on Madagascar when people first arrived there about 2,000 years ago. The birds probably were widespread on the island until the A.D. 900's. People may have contributed greatly to their extinction. Some people think legends of the giant bird called the *roc* were based on knowledge of elephant birds.

Simon James Clarke

Scientific classification. Elephant birds belong to the elephant bird family, Aepyornithidae.

Elephant man's disease. See Neurofibromatosis.

Elephant seal is the name for the two largest kinds of seals. The *southern elephant seal* lives in the Southern Ocean.The *northern elephant seal* inhabits the northeastern Pacific Ocean. A male southern elephant seal can weigh up to 8,800 pounds (4,000 kilograms). The male northern elephant seal may reach about 5,000 pounds (2,268 kilograms). Females of both types are much smaller. They weigh from 880 to 1,300 pounds (400 to 590 kilograms). Elephant seals get their name from their large size and from the male's long nose. The nose resembles an elephant's trunk.

Males establish *harems,* groups of females with whom they mate. The breeding season lasts about three months, from winter to early spring. During that time, the adults remain on land and do not eat. Males defend their harems from other males with loud noises, threatening gestures, and fights. Females usually give birth to one *pup* (baby seal).

Elephant seals swim with their hind flippers. They undertake two major migrations each year in search of food. The first occurs after the breeding season and

Daniel P. Costa

A huge male northern elephant seal defends a group of many smaller females, with whom he mates. The male has a large nose that somewhat resembles an elephant's trunk.

lasts several weeks. Elephant seals then briefly return to land to *molt* (shed their skin) before beginning a second migration that lasts up to eight months. The seals travel thousands of miles or kilometers in the ocean. They routinely dive 2,000 feet (610 meters) or more to feed on such animals as octopuses, squids, and sharks. Dives can last as long as two hours. Elephant seals may live from 14 to 20 years in the wild. Daniel P. Costa

Scientific classification. The scientific name of the northern elephant seal is *Mirounga angustirostris.* The southern elephant seal is *M. leonina.*

See also **Seal.**

Elephant shrew is a small mouselike mammal with a long, flexible nose. The nose somewhat resembles an elephant's trunk. Elephant shrews are not true shrews but are classified in their own order. They grow from 3 to 12 inches (8 to 30 centimeters) long and weigh 1 ½ to 19 ounces (42 to 540 grams). They have large eyes and ears, relatively long legs, a long tail, and normally gray or brown fur. There are about 20 *species* (kinds).

© Tom McHugh, Photo Researchers

An elephant shrew has a long, flexible nose that somewhat resembles an elephant's trunk. The animal uses its nose to find food, including insects, spiders, worms, and plants.

Elephant shrews live throughout much of Africa. They use their long, sensitive nose to find food, which includes insects, spiders, worms, and occasionally plants.

Elephant shrews usually have only one mate for life. In many species, each male and female pair establishes a territory and defends it together. The male protects the territory from other males. The female protects it from other females. Female elephant shrews usually give birth to one or two offspring at a time. The young leave their parents after one to two months. Elephant shrews can survive up to four years in the wild. Fred Koontz

Scientific classification. Elephant shrews make up the order Macroscelidea.

Elephantiasis, *EHL uh fuhn TY uh sihs,* is a skin disease that is most common in the tropics. It gets its name because the affected skin becomes rough and thickened like an elephant hide. It is usually caused by a tiny worm called the *filaria,* which is carried by mosquitoes (see **Filaria**). When the mosquito bites, the worm enters the body and eventually lodges in the lymph vessels. The disease is also called *lymphatic filariasis.* A rarer form of elephantiasis is caused by the streptococcus bacterium.

Elephantiasis is characterized by fever, roughening of the skin, and swelling of a part of the body, often the leg. There usually is a series of attacks, each increasing the swelling of the affected part. The disease is curable in early stages. However, once the part becomes permanently enlarged, there is no known cure. Drugs and surgery may give relief. Paul R. Bergstresser

Elephant's-ear is a plant with large leaves shaped like an elephant's ear or a shield. There are two types. In the South Pacific, one type is eaten like potatoes and is also known as *taro, eddo* (also spelled *eddoe*) or *dasheen.* The elephant's-ear grown in flower beds is similar, but has a smaller root and a more beautiful leaf.

David A. Francko

Scientific classification. The scientific name of elephant's-ear is *Colocasia esculenta.*

See also **Caladium; Taro.**

Eleusinian Mysteries. See Mysteries.

Elevated railroad, usually called an *el,* is an electric railroad that runs on tracks above other traffic. Steel or concrete structures support the tracks. Elevated railroads help lessen traffic on the street level, but they also block some sunlight to the street.

An elevated train gets its power through an electrified third rail, which runs beside the regular rails. Most railcars can propel themselves. A car picks up electric current through two metal plates called *shoes.* The shoes run along the third rail, delivering current through wires to two *traction motors.* The motors turn *driving wheels,* which propel the car along the track. The car operator uses a device called a controller to regulate the amount of current going to the motors and thus the train's speed. See **Electric railroad.**

Colonel Charles T. Harvey built a one-track experimental elevated line in New York City in 1867. American inventor Rufus Gilbert developed the standard elevated structure used in New York City and Chicago. The first cars were elaborate, with mahogany woodwork, carpeted floors, and plush seats. Robert C. Post

See also **Chicago** (Downtown Chicago; picture).

Elevator is a device that carries people and freight up and down the floors of a building. The word *elevator*

usually means the car in which the people or freight travel. But the term also refers to the entire system. The car travels up and down in a shaft. Steel guide rails in the shaft prevent movement sideways. In the United Kingdom and some other countries, an elevator is called a *lift.*

The development of elevators led to the construction of skyscrapers. Elevators enabled architects to design taller buildings because people no longer had to climb stairs to the upper floors.

The passenger elevators in office and residential buildings can carry from roughly 2,000 to 5,000 pounds (900 to 2,300 kilograms). Some freight elevators can carry as much as 100,000 pounds (45,000 kilograms).

How elevators work. Most elevators operate automatically. Only a few elevators are run by attendants who ride in the cars. A person brings an elevator to a certain floor by pushing a "call" button in the wall. The elevator doors open automatically after the car arrives at the floor. They close after the passenger has entered the elevator. The passenger pushes a button to indicate the floor where he or she wants the elevator to stop.

Most elevators in buildings of 10 or more floors are powered by electric traction systems. The cars are lifted by steel cables. There are two types of electric traction elevators, *gearless traction* and *geared traction.*

Gearless traction elevators are used in office buildings of more than 10 floors. They are also used in residential buildings of more than 30 floors. They travel at speeds of hundreds of feet or meters per minute. Cables called *hoisting ropes* lift the car. One end of each cable is attached to the top of the car. The other end is connected to a heavy steel counterweight. The counterweight balances the weight of the car and about half of its maximum passenger load. The counterweight reduces to a minimum the power needed to operate the elevator. The hoisting ropes fit around a *sheave* (pulley) that is connected directly to an electric motor. As the sheave turns, the ropes move and the car goes up or down. A brake holds the car in place when the elevator stops.

Geared traction elevators travel at speeds as high as 500 feet (150 meters) per minute. Geared traction elevators are similar to the gearless traction type of elevator. But the motor of a geared traction elevator operates a *reduction gear,* which turns the sheave. This gear decreases the speed at which the sheave turns.

Some elevators, called *hydraulic elevators,* are driven by a hydraulic system. They are moved by a long *ram* (piston) instead of by steel cables. Such elevators travel at speeds of 50 to 150 feet (15 to 46 meters) per minute. They serve mainly buildings of six or fewer stories. The ram rises and lifts the elevator when an electric pump forces oil into the ram cylinder. The elevator goes down when a valve opens and the oil flows into a storage tank.

Safety features. National and international standards

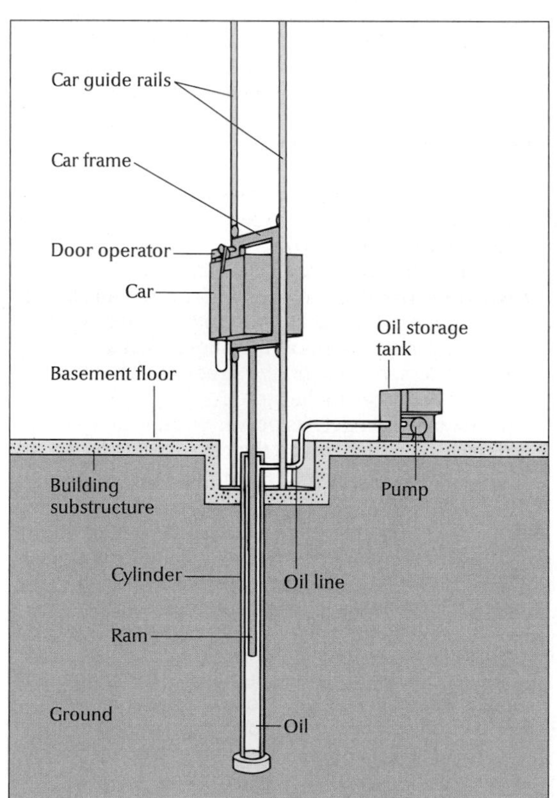

WORLD BOOK diagram by Richard Fickle

A hydraulic elevator, *shown here,* is lifted and lowered by a *ram* (piston). The car rises when a pump forces oil into the ram cylinder and descends when the oil flows into a storage tank.

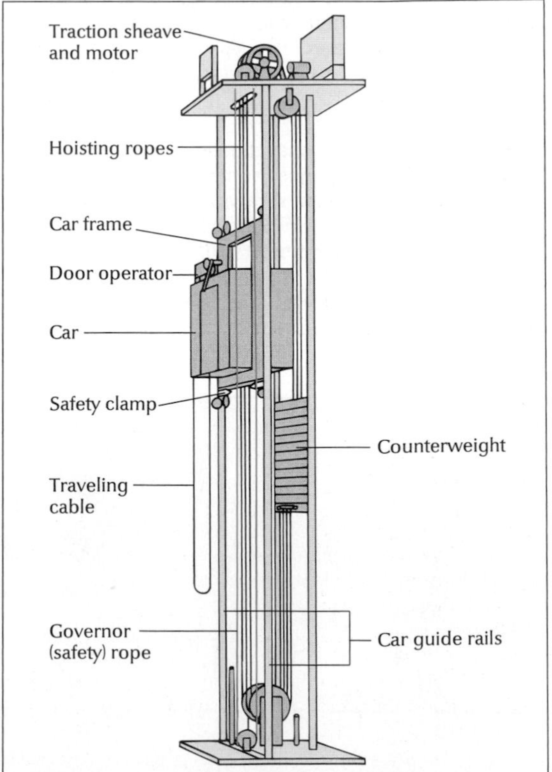

WORLD BOOK diagram by Richard Fickle

A gearless traction elevator, *shown here,* has steel cables called *hoisting ropes* that fit around a sheave. When the sheave is turned by an electric motor, the ropes lift or lower the car.

bodies have established safety codes under which elevators must operate. Local government officials inspect elevators regularly to make sure that all the safety features are functioning.

Passenger elevators must have steel doors that can withstand fire. Most have two sets of doors. One set is in the walls at each floor. The other set is part of the car itself. Both sets of doors must close and lock before the elevator can move. A special safety device causes the doors to reopen if someone is in the doorway. If an elevator goes down too fast, safety clamps grab the guide rails and stop the car. All automatic elevators have alarm bells and telephones. Passengers can use these instruments to call for help if the elevator stops between floors.

Special kinds of elevators. A few large buildings have *double-deck elevators.* These elevators have two compartments and serve two floors with each stop. People who want odd-numbered floors enter the lower compartment on the first floor. People who want even-numbered floors enter on the second floor and ride in the upper compartment.

Elevators called *observation elevators* have glass sides. They travel along the walls of interior courts or the outside walls of buildings. Passengers can view their surroundings through the glass.

Some tall buildings have express elevators that travel nonstop to certain floors called *sky lobbies.* In the sky lobby, passengers change to local elevators. The local elevators then carry the people to their floors.

Construction companies use special elevators called *hoists* that travel along the outside of buildings. These elevators carry crews and building materials, rather than the general public. Other kinds of elevators take workers and materials into mines. Hospital elevators are large enough to carry beds and stretchers.

History. The ancient Greek mathematician Archimedes invented a type of elevator before 230 B.C. Archimedes's elevator used ropes and pulleys and could lift one person.

Elevators became common in the United States and England during the early 1800's. By the 1840's, both hydraulic and steam-powered freight elevators had been invented. But the hydraulic elevators were slow. The ropes of the steam-powered elevators often broke, and the cars fell.

In the early 1850's, Elisha G. Otis of Yonkers, New York, invented the first elevator that had an automatic safety device. If the rope broke, the device prevented the elevator from falling. Otis first demonstrated the elevator in 1854. The world's first elevator designed for passenger use was installed in New York City in 1857. In 1880, the German inventor Ernst W. von Siemens introduced the first electric elevator.

Automatic elevators were introduced in residential buildings in the 1890's. Attendants operated the elevators in major office buildings until 1950. That year, an office building in Dallas became the first with automatic elevators. Kirby A. Kuntz

See also **Otis, Elisha Graves; Siemens, Ernst Werner von.**

Elevator, Grain. See **Grain elevator.**

Eleventh Amendment. See **Constitution of the United States** (Amendment 11).

Historical Pictures Service

The first elevator with a safety device was demonstrated by Elisha G. Otis in 1854. The automatic device prevented the elevator from falling if the hoisting rope broke.

Elf is an imaginary creature in northern European folklore. In some cultures, elves are called fairies. In most folk tales, elves are tiny people. However, in a few folk traditions, elves are the same size as human beings. Many folk tales describe elves as merry beings who enjoy singing and dancing all night in meadows.

Elves possess magical powers. Like other fairy creatures, such as leprechauns and pixies, elves can perform good deeds, but they can also cause misfortune, especially when they are offended. Many British and Scandinavian folk tales describe how elves steal animals and human children or lead travelers astray in forests. Elves sometimes make farm animals ill by shooting them with tiny arrows called "elf-shot." But elves can also be generous. They may grant good luck or a pocketful of gold to someone they like.

C. Scott Littleton

See also **Fairy; Gnome.**

Elgar, Sir Edward (1857-1934), a British composer, became best known for his *Pomp and Circumstance,* a set of five marches. He adapted the famous theme of the first *Pomp and Circumstance* march as the official ode for the coronation of King Edward VII in 1902. The composition generally called Elgar's masterpiece is the oratorio *The Dream of Gerontius* (1900), based on a poem by Cardinal John Newman. Elgar also became known for *The Enigma Variations* for orchestra (1899), and *Introduction and Allegro* for strings (1905). In his compositions, Elgar showed a strong sense of the harmonies and musical forms of the Romantic era.

Edward William Elgar was born on June 2, 1857, near Worcester, England. He also wrote a number of choral works, including *The Black Knight* (1893), *The Apostles* (1903), *The Kingdom* (1906), and *The Spirit of*

England (1916). Other successful works are the *Cockaigne* overture (1901), two symphonies, a violin concerto, and a cello concerto. Elgar died on Feb. 23, 1934.

Mary Vinquist

Elgin, *EHL gihn,* **Earl of** (1811-1863), served as governor general of Canada from 1847 to 1854. He is best known for recognizing the establishment of *responsible government* in Canada. Under this practice, Canada would be governed by a ministry that had the confidence of the legislature, rather than by agents of the British government.

Elgin was born in London on July 20, 1811. His given and family name was James Bruce. The eighth Earl of Elgin, he was educated at Eton and at Oxford University. He was elected to the House of Commons in 1841. From 1842 to 1846, he served as governor of Jamaica.

As governor general of Canada, Elgin was instructed by the British colonial secretary to accept responsible government. Elgin then called upon French and English Canadian reformers who had won a majority of seats in the 1848 election to form an administration. In 1849, the reformers passed the Rebellion Losses Bill. This bill was designed to compensate both rebels and loyalists who had suffered as the result of a rebellion in 1837 and 1838. Elgin approved the bill. Conservative opponents of the bill then burned the parliament buildings and stoned Elgin's carriage. Although in serious danger, Elgin refused to change his position. Elgin died on Nov. 20, 1863. D. Peter MacLeod

Elgin Marbles, *EHL gihn,* are a group of ancient Greek sculptures that originally decorated the Acropolis in Athens. They are named for Lord Elgin, a British ambassador to Constantinople, who collected them between 1802 and 1804. Most of the sculptures were part of the Parthenon. They include 56 slabs from the *frieze,* a band of horizontal relief sculpture around the top of the temple. The collection also includes statues that once stood in the *pediments* (triangular segments of the roof) and 15 slabs from the *metopes* (square panels in the frieze above the columns). The collection also contains a *caryatid* (column in the form of a statue of a woman) from the Erechtheum, another temple on the Acropolis.

In 1801, Lord Elgin received permission from the Ottoman government to remove the sculptures from Greece. Greece was then part of the Ottoman Empire, which was based in what is now Turkey. From 1803 to 1812, Elgin shipped his collection to England. The British government purchased the Elgin Marbles in 1816 for the British Museum. Marjorie S. Venit

See also **Acropolis; Parthenon.**

El Greco. See **Greco, El.**

Elijah, *ih LY juh,* was an Israelite prophet who lived in the 800's B.C. Much information about him appears in I and II Kings of the Old Testament. Elijah is also mentioned 29 times in the New Testament.

Elijah was born in Tishbe in what was then northern Israel. He gained fame as a miracle worker. For example, he miraculously increased the scarce supply of food for a poor widow (I Kings 17:8-16) and brought the widow's dead son back to life (I Kings 17:17-24). Elijah also used his powers to prove the greatness of God. He opposed King Ahab and his wife Queen Jezebel because they abandoned the *covenant* (agreement) with their God and supported the worship of the heathen god Baal. Elijah won a contest on Mount Carmel against the prophets of Baal, convincing the people of Israel of the superiority of their God (I Kings 18:17-39). Just before his death, Elijah transferred his role as a prophet to his disciple Elisha, and then ascended to heaven in a whirlwind (II Kings 2:1-15). Later references to Elijah in the Bible mention or suggest that he will return to announce the coming of the Messiah. Carol L. Meyers

Elijah Muhammad. See Muhammad, Elijah.

Elimination, also called *excretion,* is the process of removing water, waste matter, and harmful substances from the body. The skin, lungs, kidneys, and lower intestinal tract carry out this function. The kidneys eliminate most of the excess water and salt. However, an average of about 1 quart (0.95 liter) of water and ⅓ teaspoonful (1.6 milliliters) of salt are eliminated through the skin every day. When visible sweating occurs, the elimination of water and salt by the skin may be much greater. Perspiration withdraws from the body about one-fourth of all the heat produced.

The process of respiration eliminates carbon dioxide and some water. An adult eliminates about 6 ⅘ ounces (200 milliliters) of carbon dioxide each minute.

Many different substances pass out of the body through the kidneys. They eliminate daily about 1 ½ quarts (1.4 liters) of urine, consisting of water and certain solids. Urine contains the solid *urea,* a waste product of the use of protein by the body. Another solid is salt, or sodium chloride. Elimination of certain acid salts, such as acid sodium phosphate, also takes place. Excess *sodium bicarbonate* (baking soda) is sometimes eliminated in the urine by the kidneys. The body rids itself of waste products of digestion through the large intestine.

Jeffrey R. Woodside

Related articles in *World Book* include:

Colon	Kidney	Urea
Colostomy	Lung	Uric acid
Intestine	Perspiration	Urine

Elion, Gertrude Belle (1918-1999), an American biochemist, helped create important drugs used to treat cancer, malaria, and other deadly diseases. She worked with American biochemist George H. Hitchings at a research division of the Burroughs Wellcome Company. They studied how growth and reproduction in diseased cells and viruses differ from these processes in normal cells. They reasoned that identifying such differences would reveal ways to destroy unwanted cells without harming normal ones. In 1988, Elion and Hitchings shared the Nobel Prize in physiology or medicine with British scientist James W. Black for developing such logical new approaches to drug design.

In the 1950's, Elion and Hitchings designed a drug called *mercaptopurine (mur KAP toh PYUR een).* Mercaptopurine was the first drug effective in treating leukemia, a cancer in which white blood cells multiply wildly. The pair then created a related drug that helps prevent rejection of transplanted organs. In the 1960's, Elion's team developed the drug *acyclovir (ay SY kloh vihr),* the first antiviral drug used to treat genital herpes.

Elion was born in New York City on Jan. 23, 1918. She earned bachelor's and master's degrees in chemistry at New York City colleges. When she looked for work, many prospective employers refused to employ a woman chemist. After World War II pulled men away from their jobs and into combat, she was hired at Burroughs Wellcome in 1944. After her retirement, Elion served in prominent scientific advisory positions. She became a member of the National Academy of Sciences in 1990 and received the National Medal of Science in 1991. Elion died on Feb. 21, 1999. David F. Musto

Eliot, Charles William (1834-1926), an American educator, served as president of Harvard University for 40 years, from 1869 to 1909. He did much to shape the program and standards of liberal and professional education in the United States. Eliot brought outstanding scholars to Harvard as teachers and established elective courses there. He also reorganized the administration of the university and added a number of graduate and professional colleges.

Eliot served as chairman of the National Education Association's Committee on Secondary School Studies (Committee of Ten). This committee recommended an academic rather than vocational program of study for all high school students. The recommendation strongly influenced secondary education in the United States.

Eliot was born in Boston on March 20, 1834, and studied at Boston Latin Grammar School and Harvard University. He taught mathematics and chemistry at Harvard from 1858 to 1863 and then studied in Europe for two years. He taught at the Massachusetts Institute of Technology for four years and then returned to Harvard as its president. Eliot was a trustee of the Rockefeller Foundation and the Carnegie Foundation. He wrote widely on educational subjects. He died on Aug. 22, 1926.

Glenn Smith

Eliot, George (1819-1880), was the pen name of Mary Ann (or Marian) Evans, a great English novelist. Much of her fiction reflects the middle-class rural background of her youth. Eliot wrote with sympathy, wisdom, and realism about English country people and small towns. She wrote seriously about moral and social problems, but her characters are living portraits.

Eliot's masterpiece, *Middlemarch: A Study of Provincial Life* (1871-1872), is a long story of many complex characters, and their influence on and reaction to one another. *Adam Bede* (1859), her first novel, is a tragic love story in which her father serves as the model for the title character. *The Mill on the Floss* (1860) and *Silas Marner* (1861) are somber works set against country backgrounds. *Silas Marner* is the story of an embittered old miser who loses his gold but turns to a more human life through his love for a little girl. *Romola* (1863) is a historical novel set in Renaissance Florence. *Felix Holt, Radical* (1866), Eliot's only political novel, is considered one of her poorer works. *Daniel Deronda* (1876), her last novel, displays the author's knowledge of and sensitivity to Jewish culture. The book is notable for the warm portrait of its heroine, Gwendolen Harleth.

Culver
George Eliot

Eliot was born in Warwickshire on Nov. 22, 1819. She received an excellent education in private schools and from tutors. After her father's death in 1849, she traveled in Europe and then settled in London. There she wrote for leading journals and became a friend of many important people. British intellectuals regarded her as one of the leading thinkers of her day. Eliot lived with the writer George Henry Lewes from 1854 to 1878, although Lewes was married and could not obtain a divorce under existing law. Eliot died on Dec. 22, 1880. Sharon Bassett

Additional resources

Ashton, Rosemary. *George Eliot.* Penguin, 1996.
Rignall, John, ed. *The Oxford Reader's Companion to George Eliot.* Oxford, 2000.

Eliot, John (1604-1690), was an American missionary to the Indians of Massachusetts. He translated the Bible into an Indian dialect. Eliot was born in Hertfordshire, England, and came to America in 1631. He was made the teacher of the church in Roxbury, Massachusetts. Eliot organized the first village of Indian converts at Natick, near Boston, in 1651. By 1674, he had 14 villages with more than 1,000 Indians under his supervision. But King Philip's War (1675-1676) scattered his converts. Eliot died on May 21, 1690. Charles H. Lippy

Eliot, T. S. (1888-1965), ranks among the most important poets of the 1900's. In "The Love Song of J. Alfred Prufrock," *The Waste Land,* and other poems, he departed radically from the techniques and subject matter of pre-World War I poetry. His poetry, along with his critical works, helped to reshape modern literature. Eliot received the 1948 Nobel Prize in literature.

His life. Thomas Stearns Eliot was born in St. Louis, Missouri, on Sept. 26, 1888. He studied at Harvard, the Sorbonne in Paris, and Oxford. In 1914, he settled in England, where his poems came to the attention of the American poet Ezra Pound. Pound encouraged Eliot and helped him with his poetry.

Many of Eliot's views on literature appeared in *The Criterion,* a literary magazine he edited from 1922 to 1939. Eliot served as a director of a London publishing house from 1925 until his death on Jan. 4, 1965.

In 1927, Eliot became a British subject, declaring himself "Anglo-Catholic in religion, royalist in politics, and classicist in literature."

His works. Eliot's first major poem, "The Love Song of J. Alfred Prufrock" (1917), revealed his original and highly developed style. The poem shows the influence of certain French poets of the 1800's, but its startling jumps from rhetorical language to cliché, its indirect literary references, and its simultaneous humor and pessimism were quite new in English literature.

"Prufrock" created a small literary stir, but *The Waste Land* (1922) created an uproar. Some critics called the work a masterpiece, others a hoax. While this long, complex poem includes many obscure literary references, many in other languages, its main direction is clear.

Kay Bell
T. S. Eliot

It contrasts the spiritual bankruptcy Eliot saw in modern Europe with the values and unity of the past.

Eliot's "Ash Wednesday" (1930), far different from *The Waste Land* in tone and mood, is more musical, direct, and traditional, and, in its religious emphasis, tentatively hopeful. *Four Quartets,* his last major poem, is a deeply religious, often beautiful, meditation on time and timelessness. It includes four sections: "Burnt Norton" (1936), "East Coker" (1940), "The Dry Salvages" (1941), and "Little Gidding" (1942). In "Little Gidding," he wrote:

> We shall not cease from exploration
> And the end of all our exploring
> Will be to arrive where we started
> And know the place for the first time.

Eliot also wrote several verse dramas. *Murder in the Cathedral* (1935), his first major play, is based on the death of Thomas Becket, archbishop of Canterbury in the 1100's. On the surface, *The Cocktail Party* (1950) appears to be a sophisticated comedy, but it is really a deeply religious and mystical work. Eliot's other plays include *The Family Reunion* (1939), *The Confidential Clerk* (1954), and *The Elder Statesman* (1958). Eliot's book of light verse called *Old Possum's Book of Practical Cats* (1939) was adapted into the popular musical comedy *Cats* (1981).

Eliot's *Complete Poems and Plays (1909-1950)* was published in 1952. *Selected Essays* (3rd edition, 1951) is a collection of his prose. William Harmon

Elisha, *ih LY shuh,* was the follower, servant, and later the successor of the Hebrew prophet Elijah. Elisha was active from about 850 to 800 B.C., carrying on his master's policies against the pagan religion favored by King Jehoram of Israel. With this purpose, he encouraged Jehu to rebel and seize the throne. Many stories are told about Elisha in II Kings, chapters 2-9. One story describes Elisha parting the Jordan River with Elijah's mantle. Others tell how he healed the commander of the Syrian army, revived a Shunammite woman's dead son, and fed 100 men with only 20 loaves of barley and some ears of corn. Gary G. Porton

See also **Elijah.**

Elissa. See **Dido.**

Elizabeth, New Jersey (pop. 124,969), is the oldest English settlement in the state. It lies in the eastern part of New Jersey, 12 miles (19 kilometers) southwest of New York City. For location, see **New Jersey** (political map). Elizabeth is a manufacturing, transportation, and service center. Its factories make clothing, fabricated metal products, industrial machinery, paper products, pharmaceuticals, and rubber products. The city's port is a major port for container ships.

Elizabeth was settled in 1664 after England gained control of the Dutch colonies in North America. Philip Carteret (1639-1682), first English governor of New Jersey, selected the settlement as the site for his capital. He called it *Elizabethtown.* The city's industrial development began after 1835 when some New York businessmen bought land bordering Staten Island Sound, on which to build manufacturing plants. Elizabeth also became a major railroad center. The Goethals Bridge, which connects Elizabeth with Staten Island, opened in 1928. Elizabeth has a mayor-council government. It is the seat of Union County. Paul G. E. Clemens

Elizabeth, Queen Mother of England. See **George VI; Elizabeth II.**

Elizabeth, Queen of the Belgians. See **Albert I.**

Elizabeth I (1533-1603) was queen of England from 1558 until her death in 1603. Her reign is often called the Golden Age or the Elizabethan Age because it was a time of great achievement in England. Elizabeth made the Church of England, a Protestant religious group, the country's main church. At the same time, she long avoided war with Europe's leading Roman Catholic nations. The English navy defeated a powerful Spanish fleet, and English merchants and sailors challenged the Spaniards with greater confidence around the world. England's economy also prospered. Elizabeth's court became a center for musicians, scholars, and writers.

Elizabeth was a strong and clever ruler, and she succeeded in furthering England's interests despite foreign threats and religious unrest at home. Elizabeth gained the loyalty and admiration of her subjects. She reminded them of her popular father, King Henry VIII. The queen had his red hair and pale eyes. She also shared her father's gifts for music and other arts. In addition, she was an outstanding orator.

Early years. Elizabeth was born on Sept. 7, 1533, at Greenwich, an estate near London. She was the daughter of Henry VIII and his second wife, Anne Boleyn. Elizabeth's mother was executed on a charge of adultery in 1536. Henry died in 1547 and was succeeded by Elizabeth's half-brother, Edward VI. When Edward died in 1553, Elizabeth's half-sister, Mary Tudor, became queen. Mary had been raised as a Roman Catholic by her mother, Catherine of Aragon. Catherine was the first wife of Henry VIII. Mary was a devout Roman Catholic and tried to bring England back to the Roman Catholic Church. She became known as "Bloody Mary" for her persecution of Protestants. See **Mary I.**

Queen Mary distrusted Elizabeth, who was next in line to the throne. Elizabeth cautiously avoided any involvement in politics during Mary's rule. However, Elizabeth came under suspicion in 1554, following an uprising known as Wyatt's Rebellion. The rebels tried to overthrow Mary, but they failed. Elizabeth was imprisoned for a time, though no evidence was found that linked her to the rebellion. Mary died in 1558, and Elizabeth became queen.

Problems at home and abroad challenged Elizabeth as queen. The previous year, Mary had involved England in a costly war with France. Struggling Protestant forces in Scotland, France, and the Netherlands sought Elizabeth's support. But England's economy was poor, and the treasury lacked the revenue to support the routine costs of government. Elizabeth also had to decide whether England's religion would be Catholic or Protestant and to do so without causing a revolt.

With the aid of Parliament and her chief adviser, Sir William Cecil, Elizabeth ended the war with France. She also secretly sent money and weapons to the Scottish Protestants. Elizabeth hoped to satisfy most of her subjects by establishing a church that was primarily Protestant in doctrine. Elizabeth therefore signed several laws called the Religious Settlement of 1559. The main law, the Act of Supremacy, reestablished the Church of England, which her father set up and Mary tried to abolish. This church was independent of the Roman Catholic

Church but had similarities to it. The Act of Uniformity approved a new prayer book and enforced its use.

Elizabeth never married, and she used her single status as a foreign policy tool. Elizabeth encouraged both Catholic and Protestant suitors, but she committed herself to no one. By avoiding marriage to a Protestant, Elizabeth gave encouragement to her own Catholic subjects, who remained loyal with few exceptions. Elizabeth's flirtations with Catholic suitors kept King Philip II of Spain, a Catholic, from taking direct military action against her for several years while the Church of England gained popular support. For a time, Elizabeth seemed to be in love with one of her subjects, Sir Robert Dudley, the Earl of Leicester. However, Elizabeth's cautious nature kept her from entering a marriage that lacked political benefit.

Mary, Queen of Scots. Elizabeth's cousin, Mary Stuart, was forced to give up her throne as queen of Scotland in 1567. She later fled to England, where her presence caused uneasiness. Mary was a Catholic and heir to the English throne. Many English people feared that she would try to replace Elizabeth. Several plots against Elizabeth involving Catholic nobility proved unsuccessful. In 1584, the English aristocracy formed an association to protect their queen and vowed to prevent a Catholic succession in England. In 1586, Mary was accused of involvement in another plot against Elizabeth. Public reaction against Mary was strong. Elizabeth finally, though reluctantly, agreed to Mary's execution in 1587.

The Spanish Armada. In 1585, Elizabeth sent an army to help Protestants in the Dutch Netherlands fight Spanish rule. She also encouraged English ships to raid Spanish fleets. Sir Francis Drake, Sir Walter Raleigh, and other "sea dogs" looted several Spanish ships. In 1587, Drake destroyed 30 Spanish ships in port at Cádiz. These events and the execution of Mary Stuart led King Philip II of Spain to approve an invasion of England. He assembled an armada and sent it to England in 1588. But the smaller and swifter English vessels routed the Spanish fleet. Fierce storms then wrecked many of the fleeing Spanish ships off the coasts of Ireland and Scotland. Spain's power was seriously damaged, but the war went on for 16 years. See **Spanish Armada.**

A new optimism. Despite the armada's defeat, many English people still feared a Spanish invasion. But Elizabeth eased their fears in August of 1588 with a speech to soldiers assembled at Tilbury. Her words stirred national pride and confidence and scorned any European power who dared to invade England. Her optimism was typical of one of the most creative and productive periods in England's history. English literature, in particular, thrived during this period. Christopher Marlowe wrote and staged *The Tragical History of Doctor Faustus* (about 1588); Edmund Spenser wrote his epic poem, *The Faerie Queene* (1590-1596); Francis Bacon composed his *Essays* (1601); and William Shakespeare wrote some of the world's greatest poetry and drama (see **English literature** [The beginning of modern English]; **Shakespeare, William**). Already Sir Walter Raleigh had sent settlers to America, opening the way for a great colonial empire.

Later years. Problems at home marked the end of Elizabeth's reign. The Irish rebelled, and the economy soured. The Earl of Essex, an English soldier whose accomplishments Elizabeth admired, led a rebellion against the government in 1601. He was soon captured, convicted of treason, and executed. Elizabeth died on March 24, 1603. She was succeeded by James VI, the Protestant son of Mary Stuart. Gary G. Gibbs

Oil painting on canvas; the Marquess of Salisbury, Hatfield House

Queen Elizabeth I ruled England from 1558 to 1603. The English artist Nicholas Hilliard painted this portrait in 1585.

See also **England** (picture); **Furniture** (England); **Henry VIII; Leicester, Earl of; Mary, Queen of Scots.**

Additional resources

Ashworth, Leon. *Queen Elizabeth I.* Cherrytree Bks., 2002. Younger readers.
Doran, Susan. *Queen Elizabeth I.* N. Y. Univ. Pr., 2003.
Lace, William W. *Elizabeth I and Her Court.* Lucent Bks., 2003.
Loades, David. *Elizabeth I.* Hambledon, 2003.

Elizabeth II (1926-   ) is the queen of the United Kingdom of Great Britain and Northern Ireland. She became queen when her father, King George VI, died in 1952. As a *constitutional monarch,* Queen Elizabeth is formally head of state in the United Kingdom. However, Elizabeth has no power over what the British government does. Laws are formally enacted in the name of the queen, but their content is the responsibility of the government.

Early life. Elizabeth Alexandra Mary was born in London on April 21, 1926. Her father was the Duke of York, second son of King George V. Her mother—Queen Elizabeth, the Queen Mother—was the former Lady Elizabeth Bowes-Lyon, the daughter of a Scottish earl.

Elizabeth's father became king in 1936 after his older brother, King Edward VIII, gave up the throne to marry a divorced American woman. This event greatly changed the course of 10-year-old Elizabeth's life. It made her the heir to the throne, since George VI had no sons and she was the older of his two daughters.

Princess Elizabeth spent most of her childhood at

Windsor Castle, located in Windsor, near London. The castle is the British royal family's main residence outside of London. Buckingham Palace, in London, is the family's main residence. Princess Elizabeth and her sister, Princess Margaret (1930-2002), were educated at home by governesses. In March 1945, during World War II, Elizabeth joined the Auxiliary Territorial Service, a support branch of the military. She joined to train as a mechanic to repair military vehicles for the war effort. But Elizabeth served only until May, when the war in Europe ended.

Marriage and succession to the throne. Princess Elizabeth married Philip Mountbatten, a British naval lieutenant and member of the Greek royal family, on Nov. 20, 1947. Her husband became Prince Philip, Duke of Edinburgh. When King George's health began to fail, Princess Elizabeth and her husband began to undertake more public duties. The king died on Feb. 6, 1952, and Princess Elizabeth succeeded him as the British monarch that day. The coronation of Queen Elizabeth II took place on June 2, 1953, in Westminster Abbey, London.

Duties. After a general election, the queen formally appoints the prime minister. In practice, this person is the leader of the majority party in the democratically elected House of Commons. The queen has a weekly meeting with the prime minister to discuss public affairs. The prime minister is not obligated to act on her advice, but may find it useful because of her many years of experience.

The queen's chief public role is to attend ceremonial state occasions and to represent the United Kingdom in visits throughout the country and the world. Queen Elizabeth has traveled extensively. In the United Kingdom, the queen sometimes puts ceremony aside and meets informally with subjects. She hosts luncheons at Buckingham Palace, which are attended by people of many different walks of life.

The queen is also head of the Commonwealth of Nations, an association of independent countries and other political units that have lived under British law and government. Queen Elizabeth has no authority in Commonwealth nations. She serves mainly as a symbol of historical ties.

The royal family. The queen and Prince Philip have four children. The children are Charles, Prince of Wales (1948-); Anne, Princess Royal (1950-); Andrew, Duke of York (1960-); and Prince Edward (1964-). Prince Charles is heir to the throne. His oldest son, Prince William (1982-), is next in line after his father as the heir. The royal family's surname is Windsor. However, in 1960, Queen Elizabeth announced that her descendants, except for princes and princesses, will bear

The coronation of Queen Elizabeth II, *shown here,* took place on June 2, 1953. Elizabeth had become the British monarch about 16 months earlier—on Feb. 6, 1952.

British Information Service

Queen Elizabeth II serves as the monarch of the United Kingdom and as the head of the Commonwealth of Nations.

© Terry Fincher, Gamma/Liaison

The queen has traveled widely during her reign. This scene shows her on a visit to the United States in 1991.

the surname Mountbatten-Windsor. Bruce L. Kinzer

See also **Charles, Prince; Philip, Prince; United Kingdom** (Government; picture); **Windsor.**

Elizabeth, Saint, according to Luke 1 in the New Testament, was the mother of Saint John the Baptist and a kinswoman of Mary. In Luke's account, when both Elizabeth and her husband, Zechariah, were advanced in years, the angel Gabriel appeared to Zechariah and predicted that his wife would bear a son to be called John. Mary visited her at her home in Judea before the birth of Jesus. Elizabeth's feast day is November 5 in the Roman Catholic Church and September 8 in the Eastern Orthodox Churches. See also **John the Baptist, Saint.**

J. H. Charlesworth

Elizabethan Age. See **Elizabeth I.**

Elizabethan theater. See **Drama** (Elizabethan, Jacobean, and Caroline drama); **Globe Theatre; Shakespeare, William.**

Elk is a common name for two types of large deer. One type lives in North America. The other lives in Europe and Asia. Despite some similarities, the American elk and the European elk belong to different *species* (kinds) of deer. The American elk is closely related to the *red deer* found in Europe and Asia. The European elk belongs to the same species as the American moose. This inconsistent use of names results from the early days of English settlement in North America. Shawnee Indians called the American elk the *wapiti.* However, early English colonists gave the animal the name of elk, and this name is still most commonly used.

The American elk is a large deer. The *bull* (male) elk stands about 5 feet (1.5 meters) high at the shoulder and may weigh from 700 to 1,100 pounds (320 to 500 kilograms). Its rounded antlers can spread more than 5 feet (1.5 meters). The antlers of a grown bull will have a total of about 12 to 14 points. Antlers grow during the spring and summer and are shed in late winter. The *cow* (female) is smaller than the male and has no antlers. Elk have mostly brownish-gray coloring with a yellowish-tan rump. The legs, head, and neck are dark brown.

During September and October, the bulls fight one another to gain control over *harems,* or groups of cows, with whom they mate. An exceptional bull may keep a harem of 60 or more cows, but the average one keeps only a dozen or so cows at a time. As the elk travel from high mountain valleys called *parks* to the lower valleys, they gather into large herds of both sexes and all ages. In the lower valleys, where the snow is not too deep, they spend the winter.

As the snow melts in the spring, the elk move slowly back into the higher mountains. Calves are born in May or June. A cow rarely bears more than one calf. An elk calf is light tawny-brown, with many white spots that are lost during the first change of coat in August.

Michael Ederegger from Peter Arnold

The American elk has dark brown fur on its legs, head, and neck. Each summer, males of this North American species grow antlers that may spread more than 5 feet (1.5 meters).

Elk usually eat grasses. They also eat the twigs and needles of fir, juniper, and many hardwood trees and shrubs, especially during the winter. Many of the larger elk herds of the United States and Canada do not have enough winter range for feeding. Many elk die of starvation or from diseases, such as pneumonia and *necrotic stomatitis* (calf diphtheria). *Chronic wasting disease,* a deadly contagious illness of the brain, has become a major threat to American elk. Wolves and cougars are among the natural *predators* (hunting animals) of elk. Bears and coyotes kill some calves and sick adults.

Elk once roamed over most of the United States and southern Canada. But human beings wiped out the elk populations east of the Rocky Mountains, largely by overhunting them and destroying their natural habitats. Some elk have been reintroduced into parts of their former range, including areas of New Hampshire, Pennsylvania, Virginia, Michigan, and South Dakota. The largest herds live in Yellowstone National Park, on Montana's Sun River, in Colorado's Rocky Mountains, and in Washington's Olympic Mountains.

The European elk is the largest deer of Europe and Asia. It is larger and heavier than the American elk. It belongs to the same species as the huge American moose, with its scoop-shaped antlers. During the Middle Ages, Scandinavians sometimes used elk as beasts of burden. But reindeer later took the elk's place.

Elk have been well protected by law in European countries, but the animals' numbers are gradually declining in Europe. Some elk still live in parts of eastern Europe and in the forests of Norway, Sweden, and northeastern Germany. Populations of elk range eastward across Siberia, China's Northeast, and Mongolia.

Another deer species, the Irish elk, is extinct. The Irish elk was immense. It was distinguished by its huge antlers, which sometimes measured 11 feet (3 meters) from tip to tip.

The Altai wapiti and Manchurian wapiti of Asia are the largest red deer. But these species do not have such huge antlers as the American elk. Kenneth J. Raedeke

Scientific classification. The scientific name for the American elk is *Cervus elaphus.* The European elk is *Alces alces.*

See also **Deer; Moose; Red deer; Reindeer.**

Elks, Benevolent and Protective Order of, is a fraternal and charitable organization. Each year, the Benevolent and Protective Order of Elks raises millions of dollars for hospitals, youth activities, home therapy for children with disabilities, and entertainment at veterans' hospitals. The Elks National Foundation offers grants for scholarships, the study of cerebral palsy, and other health and youth activities. *Elks Magazine* is published 10 times a year for members. The Elks National Home at Bedford, Virginia, is a home for retired Elks members. Elks headquarters are in Chicago.

Critically reviewed by the Benevolent and Protective Order of Elks

Ellery, William (1727-1820), was one of the Rhode Island signers of the Declaration of Independence. He served in the Continental Congress from 1776 until 1781 and in the Congress of the Confederation from 1783 until 1785. He became commissioner of the Continental Loan Office for Rhode Island in 1786. He was collector of customs at Newport from 1790 until his death on Feb. 15, 1820. William Ellery was born on Dec. 22, 1727, in Newport, Rhode Island. Gary D. Hermalyn

Ellesmere Island, *EHLZ meer,* is part of Canada's territory of Nunavut. It lies west of Greenland. It covers 75,767 square miles (196,236 square kilometers) and is the world's 10th largest island. It has a population of about 150. Smith Sound and Kennedy Channel separate it from Greenland. The Prince of Wales Mountains rise in eastern Ellesmere. In 1616, William Baffin became the first European to reach the island. Robert Peary explored it in 1899. See also **Arctic Ocean** (map); **Baffin, William; Peary, Robert E.** M. Donald Hancock

Ellice Islands. See Tuvalu.

Ellington, Duke (1899-1974), was an American jazz bandleader, composer, and pianist. He rates as one of the greatest figures in jazz and, according to many critics, its most significant composer.

Edward Kennedy Ellington was born on April 29, 1899, in Washington, D.C. He began playing piano at the age of 7 and made his professional debut at 17. He moved to New York City in 1923 as a member of Elmer Snowden's band, the Washingtonians. Ellington soon took over the band, which grew from 5 pieces to 12 pieces by 1931. From 1927 to 1932, the Ellington band was the house band at the Cotton Club in Harlem. There, they played a rhythmic, exotic sound called *jungle music.*

The band's reputation gradually grew through many recordings of Ellington compositions. These recordings include "Mood Indigo" (1930), "Creole Rhapsody" (1931), "It Don't Mean a Thing If It Ain't Got That Swing" (1932), "Sophisticated Lady" (1933), "Solitude" (1934), and "In a Sentimental Mood" (1935).

The mid-1930's to the mid-1940's is generally considered Ellington's most creative period. Many of his most highly regarded recordings were made during this time, including "Harlem Air-shaft" (1940), "Jack the Bear" (1940), "Ko-Ko" (1940), and "Concerto for Cootie" (1940). In 1939, Billy Strayhorn joined Ellington's band as a composer, often with Ellington, and arranger. He composed "Take the A Train" (1941), which became the band's theme song.

Many of Ellington's key musicians—such as saxophonists Johnny Hodges and Harry Carney—stayed with him for several decades, contributing to the band's readily

Down Beat Magazine

Duke Ellington, *center,* was one of the leading figures in jazz history. For almost 50 years, he led an orchestra that featured many of the finest soloists in jazz. They included alto saxophonist Johnny Hodges, *left,* and clarinetist Jimmy Hamilton, *right.*

identifiable sound. Other important musicians were tenor saxophonists Ben Webster and Paul Gonsalves, trombonists Joe Nanton and Lawrence Brown, clarinetist Barney Bigard, bassist Jimmy Blanton, and trumpeters Rex Stewart, Clark Terry, Cootie Williams, and Ray Nance.

Beginning in the 1940's, Ellington composed longer works, such as *Black, Brown, and Beige* (1943). During the 1960's, Ellington wrote several film scores and began composing sacred music. *Music Is My Mistress* (1973) is Ellington's autobiography. He died on May 24, 1974. Mercer Ellington, Duke's son, was a trumpeter, composer, and record company executive. He also led the Ellington band for several years after his father's death.

Eddie Cook

See also **African Americans** (picture); **Jazz** (picture); **Popular music** (picture).

Elliot, Gilbert John Murray Kynynmond. See **Minto, Earl of.**

Ellipse, *ih LIHPS,* is a geometric figure with the shape of a flattened hoop. In geometric terms, an ellipse is one of the conic sections (see **Cone**).

An ellipse may be drawn with an *ellipsograph* (elliptic compass). But the simplest way to draw an ellipse is to fasten the ends of a string at two points, called the *foci* (see the drawings with this article). The string must be longer than the distance between the foci. Hold a pencil upright against the string so the string is stretched tight at all times. Draw half the ellipse; then lift the pencil and move the string to the other side of the pins to draw the second half. The diameter passing through the foci is called the *major axis.* The diameter running *perpendicular* (at right angles) to the major axis is the *minor axis.* To find the area of an ellipse, multiply half the length of the major axis by half that of the minor axis. Multiply the result by *pi,* which has an approximate value of 3.14159.

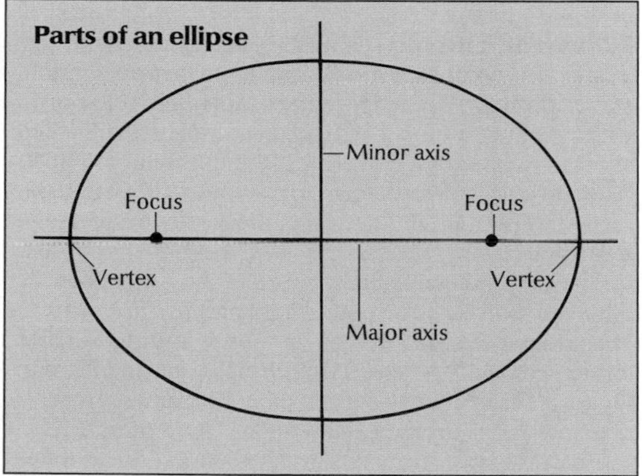

WORLD BOOK diagram by Sarah Woodward

An ellipse, in geometry, is an oval figure that resembles the shape of a flattened hoop.

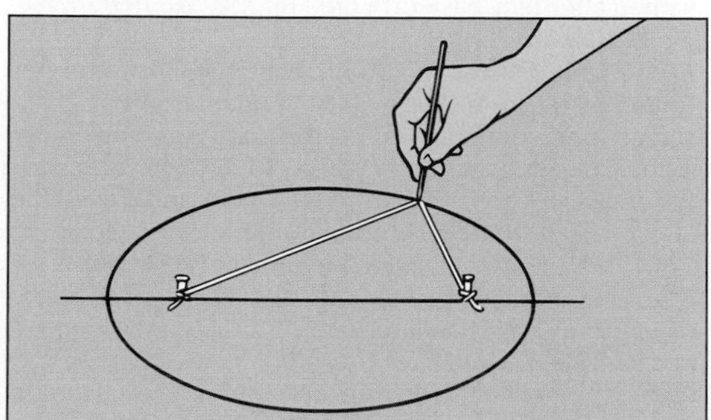

WORLD BOOK diagram by Sarah Woodward

To draw an ellipse, pin the ends of a string at the two foci. The string must be longer than the distance between the two foci. An *ellipsograph* (elliptic compass) can also be used.

The ellipse was used by the German astronomer Johannes Kepler in the 1600's to describe the orbits of the planets of the solar system. Kepler discovered that each of the planets follows an elliptical path that has the sun as one of its foci. John K. Beem

Ellis, Havelock (1859-1939), was a British writer and psychologist. His writings did much to promote the scientific study of normal adult sexuality. Ellis's most important work is his seven-volume *Studies in the Psychology of Sex* (1897-1928). In it, he tried to be both scientific and aesthetic in his approach to psychology.

Henry Havelock Ellis was born on Feb. 2, 1859, in Croydon, now part of London. He studied medicine and worked for a time as a physician. In his *The World of Dreams* (1911), Ellis used a psychoanalytic method to study his own dreams (see **Psychoanalysis**). Ellis's works include *The Philosophy of Conflict and Other Essays* (1919) and *The Dance of Life* (1923). He died on July 8, 1939. Phillip L. Rice

Ellis Island served as a United States reception center for immigrants for more than 60 years. The island is in New York Harbor, less than ½ mile (0.8 kilometer) north of Liberty Island, the home of the Statue of Liberty. Over 12 million people first entered the United States through Ellis Island. The island is named for Samuel Ellis, a merchant and farmer who owned it during the late 1700's. The United States government bought the island in 1808.

The government began using Ellis Island as an immigration station in 1892. About 35 buildings were constructed on the island. Newcomers were taken to the main building, an impressive two-story wooden structure. That building burned down in 1897 and was replaced by a three-story brick building. The immigrants were questioned by government officials and examined by doctors. Certain people were prohibited by federal law from immigrating to the United States. They included criminals, the insane, and people who had infectious diseases. But about 98 percent of those examined at Ellis Island were allowed into the country.

The island's large-scale use as an immigration station ended in 1924. The station closed completely in 1954. In 1965, the island became a national historic site, part of the existing Statue of Liberty National Monument. The site is managed and operated by the federal government's National Park Service.

The National Park Service began major repairs of the island's buildings in the 1980's. The island was reopened to the public in 1990. The main building was completely restored and is now the Ellis Island Immigration Museum. The museum's exhibits include old photographs, clothing, toys, and passports of immigrants. Visitors can listen to recordings of immigrants sharing their memories of Ellis Island. Several rooms, including the *Registry Room* or *Great Hall* (main reception area), now appear as they did between 1918 and 1924, the island's busiest years as an immigration station. The American Immi-

(©) Tony Savino, Sipa Press

Ellis Island's main building was the processing center for millions of immigrants as they entered the United States. Today, the building houses the Ellis Island Immigration Museum.

grant Wall of Honor, created in 1990, stands outside the museum. The names of hundreds of thousands of immigrants are engraved on this wall in honor of all immigrants.

Both the states of New York and New Jersey have long claimed official jurisdiction over Ellis Island. In 1834, the two states agreed to give New York official jurisdiction over the land while New Jersey got jurisdiction over the surrounding water and submerged land. At the time, the island covered only 3.3 acres (1.3 hectares). But through the years, landfill added 24.2 acres (9.8 hectares) to the total area. New Jersey sued New York to gain jurisdiction over the island. In 1998, a ruling by the Supreme Court of the United States gave New Jersey jurisdiction over all of the island except the original 3.3 acres, which New York kept. All buildings on Ellis Island are owned by the U.S. government. The National Park Service continues to manage and operate the site. Frank J. Coppa

Ellison, Harlan (1934-), is an American author best known for his science-fiction stories. He is also an important editor, essayist, and screenwriter. Ellison has gained recognition with his experiments in the form and techniques of science-fiction writing. He refuses to call himself a science-fiction writer, preferring to identify his work as "magic realism," a type of fiction that blends everyday reality with the supernatural.

Harlan Jay Ellison was born on May 27, 1934, in Cleveland. He became a full-time writer in the mid-1950's and has written more than 1,100 short stories as well as many novels and essays. Ellison has written several of the most acclaimed short stories in modern science fiction, including " 'Repent Harlequin!' Said the Ticktock Man" (1965) and "I Have No Mouth, but I Must Scream" (1967). His essays have been published in such collections as *An Edge in My Voice* (1985) and *The Harlan Ellison Hornbook* (1990).

Ellison edited two influential collections of science-fiction stories, *Dangerous Visions* (1967) and *Again, Dangerous Visions* (1972). He also wrote screenplays for many television series, including "Star Trek" and "The Twilight Zone." He writes under many pen names, including Paul Merchant and Jay Solo. William A. Kumbier

Ellison, Ralph (1914-1994), an African American author, became famous for his novel *Invisible Man* (1952). The novel won the National Book Award in 1953.

Invisible Man tells the story of a young black man's quest for identity and meaning. Born in the South, the nameless first-person narrator is expelled from a Southern conservative, all-black college. He then travels to New York City in search of greater opportunity. In the North, he briefly works as a painter and then associates with "The Brotherhood," an organization resembling the Communist Party. He defies all of the groups with which he associates because none of them allows him the power and freedom to define himself. At the novel's end, the man escapes into a hole in the ground that he furnishes as a home to live as he likes.

Ellison's novel is a complex work in which the author integrates symbolism, African American folklore, and references to music, myth, and classic literature. One of the book's themes is that white America refuses to "see" or acknowledge blacks as an equal part of American society, and thus African Americans are "invisible."

Ralph Waldo Ellison was born on March 1, 1914, in Oklahoma City. He wrote two collections of essays and nonfiction, *Shadow and Act* (1964) and *Going to the Territory* (1986). He died on April 16, 1994. Several early short stories were collected in *Flying Home*, published in 1996, after his death. An edited version of an unfinished novel was published as *Juneteenth* in 1999.

Andreá N. Williams

Ellsworth, Lincoln (1880-1951), an American civil engineer and polar explorer, became the first person to fly across both the Arctic Ocean and Antarctica. Ellsworth was a mining engineer in Canada and Alaska and a field assistant with the United States Biological Survey. In 1925, he and the Norwegian explorer Roald Amundsen made the first aerial crossing of the North Polar Basin, in a dirigible.

Ellsworth was co-leader in 1926 of the Amundsen-Ellsworth-Nobile Transpolar Flight across the North Pole. He participated in the *Graf Zeppelin* dirigible flight to the Arctic in 1931. In 1935 and 1939, Ellsworth made flights across Antarctica. Each time, he claimed large new territories for the United States (see **Antarctica**).

Ellsworth was born on May 12, 1880, in Chicago. He studied at Columbia and Yale universities. Ellsworth's books include *Search* (1932) and *Beyond Horizons* (1938). Antarctica's Ellsworth Land and Ellsworth Mountains are named after him. Ellsworth died on May 26, 1951.

William Barr

Ellsworth, Oliver (1745-1807), was chief justice of the United States from 1796 to 1800. A noted lawyer, he served in the Continental Congress and was a delegate to the Constitutional Convention of 1787. Ellsworth was a Federalist U.S. senator from 1789 to 1796 and played the major role in drafting the important Judiciary Act of 1789. This act established the federal court structure. Much of the Judiciary Act's substance is still in effect today. He was born on April 29, 1745, in Windsor, Connecticut. He died on Nov. 26, 1807. Jerre S. Williams

Elm is a beautiful, large tree that is valued for its lumber and shade. Elms are common in North America, Europe, and some parts of Asia. Some North American elms have the shape of a vase, spreading out gradually from the bottom. In other elms, the limbs branch out from the top of the trunk in the form of an umbrella. Many elms reach heights of 80 to 100 feet (24 to 30 meters). Some elms live more than 150 years.

Elms grow naturally along streams and the lower slopes of hillsides where the soil is well drained. However, they can grow in a variety of soils and terrains. In urban areas, elms are often planted along streets and in parks. They also are widely used in landscaping.

Elm wood is tough and hard, and usually light-brown in color. It does not split easily and is useful for making barrels, farm tools, fence posts, hockey sticks, furniture, and boats. It can also be used for fuel.

Kinds. There are about 20 species of elms. The *American elm,* also called the *white elm,* is the most widespread species in North America. This tree grows naturally throughout southeastern Canada and the eastern half of the United States. The small, greenish flowers of the American elm appear in the spring, before the leaves grow. The fruits, each with a little wing around it, fall to the ground as the leaves open. Most other elms produce their flowers in the spring, as well. Some species, including the *September elm* and the *cedar elm,* produce flowers and seeds in the fall.

Other important elms found in North America include the *rock elm,* the *slippery elm,* and the *English elm.* The rock elm gets its name from its extremely hard and tough wood. It is also called the *cork elm* because its bark is corky. The rock elm grows chiefly in the Great Lakes region. The slippery elm has a natural range almost as extensive as the American elm. Slippery elms have rough, hairy leaves and a gluey inner bark. The tall English elm is native to England and western Europe. The English elm has been widely planted in North America since colonial times.

Diseases. *Dutch elm disease* and *phloem necrosis* kill many elms each year. Dutch elm disease, so named because it was first observed in the Netherlands in 1919, was first noted in North America in 1930. Since then, it has spread through most of the range of the American elm, thus causing concern for the tree's future. The disease is caused by a fungus and spread primarily by native elm bark beetles and European elm bark beetles. It can also be transmitted from the roots of an infected tree to the roots of a nearby elm. Prompt removal of infected branches and trees is the most commonly used procedure for slowing the spread of the disease. See **Dutch elm disease.**

William M. Harlow, Photo Researchers

An umbrella-shaped American elm has branches that spread out. These elms make good shade trees. Elm wood is used in making furniture, boats, and other products.

Species of elms that are resistant to Dutch elm disease have been planted in the United States as a substitute for the American elm. They include the *Siberian elm* and the *Chinese elm.* Several other potentially resistant elms have been identified, most of them hybrids of European and Asian species.

Phloem necrosis is caused by a microbe carried by insects called leaf hoppers. An infected tree cannot be recognized until its leaves begin to turn yellow and fall. By then it is too late for effective treatment.

Richard C. Schlesinger

Scientific classification. Elms belong to the elm family, Ulmaceae. The scientific name for the American elm is *Ulmus americana;* the slippery elm, *U. rubra;* the rock elm, *U. thomasii;* and the English elm, *U. procera.*

See also **Hackberry.**

El Misti, *ehl MEES tee,* is a beautiful cone-shaped volcano in southern Peru. It lies in the Western Cordillera (see **Peru** [terrain map]). This mountain is 19,101 feet (5,822 meters) high. It is one of hundreds of volcanoes in the Cordillera. But none of the others surpasses it in beauty and symmetry. El Misti was of great religious significance to the ancient Inca. It figures in many Peruvian legends. The cone, snowcapped most of the year, furnishes water used to irrigate fields. Harvard University established an observatory near the summit of El Misti.

David J. Robinson

El Niño, *ehl NEEN yoh,* is a part of the interaction between the earth's atmosphere and the tropical waters of the Pacific Ocean. An El Niño occurs about every 2 to 7 years, and it can affect the climate throughout the world. In the United States, for example, the climate becomes wetter than normal in the south and drier than normal in the Pacific Northwest. Since the early 1980's, El Niños have become more frequent and more severe. A typical El Niño lasts approximately 18 months and is often followed by an opposite pattern that is called *La Niña.* The change back and forth between El Niño and conditions in which there is no El Niño is known as the *Southern Oscillation.*

In ocean science, the term *El Niño* originally referred to a current of warm water that flows southward along the coast of Ecuador and Peru every winter. The current was called El Niño because it usually occurs near Christmas. *El Niño* is Spanish for *the boy* and is used to refer to the Christ child. About every 2 to 7 years, the warm current is abnormally strong, lasts for an unusually long time, and is accompanied by changes in the winds and precipitation across the entire tropical Pacific region. For this reason, *El Niño* gradually came to refer to the entire interaction of the ocean and the atmosphere during the period of the stronger-than-normal current.

Climate without El Niño. When there is no El Niño, the warmest waters in the tropics are on the western side of the Pacific, near Indonesia. The air pressure over those waters is low. On the eastern side of the Pacific, near South America, the pressure of the overlying air is

Climate without El Niño

When no El Niño is present, the warmest waters in the Pacific Ocean are in the west, and rainfall is heavy there. Near the equator, winds and ocean currents move from east to west. To replace water that flows away in the east, cold, nutrient-rich water rises to the surface, supporting a large population of fish.

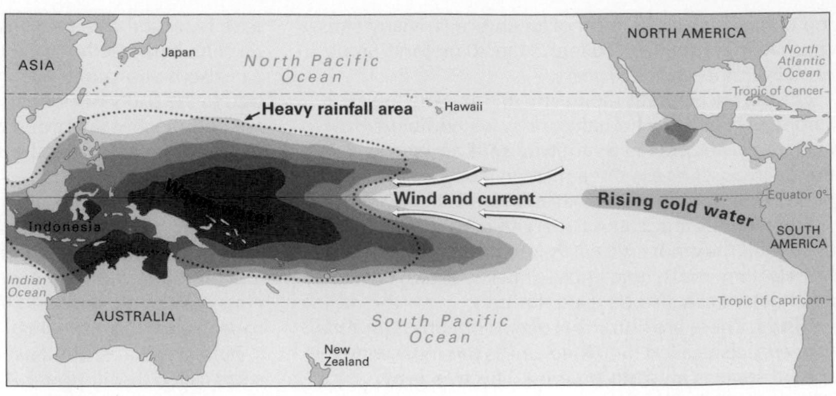

Climate with El Niño

The east-to-west winds and currents weaken—or even reverse, as shown here—when an El Niño is present. As a result, the pattern of heavy rainfall shifts eastward. Because cold water no longer rises to the surface in the east, the fish population declines there.

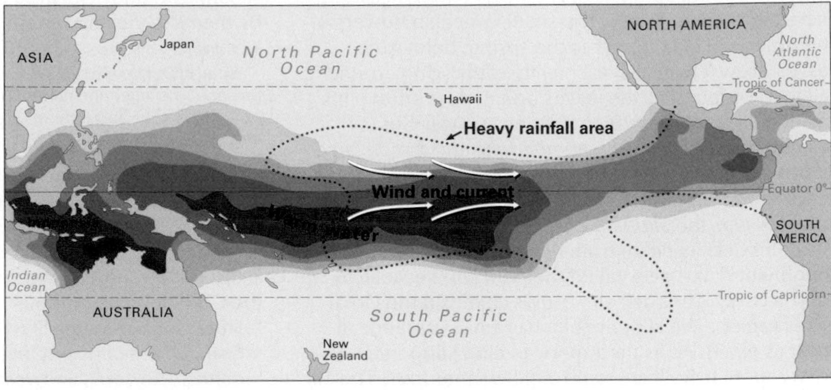

WORLD BOOK maps
Maps based on data from the National Oceanic and Atmospheric Administration

high. Winds in the tropics blow from areas of high pressure to areas of low pressure. Over the tropical Pacific, therefore, the winds normally blow from east to west.

The winds of the tropical Pacific blow the surface waters from east to west. In the east, deeper cold water rises to the surface to replace the water that is blown away. The cold water is rich in minerals and other nutrients that feed tiny organisms drifting at and near the surface. The organisms, in turn, support a huge population of fish. As a result, the waters off Ecuador and Peru are one of the world's largest commercial fishing areas.

In the west, the warm ocean waters heat the air above them. The heated air is less dense than the cooler air surrounding it. The heated air therefore rises, producing clouds that provide rain to the western Pacific.

Climate with El Niño. During an El Niño, air pressure is higher than normal in the west and abnormally low in the east. The east-to-west winds over the tropical Pacific therefore weaken—or may even reverse. In either case, the waters off Ecuador and Peru become abnormally warm. Nutrient-rich cold water does not rise to the surface there, and so the fish population declines sharply.

Also during an El Niño, clouds and heavy rainfall occur mainly over the warmer water in the eastern Pacific. Consequently, the coast of South America becomes wetter than normal. To the west, by contrast, the climate in Indonesia and other nations of Southeast Asia is unusually dry. Droughts may even occur.

Climate with La Niña. *La Niña* is Spanish for *the girl.* In general, the climate associated with a La Niña is the opposite of that associated with an El Niño. During a La Niña, the water in the western Pacific is even warmer than it is when there is no El Niño. Rajul E. Pandya

See also **Climate** (Changes in ocean circulation).

Elodea, *uh LOH dee uh,* also called *waterweed,* is a group of plants that grow submerged in water. Elodea's branching stems are densely covered with leaves that become even more crowded toward the tip. These plants are commonly used in aquariums to keep the oxygen balance in the water. They are also used to demonstrate that oxygen is a product of photosynthesis (see **Photosynthesis**). When elodea is exposed to light, oxygen bubbles appear around the leaves. David A. Francko

Scientific classification. Elodea makes up the genus *Elodea.*

Elohim, *eh loh HEEM* or *eh LOH hihm,* is a Hebrew word that means *God, a god,* or *gods,* depending on the context in which it is used. In most cases, it means *God.* In the Hebrew Bible (the Christian Old Testament), *Elohim* is one of the three most commonly used words for God. Another is the divine personal name Yahweh or Jehovah, which often is represented in translations of the Bible as "LORD." The third most commonly used word for God is *Adonai,* which describes someone who is superior and is translated as "Lord." Henry W. Morisada Rietz

El Paso, *ehl PAS oh* (pop. 649,121; met. area pop. 800,647), is a city in Texas that lies along the border between the United States and Mexico. It serves as a major gateway for travel and commerce between the two countries. It is also an important distributing and manufacturing center of the southwestern United States. El Paso sprawls along the north bank of the Rio Grande at the far western tip of Texas. It lies in a desert in a pass between the Franklin Mountains to the north and the Sierra Madre of Mexico to the south. Part of the city extends into the Franklins. For location, see **Texas** (political map). El Paso's sister city of Juárez, Mexico, lies across the Rio Grande.

In 1598, the Spanish explorer Juan de Oñate arrived at what is now El Paso. He named the area El Paso del Norte (the pass of the north). The pass became a major stop on El Camino Real (the Royal Highway) between Mexico City and the Spanish colonies of New Mexico.

The city. El Paso, the seat of El Paso County, covers 247 square miles (640 square kilometers). The El Paso metropolitan area covers 1,013 square miles (2,624 square kilometers). San Jacinto Plaza, a symbol of the city's Spanish and Mexican heritage, is in the heart of downtown El Paso. The downtown also includes the Judson F. Williams Convention Center, the Abraham Chavez Theatre, the Plaza Theatre, and the 21-story Wells Fargo Plaza, the city's tallest building. The University of Texas at El Paso, known for its Tibetan-style architecture, is northwest of downtown. Fort Bliss, a major U.S. Army post, extends from northeast El Paso into New Mexico.

About 80 percent of the people of El Paso—called El Pasoans—have Hispanic ancestry, and both English and Spanish are spoken in much of the city. Other groups include African Americans and people of English, German, and Irish descent. Indians related to the Pueblo Indians of New Mexico live on or near Ysleta del Sur Pueblo, an Indian reservation, which is in the city.

Economy. The government is a major employer in El Paso. Fort Bliss and other nearby military bases provide many civilian jobs. Hundreds of manufacturing companies operate in El Paso County. Major industries include food processing and oil refining. Factories also make electronics, machinery, metal products, wood products, and leather goods—especially Western boots. Farming, especially the growing of cotton and chiles, and cattle raising are important in the area. These activities employ thousands of El Pasoans seasonally.

Since the 1970's, the economies of El Paso and Juárez have developed a major border industry known as the *maquiladora* or *twin plants.* Assembly plants in Juárez manufacture such products as automobile parts, clothing, and electronic equipment from materials produced in the United States. Workers in El Paso help transport raw materials into Mexico and return the finished products to the United States.

Railroads and truck lines provide freight service to El Paso. Amtrak passenger trains stop in the city, and several airlines serve El Paso International Airport. Major highways connect the city with other parts of the United States and with Mexico. Four bridges span the Rio Grande between El Paso and Juárez. El Paso has one daily newspaper, the *El Paso Times.*

Education and cultural life. Public schools in El Paso are divided into three districts: the El Paso Independent School District, Ysleta Independent School District, and Socorro Independent School District. The city also has many parochial and other private schools. It is the home of a campus of the University of Texas. The El Paso Public Library operates a main library and several branches.

El Paso has a symphony orchestra, an opera company, and a number of theater companies. In addition, the city operates the El Paso Museum of Archaeology, the El Paso Museum of Art, and the El Paso Museum of History. Fort Bliss has several museums of military history.

El Paso hosts many events each year. The Sun Bowl Parade occurs each Thanksgiving, and the Sun Bowl college football game is held each December. Major Mexican holidays are widely celebrated in El Paso. The city has dozens of parks and recreation facilities. The city zoo is in Washington Park. Ascarate Park, El Paso County's largest, spreads across 448 acres (181 hectares) and includes a lake for fishing and boating.

Government. El Paso has a council-manager form of government. Voters elect a mayor and eight other council members, all to four-year terms. The council appoints a city manager to carry out its policies. The city government gets most of its revenue from property taxes.

History. Manso and Suma Indians lived in what is now the El Paso area when Europeans first arrived there. Juan de Oñate claimed the area for Spain in 1598 and named it El Paso del Norte. Spanish priests set up their first mission in the area in 1659, in what is now Juárez. In 1680, Pueblo Indians drove Spanish settlers out of northern New Mexico. The settlers, along with a group of Pueblos who later became known as the Tigua, fled to the Rio Grande. There, they founded Ysleta, now part of El Paso; and Socorro, now a suburb. Ysleta and Socorro were Texas's first towns. In 1682, the first two missions in Texas were built near the present site of El Paso.

El Paso del Norte came under Mexican control in the early 1820's after Mexico gained independence from Spain. In 1848, following the Mexican War, the Treaty of Guadalupe Hidalgo established the Rio Grande as part of the boundary between the United States and Mexico. The section of El Paso del Norte north of the river became the U.S. community of El Paso. The southern part, Mexican territory, was later renamed Juárez.

In 1848, the U.S. Army opened an infantry post, which became Fort Bliss in 1854. During the American Civil War (1861-1865), the fort surrendered to the Confederacy, and a Confederate force marched north from there to invade New Mexico. After being defeated at Glorieta Pass in New Mexico in 1862, the Confederates abandoned Fort Bliss and retreated to San Antonio.

El Paso was incorporated as a city in 1873. It had 173 residents. A railroad arrived in the city in 1881 and helped cause a land boom. By 1890, 10,338 people lived in El Paso. The city had a reputation as a rough and rowdy border town where gunfights were common.

The population of El Paso continued to grow during the 1900's. Employment opportunities with the railroad and in mining and ranching drew many people to the city. By 1910, the population had reached almost 40,000. In 1916, Elephant Butte Dam was completed across the Rio Grande about 132 miles (212 kilometers) north of El Paso. The reservoir created by the dam supplies water to parts of Texas, New Mexico, and Mexico. It helped increase agricultural activity around El Paso, and the population of the city reached 102,421 by 1930. During the 1950's, manufacturing expanded rapidly and the population more than doubled from 130,485 in 1950 to 276,687 in 1960. By 2010, the population had risen to 649,121.

Today, manufacturing partnerships largely have linked El Paso's economic fortunes with those of Juárez. The desert city continues to search for new water sources to meet the needs of its growing population. Air pollution and concerns about immigration and border security also are problems facing El Paso. Carol Roark

© Travel Pix/Alamy Images

El Salvador's Central Region, *shown here,* is the country's heartland. Rugged mountains and volcanoes extend along the region's southern border. Ilopango Lake, which lies east of San Salvador, is visible in the middle distance. The San Salvador Volcano rises beyond the lake.

El Salvador

El Salvador, *ehl SAL vuh DAWR,* is the smallest Central American country in area. However, it ranks as the third largest Central American country in population. Only Guatemala and Honduras have more people. El Salvador is a tropical land of rugged mountains, cone-shaped volcanoes, green valleys, and scenic lakes. The Pacific Ocean lies to its south, Guatemala to its northwest, and Honduras to its northeast.

El Salvador is the most densely populated nation on the mainland of the Americas. It has about nine times as many people per square mile as the United States, which has the largest population in the Americas.

The majority of El Salvador's people are of mixed *indigenous* (American Indian) and Spanish ancestry. Most Salvadorans live in central El Salvador, the agricultural and industrial heartland. San Salvador, the capital and largest city, lies in this region. About half of El Salvador's labor force works in service industries.

In 1525, Spanish soldiers led by Pedro de Alvarado conquered what is now El Salvador for Spain. Alvarado directed the founding of San Salvador that year. He named it for the Roman Catholic feast of San Salvador del Mundo (Holy Savior of the World), for which the entire country was later named.

Scarcity of fertile land has been a primary cause of turmoil and conflict in El Salvador. Beginning in the 1940's, many Salvadorans moved from rural areas to urban areas as the country's supply of land became exhausted. About 300,000 other Salvadorans who wanted land settled illegally in sparsely populated areas of neighboring Honduras. The Honduran government forced many of these settlers out of Honduras, leading to a brief war in 1969.

During the 1980's, a civil war between leftist rebels and the Salvadoran government caused many Salvadorans to leave the country. Approximately 1 million people—one-fifth of the population—sought refuge in neighboring Central American nations and the United States. Hundreds of thousands more people sought safety by moving to El Salvador's cities. The war ended in 1992.

Government

Under El Salvador's present Constitution, adopted in 1983, the country is a democratic republic with executive, legislative, and judicial branches of government. The president has executive power and is elected by the people for a five-year term. The president cannot serve two consecutive terms. The legislative branch consists of the single-chamber Legislative Assembly. The Assembly has 84 members who are elected by popular vote to three-year terms. The Supreme Court of Justice is the highest judicial authority.

Facts in brief

Capital: San Salvador.
Official language: Spanish.
Official name: República de El Salvador (Republic of El Salvador).
Area: 8,124 mi² (21,041 km²). *Greatest distances*—north-south, 88 mi (298 km); east-west, 163 mi (262 km). *Coastline*—189 mi (304 km).
Elevation: *Highest*—Cerro El Pital, 8,957 ft (2,730 m) above sea level. *Lowest*—sea level along the coast.
Population: *Estimated 2014 population*—6,321,000; density, 778 per mi² (300 per km²); distribution, 63 percent urban, 37 percent rural. *2007 census*—5,744,113.
Chief products: *Agriculture*—beans, beef, coffee, corn, milk, poultry, rice, sugar cane. *Manufacturing*—chemicals, clothing, petroleum products, processed foods and beverages, textiles.
Money: *Basic units*—Salvadoran colón and United States dollar. One hundred centavos equal one colón. One hundred cents equal one dollar.

© Fabienne Fossez, Alamy Images

San Salvador is El Salvador's capital and largest city. Street vendors sell a variety of products in the city's busy El Centro district.

El Salvador is divided into 14 administrative *departments,* which are subdivided into *municipios* (townships). Each department has a governor appointed by the president. A council governs each municipio. The people elect their council members to three-year terms.

El Salvador has an army, a navy, and an air force. The country also has a paramilitary police force called the National Civilian Police.

People

Ancestry. About 90 percent of all Salvadorans are *mestizos*—that is, people of mixed indigenous and white descent. Nearly 10 percent identify themselves as white, and about 1 percent are indigenous.

The indigenous people are mostly descended from the Pipil, the dominant group in the area when the Spanish conquerors arrived. Today, indigenous Salvadorans live mainly in the southwestern highlands near the Guatemalan border. A small number of Salvadorans still speak the Nahuatl language of the Pipil.

Religion. Over half of Salvadorans are Roman Catholics. Evangelical Protestantism has grown rapidly since the 1980's. Today, more than 20 percent of the people are evangelical Protestants.

Outline

- **I. Government**
- **II. People**
  - A. Ancestry
  - B. Religion
  - C. Housing
  - D. Food
  - E. Education
  - F. Recreation
  - G. Social problems
- **III. The land**
  - A. The Coastal Lowlands
  - B. The Central Region
  - C. The Interior Highlands
- **IV. Climate**
- **V. Economy**
- **VI. History**

Housing conditions vary greatly in El Salvador. In rural areas, some farmers own adobe houses with a dirt floor and thatched roof. Some poorer country people live in *wattle* houses. The walls of these dwellings are made of interwoven branches covered with mud. Many wealthy plantation owners live in spacious homes on their estates. But these people are increasingly moving to the cities.

In the cities, many poor families rent small apartments in crowded, decaying buildings. Homelessness is a serious problem. Natural disasters in the 1990's and early 2000's worsened El Salvador's housing shortage. Houses in the large shantytowns around San Salvador often lack electric power, running water, and adequate sanitation. These slums contrast starkly with the luxurious, modern homes and landscaped gardens of wealthy residents. Middle-class city residents live in *row houses* (houses of similar design that share a common wall) or in comfortable apartments.

Food. Most Salvadorans eat mainly beans, bread, corn, and rice. They also eat dairy products and meat when they can afford them. *Pupusas* (corn-meal tortillas stuffed with cheese, chopped meat, beans, and spices) are a popular snack. This Salvadoran specialty is sold at many roadside stands and is considered the national dish. El Salvador also imports some food from the United States, and American fast-food restaurants have be-

El Salvador's flag was adopted in 1912. The blue stripes represent unity. The white one symbolizes peace.

The coat of arms has a triangle that represents equality. The flags stand for the Central American nations.

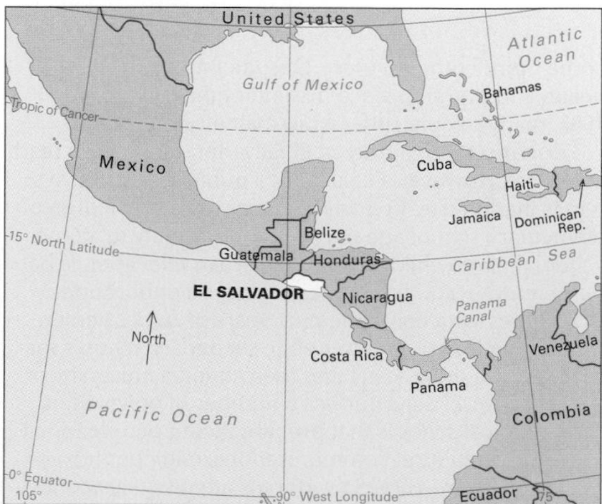

WORLD BOOK map

El Salvador is a Central American country that lies along the North Pacific Ocean. It borders Guatemala and Honduras.

Cities*

Acajutla ....52,359 ..C 1
Aguilares ....21,267 ..B 2
Ahuachapán ...110,511 ..B 1
Antiguo Cuscatlán† ....33,698 ..C 3
Apopa ....131,286 ..B 2
Armenia ....34,912 ..C 2
Atiquizaya ......33,587 ..B 1
Ayutuxtepeque† ....34,710 ..C 2
Berlín ....17,787 ..C 4
Chalatenango ...29,271 ..B 3
Chalchuapa .....74,038 ..B 1
Chinameca .....22,311 ..C 4
Chirilagua ....19,984 ..D 5
Ciudad Arce ....60,314 ..B 2
Ciudad Barrios .24,817 ..B 4
Coatepeque ....36,768 ..B 2
Cojutepeque ....50,315 ..C 3
Concepción de Ataco† .....12,786 ..B 1
Corinto ....15,410 ..B 5
Cuscatancingo† ....66,400 ..C 2
Delgado ....120,200 ..C 3
El Congo† ....24,219 ..B 2
El Tránsito ......18,363 ..C 4
Guatajiagua .....11,721 ..C 5
Ilobasco ....61,510 ..B 3
Ilopango† ......103,862 ..C 2
Intipucá ....7,567 ..D 5
Izalco ....70,959 ..B 1
Jiquilisco ....47,784 ..D 4
Juayúa ....24,465 ..B 1
La Libertad ......35,997 ..C 2
La Palma ....12,235 ..A 2
La Unión ....34,045 ..D 5
Mejicanos† ....140,751 ..C 2
Metapán ....59,004 ..A 2
Nahuizalco ......49,081 ..B 1
Nueva Concepción ..28,625 ..B 2
Nueva San Salvador (Santa Tecla) .121,908 ..C 2
Olocuilta ....29,529 ..C 3
Quezaltepeque ....52,643 ..B 2
San Alejo ....17,598 ..C 5
San Francisco Gotera ....21,049 ..C 5
San Juan Nonualco .....17,256 ..C 3
San Marcos .....63,209 ..C 3
San Miguel ....218,040 ..C 5
San Salvador ..316,090 ..C 2
San Sebastián ...14,411 ..C 3
San Vicente .....53,213 ..C 3
Santa Ana ......245,421 ..B 2
Santa Elena .....17,342 ..C 4
Santa Rosa de Lima ....27,693 ..C 5
Santiago de María ......18,201 ..C 4
Santo Tomás† ..25,344 ..C 3
Sensuntepeque ....40,332 ..B 4
Sonsonate ......71,541 ..C 1
Soyapango ....241,403 ..C 3
Suchitoto ....24,786 ..B 3
Tonacatepeque† ....90,896 ..B 3
Usulután ....73,064 ..D 4
Zacatecoluca ...65,826 ..C 3
Zaragoza ....22,525 ..C 2

Physical features

Bahía de Jiquilisco (bay) ....D 4
Cara Sucia (ruin) ....B 1
Cerro El Pital (mtn.) (highest point in El Salvador) ....B 1
Cerro Verde Natl. Park ....B 1
Cihuatán (ruin) ....B 2
El Imposible Natl. Park ..B 1
Embalse Cerrón Grande (res.) ....B 3
Embalse 15 de Septiembre (res.) ......C 4
Embalse 5 de Noviembre (res.) ......B 3
Goascorán River ....C 5
Golfo de Fonseca (gulf) ..D 5
Izalco (mtn.) ....B 1
Jiboa River ....C 3
Lago de Coatepeque (lake) .....B 2
Lago de Güija (lake) ......A 2
Lago de Ilopango (lake) ....C 3
Laguna Oloméga (lagoon) ....D 5
Lempa River ....C 4
Montecristo (mtn.) ....A 2
Montecristo Natl. Park ...A 2
Nancuchiname Natl. Park ....D 3
Paz River ....B 1
Punta Remedios (point) ..C 1
Punta San Juan (point) ...D 4
Rio Grande de San Miguel (river) .....D 4
San Andrés (ruin) ....B 2
San Miguel (mtn.) ....C 4
Santa Ana (mtn.) ....B 1
Sierra Madre (mts.) ......B 1
Sucio River ....B 2
Sumpul River ....A 3
Tazumal (ruin) ....B 2
Torola River ....B 4

*Populations are for municipalities, which may include rural areas as well as the urban center.
†Does not appear on map; key shows general location.
Source: 2007 census.

come more common there. Despite improvements in health and nutrition since the end of the civil war in 1992, many people suffer from malnutrition.

Education. A majority of El Salvador's adults can read and write. However, El Salvador's public education system is inadequate. In many poor rural areas, children of elementary school age have less opportunity to attend school than do children in urban areas. Education is better in middle- and upper-class urban neighborhoods.

Students who complete nine years of *basic* (elementary) education may go to public secondary schools for two or three more years and then attend a university or trade school. El Salvador has a number of universities and technical schools that prepare young people for careers in agriculture, communications, engineering, and other fields. Few rural Salvadorans attend postsecondary institutions because these schools are concentrated in San Salvador.

Recreation. Salvadorans love to spend their leisure time outdoors. Many people of all ages play soccer, the national sport, in neighborhood fields. Many families spend weekends at lake resorts or Pacific Ocean beaches. Los Chorros is a popular national park near Nueva San Salvador.

El Salvador's most colorful religious festival celebrates the Feast of the Holy Savior of the World. It lasts from July 24 to August 6 and includes carnival rides, fireworks, dancing, and processions. Local religious festivals include the Fiestas Julias (July Festivals) in Santa Ana and the San Miguel Carnival in that city in November.

Social problems in El Salvador include violent crime and widespread poverty. Government officials blame much of the violence on gangs that extend beyond El Salvador's borders, such as Mara Salvatrucha (also called MS-13), which originated in Los Angeles among refugees of El Salvador's civil war. Poverty has caused many workers to leave El Salvador in search of jobs, despite overall economic expansion in the country since the mid-1990's. Much of El Salvador's rural population lacks access to basic health services, and urban slums continue to grow.

The land

El Salvador has three main land regions These regions are, from south to north, (1) the Coastal Lowlands, (2) the Central Region, and (3) the Interior Highlands.

The Coastal Lowlands consist of a narrow, fertile plain along the Pacific shore. They extend 10 to 20 miles (16 to 32 kilometers) inland. Large areas of the land have been developed for farming. Many factories and a fishing industry operate near Acajutla, the leading port.

The Central Region is the heartland of El Salvador. Most of the people live there, many of them in such large cities as San Salvador and Santa Ana. The region also has most of the country's industry and fertile farmland. The Coastal Range, a band of rugged mountains and inactive volcanoes, forms the region's southern border. Coffee plantations and cattle ranches sprawl among oak and pine forests on the range's lower slopes. North of the Coastal Range is a broad plateau of gently rolling land. The plateau's volcanic soil and green pastures make it El Salvador's chief agricultural region.

The Interior Highlands in northern El Salvador rank as the most thinly populated region of the country. The Sierra Madre, a low mountain range of hardened lava, rocks, and volcanic ash, covers most of the highlands. El Salvador's largest river, the Lempa, rises in the Sierra Madre and flows 200 miles (320 kilometers) to the Pacific. A few small farms and ranches are in the area.

Climate

El Salvador has a tropical climate. Temperatures vary slightly from area to area because of differences in altitude. Average temperatures range from 80 °F (27 °C) in Acajutla along the coast to 73 °F (23 °C) in Santa Ana in the mountains.

Showers fall every afternoon in the rainy season, which lasts from May to October. Yearly rainfall ranges from 85 inches (216 centimeters) along the coast to less than 60 inches (150 centimeters) in the northwest.

Economy

For many years, El Salvador's economy depended mainly on agriculture. Today, the country has a more diverse economy. Both manufacturing and service industries are growing in importance. *Remittances* (money sent home) from Salvadorans working abroad are another important source of national income.

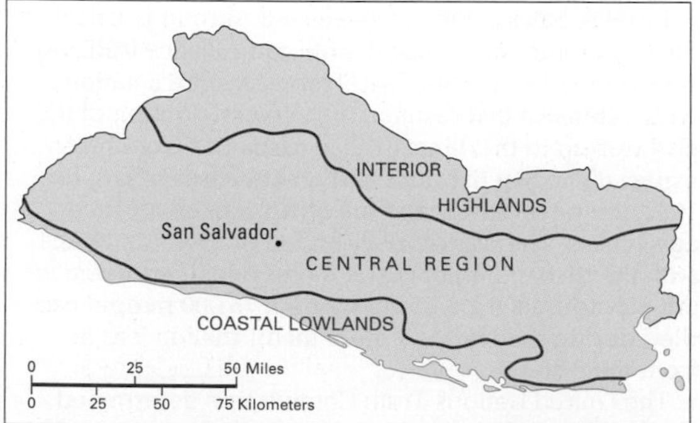

WORLD BOOK map

El Salvador has three main land regions—the Central Region, where most of the people live; the humid Coastal Lowlands; and the cool Interior Highlands.

© Luis Galdamez, Reuters/Landov

Coffee is one of El Salvador's leading crops. The children shown here are helping farmers sort coffee berries on a plantation in Comasagua. Each berry contains two coffee beans.

Cropland and pastures cover three-fourths of the country, and about one-fifth of all workers are farmers or ranchers. Livestock and livestock products, including beef and dairy cattle, hogs, and poultry products, account for much of the country's agricultural income. Many of the farmers own small farms. They cultivate beans, corn, rice, and other crops for their families and for local markets. Other farmers work on large commercial plantations called *fincas,* which raise coffee and sugar cane. Coffee, one of El Salvador's leading crops, is raised throughout the country, but it grows best at the high elevations near Santa Ana. Sugar cane thrives in the warm, humid lowlands along the coast.

The federal government has encouraged the creation of new industries to lessen the nation's dependence on agriculture. Its efforts have helped expand industrialization, and manufacturing is now one of the leading sectors in El Salvador's economy. The leading industries produce chemicals, clothing, foods and beverages, medicine, petroleum products, and textiles.

Over half of El Salvador's labor force is employed in service industries. The leading service industry group is trade, restaurants, and hotels.

El Salvador exports coffee, medicine, sugar, and textiles. Chief imports include chemicals, food, machinery, and petroleum. Costa Rica, Guatemala, Honduras, Mexico, Nicaragua, and the United States are among El Salvador's main trading partners. El Salvador belongs to the Central American Common Market, an economic union that was formed to stimulate trade among its members.

El Salvador has a good network of highways. The Pan American Highway spans the country from east to west. However, few Salvadorans own an automobile. Most people rely on public transportation. El Salvador has major ports at Acajutla and Puerto Cutuco. An international airport is at Compalapa, near San Salvador.

History

What is now El Salvador supported indigenous cultures for at least several thousand years before Europeans took control of the area in the 1500's. The ruins of huge limestone pyramids built by Maya Indians between A.D. 100 and 1000 still stand in western El Salvador. By the A.D. 900's, groups of people who spoke the Nahua language had begun to migrate into the region from what is now Mexico. These Pipil Indians seized control of the lands west of the Lempa River during the 1000's. They built cities, raised crops, and were skillful weavers. Groups that spoke a language called Lenca lived in what is now eastern El Salvador.

Colonial period. In 1524, Spanish soldiers led by the *conquistador* (conqueror) Pedro de Alvarado invaded El Salvador. The Spaniards defeated the Pipil and their allies in several years of brutal warfare. El Salvador remained a Spanish colony for about 300 years. The colony had little mineral wealth and few exports. As a result, it attracted fewer settlers than did Spain's other colonies in the Americas. The majority of the colonists and the indigenous people farmed the land and raised cattle.

Independence. In 1821, El Salvador and Spain's other Central American colonies broke away from Spanish rule. In 1823, all but Panama joined together in a *federation* (union) called the United Provinces of Central America. José Matías Delgado, a Salvadoran Catholic priest, led El Salvador's revolt against Spain and headed the convention that drafted the federation's constitution. The union began to collapse in 1838. El Salvador withdrew in 1840. In 1841, El Salvador formally declared its independence from the federation.

Political violence shook El Salvador during the rest of the 1800's. Five presidents were overthrown by force, and two others were executed. Strong dictators in neighboring countries, including Rafael Carrera of Guatemala, controlled several weak Salvadoran presidents.

The 1900's. The government became more stable in the late 1800's. From 1913 to 1931, all of El Salvador's presidents were wealthy coffee planters. The nation's prosperity centered around coffee exports, which directly and indirectly provided a large majority of the government's revenue. During this period, rich Salvadorans who made up a small percentage of the population owned most of the choice farmland. Most rural people had poor farmland or none at all.

In 1931, General Maximiliano Hernández Martínez seized the government. He ruled as a dictator for 12 years. He built many public schools, expanded social service programs, and supported labor reform. A revolution led by landowners, members of the middle class, professionals, and university students deposed Hernández Martínez in 1944. However, military governments continued to rule El Salvador through the 1970's.

In the 1940's, large numbers of landless Salvadoran farmers began to settle in the sparsely populated countryside across the border in Honduras. In 1969, Honduran land reform laws forced many of these farmers to give up their land and leave Honduras. The farmers' return to El Salvador increased population pressures and land scarcity there. Tensions created by the land reform laws and by a long-standing border dispute between El Salvador and Honduras erupted in a four-day war. The Organization of American States arranged a cease-fire, but many Salvadoran peasants had lost their land.

In the late 1970's, widespread protests broke out in El Salvador in response to economic problems and fraudulent presidential elections of 1972 and 1977. The protesters demanded that the government provide land and jobs for the poor. A few vocal members of the Roman Catholic clergy supported the protesters. Some opponents of the government kidnapped business and political leaders for ransom to raise money for their cause.

In 1979, army officers removed General Carlos Humberto Romero, the president at that time, from office. They replaced him with a *junta* (small group that rules by decree) made up of two army officers and three civilians. Meanwhile, fighting between Salvadoran military forces and leftist rebels was growing. The assassination of Archbishop Oscar Arnulfo Romero of San Salvador in March 1980 led to an escalation of the fighting and touched off widespread rioting. The archbishop had been an outspoken critic of the government. Several leftist groups formed the Farabundo Martí National Liberation Front (FMLN) in late 1980.

With the level of violence in El Salvador increasing, the junta appointed José Napoleón Duarte president in December 1980. Duarte, a civilian and a member of the Christian Democratic Party, immediately began a number of reforms, including a major program to distribute land to poor people. However, the violence continued. During the 1980's, the government of El Salvador received large-scale financial and military support from the United States to help fight the leftist rebels.

In 1983, an elected assembly completed a new constitution that restored democratic elections in El Salvador. In 1984, the voters elected Duarte president. However, Duarte was unable to negotiate a cease-fire and end the civil war with the FMLN. In 1986, an earthquake struck San Salvador. It caused more than 1,000 deaths.

In 1989, Salvadoran voters elected Alfredo Cristiani of the right-wing Nationalist Republican Alliance (ARENA) president. Also in 1989, FMLN forces staged a nationwide offensive that resulted in the worst fighting of the civil war up to that time. Civilian casualties were heavy, especially in San Salvador and other cities. On Jan. 16, 1992, the government and the FMLN signed a peace agreement. The war officially ended on Dec. 15, 1992, with the disbanding of FMLN forces and a reduction in the Salvadoran armed forces. About 75,000 people had died during the war, and more than 1 million had fled from their homes.

The United Nations Truth Commission determined that most serious acts of violence committed during the war had been carried out by Salvadoran troops, paramilitary forces, and right-wing death squads. The governments of the 1990's argued that the report had exaggerated the level of state violence against civilians.

Recent developments. Earthquakes struck El Salvador in 2001, killing about 1,200 people and leaving over 1 million homeless. In 2004, Elías Antonio (Tony) Saca was elected president. Also in 2004, El Salvador ratified the Dominican Republic-Central America-United States Free Trade Agreement (CAFTA-DR). This pact, which took effect in El Salvador in 2006, was designed to reduce trade barriers among the participating countries.

In 2009, Salvadorans elected Mauricio Funes of the leftist Farabundo Martí National Liberation Front (FMLN) president. His election marked the end of nearly two decades in power for the ARENA party.

Heavy rains caused flooding and landslides in central El Salvador in November 2009. The storm killed more than 100 people, left more than 10,000 homeless, and devastated crops. Aldo V. García-Guevara

See also **Delgado, José Matías; Maya; Romero, Oscar Arnulfo; San Salvador.**

Elton, Charles Sutherland (1900-1991), was an English biologist. He was known as a pioneer in establishing the science of *ecology,* which deals with the relation of living things to their environment and to one another.

Elton recognized that animal species and populations fit together in their environment to form communities. He defined the idea of *ecological niche*—the idea that each species has a unique function and place within the environment (see **Ecology** [The role of a species]). Elton also pointed out that a large number of plants are needed to supply food for a smaller number of plant-eating animals. Such animals, in turn, provide food for an even smaller number of meat eaters. Elton called this natural system of food relationships a *pyramid of numbers.*

Elton was born on March 29, 1900, in Manchester and graduated from Oxford University in 1922. He taught at Oxford from 1932 until he retired in 1967. Elton wrote *Animal Ecology* (1927) and *The Pattern of Animal Communities* (1966). He died on May 1, 1991. G. J. Kenagy

Elysium, *ih LIHZH uhm* or *ih LIHZ ee uhm,* in Greek and Roman mythology, was the place to which the souls of heroes were sent after death as a reward for their virtuous lives. Elysium was a land of sunshine and cool breezes, and of beautiful flowers growing in fragrant meadows. The souls lived there in perfect joy, enjoying athletics and dances, and singing hymns to the gods. Elysium was sometimes called the Elysian Fields or the Islands of the Blessed. Justin M. Glenn

Emancipation Proclamation is a historic document that led to the end of slavery in the United States. President Abraham Lincoln issued the proclamation on Jan. 1, 1863, during the American Civil War (1861-1865). It declared freedom for slaves in all areas of the Confederacy that were still in rebellion against the Union. The proclamation also provided for the use of African Americans in the Union Army and Navy, which aided the North's victory in the war. Today, the original document is in the National Archives Building in Washington, D.C.

Events leading to the proclamation

Early views on emancipation. The 11 states of the Confederacy *seceded* (withdrew) from the Union in 1860 and 1861. They seceded primarily because they feared the newly elected Lincoln would restrict their right to do as they chose about black slavery. The North entered the

By the President of the United States of America:

A Proclamation.

Whereas, on the twenty-second day of September, in the year of our Lord one thousand eight hundred and sixty-two, a proclamation was issued by the President of the United States, containing, among other things, the following, to wit:

"That on the first day of January, in the year of our Lord one thousand eight hundred and sixty-three, all persons held as slaves within "any State or designated part of a State, the people "whereof shall then be in rebellion against the "United States, shall be then, thenceforward, and "forever free; and the Executive Government of the "United States, including the military and naval "authority thereof, will recognize and maintain "the freedom of such persons, and will do no act "or acts to repress such persons, or any of them, "in any efforts they may make for their actual "freedom.

"That the Executive will, on the first day

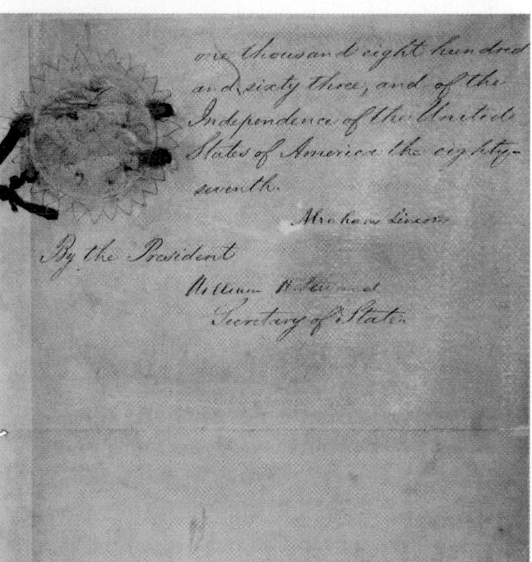

one thousand eight hundred and sixty three, and of the Independence of the United States of America the eighty-seventh.

Abraham Lincoln

By the President

William H. Seward

Secretary of State

Emancipation Proclamation was issued on Jan. 1, 1863. The first and fifth pages of the famous document are shown here.

Oil painting by Francis Bicknell Carpenter in the Senate wing, Capitol, Washington, D.C. (U.S. Capitol Historical Society; photo by George F. Mobley, National Geographic Society)

Lincoln read the preliminary Emancipation Proclamation to his Cabinet on Sept. 22, 1862. This painting by Francis B. Carpenter shows, *from left to right,* Edwin M. Stanton, Salmon P. Chase, Lincoln, Gideon Welles, Caleb B. Smith, William H. Seward, Montgomery Blair, and Edward Bates.

Civil War only to reunite the nation, not to end slavery.

During the first year and a half of the war, abolitionists and some Union military leaders urged Lincoln to take action to free the slaves. They argued that such a policy would help the North because slaves were contributing greatly to the Confederate war effort. By doing most of the South's farming and factory work, slaves made white men available to fight for the Confederate Army.

Lincoln agreed with the abolitionists' view of slavery. He once declared that "if slavery is not wrong, nothing is wrong." When he ran for president in 1860, he promised to prevent the spread of slavery to the West. But early in the war, Lincoln believed that if he freed the slaves, he would divide the North. He feared that four slave-owning border states—Delaware, Kentucky, Maryland, and Missouri—would secede if he adopted such a policy. In addition, the Constitution of the United States gave him no power to end slavery in places that remained loyal to the Union.

Lincoln's change of policy. In July 1862, with the war going badly for the North, Congress passed a law freeing all Confederate slaves who came into Union lines. But the law had limited impact. It left local federal courts to decide disputes about whether to grant a slave freedom—and in the Confederacy, such courts no longer existed. At about this time, Lincoln decided to change his stand on slavery. But he waited for a Union military victory, so that his decision would not appear desperate.

On Sept. 22, 1862, five days after Union forces won the Battle of Antietam, Lincoln issued a preliminary proclamation. It stated that if the rebelling states did not return to the Union by Jan. 1, 1863, he would declare their slaves to be "forever free." The South ignored Lincoln's warning, and so he issued the Emancipation Proclamation on Jan. 1, 1863. Lincoln took this action as commander in chief of the U.S. Army and Navy. He called it "a fit and necessary war measure." His decision provoked outrage in the South and much opposition in the North.

Effects of the proclamation

The Emancipation Proclamation did not immediately free a single slave, because it affected only areas still under Confederate control. It excluded slaves in the border states and in Southern areas under the control of the Union, such as Tennessee and parts of Louisiana and Virginia. But from 1863 to the end of the war in 1865, the proclamation meant the advancing Union armies brought freedom to the slaves in areas where the Union took military control. It also helped to encourage the border state of Maryland to end slavery and led to the 13th Amendment to the Constitution. This amendment, which became law on Dec. 18, 1865, ended slavery in all parts of the United States.

As Lincoln had hoped, the Emancipation Proclamation strengthened the North's war effort and weakened the South's. By the end of the war, more than 500,000 slaves had fled to freedom behind Northern lines. Many of them joined the Union Army or Navy or worked for the armed forces as laborers. By allowing African Americans to serve in the Army and Navy, the Emancipation Proclamation helped solve the North's problem of declining enlistments. About 200,000 African American soldiers and sailors, many of them former slaves, served in the armed forces. They helped the North win the war.

The Emancipation Proclamation also hurt the South by discouraging the United Kingdom and France from entering the war. Both of those nations depended on the South to supply them with cotton, and the Confederacy hoped that they would fight on its side. But the proclamation made the war a fight against slavery. The United Kingdom and France had already abolished slavery, and so they gave their support to the Union.

From a moral point of view, the Emancipation Proclamation transformed the United States and at last began to correct a great flaw in the Constitution. Lincoln well understood the importance of what many scholars have called his greatest presidential act. The day he signed it, Lincoln said, "If my name ever goes into history it will be for this act, and my whole soul is in it." Harold Holzer

See also **Adams, John Quincy** (The Gag Rules); **Civil War, American; Constitution of the United States** (Amendment 13).

Text of the final Emancipation Proclamation

Whereas, on the twenty-second day of September, in the year of our Lord one thousand eight hundred and sixty-two, a proclamation was issued by the President of the United States, containing, among other things, the following, to wit:

That on the first day of January, in the year of our Lord one thousand eight hundred and sixty-three, all persons held as slaves within any State, or designated part of a State, the people whereof shall then be in rebellion against the United States, shall be then, thenceforward, and forever free; and the Executive Government of the United States, including the military and naval authority thereof, will recognize and maintain the freedom of such persons, and will do no act or acts to repress such persons, or any of them, in any efforts they may make for their actual freedom.

That the Executive will, on the first day of January aforesaid, by proclamation, designate the States and parts of States, if any, in which the people thereof respectively shall then be in rebellion against the United States; and the fact that any State, or the people thereof, shall on that day be in good faith represented in the Congress of the United States by members chosen thereto at elections wherein a majority of the qualified voters of such State shall have participated, shall in the absence of strong countervailing testimony be deemed conclusive evidence that such State and the people thereof are not then in rebellion against the United States.

Now, therefore, I, Abraham Lincoln, President of the United States, by virtue of the power in me vested as Commander-in-Chief of the Army and Navy of the United States, in time of actual armed rebellion against the authority and government of the United States, and as a fit and necessary war measure for suppressing said rebellion, do on this first day of January, in the year of our Lord one thousand eight hundred and sixty-three, and in accordance with my purpose so to do, publicly proclaimed for the full period of 100 days from the day first above mentioned, order and designate as the States and parts of States wherein the people thereof, respectively, are this day in rebellion against the United States, the following, to wit:

Arkansas, Texas, Louisiana (except the parishes of St. Bernard, Plaquemines, Jefferson, St. John, St. Charles, St. James, Ascension, Assumption, Terre Bonne, Lafourche, St. Mary, St. Martin, and Orleans, including the city of New Orleans), Mississippi, Alabama, Florida, Georgia, South Carolina, North Carolina, and Virginia (except the forty-eight counties designated as West Virginia, and also the counties of Berkeley, Accomac, Northampton, Elizabeth City, York, Princess Anne, and Norfolk, including the cities of Norfolk and Portsmouth), and which excepted parts are for the present left precisely as if this proclamation were not issued.

And by virtue of the power and for the purpose aforesaid, I do order and declare that all persons held as slaves within said designated States and parts of States are, and henceforward shall be, free; and that the Executive Government of the United States, including the military and naval authorities thereof, shall recognize and maintain the freedom of said persons.

And I hereby enjoin upon the people so declared to be free to abstain from all violence, unless in necessary self-defense; and I recommend to them that, in all cases where allowed, they labor faithfully for reasonable wages.

And I further declare and make known that such persons of suitable condition will be received into the armed service of the United States to garrison forts, positions, stations, and other places, and to man vessels of all sorts in said service.

And upon this act, sincerely believed to be an act of justice, warranted by the Constitution upon military necessity, I invoke the considerate judgment of mankind and the gracious favor of Almighty God.

In witness whereof, I have hereunto set my hand and caused the seal of the United States to be affixed.

Done at the city of Washington, the first day of January, in the year of our Lord one thousand eight hundred and sixty-three, and of the independence of the United States of America the eighty-seventh.

By the President: Abraham Lincoln

William H. Seward, Secretary of State.

Embalming, *ehm BAHL mihng,* is a chemical process that preserves, sanitizes, and restores the appearance of a deceased human body. Chemicals used in embalming include formaldehyde, alcohol, and dyes that are surgically injected into a large blood vessel. Embalming keeps a body lifelike in appearance prior to a funeral. Embalming also meets the requirements of some religions, and it slows decay so that a body can be shipped or kept several days for a funeral.

Ancient embalming. Embalming was first practiced in ancient Egypt as early as 6000 B.C. Egyptians believed that the soul's survival relied on a preserved body. The embalmer dried the body by covering it with *natron,* a powdery mineral consisting of sodium carbonate and salt, and then filled the body cavities with oils, spices, and resins. The ancient Greeks, Romans, and Israelites anointed dead bodies with spices, perfumes, and oils.

Modern embalming began around A.D. 1700. A Dutch anatomist, Frederick Ruysch, devised a formula that, when injected into the arteries, would preserve a lifelike appearance of the deceased. In the United States, modern embalming began during the American Civil War (1861-1865). Officers killed in battle were embalmed, returned home, and then buried. When President Abraham Lincoln was assassinated, his body was embalmed. The body was taken across the country by train so that grieving people could see him and pay their respects. This event popularized embalming as a funeral practice in the United States.

Today, embalming is performed by a *mortician,* a person who prepares the dead for burial. To become a licensed mortician, a person must graduate from a school of mortuary science. A person then serves an apprenticeship and must pass state and national board examinations. Embalming is not nearly as common in Europe as it is in the United States. But an increased number of cremations has led to fewer embalmings throughout the world. Jody LaCourt

See also **Egypt, Ancient** (The afterlife); **Funeral customs; Mummy; Myrrh.**

Embargo is an order designed to stop the movement of goods. An embargo, issued by the government of one country, may restrict or suspend trade between that country and another nation.

One government may impose an embargo to hamper the military efforts of another. For example, the United States prohibits the export of weapons to countries that sponsor terrorism. Sometimes one government imposes an embargo to express its disapproval of actions taken by another government. The embargo is intended to pressure the offending government to change its actions. For example, the most significant embargo in U.S. history was the one authorized by Congress in 1807 to stop British and French vessels from interfering with U.S. trade (see **Embargo Act**).

In 1990, the United Nations imposed an embargo against Iraq soon after Iraq had invaded Kuwait. As a result of the embargo, trade with Iraq fell sharply. The embargo remained in place until 2003, after the fall of Saddam Hussein's Iraqi government. Ralph K. Beebe

See also **Sanctions, Economic.**

Embargo Act was a law passed by Congress in 1807 that began the most famous embargo in United States history. The act prohibited all ships from entering or leaving American ports.

Congress passed the Embargo Act to put pressure mainly on the United Kingdom and France, which were fighting a war that also involved most other European nations. The act kept the United States out of the war, but it reduced the large profits American merchants had been making by trading with both sides.

Before 1807, the United Kingdom and France had been seizing U.S. merchant ships to prevent each other from obtaining American goods. The British also searched these ships for deserters from the British Navy and forced them to return. But the British seized Americans as well and made them serve in the British Navy.

In 1807, a British ship attacked the *Chesapeake,* an American naval vessel, after it refused the British ship's request to search for deserters. This act of war greatly angered the American public. But instead of asking Congress to declare war, President Thomas Jefferson recommended a general embargo. Congress enacted the measure in December 1807.

The embargo lasted 14 months. It was unpopular in much of the nation because it hurt the economy badly. Merchants began smuggling goods and thus weakened the effectiveness of the embargo. In 1809, Congress passed the Non-Intercourse Act. This act canceled the embargo for all nations except the United Kingdom and France. Three years later, the United States went to war against the United Kingdom. Ralph K. Beebe

See also **Blockade; Jefferson, Thomas** (The embargo); **War of 1812.**

Embassy. See **Ambassador.**

Embezzlement, *ehm BEHZ uhl muhnt,* is the crime committed when someone entrusted with another's money or property illegally takes it for personal use. It is not like a robbery, in which the robber takes money or property by force or threat. In an embezzlement, the owner has turned the property over to the embezzler.

Embezzlement is a modern crime. In early English common law, a person could not be charged with theft if the property taken had been legally entrusted, even though the person did not use the property in the way its owner wanted. However, business people needed a law to protect their property while their employees handled it. So the courts devised the crime of embezzlement. The punishment for embezzlement is imprisonment. Usually the penalty is the same as for larceny—a year or more in prison for a major theft and less than a year for a minor theft (see **Larceny**). Charles F. Wellford

Emblem. See **Symbol.**

Embolism, *EHM buh lihz uhm,* is a condition in which a blood vessel is blocked by material that has been carried there by the bloodstream. The blockage, which is called an *embolus,* may consist of a blood clot, air bubbles, clumps of bacteria, small drops of fat, cancer cells, or other foreign objects. The most serious embolisms occur in the brain, kidneys, or lungs. A blood clot, the most common cause of an embolism, usually forms in a leg vein and travels to other blood vessels. Air bubbles may result from a chest or lung injury. Bacteria from a serious infection can accumulate in the blood and cause an embolism. Bone fractures may damage fat tissue, releasing drops of fat into the blood. Cancer cells that have broken loose from a tumor may cause an embolus. See also **Stroke.** M. Eileen Walsh

Embossing, *ehm BAWS ihng,* is a process in which a raised design is stamped or pressed on such materials as leather, paper, wood, or metal. One method of embossing is to press the material between two shaping tools, called *dies.* Letterheads and cards are embossed in this way. The paper is first dampened to make it more flexible. As the embossed area dries, it becomes as hard as the surrounding paper. Stamping machines are used to emboss coins because great pressure is required to raise designs on the metal (see **Die and diemaking**). Early Greek coins were embossed in dies held on an anvil. A similar process of embossing is used today.

Wood may be embossed by soaking it in water and then pressing a red-hot iron mold on it. Dies can also be used to emboss wood veneers and some plastics.
Patrick H. Ela

Embroidery is the art of stitching decorations on a fabric or similar material with a needle and thread. Stitches can be combined to make an unlimited variety of designs, including flowers, animals, people, and abstract patterns. The design may be drawn on the fabric and then embroidered. It may also be created during the embroidery process, using a chart or the embroiderer's imagination. There are many different styles of embroidery. Styles are defined by such factors as fabric structure, thread, and cultural origin.

Since prehistoric times, most cultures have developed their own embroidery styles. People embroider clothing and use embroidered furnishings to decorate their homes and public buildings. Embroidered clothing ranges from simple undergarments to royal robes decorated with gold and silver threads. Embroidered furnishings include bed linens, chair covers, tablecloths, and wall hangings. Thousands of hours may be needed to richly embroider a garment or furnishing with millions of tiny stitches.

Traditionally, craftworkers and hobbyists embroider by hand. Today, however, machines do most embroidering of factory products. Home sewing machines can be equipped with special attachments for embroidery. Computerized home embroidery machines or combination home sewing and home embroidery machines embroider digitized images.

Materials. Fabric used for embroidery is called *backing fabric* or *ground fabric.* It can be any fabric through which the embroiderer can pull embroidery thread without damaging the fabric or thread. Common backing fabrics include cotton, linen, silk, and wool. Some

WORLD BOOK photo

Embroidery uses thread and a special needle to create decorative stitches on a fabric or similar material. This example combines the four basic embroidery stitches, (1) flat, (2) knotted, (3) chained, and (4) looped, to make a colorful floral design.

people use cardboard, leather, and other materials as backgrounds as well as attachments for surface embroidery. Fabrics whose threads can be easily counted are used for such techniques as counted cross stitch. Noncountable fabrics are used for crewel, silk and metal embroidery, and surface stitchery in various forms (see **Crewel**). Embroidery threads range from thin strands to thick yarns. The most widely used threads include cotton, silk, and a variety of threads made from artificial fibers. Various sizes of sewing needles are used for embroidery. The size chosen depends on the kind of backing fabric and thread being used.

Embroiderers select materials that are best suited for the finished product. For example, embroidered chair covers that get heavy use are made from durable fabrics and sturdy threads. Wall hangings are exposed to less wear than chair covers and can be made from any materials. Some people attach buttons, shells, or other objects to their embroidery. Embroiderers often stretch their backing fabric tightly across a stretcher frame or hoop before starting to stitch. This method is especially helpful for embroidering fine, detailed work. When working with large stitches on heavy fabrics, the embroiderer can spread the fabric loosely.

Embroidery stitches. There are only a few basic embroidery stitches, but hundreds of variations of them have been developed. Most stitches belong to one of four groups: (1) flat, (2) knotted, (3) chained, and (4) looped. Flat stitches lie straight and flat against the fabric. They can be made in any length and direction to fill in an area. Knotted stitches form knots of thread on the fabric surface and give textural effects to the embroidery. Chained stitches form loops that link together. Looped stitches are curved. Chained and looped stitches are used to outline and fill in designs.

Critically reviewed by Embroiderer's Guild of America

Related articles in *World Book* include:

Appliqué
Beadwork
Crewel
Needlepoint
Petit point
Sampler

Embryo, *EHM bree oh,* is an animal or plant in an early stage of its development. The embryo is formed by sexual reproduction when a male sperm cell unites with a female egg cell, or *ovum.* This union is called *fertilization.* The fertilized egg, at first called a *zygote,* goes through a series of divisions that produce many cells. These developing cells, which form specialized structures and grow, are referred to as an embryo.

In flowering plants and conifers, the embryo is the part of the seed from which the mature plant develops. In other plants, such as ferns, the embryo is the mass of cells that develops into a new plant. See **Fern; Germination; Seed.**

In most fish and amphibians, the female releases many eggs into the water and some of the eggs are fertilized by sperm released at about the same time and place by the male. The embryo then forms and develops outside the female's body. In birds and most reptiles and insects, the embryo develops within an egg laid by the female. In almost all mammals, the egg is fertilized and the embryo develops inside the female's body. The human ovum is in an embryonic stage for about two months after fertilization. Thereafter it is called a *fetus* until birth. See **Reproduction, Human.** Julie M. Fagan

Embryo transfer. See **Breeding** (Animal breeding).

Embryology. See **Developmental biology.**

© Carl Frank, Photo Researchers

An emerald is a rich green gemstone that is a variety of the mineral beryl. An emerald with a blue tint, such as the uncut one shown here, is more valuable than one with a yellow tint.

Emerald is a rich green gemstone that is a variety of the mineral beryl. It owes its color to minute amounts of chromium in the crystals. Pure beryl is beryllium aluminum silicate. The value of an emerald lies in its color and its lack of flaws and *inclusions* (other substances enclosed in the crystals). An emerald with a blue tint is more valuable than one with a yellow tint. Most emerald crystals contain minute fractures, which are sometimes called *veils,* and various kinds of inclusions. Perfect emeralds are rare and therefore may be more expensive than diamonds. Emeralds are harder than quartz, but not as hard as sapphire.

The finest emeralds are obtained from Colombia. India, Madagascar, Russia, and Zimbabwe also produce emeralds. In the United States, North Carolina has produced some emeralds. Emeralds may be produced synthetically. Emerald is the birthstone for May.

Mark A. Helper

See also **Beryl**; **Birthstone**; **Gem** (picture).

Emerald ash borer is an Asian beetle that has become a major pest in North America. The beetle has killed millions of ash trees there. Its *larvae* (young) bore into ashes, damaging the inner bark and hindering the flow of water and nutrients inside the trees. Ashes often die from one to four years after they are infested.

Adult emerald ash borers have a hard outer body and shiny green coloring. They grow about ½ inch (1.3 centimeters) long. Females lay eggs in midsummer within the cracks of ash bark. Newly hatched larvae burrow into the tree to reach the soft inner bark. There they spend the winter and early spring feeding on the tree's sap. The insects become adults by early to middle summer. Adults die shortly after mating and laying eggs.

Emerald ash borers first spread to North America on ships during the late 1900's. To combat further spread of the insects, people have had to cut down many infested ash trees. E. W. Cupp

Scientific classification. The scientific name of the emerald ash borer is *Agrilus planipennis.*

Emerald Isle. See Ireland.

Emergency Medical Services refers to a system of emergency health care. This system involves community resources and medical workers who provide instant prehospital care to victims of injury or sudden illness.

The Emergency Medical Services (EMS) system is activated when a person calls a telephone number reserved for emergencies. In the United States, this number is 9-1-1. Some systems have a computer that displays the telephone number, address, and name of the owner of the phone used. A trained EMS dispatcher receives the call and sends an ambulance to the scene. EMS ambulances are equipped with lifesaving medical supplies and capable of ambulance-to-hospital communication.

The system includes trained ambulance workers called emergency medical technicians (EMT's). EMT's are trained to provide basic first aid and to transport the victim to the nearest or most appropriate hospital. Some EMT's are trained in advanced skills. EMT-paramedics, often called simply paramedics, can treat heart attacks and give lifesaving drugs and other advanced care.

EMS systems were introduced in the mid-1960's. Today, most U.S. families live within range of an EMS system staffed with paramedics. S. Elizabeth White

Emergency room is a hospital department that provides immediate care when any delay of treatment could cause extreme suffering or threaten life. People can go to an emergency room—commonly called an ER—at any time of the day or night without an appointment. People typically seek emergency care for such urgent matters as suspected heart attacks, strokes, broken bones, severe pain, or serious wounds. In the United States, a federal law requires an ER to examine anyone requesting care.

Evaluation of patients begins as soon as they enter the ER. In many ER's, the first person whom a patient sees is a nurse with special skill in *triage (tree AHZH).* Triage involves deciding the order in which patients should be treated based on a preliminary judgment about the seriousness of their conditions. The sickest patients receive care first. Patients whose care can safely be put off for an hour or two must wait until more urgent cases have been seen. For example, a patient with symptoms of a heart attack would be treated before a person with a sprained ankle, regardless of who arrived first.

In addition to triage specialists and other nurses, emergency rooms are staffed by doctors, doctors-in-training, clerks, and technicians. The best ER's employ doctors and nurses who are specially trained in emergency medicine. ER professionals must make rapid decisions, act quickly, and stay calm in stressful situations.

When a patient's turn arrives, a doctor performs a thorough examination and identifies the problem. Emergency rooms are outfitted with the equipment and supplies needed to diagnose and treat an extremely broad range of illnesses and injuries. In an ER, results of X rays, blood tests, and other diagnostic procedures are reported to doctors immediately.

Some patients go home after appropriate emergency treatment—for example, after a deep cut has been cleaned and stitched. These patients can see their own doctors later for any further care needed. Patients who require more extensive treatment may be admitted to other departments of the hospital.

In certain developed countries, many people rely on ER's for nonemergency care. Some of these patients seek care in an ER because they have no personal doctor and so have difficulty getting an appointment to see one when they are sick. Others feel that they are too sick or injured to wait for their doctor to see them during normal office hours. Richard M. Feldman

Emerson, Ralph Waldo (1803-1882), ranks as a leading figure in American thought and literature. He was an essayist, critic, poet, orator, and popular philosopher. He brought together elements from the past and shaped them into literature that had an important effect on later writing. He influenced the work of the American writers Henry David Thoreau, Herman Melville, Walt Whitman, Emily Dickinson, Henry James, and Robert Frost.

Emerson's essays are a series of loosely related impressions, maxims, proverbs, and parables. He has been described as belonging to the tradition of "wisdom literature" that includes Confucius of China, Marcus Aurelius of ancient Rome, Michel de Montaigne of France, and Francis Bacon of England, among others.

Despite personal hardships, Emerson developed a moral philosophy based on optimism and individualism. In "Self-Reliance" (1841), he wrote, "Nothing is at last sacred but the integrity of your own mind," and, "Whoso would be a man, must be a nonconformist."

His life. Emerson was born on May 25, 1803, in Boston. His early life was marked by poverty, frustration, and sickness. His father, a minister, died in 1811, leaving Emerson's mother to raise five sons. One of his younger brothers spent most of his life in mental institutions. Another brother, who also had a mental illness, died in 1834. A third brother died in 1836 of tuberculosis.

Until Emerson was 30, he also suffered from poor health, including a lung disease and periods of temporary blindness. His first wife, Ellen, died in 1831, and his first son, Waldo, died in 1842. Emerson wrote one of his finest poems, "Threnody" (1846), for his son.

In 1817, Emerson entered Harvard College, where he developed lifelong interests in literature and philosophy. After graduating in 1821, he taught school briefly and then returned to study theology at the Harvard Divinity School.

In 1826, Emerson was licensed to preach. In 1829, he was ordained Unitarian pastor of the Second Church of Boston. For personal and religious reasons, Emerson grew dissatisfied with this profession and resigned his pulpit in 1832. After one year's travel in Europe, Emerson began a career as a writer and lecturer.

His prose works. The sources of Emerson's thought have been found in many intellectual movements—Platonism, Neoplatonism, Puritanism, Renaissance poetry, mysticism, idealism, skepticism, and Romanticism. His prose style was active, simple, and economical.

His first book, *Nature* (1836), was received with some enthusiasm, particularly by the young people of his day. The book expressed the main principles of a new philosophical movement called Transcendentalism. Soon after its publication, a discussion group was formed with Emerson as its leader. It eventually came to be called the "Transcendental Club." The club published an influential magazine, *The Dial,* devoted to literature and philosophy. Emerson edited the periodical from 1842 to 1844. See **Transcendentalism**.

In the 1830's, Emerson gained a solid, though controversial, reputation as a public lecturer and a young man with remarkably forceful and original ideas. In 1837, he gave a famous address at Harvard called "The American Scholar," in which he outlined his philosophy of humanism. He said that independent scholars must interpret and lead their culture by means of nature, books, and action. He urged his listeners to learn directly from life, know the past through books, and express themselves through action. In this address, he proclaimed America's intellectual independence from Europe.

In the so-called "Divinity School Address" (1838), Emerson attacked "historical Christianity." He favored a new religion founded in nature and fulfilled by direct, mystical intuition of God, and opposed formal Christianity's emphasis on ritual.

Emerson's next two books, *Essays* (1841 and 1844), contain much of his most enduring prose. In "Compensation," "Spiritual Laws," and "The Over-Soul," he stated his faith in the moral orderliness of the universe and the divine force governing it. In "Experience," perhaps his best essay, Emerson allowed room for skepticism and showed how doubts are conquered through faith. In "Art" and "The Poet," he outlined his philosophy of aesthetics, and in "Politics" and "New England Reformers," he explained his social philosophy.

Emerson's later prose works are more specialized and better organized. *Representative Men* (1850) is a series of semibiographical, semicritical essays on the ancient Greek philosopher Plato; the Swedish religious leader Emanuel Swedenborg; the French emperor Napoleon; and the writers William Shakespeare of England, Michel de Montaigne of France, and Johann Wolfgang von Goethe of Germany. They are linked by Emerson's thesis that "great men" teach us to "correct the delirium of the animal spirits, make us considerate and engage us to new aims and powers." In *English Traits* (1856), Emerson recorded his two voyages to Europe and discussed English literature, character, customs, and traditions. Emerson died on April 27, 1882.

His poetry. Though in theory Emerson believed that "it is not metres, but a metre-making argument that makes a poem," he wrote his verse in traditional forms. His poetry is characterized by conventional rhythms, rhyme patterns, and stanza forms, as well as economy of phrasing and simplicity of imagery.

The two volumes of poetry that appeared during his lifetime, *Poems* (1846) and *May-Day* (1867), contain some of the finest American verse of the 1800's. He developed his mystical religion in "Each and All," "Hamatreya," and "Brahma." He celebrated nature in "The Rhodora," "The Humble-Bee," "The Snow-Storm," and the two parts of "Woodnotes." The poems "Uriel," "The Problem," and "The Sphinx" are among Emerson's most personal expressions, reflecting his frustrations, doubts, and longings. Like these poems, "Days" reveals, perhaps unintentionally, a comic portrait of himself and of his failure to fulfill his "morning wishes." "Days" is often considered Emerson's greatest poem. John Clendenning

Emery, *EHM uhr ee* or *EHM ree,* is a hard black or gray rock that consists chiefly of the minerals corundum, magnetite, and, in some cases, spinel. Its hardness depends on the amount of corundum. People use emery as an *abrasive* (grinding and polishing material). When used for grinding, emery is crushed into small grains and glued onto cloth or paper. The grains may be mixed with clay to produce grinding wheels. For use in polishing, emery is reduced to a fine powder. Certain other substances are gradually replacing emery as an abrasive. In the United States, the major use of emery is to give traction to stairs and pavement.

Emery occurs in only a few places. These include Russia, Turkey, the United States, and Cape Emeri, Greece, for which it is named. Mark A. Helper

Emetic, *ih MEHT ihk,* is a medicine used to produce vomiting. Emetics rid the stomach of poisons or irritating foods. Emetics cause vomiting in two ways: (1) They can irritate the lining of the throat and stomach and cause vomiting as a reflex action. (2) They can stimulate the vomiting center in the *medulla* (lower part of the brain) so that nerve impulses cause the muscles of the abdominal wall, diaphragm, and stomach wall to contract. The contractions push the contents out.

One widely used emetic is the drug ipecac (see **Ipecac**). Two tablespoons (30 milliliters) of dry mustard in 1 pint (0.5 liter) of water is another common emetic. An emetic should not be given to someone who has taken a petroleum product, a strong acid, or a corrosive poison, such as sodium hydroxide (also called *lye*).

Barbara M. Bayer

Emigration. See **Immigration.**

Emin Pasha, *eh MEEN pah SHAH* (1840-1892), was a German-born colonial administrator and explorer in Africa. As governor of the southern Sudanese province of Equatoria, he made important contributions to the geographical and zoological knowledge of central Africa and helped spark European colonization of the region.

Emin Pasha was born Eduard Karl Oskar Theodor Schnitzer on March 28, 1840, in Oppeln, Silesia (now Opole, Poland). He studied medicine at universities in Berlin, Breslau (now Wrocław, Poland), and Königsberg (now Kaliningrad, Russia). However, *anti-Semitism* (prejudice against Jews) blocked his career. In 1865, he became a medical officer for the Ottoman government in

Albania, then a province of the Ottoman Empire. While there, he took a Muslim Turkish name. After he went to Africa in 1875, he adopted the name Emin (faithful one).

In 1876, Emin joined the staff of Charles Gordon, the British soldier who governed the province of Equatoria under the *khedive* (ruler) of Egypt. In 1877, Gordon became governor general of Sudan. He appointed Emin as *bey* (governor) of Equatoria in 1878. Egypt later promoted Emin to *pasha,* the next administrative rank. Emin worked to end the slave trade and studied the region's plants, animals, and geography. In 1881, Muhammad Ahmad, a religious leader called the Mahdi (divinely appointed guide), began an uprising against Egyptian rule. In 1885, Emin retreated into what is now Uganda.

In 1887, King Leopold II of Belgium, with funding from English traders and the Royal Geographical Society, sent Henry Morton Stanley, a famous British-born explorer and journalist, on a mission to find Emin. Leopold and William Mackinnon, a British shipowner, portrayed Stanley's journey as a rescue but secretly hoped to claim ivory-rich Equatoria by hiring Emin. Stanley reached Emin in 1888. Emin accompanied Stanley to Africa's east coast, but chose to stay in Africa. From 1890, he worked on behalf of Germany, which controlled what is now Tanzania. On Oct. 23, 1892, slave traders killed Emin while he was on an expedition to the upper Congo River region. Timothy H. Parsons

Eminent domain, in the United States, is the power of a government to take private property for public use. According to law, the government must pay the owner a fair price for the property taken. Federal, state, and most local governments have the power of eminent domain.

Governments often use eminent domain to acquire land for such public works as roads, dams, and urban renewal. In some cases, governments give the power of eminent domain to corporations for projects that serve the public or promote economic growth. Such projects include the construction of railroads, schools, electric power plants, office buildings, and shopping malls. There is no specific law that grants governments the power of eminent domain. In the United States, the federal and state constitutions only require that a fair price be paid for property taken.

A government may take over property that an owner refuses to sell in a process called *condemnation.* A court typically appoints appraisers to set a fair price for the property or holds a jury trial to determine one (see **Appraisal**). The owner must give the property to the government in return for the price determined by the appraisers or jury. In Canada, the taking of private property for public use is called *expropriation.*

Michael J. Bushbaum

See also **City planning** (Governmental authority).

Emission control. See **Automobile** (The exhaust system; Air pollution).

Emmett, Daniel Decatur (1815-1904), an American minstrel performer and songwriter, wrote "Dixie" (1859). It became the war song of the South in the American Civil War (1861-1865). He wrote many other songs, including "Old Dan Tucker." Emmett was born in Mt. Vernon, Ohio, on Oct. 29, 1815. In 1843, he became an original member of the Virginia Minstrels, considered the first true American minstrel company. In 1859, he joined Bryant's Minstrels, for whom he wrote "Dixie." Emmett died on June 28, 1904. See also **Dixie; Minstrel show.**

Gerald Bordman

Emmett Till case was a 1955 murder case that helped launch the civil rights movement in the United States. Till, a black teenager from Chicago, was kidnapped, beaten, and killed while visiting relatives in Mississippi. Two white men were charged with the murder, but an all-white jury acquitted them. The men later admitted to the crime. The Emmett Till case sparked widespread outrage and led to increased support for the civil rights movement. Such activists as Martin Luther King, Jr., and Rosa Parks later cited the case as an example of the racially motivated violence and injustice faced by African Americans.

AP/Wide World

Emmett Till

Emmett Till was 14 years old when he was killed. On Aug. 24, 1955, he and some other black teenagers visited a country store in Money, Mississippi. A white couple, Roy and Carolyn Bryant, owned the store. Witnesses reported that Till spoke to Carolyn Bryant and may have whistled at her. On August 28, two men kidnapped Till from his great-uncle's home. His body was found in the Tallahatchie River three days later. He had been beaten and shot in the head. A metal fan had been fastened to his neck, apparently to weigh the body down.

At Till's funeral in Chicago, his mother, Mamie Till, insisted that her son's coffin be left open. She said, "Let the world see what I have seen." The funeral attracted thousands of mourners. Newspapers and magazines published photographs of the funeral.

A Mississippi grand jury charged Roy Bryant and his half-brother J. W. Milam with Till's murder. The two men had reportedly targeted Till because they objected to the way the boy spoke to Bryant's wife. The murder trial began on Sept. 19, 1955, in Sumner, Mississippi. Several days later, a jury of 12 white males acquitted both men. In 1956, Milam admitted in a magazine interview that he and Bryant had killed Till. However, neither faced further prosecution. Milam died in 1980, and Bryant in 1990.

In 2004, the U.S. Department of Justice opened a new investigation into Till's murder. The department sought to determine whether other people may have assisted Bryant and Milam with the crime. In 2005, officials *exhumed* (removed from burial) Till's body, then reburied it following an autopsy. The federal investigation concluded in 2006, and no new charges were filed. In 2007, a Mississippi grand jury found insufficient evidence to indict, and the case was closed. David J. Garrow

Emmy. See **Television** (Television awards).

Emotion, for most people, is a feeling, such as happiness, anger, or fear, that is triggered by certain events or thoughts. Emotions can cause changes in the body or behavior without personal effort or control. An emotion can be pleasant or unpleasant. People often seek out such pleasant emotions as love and happiness. They often try to avoid feeling unpleasant emotions, such as fear and grief. These experiences lead people to believe that emotions are *innate* (inborn) responses.

However, not all scientists believe that emotions are automatic responses to a trigger, or that a certain class of emotions, such as fear, anger, sadness, happiness, and disgust, are innate. For ages, philosophers, scientists, and authors have debated the nature of emotion. Today, scientists have not agreed on a formal definition that adequately distinguishes the various emotions seen in human beings and other animals. But they have developed three approaches to explaining how emotions occur. These are (1) the basic emotion approach, (2) the appraisal approach, and (3) the constructivist approach. All three have some scientific evidence to support them.

The basic emotion approach to emotion is similar to most people's understanding of emotion. It began with Charles Darwin, the British scientist who developed the theory of natural selection, who later wrote *The Expression of the Emotions in Man and Animals* (1872). In this book, Darwin proposed that all mammals express internal mental states in a similar way, through body postures and facial behaviors, that he called *expressions.* Darwin considered human emotions to be little more than remaining traces of our evolutionary past.

Other psychologists expanded on Darwin's ideas. They described emotions as complex biological reflexes that are automatically triggered by events in the environment. Scientists who believe that emotions are biologically basic do not agree on how many emotions there are or what they are called. But most agree that there are at least five basic emotions: (1) happiness, (2) anger, (3) sadness, (4) fear, and (5) disgust. They believe that each emotion issues from specific nerve networks in the brain. Thus, people are supposed to experience the same bodily sensations with a particular emotion, regardless of the situation that triggers it.

The appraisal approach to the understanding of emotions started with the work of the American psychologist David Irons in the 1890's. It was further developed by another American psychologist, Magda Arnold, in her landmark book *Emotion and Personality* (1960). According to this approach, emotions are not simply triggered by an event. Instead, they result from a person's meaningful interpretation, or *appraisal,* of an event or situation.

In some versions of the appraisal approach, an event triggers a *meaning analysis* (series of appraisals) in the person's mind. The combination of these appraisals results in an emotional experience that can be unique to that person and situation. Generally, different combinations of appraisals produce a variety of different degrees of anger, sadness, fear, and other emotions. In other versions of this approach, appraisals merely describe the situations in which emotions take place. For example, anger may occur when people feel that their goals are being blocked or their standards are being violated.

The constructivist approach to understanding emotion began when the American psychologist William James wrote his article "What Is an Emotion?" in 1884. James, along with the Danish physiologist Carl Lange, believed that emotions were physical states that are perceived or understood as telling a person something meaningful about the world. In 1962, the American psychologists Stanley Schachter and Jerome Singer proposed a popular constructivist view, where emotions are produced by two factors: (1) physical changes in a person's body and (2) the reason the person gives for those changes. For example, both pleasant and unpleasant events can trigger a person's heartbeat to increase. But memories and experience help the brain determine whether the person is experiencing fear or joy. Other scholars have since developed more complex constructivist theories of emotion.

Constructivist theories maintain that emotions are not basic elements in the mind. Instead, the mind constructs emotions by combining more basic psychological processes. This approach helps explain how the same emotion can be felt differently over time, among different people, and among different cultures.

Emotion and the brain. Research on people with brain injuries once suggested that specific locations in the brain control particular emotions, such as fear and disgust. But brain imaging studies suggest that there are no regions of the brain that are specific to emotion. Nerve connections in the brain that are involved in memory, thought, and perception, along with those that represent a person's physical state, are all active when a person experiences an emotion. Lisa Feldman Barrett

See also **Brain** (Regulating emotions); **Mood.**

Empedocles, *ehm PEHD uh KLEEZ* (495?-435? B.C.), was an early Greek philosopher. He agreed with Parmenides, an influential Greek philosopher, that what exists is eternal and unchanging. But Empedocles explained the experience of change by rejecting Parmenides's notion that the universe consists of one basic substance. Empedocles became the first philosopher to argue that what exists can be reduced to four elements—air, earth, fire, and water. He said that all other substances result from temporary combinations of these elements. The elements are eternal and unchanging, but their combining and separating appear as change.

Empedocles said that a force called *love* causes the elements to come together as compounds, and that a force called *strife* causes the compounds to break up. He believed that the universe undergoes a continuous cycle from complete unification of the elements under the domination of love to complete separation of the elements under strife. The world we live in occurs between these two extreme states. Empedocles was born in the Greek city Acragas, in Sicily. Carl A. Huffman

See also **Pre-Socratic philosophy.**

Emperor is the ruler of an *empire*—a group of nations or states. A *king* usually rules one area or people, but an emperor usually rules several areas or peoples. Both are rulers of a *monarchy.* A monarchy is a form of government in which one person who inherits, or is elected to, a throne is head of state for life. The word *emperor* comes from the Latin word *imperator,* meaning *commander. Emperor* represented a military command in early Roman times but later became the title of a ruler.

After the Roman Empire in the West fell in A.D. 476, the title passed out of use in Europe for several hundred years. In 800, Charlemagne had himself crowned "emperor of the Romans." Since 1800, emperors have ruled China, France, Germany, Japan, and Russia at one time or another. Japan's emperor, Akihito, is the only modern-day emperor, and his duties are largely ceremonial and symbolic. The wife of an emperor, or a woman who rules an empire, is called an *empress.* Thomas S. Vontz

Emperor penguin is the largest of all penguins. Adults are usually about 3 feet (1 meter) tall and weigh as much as 100 pounds (45 kilograms). An emperor penguin is heaviest just before breeding. Like other penguins, the emperor penguin does not fly. Instead, it swims by beating its flippers. It lives in Antarctica. The bird is bluish-black on its back and flippers, with a pale underside. It has bright orange-yellow ear patches.

Emperor penguins can dive to nearly 2,000 feet (600 meters) deep. They can remain underwater for 20 minutes or more, though most dives last for much less time. The birds dive to feed mainly on fish, krill, and squid. They are fed upon by leopard seals and killer whales.

Emperor penguins are among the only animals that spend the winter in Antarctica. They journey across the sea ice to nesting colonies. At these colonies, each female lays a single egg and transfers it to the male. The females then return to the sea to feed. They travel up to about 62 miles (100 kilometers) each way.

Male emperor penguins eat no food for about four months, losing half their body weight. They balance the eggs on their feet, keeping them warm with their belly. Air temperatures outside the colony may fall below -20 °F (-30 °C), with winds up to 125 miles (200 kilometers) per hour. To conserve warmth, the male birds huddle together in a group. They take turns on the group's edges, limiting each male's exposure to the cold winds. The females return shortly after the eggs hatch, allowing the males to return to the sea. The two parents then alternate trips to the sea to feed and bring back food for the newly hatched chick. Gerald Kooyman and Paul Ponganis

Emperor penguins are the largest of all penguins. Adults are usually about 3 feet (1 meter) tall. Emperor penguins breed and raise their chicks during the harsh Antarctic winter.

Scientific classification. The scientific name of the emperor penguin is *Aptenodytes forsteri.*

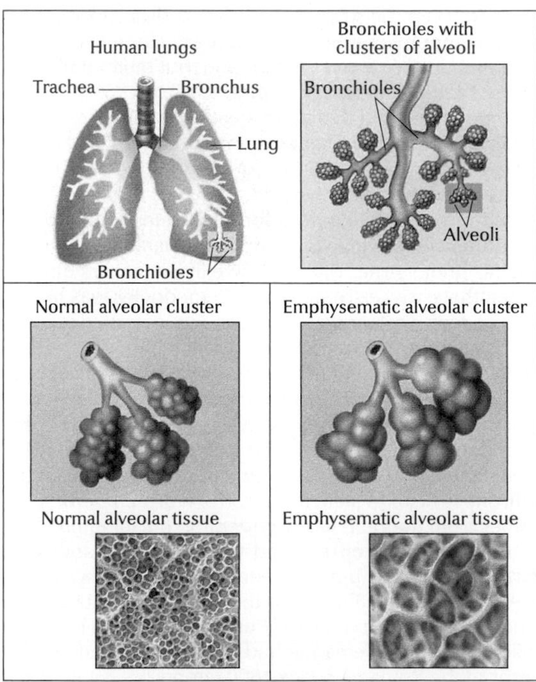

WORLD BOOK illustrations by Charles Wellek

How emphysema affects the lungs. Emphysema destroys the walls of *alveoli* (air sacs) in the lungs. This results in the formation of large air spaces that trap carbon dioxide in alveoli and obstruct the flow of oxygen. The drawings include close-ups of alveoli in a healthy lung and in one with emphysema.

Emphysema, *EHM fuh SEE muh,* is a lung disease in which patients have difficulty breathing, especially when they exhale. Emphysema is one of the two main forms of *chronic obstructive pulmonary disease* (COPD). The other is *chronic bronchitis* (see **Bronchitis**). Chronic obstructive pulmonary diseases are characterized by blockage of the *airflow*—that is, the ability to force air in or out of the lungs. Chronic obstructive pulmonary diseases are a major cause of death in many countries. Cigarette smokers are at least 12 times more likely than nonsmokers to get the diseases. Symptoms usually do not appear until about the age of 50. The diseases affect men and women equally.

How emphysema affects breathing. When fresh air is inhaled, it is carried through the airways to small air sacs, called *alveoli,* in the lungs. The walls of these air sacs contain tiny blood vessels called *pulmonary capillaries.* As the blood moves along the walls of the air sacs, oxygen from the inhaled air leaves these alveoli and enters the blood. At the same time, carbon dioxide moves from the blood into the alveoli. The oxygen in the blood is distributed to tissues throughout the body by the arteries. Carbon dioxide from the alveoli is carried through the airways to the nose and mouth and then out of the body when a person exhales. See **Respiration.**

Emphysema destroys the walls of air sacs, including the pulmonary capillaries. Because a healthy adult has several hundred million air sacs, this process may occur for many years before a person experiences difficulty breathing. As the disease progresses, the alveolar walls with their capillaries are destroyed. This destruction results in obstruction of airways because the alveolar walls help hold small airways open. It also results in the formation of large, inefficient air spaces that trap air, containing carbon dioxide, inside the lung. The lung begins to lose elasticity and becomes overinflated as more air is inhaled and trapped in the air spaces. Thus, emphysema disrupts the flow of carbon dioxide from the body and deprives body tissues of needed oxygen.

Symptoms of emphysema include difficulty breathing, especially during exhalation; shortness of breath; an enlarged chest; and a bluish skin color from a less-than-normal amount of oxygen in the blood. Emphysema patients often suffer from frequent colds and lung infections. Some develop serious heart disease over time.

Diagnosis. Physicians diagnose COPD using tests of lung function called *spirometry.* Patients with COPD often have larger lung volume because they have difficulty emptying their lungs by exhaling. Physicians can also measure the *diffusion capacity* of the lungs. Diffusion capacity is a measure of how well oxygen moves from the lungs into the bloodstream. Lung tissue damaged by emphysema shows reduced diffusion capacity.

Treatment. Emphysema cannot be cured, but treatment may help reduce further lung damage. Emphysema patients should avoid cigarette smoking and air pollution. They should receive a flu shot each year and promptly treat recurrent colds and infections. Many patients are helped by drugs, physical therapy, special breathing techniques, and by breathing oxygen-enriched air. Charles S. Dela Cruz

See also **Chronic obstructive pulmonary disease.**

Empire. See **Emperor; Imperialism.**

Empire State Building is a famous landmark in New York City. It was the tallest building in the world at the time of its completion and for many years afterward. The 102-story building measures 1,250 feet (381 meters) from the sidewalk to the roof. The Empire State Building is on Fifth Avenue between 33rd Street and 34th Street.

The architectural firm of Shreve, Lamb & Harmon designed the Empire State Building, which was completed in 1931. It is a fine example of Art Deco, a sleek geometric style popular in the 1920's and 1930's. The building rises in a series of steplike shapes called *setbacks* to a slender tower topped by a metal spire. Panels of limestone and an alloy of chrome, nickel, and steel cover the skyscraper's riveted steel framework. Leland M. Roth

Empiricism, *ehm PIHR uh sihz uhm,* is a philosophical approach that views experience as the most important source of knowledge. It is the philosophical outlook of most scientists. Empiricists try to answer as many questions as possible by using information gathered by the senses. They reject attempts to decide issues on the basis of pure reason or religious or political authority.

Empiricists disagree sharply about how experience is employed in the growth of knowledge. One group of empiricists believes that experience gained through the senses is the source of all knowledge and that all legitimate knowledge must be verifiable by sense experience. This view developed from the philosophies of George Berkeley, David Hume, John Locke, and Bertrand Russell of the United Kingdom; and Ernst Mach and philosophers called *logical positivists* in Austria. Such empiricists rely on several *presuppositions* (assumptions) that have been challenged by critics.

One presupposition is that all legitimate statements must be derivable from sense experience. However, critics have pointed out that science includes many laws that cannot be verified by experience alone. A second presupposition states that sense observations are conclusive and free from theory so that theories can reliably be built on them. However, critics say that all observations are influenced by scientific theory and so cannot provide a theory-free basis for knowledge. A third presupposition identifies what is real with what can be experienced through the senses. This idea has led many empiricists to deny the existence of a world outside our perceptions. Many scientists criticize this position because they think it runs counter to the spirit of science.

Another group of empiricists believe that the role of sense experience and experimentation is not to justify, verify, or defend knowledge. Instead, their role is to expose theories to sharp criticism. Philosophers in this group include William Whewell of the United Kingdom, Charles Sanders Peirce of the United States, and Ludwig Boltzmann and Karl Popper of Austria.

Empiricists in this group concentrate on proving theories false, rather than true. Their approach enables them to distinguish between what is real and what can be experienced. As a result, scientific discussion is not limited to what can be observed. These empiricists say that many important scientific theories have been based on factors that, at least at first, could not be perceived. The theory of the atom is one example. W. W. Bartley III

Related articles in *World Book* include:

Berkeley, George
Hume, David
Locke, John
Mach, Ernst
Philosophy (Modern philosophy)
Russell, Bertrand

Employee benefits. See **Labor movement** (Arranging contracts); **Pension; Profit sharing.**

Employee relations. See **Personnel management.**

Employment. See **Careers; Unemployment.**

Employment agency, also called a *placement office,* is a service that finds jobs for workers and workers for jobs. It arranges interviews between candidates qualified for particular jobs and employers who have those jobs available. Private agencies charge a fee paid either by the candidate or by the employer. Most colleges and universities offer free placement service to their students. Also, many governments operate public employment offices. In the United States, these offices are financed by federal taxes and are administered by each state, in cooperation with the U.S. Department of Labor.

Many private employment agencies are listed in telephone books and newspapers, and with government licensing bureaus. A number of private, public, and student employment agencies have their own Internet websites, where they advertise job opportunities, identify candidates, and contact job seekers for interviews.

Once a potential match is found, a placement counselor with the agency meets with the candidate. The agency may give vocational tests and check the job seeker's references. The agency has files, supplied by employers, which contain descriptions of available jobs. If the applicant meets the requirements for a job, the agency schedules an interview with the employer.

Employment service dates back to ancient times. Symbols scratched on lumps of clay found among the ruins of ancient Babylon indicate there was personnel placement at that time for laborers and servants. As early as 1800, Boston and New York City newspapers carried advertisements by people who found jobs for laborers, servants, and agricultural workers. Harvey A. Menden

Emu, *EE myoo,* is a large Australian bird that cannot fly. The emu stands about 5 ½ feet (1.7 meters) high and weighs about 100 pounds (45 kilograms). The ostrich is the only taller bird. The emu has thick, brownish-black feathers. Each feather has two plumes connected to a single base. The bird's small wings are hidden in feathers. The emu has long legs, and it is a swift runner.

The female emu lays between 5 and 15 green, rough-surfaced eggs in a flat nest of grass and leaves. The male sits on the eggs until they hatch. A single female may lay

WORLD BOOK illustration by Trevor Boyer, Linden Artists Ltd.

The emu can run swiftly, but it cannot fly.

eggs for several males. Emus feed on fruit and other plant matter. The emu has long been a symbol of Australia. However, farmers may consider emus pests because they eat crops and break down sheep fences.

Kevin J. McGowan

Scientific classification. The emu's scientific name is *Dromaius novaehollandiae.*

See also **Cassowary; Ostrich.**

Emulsion, *ih MUHL shuhn,* is a *colloid* (mixture) of one liquid evenly dispersed in another liquid. The two liquids do not dissolve in each other. Rather, tiny drops of the dispersed liquid stay suspended in the other liquid. These drops range in size from about 0.1 to 20 micrometers. A micrometer equals 0.001 millimeter, or $\frac{1}{25,400}$ inch.

Some common substances—such as cosmetic lotions, foods, lubricants, medicines, and paints—are emulsions. Photographic film is coated with a light-sensitive colloid that is incorrectly called an emulsion.

Emulsions are not permanently stable. The liquids separate from each other after a certain time. To help keep them mixed, an *emulsifying agent* is needed.

Oil and water form the most common emulsions. An emulsion can be formed by either droplets of oil dispersed in water or droplets of water in oil. Milk is an emulsion of butterfat in water. The emulsifying agent that keeps butterfat suspended in milk is the protein *casein.* Marianna A. Busch

See also **Colloid; Photography** (Exposing the film); **Suspension.**

Enamel is a glasslike substance used primarily to form a smooth, glossy surface on metal. It can be any of various colors and is used to decorate many kinds of articles, including metal cups, dishes, and plates. Enamel also provides a tough protective surface for bathroom fixtures, kitchen appliances, various types of industrial equipment, and many other items. Metal articles decorated or protected with enamel are called *enamelware* or, simply, *enamels.*

The word *enamel* often refers to the glasslike substance applied to ceramics. But the correct name for this substance is *glaze.* The word *enamel* also refers to a type of paint that forms a hard, glossy surface when dry. This paint can be applied over a glaze as a decoration.

Composition and application. Enamel is composed chiefly of powdered lead-soda glass or lead-potash glass. Minerals called *metallic oxides* are added to enamel to produce desired colors.

Enamel is applied to metal at a temperature of about 1500° F (816° C), and so only metals able to withstand this temperature can be enameled. Such metals include copper, gold, and platinum. Heat causes the enamel to melt and bond with the surface of metal. Enamel can be applied by sprinkling it evenly on a metal object that has been preheated. It can also be liquefied and painted on a metal article, which is then *fired* (heated).

Techniques. There are five main decorative enameling techniques. They are (1) champlevé, (2) basse-taille, (3) cloisonné, (4) plique-à-jour, and (5) painting.

Champlevé (pronounced *SHAMP luh VAY*) begins with the artist cutting a design into the metal by engraving or a similar method. The cutaway portion is filled with enamel. After the object has been fired, the enamel is polished down to the level of the surrounding uncut metal. The city of Limoges, France, was a famous center of champlevé enamelware from the 1100's to the 1300's.

Basse-taille *(bahs TY)* is a refinement of champlevé. It involves applying an almost transparent colored enamel over the raised design of a metal article, usually gold or silver. The enamel lightly colors the high parts of the design and darkens the low areas, thus creating the effect of light and shade. The method was probably developed by Italian artists in the late 1200's.

Cloisonné *(KLOY zuh NAY)* uses a design made of wire, which is bent into small, connected compartments called *cloisons.* The design is fastened to the surface of a metal article, and enamel is applied to it. After the article has been fired, the enamel is polished until the top of the wire form is exposed. The form outlines the design and keeps the colors from running together. The art of cloisonné developed in the Near East.

Plique-à-jour *(PLEEK ah ZHOOR)* is produced by forming an object out of wire and filling the spaces with colored enamel. Firing then bonds the enamel to the wire. Plique-à-jour produces a glittering stained-glass effect because there is no solid backing to stop the light. It originated in France, probably in the 1300's.

Painting involves painting a design on a metal article

Casket (early 1500's) 7 in (18 cm) long; The Art Institute of Chicago

An enameled casket made in Limoges, France, is decorated with scenes of the Biblical kings Solomon and David.

with enamel and then firing the article to make the design permanent. Metal objects painted with enamel are called *surface-painted enamels.* English enamelers of the 1700's and early 1800's made beautiful surface-painted enamels, particularly such items as gold snuffboxes and copper boxes. William C. Gates, Jr.

Enceladus, *ehn SEHL uh duhs,* the sixth largest moon of Saturn, ranks as the most reflective heavenly body known in the solar system. Enceladus reflects nearly 100 percent of the light that hits its smooth, icy surface.

Like only a few other satellites, Enceladus shows signs of ongoing geological activity. Scientists have observed a plume of particles erupting from Enceladus's south polar region. The plume is fed by several individual jets on the surface of the moon that release mostly water vapor and grains of water ice. But they also release some *organic* (carbon-containing) molecules. The jets spray material onto Enceladus's surface and into space. Some of this matter forms Saturn's broad E ring. Enceladus orbits Saturn in the densest part of the E ring at an average distance of about 148,000 miles (238,000 kilometers). Enceladus's diameter measures 313 miles (504 kilometers). The satellite orbits Saturn every 1.4 days.

Scientists do not know what process drives the eruptions on Enceladus. The moon may gain internal heat from its gravitational interactions with Saturn and the planet's other large moons. The gravitational influences of these objects pull Enceladus's interior in different directions. As a result, the interior flexes, producing heat in a process known as *tidal heating.* Enceladus also contains a greater proportion of rock than most of Saturn's moons. The rock may contain radioactive *isotopes* (forms of chemical elements). Such isotopes produce heat as they *decay* (break down to form other isotopes). The combined effects of tidal heating and radioactive decay may generate enough heat to power Enceladus's geysers. In addition, the chemistry of the interior may also contribute. If ammonia were present, for example, water that might normally freeze would remain liquid.

Enceladus has a variety of surface features. Cracks and ridges cross broad plains. Some areas show impact craters, which formed when an asteroid, comet, or other solid body struck the surface. Other areas do not. Scientists think that ice flows or particles from Enceladus's jets smoothed over the craterless areas.

The British astronomer William Herschel discovered Enceladus using a telescope in 1789. In the early 1980's, the United States space probes Voyager 1 and Voyager 2 took photographs of Enceladus. Much of what is known about the moon comes from data gathered by the U.S. Cassini spacecraft, which first visited Enceladus in 2005. Cassini flew through and sampled Enceladus's geysers in 2008. Amanda R. Hendrix

See also **Satellite** (Enceladus); **Saturn** (Satellites).

Encephalitis, *ehn* SEHF *uh LY tihs,* is an inflammation of the brain. Many victims of encephalitis suffer only mild fever and headache for a few days. But encephalitis can cause convulsions, coma, and even death. There are many kinds of encephalitis. Most result from virus infections. Bacteria, harmful chemicals, and various tiny parasites can also cause the disease.

Symptoms of encephalitis include drowsiness, fever, headache, and muscle weakness. In addition, the disease may cause jerky movements; mental confusion; paralysis; and difficulty in hearing, seeing, speaking, and swallowing. Some victims suffer permanent brain damage, but the majority do not. Treatment depends on the nature of the specific cause of the disease.

Some viruses that cause encephalitis occur in the blood of certain kinds of animals, including birds and horses. They are transmitted to a human being by the bite of a mosquito that has previously bitten an infected animal. In some cases, viruses of such diseases as measles and mumps attack the brain and cause encephalitis. The disease can also occur as a complication of a vaccination. The symptoms of a few kinds of encephalitis appear months or even years after the infecting virus has entered the body. Such viruses are called *slow viruses.*

Viruses that cause encephalitis in human beings can bring about related diseases in animals. In 1971, an outbreak of *Venezuelan equine encephalomyelitis,* an inflammation of the brain and spinal cord, killed hundreds of horses in Texas.

Encephalitis is closely related to meningitis, an inflammation of the membranes that cover the brain and spinal cord (see **Meningitis**). When both the brain and the membrane covering it are inflamed, the disease is called *meningoencephalitis.* Marianne Schuelein

See also **West Nile virus.**

Encephalograph. See **Electroencephalograph.**

Enclave, *EHN klayv* or *AHN klayv,* is a territory belonging to one country but lying within the boundaries of another country. For example, Gibraltar is a British enclave in Spain (see **Gibraltar**). Enclaves were once common in Europe and other areas. Rulers often allowed passage through their territory to the enclaves within it. Today, nations believe that the presence of foreign territories within their boundaries violates national sovereignty.

During the 1500's and 1600's, France and Portugal established several enclaves in India. India claimed these territories after it won independence from the United Kingdom in 1947. France surrendered its enclaves in 1954. But Portugal kept its enclaves until 1961, when Indian troops seized them. Today, the few remaining enclaves include the Spanish territories of Ceuta and Melilla, which lie in Morocco. Anthony D'Amato

Encyclopedia is a collection of information about people, places, events, and things. It may deal with all areas of knowledge or it may confine itself to only one area. A general encyclopedia, such as *World Book,* includes information on topics in every field of knowledge. Specialized encyclopedias provide more detailed and technical information on specific areas of knowledge, such as art, medicine, or the social sciences.

In ancient times, scholars found that the information they needed was scattered in manuscripts in various parts of the world. Some scholars made their own reference works by copying long quotations from the works of other authors. Others copied items of information from a variety of sources. These ancient collections of information were the ancestors of the encyclopedia. But they differ from encyclopedias in many ways. Early scholars presented information in any order they chose, and they had few ways to check its accuracy. In addition, they wrote only for themselves or other scholars. Encyclopedia editors, on the other hand, carefully organize their material and demand accuracy. They also present information to a large, diverse audience.

The word *encyclopedia* comes from the Greek words *enkyklios paideia,* meaning *general* or *well-rounded education.* The word did not come into common use in English until the 1700's.

An encyclopedia is concerned with the *who, what, when, where, how,* and *why* of things. For example, an article on radar tells *what* radar is and *who* developed it, as well as *when* and *where.* It also describes *how* radar operates and *why* it is important in everyday life.

No one person today can create a full-featured general encyclopedia. Such an enterprise calls for the combined talents of scholars and specialists, of editors and educators, of researchers and librarians, and of artists, mapmakers, book production and manufacturing specialists, information technologists, and electronic publishing specialists. It also calls for a large investment of money by the publisher. To keep an encyclopedia abreast of events in all fields of knowledge, the publisher must revise it on a regular basis.

Until the mid-1980's, most general encyclopedias were only available in book form. Since then, several encyclopedias have been issued in an electronic format, in which information is presented on a video screen. For information on electronic encyclopedias, see the *History* section of this article.

Preparing an encyclopedia in book form

Much work goes into the preparation of a new encyclopedia or the revision of an already existing one. The publisher must have a clear-cut idea of the encyclopedia's aims and objectives.

Aims and objectives. Before the editors decide on which subjects to include, they must know the general purpose that the encyclopedia will serve. In addition, the development of the subject matter depends on whether the encyclopedia covers one or numerous areas of knowledge.

The audience is a central factor in planning an encyclopedia. Some encyclopedias are planned primarily for children. Others are designed for scholars and specialists. Still others are family encyclopedias. Family encyclopedias aim to meet the reference and study needs of students from elementary school to college and beyond. They are also designed as everyday reference tools for the entire family, for teachers, for librarians, and for other people seeking information.

The function of the encyclopedia editor is to provide the reader with information, accurately and objectively, so that it can be readily understood. Editors bridge the gap between what there is to know and the reader who wants to know. They serve as interpreters and translators who present information so that the reader can easily understand it.

Scope of the encyclopedia. The number of pages and the number of volumes in an encyclopedia depend on the content to be covered, who will use it, and the price for which it will be sold. Regardless of the number of volumes and pages, no encyclopedia has ever contained all the information that is available on every subject. Most encyclopedias include lists of books to read and websites and other sources to consult for additional information.

Arrangement of content. Most encyclopedias use one of two basic methods of subject arrangement. These are the *alphabetical* arrangement and the *topical* arrangement.

The entries in most encyclopedias, whether the encyclopedias consist of one volume or more than one, are arranged alphabetically. The encyclopedias may have a single alphabetical arrangement from A through Z. Or they may also have a second alphabetical listing—that is, an *index.* The index may be in a single volume, or it may be divided into segments at the ends of the other volumes. An index directs the reader to information contained in the encyclopedia's entries and contributes to the usefulness of the encyclopedia.

An encyclopedia arranged on a topical basis presents its content along areas of interest. For example, one volume may be devoted to plants, another to animals, and another to history, the arts, or some other subject.

How does the publisher decide what should be put in each volume? If the publisher wants all the volumes to have the same thickness, articles that start with some letters of the alphabet may be split among two or more volumes. In this case, each volume must be marked in some way to show which part of the alphabet it contains—usually by showing the titles of the first and last articles in it. The first volume may be marked *A* to *Bib,* the second *Biboa* to *Coleman,* and so on. Such an arrangement is called the *split-letter* system.

Encyclopedias that use the *unit-letter* system have subjects beginning with the same letter of the alphabet in the same volume. In some cases, two or more consecutive letters of the alphabet may be combined into a single volume. One volume may not be large enough to hold all the articles that start with the same letter, such as C, M, P, or S. In such cases, articles starting with the same letter may be split between two volumes.

Illustrations are invaluable to the process of learning and informing. In an encyclopedia, important visual aids include pictures and diagrams. Their educational and informative value depends on the creative flair and ingenuity of editors and artists working together. The illustrations should complement and supplement the text.

Maps are also an essential feature of a good encyclopedia. Accurate, easy-to-use maps supplement the text. They present important information that can be provided in no other way. Like other illustrations, maps should lie as close as possible to the related text.

Ease of use is important to every person who wants to look up information in an encyclopedia. Young readers with little experience in using reference works may prefer a single alphabetical arrangement. However, they quickly learn the value of an index in finding items of information. The editors must exercise great care in selecting article titles. For example, John Chapman and Johnny Appleseed are the same person. Instead of including two separate articles on him, the editors must choose one place for the article and put an *entry cross-reference* at the other.

Most encyclopedias use two other kinds of cross-references. One kind occurs within an article. It tells the reader that the subject just mentioned is covered under some other title in the encyclopedia. The other kind of cross-reference appears at the end of an article. It tells readers that the encyclopedia has articles related to the one consulted.

Indexing provides access to detailed information and

draws together subjects that have significant relationships. But indexes and cross-references do the reader little good if the articles are not well organized. Ideally, the editors should give the reader ample directions to the organization of each article by using clear headings and subheadings. These headings should together form a logical outline of the subject.

Format, the physical appearance of each page, can make the encyclopedia look inviting and interesting or cluttered and dull. Artists and designers must decide the size of the page, the size of the type, the length of each line, the amount of space between lines of type, and the number of columns.

How a *World Book* article is prepared

Encyclopedia articles vary in length according to the importance and extent of the subject. Some articles may be only a few lines or a few paragraphs long. Others, such as the *World Book* article on **Painting,** may cover more than 60 pages. Methods used in preparing these short and long articles differ, depending on the kind and length of the article and on the publisher's policy.

After an encyclopedia has been published, constant revision is necessary. From printing to printing, the editors must add new articles and revise existing ones to keep the encyclopedia up to date.

Most of the steps described here also apply to the preparation of articles published in electronic forms. Web publication of an encyclopedia allows the publisher to update it continually.

The editorial staff decides on the revisions to be made in each edition. Vital information on the changing reference needs of the audience comes from recommendations by advisers and consultants. In addition, the editors review information from continual research into the curriculum and classroom use of *World Book.* Each new or extensively revised major article passes through the following steps.

Preparing specifications. *World Book* editors prepare *specifications* (a detailed outline) for each article. The "specs," as *World Book* editors call them, tell the contributor what the article should include and, in general, how it should be developed. Before preparing specifications, an editor studies the subject thoroughly to learn what information the article must contain to help a reader understand the subject. The editor also determines the grade or grades at which the material is likely to be used. All this information helps determine not only the content of the article, but also its vocabulary and sentence structure.

Selecting a contributor is vital to the *World Book* editorial process. The editors select contributors who are experts in their field. For long, complex articles, such as those on states of the United States and provinces of Canada, several contributors may be used. Each expert writes about his or her area of specialization. The contributor receives a copy of the specifications and may suggest changes for improvement.

Editing the manuscript sent in by the contributor calls for expert skill. An editor reads the manuscript to get a general grasp of what has been written. The editor then changes it, as necessary, to conform to *World Book* policies in matters of content, style, and punctuation. A researcher assists the editor in checking the facts and information. The editor clarifies any difficult concepts and adds any further facts that may be needed. The manuscript is then checked by copy editors and sometimes also by educators and readability consultants. The text is stored in a computer, where it can be revised easily. After all changes have been made, a copy of the article is returned to the contributor for final approval.

Illustrating the article calls for the skills of artists and layout experts. They work closely with the editor in selecting photographs and in planning artwork for the article. Together, the text and illustrations tell the story. The layout expert places the illustrations near the text they are designed to complement and supplement. The editor may recommend the addition of such other non-text elements as audio and video selections to articles that will be published in electronic form.

Providing cross-references to text and illustrations is the work of specially trained editors who direct readers to specific facts or articles. Information that might otherwise be missed is thus made easy to find. The cross-reference editors also check the lists of related articles at the end of new or revised articles.

Indexing requires the skills of trained indexers and computer specialists. The indexers select items to add to the index and put them into the computer system. The computer has two files—one in the page-by-page order in which the items were selected, and the other in the alphabetical order of the final index.

Preparing for the press. Editors and designers make *electronic pages,* which consist of text and illustrations in digital form. Files containing this information are then processed by computerized production systems that generate the final type and images. After final proofs have been approved, printing plates are made and printing and binding can begin. For more information about the mechanical aspects of making encyclopedias and other books, see **Printing** and its list of related articles.

How to judge an encyclopedia

If you plan to buy an encyclopedia, you should ask the following questions:

— Is it published by a reputable, experienced, and well-established company?
— Does it have a permanent editorial and art staff?
— Does it have an editorial advisory board made up of nationally known educators and scholars?
— Is it authoritative? Are the articles signed by outstanding contributors?
— Is it accurate? Look up articles in fields with which you are familiar. Are the text and pictures understandable? Do they cover all important facts?
— Is it comprehensive? Does it cover subjects in all areas of knowledge?
— Is it up to date? Check articles that deal with current events, such as United States history.
— Is it written without bias?
— Is it written clearly and simply? Can readers, young and old, easily understand it?
— Is it well illustrated?
— Is it easy to use? Check the following items:
  — Does it have a single alphabetical arrangement or some other arrangement?
  — Are the volumes numbered and lettered clearly?
  — Is there a liberal use of cross-references?

Basic steps in the preparation of a *World Book* article

Information presented in *World Book* articles must be accurate, authoritative, and up to date. Meeting these standards requires the help of educators from all fields of learning, such specialists as librarians and curators of museums, and officials in business and government. *World Book* editors, designers, and researchers collaborate to produce articles that are accurate, interesting, informative, and easy to read. The steps illustrated here refer particularly to preparing articles to appear in print.

WORLD BOOK illustrations by Jay Bensen, Jay E. Bensen and Associates

Consultants who are experts in their fields advise the editorial staff. They provide information on developments in their specialties, suggest qualified contributors, and review edited articles.

The designer, or *layout artist,* plans the layout of the article and then stores it in a computer. Later, the designer calls the text into the layout, ensuring that illustrations are placed in relation to the text.

The contributor, who is an expert on the topic, writes the article. This author also reviews the edited manuscript and makes whatever changes seem necessary before giving final approval.

The photo editor obtains photographs and other pictorial material to illustrate the article. Designers and editors work together to select illustrations that are both informative and easily understood.

The article editor revises the contributor's manuscript to present the information in a clear, direct style. The editor gears the vocabulary to the age level of the article's most likely readers.

The art director oversees the work of the designer and the photo editor. The art director also participates in the reviews of illustrations and layouts and in the selection of free-lance artists.

The copy editor polishes the edited article to make it as interesting and easy to read as possible. The copy editor also makes sure that the manuscript follows *World Book* style.

The indexer chooses items from new and revised articles to add to the index and enters them into a computer system.

The researcher checks authoritative sources to ensure that the statistics and other information in the text are accurate and up to date.

The proofreader examines the copy and marks any errors with a set of symbols called *proofreaders' marks.* The editor then keys the corrections into the article.

Cross-reference editors add references to other articles in the encyclopedia to help readers find additional information on the subject. They also add references from other articles to this one.

Preparing for the press. Proofs of the text and illustrations are output from electronic files. The approved files are then transferred onto printing plates, and the article is ready to be printed.

—Is there an accurate and comprehensive index?
—Is pronunciation given for difficult words?
—Are the article titles boldly identified?
— Do some articles have lists of related books to read?
— Does the publisher produce a yearbook that reviews the most important events of each year?
— How well are the books made? Is the paper of good quality? Is the printing clear and sharp? Is the binding sturdy?

Before you purchase an encyclopedia, make sure that you understand its basic purpose and plan. If necessary, consult a librarian to make sure that the work is standard and modern. And, after you purchase the encyclopedia, *use it!* Put it in the place, at home or in school, where it can give maximum service.

History

The first reference works. Many scholars call the ancient Greek philosopher Aristotle the father of encyclopedists. In the 300's B.C., Aristotle made one of the first attempts to bring all existing knowledge together in a series of books. He also gave his own ideas on many subjects. Marcus Terentius Varro (116-27 B.C.), a Roman writer, made the next attempt. He wrote a nine-volume work on the arts and sciences called *Disciplinae (Disciplines).* No actual copies of either Aristotle's or Varro's works exist today. Scholars know of them only from copies made at a later date. See **Aristotle.**

Pliny the Elder (A.D. 23-79), another Roman writer, wrote a set of reference books called *Historia Naturalis (Natural History).* This set is the oldest reference work in existence. It contains thousands of facts, chiefly about minerals, plants, and animals. See **Pliny the Elder.**

The Chinese compiled their first encyclopedia in the early A.D. 200's, but no physical trace of it remains. A second encyclopedia, from the late 200's, was revised in the early 1600's. The most important early Chinese encyclopedia, compiled by the scholar Du You (also spelled Tu Yu) about 800, emphasizes the things people needed to know in order to get and hold jobs in the civil service.

Isidore, the Bishop of Seville, completed his *Etymologiarum libri XX (Twenty Volumes of Etymologies)* in 623. European scholars used this collection of facts as a source book for nearly 1,000 years. But today, scholars seldom depend on it because they cannot check its accuracy. Isidore rarely gave sources for his information.

A scholar in Baghdad, Ibn Qutaiba, compiled the first Arabic reference work. He wrote the *Kitab Uyun al-Ahkbar (Book of Choice Histories)* in the 800's. A Persian scholar, al-Khuwarizmi, completed his *Mafatih al-Ulum (Key to the Sciences)* in the 990's. He separated what he considered Arab knowledge, including such fields as grammar and poetry, from "foreign" knowledge of such fields as alchemy and logic. The Brethren of Purity, a group of scholars at Basra, in what is now Iraq, during the late 900's produced an encyclopedia that tried to reconcile Greek and Arabic learning.

From the 1200's to the 1600's, some original reference works appeared, but most were copies, made slowly by hand. A Dominican friar, Vincent of Beauvais, wrote the *Speculum maius (Bigger Mirror)* in 1244 and revised it many times before he died in 1264. He organized his material under three headings—political history, natural history, and academic subjects. He chose his title because he wanted his work to reflect all human knowledge. Long afterward, scholars continued to use the term *speculum* (mirror) for a reference work.

Bartholomew de Glanville, a theology teacher in Paris during the 1200's, wrote *De proprietatibus rerum (On the Properties of Things).* This work stressed the religious and moral aspects of each topic. Bartholomew wrote in Latin, but his work was soon translated into English, French, and other languages.

In China, the scholar Ma Duanlin completed the huge *Wenxian Tongkao (General Study of the Literary Remains)* in 348 volumes in 1273. It was published in 1319. Another scholar, Wang Yinglin, completed a slightly smaller work, the *Yuhai (Sea of Jade),* in 1267. It was published in 1351.

During the late 1400's, following the European development of movable type for printing, copies and translations of written works became easier to produce than ever before. About 1481, the English printer William Caxton published *The Mirror of the World,* one of the first reference works in English (see **Caxton, William**). It was one of many translations of a French work, *Mappe Monde (The Image of the World).*

Johann Heinrich Alsted, a German theologian, published one of the last reference works written in Latin. His *Encyclopaedia septem tomis distincta (Encyclopedia in Seven Volumes),* issued in 1630, stressed geography. Louis Moréri's *Le grand dictionnaire historique (The Great Historical Dictionary),* first issued in one volume in 1671, marked a trend of the 1600's toward publishing such material in local languages.

An age of experiment in encyclopedias began in 1704 with the publication of the German *Reales Staats- und Zeitungs-Lexikon (Dictionary of Government and News).* This work was written by a German author, Sinold von Schütz, with a preface written by the scholar Johann Hübner. Schütz later changed its title to include the term *Konversations-Lexikon (Dictionary of Conversation).* This term has been used in the titles of most German encyclopedias ever since. The work, usually called simply *Hübner,* established the pattern for many later encyclopedias—all short articles, entirely the work of many contributors, with numerous cross-references.

Also in 1704, an English theologian named John Harris published his *Lexicon Technicum.* This reference work was the first that presented all articles alphabetically, used articles contributed by specialists, and included bibliographies. Ephraim Chambers, an English mapmaker, published his *Cyclopaedia, or the Universal Dictionary of Arts and Sciences,* in 1728. He based his work on Harris's but added elaborate cross-references to simplify the search for information.

Chambers's work greatly influenced two French authors, Denis Diderot and Jean d'Alembert. They founded their *Encyclopédie ou Dictionnaire raisonné des sciences, des arts et des métiers (Encyclopedia or Systematic Dictionary of the Sciences, the Arts, and the Professions)* in 1751. The work was published in 28 volumes between 1751 and 1772. Seven more volumes were added between 1776 and 1780.

Diderot and other French writers of his time were called *encyclopedists* because of their work. The *Encyclopédie* contains a number of their revolutionary opinions. Many historians believe it contributed to the movement that led to the French Revolution (1789-1799). See **Diderot, Denis.**

The *Encyclopédie* inspired a group of British scholars, who began publishing the *Encyclopædia Britannica* in 1768. The first edition was completed in 100 installments by 1771. A second edition, which included biographies, appeared between 1778 and 1783. The *Britannica* established a form that has been followed by many encyclopedias—all extensive articles, some of them more than 100 pages long, on broad topics.

Encyclopedias of the 1800's and 1900's. Pierre Larousse, a former teacher, began to publish *Le Grand Dictionnaire Universel du XIXe siècle (The Great Universal Dictionary of the 19th Century)* in Paris in 1865. His firm brought out *Larousse du XXe siècle* in 1928. *La Grande Encyclopédie* was published in 31 volumes from 1886 to 1902. It was reissued in the 1970's. The *Grand Dictionnaire Encyclopédique Larousse* was published in 1982.

In Germany, Friedrich Arnold Brockhaus, a bookseller, completed his *Konversations-Lexikon* in 1809. It was published in many editions and translations. The latest edition is called *Brockhaus Enzyklopädie.* Josef Meyer published a major *Konversations-Lexikon* in the 1840's. This work became identified with Nazi propaganda during World War II (1939-1945) and was discontinued. It reappeared in the 1950's and has been revised several times since then. The Herder *Konversations-Lexikon,* first published from 1854 to 1857, was later known as *Der Neue Herder (The New Herder).*

In Canada, the *Encyclopedia of Canada* was published in six volumes between 1935 and 1938. The 10-volume *Encyclopedia Canadiana,* which dealt only with subjects of special interest to Canadians, appeared in 1958. The first edition of *The Canadian Encyclopedia,* published as a three-volume set, appeared in 1985. *The Junior Encyclopedia of Canada,* for children, appeared in 1990.

In the United States, printers made illegal copies of the *Encyclopædia Britannica* as early as 1798. The first edition of *Encyclopedia Americana* appeared in 13 volumes from 1829 to 1833. Francis Lieber, a German American editor, translated much of it from the seventh edition of Brockhaus's *Konversations-Lexikon.* A U.S. firm, Sears, Roebuck & Co., bought *Britannica* in the 1920's. In 1943, William Benton, a former U.S. senator and advertising executive, bought a controlling interest in the encyclopedia company. After Benton died, ownership passed to a foundation set up in his name. In 1996, the Swiss investor Jacob Safra bought *Britannica* from the Benton Foundation. *Encyclopædia Britannica* ceased publishing its 32-volume print set in 2012.

In 1911, Americans published the first one-volume encyclopedia, *The Volume Library.* The *Lincoln Library of Essential Information* followed in 1924. The one-volume *Columbia Encyclopedia* appeared in 1935. *The New Columbia Encyclopedia* came out in 1975. The one-volume *Random House Encyclopedia* was published in 1977. The first edition of *Academic American Encyclopedia* (later also published as *Grolier Academic Encyclopedia)* appeared in 1980. Publication of the nine-volume *Oxford Illustrated Encyclopedia* was completed in 1993.

Other major U.S. encyclopedias of the period included Grolier's *The Book of Knowledge* (1910), the U.S. edition of the British *Children's Encyclopedia; Funk & Wagnalls* (1912-1997); *Compton's Pictured Encyclopedia* (1922-1968), later published as *Compton's by Britannica; Collier's Encyclopedia* (1949-1998), which replaced other sets first published by the company in 1902 and 1932; the restructured *Encyclopædia Britannica* (1974, consisting of three sections called the *Micropædia, Macropædia,* and *Propædia;* re-released, 1985); and *Grolier's Academic American Encyclopedia* (1980), later published as *Grolier Academic Encyclopedia.*

Today's encyclopedias may consist entirely of long articles or short articles, or they may contain both. They may appear in one volume or in many volumes. Most encyclopedias are alphabetically arranged.

Electronic encyclopedias first appeared in the mid-1980's. One type of electronic encyclopedia, the *CD-ROM* (Compact Disc Read-Only Memory) *encyclopedia,* can store the same amount of information found in a multivolume set of encyclopedias on a single compact disc. The first encyclopedia issued in this form was *The Electronic Encyclopedia* of 1986, based on *The Grolier Academic Encyclopedia.* CD-ROM and DVD-ROM encyclopedias called *multimedia encyclopedias* provide video, sound, and motion in addition to text.

Online electronic encyclopedias became increasingly popular in the late 1990's and early 2000's. Online searching involves linking a computer to a network to access information stored on databases at other locations.

Important encyclopedia dates

1244 Vincent of Beauvais arranged information by topics in his *Speculum maius (Bigger Mirror).*
1410 Domenico Bandini used many cross-references in *Fons memorabilium universi (Source of Memorable Facts of the Universe).*
1506 Raffaeli Maffei included biographies in *Comentarii Urbani (Urban Commentaries).*
1541 Ringelberg of Basel was the first to use the word *cyclopedia* in the title of a reference work.
1704 The *Reales Staats- und Zeitungs-Lexikon* was the first encyclopedia to be made up entirely of the work of many contributors.
1732 Johann Zedler, in his *Universal Lexikon,* was the first to include biographies of living persons.
1751 The first part of Denis Diderot and Jean d'Alembert's *Encyclopédie* appeared.
1768 The first part of *Encyclopædia Britannica* appeared.
1829 The first part of *Encyclopedia Americana* appeared.
1865 Pierre Larousse began *Le Grand Dictionnaire.*
1908 The British *Children's Encyclopaedia* appeared.
1910 An American version of the *Children's Encyclopaedia* appeared as *The Book of Knowledge.*
1917 The first edition of *World Book* was published.
1922 The first edition of *Compton's Pictured Encyclopedia* appeared.
1935 The one-volume *Columbia Encyclopedia* appeared.
1948 *The Oxford Junior Encyclopaedia* was published.
1949 The first edition of *Collier's Encyclopedia* appeared.
1966 *The New Book of Knowledge* was published.
1967 *Merit Students Encyclopedia* appeared.
1974 A restructured *Encyclopædia Britannica* appeared.
1977 The one-volume *Random House Encyclopedia* appeared.
1980 The first edition of *Academic American Encyclopedia* (later also published as *Grolier Academic Encyclopedia)* appeared.
1986 *The Electronic Encyclopedia,* the first CD-ROM encyclopedia, appeared. It was a compact disc version of *Academic American Encyclopedia.*
1990's Multimedia and online encyclopedias, including *World Book,* became popular.
2001 *Wikipedia* was launched.

In the first decade of the 2000's, most encyclopedias were updated and maintained only in electronic formats. But World Book continued to extensively revise its print encyclopedia as well as its online versions. Other electronic encyclopedias included variations of *Encyclopedia Americana, Encyclopædia Britannica, Compton's Interactive, Grolier Multimedia,* and *Microsoft Encarta.* In 2001, a free online encyclopedia called *Wikipedia* appeared. *Wikipedia* is a collection of interlinked web pages known as *wikis* that permit anyone to read, create, or edit articles. Later versions of free, wiki-based content included *Scholarpedia,* launched in 2006; *Citizendium,* launched in 2007; and Google's *Knol,* launched in 2008. *Encarta,* one of the earliest of the electronic encyclopedias, was discontinued by Microsoft in 2009.

World Book was first published in 1917 in 8 volumes. It grew to 10 volumes in 1918. The editors began a system of continuous revision in 1918 and a yearly revision program in 1933. They began to use analyses of contents of courses of study in 1936 and of classroom use of reference works in 1955. The set grew to 13 volumes in 1929, to 19 in 1933, and to 20 in 1960. The set expanded to 22 volumes in 1971, when an index was added.

In 1961, *World Book* became the first encyclopedia published in braille. In 1964, *World Book* was published in a large-type edition for people with visual problems. In 1980, *World Book* became the first encyclopedia reproduced as a voice recording.

In 1990, World Book produced *The World Book Information Finder.* This CD-ROM product featured text and tables from *The World Book Encyclopedia* and dictionary entries from *The World Book Dictionary. The World Book New Illustrated Information Finder,* introduced in 1994, added pictures and maps. *The World Book Multimedia Encyclopedia,* launched in 1995, added animation, videos, and audio. *World Book Online,* an online version of *World Book,* became available to schools and libraries in 1998 and to individual and home subscribers in 1999. This product, with an atlas, a dictionary, and other features, was renamed *World Book Online Reference Center* in 2003. In 2008, it was redesigned for students in upper elementary through intermediate grades and renamed *World Book Student.* World Book's collection of digital publications is known as the *World Book Web.*

In 1999, World Book launched a 13-volume general reference set, *The World Book Student Discovery Encyclopedia.* Written at a lower reading level than *World Book,* it provided a bridge to *World Book* for young readers. Later editions were titled *Discovery Encyclopedia.* This set was followed by a science reference set, *The World Book Student Discovery Science Encyclopedia* (2005). A topically organized edition of the set was published in 2013 as the *Discovery Science Encyclopedia. World Book Kids,* an online product based on the *Student Discovery Encyclopedia,* was published in 2006. *World Book Advanced,* for secondary and postsecondary students, was launched in 2007. In 2008, *World Book Discover* was added as an online product. It was designed to complement *differentiated instruction* methods. These methods are based on the idea that students vary in background knowledge, academic readiness, language, and other ways, and so should have multiple options for taking in information and understanding ideas. In 2012, *Academic World Book* was added to the *World Book Web.* The site was designed to respond to the research, independent study, and writing activities of college students. Versions of these publications adapted for use on mobile devices, such as tablet computers, began to appear in 2013. Paul A. Kobasa

Related articles in *World Book* include:

Bacon, Roger	Index	Study
Cross-reference	Reading	Vocabulary

Endangered species are living things threatened with *extinction*—that is, the dying off of all of their kind. Thousands of species of animals and plants are endangered, and the number increases each year. Some examples of endangered species are blue whales, giant pandas, orangutans, rhinoceroses, sea turtles, snow leopards, tigers, and whooping cranes. Among endangered plants are running buffalo clover, Santa Cruz cypress, snakeroot, and many species of cactuses.

Each plant and animal species plays a part in the balance of its *ecosystem,* its relation to other living things and to the environment. The extinction of many species threatens the survival of other living things, including people. As more species become endangered, ecosystems become unstable or collapsed. People have increased their efforts to protect endangered species. See **Wildlife conservation** (Values of wildlife conservation).

Most biologists consider a species endangered if they expect it would die off completely in less than 20 years if no special efforts were made to protect it, or if the rate of decline far exceeds the rate of increase. Until the last few centuries, species became rare or died out due to such natural causes as changes in climate, catastrophic movements in Earth's crust, and volcanic eruptions.

Today, species become endangered primarily due to human activities. They mainly become endangered due to (1) habitat loss, (2) wildlife trade, (3) overhunting, and (4) competition with domestic and nonnative animals.

Loss of habitat poses the greatest threat to the survival of wild species. Most animals and plants are specially adapted to live and reproduce in a specific environment or habitat and cannot survive when it is destroyed. The destruction of virgin forests by loggers and settlers and the conversion of natural grasslands into pasture for livestock have eliminated vast expanses of wildlife habitats. Marshlands have been drained for farmland and building projects. Coral reefs and many marine environments have become polluted, overfished, and even dynamited to obtain tropical fish and corals. Tropical rain forests contain the greatest variety of animal and plant life on Earth, and they are being destroyed more rapidly than any other type of wild habitat.

Wildlife trade involves the capture of animals for pets, zoo specimens, and research subjects, and the killing of animals for their fur or other body parts. The capture of wild animals for commercial use has endangered many species, including the Spix's macaw, a parrot of Brazil. Many Spix's macaws have been captured for bird collectors. Many primates, including the orangutan, have become endangered by the illegal killing of the mothers to capture their babies for zoos and pet dealers. Chimpanzees, gorillas, and other primates are killed for their meat, which is sold in African markets.

Other animals have been killed in such large numbers for their fur, hides, tusks, or horns that they are nearly extinct. Rhinoceroses, wild chinchillas, the Tibetan antelope, and snow leopards are among these. Although such animals are now protected by law in the countries where they live, they are still *poached* (hunted illegally). Poaching also has seriously reduced the number of African elephants. See **Elephant** (Protecting elephants).

Overhunting has brought many species to the brink of extinction. The West Indian manatee, Asiatic lion, and many kinds of pheasants have become endangered because people have hunted them for food and trophies.

Many species are killed by people who believe that the animals threaten their livelihoods. Livestock owners, for example, may shoot, trap, or poison wild animals that they consider a danger to their herds. Farmers and ranchers in North America have nearly eliminated the red wolf and many species of prairie dogs, while herders in Africa have almost wiped out the simian wolf. Some people in the fishing industry blame seals, which eat fish, for reductions in their catch. Fishing crews have killed so many Mediterranean monk seals that fewer than 200 survive.

Competition with domestic and nonnative animals is a major threat to much wildlife. On many islands, native birds, mammals, and reptiles have become endangered after people introduced domestic animals into the environment. Livestock overgraze vegetation, eliminating habitat. Domestic cats prey on birds and small mammals. Rats escape from ships and infest islands, killing small birds and their eggs. In mainland areas, stocking of game fish threatens native fish, and nonnative plants and animals crowd out many native species.

Protecting endangered species. Laws and conservation programs are helping to reduce endangerment worldwide. In the United States, the Endangered Species Act of 1973 protects endangered and threatened wildlife and plants from hunting, collecting, and other activities that harm them or their habitats. Since this law was enacted, the numbers of certain endangered animals, such as the alligator, bald eagle, and peregrine falcon, have increased so much that they have been removed from the endangered list or reclassified from endangered to threatened status.

Many wild species are protected by the Convention on International Trade in Endangered Species of Wild Fauna and Flora (CITES). This treaty, drawn up in 1973, aims to control trade in wild animals and plants, their parts, and products derived from them. Over 170 countries have joined the treaty. CITES bans trade in rhinoceros horn, cheetah fur, sea turtle shells and meat, and certain whale products. Elephant ivory was banned in 1989, but later CITES decisions have enabled such African nations as Botswana, Namibia, and South Africa

Some endangered species of animals and plants

Common name	Scientific name	Distribution	Survival problems
Animals			
American crocodile	*Crocodylus acutus*	Florida, Mexico, Central and South America, Caribbean islands	Overhunted for its hide; habitat destruction
Asian elephant	*Elephas maximus*	South-central and southeast Asia	Habitat destruction; illegal killing for ivory
Black-footed ferret	*Mustela nigripes*	Wyoming	Poisoning of prairie dogs, its chief prey
Black rhinoceros	*Diceros bicornis*	South of Sahara in Africa	Habitat destruction; overhunted for its horn
Blue whale	*Balaenoptera musculus*	All oceans	Overhunted for blubber, food, and whale oil
California condor	*Gymnogyps californianus*	Southern California, Arizona	Habitat destruction; hunted for sport; poisoned from lead shot and predator-control programs
Cheetah	*Acinonyx jubatus*	Africa, Iran	Habitat destruction; overhunted for sport and fur
Devils Hole pupfish	*Cyprinodon diabolis*	Nevada	Habitat destruction
Giant panda	*Ailuropoda melanoleuca*	China	Habitat destruction; illegal killing for fur; illegal capture for zoos
Imperial parrot	*Amazona imperialis*	Caribbean Islands	Habitat destruction; illegal capture for pets
Kemp's (or Atlantic) ridley sea turtle	*Lepidochelys kempii*	Tropical and temperate parts of the Atlantic	Overhunted for its leather; overcollection of eggs
Orangutan	*Pongo pygmaeus*	Borneo, Sumatra	Habitat destruction; illegal killing of mothers to obtain young for zoos and for pets
Red wolf	*Canis rufus*	Southeastern United States	Habitat destruction; killed in predator-control programs
Snow leopard	*Uncia uncia*	Central Asia	Overhunted for its fur; killed in predator-control programs
Tiger	*Panthera tigris*	Southern Asia, China, eastern Russia	Habitat destruction; illegal killing for sport and body parts
Plants			
Floating sorrel	*Oxalis natans*	South Africa	Habitat destruction
Green pitcher plant	*Sarracenia oreophila*	Alabama, Georgia	Overcollection; habitat destruction
Knowlton cactus	*Pediocactus knowltonii*	New Mexico, Colorado	Habitat destruction; overcollection
Running buffalo clover	*Trifolium stoloniferum*	Central United States	Unknown
Snakeroot	*Eryngium cuneifolium*	Florida	Habitat destruction

Endangered species

Some of Earth's most marvelous living things are endangered species. These photographs suggest the variety of species that are in danger of extinction. The greatest threat to endangered plants and animals is the destruction of their natural habitat by people. Many countries have established laws and conservation programs to protect endangered species and their habitats.

© Shutterstock

Apollo butterfly

Peggy Olwell, The Center for Plant Conservation

Knowlton cactus

Allison Leete, Los Angeles Zoo

California condor

Zig Leszczynski, Animals Animals

Tiger

Peter Weimann, Animals Animals

American crocodile

W. K. Fletcher, Photo Researchers

Sockeye salmon

to export limited amounts of ivory to Japan and other countries.

Various organizations publish lists of endangered species to improve public awareness. The IUCN (International Union for the Conservation of Nature and Natural Resources) compiles lists that include thousands of animal and plant species that are threatened or endangered.

Protecting habitat is the key method of preserving endangered species. Many governments and organizations have set aside nature preserves. Some zoos and animal research centers conduct programs that breed endangered species in hopes of returning their offspring to the wild. The programs have greatly improved the outlook for such endangered species as the black-footed ferret and the California condor. Greta Nilsson

Related articles. *World Book* has separate articles on many of the plants and animals mentioned in this article. See also:

Animal (The future of animals)
Biodiversity
Bird (Endangered species)
Coral reef
Extinction
Poaching
Wildlife conservation

Endecott, John (1588?-1665), also spelled Endicott, was an American colonial official who led about 50 people from England to what is now Salem, Massachusetts, in 1628. He governed Salem until John Winthrop arrived in 1630. Endecott remained a leader in Salem, and Winthrop established Boston. See **Winthrop, John.**

Endecott served as governor of Massachusetts Bay Colony for several terms. His zeal often led him astray. Endecott was largely responsible for causing the Pequot War in 1637 (see **Indian wars** [The Pequot War]). He slashed the red cross out of the British flag because he thought it was a symbol of the pope. Endecott persecuted the Quakers. But he used the colony's ministers to bring harmony to the community.

Endecott was born in Devonshire, England. He died on March 15, 1665. John W. Ifkovic

Enderby Land, *EHN duhr bee,* is a region on the fringe of Antarctica. The region extends from Ice Bay to Edward VIII Bay. For location, see **Antarctica** (map). Enderby Land was discovered in 1831 by the British navigator John Biscoe, who worked for a whaling company called Enderby Brothers. Ian W. D. Dalziel

Enders, John Franklin (1897-1985), a research bacteriologist, shared the 1954 Nobel Prize in physiology or medicine with Frederick C. Robbins and Thomas H. Weller. The three grew poliomyelitis viruses on living human embryonic tissue and neutralized the viruses' cell-changing action with an antibody. They later isolated and typed the three strains of poliovirus (see **Poliomyelitis**).

Enders's work showed that viruses can be grown outside the body in tissues that they do not usually attack within the body. This work provided a method for producing vaccines to combat the viruses.

In 1930, Enders helped develop typhus vaccine. He also isolated the measles virus and developed a "live" measles virus vaccine (see **Measles**). Enders was born on Feb. 10, 1897, in West Hartford, Connecticut. He died on Sept. 8, 1985. Kenneth R. Manning

Endive, *EHN dyv* or *AHN deev,* is a leafy vegetable closely related to chicory. It grows wild in the East Indies but is cultivated in other parts of the world. Endive grows close to the ground. One variety, known as *escarole,* has broad, smooth leaves. The other variety has curled or fringed leaves. Both of these plants have a slightly bitter, but pleasant, flavor and are often used in salads. Endive plants do not grow well in hot weather. Methods of cultivation are similar to those used for growing lettuce. Endive contains vitamins A, B, and C. Hugh C. Price

Scientific classification. Endive belongs to the composite family, Compositae. It is *Cichorium endivia.*

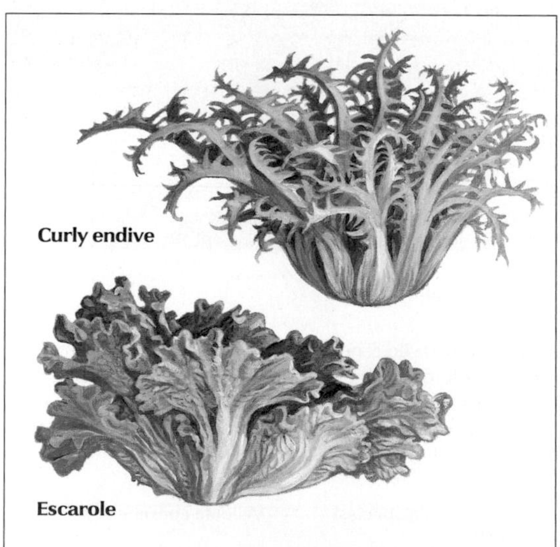

WORLD BOOK illustration by John D. Dawson

Endive is a leafy vegetable often used in salads. The two varieties of endive, *curly endive* and *escarole,* are shown here. Curly endive has curled or fringed leaves, and escarole has broad, smooth leaves. Both have a bitter, but appealing, taste.

Endocrine gland. See Gland.

Endometriosis, *EHN doh MEE tree OH sihs,* is a disease of the female reproductive system. In endometriosis, clusters of cells from the lining of the uterus grow and function outside the uterus. The areas that are most often affected are the ovaries and the walls of the pelvic and abdominal cavities. Endometriosis is most frequently diagnosed in women 20 through 40 years of age who have never been pregnant and who have experienced severe menstrual pain, infertility, or both. It can also occur in younger women.

The exact cause of endometriosis is unknown. Most physicians believe endometriosis develops when some menstrual blood from the uterus flows backward into the pelvic and abdominal cavities each month. This blood contains clusters of uterine cells. The clusters can attach to the organs, ligaments, or walls of the cavities. These endometrial clusters are stimulated to grow by *estrogen,* the hormone that stimulates the monthly growth of the uterine lining (see **Estrogen**).

Endometriosis may produce such symptoms as bladder irritation, pain during intercourse, and severe cramps during menstruation. The disease can also damage the ovaries and other reproductive organs, resulting in infertility (see **Infertility**).

Mild endometriosis may require no treatment. Physicians can treat some patients with hormones, which may relieve some of the disease's symptoms. More severe cases of endometriosis require surgery. In women who want to have children, the surgery is limited to removal of the endometrial clusters. In women who do not want to become pregnant or who are past childbearing age, the reproductive organs and all endometrial clusters may be removed. Lois Kazmier Halstead

Endorphin, *ehn DAWR fihn,* is any of a group of substances in the nervous system of human beings and animals. Endorphins, along with closely related chemicals called *enkephalins,* are part of a larger group of morphinelike compounds called *opioids.* Opioids help relieve pain and promote a feeling of well-being. Scientists believe that endorphins and enkephalins control the brain's perception of, and response to, pain and stress and may form part of the body's pain-relieving system.

Scientists have discovered several kinds of endorphins and enkephalins, all of which are *peptides* (chains of amino acids). *Beta-endorphin* is one of the most extensively studied opioid peptides. It occurs in the brain and in the pituitary gland, a small gland at the base of the brain, where it may act as a hormone. Beta-endorphin and another hormone called *adrenocorticotropin* (ACTH) are contained in larger molecules in the pituitary gland. These hormones are split and released as part of the body's coordinated response to extreme pain or stress.

Scientists believe that opioid drugs produce some of their effects by acting like endorphins and enkephalins. Research chemists have artificially produced endorphins and enkephalins and have studied their use in the control of pain. Although these substances occur naturally in the body, they produce physical dependence when administered as a drug. James N. Campbell

Endoscope, *EHN duh skohp,* is a medical instrument used to examine the interior of a hollow organ or cavity of the body. Unlike most other medical imaging devices, endoscopes are inserted directly into the organ or cavity being examined. There are several types of endoscopes. Each type has its own name and is used for viewing a specific part of the body. For example, a *gastroscope* is used to examine the stomach; a *bronchoscope,* the upper passages of the lungs; and an *arthroscope,* the small spaces within joints.

Most endoscopes consist of a flexible or rigid hollow tube with a lens at one end. Light-transmitting threads called *optical fibers* extend along the inside of some tubes. The optical fibers shed light on the tissue and permit viewing through the lens.

Various medical procedures, including certain types of surgery, can be performed through an endoscope. For example, forceps can be passed through an endoscope to obtain samples of tissue. Lasers can be inserted through an endoscope to destroy abnormal tissue or to remove fatty deposits within blood vessels.

Charles Liebow

See also **Arthroscopy; Bronchoscope; Fiber optics** (Kinds of optical fibers).

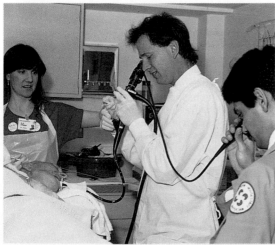

Evanston Hospital

University of Chicago Medical Center

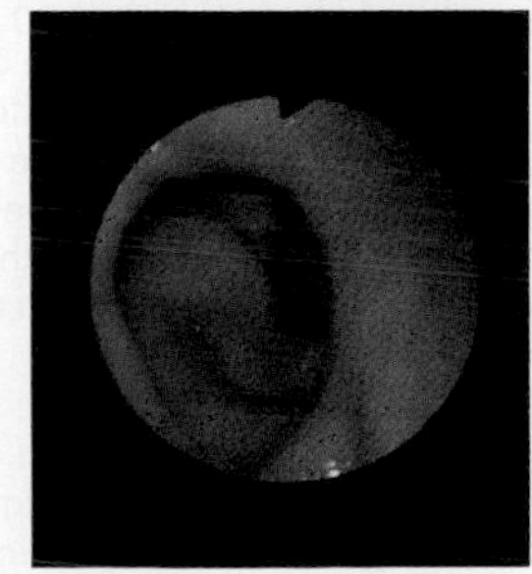

Doctors use a gastroscope to examine a patient's digestive system. This type of endoscope is passed through the mouth of the patient to the stomach. The small photograph shows a stomach ulcer as seen through a gastroscope.

Endowment is a fund that is set aside by a donor, or giver, for a specific purpose. The term *endowment* also has the same meaning as foundation, fund, or trust (see **Foundation; Trust fund**). The money for endowments may come from individuals, family estates, or business organizations. Most endowments are designed to run forever, or until all the money in the fund has been spent. Many endowments are nonprofit, tax-exempt organizations that finance numerous social welfare projects.

Endowments also refer to funds that are held by colleges, universities, hospitals, orphanages, and other institutions. The money is usually invested so that the institution has a continual income of some kind. Usually, the institution spends only the income or profit from the investments. In this way, the endowment can continue forever. Generally, the income from the endowment is used only for the general operations of the institution, or for some particular purpose for which the endowment was created. Joseph C. Kiger

Endymion, *ehn DIHM ee uhn,* in Greek mythology, was a handsome youth passionately loved by Selene (the moon). Details of Endymion's life vary from author to author in ancient Greece. According to one story, Selene put Endymion to sleep forever because she could not bear to have him die. In another version, Selene begged Zeus, the ruler of the gods, to grant Endymion a wish. He chose everlasting sleep combined with eternal youth and immortality.

The story of Endymion and Selene has inspired many artists and writers. For example, the English poet John Keats wrote *Endymion* (1818), a long poem based on the Greek myth. F. Carter Philips

See also **Selene; Keats, John** (His work).

Energy, in physics, is a quantity that is related to work. Energy has many forms. For example, you use *mechanical energy* when you toss a ball, *heat energy* warms a room, *electric energy* makes a light bulb glow, and *chemical energy* provides the driving force for an automobile.

Solar energy, energy from the sun, warms and illuminates Earth and its atmosphere. Almost all that energy arrives at the top of the atmosphere as electromagnetic waves. From the least energetic to the most energetic, those waves include radio waves; infrared rays, which we feel as heat; visible light; ultraviolet rays, which can cause sunburn; and small amounts of X rays and gamma rays. The atmosphere blocks some of the visible light and infrared rays, almost all of the radio waves and ultraviolet rays, and all of the X rays and gamma rays. The term *solar energy* additionally refers to energy supplied by solar panels and other devices that use energy from the sun.

Two forms of energy are fundamental—that is, any other form consists of one or both of them. The two forms are: (1) *kinetic energy,* which is energy of motion; and (2) *potential energy,* which can be thought of as "stored" energy. For instance, the mechanical energy involved in picking up and dropping a ball is partly potential energy and partly kinetic energy. Pick up the ball, and you give it potential energy. Drop the ball, and the potential energy of the ball is transformed into kinetic energy.

Energy conversion

Energy can be converted from one form to another. For example, our bodies change chemical energy in food to mechanical energy that we use when we move about. A coal-burning power plant converts chemical energy to electric energy.

Energy conversion at a power plant occurs in several stages. The following description of that process may help you understand various forms of energy and how they can be converted.

The coal has potential energy in the form of chemical energy. That chemical energy is stored in the electrons of atoms that make up the molecules in the coal. Each atom consists of one or more negatively charged electrons in orbit around a positive nucleus. Electrons in neighboring atoms form pairs that *bond* (join) the atoms together.

When the coal burns, its molecules change as bonds break and other bonds form. As the molecules change, electrons release energy, which is immediately converted to *heat energy.* Heat energy is the kinetic energy of the atoms and molecules of a solid object, a liquid, or a gas; the hotter an object, the greater the kinetic energy of its atoms and molecules.

In the power plant, the molecular changes that occur when the coal burns create hot gases. In the next stage of the process, heat energy in the gases changes to heat energy in the metal that makes up a boiler, then to heat energy in molecules of water inside the boiler. As the water molecules absorb heat energy, they move more and more rapidly. Eventually, they move so rapidly that water turns to steam.

The steam then flows from the boiler through pipes to a device known as a *steam turbine.* The turbine has several wheels, each with fanlike blades. The steam rushes through the blades, pushing against them and thereby spinning the wheels. In this stage, heat energy of the steam is converted to mechanical energy of the turbine.

The turbine is connected to a machine called an *electric generator.* In the final stage of the process, the generator converts mechanical energy of the spinning turbine to electric energy (see **Electric generator**). That energy is partly kinetic and partly potential.

Conservation of energy

In 1847, the British physicist James Prescott Joule demonstrated that mechanical energy can be converted into heat. Soon, scientists learned that any form of energy can be converted to any other form. They also found that, in energy conversions, the total quantity of energy is *conserved:* The quantity of energy that exists at the end of any process is the same as the quantity that existed when the process began.

Some of the energy at the end of every process is waste energy. For example, in an automobile, much heat energy goes out the exhaust pipe, and friction between parts of the engine creates heat energy that is wasted. But the automobile's heating system can use waste heat to warm the passengers on cold days.

Energy and matter

Almost 60 years after Joule's demonstration, the German-born American physicist Albert Einstein expanded the idea of conservation of energy. The expanded idea was an outgrowth of Einstein's special theory of relativity, published in 1905. Einstein explained that matter can be converted to energy and vice versa. The energy available from a conversion of matter is sometimes called the *energy-equivalent of mass.* Mass is the amount of matter in an object. An energy-equivalent of mass is potential energy.

The conversion of matter releases energy in the sun and other stars. The sun's core is so hot that atomic nuclei and electrons move about independently. The most common nucleus is that of the simplest form of hydrogen—a single proton. The protons have so much kinetic energy that they sometimes collide and *fuse* (join), producing a hydrogen nucleus consisting of a proton and an electrically neutral *neutron.* But the mass of that nucleus is less than the sum of the masses of a proton and a neutron when they are separate. The "missing matter" has been converted to energy.

Conversion of matter to energy also produces the heat energy that is used to generate electric energy in nuclear power plants. In addition, matter-to-energy conversion provides the tremendous destructive force of nuclear weapons.

Calculating quantities of energy

Scientists use *Newtonian equations* and *relativistic equations* to calculate quantities of energy. Newtonian equations are based on *Newton's laws of motion,* which were discovered by the English scientist Isaac Newton. The laws were published in 1687 in *Philosophiae Naturalis Principia Mathematica (Mathematical Principles of Natural Philosophy),* a work usually called simply *Principia* or *Principia Mathematica.*

Relativistic equations are based on Einstein's special theory of relativity, and they apply to realms of physics that were unknown in Newton's time. For example, scientists use a relativistic equation for the kinetic energy of an object traveling at more than a few percent of the speed of light in a vacuum, 186,282 miles (299,792 kilometers) per second. But a Newtonian equation will give an extremely accurate value of the kinetic energy of an object moving at a speed typical of objects seen in our everyday lives. The equations used in this article are Newtonian.

Units of work and energy. Due to the relationship between energy and work, energy is measured in units of work. In its scientific sense, *work* is the movement of an object against a resisting force. For example, a person does work by lifting an object. Lifting an object requires work because the lifter must overcome the force of gravity on the object. The amount of work done, and therefore the amount of energy used, equals that force multiplied by the distance the object is lifted. The kinetic energy used to lift the object is "stored" in the object as potential energy.

In the inch-pound system of units customarily used in the United States, work and energy are commonly measured in foot-pounds. In the International System of Units (SI), the modern metric system, work and energy

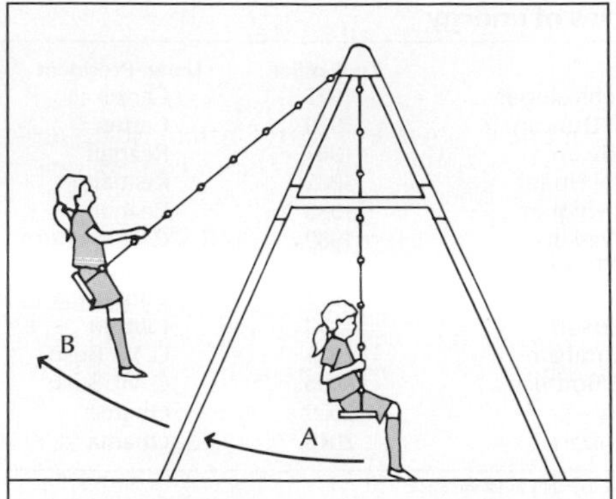

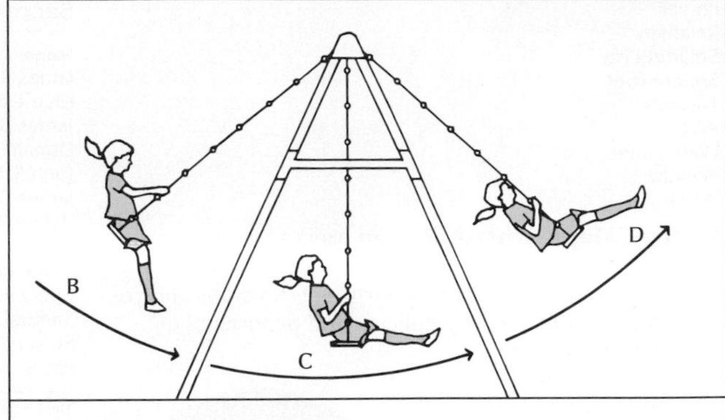

WORLD BOOK diagrams

A girl on a swing illustrates how *potential* (stored) energy becomes *kinetic* (moving) energy and vice versa. In the diagram at the left, the girl has maximum potential energy but no kinetic energy when she is in position B. In the diagram at the right, gravity swings her down from position B. At position C, she has no potential energy, but maximum kinetic energy, which swings her to D.

are measured in units known as *joules*—named for James Prescott Joule. One joule is equal to 0.738 foot-pound.

Another unit of energy is the *thermochemical calorie,* which is usually referred to as simply the *calorie.* This unit is not part of the SI, but scientists commonly use it in studying heat. The calorie equals exactly 4.184 joules. The thermochemical calorie is not the same calorie used in the field of nutrition. Instead, nutritionists use the *kilocalorie,* which equals 1,000 thermochemical calories. But the kilocalorie is also referred to as the *calorie,* and sometimes as the *Calorie*—with a capital "C" to distinguish it from the thermochemical calorie.

Energy and power. People sometimes confuse energy with *power.* Power is the rate at which energy is delivered—so power equals energy divided by time. In the inch-pound system, one unit of power is the *horsepower,* which equals 550 foot-pounds per second. In the SI, the unit for power is the *watt,* named for the Scottish inventor James Watt. One watt equals 1 joule per second. The watt is much smaller than the horsepower. One *kilowatt* (1,000 watts) equals 1.341 horsepower.

Weight and mass. The amount of energy used to lift an object can also be defined as the weight of the object multiplied by the distance the object is lifted. In this definition, *weight* is used in its scientific and technological sense to mean the force of gravity on the object. But this usage can be confusing because, in commercial and everyday use, *weight* means *mass.*

Weight, in the scientific and technological sense, is proportional to mass. The two quantities are related by the equation $F_g = mg$, where F_g is force due to gravity (that is, weight), m is mass, and g is the acceleration that a falling object undergoes due to gravity. Scientists typically work in metric units. The metric units that apply to this equation are newtons—named for Isaac Newton—for F_g, kilograms for m, and meters per second per second for g. At Earth's surface, g is about 9.8 meters per second per second.

Suppose that you wanted to find the weight of a rock that has a mass of 2 kilograms. You would insert that value of 2 kilograms and the value of g into the equation and multiply: $F_g = (2)(9.8) = 19.6$ newtons.

Potential energy of a raised object. Suppose a person raised the rock to a height of 2 meters. What would be the potential energy of the rock?

The equation for the potential energy of a raised object is $E_p = F_g s$. E_p is energy in joules, F_g is force due to gravity in newtons, and s is the distance the object has been raised in meters. We insert the values of F_g and s into the equation and multiply: $E_p = (19.6)(2) = 39.2$ joules.

Kinetic energy. Suppose the person threw the rock at a *velocity* (speed in a particular direction) of 12 meters per second. What would be the kinetic energy of the rock?

The equation for kinetic energy is $E_k = (½)mv^2$. E_k is energy in joules, m is mass in kilograms, and v is velocity in meters per second. The 2 beside the v indicates that v is to be *squared* (multiplied by itself). So the calculation for the rock's kinetic energy is $E_k = (½)(2)(12)(12) = 144$ joules.

Michael Dine

Related articles in *World Book* include:

Atom
Bond (chemical)
Calorie
Cosmic microwave background (CMB) radiation
Dark energy
Einstein, Albert
Electric generator
Electric power
Electricity
Electromagnetic waves
Energy supply
Falling bodies, Law of
Force
Friction
Fusion
Gravitation
Heat
Horsepower
Joule
Joule, James Prescott
Mass
Matter
Metric system
Molecule
Motion
Newton, Sir Isaac
Nuclear energy

http://bit.ly/12VKlRg

Power
Relativity
Solar energy
Square root
Turbine
Watt
Watt, James
Weight
Work

Energy, Department of, is an executive department of the United States government that works to meet the nation's energy needs. The department develops and coordinates national energy policies and programs.

The secretary of energy, who is a member of the president's Cabinet, directs the department. The secretary is appointed by the president, subject to the approval of the Senate. The department's official website at http://www.energy.gov offers information on the department's activities.

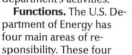

The seal of the Department of Energy

Functions. The U.S. Department of Energy has four main areas of responsibility. These four areas are (1) the development of energy resources, (2) scientific research, (3) national security, and (4) protection of the environment.

Development of energy resources. The department works to develop energy technologies that private industries are not likely to develop themselves. These technologies include ways of increasing the U.S. energy supply and of using the current supply more efficiently.

Scientific research is conducted in national laboratories supervised by the Department of Energy. Scientists in the laboratories work to develop cleaner and more economical energy sources. The scientists also work to improve the competitiveness of U.S. industries.

National security. The department manages the nation's nuclear-weapons development program. It also works to maintain a safe, reliable stockpile of nuclear weapons.

Protecting the environment. The department finds ways to reduce environmental, safety, and health risks that may result from nuclear-weapons development and production. It also works to reduce environmental damage from the development and use of energy resources.

History. Congress created the Department of Energy in 1977. The new department pulled together energy-related functions that had been scattered throughout the government. For example, it took over electric power projects and coal research programs from the Department of the Interior. In addition, the new department absorbed three independent agencies—the Energy Research and Development Administration, the Federal Energy Administration, and the Federal Power Commission.

Critically reviewed by the Department of Energy

Secretaries of energy

Name	Took office	Under President
James R. Schlesinger	1977	Carter
Charles W. Duncan, Jr.	1979	Carter
James B. Edwards	1981	Reagan
Donald Paul Hodel	1982	Reagan
John S. Herrington	1985	Reagan
James D. Watkins	1989	G. H. W. Bush
*Hazel R. O'Leary	1993	Clinton
*Federico F. Peña	1997	Clinton
*Bill Richardson	1998	Clinton
Spencer Abraham	2001	G. W. Bush
Samuel W. Bodman	2005	G. W. Bush
Steven Chu	2009	Obama
Ernest Moniz	2013	Obama

*Has a separate biography in *World Book.*

Related articles in ***World Book*** include:

Argonne National Laboratory
Brookhaven National Laboratory
Fermi National Accelerator Laboratory
Flag (picture: Flags of the United States government)
Idaho National Laboratory
Lawrence Berkeley National Laboratory
Los Alamos National Laboratory
National laboratory
Oak Ridge National Laboratory
Sandia National Laboratories
Strategic Petroleum Reserve

U.S. Department of Energy

Department of Energy headquarters are in Washington, D.C. The department conducts research on energy production, encourages energy conservation, and manages the production of the nation's nuclear weapons.

Ron Church, Tom Stack & Assoc.

U.S. Department of Energy

Georg Gerster, Rapho Guillumette

Sources of energy include petroleum, nuclear energy, and sunlight. Offshore wells, *left,* tap oil deposits that lie underwater. Nuclear reactors, *center,* produce power from the splitting of atomic nuclei. Solar furnaces, *right,* use mirrors to collect the rays of the sun.

Energy supply

Energy supply is the total amount of usable energy available to people for doing work. This energy heats and cools our homes and offices. It powers our lights, electronics, factories, and farm equipment. Energy moves our automobiles, trains, ships, and airplanes. Modern society could not exist without a plentiful and stable supply of energy.

Energy exists in several different forms. People burn fuel to produce heat energy. Batteries produce electric energy. Both batteries and fuel store energy as chemical energy. Mechanical energy is associated with the motion of objects, such as a spinning wheel or a thrown ball. In physics, *power*—as in electric power—is the rate at which energy is used or delivered.

In some cases, energy from a particular source is used directly. For example, people may burn wood to heat their homes. But energy is often transformed before use. At many power plants, for example, fuel is burned to boil water, creating steam. The energy of the expanding steam spins a device called a *turbine.* An electric generator then transforms the turbine's mechanical energy into electric energy. Wood, oil, and other fuels are called *primary sources* of energy. Electric energy, in contrast, is an *energy carrier.* It is used to move energy quickly over long distances, from power plants to homes and offices. Electric energy can easily be transformed into other kinds of energy, such as the mechanical energy of a spinning motor or light energy from a computer screen. Energy that is produced by businesses and governments and sold to the public is called *commercial energy.*

This article discusses the various sources of energy that people use, problems and challenges associated with the energy supply, and the history of humanity's use of energy. For information on the physics of energy, see the article **Energy.**

Sources of energy

About 80 percent of all commercial energy comes from coal, oil, and natural gas. These sources are called *fossil fuels* because they are the remains of long-buried ancient life. Coal comes from the remains of plants. Oil and natural gas—both forms of petroleum—come from the remains of plantlike *plankton* that lived on the ocean surface. Over millions of years, heat and pressure transformed the remains of these organisms into fuel. Fossil fuels are a *nonrenewable* source of energy, which means that they cannot be readily replaced. People burn fossil fuels much faster than they form by natural processes, and their supply may eventually run out. The nuclear fuel used in today's power plants is another nonrenewable energy source. Such fuel comes from a limited supply of the rare element uranium.

Renewable energy sources, in contrast, have potentially unlimited supplies. The energy that comes from sunlight, wind, rain, and tides, for example, need never run out. People can also regrow trees and crops after using them as fuel. Scientists and engineers are working to develop renewable energy sources to replace fossil fuels.

Fossil fuels store chemical energy that can be burned to produce great amounts of heat. This heat is used in power plants, in automobile engines, and in such home appliances as stoves and furnaces. Fossil fuels store a large amount of energy, and this energy can be released at any time. These two qualities make fossil

Sources of energy in the United States

This graph shows how the use of different energy sources in the United States has changed since 1950. The first commercial nuclear power plant in the United States began operating in 1957.

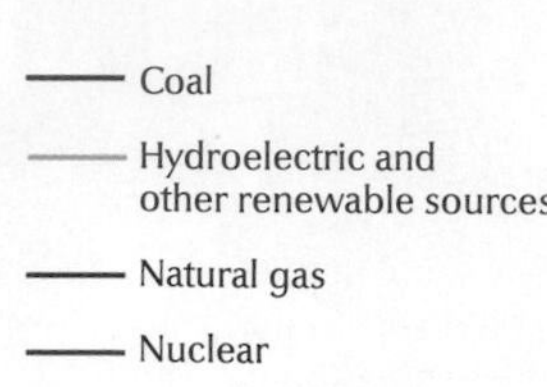

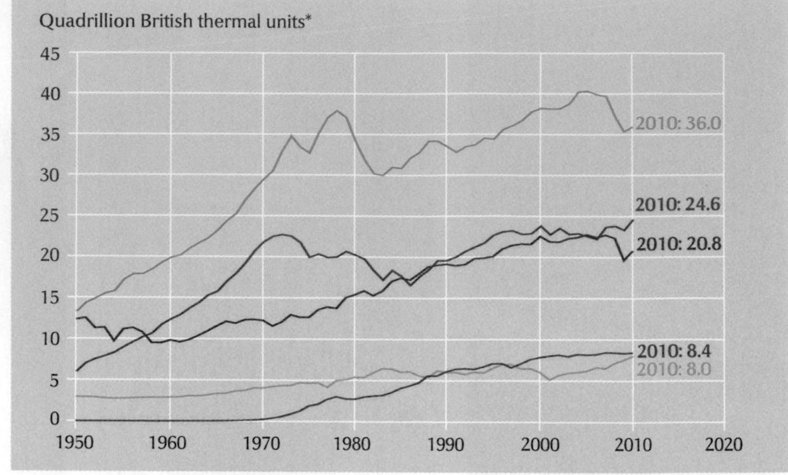

*1 quadrillion = 1,000,000,000,000,000. The *British thermal unit* (Btu) is used in the U.S. to measure energy. 1 Btu = 1,055 joules.
Source: U.S. Energy Information Administration.

fuels attractive for any number of uses. But the burning of fossil fuels is a major source of air pollution and other environmental problems.

Coal provides about 30 percent of all the commercial energy used in the world. It provides about 20 percent of the energy used in the United States. Much of the heat energy in coal is used to produce steam in boilers. The steam, in turn, is used to generate electric power or to produce motion in steam engines. Coal is also widely used in the manufacture of steel. In many Asian and European countries, people use coal to heat homes and other buildings.

There are two primary methods for mining coal. *Surface mining* removes coal less than 200 feet (60 meters) below Earth's surface. The removal is generally done by completely stripping away the material above the coal. *Underground mining* involves digging deep tunnels to reach coal buried at deeper levels.

Oil furnishes about 30 percent of the commercial energy used in the world. It accounts for about 35 percent of commercial energy used in the United States. Most of the energy in oil is used to produce transportation fuel—such as gasoline and diesel fuel—and heating oil.

Most oil is removed from deep underground as a liquid called *crude oil.* Workers pump crude oil out of the ground through wells drilled into oil-bearing formations called *reservoirs.* Because crude oil is a liquid, it is relatively inexpensive to transport long distances using pipelines. Tanker ships also carry huge quantities of oil overseas. *Refineries* process crude oil into gasoline and other petroleum products. Refining removes many impurities from crude oil.

Natural gas accounts for about 20 percent of the world's commercial energy use. It accounts for about 25 percent of U.S. energy use. Natural gas is chiefly made up of methane. Most of the heat energy contained in natural gas is used to generate steam for electric power or steam engines, to heat buildings, and for cooking and other household needs. Like oil, natural gas comes from underground deposits and can be transported long distances through pipelines. Natural gas lacks many of the pollutants associated with coal and oil.

Bituminous sands and oil shale have become important energy sources. Bituminous sands are also called *tar sands.* Each grain of sand is covered with an oil-producing substance. Oil shale is a type of rock that can be processed to yield crude oil and natural gas. The cost of obtaining fuel from tar sands and oil shale is higher than that of mining natural reservoirs of crude oil and natural gas. Since the 2000's, however, new technologies have made extracting fuel from these sources much more profitable in the United States and Canada.

Renewable energy sources include energy from the sun and from wind, water, and the heat beneath Earth's surface. They also include *biomass* (biological materials) that—unlike fossil fuels—can be quickly regrown.

Solar energy can provide a clean and almost unlimited source of energy. People capture solar energy with two basic kinds of devices. *Solar concentrators* capture or focus the sun's energy to generate heat. This heat can be used to heat water or air or to generate electric power. *Solar cells,* also called *photovoltaic cells,* on the other hand, convert solar energy directly into electric energy. Solar energy's use is limited by the high cost of such equipment and the fact that it only works when the sun is shining. But the cost of solar devices is falling. Solar plants generate significant electric power in a variety of countries, even in some such as Germany that are not particularly sunny.

Wind energy uses the spinning motion of windblown turbines to generate electric power. Such turbines generate about 2.5 percent of the electric power in the world. They produce about 4 percent of the electric power of the United States. In Spain, wind turbines generate about 15 percent of the country's electric power. China and Germany are also leading consumers of wind energy. Wind turbines are relatively cheap, and wind energy could potentially supply a large portion of the world's total energy demands. But areas with high winds are often remote, and winds themselves do not blow continuously. Thus, like solar energy, wind energy cannot generate a continuous supply of electric power.

Water power, or *hydropower,* furnishes about 2 percent of the world's commercial energy and about 3 per-

Los Alamos Scientific Laboratory

An experimental fusion device called Scyllac operates at the Los Alamos Scientific Laboratory. Scientists hope that nuclear fusion will someday provide a source of energy.

cent of the energy used in the United States. Water power is mostly used to generate electric power in *hydroelectric power plants.* Such plants are often built within dams. As water falls through the dam, its energy spins turbines connected to electric generators. Water power supplies energy without air pollution. The water itself is renewed over time by rainfall and snowmelt.

Some dams rely on *tidal energy,* the up-and-down motion of water due to the gravitational attractions of the moon and sun. Other forms of water power use energy from ocean waves or currents to power generators. But such technology is difficult to maintain in remote, saltwater environments.

Geothermal energy makes use of Earth's natural interior heat to turn water into steam. In some areas, underground water naturally comes into contact with hot rocks deep beneath the surface. The resulting steam can be captured to power generators. In other areas, engineers can pump water into the ground to be heated by hot rocks.

Geothermal electric plants have historically been limited to areas near the edges of *tectonic plates.* About 30 such plates float on a deep, fluid layer of hot rock, covering Earth's surface like the pieces of a jigsaw puzzle. Newer technology known as *hot dry rock* (HDR) *systems* or *enhanced geothermal systems* (EGS), however, can be used almost anywhere in the world, even far from tectonic boundaries. Such technology pumps water into deep wells. The wells reach a layer of hot rock that lies virtually everywhere beneath the surface. The water captures the rock's heat and can be used continuously. But high costs of drilling and concerns about causing earthquakes have limited the development and use of such systems.

Biomass includes wood, crop residues, dung, solid waste, sewage, landfill gas, and other forms of biological materials. Biomass is an increasingly important source of renewable energy. It provides around 10 percent of the world's primary energy supply. But most of this energy is used inefficiently for cooking and heating in less developed countries.

Biomass can be used to generate electricity and to produce solid, liquid, and gaseous fuels that are less harmful to the environment than are fossil fuels. Biomass can also be turned into chemicals for making plastics and other products typically made from petroleum. In the United States, biomass ranks as the largest source of renewable energy. It is used to heat buildings, to produce *biofuels* for transportation, and to generate steam and electricity. Many cities throughout the world produce usable energy by burning trash. Some cities also process liquid organic wastes, such as sewage, to produce methane gas.

Nuclear energy provides about 13 percent of the commercial energy used in the world and about 19 percent of the energy used in the United States. Nuclear power plants generate huge amounts of heat from controlled *fission*—that is, the splitting of atomic *nuclei* (cores) of certain elements, generally uranium. Uranium supplies are limited, however, and scientists and engineers are exploring methods to use uranium more effectively. Scientists also hope to eventually produce virtually unlimited nuclear energy from *fusion.* Fusion is a more powerful reaction in which atomic nuclei combine. For a detailed discussion of fission and fusion, see **Nuclear energy.**

Problems and challenges

Modern living requires massive amounts of energy

Energy use per person

This graph shows how energy use per person has risen since 1950. Energy use per person is more than four times as high in the United States as in the entire world.

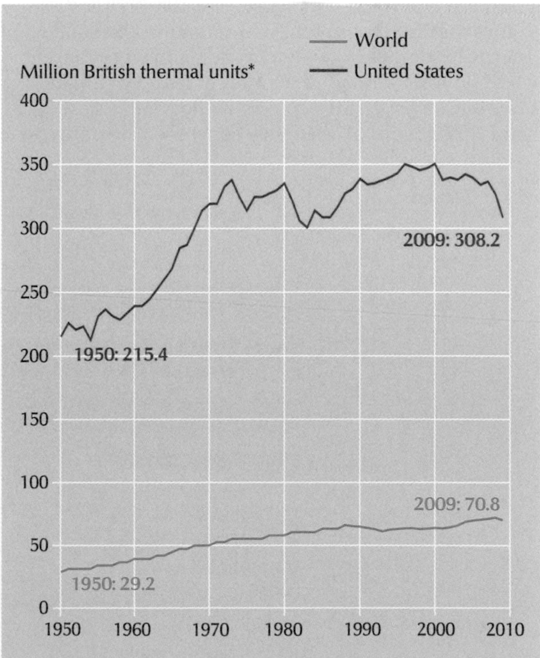

*The British thermal unit (Btu) is used in the U.S. to measure energy. 1 Btu = 1,055 joules.
Sources: United Nations; U.S. Energy Information Administration.

for transportation, the use of electric and electronic devices, heating and cooling, and the manufacture of goods. But no single source of energy can meet the world's needs without significant drawbacks. The use of some energy sources—notably fossil fuels—results in large amounts of pollution. Other sources, such as wind and solar energy, cannot generate continuous power and so must be combined with other energy sources. Balancing the demand for cheap energy with long-term supply and environmental protection is a top concern for government officials, scientists, and engineers.

Supply and demand. Wealthy countries use far more energy than do other countries. For example, the United States has less than 5 percent of the world's population. But it uses about 20 percent of the world's energy. Many developed countries engage in energy conservation. They seek to decrease—or at least stabilize—their energy consumption. But developing countries can do little to limit their energy consumption. To become developed, they need more factories, farm machinery, and transportation facilities. People in developing countries demand more heating and cooling, electric lighting, and other comforts that use energy. Thus, raising living standards around the world will likely raise demand for energy.

Even as demand increases, fossil fuel reserves are dwindling. The coal supply is expected to last about 200 years. Oil and gas supplies could run out even sooner.

As fuels become scarce—or as demand for fuels increases—the price of fuel rises. Rising energy costs can raise the cost of virtually any good or service, threatening living standards. High oil and gas costs may lead energy companies to produce more fuel from unconventional and potentially polluting sources, such as oil shale, tar sands, and low-grade deposits of coal. On the other hand, high fossil fuel costs can drive people to conserve energy or switch to renewable sources.

International conflict. Many countries lack sufficient energy resources to meet local demand. They must import fuel from abroad. A number of less developed countries, by contrast—notably in the Middle East—produce much more oil than they consume. The desire to ensure a stable supply of oil or gas from such countries can be a key factor in international conflict. Energy concerns played a role in such wars as the Iran-Iraq War (1980-1988), the Persian Gulf War of 1991, and the Iraq War (2003-2011). Such wars had causes beyond energy. But experts believe that the need to secure petroleum supplies contributed to the decisions to engage in war.

Conflicts may also arise over renewable energy technology. For example, the Chinese government heavily *subsidizes* (funds) wind and solar technology companies. The subsidies give these companies an artificial advantage in the global marketplace. These tactics risk provoking other countries to heavily tax or bar Chinese energy technology exports, potentially sparking major trade conflicts.

Environmental pollution. The use and extraction of many energy sources damages the environment. Fossil fuels cause a great deal of air pollution and other environmental problems. But other energy sources can cause environmental damage as well. Energy producers, power companies, manufacturers, and governments take various steps to limit pollution from energy use.

From fossil fuels. When burned, coal releases carbon dioxide, coal ash, sulfur *oxides* (compounds with oxygen), nitrogen oxides, mercury, and other substances that cause widespread pollution. Sulfur and nitrogen oxides can react with moisture in the air. They may eventually fall to the ground as *acid rain,* polluting lakes and rivers (see **Acid rain**). Vehicle fuels derived from oil also rank as a leading source of air pollution.

To reduce pollution, many large factories and power plants that burn coal have installed scrubbers, filters, and other cleaning devices. Coal can also be converted into a gas or a liquid. Burning either of these results in less pollution than does burning solid coal. Also, car manufacturers build cars with filtering technology. Such technology reduces the amount of pollutants released when gasoline and diesel are burned.

It is not just the burning of fossil fuels that causes environmental problems. The extraction and transportation of such fuels can also damage the environment. Both surface mining and deep underground mining of coal

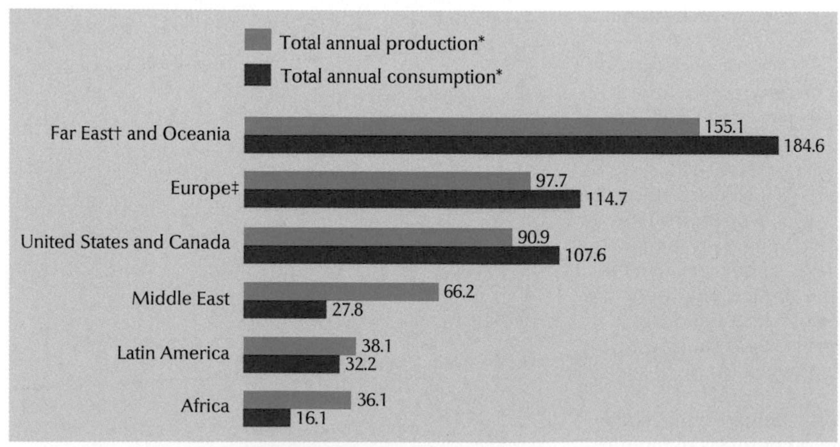

*Energy in quadrillion British thermal units (Btu), the standard measure of energy in the U.S.
1 Btu = 1,055 joules. 1 quadrillion = 1,000,000,000,000,000.
†Excludes Russia.
‡Includes both European and Asian parts of Russia.
Figures are for 2009. Source: U.S. Energy Information Administration.

World energy production and consumption

This graph shows the amount of commercial energy produced and used by various regions of the world. The oil-rich Middle East has the greatest surplus of energy.

can contaminate air and water supplies and destroy nearby habitats. Underground coal mines may cave in and release dangerous gases. Strip mining—the main method of surface mining—has exposed large areas of land to erosion. The drilling of offshore oil fields and the shipment of petroleum by tankers sometimes result in oil spills. Such spills pollute the ocean, contaminate beaches, and kill wildlife. Burying oil and gas pipelines requires changes in the environment, such as the clearing of trees along the route. Coal mining and petroleum companies have taken a number of measures to limit such environmental damage.

From nuclear power. Nuclear power plants do not release air pollution. But they may cause *thermal pollution* by heating up nearby waters, threatening wildlife that depends on them. Nuclear power plants also create *radioactive* wastes. Such wastes release harmful energy for many years as they break down. They must be kept safely sealed away. An accident at a nuclear plant can spread radioactive material far and wide in the form of fallout. Modern nuclear plants have numerous safety measures designed to prevent a release of radioactivity in case of an accident.

From renewable energy sources. Renewable sources do not result in air pollution or radioactive wastes and in general are much cleaner than fossil fuels. But they can also harm the environment. The construction and operation of large hydroelectric dams changes river conditions and disturbs local ecosystems. Geothermal power plants release heat and gases into the atmosphere. They may also cause earthquakes. Wind turbines may kill birds. Used widely enough, they may have the potential to change weather conditions in unpredictable ways.

Global warming. Burning fossil fuels produces carbon dioxide, a *greenhouse gas* that accumulates in Earth's atmosphere. Like the glass in a greenhouse, such gases allow sunlight through to warm Earth's surface. But they prevent heat from escaping back into space. Scientists think that the steady buildup of greenhouse gases from human activity has resulted in *global warming.* Global warming is an observed increase in Earth's average temperature that threatens to shift the world's climate in destructive ways (see **Global warming**).

All fossil fuels produce carbon dioxide when they are burned. Natural gas lacks many of the pollutants associated with coal and oil and releases about half as much carbon dioxide when burned. But natural gas is composed chiefly of methane, a greenhouse gas that traps heat nearly 20 times as effectively as does carbon dioxide. Thus, unburnt natural gas can greatly contribute to global warming if it leaks into the air during extraction, transport, or use.

Burning biomass generates about the same amount of carbon dioxide as does burning fossil fuels. But as a living plant grows, it removes carbon dioxide from the atmosphere. Thus, the total carbon dioxide emissions from biomass can be controlled if it is grown and transported sustainably.

History

Human beings learned to use fire over 1 million years ago. Until then, their only sources of energy had been their own strength and direct sunlight. With the heat energy released by burning wood, people warmed themselves, cooked food, and hardened pottery. By 3000 B.C., the Egyptians invented sails and used the wind to drive their boats. Water wheels, developed in ancient times, harnessed the energy of falling water.

Wood, coal, and steam. Until the late 1700's, wood ranked as the most important fuel. People used so much timber that it began to grow scarce, and coal gradually took its place as the chief fuel source. The growing demand for coal brought a search for better mining methods, including ways to keep mine shafts from flooding.

In 1698, an English inventor named Thomas Savery patented an improved pump to drain mines. The pump was powered by the first practical steam engine. People now had a device that could change heat energy into mechanical energy to do work.

The Industrial Revolution was a period of great technological and social change that began in the late 1700's. The steam engine became the chief source of power for industry and transportation during this time. People's use of energy increased tremendously during the Industrial Revolution. Power-driven machinery largely replaced hand labor, and steamboats replaced sailing ships. New uses of energy made work easier and more productive, and increased production brought greater

NASA/Science Source from Photo Researchers

Manville Sales Corporation

Reducing heat loss from buildings helps conserve energy. The colors in the thermogram at the far left represent the amount of heat that passes from a house during cold weather. Red and yellow indicate the areas of greatest heat loss. The installation of fiberglass insulation along walls, *near left,* controls the loss of heat and thus reduces the amount of fuel needed to heat the house.

wealth. This prosperity helped bring about a growth in population, and so there were more people to consume energy. At the same time, people could afford to buy more energy-consuming conveniences.

In the 1800's, inventors learned about several new sources of energy—and ways to use this energy. In the early 1830's, two physicists—Michael Faraday of England and Joseph Henry of the United States—independently discovered a way to turn mechanical energy into electrical energy. They found that magnets could be used to produce electric current in a coil of wire. Based on this principle, called *electromagnetic induction,* generators could produce electrical energy from the mechanical energy of a spinning water wheel or steam turbine.

In 1860, Jean Joseph Étienne Lenoir, a French inventor, built one of the first workable *internal-combustion engines.* These engines produce power from the explosion of a mixture of air and flammable vapors. Gasoline, which is made from oil, proved to be the most convenient fuel for such engines because it easily turns into vapor. In 1885, Karl Benz, a German engineer, built one of the first gasoline automobiles. The demand for oil soared as automobiles came into use.

The 1900's. During the 1900's, the use of energy almost doubled every 20 years. Much of the increased use stemmed from a steadily increasing—and increasingly wealthy—population. For example, the population of the United States increased about 25 percent from the late 1950's to the late 1970's. But during that period, the use of energy increased about 90 percent. The standard of living improved, and people could afford to buy such energy-using conveniences as air conditioners and cars. Such new inventions as televisions and microwave ovens consumed even more energy. People also used more of such materials as aluminum and plastic, which required huge amounts of energy to manufacture.

Many other countries followed a similar pattern during this period, putting huge demands on the world's energy supply. For most of the century, the supply of fossil fuels remained relatively plentiful, and their price remained stable—and cheap. During the late 1960's and 1970's, however, Middle Eastern oil producers acted in concert to reduce oil production and raise prices, sparking a worldwide "energy crisis." Many developed nations responded by seeking to conserve more energy. But in the 1980's, the global supply of oil stabilized, and prices remained relatively low until the 2000's.

The 2000's. During the first decade of the 2000's, energy use leveled off and then began to decline. Part of the decline was driven by increasing oil prices. In the United States, the use of *hydraulic fracturing* greatly increased the supply of natural gas. Hydraulic fracturing involves forcing fluids into the ground to break up underground rock formations, releasing petroleum trapped within. Because of hydraulic fracturing, cheap natural gas began displacing coal in U.S. power plants.

Demand for energy also decreased, in part because of a number of measures that made existing technologies more efficient. Automakers greatly increased the efficiency of modern vehicles. Consumers purchased more hybrid and electric vehicles that could use rechargeable batteries in addition to—or instead of—a gasoline engine. Highly efficient compact fluorescent lights (CFL's) and light-emitting diodes (LED's) also became popular alternatives to traditional incandescent light bulbs, which waste a great deal of electric power.

Even with such conservation measures, the goal of a reliable, clean, and affordable energy supply remained far off. Experts believe a number of steps are necessary to accomplish this goal. They emphasize developing alternatives to the modern fossil fuel-based transportation system. Such alternatives include cars that run on sustainably produced biofuels and on electric power. Another alternative is the use of hydrogen as a fuel. When burned, hydrogen emits much heat and one harmless byproduct—water. But separating hydrogen from water requires much energy. Hydrogen is also highly explosive, making it difficult to store and transport.

Solar and wind energy remain the most promising renewable energy technologies. Scientists and engineers are working to develop *energy storage systems,* such as advanced batteries, that would help stabilize the supply of energy from these sources. For example, an array of batteries could store the energy produced on windy or sunny days and release it during calm or cloudy periods.

Finally, increasing efficiency and conservation remains a major goal in energy research. New technologies, such as batterylike *fuel cells,* convert stored chemical energy into electric energy much more efficiently than do engines and power plants that use fossil fuels. In architecture and engineering, new designs and materials can cut down the energy required to heat, cool, and light buildings. Much energy can also be conserved by expanding the use of traditional methods, such as turning off lights when not in use and recycling used metal, glass, and plastic. Dalia Patino-Echeverri

Related articles in *World Book* include:

Biofuel
Biomass
Bituminous sands
Coal
Electric generator
Electric power
Electricity
Energy
Environmental pollution
Ethanol
Fossil fuel
Fuel
Fuel cell
Gas (fuel)
Gasoline
Geothermal energy
Heating (Sources of heat)
Hydraulic fracturing
Nuclear energy
Oil shale
Petroleum
Solar energy
Strategic Petroleum Reserve
Switchgrass
Synthetic fuel
Turbine
Water power
Wind power

Outline

I. Sources of energy
A. Fossil fuels
B. Renewable energy
C. Nuclear energy
II. Problems and challenges
A. Supply and demand
B. International conflict
C. Environmental pollution
D. Global warming
III. History

Questions

What are fossil fuels?
What was the first source of energy used by human beings, other than their own strength and direct sunlight?
What two resources might provide petroleum in the future?
What is the difference between fission and fusion?
What substance ranked as the most important fuel throughout most of history?
What is the most abundant fossil fuel?
What steps can people take to conserve energy?
What is the *greenhouse effect?*

Enewetak, *EH nuh WEE tahk,* is an isolated atoll in the northwest corner of the Marshall Islands, in the Pacific Ocean. It consists of 40 low, sandy *islets* (small islands) that surround a lagoon. It has a land area of 2 ¼ square miles (6 square kilometers). The lagoon covers 388 square miles (1,005 square kilometers).

In 1944, during World War II, United States naval forces captured Enewetak from Japanese troops. In 1947, the U.S. government decided to use Enewetak for testing nuclear weapons. The government moved the inhabitants to Ujelang, another atoll. From 1948 to 1958, the United States conducted nuclear tests on Enewetak, leaving it contaminated by radiation. Later, the United States conducted a cleanup operation to reduce the radiation. The inhabitants were allowed to resettle the rehabilitated parts of Enewetak in 1980. A marine laboratory built there by the United States has conducted studies of sea and land plants and animals of the atoll.

From 1947 to 1986, Enewetak and the rest of the Marshalls were part of the Trust Territory of the Pacific Islands, which was administered by the United States. In 1986, the United States granted independence to the Marshalls (see **Marshall Islands**). Scott Kroeker

Engels, *EHNG uhls,* **Friedrich,** *FREE drihkh* (1820-1895), was a German social scientist, journalist, and professional revolutionary. He is known chiefly for his long and close collaboration with Karl Marx, the founder of revolutionary Communism. Engels made important contributions to Marxist theory. The most important was his introduction of Marx to the study of economics. Marx's knowledge of military and political affairs also came largely from Engels. See **Marx, Karl.**

Historical Pictures Service

Friedrich Engels

Engels and Marx wrote many books together. The most famous is the *Communist Manifesto* (1848), of which Engels wrote the first draft. He edited the second and third volumes of Marx's influential book *Das Kapital,* published in 1885 and 1894, and wrote several articles published under Marx's name.

Engels outlived Marx by 12 years and developed some of their joint ideas in directions of his own. He was largely responsible for the Marxist preoccupation with the scientific method and the application of Marxist views to all areas of knowledge. Some scholars believe that in his philosophic writings, Engels showed a misunderstanding of his friend's ideas.

Engels was born on Nov. 28, 1820, in Barmen, Prussia, the son of a textile maker. Hunted by the police because of his revolutionary activities, he fled from Prussia in 1844. He returned during the revolution of 1848 but fled again after the revolution collapsed. He then settled in England, where he managed one of his father's factories. He earned enough to support Marx and his family.

Engels was well read in many languages and on a wide variety of topics. He was a keen observer with a creative mind, and some scholars believe that many of his works were far ahead of his time. He wrote on such diverse topics as religious history, anthropology, foreign affairs, the life of the working class, and especially military technology, his favorite subject. *The Condition of the Working Class in England* (1844) is a pioneering description of life in English working-class slums. *Herr Eugen Dühring's Revolution in Science* (1878), which is a popular presentation of Marxist theory, became the textbook for generations of Socialists and Communists. Other works by Engels dealt with German radical philosophy and the German revolution of 1848 and 1849. Engels died on Aug. 5, 1895. Stephen Schneck

Engine is a machine that converts energy into mechanical work. An engine may get its energy from any of a number of sources, including fuels, steam, and air or water under pressure.

Reciprocating gasoline engines use the chemical energy of burning gasoline to push one or more pistons. The motion of the pistons can then be converted into *rotary* (circular) motion, which can be used to turn the wheels of a car or to do other work. Gasoline engines and steam engines are called *heat engines* because they convert heat energy into mechanical work. Reciprocating gasoline engines are called *internal-combustion engines* if the gases produced by the *combustion* (burning) of the fuel push directly against the pistons.

The steam engine is an *external-combustion engine.* External-combustion engines also get their energy from hot gases produced by burning. These gases transfer heat energy to another fluid. The energy in this fluid, in turn, is converted into mechanical work. In a piston steam engine, for example, heat of combustion is transferred to water inside a boiler. The heat converts the water to steam, which pushes the engine's pistons.

In *hydraulic engines,* water pressure is used to produce mechanical work. The pressure may be created by a pump or by water flowing downward from a level above the engine. Gregory W. Davis

Related articles in *World Book* include:

Airplane (Power for flight)	Flywheel	Locomotive
Automobile (Automobile systems: Powering an internal-combustion car)	Gasoline engine	Rocket
Diesel engine	Governor	Rotary engine
Electric motor	Heat (Changing heat into motion)	Ship (How ships work)
	Hydraulic engine	Steam engine
	Internal-combustion engine	Stirling engine
	Jet propulsion	Turbine

Engine analyzer is an instrument used to determine the performance of parts of gasoline and diesel engines. An engine analyzer attaches directly to the engine. Mechanics use such analyzers to help determine problems so they can adjust or replace engine parts.

Engine analyzers range in design from simple models, which monitor a few engine functions, to complex, computerized models. An engine analyzer may consist of a number of devices, such as an *oscilloscope* and a *tachometer.* An oscilloscope evaluates the ignition system. A tachometer assists in adjusting idle speed.

Most automobiles produced today include an internal computer that controls and monitors the engine. If this computer finds a problem, it broadcasts a *diagnostic trouble code* (DTC) corresponding to that particular problem. A computerized engine analyzer, often called a *scan tool,* scans for these codes. Gregory W. Davis

See also **Diesel engine; Gasoline engine.**

© Shutterstock

Civil engineers inspecting a building site

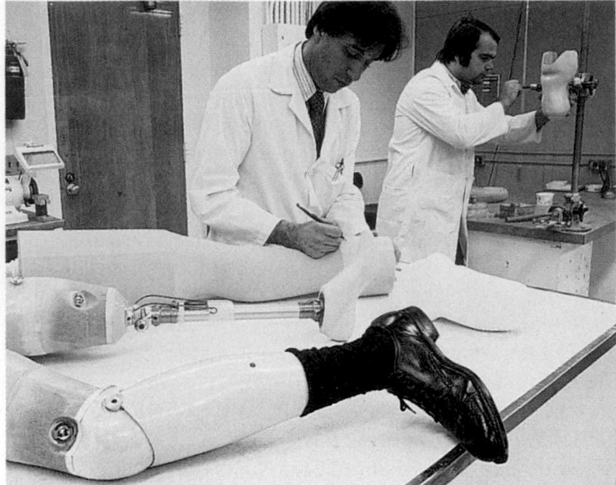

© Dan McCoy, Black Star

Biomedical engineers designing artificial limbs

The field of engineering includes a broad range of activities—from planning and supervising large construction projects to designing and producing aids for people with disabilities.

Engineering

Engineering is the profession that puts scientific knowledge to practical use. The word *engineering* comes from the Latin word *ingeniare,* which means *to design* or *to create.* Engineers use principles of science to design structures, machines, and products of all kinds. They look for better ways to use existing resources and often develop new materials. Engineers have had a direct role in the creation of most of modern *technology*—the tools, materials, techniques, and power sources that make our lives easier (see **Technology**).

The field of engineering includes a wide variety of activities. For example, engineering projects range from the construction of huge dams to the design and manufacture of tiny electronic circuits. Engineers help to produce robots for use in industry and to make artificial limbs for people with disabilities. They develop complex scientific equipment to explore the far reaches of outer space and the depths of the oceans. Engineers also plan our electric power and water supply systems and do research to improve automobiles, personal computers, and health care products. They work to reduce environmental pollution, improve the world's food supply, and make transportation faster and safer.

In ancient times, there was no formal engineering education. The earliest engineers built structures and developed tools by trial and error. Today, special college training prepares engineers to work in a certain branch or field of engineering. Standards of quality and performance guide engineers on the job.

The branches of engineering

Most of the specialized fields of engineering developed about 1750 or later. Before 1750, engineering dealt mostly with energy needs and with the construction of buildings, roads, bridges, canals, or weapons. As people gained more knowledge of science and technology during the 1700's and 1800's, engineers began to specialize in certain kinds of work.

Today, new fields of engineering are continually emerging as a result of scientific and technological breakthroughs. At the same time, the boundaries between the various fields are becoming less and less clear-cut. Numerous areas of engineering overlap, and engineers from different specialties often work closely together on projects. Because the work of engineers affects many areas of society, engineers often work with business people, government officials, doctors, lawyers, and other professionals.

Aerospace engineering involves the design, production, and maintenance of commercial and military aircraft. Engineers in the aerospace field also play an essential role in the development and assembly of guided missiles, unmanned aerial vehicles (UAV's), and all types of spacecraft. Aerospace engineers help build wind tunnels and other testing equipment with which they carry out experiments on proposed craft to determine their performance, stability, and control under flight conditions. Aerospace research ranges from efforts to design quieter and more fuel-efficient commercial aircraft to the search for materials that can withstand the high radiation levels and extreme temperatures of space flight.

To design strong, safe vehicles, aerospace engineers must know and put into practical use the principles of *aerodynamics,* the study of the forces acting on an object due to air moving past it. They must also have a thorough understanding of the strength, elasticity, and other properties of the materials they use and be able to predict how they will behave during flight. Aerospace engineers work closely with electrical engineers in developing guidance, navigation, and control instruments and with mechanical engineers in designing suitable engines. They also assist civil engineers in planning airport facilities.

Biomedical engineering applies engineering techniques to health-related problems. Biomedical engineers develop aids for people with physical disabilities.

They design artificial limbs, organs, and other devices that assist or replace diseased or damaged parts of the body. They produce such equipment as instruments that measure blood pressure and pulse rate, and *surgical lasers*—concentrated beams of light that can be used to perform delicate operations. Biomedical engineers also develop machines and techniques for viewing internal organs and methods for delivering medicines to specific internal sites. Some specialize in programming computer systems to monitor a patient's health or to process complex medical data, such as a person's genetic code.

In choosing materials for artificial aids and organs, biomedical engineers must understand the physical and chemical properties of the materials and how they interact with each other and with the human body. In their work, biomedical engineers often use principles of biology, chemistry, and medicine and of electrical, materials, and mechanical engineering. See **Biomedical engineering.**

Chemical engineering deals with the large-scale processing of chemicals and chemical products for industrial and consumer uses. Chemical engineers are concerned with the chemical processes that change raw materials into useful products. They plan, design, and help construct chemical plants and equipment and work to develop efficient and economical production methods. Many chemical engineers work for manufacturers of cosmetics, explosives, fertilizers and other agricultural chemicals, food products, fuels, *pharmaceuticals* (medical drugs), or plastics.

Chemical engineers must know how to handle and transport large quantities of chemicals. They have to understand such problems as heat transfer from one substance to another, absorption of liquids and gases, and evaporation. Chemical engineers control such processes as distillation, crystallization, filtration, mixing, drying, and crushing.

The work of chemical engineers relies heavily on principles of chemistry, physics, and mathematics, and frequently those of biology as well. Chemical engineers consult with electrical, mechanical, and industrial engineers in the design of plants and equipment. Some chemical engineers work closely with environmental engineers in seeking safe disposal methods for hazardous by-products of chemical processing.

Civil engineering, the oldest of the main branches of engineering, involves the planning and supervision of such large construction projects as bridges, canals, dams, tunnels, and water supply systems. Civil engineers also cooperate with architects to design and erect all types of buildings. Other civil-engineering projects include airports, highways, levees, irrigation and sewerage systems, pipelines, and railroads.

Civil engineers work to build strong, safe structures that meet building codes and other regulations and are well suited to their surroundings. The engineers are responsible for surveying and preparing building sites and for selecting appropriate materials. Civil engineers must also understand the use of bulldozers, cranes, power shovels, and other construction equipment.

Some civil engineers specialize in the study of the physical characteristics of soils and rocks and the design of foundations. Others concentrate on the management of water resources, including the construction of flood

© David R. Frazier

An aerospace engineer at an assembly plant checks a guided missile while a worker looks on. Aerospace engineers also play a key role in the production of airplanes and spacecraft.

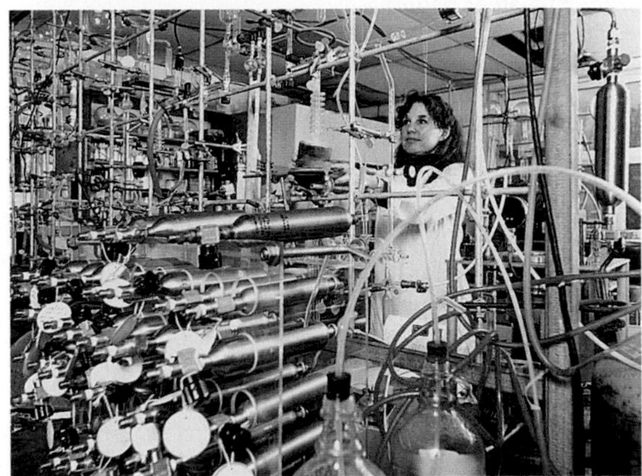

© Hans Namuth, Photo Researchers

A chemical engineer uses laboratory tests to determine which processing methods are the most economical and efficient. The best methods will be adapted to large-scale chemical plants.

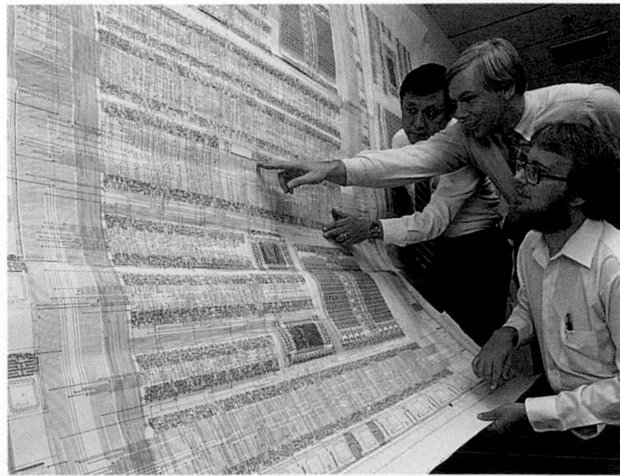

© Sepp Seitz, Woodfin Camp, Inc.

Electrical engineers develop a wide variety of electrical and electronic devices. These electrical engineers are reviewing a greatly enlarged design for a single tiny electronic circuit.

control and irrigation systems, hydroelectric power plants, and water supply and sewerage systems. Still others are concerned with designing transportation systems and methods of traffic control. Many civil engineers are involved in city planning and urban renewal programs (see **City planning; Urban renewal**).

Computer engineering deals with the design of products for electronic computation and communication. Computer engineers focus on the creation, processing, and distribution of electronic information.

Computer engineers work in virtually all industries. They build computers for home and industrial use. They also make tiny computers that are used in products that range from cellular telephones to coffeemakers. Some computer engineers write and *upgrade* (revise and improve) *software*—coded instructions that tell computers how to accomplish specific tasks. Others develop networks that connect individual computers to one another worldwide and within local regions. Still another task of computer engineers is applying computer tools to specific tasks that range from patient management in hospitals to the development of mathematical models that can predict weather patterns.

Computer engineers rely on mathematics, physics, and electrical engineering. They may be called to work with experts in virtually any other field.

Electrical engineering involves the development, production, and testing of electrical and electronic devices and equipment. Electrical engineers design equipment to produce and distribute electric power. This equipment includes generators run by water power, coal, oil, and nuclear fuels; solar energy systems; transmission lines; and transformers. Electrical engineers also design and develop electric motors and other electrical machinery as well as ignition systems used in automobiles, aircraft, and other engines. They work to improve such devices as air conditioners, food processors, and vacuum cleaners.

Electrical engineers play an essential role in the production of communications satellites; computers; industrial robots; medical and scientific instruments; missile control systems; and radar, radio, and television sets. Some engineers in the electronics field develop master plans for the parts and connections of miniature *integrated circuits,* which control the electric signals in most electronic devices. Telecommunication, which involves the transmission of messages over long distances, is another major specialty of electrical engineering.

Environmental engineering concerns efforts to prevent and control air, water, soil, and noise pollution. Environmental engineers develop equipment to measure pollution levels, and they conduct experiments to determine the effects of various pollutants. They design air pollution control devices and operate water purification systems and water treatment plants. Environmental engineers also develop techniques to protect the land from erosion and from pollution by chemical fertilizers and pesticides. They use computers to create mathematical models that help predict the results of the adoption of such techniques.

Environmental engineers are specialists in the disposal of hazardous wastes from factories, mining operations, nuclear power plants, and other sources (see **Hazardous wastes**). They work to clean up unsafe dump

Gary Milburn, Tom Stack & Assoc.

Environmental engineers are concerned with preventing and controlling pollution. These engineers are checking for leakage and contamination at a dump site for hazardous wastes.

© Cameramann International Ltd.

An industrial engineer uses a computer to design an automated robot for an assembly line. Industrial engineers work continually to improve the production of goods and services.

© Horizon International Images/Alamy Images

A materials engineer may work with metals, ceramics, or plastics and other polymers. This engineer oversees the shaping of plastic sheets.

sites created in the past and do research on new storage and recycling techniques. Environmental engineers are also involved in the development of cleaner and more reliable forms of energy and in developing ways to make the best present and future use of natural resources. Environmental engineers work with agricultural and mining engineers to develop production techniques that do the least possible damage to the land. They assist civil engineers in the design of water supply, waste disposal, and ventilation systems, and they help chemical and nuclear engineers in waste disposal.

Industrial engineering applies engineering analysis and techniques to the production of goods and services. Industrial engineers determine the most economical and effective ways for an organization to use people, machines, and materials. An industrial engineer may select the location for a plant or office, determine employee requirements, select equipment and machinery, design safe and comfortable work areas, and plan steps in operations. Industrial engineers also develop training and job evaluation programs and work-performance standards, and help determine wages and employee benefits. They work to solve such problems as high costs, low productivity, and poor product quality.

Mathematical models developed on computers enable industrial engineers to simulate the flow of work through an organization and to evaluate the effects of proposed changes. Industrial engineers also use data-processing systems to aid in financial planning, inventory control, and scheduling. Their work often requires a knowledge of mathematics, economics, psychology, physiology, and personnel management. Industrial engineers work in a variety of businesses and industries, including banks, construction and transportation firms, government agencies, hospitals, and public utilities.

Materials engineering deals with the structure, properties, production, and uses of various materials. Materials engineers work with both metallic and nonmetallic substances. They improve existing materials and develop new uses and production methods for them. They also develop new materials to meet specific needs, such as requirements for electronics and biomedical equipment. The major subdivisions of engineered materials are metals, ceramics, and *polymers* (plastics). Another important category is *composites,* which combine at least two different materials to achieve specific properties. See **Ceramics; Composite materials; Metallurgy; Plastics.**

Materials engineers are involved in nearly all industries. They help develop and determine the best materials to use for various products. Materials engineers have developed lightweight, high-strength materials for use in aircraft parts; materials to withstand high temperatures for the nuclear power industry; materials for use inside the human body; and materials designed to break down into simple compounds with minimal impact on the environment.

Materials engineers frequently work with chemical, industrial, and mechanical engineers. They may also work with aerospace, biomedical, electrical, or environmental engineers. They rely on principles of physics, chemistry, mathematics, and often those of biology.

Mechanical engineering deals with the physical behavior of solids and fluids and with systems of solids and fluids. Mechanical engineers are involved in the development of mechanical, biomechanical, and electromechanical processes; the production, transmission, and use of mechanical power; the flow of fluids and heat in systems; and the control of mechanical operations. Applications of mechanical engineering include machinery design and development and the creation of products with moving parts, which range from children's toys to automobiles to power plants.

Mechanical engineers work in many industries, including public utilities, energy production, transportation, and manufacturing. They help design products used to study the human body or to replace parts of the body. For example, mechanical engineers have developed mathematical models of human motion that have been applied to both mobile robots and biomedical devices. They have also played a key role in the development of miniature electromechanical devices, such as portable audiotape and compact disc players.

Mechanical engineers rely on the principles of physics and mathematics. Those involved in certain tasks might also rely on knowledge of biology, chemistry, electrical engineering, and materials engineering.

Nuclear engineering is concerned with the production and applications of nuclear energy and the uses of radiation and radioactive materials. Most nuclear engineers design, construct, and operate nuclear power plants that generate electric power. They handle every stage in the production of nuclear energy, from the processing of nuclear fuels to the disposal of radioactive wastes from nuclear reactors. They also work to improve and enforce safety standards and to develop new types of nuclear energy systems.

Nuclear engineers also design and build nuclear engines for ships, submarines, and space vehicles. They develop industrial, medical, and scientific uses for radiation and radioactive materials. Some nuclear engineers specialize in designing and constructing *particle accelerators,* devices used in scientific studies of the atom and in creating new elements. Others specialize in the development of nuclear weapons. Nuclear engineers also play a role in the development of radiation sources, detectors, and shielding equipment. The work of nuclear engineers frequently overlaps with that of electrical, environmental, mechanical, and materials engineers.

Other specialized fields focus on even more specific areas of engineering than do the major branches. This section describes a few important specialties.

Acoustical engineering deals with sound. The work of acoustical engineers includes designing buildings and rooms to make them quiet; improving conditions for listening to speech and music in auditoriums and halls; and developing techniques and sound-absorbing materials to reduce noise pollution.

Agricultural engineering involves the design of farm buildings and agricultural equipment, and erosion control, irrigation, and land conservation projects. Agricultural engineers are also concerned with the processing, transporting, and storing of agricultural products.

Mining engineering involves locating and appraising deposits of minerals and ores. Mining engineers decide how they can mine these materials as cheaply, efficiently, and safely as possible with minimal damage to the environment.

Mark Antman, Image Works

A mechanical engineer makes adjustments to a wind turbine. Mechanical engineers are involved in every phase in the development of a machine, from its design to its final installation.

© Cameramann International Ltd.

A nuclear engineer, *foreground,* monitors the central control room of a nuclear power plant. Nuclear engineers also help process nuclear fuels and dispose of radioactive wastes.

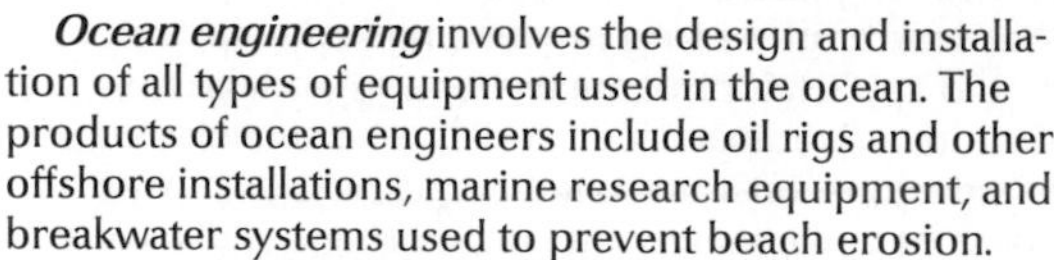

Ocean engineering involves the design and installation of all types of equipment used in the ocean. The products of ocean engineers include oil rigs and other offshore installations, marine research equipment, and breakwater systems used to prevent beach erosion.

Petroleum engineering deals with producing, storing, and transporting petroleum and natural gas. Petroleum engineers locate oil and gas deposits and try to develop more efficient drilling and recovery methods.

Sustainability engineering involves developing solutions to engineering problems that will not compromise the quality of life for future generations. Sustainability engineers devise ways to use resources and energy responsibly.

Textile engineering is concerned with the machinery and processes used to produce both natural and synthetic fibers and fabrics. Engineers in this field also work to develop new and improved textiles.

Transportation engineering involves efforts to make transportation safer, more economical, and more efficient. Engineers in this field design all types of transportation systems and develop related facilities for reducing traffic problems.

History

The history of engineering is the record of human ingenuity through the ages. Even in prehistoric times, people developed basic engineering techniques to make use of natural objects. For example, sturdy sticks became levers to lift large rocks, and logs were used as rollers to move heavy loads. The development of agriculture and the growth of civilization brought about a new wave of engineering efforts. People invented farming tools, designed elaborate irrigation networks, and built the first cities. The construction of the gigantic Egyptian pyramids at Giza during the 2500's B.C. was one of the greatest engineering feats of ancient times. In ancient Rome, engineers built large aqueducts and bridges and vast systems of roads. During the 200's B.C., the Chinese began building walls to link older walls to protect China's northern border. These links marked the start of the construction of the Great Wall of China.

Early engineers used such simple machines as the inclined plane, wedge, and wheel and axle. During the Middle Ages, a period in European history that lasted from about the A.D. 400's through the 1400's, inventors developed machines to harness water, wind, and animal power. The growing interest in new types of machines and new sources of power to drive them helped bring about the Industrial Revolution, a period of rapid industrial development in the 1700's and 1800's. The role of engineers expanded rapidly during the Industrial Revolution. The practical steam engine developed by the Scottish engineer James Watt in the 1760's revolutionized transportation and industry by providing a cheap, efficient source of power. New ironmaking techniques provided engineers with the material to improve machines and tools and to build bridges and ships. Many roads, railroads, and canals were constructed to link the growing industrial cities.

Distinct branches of engineering began to develop during the Industrial Revolution. The term *civil engineer* was first used about 1750 by John Smeaton, a British engineer. Mechanical engineers emerged as specialists in industrial machinery, and mining and metallurgical engineers were needed to supply metals and fuels. By the late 1800's, the development of electric power and advances in chemical processing had created the fields of electrical and chemical engineering. Professional schools were founded as the demand for engineers steadily increased.

During the 1900's, the number of engineers and of engineering specialties expanded dramatically. Airplanes, computers, lasers, nuclear energy, plastics, space travel, and television were among the scientific and technological breakthroughs that engineers helped achieve.

Science and technology have progressed and changed so rapidly that engineers today must learn throughout their careers to ensure that their knowledge and expertise remain current. They face the challenging task of keeping pace with the latest advances while working to shape the technology of the future.

Engineering careers

The field of engineering offers a broad range of job opportunities. Engineers may work in factories, offices, and government laboratories or at construction sites. Some engineers are involved in the research and development of new products. Others are responsible for turning plans and specifications for new structures, machines, or systems into reality. Still others use their background and training to sell and service technical equipment. Many engineers work on projects in teams that include scientists, technicians, and other engineers. But some engineers act as independent consultants who sell their services to people who need engineering assistance. Engineers may also hold teaching positions or move up into management positions in business.

Certain abilities and traits help qualify a person for an engineering career. Engineers must have technical aptitude and skill in mathematics and the sciences. They should be curious about the "how" and "why" of natural things and creative in finding new ways of doing things. Engineers need to be able to analyze problems systematically and logically and to communicate well—both orally and in writing. They should be willing to work within strict budgets and meet tight deadlines. In addition, skill in working as part of a team and in directing and supervising other workers is an important part of many engineering jobs.

Education and training. For students considering a career in engineering, the most important subjects to take in high school are mathematics and science. Typically, the mathematics courses should cover algebra, geometry, trigonometry, and introductory calculus. Chemistry and physics are important sciences for students to take. Helpful electives include biology; foreign languages; economics, history, and other social studies courses; and composition and public speaking.

To enter the engineering profession, most students complete a four-year bachelor's degree program at a college or university. In addition to a course of study in their chosen engineering fields, engineering students must take several advanced mathematics and science courses. Most undergraduate degree programs also include courses in such subjects as economics, history, languages, management, and writing to equip students with the skills that will be needed in their later work as engineers. Many programs require the completion of an independent study or design project, including a formal report, before graduation.

Undergraduate engineering students often take part in *internships* or *cooperative education* programs in which they alternate between going to school and working for companies as special engineering trainees. These programs give students the benefit of practical experience while studying for their degrees.

Graduate study offers additional preparation for a professional career. Many engineering students study for an additional year or two after receiving a bachelor's degree. They undertake a program of advanced course work in a specialized field and earn a master's degree. The completion of an original research project called a *thesis* is a requirement of most master's programs. Engineering students who want to teach at a college or university or do advanced research may then study three to five more years to earn a doctoral degree.

Some universities, junior and community colleges, and technical institutes offer two-year and four-year degree programs in certain specialized areas of engineering technology, such as computer maintenance and electronics. Engineering technology programs prepare students for basic design and production work in engineering rather than for jobs that require extensive knowledge of science or mathematical theory. *Engineering technicians,* graduates of the two-year programs, and *engineering technologists,* graduates of the four-year programs, form an important part of professional engineering teams.

Engineers continue their education after they complete their formal studies and obtain a job. Engineers, as well as engineering technicians and technologists, must continually update their knowledge by taking courses, attending workshops offered by professional societies, and reading technical journals.

Registration and licensing. Laws affecting the registration and licensing of engineers vary from country to country. In many countries, engineers must be registered if they offer their services to the public or if they are involved in construction. In the United States, each state has a board of engineering examiners that administers the licensing laws.

Professional organizations and standards. Many specialized fields of engineering have their own professional societies. The societies publish technical articles and help members keep up to date. They also grant awards to outstanding engineers, work to promote public understanding of engineering, and encourage young people to become engineers. Many engineering societies prepare standards for procedures and sponsor research of general interest.

Engineering organizations in the United States include ABET, Inc. (formerly called the Accreditation Board for Engineering and Technology) and the American Association of Engineering Societies (AAES). Both are composed of several societies. ABET reviews and accredits courses of study in engineering and engineering technology. It also provides guidance material for high

Some engineering societies

American Institute of Aeronautics and Astronautics http://www.aiaa.org
American Institute of Chemical Engineers http://www.aiche.org
American Institute of Mining, Metallurgical, and Petroleum Engineers http://www.aimehq.org
American Nuclear Society http://www.new.ans.org
American Society of Civil Engineers http://www.asce.org
American Society of Mechanical Engineers http://www.asme.org
Engineering Institute of Canada http://www.eic-ici.ca
Engineers Australia http://www.engineersaustralia.org.au
Institute of Electrical and Electronics Engineers http://www.ieee.org
Institute of Industrial Engineers http://www.iienet.org
Institution of Civil Engineers http://www.ice.org.uk
Institution of Engineering and Technology http://www.theiet.org
Institution of Engineers (India) http://ieindia.info
Institution of Mechanical Engineers http://www.imeche.org
Society of Women Engineers http://societyofwomenengineers.swe.org

school and college students. The AAES helps its member societies coordinate activities and exchange information on matters of general interest to the engineering profession. More information is available on the ABET website at http://www.abet.org and on the AAES website at http://www.aaes.org.

Many professional engineers observe codes of ethics adopted by engineering societies. The codes tell how engineers should conduct themselves in dealing with the public, with clients and employers, and with other engineers. Kristen P. Constant

Related articles in *World Book* include:

American engineers

Armstrong, Edwin H.
Armstrong, Neil A.
Corliss, George H.
Edgerton, Harold E.
Ellsworth, Lincoln
Ericsson, John
Gilbreth, Frank and Lillian
Goethals, George W.
Greenway, John C.
Hammond, John H., Jr.
Kettering, Charles F.
Latrobe, Benjamin H.
Mills, Robert
Pupin, Michael I.
Roosevelt, Nicholas J.
Steinmetz, Charles P.
Stevens, John
Stevens, Robert L.
Taylor, Frederick W.
Tesla, Nikola
Von Braun, Wernher
White, Alfred Holmes

British engineers

McAdam, John L.
Nasmyth, James
Stephenson, George
Stephenson, Robert
Stevenson, Robert
Telford, Thomas
Trevithick, Richard
Watson-Watt, Sir Robert A.
Watt, James

French engineers

Coulomb, Charles A. de
Eiffel, Gustave
L'Enfant, Pierre C.
Lenoir, Jean J. E.

German engineers

Benz, Karl
Daimler, Gottlieb
Diesel, Rudolf
Maybach, Wilhelm

Other engineers

Fleming, Sir Sandford
Gabor, Dennis
Korolev, Sergei Pavlovich
Marconi, Guglielmo
Piccard, Jacques
Piccard, Jean

Aerospace engineering

Aerodynamics
Airplane
Airship
Glider
Guided missile
Helicopter
Jet propulsion
Rocket
Satellite, Artificial
Space exploration
Streamlining
Wind tunnel

Biomedical engineering

Artificial limb
Biomedical engineering
Cryobiology
Electrocardiograph
Electroencephalograph
Hearing aid
Laser

Chemical engineering

Chemistry
Forest products
Rubber
Synthetics

Civil engineering

Aqueduct
Architecture
Bridge
Building construction
Caisson
Canal
Cantilever
City planning
Dam
Drainage
Dredging
Hydraulics
Irrigation
Reservoir
Road
Sewage
Surveying
Tunnel
Viaduct

Computer engineering

Computer
Computer-aided design
Computer chip

Electrical engineering

Electric generator
Electric light
Electric motor
Electricity
Electronics
Lighting
Radar
Radio
Servomechanism
Telegraph
Telephone
Television
Transformer

Environmental engineering

Conservation
Environmental pollution
Hazardous wastes
Waste disposal

Industrial engineering

Assembly line
Automation
Ergonomics
Manufacturing
Mass production
Microelectromechanical systems
Nanotechnology

Materials engineering

Ceramics
Composite materials
Iron and steel
Materials
Metallurgy
Plastics
Powder metallurgy

Mechanical engineering

Air conditioning
Automobile (Building an automobile)
Bearing
Brake
Engine
Heating
Machine
Machine tool
Pump
Refrigeration
Tool
Turbine

Nuclear engineering

Nuclear energy
Nuclear physics
Particle accelerator
Radiation

Other related articles

Bionics
Coal
Communication
Computer graphics (In engineering)
Cybernetics
Egypt, Ancient (Architecture; pictures)
Gas (fuel)
Great Wall of China
Greece, Ancient (The arts; pictures)
Indian, American
Industrial Revolution
Invention
Mathematics
Medicine
Mineral
Mining
National Society of Professional Engineers
Ore
Petroleum
Pyramids
Roman walls
Rome, Ancient (Transportation and communication; Architecture and engineering)
Science
Seven Wonders of the Ancient World
Technology
Transportation

Outline

I. The branches of engineering
A. Aerospace engineering
B. Biomedical engineering
C. Chemical engineering
D. Civil engineering
E. Computer engineering
F. Electrical engineering

G. Environmental engineering
H. Industrial engineering
I. Materials engineering
J. Mechanical engineering
K. Nuclear engineering
L. Other specialized fields

II. History

III. Engineering careers

A. Education and training
B. Registration and licensing
C. Professional organizations and standards

Engineers, Corps of, is the branch of the United States Army that is responsible for military engineering. It is also responsible for many kinds of civil-engineering projects. The leader of the Corps of Engineers is a lieutenant general.

In peacetime, the corps plans and directs construction of navigation and flood control works for the federal government. These works include harbors, dams, and levees. The corps also is responsible for managing and restoring U.S. wetlands.

In wartime, fighting troops depend upon the Corps of Engineers for the building of military bridges, roads, airfields, camps, and other installations. Army engineers draw and reproduce maps for the Army.

Specialists known as *combat engineers* work closely with front-line troops. For example, they handle assault boats, rafts, and bridging during river crossings. In addition, they place and clear mines and booby traps and demolish roads and bridges. Combat engineers frequently operate under enemy fire. They are prepared to fight as infantry troops if needed.

The corps as it is known today dates from 1802, when Congress authorized the president to organize the Corps of Engineers at West Point to "constitute a Military Academy." Members of the corps helped build such famous civil-engineering works as the Chesapeake and Ohio Canal and the Panama Canal. In the 1880's, the Corps of Engineers built the Washington Monument in Washington, D.C. The corps also supervised the $2-billion Manhattan Project that developed the first atomic bomb in 1945.

The Corps of Engineers has been criticized by environmental groups, which charge that the corps plans many projects with little regard for the environment. Since the 1960's, the groups have filed a number of lawsuits to delay or stop projects they consider harmful. As a result, the corps has modified many projects to minimize possible environmental damage. The corps must also prepare environmental impact statements before undertaking new projects that might have a significant impact on the environment. Joel Slackman

Engineers, International Union of Operating, or IUOE, is an international union affiliated with the American Federation of Labor and Congress of Industrial Organizations (AFL-CIO). The IUOE primarily represents operating engineers and stationary engineers. Operating engineers work as heavy equipment operators, mechanics, and surveyors in the construction industry. Stationary engineers work in operations and maintenance in building and industrial complexes, and in the service industries. The union also represents nurses and other health industry workers, along with public employees in a wide variety of occupations. The IUOE's members also include workers in a number of types of jobs in the petrochemical industry.

The union was founded in the United States in 1896. The IUOE's headquarters are in Washington, D.C. For membership, see **Labor movement** (table: Important U.S. labor unions).

Critically reviewed by the International Union of Operating Engineers

U.S. Army Corps of Engineers

The Corps of Engineers plans and supervises many civil-engineering projects. The project shown here is intended to limit the flow of the Mississippi River into the Atchafalaya River in Louisiana. The corps also handles military engineering for the United States Army.

London's Tower Bridge, completed in 1894, is one of England's many historic landmarks. Its roadway and parallel walkways extend across the River Thames on the east side of the city. London, England's capital and largest city, is a world center of culture, tourism, finance, and trade.

England

England is the largest of the four political divisions that make up the United Kingdom of Great Britain and Northern Ireland. Northern Ireland, Scotland, and Wales are the other three political divisions of the United Kingdom. The United Kingdom is often called the U.K., Britain, or Great Britain. England is the industrial and trading center of the United Kingdom.

England lies in the southern and eastern part of the island of Great Britain. It covers about three-fifths of the island. England has much charming countryside, with green pastures and neat hedges. But most of the English people live in sprawling cities. London, the capital, is England's largest city.

England has a rich history. The Industrial Revolution, a period of rapid industrialization, began there in the 1700's. English sailors, traders, explorers, and colonists helped found the British Empire—the largest empire in history. England produced Francis Bacon, one of the founders of modern philosophy; William Shakespeare, who is considered the greatest dramatist of all time; and the astronomer, mathematician, and physicist Sir Isaac Newton, one of history's most important scientists.

The English people have a long history of freedom and democracy. Their democratic ideas and practices have influenced many countries, including the United States and Canada. Most English people take great pride in their history and have deep respect for England's customs and traditions.

This article describes the people, geography, and economy of England. It also traces England's history up to 1707, when England and Wales first officially joined with Scotland to form what we now know as the United Kingdom. For a discussion of the United Kingdom as a whole and of its history since 1707, see the *World Book* article on **United Kingdom.**

Government

England is the leading political division of the United Kingdom. The government of the United Kingdom serves as England's government.

Facts in brief

Capital: London.
Official language: English.
Area: 50,301 mi² (130,279 km²). *Greatest distances*—north-south, about 360 mi (579 km); east-west, about 270 mi (435 km). *Coastline*—about 1,150 mi (1,851 km).
Elevation: *Highest*—Scafell Pike, 3,210 ft (978 m) above sea level. *Lowest*—Great Holme Fen, near the River Ouse in Cambridgeshire, 9 ft (2.7 m) below sea level.
Population: *Estimated 2014 population*—53,393,000; density, 1,061 per mi² (410 per km²); distribution, 95 percent urban, 5 percent rural. *2011 census*—53,012,456.
Chief products: *Agriculture*—barley, cattle, chickens and eggs, fruits, milk, potatoes, sheep, wheat. *Fishing*—bass, cod, crabs, lobsters, scallops, sole. *Manufacturing*—chemicals, electronic equipment, fabricated steel products, food and beverages, machinery, motor vehicles, paper, pharmaceuticals, printed materials, wool and other textiles. *Mining*—coal, natural gas, petroleum.

© Ron Oulds, Robert Harding Picture Library

An English country cottage has a garden in full bloom. Gardening is a popular activity for many English people.

© Shutterstock

Warwick Castle, in central England, overlooks the River Avon. Much of its external structure is unchanged from the mid-1300's.

The United Kingdom is both a parliamentary democracy and a constitutional monarchy. Parliament, the chief lawmaking body of the United Kingdom, meets in London. Parliament consists of the monarch, the House of Commons, and the House of Lords. Queen Elizabeth II acts as the head of state, but a group of senior members of Parliament called the Cabinet actually governs the United Kingdom. The prime minister leads the British government.

The House of Commons is the more powerful house. Its 650 members are elected from each of the four political divisions that make up the United Kingdom. England supplies a great majority of the members. The House of Lords has limited power. Most of its members are honorary appointees. For more information on British government, see **United Kingdom** (Government).

For purposes of local government, England is divided into administrative units. These units include counties, metropolitan counties, and unitary authorities. The counties are further divided into shire districts, and the metropolitan counties into metropolitan districts. The Greater London area is split into 32 boroughs and *the City.* The City is the oldest part of London and serves as London's financial district.

Each government unit has its own elected council. The government councils deal with such matters as education, housing, recreation, refuse collection, and road

England's flag is called *St. George's Cross.* The flag has never been officially adopted, but the English people have used it for over 700 years.

Royal arms of the British monarch are used in England. The sections of the shield with three gold lions on a red field represent England.

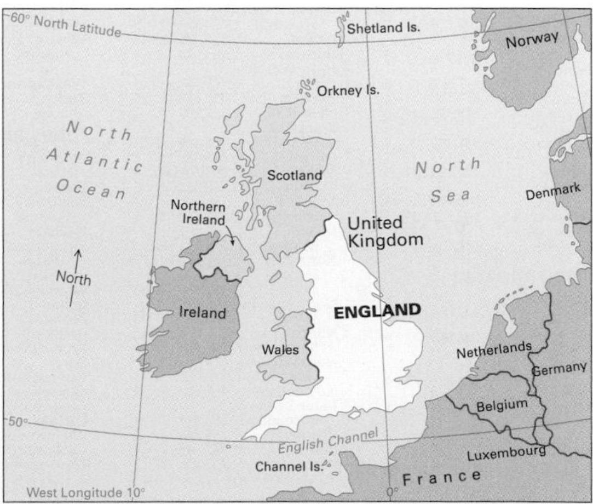

WORLD BOOK map

England, Scotland, and Wales occupy the island of Great Britain. With Northern Ireland, they make up the United Kingdom.

construction and maintenance. Most of the money for these services comes from *council taxes,* which are paid by local residents, and from grants from the national government.

People

Population. Almost all of England's people live in urban areas. More than a third live in the seven metropolitan areas.

Greater London is the largest metropolitan area in England and one of the largest such areas in the world. It covers 614 square miles (1,590 square kilometers) and has about 8 million people. The six metropolitan counties, with the largest city of each in parentheses, are (1) Greater Manchester (Manchester), (2) Merseyside (Liverpool), (3) South Yorkshire (Sheffield), (4) Tyne and Wear (Newcastle upon Tyne), (5) West Midlands (Birmingham), and (6) West Yorkshire (Leeds).

Until the mid-1800's, most of the English people lived in the countryside. During the Industrial Revolution, huge numbers of people moved to cities and towns to work in factories, mines, and mills. By the beginning of the 1900's, about four-fifths of the people lived in cities.

During the 1800's and early 1900's, millions of people left England to settle elsewhere. From the 1930's to the 1960's, the number of people moving to England outnumbered those leaving. Since the 1970's, however, the number leaving has been slightly larger than the number of people entering England. Most of the English emigrants have gone to the United States or to Canada, Australia, New Zealand, or other countries that were once part of the British Empire.

Refugees from Europe flowed into England before and after World War II (1939-1945). Since the 1950's, a large number of immigrants have come from Pakistan and from countries in Asia and the Caribbean that belong to the Commonwealth. The Commonwealth is an association of countries and other political units that were once part of the British Empire. Most of the immigrants have settled in cities and towns already facing housing shortages. During the early 1960's, the British government began restricting immigration. The wives and children of immigrants already living in England make up about half of the new immigrants who are accepted each year.

Ancestry. Celtic-speaking people lived in what is now England by the mid-600's B.C. Over the next 1,700 years, the land was invaded by the Romans, Angles, Saxons, Jutes, Danes, and Normans. The Normans, the last people to invade England, came in A.D. 1066. Each group of invaders added its own traditions and speech to English civilization and helped shape the character of the English people.

Language. English is the official language of the United Kingdom. It developed mainly from the Anglo-Saxon and Norman-French languages. For a discussion

England map index

Counties

Name	Population	Map key
Buckinghamshire	505,283	G 5
Cambridgeshire	621,210	F 6
Cumbria	499,858	C 3
Derbyshire	769,686	E 4
Devon	746,399	I 2
Dorset	412,905	I 4
East Sussex	526,671	H 6
Essex	1,393,587	G 6
Gloucestershire	596,984	G 4
Hampshire	1,317,788	H 5
Hertfordshire	1,116,062	G 6
Kent	1,463,740	H 7
Lancashire	1,171,339	D 4
Leicestershire	650,489	F 5
Lincolnshire	713,653	E 6
Norfolk	857,888	F 7
North Yorkshire	598,376	C 5
Northamptonshire	691,952	F 5
Nottinghamshire	785,802	E 5
Oxfordshire	653,798	G 4
Somerset	529,972	H 3
Staffordshire	848,489	E 4
Suffolk	728,163	F 7
Surrey	1,132,390	H 5
Warwickshire	545,474	F 4
West Sussex	806,892	H 5
Worcestershire	566,169	F 4

Metropolitan counties

Name	Population	Map key
Greater Manchester	2,682,528	E 4
Merseyside	1,381,189	E 3
South Yorkshire	1,343,601	D 4
Tyne and Wear	1,104,825	E 4
West Midlands	2,736,460	F 4
West Yorkshire	2,226,058	E 5

Unitary authorities*

Name	Population	Map key
Bath and North East Somerset	176,016	H 4
Bedford	157,479	C 4
Blackburn with Darwen	147,489	D 4
Blackpool	142,065	D 3
Bournemouth	183,491	I 4
Bracknell Forest	113,205	H 5
Brighton and Hove	273,369	I 6
Bristol	428,234	H 4
Central Bedfordshire	254,381	G 5
Cheshire East	370,127	E 4
Cheshire West and Chester	329,608	E 4
Cornwall	532,273	I 1
County Durham	513,242	C 4
Darlington	105,564	C 4
Derby	248,752	F 4
East Riding of Yorkshire	334,179	D 5
Halton	125,746	E 3
Hartlepool	92,028	C 5
Herefordshire, County of	183,477	G 3
Isle of Wight	138,265	I 5
Isles of Sicily	2,203	J 1
Kingston-upon-Hull	256,406	D 5
Leicester	329,839	F 5
Luton	203,201	G 5
Medway	263,925	H 6
Middlesbrough	138,412	C 5
Milton Keynes	248,821	G 5
North East Lincolnshire	159,616	D 6
North Lincolnshire	167,446	D 5
North Somerset	202,566	H 3
Northumberland	316,028	B 4
Nottingham	305,680	E 5
Peterborough	183,631	F 6
Plymouth	256,384	I 2
Poole	147,645	I 4
Portsmouth	205,056	I 5
Reading	155,698	H 5
Redcar and Cleveland	135,177	C 5
Rutland	37,369	F 5
Shropshire	306,129	F 3
Slough	140,205	H 5
South Gloucestershire	262,767	G 4
Southampton	236,882	H 5
Southend-on-Sea	173,658	G 6
Stockton-on-Tees	191,610	C 5
Stoke-on-Trent	249,008	E 4
Swindon	209,156	H 4
Telford and Wrekin	166,641	F 4
Thurrock	157,705	H 6
Torbay	130,959	I 3
Warrington	202,228	E 4
West Berkshire	153,822	H 5
Wiltshire	470,981	H 4
Windsor and Maidenhead	144,560	G 5
Wokingham	154,380	H 5
York	198,051	D 5

Cities and towns†

Name	Population	Map key
Aylesbury [Vale]	174,137	G 5
Barnsley	231,221	E 5
Barrow-in-Furness	69,087	C 3
Basildon	174,497	G 6
Birkenhead (Wirral District)	319,783	E 3
Birmingham	1,073,045	F 4
Bolton	276,786	E 4
Boston	64,637	E 6
Bradford	522,452	D 4
Bromsgrove	93,367	F 4
Bury‡	185,060	D 4
Calderdale‡	203,826	D 4
Cambridge	123,867	G 6
Canterbury	151,145	H 7
Carlisle	107,524	C 3
Charnwood‡	166,100	E 5
Chelmsford	168,310	G 6
Cheltenham	115,732	G 4
Chichester	113,794	I 5
Colchester	173,074	G 6
Coventry	316,960	F 4
Crawley	106,597	H 6
Doncaster	302,402	E 5
Dorchester (West Dorset District)	99,264	I 4
Dover	111,674	H 7
Dudley	312,925	F 4
Exeter	117,773	I 3
Gateshead	200,214	C 4
Glastonbury (Mendip District)	109,279	H 3
Gloucester	121,688	G 4
Great Yarmouth	97,277	F 7
Guildford	137,183	H 5
Harrogate	157,869	D 5
Hastings	90,254	H 7
Hertford (East Hertfordshire District)	137,687	G 6
Huddersfield (Kirklees District)	422,458	E 4
Ipswich	133,384	G 7
King's Lynn [and West Norfolk]	147,451	F 6
Kingston upon Thames	160,060	H 6
Knowsley‡	145,893	E 4
Lancaster	138,375	D 3
Leeds	751,485	D 5
Lewes	97,502	H 6
Lincoln	93,541	E 5
Liverpool	466,415	E 3
London (Greater London)	8,173,941	G 6
Maidstone	155,143	H 6
Manchester	503,127	E 4
Mansfield	104,466	E 5
Matlock (Amber Valley District)	122,309	E 4
Newcastle-under-Lyme	123,871	E 4
Newcastle upon Tyne	280,177	B 4
North Tyneside‡	200,801	B 5
Northallerton (Hambleton District)	89,140	C 4
Northampton	212,069	G 5
Norwich	132,512	F 7
Oldham	224,897	E 4
Oxford	151,906	G 5
Preston	140,202	D 4
Reigate [and Banstead]	137,835	H 6
Rochdale	211,699	D 4
Rotherham‡	257,280	E 5
Runnymede‡	80,510	H 5
St. Albans	140,664	G 5
St. Helens	175,308	E 3
Salford	233,933	E 4
Sandwell‡	308,063	F 4
Scarborough	108,793	C 5
Selby	83,449	D 5
Sheffield	552,698	E 5
Solihull	199,521	F 4
South Shields (South Tyneside District)	148,127	B 5
Southport (Sefton District)	273,790	D 3
Stafford	130,869	F 4
Stockport	283,275	E 4
Stratford-upon-Avon (Stratford-on-Avon District)	120,485	G 4
Stroud	112,779	G 4
Sunderland	275,506	C 5
Tameside‡	219,324	E 4
Taunton [Deane]	110,187	H 3
Tewkesbury	81,943	G 4
Trafford‡	226,578	E 4
Turnbridge Wells	115,049	H 6
Wakefield	325,837	D 4
Walsall	269,323	F 4
Warwick	137,648	F 4
Wigan	317,849	E 3
Winchester	116,595	H 5
Woking	99,198	H 5
Wolverhampton	249,470	F 4
Worcester	98,768	G 4
Worthing	104,640	H 5
Wyre‡	107,749	E 4

*Smaller unitary authorities are not labeled on the map, but their boundaries are marked.
†Populations are for districts, which may include rural areas as well as the city or town. The government of the United Kingdom does not report populations for individual cities and towns.
‡Does not appear on map; key shows general location.
Source: 2011 census.

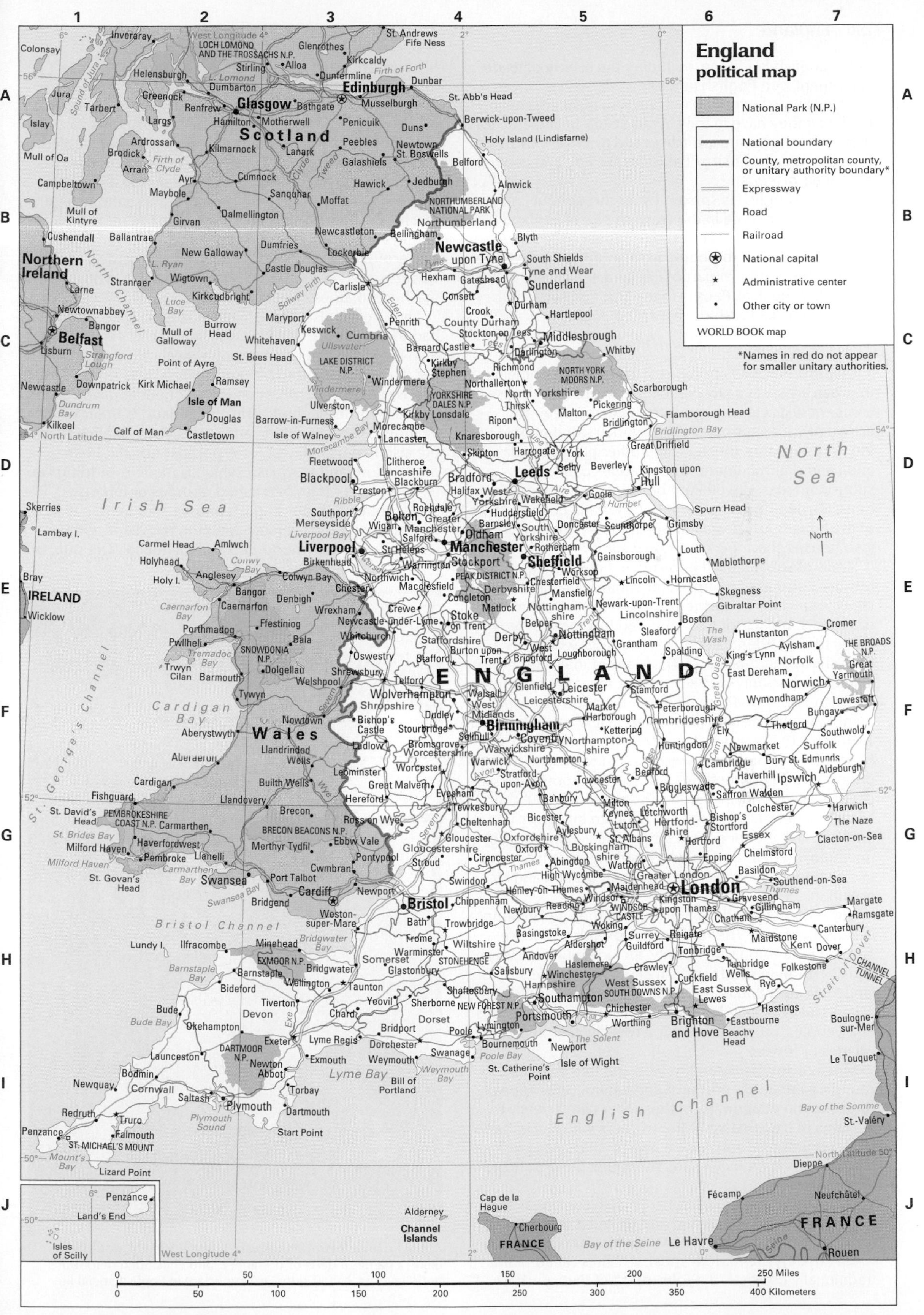
England
political map
National Park (N.P.)
National boundary
County, metropolitan county, or unitary authority boundary*
Expressway
Road
Railroad
National capital
Administrative center
Other city or town
WORLD BOOK map
*Names in red do not appear for smaller unitary authorities.
1
2
3
4
5
6
7
A
B
C
D
E
F
G
H
I
J
West Longitude 4°
North Latitude 50°
54° North Latitude
Colonsay
Inveraray
LOCH LOMOND AND THE TROSSACHS N.P.
Glenrothes
St. Andrews
Fife Ness
Kirkcaldy
Stirling
Alloa
Firth of Forth
Helensburgh
L. Lomond
Dunfermline
Dunbar
Jura
Sound of Jura
Greenock
Dumbarton
Edinburgh
St. Abb's Head
Tarbert
Renfrew
Glasgow
Bathgate
Musselburgh
Islay
Largs
Hamilton
Motherwell
Berwick-upon-Tweed
Scotland
Penicuik
Duns
Ardrossan
Lanark
Peebles
Holy Island (Lindisfarne)
Mull of Oa
Brodick
Kilmarnock
Newtown St. Boswells
Firth of Clyde
Galashiels
Arran
Tweed
Belford
Clyde
Campbeltown
Ayr
Cumnock
Hawick
Jedburgh
Alnwick
Maybole
Sanquhar
Moffat
NORTHUMBERLAND NATIONAL PARK
Mull of Kintyre
Dalmellington
Northumberland
Girvan
Newcastleton
Bellingham
Blyth
Cushendall
Ballantrae
Dumfries
Newcastle upon Tyne
Northern Ireland
New Galloway
Lockerbie
South Shields
North Channel
L. Ryan
Castle Douglas
Tyne and Wear
Larne
Stranraer
Wigtown
Hexham
Gateshead
Sunderland
Carlisle
Solway Firth
Kirkcudbright
Consett
Durham
Newtownabbey
Luce Bay
Eden
Crook
Bangor
Burrow Head
Maryport
Penrith
County Durham
Hartlepool
Belfast
Mull of Galloway
Keswick
Cumbria
Stockton on Tees
Middlesbrough
Lisburn
Strangford Lough
Whitehaven
Ullswater
Barnard Castle
Darlington
Whitby
St. Bees Head
LAKE DISTRICT N.P.
Kirkby Stephen
Richmond
NORTH YORK MOORS N.P.
Point of Ayre
Ramsey
Windermere
Northallerton
Newcastle
Downpatrick
Kirk Michael
Scarborough
Isle of Man
YORKSHIRE DALES N.P.
North Yorkshire
Dundrum Bay
Ulverston
Thirsk
Pickering
Douglas
Barrow-in-Furness
Kirkby Lonsdale
Malton
Kilkeel
Morecambe
Ripon
Flamborough Head
Calf of Man
Castletown
Isle of Walney
Morecambe Bay
Lancaster
Bridlington
Knaresborough
Bridlington Bay
Great Driffield
Fleetwood
Skipton
Harrogate
York
North Sea
Clitheroe
Lancashire
Blackpool
Bradford
Leeds
Selby
Beverley
Kingston upon Hull
Preston
Blackburn
Halifax
West Yorkshire
Ouse
Aire
Goole
Ribble
Wakefield
Humber
Skerries
Irish Sea
Spurn Head
Southport
Rochdale
Huddersfield
Merseyside
Bolton
Greater Manchester
Barnsley
Doncaster
Scunthorpe
Grimsby
Wigan
South Yorkshire
North
Lambay I.
Liverpool Bay
Salford
Oldham
Carmel Head
Amlwch
Liverpool
St. Helens
Manchester
Rotherham
Louth
Holyhead
Conwy Bay
Birkenhead
Stockport
Sheffield
Gainsborough
Mablethorpe
Anglesey
Warrington
Worksop
Holy I.
Colwyn Bay
Northwich
PEAK DISTRICT N.P.
Lincoln
Horncastle
Bray
Bangor
Macclesfield
Chesterfield
Chester
Derbyshire
Mansfield
Skegness
IRELAND
Caernarfon
Denbigh
Congleton
Newark-upon-Trent
Gibraltar Point
Caernarfon Bay
Crewe
Matlock
Lincolnshire
Wicklow
Wrexham
Nottinghamshire
Boston
Ffestiniog
Newcastle-under-Lyme
Stoke on Trent
Porthmadog
Belper
Sleaford
Cromer
Bala
Whitchurch
Derby
Nottingham
The Wash
Hunstanton
Pwllheli
SNOWDONIA N.P.
Staffordshire
West Bridgford
Grantham
Aylsham
THE BROADS N.P.
Tremadoc Bay
Oswestry
Burton upon Trent
Loughborough
Spalding
King's Lynn
Norfolk
Great Yarmouth
Stafford
Trwyn Cilan
Barmouth
Dolgellau
Shrewsbury
ENGLAND
East Dereham
Norwich
Welshpool
Telford
Glenfield
Leicester
Stamford
Tywyn
Wolverhampton
Walsall
Leicestershire
Wymondham
Lowestoft
Cardigan Bay
Shropshire
West Midlands
Market Harborough
Peterborough
Bungay
Newtown
Severn
Dudley
Cambridgeshire
Bishop's Castle
Thetford
Aberystwyth
Wales
Stourbridge
Birmingham
Kettering
Ely
Southwold
Llandrindod Wells
Ludlow
Solihull
Coventry
Northamptonshire
Huntingdon
Newmarket
Suffolk
Bromsgrove
Worcestershire
Warwickshire
Aberaeron
Warwick
Northampton
Cambridge
Dury St. Edmunds
Aldeburgh
Worcester
Leominster
Stratford-upon-Avon
Towcester
Bedford
Haverhill
Cardigan
Builth Wells
Great Malvern
Biggleswade
Ipswich
Wye
Avon
Fishguard
Llandovery
Hereford
Evesham
Banbury
Saffron Walden
Milton Keynes
Letchworth
St. David's Head
PEMBROKESHIRE COAST N.P.
Brecon
Tewkesbury
Bicester
Colchester
Harwich
Carmarthen
Ross on Wye
Cheltenham
Hertfordshire
Bishop's Stortford
The Naze
St. Brides Bay
BRECON BEACONS N.P.
Gloucester
Oxfordshire
Aylesbury
Luton
Essex
Clacton-on-Sea
Milford Haven
Haverfordwest
Merthyr Tydfil
Ebbw Vale
Gloucestershire
Oxford
St. Albans
Hertford
Chelmsford
Llanelli
Pontypool
Buckinghamshire
Pembroke
Stroud
Cirencester
Abingdon
Epping
Basildon
Carmarthen Bay
Cwmbran
Thames
Watford
Greater London
St. Govan's Head
Swansea
Port Talbot
Swindon
High Wycombe
Southend-on-Sea
Cardiff
Newport
Henley-on-Thames
Maidenhead
London
Swansea Bay
Bridgend
Bristol
Chippenham
Windsor
Gravesend
Margate
Weston-super-Mare
Newbury
Reading
WINDSOR CASTLE
Kingston upon Thames
Gillingham
Ramsgate
Bristol Channel
Bath
Trowbridge
Chatham
Bridgwater Bay
Woking
Maidstone
Canterbury
Lundy I.
Ilfracombe
Minehead
Frome
Basingstoke
Surrey
Reigate
Kent
Dover
Wiltshire
Aldershot
Guildford
Warminster
Tonbridge
EXMOOR N.P.
Somerset
STONEHENGE
Andover
Tunbridge Wells
Folkestone
Barnstaple Bay
Bridgwater
Barnstaple
Glastonbury
Haslemere
Crawley
Salisbury
Winchester
Strait of Dover
CHANNEL TUNNEL
Bideford
Wellington
Taunton
West Sussex
Cuckfield
Hampshire
Rye
Shaftesbury
East Sussex
SOUTH DOWNS N.P.
Tiverton
Yeovil
Sherborne
Lewes
Bude
Southampton
NEW FOREST N.P.
Chichester
Hastings
Devon
Bude Bay
Chard
Dorset
Portsmouth
Brighton and Hove
Eastbourne
Exe
Boulogne-sur-Mer
Okehampton
Bridport
Worthing
Lymington
Exeter
Lyme Regis
Poole
Beachy Head
The Solent
Bournemouth
DARTMOOR N.P.
Dorchester
Swanage
Newport
Launceston
Exmouth
Poole Bay
Weymouth
Le Touquet
Isle of Wight
Newton Abbot
St. Catherine's Point
Bodmin
Lyme Bay
Weymouth Bay
Bill of Portland
Newquay
Cornwall
Torbay
Saltash
Plymouth
English Channel
Bay of the Somme
Dartmouth
Redruth
Truro
Plymouth Sound
St.-Valéry
Start Point
Penzance
Falmouth
ST. MICHAEL'S MOUNT
Mount's Bay
Lizard Point
Dieppe
Penzance
Cap de la Hague
Fécamp
Neufchâtel
Land's End
Alderney
Channel Islands
Cherbourg
FRANCE
Isles of Scilly
FRANCE
Bay of the Seine
Le Havre
Seine
Rouen
0
50
100
150
200
250 Miles
0
50
100
150
200
250
300
350
400 Kilometers

of the English language, including the history of its development, see **English language.**

Many English words have different meanings in England than they have in the United States. In England, for example, freight cars are *trucks* and trucks are *lorries.* Gasoline is called *petrol.* Elevators are *lifts,* and cookies are called *biscuits.*

The way English is spoken varies throughout England. For example, people in the western part of England speak with a flatter accent and pronounce the letter *r* more clearly than do people in other areas. In east Yorkshire, in the northern part of England, the accent is soft and rather musical. People in the East End section of London speak a harsh dialect called *cockney.*

Way of life

City life. About 95 percent of the English people live in urban areas. The city centers are business and entertainment districts with modern buildings. They are crowded with shoppers, office workers, and people going to restaurants, theaters, and other places of relaxation and entertainment. On the edges of the cities lie suburban areas of well-kept brick houses with neat gardens. Gardening is a favorite hobby of the English. Most of the houses are *detached* (separate) or *semidetached* (two houses sharing a common wall).

Areas of substandard housing lie between the central business districts and the outer suburbs of many English cities, especially in northern England. Some of these areas consist of factories surrounded by blocks of *terraced houses* (identical houses in a row), which were built cheaply in the late 1800's. Many of the factories are abandoned or only partially used, and many of the houses are in poor condition. Some of the areas have apartment buildings called *council flats* that were built in the 1960's and 1970's by local authorities as public housing. Many of these buildings were built inexpensively, using poor construction methods, and have become rundown. Lack of housing and an increase in the number of homeless people are issues of concern in many cities in England. Other concerns in large urban areas include unemployment and problems resulting from the heavy use of automobiles, such as traffic congestion and air pollution.

Rural life. Only about 5 percent of the English people live in rural areas. The rural areas of England, where farming is an important activity, include much of Devon and Cornwall in southwestern England; a broad strip of land in eastern England around a bay of the North Sea called The Wash; and the northern Pennines mountains. The people live in isolated rural dwellings or in country villages or towns.

Much of southeastern England and the areas surrounding England's northern and central cities appear rural. But the economies of these areas are actually extensions of cities. Most of the workers who live in these areas commute to jobs in the nearby cities. Area residents often visit the cities for shopping, dining, and entertainment.

Food and drink. Traditional English cooking is simple. The English like roasted and grilled meats and use fewer spices and sauces than do other Europeans.

On Sunday, the midday meal, which is called *dinner,* traditionally consists of a *joint* (roast) of beef, pork, or lamb; roasted or boiled potatoes; a vegetable; and a *sweet* (dessert)—often fruit pie topped with hot custard sauce. *Yorkshire pudding,* a batter cake baked in meat fat, is often served with beef. Cabbage, Brussels sprouts, cauliflower, peas, and carrots are common vegetables because they are easily grown in England's climate.

Other popular English dishes include roast chicken, steak and kidney pie, shepherd's pie, and bangers and mash. *Steak and kidney pie* is a stew made of beef and kidneys and topped by a pastry crust. *Shepherd's pie* is a casserole of ground meat and mashed potatoes. *Bangers and mash* are thick sausages served with mashed potatoes.

The English also like fish, especially cod, Dover sole, haddock, herring, and plaice. *Fish and chips* is a favorite dish for lunch, the late afternoon meal called *tea,* or supper. It consists of fried fish and French fried potatoes and is sold at specialty shops throughout England.

The favorite alcoholic drink in England is beer, which includes lager, ale, bitter, and stout. Many English people also like Scotch whisky. A popular nonalcoholic drink in England is *squash,* which is made by adding water to a concentrate of crushed oranges or lemons.

Recreation. Many English people, like people elsewhere, spend the evening watching television. Others visit their neighborhood *pub* (public house). The pub, or

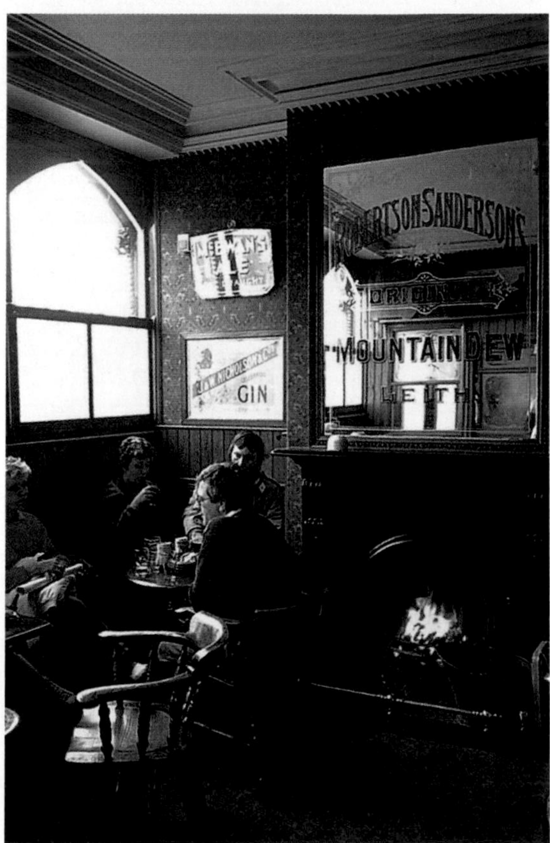

© Davies, ZEFA

A public house provides a place to meet friends, drink beer, enjoy a game of darts or dominoes, and chat. Such neighborhood taverns, called *pubs,* are important in English social life.

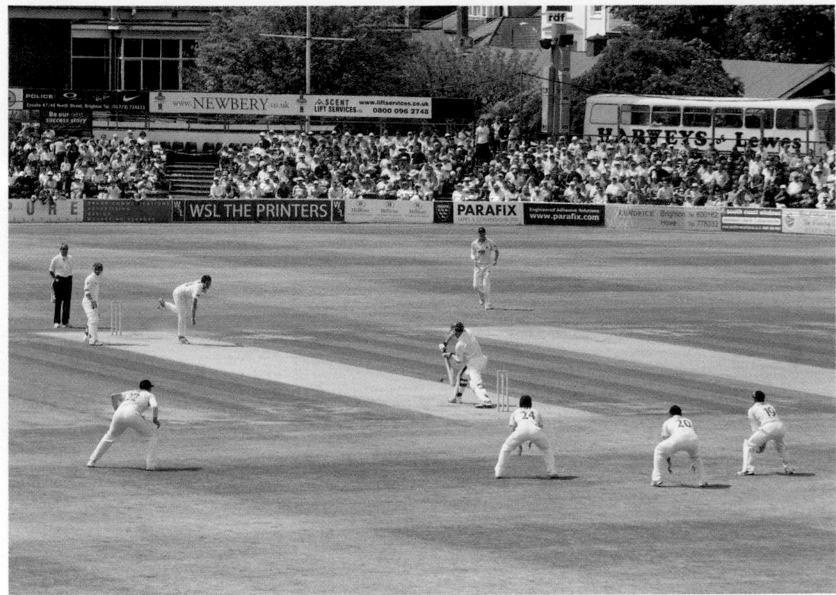

Cricket is one of England's most popular sports. Almost all towns and villages have cricket teams. The English have been playing cricket since at least the 1300's. The game became a major sport in England in the 1700's.

© Lance Bellers/Shutterstock.com

the local, as many people call it, is an important part of social life in England. At a pub, people may drink beer or other beverages, talk with friends, or play a game of darts or dominoes.

Many English people enjoy sports and outdoor activities, and they have many opportunities to participate in and watch organized sports. Others enjoy simply taking long hikes through the woods or countryside or working in their gardens.

England's most popular organized sport is *football,* the game Americans call soccer. During the football season, which lasts from August to May, about 20 million spectators watch the games. Millions of English people bet on the results of each week's football games by filling out *pools coupons.* The chances of winning are small, but winners have collected large amounts of money. At the end of the season, two teams battle for the Football Association Cup. International matches are held in England throughout the season.

Cricket has been popular in England for hundreds of years. It is played by two 11-member teams using bats and a ball. The English probably began playing cricket as early as the 1300's. Today, almost all towns and villages have cricket teams. Highlights of the cricket season are the international competitions called *test matches* between a team representing England and a team from Australia, India, New Zealand, Pakistan, Sri Lanka, or the West Indies.

Rugby, a game that uses an oval ball, is played in England from late summer to late spring. People of all ages, but especially older people, enjoy *bowls,* a sport similar to bowling. There are thousands of bowls clubs in England. Other favorite sports include golf, horse racing, rowing, sailing, swimming, and tennis.

Hunting, horseback riding, fishing, and shooting are popular in the English countryside. Some wealthy people shoot game birds such as grouse, partridge, pheasant, snipe, and woodcock. Fox hunting, a traditional English sport in which hunters on horses follow a pack of hounds chasing a wild fox, was popular among the wealthy. However, a law restricting hunting with dogs, which included a ban on using the dogs to kill the fox, took effect in 2005.

Education. All English children between the ages of 5 and 16 must attend school. About 90 percent of the students go to schools supported entirely or partly by public funds. The rest attend private schools. The Department of Education and Science and local education authorities supervise England's school system.

For many years, every child had to take an *11-plus* examination after attending elementary school from ages 5 through 11. This test determined which of three specialized high schools—*grammar, secondary-modern,* or *technical*—a child would attend from ages 11 through 16. Grammar schools prepared students for college entrance. Secondary-modern schools provided a general education. Technical schools offered vocational training. But in the 1960's and 1970's, the English educational system gradually changed. Most of the specialized high schools have been replaced by *comprehensive* schools. These schools provide all three types of education.

England's *public schools* are actually private schools. But they are called *public schools* because the earliest of them were established for the children of the middle classes. Most of the public schools are boys' boarding schools. Students generally attend from about ages 11, 12, or 13 up to 18 or 19. The leading public schools include Charterhouse, Eton, Harrow, St. Paul's, and Winchester. Such schools traditionally have helped train students for high-ranking positions in the government, the Church of England, the armed forces, or the practice of law. To pass the difficult entrance examinations of the public schools, some young boys attend private *prep* (preparatory) schools from about age 5 to 11, 12, or 13.

Institutions of higher education in England include two of the most famous universities in the world, Oxford

© Thinkstock

Hiking through the countryside is a favorite English pastime. A number of people take walking vacations. These hikers are making their way along Ullswater, in northwestern England's Lake District.

and Cambridge. The largest traditional university in England is the University of London. England's Open University has more students, but it has no regular classrooms. Instruction is carried out through correspondence, TV, the Internet, and other distance learning technologies.

Religion. The Church of England, or Anglican Church, is the official church in England. The British monarch must belong to it and is its worldly head. All other English people may worship as they choose. The spiritual head of the Church of England is the archbishop of Canterbury, who is known as the *primate of all England.* The archbishops of Canterbury and York and 24 bishops have seats in the House of Lords. This gives the Church of England an official link with the British government. About 20 percent of England's people identify themselves as belonging to the Church of England.

Many people in England belong to other Protestant churches, called *Free Churches.* The largest Free Churches include the Baptist, Methodist, Presbyterian, and United Reformed churches. About 9 percent of England's population is Roman Catholic. The Catholic Church is headed by the archbishop of Westminster.

About 5 percent of England's population is Muslim. Most Muslims live in London and other large cities. England is also home to large Hindu, Jewish, and Sikh populations.

The arts. The English enjoy motion pictures, plays, and concerts. London is the center of English music and drama. But Birmingham and other major cities also have a growing number of music and theater companies.

England has a history of producing outstanding artists. It has been the birthplace of many noted architects, painters, and composers. But its greatest artists have probably been writers. Geoffrey Chaucer, Charles Dickens, William Shakespeare, and many other English authors wrote masterpieces of literature.

English architects have developed many different styles over the years. The Norman style began after the Norman Conquest of 1066. Buildings designed in the Norman style have heavy columns and semicircular arches. The Tudor style became popular for houses in the late 1500's, during the reign of Queen Elizabeth I.

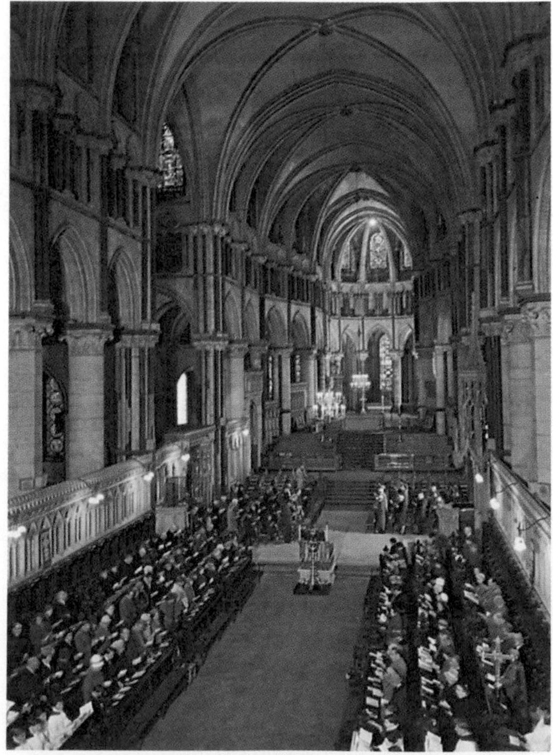

George Rodger, Magnum; courtesy National Geographic Society

Canterbury Cathedral is the church of the archbishop of Canterbury, the spiritual head of the Church of England.

Tudor was the family name of the queen. Characteristics of the Tudor style include flat arches; many windows, gables, and chimneys; and timber frames filled in with brick and plaster.

During the 1600's, two of England's greatest architects were Inigo Jones and Sir Christopher Wren. Jones designed the Queen's House in Greenwich and remodeled St. Paul's Cathedral in London. Wren rebuilt St. Paul's and many other churches after they were destroyed by the Great Fire of London in 1666. Georgian architecture, which began during the 1700's, uses much brick and stone and has a simple, balanced design.

For hundreds of years, English painters followed the styles of other European artists. But during the 1700's, such painters as Thomas Gainsborough, William Hogarth, and Sir Joshua Reynolds began to develop their own individual styles. During the 1800's, John Constable and Joseph Turner produced beautiful landscapes. Important English painters of the 1900's included Duncan Grant, David Hockney, Paul Nash, Ben Nicholson, John Piper, and Graham Sutherland.

The English have always loved music, and many of their old folk songs are still sung throughout the English-speaking world. During the 1500's and early 1600's, such composers as Thomas Tallis and William Byrd wrote excellent church music. Henry Purcell, who lived in the late 1600's, is considered one of England's greatest classical composers. In the 1870's and 1880's, Sir William S. Gilbert and Sir Arthur Sullivan wrote many popular satirical operettas. Leading English composers of the 1900's included Benjamin Britten, Frederick Delius, Sir Edward Elgar, Gustav Holst, Ralph Vaughan Williams, and Sir William Walton. Two English groups, the Beatles and the Rolling Stones, had enormous influence on the development of rock music.

English furniture makers were the best in Europe during the 1700's. Furniture collectors today prize the beautifully designed works of Thomas Chippendale, George Hepplewhite, and Thomas Sheraton. Also during the 1700's, Josiah Wedgwood and Josiah Spode produced lovely chinaware. Wedgwood and Spode pottery is still one of the United Kingdom's important exports.

For more information, see the separate articles on **Architecture; Classical music; Drama; English literature; Furniture; Painting; Rock music;** and **Theater.**

The land

England, Scotland, and Wales occupy the island of Great Britain. The River Tweed and the Cheviot Hills form England's northern border with Scotland. Wales lies west of England. The Irish Sea separates England and the island of Ireland, and the English Channel and the North Sea divide England from Europe's mainland.

Land regions. England has three main land regions. They are the Pennines, the Southwest Peninsula, and the English Lowlands.

The Pennine Chain is a long line of uplands that runs like a backbone through northern and central England. The chain is rich in a number of minerals, and it is an important recreational area.

The Lake District is one of England's most scenic areas. It is a region of clear, quiet lakes and low mountains. The Lake District lies in northwestern England, west of the Pennine Chain.

© Shutterstock

The white cliffs of Dover rise on the southeastern coast of England. The cliffs are composed of chalk. They border the Strait of Dover, a narrow channel that separates England from France.

© Telegraph Colour Library from FPG

The Pennines are England's main mountain system, often called the *backbone of England.* They extend from the Scottish border about halfway down the length of England. They are also known as the Pennine Chain or Pennine Hills. The flanks of the Pennines are rich in coal. West of the Pennines lies the Lake District, an area known for its beautiful mountain scenery and its many lakes. The highest point in England, 3,210-foot (978-meter) Scafell Pike, is in the Lake District.

The Southwest Peninsula consists of a low plateau with highlands rising above it. Several of the highlands are composed of granite. Near much of the coast, the plateau ends sharply in cliffs that tower above the sea. The westernmost point in England, Land's End, and the southernmost point in the United Kingdom, Lizard Point, are both on the peninsula.

The English Lowlands cover all of England outside the regions of the Pennines and the Southwest Peninsula. The Lowlands have most of England's farmable land, industry, and people.

The rich plains of Lancashire lie in the northwestern part of the region, and those of Yorkshire lie in the northeastern part. A large plain called the Midlands occupies the center of the English Lowlands. England's chief industrial cities are in the Midlands. South of the Midlands, a series of hills and valleys crosses the land to the valley of the River Thames.

Most of the land north of the Thames and up to a bay

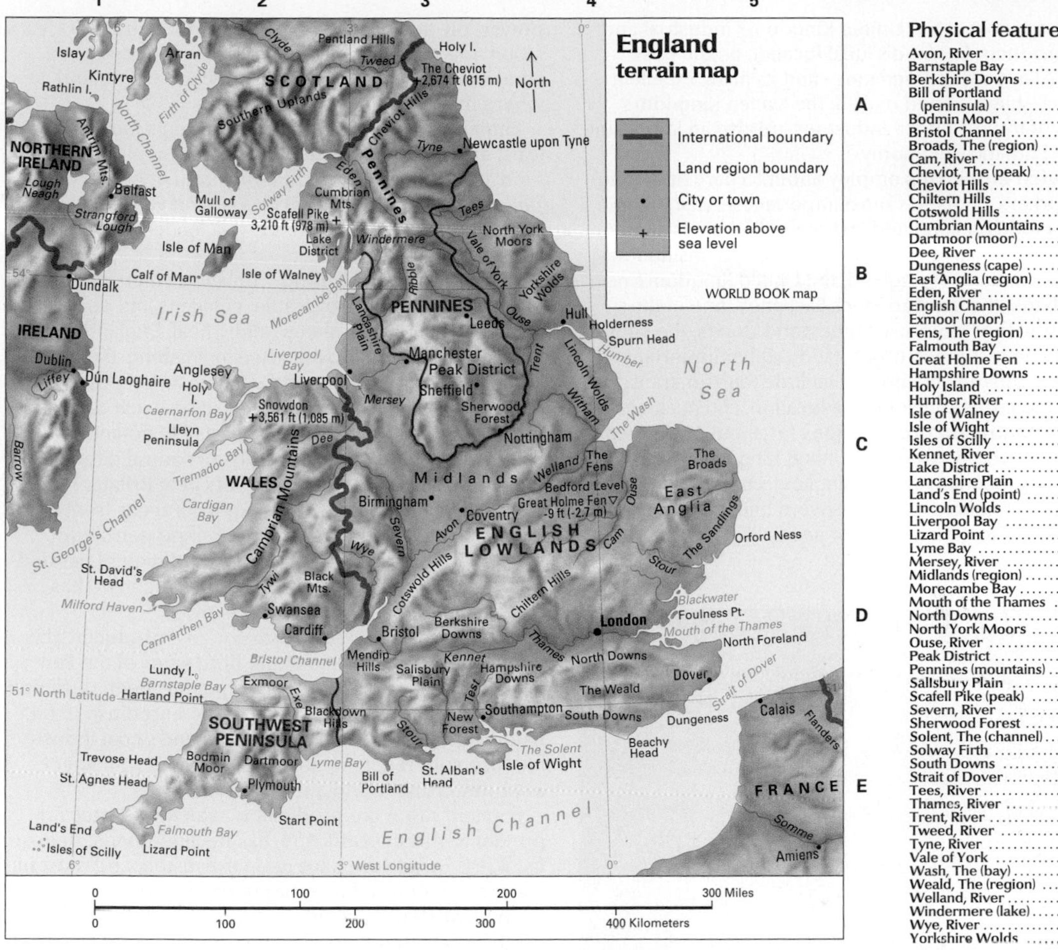

Physical features

Avon, River	D	3
Barnstaple Bay	D	2
Berkshire Downs	D	3
Bill of Portland (peninsula)	E	3
Bodmin Moor	E	2
Bristol Channel	D	2
Broads, The (region)	C	5
Cam, River	D	4
Cheviot, The (peak)	A	3
Cheviot Hills	A	3
Chiltern Hills	D	4
Cotswold Hills	D	3
Cumbrian Mountains	B	2
Dartmoor (moor)	E	2
Dee, River	C	2
Dungeness (cape)	E	4
East Anglia (region)	C	4
Eden, River	A	2
English Channel	E	3
Exmoor (moor)	D	2
Fens, The (region)	C	4
Falmouth Bay	E	2
Great Holme Fen	C	4
Hampshire Downs	D	3
Holy Island	A	3
Humber, River	B	4
Isle of Walney	B	2
Isle of Wight	E	3
Isles of Scilly	E	1
Kennet, River	D	3
Lake District	B	2
Lancashire Plain	B	3
Land's End (point)	E	1
Lincoln Wolds	C	4
Liverpool Bay	D	2
Lizard Point	E	2
Lyme Bay	E	2
Mersey, River	C	3
Midlands (region)	C	3
Morecambe Bay	B	2
Mouth of the Thames	D	4
North Downs	D	4
North York Moors	B	3
Ouse, River	B	3
Peak District	C	3
Pennines (mountains)	A	3
Salisbury Plain	D	3
Scafell Pike (peak)	B	2
Severn, River	C	3
Sherwood Forest	C	3
Solent, The (channel)	E	4
Solway Firth	A	2
South Downs	E	4
Strait of Dover	D	5
Tees, River	B	3
Thames, River	D	4
Trent, River	B	4
Tweed, River	A	3
Tyne, River	A	3
Vale of York	B	3
Wash, The (bay)	C	4
Weald, The (region)	D	4
Welland, River	C	4
Windermere (lake)	B	3
Wye, River	C	4
Yorkshire Wolds	B	4

of the North Sea called The Wash is low and flat. This area has rich farmland. A great plain called The Fens borders The Wash. South of the Thames, long, low lines of hills called *scarplands* cross the land. Between the scarplands are lowlands of clay. The scarplands consist of layers of chalk and other forms of limestone. Along the English Channel, the hills drop sharply and form steep cliffs. The most famous are the white cliffs of Dover.

Rivers and lakes. England's rivers flow from the central uplands to the seas. The rivers that flow east to the North Sea include the Tees, Thames, Tyne, and a group of rivers that join and form the Humber. The rivers that flow west into the Irish Sea and the Bristol Channel include the Mersey, Dee, Severn, and Avon. Several shorter streams flow south from the uplands into the English Channel.

The Thames is the longest river entirely in England. It is 210 miles (340 kilometers) long. The Severn is approximately the same length. Most of it is in England, but part is in Wales. England's third longest river, the Trent, is 170 miles (274 kilometers) long. All three rivers are navigable for part of their length and are connected by canals. England has more than 2,000 miles (3,200 kilometers) of inland waterways. Many of England's rivers empty into broad inlets that make excellent harbors. London, Liverpool, and other English ports are on or near such inlets.

England's largest natural lakes are in the Lake District, where 16 lakes lie within a circle about 30 miles (48 kilometers) in diameter. The largest lake, Windermere, is about $10\frac{1}{2}$ miles (17 kilometers) long and about 1 mile (1.6 kilometers) wide at its widest point.

Islands. England has a number of offshore islands. One of the most important is the lovely Isle of Wight, near the southern coast. The colorful Isles of Scilly lie off Land's End in southwestern England. The Isle of Man, in the Irish Sea, and the Channel Islands, in the English Channel, are British crown dependencies but are not part of England. These islands are largely self-governing, though the British government takes responsibility for their defense and foreign affairs.

For more information about the geography of England, see *The land* section of **United Kingdom.** For information on England's climate, see the *Climate* section of **United Kingdom.**

Economy

England has been a leader in manufacturing since the Industrial Revolution began there in the 1700's. England produces most of the United Kingdom's industrial and farm products. England's ideal location on the busy North Atlantic shipping lanes—and its many excellent harbors—have helped make it the United Kingdom's center of trade. Service industries are also an important part of England's economy.

Service industries employ about 85 percent of English workers. England's most important service industries include banking and insurance. London is an international financial center. Its major financial institutions include the Bank of England, the United Kingdom's national bank; the London Stock Exchange, one of the world's busiest stock exchanges; and Lloyd's, the famous worldwide insurance organization. Other important service industries in England include tourism, transportation and communications, education, and health care.

Manufacturing provides jobs for about 10 percent of the work force. Most of the United Kingdom's exports are goods manufactured in England. For many years, almost all of England's factories were built near coal fields, close to their source of power. Today, electric power, oil, and gas are being used more and more. As a result, many new industries have developed around London and in the southeastern section of England, where there is little coal.

© J. Reznicki, The Stock Market

Harrods, a well-known English department store, includes a meat market with a cathedral ceiling. Wholesale and retail trade and other service industries employ most English workers.

England's chief manufactured products include chemicals, electronic equipment, fabricated steel products, food and beverages, machinery, motor vehicles, paper, *pharmaceuticals* (medicinal drugs), and woolen cloth and other textiles. England is also a leader in printing and publishing.

Agriculture and fishing. England's chief agricultural products include barley, cattle, chickens and eggs, fruits, milk, potatoes, sheep, and wheat. England's shallow coastal waters provide excellent fishing. Bass, cod, crabs, lobsters, scallops, and sole are among the principal fishing catches. Much of the fishing catch comes off the eastern and southwestern coasts of England.

Mining. Oil deposits and fields of natural gas lie in the North Sea, east of the island of Great Britain. The United Kingdom began pumping natural gas from North Sea wells in 1967, and it began pumping petroleum from the sea in 1975. The production of natural gas and petroleum has increased rapidly since then and has greatly benefited England's economy.

England once ranked as a major coal producer. The largest coal fields extend along both sides of the Pennines into the Midlands. Coal output has been declining steadily, however, because of the increased use of oil, natural gas, and nuclear power. England's coal industry has also suffered competition from lower-priced coal imported from Poland and South Africa.

England's iron ore production, which was once important to the steel industry, has declined. Most deposits of high-grade ore have been exhausted, and most of the ore that England uses has to be imported.

Southwestern England has fine china clay, which is used in making pottery. Southeastern England has deposits of chalk, which is used to make cement.

Transportation and communication. England has an extensive system of *motorways* (expressways) that link London with other major industrial centers. Roads and railroads carry passenger and freight traffic. England has dozens of ports of commercial significance. The most important are London, Tees and Hartlepool, Grimsby and Immingham, Southampton, and Liverpool. England also has a widespread inland waterway system, but these rivers and canals are more important for recreational boating than for transporting freight.

Ferry services and *hovercraft* (vehicles that ride over water on a cushion of air) carry passengers across the English Channel between England and France. In 1987, the United Kingdom and France began construction of a railroad tunnel beneath the English Channel. The tunnel was completed in 1994 (see **Channel Tunnel**).

England has dozens of daily newspapers. A number of them, including the *Daily Mail,* the *Daily Mirror, The Daily Telegraph,* and *The Sun,* circulate throughout the United Kingdom.

The British Broadcasting Corporation (BBC), a public corporation, provides radio and television services. The BBC has no commercials. It is financed chiefly by yearly license fees paid by television owners. Commercial radio and television stations also broadcast throughout England.

© Shutterstock

Fishing is an important economic activity in England. England's shallow coastal waters provide excellent fishing. These fishing boats are moored along the Cornish coast in southwestern England.

For more information on England's economy, see the *Economy* section of the **United Kingdom** article.

History

Scholars do not know when the first people arrived in what is now England. But they do know that prehistoric people lived in caves in the region during the Old Stone Age, which ended about 10,000 years ago. Scientists believe that the sea was lower at that time, and what is now the island of Great Britain was part of the European mainland.

By about 6000 B.C., Great Britain had become an island. In the mid-3000's B.C., people in England began to grow crops and raise cattle, pigs, and sheep. The knowledge of farming and livestock raising probably came from people who lived along the lower Rhine River in what are now Germany and the Netherlands and in present-day Brittany in northwestern France.

In the early 1000's B.C., people in England mined tin and made bronze tools. They also built large circular monuments with stones. Scholars believe these monuments were religious structures. Stonehenge, the most famous monument, still stands near Salisbury.

Historians are not certain when the Celtic language was first used in England, but it had been introduced there by about the mid-600's B.C. A form of Celtic called Brythonic was spoken throughout the island of Great Britain.

The Celtic-speaking people worshiped nature gods through priests who belonged to the learned *Druid* class. They used iron and mined tin. They probably brought the knowledge of ironmaking to England in the mid-600's B.C. from continental Europe. They also made woolen cloth, which they dyed bright colors. They traded with the Gauls in what is now France and with other Celtic-speaking tribes in Ireland.

The Roman conquest. In 55 B.C., the great Roman general Julius Caesar sailed across the English Channel from Gaul with a small force to explore England. He returned the next year with an invading army and defeated some of the native tribes before returning to Rome.

In A.D. 43, the Roman emperor Claudius ordered Roman armies to invade Britannia, as the island was then called. The Romans easily conquered the native tribes in the southeast. In A.D. 61, the Roman forces put down a revolt led by Boadicea (or Boudicca), queen of a tribe of Britons called the Iceni. During the A.D. 80's, the Romans completed the conquest of the southern part of the island of Great Britain, including present-day England and

Important dates in England

A.D. 43	Roman armies invaded Britannia.
400's	Germanic tribes invaded England.
597	Saint Augustine of Canterbury brought Christianity to the people of southern England.
1066	Norman forces won the Battle of Hastings, and William the Conqueror became king of England.
1215	English barons forced King John to agree to Magna Carta.
1282-1283	England conquered Wales.
1295	Edward I called together the Model Parliament.
1314	Scotland assured its independence from England by winning the Battle of Bannockburn.
1337-1453	England fought the Hundred Years' War with France and lost most of its lands on the European mainland.
1455-1480's	Two royal families fought for the throne in the Wars of the Roses.
1534	At the urging of Henry VIII, Parliament made the king supreme head of the Church in England.
1536	Henry VIII united England and Wales.
1588	An English fleet defeated the Spanish Armada.
1603	England and Scotland were joined in a personal union under one king, James I.
1642-1648	Supporters of the king fought supporters of Parliament in a civil war.
1649-1659	England became a commonwealth and then a protectorate.
1660	Parliament restored the monarchy in England.
1688	The Glorious Revolution ended James II's rule.
1689	Parliament passed the Bill of Rights.
1707	England and Wales were united politically with Scotland, forming a united kingdom of Great Britain. (For later dates, see **United Kingdom** [History]).

© ZEFA

Hadrian's Wall, built by the Romans in the A.D. 120's, protected England from northern raiders. It extended from Solway Firth to the North Sea. Parts of the wall, such as that shown here, still stand.

Wales. They were never able to completely subdue what is now Scotland.

The Romans made the part of the island under their control a province of their huge empire. They built camps and forts throughout the land and constructed roads to connect the camps. The most famous road, which became known as Watling Street, ran from Richborough, near Dover, to Chester and passed through the settlements that became Canterbury and London. The Romans also built walls and forts across northern England to protect the province from the warlike peoples of Scotland. The most famous of the walls was Hadrian's Wall, named after the Emperor Hadrian. It was built in the A.D. 120's and extended from Solway Firth to the mouth of the River Tyne.

England prospered under the Romans. Trade flowed along the Roman roads, and towns sprang up around the armed camps. London, then called Londinium, began to develop as a port city. During the Roman period, Christianity came to England. Some items bearing Christian symbols and dating from the A.D. 300's have been found in various places in England. Also, an early Christian chapel has been discovered in a Roman villa in Kent.

The Germanic invasions. The Roman soldiers left England in the early 400's to help defend Rome against Germanic invaders. With the Romans gone, the Britons could not protect themselves against invasion by people from Scotland called *Picts* and people from Ireland called *Scots.* But the greatest danger came from seafaring Germanic tribes, especially the Angles, Saxons, and Jutes. These tribes first raided the coast. In the mid-400's, they began to establish permanent settlements. The Jutes were probably the first tribe to land. They settled in southeastern England, in what is now the county of Kent, and in south-central England on the Isle of Wight and in what is now southern Hampshire. The Angles and Saxons followed the Jutes and set up kingdoms throughout southern and eastern England. The name *England* comes from the Anglo-Saxon words meaning the *Angle folk* or *land of the Angles.*

The Germanic tribes gradually pushed the Britons north and west. The Britons held out for a number of years under a tribal chief who may have been the inspiration for the King Arthur legends. However, the Britons were beaten repeatedly until they controlled only the mountain areas of the extreme western and northern parts of England. Those Britons remaining in southern, eastern, and central Britain were gradually absorbed into the culture of their Anglo-Saxon conquerors.

In 597, Saint Augustine of Canterbury traveled from France to Kent and converted Kent's King Ethelbert, also spelled Aethelberht, to Christianity. Christianity had died out in most of England as a result of the Germanic invasions. The Germanic invaders were not Christians. Augustine built a monastery near Canterbury. Canterbury eventually became the main religious center in England. Augustine's followers spread Christianity in southern and central England. Celtic missionaries, who had begun converting tribes in Scotland during the 500's, converted many people in northern England.

The Anglo-Saxon period. The Angles and Saxons soon became the most powerful tribes in England. Each tribe became divided into separate nations. The Saxons, who occupied much of southern England, were organized into East Saxons, Middle Saxons, South Saxons, and West Saxons. The Angles lived mainly in northern, central, and eastern England. Their nations were called Mercia, East Anglia, and Northumbria.

In time, the tribal nations developed into seven main kingdoms called the *Heptarchy.* These kingdoms were East Anglia, Essex, Kent, Mercia, Northumbria, Sussex, and Wessex. In the 800's, under King Egbert, also spelled Ecgbehrt, Wessex became the most powerful kingdom in the Heptarchy.

Danish raiders began to attack England in the late 700's. During the 800's, they easily conquered all the Anglo-Saxon kingdoms except Wessex. Alfred the Great, the king of Wessex, resisted most of the attacks. In 886, he defeated the Danes and forced them to withdraw to the northeastern third of England. The area ruled by the Danes became known as the *Danelaw.*

Alfred was an effective ruler who made his territory a united country. He supported Christianity, encouraged education, and issued a code of laws. He also built a fleet of ships, established fortified towns, and reorganized the army to protect his kingdom from the Danes.

Alfred died in 899. During the early 900's, Alfred's successors reconquered the Danelaw. But in the late 900's, during the reign of King Ethelred II, Danish attacks resumed. In 1016, Canute, a brother of the king of Denmark, became king of England. Canute, like Alfred, ruled as a wise and just king until his death in 1035. Two of Canute's sons followed him on the throne before the old Anglo-Saxon dynasty was restored.

The last great Anglo-Saxon king was Edward the Confessor, son of Ethelred II. He ruled from 1042 until his death in 1066. Edward built the first church on the site of what is now Westminster Abbey in London.

The Norman Conquest. Edward the Confessor died without a direct heir to the throne. The English nobles chose Harold, Earl of Wessex, as king. But a French nobleman, William, Duke of Normandy, claimed that Edward had promised him the throne. Soon after Harold became king, William invaded England. His Norman knights killed Harold and defeated his forces in the historic Battle of Hastings on Oct. 14, 1066. On Christmas Day, William, who became known as William the Conqueror, was crowned king of England.

William I established a strong central government in England. He formed an advisory council, the *curia regis,* to help him govern. William appointed Norman nobles to the council and to other high positions. He kept some of the conquered land for himself and divided most of the rest among his Norman followers.

During William's reign, many cathedrals and castles were built. The construction of the Tower of London began. Shortly before his death in 1087, William ordered a survey conducted to determine how much land and other property there was in England, who held it, and what taxes and services the landholders owed the king for their property. The record of William's survey became known as the *Domesday Book* and is a rich source of information about medieval England.

Although most Anglo-Saxons became serfs under the Normans, they kept their language and many of their customs. Through the years, the differences between the Anglo-Saxons and the Normans gradually decreased. For example, the Normans spoke French at first. But eventually, their language blended with that of the Anglo-Saxons. In time, the Normans and Anglo-Saxons became a united people. The modern English language developed from their blended languages.

Struggles for power. During the late 1000's and early 1100's, a struggle developed in England between the kings and the nobles. The nobles tried to increase their own power. However, the kings wanted to keep supreme authority over the country. Similar disputes occurred in most other European nations. But in England, unlike in the other countries, the kings at first won the struggle.

In 1088, William II, son of William the Conqueror, put down a revolt of Norman barons. Henry I, William II's brother, became king in 1100. He was also determined to keep the nobles in check and, in fact, strengthened the king's control over the country. But civil war broke out after Stephen, William the Conqueror's grandson, became king in 1135. The nobles and religious leaders became almost independent during the conflict.

Henry II, Henry I's grandson, followed Stephen as king in 1154. He regained the power that Henry I had held, and he increased it. He kept the Norman tradition of a powerful king. But he combined the tradition with the Anglo-Saxon system of local rule and expanded the system of jury trials. Under the Anglo-Saxons, each local court had decided cases mainly on the basis of local laws and customs and earlier cases. Henry sent judges to all parts of England to administer the same laws throughout the land. The judges' decisions became

Detail of the Bayeux Tapestry (late 1000's), embroidery on linen by unknown artists; total length, 230 feet (70 meters); William the Conqueror Center, Bayeux, France (Barnaby's Picture Library, London)

The Battle of Hastings in 1066, pictured on the Bayeux Tapestry, ended with the defeat of the English by the Normans. The Norman leader, William the Conqueror, became king of England.

the basis for the English system of *common law*—that is, law that applied equally anywhere in England. Today, English common law is the basis of the legal system in the United Kingdom, the United States, Canada, and many other countries.

Henry II wanted to control the Church in England. This led to a bitter and famous conflict between Henry and Thomas Becket, archbishop of Canterbury. The quarrel ended when four of Henry's knights killed Becket in 1170 while he was at prayer in his cathedral. The people were so angered by the murder that Henry granted many special rights to religious leaders.

Magna Carta. Henry II's son Richard I, who was called Richard the Lion-Hearted, reigned from 1189 to 1199. But he spent only six months of his reign in England. Richard went to the Holy Land to fight in a military campaign called the Third Crusade, and he fought a war with France. He forced the people to pay high taxes to support his armies.

During his absence, Richard left the government in the care of ministers, but his brother John plotted to gain power. John was cruel and treacherous. The legendary Robin Hood supposedly fought against John's officers. John became king after Richard's death in 1199. During his reign, John made enemies among the barons and religious leaders, lost much of the land England held in France, and quarreled with Pope Innocent III. In an attempt to reduce John's power, a group of barons and church leaders demanded reform and then rebelled. They forced John to agree to a settlement in 1215 that became known as *Magna Carta* (Great Charter). It placed the king under English law and limited his power.

The beginnings of Parliament. Parliament became important in the late 1200's, during the reign of John's grandson Edward I. Like earlier kings, Edward called meetings of leading nobles and church leaders to discuss government problems. But Edward enlarged the meetings to include knights from the shires, less important church leaders, and representatives of the towns. In 1297, Edward agreed not to collect certain taxes without the consent of the realm. He also strengthened the royal court system.

Edward I brought Wales under English control. His army conquered the Welsh in 1283 after killing their leader, the Prince of Wales, late in 1282. In 1284, Edward issued the Statute of Rhuddlan, which reorganized Welsh lands and placed them under the control of the king and English nobles. In 1301, Edward gave the title Prince of Wales to his son, who had been born in Caernarfon, Wales, and who later became Edward II. Since then, nearly all male heirs to the throne have received that title.

Edward I also tried to conquer Scotland. In 1296, he invaded the country and proclaimed himself king of Scotland. But the Scots rebelled continually. Edward II's disastrous defeat in the famous Battle of Bannockburn in 1314 assured Scotland's independence for more than 300 years.

England became an important center of learning during the 1200's. Oxford and Cambridge universities received royal charters, and students from many countries flocked to them. During the 1200's, England also produced two of the greatest thinkers of the Middle Ages, Roger Bacon and John Duns Scotus.

The Hundred Years' War broke out between England and France in 1337. It lasted until 1453. Edward II's son Edward III became king in 1327. His mother was the sister of three French kings. The war began in 1337, when the French king, Philip VI, declared he would take over lands held by Edward in France. Edward, in turn, formally claimed the French throne. The first important battle of the Hundred Years' War was fought in 1346 at Crécy, in France, where Edward won a brilliant victory over the French. His son Edward, who was called the Black Prince, won the next great English victory, at Poitiers in 1356.

In spite of England's victories, the war dragged on. The English people began to oppose the long war, and Parliament refused to approve the high taxes needed to support it. In 1381, a man named Wat Tyler led a peasants' revolt against forced labor and heavy taxation. Forces of King Richard II, a son of the Black Prince, put down the rebellion.

During the 1390's, Richard tried to undermine the power of Parliament. However, he governed so badly that the country turned against him. In 1399, Richard was forced to *abdicate* (give up the throne). Parliament then chose his rival, the Duke of Lancaster, to rule as Henry IV.

Henry IV spent much of his time fighting small wars against English nobles and paid little attention to the war with France. But his son Henry V gained popular support for continuing the Hundred Years' War.

Henry V won a great victory at Agincourt in 1415. He then forced the king of France to accept him as *regent* (temporary ruler) and heir to the French throne. After Henry died in 1422, the French disputed the English claim to the throne, and the war flared again. By 1428, the English had swept through northern France. But the tide turned in 1429, when French forces led by a young peasant woman, Joan of Arc, defeated the English army in the Battle of Orléans. French successes continued. By the time the war ended in 1453, the English held only the city of Calais.

Great advances in literature and education occurred in England during the Hundred Years' War. English poetry became important for the first time. William Langland wrote *The Vision of Piers Plowman,* one of the first major poems in English. Geoffrey Chaucer helped shape the English language with such works as *The Canterbury Tales.* In 1440, Henry V's son, Henry VI, established Eton College.

The Wars of the Roses. A struggle for the throne began to develop near the end of the Hundred Years' War. Henry VI of the House (family) of Lancaster had become king in 1422. He was a weak ruler, and the nobles of the House of York decided to overthrow him. The wars that resulted came to be called the Wars of the Roses because York's emblem was a white rose and Lancaster's a red rose. The wars began in 1455. Edward IV of York won the throne from Henry VI in 1461, but Henry won it back in 1470. In 1471, Edward again defeated Henry and became king. Henry was imprisoned in the Tower of London, where he died.

When Edward died in 1483, his two sons were still children. His brother, Richard of York, imprisoned the boys in the Tower of London and declared himself King

The Battle of Crécy, fought in France in 1346, was the first important battle of the Hundred Years' War. English troops, *left,* led by Edward III, defeated the French forces, *far left,* in this battle.

Detail of an illuminated manuscript (1300's) by an unknown artist; Bibliothèque Nationale, Paris

Richard III. Some historians believe he had the boys murdered. But there is no proof of such a crime, and no one knows what happened to the boys.

Soon after Richard became king, Henry Tudor claimed the throne as heir of the House of Lancaster. His forces killed Richard and defeated the Yorkists in the Battle of Bosworth Field in 1485. Many historians consider this battle as marking the wars' end. Other scholars view the Battle of Stoke, won easily by Henry in 1487, as the wars' final engagement.

Henry Tudor ruled as King Henry VII. In 1486, he helped ensure future peace by marrying Edward IV's daughter, and so uniting the houses of Lancaster and York.

Henry VII was a stern, clever ruler. He held strong control over the nobles, cooperated with Parliament, and respected the interests of England's growing middle class. He also strengthened England's position among other nations by arranging marriages between his daughter and James IV of Scotland and between his son Arthur and Catherine of Aragon of Spain. After Arthur died, the king arranged Catherine's marriage to his second son, Henry.

The English Reformation. Henry VIII inherited great wealth when he became king in 1509. His father, Henry VII, had been a thrifty ruler. Henry VIII was talented and popular, but he was also selfish and wasteful. He enjoyed luxury, sports, good food, and music.

Early in his reign, Henry VIII made Thomas Cardinal Wolsey, archbishop of York, responsible for much of the country's management. But then, Henry wanted to annul his marriage to Catherine of Aragon, the first of his six wives. Wolsey was unable to get the pope to dissolve the marriage, so in 1529, Henry took away Wolsey's authority. During the 1530's, Thomas Cromwell became Henry's chief adviser. In 1534, Henry had Parliament pass a law declaring that the king, not the pope, was supreme head of the Church in England. These actions occurred while the Reformation, the religious movement that gave birth to Protestantism, was spreading across northern Europe.

Following Henry's actions, English church leaders made changes in Roman Catholic services that gradually led to the formation of the Church of England. A number of Henry's subjects who opposed him were imprisoned or executed for treason.

During Henry VIII's reign, England and Wales were finally united. The Welsh people had revolted against the English several times after Edward I had conquered Wales in the 1280's. But the Welsh gradually accepted the idea of union with England. In acts of 1536 and 1543, Henry joined both countries under one system of government.

Parliament passed more church reforms during the short reign of Edward VI, Henry's son. But in 1553, Edward's half sister Mary became queen. Mary was the daughter of Catherine of Aragon and was a Roman Catholic. As queen, she reestablished Catholicism as the state religion.

The reign of Elizabeth I is often called the Golden Age of English history. Elizabeth became queen in 1558 after Mary, her half sister, died. Elizabeth was a strong but cautious ruler who played her enemies off against one another. One of her first acts was to reestablish the Church of England.

Under Elizabeth, England advanced in many areas. Merchants formed a great trading company, the East India Company, in 1600. Sir Francis Drake, Sir Walter Raleigh, and other daring English adventurers explored the West Indies and the coasts of North and South America. English literature flowered during Elizabeth's reign with the works of such great writers as Francis Bacon, Ben Jonson, Christopher Marlowe, Edmund Spenser, and—above all—William Shakespeare.

In 1588, England won a great sea battle against Spain, the most powerful nation in Europe. King Philip II of Spain built a huge fleet called the *Armada* to conquer England. But an English fleet led by Admiral Lord Howard of Effingham defeated the Armada.

The first Stuarts. After Elizabeth I died in 1603, her cousin James VI of Scotland inherited the English throne. James belonged to the House of Stuart, which had ruled Scotland since 1371. As king of England, he took the title of James I. Although England and Scotland became joined in a *personal union* under James, he ruled each country as a separate kingdom. During his reign, English colonists founded the Jamestown and Plymouth settlements in America.

The English people disliked James. He increased royal spending, went into debt, and raised taxes. He quarreled frequently with Parliament because he wanted to rule as an absolute monarch. He believed in the *divine right of kings*—that is, that kings got their right to rule solely and directly from God.

Under James's son, Charles I, the struggle between the king and Parliament became more intense. Three groups—Puritans, lawyers, and members of the House of Commons—united against the king. In 1628, Charles reluctantly agreed to the *Petition of Right,* a document that limited the power of the king. However, Charles had no intention of keeping the agreement.

The Civil War. Charles I did not call Parliament into session from 1629 to 1640. When Parliament finally met in 1640, it refused to grant the king any funds unless he again agreed to limit his power. Charles reacted angrily, and civil war broke out in 1642.

The rulers of England

Name	Reign
Saxons	
*Egbert	802-839
Ethelwulf	839-858
Ethelbald	858-860
Ethelbert	860-865?
Ethelred I	865?-871
*Alfred the Great	871-899
Edward the Elder	899-924
Athelstan	924-939
Edmund I	939-946
Edred	946-955
Edwig	955-959
Edgar	959-975
Edward the Martyr	975-978
Ethelred II	978-1016
Edmund II	1016
Danes	
*Canute	1016-1035
Harold I	1035-1040
Hardecanute	1040-1042
Saxons	
*Edward the Confessor	1042-1066
*Harold II	1066
Normans	
*William I	1066-1087
*William II	1087-1100
*Henry I	1100-1135
*Stephen	1135-1154
Plantagenet family	
*Henry II	1154-1189
*Richard I	1189-1199
*John	1199-1216
Henry III*	1216-1272
*Edward I	1272-1307
*Edward II	1307-1327
*Edward III	1327-1377
*Richard II	1377-1399
House of Lancaster	
*Henry IV	1399-1413
*Henry V	1413-1422
*Henry VI	1422-1461
House of York	
*Edward IV	1461-1470
House of Lancaster	
*Henry VI	1470-1471
House of York	
*Edward IV	1471-1483
*Edward V	1483
*Richard III	1483-1485
House of Tudor	
*Henry VII	1485-1509
*Henry VIII	1509-1547
*Edward VI	1547-1553
*Grey, Lady Jane	1553
*Mary I	1553-1558
*Elizabeth I	1558-1603
House of Stuart	
*James I	1603-1625
*Charles I	1625-1649
Commonwealth	
*Long Parliament	1649-1653
Protectorate	
*Oliver Cromwell	1653-1658
Richard Cromwell	1658-1659
House of Stuart	
*Charles II	1660-1685
*James II	1685-1688
*William III and *Mary II	1689-1702 1689-1694
*Anne	1702-1714

(For monarchs after 1714, see **United Kingdom.**)

*Has a separate article in *World Book.*

People who supported the king in the war were called *Royalists* or *Cavaliers.* Many of Parliament's greatest supporters were Puritans, who were called *Roundheads* because they cut their hair short. The Puritans closed the theaters, changed the structure of the Church of England, and tried to force many of their religious beliefs on the people. During the war, Oliver Cromwell emerged as a leader in the army and in Parliament. In 1646, Charles surrendered to Scottish troops, but the next year, they turned him over to the English Parliament. Attempts to negotiate a settlement between the king and Parliament failed. In 1647 and 1648, the army removed the more moderate members from Parliament. The remaining members set up a special court, which condemned Charles to death. He was beheaded in 1649.

Detail of enamel portrait (late 1700's-early 1800's) by Henry Bone from an original painting of the late 1500's; National Trust/Art Resource, NY

Queen Elizabeth I ruled England from 1558 until her death in 1603. Her reign is often called the Golden Age of English history because it was a time of great achievement.

The trial of Charles I in 1649, after England's Civil War, resulted in a death sentence for the king. After Charles was beheaded, England became a republic called the Commonwealth of England.

© Bettmann

After Charles's execution, England became a republic called the Commonwealth of England. A committee of Parliament ruled the country. Cromwell ended the Commonwealth of England in 1653 by forcibly disbanding the Long Parliament. The Parliament was called *Long* because part of it had been meeting since 1640. England then became a dictatorship called the Protectorate, with Cromwell as *lord protector.* During his rule, Cromwell brought Scotland and Ireland under the control of England. His armies swept through both countries and put down all resisting forces.

The Restoration. Oliver Cromwell died in 1658, and his son Richard was named lord protector. But Richard could not handle the affairs of government. In addition, the people were dissatisfied with the Protectorate and wanted a monarchy again. George Monck, a general who had served under Oliver Cromwell, overthrew the government in 1660. A new Parliament, elected in 1660, restored the monarchy under Charles II, the son of Charles I.

Under Charles II, Parliament kept most of the powers it had won, and authority was divided between the king and Parliament. Charles died in 1685, and his brother became King James II. James, a Roman Catholic, wanted to restore Catholicism and absolute monarchy in England. The people disliked his ideas but put up with him. They expected James's Protestant daughter, Mary, to become queen after he died. Above all, they did not want another civil war. But when James had a son, people realized the restoration of Catholicism would be permanent. Leading politicians invited William of Orange, Mary's husband and ruler of the Netherlands, to invade England with Dutch forces and restore English liberties. In 1688, he landed in England. James fled to France and lost his throne in what is called the Glorious Revolution.

In 1689, William and Mary became joint rulers of England after accepting what became known as the Bill of Rights. This document assured the people certain basic civil rights. In addition, the Bill of Rights made it illegal for the king to keep a standing army, to levy taxes without Parliament's approval, or to be a Roman Catholic.

War with France. During the late 1660's, France became the strongest nation on the European mainland. William III had fought against France when he ruled the Netherlands. As king of England, he made alliances with other countries to keep France from growing even more powerful. William died in 1702. His wife's sister Anne, who was also a daughter of James II, became queen. In 1701, the War of the Spanish Succession had broken out, with England and most other European countries joining forces against France and Spain. The allied armies, led by England's Duke of Marlborough, defeated France. Under the peace treaty, signed at Utrecht in 1713, England won Newfoundland, mainland Nova Scotia, and the territory around Hudson Bay from France. England also got full control of the Caribbean island of St. Kitts, previously divided with France, and gained Gibraltar and the island of Minorca from Spain.

The Augustan Age. During Queen Anne's reign, literature reached a height that many scholars considered similar to that reached in ancient Rome under Emperor Augustus. For this reason, her reign is said to mark the start of the Augustan Age. The literary masters of the period included Joseph Addison, Alexander Pope, Richard Steele, and Jonathan Swift. During Anne's reign, England's commercial prosperity also continued to grow, and Parliament won unquestioned control over the monarchy.

In 1707, the Act of Union joined the Kingdom of England and Wales with the Kingdom of Scotland to form a "united kingdom of Great Britain." The history of England then became part of the United Kingdom's history. For the story of the United Kingdom, see **United Kingdom.**

Peter R. Mounfield, Anthony Sutcliffe, and Rodney Barker

Related articles in *World Book.* See **United Kingdom** and its list of *Related articles.* See also the following articles:

Biographies

See the biographies of the rulers whose names are marked by an asterisk in the table *The rulers of England* with this article. See also the following biographies:

Bacon, Francis
Bacon, Roger
Baffin, William
Becket, Saint Thomas
Boleyn, Anne
Boudicca
Buckingham, Duke of
Burghley, Lord
Cabot, John
Cabot, Sebastian
Calvert, George
Catherine of Aragon
Cromwell, Thomas
Drake, Sir Francis
Duns Scotus, John
Edward (the Black Prince)
Frobisher, Sir Martin
Gilbert, Sir Humphrey
Grenville, Sir Richard
Guy of Warwick
Hawkins, Sir John
Hudson, Henry
John of Gaunt
Laud, William
Marlborough, Duke of
Monck, George
More, Sir Thomas
Pym, John
Raleigh, Sir Walter
Russell, Lord John
Strafford, Earl of
Warwick, Earl of
Wolsey, Thomas

Cities and towns

Bath
Birmingham
Brighton and Hove
Bristol
Cambridge
Canterbury
Coventry
Dover
Durham
Glastonbury
Hull
Leeds
Leicester
Lincoln
Liverpool
London
Manchester
Newcastle upon Tyne
Nottingham
Oxford
Plymouth
Portsmouth
Salisbury
Sheffield
Southampton
Stoke-on-Trent
Stratford-upon-Avon
Winchester
York

Physical features

Avon, River
Bristol Channel
Channel Islands
Dover, Strait of
English Channel
Irish Sea
Mersey, River
Pennines
Severn, River
Thames, River
Wight, Isle of
Windermere

Colleges, schools, and universities

Cambridge, University of
Charterhouse
Eton College
Harrow School
London, University of
Oxford, University of
Rugby School
Westminster School
Winchester College

Battles and wars

Agincourt, Battle of
Bannockburn, Battle of
Crécy, Battle of
Crusades
Hastings, Battle of
Hundred Years' War
Poitiers, Battle of
Succession wars (The War of the Spanish Succession)
Wars of the Roses

Important documents

Anglo-Saxon Chronicle
Bill of rights
Domesday Book
Magna Carta
Petition of Right

Peoples

Angles
Anglo-Saxons
Celts
Jutes
Normans
Saxons
Vikings

History

Archbishop of Canterbury
Cabal
Coffee house
Colonial life in America (Why the colonists came to America)
Coronation
Divine right of kings
Druids
East India Company
Glorious Revolution
Gunpowder Plot
Hampton Court Conference
Lancaster
Levellers
Long Parliament
Model Parliament
New England, Dominion of
Norman Conquest
Plymouth Colony
Plymouth Company
Prince of Wales
Puritans
Reformation (In England)
Restoration
Roman walls
Rump Parliament
Runnymede
Spanish Armada
Star Chamber
Stonehenge
Stuart, House of
Test Acts
Thane
Toleration Act
Wat Tyler's Rebellion
Yeoman
York

Other related articles

Bayeux Tapestry
Beatles
Bodleian Library
Boxing Day
British Isles
British Museum
Church of England
Classical music (History)
Cockney
Cricket
Democracy (Democracy in England)
English language
English literature
Europe (pictures)
Fleet Prison
Fox hunting
Furniture
George, Saint
Humberside
Masque
Newgate Prison
Old Bailey
Painting
Postal services (The creation of the Penny Post)
Rolling Stones
Rugby football
Soccer
Sulgrave Manor
Theater (Theater in other countries)
Tower of London
Victoria and Albert Museum
Westminster Abbey
Weights and measures (Development of units of measure)
Windsor Castle

Outline

I. Government
II. People
A. Population
B. Ancestry
C. Language
III. Way of life
A. City life
B. Rural life
C. Food and drink
D. Recreation
E. Education
F. Religion
G. The arts
IV. The land
A. Land regions
B. Rivers and lakes
C. Islands
V. Economy
A. Service industries
B. Manufacturing
C. Agriculture and fishing
D. Mining
E. Transportation and communication
VI. History

Questions

How has England's location helped make it an important trading center?
What is the *backbone of England?*
What is England's most popular organized sport?
What was the Glorious Revolution?
What are the two houses of Parliament?

How many metropolitan areas does England have?
Who were the Roundheads? Who was their leader?
Where is the point of land called Land's End?
To what church must the British monarch belong?
Why was the reign of Elizabeth I called the Golden Age?

Additional resources

Level I

Allport, Alan. *England.* 2nd ed. Chelsea Hse., 2007.
Aronson, Marc. *If Stones Could Speak: Unlocking the Secrets of Stonehenge.* National Geographic Children's Bks., 2010.
Blashfield, Jean F. *England.* Rev. ed. Children's Pr., 2007.

Level II

Black, Jeremy. *A New History of England.* 2nd ed. Hist. Pr., 2008.
Cannon, John A., and Hargreaves, Anne. *The Kings and Queens of Britain.* 2nd ed. Oxford, 2009.
Flanders, Judith. *Inside the Victorian Home.* 2003. Reprint. Norton, 2006.
Mortimer, Ian. *The Time Traveler's Guide to Medieval England: A Handbook for the Visitors to the Fourteenth Century.* 2008. Reprint. Simon & Schuster, 2010.

England, Bank of. See **Bank of England.**

England, Commonwealth of. See **England** (The Civil War).

English, language. See **English language.**

English, William Hayden (1822-1896), was the Democratic candidate for vice president of the United States in 1880. He and presidential candidate Winfield S. Hancock were defeated by Republicans James A. Garfield and Chester A. Arthur. English was a member of the U.S. House of Representatives from Indiana from 1853 to 1861. He also served as a member of the Indiana house of representatives in 1851 and 1852. English was born on Aug. 27, 1822, in Lexington, Indiana. He died on Feb. 7, 1896. Irving G. Williams

English-Canadian literature. See **Canadian literature.**

English Channel is a body of water between England and France that connects the Atlantic Ocean and the North Sea. The channel is about 350 miles (563 kilometers) long. It ranges from about 21 to 100 miles (34 to 160 kilometers) in width. The narrowest part of the channel—between the English city of Dover and the French city of Calais—is called the Strait of Dover.

The English Channel is the world's busiest sea passage. About 600 vessels sail through or across the Strait of Dover daily. Ferryboats and hovercraft carry passengers and vehicles across the channel between England and France.

Major ports on the English coast include Dover, Plymouth, Portsmouth, and Southampton. Ports on the channel's French coast include Boulogne-sur-Mer, Calais, Cherbourg, Dieppe, and Le Havre. Popular resorts line the channel coast, including Brighton and Hove, the Isle of Wight, and Bournemouth in England, and Deauville and Le Touquet in France. Islands in the channel include the United Kingdom's Channel Islands, near the French coast, and the Isle of Wight, near the English coast.

Vessels in the English Channel must often battle rough seas. Currents from the North Sea and the Atlantic Ocean meet in the channel. The currents and strong winds cause the roughness. About 25 dense fogs occur in the channel annually.

Most geologists believe that what are now England and France were joined by a low-lying plain at the end of the Ice Age, about 10,000 years ago. They believe that about 7,000 years ago, large amounts of ice melted nearby. The water from the melting ice raised the level of the sea, flooding the low-lying plain and creating the English Channel.

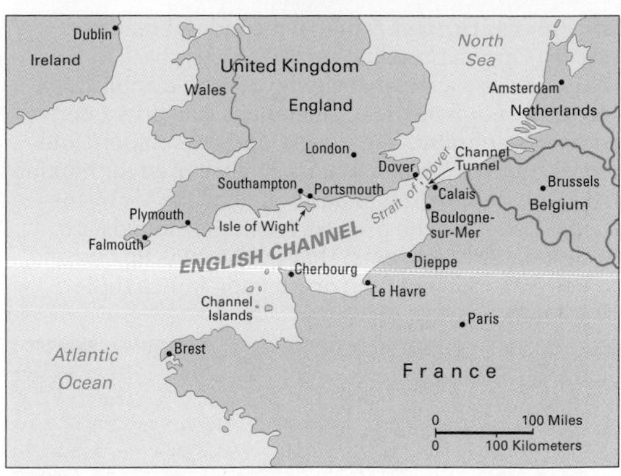

WORLD BOOK map

The English Channel separates England and France.

The channel has long protected England from invasions. The Spanish Armada in the 1500's, Napoleon's fleet in the 1800's, and Adolf Hitler's warships in the 1940's all failed to cross the channel and conquer England.

Since the mid-1700's, there has been interest in building a tunnel beneath the English Channel. Albert Mathieu, a French mining engineer, presented the first plan for a tunnel in 1802. In 1986, the United Kingdom and France announced plans to build a railroad tunnel under the Strait of Dover. Construction on the tunnel began in 1987 and was completed in 1994. Passenger trains and freight trains use the tunnel. Also, the tunnel accommodates special trains that carry automobiles, buses, and trucks through it. See **Channel Tunnel.**

The English Channel has long been a challenge for swimmers. In 1875, Matthew Webb of the United Kingdom made the first recorded crossing of the channel, swimming from England to France in 21 hours 45 minutes. In 1926, Gertrude Ederle of the United States became the first woman to cross the English Channel, swimming from France to England in 14 hours 39 minutes (see **Ederle, Gertrude C.**).

Swimmers continue to prove themselves by swimming across the channel. Some swimmers cross the channel two or even three times without stopping. Current records for swimming once across the channel have dropped to about 8 hours or less. D. Ian Scargill

See also **Dover, Strait of.**

English Civil War. See **England** (History [The Civil War]).

English cocker spaniel is a popular sporting dog. Outside the United States, it is known as the *cocker spaniel.* The English cocker is alert, well balanced, and strongly built. It is noted for its endurance and intelligence and is a responsible and willing dog, both in the field and as a companion. It differs from other cockers chiefly in size, weighing from 26 to 34 pounds (12 to 15 kilograms) and standing 16 inches (41 centimeters) tall at the shoulder. See also **Dog** (picture: Sporting dogs).

Critically reviewed by the English Cocker Spaniel Club of America

English foxhound is one of the oldest breeds of hounds. Careful breeding records, dating back to the 1700's, give the ancestry of some purebred English foxhounds through 50 to 60 generations. The breed derives from the staghound, the beagle, and the southern (old English) hound. It has traditionally been used for hunting foxes. The hounds run in packs, trailing the fox by the scent it leaves on the ground. English foxhounds are rarely kept as house pets. They are not affectionate and do not seek much petting or attention from people.

WORLD BOOK photo

The English foxhound has a sturdy body with straight legs. Its smooth coat is white with patches of black and tan.

They were first brought to North America in 1738.

The English foxhound is sturdy and heavy-boned, with very straight legs. The dog's height is about 23 inches (58 centimeters), and it weighs from 60 to 75 pounds (27 to 34 kilograms). Its smooth, hard coat is white with patches of black and tan.

Critically reviewed by the American Kennel Club

See also **Fox hunting; Harrier.**

English grammar. See **Grammar.**

English horn is a woodwind instrument. It is actually an alto oboe, not a horn. An English horn consists of a wooden tube 30 inches (76 centimeters) long with a pear-shaped bell at one end. A short metal tube with a double reed is attached to the other end. The player blows on the reed through the short metal tube and plays different notes by pressing keys that open and close holes along the length of the instrument. See also **Music** (picture: Wind instruments). André P. Larson

English language is, along with Chinese, one of the two most widely spoken languages in the world. It is used as either a primary or secondary language in many countries.

During the 1500's, fewer than 2 million people spoke English. All of them lived in what is now the United Kingdom. Through the centuries, as the result of various historical events, English spread throughout the world. Today, it is estimated that about 400 million people speak English as their native language. Most of them live in Australia, Canada, Ireland, New Zealand, South Africa, the United Kingdom, and the United States.

Another 400 million people, chiefly living in Bangladesh, India, Pakistan, and many African countries, speak English in addition to their own language. An additional 750 million people probably speak English as a foreign language.

Characteristics of English

Vocabulary. English has a larger vocabulary than any other language. There are more than 600,000 words in the largest dictionaries of the English language.

Some English words have been passed on from generation to generation as far back as scholars can trace. These words, such as *woman, man, sun, hand, love, go,* and *eat,* express basic ideas and feelings. Later, many words were borrowed from other languages, including Arabic, French, German, Greek, Italian, Latin, Russian, and Spanish. For example, *algebra* is from Arabic, *fashion* from French, *piano* from Italian, and *canyon* from Spanish.

A number of words, such as *doghouse* and *splashdown,* were formed by combining other words. New words are also created by blending words. For example, *motor* and *hotel* were blended into *motel.* Words can be shortened to form new words, as was done with *history* to form *story.* Words called *acronyms* are formed by using the first letter or letters of several words. The word *radar* is an acronym for *ra*dio *d*etection *a*nd *r*anging.

Pronunciation and spelling in English sometimes seem illogical or inconsistent. Many words are spelled similarly though pronounced differently. Examples include *cough, though,* and *through.* Other words, such as *blue, crew, to, too,* and *shoe,* have similar pronunciations but are spelled differently. Many of these variations show changes that occurred during the development of English. The spelling of some words remained the same through the centuries, though their pronunciation changed.

Grammar is the set of principles used to create sentences. These principles define the elements used to assemble sentences and the relationships between the elements. The elements include *parts of speech* and *inflections.*

Parts of speech are the word categories of the English language. Scholars do not all agree on how to describe the parts of speech. The traditional description lists eight classes: nouns, pronouns, verbs, adjectives, adverbs, prepositions, conjunctions, and interjections. The most important relationships of the parts of speech include subject and verb, verb and direct object, and modifier and the word modified.

Some modern scholars also divide the parts of speech into two categories, *content words* and *function words.* Content words are the main parts of speech—nouns, verbs, adverbs, and adjectives—and carry the basic vocabulary meanings. For example, *dog, write, happy,* and *seldom* are content words. These words are also called *form classes.* Function words express relationships between content words in a sentence. For example, *in, because, the, very,* and *not* are function words. They show the grammatical, or structural, meanings of the sentence and are also called *structure classes.* Function words include articles, prepositions, pronouns, and conjunctions. See **Parts of speech.**

English has fewer inflections than most other European languages. An inflection is a variation of the form of a word that gives the word a different meaning or function. An English noun has only two inflections, the plural and the possessive. Inflections are used to change the tense and number of a verb or the case of a pronoun. Inflections can also change adjectives to the comparative or the superlative—for example, *big, bigger, biggest.*

Grammar also defines the order in which parts of speech may be used. The subject of a sentence usually comes first in the word order in English. It is generally followed by the verb and then the object. Single words that modify nouns are usually placed before the noun, but phrases that modify nouns are usually placed after the noun. Words that modify verbs can be put before or after the verb. For more information on word order and sentence patterns, see **Sentence.**

The development of English

Origins. The earliest source of the English language was a prehistoric language that modern scholars call Proto-Indo-European (PIE). PIE was probably spoken about 5,000 years ago by people who lived in the region north of the Black Sea, in southeastern Europe. These people migrated through the centuries and gradually developed new languages.

One group of people who spoke PIE migrated west and divided into groups who spoke languages that were the ancestors of the Germanic, Greek, and Latin tongues. The Germanic languages developed into English, Danish, Dutch, German, Norwegian, and Swedish. The ancient Greek language became modern Greek, and early Latin grew into French, Italian, and Spanish.

The earliest known language in what is now the United Kingdom was spoken by a people called the Celts. The Romans started to conquer the Celts in A.D. 43 and ruled much of Britain until the early 400's, when they returned to Rome. During the mid-400's, Germanic people who lived along the North Sea invaded Britain. The invaders belonged to three main tribes—the Angles, the Jutes, and the Saxons. All three tribes spoke their own Germanic dialect, but they probably understood one another. The Angles settled in central Britain. The word *England* came from a word meaning the *Angle folk* or *land of the Angles,* which was used by the late 800's to encompass all the Anglo-Saxon people and their lands. The language of the Angles, Saxons, and Jutes became known as English.

The history of the English language can be divided into three main periods. The language of the first period, which began about 500 and ended about 1100, is called *Old English.* During the next period, from about 1100 to 1485, the people spoke *Middle English.* The language of the period from about 1485 to the present is known as *Modern English.*

Old English was mainly a mixture of the Germanic languages of the Angles, Jutes, and Saxons. Old English resembles modern German more than it does modern English. Old English had many inflections, as does modern German, and its word order and pronunciation resembled those of modern German.

The vocabulary of Old English was chiefly Germanic, though some words came from the language of the Celts. The Germanic people had learned some Latin words while they lived on the European continent. These people brought some of those words to England and added them to Old English. More Latin words were added during the 500's and the 600's, when Christianity spread in England.

During the late 800's, Viking invaders from Denmark and Norway settled in northeast England. As a result, many words from Scandinavian languages became part of Old English. Gradually, many inflections of Old English were dropped. People also began to put words into a more regular order and to use more prepositions to indicate relationships between words.

Middle English. In 1066, England was conquered by the Normans, a people from the area in France that is now called Normandy. Their leader, William the Conqueror, became king of England. The Normans took control of all English institutions, including the government and the church.

Most of the English people continued to speak English. But many of the members of the upper class in England learned Norman French because they wanted influence and power. The use of French words eventually became fashionable in England. The English borrowed thousands of these words and made them part of their own language. The French-influenced language of England during this period is now called Middle English.

The Normans intermarried with the English and, through the years, became increasingly distant—socially, economically, and culturally—from France. The Normans began to speak English in daily life. By the end of the 1300's, the French influence had declined sharply in England. English was used again in the courts and in business affairs, where French had replaced it.

Modern English. By about 1485, English had lost most of its Old English inflections, and its pronunciation and word order closely resembled those of today. During this period, the vocabulary of English expanded by borrowing words from many other languages. Beginning in the 1600's, the language spread throughout the world as the English explored and colonized Africa, Australia, India, and North America. Different dialects of the English language developed in these areas.

Today, English is the international language of science and technology. In addition, the English language is used throughout the world in business and diplomacy.

Josh Ard

Related articles in *World Book* include:

Case
Celts
Conjugation
Declension
Dialect
Dictionary
England (Language)
English literature
Etymology
Gender
Grammar
Inflection
Language
Linguistics
Mood (grammar)
Number (grammar)
Person
Phonetics
Pidgin English
Pronunciation
Sentence (grammar)
Shakespeare, William (introduction)
Spelling
Tense
Teutons
Vocabulary
Voice (grammar)

Additional resources

Bragg, Melvyn. *The Adventure of English: The Biography of a Language.* Arcade Pub., 2004.
Crystal, David. *The Stories of English.* Overlook, 2004.
Strumpf, Michael, and Douglas, Auriel. *The Grammar Bible.* 1999. Reprint. Owl Bks., 2004.

English literature

English literature consists of the poetry, prose, and drama written in the English language by authors in England, Scotland, and Wales. These three lands occupy the island of Great Britain and are political divisions of the United Kingdom of Great Britain and Northern Ireland. They have produced many outstanding writers.

English literature is a rich, varied literature. It includes masterpieces in many forms, particularly the novel, the short story, epic and lyric poetry, the essay, literary criticism, and drama.

English literature is also one of the oldest national literatures in the Western world. English authors wrote important works as early as the A.D. 700's.

This article traces the history of English literature from its earliest period to the present. The dates given for each period in the development of the literature are approximate. The article deals with works written in English by authors whose lives and careers have been based in England, Scotland, and Wales. For information on the literature of the United States, Canada, and Ireland, see the articles **American literature, Canadian literature**, and **Irish literature.**

Old English literature (500-1100)

During the A.D. 400's and 500's, three Germanic tribes—the Angles, Jutes, and Saxons—settled in England and established powerful kingdoms. Together, these tribes are called Anglo-Saxons. They used dialects that became known as Old English or Anglo-Saxon. Old English was the chief literary language of England until about 1100. In 597, Saint Augustine of Canterbury began converting the Anglo-Saxons to Christianity. English literature began through the combined influence of the Anglo-Saxon kingdoms and the Christian church.

Old English poetry. Many Old English poems glorified a real or imaginary hero and tried to teach the values of bravery and generosity. Poets used *alliteration* (words that begin with the same sound) and *kennings* (elaborate descriptive phrases). They also used *internal rhyme,* in which a word within a line rhymes with a word at the end of the line.

The first English poet known by name is Caedmon, who lived during the 600's. His only authentic surviving work is a nine-line poem that praises God.

Masters of English literature

The masters of English literature from the 1300's to the present rank among the world's greatest literary figures. The writers in this table appear in chronological order. The table also lists early types of dramas and specific works that played an important part in the development of English literature. Major works written before the 1300's include the epic poem *Beowulf* and adventure stories, called *romances,* about heroes and battles.

Gulliver's Travels **(1726) by Jonathan Swift**

Romeo and Juliet **(about 1596) by William Shakespeare**

WORLD BOOK illustrations by Konrad Hack

John Bunyan (1628-1688)
Henry Vaughan (1622-1695)
Andrew Marvell (1621-1678)
John Evelyn (1620-1706)
Abraham Cowley (1618-1667)
Richard Lovelace (1618-1658)
Jeremy Taylor (1613-1667)
King James Bible (1611)
Sir John Suckling (1609-1642)
John Milton (1608-1674)
Sir Thomas Browne (1605-1682)
Izaak Walton (1593-1683)
George Herbert (1593-1633)
Robert Herrick (1591-1674)
Francis Beaumont (1584?-1616)
John Webster (1580?-1625?)
Robert Burton (1577-1640)
Ben Jonson (1572-1637)
John Donne (1572-1631)
Thomas Campion (1567-1620)
Thomas Nash (1567-1601)
William Shakespeare (1564-1616)
Christopher Marlowe (1564-1593)
George Peele (1558?-1597?)
Thomas Kyd (1558-1594)
Robert Greene (1558-1592)
John Lyly (1554?-1606)
Sir Philip Sidney (1554-1586)
Edmund Spenser (1552?-1599)
Earl of Surrey (1517?-1547)
Sir Thomas Wyatt (1503?-1542)

Geoffrey Chaucer (1340?-1400)
John Gower (1330?-1408)
Miracle plays (1300's)
Mystery plays (1300's)
Le Morte Darthur (about 1469)
Morality plays (1400's)

1300 | 1400 | 1500 | 1600

The first major work of English literature is the epic *Beowulf.* Epics are long narrative poems that focus on heroic and extraordinary actions. Many are based on legend or myth, and their language is dignified and serious. One or more unknown authors wrote *Beowulf* some time between 750 and 1100. The poem tells about the adventures of a warrior named Beowulf.

After about 750, poetry flourished in Northumbria, an Anglo-Saxon kingdom in the north. There, poets wrote verses about the lives and hardships of saints. The leading Northumbrian poet was Cynewulf.

Old English prose. Most prose writers wrote in Latin until the late 800's, when Alfred the Great became king of Wessex in southwestern England. Alfred translated or ordered the translation of several works from Latin into Old English. One of the most important of these works was the *Ecclesiastical History of the English People* (731) by a monk called Saint Bede or the Venerable Bede. This is the first history of the English people and a valuable source of information about English life from the late 500's to 731. A monk named Aelfric wrote *homilies* (short moral essays) in Old English during the 990's. From about 892 to 1154, a number of authors contributed to the *Anglo-Saxon Chronicle,* which was a record of current events in England.

Middle English literature (1100-1485)

In 1066, Norman invaders from France conquered England. For more than 200 years thereafter, members of the royal court and the upper class spoke French. Only the common people continued to speak English. By about 1300, however, English had again become the chief national language, but in an altered form now called Middle English.

The development of English romances. Medieval romances originated in France during the 1100's. By the end of the 1200's, they had become the most popular literary form in England. Like epics, romances described the adventures of heroes, but their plots depended more on supernatural events and featured stories of love and high-born ladies. Romances were written in prose as well as verse.

In 1155, a Norman poet named Wace completed the first work that mentioned the Knights of the Round Table, who were led by the legendary British ruler King Arthur. King Arthur and his knights became a favorite subject in English romances. During the 1400's, Sir Thomas Malory wrote a prose work called *Le Morte Darthur (The Death of Arthur).* Malory's romance is the most complete English version of stories about Arthur.

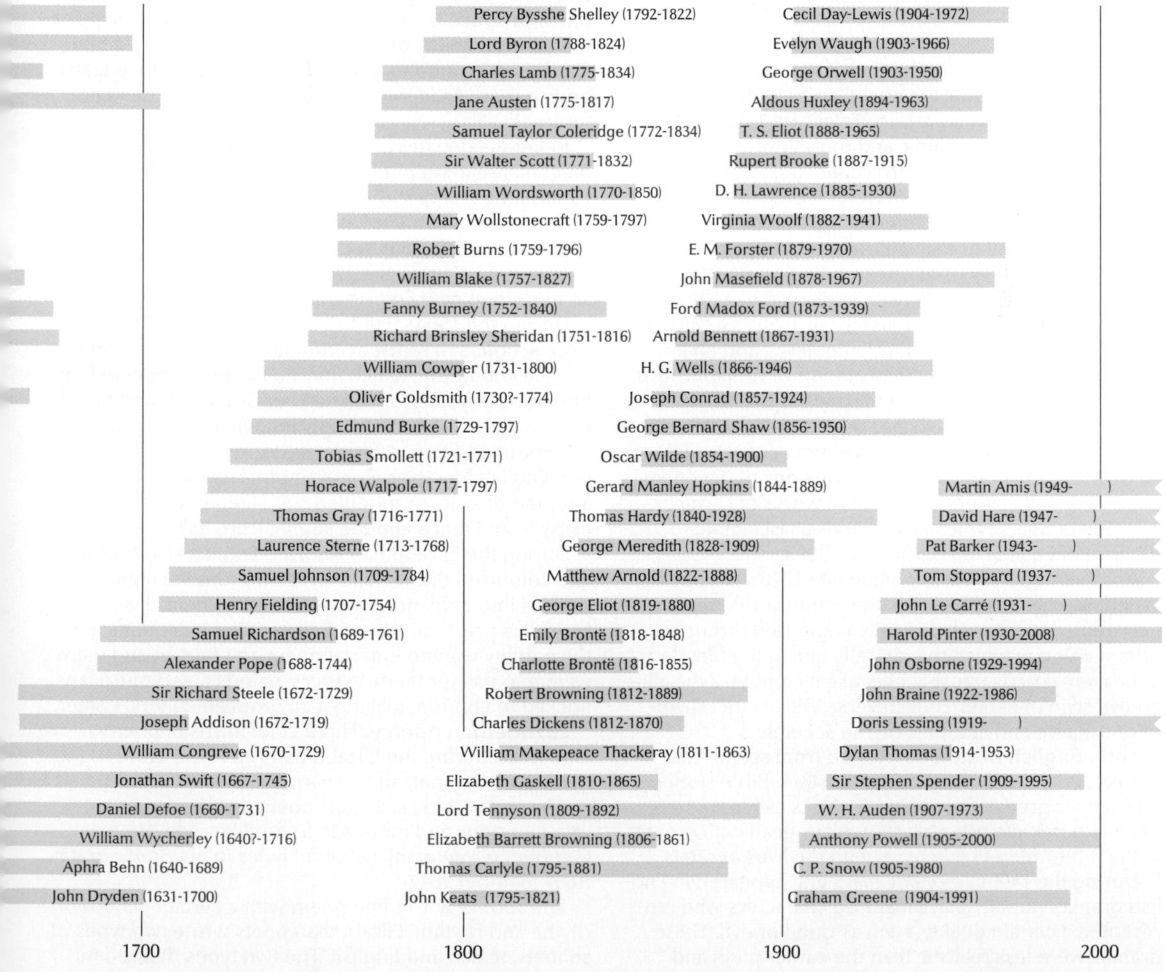

Percy Bysshe Shelley (1792-1822)
Lord Byron (1788-1824)
Charles Lamb (1775-1834)
Jane Austen (1775-1817)
Samuel Taylor Coleridge (1772-1834)
Sir Walter Scott (1771-1832)
William Wordsworth (1770-1850)
Mary Wollstonecraft (1759-1797)
Robert Burns (1759-1796)
William Blake (1757-1827)
Fanny Burney (1752-1840)
Richard Brinsley Sheridan (1751-1816)
William Cowper (1731-1800)
Oliver Goldsmith (1730?-1774)
Edmund Burke (1729-1797)
Tobias Smollett (1721-1771)
Horace Walpole (1717-1797)
Thomas Gray (1716-1771)
Laurence Sterne (1713-1768)
Samuel Johnson (1709-1784)
Henry Fielding (1707-1754)
Samuel Richardson (1689-1761)
Alexander Pope (1688-1744)
Sir Richard Steele (1672-1729)
Joseph Addison (1672-1719)
William Congreve (1670-1729)
Jonathan Swift (1667-1745)
Daniel Defoe (1660-1731)
William Wycherley (1640?-1716)
Aphra Behn (1640-1689)
John Dryden (1631-1700)

Cecil Day-Lewis (1904-1972)
Evelyn Waugh (1903-1966)
George Orwell (1903-1950)
Aldous Huxley (1894-1963)
T. S. Eliot (1888-1965)
Rupert Brooke (1887-1915)
D. H. Lawrence (1885-1930)
Virginia Woolf (1882-1941)
E. M. Forster (1879-1970)
John Masefield (1878-1967)
Ford Madox Ford (1873-1939)
Arnold Bennett (1867-1931)
H. G. Wells (1866-1946)
Joseph Conrad (1857-1924)
George Bernard Shaw (1856-1950)
Oscar Wilde (1854-1900)
Gerard Manley Hopkins (1844-1889)
Thomas Hardy (1840-1928)
George Meredith (1828-1909)
Matthew Arnold (1822-1888)
George Eliot (1819-1880)
Emily Brontë (1818-1848)
Charlotte Brontë (1816-1855)
Robert Browning (1812-1889)
Charles Dickens (1812-1870)
William Makepeace Thackeray (1811-1863)
Elizabeth Gaskell (1810-1865)
Lord Tennyson (1809-1892)
Elizabeth Barrett Browning (1806-1861)
Thomas Carlyle (1795-1881)
John Keats (1795-1821)

Martin Amis (1949-)
David Hare (1947-)
Pat Barker (1943-)
Tom Stoppard (1937-)
John Le Carré (1931-)
Harold Pinter (1930-2008)
John Osborne (1929-1994)
John Braine (1922-1986)
Doris Lessing (1919-)
Dylan Thomas (1914-1953)
Sir Stephen Spender (1909-1995)
W. H. Auden (1907-1973)
Anthony Powell (1905-2000)
C. P. Snow (1905-1980)
Graham Greene (1904-1991)

1700 1800 1900 2000

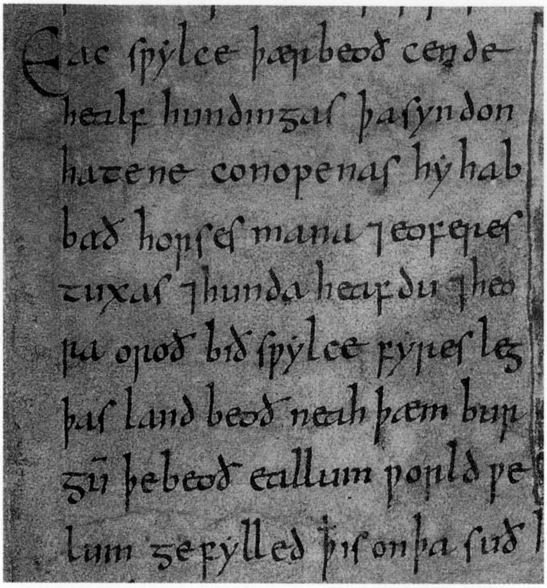

The British Library, London

Beowulf was the first major work in English literature. The poem was written in Old English, the earliest form of English. This detail is from a manuscript produced about 1000.

The age of Chaucer. The greatest writer of the Middle English period was the poet Geoffrey Chaucer. His masterpiece is *The Canterbury Tales* (late 1300's), an unfinished collection of comic and moral stories. Chaucer introduced a rhythmic pattern called *iambic pentameter* into English poetry. This pattern, or meter, consists of 10 syllables alternately unaccented and accented in each line. The lines may or may not rhyme. Iambic pentameter became a widely used meter in English poetry.

Chaucer's friend John Gower wrote verse in Latin and English. His *Confessio Amantis* (about 1390) is a Middle English poem that uses Biblical, medieval, and mythological stories to discuss the problems of romantic love. A religious and symbolic poem called *Piers Plowman* has been attributed to William Langland. It describes a series of dream visions that show humanity's struggle to arrive at spiritual salvation. Three versions of the poem appeared in the late 1300's. Like the works of Chaucer and Gower, *Piers Plowman* provides a fascinating glimpse of English life during the 1300's.

Another important work of the late 1300's is a poem called *Pearl.* In this poem, a father mourns the death of his young daughter. He is finally comforted through a dream vision in which the girl tells him of the blessings of heaven. *Pearl* is unusual because it combines the alliterative style of earlier English verse with a strict rhythmic structure and complex rhyme scheme.

Early English drama developed from scenes that monks acted out in churches to illustrate Bible stories. The scenes grew into full-length works called *mystery plays* and *miracle plays.* Mystery plays dealt with events in the Bible, and miracle plays with the lives of saints.

During the 1400's, *morality plays* first appeared in English drama. Morality plays featured characters who represented a certain quality, such as good or evil. These dramas were less realistic than the earlier plays and were intended to teach a moral lesson.

Middle English prose consists mainly of religious writings. Often such works were intended for women readers, because women were much less likely than men to be taught Latin. One well-known work of the period is *The Book of Margery Kempe,* dictated during the 1430's by a woman who could not read or write. It is an autobiography that describes Kempe's mystical visions, her pilgrimages, and her struggles with the official church of her time.

The beginning of Modern English (1485-1603)

During the late 1400's, Middle English began to develop into Modern English. By the late 1500's, people in England were speaking and writing English in a form much like that used today.

Queen Elizabeth I reigned from 1558 to 1603. During this period, usually called the Elizabethan Age, English writers produced some of the greatest poetry and drama in world literature.

A number of developments contributed to the brilliant literary output of the Elizabethan Age. One of the most important occurred in 1476, when William Caxton set up the first printing press in England. Before that time, books and all other literary works had to be slowly and laboriously copied by hand. Printing made it possible to produce far more books and at far lower cost. The greater availability of books and their lower cost stimulated a desire among a large number of people to learn how to read. As literacy increased, so did the demand for books.

Religious debates also played a role in the development of a reading public. During the reign of Elizabeth's father, King Henry VIII, the English church became independent of the Roman Catholic Church. Under the influence of the Protestant Reformation, Bible reading was encouraged. During the 1520's, William Tyndale made an important new English translation of the Bible.

During the 1500's, English scholars joined other European scholars in rediscovering the cultures of ancient Greece and Rome, which they had largely neglected for hundreds of years. Translations of Greek and particularly Roman literary works strongly influenced Elizabethan writers. In addition, new literary forms were introduced into English literature. For example, English authors adopted directly or modified such literary forms as the essay from France and the sonnet from Italy.

During the Elizabethan Age, the English also explored and colonized distant lands. Wealth from the colonies poured into England. A newly rich merchant class made London a great commercial center. The merchants and the nobility wanted entertainment and fine art and were willing to pay for them. Writers, painters, and musicians flocked to London, making it a European cultural center.

Elizabethan poetry. Three chief forms of poetry flourished during the Elizabethan Age. They were (1) the lyric, (2) the sonnet, and (3) narrative poetry.

The lyric. A lyric is a short poem that expresses private emotions and moods in a songlike style. Thomas Campion wrote many beautiful lyrics in his *Books of Airs* (1601 to about 1617).

The sonnet is a 14-line poem with a certain pattern of rhyme and rhythm. Elizabethan poets wrote two types of sonnets, Italian and English. The two types differed in the arrangement of the rhymes. Sir Thomas Wyatt introduced the sonnet from Italy into English literature in the early 1500's. The Earl of Surrey modified the form into the English sonnet. Their verses were published in a collection commonly called *Tottel's Miscellany* (1557).

Edmund Spenser and William Shakespeare wrote *sonnet sequences,* groups of sonnets based on a single theme. Spenser and Sir Philip Sidney wrote sequences of love sonnets. Shakespeare wrote a sequence addressed to a nobleman who was his patron and to an unknown "dark lady."

Narrative poetry. A narrative poem tells a story. In addition to sonnets, Shakespeare and Spenser wrote narrative poems. Shakespeare based his *Venus and Adonis* (1593) on a Roman myth and *The Rape of Lucrece* (1594) on an event from Roman history.

Perhaps the most ambitious Elizabethan narrative poem is *The Faerie Queene* by Spenser. The poet borrowed heavily from medieval romances to invent an imaginary land representing British and Christian ideals. The style of the poem is *allegorical.* In allegorical writing, people and objects are used to represent abstract ideas, such as holiness and justice. *The Faerie Queene* combines those abstract moral meanings with striking visual imagery.

Elizabethan drama. In 1576, James Burbage built England's first playhouse, called The Theatre, in a suburb of London. Until this time, drama had been performed in the streets, in homes and palaces, and at universities. After Burbage's theater, other playhouses opened and the popularity of drama rapidly increased.

Elizabethan drama was noted for its passion and vitality. Thomas Kyd's play *The Spanish Tragedy* (1580's) was one of the earliest Elizabethan dramas. It is filled with scenes of violence and madness and set a pattern for themes of murder and revenge in later plays.

A group of leading Elizabethan playwrights were known as the "University Wits" because they had attended the famous English universities at Oxford or Cambridge. These playwrights included Robert Greene, Christopher Marlowe, and George Peele. Marlowe was the most important dramatist among the Wits. He wrote tragedies that center on strong personalities. These works include *Tamburlaine the Great* (about 1587) and *The Tragical History of Doctor Faustus* (about 1588).

The greatest Elizabethan playwright was William Shakespeare. No other English author has equaled his brilliant verse and characterizations. For detailed information about his writings, see **Shakespeare, William.**

Elizabethan fiction. The Elizabethan Age produced some of the first works of prose fiction in English. Readers especially liked fanciful, elaborately told stories of love and adventure. John Lyly popularized an artificial, elegant style in *Euphues: The Anatomy of Wit* (1578). Sir Philip Sidney wrote in Lyly's style in *Arcadia* (1580). Both works are *pastorals* (stories that idealize the lives of shepherds). Thomas Nashe wrote in a more realistic style. In *The Unfortunate Traveller* (1594), he described the adventures of one of King Henry VIII's pages.

The early and middle 1600's

King James I, who ruled from 1603 to 1625, and his son Charles I, who took the throne in 1625, quarreled often with Parliament. Civil war broke out in 1642 between the king's followers, called Cavaliers, and Parliament's supporters, including many of the religious reformers known as Puritans. In 1648, Parliament's supporters won the war. They beheaded Charles in 1649 and ruled England until 1660.

Metaphysical and Cavalier poets were two major groups of poets during the 1600's. The Metaphysical poets included John Donne, their leader; Abraham Cowley; Richard Crashaw; George Herbert; Andrew Marvell; and Henry Vaughan. The Cavalier poets, who were associated with the court of Charles I, included Thomas Carew, Robert Herrick, Richard Lovelace, and Sir John Suckling.

The Metaphysical poets used comparatively simple language, but they often created elaborate images called *conceits.* Donne wrote passionate love poetry until he converted from Roman Catholicism to the Anglican faith. He became an Anglican priest in 1615. After his conversion, Donne wrote equally passionate religious poetry. Several other Metaphysical poets also wrote religious verse. In contrast to the serious Metaphysical poets, the Cavalier poets were best known for their dashing love poetry.

Jacobean drama is the name given to the plays written during the reign of James I. Jacobean tragedies reflected Elizabethan drama, especially in such characteristics as violent action, spectacle, and the revenge theme. John Webster's drama *The Duchess of Malfi* (about 1613) is a masterpiece of revenge tragedy. *Satiric comedies,* which poked fun at various subjects, were also popular. In *The Knight of the Burning Pestle* (1607?), for example, Francis Beaumont ridiculed earlier dramas and romances about elegant heroes and also satirized the newly rich merchant class.

Ben Jonson wrote plays that showed the influence of ancient Roman drama. His comedies *Volpone* (1606) and *The Alchemist* (1610) satirize universal human failings, such as greed, ignorance, or superstition.

In 1642, the Puritans ordered the closing of the theaters, claiming that plays were wicked. The order remained in effect for 18 years.

Prose writings. In 1604, King James I authorized a group of scholars to prepare a new English version of the Bible. It appeared in 1611 and became known as the King James Version or Authorized Version. Although it borrowed from earlier translations, such as Tyndale's, the King James Version was a landmark in the development of English prose. Its eloquent yet natural style had enormous influence on English-speaking writers.

Lady Mary Wroth, Sir Philip Sidney's niece, continued the tradition of writing in her uncle's elegant, artificial style. She combined prose and poetry in *Urania* (1621). Robert Burton's *The Anatomy of Melancholy* (1621) was written as a psychological study of the causes, symptoms, and cures of melancholy, which Burton believed all people experienced. But at the same time Burton explored a wide range of human learning and effort.

Many authors wrote philosophical works during the early and middle 1600's. Donne composed a series of meditations on sickness, sin, and death in *Devotions upon Emergent Occasions* (1624). Sir Thomas Browne, a physician, and Jeremy Taylor, an Anglican bishop, wrote works noted for their beautiful prose style. In *Religio Medici* (1642), Browne gave his learned opinions on a variety of subjects, including miracles and witchcraft.

Taylor is best known for two religious essays, *Holy Living* (1650) and *Holy Dying* (1651). In contrast to these serious works, Izaak Walton wrote *The Compleat Angler* (1653), a light-hearted but thoughtful book on fishing.

John Milton was the greatest English writer of the mid-1600's. Milton was deeply involved in the political and religious debates of his time and supported the Puritans during the English Civil War. He wrote prose and verse on many subjects before, during, and after the war. These writings include an attack on censorship, *Areopagitica* (1644). In this piece, Milton argued that knowledge and virtue can only grow when different opinions have a chance to be openly debated.

Milton's greatest achievement is *Paradise Lost* (1667), an epic based on the story of Adam and Eve. Its vivid descriptions of heaven, hell, and the Garden of Eden, and its rich and musical blank verse, make it one of the most admired and imitated works in English literature.

Restoration literature (1660-1700)

In 1660, Parliament restored the monarchy under Charles II. The period from 1660 to 1700 is known as the Restoration.

The Puritans had attempted to enforce a strict moral code during their years in power. The Restoration brought a strong reaction against this code. The nobility and upper class, in particular, became known for carefree and often morally loose living. Restoration writers reflected this relaxed morality in their works.

John Dryden followed Milton as the outstanding literary figure of the Restoration. Dryden wrote poetry, popular dramas, and literary criticism. During his career, he shifted his support from the Puritans to the restored monarchy. Late in life, he converted from the Anglican faith to Roman Catholicism. Many of Dryden's poems reflect these political and religious shifts. His political satire *Absalom and Achitophel* (1681) attacks the enemies of the future James II. In *The Hind and the Panther* (1687), Dryden justified his conversion to Catholicism.

Dryden's best plays include *Marriage à la Mode* (1672), a comedy, and *All for Love* (1677), a tragedy. Dryden also wrote some of the finest literary criticism in English.

Restoration drama. After Charles II became king in 1660, the theaters reopened and an important period in English drama began. Two types of plays rapidly dominated Restoration stages: (1) the comedy of manners and (2) the heroic tragedy.

The comedy of manners was witty, sometimes cynical, and occasionally indecent. It treated love and romantic intrigue in a light, often broadly humorous way. The best comedies of manners included *The Country Wife* (1675) by William Wycherley and *The Way of the World* (1700) by William Congreve.

The heroic tragedy had a complicated plot that dealt with the conflict between love and honor. Most of these plays were set far from England. Little action took place on the stage, and the characters spoke in elegant, noble-sounding *heroic couplets.* A heroic couplet is a verse form consisting of two rhymed lines of 10 syllables each. Dryden wrote several heroic tragedies, including *The Conquest of Granada* (1670, 1671).

Restoration prose. During the Restoration, prose became less elaborate than had been fashionable earlier in the 1600's. Writers tried to express themselves in a style that was clear, simple, and direct.

Aphra Behn's *Oroonoko* (first published about 1678) tells the story of an African prince sold into slavery who leads a tragic rebellion against his English captors. In the novel's descriptive passages, Behn drew on her experiences in the English colony of Surinam. Her interest in factual, realistic background was new to English fiction.

John Bunyan wrote the popular Christian allegory *The Pilgrim's Progress* (1678, 1684). The work shows the journey of its hero, Christian, through this world to the heavenly city of salvation in the world beyond. The diaries of Samuel Pepys and John Evelyn are also vividly written. They provide a delightful and detailed view of English life in the late 1600's.

The Augustan Age (1700-1750)

The period in English literature from 1700 to about 1750 is called the Augustan Age, named for the Roman emperor Augustus, who reigned from 27 B.C. to A.D. 14. English authors tried to imitate or recapture many of the philosophic and literary ideals of Augustan Rome. In particular, they admired the ideals of reason and common sense, and they tried to achieve balance and harmony in their writings. The Augustan Age of English literature is also known as the Neoclassical period.

Swift and Pope. Satire was one of the most common types of literature during the Augustan Age. In spite of the Augustan emphasis on reason, many satires were extremely bitter and personal. The leading satirists were Jonathan Swift in prose and Alexander Pope in poetry.

Swift attacked hypocrisy in *Gulliver's Travels* (1726), the most famous satire in English. In *A Modest Proposal* (1729), Swift, who was born and lived much of his life in Ireland, satirized the harshness and indifference that he saw in England's rule of Ireland.

Pope perfected the heroic couplet, giving its two rhymed lines a quality of balance and wit that often echoed his themes. In *The Rape of the Lock* (1712-1714), he ridiculed fashionable society. In *An Essay on Man* (1733-1734), he advised readers to take the middle way—avoid extremes—in all things. He wrote with especially cutting brilliance about the authors of his time and their weaknesses in *The Dunciad* (1728-1743). One of Pope's most important nonsatirical poems is *Windsor Forest* (1713). It uses England's Windsor forest as a symbol of social harmony, weaving patriotic reflections on history, politics, and morality into a description of the landscape.

Addison and Steele. Joseph Addison and Sir Richard Steele were the outstanding essayists of the Augustan Age. They published many of their essays in two periodicals, *The Tatler* (1709-1711) and *The Spectator* (1711-1712). Both writers described and criticized the social customs and attitudes of their day. Their essays helped form middle-class tastes in manners, morals, and literature. In addition, Addison's pure and elegant prose style served as a model throughout the 1700's.

The rise of the novel. The development of the novel is one of the great achievements of English literature. With the novel, English prose fiction became more realistic and addressed a wider, middle-class audience. One of the major figures in the development was Daniel Defoe. He wrote realistic stories consisting of loosely connected incidents that were presented as actual happenings. Defoe's *Robinson Crusoe* (1719) and *Moll Flanders* (1722) are early examples of the novel, but they lack the unified plot that became typical of that literary form.

Many scholars consider Samuel Richardson the first true novelist in English. He wrote *epistolary novels,* which take the form of letters exchanged between the novel's characters. Richardson's novels are highly moralistic. His first novel, *Pamela* (1740), tells about a servant girl whose virtuous refusal to be seduced by her master eventually leads him to marry her. Richardson's masterpiece is *Clarissa* (1748), a tragic story of a young woman tricked into leaving her home and raped by a villainous nobleman. It is remarkable for the detailed exploration of the characters' states of mind.

The novels of Henry Fielding and Tobias Smollett emphasize vigorous humor and satire. Fielding ridiculed *Pamela* in *An Apology for the Life of Mrs. Shamela Andrews* (1741). Fielding was a master at putting together a complex plot. His *Tom Jones* (1749) is perhaps the greatest comic novel in English. Smollett's *The Expedition of Humphry Clinker* (1771) gives a humorous account of a family's travels through England and Scotland.

Laurence Sterne was another leading novelist. His *The Life and Opinions of Tristram Shandy, Gentleman* (1760-1767) has almost no story. The narrator, Tristram, tries to write his life story but keeps breaking off to discuss other topics. The work inspired many experimental novelists of the 1900's.

The Age of Johnson (1750-1784)

Samuel Johnson dominated English literature from about 1750 until his death in 1784. He was as famous for his conversation—in which he sometimes voiced outrageous opinions—as he was for his writings.

Johnson's literary achievements are remarkable. His *Dictionary of the English Language* (1755) is noted for its scholarly definitions of words and the use of excellent quotations to illustrate the definitions. In *The Lives of the English Poets* (1779-1781), Johnson critically examined the work of 52 poets and did much to establish literary criticism as a form of literature. Johnson also wrote articles, reviews, essays, and poems. His prose work *Rasselas* (1759) is a philosophical attack on people who seek an easy path to happiness.

The Johnson circle. Johnson's friends were the most important writers of the late 1700's. They included Oliver Goldsmith; Richard Brinsley Sheridan; Edmund Burke; and Johnson's biographer, James Boswell.

Goldsmith's novel *The Vicar of Wakefield* (1766) tells about the misfortunes of a kindly clergyman and his family. *The Deserted Village* (1770) is a poem that movingly describes the decline of an English village. Goldsmith's great play is the classic comedy *She Stoops to Conquer* (1773). Sheridan wrote two clever comedies of manners, *The Rivals* (1775) and *The School for Scandal* (1777). Burke composed essays on government, history, and beauty. His *Philosophical Enquiry into the Origin of Our Ideas of the Sublime and Beautiful* (1757) anticipates many ideas of Romantic writers of the 1800's. His attack on the French Revolution, *Reflections on the Revolution in France* (1790), quickly became one of the most influential books on politics ever written.

Fanny Burney became part of Johnson's circle through her father, the music historian Dr. Charles Burney. In such novels as *Evelina* (1778) and *Cecilia* (1782), she combined Richardson's moral concerns and psychological insight with Fielding's satirical, humorous tone. Boswell brilliantly recorded Johnson's eccentricities and witty conversations in *The Life of Samuel Johnson* (1791), one of the great biographies in literature.

Detail of an engraving by R. B. Parkes from a lost oil painting (1860) by Eyre Crowe; Radio Times Hulton Picture Library

Samuel Johnson, *right,* was the most influential English author and critic of the late 1700's. Johnson often exchanged opinions on literature in London's Mitre Tavern with such writers as Oliver Goldsmith, *left,* and James Boswell, *center.*

Ignatius Sancho was the first African prose writer published in England. Sancho was born on a slave ship on its way to America. When he was 2 years old, he was taken to England. Sancho was especially admired as a letter writer. His *Letters* (1782) were published two years after his death. During the late 1700's and early 1800's, several former slaves wrote memoirs of their experiences, notably Olaudah Equiano's *The Interesting Narrative of the Life of Olaudah Equiano* (1789). Equiano offers a vivid account of his childhood, enslavement, and eventual freedom.

Romantic literature (1784-1832)

English writers of the late 1700's and early 1800's believed that the Augustan ideals of harmony and moderation were narrow and artificial. These writers are called Romantics. The Romantics emphasized the creative power of the human imagination and placed increasing value on private experience and the natural world.

In 1789, the French Revolution began, and from 1792 through 1815, England was often at war with France. Romantic writers responded to these events with a complex mixture of sympathy for the democratic ideals of the revolution and patriotic support for the English war effort. England's colonial interests overseas also grew at this time, and many of the most popular Romantic works were set in distant lands associated with those interests.

The Preromantics is the name given to a group of poets of the mid-1700's whose work first touched on important Romantic themes and ideas. Their writing reflected the awareness of social problems, the love of nature, and the fascination with myth and mystery that became typical of Romanticism.

The Scottish poet Robert Burns wrote about rural characters. He often used Scots dialect. Burns's most popular verses include "Auld Lang Syne" (about 1788) and "Comin Thro' the Rye" (about 1796).

The leading Preromantic poet was William Blake. Blake was an important printer and engraver as well as a poet. His work expresses an intensely personal vision and, partly for this reason, was barely known when he was alive. Many of his most direct lyrics are collected in *Songs of Innocence* (1789) and *Songs of Experience* (1794). His poetry combines anger at the social injustices of his time with richly imagined portraits of a freer, more just society.

Romantic poetry. William Wordsworth and Samuel Taylor Coleridge were the first important English Romantic poets. They produced a joint volume of poems titled *Lyrical Ballads* (1798). Wordsworth's preface to the second edition (1800) is an important statement of Romantic ideas about the continuing value of poetry. He explained that his poetry used everyday language rather than the elevated poetic language of such earlier writers as Dryden and Pope because everyday language comes closer to expressing genuine human feeling. For the same reason, he wanted to write about everyday topics, especially rural, unsophisticated subjects.

Wordsworth and Coleridge lived most of their lives in the scenic Lake District of northwestern England and wrote expressively about the beauties of nature and the thoughts that natural beauty inspires. Many of their blank verse poems are written in a meditative, conversational tone new to English poetry.

Wordsworth's poems also emphasize the mind of the poet. His memories of his childhood and his experiences in France during its revolutionary period are the subject of his great autobiographical poem, *The Prelude*, published in 1850, shortly after his death.

Coleridge's most famous poems are "The Rime of the Ancient Mariner" (1798) and "Christabel" (written in 1799 and 1800 but not published until 1816). Both deal with supernatural subjects. Coleridge was also an important literary critic and philosopher. In *Biographia Literaria* (1817), he argued that the imagination is the active power in the creation of human experience.

The next generation of romantic poets included Lord Byron, Percy Bysshe Shelley, and John Keats. They criticized Wordsworth and Coleridge for giving up on the ideals of the French Revolution. These poets were interested in reviving classical subject matter in the manner of Renaissance poets. Byron and Shelley especially admired the ideal of ancient Greek democracy, and Byron died participating in the fight for Greek independence.

Byron wrote a series of "Eastern" tales set mainly in Turkey and Greece. He created a partly autobiographical hero in such lengthy works as *Childe Harold's Pilgrimage* (1812-1818) and the unfinished *Don Juan* (1819-1824). While much of Byron's poetry is dark and self-dramatizing, *Don Juan* is written in a comic style. The poem makes fun of many aspects of society, including Byron's own success as a celebrity author.

Shelley wrote poetry that was both politically involved and intensely lyrical. Many of his poems call for political and social reforms in language that is melodious and complex. In his long drama *Prometheus Unbound* (1820), Shelley argued that reform needs to be based on inner transformation. For the world to change, people's beliefs must change.

John Keats wrote intense, vivid poems that capture the experience of beauty and its inevitable passing. He wrote some of his most important poems in response to other works of art. His major works include "Ode on a Grecian Urn" (1819) and "Ode to a Nightingale" (1819).

Romantic prose included essays, criticism, journals, and novels. During the 1790's, many important prose works were written in response to the French Revolution. They included Mary Wollstonecraft's *A Vindication of the Rights of Men* (1790), which supported the revolution against Edmund Burke's attacks. Wollstonecraft also wrote one of the first feminist works, *A Vindication of the Rights of Woman* (1792). In it, she argued for a woman's right to education and independence.

The leading Romantic essayists were Thomas De Quincey, William Hazlitt, and Charles Lamb. De Quincey's *Confessions of an English Opium Eater* (1821) is typical of the personal, revealing essay that was popular during the early 1800's. Hazlitt wrote outstanding critical studies of English literature. His writings helped revive interest in the plays of the Elizabethan Age. He also wrote political and personal essays in a sparkling, forceful prose that seems to speak directly to his readers. Lamb's warm, humorous essays were collected in *Essays of Elia* (1823) and *Last Essays of Elia* (1833).

Horror stories called *Gothic novels* became popular during the late 1700's and early 1800's. Most of these tales deal with supernatural or seemingly supernatural events. Horace Walpole wrote the first Gothic novel, *The Castle of Otranto* (1764). Another Gothic novelist, Ann Radcliffe, used detailed landscape descriptions to show her characters' mood and attitude. Mary Wollstonecraft Shelley, the daughter of Mary Wollstonecraft and the wife of Percy Bysshe Shelley, wrote *Frankenstein* (1818), one of the most daring and popular Gothic novels.

The two greatest novelists of the Romantic period were Jane Austen and Sir Walter Scott. Austen wrote about middle-class life in small towns and in the famous resort city of Bath. Her writing is elegant and playful, but below the surface it has a surprising bite. The heroines in such Austen novels as *Pride and Prejudice* (1813) and *Emma* (1816) are known for their independence and wit.

Scott wrote many novels that take place in the Scottish Highlands or Edinburgh. He also used historical settings to comment on important issues of his time. These are the first truly historical novels in English literature.

Victorian literature (1832-1901)

Victoria became queen of the United Kingdom in 1837. Her reign, the longest in English history, lasted until 1901. This period is called the Victorian Age.

During the Victorian Age, the British Empire reached its height and covered about a fourth of the world's land. Industry and trade expanded rapidly, and railroads and canals crisscrossed the country. Science and technology made great advances. The middle class grew enormously. In spite of this prosperity, factory laborers and farmworkers lived in terrible poverty.

The Victorian Age's new scientific theories seemed to challenge many religious beliefs. The most controversial theory appeared in *The Origin of Species* (1859) by the biologist Charles Darwin. In the book, he stated that every species of life develops from an earlier one, which seemed to contradict the Biblical account of the creation of life. The theories of Darwin and other scientists led many people to feel that traditional values could no longer guide their lives.

Victorian writers dealt with the contrast between the prosperity of the middle and upper classes and the wretched condition of the poor. In the late 1800's, they also analyzed the loss of faith in traditional values.

Early Victorian literature includes some of the greatest and most popular novels ever written. Most novelists of the period wrote long works with numerous characters. In many instances, the authors included actual events of the day in their tales.

The novels of Charles Dickens are noted for their colorful—and sometimes eccentric—characters. In *Oliver Twist* (1837-1839) and *David Copperfield* (1849-1850), Dickens described the lives of children made miserable by cruel or thoughtless adults. Many of his later novels picture the grim side of Victorian life. In *Bleak House* (1852-1853), Dickens criticized the courts, the clergy, and the upper class neglect of the poor. His novels often balance their harsh social criticism with satirical humor, idealized heroines, and sentimental scenes of family life.

William Makepeace Thackeray created a masterpiece of Victorian fiction in *Vanity Fair* (1847-1848). The story follows the lives of many characters at different levels of English society during the early 1800's.

The novels of the three Brontë sisters—Emily, Charlotte, and Anne—have many Gothic and Romantic elements. The novels are known especially for their psychologically tormented heroes and heroines. Emily's *Wuthering Heights* (1847) and Charlotte's *Jane Eyre* (1847) are among the best-loved works of Victorian fiction.

Engraving (1838) by George Cruikshank; The Newberry Library, Chicago

Oliver Twist is one of Charles Dickens's novels that attacked social injustice during the Victorian Age. In this scene, the orphan Oliver begs the cruel head of his orphanage for more food.

Elizabeth Gaskell wrote about confrontations between factory workers and owners in *Mary Barton* (1848) and *North and South* (1854-1855). She also wrote an important biography of author Charlotte Brontë (1857).

Several writers wrote nonfiction that dealt with what they believed to be the ills of the time. For example, Thomas Carlyle attacked greed and hypocrisy in *Sartor Resartus* (1833-1834). John Stuart Mill discussed the relationship between society and the individual in his long essay *On Liberty* (1859). In a later essay, *The Subjection of Women* (1869), he argued that women should have the same political rights as men.

Later Victorian literature. During the late 1800's, an uneasy tone appeared in much of the best Victorian poetry and prose. Matthew Arnold described his doubts about modern life in such poems as "The Scholar-Gypsy" (1853) and "Dover Beach" (1867). His most important literary achievements are his critical essays on culture, literature, religion, and society. Many of them were collected in *Culture and Anarchy* (1869).

John Ruskin and Walter Pater were other important critics. Ruskin was a major critic of painting and architecture. In *Unto This Last* (1862), Ruskin argued that the modern industrial economy was ruining England. He believed that the Middle Ages offered more humane and spiritually satisfying ideals because they allowed for individual development and craftsmanship. Pater's *Studies in the History of the Renaissance* (1873 is a collection of his essays about Renaissance writers and painters.

Alfred, Lord Tennyson and Robert Browning were the two most important late Victorian poets. In *In Memoriam* (published in 1850), Tennyson tried to reconcile traditional Christian faith with modern science. *Idylls of the King* (1842-1885) returned to medieval legends of King Arthur and his knights.

Browning created finely drawn character studies in poems called *dramatic monologues.* In these poems, a real or imaginary character narrates the story. Browning's best-known work is *The Ring and the Book* (1868-1869). He based the poem on an Italian murder case of 1698. Twelve characters discuss the case, each from his or her own point of view. Elizabeth Barrett Browning, Browning's wife, wrote a famous sequence of love poems called *Sonnets from the Portuguese* (1850). In her long "novel in verse" *Aurora Leigh* (1857), she commented on the social role of women and poetry in the 1800's.

The Pre-Raphaelites were a group of poets and painters who followed Ruskin and took their inspiration from the Middle Ages. The most important Pre-Raphaelite poet, Dante Gabriel Rossetti, was also an important painter. His partly autobiographical sonnet sequence *The House of Life* (1881) draws connections between experiences of love, death, and art.

Gerard Manley Hopkins wrote experimental religious verse. His poems were not published until 1918, almost 30 years after his death. Hopkins filled his poetry with rich word pictures and unusual word combinations. The "Terrible" sonnets (written in 1885) express experiences of extreme spiritual loneliness and suffering.

The leading late Victorian novelists were George Eliot (the pen name of Mary Ann Evans), Wilkie Collins, George Meredith, Anthony Trollope, and Thomas Hardy. Eliot's novels address social and moral problems. Her masterpiece is *Middlemarch* (1871-1872). Collins wrote stories of crime and suspense. His book *The Moonstone* (1868) is one of the first mystery novels.

Meredith's novels are noted for their witty style and sophisticated psychological treatment of character. His works include the novels *The Ordeal of Richard Feverel* (1859) and *The Egoist* (1879). The six "Barsetshire Novels" of Trollope are satires of life in rural England. They often tell of conflicts within the Church of England, usually in a humorous way. Hardy wrote about characters defeated by an apparently hostile fate. He used the landscape of the imaginary county of Wessex to help create the brooding atmosphere of such novels as *The Mayor of Casterbridge* (1886) and *Jude the Obscure* (1895).

From the late 1700's to the late 1800's, almost no important dramas were produced in England. But by 1900, a number of playwrights had revived the English theater both with witty comedies and with realistic dramas about social problems of the time.

Oscar Wilde recalled the glittering Restoration comedy of manners in *The Importance of Being Earnest* (1895). George Bernard Shaw wrote plays exposing the faults he saw in society. Shaw, like Wilde an Irishman who settled in England, addressed England's relation to Ireland in the play *John Bull's Other Island* (1904).

Literature before and after the world wars

Literature before World War I. Several outstanding authors gained fame during the period that began with Queen Victoria's death in 1901 and ended with the outbreak of World War I in 1914. A number of these authors wrote novels and plays of social criticism. Late in the period, a group of poets returned to the values of the Romantics, writing verse in the style of Wordsworth.

After Victoria died, her oldest son became King Edward VII. The term Edwardian is often applied to the period of Edward's reign—1901 to 1910. The leading Edwardian novelists included Arnold Bennett and H. G. Wells. In *The Old Wives' Tale* (1908) and other realistic novels, Bennett wrote about the dull, narrow lives of the middle class in the small towns of central England. Wells became famous for *The War of the Worlds* (1898) and other science-fiction novels. However, he also wrote political and satirical fiction. Shaw continued to attack uncritically accepted social values in such plays as *Major Barbara* (1905) and *The Doctor's Dilemma* (1906).

Joseph Conrad wrote probing novels on such themes as guilt, heroism, and honor. Many of his novels depict life at sea and show insight into the physical and psychological impact of imperialism.

Beginning about 1905, a group of writers and artists met frequently in a section of London called Bloomsbury to discuss intellectual questions. They were known as the Bloomsbury Group. The leading Bloomsbury writer was Virginia Woolf. In such novels as *Mrs. Dalloway* (1925) and *To the Lighthouse* (1927), she wrote with great insight about the collapse of belief systems of the 1800's and its transforming effect on the lives of her characters. Woolf used a technique called *stream of consciousness* to reveal the inner thoughts of her characters, capturing even their most fleeting experiences. Woolf also wrote critical essays on literature and society. In *A Room of One's Own* (1929), she discussed many of the social, economic, and psychological disadvantages facing women writers.

The leading poets of the early 1900's belonged to a group called the Georgians. The group's name came from George V, who became king on the death of his father, Edward VII. The Georgians wrote poetry about nature and the pleasures of rural living. Their work was idealistic and traditional. The most important members of the group included Rupert Brooke and John Masefield. Brooke was one of several promising young writers who died during World War I.

Poetry between the wars. English poetry changed in both form and subject matter between the end of World War I in 1918 and the outbreak of World War II in 1939. The horrifying battlefield experiences of World War I had an enormous impact on English literature. A number of poets serving in the British Army expressed their disillusionment with conventional patriotic ideas and imagery. Their poetry describes scenes of warfare with unusual realism. Siegfried Sassoon and Wilfred Owen were among the most important of these war poets. Owen, like Brooke, died in the war.

The destructiveness of the war left many people with the feeling that society was falling apart. T. S. Eliot best summarized their despair in *The Waste Land* (1922), the most influential poem of the period. Its jagged style, complex symbols, and references to other literary works set a new pattern for poetry. Eliot was conservative in politics and religion. But W. H. Auden, Stephen Spender, and Cecil Day-Lewis expressed radical political ideals in their verse. All three criticized injustices they saw in an unequal society. For all of these poets, society suffered from feelings of rootlessness and isolation.

Hugh MacDiarmid was a Scottish nationalist and political radical who wanted to capture a specifically Scottish cultural identity in his poetry. Dylan Thomas became the greatest Welsh poet of the 1900's. Thomas was known for his lyrical poems, which expressed his passionate love of life in vivid and melodious verse.

Fiction between the wars. Virginia Woolf remained the outstanding novelist of this period until her death in 1941. Another important novelist was D. H. Lawrence. He explored relationships between men and women in *Women in Love* (1920) and other autobiographical novels. Ford Madox Ford described changes in English society after World War I in four novels titled *Parade's End* (1924-1928). Graham Greene wrote about people troubled by difficult moral or religious problems in *The Power and the Glory* (1940) and other novels.

Several writers wrote humorous, satirical novels. Evelyn Waugh satirized wealthy and fashionable young people in *Vile Bodies* (1930) and *A Handful of Dust* (1934). Aldous Huxley also made fun of fashionable society in *Crome Yellow* (1921) and *Point Counter Point* (1928). But Huxley's best-known novel is *Brave New World* (1932), which describes a terrifying future society that eliminates individuality and personal liberty.

Literature after World War II. After World War II, the United Kingdom gradually lost most of its overseas empire. A sense of shrinking power in the world contributed to the anger and pessimism of much English literature in the years following the war. At the same time, many authors from the former English colonies settled in the United Kingdom and made important and original contributions to English literature.

Writers from the pre-war period, such as Greene and Auden, continued to produce important works after World War II. George Orwell began his literary career in the 1930's, but his most famous novel, *1984,* appeared in 1949. This frightening story describes a future society that distorts truth and deprives the individual of privacy.

During the 1950's, a number of younger writers expressed their discontent with traditional English politics, education, and literature. These writers were labeled the *Angry Young Men.* They included the playwright John Osborne and the novelist John Braine. Osborne's drama *Look Back in Anger* (1956) describes a young working-class man's resentment of the English class system. In *Room at the Top* (1957), Braine created an ambitious working-class hero who has little respect for traditional English ways of life. Kingsley Amis's novel *Lucky Jim* (1954) satirized the self-satisfied and pretentious society of an English university.

Amis was also associated with the Movement, a name given to a group of writers in the 1950's who shared an interest in bringing clarity, restraint, and traditional craftsmanship to their writing. The Movement included novelists and playwrights, but the term usually refers to poets. The leading Movement poet was Philip Larkin. He combined traditional lyric forms with modern, everyday, and sometimes even vulgar vocabulary. Many of his poems explore change, loss, and death. Larkin grew increasingly conservative in later years. He and Amis were typical of several post-war British writers who felt great unease at the changes in British society following the loss of its empire.

Several authors wrote about such changes in society in multivolume works that follow many characters over a long period. Anthony Powell wrote 12 novels titled *A Dance to the Music of Time* (1951-1975). They portray upper middle-class society from the 1920's to the 1970's. Paul Scott wrote about the final years of British rule in India in the four-volume *Raj Quartet* (1966-1975). Doris Lessing wrote the five-volume *Children of Violence* (1952-1969). It deals with a British woman who grows up in Rhodesia (now Zimbabwe), moves to England, and becomes involved in radical politics.

William Golding wrote one of the most disturbing novels of the 1950's, *Lord of the Flies* (1954). In the novel, a group of English schoolboys are marooned on a deserted island and establish a rule of violence and terror.

Harold Pinter was the most important playwright of the postwar period. He wrote comic dramas that seem commonplace on the surface but have an underlying sense of menace. His most important early plays are *The Caretaker* (1960) and *The Homecoming* (1965). In the 1960's, Joe Orton wrote several farces, including *Entertaining Mr. Sloane* (1964) and *Loot* (1966) that dealt with sexual themes that had never before been treated so openly on the English stage.

English literature today

Recent English poetry has moved away from the restraint and traditionalism of the Movement. One of the period's most important poets, Ted Hughes, wrote on darker, mythical subject matter. His poetry often includes violent imagery, as in *Crow* (1970). In 1998, shortly before his death, Hughes published *Birthday Letters,* a group of poems looking back on his failed marriage to American poet Sylvia Plath.

Geoffrey Hill writes difficult, complex verse that often focuses on religious and historical themes. Douglas Dunn's earliest poetry shows the influence of Larkin. However, some of his later work moves toward fantastic and Scottish-influenced themes. Linton Kwesi Johnson's poetry combines the rhythms of English verse with those of Caribbean music and slang. This combination, called *dub,* has influenced many young black British writers. Fred D'Aguiar's verse collection *British Subjects* (1993) emphasizes how Caribbean experience and culture have become part of recent British cultural identity.

Recent English fiction. During the 1960's and 1970's, Iris Murdoch, Muriel Spark, and Anthony Burgess emerged as important novelists. Murdoch was a professor of philosophy who often treated questions of moral philosophy in her fiction. Spark's novels are often comic but with disturbing and even Gothic undertones. Burgess wrote experimental novels of great verbal complexity and wit. In *A Clockwork Orange* (1962), he told the story of a violent juvenile delinquent who is brainwashed into numb social conformity.

More recent significant English novelists have often come from the United Kingdom's different immigrant communities. They include Salman Rushdie from India, Kazuo Ishiguro from Japan, and Caryl Phillips from the Caribbean. Rushdie is the outstanding figure of this group. His writing has been described as an example of *magic realism,* a style that combines realism with fantastic or apparently supernatural events. His novels overflow with multiple characters and stories. Ishiguro's novels offer subtle psychological explorations of memory and history. Phillips's novels show the experience of ethnic hatred, slavery, and exile through the use of historical settings and multiple narrators,.

Other notable English novelists include A. S. Byatt, Pat Barker, and Martin Amis, the son of Kingsley Amis. Byatt's novels often develop through clever references to other works of literature and art. Barker's *Regeneration* trilogy (1991-1995) is based on the experiences of a psychologist who worked with soldiers during World War I. Many of Amis's novels treat violent and controversial subject matter.

Recent English drama. Harold Pinter continued to write highly individual plays. Many of his later dramas deal with power relationships among friends or lovers. Tom Stoppard writes original and complex plays with philosophical themes. His works often experiment with imaginary historical situations and are remarkable for their verbal brilliance. Peter Shaffer has written a number of plays about the psychology of artists, outsiders, and nonconformists.

Several playwrights have engaged political issues in their work. Edward Bond has written plays about class conflict and oppression throughout British history. Caryl Churchill draws on such themes as the connection between colonial and sexual oppression in British history. David Hare has examined key British institutions—the Anglican church, the legal system, and political parties—in three related plays. In *Amy's View* (1997), Hare reflected on differences between theater and the newer, more popular media of film and television. D. E. White

Related articles. For a list of British playwrights, see the *Re-*

lated articles in **Drama.** For a list of British poets, see the *Related articles* in **Poetry.** See also:

Old English literature (500-1100)

Alfred the Great
Anglo-Saxon Chronicle
Anglo-Saxons
Bede, Saint
Beowulf

Middle English literature (1100-1485)

Arthur, King
Brut
Canterbury Tales
Geoffrey of Monmouth
Guy of Warwick
Malory, Sir Thomas
Miracle play
Morality play
Mystery play
Robin Hood
Round Table

The beginning of Modern English (1485-1603)

Bacon, Francis
Caxton, William
Gascoigne, George
Greene, Robert
Jonson, Ben
Lyly, John
More, Sir Thomas
Nashe, Thomas

The early and middle 1600's

Metaphysical poets
Milton, John
Walton, Izaak

Restoration literature (1660-1700)

Behn, Aphra
Bunyan, John
Pepys, Samuel
Restoration

The Augustan Age (1700-1750)

Addison, Joseph
Burke, Edmund
Classicism
Defoe, Daniel
Enlightenment
Fielding, Henry
Gay, John
Gulliver's Travels
Richardson, Samuel
Robinson Crusoe
Smollett, Tobias G.
Steele, Sir Richard
Sterne, Laurence
Swift, Jonathan

The Age of Johnson (1750-1784)

Boswell, James
Burke, Edmund
Burney, Fanny
Chesterfield, Earl of
Goldsmith, Oliver
Johnson, Samuel

Romantic literature (1784-1832)

Austen, Jane
De Quincey, Thomas
Frankenstein
Gothic novel
Hazlitt, William
Lamb, Charles
Romanticism
Scott, Sir Walter
Shelley, Mary W.
Thomson, James
Walpole, Horace

Victorian literature (1832-1901)

Brontë sisters
Bulwer-Lytton, Edward G. E. L.
Carlyle, Thomas
Carroll, Lewis
Collins, Wilkie
Dickens, Charles
Doyle, Arthur Conan
Dracula
Du Maurier, George
Eliot, George
Gaskell, Elizabeth
Haggard, H. Rider
Hardy, Thomas
Holmes, Sherlock
Hughes, Thomas
Kingsley, Charles
Kipling, Rudyard
Macaulay, Thomas Babington
Marryat, Frederick
Newman, John Henry
Pater, Walter
Pre-Raphaelite Brotherhood
Ruskin, John
Stevenson, Robert Louis
Stoker, Bram
Thackeray, William Makepeace
Trollope, Anthony
Wilde, Oscar

Literature before and after the world wars

Ambler, Eric
Amis, Kingsley
Barrie, J. M.
Beerbohm, Max
Belloc, Hilaire
Bennett, Arnold
Bloomsbury Group
Bowen, Elizabeth
Buchan, John
Cary, Joyce
Chesterton, G. K.
Christie, Agatha
Clarke, Arthur C.
Compton-Burnett, Ivy
Conrad, Joseph
Cronin, A. J.
Dahl, Roald
Douglas, Norman
Du Maurier, Daphne
Durrell, Lawrence
Fleming, Ian
Ford, Ford Madox
Forester, Cecil Scott
Forster, E. M.
Galsworthy, John
Golding, William
Greene, Graham
Heyer, Georgette
Hilton, James
Hudson, William Henry
Huxley, Aldous
Isherwood, Christopher
Knight, Eric
Larkin, Philip
Lawrence, D. H.
Lawrence, T. E.
Leavis, F. R.
Lessing, Doris
Lewis, C. S.
Lord of the Flies
Lowry, Malcolm
Mansfield, Katherine
Maugham, W. Somerset
Munro, Hector Hugh
Orczy, Baroness
Orwell, George
Powell, Anthony
Priestley, John Boynton
Sackville-West, V.
Sayers, Dorothy L.
Sillitoe, Alan
Sitwell, Edith
Snow, C. P.
Strachey, Lytton
Tolkien, J. R. R.
Walpole, Hugh Seymour
Waugh, Evelyn
Wells, H. G.
West, Rebecca
Wilson, Angus
Wodehouse, P. G.
Woolf, Virginia

English literature today

Burgess, Anthony
Deighton, Len
Drabble, Margaret
James, P. D.
Le Carré, John
McEwan, Ian
Murdoch, Iris
Rushdie, Salman
Spark, Muriel

Other related articles

Ballad
Bard
Biography
Blank verse
Criticism
Detective story
Drama
English language
Epic
Essay
Ghost story
Irish literature
Literature for children
Minstrel
Novel
Poetry
Romance
Satire
Science fiction
Scotland (The arts)
Sonnet
Wales (The arts)

Outline

I. Old English literature (500-1100)
A. Old English poetry
B. Old English prose

II. Middle English literature (1100-1485)
A. The development of English romances
B. The age of Chaucer
C. Early English drama
D. Middle English prose

III. The beginning of Modern English (1485-1603)
A. Elizabethan poetry
B. Elizabethan drama
C. Elizabethan fiction

IV. The early and middle 1600's
A. Metaphysical and Cavalier poets
B. Jacobean drama
C. Prose writings
D. John Milton

V. Restoration literature (1660-1700)
A. John Dryden
B. Restoration drama
C. Restoration prose

VI. The Augustan Age (1700-1750)
A. Swift and Pope
B. Addison and Steele
C. The rise of the novel

VII. The Age of Johnson (1750-1784)
A. Samuel Johnson
B. The Johnson circle

VIII. Romantic literature (1784-1832)
A. The Preromantics
B. Romantic poetry
C. Romantic prose

IX. Victorian literature (1832-1901)
A. Early Victorian literature
B. Later Victorian literature

X. Literature before and after the world wars
A. Literature before World War I
B. Poetry between the wars
C. Fiction between the wars
D. Literature after World War II

XI. English literature today
A. Recent English poetry
B. Recent English fiction
C. Recent English drama

Questions

What was the Augustan Age in English literature?
Who were the Angry Young Men?
What were some characteristics of Old English poetry?
What subjects did Victorian writers deal with?

How did Geoffrey Chaucer influence English poetry?
What is a *sonnet?* A *sonnet sequence?*
Who was the leading Preromantic poet?
When was heroic tragedy important in English drama?
What was the Movement in modern English literature?

Additional resources

Abrams, Meyer H., and others, eds. *The Norton Anthology of English Literature.* 2 vols. 7th ed. Norton, 2000.
British Writers. 8 vols., 9 supplements. Scribner, 1979-2003.
Drabble, Margaret, ed. *The Oxford Companion to English Literature.* 6th ed. Oxford, 2000.
Lambdin, Laura C. and Robert T., eds. *A Companion to Old and Middle English Literature.* Greenwood, 2002.
Ricks, Christopher, ed. *The Oxford Book of English Verse.* Oxford, 1999.
Sanders, Andrew. *The Short Oxford History of English Literature.* 2nd ed. Oxford, 2002.
Schlueter, Paul and June, eds. *An Encyclopedia of British Women Writers.* Rev. ed. Rutgers, 1999.
Stringer, Jenny, ed. *The Oxford Companion to Twentieth-Century Literature in English.* Oxford, 1996.

English setter is a popular dog because of its handsome face and sleek coat. Its hunting skill also makes it a popular gundog. The setter has a fairly long, flat coat, colored white, black, and tan or in mixtures of white, black, lemon, orange, and chestnut. Long hairs called *feathers* cover the dog's legs and tail. Many owners prefer setters that have a white coat with little flecks of color instead of coats with large, solid-colored patches. The setter is quick and graceful and has a fine sense of smell. It shows where game is by pointing with its nose toward the game. It also may lift one of its front paws. An English setter stands about 25 inches (64 centimeters) high and weighs from 50 to 70 pounds (23 to 32 kilograms).

Critically reviewed by the English Setter Association of America

See also **Dog** (picture: Sporting dogs).

English sparrow. See **House sparrow.**

English springer spaniel is a sporting dog that forces game to spring from hiding places. Hunters use this dog more often than the cocker spaniel because it is larger and stronger. It stands about 18 to 21 inches (46 to 53 centimeters) high at the shoulder and weighs from 37 to 55 pounds (17 to 25 kilograms). The dog's coat is fairly long and grows thick enough to resist water and brambles. The coat may be reddish-brown and white, black and white, or a combination of white, tan, and black or reddish-brown. The dog is also a popular pet. See also **Dog** (picture: Sporting dogs).

Critically reviewed by the English Springer Spaniel Field Trial Association

English toy spaniel is a breed of dog that was a favorite with English nobility in the 1600's. It weighs from 9 to 12 pounds (4 to 5.4 kilograms) and has a round head, with a short, turned-up nose. The dog's silky coat grows thickly, with longer fringes of hair on the chest, legs, tail, and feet. There are four varieties of English toy spaniels. The *King Charles* is black and tan. The *Prince Charles* is black, tan, and white. The *Blenheim* is red and white, and the *Ruby* is solid red.

Critically reviewed by the English Toy Spaniel Club

Engraving is a process of *incising* (cutting) a design or image into a flat metal plate. The engraved plate is then used to print the design. Engraving has importance both in the fine arts and in commercial printing. This article discusses engraving as a fine art. For information about engraving in commercial printing, see **Printing** (Methods of printing).

Engraving the plate. Most plates used in engraving are made of copper or zinc. To engrave an image into the plate, the artist uses a *burin,* a slim bar of tempered steel. One end of this tool is cut and sharpened to a 45-degree angle. The other end is set into a round wooden handle.

Engraving a plate requires great skill and patience. With one hand, the artist slowly and carefully moves the plate against the point of the burin. At the same time, the artist uses the other hand to guide and drive the burin in the desired direction. The depth and width of the incisions help determine the appearance of the line and thus the character of the picture. The artist removes the metal shavings from the incisions with a scraper. Lines can be altered or erased with special tools and materials. The artist can even eliminate all the incisions and begin a new engraving on the same plate.

Printing the engraving also requires considerable skill because the artist wants to produce pictures that are as identical as possible. Each picture *pulled* (printed) from a single plate is called an *impression.* To pull an impression, the artist needs ink, paper, and a press. First the engraved plate is warmed over an appliance called a hot plate. The heated metal holds the thick printing ink more firmly than cold metal could. A piece of cardboard or a small roller is then used by the artist to put a layer of ink on the engraved surface. The artist rubs and pushes the ink across the plate, forcing ink into the incisions.

After the incisions have been filled with ink, the plate is wiped several times with a pad of stiff fabric. The artist wipes in a circular motion, varying the pressure to distribute the ink evenly over the entire plate. Additional wiping eliminates all except a thin film of ink from the plate's surface. The plate is usually wiped a final time with the hand to create highlights and delicate tonal effects. The plate is then ready for the press.

The English toy spaniel has a long, silky coat.

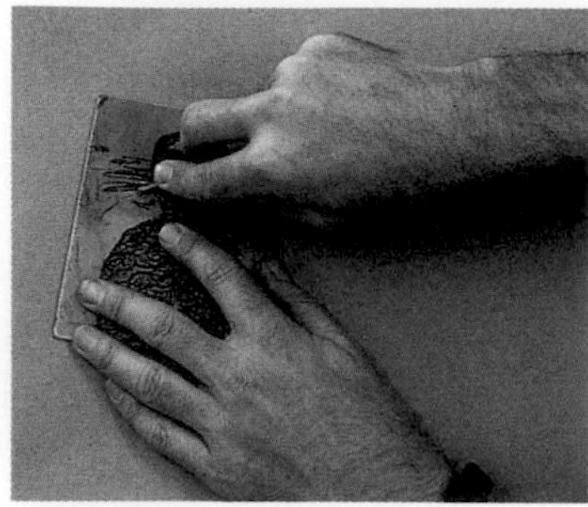

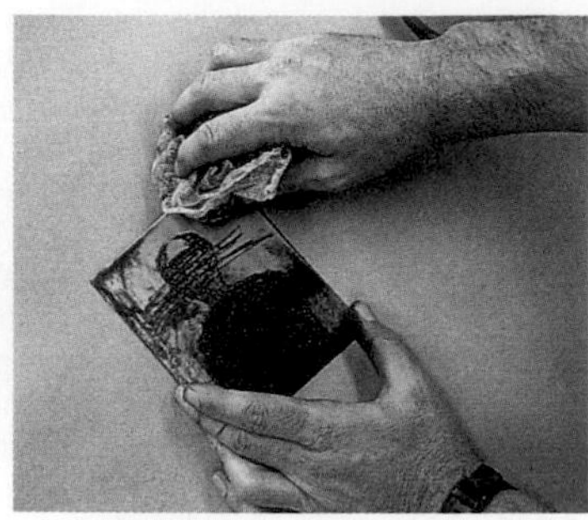

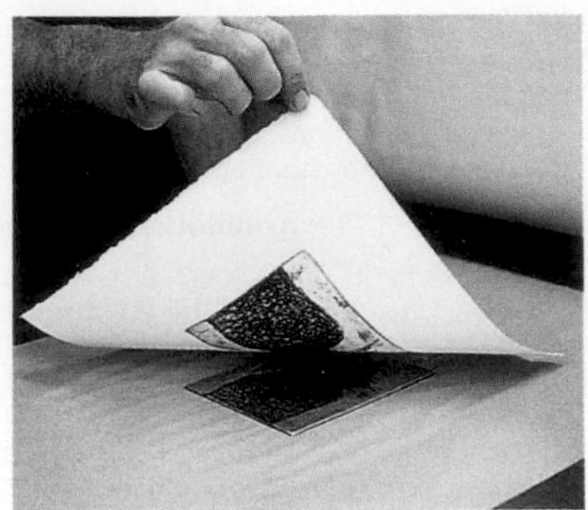

WORLD BOOK photos by Dan Miller

Making an engraving. The artist cuts a design into a metal plate, *left,* with a sharp tool called a *burin.* Then ink is put on the plate, *center.* The artist runs the inked plate and a piece of paper through a press. The ink transfers onto the paper, creating the finished print, *right.*

Artists usually print engravings on handmade paper because of its superior quality. They soak or sponge the paper with water so it becomes more pliable and receives the ink better. They then adjust the press to obtain the desired pressure from the metal roller. They place the plate on the press and put the dampened paper on the inked plate. Next, they cover the paper with two or more felt blankets and run the plate through the press. The pressure of the roller causes the ink to transfer onto the paper, creating an impression or print.

After the plate has passed through the press, the artist removes the blankets and carefully lifts the paper so that it does not tear. The freshly pulled impression is placed between white blotters to dry. The artist puts flat boards on the blotters to make sure that the paper lies flat and does not wrinkle. Inking and printing are repeated for each impression. After pulling the impressions, the artist removes all ink from the plate with turpentine and carefully wraps and stores the plate.

Dry point is a variation of the basic engraving process. Like engraving, dry-point prints are made by cutting a design into a metal plate. But instead of a burin, the artist uses a metal tool called a *needle* with a diamond or hard steel point. As the needle cuts into the plate, it throws up a soft ridge of metal called a *burr.* Depending on the angle, the artist can create a burr on one or both sides of the incision. The burr, rather than the incision, holds the ink and thus forms the lines of the image. Dry-point plates are printed in the same way as other engraved plates. Dry-point lines are softer than those in burin engravings. Dry point is often combined with etching and engraving to obtain special effects.

History. Engraving ranks as one of the earliest forms of artistic expression. The first engravings were carved during prehistoric times. The oldest surviving metal engravings date back to the 1400's.

The German artist Albrecht Dürer, who lived from 1471 to 1528, became the first great engraver. Other

Madonna and Child (about 1470) by Andrea Mantegna; the Metropolitan Museum of Art, New York City, Elisha Whittelsey Fund, 1952

A Renaissance engraving by Andrea Mantegna of Italy has the solid quality of a statue. The artist captured this sculptural feeling by shading the folds of the robe with parallel lines.

Detail of *The Two Sisters* (1932) by Étienne Cournault; Bibliothèque Nationale, Paris (Mme. Simon-Cournault)

A modern engraving shows how texture can be created. The French artist Étienne Cournault produced different textures in a small area through concentrations of dots, dashes, and lines.

early masters included Martin Schongauer of Germany, Lucas Van Leyden of the Netherlands, and Andrea Mantegna and Antonio del Pollaiuolo of Italy. William Hogarth was a leading English engraver of the 1700's. William Blake of England was a major engraver in the 1800's. Leading engravers of the 1900's included Stanley William Hayter and Gabor Peterdi. Andrew J. Stasik, Jr.

Related articles in *World Book* include:

Blake, William	Mantegna, Andrea
Dürer, Albrecht	Printing
Etching	Schongauer, Martin
Hogarth, William	Van Leyden, Lucas
Intaglio	

Engraving and Printing, Bureau of, designs, engraves, and prints the paper money issued by the United States government. The bureau also makes commissions, certificates, permits, and internal revenue and customs stamps. In addition, it produces hundreds of other kinds of U.S. government security documents, including Treasury bills, bonds, and notes. The Bureau of Engraving and Printing also helps other federal agencies design and print documents that require safeguards against counterfeiting. These include military identification cards and other items.

The bureau is a division of the Department of the Treasury in Washington, D.C. It is the world's largest printer of security documents, producing many billions of items each year. Congress passed legislation authorizing the bureau's work in July 1862. A director appointed by the secretary of the Treasury heads the bureau.

Critically reviewed by the Bureau of Engraving and Printing

See also **Money** (How money is manufactured).

Enid, *EE nihd* (pop. 49,379), a city in north-central Oklahoma, is the center of a wheat-growing district (see **Oklahoma** [political map]). Enid has grain elevators and flour mills, including the largest flour mill in the state. The city produces portable drilling equipment and processed meat products. Northern Oklahoma College and Northwestern Oklahoma State University have campuses in Enid. The city is the home of Vance Air Force Base. Enid was incorporated in 1894. It is the seat of Garfield County, and it has a council-manager form of government. Kevin Hassler

Eniwetok. See Enewetak.

Enlightenment was a period in history when philosophers emphasized the use of reason as the best method of learning truth. The period of the Enlightenment began in the 1600's and lasted until the late 1700's. The Enlightenment is also called the Age of Reason or the Age of Rationalism. Its leaders included several French philosophers—the Marquis de Condorcet, René Descartes, Denis Diderot, Jean-Jacques Rousseau, and Voltaire—and the English philosopher John Locke.

The leaders of the Enlightenment relied heavily on the scientific method, with its emphasis on experimentation and careful observation. The period produced many important advances in such fields as anatomy, astronomy, chemistry, mathematics, and physics. Philosophers of the Enlightenment organized knowledge in encyclopedias and founded scientific institutes.

The philosophers believed that the scientific method could be applied to the study of human nature. They explored issues in education, law, philosophy, and politics and attacked tyranny, social injustice, superstition, and ignorance. Many of their ideas were taken up as the ideals of the American and French revolutions during the late 1700's.

The worship of reason. The philosophers of the Enlightenment believed that human beings have a unique advantage over all other creatures because they can reason. These philosophers credited reason for all the achievements made in science and philosophy. They contrasted reason with ignorance, superstition, and uncritical acceptance of authority—all of which they felt had dominated the Middle Ages, the period from about the 400's through the 1400's. Enlightenment thinkers blamed people in authority, particularly the leaders of the Roman Catholic Church, for keeping others in ignorance to maintain their own personal power.

The philosophers of the Enlightenment were greatly influenced by discoveries in the physical sciences, such as the law of falling bodies discovered by Galileo in Italy and the laws of gravitation and motion formulated by Isaac Newton in England. The philosophers saw that great discoveries like these were made through the use of mathematics. They believed that mathematics yielded absolutely certain conclusions because the mathematical process started with simple *axioms* (self-evident truths) and moved from one self-evident step to another. Using this method, scholars discovered laws of nature that otherwise would have remained unknown. As a result, the philosophers of the Enlightenment believed mathematics was the model that all other sciences should follow.

The philosophers of the Enlightenment believed that each person has a rational will, which makes it possible to make and carry out plans. Animals, they declared, are slaves of their emotions. When an animal is afraid of something, it tries to escape. When an animal is angry, it fights. However, people can figure out the best course of action when they are afraid, angry, or in trouble. In addition, people can make themselves do the right thing, instead of doing only what may seem easier or more appealing.

The philosophers realized that people do not always plan ahead but often act on impulse, which they attributed to inadequate education. All people, the philosophers believed, are born with the capacity to reason. Descartes wrote that "the power of forming a good judgment and of distinguishing the true from the false, which is properly speaking what is called good sense or reason, is by nature equal in all men." Descartes therefore thought that to become rational, a person need only acquire an education that teaches a good method of reasoning.

Locke wrote that reason is "the candle of the Lord set up by Himself in men's minds" and "must be our last judge and guide in everything." Locke believed reason teaches that people must unite and form a state to protect their "lives and liberty and property." He noted that although people must give up some rights when they form a state, they gain more in protection than they lose.

Locke believed that anyone can reason, providing the capacity is allowed to develop. He therefore emphasized the importance of education and insisted on the right of free speech and on toleration of conflicting ideas.

The orderliness of nature. Philosophers of the Enlightenment believed that nature is vast and complex but well ordered. The English poet Alexander Pope described nature as "a mighty maze, but not without plan." The philosophers of the period felt that everything in the universe behaves according to a few simple laws, which can be explained mathematically. Their favorite example of such a law was Newton's law of gravity.

Human nature, the philosophers believed, is as well ordered as the physical universe. In *The Spirit of the Laws* (1748), the French philosopher Montesquieu wrote: "The material world has its laws, the intelligences superior to man have their laws, the beasts their laws, and man his laws." Montesquieu thought that a science of human nature was possible, and he became one of the first philosophers to try to formulate the basic uniformities of all human behavior.

Montesquieu believed that climate has an important influence on temperament and thus on conduct. According to Montesquieu, different kinds of government are appropriate for peoples who are living in different parts of the world. The best government for each nation could be planned, he felt, by considering the country's climate. Montesquieu thought, for example, that free governments are possible in northern latitudes. "People are more vigorous in cold climates," he wrote, and they have a "greater share of frankness and sincerity." But, Montesquieu said, the only workable form of government in a hot climate is *despotism* (rule by a dictator). Although his conclusions were discarded as mere speculation, they are typical of the Enlightenment's faith in reason.

Literature in the Enlightenment questioned accepted thinking. Writers portrayed human life as changeable and human understanding as partial. Much of the literature was written with self-consciousness and irony. It called attention to conventions and provoked skeptical awareness. The period reached its peak with works such as Pierre de Laclos's *Dangerous Liaisons* (1782) and the Marquis de Sade's *Philosophy in the Bedroom* (1795). In these novels, rational thought goes as far as possible toward separating the thinking individual from conventional influences and limitations.

Deism. The philosophers of the Enlightenment were convinced that the universe can be understood by the human mind. This is not an accident, the philosophers emphasized, because God could have created a universe too complex to be grasped by human beings. Instead, God created a universe ideally adjusted to the reasoning powers of people.

Most of the philosophers believed that after God had created the universe, he left it strictly alone. This theory, called *deism,* rules out the possibility of miracles or other special acts by God. According to deism, God regulated nature so that it proceeds mechanically. Future events are therefore fully predictable on the basis of earlier events. The philosophers liked to think of the universe as a clock that keeps perfect time because it was designed by a superior clockmaker. See **Deism.**

Influence of the Enlightenment. The thinkers of the Enlightenment formulated ideals of human dignity and worth. In France, a group of philosophers known as the *philosophes* criticized unjust social and political conditions. This group, which included Diderot, Rousseau, and Voltaire, greatly influenced leaders of the French Revolution (1789-1799). The philosophes and, more importantly, Locke also influenced the leaders of the Revolutionary War in America (1775-1783).

Philosophers of the Enlightenment sometimes disagreed on minor matters, but they all accepted the idea of the English philosopher Francis Bacon that "knowledge is power." Because they aimed, in Bacon's phrase, at "the improvement of man's estate," they concentrated their efforts on the advancement of knowledge. Their action explains why so many scientific institutes, including the famous Royal Society in England, were founded during the Enlightenment.

The urge to advance knowledge also explains why scholars made great efforts to organize and circulate the results of the scientific research of the time. Many learned people gathered, organized, and published this knowledge. In fact, the Enlightenment could be called the "age of the encyclopedia." The most famous reference work was the French *Encyclopédie,* edited by Diderot and Jean d'Alembert, and completed between 1751 and 1772.

To the philosophers of the Enlightenment, progress in human affairs seemed assured. It was only a question of time, they believed, until people learned to let reason—not ignorance, emotion, or superstition—guide them. When people did so, they would be happy. Condorcet expressed this optimism in his *Sketch for a Historical Picture of the Progress of the Human Mind* (1793-1794).

Criticism of the Enlightenment. Today, many beliefs of the Enlightenment seem naive. Most philosophers now believe that truths discovered by reason are universal only because they are *tautologies.* A tautology is a statement that merely repeats an idea in different words, without giving any new information. We can say, for example, that "all cats are felines." The statement is universally true, but only because *cat* means *feline.*

If the rational truths of the Enlightenment are tautologies, they do not tell us anything about nature. They tell us only how words are used. Most philosophers today believe that factual statements about the world are never certain. Such statements are only probable at best, and they may even be false.

The philosophers of the Enlightenment felt it was self-evidently true that governments should preserve their citizens' property. But in the 1800's, the German philosopher Karl Marx argued that this view merely reflected the prejudices of the middle class. These people own the property, said Marx, and thus want to preserve it.

The argument that universal truths are only tautologies was stated early in the Enlightenment by the English philosopher Thomas Hobbes. He wrote that reasoning is "nothing but reckoning, that is, adding and subtracting of the consequences of general names." But few people paid any attention to Hobbes's views, except to condemn them.

The Enlightenment's optimistic belief in a rational human will has also been challenged. In the early 1900's, for example, the Austrian physician Sigmund Freud stated that what we like to consider as "sound reasons" for our actions are only excuses. We act the way we do, Freud said, because of unconscious drives arising from a part of our subconscious mind called the *id.* We then attribute socially acceptable motives to ourselves to please another part of our subconscious, the *superego.*

The Enlightenment, however, ended long before

Marx and Freud attacked its basic beliefs. Toward the end of the 1700's, a great change in people's outlook occurred. They came to value feeling rather than reason and to prefer passion, individuality, and spontaneity to discipline, order, and control. This change marked the beginning of the Romantic movement and the end of the Enlightenment. James Creech

Related articles in *World Book* include:

Biographies

Bacon, Francis	Locke, John
Condorcet, Marquis de	Montesquieu
Descartes, René	Rousseau, Jean-Jacques
Diderot, Denis	Voltaire
Hobbes, Thomas	

Other related articles

French literature (The Age of Reason)
Government (The Enlightenment)
Philosophes
Philosophy (Modern philosophy)
Rationalism
Science (The Age of Reason)

Enright, Elizabeth (1909-1968), was an American author who is best known for her books for children. She won the 1939 Newbery Medal for *Thimble Summer* (1938), a story of life on a Wisconsin farm in summer. Her other books include *Kintu: Congo Adventure* (1935), *The Saturdays* (1941), *Gone-away Lake* (1957), and *Tatsinda* (1963). Enright also wrote adult books. She illustrated most of her own works.

Enright was born on Sept. 17, 1909, in Oak Park, Illinois. She died on June 8, 1968. Virginia L. Wolf

Enron Corporation was once one of the world's largest energy companies. In November 2001, Enron revealed that it had overstated its earnings by several hundred million dollars since 1997. The following month, Enron filed one of the largest corporate bankruptcy claims in United States history. The financial collapse led to numerous investigations into complicated financial transactions and accounting procedures by both Enron and Arthur Andersen, Enron's accounting firm. Investigators focused on charges that Enron deliberately concealed its financial problems from investors. Arthur Andersen admitted to destroying documents that might have been significant to the Enron investigations.

Prior to the company's downfall, some top Enron executives sold their shares of company stock. However, Enron's employees were not allowed to sell shares from their retirement accounts for several weeks as the stock value dropped. As a result, thousands of employees lost much of their retirement savings. Many of these employees and other shareholders brought lawsuits against Enron officials, and against Arthur Andersen. In addition, because Enron and some of its executives contributed money to politicians, some people charged that Enron received special treatment from the U.S. government.

In January 2002, Kenneth L. Lay, Enron's founder, resigned as the company's chairman. Arthur Andersen's accounting business collapsed due to the scandal. In May 2006, Lay and former Enron chief executive Jeffrey Skilling were found guilty of conspiracy and fraud. Lay died in July 2006. Skilling began serving a prison sentence of 24 years 4 months in December 2006. In 2013, Skilling was resentenced to 14 years. The new term was part of a court-ordered reduction in Skilling's sentence and a separate deal with the U.S. Justice Department.

Enron originated with the 1985 merger of Houston Natural Gas and InterNorth of Omaha, Nebraska. Based in Houston, Enron evolved from a utility that produced and transported natural gas into an energy trading firm. Before its collapse, Enron was, by some calculations, the seventh largest U.S. corporation. In 2007, Enron's name was changed to Enron Creditors Recovery Corporation. The goal of the new company was to repay the old Enron Corporation's remaining creditors and to end Enron's operations. James R. Barth

Ensor, James (1860-1949), was a Belgian painter and printmaker. He created his most important pictures between 1880 and 1900. Masks were a favorite subject. His figures often wear brightly colored but devilish masks that serve to both threaten the viewer and hide the wearer's identity. Skeletons and demons also appear in many of Ensor's paintings and etchings. In his most famous painting, *The Entry of Christ into Brussels* (1888), Ensor combined three of his most common themes—the mask, the crowd, and Jesus Christ.

Detail of *Demons Tormenting Me* (1888), a pencil and black chalk drawing; The Art Institute of Chicago, the Ada Turnbull Hertle Fund

A self-portrait of James Ensor is featured in this drawing. Ensor included images of demons and freakish figures in many of his works.

Ensor's fantastic subjects have been compared to the paintings of two earlier Belgian artists, Pieter Bruegel the Elder and Hieronymus Bosch. His paintings also anticipate two art movements of the early 1900's—Expressionism and Surrealism.

Ensor was born on Oct. 13, 1860, in Ostend, a resort town on the North Sea. His paintings reflect the carnival masks, toys, and sea shells that his parents sold from their souvenir shop to the tourists. He died on Nov. 19, 1949. Pamela A. Ivinski

Entebbe, *ehn TEHB ay* (pop. 55,086), is a major city in Uganda. It lies on Lake Victoria's northwest shore south of Kampala, Uganda's commercial center and capital (see **Uganda** [map]).

Entebbe was founded in 1893 as the British colonial headquarters of Uganda. It was the capital from 1894 until Uganda won independence in 1962, and it is still the site of many government departments. The city also has botanical gardens, the president's official residence, and Uganda's international airport. Sources of employment include construction, fishing, government, small-scale industry, tourism, and transportation. Ronald R. Atkinson

Entomology, *EHN tuh MAHL uh jee,* is the scientific study of insects. Scientists who specialize in insects are called *entomologists.* Entomologists also study animals related to insects, such as ticks, mites, spiders, and centipedes. All these creatures are types of *arthropods,* a group of animals distinguished by their jointed legs. Entomology developed rapidly after the 1750's, when the Swedish naturalist Carolus Linnaeus provided a useful system of classifying and naming plants and animals.

What entomologists do. Entomologists investigate the anatomy, physiology, development, life history, behavior, ecology, and classification of insects and related arthropods. This group of creatures includes about 1 ½ million known *species* (kinds), though scientists estimate that millions of additional species have not yet been described and named. Insects make up the largest group of animals, and they live on every continent. Entomologists study insects and similar animals in part because these creatures are vital to the health of *ecosystems* on land. An ecosystem consists of all the living and nonliving things in an area and the relationships among them. People also study insects because some species are pests that can damage crops, stored goods, or even buildings. Other insect species can transmit diseases.

Most entomologists work in the field of *economic entomology,* also called *applied entomology.* They study insect pests that cause damage or endanger the health of people and animals. *Agricultural entomologists* study insect pests that damage crops. *Forest entomologists* study pests of timber. *Medical entomologists* and *veterinary entomologists* seek to decrease the threat of insects that spread disease among people and animals.

Entomologists work to reduce the numbers of insect pests through a variety of controls. These include *cultural controls,* such as planting insect-resistant crops; *chemical controls,* such as the use of insecticides and insect repellents; and *biological controls,* such as the use of animals that naturally prey on insect pests.

Many insects benefit people. Silkworms produce a valuable fiber. Honey bees provide honey and are one of many insects that pollinate plants, including many crops. Other insects and similar animals prey on pests.

Careers in entomology. People pursuing a career in entomology must have at least a bachelor's degree in entomology or biology. Most teaching and research positions require a master's or doctor's degree in entomology. Entomologists are employed by state and federal agricultural experiment stations and in public health agencies. They may work for universities or museums. Some also work in industry. David L. Denlinger

Related articles in *World Book.* For more information on the animals that entomologists study, see **Arachnid** and **Insect** with their lists of *Related articles.* See also **Centipede; Insecticide; Millipede; Swammerdam, Jan.**

Entrepreneur. See **Industrial Revolution** (Life before the Industrial Revolution).

Entropy, *EHN truh pee,* is a measure of the amount of disorder or randomness in a system. Because there are many more random ways of arranging a group of things than there are organized ways, disorder is much more probable. For example, shuffling a deck of cards always leads to a jumbled distribution of cards, and never to an ordered sequence.

The idea of entropy is the basis of the second law of thermodynamics. According to this law, the direction of spontaneous change in isolated systems is toward maximum disorder. Thus, heat flows of its own accord only from a hotter substance to a cooler one. As the cooler substance gains heat, the motion of its molecules becomes more disorderly and its entropy increases (see **Heat** [Disorder]).

Furthermore, a gas will always expand to fill its container but will never contract to occupy only a fraction of the container. The entropy of the gas increases as the gas expands because more positions are available for the molecules to occupy. Every substance has greater entropy as a gas than as a liquid.

Some changes may decrease entropy in a system. But this decrease is more than offset by an entropy increase in connected systems. For example, the entropy of water decreases as the liquid freezes, but heat released in the process increases the entropy of the surrounding air.

The entropy of a substance increases whenever the substance loses some of its ability to do work. For example, air forced into an empty balloon has low entropy because the air molecules are compressed in a small volume. The compressed air does work by expanding to inflate the balloon. In the inflated balloon, the molecules can occupy a larger number of positions and thus have greater entropy. But they have lost the ability to do more work by expanding the balloon further.

Taken together, all processes occurring now will result in a universe of greater disorder. Because the entropy of the universe is always increasing, a state of greater entropy must be one that occurs later in time. For this reason, entropy has been called "time's arrow."

Robert B. Prigo

See also **Time** (Arrows of time).

Enunciation. See **Pronunciation.**

Envelope is a piece of folded, sealed paper. It serves as a wrapper to hold letters and other papers to be mailed, or it acts as protection against loss or damage. Envelopes are made of a single sheet of paper folded so that one flap remains open. This flap is gummed so the envelope may be sealed after the letter or papers have been inserted. Self-sealing envelopes make use of a gum that need not be moistened to stick.

Envelopes were first manufactured in 1839 by a New York City man named Pierson. Before that time, all letters were folded so that a blank portion of the paper could be used for the address. The edges of the paper were sealed with sealing wax. For about 10 years after envelopes were invented, they were cut, folded, and pasted by hand. A worker could make about 3,000 envelopes a day. The first successful machine for making envelopes was patented in 1849 by J. K. Park and C. S. Watsen of New York City. A greatly improved envelope machine, patented in 1898 by John Ames Sherman, lowered the cost of making gummed envelopes.

Envelopes are numbered from 5 to 14 according to size. The No. 10 envelope is the most popular size for business letters. It measures 9 ½ inches (24.1 centimeters) long and 4 ⅛ inches (10.5 centimeters) wide.

Some standardization of envelope sizes is necessary for the efficient operation of mechanical mail-sorting devices. The U.S. Postal Service requires that envelopes sent through the mail be rectangular and no smaller than 5 inches (12.7 centimeters) long and 3 ½ inches (8.9 centimeters) wide. The Universal Postal Union, a United Nations agency, has a metric size range to make the handling of international mail more efficient. Envelopes should be at least 14 centimeters (5 ½ inches) long and 9 centimeters (3 ½ inches) wide, but no more than 23.5 centimeters (9 ¼ inches) long and 12 centimeters (4 ¾ inches) wide. Larry L. Graham

Environment is everything that is external to a living thing. A human being's environment includes such factors as temperature, food supply, and other people. A plant's environment includes soil, sunlight, and animals that may eat the plant. Nonliving environmental factors, such as temperature and sunlight, make up the *abiotic environment.* Living or recently living things, such as seaweed and fallen leaves, make up the *biotic environment.* The abiotic and biotic environments interact to make up the environment of a living thing. *Ecology* is the study of the relationships between *organisms* (living things) and their environment.

Abiotic environment includes such factors as soil, water, atmosphere, and radiation. This environment is made up of many objects and forces that influence one another and living things. For example, a river's current, temperature, clearness, and chemical composition influence what kinds of organisms are found there and how they live.

One important group of abiotic environmental factors make up what is called the weather. Living and nonliving things are influenced by rain, snow, hot or cold temperature, evaporation of water, *humidity* (amount of water vapor in the air), wind, and many other weather conditions. Many plants and animals die each year because of weather conditions. Human beings build homes and wear clothes to protect themselves from harsh weather.

Other abiotic factors include the amount of living space and *nutrients* (nourishing substances) available to an organism. All organisms need a certain amount of space in which to live. They also must have nutrients, such as phosphorus, to grow and live.

Biotic environment includes plants, animals, and other organisms and their interactions with one another. For example, animals must feed on plants or on animals that eat plants. Thus, the plants that grow in an area strongly influence which animals can live there. Similarly, a person's well-being depends in part on the quality and variety of foods available, such as fruit and vegetables from plants and meat from animals. Organisms also have associations apart from feeding relationships. For example, a person houses trillions of bacteria in the digestive tract. These bacteria help the person digest food.

Some living things are able to control their environment to some degree. For example, beavers cut down trees to make dams. These dams cause ponds to form, which influences the kinds of plants and animals that grow there. In this way, beavers help shape both their abiotic environment and their biotic environment. Human beings have advanced beyond any other animal in controlling their environment. They have greatly changed many natural environments, such as by cutting down forests to plant crops. People also can create artificial environments. For example, spacecraft provide the environment people need to survive in the harsh conditions of outer space. Lawrence C. Wit

Related articles in *World Book* include:

Adaptation
Biome
Child (Individual differences among children)
Ecology
Engineering (Environmental engineering)
Environmental pollution
Gaia
Heredity (Heredity and environment)

Environmental Defense Fund is a private organization in the United States that works to protect the environment. It has achieved many of its goals through legal action. The organization sues private companies and federal, state, and local government agencies to make them stop polluting the environment. Its cases are based on the belief that Americans have a constitutional right to a healthy environment.

A lawsuit by the fund strongly influenced the U.S. government's decision to phase out all uses of DDT, an insecticide. This decision took effect in 1972. Other suits caused companies and government agencies to abandon or modify a number of projects that could have harmed the environment. These projects included the construction of canals, dams, and highways. A group of lawyers and scientists founded the fund in 1967. It has headquarters in New York City. Alan McGowan

Environmental impact statement is a report that evaluates the likely environmental effects of a planned government project or program. A number of countries have laws requiring environmental impact statements.

The purpose of an environmental impact statement is to ensure that a government agency considers the environmental damage that may result from a project over which it has authority. The agency must identify ways of reducing harm and consider alternatives to the project that may be less damaging. Normally, other interested parties—such as state and local agencies, businesses, or individuals—can comment on the project during the environmental impact review process. After a final report is issued, the agency itself decides whether to go ahead with the project or whether to alter or abandon it.

The world's first law requiring environmental impact statements was the National Environmental Policy Act, a United States law that went into effect in 1970. Under the law, any U.S. agency that plans to build a dam, power plant, or other facility must issue an environmental impact statement. A federal agency also must issue a statement for any large state, local, or private project that it will fund or regulate. Several states have similar laws for projects by state agencies or local governments.

In 1992, the United Nations Conference on Environment and Development—also known as the Earth Summit—was held in Rio de Janeiro, Brazil. As a result of the summit, more than 170 countries approved Agenda 21, a plan to achieve worldwide economic development in an environmentally responsible way. Since then, several countries have begun to require environmental impact statements. John R. Nolon

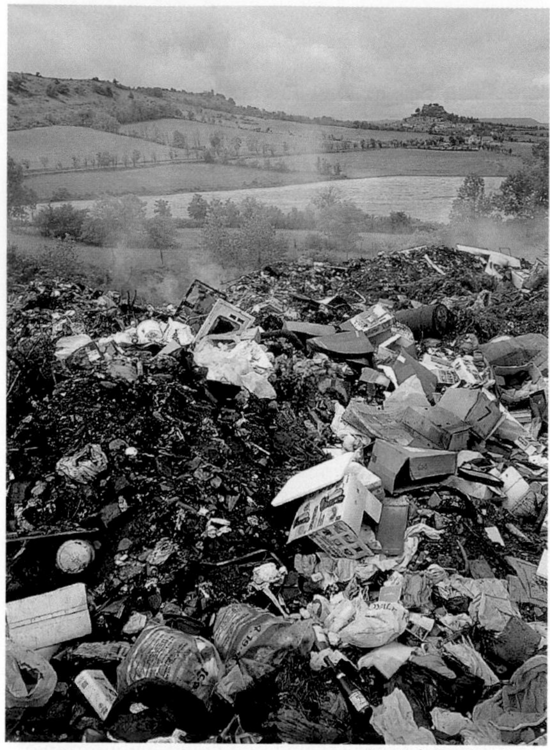
Peter Cade, Tony Stone Images
Solid waste in France

Sergio Dorantes, Sygma
Air pollution in Mexico City

Bob Stern, Gamma/Liaison
Water pollution in Estonia

Environmental pollution is one of the most serious problems facing the world today. It threatens the health of all living things and damages the natural beauty of Earth.

Environmental pollution

Environmental pollution refers to harmful chemicals and other contaminants that damage the natural environment. Some pollution can easily be seen. Examples include an open garbage dump or an automobile pouring out black smoke. However, pollution can also be invisible, odorless, and tasteless. Such forms of pollution do not obviously dirty the land, air, or water. But they reduce the quality of life for people and other living things. Noise pollution from traffic and machinery is one such example.

Environmental pollution is one of the most serious problems facing humanity and other life forms today. Badly polluted air can harm crops and cause life-threatening illnesses. Some air pollutants have reduced the capacity of the atmosphere to filter out the sun's harmful ultraviolet radiation. Most scientists believe that these and other air pollutants have begun to change climates around the world. Water and soil pollution threaten the ability of farmers to grow enough food. Ocean pollution endangers many marine organisms.

Many people think of air, water, and soil pollution as distinct forms of pollution. However, each part of the environment—air, water, or soil—is related to the others. All living and nonliving things in an environment interact to make up an *ecosystem.* All the ecosystems of Earth are connected. Thus, pollution that seems to affect only one part of the environment may also affect other parts. For example, sooty smoke from a power plant might appear to harm only the atmosphere. But rain can wash some harmful chemicals in the smoke out of the sky and onto land or into waterways.

Some pollution comes from one specific point or location, such as a sewage pipe spilling dirty water into a river. Such pollution is called *point source pollution.* Other pollution comes from large areas. Water can run off farmland and carry pesticides and fertilizers into rivers. Rain water can wash gasoline, oil, and salt from highways and parking lots into the wells that supply drinking water. Pollution that comes from such large areas is called *nonpoint source pollution.*

Most of the pollution that now threatens the health of our planet comes from products that many people want and need. For example, automobiles provide the convenience of personal transportation, but they create a large percentage of the world's air pollution. Factories make products that people use and enjoy, but industrial processes can also pollute. Pesticides and fertilizers aid in growing large quantities of food, but they also poison the soil and water.

To end or greatly decrease pollution, people would need to reduce their use of polluting cars and other modern conveniences. Some factories might have to close or change production methods. Because many jobs are dependent on industries that contribute to environmental pollution, shutting down these industries would potentially increase unemployment. In addition, if farmers suddenly stopped using chemical fertilizers and pesticides, there might be less food available to feed people.

Over time, however, pollution can be reduced in many ways without seriously disrupting people's lives. For example, governments can pass laws that encourage businesses to adopt less polluting methods of operation. Scientists and engineers can develop products and processes that are cleaner and safer for the environment. And individuals around the world can themselves find ways to reduce environmental pollution.

Types of pollution

The chief types of environmental pollution include air pollution, water pollution, soil pollution, pollution caused by solid waste and hazardous waste, and noise pollution.

Air pollution is the contamination of the air by such substances as fuel exhaust and smoke. It can harm the health of plants and animals and damage buildings and other structures. It can potentially cause a change in the worldwide climate. Air pollution also causes a variety of health problems, such as asthma and other lung diseases and coronary artery disease. According to the World Health Organization, about 3 million people die each year as a result of air pollution.

The atmosphere normally consists of nitrogen, oxygen, and small amounts of carbon dioxide and other gases and *particulates* (tiny particles of liquid or solid matter). A number of natural processes work to keep the parts of the atmosphere in balance. For example, plants use carbon dioxide and produce oxygen. Animals, in turn, use up oxygen and produce carbon dioxide through respiration. Forest fires and volcanic eruptions shoot gases and particulates into the atmosphere. Over time, rain and wind can wash them out or scatter them.

Air pollution occurs when industries and vehicles release such large amounts of gas and particulates into the air that natural processes can no longer keep the atmosphere in balance. There are two chief types of air pollution: (1) outdoor and (2) indoor.

Outdoor air pollution. Each year, hundreds of millions of tons of gases and particulates pour into the atmosphere. Most of this pollution results from the burning of fuel to power motor vehicles and to heat buildings. Some air pollution also comes from business and industrial processes. The burning of garbage may discharge smoke and heavy metals, such as lead and mercury, into the atmosphere. Most heavy metals are highly poisonous.

One of the most common types of outdoor air pollution is *smog.* Smog is a brown, hazy mixture of gases and particulates. It develops when certain gases released by the combustion of gasoline and other petroleum products react with sunlight in the atmosphere. This reaction creates hundreds of harmful chemicals.

One of the chemicals in smog is a toxic form of oxygen called *ozone.* Exposure to high concentrations of ozone causes headaches, burning eyes, and irritation of the respiratory tract in many individuals. In some cases, ozone in the lower atmosphere can cause death. Ozone can also damage plant life and even kill trees.

Particulates also contribute to air pollution. Some particles of fossil fuels escape from boilers in factories and from engines in cars and trucks when fuels do not burn completely. These particles pollute in many ways. They fall onto vegetation and the surfaces of buildings. Particulates can mix with other chemicals to create smog. They can also enter people's lungs and contribute to the development of asthma or other diseases.

Acid rain is a term for rain and other precipitation that is polluted mainly by sulfuric acid and nitric acid. These acids form when gases called sulfur dioxide and nitrogen oxides react with water vapor in the air. A major source of both gases is the burning of coal, gas, and oil by cars, factories, and power plants. Because rain storms often affect large areas, acid rain can harm large areas of the environment. Acid rain has killed entire fish populations in a number of lakes. It has also damaged many buildings, bridges, and statues. Scientists believe high concentrations of acid rain can harm forests and soil. Regions affected by acid rain include large parts of eastern North America, Scandinavia, and central Europe.

Chemicals called *chlorofluorocarbons* (CFC's) are pollutants that destroy the ozone layer in the upper atmosphere. CFC's have been used as refrigerants in air conditioners and refrigerators and to make plastic foam insulation. Ozone, the same gas that is a harmful pollutant in smog near the ground, forms a protective layer in the upper atmosphere. It shields Earth's surface from more than 95 percent of the sun's ultraviolet radiation. As CFC's thin the ozone layer, more ultraviolet radiation reaches the surface of Earth. Overexposure to such radiation damages plants and greatly increases people's risk of skin cancer.

The *greenhouse effect* is the warming that results when Earth's atmosphere traps the sun's heat. Certain gases, called *greenhouse gases,* let the sun's energy through to reach Earth's surface, but prevent heat from leaving—much like the glass walls of a greenhouse. Carbon dioxide and methane are major greenhouse gases.

Fuel burning and other human activities increase the amount of greenhouse gases in the atmosphere. Many scientists believe such an increase is intensifying the greenhouse effect and raising temperatures worldwide. The increase in temperature, called *global warming,* may cause many problems. A strong greenhouse effect could melt glaciers and Arctic ice, flooding coastal areas. It could also shift rainfall patterns, leading to more droughts. In addition, global warming may lead to more extreme weather conditions.

Indoor air pollution occurs when buildings with poorly designed ventilation trap pollutants inside. Indoor pollutants include tobacco smoke, gases from stoves and furnaces, household chemicals, small fiber particles, and hazardous fumes given off by such building materials as insulation, glue, and paint. In some office buildings, significant amounts of these substances cause headaches, eye irritation, and other health problems in workers. Such health problems are sometimes called *sick building syndrome.*

Radon, a radioactive gas given off through the decay of uranium in rocks within Earth, is another harmful indoor pollutant. It can cause lung cancer if inhaled in

Text continued on page 334.

Kinds of environmental pollution

There are many kinds of environmental pollution that harm our planet in a wide variety of ways. Because all the parts of the environment are connected with one another, a pollutant that chiefly damages one natural system may also affect others.

WORLD BOOK illustration by Michael Yurkovic

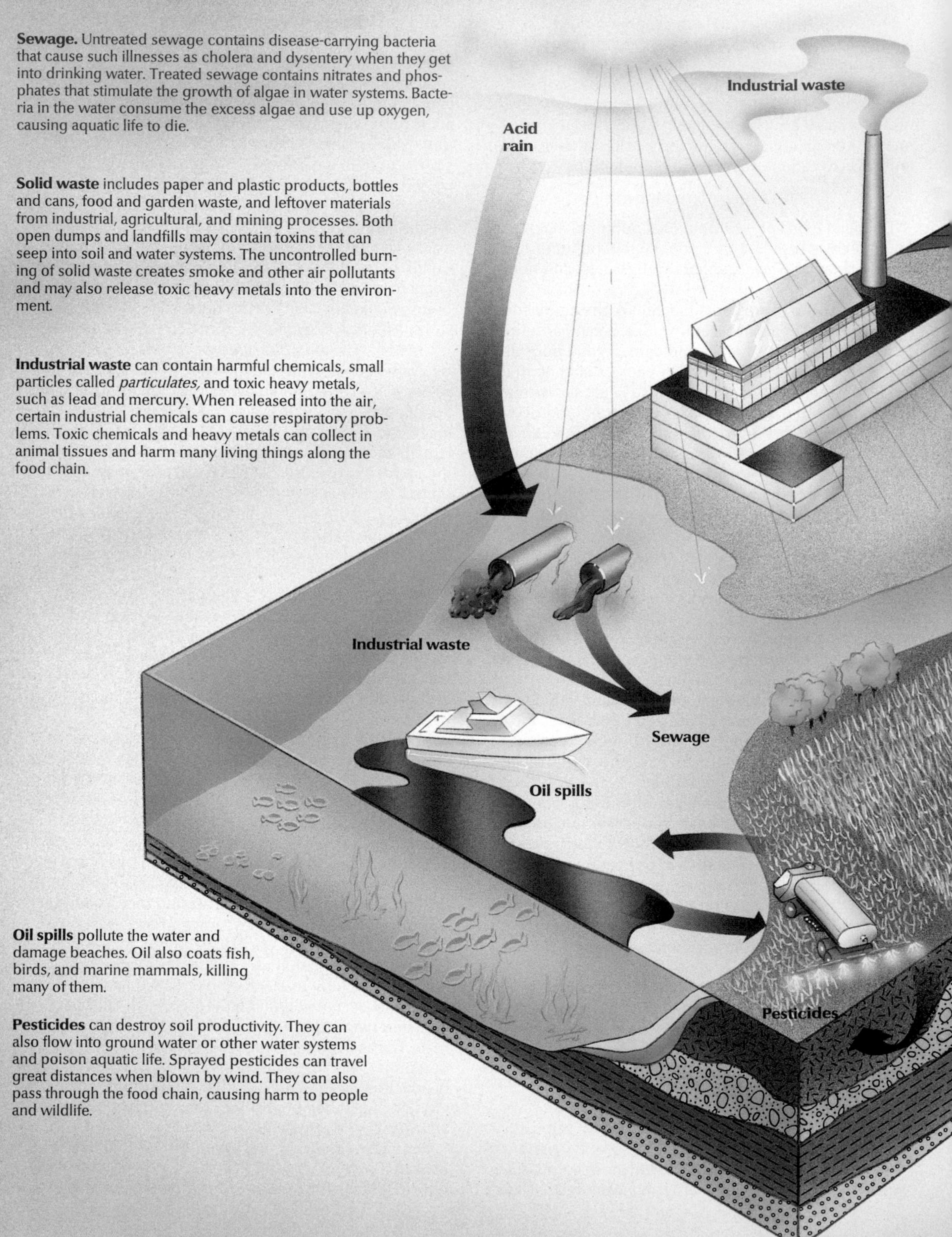

Sewage. Untreated sewage contains disease-carrying bacteria that cause such illnesses as cholera and dysentery when they get into drinking water. Treated sewage contains nitrates and phosphates that stimulate the growth of algae in water systems. Bacteria in the water consume the excess algae and use up oxygen, causing aquatic life to die.

Solid waste includes paper and plastic products, bottles and cans, food and garden waste, and leftover materials from industrial, agricultural, and mining processes. Both open dumps and landfills may contain toxins that can seep into soil and water systems. The uncontrolled burning of solid waste creates smoke and other air pollutants and may also release toxic heavy metals into the environment.

Industrial waste can contain harmful chemicals, small particles called *particulates,* and toxic heavy metals, such as lead and mercury. When released into the air, certain industrial chemicals can cause respiratory problems. Toxic chemicals and heavy metals can collect in animal tissues and harm many living things along the food chain.

Oil spills pollute the water and damage beaches. Oil also coats fish, birds, and marine mammals, killing many of them.

Pesticides can destroy soil productivity. They can also flow into ground water or other water systems and poison aquatic life. Sprayed pesticides can travel great distances when blown by wind. They can also pass through the food chain, causing harm to people and wildlife.

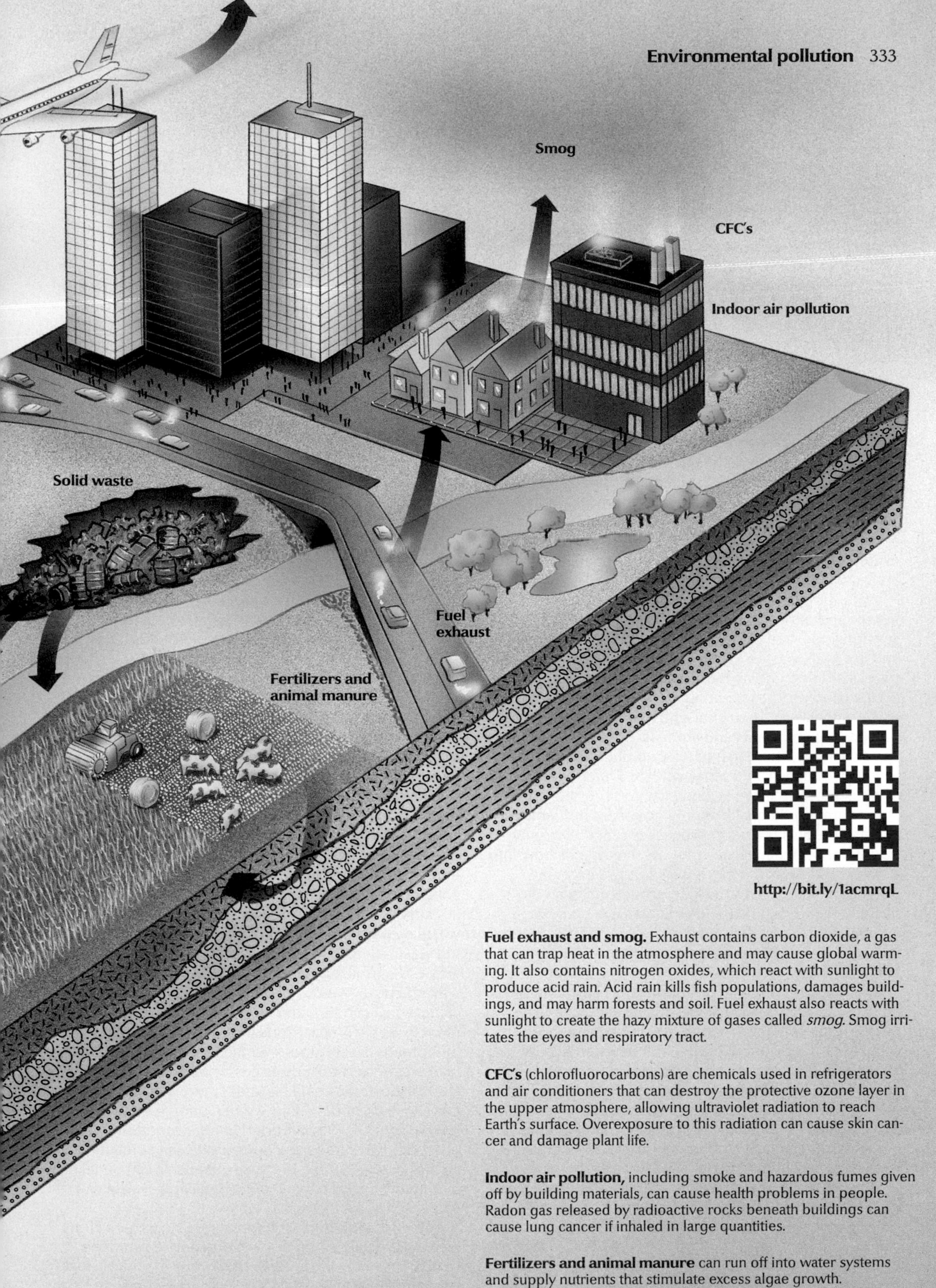

http://bit.ly/1acmrqL

Fuel exhaust and smog. Exhaust contains carbon dioxide, a gas that can trap heat in the atmosphere and may cause global warming. It also contains nitrogen oxides, which react with sunlight to produce acid rain. Acid rain kills fish populations, damages buildings, and may harm forests and soil. Fuel exhaust also reacts with sunlight to create the hazy mixture of gases called *smog.* Smog irritates the eyes and respiratory tract.

CFC's (chlorofluorocarbons) are chemicals used in refrigerators and air conditioners that can destroy the protective ozone layer in the upper atmosphere, allowing ultraviolet radiation to reach Earth's surface. Overexposure to this radiation can cause skin cancer and damage plant life.

Indoor air pollution, including smoke and hazardous fumes given off by building materials, can cause health problems in people. Radon gas released by radioactive rocks beneath buildings can cause lung cancer if inhaled in large quantities.

Fertilizers and animal manure can run off into water systems and supply nutrients that stimulate excess algae growth.

large quantities. People can be exposed to radon when the gas leaks into basements of homes built over radioactive soil or rock. Energy-efficient buildings, designed to keep in heated or cooled air, can trap radon indoors and lead to high concentrations of the gas.

Water pollution is the contamination of water by sewage, toxic chemicals, metals, oils, or other substances. Water pollution can affect rivers, lakes, and oceans, as well as the water beneath Earth's surface, called *ground water.* Water pollution can harm many species of plants and animals. According to the World Health Organization, nearly one-sixth of the world's people have no access to safe drinking water.

In a healthy water system, a cycle of natural processes turns wastes into useful or harmless substances. The cycle begins when organisms called *aerobic bacteria* use the oxygen dissolved in water to digest wastes. This digestion process releases nitrates, phosphates, and other *nutrients* (chemical substances that living things need for growth). Algae and aquatic green plants absorb these nutrients. Microscopic animals called *zooplankton* eat the algae, and small fish eat the zooplankton. These fish, in turn, may be eaten by larger fish, birds, or other animals. These larger animals produce body wastes and eventually die. Bacteria break down dead animals and animal wastes, and the cycle begins again.

Water pollution comes from businesses, farms, homes, industries, and other sources. It includes sewage, industrial chemicals, agricultural chemicals, and livestock wastes. Water pollution occurs when people put so much waste into a water system that its natural cleansing processes cannot function properly. Some waste, such as oil, industrial acids, or farm pesticides, poisons aquatic plants and animals. Chemical and oil spills can cause devastating water pollution that kills water birds, shellfish, and other wildlife. Other waste, such as phosphate detergents, chemical fertilizers, and animal manure, pollutes by supplying excess nutrients for aquatic life. This pollution process is called *eutrophication.* It begins when large amounts of nutrients flow into a water system. These nutrients stimulate excessive growth of algae. As more algae grow, more also die. Bacteria that consume the dead algae use up large amounts of oxygen dissolved in the water. The oxygen level of the water then drops, causing many aquatic plants and animals to die.

Another form of water pollution is the clean but heated water discharged by power plants into waterways. Such *thermal pollution* harms fish and aquatic plants by reducing the amount of oxygen in the water. In addition, it may affect fish that rely on seasonal temperature changes to locate their breeding grounds.

Some water pollution occurs when wastewater is improperly separated from clean drinking water. In parts of the world that lack modern sewage treatment plants, water carrying human waste can flow into drinking water supplies. Disease-carrying bacteria in the waste can then contaminate the drinking water and cause such illnesses as cholera and dysentery. In areas with good sanitation, most human waste flows through underground pipes to special treatment plants that kill the harmful bacteria and remove the solid waste.

Water pollution also occurs when chemicals seep through the ground and enter *aquifers,* areas where ground water is stored in porous rock. Such pollution is of major concern because aquifers supply much of the drinking water and water for farms in some areas. The lack of oxygen in aquifers stops bacteria from breaking down contaminants, and the isolation of aquifers underground makes it difficult to locate and remove pollutants from them. Thus, chemicals that enter ground water can remain there for long periods and continue to contaminate local water supplies.

Soil pollution is the destruction of Earth's thin layer of healthy, productive soil, where much of our food is grown. Without fertile soil, farmers could not grow enough food to support the world's people.

Healthy soil depends on bacteria, fungi, and small animals to break down wastes in the soil and release nutrients. These nutrients help plants grow. However, fertilizers and pesticides can limit the ability of soil organisms to process wastes. As a result, farmers who overuse fertilizers and pesticides can destroy the soil's productivity.

Soil can be damaged in other ways. When soil is irrigated in dry areas with poor drainage, standing water may remain in fields. When this standing water evaporates, it leaves salt deposits behind, making the soil too salty for growing crops. Mining operations and smelters contaminate soil with toxic heavy metals. Many scientists believe acid rain can also reduce soil fertility.

Solid waste is probably the most visible form of pollution. Every year, people dispose of billions of tons of solid garbage. Industrial wastes account for the majority of the discarded material. Solid waste from homes, offices, and stores is called *municipal solid waste.* It includes paper, plastic, glass, metal cans, food scraps, and yard trimmings. Other waste consists of junked automobiles, scrap metal, leftover materials from agricultural processes, and mining wastes known as *spoil.*

The handling of solid waste is a problem because most disposal methods damage the environment. Open dumps ruin the natural beauty of the land and provide a home for rats and other disease-carrying animals. Both open dumps and *landfills* (areas of buried wastes) may contain toxins that seep into ground water or flow into streams and lakes. The uncontrolled burning of solid waste creates smoke and other air pollution. Even burning waste in incinerators can release toxic chemicals, ash, and harmful metals into the air.

Hazardous waste is composed of discarded substances that can threaten human health and the environment. A waste is hazardous if it *corrodes* (wears away) other materials; explodes; ignites easily; reacts strongly with water; or is toxic. Sources of hazardous waste include industries, hospitals, and laboratories. Such waste can cause immediate injury when people breathe, swallow, or touch it. When buried in the ground or left in open dumps, some hazardous waste can contaminate air and ground water. Because chemicals can be taken into plants through their roots, hazardous waste can contaminate food crops.

The mishandling or accidental release of hazardous waste has caused a number of disasters around the world. For example, in 1978, hazardous chemicals leaking from a waste disposal site in the Love Canal area of western New York threatened the health of nearby residents. Hundreds of people were forced to abandon their homes. In 1984, a leak of poisonous gas from a pesticide plant in Bhopal, India, killed about 3,000 people and caused serious injuries to about 50,000.

Some hazardous waste can seriously harm the health of people, wildlife, and plants. These pollutants include radiation, pesticides, and heavy metals.

Radiation is an invisible pollutant that can contaminate any part of the environment. Most radiation comes from natural sources, such as minerals and the sun's rays. Scientists can also produce radioactive elements in their laboratories. Exposure to large amounts of radiation can harm cells and result in cancer.

Radioactive waste produced by nuclear reactors and weapons factories poses a potentially serious environmental problem. Some of this waste will remain radioactive, giving off harmful radiation, for thousands of years. The safe storage of radioactive waste is both difficult and expensive.

Pesticides are used to protect plants from weeds, insects, and other unwanted pests. However, they can travel great distances through the environment. When sprayed on crops or in gardens, pesticides can be blown by the wind to other areas. They can also flow with rain water into nearby streams or can seep through the soil into ground water. Some pesticides can remain in the environment for many years and pass from one organism to another. For example, when pesticides are present in a stream, small fish and other organisms can absorb them. Larger fish who eat these contaminated organisms build up even larger amounts of pesticides in their flesh. This process is called *bioaccumulation.*

Heavy metals include cadmium, mercury, and lead. Mining operations, solid waste incinerators, industrial processes, and motor vehicles can all release heavy metals into the environment. Coal-burning power plants can release mercury. Like pesticides, heavy metals are long lasting and can spread through the environment. Also, like pesticides, they can collect in the bones and other tissues of animals. In human beings, heavy metals can damage bones, various internal organs, and the nervous system. Many can also cause cancer.

Noise pollution comes from such machines as airplanes, motor vehicles, construction machinery, and industrial equipment. Noise does not dirty the air, water, or land, but it can cause discomfort, anxiety, and hearing loss in human beings and other animals.

Controlling pollution

Controlling pollution depends on the efforts of governments, scientists, business and industry, agriculture, environmental organizations, and individuals.

Government action. In many countries around the world, governments work to help clean up pollution. Such environmental efforts come from both local and national governments, but they also depend on international cooperation. A number of international groups have been established to protect Earth's resources.

Local efforts. Many local governments have enacted laws to help clean up the environment. For example, in 1989, California adopted a 20-year plan to reduce air pollution in the Los Angeles area, which had the worst air quality in the United States. The plan introduced measures to restrict the use of gasoline-powered vehicles and to encourage the use of mass transportation.

Paul Howell, Gamma/Liaison

A government cleanup project called Superfund works to eliminate unsafe toxic waste dumps in the United States. Inspectors from the Environmental Protection Agency collect mud samples, *shown here,* to check for chemical contamination.

National efforts. Most countries have national pollution control agencies. In the United States, for example, the Environmental Protection Agency (EPA) sets and enforces pollution control standards. It also assists state and local governments with pollution control.

Many national governments pass legislation to help limit and prevent pollution. Some pollution control laws limit or ban the release of pollutants into the environment. In the United States, the Clean Water Act of 1972 and its amendments have reduced the discharge of untreated water and harmful chemicals into rivers and other waterways. The Clean Air Act of 1972 and the Clean Air Act Amendments of 1990 restrict the release of hazardous air pollutants and require measures to control the release of common pollutants such as those that make up urban smog. The Resource Conservation and Recovery Act of 1976 requires that hazardous wastes be specially treated before disposal. The act also requires landfills to be constructed with double liners and collection systems to prevent hazardous chemicals from entering water supplies.

Some pollution prevention laws require that polluters be issued an *emission permit.* Such a permit limits the amount of a pollutant a facility can legally release. The Clean Water Act of 1972 requires facilities releasing pollutants into surface water to do so within the limits of a permit. If a facility releases pollutants without a permit or above the limits of its permit, it may receive a fine or be shut down.

Other laws are designed to clean up pollution. In 1980, for example, the U.S. Congress enacted the Comprehensive Environmental Response, Compensation, and Liability Act. The act, also known as "Superfund," began a government cleanup of hazardous waste dumps in the United States. This law and others hold polluters responsible for repairing the environmental damage they cause.

National governments may also levy taxes on the release of pollutants or substances that create pollution. Beginning in 1990, the United States imposed taxes on the use of CFC's to help phase out their production.

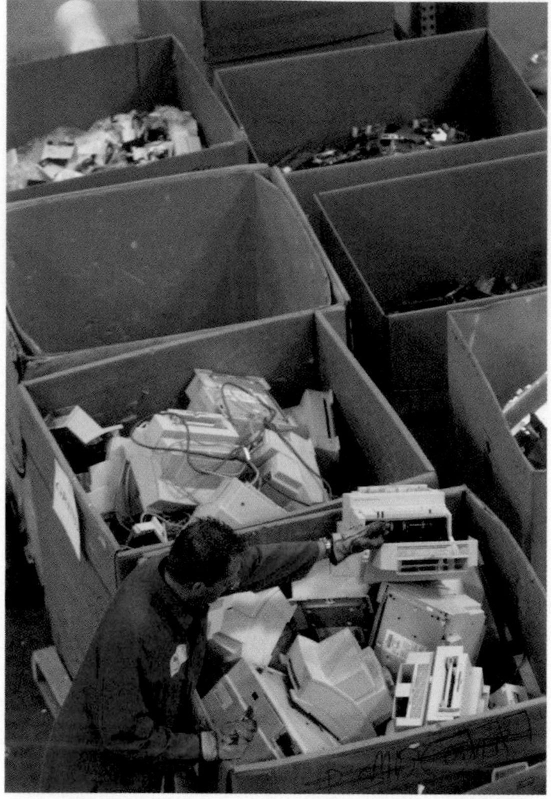

AP/Wide World

Recycling helps prevent pollution by reducing the amount of solid waste that must be dumped or burned. At a computer recycling center, workers remove reusable components and materials from computer equipment cases, which are then crushed.

High taxes gave companies an incentive to develop alternatives to CFC's in their processes. By 1996, the production of CFC's had ended in the United States. High gasoline taxes may encourage people to drive less, to carpool, and to use public transportation, thus reducing air pollution from automobiles.

The forces of a free market can be used to help control pollution. A national government may set a total amount of pollutant emissions allowed over all industries and permit companies to buy or sell emissions credits. For example, 1990 amendments to the Clean Air Act established *tradeable emission credits* for the release of sulfur dioxide from such major sources as power plants. A facility was allowed to release only as much sulfur dioxide as it had credits for. But it could buy credits from a facility whose emissions were so low that it had unused credits. To avoid buying emission credits, many power plant operators decided to burn cleaner fuels or to install pollution control devices.

Some government regulations simply require businesses to tell the public how many pollutants they release into the environment. This type of regulation has caused some companies to find ways to reduce pollution so that consumers do not develop an unfavorable impression of them and perhaps refuse to purchase their products. The Emergency Planning and Community Right-to-Know Act, established in the United States in 1986, is an example of such a regulation.

Global efforts. Pollutants often move across national boundaries. In addition, much pollution occurs in Earth's oceans and atmosphere, which do not belong to any nation or individual. For these reasons, the people of the world must work together to control pollution.

Since the 1970's, representatives of many nations have entered into environmental treaties. The treaties aim to control such problems as acid rain, the thinning of the ozone layer, and the dumping of waste into oceans.

In 1992, representatives of member countries of the United Nations (UN) met in Rio de Janeiro, Brazil, for the UN Conference on Environment and Development, also known as the Earth Summit. UN members signed agreements on the prevention of global warming, the preservation of forests and endangered species, and other issues. In 2002, UN countries met for the World Summit on Sustainable Development, in Johannesburg, South Africa. At that meeting, UN members committed themselves to reversing environmental damage. They set target dates by which to complete the restoration of depleted fisheries and to end the production of certain hazardous chemicals.

In 2001, 127 countries formed a treaty to ban or phase out the use of 12 *persistent organic pollutants* (POP's). These chemicals, which include the pesticide DDT, are carried across national boundaries by air and water, and they threaten the health of human beings and other animals. The treaty is expected to promote cooperation among scientists, industries, and governments to reduce the presence of POP's in the environment.

Scientific efforts. Increasing concern over environmental protection has caused scientists and engineers to look for technological solutions. Some research seeks ways to clean up or manage pollution. Other research aims to prevent pollution. Many industrial researchers are finding more economical ways to use fuels and other raw materials. As a result, some European cities now use waste heat from power plants or trash incinerators to warm homes. New automobile engines burn gasoline much more cleanly and efficiently than older engines. Researchers have also developed automobiles that can use natural gas, which burns more cleanly than does gasoline. In Brazil, some cars use a type of alcohol called *ethanol* as fuel. Scientists are also developing cars that can use hydrogen gas as fuel. Hydrogen creates almost no pollution when it is burned. In addition, an increasing number of cars use electric batteries in addition to—or instead of—fuel-burning engines.

Scientists and engineers are also researching ways to generate electric power more cheaply from such renewable energy sources as the wind and the sun, causing little or no pollution. Large fields of windmills, known as *wind farms,* supply about 1 percent of California's electric power and more than 2 percent of Germany's. Devices called *photovoltaic cells* convert sunlight directly into electric power. Using such cells, a photovoltaic power plant in Sacramento, California, produces enough power for 1,000 homes.

Business and industry. Many companies believe that it makes good business sense to pollute less. Some have found that reducing pollution improves their public image and saves money. Others have met consumer

Environmental do's and don'ts

Reducing environmental pollution will require the efforts of people all over the world. The following illustrations show some of the ways individuals can help protect the environment.

WORLD BOOK illustrations by Yoshi Miyake

Buy sensibly, choosing products with minimal packaging to help reduce solid waste.

Insulate windows and use efficient appliances to conserve energy and reduce air pollution.

Ride a bike or use public transportation to avoid polluting the air with auto exhaust.

Turn off lights and appliances when not in use to save electric power.

Recycle as many different materials as possible instead of throwing them away.

Compost yard trimmings and food waste to keep garbage out of landfills and improve the soil.

Don't pour harmful chemicals down the drain. Take toxic materials to a drop-off center instead.

Don't overheat or overcool your home. Save energy by setting the thermostat appropriately.

demands for environmentally safe products or packaging. Still others develop pollution control systems because they believe that laws will eventually force them to do so anyway. Some companies limit pollution merely because the people running them choose to do so.

In the past, waste disposal was relatively inexpensive for most businesses. Today, however, legal waste disposal sites have become increasingly scarce in many areas. Regulation of certain types of waste has made their continued production extremely costly. As a result, many businesses have found ways to produce less waste or to recycle materials that they use. Manufacturers may use a minimum of packaging and choose packing materials that can be recycled. Lighter and less bulky packaging means distributors use less fuel transporting the products. In addition, the consumer throws out less packaging and creates less garbage.

Many businesses specialize in different types of pollution management. For example, some pollution management firms develop devices that remove harmful particulates from smokestack emissions. Particulates can be captured by filters, by traps that use static electricity, or by devices called *scrubbers* that wash out particulates with chemical sprays.

Other businesses assist companies in following government orders to clean up pollution. Some firms manage recycling or energy conservation programs. Still others help businesses devise less-polluting processes.

Regardless of why or how industries begin to clean up pollution, it is a slow, expensive process. Many businesses rely on the cheapest production methods available, even though such methods pollute. If the cost of cleaning up the pollution created by current production methods is added to manufacturing costs, however, methods that pollute less may prove more economical.

Some businesses work together to reduce their pollution. Waste materials from one industry can be used as a raw material by another industry. For example, a power plant in Kalundborg, Denmark, sells gypsum captured from burning fossil fuels to a nearby wallboard factory. It also sells ash to a cement manufacturer and steam to other nearby factories and homeowners. By sharing materials, industries can reduce pollution and waste while profiting from the exchange of resources. A field of study called *industrial ecology* explores these and similar opportunities related to reducing the impact on the environment from industrial and economic sources.

Agriculture. Scientists and farmers are developing ways to grow food that require less fertilizer and pesticides. Many farmers rotate their crops from year to year to reduce the need for chemical fertilizers. The rotation of corn, wheat, and other crops with legumes, such as alfalfa and soybeans, helps replace nitrogen lost from the soil. Crop rotation also helps control pests and plant diseases. Some farmers use compost and other fertilizers that are less harmful to the soil. Instead of spraying their crops with harmful pesticides, some farmers combat damaging insects by releasing other insects or bacteria that prey upon the pests. Scientists are also developing genetically engineered plants that are resistant to certain pests.

The rotation of crops and the use of natural pest enemies are called *natural pest control.* Combining a limited use of chemical pesticides with natural controls is known as *integrated pest management* (IPM). Farmers using IPM apply chemical pesticides in smaller amounts and only when they will have the most effect.

Environmental organizations attempt to help control pollution by working to influence lawmakers and elect political leaders who care about the environment. Some groups raise money to buy land and protect it from development. Other groups study the effects of pollution on the environment and develop systems for pollution prevention and management. Such groups use their findings to persuade government and industry to prevent or reduce pollution. Environmental organizations also publish materials to persuade people to prevent pollution.

Political parties representing environmental concerns have formed in many industrial nations. These organizations, often known as *Green parties,* have had a growing influence on environmental policies. Countries with active Green parties include Australia, Austria, Germany, Finland, France, New Zealand, Spain, and Sweden.

Individual efforts. One of the most important ways an individual can reduce pollution is by conserving energy. Conserving energy reduces the air pollution created by power plants. Reduced demand for oil and coal might also result in fewer oil spills and less destruction of coal-bearing lands. Driving less is one of the best ways to save energy and avoid polluting the air.

Using more efficient light bulbs and home appliances conserves electric power. For example, a *compact fluorescent lamp* (CFL) or *light-emitting diode* (LED) uses a fraction of the electric power that is used by a traditional incandescent bulb. People can also conserve by using appliances less often, by turning off appliances and lights when not in use, and by setting home thermostats at or below 68 °F (20 °C) in winter and at or above 78 °F (26 °C) in summer. Buildings with specially treated windows and good insulation need less fuel or electric power to heat or cool than do buildings without such materials.

People can also buy products that are safe for the environment. For example, households can help reduce water pollution by using fewer toxic cleaning products and by properly disposing of any toxic products they do use. If consumers refuse to purchase harmful products, manufacturers will stop making them.

Many cities and towns have recycling programs. Recycling saves energy and raw materials, and it prevents pollution. Many different waste products can be recycled. Commonly recycled wastes include metal cans, glass, paper, plastic containers, and old tires. Cans can be melted and used to make new ones. Glass can be ground up and made into new containers or used as a substitute for sand in road pavement. Paper can be reprocessed into different paper products. Plastics can be melted and re-formed into plastic lumber for such uses as fences, decks, and benches. They can also be reused to make carpeting. Old tires can be ground up and added to asphalt or some other adhesive to make roadbeds or such molded products as floor mats and playground equipment.

The most important way people can fight pollution is to learn as much as possible about how their actions affect the environment. Then they can make intelligent choices that will reduce damage to the planet.

History

Human beings have always caused some environmental pollution. Since prehistoric times, people have created waste. Like garbage today, this waste was either burned, tossed into waterways, buried, or dumped aboveground. However, the waste of early peoples was mostly food scraps and other substances that broke down easily by natural decay processes. Prehistoric populations were also much smaller and were spread out over large areas. As a result, pollution was less concentrated and caused few problems.

The growth of pollution started during ancient times when large numbers of people began living together in cities. As cities grew, pollution grew with them. Environmental problems became even more serious and widespread in the 1800's, during a period called the Industrial Revolution. This period was characterized by the development of factories and the overcrowding of cities with factory workers.

During the Industrial Revolution, coal powered most factories. Most city homes also relied on coal as a heating fuel. The burning of coal filled the air with smoke and soot. Poor sanitation facilities also allowed raw sewage to get into water supplies in some cities. The polluted water caused typhoid fever and other illnesses.

In the United States, air pollution problems became particularly serious in the early 1900's. By the 1930's, smoke and soot from steel mills, power plants, railroads, and heating plants filled the air over many Eastern and Midwestern cities. In some industrial cities, such as Pittsburgh, Pennsylvania, and St. Louis, Missouri, pollution frequently became so thick that drivers needed streetlights and headlights to see during the day.

Progress in controlling pollution has gained speed since the 1960's. Nearly all the railroads, industries, and homes of western Europe and the United States have switched from coal to cleaner-burning fuels, such as oil and natural gas. In many other places, pollution controls effectively limit the air pollution created by coal burning. Today, cities in many parts of the world also treat their water and process their sewage, thus reducing the problems caused by harmful bacteria.

Important progress has been made in other areas of pollution management. Industrial waste, sewage, fertilizers, and other contaminants have polluted the Great Lakes since the mid-1800's. By the early 1970's, Lake Erie, Lake Ontario, and shallow regions of Lake Huron and Lake Michigan were so polluted that the waters had turned green and smelled foul, and huge fish kills were common. In 1972, Canada and the United States signed the Great Lakes Water Quality Agreement. Since then, local governments around the lakes have improved sewage treatment plants, controlled the runoff of chemical fertilizers from farms, and worked to reduce the use of phosphate detergents. They have also forced industries to reduce the pollutants they dump into the lakes. Today, the Great Lakes are much cleaner.

Current environmental issues

Current environmental issues include the need to weigh the benefits and risks of pollution controls, and the effects of population growth and of wastefulness in the industrialized world.

Weighing benefits and risks. Increased concern

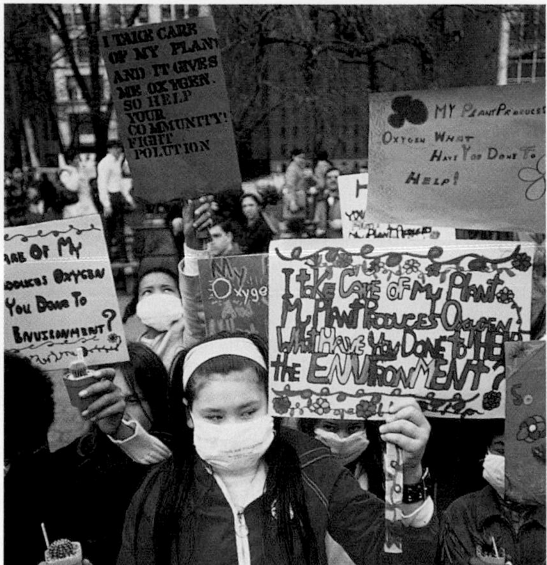

Paul Fusco, Magnum

The first Earth Day was celebrated in April 1970. Its purpose was to increase public awareness of environmental problems.

about the environment has caused people to protest many products and practices. However, few choices are clear cut. It is often difficult to determine the relative risks and benefits to the environment of various products and practices. For example, nuclear power plants generate energy without creating air pollution. In this respect, nuclear power plants are safer for the environment than plants that burn coal, oil, or natural gas. But nuclear plants produce radioactive waste, which is difficult to dispose of safely. And the mining of uranium, a nuclear fuel, can pollute large areas of land and water. Business, environmental groups, and scientists work to determine which products, materials, and processes produce the most pollution.

When creating pollution laws, government officials must consider both the dangers of the pollutant and the possible financial effects of regulation. Regulations often require that an industry purchase pollution control devices, make costly production changes, or discontinue manufacturing certain products. These measures may be expensive, and many believe that such expenses might cause some businesses to fail, creating unemployment. As a result, the effects of certain proposed pollution laws could harm people more than the pollutant would. On the other hand, pollution control measures can also create jobs for the specialists required to implement them. In addition, consumers may be willing to absorb the additional costs of such measures, enabling affected industries to remain profitable.

Effect of population growth. Despite progress in protecting the environment, the problem of pollution has become increasingly widespread and potentially more harmful. The main cause for the increase in pollution is that Earth's population grows larger every day. More people means more waste of every kind. As a result, one of the most important ways to begin controlling environmental pollution is to slow population growth. A reduction in population growth would slow the destruction and give people more time to develop effective pollution control systems.

Most of the world's population growth occurs in the poorest parts of the world, including certain nations in Africa, Asia, and Latin America. In these areas, people use what little resources they have just trying to stay alive. Governments in developing countries struggle to build modern industries and agricultural systems to provide a basic standard of living for their citizens. However, many developing countries use old technology that tends to pollute because they cannot afford modern, efficient machinery. Even if they could afford pollution controls, pollution in the developing world would continue to rise simply because these nations are industrializing. And more industry means more pollution.

Wastefulness in the industrialized world. Many people in Japan and in wealthy North American and European nations have become accustomed to comfortable lifestyles that consume large amounts of energy and raw materials and produce many wastes. A person living in an industrialized nation uses about 10 times the amount of fossil fuels and electric power and produces 2 to 3 times as much municipal waste as a person in a developing country. For a true reduction in pollution, people in the industrialized world would probably have to accept less convenience and luxury in their lives. Solving the problems of global environmental pollution will require the cooperation of governments and industry in all countries, rich and poor, as well as the efforts of individuals all over the world.

Martha E. Richmond

Related articles. See **Air pollution** and **Water pollution** and their lists of *Related articles.* See also:

- Acid rain
- Animal (How human beings endanger animals)
- Chlorofluorocarbon
- City (Physical problems)
- Conservation
- Earth Day
- Ecology
- Energy supply (Environmental pollution)
- Environment
- Environmental Defense Fund
- Environmental impact statement
- Environmental Protection Agency
- Fallout
- Fossil fuel
- Green party
- Hazardous wastes
- Industry (Social costs)
- Landfill
- National park (Changes in the environment)
- Nitrogen (Nitrogen and pollution)
- Nuclear energy
- Nuclear winter
- Ocean (Marine pollution)
- Oil spill
- Ozone
- Ozone hole
- Pest control
- Plastics (Plastics and the environment)
- Radiation
- Radon
- Recycling
- Thermal pollution
- Waste disposal

Outline

I. Types of pollution
- A. Air pollution
- B. Water pollution
- C. Soil pollution
- D. Solid waste
- E. Hazardous waste
- F. Noise pollution

II. Controlling pollution
- A. Government action
- B. Scientific efforts
- C. Business and industry
- D. Agriculture
- E. Environmental organizations
- F. Individual efforts

III. History

IV. Current environmental issues
- A. Weighing benefits and risks
- B. Effect of population growth
- C. Wastefulness in the industrialized world

Questions

How can consumers encourage manufacturers to produce less polluting products?
What causes most air pollution?
What natural processes cleanse water systems?
How does the desire for convenience contribute to environmental pollution?
What are some ways governments work to control environmental pollution?
Why is solid waste difficult to eliminate?
How does population growth contribute to environmental pollution?
What are the hazards and benefits of ozone in Earth's atmosphere?
How can businesses help reduce pollution?
How do pesticides build up in the flesh of certain animals?

Additional resources

Level I
Alper, Ann F. *A Brief Green History of Planet Earth.* PPI Pub., 1995.
Brown, Paul. *Global Pollution.* Raintree, 2003.
Protecting Our Planet. 6 vols. Raintree Steck-Vaughn. 1998. Each volume looks at a different type of pollution.

Level II
Goudie, Andrew. *The Human Impact on the Natural Environment.* 6th ed. Blackwell, 2005.
McNeill, J. R. *Something New Under the Sun: An Environmental History of the Twentieth-Century World.* Norton, 2000.
Stapleton, Richard M., ed. *Pollution A to Z.* 2 vols. Macmillan Reference, 2004.

Environmental Protection Agency (EPA) is an independent agency of the United States government. It was established in 1970 to protect the nation's environment from pollution. Creation of the Environmental Protection Agency brought under single management the functions of a number of federal programs dealing with pollution.

The EPA establishes and enforces environmental protection standards and conducts research on the effects of pollution. It provides grants and technical assistance to states, cities, and other governmental units that seek to prevent pollution. The agency also helps the Council on Environmental Quality develop environmental protection policies and recommend them to the president.

Upon its establishment, the EPA took over a number of programs previously managed by such governmental bodies as the Department of the Interior; the Department of Agriculture; the Department of Health, Education, and Welfare; and the Atomic Energy Commission.

EPA personnel have worked to enforce many important environmental laws, including the Clean Air Act of 1970, the Clean Water Act of 1972, and congressional amendments to those acts, as well as the Resource Conservation and Recovery Act of 1976. The EPA also administers provisions of the Comprehensive Environmental Response, Compensation, and Liability Act of 1980, also called "Superfund." The act has provided billions of dollars of federal funds to clean up hazardous toxic waste sites and to prosecute violators.

Notable accomplishments of the EPA include the banning of such dangerous pesticides as DDT; the removal of lead from paints and gasoline; the phasing out of chlorofluorocarbons (CFC's) used in aerosols; the establishment of efficiency standards for automobiles and appliances; and the reduction of pollutants emitted by oil refineries and chemical plants. Lee Thornton

Enzyme, *EHN zym,* is a molecule that speeds up chemical reactions in all living things. Without enzymes, these reactions would occur too slowly or not at all, and no life would be possible.

All living cells make enzymes, but enzymes are not alive. Enzyme molecules function by altering other molecules. Enzymes combine with the altered molecules to form a complex molecular structure in which chemical reactions take place. The enzyme, which remains unchanged, then separates from the product of the reaction. Enzymes thus serve as *catalysts* (see **Catalysis**). A single enzyme molecule can perform its entire function a million times a minute. The chemical reactions occur thousands or even millions of times faster with enzymes than without them. Most enzymes are proteins. A small number of RNA (ribonucleic acid) molecules also function as enzymes.

The human body has thousands of kinds of enzymes. Each kind does one specific job. Without enzymes, a person could not breathe, see, move, or digest food. Photosynthesis in plants also depends on enzymes.

Many enzymes break down complex substances into simpler ones. Others build complex compounds from simple ones. Most enzymes remain in the cells where they were formed. However, some enzymes work in other places. For example, the pancreas secretes the enzyme *lipase,* which travels to the small intestine to break down fats.

The word *enzyme* comes from two Greek words meaning *in yeast.* Many scientists who studied enzymes during the 1800's investigated reactions caused by yeast enzymes.

An American biochemist, James B. Sumner, was the first person to isolate a pure enzyme in the form of crystals. In 1926, he extracted the enzyme *urease* from beans

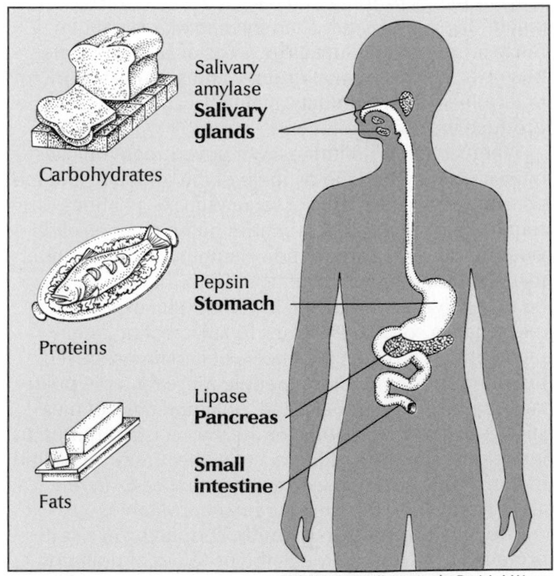

WORLD BOOK illustration by Patricia J. Wynne

Enzymes in the digestive system break down food for use in the body. Each enzyme performs a specific job. For example, *salivary amylase,* an enzyme produced by the salivary glands, splits carbohydrates into simpler chemicals. *Pepsin,* secreted by the walls of the stomach, acts on proteins. *Lipase* is secreted by the pancreas into the small intestine, where it breaks down fats.

and proved that enzymes are protein molecules. In 1969, scientists first chemically synthesized an enzyme, *ribonuclease,* from amino acids. This enzyme breaks down ribonucleic acid into molecules of other amino acids (see **RNA**). Today, scientists are trying to make new synthetic enzymes that carry out reactions not found in nature.

Structure. Enzymes are too tiny to be seen even with the most powerful light microscopes. However, scientists know through various research techniques that enzymes occur in a number of shapes and sizes. Although enzymes of different plants and animals have different protein structures, they function in similar ways. The structure of any particular enzyme enables it to cause chemical reactions in other molecules. Scientists sometimes change the structure of enzyme molecules to study how altered enzymes function or to make enzymes carry out different chemical reactions.

An enzyme's structure can easily be destroyed by heat, acids, or alkalis. Many deadly poisons act by damaging important enzymes. Hereditary diseases may occur in people born without certain enzymes. These diseases include such brain-damaging disorders as *galactosemia* and *phenylketonuria* (PKU). In many cases, tests can detect these enzyme deficiencies. Physicians can sometimes treat them with diet and drugs to prevent deformities, intellectual disability, and even death.

Although most enzymes are proteins, some must be attached to certain nonprotein molecules to function. Many of these nonprotein molecules are metals, such as copper, iron, or magnesium. They occur within the body as *trace elements* (see **Trace elements**). Others are organic compounds called *coenzymes.* If a coenzyme is tightly attached to the protein part of the enzyme, the unit is called a *prosthetic group.* Neither the coenzyme nor the protein part of a prosthetic group can function alone.

Many coenzymes consist of vitamins, especially B vitamins. If a person's diet lacks adequate amounts of these vitamins, the enzymes cannot function properly, and various body disorders may develop. See **Vitamin** (How vitamins work).

Uses. Enzymes have many uses in addition to their natural functions in the body. Manufacturers use enzymes in making a wide variety of products. For example, some detergents contain enzymes that break down protein or fats that cause stains. Enzymes are also used in the manufacture of antibiotics, beer, bread, cheese, coffee, sugars, vinegar, vitamins, and many other products. Physicians use medicines containing enzymes to help clean wounds, dissolve blood clots, relieve certain forms of leukemia, and check allergic reactions to penicillin. Doctors also diagnose some diseases by measuring the amount of various enzymes in blood and other body fluids. Such diseases include anemia, cancer, leukemia, and heart and liver ailments.

In the future, enzymes may be widely used to change raw sewage into useful products. Enzymes also may be used to help get rid of spilled oil that harms lakes and oceans. The enzymes would turn the oil into food for sea plants. Frederick B. Rudolph

Related articles in ***World Book*** include:

Biochemistry	Digestive system	Food preservation
Cell	Fermentation	Pepsin

Eohippus. See **Horse** (Origins of the horse; diagram).

Eon. See **Earth** (Age of Earth).

Eoraptor, *EE oh RAP tuhr,* was one of the earliest dinosaurs. This small creature lived about 230 million years ago in what is now northwestern Argentina. Scientists believe *Eoraptor* is one of the most primitive *theropods,* a group that includes *Tyrannosaurus rex* and other meat-eating dinosaurs.

Eoraptor had a slender body that grew about 3 feet (90 centimeters) long. Like many early dinosaurs, it ran upright on its hind legs, which were more than twice as long as its arms. *Eoraptor's* hands had five fingers, unlike the three-fingered hands of other theropods. However, it used only the three longest fingers on each hand to handle prey. These three fingers ended in large claws. The fourth and fifth fingers were probably too small to be of use.

The only known skeleton of *Eoraptor* was discovered in 1991. The animal lacked most of the specialized features found in later meat-eating dinosaurs. For example, it did not have a joint within its lower jaw that may have helped to hold struggling prey. In addition, not all of its teeth were curved and *serrated* (saw-edged) like those of meat-eaters. *Eoraptor* only had such teeth in the back of its jaw. At the front of the jaw, its teeth were leaf-shaped like those of some plant-eating dinosaurs. *Eoraptor* probably ate small animals, but it also may have eaten plants. James M. Clark

EPA. See **Environmental Protection Agency.**

Ephesians, *ih FEE zhuhnz,* **Epistle to the,** is the 10th book of the New Testament. The book is a letter that claims to have come from the apostle Paul. However, many scholars believe this letter was written in Paul's name by one of his followers. If Paul wrote Ephesians, he did so while in prison, possibly in Rome, about A.D. 60. The first half of Ephesians describes the hope for the unification of all of God's creation in Christ and in the church. The second half urges Christians to live in a manner worthy of this calling.

According to Christian tradition, the letter was addressed to the church in Ephesus, in present-day Turkey. However, the earliest copies of the letter do not mention Ephesus, or any other place. Some scholars believe the letter may have been sent to several churches with the address left blank. The reader of the letter would have then filled in the appropriate name at each destination.

Terrance D. Callan

Ephesus, *EHF ih suhs,* was an ancient Greek city that stood about 35 miles (56 kilometers) south of modern-day İzmir, Turkey. It was founded by colonists from Athens in the early 1000's B.C. The city became famous for its Temple of Artemis, dedicated to the Greek goddess Artemis and considered one of the Seven Wonders of the Ancient World. The temple was built in the 500's B.C. over the remains of a structure from the 600's B.C. During the 500's B.C., the Lydians and then the Persians conquered Ephesus.

The city became an important trading and banking center under the Greeks during the 300's B.C. Later, Ephesus was the capital of the Roman province of Asia. Saint Paul and Saint John helped establish a flourishing Christian church in Ephesus. The city became the leading Christian community of Asia. Ephesus later was looted by the Goths, Arabs, Turks, and finally the Mongols in

A.D. 1403. The city was finally abandoned. Archaeologists uncovered its ruins in the late 1800's.

Donald Kagan

See also **Seven Wonders of the Ancient World; Turkey** (picture).

Ephron, Nora (1941-2012), was an American journalist, essayist, screenwriter, and director. She first gained fame for her fresh and witty magazine essays about modern life. These writings were collected in her first three books—*Wallflower at the Orgy* (1970), *Crazy Salad: Some Things About Women* (1975), and *Scribble, Scribble: Notes on the Media* (1978). Other collections were published as *Nora Ephron Collected* (1991), *I Feel Bad About My Neck* (2006), and *I Remember Nothing* (2010). Her 1983 novel *Heartburn,* the story of a failing marriage, was widely assumed to be based on her relationship with journalist Carl Bernstein, her second husband.

Ephron was born on May 19, 1941, in New York City but raised in Beverly Hills, California, where her parents, Henry and Phoebe Ephron, were screenwriters. Ephron was coauthor of scripts for such films as *Silkwood* (1983) and adapted *Heartburn* into a 1986 movie. Ephron also wrote the screenplay for *When Harry Met Sally* (1989). She co-wrote and directed the films *You've Got Mail* (1998), *Hanging Up* (2000), and *Julie & Julia* (2009). She also directed the films *This Is My Life* (1992), *Sleepless in Seattle* (1993), *Michael* (1996), and *Lucky Numbers* (2000). She wrote the play *Imaginary Friends* (2002). Ephron died on June 26, 2012. Barbara M. Perkins

Epic is a long narrative poem. Almost all epics tell about the heroic deeds of divine beings and people in war or travel. In many epics, the hero is a *demigod,* born of one human parent and one divine parent. Some *cycles* (series) of epic poems developed around a hero or event. Many epics tell how a nation or people began. Some were created by several unknown authors over a long time. Other epics were written by one author.

Epics date back to prehistoric times. The earliest ones were sung by poets who accompanied themselves on a stringed instrument. These epics had no established text. The singers composed each line as they sang it, following the outline of a traditional tale. But every singer memorized certain descriptions, incidents, phrases, and scenes that could be used in making up verses. This method of composition is called *oral formulaic.*

In European literature, epic poetry began with the *Iliad* and the *Odyssey.* Scholars believe that Homer, a blind Greek poet who may have lived during the 700's B.C., composed these two works. Both epics belonged to a cycle of poems based on the partly historical, partly mythical Trojan War. Homer's works served as models for later poets.

Greek and Roman literary critics prescribed rules for epics based on the style of Homer and his most important follower, the Roman poet Virgil. These rules stated that epics must begin *in medias res* (in the middle of things). That is, the story had to begin after much of the action had already taken place. Poets also had to write in a dignified style and begin with an "invocation" in which they asked a Muse for divine inspiration (see **Muses**).

During the Middle Ages, from about A.D. 400 through the 1400's, Greek and Roman epics and their rules were largely forgotten. Poets wrote epics in a more natural style. By the 1600's, the Greek and Roman models had been rediscovered. The English poet John Milton imitated Homer and Virgil in his epic *Paradise Lost* (1667). Beginning in the 1700's, the acceptance of realistic prose fiction, especially novels, helped lead to the decline of epic poetry. Paul B. Diehl

Related articles in *World Book* include:

Aeneid	Mahabharata
Ariosto, Ludovico	Nibelungenlied
Beowulf	Odyssey
Cid, The	Ramayana
Divine Comedy	Roland
Gilgamesh, Epic of	Spenser, Edmund
Iliad	Tasso, Torquato

Epictetus, *EHP ihk TEE tuhs* (A.D. 50?-138?), was a Greek Stoic philosopher. He taught that we should not demand that events happen as we want. We should instead want them to happen as they do. A wise, divine Providence governs all things, so that what seem to be calamities are really parts of a divine plan that orders everything for the best. Epictetus thought that only foolish people are upset by events they cannot control. The true Stoic can face even death and all so-called misfortunes with perfect calm (see **Stoic philosophy**).

Epictetus was born in Asia Minor and was a slave in his youth. He became free, and lived and taught in Rome until A.D. 89, when the Emperor Domitian expelled the philosophers. Epictetus spent the rest of his life teaching in Nicopolis, Greece. S. Marc Cohen

Epicurus, *EHP uh KYUR uhs* (342?-270 B.C.), was a Greek philosopher. His views on pleasure, freedom, and friendship had a great influence in the Greco-Roman world. The word *epicurean* comes from his name.

Epicurus believed the human mind was disturbed by two main anxieties: fear of *deities* (gods and goddesses) and fear of death. He believed both fears could be overcome by the study of physics. Epicurus said that physics proves that the movements of the heavens and meteorological phenomena are caused by the motions of atoms, not by deities. He said deities should not be feared because they are not concerned with human affairs.

Epicurus said that death should not be feared because good and evil lie in sensation, and death ends sensation. According to Epicurus, the soul is made of atoms that disperse at death. Freed from anxieties over death, a person can live a good life by seeking moderate pleasures and avoiding pain. The modern term *epicurean* suggests excessive bodily pleasures, but Epicurus taught that pleasure comes from living with prudence, moderation, courage, and justice, and from friendship.

Epicurus was born on the island of Samos. Except for three letters that summarize his teachings, his philosophy has been reconstructed from fragments of his many works and the poem *On the Nature of Things* (about 50 B.C.) by Lucretius (see **Lucretius**). Carl A. Huffman

Epidaurus, *EHP ih DAWR uhs,* was a small ancient city on the east coast of the Peloponnesus, a large peninsula of southern Greece. Sources mention Epidaurus as early as the 700's B.C. and as late as the A.D. 500's. It is best known for its *sanctuary* (sacred place) of Asclepius, the Greek god of healing (see **Asclepius**). The sanctuary was about 6 miles (10 kilometers) southwest of the city. The ruins of the sanctuary include a temple, a stadium, and many facilities for visitors, including baths and a hotel with 160 rooms. The best preserved of all ancient Greek theaters is also at the site. Built in the 320's B.C., it seats about 14,000 people and has excellent acoustics. See **Drama** (picture: Ancient Greek theaters).

The *cult* (worship) of Asclepius, centered at Epidaurus, reached its height in the 300's B.C. The worshipers of Asclepius believed in the god's healing powers. The temple was built in the 370's B.C. Many inscriptions at the sanctuary say that Asclepius cured sick people while they slept in a special guesthouse. Peter Krentz

Epidemic is an outbreak of disease that attacks many people at about the same time. An epidemic may last a few hours, a few weeks, or a number of years. When a disease exists permanently in a region, it is said to be *endemic.* A disease that spreads throughout the world is *pandemic.* The term *epidemic* traditionally has been used to describe outbreaks of infectious diseases, such as measles, cholera, and influenza. People now often use the term to describe increased incidences of such noninfectious diseases as lung cancer or heart disease. Scientists called *epidemiologists* study epidemics to understand their causes and to stop epidemics from spreading.

Methods of preventing epidemics can sometimes be found before the cause of the disease is known. For example, in the 1850's, English physician John Snow found that many Londoners with cholera obtained their water from a certain pump. He concluded that the water from the pump somehow caused the cholera. When officials closed down the pump, the incidence of cholera dropped. The bacterium that causes cholera, however, was not identified until the 1880's. Researchers studying AIDS during the early 1980's determined that the disease spread through sexual intercourse, through direct contact with infected blood, and from a pregnant woman to her fetus. Therefore, even though HIV, the virus that causes AIDS, had not yet been identified, epidemiologists were able to recommend methods of AIDS prevention, such as the use of condoms during sexual intercourse.

Public health agencies are responsible for the control of epidemics. Immunizations can prevent epidemics of some infectious diseases, such as measles. Other epidemics are prevented by maintaining clean food and water supplies, or by controlling insects and other animals that spread disease. Informing people about the causes of epidemics and methods of prevention is crucial in the control of epidemics. Jane McCusker

See also **Black Death; Plague** (History of plague).

Epidermis. See **Skin.**

Epiglottis. See **Throat.**

Epigram, *EHP uh gram,* is a short, witty poem or pointed saying. Its important features are compression, polish, balance, and clarity. Often in verse form, it is sometimes satirical. The English poet Samuel Taylor Coleridge wrote:

What is an epigram? A dwarfish whole,
Its body brevity, and wit its soul.

For the ancient Greeks, the epigram was a simple and brief inscription for a statue, a building, or a coin, or the epitaph for a tomb. But it changed from its original form and content. The Roman poet Martial developed the sharp and stinging epigram that we know today. Two English poets, Ben Jonson in the 1600's and Alexander Pope in the 1700's, perfected the form.

But epigrams are not always in verse. Popular sayings are really epigrams, as in "It never rains but it pours." H. George Hahn

Epilepsy, *EHP uh LEHP see,* is a brain disorder characterized by sudden attacks, or seizures. This condition is said to exist when an individual has two or more seizures not resulting from infection, injury, a tumor, or other known cause. Doctors believe epileptic seizures occur when nerve cells in the brain suddenly release a large burst of electrical energy. Normally, brain cells produce some electrical energy. This energy flows through the nervous system and activates the muscles. At times, an epileptic patient's brain fails to control this energy release.

Doctors classify epileptic seizures as either *generalized* or *partial.* Generalized seizures affect the whole brain at the same time. Two types of generalized seizures are *grand mal* and *petit mal.* Partial seizures begin in one area of the brain and sometimes spread to other areas. *Psychomotor epilepsy* is one type of partial seizure.

In a grand mal seizure, the most dramatic type of epileptic seizure, the patient suddenly loses consciousness. The person falls unless he or she is supported, and the muscles jerk. Most grand mal seizures last a few minutes, after which the patient goes into a deep sleep.

During a petit mal episode, the patient has a blank look and loses awareness of his or her surroundings for some seconds. The patient may appear confused but does not fall. Many of these episodes are not even noticed. Most petit mal seizures occur in children.

In a psychomotor seizure, the patient acts withdrawn and behaves strangely for a few minutes. The patient may roam around the room or tug at his or her clothes.

A person with epilepsy can have a seizure at any time of the day or night. Some patients have frequent attacks, but others rarely have them. Seizures seem to occur for no apparent reason, but fatigue and emotional stress can make them occur more often. In most cases, the first seizure occurs during childhood.

Scientists do not know what causes most cases of epilepsy. Some types are caused by defects in *genes,* the microscopic units of heredity. Epilepsy is not contagious. About 0.5 percent of all the people in the world have epilepsy.

Doctors treat epilepsy with drugs that either reduce the number of seizures or prevent them entirely. In certain cases, special diets have also been helpful. In cases where only one area of the brain triggers epileptic attacks, surgical removal of that area can lead to a complete cure. Most people with epilepsy can lead normal lives. The earlier treatment begins, the better the results.
Marianne Schuelein

See also **Electroencephalograph.**

Epinephrine, *ehp uh NEHF rihn,* is a hormone that is secreted by the adrenal glands. It is also called *adrenalin.* Epinephrine helps the body adjust to sudden stress. When a person becomes angry or frightened, the adrenal glands release large amounts of epinephrine into the blood. The hormone causes changes in the body to make it more efficient for "fight or flight." For example, epinephrine increases the strength and rate of the heartbeat and raises the blood pressure. In addition, epinephrine speeds up the conversion of glycogen into glucose, which provides energy to the muscles.

Epinephrine can be extracted from the adrenal glands of animals or it can be chemically synthesized. The drug stimulates the heart and relaxes muscles in the *bronchioles,* the small air passages in the lungs. Doctors use epinephrine to treat severe allergic reactions and to restore the heartbeat in patients who are suffering cardiac arrest. Epinephrine was once widely used to treat asthma attacks, but doctors now usually treat asthma with drugs that do not excite the heart. Eugene M. Johnson, Jr.

Epiphany, *ih PIHF uh nee,* is a Christian festival. In Roman Catholic and Protestant churches, it commemorates the adoration of the infant Jesus by the Three Wise Men who had come from the East. In Eastern churches, it celebrates the baptism of Jesus. *Epiphany* comes from a Greek word that means *to appear* or *to show oneself.*

Most Christians celebrate Epiphany on January 6. Roman Catholics in the United States observe the festival on any Sunday from January 2 through January 8. During Epiphany in Western churches, Biblical texts are read in church that describe the various appearances of Jesus. In Eastern churches, the major observance is the blessing of baptismal water. Jill Raitt

See also **Twelfth Night.**

Epiphyte, *EHP uh fyt,* also called *air plant,* is any plant that grows on another plant but makes its own food. Most plants send roots into the soil and use them to get the moisture and chemicals they need for growth. But epiphytes take most of the moisture and raw materials they need for food directly from the air or from plant debris accumulated around their roots. Epiphytes have no underground roots. Some of them receive moisture from the air through their leaves. Others have fleshy roots that dangle in the air to extract moisture from it.

Epiphytes are not parasitic plants. Parasitic plants fasten themselves to other plants and injure their hosts by feeding on their juices and tissues (see **Parasite**). But epiphytes may harm the plants they live on if they grow so abundantly as to deprive the host plants of light and air. Some take salts from the decaying bark of the trees upon which they live. Many epiphytes do not need to live on living plants. They thrive attached to stones, buildings, or timbers.

Some epiphytes are found in *temperate* (mild) and cold climates, but most grow in tropical forests. Temperate epiphytes include such small, inconspicuous plants as certain mosses and liverworts. Spanish moss is a well-known epiphyte of the southern United States. The largest and most beautiful of the epiphytes live in tropical rain forests. The most common epiphytes include aroids, bromeliads, ferns, and orchids. These plants may grow on any part of a tree but survive best on the trunk, in forks of limbs, and on large branches.

Thomas B. Croat

Epiphytes grow on other plants, especially trees. Some epiphytes, such as Spanish moss, *shown here,* hang from branches.

Related articles in *World Book* include:

Bromeliad	Lichen	Monstera	Orchid
Fern	Liverwort	Moss	Spanish moss

Episcopal Church, *ih PIHS kuh puhl,* is a Christian church based in the United States. It makes up a *province* (administrative district) of the Anglican Communion, a global association of churches that includes the Church of England and churches that developed from it. The Episcopal Church has more than 2 million members.

Bishops, priests, and deacons, together with some members of the *laity* (regular church members), lead the church. Every three years, all active bishops plus elected clerical and lay representatives meet as a two-house governing body at the church's General Convention. Between conventions, an elected Executive Council carries out the General Convention's policies and programs. The church is divided into about 100 *dioceses* (regional districts). A bishop heads each diocese.

The Episcopal Church began in the early 1600's among members of the Church of England who settled in the American Colonies. In 1789, after the American Revolution, the Episcopal Church was founded as an independent church. Episcopalians have held many positions of political and social power in U.S. history. Today, the church's membership is socially diverse. The Episcopal Church maintains the Washington National Cathedral in Washington, D.C.

The Episcopal Church has been a leader in allowing women to join the clergy. The church began ordaining women as priests in the 1970's. In 1989, it ordained the first female bishop in the Anglican Communion. In 2006, the Episcopal Church elected the first woman to serve as presiding bishop of an Anglican province.

In 2012, the Episcopal Church approved a religious ceremony for blessing committed same-sex relationships. It became the largest U.S. denomination to do so.

Christopher A. Beeley

See also **Anglican Communion.**

Episcopalians. See **Anglican Communion; Episcopal Church.**

Epistle, *ih PIHS uhl,* can refer to any letter to a person or a group. But the word usually describes a letter that is formal and serious in tone, impersonal, and instructive.

The term *epistle* is particularly associated with 21 books of the New Testament. The Roman orator and statesman Cicero wrote epistles on subjects ranging from politics to philosophy. More than 800 of his letters have survived and remain a major source for the study of Roman history and thought. A number of poets have used the epistle form for their verses. The Roman poet Horace composed many verse epistles between 20 and 8 B.C. The English poet Alexander Pope imitated Horace in such satirical poems as "An Epistle to Dr. Arbuthnot" (1735) and "An Epistle to Augustus" (1737). Pope's verse epistles gained a new popularity for the form during the

1700's. Epistolary novels such as Samuel Richardson's *Pamela* (1740) and Alice Walker's *The Color Purple* (1982) take the form of letters exchanged between fictional characters. William H. Epstein

For a list of articles on New Testament epistles, see the *Related articles* in **Bible**. See also **Pope, Alexander.**

Epithelioma, *EHP uh THEE lee OH muh,* is any tumor of the *epithelium,* the tissue that lines the body cavities and covers the body surface and the internal organs. These tumors may be either benign or malignant. However, most doctors use the term *epithelioma* to denote *basal cell carcinoma,* a common skin cancer. Such a cancer often begins as a small sore that will not heal. But sometimes it will seem to heal over and then reappear. These tumors may be caused by prolonged exposure to the sun, X rays, or by materials containing tars or arsenic. Unlike most cancers, malignant epitheliomas usually do not spread to other parts of the body. They can be cured by surgery. Martin D. Abeloff

Epithelium, *EHP uh THEE lee uhm,* is one of the major kinds of tissue formed in the bodies of human beings and some animals. It covers the body surface and lines the channels of the body that have openings to the outside. For example, the respiratory tract, alimentary tract, and the urinary tract are lined with epithelium.

Three types of cells make up the epithelium. They are the *squamous, cuboidal,* and *columnar* cells. These cells are differentiated by their shape. The squamous cells are thin and scalelike. They have irregular edges. These cells make up the tissue that covers the body surface and lines the mouth and esophagus. Cuboidal cells look like tiny cubes. They are almost as tall as they are broad. These cells line some of the body cavities and are found in many of the glands. Columnar cells resemble columns. They are much taller than they are broad. Tissue made up of these cells lines the stomach and intestines, and the innermost layer of the *epidermis* (skin). A form of columnar epithelium equipped with cilia lines the respiratory passages. Paul R. Bergstresser

See also **Epithelioma.**

Epsom salt, *EHP suhm,* is a white powder that in the past was commonly used as a laxative. It was also mixed with water to make a solution for soaking *inflamed* (red and swollen) body parts. Epsom salt is now rarely used.

As a laxative, Epsom salt prevents the *bowels* (intestines) from absorbing water. The water creates bulk, causing the bowels to discharge their contents. Epsom salt should not be taken frequently because it interferes with the absorption of food materials. It should never be taken when there is abdominal pain.

Epsom salt is a powder form of the chemical magnesium sulfate. It is named for the springs in Epsom, England, where it was first obtained. Brian V. Reed

Epstein, *EHP styn,* **Sir Jacob** (1880-1959), was an American-born sculptor who spent most of his life in London and became a major figure in British sculpture. Epstein worked mainly in bronze and stone. Most of his sculpture has recognizable subject matter that is modified by his own individual style. At first, Epstein's sculpture aroused hostile criticism. But later in his life, his work became more popular.

Much of Epstein's early work, such as *The Rock Drill* (1913), was influenced by primitive art. Many of his human figures are long and thin with coarse surfaces and have a tormented appearance. Many of his public commissions are devoted to religious themes. Epstein also executed many portraits that are noted for their emotional emphasis and rough surfaces. Examples include *Albert Einstein* (1933) and *Lord Russell* (1953).

Epstein was born in New York City on Nov. 10, 1880, and moved to London in 1905. He became a British subject in 1910, and Queen Elizabeth II knighted him in 1954. Sir Jacob died on Aug. 19, 1959. Joseph F. Lamb

Epstein-Barr virus, *EHP styn BAHR,* often called EBV, is a type of herpesvirus that causes infectious mononucleosis. EBV infects white blood cells called *B lymphocytes* and reproduces in mucous membranes, especially in the throat. Most people will become infected with EBV during their lives. Infection with EBV before age 15 usually causes no symptoms, or a mild flulike illness. Infection during adolescence or early adulthood usually causes infectious mononucleosis. Like other herpesviruses, EBV can persist in the body for years, alive but dormant, and later become activated.

The virus was first isolated by British scientists M. Anthony Epstein, Yvonne M. Barr, and Bert G. Achong in 1964. Scientists have linked the virus to a type of cancer called *Burkitt's lymphoma,* and to cancers of the nose and throat among certain populations. Nelson M. Gantz

See also **Herpesvirus; Mononucleosis.**

Equal Employment Opportunity Commission (EEOC) is a United States government agency. It enforces laws that prohibit job discrimination because of race, color, religion, sex, national origin, age, or disability. These laws include the Equal Pay Act of 1963; Title VII of the Civil Rights Act of 1964; the Age Discrimination in Employment Act of 1967; sections of the Rehabilitation Act of 1973; Titles I and IV of the Americans with Disabilities Act of 1990; and the Civil Rights Act of 1991. The commission investigates complaints of job discrimination by public and private employers, labor unions, and employment agencies. If an investigation shows reasonable cause to believe that discrimination has occurred, the EEOC works to help negotiate a settlement. If negotiations fail, the EEOC may sue in federal court.

The EEOC was set up under the Civil Rights Act of 1964 and began operating in 1965. The Equal Employment Opportunity Act of 1972 broadened its powers.

Critically reviewed by the Equal Employment Opportunity Commission

See also **Civil Rights Act of 1964.**

Equal Rights Amendment is a proposed amendment to the United States Constitution calling for equal treatment of men and women. It reads: "Equality of rights under the law shall not be denied or abridged by the United States or any state on account of sex."

The amendment, often called the ERA, was first introduced in Congress in 1923 through the efforts of the National Woman's Party. This party, led by Alice Paul, worked for equality for women. In 1972, after years of nationwide controversy involving state labor laws, Congress passed the ERA. But to become law, a constitutional amendment must also be *ratified* (approved) by the legislatures of three-fourths of the states.

Congress required that the ERA, like most amendments passed by Congress since the early 1900's, be ratified within seven years. Supporters of the amendment had until March 22, 1979, to obtain ratification by 38 states. But in 1978, Congress voted to extend that deadline until June 30, 1982. By the 1982 deadline, only 35 of the necessary 38 states had ratified the amendment. Since 1983, the ERA has been reintroduced in Congress a number of times, but it has not been passed.

Critics of the amendment argue that the Constitution already guarantees equal rights to women. They claim the ERA would *undermine,* or weaken, the institution of marriage, require women to register for the military draft, and outlaw protective labor legislation. Supporters of the ERA, including the National Organization for Women (NOW), argue that the amendment would not affect personal relationships within marriage. Supporters also argue that, despite the guarantees of the Constitution, women do not always receive equal treatment in education and in the workplace. Passage of the ERA would make unconstitutional all state and local laws that discriminate on the basis of sex.

Melanie S. Gustafson

See also **National Organization for Women; Paul, Alice; Schlafly, Phyllis Stewart; Sex discrimination; Women's movement** (Legal gains).

Equator is the great circle of Earth that lies halfway between the North and South poles. This imaginary line divides Earth into two equal parts called the Northern Hemisphere and the Southern Hemisphere. It is the starting point for the degrees of latitude that measure distances north and south from the equator to the poles (see **Latitude**). The latitude of the equator is zero. On a globe, the equator is also a line on which equal distances are marked to show degrees of longitude, which measures east and west distances (see **Longitude**). The circumference of Earth at the equator is 24,901.55 miles (40,075.16 kilometers). Each degree of longitude at the equator equals 69.17 miles (111.32 kilometers).

The location of the equator can be determined by observing the elevation of the North Star or the sun above the horizon. Allowing for slight corrections, the angle of elevation of the North Star at any given place equals the latitude of that place. Thus, at the equator, the North Star is barely visible above the horizon and has an elevation of nearly zero degrees.

The equatorial climate. The climate along the equator varies according to altitude and the distance from the sea. In most equatorial lowlands, heavy rains and average temperatures are uniform all year. However, the east coast of Africa has only light rain and a long dry season. Quito, Ecuador, which lies almost exactly on the equator, has an elevation of 9,350 feet (2,850 meters). Quito has a uniform temperature that is about 25 Fahrenheit degrees (14 Celsius degrees) cooler than nearby lowlands.

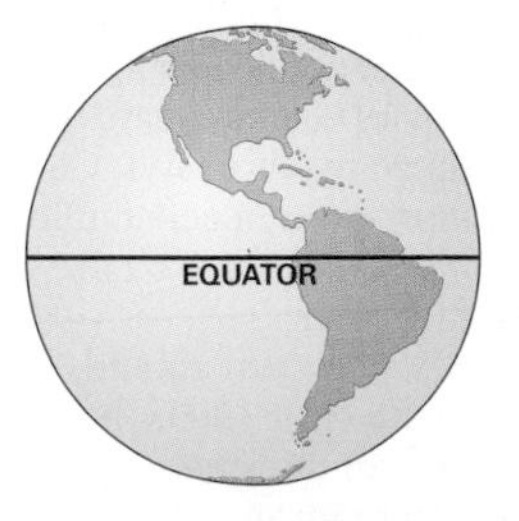

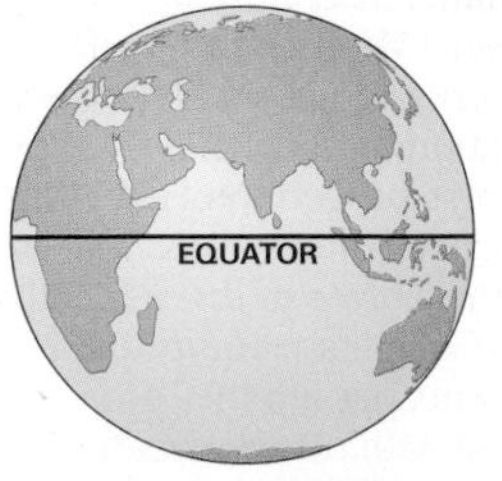

WORLD BOOK maps

The equator circles Earth.

The celestial equator is an imaginary circle that goes around the sphere in which Earth and heavenly bodies lie. It helps locate stars and planets. See **Astronomy** (Locating objects in space).

The magnetic equator is an irregular imaginary line near the geographic equator. At any point on the magnetic equator, a magnetized needle balances horizontally. See **Magnetic equator.** Paul R. Bierman

Equatorial Guinea, *GIHN ee,* is a small country in western Africa. It consists of a territory on Africa's west coast, plus five offshore islands. The territory, Río Muni, lies between Cameroon and Gabon. The largest island, Bioko (formerly Fernando Po), is in the Gulf of Guinea, about 100 miles (160 kilometers) northwest of Río Muni. The other islands—Corisco, Elobey Chico, Elobey Grande, and Annobón—are southwest of Río Muni. Malabo is the nation's capital. Bata is the largest city.

Equatorial Guinea became independent in 1968. It had been ruled by Spain since the mid-1800's.

Government. A president, elected by the people to a seven-year term, is the most powerful official in Equatorial Guinea. A House of People's Representatives makes the country's laws. The people elect its members to five-year terms.

People. About 80 percent of Equatorial Guinea's people live in Río Muni. Most people in Río Muni belong to the Fang ethnic group. The Fang are closely related to the people of Cameroon and Gabon. Most people of Bioko belong to the Fernandino or Bubi ethnic groups.

Most of the people who live in Equatorial Guinea's rural areas are farmers. Others fish or work in lumber camps for a living. Many of the urban people work in small industries or in import-export activities.

Spanish and French are the official languages of Equatorial Guinea. Spanish is used in government and commerce and in the country's schools. The most widely spoken African language is Fang. Roman Catholicism is

WORLD BOOK maps

Equatorial Guinea

International boundary
Road
Railroad
National capital
Other city or town
Elevation above sea level

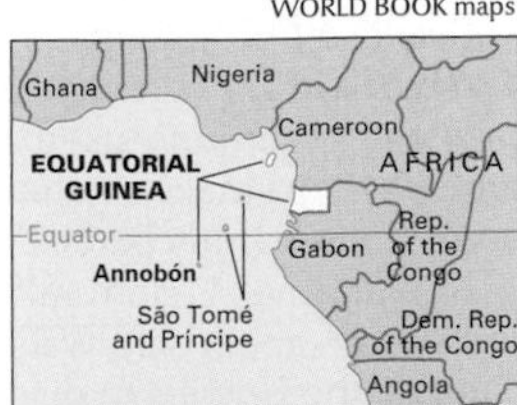

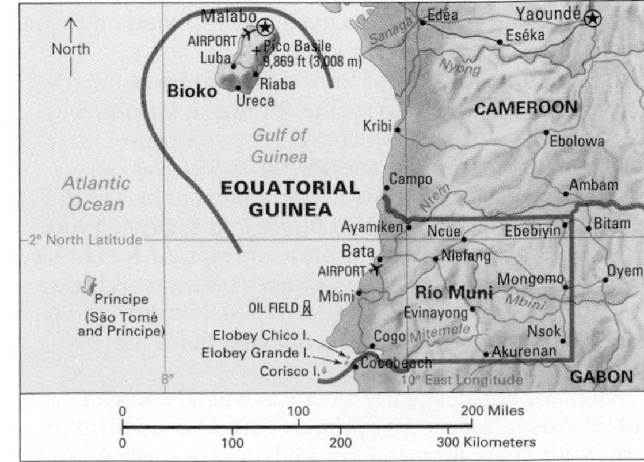

Facts in brief

Capital: Malabo.
Official languages: Spanish and French.
Official name: República de Guinea Ecuatorial (Republic of Equatorial Guinea).
Total land area: 10,831 mi² (28,051 km²).
Elevation: *Highest*—Pico Basile, 9,869 ft (3,008 m). *Lowest*—sea level along the coast.
Population: *Estimated 2014 population*—780,000; density, 72 per mi² (28 per km²); distribution, 60 percent rural, 40 percent urban.
Chief products: Bananas, cacao, cassava, coffee, natural gas, petroleum, sweet potatoes, timber.
Flag: The flag has green, white, and red horizontal stripes, and a blue triangle at the staff. The national coat of arms is on the white stripe. See **Flag** (picture: Flags of Africa).
National anthem: "Caminemos pisando la senda de nuestra inmensa felicidad" ("Let's walk down the path of our immense happiness").
Money: *Basic unit*—CFA franc. CFA stands for Coopération Financière en Afrique Centrale (Financial Cooperation in Central Africa).

the most widespread religion in Equatorial Guinea. Most of the people are Catholics.

The law requires children in Equatorial Guinea to go to school until the age of 12. However, many do not attend because of a shortage of teachers. The National University of Equatorial Guinea is in Malabo.

Limited health service is a major problem. The nation has only a few physicians, and the lack of health care has caused malaria, measles, and other diseases to spread.

Land and climate. Dense tropical rain forests cover much of Equatorial Guinea, but plains line the coasts of Río Muni and Bioko. Crops of bananas, *cacao* (beans from which cocoa is made), and coffee beans thrive in the rich volcanic soil of Bioko. The soil of Río Muni is poor for agriculture, but coffee is grown in the territory, and wood from Río Muni's forests is used for lumber.

Equatorial Guinea has a hot, humid climate. Temperatures average higher than 80 °F (27 °C). The annual rainfall varies from 76 inches (193 centimeters) in Malabo to 430 inches (1,090 centimeters) in Ureca.

Economy of Equatorial Guinea is based chiefly on oil and natural gas production. Large oil and gas deposits were discovered near Bioko in the mid-1990's. Since then, Equatorial Guinea's economy has grown rapidly. Petroleum accounts for most of the country's exports.

Agriculture and forestry are also important to the nation's economy. The main food crops include bananas, cassava, and sweet potatoes. Equatorial Guinea produces much cacao for export. Most of the cacao comes from Bioko. The okoumé tree, used to make plywood, is the country's most important timber tree. The country has some food-processing plants and sawmills, but little manufacturing. It also has many undeveloped mineral resources, such as gold, iron, and manganese.

The chief ports include Bata, Luba, Malabo, and Mbini. Malabo has an international airport. The government operates radio and television stations.

Equatorial Guinea exports more than it imports. In addition to petroleum and cacao, the country exports chemicals and timber. Equatorial Guinea imports machinery, petroleum products, and transportation equipment. The country's important trade partners include China, Spain, and the United States.

History. Pygmies were probably the earliest people who lived in what is now Río Muni. They inhabited the area before the 1200's. Various ethnic groups, including the Benga, Bubi, and Fang, then occupied the Río Muni area until the 1700's. Bubi from the mainland settled on Bioko during the 1200's. They were the first people to live on the island. The Portuguese landed on Annobón in 1471. They later claimed Annobón, Bioko, and part of the mainland coast. Spain gained control of these territories in the mid-1800's and made them a colony in 1959.

Equatorial Guinea became an independent nation on Oct. 12, 1968. Later that year, Francisco Macías Nguema took control of the government as president and dictator. In 1970, he dissolved all political parties and formed a single organization to replace them. During the 1970's, most of Macías's political opponents fled the country or were imprisoned or killed. In 1979, army officers led by Lieutenant Colonel Teodoro Obiang Nguema Mbasogo overthrew Macías and set up a military government with Obiang as president. In 1989, Obiang won a presidential election in which only his party was allowed. A new constitution providing for a multiparty system was adopted in 1991. In 1996, 2002, and 2009, Obiang was reelected president. Opposition candidates called all three elections fraudulent. Florence Bernault

See also **Malabo.**

Equatorial Islands. See **Line Islands.**

Equestrian order, *ih KWEHS tree uhn,* was a class of prominent citizens in ancient Rome. Most of the order's members were aristocrats. Originally, they served in the cavalry of the Roman legions. The members were called *equites* (pronounced *EHK wuh teez),* a Latin word meaning *horsemen* or *knights.* The order's military significance declined as more effective cavalry was recruited from among Rome's allies. But the equites retained their political, social, and economic importance.

In the 100's B.C., the equestrian order expanded, and many nonaristocrats were admitted to it. Over time, the increasing power of the order reduced that of the Roman Senate. The equites gained control of important courts that could try senators. They also engaged in business activities from which senators were excluded.

Although the equites sometimes opposed the Senate, they belonged to the same level of Roman society as the senators. They intermarried with senatorial families and shared the interests and attitudes of most senators. During the Roman Empire, equites were appointed to high civil and military offices, including viceroy of Egypt and commander of the Praetorian Guard. D. Brendan Nagle

Equestrian sports. See **Horse** (Horse shows and sports).

Equilibrium, in physics. See **Gravity, Center of; Lever; Statics.**

Equilibrium, *EE kwuh LIHB ree uhm,* **Chemical,** is a state of balance between a pair of *forward* and *reverse* chemical reactions. A double arrow in a chemical equation such as the one below indicates equilibrium. At equilibrium, the rate of the forward reaction (left to right in the equation) is equal to the rate of the reverse reaction (right to left).

$$N_2 + 3H_2 \rightleftharpoons 2NH_3$$

In the forward reaction illustrated by the above equation, nitrogen, N_2, is combining with hydrogen, H_2, to form ammonia, NH_3. In the reverse reaction illustrated by the equation, ammonia is breaking up into nitrogen and hydrogen. At equilibrium, the concentrations of the various substances do not change. In general, temperature and pressure affect the concentrations of chemicals in an equilibrium mixture. Peter A. Rock

Equinox, *EE kwuh nahks,* is either of the two moments each year when the sun is directly above Earth's equator. On the days of the equinoxes, all places on Earth receive approximately 12 hours of sunlight. The term *equinox* comes from a Latin word meaning *equal night.*

The equinoxes occur on March 19, 20, or 21 and on September 22 or 23. In the Northern Hemisphere, the March equinox marks the start of spring and is often called the *vernal equinox.* The position of the vernal equinox is called the *first point of Aries.* The word *vernal* means *of spring.* The September equinox marks the beginning of autumn and is called the *autumnal equinox.* The seasons are reversed in the Southern Hemisphere.

The time interval from the March equinox to the September equinox is longer than that between the September equinox and the next March equinox. This difference results from Earth's *elliptical* (oval-shaped) orbit around the sun. Earth moves faster in its orbit when it is closer to the sun. The distance between Earth and the sun is shortest in January. Therefore, Earth completes the semicircle from the September equinox to the March equinox faster than it does the opposite semicircle.

Astronomers also use the term *equinox* for either of two imaginary points where the sun's apparent path among the stars crosses the *celestial equator,* an imaginary line through the sky directly over the equator.

The positions of the two equinoctial points do not remain the same from year to year. They shift westward extremely slowly—about 1 degree every 70 years. This gradual movement of the points, called the *precession of the equinoxes,* is caused by a slight change in the direction of Earth's axis of rotation. The change results mainly from the gravitational pull of the moon and the sun on Earth's equatorial bulge. Lee J. Rickard

See also **Solstice.**

Equity, *EHK wuh tee,* in law, usually refers to a set of rules developed from broad principles of reason and justice. The rules became important in England during the Middle Ages (about A.D. 400 through the 1400's). They replaced English common law in cases in which following common law would have produced an unfair judgment. Equity was later adopted in the United States, Canada, and many other countries. The term *equity* comes from a Latin word meaning *even* or *fair.*

Equity allows the law to adjust to the circumstances of a case. For example, a person may borrow money and give the lender a *mortgage* (claim on the borrower's property) as security. The borrower agrees to repay the loan by a certain date and to forfeit the mortgaged property if the loan is not repaid on time. Normally, a court would enforce the agreement. Sometimes, however, the value of the property greatly exceeds that of the loan. In such cases, the court may use principles of equity to order the property sold. If the court orders the property sold, the debt and the court costs are paid from the proceeds and the rest of the money is returned to the borrower. This result is fairer than the borrower's forfeiture of the total value of the property.

Equity came into use in England because the English courts had applied common law so strictly that injustices were created in many cases. In some cases, a party to the lawsuit asked the king to step in and provide relief by judging the case according to broad principles of justice rather than to the strict letter of the law. A minister of the king called the *chancellor* reviewed petitions to hear such cases. The chancellor eventually became head of a court of equity called the Court of Chancery.

The Court of Chancery and other courts of equity differed from England's courts of common law. The courts of common law used juries, but the courts of equity did not. The two kinds of courts also had different powers. Courts of common law could only award compensation for damages after an injury was done. Courts of equity could also issue *injunctions,* which required one or more persons to do, or not to do, something.

In England, the Court of Chancery was once the highest court next to the House of Lords. But from 1873 to 1875, new laws merged the Court of Chancery with the common law courts to form the High Court of Justice.

Many U.S. states once had both courts of equity and *courts of law.* But in most of these states today, the two kinds of courts have been merged into one court called

WORLD BOOK map

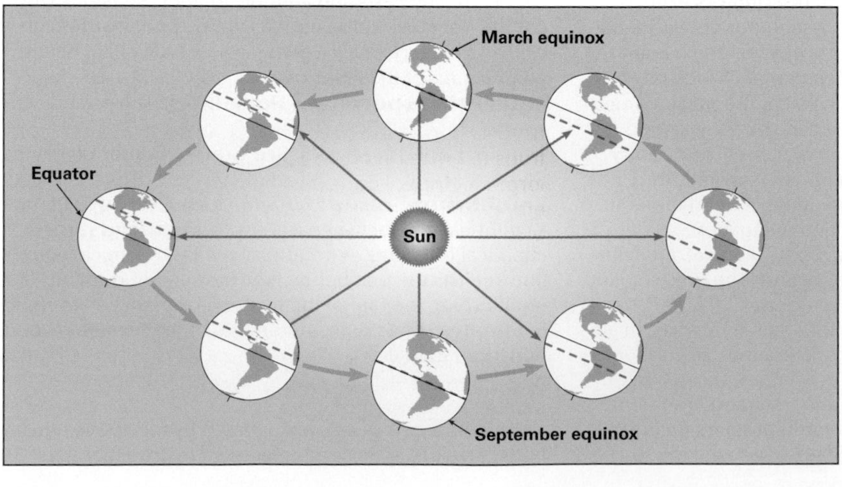

March equinox
Equator
Sun
September equinox

The equinoxes are the two moments of the year when the sun is directly above the equator. As Earth moves in its orbit around the sun, the position of the sun changes in relation to the equator, as shown in this map by the dotted lines. The sun appears north of the equator between the March equinox and the September equinox. It is south of the equator between the September equinox and the next March equinox.

a court of law. Unlike a suit in common law, where the case may be tried before a jury, a suit in equity is tried before a judge. A court of equity will rarely try a criminal case. In some states, an unmerged court of equity is called a *court of chancery,* and its presiding judge is called a *chancellor.* Federal equity courts and federal law courts in the United States have also been merged.

The term *equity* has special meanings in bookkeeping, taxation, and real estate law. For information on these types of equity, see **Bookkeeping; Mortgage;** and **Taxation** (Principles of taxation). Michael J. Bushbaum

See also **Common law; Injunction.**

ERA. See **Equal Rights Amendment.**

Eraser is a device for removing marks from paper or some other surface. Pencil erasers remove pencil marks by rubbing. Most pencil erasers are made of soft rubber that crumbles gradually when used. A compound called *gum eraser* crumbles more easily and is used on surfaces easily damaged by rubbing. Ink erasers contain powdered pumice or a similar material that removes some of the paper, exposing a clean surface. Some inks can be removed with erasing fluids. Erasing fluids may consist of a bleach called *hypochlorite* and an acid applied in succession, and then removed by blotting.

Chalkboard erasers remove chalk marks by wiping. Most such erasers are made of strips of felt attached to a stiff backing. Erasers for *dry-erase boards* are made of nylon or other synthetic fibers. Dry-erase boards are nonporous, and special markers are used to write or draw on them. The marks become a dust that is attracted to the eraser. Critically reviewed by Sanford

Erasmus, *ih RAZ muhs,* **Desiderius,** *DEHZ ih DEER ee uhs* (1466?-1536), was a Dutch priest and scholar who sought to reform the Roman Catholic Church. At first, he supported the German theologian Martin Luther and other leaders of the Reformation, the movement that gave birth to Protestantism. These leaders opposed the corruption and dogmatism they and Erasmus saw in the church. But Erasmus, believing in the unity of Christianity, refused to endorse the creation of a separate church. He tried but failed to create a humane middle ground in the fierce conflict between Catholics and Protestants.

Erasmus was born in Rotterdam, the Netherlands. He was ordained a priest in 1492. In 1499, he visited England and met scholars John Colet and Thomas More. They persuaded him to focus on Biblical studies.

In his *Handbook of a Christian Soldier* (1503), Erasmus presented what he called the *philosophy of Christ,* which stressed piety, morality, and dedication to truth. In his satire *The Praise of Folly* (1511), he criticized the clergy for neglecting these values and instead emphasizing ceremonies and the letter of the law. Erasmus's 1516 edition of the New Testament in Greek made the original text available for the first time. He died on July 12, 1536. Jill Raitt

Eratosthenes, *ehr uh TAHS thuh neez* (276?-195? B.C.), was a Greek mathematician. He found a way of measuring the distance around Earth without leaving northern Africa, where he lived. Eratosthenes also developed the *Sieve of Eratosthenes*—a method of identifying prime numbers (see **Sieve of Eratosthenes**).

Eratosthenes was born in Cyrene, a Greek town in northern Africa. Like other Greek scientists of his time, he knew that Earth was round. He observed that shadows at noon grew shorter as he got closer to the equator. He also knew that at noon on the day of the summer solstice in Alexandria, Egypt, a vertical post casts a shadow. But at noon in Syene, a town to the south, a vertical post casts no shadow. Eratosthenes based his calculation on geometry. He measured the angle formed by the post and an imaginary line from the end of the shadow to the top of the post. Treating the sun's rays as parallel, he could assume that the measured angle equaled the angle formed at Earth's center by imaginary lines from the two towns. He then calculated Earth's circumference by measuring the distance between Alexandria and Syene, multiplying it by the number of times the angle at Earth's center goes into 360°. His measurement of Earth's polar circumference was between 28,000 and 29,000 miles (45,000 and 47,000 kilometers). The actual value is 24,860 miles (40,008 kilometers). Judith V. Grabiner

Erbium, *UR bee uhm* (chemical symbol, Er), is one of the lanthanide metals. Its *atomic number* (number of protons in its nucleus) is 68. It has a *relative atomic mass* of 167.259. An element's relative atomic mass equals its *mass* (amount of matter) divided by $\frac{1}{12}$ of the mass of carbon 12, the most abundant form of carbon. Erbium has six known relatively stable *isotopes,* atoms with the same number of protons but different numbers of neutrons. The Swedish scientist Carl Mosander discovered it in 1843. Erbium occurs with the heavier lanthanides, such as europium and gadolinium, chiefly in the yttrium minerals. Erbium of high purity is available commercially. The metal is grayish-silver. It melts at 1529 °C and boils at 2868 °C. It has a density of 9.066 grams per cubic centimeter at 25 °C. Erbium forms a rose-pink oxide used to make pink glass. Erbium is also used in laser technology and is added to certain *alloys* (metal mixtures) to improve hardness. See also **Element, Chemical** (table); **Lanthanide; Yttrium.** Marianna A. Busch

Erectile dysfunction is the inability to obtain or maintain an erection satisfactory for sexual activity. As many as half the men over age 40 may have some degree of erectile dysfunction, also called *impotence.*

A penis is usually soft and limp. Sexual excitement relaxes muscles in the organ and reduces the flow of blood from it. As a result, bodies in the penis called corpora cavernosa fill with blood, making the organ rigid and erect. Any condition that reduces muscle relaxation, blocks blood flow into the penis, or increases the outward flow of blood may result in erectile dysfunction.

Erectile dysfunction may be caused by tobacco use, diabetes, diseases of the arteries or other blood vessels, excess fat in the blood, surgery, or injury to the pelvis. It may result from use of certain medications, such as drugs to lower blood pressure, antidepressants, and hormone drugs. Low levels of the male hormone testosterone in the blood may also cause erectile dysfunction. In addition, impotence may have psychological causes.

To help a patient with erectile dysfunction, a doctor begins by analyzing the patient's medical and sexual history. The doctor may order laboratory testing of blood sugar, cholesterol, and testosterone levels. Some patients may undergo *arteriography,* a technique that makes arteries visible on an X-ray image; ultrasound examination to measure blood flow to the penis; or studies to monitor erections during sleep.

Treatment may involve lifestyle changes, such as reducing cholesterol levels, quitting smoking, or, for diabetics, treating high blood sugar. Physicians may prescribe testosterone for patients with low hormone levels. Other patients may use oral medications, such as sildenafil (sold under the trade name Viagra) and apomorphine, to stimulate erection. If other treatments fail, certain patients may be treated with injections to increase blood flow to the penis, or by surgically implanting a device to produce erections. Culley C. Carson

Ergonomics, *UR guh NAHM ihks,* is the science of designing machines, objects, and environments to match the physical and psychological needs of human beings. One example of ergonomic design is a type of computer keyboard that features special shaping and support to prevent strain on hands and wrists. Such strain can lead to muscle or nerve damage when people spend long hours typing. The most widespread use of ergonomics is in workplaces. Many ergonomic products are also used in homes. Ergonomics is also known by the terms *human factors engineering* and *human engineering.*

The science of ergonomics developed from studies conducted during the early 1900's. At that time, engineers discovered that the efficiency of a machine often depends on the mood and comfort of the person operating it. At the same time, sociologists, psychologists, and other social scientists studied human behavior to learn how psychological factors affect production. Today, scientists and designers use ergonomic principles to create workplaces and equipment that are safe, comfortable, and satisfying for people. Thomas T. Liao

See also **Repetitive strain injury.**

Ergot, *UR guht,* is a parasitic fungus that attacks wheat, barley, rye, and many wild and cultivated grasses. It most commonly infects rye. Ergot attacks the grain of the plant. Long purple structures of the fungus called *sclerotia* form in place of the seeds of the host plant. In the spring, these sclerotia grow and produce stalks and spores. The spores ripen and are scattered by the wind to infect new plants. Ergot infection can be reduced or prevented by rotating crops, using clean seed, and cutting grasses that may harbor the disease.

Ergot also causes a disease called *ergotism* in human beings and cattle. This disease was common among people who ate bread made from rye grain that contained ergot sclerotia. The symptoms were often gangrene and convulsions. The disease has practically disappeared because of improved ways to clean grain.

Ergot sclerotia are the source of a number of drugs, such as *ergonovine, ergotoxine,* and *ergotamine.* These drugs are used to ease migraine headaches and to prevent hemorrhage after childbirth. Joe F. Ammirati

Scientific classification. Ergot fungi make up the genus *Claviceps.* The most prominent species is *Claviceps purpurea.*

Eric the Red. See Erik the Red.

Erickson, Arthur Charles (1924-2009), a Canadian architect, became noted for buildings that dramatically harmonize with the landscape. Many of Erickson's designs were built in or near Vancouver, British Columbia, and reflect the English, American Indian, and Japanese traditions of western Canada.

In the 1960's, Erickson designed Simon Fraser University on a mountaintop overlooking Vancouver. Erickson used simple geometric forms that recall Japanese design, but the colors and some of the shapes capture the feeling of the hills and mountain peaks of western Canada. Erickson's use of concrete, glass, and wood in the buildings further unites the structures with their natural surroundings. A picture of part of the campus appears in the introduction to the **Architecture** article.

In 1969, Erickson designed the main building of the University of Lethbridge in Alberta. It resembles a horizontal ribbon of concrete that blends with the flat natural surroundings. In the 1970's, he designed Robson Square, a government center including law courts for downtown Vancouver. It has waterfalls, landscaped hills, and parks. His Canadian Embassy (1989) in Washington, D.C., features a series of elemental shapes set within a giant open cage. Erickson was born on June 14, 1924, in Vancouver. He died on May 20, 2009. Nicholas Adams

Ericson, Leif. See **Leif Eriksson.**

Ericsson, John (1803-1889), was a Swedish-born American engineer. He made many improvements in heating engines, ships, and locomotives. Ericsson's chief accomplishment was introducing screw propellers for use in place of paddle wheels on ships.

Ericsson was born on July 31, 1803, in Värmland province, Sweden. He showed great mechanical ability at an early age. From ages 13 to 17, Ericsson worked as an engineering apprentice on the Göta Canal in Sweden. He then served as a surveyor in the Swedish army.

In 1826, Ericsson went to London, where he attempted to develop an engine that used heated air instead of steam. This effort failed, but he succeeded with other projects. Ericsson developed improved boilers and condensers for steam engines, designed an early steam-powered locomotive, and devised a machine for automatically cutting metal files. In 1833, he began experimenting with screw propellers, and in 1837, he built the first propeller-driven commercial ship.

Ericsson came to the United States in 1839 and became a U.S. citizen in 1848. There he designed a number of vessels, including the *Princeton* (1844), the first propeller-driven warship. He won fame for his design and construction of the *Monitor* (1862), one of the earliest ironclad warships. The ship also had a revolving gun turret. Its clash in the American Civil War (1861-1865) with the *Merrimack,* then called the *Virginia,* marked the first battle between ironclad ships. Ericsson died on March 8, 1889. Terry S. Reynolds

See also **Monitor and Merrimack; Propeller.**

Erie, *EER ee* (pop. 101,786; met. area pop. 280,566), is the fourth largest city in Pennsylvania. Only Philadelphia, Pittsburgh, and Allentown have more people. Erie is in northwestern Pennsylvania, on the south shore of Lake Erie. It is the state's only lake port. For location, see **Pennsylvania** (political map).

Erie is laid out in a series of squares. Perry Square, the most prominent one, includes the City Hall and a federal courthouse. Many stately mansions stand near the square. One is the main building of Gannon University. Mercyhurst College is also in Erie, as is a campus of Pennsylvania State University called Penn State Erie, the Behrend College. Erie's industries include shipping, tourism, and the manufacture of locomotives and plastics. Presque Isle State Park, on a peninsula near the city, has beaches, boating areas, hiking trails, and picnic areas. The park attracts many tourists to Erie.

Erie was founded as a town in 1795. Most of the ships

of Commodore Oliver Hazard Perry's fleet, which defeated the British on Lake Erie during the War of 1812, were built in Erie. A restoration of Perry's flagship, the *Niagara,* is on exhibit in the city. Erie became a city in 1851. It is the county seat of Erie County. William C. Rense

Erie, Lake. See **Lake Erie.**

Erie Canal, *EER ee,* was the first important national waterway built in the United States. It crossed upstate New York from Buffalo on Lake Erie to Albany and Troy on the Hudson River. Completed in 1825, the canal joined the Atlantic Ocean with the Great Lakes system. It provided a route over which manufactured goods and settlers could flow into the Midwest without passing through Canada, and over which timber and agricultural products could be transported to the East.

For a hundred years before the Erie Canal was built, people had been talking about a canal that would join the Great Lakes and the Atlantic Ocean. The man who planned the Erie Canal and carried the plans through was De Witt Clinton. Clinton was mayor of New York City for most of the period between 1803 and 1815. He was governor of the state from 1817 to 1822 and again from 1825 until his death in 1828. Those who opposed the canal laughingly called it "Clinton's Ditch."

Clinton and Gouverneur Morris went to Washington in 1812 to ask for federal help for the project, but they were unsuccessful. In 1816, Clinton petitioned the New York State Legislature to build the canal. His petition won so much support that the governor appointed a canal commission and made Clinton its head. Clinton became governor in 1817, and shortly afterward, on July 4, 1817, broke ground for the canal in Rome, New York, then a village on the Mohawk River. Construction took eight years. The canal formally opened on Oct. 26, 1825. The first barge to travel its entire length, the *Seneca Chief,* left Buffalo with Clinton on board on Oct. 26, 1825. It arrived in New York City on November 4 and was greeted all along the way by enthusiastic crowds.

The building of the canal was paid for by the state of New York. It cost $7,143,789, but it soon earned its price many times over. The canal cut freight rates between Buffalo and New York City by more than 90 percent and strengthened New York City's position as the nation's largest city and principal port. As the canal traffic grew, towns along its course prospered. Albany, Utica, Syracuse, Rochester, and Buffalo became major cities.

The original canal was 363 miles (584 kilometers) long. It was 28 feet (8.5 meters) wide at the bottom, 40 feet (12 meters) wide at the top, and 4 feet (1.2 meters) deep. It could carry barges that were 80 feet (24 meters) long and 15 feet (4.6 meters) wide, with a draft of 3 ½ feet (1.1 meters). The canal had 83 locks, which raised vessels on the canal about 565 feet (172 meters) from the Hudson River to Lake Erie. Barges were towed along the canal by horses and mules on shore. At first, travel on the canal was slow. The famous editor Horace Greeley wrote that passengers traveled a mile and a half an hour on the Erie Canal for a cent and a half a mile. But fast passenger boats could travel 100 miles (160 kilometers) a day.

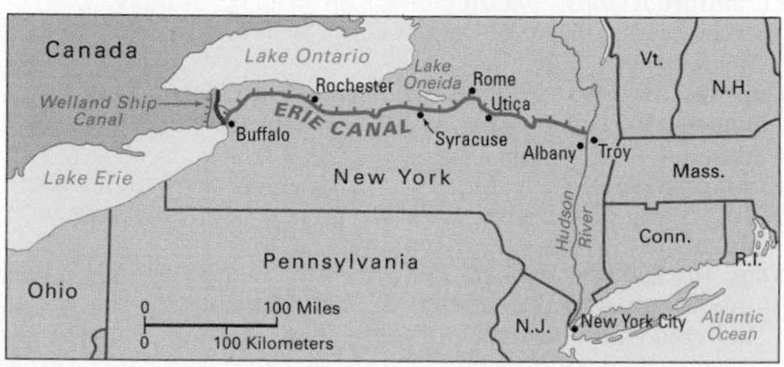

WORLD BOOK map

Location of the Erie Canal

The canal was enlarged several times between 1835 and 1862. But business began to fall off in the 1870's as railroads became the main long-distance carriers of freight and passengers. In 1903, the people of New York voted to build a great modern waterway, linking the Erie Canal with three shorter canals in the state to form what now is called the New York State Canal System. This system, which is 524 miles (843 kilometers) long, opened in 1918. See **New York State Canal System.** Ray Bromley

See also **Clinton, De Witt.**

Erik the Red (A.D. 950?-1000?) was a Viking explorer who colonized Greenland. His name was Erik Thorvaldson, but he was called Erik the Red because of his red hair. His name is also spelled Eric or Eirik.

Erik was born in Jaeren, in southern Norway. He and his father left Norway because one or both of them had been involved in some killings. Erik and his father then moved to Iceland. After his father died, Erik became involved in several more quarrels and killings. In 982, he was exiled from Iceland for three years. During his exile, Erik explored the waters west of Iceland for land that the Icelander Gunnbjorn Ulfsson had sighted about A.D. 900. Erik reached Greenland and spent the rest of his exile there. He then returned to Iceland. Erik named the new land Greenland to attract people to it.

About 985, Erik sailed for Greenland with 25 ships of colonists, but only 14 of the vessels completed the voyage. Two settlements, with a total of about 450 people, were established the Eastern Settlement on the southwest coast and the Western Settlement about 300 miles (480 kilometers) north. Erik lived in the Eastern Settlement at Brattahlid, in Eiriksfjord, near what is now Qaqortoq. He was the principal leader of both communities. The settlers farmed the land; raised cattle, hogs, and sheep; and hunted bears, caribou, walruses, and other animals. Erik's wife, Thjodhild, converted to Christianity and built the first Christian church in Greenland. Erik himself did not adopt Christianity.

Erik planned to lead an expedition west from Greenland to find more land. But he refused to make the journey after falling from his horse on the way to his ship. Erik feared the accident was a sign of misfortune. About 1000, his son Leif Eriksson led what was probably the first voyage to the mainland of North America.

Most information about Erik the Red comes from two Icelandic stories written in the late 1100's or the 1200's, *The Saga of Erik the Red* and *The Saga of the Greenlanders.* The sagas were based on oral traditions nearly 200 years old. During the 1960's, archaeologists uncovered several stone and turf buildings from the early colonies. They included Erik's house at Brattahlid and Thjodhild's church, about 600 feet (183 meters) away. Marvin G. Slind

See also **Leif Eriksson.**

Erikson, Erik Homburger (1902-1994), was an American psychoanalyst. He became best known for his ideas on how human beings develop a sense of *identi-*

ty—that is, the awareness of oneself as a whole person.

Erikson based his ideas on the theories of the Austrian psychoanalyst Sigmund Freud, who emphasized the importance of early childhood for all later development. But Erikson modified Freud's ideas, stressing the continual development of human beings throughout an eight-stage life cycle. Freud focused on the psychological and biological aspects of development. Erikson said social and cultural influences also affect development.

Erikson became widely known for his studies of adolescence, chiefly the idea of an adolescent *identity crisis.* Such a crisis may occur when an adolescent struggles with inner conflicts before gaining a sense of purpose and moving into adulthood. Erikson expressed his central ideas on adolescence in the books *Childhood and Society* (1950) and *Identity: Youth and Crisis* (1968).

Erikson also gained praise for biographies that examine the psychological development of well-known historical figures. These books include *Young Man Luther* (1958), which depicts German religious reformer Martin Luther, and *Gandhi's Truth* (1969), which focuses on the Indian spiritual and political leader Mohandas K. Gandhi.

Erikson was born on June 15, 1902, in Frankfurt (am Main), Germany. His parents were of Danish ancestry. In 1933, Erikson graduated from the Vienna Psychoanalytic Institute. Then he moved to the United States. Erikson taught at Harvard University, Yale University, and the University of California at Berkeley. He died on May 12, 1994. Hannah S. Decker

Eriksson, Leif. See **Leif Eriksson.**

Erin. See **Ireland.**

Eris is a nearly planet-sized object that orbits the sun in the outer solar system. The International Astronomical Union (IAU), a widely recognized authority in naming heavenly bodies, classifies Eris as a *dwarf planet.* Eris has a diameter about equal to that of Pluto. First identified in 2005, Eris became the largest sun-orbiting object found since the discovery of the planet Neptune in 1846. The Minor Planet Center, part of the IAU, assigned the newly discovered object the temporary designation 2003 UB_{313} based on the date when it was first photographed. People sometimes informally referred to 2003 UB_{313} as Xena, a nickname used by the object's discoverers.

Observations made by astronomers in 2010 suggest that Eris is about 1,450 miles (2,350 kilometers) in diameter, roughly the size of Pluto. The orbit of Eris is *elongated* (oval), ranging from 3.5 billion to 9 billion miles (5.6 billion to 14.5 billion kilometers) from the sun. One complete orbit takes about 557 years. Because of its distance from the sun, Eris has extremely low surface temperatures, around 30 K (−243 °C or −406 °F). Its surface includes methane ice. The surface is shiny, reflecting almost all starlight back into space. Eris has a small moon, Dysnomia, that measures about ⅛ Eris's diameter.

The American astronomers Michael E. Brown, Chadwick A. Trujillo, and David L. Rabinowitz announced the discovery of Eris on July 29, 2005. They found it in pictures taken in 2003 using the Samuel Oschin Telescope at Palomar Observatory in southwestern California. Astronomers first detected the object's moon on Sept. 10, 2005, at Keck Observatory in Hawaii. In 2006, they named the object Eris for the Greek goddess of chaos and strife.

The discovery of Eris intensified an ongoing debate over the definition of the term *planet.* Some astronomers proposed that the object should be classified as a planet because it is about the size of Pluto, then considered the ninth planet. Other astronomers argued that Eris and Pluto should not be considered planets, grouping them instead with thousands of similar but smaller objects in a region of the solar system called the Kuiper belt. In 2006, the IAU created the term *dwarf planet* to describe Pluto, Eris, and other similar objects. Many astronomers welcomed the IAU's decision. But some considered the term vague and declined to adopt it. In 2008, the IAU also classified Eris, Pluto, and the other dwarf planets beyond Neptune as *plutoids.* Chadwick A. Trujillo

See also **Dwarf planet; Kuiper belt.**

Eritrea, *EHR ih TREE uh,* is a small country on the northeast coast of Africa. It stretches along the Red Sea, between Sudan and Djibouti. Ethiopia lies to the south. Most of Eritrea's people are farmers or herders. The country has little industry. Asmara is the capital and largest city. The country's official name is the State of Eritrea.

Eritrea was once a part of the Aksum Kingdom. The kingdom reached its height as a trading and cultural center between the A.D. 300's and 600's. Italy gained control of Eritrea in the late 1800's. The United Kingdom took over the area in 1941, during World War II (1939-1945). In 1952, Eritrea became part of Ethiopia.

In 1961, civil war broke out between Eritrean rebels, who wanted independence for their land, and Ethiopian government troops. The war finally ended in 1991, with a victory by Eritrean and other rebels. Eritrea formally achieved independence in 1993.

Government. Eritrea has had a *transitional* (temporary) government since it gained independence. The People's Front for Democracy and Justice (PFDJ), Eritrea's only legal political party, dominates the government. Formerly called the Eritrean People's Liberation Front (EPLF), the party led the fight for independence. In 1997, Eritrea approved a new constitution providing for an elected legislature. But the constitution has not yet been implemented. A president heads the transitional government. The president is chosen by a transitional legislature called the National Assembly.

People. Most Eritreans are descendants of people from the Arabian Peninsula and from the Nile River region of Sudan who came to the area starting about 2000 B.C. Tigrinya is Eritrea's chief language. Tigre is the sec-

Facts in brief

Capital: Asmara.
Principal language: Tigrinya.
Area: 45,406 mi² (117,600 km²). *Greatest distances*—northwest-southeast, 510 mi (821 km); northeast-southwest, 290 mi (467 km). *Coastline*—620 mi (1,000 km).
Elevation: *Highest*—Mount Soira, 9,885 ft (3,013 m) above sea level. *Lowest*—Denakil Depression, 246 ft (75 m) below sea level.
Population: *Estimated 2014 population*—5,902,000; density, 130 per mi² (50 per km²); distribution, 78 percent rural, 22 percent urban.
Chief products: *Agriculture*—barley, beef and dairy cattle, millet, sorghum, teff, wheat. *Manufacturing*—construction materials, leather goods, processed foods.
Flag: The flag has a red triangle across the middle, bearing a yellow wreath and olive branch; a green triangle at the top; and a light blue triangle at the bottom. Adopted in 1993. See **Flag** (picture: Flags of Africa).
Money: *Basic unit*—nakfa. One hundred cents equal one nakfa.

ond most common language. Arabic is spoken on the coast. Groups of herders speak Afar or other languages.

About 80 percent of the people of Eritrea are farmers or herders. Farming families live in walled or fenced settlements. The homes have flat thatched roofs or peaked roofs made of corrugated iron. Most farm households consist of an extended family that may include up to several dozen relatives. Farmers meet for occasional market days, for festivals, or at regional village towns. Herders move from place to place with their livestock.

About half the Eritreans are Christians. Most of the others, including many herders, are Muslims. Coptic Christianity, which originated in Egypt, was brought to Eritrea in the A.D. 300's. Islam came to Eritrea in the 600's.

Eritrea's educational system was shaped under Italian rule and expanded under British rule. The long civil war disrupted the educational system. As a result, a majority of Eritrea's children have little formal education. Illiteracy remains a serious problem in the country.

Land and climate. Eritrea stretches along the Red Sea from Cape Kasar to the Strait of Bab el Mandeb—a distance of about 620 miles (1,000 kilometers). A coastal plain along the Red Sea ranges from 10 to 40 miles (16 to 64 kilometers) in width. The plain rises to highlands in central Eritrea. Mount Soira, in the highlands, is the country's highest peak. It rises 9,885 feet (3,013 meters) above sea level. The highlands drop to lowlands in the west. Denakil Desert covers southeastern Eritrea.

The country's main rivers flow westward, cutting valleys through the central highlands and western lowlands. Eritrea's main rivers include the Baraka and the Gash. The Gash is called the Marab for part of its length.

Temperatures average 86 °F (30 °C) along the coast and 60 °F (16 °C) in the highlands. The coast gets about 6 to 10 inches (15 to 25 centimeters) of rain a year, and the highlands get up to 24 inches (61 centimeters). In most parts of Eritrea, the heaviest rains occur in June and July.

Economy. Eritrea faces a number of economic problems. It is a poor country, and many of its people live in poverty. Eritrea's economy suffered severely during the Ethiopian civil war from 1961 to 1991. The economy improved somewhat after the war. However, it was devastated again by a border conflict between Eritrea and Ethiopia from 1998 to 2000.

Eritrea's people largely depend on subsistence agriculture. However, the country's agriculture has suffered from recurring periods of drought. Crops are primarily grown in the central highlands. The country's main crops include barley, millet, sorghum, and wheat. Farmers also grow *teff,* a grain that is common only in Eritrea and Ethiopia. Livestock raising is concentrated along the coast and in the western lowlands. Herders raise beef and dairy cattle, goats, and sheep.

Manufacturing contributes a small amount to Eritrea's economy. Eritrea's chief manufactured or processed products include construction materials, leather goods, and processed foods. Eritrea's deposits of gold, petroleum, and other mined products are underdeveloped.

Eritrea is strategically located for trade. The country imports more than it exports. Eritrea's main trading partners include China, Italy, and Saudi Arabia. Massawa and Assab rank as its chief ports.

History. About 2000 B.C., people from the interior of Africa settled in what is now Eritrea. About 1000 B.C., people began arriving from the Arabian Peninsula.

Eritrea

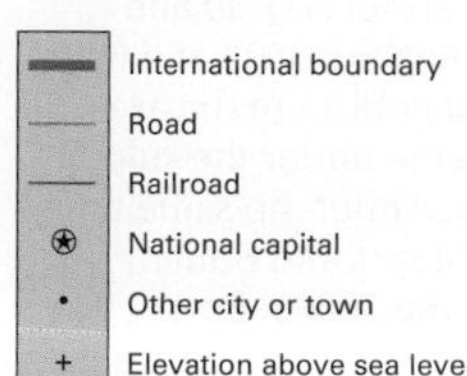

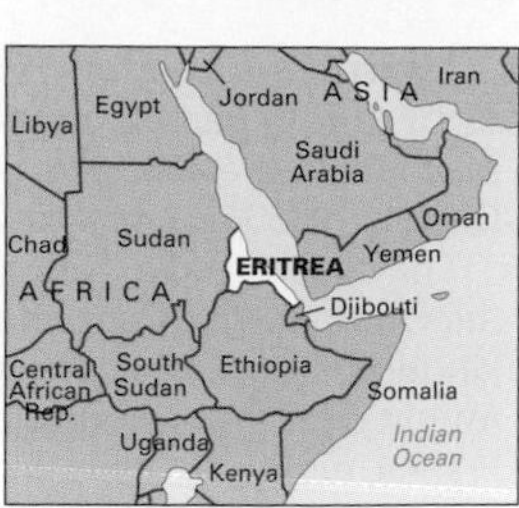

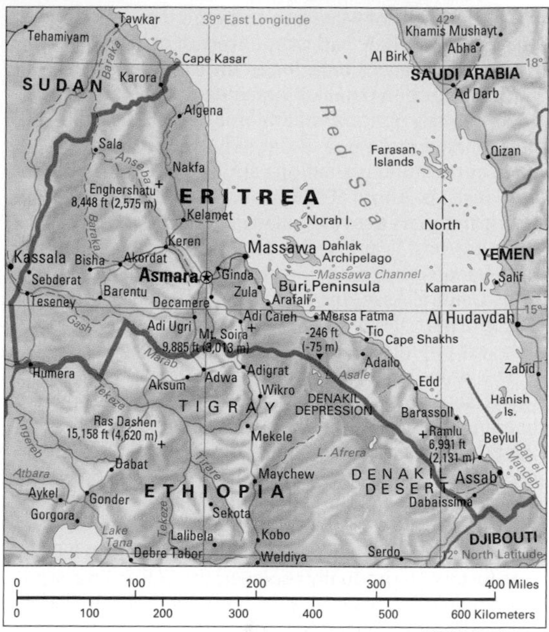

WORLD BOOK maps

© Patrick Lages, Gamma/Liaison

Asmara is the capital and largest city of Eritrea. The city has many European-style buildings dating from the early and middle 1900's, when Eritrea was a colonial possession of Italy's.

The Aksum Kingdom became the first important state in the area. It gained importance about A.D. 50 and reached its greatest power between the 300's and 600's. During the 600's, Muslims gained control of the area.

The coastal region of Eritrea came under the rule of the Ottoman Empire in the 1500's. About the same time, kingdoms from what are now Ethiopia and Sudan fought over the rest of Eritrea. In the 1800's, Egypt, France, and Italy attempted to gain control of Eritrea.

In 1882, Italy occupied the port of Assab. In 1885, it occupied the port of Massawa and other regions along the coast. By 1889, Italy had conquered all of Eritrea. Italy used Massawa as a base for an invasion of Ethiopia. Ethiopian Emperor Menelik II defeated the Italian forces in 1896. But Italy conquered Ethiopia in 1935. During the period that Eritrea was under Italy's control, Italy invested in agricultural plantations and established a number of industries. About 60,000 Italians settled in Eritrea.

British forces drove the Italians out of Africa in 1941, during World War II. A British military administration then began governing Eritrea. In 1950, the United Nations General Assembly adopted a resolution that Eritrea become part of Ethiopia, but govern itself. The resolution was put into effect in 1952.

The Ethiopian government, led by Emperor Haile Selassie, sought to undermine Eritrea's self-government by banning political parties and trade unions in Eritrea. But the Eritreans started a political movement called the Eritrean Liberation Front (ELF). In 1961, civil war broke out between the ELF and the Ethiopian government. In 1962, Ethiopia declared Eritrea to be a province of Ethiopia.

In 1970, the Eritrean People's Liberation Front (EPLF) was formed. It gradually replaced the ELF as Eritrea's main political organization. In 1974, Ethiopian military leaders removed Haile Selassie from power. They set up a government called the Dergue. The EPLF tried to negotiate with the Dergue for Eritrean independence. But the talks failed, and civil war continued. In 1987 and 1988, victories against Ethiopian forces by EPLF forces and forces from the Tigray region, south of Eritrea, led to a collapse of central government rule in much of Ethiopia.

In 1991, Eritrean rebels joined with a group of rebels led by Tigrayans to overthrow Ethiopia's government. The group led by Tigrayans set up a new government for all of Ethiopia except Eritrea. The Eritreans formed their own government. They formally declared independence on May 24, 1993, after a *referendum* (popular vote) in favor of it. EPLF leader Issaias Afewerki became president of the new country. In 1994, the EPLF became a political party called the People's Front for Democracy and Justice. Eritrea adopted a new constitution in 1997.

When Eritrea achieved independence, a section of the border with Ethiopia had not been clearly defined. Eritrea and Ethiopia fought a bloody war over this area from May 1998 until June 2000, when they signed a cease-fire deal. They signed a formal peace treaty in December 2000. A commission established by the treaty to identify the border issued a ruling in 2002. However, Ethiopia objected to the ruling, and the border has not yet been marked. In 2005, an international court in The Hague, Netherlands, blamed Eritrea for starting the border war. In 2009, the court ruled that Eritrea owed Ethiopia $10 million for war damages. Stephen K. Commins

See also **Asmara; Ethiopia** (History).

Ermine, *UR muhn,* is a small animal that lives in North America, Europe, Asia, and northern Africa. In North America, ermines are sometimes called short-tailed weasels. In Europe, they are called stoats. North American ermines are found from the Arctic south to Pennsylvania and northern Virginia in the east and to central California and New Mexico in the west. The ermine is a member of the weasel family, which also includes badgers, minks, otters, and wolverines.

Most ermines measure about 7 to 13 inches (18 to 33 centimeters) long and weigh about 2 to 10 ounces (57 to 285 grams). The males are larger than the females. An ermine has silky fur. During the late spring and summer, the color of the fur is brown above and white below. The tail has a black tip. The ermine sheds its fur each autumn and grows a new coat that is pure white, except for the black tip on the tail. During the white color phase, the animal is often trapped for its fur. In the Middle Ages, from about the 400's through the 1400's, nobles used ermine fur for full-length coats and capes. Today, the fur is rarely used in clothing.

Ermines live in a variety of habitats, including riverbanks, the edges of forests, and wet meadows, marshes, and ditches. Ermines feed primarily on small rodents and rabbits. They generally live alone as adults.

A female ermine has one litter of 3 to 13 young each year, usually in April. The mother usually raises the young by herself. Ermines grow rapidly. Some females are fully grown and able to mate during their first summer. Males mature later than females. Ermines can live for 4 to 7 years. The chief enemies of ermines include cats, dogs, foxes, hawks, and owls. Gary A. Heidt

Scientific classification. The ermine's scientific name is *Mustela erminea.*

See also **Fur; Weasel.**

Ernst, Max (1891-1976), was a German artist associated with the development of the Dada and Surrealist movements. He joined with several other artists and writers as a leader of the Dada movement, founded in 1916. He created Dada works by combining photographs, scientific and technical illustrations, and newspaper clippings into pasted compositions called *collages.* His images often deal with symbolic meanings taken from philosophy and psychiatry, which he studied as a young man. Ernst moved to Paris in 1924 and helped to found the Surrealist movement there. His Surrealist works suggest nightmares and hallucinations. They often portray mysterious and menacing forests. Ernst was born on April 8, 1891, in Brühl. He lived in the United States in the 1940's. Ernst died on April 1, 1976. See also **Dadaism; Surrealism** (picture). Pamela A. Ivinski

Eros is one of the largest asteroids that come close to Earth. Eros's distance from the sun ranges from 105 million to 166 million miles (169 million to 267 million kilometers)—1.13 to 1.78 times Earth's average distance from the sun. The asteroid completes one orbit around the sun every 1.76 Earth years. Although its orbit does cross that of Earth, scientists estimate that Eros has only a tiny chance of hitting Earth in the next 100 million years.

Eros is shaped like a potato, and it is 21 miles long, 7 miles wide, and 7 miles high (34 by 11 by 11 kilometers). It is made up of rocky material. The average density of Eros is 2.67 grams per cubic centimeter, slightly less than half that of Earth. Eros's low density suggests that about 30 percent of the asteroid's volume consists of crevasses and cracks. Eros spins end-over-end, rotating once every 5 hours 16 minutes. Areas of the surface in sunlight have a temperature of about 210 °F (100 °C), while areas in darkness are as cold as −240 °F (−150 °C).

Impacts of meteorites and other asteroids have created countless craters on Eros and have broken the surface into a network of cracks and troughs. Strewn across the surface are boulders that range from the size of a chair to the size of a house.

The German astronomer Gustav Witt and the French astronomer August H. P. Charlois independently discovered Eros in 1898. The space probe Near Earth Asteroid Rendezvous-Shoemaker (NEAR Shoemaker) landed on Eros in 2001. Louise M. Prockter

Eros, in mythology. See **Cupid.**

Erosion, *ih ROH zhuhn,* is a natural process by which rock and soil are broken loose from the surface at one location and moved to another. Erosion changes land by wearing down mountains, filling in valleys, and making rivers appear and disappear. It is usually a slow and gradual process that occurs over thousands or millions of years. But erosion can be speeded up by such human activities as farming and mining.

How erosion occurs. Erosion begins with a process called *weathering.* In this process, environmental factors break rock and soil into smaller pieces and loosen them from the surface. A chief cause is the formation of ice. As water freezes, it expands with great force. As a result, when it freezes inside the crack of a rock, it can break the rock apart. Other major agents of weathering include chemicals; living organisms; the movement of air, ice, and water; and heat from the sun.

After materials have been loosened by weathering, they are moved to new locations. For example, winds lift particles from the surface and can carry them over great distances. Glaciers transport materials embedded in them. Raindrops that splash against sloping land move soil particles downhill. Water currents carry materials down a riverbed or out to sea.

Effects of erosion. Erosion can be both helpful and harmful. It benefits people by contributing to the formation of soil through the breaking up of rock. It causes rich soil to be deposited on valley floors and at the mouths of rivers. Erosion also has produced some of the world's most spectacular geological formations. The Grand Canyon, for instance, has been created over the course of millions of years by erosion from the Colorado River. See **Grand Canyon.**

One of the most harmful effects of erosion is that it robs farmland of productive topsoil. For this reason, it is one of the leading threats to the food supply. Erosion can also wash valuable fertilizers from farmland and carry pollution-causing agricultural chemicals into lakes and rivers. Eroded soil can clog irrigation ditches, ponds, and reservoirs. Gullies caused by flowing water may ruin fields by making them too small to farm with tractors and other modern equipment.

Controlling erosion. Although erosion is a natural process, people can influence the extent to which it occurs. Soil erosion increases, for example, when land is cleared and cultivated, because trees and other plants shield soil from wind and rain. Plant roots and the remains of dead plants also help to hold soil in place. Farmers can thus reduce erosion by keeping idle fields planted with such thickly growing *cover crops* as alfalfa or grass. Many farmers also decrease erosion through the use of *no-till* and *conservation tillage* techniques, in which remains of the previous crop are left on the soil surface. Other conservation methods include *contour plowing, strip cropping,* and *terracing.* See **Conservation** (Soil conservation). John M. Laflen

Related articles in *World Book* include:

Badlands	Farm and farming (Soil management)	Soil
Canyon	Glacier	Water (How water shapes Earth)
Dust storm	River	Windbreak
Earth (Earth's rocks)		

Erving, Julius (1950-), became one of the most exciting and popular players in the National Basketball Association (NBA). Erving, who was 6 feet 6 inches (198 centimeters) tall, played forward and guard. He became noted for his outstanding jumping ability and spectacular dunk shots. Erving was nicknamed Dr. J.

Julius Winfield Erving, Jr., was born on Feb. 22, 1950, in East Meadow, New York. He attended the University of Massachusetts from 1968 until 1971, when he left to play for the Virginia Squires of the American Basketball Association (ABA). In 1973, Erving was traded to the New York Nets of the ABA. In 1976, the Nets sold Erving to the Philadelphia 76ers of the NBA. Erving was named the NBA's Most Valuable Player for the 1980-1981 season. He retired after the 1986-1987 season. Bob Logan

See also **Basketball** (picture).

Eryops, *EH ree ahps,* was a prehistoric amphibianlike animal that inhabited swamps of what is now North America. It lived about 270 million years ago, during the Permian Period and long before the dinosaurs. The name *Eryops* means *long face.* It describes the animal's broad, elongated head.

Eryops ranked among the larger land animals of its time, growing more than 5 feet (1.5 meters) in length. Four short, strong legs supported the creature's thick body. Its powerful jaws held many sharp teeth.

Eryops resembled modern amphibians in living part of its life in the water and part on land. It probably laid its eggs in water. A young *Eryops* likely breathed by means of gills, but it lost its gills as an adult and breathed with lungs. In other respects, *Eryops* resembled a crocodile. Scientists believe *Eryops* may have been more capable of life on land than were other amphibianlike animals. *Eryops* ate mostly fish, but it also preyed on small *tetrapods* (four-legged animals). It probably captured its prey both on land and in water.

American paleontologist Edward Drinker Cope named *Eryops* in 1887. Its fossils have been found in New Mexico, Oklahoma, and Texas. Kenneth Carpenter

See also **Prehistoric animal** (picture: Animal life of the Paleozoic Era).

Erysipelas, *EHR uh SIHP uh luhs,* is a skin infection that chiefly affects infants, young children, and elderly people. It causes a painful thickening and tightening of the skin and spreads rapidly during one or two days. The infected area appears red and shiny, with a slightly raised border. If left untreated, erysipelas can lead to serious internal infections, especially in newborns.

Most cases of erysipelas are caused by bacteria of a type called *group A beta-hemolytic streptococci* (see

Streptococcus). The infection begins when the bacteria enter the skin, typically through an open cut or scratch. The bacteria then invade the surrounding skin. Erysipelas most often affects the face, but it may affect any area of skin. The infection may also cause fever and vomiting. The infection normally clears up a few days after treatment with an antibiotic, usually penicillin or erythromycin. Untreated cases may last several weeks.

Serious complications can occur if erysipelas spreads inside the body. The infection may lead to *septicemia* (blood poisoning) or to a kidney disease called *acute glomerulonephritis* (see **Blood poisoning; Nephritis**).

Paul R. Bergstresser

Erythema, *EHR uh THEE muh,* is a redness of the skin. It is related to an increase in the amount of blood present in the *capillaries* (small blood vessels) of the skin. The skin reacts to slight injury or irritation with erythema, which can be produced in many ways. For example, exposure of the skin to sunlight for a short time will cause erythema. Longer exposure results in the formation of blisters. A sharp slap will also produce erythema in the contacted area. Erythema is also a symptom of some diseases. Paul R. Bergstresser

Erythromycin, *ih RIHTH roh MY sihn,* is an antibiotic used to treat scarlet fever, strep throat, and many other bacterial infections. Erythromycin is also effective against Legionnaires' disease and certain other types of pneumonia (see **Legionnaires' disease**). Many of these infections are more commonly treated with one of the penicillins, but erythromycin is useful for patients allergic to penicillins. Erythromycin fights bacteria by blocking the process by which they produce proteins. This blockage prevents the bacteria from multiplying, and the body eventually destroys them. Erythromycin was discovered in 1952. It is relatively safe and seldom causes serious side effects. See also **Antibiotic.** N. E. Sladek

Esau, *EE saw,* was the son of Isaac and Rebecca, and the twin brother of Jacob in the Bible. He is a main character in stories in Genesis 25-33. The best known are Jacob's buying Esau's birthright for a bowl of stew (Genesis 25: 27-34) and the loss of his blessing through the plotting of Rebecca and Jacob (Genesis 27). Angered by Jacob's trickery, Esau planned to kill him. Jacob fled, but 20 years later Esau graciously welcomed him back. Biblical history regards Esau as the founder of the Edomite nation. Carole R. Fontaine

See also **Edom; Isaac; Jacob.**

Escalator is a moving stairway that transports people from one floor or level to another. Escalators are found in airports, subway stations, stores, and other commercial and public buildings. *Moving sidewalks* are similar to escalators but run on flat or slightly inclined surfaces.

An escalator resembles a conveyor belt with steps attached. Each step has two pairs of wheels on the underside. The wheels travel on two sets of tracks. The steps are pulled along the tracks by chains that move around gears located at the top and bottom of the escalator. An electric motor powers the steps. The steps of an escalator are formed where the two sets of tracks run alongside each other. At the top and bottom of an escalator, the two sets of tracks level off and separate, causing the steps to flatten. The steps form a moving platform that enables passengers to get on or off at the landing without tripping. Other safety features include moving handrails and a grooved tread on the steps. Safety devices stop an escalator if anything gets caught in the steps.

Some escalators can carry up to 4,500 people an hour. The movement of the steps can be reversed during rush hours, when most traffic moves in one direction. Modern escalators have sensors and can slow down to save energy when no people are nearby.

The escalator developed chiefly from the work of two American inventors, George H. Wheeler and Jesse W. Reno. In 1892, Wheeler patented a design for a moving stairway that had flat steps and landings at the sides. He later sold the patent to another inventor, who improved the design. Reno developed an inclined conveyor belt with a grooved tread for steady footing. The first operating escalator, based on Reno's design, was used in a New York City elevated train station in 1900. In 1922, the

How an escalator works An escalator is a series of steps that move on two pairs of tracks. An electric motor pulls chains around the outer pair of tracks. The steps move around gears located at the top and bottom.

WORLD BOOK illustrations by Steven Liska

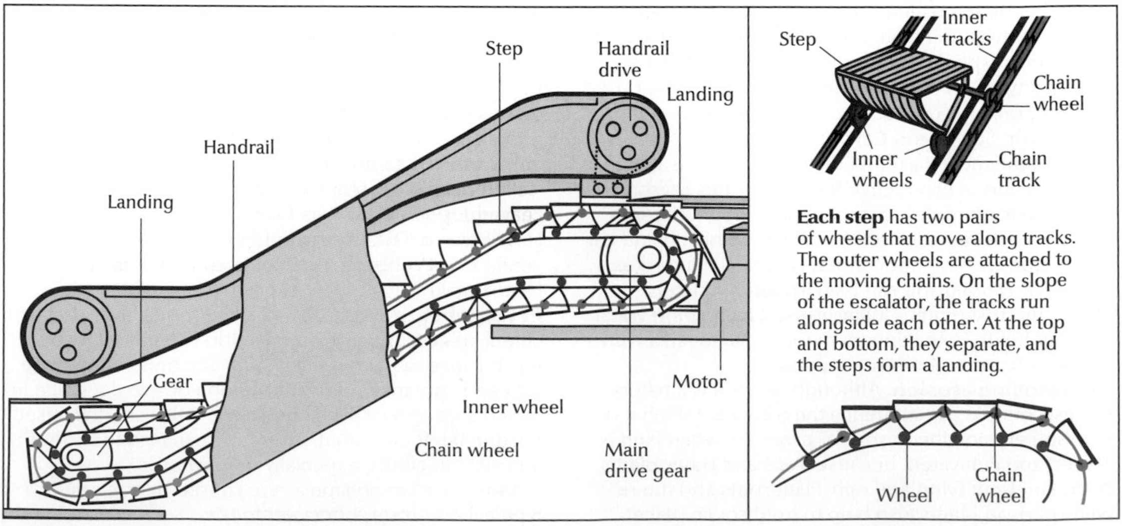

Each step has two pairs of wheels that move along tracks. The outer wheels are attached to the moving chains. On the slope of the escalator, the tracks run alongside each other. At the top and bottom, they separate, and the steps form a landing.

Otis Elevator Company combined the flat steps and the grooved tread to form the modern escalator.

Kirby A. Kuntz

Escheat. See Estate; Heir; Will.

Eschenbach, Wolfram von. See Wolfram von Eschenbach.

Escher, M. C. (1898-1972), was a Dutch artist known for his intricate, detailed prints. Most of his work consists of black-and-white lithographs and woodcuts. In his graphic art, Escher explored the complex relationship of shapes and figures to space. He often experimented with the repetition of interlocking figures, using black and white to create dimension. His prints also portray mirror images of cones, spheres, and cubes as well as connecting rings and continuous spirals. Escher used these designs to create such illusory images as circular waterfalls and endless staircases.

Lithograph (1961); © 1994 M. C. Escher/Cordon Art-Baarn-Holland

An M. C. Escher print shows the geometric designs and optical illusions that are typical of his style. In *Waterfall, shown here,* a continuous waterfall seems to flow from water moving uphill.

Maurits Cornelis Escher was born on June 17, 1898, in Leeuwarden, the Netherlands. He studied at the School for Architecture and Decorative Arts in Haarlem, intending to become an architect. In a short time, however, he turned to the decorative and graphic arts. Escher died on March 27, 1972. Roger Ward

Escherichia coli. See E. coli.

Escobar, Marisol. See Marisol.

Escobedo v. Illinois, *ehs koh BEE doh,* was a landmark decision of the Supreme Court of the United States concerning the rights of people accused of crimes. In this 1964 ruling, the court stated that police who question suspects must advise them of their right to consult a lawyer. If the police do not do so, the suspects' answers may not be used as evidence.

In 1960, Danny Escobedo, a Mexican American laborer, had been arrested in connection with a murder. While questioning Escobedo, Chicago police refused to let him confer with his attorney. They also did not inform him of his constitutional right to remain silent. A jury convicted Escobedo chiefly because of answers he gave during this interrogation.

The Supreme Court ruled that Escobedo's statements could not be used to convict him. The court based its decision on the defendant's right to "assistance of counsel," guaranteed by the Sixth Amendment to the Constitution of the United States. The ruling became controversial, partly because the court had failed to establish clear guidelines for police procedures. The court clarified its position in a 1966 case, *Miranda v. Arizona* (see **Miranda v. Arizona**). Gregg Ivers

Escorial, *ehs KAWR ee uhl,* is a large complex of buildings and courtyards about 30 miles (48 kilometers) northwest of Madrid, Spain. The Escorial consists of a domed church, a college, a monastery, and a palace surrounded by a wall. The Escorial was erected during the reign of Philip II. Construction began in 1563 and was completed in 1584. The complex stands as a monument to Roman Catholicism and serves as the burial place of Philip II and many other kings of Spain.

The Escorial is noted for its order, simplicity, and austerity. It is built of yellow-gray granite from a nearby quarry. The church and a monastery cloister called the Court of the Four Evangelists are especially grand in scale and character. J. William Rudd

See also **Spain** (Architecture).

Esfahan. See Isfahan.

Eskimo. See Inuit.

Eskimo dog. See American Eskimo dog.

Esophagus, *ee SAHF uh guhs,* also called *gullet,* is the muscular tube that carries food from the mouth to the stomach. The muscles in the walls of the esophagus contract in a wavelike manner, moving the food down to the stomach. Glands in the walls secrete mucus that helps the movement of food by providing lubrication.

A muscular ring called the *lower esophageal sphincter* surrounds the opening between the esophagus and the stomach. The sphincter normally keeps the stomach contents from flowing back into the esophagus. The stomach produces a digestive juice that contains a strong acid called *hydrochloric acid.* If the sphincter fails to function properly, stomach acid may rise back into the esophagus, causing a painful burning sensation called *heartburn.* The acid may damage the esophagus, leaving open sores in its lining.

The human esophagus is about 10 inches (25 centimeters) long. The length varies greatly in different animals. The esophagus of fish is short, while that of giraffes is extremely long. Many birds have a saclike part of the esophagus called the *crop* for the temporary storage of food. Charles Liebow

Related articles in *World Book* include:

Acid reflux
Alimentary canal
Digestive system
Heartburn
Human body (Anatomy of the human body)
Stomach

ESP. See Extrasensory perception.

Esperanto, *EHS puh RAHN toh,* is the most widely used international language. L. L. Zamenhof, a Polish physician, devised Esperanto. He published a book about the language, *Lingvo Internacia* (1887), under the pen name Dr. Esperanto. The word *esperanto* means *one who hopes* in that language.

Esperanto uses a roman alphabet, in which each letter represents a single sound. The language also has a simple, uniform structure. For example, a word's accent always falls on the next-to-last syllable. Adjectives end in *a*, adverbs end in *e*, and nouns end in *o*. But when a noun is an object, an *n* is added at the end of the word. Plurals end in *j*. The basic vocabulary of Esperanto consists mainly of root words common to the Indo-European languages. The following sentence is written in Esperanto: *La astronaŭto, per speciala instrumento, fotografas la lunon.* The translation: *The astronaut, with a special instrument, photographs the moon.*

Critically reviewed by The Esperanto League for North America, Inc.

Espionage, *EHS pee uh NAHZH,* is the act of spying on a country, organization, movement, or person. It involves a network of agents and those who recruit and supervise them—called case officers—serving *clandestinely* (secretly). These people are known as spies.

Spies seek timely and accurate military, political, scientific, economic, and technical information called *intelligence.* This information can be *classified* (obtained from secret documents or missions) or *open source* (obtained from media outlets, including social media). Agents engage in espionage for a variety of reasons, including for money; because of ideology (to advance a particular cause); to compromise (because of blackmail); and for ego purposes (as a result of flattery).

There are two principal kinds of intelligence gathered by agents: (1) information obtained from people directly and (2) information obtained from *wiretapping* and other electronic eavesdropping methods. A wiretap is a concealed listening or recording device that is attached to a communications system such as a telephone wire. The gathered information is evaluated by analysts with special knowledge in a particular topic. Depending on the threat or need, the information can be included in *briefing books* (formal reports prepared for policymakers).

Counterespionage consists of efforts to deceive, *subvert* (destroy), monitor, or neutralize the clandestine activities of another spy agency or foreign government.

History. Espionage is older than war. The first spies were probably prehistoric people who were curious about their neighbors' hunting techniques. The Bible tells of Moses sending spies into Canaan. More than 4,000 years ago, the first known intelligence dispatch was written on a clay tablet. It described a *covert* (secret) mission along the Euphrates River in southwestern Asia.

George Washington's extensive network of spies obtained intelligence and conducted secret missions for the Continental Army during the American Revolution (1775-1783). Allan Pinkerton directed espionage and counterespionage for the Union Army during the early days of the American Civil War (1861-1865). One of the most productive secret agents on either side was Union sympathizer Elizabeth Van Lew of Richmond, Virginia. Van Lew ran an underground network of men and women who served as spies. Van Lew reported to Union authorities on Confederate activities in Richmond, the Southern capital, and supervised covert missions from her home.

During World War II (1939-1945), the Office of Strategic Services (OSS) conducted overseas espionage and intelligence operations for the Allies. Created as a result of the surprise attack at Pearl Harbor, the OSS is considered America's first intelligence agency. President Harry Truman disbanded the OSS after the war ended.

The National Security Act of 1947 established the U.S. Central Intelligence Agency (CIA) to coordinate the nation's postwar intelligence activities. During this time, the CIA's principal adversary was the Soviet Union's KGB. *KGB* stands for Russian words meaning *Committee for State Security.* Following the Sept. 11, 2001, terrorist attacks against the United States, Congress created the Office of the Director of National Intelligence to oversee the intelligence-gathering operations of the CIA and other government agencies.

Since the mid-1990's, global reliance on information technology has resulted in major opportunities for hackers who target military, government, and corporate computer systems. This development has led to computer espionage, called *cyber espionage.* Linda McCarthy

See also **Central Intelligence Agency; Codes and ciphers; Cold War; Intelligence service; Spy.**

Esposito, *EHS puh ZEE toh,* **Phil** (1942-), was one of the greatest scorers in National Hockey League (NHL) history. A center, Esposito led the NHL in goals six straight years, from 1969-1970 through the 1974-1975 season. During the 1970-1971 season, he scored 76 goals and 152 points (goals plus assists). Both marks were NHL records until Wayne Gretzky broke them.

Esposito played with the Chicago Black Hawks (later Blackhawks) from the 1963-1964 season through the 1966-1967 season, before being traded to the Boston Bruins. In 1975, he was traded to the New York Rangers, where he played until his retirement in 1981. He was general manager of the Rangers from 1986 to 1989 and also coached the team for portions of those years. From 1990 to 1998, Esposito served as president and general manager of the Tampa Bay Lightning. Philip Anthony Esposito was born on Feb. 20, 1942, in Sault Ste. Marie, Ontario. Larry Wigge

Espy, Mike (1953-), became the first African American to serve as United States secretary of agriculture. He was appointed by President Bill Clinton in 1993 and served until the end of 1994. Before his appointment, Espy had represented Mississippi as a Democrat in the U.S. House of Representatives since 1987. He was the first African American representative from that state since the Reconstruction era of the 1860's and 1870's. In Congress, Espy served on the House Agriculture Committee, where he became known for his proposals to help farmers living in poverty.

In 1997, Espy was charged with accepting gifts from companies regulated by the Department of Agriculture while he was its secretary. Espy pleaded innocent to the charges. A trial was held in 1998. Espy was found not guilty on all of the 30 charges brought against him. The trial judge had earlier dismissed eight other charges.

Alphonso Michael Espy was born in Yazoo City, Mississippi, on Nov. 30, 1953. He received a law degree from Santa Clara University in 1978. Espy became an assistant secretary of the state of Mississippi in 1978. In

1984 and 1985, he was an assistant state attorney general.
Barbara A. Reynolds

Essay is a short, nonfictional composition that presents the writer's opinion or analysis of a particular subject. Essays make up a major form of literature that includes many types of writing, such as book reviews, magazine articles, and newspaper editorials.

There are two main kinds of essays, *personal essays* and *formal essays.* A personal essay is written in a casual, conversational style. A formal essay is carefully organized and more serious than a personal essay.

Personal essays were originated by Michel de Montaigne, a French writer of the 1500's. He was the first to establish the essay as a distinct form of literature. The word *essay* comes from *Essais* (1580), Montaigne's two-volume collection of writings. Montaigne called this collection *Essais,* a French word meaning *trials* or *attempts,* because his compositions are exploratory and informal. They are based mainly on personal experience and discuss such topics as idleness, judgment, and lying.

Joseph Addison and Sir Richard Steele, two English essayists of the early 1700's, wrote about the opinions and tastes of the English people. Addison composed clear, compactly written essays. Steele's essays are more spontaneous and conversational. Addison and Steele published and wrote essays for two periodicals, *The Tatler* (1709-1711) and *The Spectator* (1711-1712). These periodicals helped make the personal essay popular.

Charles Lamb, an English author of the early 1800's, wrote essays about the people and events in his life. Lamb's essays contain interesting insights and are written in a casual, sometimes humorous style.

Oliver Wendell Holmes, an American writer of the 1800's, composed witty personal essays. His best-known book, *The Autocrat of the Breakfast-Table* (1858), consists of 12 essays that combine imagination, humor, and scientific fact. These essays supposedly describe a breakfast conversation at a boarding house. However, they actually express Holmes's opinions on human nature, religion, science, and other topics.

H. L. Mencken was an American critic, journalist, and editor whose major essays were published in the early 1900's. His essays, written in a colorful, aggressive style, criticized the attitudes of the American middle class.

The American author E. B. White became one of the few writers of the middle and late 1900's to concentrate on personal essays. His writings have an informal, conversational style and deal with many topics.

Formal essays were developed by Sir Francis Bacon, an English philosopher and statesman of the late 1500's and early 1600's. Bacon was the first English essayist. One of his major works was *Essays* (1597), a collection of 10 essays that explain how to lead a sensible life. These essays are short, impersonal, and informative, and they discuss such subjects as death, fear, truth, and wealth.

The English poet and essayist John Milton wrote the *Areopagitica* (1644), one of the finest examples of a formal essay. It is a persuasive appeal to Parliament to protect freedom of speech and of the press. It was printed as a pamphlet and distributed in London.

Alexander Pope, an English poet of the 1700's, wrote formal essays in verse. In *An Essay on Criticism* (1711), Pope used verse to explain how poetry should be criticized. He also discussed the works of several major poets in this informative, clearly written essay. Pope's other works include *An Essay on Man* (1733-1734) and *Moral Essays* (1731-1735). One of the most important sets of formal essays in the United States was *The Federalist* (1787-1788) by James Madison, Alexander Hamilton, and John Jay. Their 85 essays argued for the ratification of the United States Constitution.

The English critic William Hazlitt was one of the best writers of formal essays during the late 1700's and early 1800's. His collection of critical essays called *Characters of Shakespeare's Plays* (1817) discusses the personalities of various characters in the dramas of William Shakespeare. Hazlitt also wrote many fine personal essays.

Ralph Waldo Emerson was an important American essayist of the 1800's. He wrote many formal essays about morals and philosophy. Emerson's book *Nature* (1836) is an essay that explains the complex principles of transcendentalism, a philosophical movement that he helped establish in the United States.

Major American essayists of the late 1900's and early 2000's included Stephen Jay Gould and Susan Sontag. Gould discussed scientific subjects. Sontag wrote about many subjects, including politics, the arts, and popular culture. H. George Hahn

Each of the writers mentioned in this article has a biography in *World Book.*

Essen (pop. 566,201), a city in western Germany, is in a major industrial region called the Ruhr (see **Germany** [political map]). The city was home to the Krupp steelworks company, a major weapons manufacturer during World War I (1914-1918) and World War II (1939-1945). In the 1990's, Krupp merged with another industrial giant, Thyssen, to form ThyssenKrupp, which continues to be a major employer in Essen. Other economic activity includes coal and electric power production, transportation, and commerce. Essen's landmarks include a cathedral that dates from the 800's; and Borbeck Castle, built in the 1200's. Essen dates from the 800's, when it was the site of a convent. Peter H. Merkl

Essenes, *EHS eenz* or *eh SEENZ,* were members of a Jewish sect living in Palestine from about 150 B.C. to A.D. 68. They numbered about 4,000 and had a communal life. Essenes were *ascetics* who tried to avoid contamination by worldly impurity (see **Asceticism**). According to the Jewish historian Josephus, the Essenes believed in the immortality of the soul, but rejected the idea of the resurrection of the body. They apparently objected to animal sacrifices. In the late 1940's and the 1950's, the remains of a settlement and several jars of scrolls were found at and around Khirbat Qumran near the Dead Sea. Many of these scrolls, which include the oldest Biblical manuscripts yet found, probably belonged to a group of Essenes. See also **Dead Sea Scrolls.** Gary G. Porton

Estate is a legal term that refers to a person's total property. The term once referred mainly to a person's land. But today the term is usually associated with the property a person owns at death. Thus, an estate may consist of land, money, stocks, cars, and collections of value, among other items. An estate can also be responsible for paying the debts the person left at the time of death. The United States government levies an *estate tax* on estates above a certain size. The tax is based on the estate's value at the time of the owner's death. There are two main kinds of estates—*leasehold* and *freehold.*

A leasehold estate is property specified in a contract or a lease by which the owner agrees to let another person use the property. The lease specifies how the property may be used, how long it may be used, and what rent will be given to the owner. A lease may last for life, for many years, or for a shorter period. Some leases specify that they may be ended at will. The holder of a leasehold estate may use the property as he or she sees fit, subject to lease terms and local laws, but that person does not own the property. See **Lease.**

A freehold estate involves some level of ownership. In the United States, there are two principal kinds of freehold estates. One is the *life estate,* which restricts the possessor's interest in a property to his or her lifetime. The other is the estate in *fee simple,* which entails absolute ownership. However, use of an estate in fee simple is subject to zoning laws and other legal restrictions.

Another form of estate, known as an estate in *fee tail,* is an old kind of freehold estate. At one time, the owners of such an estate could not sell or dispose of it. They had to leave it to a specified descendant. In most U.S. states today, however, the fee tail estate has become equivalent to an estate in fee simple.

The term *estate* meant the same thing as *status* in the days of the feudal system. The king owned the land in his realm. Private landowners were his tenants. They agreed to certain terms. Their *estate,* or status, in connection with the land they held, was the whole set of conditions of their tenancy. Michael J. Bushbaum

See also **Dower; Fee.**

Estates-General was a French representative assembly that met irregularly between 1302 and 1789. It consisted of the delegates of three groups called *estates.* The first estate was the clergy, the second the nobility, and the third the common people. The Estates-General came into being as French kings began to invite leaders from each of the three estates to meet and discuss financial matters. The assembly never won the power to make laws, nor did it ever establish itself permanently.

The Estates-General was summoned repeatedly in the late 1500's, during the Wars of Religion—a series of civil wars between French Catholics and Protestants. However, King Henry IV, who ruled from 1589 to 1610, never called the Estates. Under his son Louis XIII, the Estates met only once, in 1614. The Estates was not called again until May 1789, shortly before the French Revolution began. That year, the government was almost bankrupt, and King Louis XVI could borrow more money or raise taxes only by calling a meeting of the Estates-General.

The royal government, in response to popular pressure, asked the French people to elect delegates to the Estates-General and to prepare lists of grievances along with suggestions for reforms. The government granted the third estate, which represented more than 95 percent of the people, twice as many delegates as each of the other estates. But the third estate also demanded that all delegates receive the right to vote individually, rather than each estate receiving one vote. The king and the first and second estates resisted this demand.

On June 17, 1789, the third estate declared itself the National Assembly of France. It was soon joined by representatives of the other two estates. On June 20, the members of the new Assembly found themselves locked out of their meeting room. They then met on an indoor tennis court and swore that they would not disband until they had written a constitution for France. This vow became known as the Oath of the Tennis Court. Eventually, King Louis realized that he had to accept popular pressure for change, and the National Assembly gained control of France. Maarten Ultee

See also **French Revolution.**

Estéban. See **Estevanico.**

Ester is any of an important group of *organic* (carbon-containing) compounds. Esters belong to a class of oily or fatty substances called *lipids.* Lipids occur widely in plant and animal cells. Like other lipids, esters do not dissolve in water. Esters have the general formula RCOOR', where R and R' stand for groups of atoms that include carbon atoms. Esters form when alcohols react chemically with acids. For example, ethyl alcohol (C_2H_5OH) reacts with acetic acid (CH_3COOH) to form the ester *ethyl acetate* ($CH_3COOC_2H_5$) and water (H_2O).

Waxes are esters that act as protective, waterproof coatings on skin, feathers, and leaves. Esters called *phosphoglycerides* serve as "building blocks" of cell membranes. Fats are esters of an alcohol called *glycerol* and fatty acids. Much of *cholesterol*—a fatty substance found in animal tissues—consists of esters of fatty acids. Other esters give fragrance to flowers and flavor to fruits. *Menthyl acetate* is an ester found in peppermint oil. Esters are used to make *polyesters,* a group of materials that are commonly used in fabrics. Roger D. Barry

Estevanico, *ehs tay vahn EE koh* (1500?-1539), also called Estéban, was a black slave from Morocco who became one of the first explorers of the southwestern United States. His tales of the fabled Seven Cities of Cíbola led to the famous expedition of Francisco Coronado in 1540. See **Cíbola, Seven Cities of.**

Estevanico was a servant of the Spanish explorer Andrés Dorantes de Carranza on an expedition that landed at Tampa Bay, Florida, in 1528. Some of the group, including Estevanico and the expedition's treasurer, Álvar Núñez Cabeza de Vaca, eventually reached what is now Texas. American Indians there told Estevanico about seven cities to the north that were built of gold. Years later, in 1539, Estevanico guided Marcos de Niza's expedition to the Southwest. He explored ahead into what are now Arizona and New Mexico. He reached Cíbola, where the inhabitants of Hawikuh, a Zuni Indian pueblo, killed him. Later, Coronado found that Cíbola consisted of adobe pueblos that shone like gold from afar. Jon L. Brudvig

Esther, Book of, is a book of the Bible. It tells the story of Esther, a young Jewish woman, during the reign of the Persian King Ahasuerus. The king selects the attractive Esther as his queen. Haman, the evil prime minister, persuades the king to issue an order condemning all Jews to death. With the advice of her guardian, Mordecai, Esther persuades Ahasuerus to issue another order permitting the Jews to defend themselves on the day Haman's plan is to occur. Thus, Esther saves her people.

The Book of Esther was written between 400 and 200 B.C. It deals with Jewish survival in the face of hardship. Each February or March, Jews celebrate their deliverance from Haman in a festival called Purim (see **Purim**).

About 100 B.C., 107 additional verses were composed and inserted into the story of Esther. They are called the Additions to the Book of Esther. In some Bibles, the Additions are part of the *canon* (officially accepted writings). In others, they are part of noncanonical writings called the Apocrypha. Unlike the Book of Esther, which omits any reference to God and religious practices, the newer verses are filled with a sense of devotion and prayer. Eric M. Meyers

Esthetics. See **Aesthetics.**

Estivation, *EHS tuh VAY shuhn,* is an inactive state that occurs in the life of some animals during hot, dry periods. The word is also spelled *aestivation.* Animals that estivate are protected from dryness in much the same way as those that hibernate are protected from cold. When an animal estivates, its breathing, heartbeat, and other body processes slow down. This reduction in activity decreases the need for water. The animal can thus survive hot, dry periods in which it otherwise might die.

Many amphibians and reptiles estivate, as do some insects, snails, and fish. Fish that estivate live in ponds and streams that evaporate during the dry season. Some estivators, including various kinds of frogs, lungfish, and salamanders, form a cocoon just before entering estivation. The cocoon helps prevent water loss from the skin. The animal awakens from estivation after the dry season and emerges from its cocoon. Larry L. Wolf

See also **Hibernation; Lungfish.**

Estonia, *eh STOH nee uh,* is a country on the Baltic Sea in northeastern Europe. The country's name in Estonian, the official language, is Eesti Vabariik (Republic of Estonia). Tallinn is Estonia's capital and largest city.

Through the centuries, Germans, Danes, Swedes, Poles, and Russians controlled Estonia, but Estonians continued to foster their own culture and language. Estonia was independent from 1918 until 1940, when the Soviet Union occupied it and made it one of the 15 Soviet republics. Estonia regained its independence in 1991.

Government. Estonia has a parliamentary democracy. The parliament has 101 members, elected by the people to four-year terms. The president, the head of state, is chosen by the parliament for a five-year term. The prime minister, recommended by the president and approved by the parliament, heads government operations.

People. About 70 percent of the population are Estonians, a people related to the Finns. Russians make up about a quarter of the population. Estonia also includes small groups of Ukrainians, Belarusians, and Finns. The Estonian language is closely related to Finnish.

Most Estonians are urban dwellers and live in apartments in cities or towns. Many Estonians have colorful traditional costumes, which they wear on festive occasions. Folk songs have a long tradition in Estonia. A song festival is held every five years in Tallinn. It attracts thousands of singers and hundreds of thousands of visitors.

Many people in Estonia belong to the Lutheran and Eastern Orthodox churches. Estonia has several colleges and universities. The oldest and best known is the University of Tartu, founded in 1632.

Land and climate. Estonia consists chiefly of a low plain. Farmland covers about 25 percent of the country, and forests about 50 percent. Lake Peipus and the Narva River form much of the eastern boundary.

Estonia, Latvia, and Lithuania are often called the Baltic States. Estonia has a total of 481 miles (774 kilometers) of coastline on the Baltic Sea, the Gulf of Finland, and the Gulf of Riga. The sandy western coast is a favorite resort area. Estonia has more than 1,500 islands, the largest of

Tass from Sovfoto

Tallinn, the capital of Estonia, has many beautiful churches, castles, and other structures that were built from the 1200's to the 1500's. The city lies on Estonia's northern coast.

Symbols of Estonia. Estonia's flag has three horizontal stripes. The blue stripe at the top of the flag represents the sky. The middle stripe of black stands for the land. The white stripe at the bottom symbolizes hope in the future. The Estonian coat of arms features three blue lions on a golden shield.

Facts in brief

Capital: Tallinn.
Official language: Estonian.
Official name: Eesti Vabariik (Republic of Estonia).
Area: 17,462 mi² (45,227 km²). *Greatest distances*—north-south, 150 mi (240 km); east-west, 230 mi (370 km). *Coastline*—481 mi (774 km).
Elevation: *Highest*—Munamagi, 1,043 ft (318 m). *Lowest*—sea level along the coast.
Population: *Estimated 2014 population*—1,338,000; density, 77 per mi² (30 per km²); distribution, 70 percent urban, 30 percent rural. *2011 census*—1,294,236.
Chief products: *Agriculture*—barley, beef cattle, chickens, eggs, hogs, milk, potatoes, rye, wheat. *Manufacturing*—electronics, processed foods and beverages, textiles, wood products.
Money: *Basic unit*—euro. One hundred cents equal one euro. The Estonian kroon was taken out of circulation in 2011.

which is Saaremaa Island.

Estonia has a surprisingly mild climate for an area so far north. Sea winds help keep the weather from becoming extremely cold or hot. Temperatures average from about 24 to 29 °F (–4 to –1 °C) in January to 63 to 65 °F (17 to 18 °C) in July. Estonia receives an average of 21 to 26 inches (55 to 65 centimeters) of rain annually.

Economy. Service industries employ more than half of Estonia's workers. The main service industries are real estate, transportation and communication, and wholesale and retail trade.

Manufacturing employs about a fourth of the workers. Estonia's manufactured products include chemical fertilizer, electronics, processed foods and beverages, textiles, and wood and wood products. Tallinn is an important center for fashion and design.

Oil shale is the country's most important mineral resource. It is used extensively as fuel for electrical power plants. It is also refined into petrochemicals.

Estonia's chief agricultural products include barley, beef cattle, chickens, eggs, hogs, milk, potatoes, rye, and wheat. Commercial fishing is also important.

History. Scientists have found evidence that human settlements existed in Estonia as early as 9000 B.C. The ancestors of the Estonians settled there several thousand years ago. They formed several independent states headed by elected elders.

Early rulers. During the early 1200's, the Teutonic Knights, an organization of German crusaders, converted the Estonians to Christianity by force (see **Teutonic Knights**). They took control of southern Estonia, and Danish forces conquered the north. The Danes sold their Estonian holdings to the Teutonic Knights in 1346.

By the 1500's, German nobles owned much of Estonia's land and controlled thousands of Estonian *serfs.* Serfs worked on the estates of the nobles. In 1561, Sweden took over northern Estonia, and Poland conquered the southern part of the country. Sweden controlled all of Estonia from 1625 to 1721, when the area fell to Russia. But German nobles kept estates there until 1919.

The serfs were freed in 1816, but most of the land remained in the hands of German nobles. In 1868, former serfs gained the right to buy land. Some became successful landowners and educated their children well. Others found industrial employment in cities.

Independence. A national revival begun in the mid-1800's led to the establishment of Estonia as an independent country. Estonia proclaimed its independence on Feb. 24, 1918. Russia recognized Estonia's independence in 1920. The Estonian Constitution established a democratic form of government. In 1919, the government took over the country's large estates and began distributing the land to thousands of Estonian citizens.

Soviet rule. The Soviet Union was formed in 1922 under Russia's leadership. In 1939, the Soviet Union and Nazi Germany agreed secretly to take over a number of eastern European countries between themselves. The Soviet Union established military bases in Estonia. Soviet forces occupied Estonia in June 1940. In August, the Soviets forcibly made Estonia part of the Soviet Union. Germany occupied Estonia in 1941, during World War II, but the Soviet Union regained control of Estonia in 1944.

Estonia went through great social and economic changes under Soviet rule. At the time of the Soviet take-over in 1940, Estonians made up about 90 percent of the country's population. When Estonia regained independence in 1991, Estonians made up about 60 percent of the population. Most Estonians opposed Soviet rule, and in 1941, before the German occupation, the Soviet government deported about 10,000 Estonians to Siberia. About 100,000 Estonians fled to Western countries after the Soviet take-over. Hundreds of thousands of Russians settled in Estonia during Soviet rule.

Before Estonia became a Soviet republic, almost two-thirds of the Estonians farmed and lived in rural villages. But during Soviet rule, many people moved to the cities

Estonia

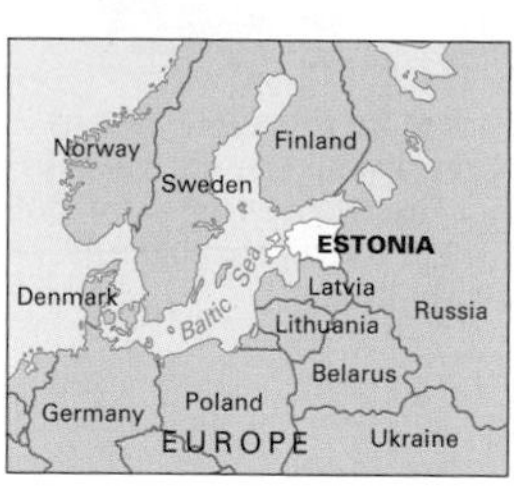

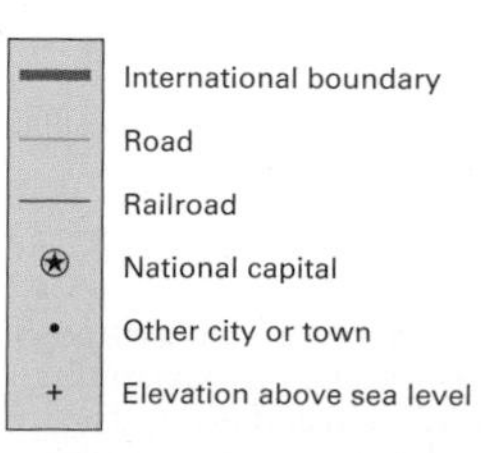

WORLD BOOK maps

© Gary Matoso, Contact Press

Estonians celebrated independence in September 1991, when the Soviet Union recognized Estonia as an independent nation. Estonia had been part of the Soviet Union since 1940, when the Soviets forcibly made it a Soviet republic.

to find industrial jobs. The Soviets prohibited private factories and farms, and they established government-controlled enterprises. They created economic plans that emphasized industrial growth. Thus, Estonia experienced much industrial development. Although its economy was advanced by Soviet standards, there were widespread complaints about the shortages and poor quality of goods and services. Economic development brought many Soviet immigrants to work in Estonia. Industrial pollution became a major problem.

Resistance to Soviet rule. After World War II ended in 1945, movements against Soviet control appeared periodically. A strong guerrilla resistance against the Soviets lasted for several years after the war. In 1949, about 20,000 Estonians were deported to Siberia. A movement to promote human rights began in the 1960's.

During the late 1980's, a new wave of Estonian nationalism appeared. It was fueled in part by Soviet leader Mikhail Gorbachev's call for openness of expression in the Soviet Union. Most Estonians demanded greater control over their government and economy. Many demanded complete independence from the Soviet Union.

Independence regained. In 1990, the Estonian parliament declared the 1940 Soviet annexation illegal and Soviet rule in Estonia invalid. The parliament called for the restoration of Estonian independence through a gradual separation from the Soviet Union. The Soviet Union called the parliament's action illegal.

In August 1991, hard-line Communist officials attempted but failed to remove Gorbachev and take over the Soviet government. In the resulting upheaval, Estonia declared independence. In September, the Soviet Union recognized Estonia's independence. In December, most of the republics formed the Commonwealth of Independent States. Estonia declined to join because it feared that Russia would control the group.

After becoming independent, Estonia moved forward with economic reform and reduced government control of most economic activities. By the mid-1990's, most businesses had become privately owned.

In 2004, Estonia joined both the European Union (EU) and the North Atlantic Treaty Organization (NATO). The EU is a group of European countries that promotes economic and political cooperation among its members. NATO is a military alliance that includes the United States, Canada, and many European countries.

Jaroslaw Bilocerkowycz

See also **Baltic States; Lake Peipus; Tallinn.**

Estrogen, *EHS truh juhn,* is any of a group of chemically similar hormones that cause the growth and development of female sexual characteristics in human beings and other animals. Estrogens also influence the female reproductive cycle. Of several forms produced in a woman's body, *estradiol* is the strongest.

During a girl's preteen or early teenage years, her ovaries begin to secrete increasing amounts of estrogens into the bloodstream. Estrogens cause the girl to develop breasts and rounded hips and cause the genital organs to enlarge and mature. Estrogens also stimulate the lining of the uterus to thicken. The hormone *progesterone* limits this growth. The uterine lining is shed during menstruation each month. The amount of estrogens secreted by the ovaries changes during the menstrual cycle. As the woman grows older, her ovaries secrete smaller amounts of estrogens. After the level of estrogens in the blood becomes too low to stimulate the uterine lining, menstruation no longer occurs. The woman is then said to have reached *menopause.*

In both women and men, small amounts of estrogens are produced in fat tissue, muscles, and many other parts of the body. In males, the *testes* (sex organs) also produce estrogens. The function of estrogens in the male is unclear.

The drug industry makes synthetic estrogens for use in birth control pills and for certain medical therapy. Use of large amounts of synthetic estrogens may harm some patients. Using birth control pills has been associated in some women with blood clots, high blood pressure, and diabetes. Women who take estrogen without progesterone are at higher risk for cancer of the *endometrium* (inner lining of the uterus). After menopause, many women receive treatment with estrogens to relieve *hot flashes* (sudden episodes of intense heat) and other symptoms associated with menopause. Women considering such treatment should discuss the possible risks with a physician. Mona M. Shangold

Related articles in ***World Book*** include:

DES
Hormone (Growth and sex hormones)
Hormone replacement therapy
Menopause
Menstruation
Progesterone
Steroid
Tamoxifen

Estrous cycle, *EHS truhs,* is the process that prepares the females of most species of mammals for mating and bearing young. It is also called the *breeding cycle.* Among many mammals, the estrous cycle occurs during a certain period, called the *breeding season.* The cycle is timed so that the young are born at the time of year when they have the best chance of survival.

During the estrous cycle, a period called *estrus,* or *heat,* occurs. The female is sexually excited throughout estrus and, among most species of mammals, will mate only during this period. The length of both the estrous cycle and estrus varies among the species. In most rats, the cycle lasts about 4 days, and estrus lasts about 14 hours. Among most breeds of dogs, the cycle lasts about six months and estrus lasts about three weeks.

Some mammals, including humans and most apes, do not have such an estrous cycle. The females of these species have a *menstrual cycle,* which prepares them to bear young (see **Menstruation**). George B. Johnson

See also **Mammal** (How mammals reproduce).

Estuary is a coastal river valley flooded by an ocean. Most estuaries are funnel-shaped, with the wide end toward the sea. Chesapeake Bay on the Atlantic Coast is an estuary in the United States. The Rio de la Plata is a major estuary on the Atlantic in South America. Estuaries in Europe include the Gironde in France and the Humber, Severn, and Thames estuaries in the United Kingdom.

Most estuaries formed as the seas rose during the past 11,500 years. The water level rose because of the melting of vast ice sheets that had accumulated during the most recent ice age.

Within an estuary, currents created by the tides mix the salty seawater with the fresh water of the river. Where those currents are weak, little mixing occurs. Because the seawater is salty, it is denser than the river water. Therefore, the river water overlies the seawater, and there are large differences in *salinity* (saltiness). But where the currents are strong, much mixing occurs, and so the salinity is the same throughout the estuary.

The river erodes soil from the land and deposits much of it in the estuary as *sediment.* Waves and tidal currents can redistribute the sediment and deposit it around the edges of the estuary. The sediment can accumulate as *mudflats,* stretches of muddy land that are uncovered at low tide. David S. McArthur

See also **River** (The mouth of a river); **Tide.**

Etching is a process of creating a design on a metal plate with the use of acid. Etching has importance both in the fine arts and in commercial printing. This article discusses etching as a fine art. For information about etching in commercial printing, see **Printing** (Methods of printing).

How etching works. Most plates used in etching are made of copper, zinc, or iron. First, the artist polishes the plate to remove any scratches. The plate is then covered with *ground,* an acid-resistant coating of beeswax, bitumen, and resin. After the ground dries, the artist draws a design or image into the ground using a sharp metal tool. The artist covers the edges and back of the plate with a tough, acid-resistant varnish and places the plate in an acid bath.

The acid *etches* (eats away) the exposed areas of metal, creating indentations. The depth of an indentation determines the appearance of a line in the finished picture. To make lines and dots of different depth and size, the artist gives the plate several acid baths, varying the time the plate is bathed. Before the second and each successive bath, the artist uses ground or varnish to *stop out* (cover) areas of the plate having the desired depth.

After finishing the etching process, the artist removes the ground and varnish. The plate is warmed and covered with a layer of oily ink. The artist wipes the plate with a pad of coarse buckram cloth until a deposit of ink has been forced into the etched indentations. The artist then places the inked plate on a press. He or she puts a sheet of dampened paper on the plate and covers the paper and plate with felt blankets. The press's heavy rollers exert great pressure on the felt, pushing the paper into the ink-filled grooves. This causes the ink to transfer onto the paper, creating the finished print.

Artists can achieve special effects by various methods, such as the way they apply and wipe the ink and the type of paper they use. Various tones can be created by roughening the plate's surface so it holds different amounts of ink. To combine tonal areas with an etched line, artists use a method that is called *aquatint.*

History. In western Europe, etching began in the early 1500's. It became an independent, creative art form in the 1600's, especially through the work of the Dutch artist Rembrandt. Pablo Picasso ranks as perhaps the greatest etcher of the 1900's. Andrew J. Stasik, Jr.

See also **Glass** (Etching); **Rembrandt.**

Ethane, *EHTH ayn,* is an important industrial gas. It is obtained directly from natural gas or by refining petroleum. Its most important use is in preparing ethylene. Ethane is sometimes used as a fuel. Industries also prepare important organic compounds from it. Ethane is a colorless, odorless, flammable gas, slightly heavier than air. It is soluble in alcohol, but only slightly soluble in water. Ethane has the chemical formula C_2H_6 and is the second member of the *paraffin* series of hydrocarbons. See also **Ethylene; Hydrocarbon.** Geoffrey E. Dolbear

Ethanol, *ETH uh nohl* or *ETH uh nol,* is a type of alcohol found in alcoholic beverages and used as an automobile fuel. It is a clear, colorless liquid that mixes read-

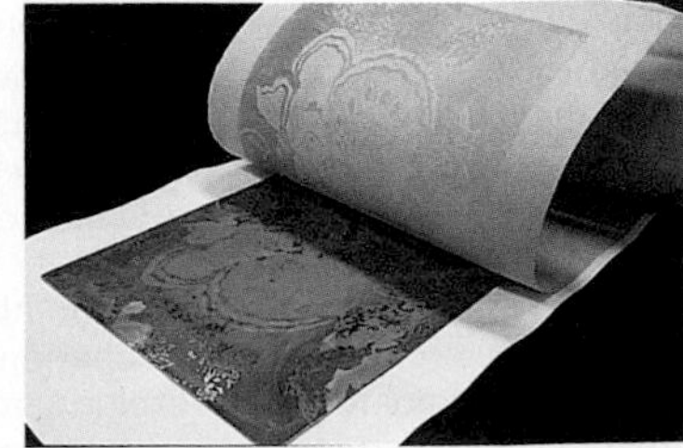

WORLD BOOK photos by Dan Miller

Making an etching. The artist draws a picture by cutting through an acid-resistant coating on a metal plate, *left.* Then, the plate is placed in an acid bath, *center.* The acid eats away the exposed metal, creating indentations. The artist forces ink into the indentations and runs the plate and a piece of paper through a press. The ink transfers onto the paper, *right,* creating the finished print.

ily with water. Ethanol dissolves a number of chemicals, making it valuable to chemical manufacturers as a *solvent* (substance that dissolves other substances). It is sometimes called *ethyl alcohol* or *grain alcohol.*

Ethanol's chemical formula is CH_3CH_2OH. It has a *relative molecular mass* of 46.07. A molecule's relative molecular mass, sometimes called its *molecular weight,* is the amount of matter in the molecule. Ethanol boils at 172 °F (78 °C) and freezes at −173 °F (−114 °C). At 20 °C, its density is 0.7893 grams per cubic centimeter.

There are two ways to manufacture ethanol. In one method, *ethylene* (a gas made from petroleum) is combined with water. The other method uses *fermentation,* a biological process in which tiny organisms called *yeast* convert sugars into ethanol. The sugars used typically come from crops also grown for food. Ethanol fermentation was one of the first chemical processes developed by people. Today, it ranks as the most common method for making ethanol.

People use most ethanol for fuel. The United States and Brazil produce about three-fourths of the world's ethanol. The United States makes most of its ethanol by fermenting corn. Brazil uses sugar cane instead.

In the late 1970's, the U.S. fuel industry introduced ethanol to reduce dependence on foreign oil. Fuel producers developed a mixture of 90 percent gasoline and 10 percent ethanol. This mixture, then called *gasohol,* is now known as *E10.* At the same time, Brazil introduced a fuel of 100 percent ethanol, E100. Traditional automobiles can use E10 without modification, but E100 requires specially designed vehicle fuel systems. In the 1990's, U.S. automakers introduced *flexible fuel vehicles* (FFV's), which use any ethanol-gasoline mixture with up to 85 percent ethanol, or E85. People in the United States drive millions of FFV's, but E85 fuel is not yet widely available. Brazil's automobiles are mostly FFV's. They run on gasoline with up to 25 percent ethanol, or E25.

Ethanol, unlike gasoline, comes from *renewable resources* that can be regrown again and again. However, many people have questioned how farmers should balance demand for ethanol fuel with the need to grow crops for food. In the United States, some byproducts of corn used in ethanol production are fed to livestock. Scientists are also developing technologies to produce ethanol from plant wastes rather than from food crops. For example, *cellulosic ethanol* is produced from woody plant wastes. Gregory W. Davis

See also **Alcohol** (Ethanol); **Alcoholic beverage.**

Ether, in chemistry, is a colorless, highly flammable liquid with a strong, sweet smell. Ether vapor causes unconsciousness when inhaled. For many years, physicians used ether as a general anesthetic during surgery. General anesthetics make patients unconscious and insensitive to pain. Ether was one of the first general anesthetics to be developed.

Credit for the first use of ether as a surgical anesthetic is given to Crawford W. Long, a Georgia doctor. Long used ether during surgery as early as 1842. However, ether anesthesia did not come into wide use until after 1846, when William T. G. Morton, a Boston dentist, first publicly demonstrated it at the Massachusetts General Hospital. For the next hundred years, ether served as the standard to which all other anesthetics were compared.

Ether's popularity declined during the mid-1900's, largely because of the increasing use of electrical equipment in the operating room. The concentrated ether vapor needed for anesthesia produced a danger of fire and explosions when used around electrical equipment. In addition, many patients took a long time to wake up from ether anesthesia, and they frequently experienced nausea and vomiting afterward. To avoid these problems, scientists developed halothane and other general anesthetics that are nonflammable and less irritating.

Today, ether is rarely used as an anesthetic. It does serve, however, as a solvent in the manufacture of perfumes, explosives, and many other products. Ether's chemical name is *ethyl ether* or *diethyl ether.* Its chemical formula is $(C_2H_5)_2O$. Edwin S. Munson

See also **Anesthesia; Halothane; Long, Crawford W.; Morton, William T. G.**

Ether, in physics, was once believed to be a substance that filled all space. By the late 1600's, some physicists believed that light traveled in waves. They knew that light could travel through artificially created vacuums and through the void of outer space. But they could not explain how light could travel without a *medium* (substance) to travel through. As a result, they assumed the presence of a *luminiferous* (light-carrying) ether, a substance that differed from all other matter. It could not be seen, felt, or weighed and was present in vacuums, outer space, and all matter. The ether was stationary, and Earth and other bodies in space moved through it.

In 1864, the British physicist James Clerk Maxwell correctly suggested that light waves are electromagnetic and travel as disturbances of an electromagnetic field. Therefore, they do not need a medium to travel through. But Maxwell and other physicists still believed in the existence of ether.

In 1887, two American scientists, Albert A. Michelson and Edward W. Morley, conducted an experiment to measure the speed of Earth relative to the ether. Their findings suggested that Earth did not move through ether. However, Hendrik A. Lorentz, a Dutch physicist, explained the finding by assuming that ether affected matter in a complicated way. In 1905, the German-born physicist Albert Einstein published his special theory of relativity, which shows how light behaves and does not rely on the existence of ether. Robert B. Prigo

See also **Light** (Electromagnetic waves); **Relativity** (Special relativity).

Etherege, Sir George (1635?-1692?), was an English playwright. Little is known of his early life, but during the Restoration period (1660-1700), he wrote *comedies of manners.* These plays were clever satires of upper-class society. Etherege provided comic portraits of London society in *The Comical Revenge, or Love in a Tub* (1664) and *She Would if She Could* (1668). But his fame rests on his only other play, *The Man of Mode, or Sir Fopling Flutter* (1676). The play is full of witty dialogue and sparkling language. Sir Fopling Flutter, a pretentious fool, is one of the most popular characters in English comedy. Etherege also created brilliant comic figures in Dorimant, an attractive young man who wins the affections of all the women in the play, and Loveit, his aging and abandoned mistress. See also **Drama** (European drama: 1660-1800). Michael Seidel

Ethics is a branch of philosophy that attempts to help us understand which ways of life are worth following and which actions are right or wrong. Ethics addresses questions of right and wrong using reason rather than faith or tradition.

Ethical issues

Some ethical theories seem complicated, but they are simply attempts to settle issues that we all think about. Usually, we think about these issues because we find ourselves faced with a tough decision.

For example: Alice knows that her friend Max has been using a harmful drug. She has tried to persuade him to stop, but he does not listen. She has begun to wonder if she should tell someone what he is doing, someone with authority who might make him stop. To some people facing such a choice, it might seem obvious that one should inform on Max. To others, it would seem equally obvious that they should say nothing.

If Alice is like most people, though, she will have conflicting thoughts. If she tells somebody, she would be violating her friend's trust in her. Max never would have let her know his secret if he had thought she would use it to get him into trouble. On the other hand, it may be best for him if she tells what she knows so that he can be helped. Alice's choice is difficult because she has more than one idea about what she should do, and these ideas lead her in opposite directions. Some philosophers would say that these conflicts arise because some of the ideas she is considering do not really apply to the question of what she should do.

Ethics tries to introduce order into the way people think about life and action. Often this means replacing the vast confusion of everyday ideas with a single general theory. Ethical theories aim to bring order into ordinary thinking by telling us which of our conflicting ideas apply to what we should do and which ones do not apply.

Ancient ethics

Before the year 1500, many ethical theorists were followers of the ancient Greek philosophers, especially Plato and Aristotle. These two influential thinkers brought order into thinking about ethical problems by defining the sort of life that is worth living and the sort of person who can live such a life. We can understand what such an admirable person would be like, Plato and Aristotle thought, by understanding the good character traits, or virtues, that such a person would possess.

Plato thought there are four virtues: (1) wisdom, (2) courage, (3) temperance, or self-control, and (4) justice. The most important of these is wisdom, which is knowledge of what is truly good. People who have wisdom and, as a result, know what is truly good will tend to do what is right. These people will act in their own true interest and be in harmony with themselves. This harmony is the basis of all justice. People who have justice, in Plato's view, will tend to have other virtues as well. Plato did not try to tell us, in a neat and easy formula, what is truly good. Instead, he wrote books in which he described the life and death of one man who, he believed, did understand goodness—his teacher Socrates. See **Plato** (Ethics).

Aristotle, Plato's most distinguished student, had views that were similar but more complicated. Aristotle disliked oversimplification. Although he agreed with Plato's four virtues, he considered other traits to be important also. These traits included friendliness, generosity, gentleness, truthfulness, and wit.

Like Plato, Aristotle thought there is one trait that is the source of all the other virtues. He called it *phronesis,* meaning *prudence* or *good judgment.* Prudence is the ability to know what we should do by figuring out which course of action would lead to a good life.

Aristotle tells us much about what the good life is like. He says that it involves such things as having friends, acting justly, and participating in community affairs. However, like Plato, Aristotle did not specify which courses of action are right and which ones are wrong. People who are properly brought up and who make full use of their own minds will, he thought, usually see the right course and take it. See **Aristotle** (Ethics and politics).

Limitations of ancient ethics. Neither Plato nor Aristotle seems to offer help to people who, like Alice, face a tough decision and do not find the solution to be obvious. Perhaps in ancient Greece people faced fewer critical decisions in which clashing ideas pulled in opposite directions. Perhaps when the ancient thinkers developed their systems of ethics, such dilemmas seemed unusual and not important for discussion. Even in a complex society like ours, with all of its conflicting traditions and theories, most ethical decisions do not present us with such dilemmas.

For whatever reason, ancient ethics did not try to provide rules to guide us in making difficult choices. Modern ethics—beginning about 1500—does, on the contrary, try to provide such rules. Ancient ethics is a theory of normal life, while modern ethics is a theory of life in crisis. Modern ethics aims to help us sort out the conflicting reasons for different courses of action. Modern ethics tries to help us decide which reasons are important or fundamental and which are less important or not valid at all.

Modern ethics

When people face a critical choice like Alice's and hesitate between different courses of action, they think of reasons for the different things they might do. Modern thinkers have observed that the reasons people produce in such situations can be sorted into different categories. There are considerations of *benefits* and considerations of *obligations.* On one hand, Alice may think she has an obligation to Max to keep quiet about what he does. On the other hand, she may think he might benefit if she violates this obligation by speaking up. In this case, as in others, considering one's obligations may lead to different conclusions than considering what is beneficial to people. A person who always takes obligations seriously will make different decisions than a person who is committed to doing what is most beneficial to people. After hundreds of years of thinking about conflicts among moral ideas, theorists have reached at least one conclusion. This conclusion is that it is difficult to give equal importance to both obligations and benefits.

Modern ethical theory is roughly divided into two schools of thought: (1) *deontology* and (2) *teleology.* Deontology holds that what really matters, ethically, is what your obligations are. Teleology claims that what really matters is which actions or policies would be most beneficial to people.

Kant. The greatest of the deontologists was Immanuel Kant, a German philosopher of the 1700's. He believed that the only test of whether a decision is right or wrong is whether it could be applied to everyone. Would it be all right for everyone to do what you are doing? If not, your decision is wrong. It would be wrong, for example, to make a promise with the intention of breaking it because if everyone did that, no one would believe anyone's promises. As a result, no one would make promises at all.

Kant thought that the difference between right and wrong is simply a matter of consistency: can you apply the same standard to others that you apply to yourself? You must ask if it would be acceptable if everyone were to act in the way that you propose to act. Using this test, Kant would probably say that Alice should inform the authorities about Max's drug use. To Kant, whether a person's decisions are useful, whether they bring about desirable results for oneself or anyone else, is not ethically important. See **Kant, Immanuel.**

Bentham and Mill. Arguing against Kant, teleologists have often pointed out that most moral rules are actually useful or beneficial. Rules against murder and theft serve to protect our interests. If there were no such rules, we would be faced with a constant threat of violent injury and death.

Moral rules protect us from misery and chaos, and it is hard to imagine anything more useful than that. Teleologists have asked what followers of Kant would say if a moral rule that they believe in was found to make people unhappy and do no good at all. They would immediately decide that the rule was a bad one. The reason for this, teleologists say, is that deontologists are like everyone else. Despite their theories, what matters in the end is what is beneficial or useful.

The most influential teleologists are the *utilitarians,* who include the English philosophers Jeremy Bentham during the 1700's and John Stuart Mill in the 1800's. The utilitarians claim that the test of whether a policy or action is right is not whether it brings happiness to a particular individual, but whether it increases happiness for society as a whole. We should have rules against murder and theft, though they frustrate murderers and thieves, because most people are happier with such rules.

Mill argued that the code of rules that is best for humanity is one that prevents people from harming one another but otherwise lets them do what they want. Mill believed that people are happiest if they develop their ability to make choices and learn from their mistakes, provided they injure no one but themselves. Mill might tell Alice that she should think again about how beneficial it would be for Max if she were to inform on him. Being forced to quit drugs when he did not want to might cause more harm than good. According to Mill, we only reach full potential for happiness if society and government allow individuals to pursue their own experiments in living.

On the other hand, Kant's followers have asked what Mill would think of a system ruled by masterminds. These superior beings would persuade people to want what was best for them and thus would leave them unable to make their own choices. Of course, Mill would find such a system horrifying. But the followers of Kant say that this shows that even for Mill there is something more important than satisfaction or happiness. That something is the dignity people have as rational beings, who are able to grasp moral law and make decisions based on it.

Nietzsche. Most modern ethical theorists have been either deontologists or teleologists, but some have criticized both of these positions. The most famous of these critics was the German philosopher Friedrich Nietzsche, who lived in the 1800's. Nietzsche thought that the ideas of the ancient Greeks were closer to the truth than those of the moderns. He believed that the problem the deontologists and teleologists argued about—the problem of which actions are right and which are wrong—cannot be solved and is not really that important. Different nations and cultures make up their own ethical rules to suit their own unique circumstances. According to Nietzsche, what is held to be right and good in one culture or historical period could be considered bad or evil in another culture or historical period.

Like Plato and Aristotle, Nietzsche thought that human beings should concern themselves with attaining virtue rather than with the correctness of their particular actions. His notion of virtue, however, was different from theirs. For him, attaining virtue was essentially a matter of achieving more power, especially power over oneself. Virtue does not depend upon believing some rational notion of the good life. There is no such thing as *the* good life. There are only a "thousand and one goals" that different people pursue. It is not one's choice of goals that determines one's virtue. It is rather the power with which one pursues whatever goals one has chosen. See **Nietzsche, Friedrich.**

What can ethics do for us?

Faced with the great variety of ethical theories, people may still lack answers to such questions as "How should I live?" and "What should I do?" Such questions probably ask too much of ethics. Perhaps ethics can do no more than help us make our own ideas clearer, more rational, and more responsive to the realities of life. Ethical theory might not tell Alice what to do. But it might help her to think clearly and critically about her values, and to decide whether she needs to develop better ones. That is probably a process that never ends. Lester H. Hunt

Related articles in ***World Book*** include:

Aristotle (Ethics and politics)
Bioethics
Business ethics
Kant, Immanuel
Medical ethics
Moral education
Philosophy (Ethics and political philosophy)
Plato (Ethics)
Religion (A code of conduct)

Additional resources

Becker, Lawrence C. and Charlotte B., eds. *Encyclopedia of Ethics.* 3 vols. 2nd ed. Routledge, 2001.
Blackburn, Simon. *Being Good: An Introduction to Ethics.* Oxford, 2001.
Grenz, Stanley J., and Smith, J. T. *Pocket Dictionary of Ethics.* InterVarsity, 2003.
Roth, John K., ed. *Ethics.* 3 vols. Rev. ed. Salem Pr., 2004.

© Robert Harding Picture Library/SuperStock

Addis Ababa, the capital and largest city of Ethiopia, has many modern buildings. An important Ethiopian economic center, the city also hosts many international African conferences.

Ethiopia, *ee thee OH pee uh,* is a country in northeastern Africa. Much of Ethiopia consists of rugged mountains and a high plateau. Addis Ababa is Ethiopia's capital and largest city.

The name *Ethiopia* comes from a Greek word meaning *burned faces.* The ancient Greeks used the word to refer to lands south of Egypt—including modern Ethiopia—where people had darker skin than the Greeks or most Egyptians. Ethiopia was formerly called Abyssinia, a name derived from the Yemeni term *Habashat,* which means *the country of mixed population.* More than 80 ethnic groups, speaking dozens of different languages, live in Ethiopia.

Ethiopia is one of the oldest nations. According to tradition, the first emperor of Ethiopia, Menelik I, was the son of the Biblical queen of Sheba and King Solomon of ancient Israel. Later Ethiopian rulers of the Solomonic dynasty claimed descent from the queen of Sheba and Solomon. This dynasty ruled Ethiopia until 1974, when a military *coup* (take-over) established a socialist government. Military leaders controlled the government until they were overthrown by rebels in 1991. A new constitution came into effect in 1994.

Government

National government of Ethiopia consists of a two-house legislature, a prime minister, and a president. The legislature is called the Federal Parliamentary Assembly. It consists of the Council of the Federation and the Council of People's Representatives. Ethiopia's states elect the members of the Council of the Federation. The people elect the members of the Council of People's Representatives. The Council of People's Representatives chooses the prime minister, who heads the government. Both houses of the Federal Parliamentary Assembly choose the president, who serves a mainly ceremonial role.

Local government. Ethiopia is divided into nine states and two cities, Addis Ababa and Dire Dawa. The states were created on the basis of the ethnic groups living in them. Each state has its own parliamentary assembly chosen through local elections.

Courts. The Federal Supreme Court is Ethiopia's highest court. It hears appeals from the Federal High Court, the second highest court.

Armed forces. Ethiopia has an army and an air force. Members of the armed forces must be at least 18 years of age.

People

Ethnic and language groups. The government classifies Ethiopians into groups based on the main language they speak. Major ethnic and language groups include the Oromo, Amhara, and Tigrayan peoples.

The Oromo make up the largest ethnic and language group. They speak a language called Oromiffa or Afaan Oromo, an African language related to Somali. The Oromo live in nearly every part of the country. Amhara and Tigrayan peoples of the northern plateau speak Amharic—the nation's official language—and Tigrinya, respectively. These languages belong to the same language family as Arabic and Hebrew.

Other important ethnic and language groups in Ethiopia include the Somali, who live in the southeast, and the Afar, who live in the east and northeast. Many Ethiopians speak more than one language, including English and other Ethiopian and European languages.

Ge'ez (also called Ethiopic) is an ancient Ethiopian language. In the past, all Ethiopian Bibles were written in the language. The Ethiopian Orthodox Church still uses Ge'ez in ceremonies.

Way of life. Most Ethiopians live in rural areas as either farmers or livestock herders. Many small farmers use an ancient wooden plow called a *maresha* and oxen to plow their fields. They grow crops for sale, such as coffee, and various cereal crops, such as barley, corn, wheat, and a tiny local grain called *teff.* Livestock herders raise camels, cattle, goats, and sheep. They travel from place to place to find food for their animals. Ethiopians in cities and towns work for the government, hold jobs in businesses and industries, or run shops.

Poverty in Ethiopia is widespread. Each year, many rural men and women move to towns and cities to seek jobs and a better life. Medical care, electric power, schools, and clean water supplies are part of what attracts rural Ethiopians to cities.

Styles of houses vary widely in Ethiopia. Many houses in rural areas are round with walls constructed of wooden poles and mud plaster. These houses have roofs of thatch or iron. In Tigray areas, many dwellings are rectangular and made of stone. Addis Ababa and other cities have tall office buildings, multistory apartment houses, large villas, and mixed neighborhoods of stone, brick, mud, and cement houses.

© SuperStock

A typical Ethiopian village, such as this one in the north, consists of a number of round houses with thatched roofs. Most rural Ethiopians live in villages or isolated homesteads.

In rural areas, many men and women wear a white cotton cloth called a *shamma.* Men wear a shamma over a shirt, and women wear it over a dress. In towns and cities, many people wear clothing similar to that worn in Europe and North America. In southern Ethiopia, some people wear traditional clothing made of leather or a colorful cloth used as a shawl and a waist wrap.

Ethiopians eat a wide variety of foods based on a diet of *injera.* This large flat bread is made of fermented flour from teff or other grains. Ethiopians also eat barley, corn, or wheat, which are roasted or boiled. Ethiopians in some areas eat a bread made from the root of *ensete,* a plant that resembles a banana tree. Popular beverages include beer, coffee, tea, and thin yogurt.

Favorite sports in Ethiopia include soccer, volleyball, and *genna,* a game similar to field hockey. Ethiopians also enjoy playing card games, as well as a local kind of chess and other board games. Holidays include special celebrations from both the Christian and Islamic faiths.

Religion. Most Ethiopians are either Christians or Muslims. About 40 percent of the people belong to the Ethiopian Orthodox Church, a Christian faith related to the Coptic, Greek, and Russian Orthodox churches.

A small group of Jewish Ethiopians called the Falasha or Beta Israel lived in the northeast highlands. The group practiced an old form of Judaism. The Falasha left Ethiopia to take up citizenship in the Jewish state of Israel. They left in two main waves, one in the mid-1980's and the other in the 1990's. However, other Jews known as Falash Mura remained in Ethiopia. These people are descendants of Jews who converted to Christianity in the 1800's to avoid persecution. Beginning in the late 1990's, the government of Israel began to allow some Falash Mura to immigrate to Israel.

Education. Ethiopian children are not required by law to attend school. About 45 percent of the children attend elementary school, but less than 15 percent attend high school. The main national university is Addis Ababa University. There are also several regional, state, and private universities.

The arts. Much of the country's art is related to the Ethiopian Orthodox religion. In the past, many artists painted church walls with Biblical scenes and pictures of saints. Artists also illustrated religious manuscripts with elaborate decorations. Writers created religious poetry and other sacred works in the Ge'ez language.

Since the early 1900's, Ethiopian writers have produced novels, plays, and poetry in Amharic and other modern Ethiopian languages. Modern artists have created murals, paintings, and stained-glass windows that incorporate European and American styles.

Land and climate

The Ethiopian Plateau covers much of the western and central parts of the country. Lowlands surround the plateau.

The Ethiopian Plateau spreads out over about two-thirds of the country. It lies between 6,000 and 10,000 feet (1,800 and 3,000 meters) above sea level. Most of Ethiopia's people live on the plateau, which has the

Facts in brief

Capital: Addis Ababa.

Official language: Amharic.

Official name: Federal Democratic Republic of Ethiopia.

Area: 426,373 mi² (1,104,300 km²). *Greatest distances*—north-south, 800 mi (1,290 km); east-west, 1,035 mi (1,666 km).

Elevation: *Highest*—Ras Dashen, 15,158 ft (4,620 m) above sea level. *Lowest*—Denakil Depression, 381 ft (116 m) below sea level.

Population: *Estimated 2014 population*—91,226,000; density, 214 per mi² (83 per km²); distribution, 83 percent rural, 17 percent urban. *2007 census*—73,750,932.

Chief products: *Agriculture*—cattle, coffee, corn, khat, oilseeds, sheep, sorghum, sugar cane, teff, wheat. *Manufacturing*—cement, leather products, processed food, textiles.

National anthem: "Whedefit Gesgeshi Woude Henate Ethiopia" ("March Forward, Dear Mother Ethiopia").

Flag: The flag has three horizontal stripes—green, yellow, and red (from top to bottom). The country's coat of arms appears in the center. It has a yellow star design on a round blue field. See **Flag** (picture: Flags of Africa).

Money: *Basic unit*—birr. One hundred cents equal one birr.

Outline

I. Government
- A. National government
- B. Local government
- C. Courts
- D. Armed forces

II. People
- A. Ethnic and language groups
- B. Way of life
- C. Religion
- D. Education
- E. The arts

III. Land and climate
- A. The Ethiopian Plateau
- B. The lowlands
- C. Rivers and lakes
- D. Animal life and vegetation

IV. Economy
- A. Agriculture
- B. Manufacturing
- C. International trade
- D. Transportation and communication

V. History

country's best agricultural land. Most of the plateau receives more than 40 inches (102 centimeters) of rain annually. Average temperatures on the plateau range from about 72 °F (22 °C) in areas below 8,000 feet (2,400 meters) to less than 60 °F (16 °C) at higher altitudes.

The Great Rift Valley, which runs north and south through eastern Africa, divides the plateau into two large sections. The sections are further divided by deep, spectacular river gorges and high mountain ranges. Ethiopia's highest mountain, Ras Dashen, rises 15,158 feet (4,620 meters) above sea level on the plateau.

The lowlands. The Ethiopian Plateau slopes downward in all directions toward lowland regions. Most of the lowland areas have an average temperature of about 80 °F (27 °C) and receive less than 20 inches (51 centimeters) of rain a year. The Denakil Depression, which lies below sea level in northeastern Ethiopia, is one of the hottest places in the world. Temperatures there sometimes rise above 120 °F (49 °C). The lowlands are thinly populated because of the hot, dry climate and because the soil is poor for farming.

Rivers and lakes. Ethiopia's chief rivers include the Awash, Baro, Blue Nile (called Abay in Ethiopia), Genale, Omo, and Wabe Shebele. Lake Tana, the country's largest lake, lies in the northwest. A number of lakes extend through southern Ethiopia along the Great Rift Valley. The lakes include Abaya and Ziway.

Animal life and vegetation. A wide variety of animals live in Ethiopia. Some of these animals live nowhere else. They include an antelope called the walia ibex and the Simien fox, also known as the Simien jackal or Ethiopian wolf. Coffee originated in the forests of southwest Ethiopia. Teff and several other types of crops also had their origins in the country. The most common tree in Ethiopia is the eucalyptus, which was imported from Australia in the 1890's.

Economy

Ethiopia is one of Africa's poorest and least developed countries. Agriculture is the country's chief economic activity and employs most of its workers. Service industries, especially banking, government, insurance, retail trade, tourism, and transportation, also contribute much to Ethiopia's economy.

Agriculture. Many Ethiopian farmers produce goods chiefly for their own use. Grain crops include corn, sorghum, teff, and wheat. Many farmers in the southwest grow coffee plants. Other crops grown for sale include khat, oilseeds, and sugar cane. The leaves of khat produce a feeling of well-being when chewed. Most

Ethiopia

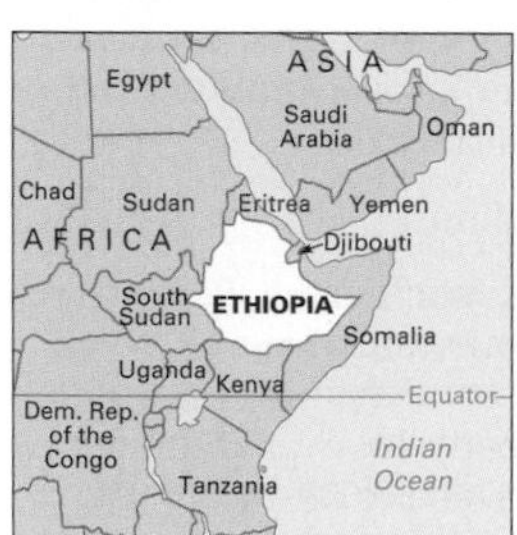

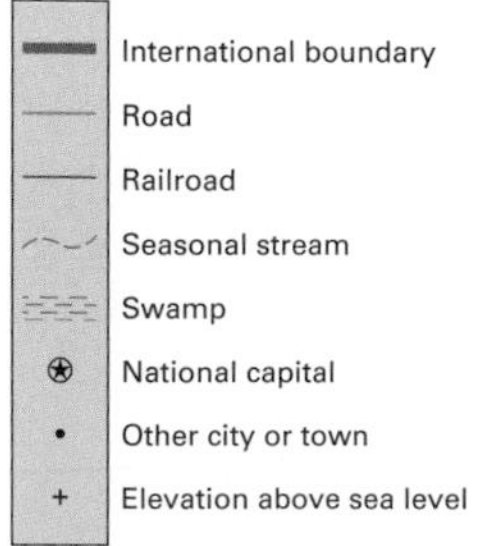

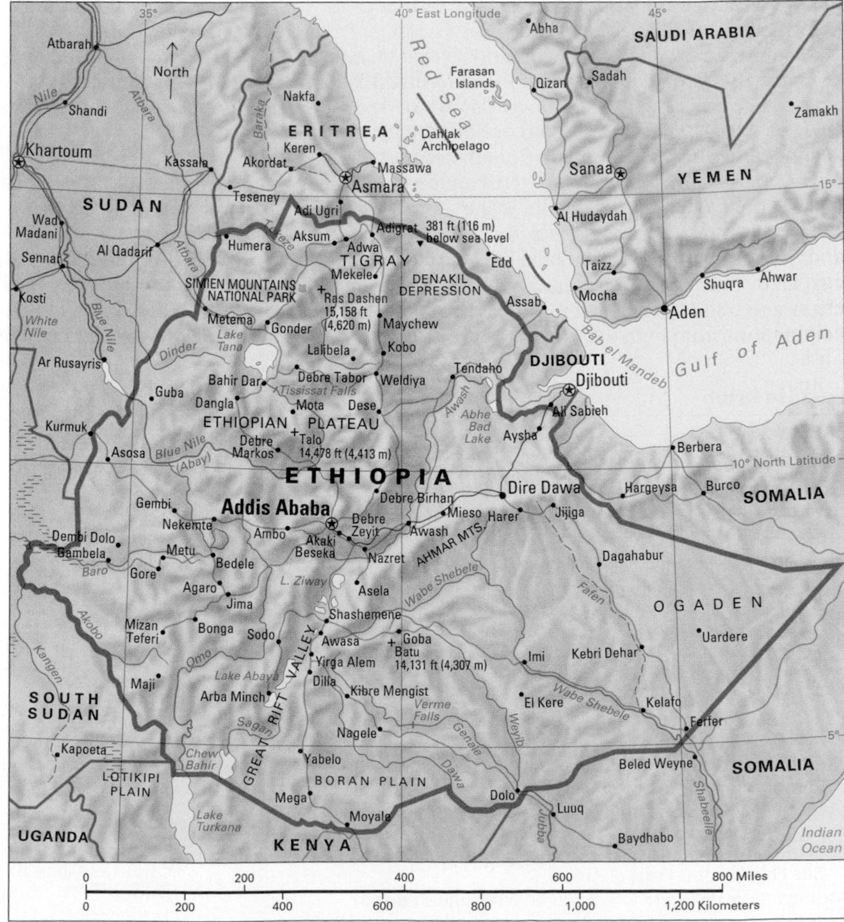

WORLD BOOK maps

farmers also raise cattle, chickens, goats, and sheep.

Although agriculture is widespread in Ethiopia, farming methods are inefficient. Many farmers struggle just to raise enough food for their families. Droughts occur from time to time and sometimes result in famine.

Manufacturing accounts for a small percentage of both Ethiopia's economic production and its employment. The country produces cement, leather products, processed foods, and textiles.

International trade. Ethiopia imports much more than it exports. Coffee, gold, leather products, oilseeds, and vegetables rank among Ethiopia's chief exports. Imports include food, machinery, motor vehicles, and petroleum products. Ethiopia's chief trading partners include China, Germany, India, Italy, and Saudi Arabia.

Transportation and communication. Most of Ethiopia's roads are unpaved. A railroad connects Addis Ababa with the port city of Djibouti, in the country also called Djibouti. Addis Ababa also has an international airport. Much of Ethiopia's international trade takes place through Djibouti.

Several daily newspapers are published in Amharic, English, and Tigrinya. The government controls the country's television station and most of its radio stations.

History

Early days. Some of the oldest fossil fragments of human ancestors have been found in Ethiopia. They date from about 5 million years ago.

By about 1000 B.C., farmers in Ethiopia had domesticated a number of crops, including such grains as millet, sorghum, and teff. The plow was already the major agricultural tool by that time. In addition, there is evidence that Ethiopians controlled water and used irrigation.

The Aksum Kingdom was the first important state in what is now Ethiopia. It was well established by the A.D. 200's. Its capital was the city of Aksum. The Aksum Kingdom gained much wealth through trade with Arabia, Egypt, Greece, India, Persia, and Rome. The Aksumites exported gold, ivory, and spices. Aksum reached its height of power in the 300's under King Ezana. He made Christianity the official religion of Aksum.

In the late 600's, Aksum's power fell sharply after Muslims gained control of Arabia, the Red Sea, and the coast of northern Africa. The Muslims put an end to the foreign trade of Christian Aksum.

The Zagwé dynasty. In 1137, the Zagwé dynasty rose to power on the Ethiopian Plateau. The Zagwé rulers had their capital at Roha—now called Lalibela. During the reign of the Zagwé emperors, 11 magnificent churches were carved out of solid rock at Roha. The churches still stand. In 1270, Yekuno Amlak overthrew the Zagwé dynasty. After the 1500's, the Ethiopian Empire broke up into a number of small kingdoms.

Menelik II, who became emperor in 1889, reunified the old Ethiopian Empire by gaining control of many of the small kingdoms. In 1896, at the Battle of Adwa, Menelik defeated an Italian army that had occupied a part of Ethiopia called Eritrea. This victory earned him much respect and increased his power in Ethiopia.

Under Menelik, Ethiopia engaged in its own colonial expansion and nearly doubled its territory to the south and east. Menelik made Addis Ababa the capital of Ethiopia. He began the construction of the railway that links Addis Ababa to Djibouti. Menelik also established the first modern schools and hospitals in Ethiopia.

© George Holton, Photo Researchers

The spectacular Tissisat Falls is formed by waters of the Blue Nile River. The falls is on the Ethiopian Plateau, about 20 miles (32 kilometers) southeast of Lake Tana.

In 1913, Lij Iyasu, Menelik's grandson, became emperor of Ethiopia. He introduced political reforms that threatened the power of the traditional ruling class. A military coup removed Lij Iyasu from power in 1916. France, Italy, and the United Kingdom supported the coup because they feared Lij Iyasu might side against them in World War I (1914-1918). Zawditu, Menelik's daughter, then became empress of Ethiopia. She ruled with the help of Ras Tafari, the son of Menelik's cousin. Tafari was named heir to the throne.

Haile Selassie. Zawditu died in 1930. Tafari then became emperor and took the name Haile Selassie I. He continued Menelik's policy of modernizing Ethiopia. In 1931, he gave the country its first written constitution.

Italy invaded Ethiopia in 1935 in an attempt to expand its colonies in Africa. In 1936, the Italians conquered Addis Ababa, and Haile Selassie fled to the United Kingdom. Italy aided Ethiopia's development by building a network of roads. However, Italian rule was harsh, and Ethiopians rose up against it. Some Ethiopians used *guerrilla* tactics, such as sudden raids and other small-scale attacks. In 1941, during World War II, British troops helped the Ethiopians drive the Italians out of Ethiopia. Haile Selassie then returned to the throne.

Eritrea, a province along the Red Sea, had been captured by Italy in the 1880's. In the late 1940's, Eritrean and Ethiopian nationalists debated whether Eritrea should be an independent nation or a federation with Ethiopia. In 1952, Ethiopia regained control of the area when Eritrea was joined with Ethiopia in a federation. In 1961, civil war broke out in Eritrea. The following year, the Eritrean parliament dissolved the federation under pressure from Ethiopia.

The Ogaden region of southeastern Ethiopia also became a trouble spot in the 1960's. The government of neighboring Somalia claimed the region, which Menelik had conquered in the 1890's. Many Somali people had always lived there, and they revolted against Ethiopian rule. In the late 1970's, Ethiopia and Somalia fought over the Ogaden region.

Military take-over. In the 1960's, many Ethiopians became dissatisfied with Haile Selassie's government. They demanded better living conditions for the poor and an end to government corruption. In 1972 and 1973, severe drought led to famine in northern Ethiopia. Haile Selassie's critics claimed that he ignored victims of the famine. In 1974, Ethiopian military leaders removed the emperor from power and took over the government.

The military government adopted socialist policies and established close relations with the Soviet Union. In 1975, the government began large-scale land reform, breaking up the huge estates of the former nobility. The government claimed ownership of this land. The military leaders killed many of their Ethiopian opponents. In the late 1970's, insurgents in the Tigray region in the north called for independence from the central government.

Severe drought again led to famine in the mid-1980's, mainly in the northern part of the country. About 1 million people died as a result. In 1987, Ethiopia adopted a constitution that provided for a return to civilian government. A parliament was elected, but the country's military leaders continued to hold power. Lieutenant Colonel Mengistu Haile Mariam became president.

The late 1900's. In the 1980's, Ethiopia's government continued to face rebellions in the Eritrea and Tigray regions. In 1991, rebels consisting of Eritrean, Tigrayan, and Oromo liberation forces defeated President Mengistu and his army. In May 1991, the rebels, chiefly from the province of Tigray, established the Transitional Government of Ethiopia. The Eritrean rebels established a separate government, and Eritrea gained independence in 1993. At that time, however, part of the border between the two countries was not clearly defined.

In 1994, Ethiopia adopted a new constitution. In 1995, the country held its first multiparty parliamentary elections. The Ethiopian People's Revolutionary Democratic Front, which had dominated the government since 1991, won elections in 1995 and in 2000. Party leader Meles Zenawi was chosen prime minister after both elections.

Ethiopia and Eritrea fought a war over disputed land from May 1998 to June 2000, when the two sides signed a cease-fire agreement. They signed a formal peace treaty in December 2000. The treaty established a commission to determine the border between the two countries. The commission issued a border ruling in 2002. But Ethiopia objected to the ruling, and the border has not yet been marked. In 2005, a commission of an international court blamed Eritrea for starting the border war. Both Eritrea and Ethiopia began troop build-ups along the border. In 2009, the commission ruled that Eritrea owed Ethiopia $10 million. Both countries accepted the ruling.

Hulton Getty/Archive Photos

Haile Selassie I ruled Ethiopia as emperor beginning in 1930. He gave the country its first written constitution in 1931. His reign ended in 1974, when military leaders overthrew him.

AP Photo

Ethiopian soldiers withdraw from Eritrea in 2001 after the two countries reached a cease-fire agreement. Ethiopia and Eritrea went to war in 1998 over a border dispute.

Recent developments. Droughts again struck Ethiopia during the early 2000's. Millions of people faced starvation.

Zenawi's party claimed victory in elections held in May 2005. However, opponents argued that the election had been rigged, and protests erupted. On June 8, security forces in Addis Ababa opened fire on protesters, killing dozens of them. The opposition continued to dispute the results. About 100 members of the Federal Parliamentary Assembly boycotted the Assembly. In November, more election protests turned violent. Over 190 people died in the June and November protests.

In 2006, an Ethiopian court convicted former President Mengistu *in absentia* (while absent) of genocide. Mengistu has been living in Zimbabwe since 1991.

In December 2006, Ethiopian forces assisted the United Nations-backed Somali government forces in fighting back an Islamic militia that had gained control of southern Somalia. In March 2007, African Union peacekeeping forces began entering Somalia. Occasional fighting continued between Ethiopian and African Union troops, the Islamic militia, and clan factions. Ethiopian troops pulled out of Somalia in January 2009. But fighting continued, and Ethiopian troops again fought Islamic militants in Somalia in late 2011 and in 2012.

Zenawi's party increased its parliamentary majority following May 2010 elections. Opposition parties again claimed that the results were fraudulent. Zenawi died in August 2012. Ezekiel Gebissa

Related articles in *World Book* include:

Addis Ababa
Aksum
Bruce, James
Clothing (picture: Traditional costumes)
Eritrea
Great Rift Valley
Haile Selassie I
Italo-Ethiopian War
Lake Tana
Menelik II
Prester John

Additional resources

Metaferia, Getachew. *Ethiopia and the United States.* Algora Pub., 2007.

Teferra, Daniel. *Lessons of Peace and Development.* Univ. Pr. of Am., 2008.

Tronvoll, Kjetil. *War & the Politics of Identity in Ethiopia.* Oxford, 2009.

Ethnic group is a group of people with common characteristics that distinguish them from most other people of the same society. Members may have ties of ancestry, culture, language, nationality, or religion, or a combination of these things. Most ethnic groups are minority groups with at least some values or institutions that differ from those of the larger society. Since ancient times, ethnic groups have resulted from migrations, wars, slavery, changed political boundaries, and other significant movements of peoples. In some nations, ethnic identification may affect social standing and access to power. In Japan, for example, people of Korean ancestry have been discriminated against by the Japanese.

In the United States, the term *ethnic group* refers to groups that immigrated to America since about 1840. These include Chinese, Dutch, Germans, Greeks, Irish, Italians, Japanese, Jews, Mexicans, and Poles. Others include African Americans, whose ancestors were brought to America as slaves, and American Indians.

Ethnic groups can bring variety and richness to a society by introducing their own ideas and ways of life. But ethnic groups who promote their own interests above others in a multiethnic nation or state can also threaten national unity. In many places, neighboring ethnic groups dislike and distrust one another.

The United States is one of the world's most ethnically mixed societies. Some social scientists call the nation a *melting pot,* meaning its different ethnic groups have joined to form a unified culture and have given up their ethnic ties. Others believe the country consists of many separate ethnic groups. Their view is called *ethnic pluralism.* Most social scientists believe that there has been considerable "melting" in the United States but that the nation also reflects much pluralism. Russell Zanca

See also the *People* section of the continent and country articles in *World Book,* such as **Africa** (People).

Ethnocentrism, *EHTH noh SEHN trihz uhm,* is the belief that one's own culture is the best and most natural. William Graham Sumner, an American sociologist, introduced the term in 1906. He defined it as "the tendency to view one's own group as the center of everything, and all others are scaled and rated with reference to it."

As a result of growing up within a culture, people view their society's ways as the normal and proper ways of thinking, feeling, and acting. Ethnocentrism probably cannot be avoided. It gives people a sense of belonging and pride, and a willingness to sacrifice for the good of the group. But ethnocentrism is harmful if carried to extremes. It may cause prejudice, automatic rejection of ideas from other cultures, and even persecution of other groups. Exposure to other cultures may lessen such reactions, but they can never be completely overcome.

Many social scientists consider ethnocentrism a problem in their work. A researcher's observations should be impartial. However, a tendency to judge other people by the standards of one's own group may distort these observations. James W. Vander Zanden

See also **Ethnic group; Minority group; Racism.**

Ethnography is the scientific description of contemporary cultures. The term also refers to a written, photographic, or motion-picture report that provides such a description. An ethnography deals with one group of people or, at most, several neighboring peoples. Anthropologists compare ethnographies to determine similarities and differences in how human groups behave. This comparative study is called *ethnology.* Ethnography and ethnology provide the basis for *cultural anthropology,* also called *social anthropology.*

An anthropologist gathers information for an ethnography by doing *field work*—that is, by living with a group of people and studying their culture. The ethnographer studies the people's values, daily life, and social relationships. He or she obtains information in a variety of ways, including talking with the people and filming them.

Ethnography requires sensitivity and an ability to speak the language of the people being studied. An ethnographer must become involved with the people to understand their culture. At the same time, he or she must remain a detached, scientific observer.

Most ethnographers are trained in anthropology, particularly cultural anthropology. But other scientists also do ethnographic research. Two classic ethnographies are *Argonauts of the Western Pacific* (1922), by the Polish-born anthropologist Bronisław Malinowski, and *The Nuer* (1940), by the British anthropologist E. E. Evans-Pritchard. Russell Zanca

Ethnology. See **Ethnography.**

Ethology, *ih THAHL uh jee,* is the branch of zoology that deals with animal instincts. Ethologists study such instinctive behavior as courtship, mating, and care of young. They also study how animals communicate and how animals establish and defend their territories.

Ethologists seek to determine what causes instinctive behavior, how such behavior developed over millions of years, and how it helps a species survive. For each kind of animal studied, ethologists prepare an *ethogram,* a list that describes the known behavior patterns of the species. In the ethogram, ethologists also try to specify conditions under which each instinctive act occurs. Ethologists have developed ethograms for various species of insects, fishes, birds, and mammals.

Duane M. Rumbaugh

Related articles in *World Book* include:

Dominance	Lorenz, Konrad Z.
Frisch, Karl von	Morris, Desmond
Hamilton, William Donald	Sociobiology
Instinct	Tinbergen, Nikolaas

Ethyl alcohol. See **Alcohol.**

Ethylene, *EHTH uh leen,* an *organic* (carbon-based) gas, is one of the most important industrial chemicals. Tens of millions of tons of ethylene are produced worldwide each year.

The chemical industry uses ethylene to prepare compounds, such as ethylene oxide, polyethylene, ethyl alcohol, ethylbenzene, ethyl chloride, and ethylene dichloride. Ethylene oxide is used to make ethylene glycol (antifreeze). The plastics industry uses polyethylene. Plastics manufacturers also convert ethylbenzene to styrene, which is used for plastics and synthetic rubber. Ethylene is also used to help ripen fruit. Ethylene is prepared by heating ethane and propane to high temperatures in the presence of steam. Ethylene is also obtained as a by-product of petroleum refinery processes.

Ethylene is a colorless, flammable gas that has a faint, sweet odor. It is slightly lighter than air. Its chemical formula is C_2H_4, and it is the first member of the *olefin* series of aliphatic hydrocarbons. Ethylene mixed with air is explosive. Geoffrey E. Dolbear

Etiquette, *EHT uh keht,* is a code of behavior that helps people get along with one another. Some people think of it as a set of rigid rules concerning such subjects as the proper dress for a party, the organization of a wedding, or the setting of a dinner table. But etiquette deals with a much wider range of behavior—everything from being a guest to blowing your nose, riding an elevator to sending a text message.

Each culture has its own system of etiquette. Behavior considered proper in one culture may be considered improper in another. In Japan, for example, people take off their shoes before entering a house. In the United States, guests might be regarded as impolite if they removed their shoes. In general, this article discusses etiquette in Western society.

Etiquette also varies within a culture. People in large cities have customs that differ from those of residents of small towns. For example, in large U.S. cities, most people do not drop in on each other uninvited. But in small U.S. towns, an occasional unannounced visit is considered friendly. Many of society's subgroups—such as teenagers, politicians, or sports teammates—have their own rules to guide behavior, language, and dress within the group. Thus, a greeting considered appropriate between two surfers may be inappropriate for two judges.

A special form of etiquette called *protocol* is observed at social functions attended by government officials, military officers, foreign diplomats, and high-level professional people. For example, protocol specifies that such individuals be seated at dinner in a definite order according to their rank or position. Protocol also indicates the titles that should be used when speaking or writing to these people (see **Address, Forms of**).

Etiquette in daily life

Introduction etiquette. Proper etiquette requires that introductions be made whenever necessary. If someone you know joins your conversational group, you should introduce that person to the group. Etiquette guidelines state that you introduce the person of *lesser* status to the person of *greater* status. In other words, you present children to adults, employees to bosses, students to teachers, and new friends to old friends. You do this by saying the name of the person of greater status first. For example, "Grandma, this is my friend Anthony from soccer camp. Anthony, this is my grandmother, Mrs. Jones." Or, "Your honor, I would like to introduce my law partner Steven Strong. Steven, this is Judge Elena Rivera." When introducing someone, include some information about that person. This helps the people being introduced to engage in further conversation.

Always shake hands when you are introduced to someone. Look the person in the eyes and use a firm grip. If you are seated when a newcomer enters the room, stand up to be greeted or introduced.

Invitation etiquette. Invitations may be extended electronically (through e-mail, social media, or the website Evite), or by a written note, printed or engraved card, or telephone call. Your choice of form may depend on the size and formality of the event and the time available for organizing it. For example, a person might use the telephone to invite six friends to dinner a week later but a text message to see if a friend is free that evening. For a wedding, a person may use printed or engraved invitations and mail them six weeks before the event.

Reply promptly to any invitation, because the host needs to know how many people will be attending. The sooner the event, the more quickly you should respond.

Dating etiquette. In the past, dating followed a set of specific rules. For example, the man chose the activities for the date and paid all the expenses. Today, the rules of dating etiquette are much more flexible. Women can ask men out and pay the bill. Many couples share the cost of the date and decide together what they will do.

Telephone etiquette. Courtesy is as important over the telephone as it is when talking face to face. A person should answer the phone with a pleasant "hello." When taking a message, write down the caller's full name and phone number, as well as the time of the call. When using voice mail, keep greetings and messages brief.

The use of *cell phones, smartphones,* and *pagers* has generated new rules of etiquette. For instance, it is impolite to text or talk on a cell phone while in a restaurant or motion-picture theater. If you are with others and must take a call, move to a private spot where your conversation will not be an intrusion. Silence your phone or pager when quiet or respect is required, such as in a library, classroom, or place of worship. When socializing, give people your full attention. It is impolite to text, play computer games, or focus on your smartphone when others are present and want your company.

Internet etiquette. Internet etiquette is based on the same rules of courtesy and respect observed in face-to-face social interactions. For example, be thoughtful and considerate when sending e-mail or other electronic messages. Do not say anything you would not say in person. Do not forward private messages or photos without getting permission. Keep in mind that written electronic communications do not provide visual or vocal clues to their meaning. Such messages are prone to misinterpretation without facial expressions, body language, or the sound of a person's voice. Although it is polite to reply as promptly as you can, with instant communications it is often a good idea to wait before responding so that you do not impulsively send a message you later regret. Remember, electronic communications and posts cannot be taken back. Once they are sent, they exist electronically forever.

Be sensible when using acronyms, abbreviations, and *emoticons.* Emoticons are combinations of keyboard symbols used in messages, especially e-mail, to indicate such facial expressions as a smile or frown. Although such symbols can save time and help to convey meaning and intent, they can also be confusing, especially for people who do not understand Internet shorthand. Electronic messages are best for brief and informal communications. Whenever possible, avoid using them for bad or sad news, condolences, confrontations, or issues with heavy emotional content.

When using social media, be kind. Do not gossip, bully, spread rumors, or send hurtful messages. Do not post photographs or comments that invade someone else's privacy. Be careful about revealing intimate details of your or anyone else's life in a public forum.

How etiquette develops and changes

The origins of etiquette. As prehistoric people began to interact with one another, they learned to behave in ways that made life easier and more pleasant. For example, as people learned to plant crops and farm, the ability to store food led to communal eating. Rituals developed for the preparation and sharing of meals and, over time, evolved into the table manners of today.

Early civilizations, such as ancient Greece and Rome, also developed rules for proper social conduct. Such rules became more formal during the Middle Ages, a period from about the A.D. 400's through the 1400's in Europe. During this time, boys training to be knights learned a code of conduct called *chivalry.* According to this code, a knight was devoted to the Christian church and his country and treated women with great respect. Some aspects of chivalry, particularly the special treatment of women, became a traditional part of manners.

Much of today's formal etiquette originated in the French royal courts during the 1600's and 1700's. King Louis XIV drew up a daily list of events, giving time, place, and proper dress. It was posted in his palace at Versailles as an *étiquette,* a French word meaning *ticket,* to help the nobles know what to do. It brought order to court society, and other monarchs adopted the code of behavior for their own courts. In time, upper classes throughout the Western world adopted the code, which then spread to more and more people.

Etiquette today concerns itself less with rigid rules for formal occasions, and more with everyday living. The goal is to help people of all lifestyles get along by respecting one another's rights, feelings, beliefs, privacy, and property. Etiquette today is based on common sense and consideration of others, regardless of gender, social status, race, ethnicity, or sexual orientation.

Etiquette also evolves along with changes in society and technology. For example, since 1950, the roles of women have changed dramatically. What used to be considered correct behavior for men—emphasizing male gallantry, chivalry, leadership, and dominance—no longer has a place in public life. Child-rearing and household responsibilities are shared more equally between parents. When men and women work, socialize, or raise a family together, good manners demand that they help each other when help is needed, without any reference to a person's gender.

Books on etiquette

The first known guide to courteous behavior was written by Ptah-hotep, a government official in ancient Egypt. His work, *The Instruction of Ptah-hotep,* dates from about 2400 B.C. One of the earliest European etiquette books, *A Treatise on Courtesy,* was compiled by the German writer Thomasin von Zerclaere in about A.D. 1200. A hugely popular guide to manners, *On Civility in Children,* by the Dutch scholar Erasmus, appeared in 1530. It became required reading for young people throughout Europe for more than two centuries. The first established etiquette guide in the United States was *Etiquette* (1922), by the American author Emily Post (see **Post, Emily**). Alex J. Packer

Etna, Mount. See **Mount Etna.**

Eton College, *EE tuhn,* is the most famous of the English private secondary schools called *public schools.* The full name of Eton, a boys school, is the King's College of Our Lady of Eton Beside Windsor. Many English statesmen, including a large number of prime ministers, have graduated from Eton. The school is in the town of Eton, about 20 miles (32 kilometers) west of London.

Around 1,300 boys, from 13 through 18 years old, live and study at Eton College. Eton offers courses in such subjects as ancient history, divinity, Greek, Latin, modern languages, mathematics, and science. Each student is assigned a tutor who provides assistance and instruction outside of classes.

King Henry VI founded Eton in 1440 for 70 *Scholars.* These boys, most of whom were poor, received scholarships and lived in the college. Soon, it also began to admit *Oppidans,* who came from prosperous families and paid for their room and board in the town of Eton. Today, all students live at the college. P. A. McGinley

See also **England** (Education).

Etruscans, *ih TRUHS kuhnz,* were an ancient Italian people who lived in Etruria (present-day Tuscany, Umbria, and Latium). Etruria extended from the Arno River in the north to the Tiber River in the south, and from the Apennine Mountains in the east to the Tyrrhenian Sea in the west. Archaeologists have shown that a continuous settlement existed in Etruria from prehistoric times. The Etruscans also spread north to the Po Valley and south to Campania. The early Etruscans maintained close commercial ties with other peoples throughout the Mediterranean, beginning in the 700's B.C. Intense trading with the ancient Greeks and Phoenicians in the 500's B.C. influenced Etruscan culture and technology.

The Etruscans ruled Rome for more than 100 years, from 616 to 509 B.C. Etruria then suffered an economic and social crisis that lasted until about 400 B.C. In 396 B.C., Rome conquered the Etruscan city of Veii. But Rome did not take complete control of Etruria until the mid-200's B.C.

Government and economy. The political unit of the Etruscans was the city. A *lucumo* (king) ruled each city. Officials called *magistrates* handled the daily business of cities. Magistrates belonged to a wealthy class and often promoted their own interests at the expense of a large body of poorer citizens.

Twelve major cities of Etruria formed a loose organization, the League of Twelve Cities. One of the most important cities was Felsina (present-day Bologna), in the

WORLD BOOK map

Etruria, shown in yellow, was the home of the Etruscans. They gained control over much of the surrounding area, shown in tan.

Po Valley. Religion, rather than politics, probably held the league together. Relations between the cities were not always peaceful, and wars sometimes broke out.

The wealth and power of Etruria came largely from copper and iron mining and metalworking, and from the Etruscans' control of trade in the western Mediterranean Sea. Agriculture, fishing, hunting, and logging also provided income.

Language and culture. Today, about 13,000 written specimens remain of the Etruscan language, which is written in a script much like ancient Greek. Although modern scholars can interpret individual words and phrases, they cannot fully understand the language.

Etruscan wallpaintings provide some of the finest examples of ancient Etruscan artwork. The wallpainting shown here, from an Etruscan tomb in Tarquinia, Italy, dates from around 490 B.C.

Etruscan art is characterized by a simple and lively style. The most spectacular examples of Etruscan art are the wallpaintings in Etruscan tombs. The Etruscans were also skilled in making bronze and *terra cotta* (molded and baked clay) sculpture.

Individuals called *haruspices* oversaw Etruscan religion. They primarily observed the natural world for signs from the gods and made predictions about the future. The Etruscans believed in life after death. They put clothing, food, furniture, jewelry, and pottery inside tombs to ease the dead's passage to the afterlife. Duels to the death, which provided entertainment at festivals, served as human sacrifices to the underworld gods.

Influence on Rome. During the period of Etruscan rule, Rome prospered and became powerful. Some of Rome's political symbols were probably inherited from the Etruscans. The Romans also adopted elements of Etruscan theater and religion. During the period of the Roman Republic (509-27 B.C.), the Roman Senate sometimes consulted the Etruscan haruspices. The Etruscan nobility held considerable influence in Rome until the time of Julius Caesar, who died in 44 B.C. Alex T. Nice

See also **Rome, Ancient** (The regal period); **Sculpture** (Etruscan and Roman sculpture).

Étude, *AY tood* or *ay TOOD,* is a short musical composition written especially to enable students to practice a particular technique. Its purpose may be to strengthen certain fingers, to improve rhythm or accent, or to develop musical style. The word *étude* is French for *a study.* Études are also written as compositions to be played for their own beauty. Among the most beautiful études are those written for piano by the Polish-born composer Frédéric Chopin. Thomas W. Tunks

Etymology, *eht uh MAHL uh jee,* is the study of the origin and development of words. Words, like peoples and nations, have histories that can be traced and recorded. Etymologists attempt to identify each change in a word's meaning and pronunciation for which there is historical evidence.

The modern study of etymology rests upon three basic principles that apply to all languages, past or present. First, the association between the sound and meaning of most words is random and not governed by any rules. In most cases, languages do not share the same word for an object or idea. For example, the word for *dog* is *chien* in French, *Hund* in German, *kutya* in Hungarian, and *inu* in Japanese. Second, because children learn to talk by imitating their elders, words are passed from generation to generation by imitation. Third, since languages are a form of social behavior, they always change gradually from generation to generation.

Etymons and cognates. Although there is no connection between the sound and meaning of most words, certain words in different languages resemble one another in both respects. The word for *father,* in certain languages, is an example. It is *padre* in Italian, *padre* in Spanish, *père* in French, and *pai* in Portuguese. These similarities occur because each word is a form of a single, earlier form—the Latin word *pater.* This earlier form is called an *etymon.*

The various words derived from an etymon are called *cognates* of one another. Sometimes the etymology of a word will reveal that it is cognate with words in another language. The various words for *father* already mentioned are examples. Another example is the English word *new,* which is cognate with the Latin word *novus* and the ancient Greek word *neos.* The etymon for these three words is *newos,* a form reconstructed from the prehistoric language called Proto-Indo-European. This language is the ancestor of English, Latin, Greek, and most other European languages.

Different types of etymologies provide interesting perspectives on a word. The etymology for *scholar* is ultimately connected with the ancient Greek word *schole,* which means *leisure.* Thus, scholars are people who need leisure time to pursue their studies. Many words in English are derived from proper nouns. For example, the flower called the dahlia is named for a Swedish botanist of the 1700's named Andrew Dahl.

Some words are modifications of one or more other words. *Smog* is a blend of *smoke* and *fog.* The word *radar* comes from letters in the phrase "*ra*dio *d*etection *a*nd *r*anging." *Pep* is a shortened form of *pepper. Alone* is a combination of *all* and *lone. Scribble* is based on the Latin word *scribere,* which means *to write.* This Latin word is associated with such English words as *scripture, description, scribe,* and many other words that have *script-* or *scribe-* in their makeup. Robert J. Kispert

See also **Linguistics; Slang.**

Eucalyptus, *YOO kuh LIHP tuhs,* is a large group of trees native to Australia. These trees are useful for their oil, gum, and timber. Most eucalyptuses grow best in warm climates that have alternate wet and dry seasons. They have been successfully grown in Florida, southern California, and other parts of the southern United States.

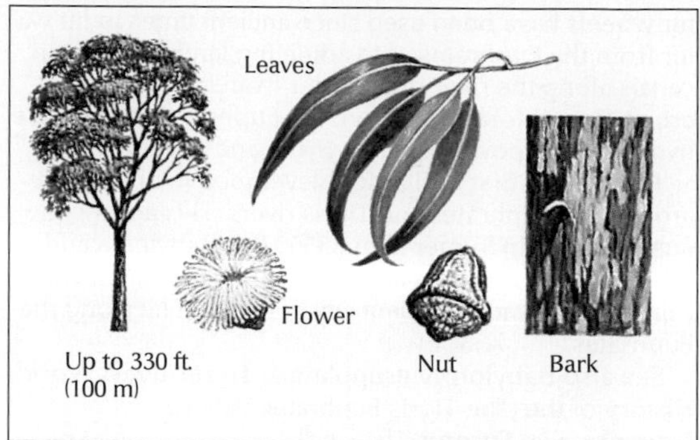

WORLD BOOK illustration by John D. Dawson

The eucalyptus is an important commercial tree.

The type most frequently planted in North America is the *blue gum.* The trees grow rapidly and reach a gigantic size. The mature leaves are long, narrow, and leathery. The flowers are filled with nectar.

In Australia, eucalyptuses are the most important timber trees. The *jarrah* is an Australian eucalyptus with red wood much like mahogany. In California, eucalyptuses are planted around orange and lemon groves to break the force of the wind.

Manufacturers use eucalyptus lumber for ships, railroad ties, paving blocks, utility poles, fences, and piers. The trees furnish a resin, called *Botany Bay kino,* that protects wood against shipworms and other borers. The bark of some species of eucalyptus trees furnishes tannin, which is used in medicine. The leaves contain a valuable oil that is used as an antiseptic, a deodorant, and a stimulant. Christopher W. Dick

Scientific classification. Eucalyptus trees make up the genus *Eucalyptus.* The scientific name for the blue gum is *E. globulus.* The jarrah is *E. marginata.*

See also **Australia** (Native plants).

Eucharist. See **Communion; Transubstantiation.**

Euclid, *YOO klihd* (330?-270? B.C.), a Greek mathematician, is often called the father of geometry. He compiled, systematically arranged, and wrote portions of the mathematics textbook *Elements* (about 300 B.C.). Euclid began with accepted mathematical truths called *axioms* and *postulates* (see **Axiom**). From them, he logically demonstrated 467 propositions of plane and solid geometry.

Euclid's textbook has probably had a greater influence on scientific thinking than any other work. It includes the *parallel postulate* and a well-known proof of the *Pythagorean theorem* (see **Geometry; Pythagorean theorem**).

Euclid wrote on most branches of mathematics that were known in his time. But only a few of his other writings have survived. They include works on conic sections, perspective, and pitfalls in geometry.

The place and date of Euclid's birth are uncertain, though it is known that he taught mathematics at the Museum, an institute in Alexandria, Egypt. Euclid probably studied in Athens and came to Alexandria shortly after 300 B.C. at the invitation of the Egyptian ruler Ptolemy I. According to the Greek philosopher Proclus, when Ptolemy I asked if there was a shorter way to the study of geometry than the *Elements,* Euclid replied, "There is no royal road to geometry." Ronald S. Calinger

Eugene (pop. 156,185; met. area pop. 351,715) is the second largest city in Oregon. Only Portland has more people. Eugene lies in a timber-rich area at the head of the fertile Willamette Valley in the western part of the state. For location, see **Oregon** (political map).

Downtown Eugene includes government buildings, retail stores, a conference center, and the Hult Center for the Performing Arts. Valley River Center, a large shopping mall, stands northwest of downtown, across the Willamette River. Nearby stand a convention center and a performing-arts center. Eugene is the home of the University of Oregon and Northwest Christian University. Eugene's major industries are the processing of lumber and the making of wood products. Other industries include food processing, the manufacture of machinery, metal production, and tourism.

Eugene developed from a village named for Eugene F. Skinner, a pioneer who settled in the area in 1846. It became an incorporated city in 1862. Eugene grew rapidly after the Oregon and California Railroad was built in 1871. It is the county seat of Lane County and has a council-manager form of government. Alton F. Baker III

Eugenics, *yoo JEHN ihks,* is a method that aims at improving the human race by selection of parents based on their inherited characteristics. *Eugenists* (people who study eugenics) want to improve future generations by encouraging people who are above average mentally and physically to have more children. This is called *positive eugenics.* Eugenists also propose that people who are below average mentally or physically have fewer children. This is called *negative eugenics.*

Scientists still cannot predict with great accuracy the presence of desirable traits, such as intelligence and physical fitness. However, they understand the inheritance of certain physical and mental abnormalities. They can identify people who are healthy themselves but carry a weakness for certain diseases in their *genes* (see **Gene**). For example, a blood test will reveal the presence of a hidden defective gene that causes the blood disease *sickle cell anemia.* Eugenists warn against a marriage of two people who are carriers of the defective gene because some of the couple's children may have the disease. In many inherited diseases, children show the defect that their parents only carried.

Eugenics began with the research of Sir Francis Galton in the 1880's, but it has not won widespread acceptance. Many people fear that a eugenics program would take away basic human rights, such as people's rights to marry whom they choose. They also fear that control of reproduction might be misused. Many people object to such controls because of religious beliefs.

Some states have laws that are aimed at preventing people with known defects from having children. However, most eugenic action comes from educational programs and voluntary decisions. Daniel L. Hartl

Related articles in *World Book* include:

Breeding	Genetics	Reproduction, Human
Environment	Heredity	
Galton, Sir Francis	Pearson, Karl	

Euglena, *yoo GLEE nuh,* is a microscopic, single-celled water organism. It lives in fresh water. Euglenas are especially common in warm seasons, when they may form a green scum on the surfaces of small ponds or drainage ditches.

Euglenas have spindle-shaped bodies and range in

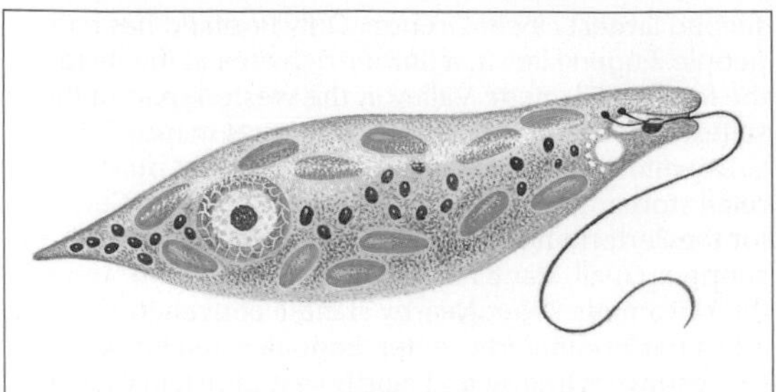

WORLD BOOK illustration by James Teason

Euglenas are tiny freshwater organisms.

size from $\frac{1}{1,000}$ to $\frac{1}{100}$ of an inch (0.025 to 0.254 millimeter) long. Most *species* (kinds) are green because they contain *chlorophyll,* the green coloring material found in most types of plants. These species get energy from sunlight. Some species also eat tiny particles of living matter. Euglenas use a *flagellum* (whiplike appendage) that sticks out from the body to move.

Euglenas are often used in classrooms for study and in laboratory research because they are easy to find, grow, and keep. They reproduce rapidly and can be studied under an ordinary microscope. Diana L. Lipscomb

Scientific classification. Euglenas make up the genus *Euglena.*

Euler, *OY lur,* **Leonhard,** *LAY ahn hahrt* (1707-1783), a Swiss mathematician, contributed to nearly every branch of mathematics known during his time. There are probably more formulas, theorems, and other concepts named for Euler than for any other mathematician or scientist in history.

One of Euler's most famous formulas elegantly relates five of the most important numbers in mathematics: e, π, i, 1, and 0. The formula is:

$$e^{\pi i} + 1 = 0$$

The number *e*, also called *Euler's number,* is the base of special numbers called *natural logarithms* (see **Logarithms** [Natural logarithms]). The value of *e* cannot be written exactly as a decimal, but it is approximately 2.718281. The number π is the ratio of a circle's circumference to its diameter (see **Pi**). The number *i*, called the *imaginary unit,* is equal to the square root of −1.

Euler was born in Basel, Switzerland, on April 15, 1707. He did most of his work in St. Petersburg, Russia, and in Berlin. He died on Sept. 18, 1783. Eli Maor

Euphorbiaceae. See **Spurge.**

Euphrates River, *yoo FRAY teez,* is the longest river in southwestern Asia. It is about 1,700 miles (2,736 kilometers) long and forms part of the historic Tigris-Euphrates river system. The Euphrates rises in a mountainous area of eastern Turkey and flows southwest into Syria. In Syria, it turns southeast and gradually descends until it reaches low, flat land. After leaving Syria, the Euphrates cuts across Iraq. At the town of Al Qurnah, Iraq, it joins the Tigris, forming a river called the Shatt al Arab, which flows into the Persian Gulf.

The area near and between the Euphrates and Tigris rivers in Iraq has the country's most fertile soil. Most of Iraq's people live there. Large ships cannot navigate the Euphrates because of its shallow waters and shifting sandbars. The river serves chiefly as a source of irrigation water and hydroelectric power. In some places, water wheels have been used since ancient times to lift water from the Euphrates onto adjoining land. In addition, canals along the river drain water from it to irrigate crops. Dams store water from the Euphrates to generate hydroelectric power for Iraq, Syria, and Turkey.

The world's first civilization developed in the region around the Euphrates and Tigris rivers. This advanced culture arose in Sumer about 3500 B.C. Babylonia and other early civilizations also thrived in this region. The ruins of the famous ancient city of Babylon lie along the Euphrates. Aaron T. Wolf

See also **Babylon; Mesopotamia; Tigris River; World, History of the** (The Tigris-Euphrates Valley).

Eurasia. See **Europe** (The land).

Euripides, *yoo RIHP uh deez* (about 480-406 B.C.), was the third of the three great writers of Greek tragedy. He dealt with the same mythological heroes as the other two, Aeschylus and Sophocles. But he showed the heroes as ordinary people and used his plays to criticize political, social, and religious ideas of the time. He used much simpler language than the earlier playwrights, but his plots were more complicated.

Euripides was not popular during his lifetime. His ideas were not always the accepted ones, and he sometimes offended writers and politicians. The Greek playwright Aristophanes satirized Euripides in several comedies (see **Aristophanes**). But Euripides's plays have been revived more frequently than those of his rivals.

Euripides wrote about 90 plays. Eighteen tragedies and a *satyr play* survive. A satyr play is a type of comedy presented at the conclusion of a trilogy. Euripides's satyr play, *Cyclops,* is probably one of his later works. The tragedies are *Rhesus,* Euripides's earliest existing play; *Alcestis* (438 B.C.); *Medea* (431); *The Children of Heracles* (about 430); *Hippolytus* (428); *Andromache* (about 426); *Hecuba* (about 424); *The Suppliants* (about 422); *Heracles* (about 417); *Electra* (about 417); *The Trojan Women* (415); *Iphigenia in Tauris* (about 412); *Helen* (412); *Ion* (about 412); *The Phoenician Women* (about 410); *Orestes* (408); and two plays performed after his death, *Bacchae* (405?) and *Iphigenia in Aulis* (405?).

Euripides was born on the island of Salamis. He grew up in Athens. As a youth, Euripides was trained to be an athlete. He also studied philosophy and literature. His instructors included the philosophers Anaxagoras and

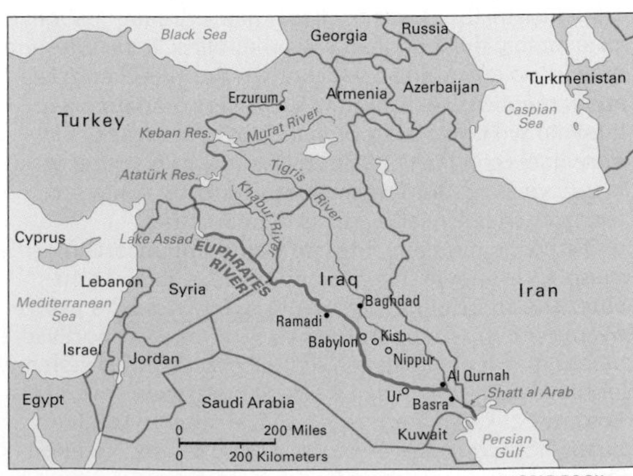

WORLD BOOK map

Location of the Euphrates River

Protagoras. Euripides began to write plays before the age of 20 and entered a contest for playwrights when he was 25. From this time on, he wrote plays steadily. Euripides became a friend of the philosopher Socrates, and some critics believe Socrates influenced his writing.

Unlike Aeschylus and Sophocles, Euripides seems to have played no active role in Athenian public life. In about 408, Euripides went to Thessaly, in northern Greece. He later went to Macedonia, where he wrote *Bacchae* and *Iphigenia in Aulis.* Luci Berkowitz

See also **Drama** (Greek drama); **Greek literature.**

Euro, *YUR oh,* is the basic monetary unit of 18 member countries of the European Union (EU). These countries are Austria, Belgium, the Republic of Cyprus, Estonia, Finland, France, Germany, Greece, Ireland, Italy, Latvia, Luxembourg, Malta, the Netherlands, Portugal, Slovakia, Slovenia, and Spain. The countries of Andorra, Kosovo, Monaco, Montenegro, San Marino, and Vatican City also use the euro. The euro is divided into 100 cents.

European Central Bank

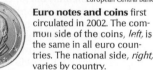

Euro notes and coins first circulated in 2002. The common side of the coins, *left,* is the same in all euro countries. The national side, *right,* varies by country.

Most of the countries that use the euro adopted it on Jan. 1, 1999. The euro replaced such traditional currencies as the French franc, the German mark, and the Italian lira. Euro notes and coins fully replaced the traditional currencies in 2002. Additional European countries could adopt the euro in the future. C. Randall Henning

Eurodollar, *YUR oh DAHL uhr,* refers to a transfer of credit designated in United States dollars from a U.S. bank to a foreign bank. Banks that handle Eurodollars are sometimes called Eurobanks. Most of them are in Europe, but Eurobanks also operate in international financial centers in Asia and even in New York City.

Eurodollar deposits are subject to few restrictions. For example, banks outside the United States are not required to keep reserves against such deposits. Furthermore, interest rates are unregulated. Critics are concerned that the Eurodollar market limits national control over money and credit. But the Eurodollar system has helped reduce the differences in interest rates between lending and borrowing countries. Robert M. Stern

Europa, *yu ROH puh,* in Greek mythology, was the beautiful daughter of Agenor, king of the city of Tyre in Phoenicia. The god Zeus fell in love with her. He disguised himself as a handsome white bull and tempted Europa to climb onto his back. Zeus then swam to the island of Crete and made love to her. Zeus and Europa had three sons: Minos, Rhadamanthys, and Sarpedon.

Agenor ordered his sons to search for Europa, but they never found her. Agenor's son Cadmus founded the Greek city of Thebes while searching (see **Cadmus**). Europa eventually married Asterius, the king of Crete.

The continent of Europe is named for Europa. Zeus's disguise as a bull is commemorated by the constellation Taurus and as a sign of the zodiac. Justin M. Glenn

Europa, *yu ROH puh,* is a large moon of Jupiter. Its surface is made of ice, which may have an ocean of water beneath it. Such an ocean could provide a home for living things. The surface layer of ice or ice and water is 50 to 100 miles (80 to 160 kilometers) deep. Europa has an extremely thin atmosphere. Electrically charged particles from Jupiter's radiation belts continuously bombard it.

Europa is one of the smoothest bodies in the solar system. Its surface features include shallow cracks, valleys, ridges, pits, blisters, and icy flows. None of them extend more than a few hundred yards or meters upward or downward. In some places, huge sections of the surface have split apart and separated. The surface of Europa has few *impact craters* (pits caused by collisions with asteroids or comets). The splitting and shifting of the surface and disruptions from below have destroyed most of the old craters.

Europa's interior is hotter than its surface. This internal heat comes from the gravitational forces of Jupiter and Jupiter's other large satellites, which pull Europa's interior in different directions. As a result, the interior flexes, producing heat in a process known as *tidal heating.* The core of Europa may be rich in iron, but most of the satellite is made of rock.

The diameter of Europa is 1,940 miles (3,122 kilometers), slightly smaller than Earth's moon. Europa orbits Jupiter every 3.55 days at a distance of 416,900 miles (670,900 kilometers). The Italian astronomer Galileo discovered Europa in 1610. Much knowledge about it is from data gathered by a space probe, also named Galileo, that orbited Jupiter from 1995 to 2003.

William B. McKinnon

See also **Jupiter; Satellite.**

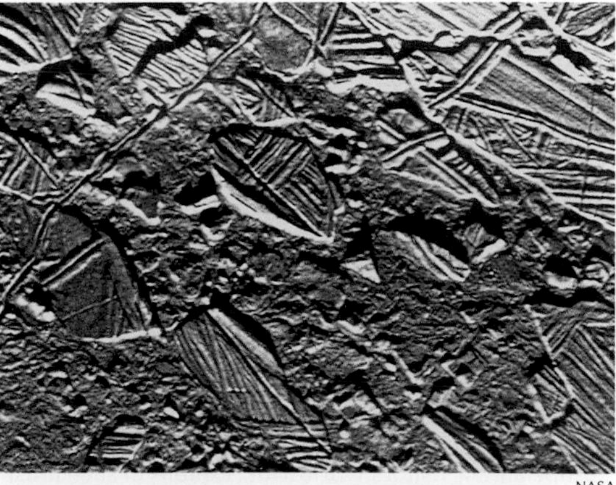

NASA

The surface of Europa, a moon of Jupiter, consists mostly of huge blocks of ice that have cracked and shifted about, suggesting that there may be an ocean of liquid water underneath.

© Steve Vidler, SuperStock

The great cities of Europe rank among the world's centers of art, culture, tourism, and trade. London, *shown here,* is the capital of the United Kingdom and one of Europe's busiest urban centers. The River Thames flows through the heart of London.

Europe

Europe is one of the smallest of the world's seven continents in area but one of the largest in population. All of the continents except Australia have more land than Europe. But only Asia and Africa have more people. About one-tenth of the world's people live in Europe. Europe is more densely populated than all the other continents except Asia.

Europe extends from the Arctic Ocean in the north to the Mediterranean Sea in the south and from the Atlantic Ocean in the west to the Ural Mountains in the east. The continent of Europe occupies the western fifth of the world's largest land mass. Asia occupies the rest of this land.

The countries of Europe include the world's largest country, Russia, as well as the world's smallest, Vatican City. Russia lies partly in Europe and partly in Asia. By world standards, most European countries are average or small in size. The five smallest countries—Liechtenstein, Malta, Monaco, San Marino, and Vatican City—are smaller in area and population than many cities.

Europe has long ranked among the world's leading industrial and agricultural centers. The continent has many rich deposits of coal and iron ore. It also has some of the richest farmland in the world.

The many cultural landmarks and natural beauties of Europe attract visitors worldwide. Exhibits in such museums as the Louvre in Paris and the Hermitage Museum in Russia thrill art lovers. Masterpieces of architecture include the temples of ancient Greece and Rome and the Gothic cathedrals of France, Germany, Spain, and the United Kingdom. Europe's historic Rhine River winds past steep cliffs dotted with the ruins of castles built hundreds of years ago. Other attractions on the continent include the snow-covered Alps of Switzerland, the colorful tulip fields of the Netherlands, the canals of Venice in Italy, and the sunny beaches of the Riviera of France and Italy.

Europe has had a great impact on the history of the world. It is the birthplace of Western civilization. From the time of the ancient Greeks, Europe's political ideas, scientific discoveries, arts and philosophies, and religious beliefs have spread to other parts of the world. The civilizations of Australia, Canada, New Zealand, the United States, and the Latin American countries largely developed from European civilization.

The most important European civilizations of ancient times developed in the region around the Mediterranean Sea. The earliest of these civilizations began about 3000 B.C. on islands in the Aegean Sea, east of Greece. The two most influential ancient European civilizations were those of the Greeks and the Romans. Greek civilization reached its height in the 400's and 300's B.C. The Greeks made lasting contributions to art, science, philosophy, and government. The Romans, who lived on the Italian Peninsula, adopted much of Greek civilization. They began to expand their territory in the 200's B.C., and they eventually built an empire that included much of Europe and parts of Africa and Asia.

The Roman Empire ended in western Europe in the A.D. 400's, and a period of European history called the Middle Ages began. During this era, the Roman Catholic

© Vera Bogaerts, Shutterstock

The natural beauty of Europe attracts visitors from all parts of the world. The villages of Saanen and Gstaad in Switzerland, *shown here,* sit among rolling hills, picturesque valleys, and the snow-capped mountains of the Alps. The Alps are the largest mountain system in Europe.

Church had enormous influence in the politics, education, arts, and religion of western and central Europe. In eastern Europe, the Eastern Orthodox Churches gained great influence.

The early 1300's marked the beginning of the Renaissance, a period in which Europeans made great achievements in the arts and learning. By the time the Renaissance ended, about 1600, Europe was moving into an age of rapid economic, political, and scientific progress. By the early 1700's, Great Britain (now also called the United Kingdom), France, and several other European nations had become the world's leading powers. These nations established colonies in Africa, Asia, and North and South America, and they gained great wealth through trade with the colonies.

The Industrial Revolution, which marked the start of modern industry, began in Europe during the 1700's. The continent soon became the manufacturing center of the world, and European nations established more and more overseas colonies. Colonies supplied raw materials to European industry and served as markets for Europe's manufactured goods. Most of Africa and about a third of Asia came under European colonial rule. But during the 1900's, European nations lost almost all their colonies.

World War I (1914-1918) and World War II (1939-1945) started in Europe. The wars brought great destruction to the continent. They also led to changes in the form of government in many European nations and to the creation of several countries.

Communist governments were set up in much of Europe after World War II. The continent became divided between Communist countries of eastern Europe and non-Communist countries of western Europe. From the late 1940's through the early 1960's, Europe was a center of the Cold War struggle between the world's Communist and non-Communist forces. The mutual fear and suspicion inspired by the Cold War lasted until at least 1989, when countries in eastern Europe began to end one-party rule. In 1991, the Soviet Union, then the world's most powerful Communist country, dissolved. It split into several independent, non-Communist nations.

During the late 1900's and early 2000's, many of the continent's countries took steps toward unity. A number of them formed an association called the European Union (EU). Through the EU, they cooperate with one another in some political matters and work to unite their resources into a single economy.

Facts in brief

Area: 4,033,000 mi² (10,445,000 km²). *Greatest distances*—east-west, about 4,000 mi (6,400 km); north-south, about 3,000 mi (4,800 km). *Coastline*—37,887 mi (60,973 km).

Population: *Estimated 2014 population*—722,305,000; density, 179 per mi² (69 per km²).

Elevation: *Highest*—Mount Elbrus, 18,510 ft (5,642 m) above sea level. *Lowest*—shore of the Caspian Sea, 92 ft (28 m) below sea level.

Physical features: *Chief mountain ranges*—Alps, Apennines, Balkans, Carpathians, Caucasus, Pyrenees. *Chief rivers*—Danube, Don, Elbe, Oder, Rhine, Rhône, Seine, Volga. *Chief lakes*—Caspian Sea, Lake Ladoga. *Chief islands*—Balearic Islands, Corsica, Crete, Faroe Islands, Great Britain, Iceland, Ireland, Malta, Sardinia, Sicily.

Number of countries: 49.

Article outline

I. People
A. Population
B. Ethnic groups
C. Languages
D. Religions
II. Ways of life
A. City life
B. Rural life
C. The family
D. Recreation
E. The role of government
F. Education
III. The arts
A. Ancient Greek and Roman art
B. Medieval art
C. Renaissance art
D. From 1600 to 1900
E. The early 1900's
F. Since the mid-1900's
IV. The land
A. Land regions
B. Coastline and islands
C. Rivers
D. Lakes
V. Climate
VI. Plant and animal life
A. Plants
B. Animals
VII. Economy
A. Agriculture
B. Manufacturing
C. Mining and energy
D. Forestry and fishing
E. International trade
F. Service industries
G. Transportation
H. Communication
VIII. History

The contributors of this article are Daniel P. Barbezat, Professor of Economics at Amherst College; David Cast, Professor of History of Art at Bryn Mawr College; Andreas Erhardt, Professor of Biology at the University of Basel; Charles W. Ingrao, Professor of History at Purdue University; and George W. White, Professor of Geography at Frostburg State University.

This article provides a broad overview of the people, ways of life, arts, land, climate, wildlife, economy, and history of Europe. Many separate *World Book* articles have more detailed information. A list of these articles appears at the end under *Related articles.*

People

The people of Europe represent a variety of cultural backgrounds. For centuries, they have spoken different languages and followed different cultural traditions.

Most Europeans are descended from nomadic peoples who lived on the continent in ancient times. Many of these groups moved from place to place and mixed with other groups they met, sometimes through trade and other times through conquest. For example, the ancestors of the British people included such groups as the Angles, Danes, Jutes, Romans, and Saxons.

In the last half of the 1900's, large numbers of people from former European colonies in Asia and Africa migrated into Europe. Large migrations from other parts of the world also flowed into Europe, including large numbers of Turks into Germany. In urban areas in France, Germany, and other nations, ethnic minorities have gained more political and economic influence. However, people of Asian or African descent still make up only a small percentage of the continent's population.

Population. Europe ranks as the third largest continent in population, behind Asia and Africa. About 720 million people, or about a tenth of the world's population, live in Europe.

Approximately 110 million people live in the part of Russia that lies in Europe. No other European country has nearly as many people. Vatican City ranks as the smallest country in Europe and in the world. It has only about 1,000 inhabitants.

Europe has an average of about 179 people per square mile (69 people per square kilometer). Europe and Asia rank as the two most densely populated continents in the world. In Europe, as in all continents, the people are not distributed evenly. For example, large stretches of northern Europe are nearly uninhabited. In much of western Europe, however, people live close to one another. For example, the Netherlands has about 1,050 people per square mile (405 per square kilometer), making it one of the world's most densely populated countries.

Ethnic groups. The peoples of Europe include widely varying *ethnic groups.* An ethnic group consists of a large number of people with the same cultural background. Members may be united by the same language, the same religion, a common ancestry, or all of these characteristics. Ethnic groups can provide their members with a sense of belonging. They can establish standards of behavior for their members and can also preserve artistic, religious, and other traditions.

Many European countries now have several different ethnic groups living in them. Since the mid-1900's, for example, people from northern and western Africa have moved to France, while Indonesians have migrated to the Netherlands. Large numbers of people from Turkey, Morocco, and Suriname also live in the Netherlands.

In some cases, members of neighboring ethnic groups dislike and distrust each other. These feelings of dislike often lead to fighting among groups, both within and between countries. Such conflicts in modern Europe have included fighting between the English and the Irish in Northern Ireland, between the Spanish and the Basques of northern Spain, and between Serbs and ethnic Albanians in Kosovo.

Violence also has arisen between Europeans and immigrants from other parts of the world. For example, conflicts have occurred in French cities between certain groups of French people and Muslim immigrants from northern Africa.

However, many European ethnic groups have gradually forgotten their differences and now think of themselves as members of a national group, such as Germans or Italians. Because of the closer economic and political ties created within the European Union, some people have even begun to think of themselves less as members of national groups and more as Europeans.

Languages. About 50 languages and more than a hundred *dialects* (local forms of languages) are spoken in Europe. Languages have caused both unity and division throughout the continent. People generally feel a sense of unity with others in their language group and feel separated from people who speak other languages.

Almost all European languages belong to the Indo-European language family. No one knows where the first Indo-European languages originated, but they prob-

Independent countries of Europe*

Map key	Name	Area in mi²	Area in km²	Population	Capital
J 8	**Albania**	11,100	28,748	3,248,000	Tiranë
I 5	**Andorra**	181	468	86,000	Andorra la Vella
H 7	**Austria**	32,383	83,871	8,486,000	Vienna
I 14	**Azerbaijan (European)**	5,521	14,300	2,837,000	Baku
G 10	**Belarus**	80,155	207,600	9,431,000	Minsk
G 6	**Belgium**	11,787	30,528	11,047,000	Brussels
I 8	**Bosnia-Herzegovina**	19,772	51,209	3,785,000	Sarajevo
I 10	**Bulgaria**	42,811	110,879	7,264,000	Sofia
H 8	**Croatia**	21,851	56,594	4,385,000	Zagreb
G 8	**Czech Republic**	30,451	78,867	10,598,000	Prague
E 7	**Denmark**	16,639	43,094	5,639,000	Copenhagen
E 9	**Estonia**	17,462	45,227	1,338,000	Tallinn
D 9	**Finland**	130,669	338,432	5,437,000	Helsinki
H 5	**France**	212,935	551,500	64,097,000	Paris
I 13	**Georgia (European)**	5,651	14,637	439,000	Tbilisi
G 7	**Germany**	137,882	357,114	81,310,000	Berlin
J 9	**Greece**	50,949	131,957	10,850,000	Athens
H 8	**Hungary**	35,919	93,030	9,907,000	Budapest
B 4	**Iceland**	39,769	103,000	330,000	Reykjavík
F 4	**Ireland**	27,133	70,273	4,747,000	Dublin
I 7	**Italy**	116,346	301,336	61,374,000	Rome
G 13	**Kazakhstan (European)**	46,603	120,700	517,000	Astana
I 9	**Kosovo**	4,212	10,908	2,235,000	Priština
E 9	**Latvia**	24,926	64,559	2,165,000	Riga
H 7	**Liechtenstein**	62	160	37,000	Vaduz
F 9	**Lithuania**	25,212	65,300	3,264,000	Vilnius
G 6	**Luxembourg**	998	2,586	534,000	Luxembourg
J 9	**Macedonia**	9,928	25,713	2,076,000	Skopje
K 7	**Malta**	122	316	422,000	Valletta
H 10	**Moldova**	13,070	33,850	3,473,000	Chisinau
I 6	**Monaco**	0.75	1.95	33,000	Monaco
I 8	**Montenegro**	5,333	13,812	634,000	Podgorica
F 6	**Netherlands**	16,040	41,543	16,805,000	Amsterdam
D 7	**Norway**	148,721	385,186	5,087,000	Oslo
G 8	**Poland**	120,726	312,679	38,345,000	Warsaw
I 3	**Portugal**	34,397	89,089	10,210,000	Lisbon
H 9	**Romania**	92,043	238,391	21,288,000	Bucharest
F 10	**Russia (European)**	1,663,869	4,309,400	111,078,000	Moscow
I 7	**San Marino**	24	61	34,000	San Marino
I 9	**Serbia**	29,913	77,474	7,183,000	Belgrade
H 8	**Slovakia**	18,933	49,035	5,498,000	Bratislava
H 8	**Slovenia**	7,827	20,273	2,066,000	Ljubljana
I 4	**Spain**	195,365	505,992	47,324,000	Madrid
D 8	**Sweden**	173,860	450,295	9,659,000	Stockholm
H 6	**Switzerland**	15,940	41,285	8,048,000	Bern
J 10	**Turkey (European)**	9,120	23,621	8,381,000	Ankara
H 10	**Ukraine**	233,032	603,550	45,060,000	Kiev
F 5	**United Kingdom**	93,628	242,495	63,643,000	London
I 7	**Vatican City**	0.17	0.44	1,000	—

Dependencies in Europe*

Map key	Name	Area in mi²	Area in km²	Population	Capital	Status
†	**Azores**	897	2,322	244,000	Ponta Delgada	Autonomous region of Portugal
G 5	**Channel Islands**	75	194	160,000	St. Peter Port; St. Helier	British crown dependencies
C 5	**Faroe Islands**	538	1,393	50,000	Tórshavn	Self-governing community of Denmark
J 3	**Gibraltar**	2.5	6.5	30,000	Gibraltar	British overseas territory
E 5	**Man, Isle of**	221	572	86,000	Douglas	British crown dependency

*Each country and dependency in Europe has a separate article in *World Book*. †Not on map; about 800 miles (1,300 kilometers) west of Lisbon, Portugal.
Populations are current estimates based on the latest figures from official government, United Nations, and other sources.

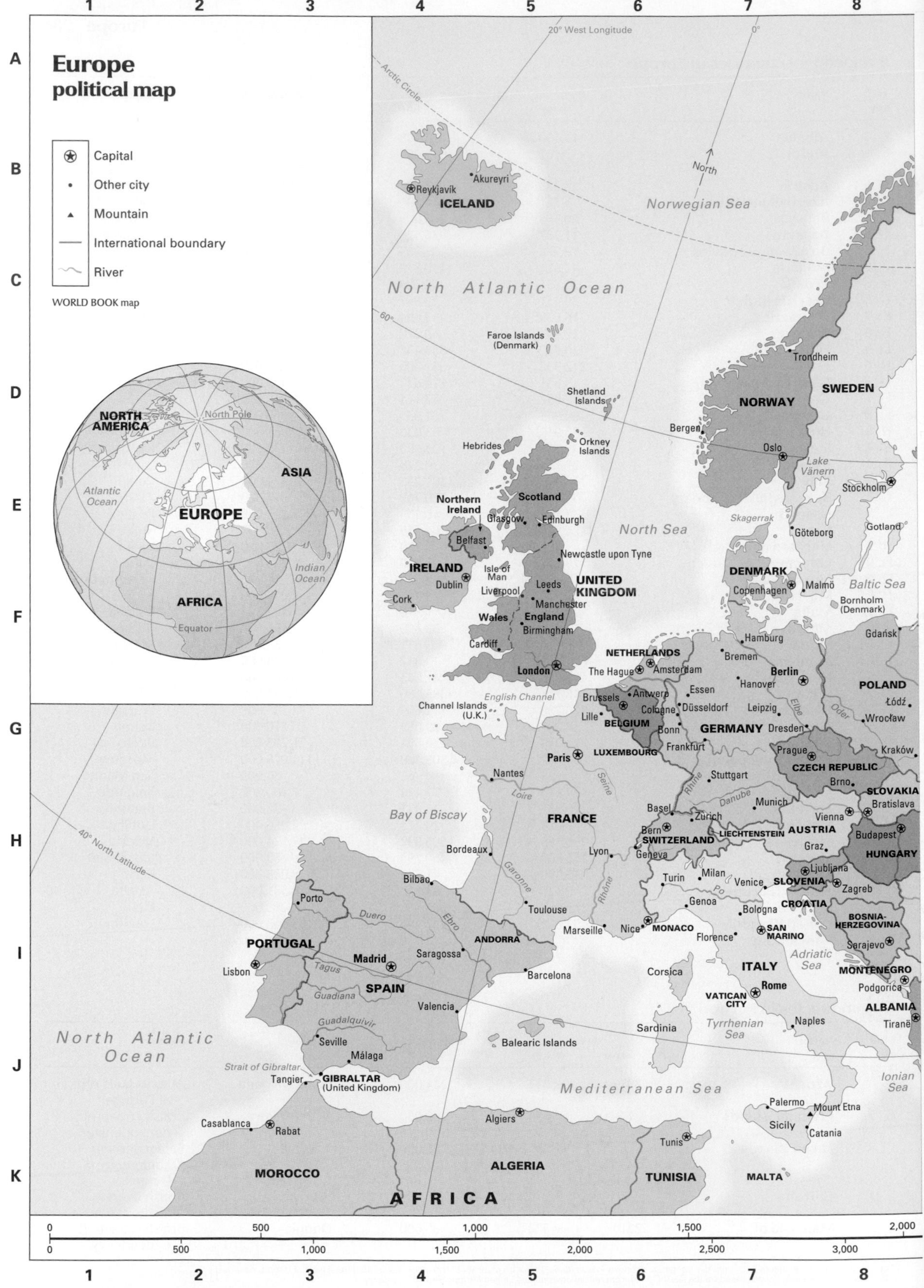

Europe
political map
Capital
Other city
Mountain
International boundary
River
WORLD BOOK map
NORTH AMERICA
North Pole
ASIA
Atlantic Ocean
EUROPE
Indian Ocean
AFRICA
Equator
20° West Longitude
0°
Arctic Circle
North
Reykjavík
Akureyri
ICELAND
Norwegian Sea
North Atlantic Ocean
60°
Faroe Islands (Denmark)
Shetland Islands
Orkney Islands
Hebrides
Trondheim
NORWAY
SWEDEN
Bergen
Oslo
Lake Vänern
Stockholm
Scotland
Northern Ireland
Glasgow
Edinburgh
North Sea
Skagerrak
Göteborg
Gotland
Belfast
Newcastle upon Tyne
IRELAND
Dublin
Isle of Man
UNITED KINGDOM
DENMARK
Copenhagen
Malmö
Baltic Sea
Cork
Liverpool
Leeds
Manchester
Bornholm (Denmark)
Wales
England
Birmingham
Hamburg
Gdańsk
Cardiff
NETHERLANDS
Bremen
London
The Hague
Amsterdam
Berlin
Hanover
POLAND
English Channel
Brussels
Antwerp
Essen
Channel Islands (U.K.)
Cologne
Düsseldorf
Leipzig
Łódź
Lille
BELGIUM
Elbe
Oder
Wrocław
Bonn
GERMANY
Dresden
Frankfurt
Paris
LUXEMBOURG
Prague
Kraków
CZECH REPUBLIC
Nantes
Stuttgart
Seine
Loire
Rhine
Brno
SLOVAKIA
Danube
Munich
Bratislava
Bay of Biscay
Basel
Zurich
Vienna
FRANCE
Bern
LIECHTENSTEIN
AUSTRIA
Budapest
SWITZERLAND
Graz
Bordeaux
Lyon
Geneva
HUNGARY
40° North Latitude
Ljubljana
Garonne
Milan
Bilbao
Turin
Venice
SLOVENIA
Zagreb
Porto
Rhône
Po
Genoa
Duero
Toulouse
Bologna
CROATIA
Ebro
BOSNIA-HERZEGOVINA
Marseille
Nice
MONACO
SAN MARINO
ANDORRA
Florence
PORTUGAL
Sarajevo
Madrid
Saragossa
Adriatic Sea
Lisbon
ITALY
MONTENEGRO
Tagus
Barcelona
Corsica
Rome
SPAIN
VATICAN CITY
Podgorica
Guadiana
Valencia
ALBANIA
Guadalquivir
Naples
Tiranë
Sardinia
Tyrrhenian Sea
North Atlantic Ocean
Seville
Balearic Islands
Málaga
Strait of Gibraltar
Tangier
GIBRALTAR (United Kingdom)
Mediterranean Sea
Ionian Sea
Palermo
Mount Etna
Algiers
Casablanca
Rabat
Sicily
Catania
Tunis
MOROCCO
ALGERIA
TUNISIA
MALTA
AFRICA
0
500
1,000
1,500
2,000
0
500
1,000
1,500
2,000
2,500
3,000
1 2 3 4 5 6 7 8
A B C D E F G H I J K

9
10
11
12
13
14
15
16
A
B
C
D
E
F
G
H
I
J
K
40° East Longitude
60°
80°
Novaya Zemlya
Barents Sea
Kolguyev Island
North
Murmansk
Lapland
White Sea
Arkhangelsk
Northern Dvina
Ural Mountains
ASIA
EUROPE
Ob
West Siberian Plain
Irtysh
ASIA
Omsk
Gulf of Bothnia
RUSSIA
Lake Onega
Lake Ladoga
FINLAND
Tampere
Turku
Helsinki
St. Petersburg
Yekaterinburg
Perm
Chelyabinsk
Kama
Magnitogorsk
Tallinn
ESTONIA
Lake Peipus
Rybinsk Reservoir
Gorki Reservoir
Kazan
Nizhniy Novgorod
Volga
Kuybyshev Reservoir
Ural
Riga
LATVIA
Moscow
Orenburg
Samara
Western Dvina
Oka
KAZAKHSTAN
LITHUANIA
RUSSIA
Vilnius
Minsk
Neman
BELARUS
Saratov
Volgograd Reservoir
Don
Syr Darya
Aral Sea
Warsaw
Vistula
Kiev
Kharkiv
Volgograd
UZBEKISTAN
Amu Darya
Lviv
UKRAINE
Dnieper
Donetsk
Dnipropetrovsk
Astrakhan
Rostov-on-Don
Dniester
Miskolc
MOLDOVA
Chisinau
Sea of Azov
Odessa
Cluj-Napoca
ROMANIA
Brasov
Crimea
Yalta
Mount Elbrus
Caspian Sea
TURKMENISTAN
Ashgabat
Belgrade
Bucharest
Danube
SERBIA
Black Sea
GEORGIA
Tbilisi
Batumi
AZERBAIJAN
Baku
ARMENIA
Yerevan
Mount Ararat
Priština
KOSOVO
BULGARIA
Sofia
Plovdiv
Bosporus
Skopje
MACEDONIA
Istanbul
TURKEY
Ankara
Lake Van
Lake Urmia
Tehran
Thessaloniki
Aegean Sea
GREECE
TURKEY
IRAN
Athens
ASIA
Tigris
Baghdad
Euphrates
SYRIA
Rhodes
Nicosia
CYPRUS
Beirut
LEBANON
Damascus
IRAQ
Crete
Persian Gulf
Mediterranean Sea
2,500
3,000
3,500
4,000 Miles
3,500
4,000
4,500
5,000
5,500
6,000 Kilometers

ably began in the area north of the Black Sea. This family of languages has three major branches in Europe: Balto-Slavic, Germanic, and Romance. Most people in eastern Europe speak Balto-Slavic languages, which include Bulgarian, Czech, Polish, and Russian. The Germanic languages—such as Danish, English, German, and Swedish—are spoken chiefly in northwestern Europe. The Romance languages, spoken mostly in southwestern Europe, include French, Italian, and Spanish.

A few countries in Europe speak languages outside the Indo-European family. Hungarian, known as Magyar, belongs to the Finno-Ugric language group. This group also includes Estonian, Finnish, and Sami. People in the European part of Turkey speak Turkish, a Turkic language. Most people on the island country of Malta speak Maltese, which developed from West Arabic and has many words borrowed from Italian. The Basque language of northern Spain, known as Euskara, has an unknown origin and is called a *language isolate.* See also **Language** (Language families; chart; map).

Religions. Christianity has long served as Europe's major religion. This faith began in the Middle East, but it developed primarily in Europe. Since the mid-1900's, however, Christianity and other religions have become less influential in many parts of Europe. Only a small percentage of Europeans now attend religious services regularly.

Roman Catholics make up most of Europe's Christians. Catholics live chiefly in southwestern and northeastern Europe. The continent's other Christians are about evenly divided between the Eastern Orthodox and Protestant faiths. Members of the Eastern Orthodox Churches live chiefly in Greece, Russia, and in southeastern Europe. Protestantism remains the chief form of Christianity in most of northwestern Europe.

The languages of Europe

This map shows where the major European languages are spoken. Most Europeans speak languages of the Balto-Slavic, Germanic, and Romance branches of the Indo-European family.

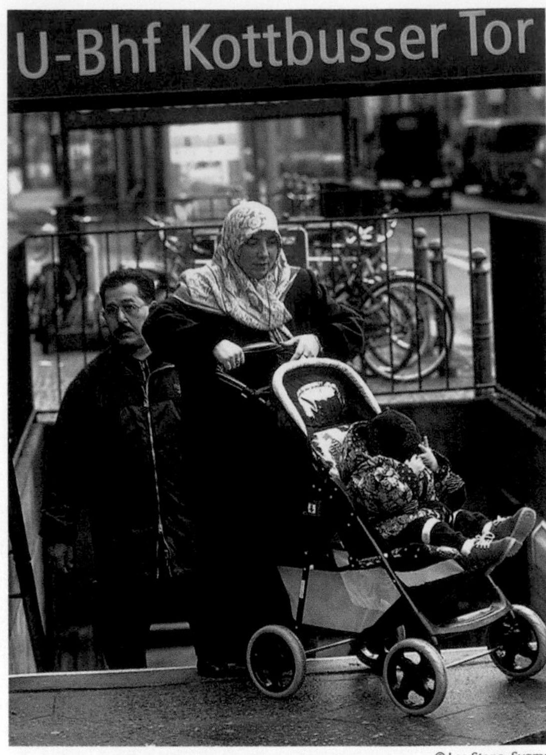

© Les Stone, Sygma

Turkish residents of Germany are an example of the ethnic diversity found in many European countries. A large number of people from Asia and northern Africa have moved to Europe.

Europe also has several million Jews and Muslims. Jews live in most parts of the continent. Muslims make their homes chiefly in southeastern European countries, including Albania and Bosnia-Herzegovina, and in Azerbaijan, Kazakhstan, and Turkey, which are considered both European and Asian. Large populations of Muslim immigrants inhabit many western European cities, mainly in France and Germany.

During the Middle Ages, Christian monasteries and universities were centers of learning and preserved much of the heritage of the Greek and Roman cultures. In addition, medieval Islamic and Jewish scholars contributed to the preservation and advancement of learning in Europe, especially in Spain and Sicily. Through the centuries, religious organizations supported schools for young people and sponsored many of Europe's greatest artists.

Christianity, in particular, helped to shape European culture, philosophy, and law. The Christian idea of the equality of every person before God eventually became a foundation of the modern social and political concepts of equality.

Many problems also have been caused in the name of religions. A number of violent and bloody events in

European history have resulted, in part, from religious conflict, though they had political and social causes as well. During the Middle Ages, for example, the Roman Catholic Church conducted wars known as the Crusades against Muslims.

After the birth of Protestantism in Germany in the early 1500's, Europe experienced more than 100 years of warfare between Catholics and Protestants. Bitterness between Catholics and Protestants still exists in a few parts of Europe today. For example, disputes between Catholics and Protestants in Northern Ireland helped produce much violence in the last half of the 1900's.

In World War II (1939-1945), the Nazi government of Germany killed more than two-thirds of the Jews in Europe—about 6 million people—in what is called the Holocaust. During the break-up of Yugoslavia in the 1990's, violence erupted between the Roman Catholic, Eastern Orthodox, and Muslim groups that lived there.

Ways of life

Ways of life—including customs, languages, religions, and educational systems—have long varied throughout Europe. Even within individual countries, ways of life can differ greatly from one region to another.

The northern areas of Europe generally are more industrial and urbanized than the southern areas, which tend to be more agricultural. In Italy, for example, the rural southern part of the country remains less economically developed than the industrialized northern part.

Beginning in the last half of the 1900's, these regional differences have lessened. Reasons for the decreased difference include industrialization, migration from rural areas to cities, and rising standards of living. People generally begin to follow similar ways of life after they move to cities, find industrial jobs, and increase their earnings. Today, moreover, even rural communities have adopted many urban ways of life. For example, the spread of cellular telephones, computers, and other communication devices has brought rural and urban communities closer together.

Europeans have long shared several basic attitudes and beliefs. For example, many Europeans believe strongly in the importance of social class, and social mobility has generally proved more difficult in Europe than in the Americas. Europeans have long paid high taxes, and they expect the government to provide a wide array of services and to play a central role in managing their countries' economies.

© Shutterstock

Masterpieces of architecture are among the many cultural attractions of Europe. The famous St. Basil's Cathedral, *shown here,* stands on Red Square in the heart of Moscow.

Europeans often have a deep respect for history and tradition, both in their private and public lives. They take great pride in the outstanding artistic, educational, and political achievements of Europe's past.

City life. Europe has some of the world's largest and most famous cities. Moscow, the capital of Russia, is the

AP/Wide World

Conflict among ethnic groups has often broken out in Europe when members of neighboring ethnic groups dislike or distrust one another. In this photo, ethnic Albanians in what was then the Serbian province of Kosovo protest the Serbs' violence against them. Kosovo became an independent nation in 2008.

largest city in Europe. London, the capital of the United Kingdom, and Paris, the capital of France, also rank among the largest urban centers of the world. London is an important center of international finance. Paris has long been a world capital of fashion, art, and learning.

Cities in Europe show great differences between the old and the new. Many European cities have cathedrals built during the Middle Ages, and some, including Athens and Rome, have ruins of buildings constructed over 2,000 years ago. Yet these ancient structures stand near modern supermarkets, glass-and-steel skyscrapers, department stores, and fast-food restaurants.

The rapid growth of industry and business in many large cities of Europe has drawn many people from rural areas and from foreign countries. As a result, these cities have become crowded, and suburbs have grown up around them.

Rural life varies throughout Europe. Generally, people in rural areas have a lower standard of living and follow a more traditional way of life than people in urban areas.

Some European farmers live on their farms. But most live in villages and travel to their fields each day. On a typical family-owned farm, the father, mother, and chil-

Where the people of Europe live

Europe is the third largest continent in population, after Asia and Africa. Most of the people of Europe live in cities. This map shows where Europeans live and the location of most of the largest cities. Heavily populated areas are shown in the darker colors.

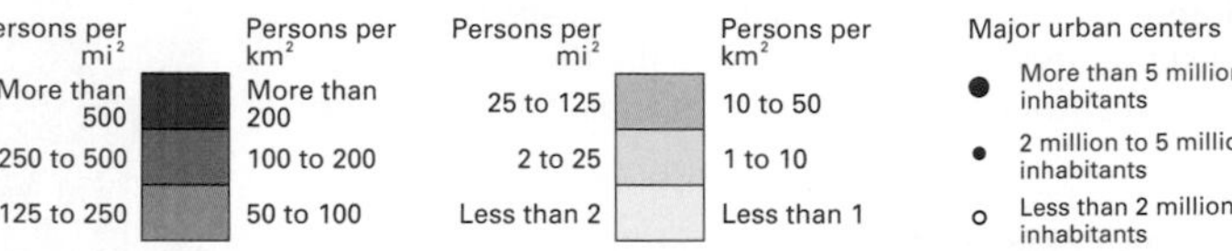

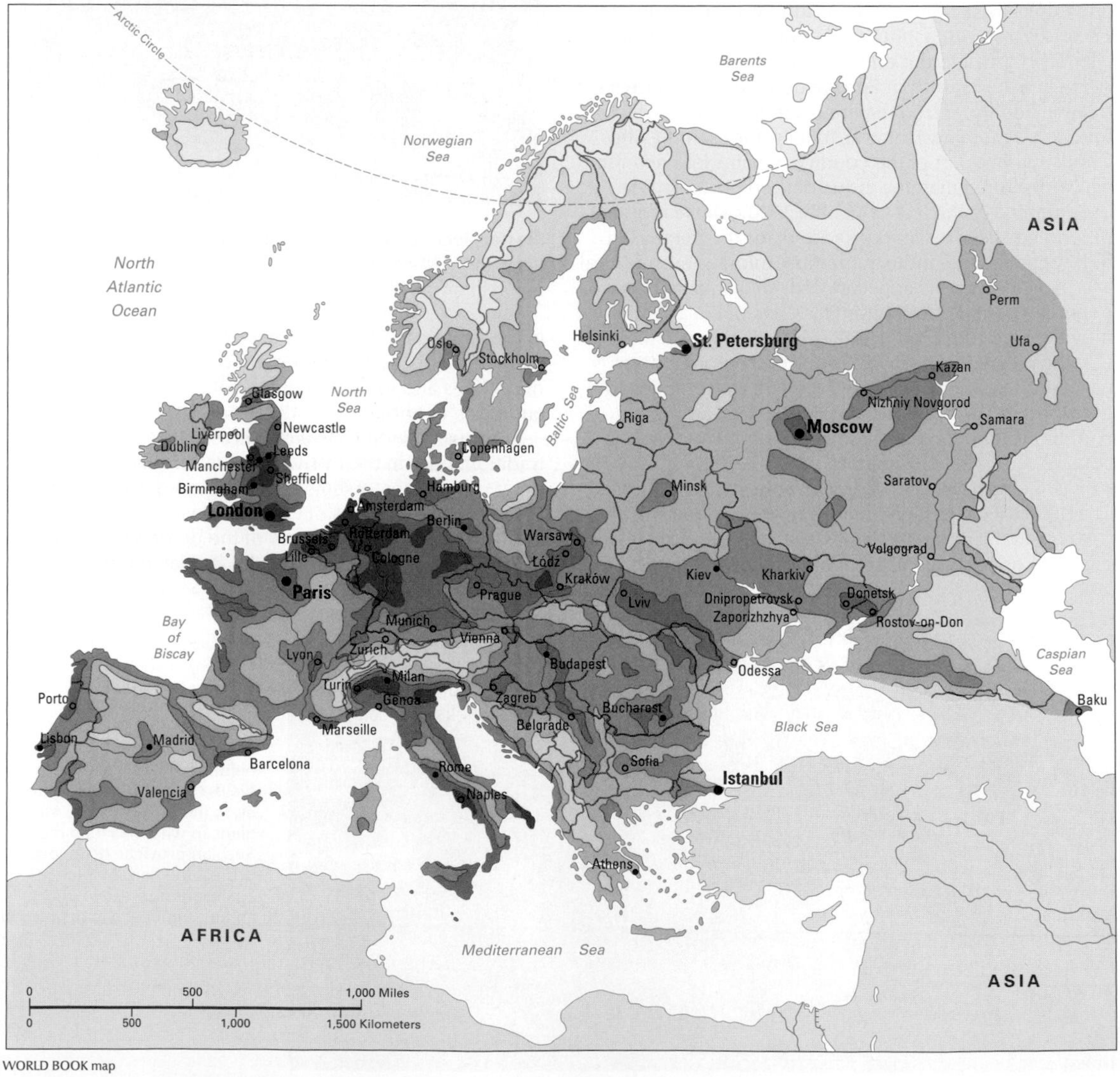

WORLD BOOK map

European stores carry a wide variety of clothing, electronics, and other goods. This indoor mall in Bucharest, Romania, is one of the numerous modern shopping centers across Europe.

© Rainer Unkel, Vario/Alamy Images

Rural life in many European communities is based on agriculture. This farm near Bratislava, Slovakia, uses modern machinery to harvest grain.

© Peter Hudec, EPA Photo/ČTK/European Commission

dren provide most of the labor. Farmers in the northwestern regions of Europe, including Denmark, the Netherlands, and the United Kingdom, generally use advanced agricultural methods and equipment. As a result, they have generally achieved the highest standards of living of any European farmers.

In parts of southern Europe, especially in Greece and Portugal, some farmers work in much the same way as their ancestors did hundreds of years ago. They use traditional agricultural methods and equipment. But even in such regions, more and more farmers have begun to use modern machinery and methods. Funds from the European Union have greatly benefited these farmers.

The family has held an important place in European life for hundreds of years. For many Europeans, the family remains the most important unit of society because it protects the individual and teaches a person about life. Many Europeans owe their first loyalty to the family and regard the extended family as the center of their social lives. In many parts of Europe, people remain near their families, and children frequently live with parents well into adulthood. However, commitment to the family is not as strong among young Europeans as it is among older people.

Family ties remain strongest today in southern Europe and parts of eastern Europe. Most of the countries in these areas have the least industrialized and urbanized societies of Europe. The role of the family has become less important in northwestern Europe, which generally is more urban and industrialized. There, workers move to the places where they can find the best jobs, regardless of their family ties.

In such countries as France, Germany, and Italy, many families have fewer than two children. As a result, the native populations of those countries are decreasing.

Recreation. Europeans take part in a broad variety of pastimes. Many European governments have legislated workweeks of less than 40 hours. Workers in the United States and other industrialized countries have longer workweeks than do most Europeans. In addition to having shorter workweeks, Europeans receive longer vacation periods than do workers in other areas.

Europeans travel all over the world. Favorite vacation spots within Europe include southern Spain and the islands off Greece and southern Italy.

The most popular European sport is soccer, known in Europe as football. Numerous European cities field soccer teams in major national and international tournaments. People throughout Europe also play such sports as basketball, rugby, team handball, tennis, and volleyball. Other sports flourish only in parts of Europe, such as cricket in the United Kingdom and hurling in Ireland.

Europe boasts some of the world's greatest museums, including the Prado in Madrid, Spain; the Louvre in

© Steve Vidler, SuperStock

Public squares are popular gathering places in many European cities. Such squares often include shops, sidewalk cafes, and areas to relax. The Piazza del Campo, *shown here,* is a famous square in Siena, Italy.

The role of government. European governments play a major part in running the economies of their countries and providing for the welfare of the people. In almost all western European countries, the government is a part or sole owner of such public service businesses as airlines, electric companies, railroads, and telephone companies. In most of these countries, the government also provides many types of social welfare programs. For example, the Swedish government gives every family an allowance for each child under 16 years of age. In addition, European governments regulate the workplace closely, setting limits on the workweek and guaranteeing minimum vacation time for workers.

Education. As a group, Europeans rank among the best-educated people in the world. In almost all the countries of Europe, 90 percent or more of the people can read and write.

In general, the level of education in Europe has been higher in the north than in the southernmost regions. In most northern countries—such as Norway, Sweden, and the United Kingdom—all children generally receive the same education until they are about 15 or 16 years old. At that age, young people may quit school, enroll in vocational schools, or go to college. Children in southern countries attend school for fewer years, on average, than do children in the north. Moreover, fewer young people in southern Europe attend college than do young people in northern Europe.

Government control over education also varies. France, for example, has a highly centralized educational

Paris; the Hermitage in St. Petersburg, Russia; the National Gallery in London; and the Uffizi Palace in Florence, Italy. Europeans also enjoy some of the world's greatest theater, music, and dance. Such cultural institutions include the Royal National Theater in London; La Scala opera house in Milan, Italy; and the Bolshoi Ballet in Moscow. Many European cities also host famous festivals that draw thousands of visitors from around the world. Famous examples include La Feria de Abril in Seville, Spain, and Oktoberfest in Munich, Germany.

Some European countries, including France and Germany, have long had important national film industries. However, American films rank as the most popular and widely shown movies throughout Europe. Television in Europe consists of a mix of local or national programs, along with programs imported from the United States. Europeans commonly listen to popular music groups from such countries as the United Kingdom and Germany, but American popular music is also common throughout the continent.

People in Europe read a variety of magazines and local and national newspapers. Popular kinds of books in Europe include novels and detective stories. Many European authors have large readerships in their native countries, and their works often appear translated into various languages around the world.

A growing number of Europeans spend recreational time on the Internet. Many people read Internet websites devoted to news or entertainment. They also create personal web pages and participate in online discussion groups.

© Alistair Berg, Alamy Images

Oxford University, founded in England in the 1100's, is one of several European universities that date from the Middle Ages. These school officials are taking part in an enrollment ceremony.

system controlled by the national government. In Switzerland, the *cantons* (states) chiefly direct their own educational systems.

Since the mid-1900's, with the increasing economic and political integration of Europe, educational programs in many poorer European countries have been improving. More children in these countries have opportunities to attend colleges or vocational schools.

Europe has many of the world's oldest and most respected universities. The oldest European university is the University of Bologna in Italy, founded in about 1100. Other famous European universities include the University of Paris; Oxford University in Oxford, England; Cambridge University in Cambridge, England; Charles University in Prague, the Czech Republic; and the Jagiellonian University in Kraków, Poland.

In addition, Europe has some of the world's leading libraries. They include the Bibliothèque Nationale de France in Paris, the Bodleian Library of Oxford University, the Russian State Library in Moscow, and the Vatican Library in Vatican City. For more information on libraries in Europe, see **Library** (Libraries of the world).

The arts

European art has had a far greater influence around the world than has the art of any other continent. This influence began during the 1500's, when the nations of western Europe established colonies in North and South America. It spread as Europeans colonized Australia and much of Africa and Asia by the early 1900's. Even after most colonies achieved political independence, the influence of European art remained strong.

Ancient Greek and Roman art. Many ancient European cultures produced beautiful works of art. But the Greeks developed the most enduring European art of ancient times. This art influenced European artists for more than 2,000 years. The Greeks strove to achieve an ideal of beauty based on harmonious proportions. They applied this ideal to their graceful columned temples and to their lifelike sculptures and paintings of gods, goddesses, and human beings. The Greeks also wrote the first substantial literature of Europe, developing such literary forms as lyric and epic poetry, tragic and comic drama, and history.

The Romans based much of their art and literature on that of the Greeks. But in their architecture, with the use of the arch and concrete, the Romans created larger and more complex structures than anything produced before. They designed aqueducts and water systems and built roads and bridges that helped tie together their vast empire.

Medieval art. The arrival of Christianity in Europe inspired new types of architecture, sculpture, and painting. Biblical images replaced depictions of Greek and Roman gods and goddesses. Churches, and especially cathedrals, became the most important and creative form of architecture.

Beginning in the early Middle Ages, Byzantine architects of southeastern Europe created beautiful domed churches. Multicolored marble and elaborate *mosaics* decorated the interiors of many of these churches. Mosaics consist of small pieces of glass or stone fitted together to form a picture. Byzantine mosaics commonly depicted Biblical figures, but they sometimes included portraits of Byzantine emperors and their wives. Byzantine images appear flat and somewhat abstract, rather than lifelike.

Beginning in the A.D. 700's, with the Muslim conquest of Spain, Islamic art spread to Europe. The abstract forms found in Muslim decorative arts greatly influenced medieval Spanish art. It also influenced medieval artists in southern Italy and elsewhere in Europe.

During the 1000's and 1100's, an artistic style that came to be known as Romanesque appeared in Europe. Romanesque architecture featured solid, heavy forms with thick walls and supports and low, wide arches. The religious paintings of this time used strong colors and simplified shapes. Romanesque sculptors decorated many church portals and *capitals* (tops of columns) with expressive, though nonrealistic, figures of saints and other Biblical characters.

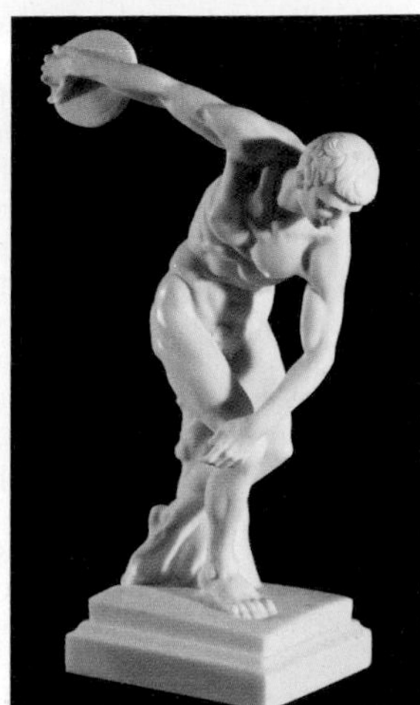

© Shutterstock

Ancient Roman sculpture was based on Greek art. Figures were lifelike and often sculpted in athletic poses.

David Moore, Black Star

Ancient Greek drama was the first drama of the Western world. It was performed in theaters like the one in Athens shown here. The lighted temple in the background is the Parthenon.

In the 1200's, Gothic became the major style of art throughout much of Europe. Medieval engineers carefully designed Gothic cathedrals so they would not require thick walls for support. These buildings featured pointed arches and huge windows filled with stained glass. Gothic windows usually depicted stories from the Bible in a series of images. Gothic cathedrals also featured rich sculptural decoration. Many Gothic sculptors created larger than life-sized, and sometimes highly lifelike, images of religious figures.

Renaissance art began in the early 1300's in Italy and spread throughout Europe over the next two centuries. This art was directly inspired by the ideas of proportion and order found in ancient Greek and Roman art. Renaissance sculptors revived the tradition of sculpting the naked human body in a realistic way. Painters developed the technique of *perspective,* which gave their pictures the illusion of depth and distance. Architects studied Roman ruins and used Classical architectural forms and proportions in their buildings. Moreover, many artists began creating more nonreligious works, such as portrait paintings or private villas.

Artists of the Renaissance acquired far more fame than did those of medieval times. Such artists as Raphael and Michelangelo became appreciated more for the qualities of their artworks than for the subjects or uses of the works.

© Shutterstock

The Chartres Cathedral in France is an example of Gothic architecture, which flourished in medieval Europe.

From 1600 to 1900, art reflected the many fundamental changes that occurred in European society. Many new forms of art developed. Opera was first composed and performed in the 1590's, and the first symphonies appeared in the 1700's. In literature, the modern novel took shape during the 1600's and 1700's. Ballet, which had originated in Italy during the Renaissance, became a professional art form at this time.

During the 1600's, the rise of powerful European countries helped create a dramatic, emotional style known as Baroque. Architects, sculptors, and painters worked together to design and decorate grand Baroque palaces and churches. European monarchs and church leaders used these buildings, in part, to show their authority over their own people and to impress leaders of other countries.

Beginning in the 1700's, rapid industrial and urban growth, together with advances in science and technology, brought great changes to Europe. These changes made artists more concerned with humanity's place in the world than with religion. During the late 1700's and early 1800's, Romanticism appeared in both in art and literature. This personal, emotionally charged style often turned for its subject to nature, political change, and even fantasy. Many Romantic artists protested against the standardized character of an increasingly industrial society. Many also objected to the social injustices and political tyranny of the time.

In the mid-1800's, a movement called Realism developed in literature and the visual arts. Realism attempted to portray life as it really was, presenting both the good and the bad. During the 1860's, another style called Impressionism developed, mostly in France. Impressionist painters often used rapid, impulsive brushwork and vivid colors to present an immediate impression of an object or event.

The early 1900's saw the birth of many new styles of art in Europe. Artists during this period became less openly concerned with telling a story or representing political ideas. Instead, they focused on exploring the possibilities of the materials with which they worked and engaging the spectator on a deeper emotional level. To an increasing extent, they incorporated art styles from other parts of the world, including Africa and the Pacific Islands.

Painters often created abstract works without actual figures or objects to express feelings or moods. Sculptors worked with new materials, including aluminum or plastic, to create similarly abstract forms. Architects, especially those associated with the Bauhaus school in Germany, created simple, unornamented, functional buildings designed to serve all members of society. Composers often abandoned traditional harmonies to explore *dissonance,* the combining of notes and chords to create harsh or restless sounds. In literature, authors explored more deeply the internal feelings and emotions of people, often by using fragmented or abstract writing. Modern dancers abandoned the formal movements of ballet to explore the artistic possibilities of more natural movements.

Two technological inventions of the 1800's, photography and film, developed into important art forms during

Oil painting on wood panel (1506); Museum of Art History, Vienna, Austria

Renaissance painting emphasized lifelike figures and realistic settings. Raphael's *Madonna of the Meadow, shown here,* illustrates the Italian artist's skill at portraying beauty and gentleness.

the early 1900's. European photographers and filmmakers began using these technologies to express ideas that others were exploring in the traditional arts.

Since the mid-1900's. After the mid-1900's, new forms and styles of art appeared in Europe. European artists had become more influenced by the art of the United States. They also reflected the ever closer intellectual and political ties between Europe and the rest of the world.

Beginning in the 1960's, the growth of feminism led to the emergence of many more women artists. These artists produced works exploring the emotions and attitudes of women and the changing roles of women in society. Also in the 1960's, a new style called Pop Art developed. It commented, often humorously, on such aspects of modern culture as mass media and the power of celebrities.

Contemporary European artists continue to explore new materials for creating art. Today, such materials may include videos, computers, and even entire landscapes.

The land

Europe is a huge peninsula that extends westward from northwestern Asia. No body of water separates Europe and Asia completely, and so many geographers consider them to be one continent called *Eurasia.* Europe's status as a continent sprung from the belief in ancient and medieval times that Europe was separated from Asia by mostly water. Cultural differences between Europeans and Asians reinforced the belief that Europe was a true continent.

Europe covers 4,033,000 square miles (10,445,000 square kilometers), or about one-fifteenth of the world's land area. It is smaller than every other continent except Australia.

The Atlantic Ocean forms the western boundary of Europe. The Ural Mountains, the Ural River, and the Caspian Sea form the eastern boundary of the continent. Europe extends from the Arctic Ocean in the north to the Mediterranean Sea, the Black Sea, and the Caucasus Mountains in the south. Iceland, Great Britain, Ireland, and thousands of other smaller islands near Europe's coastline are usually included as part of the continent.

Land regions. Europe has four major land regions: (1) the Northwest Mountains, (2) the Central Uplands, (3) the Alpine Mountain System, and (4) the Great European Plain.

The Northwest Mountains region includes northwestern France, Ireland, the northern United Kingdom, Norway, Sweden, northern Finland, and the northwest corner of Russia. This region includes some of the oldest rock formations on Earth. The mountains have worn down over the years, so even the highest peak, Galdhøpiggen in Norway, rises only 8,100 feet (2,469 meters). The thin soil of the mountain slopes combined with cold climates makes for poor farming in the region. Consequently, most of the Northwest Mountains is sparsely populated.

The Central Uplands region includes low mountains and high plateaus that extend across central Europe. Elevations vary from about 1,000 to 6,000 feet (300 to 1,800 meters). Major features of the uplands include the Meseta, or central plateau, of Portugal and Spain; the Massif Central, or central highlands, in France; and the plateaus and low mountains of central Germany and most of the Czech Republic. Some of the Central Uplands have forests, but most of the land is rocky with poor soils for farming. River valleys provide the best farmland. Parts of the Central Uplands—especially in Germany and the Czech Republic—have rich deposits of minerals. The most densely populated areas of this region lie in parts of Germany and the Czech Republic.

The Alpine Mountain System consists of several mountain chains that run across southern Europe from Spain to the Caspian Sea. The Sierra Morena and Cantabrian Mountains lie in Spain, while the Pyrenees form a natural border between Spain and France. The world-famous Alps cover part of southeastern France and northern Italy, most of Switzerland, and part of southern Germany, Austria, and northern Slovenia. The Apennines run the length of Italy. Farther east, the Dinaric Alps stretch from Croatia to northern Greece, where they continue as the Pindus Mountains. The Carpathians curve from northern Slovakia through southern Poland, far western Ukraine, and Romania. The Balkan Mountains lie in northern Bulgaria, and the Rhodope Mountains run from southern Bulgaria to northern Greece. The Caucasus Mountains lie at the eastern end of the region between the Black Sea and Caspian Sea.

The Alpine Mountain System includes the highest mountains in Europe. The highest peak, Mount Elbrus in the Caucasus Mountains, rises 18,510 feet (5,642 meters). Other high peaks include Mont Blanc in the French Alps and the Matterhorn in the Swiss Alps. Heavy forests cover many of the higher slopes in the region. Meadows

Adam Woolfit, Woodfin Camp, Inc.

The Northwest Mountains region covers much of northwestern Europe. Many beautiful lakes, including Scotland's Loch Tay, *shown here,* lie in this mountainous region.

H. Herfort, Bruce Coleman Inc.

The Alpine Mountain System covers much of southern Europe. Beautiful scenes like this one in southern Germany help make the region a popular vacationland.

© Herve Champollion, Cephas Picture Library/Alamy Images

The Central Uplands region extends from Portugal to the Czech Republic. Cattle graze in a meadow in the Massif Central, or central highlands, in France, *shown here.*

© Shutterstock

The Great European Plain stretches from the Atlantic Ocean to the Ural Mountains. It has most of Europe's best agricultural areas, including farmland in Ukraine, *shown here.*

above the timber line yield pastures for livestock. The lower mountain slopes and valleys provide the best farmland. Many parts of this region are popular vacation destinations.

The Great European Plain extends from southern France to the Ural Mountains in Russia and includes southeastern England. At its narrowest point, in Belgium, it is only about 50 miles (80 kilometers) wide. The plain widens through Germany and Poland. At its greatest width, in Russia, it extends from the Arctic Ocean to the Caucasus Mountains, a distance of more than 1,500 miles (2,410 kilometers).

This region consists chiefly of flat and rolling land with some hills. Glaciers shaped the northerly and easterly sections, leaving an uneven ground surface marked by lakes and marshes, such as the Pripyat Marshes in southwestern Belarus and northwestern Ukraine. The region has an average elevation of about 600 feet (180 meters) above sea level in Russia, and less than 500 feet (150 meters) elsewhere.

The Great European Plain has some of the world's most fertile farmland. It also supports densely populated areas, especially in the western regions. But most of the Russian part is sparsely populated.

Coastline and islands. Europe has a highly irregular coastline. The coastline penetrates deeply inland in many places, leaving a series of large and small peninsulas. The major peninsulas are the Scandinavian Peninsula (Norway and Sweden), Jutland (Denmark), the Iberian Peninsula (Portugal and Spain), the Italian Peninsula, and the Balkan Peninsula (Albania, Bosnia-Herzegovina, Bulgaria, Greece, Macedonia, Montenegro, and parts of Croatia, Romania, Serbia, Slovenia, and Turkey).

The irregularity of Europe's coastline makes it unusually long, about 37,877 miles (60,957 kilometers). Along the coastline are numerous seas, bays, gulfs, and natural harbors. Most of Europe—except for the heart of European Russia—lies within about 300 miles (480 kilometers) of a seacoast.

Thousands of islands lie off the coast of Europe. The largest and most important of these is Great Britain, which lies north and west of the European mainland. Other major islands in this area include Ireland, Iceland, and the Channel, Faroe, Orkney, and Shetland islands. Major islands south of the mainland include, from west to east, the Balearic Islands, Corsica, Sardinia, Sicily, and Crete.

Rivers. Europe's many rivers serve as major industrial transportation routes. They also supply water to irrigate farmland and provide power to generate electric power.

Europe's longest river, the Volga, flows 2,194 miles (3,531 kilometers) through Russia to the Caspian Sea. Canals link the Volga with the Arctic Ocean, the Baltic Sea, and the Don River. The Don flows into the Sea of Azov, which is connected to the Black Sea. The Danube, 1,770 miles (2,850 kilometers) long, is Europe's second longest river. It winds from southern Germany through Austria, Slovakia, Hungary, Serbia, Bulgaria, and Romania to the Black Sea. The Rhine River flows for 820 miles (1,320 kilometers) from the Swiss Alps through western Germany and the Netherlands to the North Sea. It ranks among the world's busiest waterways.

Other important European rivers include the Dnieper in Russia, Belarus, and Ukraine; the Northern Dvina in Russia; the Western Dvina in Russia and Latvia; the Oder and Vistula in Poland; the Elbe in the Czech Republic and Germany; the Po in Italy; the Rhône and Seine in France; the Ebro in Spain; the Tagus in Spain and Portugal; and the Thames in England.

Lakes. The world's largest lake, the saltwater Caspian Sea, straddles the boundary of Europe and Asia. Although called a sea, the Caspian is really a lake because land completely surrounds it. The Caspian covers 143,250 square miles (371,000 square kilometers). With its northern shore 92 feet (28 meters) below sea level, it ranks as Europe's lowest point.

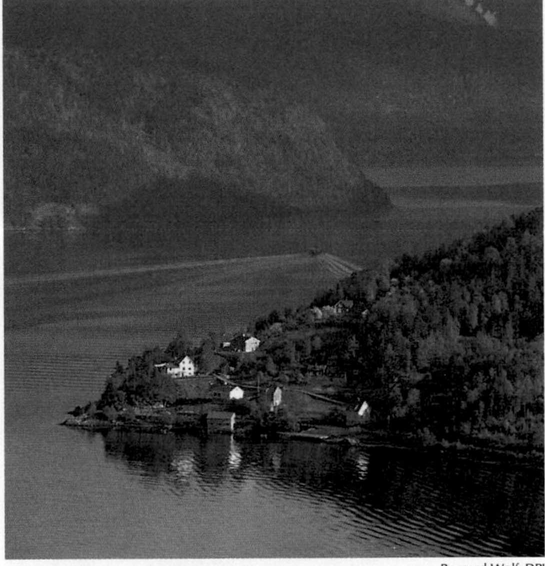

Bernard Wolf, DPI

Fiords are long, narrow inlets of the sea that cut into the Norwegian coast. Steep, wooded mountains line most fiords, creating beautiful scenes. Many tiny villages lie along the banks.

The area of freshwater lakes totals only about 53,000 square miles (137,000 square kilometers). The largest, Lake Ladoga in northwestern Russia, covers 6,835 square miles (17,703 square kilometers). Finland, which has about 60,000 lakes, is known as *the land of thousands of lakes.*

Climate

Europe has a variety of climates, as illustrated by the large climate map in this article. The small maps provide information about temperatures and precipitation.

Europe generally has milder climates than parts of Asia and North America at the same latitude. For example, Berlin, Germany; Calgary, Canada; and Irkutsk, in the Asian part of Russia, lie at about the same latitude. But

© Harvey Lloyd, The Stock Market

Canals and rivers form an important transportation system in many parts of Europe. Boats called *gondolas, shown here,* carry people throughout the city of Venice, Italy.

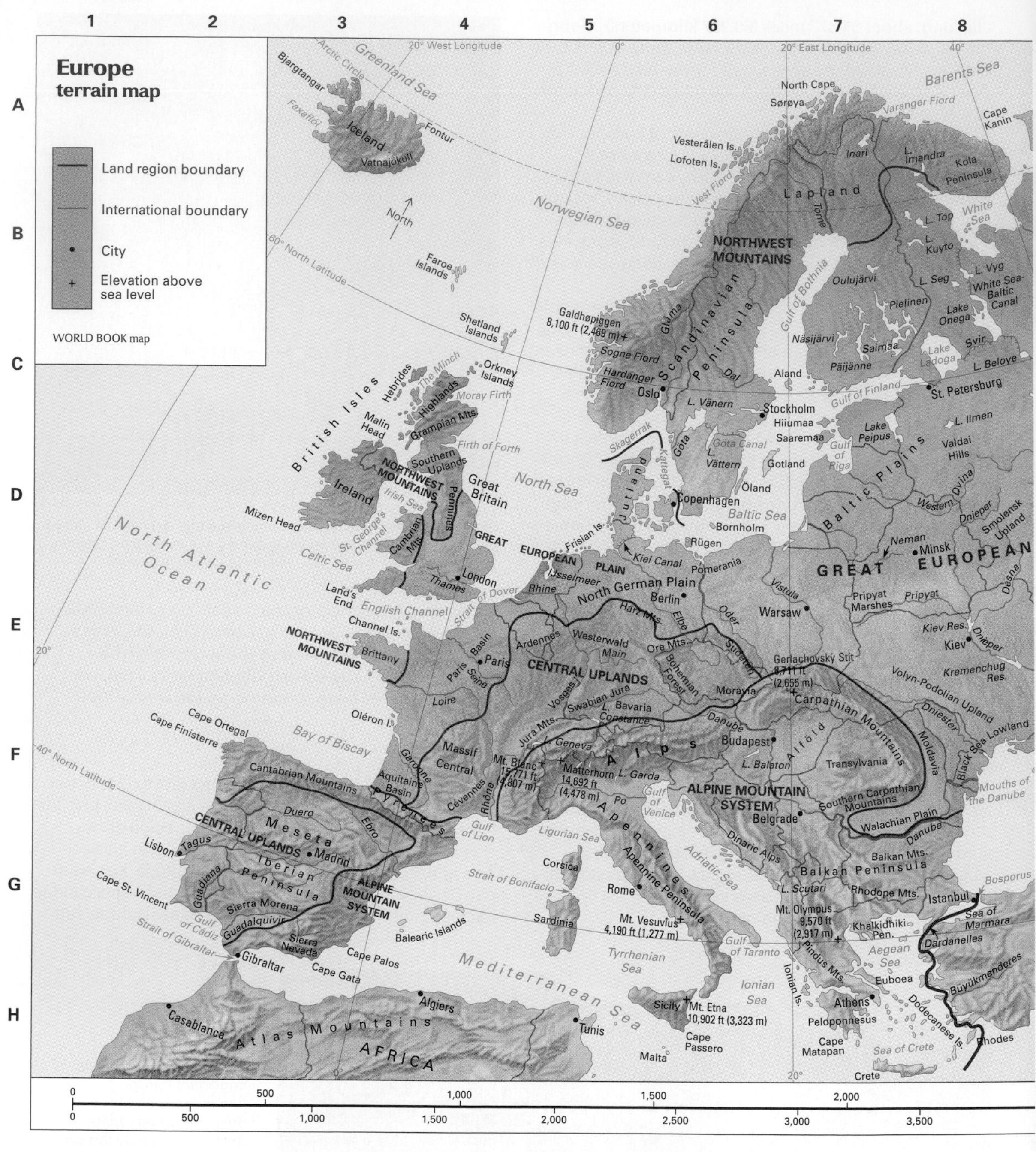

Physical features

Feature	Grid	
Adriatic Sea	G	6
Aegean Sea	G	7
Alps (mountains)	F	5
Apennine Peninsula	G	6
Apennines (mountains)	G	5
Balearic Islands	G	4
Balkan Mountains	G	7
Balkan Peninsula	G	7
Baltic Sea	D	6
Barents Sea	A	8
Bay of Biscay	F	3
Black Sea	G	9
Bosporus (strait)	G	8
Cantabrian Mountains	F	3
Carpathian Mountains	F	7
Caspian Sea	F	11
Caucasus Mountains	F	10
Celtic Sea	D	3
Channel Islands	E	3
Corsica (island)	G	5
Crete (island)	H	7
Dal River	C	6
Danube River	F	6
Dardanelles (strait)	G	8
Dnieper River	E	8
Dniestr River	F	8
Dodecanese Islands	H	8
Don River	E	10
Donets River	E	9
Ebro River	G	3
Elbe River	E	6
English Channel	E	3
Faroe Islands	B	4
Firth of Forth	D	4
Galdhøpiggen (mountain)	C	5
Gerlachevsky Stit (mountain)	E	7
Gulf of Bothnia	B	7
Gulf of Cádiz	G	2
Gulf of Lion	G	4
Gulf of Riga	D	7
Gulf of Taranto	G	6
Gulf of Venice	F	5
Hebrides (islands)	C	3
Iberian Peninsula	G	2
Iceland (island)	A	3
Ionian Sea	H	6
Irish Sea	D	3
Jutland (peninsula)	D	5
Khalkidhiki Peninsula	G	7
Kola Peninsula	A	8
Lake Geneva	F	5
Lake Ladoga	C	8
Lake Onega	C	8
Lake Peipus	D	7
Land's End (point)	E	3
Lapland	B	7
Ligurian Sea	G	5
Lofoten Islands	A	6
Loire River	F	4
Malta (island)	H	5
Matterhorn (mountain)	F	5
Mediterranean Sea	H	5
Minch, The (strait)	C	4
Mont Blanc	F	4
Mount Elbrus	F	10
Mount Etna (volcano)	H	6
Mount Narodnaya	A	10
Mount Olympus	G	7
Mount Vesuvius (volcano)	G	6
Neman River	D	7
North Cape	A	7
North Sea	D	5
Northern Dvina River	B	9
Norwegian Sea	B	5
Oder River	E	6
Orkney Islands	C	4
Pechora River	A	9

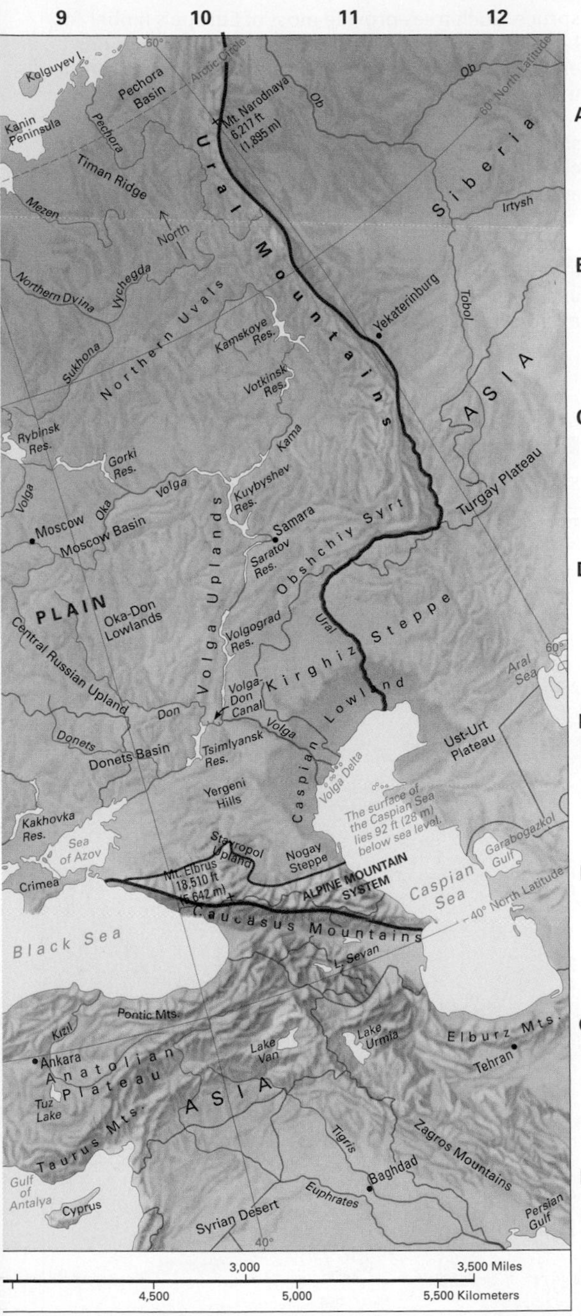

Peloponnesus (peninsula)	H	7
Po River	F	5
Pyrenees (mountains)	F	3
Rhine River	E	5
Rhodes (island)	H	8
Rhône River	F	4
St. George's Channel	D	3
Sardinia (island)	G	5
Scandinavian Peninsula	C	6
Sea of Azov	F	9
Sea of Marmara	G	8
Seine River	E	4
Shetland Islands	C	4
Sicily (island)	H	6
Sogne Fiord	C	5
Strait of Dover	E	4
Strait of Gibraltar	H	2
Tagus River	G	2
Thames, River	E	4
Torne River	B	7
Tyrrhenian Sea	H	5
Ural Mountains	B	10
Ural River	D	11
Varanger Fiord	A	8
Vest Fiord	B	6
Vesterålen Islands	A	6
Vistula River	E	7
Volga River	C	10
Western Dvina River	D	8
White Sea	B	8

January temperatures in Berlin average about 19 °F (11 °C) higher than those in Calgary and about 40 °F (22 °C) higher than those in Irkutsk.

Europe's mild climates result from winds that blow across the continent from the Atlantic Ocean. These winds are warmed and given moisture by the Gulf Stream, a powerful ocean current that carries warm water from the Gulf of Mexico to Europe's western coast. The most spectacular effect of the Gulf Stream occurs along the Norwegian coast. Though much of Norway's coast lies in the Arctic region, almost all of Norway's coast remains free of ice and snow through the winter.

In general, western Europe has shorter and warmer winters and longer, cooler summers than eastern Europe. The farther away an area is from a coast, the greater the variations in temperature and moisture are from summer to winter. This phenomenon is known as *continentality.*

Europe's climates also vary from north to south. Southern Europe generally has shorter, milder winters and longer, hotter summers than northern Europe. Moreover, an area of high air pressure in the Atlantic called the Azores High prevents winds from bringing moisture into much of southern Europe during the summer. This phenomenon frequently causes drought in the region.

Most of Europe receives from 20 to 60 inches (50 to 150 centimeters) of precipitation each year. More than 80 inches (200 centimeters) usually occurs in areas just west of mountains. Such regions include parts of western England and western Norway. Less than 20 inches (50 centimeters) of precipitation usually falls in three general areas: (1) east of high mountains, (2) far inland from the Atlantic Ocean, and (3) along the Arctic coast. Such regions include central and southeastern Spain, northern Scandinavia, northern and southeastern parts of European Russia, and western Kazakhstan.

Plant and animal life

Europe's wildlife includes many *species* (kinds) of plants and animals that also inhabit other continents. But some species of wildlife, including the nightingale and the Norway lemming, are native only to Europe. Some European species of wild plants and animals share the same name, yet differ from the wildlife of other continents. For example, the European robin is only about half the size of the American robin.

The activities of human beings have threatened, and even wiped out, many of Europe's wild plants and animals. People have cut down vast forests that once covered much of Europe to make way for farms and cities. Industrialization has polluted both air and water. Overhunting, trapping, and overfishing have threatened numerous European animals. Moreover, global warming, a phenomenon probably caused in part by human activities, could threaten the survival of many species in the cold regions of Europe, including the high Alps.

People also have introduced a number of plant and animal species into Europe that are now threatening native species. For example, North American gray squirrels pose a serious threat to the native Eurasian red squirrel in the United Kingdom. Among plants, the Canada goldenrod can grow in such dense patches in Europe that it hinders the growth of most native plants.

Since the mid-1900's, conservation efforts have helped save some animal and plant species from extinction. These species include the white-tailed eagle and the European brown bear.

Plants in Europe grow in three basic types of areas: (1) forests, (2) grasslands, and (3) tundra and high mountains.

Forests. Most of the forests of central and southern Europe have been cut down, but northern Europe still has large woodlands. These northern forests, known as *needleleaf forests,* consist mostly of cone-bearing trees called *conifers* or *evergreens,* which have narrow, needlelike leaves. Conifers include the fir, larch, pine, and spruce. Such trees provide most of Europe's timber for building and for manufacturing paper. European governments regulate the cutting of these trees to protect the forests.

The central and southern regions of Europe have some *broadleaf forests.* A broadleaf forest consists chiefly of trees with broad, flat leaves that fall off each autumn. Such trees include the ash, beech, birch, elm, maple, and oak. The central and southern regions also have some *mixed forests* of broadleaf and needleleaf trees. In addition, needleleaf forests cover many of the upper slopes of mountains in these regions. *Broadleaf evergreens* remain common along the Mediterranean

What the climate in Europe is like

Tundra–Always cold, with a brief, chilly summer. Little precipitation in all seasons.

Subarctic–Short, cool summers and long, cold winters. Light to moderate precipitation, mostly in summer.

Humid continental–Mild summers and cold winters. Moderate precipitation in all seasons.

Humid oceanic–Moderately warm summers and generally cool winters. Moderate precipitation in all seasons.

Humid subtropical–Warm to hot summers and cool winters. Moderate precipitation in all seasons.

Subtropical dry summer–Hot, dry summers and mild, rainy winters. Moderate precipitation in winter.

Semiarid–Hot to cold. Great changes in temperature from day to night except in coastal areas. Light precipitation.

Highland–Climate depends on altitude. Climates at various altitudes are like those found in flat terrain.

WORLD BOOK map

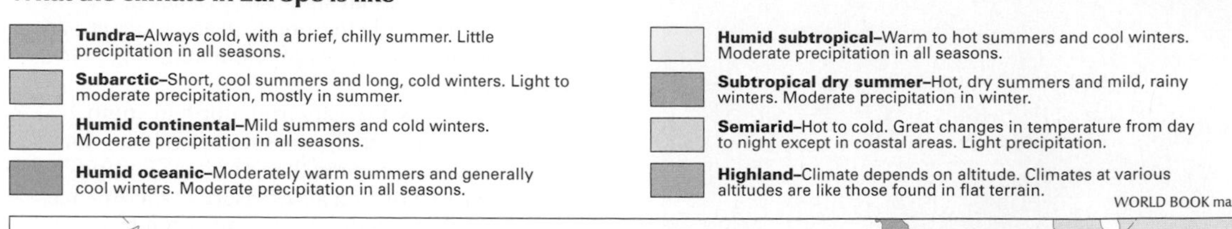

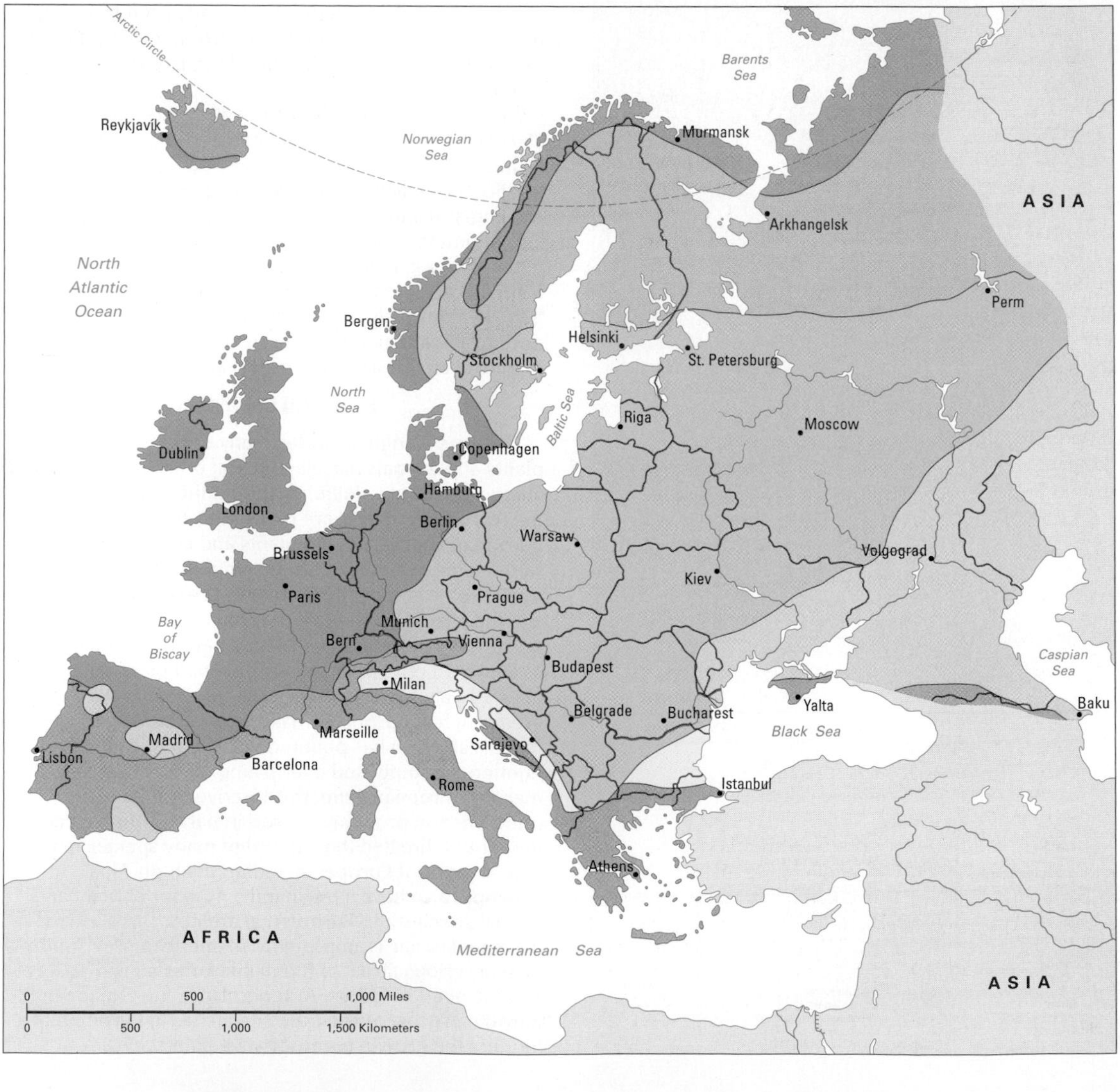

Average January temperatures

This map shows the range of average January temperatures in Europe. Most of Europe has average temperatures below freezing. The southern and western coastal areas have the warmest winters.

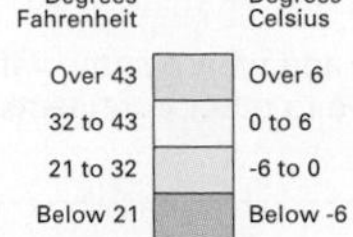

Average July temperatures

This map shows the range of average July temperatures in Europe. Northeastern Europe and the high mountains are the coolest areas, and the Mediterranean and Caspian seacoasts are the warmest.

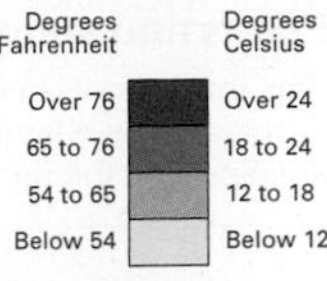

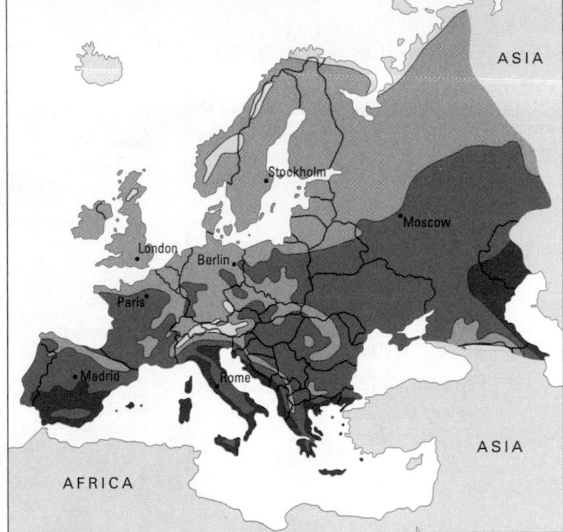

coast. Trees of this type include cork and olive trees. These trees do not lose their leaves in the fall, and many have tough, wax-coated leaves that hold moisture well.

Grasslands are open areas where grasses rank as the most plentiful plant life. Europe has both natural grasslands, known as *steppes,* and artificial grasslands created by people. Steppes are dry areas where only short grasses grow. They cover most of southwestern Russia and western Kazakhstan. Artificial grasslands cover most of the smaller plains of Europe. Today, farmers use most of these grasslands for cropland and grazing land.

Tundra and high mountains are cold, treeless areas. Tundra covers much of the region near Europe's Arctic coast. Land in this region remains frozen throughout most of the year. The top 1 to 2 feet (30 to 61 centimeters) of tundra thaws in the short Arctic summer, and many small marshes, ponds, and swamps form on the land. Mosses, small shrubs, wildflowers, and lichens also cover the tundra during the summer. The upper slopes of Europe's highest mountains resemble tundra. Farmers use parts of the tundra and high mountains as grazing land.

Animals. Many of Europe's wild animals live in areas that are difficult for people to reach. Many others inhabit special areas where people may not kill them, including preserves, national parks, or zoos.

Foxes and wolves roam throughout much of Europe, as do elk, reindeer, and several other kinds of deer. The European brown bear, one of the largest bears, lives mostly in Russia and northern Scandinavia. The chamois and ibex, two goatlike animals, make their homes in the high mountains of southwestern Europe. Seals live off the Arctic, Atlantic, and Mediterranean coasts. Other wild animals of Europe include badgers, hares, hedgehogs, lemmings, moles, otters, rabbits, and wild boars.

Average yearly precipitation

(Rain, melted snow, and other forms of moisture)

This map shows the average yearly precipitation in Europe. Most of Europe has moderate precipitation.

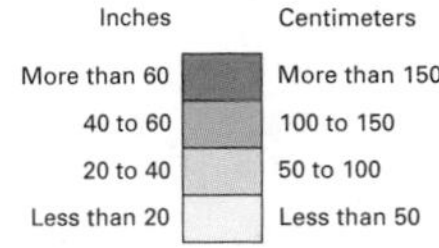

European birds include eagles, falcons, finches, house sparrows, owls, ravens, robins, storks, thrushes, and wood pigeons. European reptiles include adders and wall lizards. The continent's amphibians include numerous types of frogs and salamanders. European amphibians have declined greatly since the mid-1900's, with many species near extinction.

Plants and animals of Europe

This map shows in general where some of Europe's wild animals live and where some wild plants of Europe grow. Many species of wildlife found in Europe are also native to other continents. But some species, like the nightingale, can be found only in Europe.

WORLD BOOK illustration by John Wood

Fish inhabit the waters off the Atlantic coast and in the Baltic, Black, Caspian, Mediterranean, and North seas. Fishing crews catch anchovies, flounders, herrings, mackerels, salmon, sardines, trout, and tuna in these areas. Since the mid-1900's, especially in the Mediterranean Sea, overfishing has caused severe declines in cod and other fish. Such declines threaten not only the survival of the fish but also whether traditional fishing will continue in these areas.

As in other parts of the world, insects make up most of Europe's animal species. Insects often play vital roles in maintaining the health of environments that support other living things.

Economy

The majority of the countries in Europe belong to the European Union, which has developed a highly integrated *common market,* or economic union. EU member countries trade among themselves without such barriers as tariffs, import quotas, and other regulations or restrictions. EU members also invest freely in one another's economies. In addition, the EU promotes a common trade policy with countries outside Europe. The combined value of the EU's imports and exports is greater than that of any single country in the world. As a result, European countries have some of the world's highest standards of living. The EU also regulates its members' industrial policy, transportation policy, and agricultural policy. Many EU countries use a common currency called the euro.

Agriculture. Europe has some of the world's richest farmland. European farmers produce most of the food consumed within the continent. Much of the food imported into Europe comes from tropical countries, in-

Dennis Brack, Black Star

The Black Forest, in Germany, is made up mostly of dark fir and spruce trees. Forests of such trees are common throughout northern Europe and in mountain areas of southern Europe.

Dan Budnik, Woodfin Camp, Inc.

Reindeer live in far northern Europe. Some wander wild, but the Sami (also called Lapps) herd many reindeer. Sami raise reindeer for food, clothing, and transportation.

© Argus from Peter Arnold, Inc.

Storks live in many parts of Europe during the summer and often nest on roofs and chimneys. The storks shown here are nesting on the top of a church in Lwówek, near Poznań, Poland.

cluding such goods as cocoa, coffee, and tropical fruits.

The main European crops include grains—such as barley, oats, rye, and wheat—as well as corn, flax, potatoes, sugar beets, and tobacco. Most of the world's olives come from farms in the Mediterranean areas of Europe. These farms also produce citrus fruits, dates, figs, and grapes.

Farmers in most of Europe raise cattle, hogs, sheep, and poultry for meat. Dairy farming is important in such countries as Denmark, Ireland, the Netherlands, Switzerland, and the United Kingdom. Grazing lands exist throughout Europe. Some of the world's best breeds of cattle and sheep originated in Europe. The United Kingdom has produced many of these breeds, including Hereford and Jersey cattle and Hampshire, Shropshire, and Suffolk sheep.

Manufacturing. Leading industrial areas of Europe have traditionally included parts of France, Germany, northern Italy, the Netherlands, Norway, Spain, Sweden, and the United Kingdom. Since the late 1900's, major industrial areas have also developed in Ireland and in such central and eastern European countries as the Czech Republic, Hungary, Poland, Russia, and Ukraine.

Europe leads the rest of the world in the production of certain goods, such as automobiles and automobile products. Many European automobile manufacturers, including Volkswagen in Germany and Fiat in Italy, market their cars worldwide. However, such industries face growing competition from countries in North America and Asia. Other industrial products made in Europe include aerospace equipment, cement, construction equipment, electronics and telecommunications equipment, motor vehicles, *pharmaceuticals* (medicinal drugs), rail transportation equipment, and textiles.

Increased international competition has provided great challenges for Europe's traditional industrial centers, such as the Ruhr region of western Germany. European countries have responded by working to increase industrial productivity. They also have moved resources from formerly productive industries, such as steel and shipbuilding, to more rapidly growing industries, such as telecommunications and electronics.

New industries that utilize Europe's highly skilled labor force and highly developed research and development programs have grown and spread. For example, the electronic components industry, which produces parts for computers and other electronic goods, has spread from western Europe to many countries in eastern Europe.

Mining and energy. Although Europe imports most of its raw materials, many parts of the continent have large deposits of minerals and other resources. Coal fields exist in Germany, Poland, and Russia. Substantial iron ore deposits occur in both Russia and Ukraine. The chief petroleum producers are Norway, Russia, and the United Kingdom. Natural gas is taken from the Netherlands, Russia, and the United Kingdom. Many of the other mined products of Europe, including diamonds, nickel, platinum, potash, silver, and zinc, exist primarily in Russia.

Energy comes from many sources, including coal, natural gas, nuclear energy, oil, and renewable energy sources. Coal-burning power plants, *hydropower* (water power) facilities, and nuclear power plants rank as the chief sources of the continent's electric power. Beginning in the late 1900's, Europe invested in methods of generating energy from renewable sources. These projects have sought to harness the power of ocean tides, rivers, sunlight, and wind.

Forestry and fishing. Northern Europe ranks among the most important areas in the world for forestry. Austria, Finland, Germany, Norway, and Sweden have vast forested areas that supply Europe with lumber, wood pulp, and paper. Pine and other softwoods account for most of the lumber consumed in Europe.

Fishing boats sail all the waters that border Europe. However, the most important fisheries lie in the North Sea, the Atlantic Ocean, and the Arctic Ocean. Norway, Spain, and Russia run the largest fishing fleets in Europe. The European Union created its Common Fisheries Policy to coordinate fishing efforts and attempt to manage overfishing, which has threatened the survival of many fish species. Such fish as hake and cod, once abundant in northern waters, have become severely threatened in those areas.

International trade. The development of the European Union common market has stimulated trade in Europe. The EU hopes to increase employment throughout the continent and to make more goods and services available to European consumers. Moreover, the EU works to ensure that the wealth generated by Europe's economy is spread fairly among all its member states.

Agriculture and fishing in Europe

This map shows the chief uses of land in Europe. The continent has some of the world's richest farmland, and farmers in western Europe produce some of the highest crop yields. The most important crops—such as wheat in Ukraine and potatoes in Poland—are shown in larger type. The map also shows the major fishing areas in surrounding waters.

Mostly cropland
Grazing land
Forest land
Generally unproductive land
Major fishing areas

WORLD BOOK map

Some countries that do not belong to the EU belong to other trade groups, such as the European Free Trade Association (EFTA). EFTA is a *free trade area*—that is, its members have agreed to eliminate trade barriers on certain products and allow for differences in how they conduct trade with nonmember countries. Three EFTA members—Iceland, Liechtenstein, and Norway—have entered into an agreement with the EU called the European Economic Area (EEA). The EEA has removed most trade barriers between these three countries and the European Union.

EU members also trade with many non-European countries. Europe's major trading partners are the United States, China, and Japan. The EU also has a number of regional trade agreements with Latin America, with the non-EU countries of the Mediterranean, and with developing countries in a group called the African, Pacific, and Caribbean (APC) states.

Service industries produce services rather than goods. They include health care, finance, and government. Collectively, these industries employ more European workers than does any other economic sector.

Health care. In some European countries, including the United Kingdom, the government pays the health care expenses of almost all of the country's people. Under this system, all medical facilities are publicly owned and all medical personnel are paid from public funds. Citizens receive health care for free or at a low cost.

John Launois, Black Star

Coal mining has long been a major industry in Europe. About a fifth of the world's coal comes from the continent. The industry uses modern technology, such as this huge digging machine.

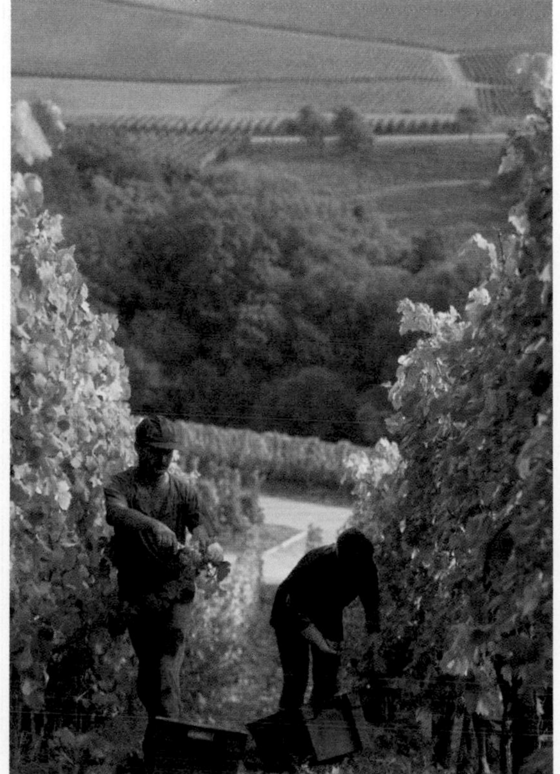

© Rob Kieffer, eu2005.lu

Grapes from various regions of Europe are used to make much of the world's wine. These workers are collecting grapes near the Moselle River in Luxembourg.

© David Veis, EPA Photo/CTK/European Commission

Fishing is an important industry in many European countries. These fishermen are pulling carp from a pond in the Bohemia region of the Czech Republic.

However, medicine in most of Europe is only partly provided by national governments. The governments do not own most medical facilities, nor do they directly pay doctors, who are self-employed. Yet these countries do provide health insurance, which ensures free medical care for those unable to pay and refunds most of the payments made by patients who do pay. European countries finance these plans through high tax rates.

Many European countries rank among the leading countries in medical research. The Pasteur Institute in Paris is a world center for the study, prevention, and treatment of disease. The United Kingdom's Medical Research Council, a government agency, supports biomedical research.

Since the late 1900's, Europe's pharmaceutical industry has grown rapidly. European drug companies are developing new medications to treat or prevent a variety of diseases.

Finance. Europe has for centuries played a leading role in international finance. The EU ranks as the top investor in such countries as India and China.

Major stock exchanges of Europe include those in Amsterdam, the Netherlands; Frankfurt, Germany; London; Paris; and Zurich, Switzerland. The London Bullion Market Association is the center of the world's gold market, and Amsterdam is the center of the world's diamond market. Frankfurt, the site of the European Central Bank, has become a major center for the European bond market.

Mining and manufacturing in Europe

This map shows the locations of the chief mineral resources of Europe. The most important minerals—such as coal in Russia and bauxite in France—are shown in larger type. The map also shows Europe's major manufacturing centers. The four main industrial areas—the Donets Basin, the Midlands, the Ruhr, and the Urals—are labeled in large red type.

Coal Major mineral deposit
Lead Other mineral deposit
Lille Manufacturing center

WORLD BOOK map

AP/Wide World

Major stock exchanges operate in many parts of Europe. Euronext, which provides a transaction system across international borders, is one of the largest European stock markets. These analysts in Amsterdam, the Netherlands, are monitoring Euronext activity on their computers.

Some of the world's largest banks have their headquarters in France, Germany, Switzerland, and the United Kingdom. These banks receive much foreign investment because they offer security and high rates of return. The spread of the euro has made such large banks even more important, as more and more international investors have acquired funds in euros.

Government plays a vital role in the economies of European countries. Governments provide such public services as education, highway systems, and military protection. European central governments employ large numbers of people and regulate much of their countries' economies.

Transportation. Europe has highly developed transportation networks. Airlines, highways, railways, and waterways provide efficient systems for the movement of people and goods.

European airlines fly throughout the continent and the world. National airlines—which include British Airways in the United Kingdom, Lufthansa in Germany, and Air France in France—receive financial support from government funds. The national airlines of Denmark, Norway, and Sweden combined to form Scandinavian Airlines (SAS).

A well-developed network of highways and roads serves most of Europe. Private ownership of automobiles is widespread. Trucks carry goods throughout the continent. Among the best-known European highways are the four-lane superhighways in Germany known as *autobahns.*

Many long road tunnels enable traffic to flow easily through Europe's mountains. The world's longest tunnel, the Lærdal Tunnel, connects Oslo to Bergen in Norway. It runs 15.2 miles (24.5 kilometers) long. The St. Gotthard Road Tunnel, which cuts through the Alps in central Switzerland, is 10.5 miles (16.9 kilometers) long.

People and goods also travel on Europe's highly developed train networks. European express trains—including the fast passenger trains called InterCity trains, which stop only at large stations—rank among the most efficient in the world. They can travel 150 miles (240 kilometers) per hour. European governments typically operate such train systems.

Europe has some of the world's longest railroad tunnels. The Channel Tunnel, or Chunnel, runs under the English Channel and connects the United Kingdom and France. The Chunnel, which is 31.4 miles (50.5 kilometers) long, carries passenger trains, freight trains, and shuttle trains for motor vehicles (see **Channel Tunnel**). The 21.5-mile (34.6-kilometer) Lötschberg Base Tunnel carries rail traffic through the Alps in Switzerland.

The rivers and canals of Europe provide a network for sending goods on barges and other ships. Major European waterways include the Danube, Moselle, Rhine and Volga rivers.

Europe handles more than half the world's international shipping. Some of the world's largest merchant fleets belong to European nations. Such countries as Greece, Norway, and the United Kingdom have huge fleets. Rotterdam ranks as Europe's major port, taking in much of the goods from non-European countries. Other European ports include those in Barcelona, Spain;

© age fotostock/SuperStock

High-speed trains carry much of the long-distance passenger traffic throughout Europe. These trains have arrived at the Delicias train station in Saragossa, Spain.

Adam Woolfitt, Woodfin Camp, Inc.

The port of Rotterdam, the Netherlands, *shown here,* ranks as one of the busiest ports in the world. Several other European ports are also leading shipping centers.

Copenhagen, Denmark; Gdańsk, Poland; Hamburg, Germany; Helsinki, Finland; Le Havre, France; Lisbon, Portugal; London; Naples, Italy; Piraeus, Greece; Riga, Latvia; and Stockholm, Sweden.

Communication. Europe plays a leading role in the international telecommunications industry, especially cellular telephone service. Nokia, headquartered in Finland, ranks as the world's top provider of cell phones.

Most Europeans own televisions, which air channels run by governments and private companies. Large international TV networks link European countries to one another and to the rest of the world. The European Broadcasting Union operates Eurovision, the world's largest provider of international sports and news broadcasts.

Mail, telephone, and telegraph services are mainly run by European governments. Newspapers are published throughout Europe, with both national and local papers available in most European cities. Some of the national papers, such as *The Times* and the *Financial Times* of the United Kingdom and *Le Monde* of France, appear in many countries throughout the world.

The Internet plays an increasingly important role in the European communication industry. More and more Europeans have access to computers, making the use of e-mail and other electronic communication techniques more widespread.

History

Prehistoric times. Scientists have found fossils and stone tools that indicate early human beings lived in Europe more than 700,000 years ago. The best-known prehistoric people in Europe are the Neandertals (also spelled Neanderthals) and the Cro-Magnon people. Neandertals lived from about 150,000 years ago to 35,000 years ago. Cro-Magnon people lived from about 35,000 years ago to 10,000 years ago. The Cro-Magnons were an early type of modern human being. Cro-Magnons lived in small groups, wandering from place to place to hunt and gather food.

About 6000 B.C., people in southeastern Europe learned to raise food by farming. This development made it possible for early human beings to take the final steps toward civilization. People no longer had to move from place to place in search of food. They could settle in one place and form villages. Some of these villages eventually developed into Europe's first cities. After 6000 B.C., more and more people in Europe turned to farming for their chief source of food. By the end of prehistoric times—about 3000 B.C.—farming had spread to all parts of Europe except the dense northern forests.

Early civilizations. The first European civilizations developed on islands in the Aegean Sea, east of Greece. Aegean civilization flourished from about 3000 to 1200 B.C. On some Aegean islands, especially Crete, the people used a system of writing and became skilled architects, craftworkers, and painters. They also were adventurous sailors and traders. A similar civilization developed on the island of Malta, south of Italy. After about 2500 B.C., seafarers from the Aegean islands and Malta sailed along the southern and western coasts of Europe. They introduced their way of life to people they met on the way.

Great European empires, 300's B.C. - A.D. 500's

These maps show the European empires that flourished between the 300's B.C. and the A.D. 500's. The empire of Alexander the Great was the first great empire that began in Europe. It spread Greek civilization into Asia. The maps show each empire at its height.

Alexander's empire, 323 B.C.

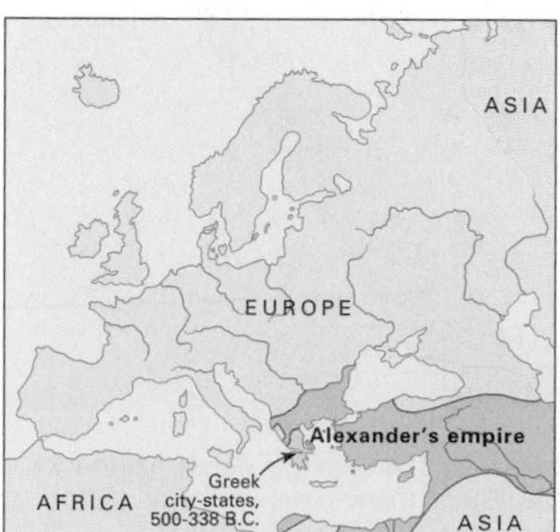

Roman Empire, A.D. 117

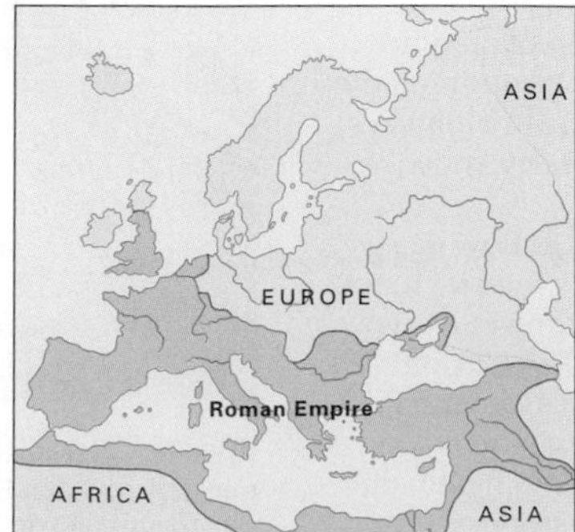

Byzantine Empire, A.D. 500's

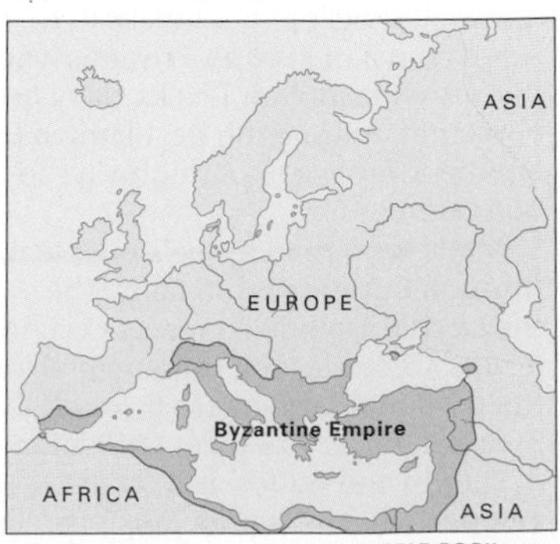

WORLD BOOK maps

Important dates in Europe

c. 3000 B.C. Civilization developed on Crete and other islands in the Aegean Sea.

c. 500 to 300 B.C. Greek civilization reached its height.

27 B.C. to A.D. 180 Rome achieved its greatest power.

A.D. 300's Romans granted the Christians freedom of religion. The Roman Empire split into two parts: the West Roman Empire and the East Roman, or Byzantine, Empire.

400's The West Roman Empire fell, and the Middle Ages began.

732 A Frankish army defeated Muslim forces in Spain.

768-814 Charlemagne built an empire in western Europe.

1054 The Christian Church split into the Roman Catholic Church and the Eastern Orthodox Churches.

Late 1000's Europeans began the Crusades.

1347-1352 The Black Death killed many of Europe's people.

1300's The Renaissance began in Italy.

1500's The Reformation brought Protestantism to Europe.

1689 The English Parliament passed the Bill of Rights.

1789-1799 The French Revolution ended absolute monarchy in France.

1815 Napoleon was defeated in the Battle of Waterloo.

1700's to mid-1800's The Industrial Revolution swept through Europe.

1914-1918 World War I raged in Europe.

1917 The Bolshevik Revolution led to the establishment of a Communist dictatorship in Russia.

1920's Joseph Stalin became dictator of the Soviet Union, and Benito Mussolini became dictator of Italy.

1933 The Nazis under Adolf Hitler took control of the German government.

1939-1945 The Allies defeated Germany, Italy, and the other Axis powers in World War II.

1940's Soviet-controlled Communist dictatorships seized control of governments in eastern Europe after World War II.

1949 Canada, the United States, and 10 western European countries formed the North Atlantic Treaty Organization.

1950's Western European countries began economic associations that later merged to form the European Union.

1975 Most European countries signed the first of the Helsinki Accords, pledging increased cooperation and promotion of human rights.

1989-1990 Most of eastern Europe ended Communist rule and began reforms toward giving the people more freedom.

1990 East and West Germany were unified.

1991 Most of the republics of the Soviet Union declared their independence, and the Soviet Union was dissolved. Three of Yugoslavia's six republics declared their independence.

2002 The euro replaced the traditional currencies of many European countries.

Tribes of horseback riders from the region northeast of the Black Sea swept south and west through Europe around 2000 B.C. These warriors had been herders on the grassy plains of their homeland. They spread their warrior culture throughout much of Europe as they conquered large numbers of villages.

Ancient Greece made great advancements in the development of civilization. Tribes from the north moved to the Greek Peninsula about 2000 B.C. They developed a way of life based chiefly on the Cretan civilization. The Greeks became the most powerful people in the Aegean area, and, in the 1400's B.C., they took control of the region from the Cretans. During the 1100's B.C., another wave of invading tribes swept into Greece from the north. They conquered most of southern Greece and drove out the people who were living there. During the next several hundred years, groups of these tribes united to form a new type of independent governmental unit. Each of these units, called a *polis* or *city-state*, consisted of a city and its outlying areas. The word *political* comes from this ancient Greek word.

Ancient Greek civilization reached its height in the 400's and 300's B.C. with the rise of Athens, Sparta, and other powerful city-states. The idea of democracy spread during this period, and Greek art and learning flourished. But about the same time, Greece entered a long period of warfare. First, the Greeks defeated attacking forces from the Persian Empire to the east. Then the Greek city-states began to fight among themselves. As this fighting continued, Greece's political strength began to decay. But Athens remained a cultural center of the ancient world.

Macedonia, a kingdom north of Greece, grew stronger during this period, and it seized control of Greece in 338 B.C. Beginning in 336 B.C., Alexander the Great ruled Macedonia. He built a huge empire—partly in Europe but mostly in Asia. Alexander admired the Greeks and spread their culture throughout his empire. Macedonia became weaker after Alexander's death in 323 B.C., but its rulers continued to control Greece.

Ancient Rome was the next major European civilization. Rome grew into an important city during the 500's B.C., under the leadership of Etruscan kings. The Etruscans had the most advanced civilization in Italy during that time. At the end of the 500's B.C., Roman nobles expelled the last Etruscan king and established the independent Roman Republic. By the early 200's B.C., Rome had conquered all of the Italian Peninsula south of what is now Florence.

Over the next 200 years, the Romans built an empire across the Mediterranean Sea, extending from what is now Spain into southwestern Asia and along Africa's northern coast. Although they soon added much of the rest of Europe to their empire, the Mediterranean remained the center of the Roman world. The Roman Republic ended in 27 B.C., when Augustus became the first emperor of the Roman Empire.

The Roman Empire reached the height of its power during a time known as the *Pax Romana* (Roman Peace), which lasted from 27 B.C. to A.D. 180. No country was strong enough to threaten the empire in this period, and so the era was a time of peace. Roman art and learning reached a high point, and commerce flourished.

The Romans borrowed many ideas from the Greeks, and they spread much of the Greek culture throughout the empire. In fact, historians frequently refer to the culture of the Roman Empire as *Greco-Roman.* But the Romans also made many contributions of their own to European life. For example, they built carefully planned cities and vast systems of well-constructed roads. Latin, the Roman language, became the basis of the Romance languages spoken in Europe today. Many legal principles developed by the Romans became part of legal systems in Europe. These principles later helped shape legal systems in other parts of the world, including North and South America.

Christianity began in Palestine, a land in southwestern Asia that was part of the Roman Empire. It soon spread to the European part of the empire. The Romans persecuted the early Christians. But in the early A.D. 300's, the Roman Emperor Constantine the Great granted the Christians freedom of religion. Christianity became the official religion of the empire in the late 300's.

The decline of Rome. By the late A.D. 100's, powerful tribes from the north and east threatened the Roman Empire. Rome could not defend all of its territory. Disagreement broke out within the empire, and it began to break apart. Constantine reunited the empire in 324. But it began to break apart again after his death in 337.

The Roman Empire split permanently into two parts in 395. The eastern half became the East Roman, or Byzantine, Empire. Constantinople (now Istanbul, Turkey) was its capital. The rest of the empire became the West Roman Empire, with Rome as its capital.

Germanic invasions. Germanic tribes lived throughout much of Europe north of the Roman Empire. These tribes included the Angles, Franks, Jutes, Saxons, Vandals, and Visigoths. Some of these peoples adopted the civilization of their Roman neighbors. But most of the tribes were rough, uncivilized people whom the Romans called *barbarians.*

During the late 300's and the 400's, Mongolians from central Asia, called Huns, attacked the Germanic tribes and drove them into the empire. The Vandals moved into what is now Spain. The Visigoth general Alaric invaded the Italian Peninsula and looted Rome in 410, then moved westward and eventually defeated the Vandals. The Angles, Jutes, and Saxons invaded Britain, and the Franks conquered most of what is now France. The Germanic chieftain Odoacer overthrew the last West Roman emperor, Romulus Augustulus, in 476.

The Germanic tribes were followed by Slavic peoples from Asia who settled eastern Europe from the Baltic Sea south to northern Greece. Next came the Magyars, a Central Asian people who settled the Hungarian plain in the 900's.

The Byzantine Empire. Most of the East Roman Empire survived the barbarian invasions and lasted through the Middle Ages. By the 500's, it recovered much of southeastern Europe, parts of what are now Italy and Spain, much of the Middle East, and lands along the northern African coast. For hundreds of years, the Byzantine Empire served as a barrier against barbarian attacks and invasion by Muslim peoples from southwestern Asia. It also preserved much of ancient Greek and Roman culture. Constantinople became the center of eastern Christendom, which spread through most of eastern Europe.

Stone relief (A.D. 200's or 300's) from the tomb of the Haterii family; Museo Gregoriano Profano, Rome (SCALA/Art Resource)

The ancient Romans were skillful builders. They constructed many large buildings throughout their empire. This relief sculpture shows a Roman tomb under construction.

After the death of its greatest emperor, Justinian, in 565, the Byzantine Empire began to lose territory to a series of Asiatic peoples, including the South Slavs, Arabs, Mongols, and Turks. Even western Europeans became adversaries of the Byzantines after the 1000's, when the

Great European empires, A.D. 800 - 1812

These maps show the great empires that flourished in Europe from the time of Charlemagne around 800 to that of Napoleon around 1812. The Ottoman Empire began in Asia and gained control of a large part of southeastern Europe. The maps show each empire at its height.

Charlemagne's empire, 800

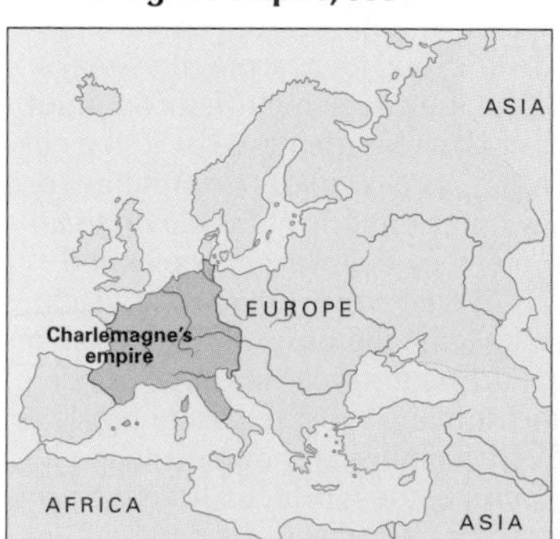

The Holy Roman Empire, 1000's

Ottoman Empire, 1500's

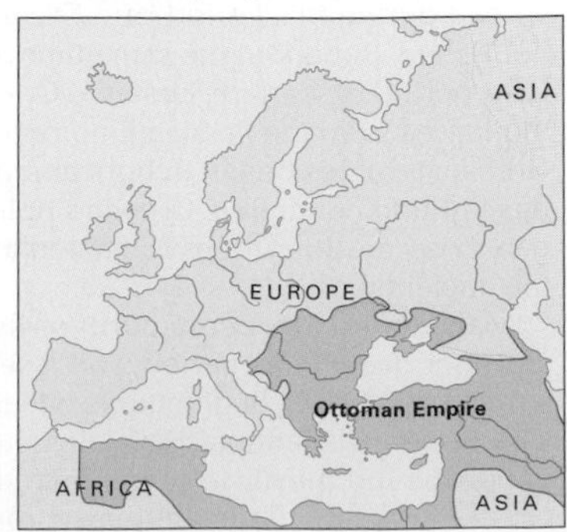

Christian church split into two main groups. These groups would become the western Roman Catholic Church and the Eastern Orthodox Churches. By 1400, all that remained of the once mighty Byzantine Empire barely extended beyond the area of Constantinople.

The Middle Ages. The fall of the West Roman Empire brought great changes to the rest of Europe. These changes ushered in the Middle Ages, a period that lasted until about 1500. The strong, united government established by the Romans quickly disappeared. It was replaced by many small kingdoms and states. The church survived as the most powerful and unifying force on the continent, not only in religious matters, but also in politics, learning, and the arts.

Most European trade that had developed under Roman rule collapsed. As a result, people depended more and more on farming to make a living. Towns lost their importance as people moved to rural areas. Townspeople who had managed most of the trade and industry almost disappeared. Much of the knowledge that had been acquired by Greek and Roman civilization was lost or ignored.

The *manorial system* dominated the economy in rural areas. Noble families ruled estates called *manors,* and they organized and supervised life on the manors. They provided basic protection and local government services to the peasants. Peasant families farmed their plots of land from generation to generation. In return, they paid dues and performed various duties without pay. The heaviest burden among these tasks was farming the nobles' land. During the 700's, a majority of peasants in western Europe lost many of their personal freedoms. Known as *serfs,* these peasants could not leave the manor, change jobs, or even marry without the nobles' permission.

Although the manorial system brought stability, most of Europe remained poor and thinly populated. Large areas covered with swamps or thick forests could not be farmed. Disease, famine, war, and a low birth rate kept the population small. The average person lived about 30 to 40 years, with over half of all children dying before they reached adulthood.

The Franks created the most powerful kingdom in medieval Europe. The kingdom included what is now

Napoleon's empire, 1812

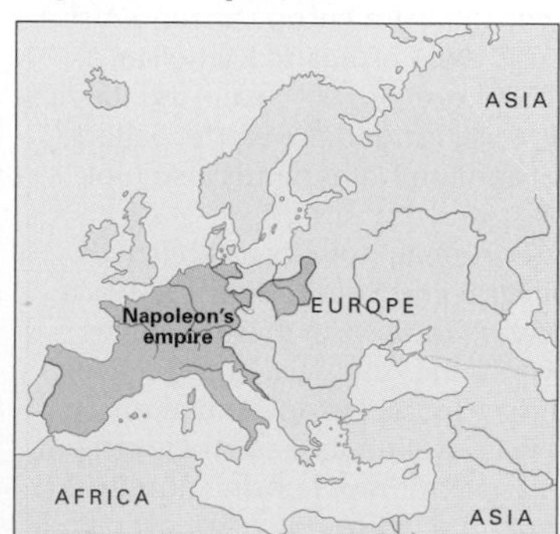

WORLD BOOK maps

"September" by the Limbourg brothers, from the Duc de Berry's *Très Riches Heures,* an illuminated French manuscript of the 1400's Musée Condé, Chantilly, France (Bibliothèque Nationale, Paris)

During the Middle Ages—the A.D. 400's to the 1500's—wealthy lords owned most of the land in western Europe. They also ruled the peasants who worked in their fields.

France, Belgium, the Netherlands, Luxembourg, and the western half of Germany. The Frankish empire achieved its greatest power under Charlemagne, who ruled from 768 to 814. Charlemagne's empire extended from central Italy north to Denmark and from eastern Germany west to the Atlantic Ocean. He supported the Roman Catholic Church and tried to reestablish the West Roman Empire. The pope crowned him emperor in 800. Charlemagne died in 814. His sons, after fighting among themselves, divided the empire into three parts.

In the 900's, Otto I, a German king, took control of the northern half of the Italian Peninsula. The pope crowned Otto emperor in 962, marking the start of what later was called the Holy Roman Empire. Otto hoped his empire would become as powerful as Charlemagne's had been. But it began to break apart in the 1000's.

Under the Franks and their successors, a new military and political system called *feudalism* developed in much of western and central Europe. In this system, powerful lords called *magnates* controlled most of the land. They gave land to less powerful nobles called *vassals* in return for military and other services. The peasants worked for the nobles.

Advances and setbacks. Beginning in the 1000's, merchants again began to travel the old land routes and waterways of Europe. Towns grew along the trade routes. The peasants learned better farming methods and gained new land for farming by clearing forests and draining swamps. Such improvements enabled the population to begin to grow.

In 1215, English barons forced King John to approve the Magna Carta (Great Charter), in which the king granted many rights to the English aristocracy. This event

Detail of an illuminated French manuscript of the 1500's; Bibliothèque Nationale de France, Paris

During the Renaissance—about 1300 to 1600—movable printing type was invented in Europe. By 1500, Europe had more than a thousand print shops. This picture shows a shop in Paris.

marked an early step in the development of constitutional government and of trial by jury. Magna Carta limited royal power and made it clear that the king had to obey the law.

Around 1300, climate changes made weather in western Europe cooler and wetter. As a result, the agricultural practices that had developed in Europe could not sustain the increased population. Famines and floods caused widespread hardship. An outbreak of plague later called the *Black Death* lasted from 1347 to 1352. It killed at least a fourth of Europe's people.

Muslims in medieval Europe. During the early 600's, the Arab prophet Muhammad began to preach in Arabia. His teachings and life formed the basis for the Islamic religion. By the early 700's, his followers had conquered the Middle East, except for Asia Minor, as well as northern Africa and most of Spain. In 732, a Frankish army stopped the Arab advances in western Europe by defeating them in a battle at Tours, in what is now France. But the Muslims remained in Spain and established a flourishing culture there. In the 1000's, the Muslim kingdom in Spain weakened and splintered. It gradually lost more and more territory to Christian kingdoms. In 1492, the Muslims lost Granada, their last center of control in Spain.

During the 1000's, a Muslim Turkish tribe from central Asia called the Seljuks conquered most of Asia Minor (now part of Turkey) and much of the Middle East. In the 1300's, a Turkish tribe known as the Ottomans gradually gained control. By the mid-1500's, the Ottoman Empire had conquered most of the Middle East, northern Africa, and much of southeastern Europe.

Beginning in the late 1000's, western Europeans launched a series of military expeditions called Crusades to free Palestine—where Jesus Christ had lived—from Muslim rule. Crusader armies held parts of Palestine for nearly 200 years. Moreover, the Crusades helped open up trade between Europe and Asia. Europeans imported such luxuries as porcelain, silk, and spices from as far away as China.

The Muslim world contributed much to the culture of Europe. The Muslims preserved many ancient Greek writings, which thus remained available to European scholars. Muslim poets produced works of great lyrical beauty. The Muslims made numerous advances in such areas as astronomy, medicine, and mathematics, including the development of the system of Arabic numerals used today.

The Renaissance was a period of great advancement in the arts and learning in Europe. It began during the early 1300's in northern Italy, where many large cities had become rich from trade. The Renaissance, which means *rebirth,* tried to revive aspects of ancient Greek and Roman culture. In the 1300's, the Italian scholar Petrarch began a cultural movement called *humanism,* which sought to study human nature through literature, history, and philosophy. Scholars of Petrarch's time were the first to divide European history into ancient, medieval, and modern periods. They considered the medieval period a time of ignorance—the Dark Ages.

Renaissance writers and artists often copied ancient Greek and Roman styles in their works. Many artists studied the human body to create more lifelike human images. Around 1450, the German printer Johannes Gutenberg invented metal movable type and several processes that made printing with movable type practical for the first time. The Chinese and Koreans had known of movable type for centuries, but had not fully developed the practical use of it on a large scale. This method of printing helped spread Renaissance learning and culture through most of Europe in the 1500's.

The Renaissance also helped initiate the great age of European exploration. During this era, Europe's influence began to spread around the world. Portuguese and Spanish sailors were the leading European explorers of the 1400's and 1500's. Christopher Columbus, an Italian navigator in the service of Spain, reached America when he sailed from Spain to the West Indies in 1492. In 1497 and 1498, the Portuguese explorer Vasco da Gama made the first voyage from Europe around Africa to India. About 20 years later, Ferdinand Magellan, a Portuguese navigator in the service of Spain, led the first European expedition to sail around the world. Sailors from England, France, and the Netherlands also took part in exploration.

During this period, European powers established their first colonies in North and South America, Africa, and Asia. Steadily growing trade with these colonies and the mining of silver in the Americas brought even greater wealth and power to the European nations.

The Reformation was a religious reform movement of the 1500's. It began as an attempt to bring about changes in the Roman Catholic Church, but it eventually led to the birth of Protestantism. In the centuries leading up to this movement, the Catholic Church had become deeply divided by internal disputes. These disputes weakened the authority of the pope. European kings took advantage of the popes' weakness. Throughout Europe, the church was criticized for neglecting its spiritual responsibilities.

In 1517, Martin Luther, a German monk and theology professor, set off the reform movement by challenging a number of church teachings and practices. He spread his message by publishing his views. He also translated the Bible from Latin into German, so that the people of his country could read it themselves. By 1555, about half of Germany's people had become followers of Luther or other Protestant religious leaders. Much of northern Europe had also adopted Protestantism in some form. Most Catholics in southern Europe remained Catholic.

The spread of Protestantism inspired Catholic leaders to initiate a reform movement called the Counter Reformation, which won back many Protestants in central Europe, including Germany, Poland, and Hungary. A series of religious wars between Protestants and Catholics broke out during this time. The last of these religious wars, the Thirty Years' War (1618-1648), involved much of Europe and devastated most of what is now Germany.

The development of the great powers in Europe began during the Middle Ages. The first great contest, a series of wars known as the Hundred Years' War, had taken place from 1337 to 1453, when English and French kings fought for control of France. France won and soon began another power struggle by invading Italy in 1494. Its success alarmed many of France's neighbors. The rulers of Spain formed an alliance with the Habsburg ruler of Austria, who was the emperor of the German-based Holy Roman Empire and who also controlled the Low Countries (now the Netherlands, Belgium, and Luxembourg). The alliance sought to create a *balance of power* against France—that is, to maintain peace by ensuring that no nation became strong enough to take over. The ruling families of Spain and Austria intermarried. Between 1506 and 1530, Charles, the eldest son of that union, became ruler of the Low Countries, the Holy Roman Empire, Spain, the growing Spanish empire in America, and about half of Italy. Charles is usually known by his imperial title, Emperor Charles V. In the 1550's, he split his lands between his son, Philip, and his brother, Ferdinand.

With the discovery of lands overseas, Europe's seafaring countries built overseas empires. By 1600, Spain controlled most of Central and South America. The Portuguese held Brazil and numerous trading posts along the African coast and Indian Ocean. The Netherlands became a top sea power in the 1600's, but it was weakened by wars with England and France from 1652 to 1713. England settled the east coast of North America. France established North American colonies that included, by the early 1700's, much of what is now eastern Canada and the Mississippi Valley of the United States.

These European nations began to compete fiercely with one another for power. Europe's monarchs had to raise large amounts of money to pay for armies and the wars they fought. They also needed the armies to put down internal religious conflicts caused by the Reformation. They accomplished these goals, in part, by reducing the power of the clergy and feudal lords. The monarchs also got support from the growing towns and cities, which enlisted them as allies against the feudal lords. Townspeople agreed to pay taxes to the monarch in return for royal protection and the freedom to develop their businesses. Meanwhile, the monarchs promoted trade and industry as a new source of tax revenue.

By the 1600's, the power of many monarchs was regarded as *absolute*—that is, nearly unlimited. The monarch and the royal ministers directed thousands of officials throughout the kingdom. These officials enforced the law and collected taxes for armies.

Some countries, especially England and the Netherlands, successfully resisted the trend toward absolute monarchy. In England, a Civil War abolished the monarchy for 10 years during the mid-1600's. In 1689, the Eng-

Detail of *Opening of the Glasgow and Garnkirk Railway,* 1831, a lithograph by David Octavius Hill; Science Museum, London

The Industrial Revolution, which began in Britain in the 1700's, led to the first use of steam-powered railroad trains. This picture shows the opening of a railway in Scotland in 1831.

lish Parliament passed a document that increased its own authority and limited the monarch's power. This document later became known as the Bill of Rights.

The scientific revolution and the Enlightenment helped increase human knowledge in the 1600's. In the 1500's and 1600's, scientists increasingly realized the importance of experimentation and mathematics to scientific advances. From all over Europe, scientists made important discoveries in anatomy, astronomy, chemistry, geometry, and physics. For example, the Italian scientist Galileo used mathematics to prove the law of falling bodies, which says that all objects fall at the same speed, regardless of weight. William Harvey, an English physician, performed careful experiments to show how blood circulates in the human body. The scientific revolution led Europeans to believe that people could begin to gain control over the natural world.

By the late 1600's, philosophers had begun making similar breakthroughs. Historians refer to this period as the Enlightenment. Philosophers of the era began arguing for the removal of restrictions on human freedom and equality, so that people could pursue the goal of happiness. These scholars even questioned religious teachings. For example, some cast doubt on the miracles described in the Bible because they could not be proved scientifically. Others studied the history of words and suggested that parts of the Bible, though still divinely inspired, had been revised over time. Some thinkers urged the toleration of all religions because none could be proved true or false.

Enlightenment thinkers attacked Europe's economic systems and governments. Many called for fewer government restrictions on trade and other aspects of national economies, as well as a reduction of taxation. Others criticized governments for not taking into account the welfare of ordinary people.

Revolution, democracy, and nationalism. In the late 1700's, the ideas of the Enlightenment initiated a series of revolutionary political movements. These movements included the American Revolution (1775-1783), as well as several revolutions in Europe.

The French Revolution, which took place from 1789 to 1799, was the most important democratic revolution in Europe during this period. In 1789, representatives of the three *estates* (classes) in France—the clergy, the nobility, and the commoners—formed a National Assembly and seized control of the government. They adopted the Declaration of the Rights of Man and of the Citizen, a document that set forth the principles of human liberty and the rights of individuals. By 1792, the revolution turned radical and violent. The king was beheaded in January 1793. Thousands more, including the queen, followed him to their deaths in a period called the Reign of Terror. The revolution finally ended in 1799, when the young general Napoleon Bonaparte seized power.

The Napoleonic wars. During this period, war had broken out between France and many other European countries. Under Napoleon's leadership, the French armies at first seemed unbeatable. By 1812, they controlled most of mainland Europe, except Russia and the Ottoman Empire. But Napoleon lost most of his army that same year when he invaded Russia. Napoleon suffered his final defeat in 1815 at the Battle of Waterloo and was exiled to a small island in the South Atlantic. But the ideas of the French Revolution continued to spread throughout Europe.

France's revolutionaries had drawn inspiration from the democratic belief that all people were equal and were entitled to rule themselves. In the process of fighting against most of Europe, the French people also had bonded as a single nation. This common identity and loyalty to a nation of people is called *nationalism.*

Europe before World War I

This map shows Europe in 1914, before World War I. By that time, most of the Balkan nations had gained independence from the Ottoman Empire. Other nations had begun to demand independence from Austria-Hungary, Germany, and Russia.

Europe after World War I

This map shows Europe about 1923, after the treaties that ended World War I had taken effect. As a result of those treaties, many central and eastern European nations won their independence from what had been Germany, Russia, and Austria-Hungary.

WORLD BOOK maps

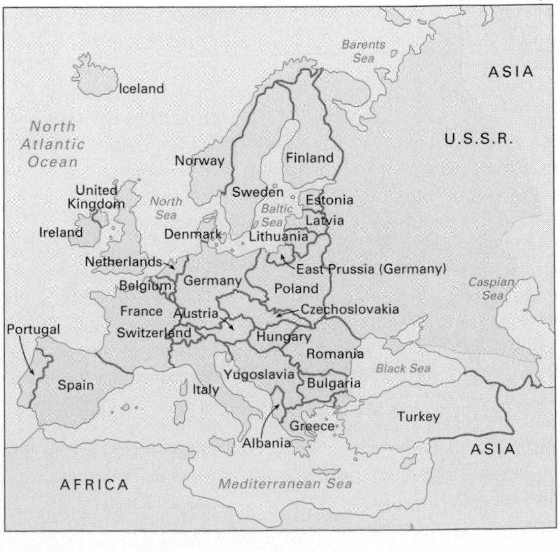

Other European governments blamed democratic ideas for the terrible violence and destruction of the French Revolution and Napoleonic wars. Nationalism also threatened the unity of such European empires as Austria, which consisted of many diverse cultures that spoke different languages.

In 1814 and 1815, Europe's political leaders met at the Congress of Vienna. Led by the Quadruple Alliance of Austria, Prussia, Russia, and the United Kingdom, the Congress sought to restore much of the European political system to the way it had been before the French Revolution. The Congress restored most of the borders that had existed before the Revolution. It also brought back many of the monarchs who had been toppled by the revolutionary armies. The Austrian statesman Metternich encouraged European powers to suppress democratic and nationalist activity throughout Europe. But the "Metternich System" failed to halt the spread of democracy and nationalism on the continent.

New governments. Other revolutions broke out during the 1800's. In the 1820's, France, Russia, and the United Kingdom supported a Greek war of independence against the Ottoman Empire. Democratic revolts took place in Belgium and France in 1830. Italy was founded as a national state in 1861, and Germany in 1871. Both states adopted constitutions, though they kept a monarchy. By 1900, nearly every European country except Russia had a constitution and at least some institutions of democratic government.

The Industrial Revolution began in the United Kingdom during the 1700's and spread to other parts of western Europe in the 1800's. Industry grew rapidly with the development of power-driven machinery and new methods of production.

Before the Industrial Revolution, most people had worked as farmers in the countryside. But as factories appeared, towns grew rapidly into industrial cities. People streamed into these cities to take factory jobs.

Industrial growth brought social changes. The middle class of business leaders and industrialists grew rapidly. They owned most of the factories, hired the workers, and operated the banks, mines, railroads, and shops. At the same time, new production methods threatened the occupations of some skilled craftworkers. Many women and children began to work outside the home. Most laborers were unskilled and earned low salaries. They worked and lived under dreadful conditions. Even so, the typical factory worker earned more money, ate better, and lived longer than their farmer ancestors had managed to do.

Industrialization also changed European politics. The growing number of industrial workers demanded not only a voice in government but also a political party to represent them. In the mid-1800's, a new philosophy called *socialism* argued for better treatment of factory workers and other poor people. The German philosopher Karl Marx even called for workers to rise up against the wealthy and to establish state-controlled economic systems. Marx desired a "classless" society with no distinctions based on social class. Many of his followers later became known as Communists.

These developments led some governments to pass laws regulating conditions in factories. In the mid-1800's, workers in the United Kingdom and some other western European countries won the right to form labor unions. The unions could negotiate better wages and working conditions for factory workers.

United Press Int.

World War II began with the German invasion of Poland on Sept. 1, 1939, *shown here.* The war ended in 1945. It brought great destruction to many European cities and towns.

Colonial expansion. The Industrial Revolution helped begin a new age of colonial expansion. The industrial nations needed such raw materials as *copra* (dried coconut meat) and cotton for their factories, and Africa and Asia had great quantities. These continents also provided vast markets where the industrial nations could sell their manufactured goods. With Europe's population expanding, many countries sought new colonies to settle their surplus population. During the 1870's, several European powers began establishing control over most of Africa, Asia, and Pacific Islands. By 1914, virtually the entire world was either under the control or influence of the European powers or was populated by descendants of earlier European settlers.

World War I began in 1914. The war resulted mainly from the desire by national groups to gain independence and from competing military alliances among nations of Europe.

World War I began as a regional conflict between Austria-Hungary and Serbia. The killing of Austria-Hungary's Archduke Franz Ferdinand by a Serbian assassin from Bosnia-Herzegovina sparked the conflict, which quickly became a war between Europe's two major military alliances. The United Kingdom, France, and Russia led one group of countries (known as the Allies) against a group led by Germany and Austria-Hungary (known as the Central Powers). In 1917, the United States joined the Allies and helped them win the war the following year.

The victorious Allies met in Paris in 1919 to impose separate peace treaties on each of the defeated Central

© Tom Stoddart, Getty Images

The Berlin Wall, which had divided Communist East Berlin and non-Communist West Berlin since 1961, was knocked down in 1989. The removal of the wall symbolized the collapse of Communism in Eastern Europe. This photograph shows cheering crowds and East German border guards on the day the first section was taken down.

Powers. The most famous treaty, signed with Germany, was the Treaty of Versailles.

World War I brought numerous changes of government in Europe. The successful Bolshevik Revolution in 1917 led to the founding of a Communist dictatorship in Russia. Austria-Hungary was divided into several countries. Six countries in Europe won their independence: Czechoslovakia, Estonia, Latvia, Lithuania, Poland, and what later became Yugoslavia. Germany remained largely intact, but it paid a high price for the war. It lost Alsace-Lorraine to France, additional territory to Poland, and all of its overseas colonies. The once powerful German army was greatly reduced in size. The new democratic German government had to pay heavy fees, called *reparations,* to the victorious Allies.

Europe between the world wars. The Paris peace settlements left many of Europe's problems unsolved and created some new problems. Many Germans blamed their new government for signing the Treaty of Versailles and paying the huge reparations. Most of the newly created countries contained unhappy minorities who wanted either independence or the right to join a neighboring country.

The war had also badly hurt Europe's once thriving economies. Governments needed to levy high taxes to pay off their war debts, and inflation became rampant in the 1920's. During the 1930's, a worldwide economic slump called the Great Depression caused massive unemployment. Hard times created an opportunity for a new antidemocratic movement called *fascism.* The first fascist political party developed in Italy under Benito Mussolini. Eventually, fascist parties gained control over most of the countries in central and southern Europe.

In 1933, Adolf Hitler set up the fascist Nazi dictatorship in Germany. Ignoring the Treaty of Versailles, he began rearming Germany for a new war. In 1935, he formed a fascist alliance called the Axis with Italy and Japan. He and Mussolini sent troops, tanks, and warplanes to help the fascist leader Francisco Franco win the bloody Spanish Civil War (1936-1939).

The Russian Bolshevik government, under the leadership of V. I. Lenin, formed the Soviet Union in 1922. By the end of the 1920's, Lenin had died and Joseph Stalin had become dictator of the Soviet Union. Stalin industrialized the country in the 1930's, but he also executed and imprisoned millions of his own people.

World War II. By 1938, Adolf Hitler began to demand changes in the borders created by the Treaty of Versailles. Germany seized Austria and Czechoslovakia without resistance from other European powers. But when Hitler's armies invaded Poland in 1939, the United Kingdom and France declared war on Germany. Germany's armies rapidly conquered Belgium, Denmark, France, Luxembourg, the Netherlands, and Norway in 1940. Italy entered the war on Germany's side in June of that year. Germany conquered much of eastern Europe in 1941.

At the end of 1941, the United States entered the war after Japan attacked Pearl Harbor in Hawaii. Japan, Germany, and Italy were the three main powers in an alliance called the Axis. American forces also joined those of the United Kingdom and the Soviet Union to fight in Europe. The United Kingdom, the United States, and Russia were soon leading a worldwide alliance of over 40 countries known as the Allies.

In 1942, Allied forces won major victories against Germany in the Soviet Union and North Africa. British and United States troops invaded Italy in 1943 and forced it to surrender. In June 1944, a much larger Allied army landed in Normandy, France, and began the eastward march toward Germany. Soviet forces marched west to meet them, conquering most of eastern Europe in the process. Allied forces found many concentration camps where the Nazis had murdered millions of Jews and other Europeans.

Postwar Europe. World War II had cost the lives of about 40 million Europeans. Many cities lay in ruins, leaving millions homeless and in poverty. The Soviet Union and the United States took Europe's place as the leaders of the postwar period.

Germany and its capital of Berlin were divided into four zones occupied by the Soviet Union, the United States, the United Kingdom, and France. Stalin gave half of the Soviet zone to Poland. The remainder of this zone became East Germany, a Communist dictatorship. The other three zones joined to form a democratic country known as West Germany. The presence of Soviet troops throughout eastern Europe helped ensure the creation of Communist dictatorships in all the countries there during the late 1940's.

Western European countries restored their democratic governments. But the devastation of World War II made these countries economically and militarily dependent on the United States. The U.S. government set up the European Recovery Program—known as the Marshall Plan—to help these countries rebuild their economies. Other U.S. assistance programs followed the Marshall Plan. By the early 1950's, the economies of most western European countries had become more productive than they were before the war.

Eastern Europe took much longer to recover from World War II. Stalin forbade the Communist European states to accept Marshall Plan aid. Yet the equally devastated Soviet Union could not afford to offer much assistance of its own. Many people wanted to go to western Europe in search of greater freedom and prosperity. The Soviet Union fortified eastern European borders with barbed wire, land mines, and watch towers. They put in place barriers to free communications, trade, and travel along borders extending from the Baltic Sea to the Mediterranean. This "Iron Curtain" became the new symbol of a divided continent.

The Cold War. To many, the erection of the Iron Curtain marked the beginning of the Cold War, a tense period of international rivalry between the Western democracies, led by the United States, and the Communist countries, led by the Soviet Union. Both sides feared invasion from the other. Many leaders on both sides became convinced that it was their duty to spread their system of government throughout the world.

The Western powers tried to prevent Soviet expansion by a policy called *containment.* They built a series of defensive military alliances around the world. In 1949, the United States, Canada, and most of Europe's democracies formed the North Atlantic Treaty Organization (NATO). In 1955, the Soviet Union and its eastern European *satellites* (nations controlled by the Soviet Union) signed a similar agreement known as the Warsaw Pact. The Iron Curtain now separated two huge armies, backed by thousands of nuclear weapons, in a tense standoff.

Stalin's death in 1953 marked the beginning of a gradual reduction in Cold War tensions. The new Soviet leader Nikita Khrushchev advocated peaceful coexistence between the two alliances.

But the Soviet Union retained an iron grip on eastern Europe. In 1956, Soviet forces crushed Hungary's attempt to establish democracy. In 1961, East Germany built a wall around West Berlin to prevent East Germans from escaping Communism. Warsaw Pact troops put down another democratic reform movement in Czechoslovakia in 1968.

The 1970's witnessed a further relaxation of Cold War tensions. In 1970, government leaders of East and West Germany conferred for the first time since the division of Germany. That same year, West Germany signed nonaggression treaties with the Soviet Union and Poland. In 1975, representatives from the United States, Canada, and most European countries met in Helsinki, Finland, to form the Conference on Security and Cooperation in Europe (CSCE). These countries signed the first of the Helsinki Accords, called the Helsinki Final Act. In this agreement, the signers pledged to work for increased cooperation in matters of economics and peacekeeping and to promote human rights.

Toward European unity. While the Cold War divided Europe between east and west, Europe's democracies had worked to strengthen ties with one another. The massive destruction and suffering from two world wars had convinced them of the evils of international conflict. They formed the Council of Europe in 1949 to create stronger cultural, social, and economic ties with one another. The European Coal and Steel Community (ECSC), organized in 1951, sought to unify the coal, iron, and steel industries of Belgium, France, Italy, Luxembourg, the Netherlands, and West Germany.

In 1957, the six ECSC members formed the European Economic Community (EEC). The organization was created to begin removing barriers to the movement of goods, services, workers, and capital among its members. Also in 1957, the same six countries agreed to establish the European Atomic Energy Community (Eur-

European leaders signed the Treaty of European Union, or Maastricht Treaty, in 1992 in Maastricht, the Netherlands. The treaty, effective in 1993, provided for the creation of the European Union and European Central Bank and the adoption of a common currency, later named the euro.

atom) to work together to develop nuclear energy for peaceful uses. The EEC and Euratom went into effect in 1958. The six member countries became known as the European Community. The European Community admitted Denmark, Ireland, and the United Kingdom in 1973. Greece joined in 1981, and Portugal and Spain in 1986.

In 1987, the European Community ratified the Single European Act. It set the end of 1992 as the deadline for eliminating all customs controls and most other obstacles to the free movement of goods, services, workers, and capital among members. In 1992, representatives of the European Community's countries signed the Treaty on European Union in Maastricht, the Netherlands. This pact, known as the Maastricht Treaty, went into effect in 1993. The European Community was then incorporated into the European Union (EU). The EU was formed to extend cooperation among members to such areas as military policy, crime control, and immigration. The EU also later worked to establish closer monetary and economic ties by founding a central bank and moving toward the adoption of a common currency.

The collapse of Communism. Mikhail Gorbachev became leader of the Soviet Union in 1985. He recognized that the Communist government did not satisfy the needs of his country's people, either economically or politically. Gorbachev proposed reforms to the Soviet government that would reduce the power of the Communist Party, increase the power of elected government bodies, and reduce government control over the economy. He called these reforms *perestroika.* Gorbachev also promoted more freedom of speech and other forms of public openness. He called this reform *glasnost.*

Gorbachev's reforms sparked calls for greater democratization and independence across eastern Europe. In 1989, Hungary opened its border with Austria to allow thousands of eastern Europeans to leave for western Europe. Later that year, crowds in Berlin tore down the wall that had divided the city. All over eastern Europe, mass demonstrations demanded more freedom and an end to Communist rule. In 1989 and 1990, free elections were held in these countries, and non-Communist parties gained control. The governments lifted restrictions on such civil liberties as freedom of speech, religion, and the press. They began to replace their socialized economies with free enterprise economies.

In 1990, West Germany and East Germany united to form the single non-Communist nation of Germany. Later that year, leaders of the CSCE countries signed the Charter of Paris for a New Europe, in which they declared an end to the Cold War. In 1991, the Warsaw Pact countries formally dissolved the pact, and the Soviet Union itself broke apart into 15 independent republics, marking the end of the Cold War.

The new nationalism. Even as Europe united, several countries became divided by old national and ethnic rivalries. Ethnic minorities in several former Soviet republics demanded independence, which resulted in rebellions in Moldova, Azerbaijan, Georgia, and the Russian province of Chechnya.

Two former countries of Communist eastern Europe dissolved. One of them, Czechoslovakia, broke up peacefully in 1993 into two new states, the Czech Republic and Slovakia. But the other country, Yugoslavia, endured a breakup that involved some of the bloodiest European conflict since World War II. In 1948, Yugoslav leader Josip Broz Tito had declared his country independent of the Soviet Union, the first Communist country to do so. Tito established a delicate political balance among Yugoslavia's nationalities, including Eastern Orthodox Serbs, Roman Catholic Croatians, and Muslim Bosnians. In the late 1980's, after the death of Tito, Serb leader Slobodan Milošević upset that balance in favor of the Serbs.

In 1991 and early 1992, four of the country's six republics—Slovenia, Croatia, Bosnia-Herzegovina, and Macedonia—declared their independence from Yugoslavia. The two other republics—Serbia and Montenegro—formed a new Yugoslavia and fought hard to keep control of the parts of Croatia and Bosnia where Serb minorities lived. They often did so by expelling non-Serbs from the areas they wanted to retain, a policy called *ethnic cleansing.*

Representatives of Bosnia, Croatia, and Serbia signed a peace plan for Bosnia in 1995. But a new conflict broke out in 1998 in the Serbian province of Kosovo, where the ethnic Albanian majority wanted independence. After Serbian forces forced tens of thousands of people to leave their homes, NATO threatened to intervene unless Kosovo was granted autonomy. When Milošević refused, NATO aircraft bombed targets in Serbia in 1999 until Milošević agreed to withdraw all his troops from Kosovo. NATO forces then occupied Kosovo, which came under United Nations (UN) administration.

In 2003, Yugoslavia changed its name to Serbia and Montenegro. In 2006, Serbia and Montenegro separated and became independent countries. Kosovo declared its independence in 2008, without Serbia's recognition. Other countries were divided over accepting Kosovo's independence.

Recent developments. NATO's victory in Kosovo strengthened confidence in the future of European unity and encouraged further efforts at unification. Since 2002, many EU countries have adopted a common currency, known as the euro. Since 2004, several more European countries—including some of the former Communist eastern European countries and Soviet republics—have joined the EU.

Beginning in 2008, a global economic downturn caused problems for much of Europe. By the spring of 2013, Cyprus, Greece, Ireland, Portugal, and Spain had all accepted emergency loans from the countries that use the euro and from the International Monetary Fund (IMF), a specialized agency of the United Nations.

In the 1990's and the early 2000's, millions of Muslims immigrated to western Europe, and tensions arose between the immigrants and their host countries. Terrorist attacks by Islamic extremists in Europe, Russia, and the United States increased the tensions. With native populations declining in certain European countries, many Europeans feared that non-Western peoples would not embrace Western values and might threaten the democratic cultures of those countries.

Daniel P. Barbezat, David Cast, Andreas Erhardt, Charles W. Ingrao, and George W. White

Related articles. *World Book* has articles on all the European countries and on other political units, which are listed in the tables at the beginning of this article. Articles on many European cities are listed at the end of each country article. See also:

History

Aegean civilization
Alexander the Great
Byzantine Empire
Charlemagne
Churchill, Sir Winston L. S.
Cold War
Communism
Counter Reformation
Crusades
Eastern Orthodox Churches (History)
Enlightenment
Exploration (The age of European exploration)
Feudalism
Franco-Prussian War
French Revolution
Greece, Ancient
Helsinki Accords
Hitler, Adolf
Holy Roman Empire
Humanism
Hundred Years' War
Industrial Revolution
Islamic Empire
Knights and knighthood
Manorialism
Marshall Plan
Marx, Karl
Middle Ages
Napoleon I
Napoleonic Wars
Reformation
Renaissance
Revolution of 1848
Rome, Ancient
Seven Years' War
Stalin, Joseph
Succession wars
Thirty Years' War
Versailles, Treaty of
Vienna, Congress of
Vikings
Warsaw Pact
World War I
World War II

Peoples

Angles
Basques
Celts
Cossacks
Franks
Goths
Jutes
Magyars
Roma
Sami
Saxons
Slavs
Vandals
Walloons

Organizations

Benelux
Common market
Europe, Council of
European Economic and Monetary Union
European Free Trade Association
European Space Agency
European Union
North Atlantic Treaty Organization
Organisation for Economic Co-operation and Development
Organization for Security and Co-operation in Europe
Western European Union

Physical features

Adriatic Sea
Aegean Sea
Alps
Arctic Ocean
Atlantic Ocean
Baltic Sea
Bay of Biscay
Black Sea
Bosporus
Caspian Sea
Danube River
Dardanelles
English Channel
Marmara, Sea of
Mediterranean Sea
Mount Elbrus
North Sea
Rhine River
Volga River
White Sea

Regions

Abkhazia
Balkans
Baltic States
Bessarabia
Caucasus
Crimea
Galicia
Iberia
Karelia
Lapland
Macedonia (historical region)
Ruthenia
Scandinavia
Siberia
Slavic countries
Transylvania
Turkestan
Wallonia

Other related articles

Bank (Europe)
Clothing (Clothing of Europe)
Communism
Democracy (The development of democracy)
Economics
Education (History)
Euro
Flag (pictures: Flags of Europe; Historical flags of the world)
Food
Furniture
Government
Language
Law (The development of law)
Literacy (table)
Philosophy (The history of Western philosophy)
Political science (The development of political science)
Postal services (The history of postal services)
Prehistoric people
Races, Human
Science (The history of science)
Socialism
Television (In Europe)

Europe, Council of, is an organization of European nations that seeks to promote unity among its members to achieve economic and social progress. It has no real power and can only advise on economic, social, legal, cultural, scientific, and other matters.

The council consists of a joint committee, a secretariat-general, a committee of ministers with a representative from each member nation, and a parliamentary assembly with several members from each nation. The assembly makes recommendations to the ministers. The council's main areas of activity include culture and sport, education, human rights, and public health.

The Council of Europe was formed in 1949. Its founding members were Belgium, Denmark, France, Ireland, Italy, Luxembourg, the Netherlands, Norway, Sweden, and the United Kingdom. The organization's headquarters are in Strasbourg, France. M. Donald Hancock

European Community. See European Union.

European Economic and Monetary Union was established as the final step in the process of creating a single economic market among member nations of the European Union (EU). A major task of Economic and Monetary Union, also called EMU, was replacing the many national currencies in the EU with one currency, called the *euro.* See **Euro.**

Eleven EU members began phasing in the euro in 1999 by fixing the values of their traditional currencies to the value of the euro. As of 2014, 18 member countries of the European Union (EU) had converted their currency to the euro. These countries were Austria, Belgium, the Republic of Cyprus, Estonia, Finland, France, Germany, Greece, Ireland, Italy, Latvia, Luxembourg, Malta, the Netherlands, Portugal, Slovakia, Slovenia, and Spain. The EMU process is still used, however, to help such EU countries as Lithuania in their attempt to adopt the euro as their currency. David L. Cleeton

European Free Trade Association (EFTA) is a trade group of four European nations. It works to remove tariffs and other trade obstacles in Western Europe and to uphold fair trade practices. Norway and Switzerland have been full members of EFTA since it began in 1960. Iceland joined in 1970. Liechtenstein became a full member in 1991.

Five founding members—Austria, Denmark, Portugal, Sweden, and the United Kingdom—have left EFTA. Denmark and the United Kingdom left in 1972, Portugal in 1985, and Austria and Sweden in 1995. Denmark, Portugal, and the United Kingdom left to join the European Community (EC), another economic association. The EC later became part of the European Union (EU). Austria and Sweden left EFTA to join the EU. Finland also left to join the EU in 1995. It had been an associate member of EFTA since 1961 and a full member since 1986.

EFTA achieved free trade in industrial goods among its members in 1966. Tariffs on industrial goods traded between EFTA and the EC were abolished by 1984.

In 1994, a treaty providing for a European Economic Area (EEA) went into effect. The EEA prohibited most trade barriers between the EU and two EFTA members—Norway and Iceland. In 1995, Liechtenstein joined the EEA. EFTA headquarters are in Geneva, Switzerland.

Critically reviewed by the European Free Trade Association

European Organization for Nuclear Research. See **CERN.**

European Space Agency (ESA) promotes the development of a cooperative space program among the nations of Europe. It was created in 1975 by merging the European Launch Development Association and the European Space and Research Organization (ESRO). ESRO had been formed in 1962. ESA members are Austria, Belgium, the Czech Republic, Denmark, Finland, France, Germany, Greece, Ireland, Italy, Luxembourg, the Netherlands, Norway, Poland, Portugal, Romania, Spain, Sweden, Switzerland, and the United Kingdom.

The ESA combines parts of the space programs of its member countries. It has a council of representatives from each member nation and a director-general who represents the agency's interests. The council must approve all ESA programs. In 1980, the ESA formed a private firm, Arianespace, which launches satellites aboard Ariane rockets from a launch site in French Guiana.

The ESA supervised the building of Spacelab, an orbiting laboratory module carried into space aboard the United States space shuttles. The shuttles carried Spacelab on various missions between 1983 and 1998. The ESA then began constructing Columbus, a permanent laboratory module for the International Space Station. The space shuttle Atlantis delivered Columbus in 2008.

In 1985, the ESA launched the space probe Giotto, which took photographs and collected data as it passed within 370 miles (600 kilometers) of Halley's Comet. In 1990, the ESA and the United States launched the probe Ulysses. The probe made observations over the sun's south pole in 1994 and over the sun's north pole in 1995.

During the first decade of the 2000's, the ESA launched a number of space probes. These probes included the Mars Express probe in 2003, the SMART-1 probe to the moon in 2004, and the Venus Express probe in 2005. The ESA also built the Huygens probe, which was carried to a position near Saturn's moon Titan by the U.S. Cassini spacecraft. Huygens descended through Titan's atmosphere in 2005, becoming the first craft to land on a satellite of a planet other than Earth.

In 2009, the ESA launched two space observatories aboard the same rocket. The Herschel Space Observatory explores early galaxy formation and planet formation around distant stars. The Planck mission mapped the *cosmic microwave background* (CMB) *radiation,* energy left over from the early universe. James Oberg

See also **Cosmic microwave background (CMB) radiation; Mars** (picture: A channel on Mars); **Space exploration** (European nations); **Titan** (picture: Dark channels cross the surface of Titan).

European Union (EU) is an economic and political partnership between 28 European countries. The EU member countries have successfully created a single economic market without internal barriers to trade, labor, and investment. The union's members are Austria, Belgium, Bulgaria, Croatia, Cyprus, the Czech Republic, Denmark, Estonia, Finland, France, Germany, Greece, Hungary, Ireland, Italy, Latvia, Lithuania, Luxembourg, Malta, the Netherlands, Poland, Portugal, Romania, Slovakia, Slovenia, Spain, Sweden, and the United Kingdom. The union's principal seat is in Brussels, Belgium. Its judicial seat is in the city of Luxembourg, and its parliamentary seat is in Strasbourg, France.

The European Union evolved from economic cooperation that began among Western European countries in the early 1950's. These countries eventually cooperated in economic affairs as members of the European Community (EC). In 1993, the EC members extended their cooperation into the areas of law enforcement and military and foreign policy. The EU was officially created when cooperation was extended to these new areas.

The European Union is a major economic unit. Together, its members have more people than the United States. In addition, the value of the goods and services produced by its members exceeds that of the goods and services produced by the United States. The combined value of the union's imports and exports is greater than that of any single country in the world. The United States is the union's main trading partner.

Working for cooperation

Internal affairs. The European Union works to improve the economies of its members by encouraging trade, investment, and economic competition. Union members impose no tariffs on one another and give *European citizenship* to their people. This means that citizens of member countries can live and work anywhere in the union. They may also vote in local and European Union elections in any member country in which they live, even if they are not citizens of that country.

The European Union also fosters economic development by adopting common policies and regulations in such areas as agriculture, transportation, health and safety, antitrust matters, and industrial standards. One such policy, the common agricultural policy (CAP), controls the prices of farm goods, limits agricultural production, and gives *subsidies* (cash grants) to farmers. In addition, the union determines common policies for its members in such areas as immigration and the control of illegal drug trafficking and other international crimes.

The European Union administers programs in education and training and in science and technology. It also provides money for economic development in its poorer regions. This aid is aimed at achieving economic and social equality. The union's revenue comes from a general sales tax, levies on imports from nonmember countries, and contributions from members.

In 1999, many member states began to phase in a single currency, the *euro,* as part of a process called European Economic and Monetary Union (EMU). A central bank, called the European Central Bank, conducts *monetary policy* for all EMU members. Officials use monetary policy to influence such economic factors as interest rates and the availability of money and loans. Denmark, Sweden, the United Kingdom, and some eastern European states have not accepted the single currency.

Eighteen European Union member countries have joined the EMU and adopted the euro. In 1999, companies, banks, and stock exchanges in 11 of these countries—Austria, Belgium, Finland, France, Germany, Ireland, Italy, Luxembourg, the Netherlands, Portugal, and Spain—began to carry out many of their noncash transactions in euros. The value of the traditional currencies of each of these countries was firmly tied to that of the euro. In 2001, Greece became the 12th EU member to adopt the euro. The euro began circulating as coins and paper money on Jan. 1, 2002. The traditional currencies of the 12 countries were withdrawn from circulation that same year. Slovenia adopted the euro in 2007. Cyprus

The European Union consists of 28 nations in Europe that co-operate with one another economically and politically.

and Malta followed in 2008, Slovakia in 2009, and Estonia in 2011. Latvia adopted the euro in 2014.

Relations with other countries. The European Union is the main partner of the United States in efforts to negotiate and manage world trade rules. The EU also cooperates with the United Nations (UN) and such agencies as the International Monetary Fund and the World Bank. The European Union belongs to the Food and Agriculture Organization, a UN agency. It also gives economic help to struggling nonmember nations.

The European Union sometimes helps resolve the military conflicts of nonmember countries. A defense alliance among several EU nations called the Western European Union performed these duties for many years. The European Union gradually took over these responsibilities in the early 2000's. The EU also works closely with the North Atlantic Treaty Organization (NATO). NATO is a larger defense alliance among whose members are the United States, Canada, and numerous European countries, including most members of the EU.

Governing institutions

The European Union is governed by seven institutions. These institutions are (1) the European Parliament, (2) the European Council, (3) the Council of the European Union, (4) the European Commission, (5) the Court of Justice of the European Union, (6) the European Central Bank, and (7) the Court of Auditors.

The European Parliament shares legislative and budgetary powers with the Council of the European Union. The Parliament has over 700 members. They are directly elected by EU citizens to five-year terms. The Parliament elects a president from among its members. Most EU laws are adopted jointly by the Parliament and the Council. The Parliament cannot propose legislation, but it can accept, amend, or reject legislation proposed by the European Commission. In addition, the Parliament has the power to expel the entire Commission. The Parliament meets in Strasbourg and Brussels. Its *secretariat* (administrative body) is based in Luxembourg.

The European Council establishes the general political goals of the EU. It consists of the heads of state or government of each member nation; the president of the European Council; and the president of the European Commission. The European Council elects its president for a term of 2 ½ years. He or she must not hold a national office. Meetings of the European Council generally take place four times a year in Brussels.

The Council of the European Union, also known as the Council of Ministers or simply the Council, is the EU's main decision-making body. The Council, usually acting jointly with the Parliament, passes laws and adopts the EU budget. The Council coordinates the economic policies of EU member nations, establishes the EU's common foreign and security policy, and adopts measures relating to police and judicial cooperation. The Council consists of people who serve as cabinet ministers in the government of their home nation. The presidency of the Council rotates every six months among the EU member nations. Most Council meetings are in Brussels, but some meetings are in Luxembourg.

The European Commission is the EU's executive body. It proposes legislation to the Parliament and the Council of the European Union. It also oversees the carrying out of the treaties on which the EU is based, as well as the laws, the budget, and other measures adopted by EU institutions. The Commission consists of one member from each EU member nation. One of the commissioners is the president, and another commissioner holds the position of high representative for foreign affairs and security policy. All the commissioners must be approved by the Parliament. They serve five-year terms. The Commission is based in Brussels and holds most of its meetings there.

The Court of Justice of the European Union, based in Luxembourg, decides whether the actions of EU institutions and member governments comply with EU law. It also interprets EU law at the request of the national courts. The Court of Justice of the European Union consists of three courts: (1) the Court of Justice, which is the highest court; (2) the General Court; and (3) the Civil Service Tribunal, a specialized court for disputes involving EU employees. The Court of Justice and the General Court include judges from each member nation. Judges of all three courts are appointed for six-year terms.

The European Central Bank, based in Frankfurt, Germany, administers monetary policy for the EU member nations that have adopted the euro as their currency. The bank's primary goal is to maintain price stability.

The Court of Auditors, based in Luxembourg, examines the EU's accounts to ensure that EU funds are collected, managed, and spent in a manner that is legal and financially sound. The Court of Auditors consists of one member appointed from each EU member nation. Members serve six-year terms.

History

Beginnings. After World War II ended in 1945, Jean Monnet, a French statesman, promoted the idea of gradually uniting the democratic European nations both economically and politically (see **Monnet, Jean**). As a result, in 1951, Belgium, France, Italy, Luxembourg, the Netherlands, and West Germany signed the Treaty of Paris, which established the European Coal and Steel Community (ECSC). The ECSC united its six member nations in a single common market for the production and trade of coal, steel, iron ore, and scrap metal. It abolished all trade barriers among the members for these products. It allowed coal and steel workers from any member nation to work anywhere in the ECSC countries. The ECSC began operating in 1952.

Formation of the European Community. The ECSC's success led its six members to sign the Treaties of Rome in 1957. The treaties broadened the nations' cooperation by establishing the European Atomic Energy Community (Euratom) and the European Economic Community (EEC). Through Euratom, the nations pooled resources to develop nuclear energy for electric power production and other peaceful uses. The EEC worked to combine the members' economic resources. Euratom and the EEC began operating in 1958. They shared the ECSC's judicial and legislative bodies but had separate executive agencies. In 1967, the three executive agencies were merged, and the three organizations together became known as the European Community (EC).

Increasing cooperation. By mid-1968, the EC members had eliminated all tariffs affecting trade among themselves and had established a common tariff on goods from other countries. As a result, the volume of trade among member countries rose quickly. The elimination of tariffs on trade within the EC allowed member countries to increase their economic efficiency and substantially raise their citizens' standard of living.

In the early 1970's, the EC began managing the exchange rates of the currencies of some of its members, notably West Germany and France. EC efforts to stabilize exchange rates were strengthened in 1979 when its members formed the European Monetary System (EMS). The EMS required that the value of member countries' currencies stay at set limits in relation to each other.

Over the years, the European Community admitted six new members. Denmark, Ireland, and the United Kingdom were admitted in 1973. Greece joined the EC in 1981, and Portugal and Spain became members in 1986.

Starting in 1989, many Communist nations in Eastern Europe moved away from Communist rule. They held democratic elections and reduced government control of their economies. The EC made special agreements with these nations on trade, economic aid, and political relations. In 1990, West and East Germany united. The new, united Germany replaced West Germany in the EC.

In 1987, the EC completed ratification of the Single European Act. This act called for ending all customs controls and most other obstacles to the free movement of goods, services, workers, and capital among EC members. It took effect on Jan. 1, 1993.

Formation of the European Union. In 1992, representatives of the 12 EC members signed the Treaty on European Union in Maastricht, the Netherlands. This pact, also called the Maastricht Treaty, took effect in November 1993. It provided for creation of the European Union (EU), which took the place of the EC. In 1995, Austria, Finland, and Sweden joined the EU as full members.

The Maastricht Treaty also called for establishing the European Central Bank and adopting a single currency—the euro. The central bank began operations in 1998.

Recent developments. In 2002 and 2003, a convention of delegates from across Europe drafted a constitution for the EU. The document was designed, in part, to define the balance of power between the central EU government and the member countries. In 2004, European leaders approved the constitution. To go into effect, the document needed to be ratified by the voters or legislature of every member nation. Many countries did approve the constitution, but French and Dutch voters rejected it in referendums in 2005.

Also in 2004, 10 more countries joined the EU. They were Cyprus, the Czech Republic, Estonia, Hungary, Latvia, Lithuania, Malta, Poland, Slovakia, and Slovenia. In 2007, Bulgaria and Romania joined the organization.

While the European Union has proven itself highly effective on a variety of levels, there are sharp differences in the economic well-being of the member nations and differing approaches to law within them. On Dec. 1, 2009, the Treaty of Lisbon amending the existing EU and EC treaties went into effect. The treaty improved EU cooperation on defense, security, and external policy. It also strengthened the role of the European Parliament and gave full legal force to the Charter of Fundamental Rights for EU citizens.

In 2012, the EU, while struggling to overcome a number of economic and social difficulties, was awarded the Nobel Peace Prize. The Nobel committee cited the EU's efforts to promote "peace and reconciliation, democracy and human rights in Europe." Croatia became a member of the EU in 2013. Neil Kent

See also **Euro; Europe** (picture: European leaders signed the Treaty of European Union); **European Economic and Monetary Union.**

Europium, *yu ROH pee uhm* (chemical symbol, Eu), is one of the lanthanide metals. It is soft and silver in color. Its *atomic number* (number of protons in its nucleus) is 63. Its *relative atomic mass* is 151.964. An element's relative atomic mass equals its *mass* (amount of matter) divided by $\frac{1}{12}$ of the mass of carbon 12, the most abundant form of carbon. Europium has two naturally occurring *isotopes,* atoms with the same number of protons but a different number of neutrons. One isotope is stable and one is weakly radioactive. Europium's density is 5.245 grams per cubic centimeter at 25 °C (see **Density**). The French scientist Eugène Demarçay discovered the element in 1901. He named it *europium* in honor of Europe. Europium occurs in cerium minerals. It melts at 822 °C and boils at 1529 °C. Europium is used in laser technology, *alloys* (metal mixtures), some fluorescent light bulbs, and nuclear reactor control rods. See also **Element, Chemical** (table); **Lanthanide.** Marianna A. Busch

Eurydice, *yoo RIHD ih see,* in Greek mythology, was a tree nymph loved by Orpheus, who was a legendary Greek musician. On their wedding day, Eurydice accidentally stepped on a snake and died from its bite. Another version of her death tells that she tripped over the snake as she fled from the amorous advances of Aristaeus, a rural divinity. After her death, Eurydice descended into the underworld, which was ruled by the god Hades and his wife, Persephone. Orpheus was determined to rescue Eurydice. He went to the underworld and charmed the ghosts of the dead with his music.

Hades and Persephone agreed to release Eurydice

only if Orpheus would walk ahead and not look back at her until they both reached the upper world. As they approached the light, Orpheus turned around to look at Eurydice because he did not hear her footsteps. Eurydice was immediately drawn back to the underworld forever. Luci Berkowitz

Euthanasia, *yoo thuh NAY zhuh,* is the practice of intentionally and directly ending the life of a person who has a severe and incurable disease or medical condition. Euthanasia most commonly occurs when a person with a *terminal* (fatal) illness asks a doctor for a lethal injection. The practice is sometimes called *mercy killing.*

Active euthanasia involves deliberate actions by a physician who administers a lethal dose of a drug to end a person's life. In the past, the term *euthanasia* was used to refer both to active euthanasia and to termination of life-sustaining treatment, sometimes called *passive euthanasia.* But this dual use of the term was confusing, so *euthanasia* now usually refers only to active euthanasia.

People differ in their beliefs regarding active euthanasia. Supporters believe that terminally ill people have a right to a lethal injection or other intervention by a physician to end their lives. Many opponents, however, consider active euthanasia to be a violation of medical ethics and, in some cases, the equivalent of murder. Most countries do not allow active euthanasia.

Termination of life-sustaining treatment. Stopping the use of life-sustaining medical treatment may also result in a patient's death. However, this practice is usually distinguished from active euthanasia by the fact that the doctor does not administer a lethal drug or other intervention to directly cause death. By removing the life-sustaining treatment, the doctor lets the underlying disease take its course. Termination of life-sustaining treatment is legal in the United States and in many other countries. The Supreme Court of the United States ruled in *Cruzan v. Director, Missouri Department of Health* (1990) that people may refuse life-sustaining treatment. Patients also have the right to stop treatment already started.

In some cases, a patient, because of injury or disease, may be unable to express his or her wishes about medical treatment. For this reason, many people make their wishes known in advance through the use of *living wills* or by granting *durable powers of attorney* to a family member or a friend. In living wills, people state what kind of care they would want if, because of injury or disease, they could not express their wishes themselves. In granting durable powers of attorney, individuals designate a person to make decisions about their medical care if they should lose the ability to communicate such decisions themselves. Living wills and durable powers of attorney are types of *advance directives* for the planning of future medical treatment.

Physician-assisted suicide occurs when a physician provides medication or a prescription to help a patient commit suicide. Physician-assisted suicide differs from active euthanasia because the patient takes the last step to end his or her own life. Physician-assisted suicide is controversial. Many people believe terminally ill people should be able to use physician-prescribed drugs to kill themselves. Others argue that a doctor should not help patients kill themselves because a physician's job is to preserve life and to improve the patients' condition.

In the United States, Jack Kevorkian, a Michigan doctor, focused attention on physician-assisted suicide in the 1990's by helping seriously ill people kill themselves. In 1999, he was convicted of murder in a case in which he performed active euthanasia. Most states have laws against physician-assisted suicide. Montana, Oregon, and Washington, however, permit some forms of this practice. Susan M. Wolf

See also **Death** (The right to die); **Living will; Medical ethics; Suicide.**

Eutrophication, *yoo truh fuh KAY shuhn,* is a process that affects lakes and other bodies of water. During eutrophication, the quality of the affected water deteriorates until it is unfit for human use. Lakes and rivers become foul smelling and can no longer support many fish and other animals. Some lakes naturally become eutrophic over hundreds of thousands of years. But in the 1900's, many lakes and rivers became eutrophic because people polluted them. This accelerated process caused by human activities is called *cultural eutrophication.*

How eutrophication occurs. Water bodies support a natural cycle of life. The bacteria of decay break down the wastes of fish and other organisms, releasing such *nutrients* (nourishing substances) as carbon dioxide, nitrate, and phosphate. Simple plantlike organisms called *algae* feed on the nutrients. Microscopic animals called *zooplankton* eat the algae, and fish eat the zooplankton. When this cycle is in balance, each member of the cycle supports the others. Fish get food and oxygen from algae. Bacteria use organic matter from fish and oxygen from algae, and algae feed on the products of decay.

People upset the balance when they pollute the water with wastes, which provide many nutrients. Algae consume the excess nutrients. They become so well nourished that they grow faster than fish can eat them. Thick layers of algae, called *algal blooms,* spread over the water. The lower layers of algal blooms cannot get the light they need for photosynthesis. These algae soon die and decay, using up huge quantities of oxygen in the water.

Fish and other water animals die when the oxygen supply in the water becomes too small to sustain them. As the bodies of the animals decay, they consume still more oxygen. Without oxygen, the bacteria of decay can no longer function, and foul-smelling wastes accumulate. The dead fish and plants and other wastes sink to the bottom of the water and form a layer of soft mud. As the mud becomes thicker, the lake gradually shrinks. Some lakes eventually fill and become swamps.

Eutrophication and water pollution. Eutrophication is a major pollution problem. Many of the excess nutrients that enter bodies of water and cause the problem come from sewage treatment plants. In particular, the use of detergents that contain phosphate greatly increases the quantity of phosphate entering rivers and lakes through sewage. Rain also washes the nitrate from fertilizers used on farmland, gardens, and lawns into ponds and streams. Nitrates from automobile exhaust enter the water in rain and snow, and industrial plants discharge nutrients in wastewater. Melody J. Hunt

See also **Environmental pollution** (Water pollution); **Water pollution** (Effects; diagram).

Evangelical Lutheran Church in America, also known as the ELCA, is the largest Lutheran denomination in the United States. It was formed by the merger of the Lutheran Church in America, the American Lutheran

Church, and the Association of Evangelical Lutheran Churches. The ELCA officially came into being in 1988.

The church is organized into 65 regional jurisdictional units called *synods,* each headed by a bishop. The leader of the denomination is a bishop elected for a six-year term. The church ordains women, as well as people in committed same-sex relationships; maintains ecumenical ties with other churches; supports an extensive international and domestic mission program; and seeks increased participation from people of color.

The Evangelical Lutheran Church in America traces its roots back to Lutheran immigrants who came from Germany and Scandinavian countries in colonial times and in the 1800's. The church's headquarters are in Chicago.

In 2009, the Churchwide Assembly of the ELCA voted to permit the ordination of people in committed, long-term, same-sex relationships. In response, some conservative congregations voted to leave the ELCA.

Critically reviewed by the Evangelical Lutheran Church in America

See also **Lutherans.**

Evangelicalism is a Protestant religious movement that stresses religious conversion, personal religious experience, and the Bible as God's revelation to humanity and the only authority in matters of faith. In North America and the United Kingdom, and increasingly throughout the world, evangelicalism has worked as a renewal movement within Christianity.

The term *evangelical* comes from a Greek word meaning *gospel.* It refers generally to the New Testament, the part of the Bible that contains the Gospels. It also refers to the German theologian Martin Luther's teachings in the 1500's. Luther asserted that the Bible should be the sole authority in the Christian church.

In the United States, evangelicals provided support for the patriot cause during the American Revolution (1775-1783). In the 1800's, they shaped U.S. politics and society by working for such causes as abolition, *temperance* (limiting alcohol consumption), education, and literacy and equal rights for women.

By the start of the 1900's, evangelicals had begun to divide among themselves. Pentecostals, who believed in the spiritual gifts of divine physical healing and *speaking in tongues* (speaking in languages unknown to the speakers), emerged as a distinct group in 1901. A series of pamphlets called *The Fundamentals* (1910-1915) expressed extremely conservative beliefs on such matters as the Bible's freedom from error, the virgin birth and resurrection of Jesus, and the genuineness of miracles. The 1920's saw Protestant "fundamentalists" defending these beliefs against more liberal "modernists." Many fundamentalists left moderate churches, sometimes called the *mainline* churches, to form new ones.

Believing that American culture had turned against them, evangelicals retreated from public life in the early to middle 1900's. They set about building a huge network of churches, schools, Bible camps, mission societies, radio stations and programs, and publishers. Evangelicals returned to public life in the 1970's. Led by such preachers and activists as Pat Robertson and Jerry Falwell, they became an important presence in American politics and society. In particular, a conservative Protestant movement called the Religious Right has won considerable influence in U.S. politics since the late 1970's.

Randall Balmer

See also **Christianity** (Christianity today; picture: Evangelical Protestants); **Fundamentalism; Luther, Martin; Pentecostal churches; Protestantism.**

Evangeline. See **Longfellow, Henry Wadsworth.**

Evans, Sir Arthur John (1851-1941), a British archaeologist, is known for his excavations at Knossos on the island of Crete. Beginning in 1900, he uncovered the Palace of Minos at Knossos, on which most knowledge of pre-Greek Minoan civilization is based. He also found clay tablets bearing the earliest form of Greek writing. This form preceded the writing of the Phoenicians.

Evans was born on July 8, 1851, in Hertfordshire, England. He graduated from Oxford and Göttingen (Germany) universities. His discoveries were published in the multiple volume *Palace of Minos* (1922-1935). Evans was knighted in 1911. He died on July 11, 1941. Ruth Palmer

See also **Knossos.**

Evans, Mary Ann. See **Eliot, George.**

Evans, Oliver (1755-1819), an American engineer, inventor, and manufacturer, built what was likely America's first self-propelled land vehicle (see **Automobile** [The steam car]). The vehicle, a steam-powered dredge to be used in the Philadelphia harbor, was completed in 1805. Evans had built one of the first high-pressure steam engines in 1802. These engines became highly successful, and Evans manufactured large numbers of them for use in flour mills, locomotives, and steamboats. Evans was born on Sept. 13, 1755, near Newport, Delaware. He died on April 15, 1819. Joel Webb Eastman

Evans, Walker (1903-1975), was an American photographer who became best known for his pictures of Southern sharecroppers of the 1930's. Evans's photographs capture the poverty and desolation of rural life in the southern United States during the Great Depression. A group of 31 of his pictures and a text by James Agee were published in *Let Us Now Praise Famous Men* (1941). The book portrays the lives of three poor sharecropper families in Alabama.

Evans was born on Nov. 2, 1903, in St. Louis. He took up photography in 1928 after failing as a writer. Evans often photographed such common subjects as billboards, pedestrians, and subway riders. In the 1930's, he took pictures of farms, towns, and cities in the East and the South for the government. Many of these pictures appear in his book *American Photographs* (1938).

From 1945 to 1965, Evans worked for *Fortune* magazine. He taught at Yale University from 1965 until his death on April 10, 1975. John G. Freeman

See also **Photography** (picture).

Evaporation is the conversion of a liquid or solid to a gas. Energy in the form of heat causes evaporation. For example, evaporation occurs when water in an open pan in a warm room disappears, leaving a dry pan. Sometimes solids may change directly into *vapor* (a gaseous form) without first becoming a liquid. This process is called *sublimation.* The vaporization of dry ice (solid carbon dioxide) is an example of sublimation.

How evaporation occurs. The molecules of all substances have a certain amount of *kinetic energy* (energy of motion). This energy is provided by heat from the surroundings, including other nearby molecules. The more energy molecules have, the faster they move, making it possible for them to break the bonds that hold them together. Evaporation occurs when the molecules of a

How evaporation occurs

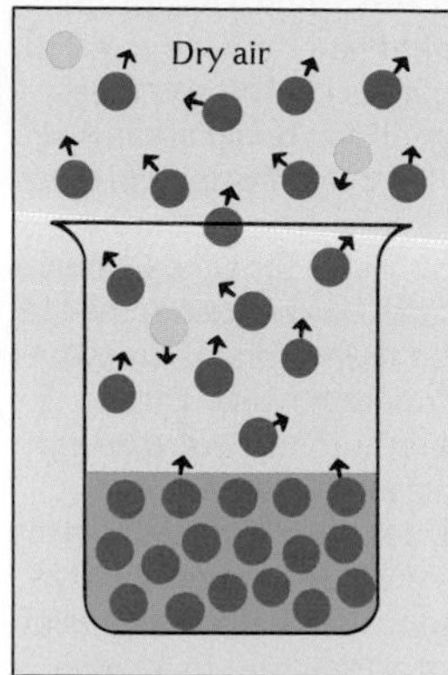

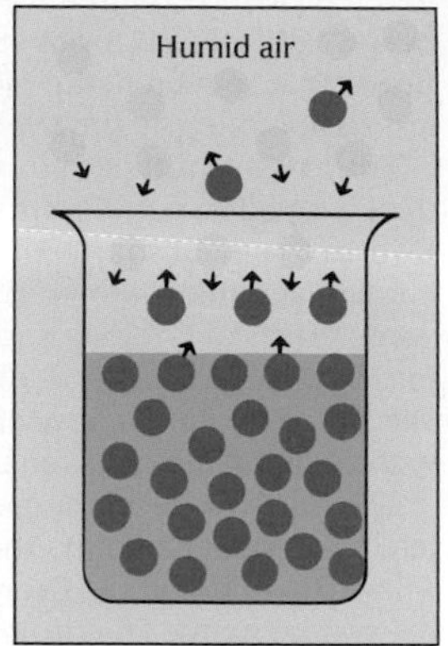

WORLD BOOK diagrams

In dry air, water evaporates readily. Many molecules escape from the container as vapor, but few enter to become liquid. Dry air contains so little moisture that condensation hardly occurs.

In humid air, water evaporates slowly, if at all. The vaporization occurring at the surface of the water in the container is quickly matched by the condensation of moisture in the humid air.

substance have enough kinetic energy to escape from the substance's surface as vapor. The escaping molecules absorb heat energy from the remaining molecules and cause the substance to become cooler.

Evaporation occurs more rapidly when temperature is increased. An increase in temperature increases the energy of a substance's molecules, enabling them to escape at a faster rate. Different substances vary greatly in the speed at which they evaporate at a given temperature. For example, alcohol, ammonia, and the anesthetic diethyl ether evaporate quickly when poured onto an open surface at room temperature. Such substances are said to be *volatile.* Other substances, such as table salt (sodium chloride), evaporate extremely slowly, if at all, at room temperature. They are said to be *nonvolatile.*

A substance that is nonvolatile at one temperature may become volatile if it is heated. In this sense, the boiling point of a substance is a measure of its volatility. The lower the boiling point of a substance, the more easily it evaporates. See **Boiling point.**

The *vapor pressure* of a substance also helps determine how readily the substance evaporates. Vapor pressure is the pressure produced by vapor molecules escaping from the surface of a liquid or solid. The greater a substance's vapor pressure, the faster the substance evaporates. As a substance gains heat, more and more molecules escape. Vapor pressure increases until the number of molecules escaping from the liquid or solid equals the number returning to it. When these numbers are equal, the amount of the liquid or solid does not change. For example, water evaporates slowly, if at all, when exposed to humid air because the vaporization occurring at the surface of the water is almost matched by the condensation of moisture in the air. But water evaporates rapidly in dry air because dry air has only a fraction of the maximum vapor pressure of water.

Uses of evaporation. Evaporation plays an important part in the earth's water cycle. Water evaporated from the earth by the heat of the sun later falls as precipitation. Because evaporating molecules absorb heat from their surroundings, evaporation functions as a cooling process. Air-conditioning and refrigeration systems contain evaporators that remove heat and moisture from the surrounding air and so reduce the temperature. The evaporation of perspiration cools the skin.

Evaporation provides a way to separate mixtures. In distillation, mixtures of liquids that differ in *volatility* (ease of evaporation) are heated to form a vapor that is then condensed. The resulting liquid contains a greater proportion of the more volatile substance than does the original mixture. Such products as alcoholic beverages and gasoline are manufactured by distillation.

Evaporation also serves as a means of concentrating nonvolatile substances. For example, the juice from sugar cane is heated until nearly all the liquid evaporates. This process produces a concentrated sugar solution from which sugar crystals form. Marye Anne Fox

See also **Cloud; Steam; Sublimation; Vapor.**

Evarts, William Maxwell (1818-1901), an American lawyer, gained fame for successfully handling important trials. He helped President Andrew Johnson gain acquittal in his impeachment trial in 1868 (see **Johnson, Andrew** [Impeachment]). Evarts served as attorney general of the United States in 1868 and 1869, as U.S. secretary of state from 1877 to 1881, and as U.S. senator from New York from 1885 to 1893. As president of the New York City Bar Association, he led movements for law reform and helped smash the "Tweed Ring" (see **Tweed, William M.**). His closing argument for the defense in a case against Henry Ward Beecher lasted eight days. Evarts was born in Boston on Feb. 6, 1818. Daniel J. Dykstra

Eve. See **Adam and Eve.**

Evening primrose is any of several related wild flowering plants that grow from Labrador to Florida and westward to Wyoming and New Mexico. The plants may be 1 to 8 feet (30 to 240 centimeters) high, and often have shrubby bases. The hairy leaves grow 2 to 6 inches (5 to 15 centimeters) long. Saucer-shaped flowers grow among the upper leaves. They may be white, bright yellow, or rosy-pink. The blossoms may be 1 to 4 inches (3 to 10 centimeters) wide. One species, called the *small-flowered evening primrose,* has flowers that grow no more than $\frac{1}{2}$ inch (13 millimeters) wide.

Melinda F. Denton

Scientific classification. Evening primroses are in the family Onagraceae. The common evening primrose is *Oenothera biennis.* The small-flowered plant is *O. cruciata.*

Evening star is any planet that can be seen after sunset. The planets Venus and Mercury are most often seen as evening stars. Because these two planets move in orbits closer to the sun than the earth's orbit, they appear to move from one side of the sun to the other. The two planets can be seen only in the western sky after sunset or in the eastern sky before sunrise. When either of the planets is seen at sunrise, it is called a *morning star.*

Planets are not really stars, but solid bodies in our own solar system. They do not give off their own light as stars do. They shine by reflecting sunlight. Ancient people thought planets were wandering stars. By Roman times, they recognized that the morning stars and evening stars were the same. But it was not until 1543 that the Polish astronomer Nicolaus Copernicus identified their positions in the solar system. C. R. O'Dell

Everest, Mount. See Mount Everest.

Everett, Edward (1794-1865), an American statesman, was considered one of the greatest orators of his day. He was the chief speaker in Gettysburg, Pennsylvania, on Nov. 19, 1863, the day that Abraham Lincoln delivered his famous Gettysburg Address (see **Lincoln, Abraham** [The Gettysburg Address]). Lincoln's logic and ability to say so much in so few words impressed Everett. He declared Lincoln's speech would live for generations.

Everett was born on April 11, 1794, in Dorchester, Massachusetts. He became a Unitarian minister at 19. In less than two years, he resigned from his first pastorate. He studied in Germany and England and returned to become professor of Greek literature at Harvard College. For four years, Everett edited the *North American Review.* Then he served five terms in Congress. Everett was governor of Massachusetts from 1836 to 1840, U.S. minister to the United Kingdom from 1841 to 1845, and president of Harvard from 1846 to 1849. In 1852, he became secretary of state in President Millard Fillmore's Cabinet and was soon elected U.S. senator from Massachusetts. He resigned from his Senate post in 1854. In 1860, he was the Constitutional Union Party's candidate for vice president (see **Constitutional Union Party**). Everett died on Jan. 15, 1865. James M. McPherson

Everglades, in southern Florida, are one of the most interesting and unusual wetland areas in the world. Everglades National Park makes up about one-fifth of the Everglades' original area and covers about 1,500,000 acres (610,000 hectares). The Everglades extend from Lake Okeechobee to Florida Bay and the Gulf of Mexico.

The northern part of the Everglades consists of a prairie covered by shallow water and by saw grass, a grasslike plant with sharp, jagged edges that grows as high as 12 feet (3.7 meters) in some places. Bustic, gumbo limbo, live oak, mastic, and royal palm trees grow on mounds of higher land called *tree islands.* Near the southern coast, the Everglades become salt marshes and mangrove swamps, where the spreading roots of mangrove trees catch and hold soil. Many animals live in the Everglades. They include alligators, deer, fish, herons, pelicans, snakes, and the rare Florida panther.

Development of the Everglades. The Everglades were created after the most recent ice age, which ended approximately 11,500 years ago. The ice melting from glaciers raised the level of the sea, which flooded the outlets of Everglades streams and turned the area into a wetland. Various peoples have lived in the Everglades. The Seminole Indians fled the area in the early 1800's during a period of wars against U.S. troops.

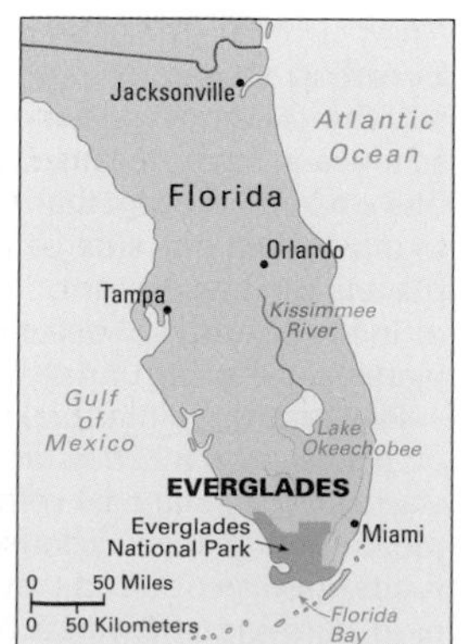

WORLD BOOK map
Location of the Everglades

In 1906, the state of Florida began draining parts of the Everglades to make the land suitable for farming. After World War I ended in 1918, farmers moved in and began growing vegetables and sugar cane. Canals were built southeast from Lake Okeechobee to supply water to the growing communities in and around Miami. But by the 1940's, the U.S. government had decided to try to preserve a section of the Everglades. So the southwestern region became the Everglades National Park in 1947.

Environmental problems. Despite efforts to protect the Everglades, conditions worsened. The Kissimmee River is the main source of fresh water for Lake Okeechobee and the southern wetlands. In the 1960's, the U.S. Army Corps of Engineers forced the waters of the winding Kissimmee into a straight concrete canal. This sharply reduced the flow of water into the Everglades, with disastrous results for plants and wildlife.

The massive development of southern Florida in the late 1900's also damaged the Everglades' water supply. Cities surrounding the Everglades use huge amounts of the water supply. The growth of agriculture in an area just south of Lake Okeechobee has also contributed to the water problem. Sugar plantations and vegetable farms consume much water, and harmful chemicals used in agriculture run off into the water supply.

Plant species that are not native to the Everglades also pose problems for the area. Seeds from plants, including paperbark trees and Brazilian pepper trees, have been dispersed to the Everglades by high winds. When such seeds take root and develop into plants, they can overpower and replace native Everglades species.

Saving the Everglades. Many groups have joined the fight to save the Everglades. The state of Florida has bought land around Lake Okeechobee to create new marshes that will store water and filter out toxic chemicals before releasing the additional water into the wetlands to the south. The U.S. Army Corps of Engineers is working on restoring the Kissimmee to its original course. In 1999, the Corps also introduced a 20-year plan to reconnect the various parts of the Everglades that have been fragmented by the building of artificial barriers and drainage canals. Peter O. Muller

See also **Everglades National Park; Florida** (picture); **Lake Okeechobee.**

Everglades National Park is one of the few subtropical regions in the United States. The park, on the southwestern tip of the Florida peninsula, includes Ten Thousand Islands along the Gulf of Mexico and parts of the Everglades and the Big Cypress Swamp. Its junglelike plant life includes saw grass, delicate orchids, lacy cypress trees, pines, palms, and mangrove trees that form a thick tangle as high as 70 feet (21 meters). Crocodiles, alligators, manatees, swamp birds, and many other species live there. The park was established in 1947. For its area, see **National Park System** (table: National parks). Critically reviewed by the National Park Service

Evergreen is a plant that remains green throughout the year. It grows new leaves before shedding the old ones. Many evergreens keep their leaves for several years. The leaves of some of them are tougher and more leathery than those of other plants. Some evergreens, such as the cone-bearing trees, have needle-shaped leaves. These leaves have less surface area than broad, flat leaves and can resist changes in temperature more easily. Many tropical plants are called broadleaf evergreens to distinguish them from needle-leaved ones. Both kinds of leaves contain *chlorophyll,* the green coloring matter used by plants to make food.

The best-known North American evergreen trees include pine, fir, spruce, hemlock, cedar, cypress, and yew. Holly, box, ivy, and myrtle are other common evergreens. Rhododendron, laurel, some magnolias, and most tropical plants are evergreens. Pines and spruces are valuable timber trees. Ross W. Wein

Related articles in *World Book* include:

Beefwood	Douglas-fir	Monkey puzzle tree	Sequoia
Box	Fir	Myrtle	Spruce
Bristlecone pine	Hemlock	Pine	Tamarind
Cedar	Holly	Redwood	Traveler's-tree
Conifer	Ivy	Rhododendron	Tree (Kinds)
Cycad	Juniper		Wax myrtle
Cypress	Laurel		Yew
	Magnolia		

Evers, Medgar (1925-1963), was an African American civil rights leader. He fought against segregation and racial discrimination in Mississippi during the 1950's and early 1960's. Evers was shot and killed outside his home in Jackson, Mississippi, on June 12, 1963.

Medgar Wiley Evers was born on July 2, 1925, in Decatur, Mississippi. He enlisted in the U.S. Army in 1942 during World War II. He received a bachelor's degree from Alcorn Agricultural and Mechanical College (now Alcorn State University) in 1952. From 1954 to 1963, he served on the staff of the National Association for the Advancement of Colored People (NAACP) as field secretary for Mississippi. Evers traveled throughout the state, encouraging blacks to register to vote. He also organized African American *boycotts* (buyers' strikes) against white-owned firms that practiced racial discrimination.

Evers soon became Mississippi's best-known champion of civil rights and a target of white supremacists, who violently opposed programs designed to guarantee blacks' rights. Ten days after Evers's murder, police arrested white supremacist Byron De La Beckwith for the crime. Beckwith, whose fingerprints were on the rifle that killed Evers, was tried twice in 1964 for the slaying. But each time, an all-white jury could not reach a verdict. The charges against Beckwith were dropped in 1969. In 1989, the case was reopened after new evidence was found. In 1994, a jury of eight African Americans and four whites convicted Beckwith of Evers's murder.

Medgar's brother Charles succeeded him as field secretary. In 1969, Charles was elected mayor of Fayette, Mississippi. He held that office until 1981 and again from 1985 to 1989. Medgar's widow, Myrlie Evers-Williams, served as chairwoman of the NAACP's board of directors from 1995 to 1998. In 1998, she set up the Medgar Evers Institute to work for civil rights. David J. Garrow

See also **Evers-Williams, Myrlie.**

Evers-Williams, Myrlie (1933-), served as chairwoman of the board of the National Association for the Advancement of Colored People (NAACP) from 1995 to 1998. She won election to the position by defeating William F. Gibson, who had been board chairman since 1985. The election followed months of public disagreement over the NAACP's financial and personnel practices under both Gibson and executive director Benjamin Chavis, who was dismissed in 1994. Evers-Williams did not seek reelection in 1998.

Evers-Williams was born Myrlie Louise Beasley on March 17, 1933, in Vicksburg, Mississippi. In 1951, she married Medgar Evers, who later became the NAACP's Mississippi field secretary. In 1963, Evers was assassinated. More than 30 years later, in 1994, Evers-Williams played a key role in winning the conviction of white supremacist Byron De La Beckwith for the murder. After her husband's assassination, Mrs. Evers moved to California, where she graduated from Pomona College in 1968. She then held a series of positions as a business executive. From 1987 to 1990, she was commissioner of the Los Angeles Board of Public Works. In 1976, she married Walter Williams, a dockworker and civil rights worker. In 1998, Evers-Williams set up the Medgar Evers Institute to promote civil rights. David J. Garrow

Evert, Chris (1954-), an American tennis champion, ranks as one of the greatest female tennis players in the history of the sport. Evert never ranked lower than fourth from the year she turned professional in 1972 until her retirement in 1989. She was noted for her technically perfect forehand and two-handed backhand, both delivered with accuracy, power, and depth. She was at her best on clay court surfaces and won 125 consecutive matches on clay from August 1973 to May 1979. Evert won 18 Grand Slam titles, winning Wimbledon in England three times, the French Open seven times, the United States Open six times, and the Australian Open twice.

Christine Marie Evert was born on Dec. 21, 1954, in Fort Lauderdale, Florida. From 1979 to 1987, she was married to the British tennis player John Lloyd and competed under the name Chris Evert Lloyd. She was married to Andy Mill, a former U.S. Olympic skier, from 1988 to 2006, and to the Australian golf star Greg Norman from June 2008 to December 2009.

Evert won 154 professional singles titles during her career. After retiring as a player in 1989, she served as a tennis analyst for NBC television from 1990 to 2003. She became the publisher of *Tennis* magazine in 2001. Evert also runs a tennis academy in Florida. Tony Lance

See also **Tennis** (picture: Modern women tennis stars).

Eviction, in law, is an action that deprives a tenant of the use of leased premises, such as an apartment or an office. An eviction can occur if either the tenant or the landlord violates the lease. A landlord may evict a tenant who owes rent or has substantially failed in some other way to meet the lease obligations. Such obligations include not disturbing other tenants. On the other hand, the landlord may have made the premises unfit for the tenant's use. For example, the landlord may have refused to make repairs that were necessary for the tenant's comfort and safety. In such cases, the tenant no longer must pay rent if he or she abandons the premises within a reasonable time. James E. Krier

Evidence is information that tends to prove or disprove a fact in question. Evidence may consist of documents, public records, or the testimony of witnesses. It may be an object, such as a murder weapon or a signed contract, the existence or appearance of which provides information about the fact in question. Most evidence is presented through witnesses whom a judge declares *competent* (mentally able) to testify. Insane people and some children may be declared incompetent.

Each party to a legal dispute presents evidence to the court. The *trier of fact* considers the evidence and decides the disputed facts. In a jury trial, the trier of fact is the jury. In a nonjury trial, it is the judge.

Evidence is used in other fields besides law. For example, scientists gather evidence to support theories.

This article chiefly discusses court evidence.

Burden of proof is the obligation to provide evidence, and it falls on one of the parties to a lawsuit. In a criminal case, the prosecuting attorney has the burden of proving the defendant's guilt "beyond a reasonable doubt." In civil trials, the party that is suing, called the *plaintiff,* need only prove a fact by a *fair preponderance* (greater weight) of the evidence.

The burden of proof may shift during a trial. For example, a plaintiff suing a defendant for injuries suffered in an automobile accident must prove that the defendant was negligent. But the burden of proof shifts to the defendant if the defendant claims that the plaintiff's actions contributed to the accident.

Kinds of evidence. There are two general kinds of evidence—*direct evidence* and *circumstantial evidence.* Direct evidence tends to prove a fact without the help of other evidence. For example, an eyewitness to a murder gives direct evidence by testifying that he or she saw the defendant kill the victim. Circumstantial evidence tends to prove facts that support the main fact in question, but such evidence does not tend directly to prove the main fact itself. Witnesses may give circumstantial evidence by testifying that they saw the defendant leave the murder scene. This evidence indicates that the defendant could have killed the victim, but does not prove it.

Rules regulate the admission of evidence in court. The judge decides whether evidence is admissible under the rules. In 1975, United States federal courts began to operate under uniform rules. Many state rules of evidence closely follow the federal rules, but a state court is not required to follow federal rules. Thus rules of evidence may vary from state to state.

One type of evidence that generally is not admitted is *hearsay.* Such evidence is testimony in which a witness tells the court what he or she heard others say, rather than what the witness knows from firsthand experience.

Relevancy. Evidence must be *relevant* to be admitted in court—that is, it must relate to, and help resolve, a significant question in a case. Evidence that seems relevant may be excluded because it might prejudice or mislead a jury. For example, evidence that a defendant has previously committed crimes is not ordinarily admitted.

Privilege is the right to withhold evidence to protect an important interest or relationship. The U.S. Constitution provides some privileges. For example, accused people cannot be forced to give evidence against themselves at a criminal trial. Other privileges include the right not to reveal confidential communication between husbands and wives, attorneys and clients, or priests and the people whose confessions they hear. The federal government has also claimed privilege on the grounds of national security or defense.

Presumptions. If evidence about a fact is lacking, a rule of law may state that the fact is proved by other facts. Such a statement is called a *presumption.* For example, proof that a person has been missing for at least seven years may result in the presumption that he or she is dead. Michael J. Bushbaum

See also **Crime scene investigation; DNA fingerprinting; Forensic science; Trial; Witness.**

Evil eye is the supposed power to harm people by merely looking at them or by speaking ill of them. According to particular belief systems, an evil person who has this power may use it to cause such misfortune as death, illness, or property damage. A person may also unknowingly have the evil eye and cause harm unintentionally. To avoid the evil eye, many people utter such phrases as "God bless you" or wear blue beads or protective charms. For thousands of years, people in many parts of the world have believed in the evil eye. Today, the belief remains common in India and in Mediterranean countries. See also **Amulet.** Russell Zanca

Evolution is a process of change over time. The word *evolution* may refer to various types of change. For example, scientists generally describe the formation of the universe as having occurred through evolution. Many astronomers think that the stars and planets evolved from a huge cloud of hot gases. Anthropologists study the evolution of human culture from hunting and gathering societies to complex, industrialized societies.

Most commonly, however, *evolution* refers to the formation and development of life on Earth. The idea that all living things evolved from simple organisms and changed through the ages to produce millions of species is known as the *theory of organic evolution.* Most people call it simply the *theory of evolution.*

The French naturalist Chevalier de Lamarck proposed a theory of evolution in 1809. But evolution did not receive widespread scientific attention until the late 1850's, when the British naturalist Charles Darwin presented his theory of evolution. Since then, advances in various scientific fields have refined the theory. The main ideas of evolution, however, have remained largely unchanged.

This article discusses the main ideas of evolutionary theory and the scientific evidence that supports the theory. For information about other types of evolution, see the *World Book* articles on **Universe** (Changing views of the universe) and **Earth** (History of Earth).

Main ideas of evolutionary theory

The theory of evolution consists of a set of interrelated ideas. The basic idea states that species undergo changes in their inherited characteristics over time. The most important mechanism of evolution is *natural selection,* a process by which the individuals better suited to their environment tend to leave more descendants. All living organisms must compete for a limited supply of food, water, space, mates, and other things they need to successfully reproduce. Scientists use the term *fitness* to refer to an individual's overall ability to reproduce.

There are two main types of change in organic evolution: *anagenesis* and *cladogenesis.* Anagenesis refers to changes that occur within a species over time. Because of anagenetic change, the forms and traits of many species today differ from the forms and traits of their ancestors. Cladogenesis refers to the splitting of one species into two or more descendant species. This branching process, also called *speciation,* can be repeated to create many species. Current evolutionary theory holds that all species evolved from a single form of life which lived more than 3 ½ billion years ago. Over time, repeated speciation events and anagenetic changes have produced the more than 10 million species on Earth today.

Related to speciation is the idea of *common ancestry.* Because all organisms evolved from one basic life form, any two species once had a common ancestor. Closely related species share a more recent common ancestor,

© Shutterstock

Evolution has produced a stunning variety of living things, each adapted to a different way of life. Mangrove trees, *left,* are able to live in shallow water along coasts. The tree's many stiltlike roots anchor it to the bottom. The roots also provide shelter for fish and other ocean life. A hummingbird, *below,* feeds on sweet nectar made by a flower. The delicate hummingbird can hover in place, its long bill and tongue enabling it to reach deep inside the flower. As it feeds, the hummingbird picks up tiny grains of pollen, which the flowers exchange to reproduce. In this way, flowers and the hummingbirds have evolved to depend on each other.

© Shutterstock

but distantly related species must trace their ancestry far into the past to find a common ancestor. For example, human beings, chimpanzees, and gorillas evolved from a common ancestor that lived between 4 million and 10 million years ago, while the common ancestor of human beings and reptiles lived about 300 million years ago.

Other ideas relate to the tempo of evolutionary change. *Gradualism* is the idea that some evolutionary changes occur continuously over long stretches of time. *Punctuated equilibrium* is the idea that some evolutionary changes take place in relatively short periods, from tens to hundreds of generations, followed by longer periods of little change called *stasis.* Both gradual and punctuated patterns can occur for different traits. The theory of evolution holds that evolution continues today at rates comparable to those of the past.

Although evolution is called a "theory," this term does not mean that evolutionary biology is guesswork or is not supported by evidence. In science, a *theory* is a set of ideas based on observations about nature that explains many related facts. The theory of evolution is supported by evidence from many scientific fields. When a theory is supported by so much evidence, it becomes accepted as a scientific fact. Almost all scientists consider the theory of evolution to be a scientific fact.

Many people, however, reject the theory of evolution because of their religious beliefs. They believe the theory conflicts with the Biblical account of the Creation, which they interpret to mean that all forms of life were created essentially as they exist today.

Causes of evolutionary change

Much evolutionary change results from the interaction of two processes: (1) *mutation* and (2) *natural selection.* Mutation produces *random* (chance) variation in the biological makeup of a species or a *population*—that is, individuals of the same species living in the same area. Natural selection sorts out these random changes according to their value in enhancing reproduction and survival. Such selection ensures that variations which make individuals better adapted to their environment will be passed on to future generations. At the same time, natural selection eliminates variations that make individuals less able to survive. A third process called *genetic drift* also helps create evolutionary change.

Mutation is a permanent change in the hereditary material of an organism. By altering this material, a mutation may produce changes in an organism's traits. To understand how mutations produce these changes, one must understand how characteristics are inherited.

How characteristics are inherited. Hereditary characteristics of organisms are carried by threadlike structures called *chromosomes* in cells. Chromosomes carry large numbers of *genes,* the basic units of heredity. Genes consist of a substance called *DNA* (deoxyribonucleic acid). DNA contains the coded information that influences hereditary characteristics.

Among most animals and plants, each body cell has a

full set of paired chromosomes. Human body cells, for example, have 46 chromosomes arranged in 23 pairs. Offspring inherit half a set of chromosomes from each parent. Parents pass on their chromosomes to their offspring during sexual reproduction. Egg cells and sperm cells form in a special process called *meiosis* that gives them one chromosome at random from each pair of the parent's set. As a result, egg and sperm cells have half the number of chromosomes found in all other cells in the body. During reproduction, a sperm and an egg unite in the process called *fertilization,* and the fertilized egg then has the full number of chromosomes.

Sometimes, the genes from one of a pair of chromosomes change places with genes on the other pair as a sperm or egg cell forms. This change in the arrangement of genes, called *recombination,* can result in new combinations of inherited traits.

As the fertilized egg cell begins to grow, it also begins a process of division. Each chromosome in the nucleus of the cell duplicates itself. The chromosome and its duplicate lie next to each other in pairs. During normal cell division, called *mitosis,* one of each pair of chromosomes goes into each of two new cells. Thus, the new cells contain chromosomes that are identical with those in the original cell. This process of growth through cell division continues until it has produced all the cells that make up an organism.

How mutations change a species. Mutations may be caused by environmental factors, such as chemicals and radiation, which alter the DNA in genes, or by errors in the copying of DNA during cell division. After a gene has changed, it duplicates itself in its changed form. If these *mutant genes* are present in the egg or sperm cells of an organism, they may alter some inherited characteristics. Only such mutations can introduce new hereditary characteristics. For this reason, mutations are the building blocks of evolutionary change and of the development of new species.

Mutations occur regularly but are usually infrequent, and most of them produce unfavorable traits. *Albinism* is one such mutation. Albino animals have mutant genes that lack the ability to produce normal skin pigment. These animals do not survive and reproduce as well as normal animals. In most cases, such mutant genes are eliminated by natural selection because most individuals that inherit them die before producing any offspring.

Some mutations, however, help organisms adapt better to their environment. A plant in a dry area might have a mutant gene that causes it to grow longer roots. The plant would have a better chance of survival than others of its species because its roots could reach deeper for water. This type of beneficial mutation provides the raw material for evolutionary change.

Natural selection can involve any feature that affects an individual's ability to leave offspring. These features include appearance, body chemistry, and *physiology* (how an organism functions), as well as behavior.

For natural selection to operate, two biological conditions must be met. First, the individuals of a population must differ in their hereditary characteristics. Human beings, for example, vary in almost every aspect of their appearance, including height, weight, and eye color. People also differ in less obvious ways, such as brain size, thickness of bones, and amount of fat in the blood.

Sexual selection has caused the evolution of features that give an animal an advantage in finding a mate. The colorful plumage of a peacock, *shown here,* helps it attract the female bird.

Many of these differences have some genetic basis.

The second requirement for natural selection is that some inherited differences must affect chances for survival and reproduction. When this occurs, the individuals with higher fitness will pass on more copies of their genes to future generations than will other individuals. Over time, a species accumulates genes that increase its ability to survive and reproduce in its environment.

Natural selection is a group process. It causes the evolution of a population or a species as a whole—not the evolution of an individual—by gradually shifting the average characteristics of the group over time.

There are several types of natural selection. They include (1) directional selection, (2) stabilizing selection, (3) balancing or diversifying selection, and (4) sexual selection.

Directional selection favors changes in traits that help a species adapt to its environment. Lizards called *anoles* provide an example of directional selection. These lizards live on many Caribbean islands. In the late 1900's, scientists moved populations of one anole species from their native habitat to several uninhabited islands. Some of these islands had little vegetation, and the lizards had to perch on twigs and small branches. Other islands had large trees. After just 10 to 14 years, the anoles on islands without large trees had evolved smaller hindlimbs, which gave them needed agility on their small perches. The anoles on islands with large trees developed longer hindlimbs, giving them the speed they needed to catch prey and avoid predators in their new habitat. These changes showed that anoles with shorter-than-average hindlimbs had left more offspring than average on islands without large trees. At the same time, anoles with larger-than-average hindlimbs had left more offspring than average on forested islands. Such natural selection helps species adapt to new environments by favoring more extreme traits. Over time, continued mutation and directional selection can produce species that differ significantly from their ancestors.

Stabilizing selection occurs if a species is already well adapted to its environment. In such cases, the individuals with average characteristics leave the most offspring, and individuals that differ most from the average leave fewest. One example of stabilizing selection is the survival rate of human babies according to birth weight. Babies of average weight tend to survive better than those who are either heavier or lighter. Unlike directional selection, stabilizing selection eliminates extreme traits.

Balancing or diversifying selection occurs when natural selection maintains two or more alternative traits in the population. The gene that causes *sickle cell anemia,* a blood disease, provides an example of balancing selection. An individual who inherits the sickle cell gene from both parents may develop fatal anemia. But people who inherit the gene from only one parent do not get anemia and become more resistant to malaria, a common tropical disease. Thus, in areas threatened by malaria, the beneficial effects provided by a single copy of the sickle cell gene balance the harmful effects of inheriting two copies of the gene. Because of this balance, natural selection maintains the sickle cell gene in the population, along with the traits of both anemia and malaria resistance.

Sexual selection occurs primarily among animals. Adults of many species prefer mates who display certain behaviors or have certain external features. Over time, this process can lead to the evolution of complicated courtship rituals, bright coloring to attract mates, and other features. Sexual selection explains, for example, why males of many bird species have more-colorful feathers than do the females.

Genetic drift is a random change in the frequencies of genes in populations. It is caused by the random way that egg and sperm cells receive some chromosomes from each parent as they form. Because these reproductive cells contain only half a set of chromosomes, only half of a parent's genes exist in an egg or sperm. If the parents produce a limited number of offspring, some of their genes may not be passed on. Genetic drift alone does not enable species to adapt to their environment. But just as random mutations may lead to evolutionary change, so may the changes caused by genetic drift.

In small populations, genetic drift can bring about large evolutionary changes. For example, in Lancaster County, Pennsylvania, members of the Protestant Old Order Amish group have a high occurrence of Ellis-Van Creveld syndrome, a rare inherited disorder that causes people to become *dwarfs* (unusually small adults) with malformed hearts. These people are descendants of about 200 immigrants from Europe in the 1700's. A few of the immigrants probably carried the harmful trait. Biologists attribute the high frequency of this syndrome to genetic drift in the founding Amish population.

Evolution of new species

A *species* is a group of organisms that has become a *distinct evolutionary lineage*—that is, its members share critical adaptations required for successful reproduction. Various devices in nature maintain the distinct evolutionary lineages of species. In species that reproduce sexually, *reproductive isolating factors* play major roles. They include factors that prevent different species living in the same area from mating. For example, many species of birds have unique courtship rituals, and females

The evolution of mammals from early synapsids

WORLD BOOK illustrations by Oxford Illustrators Limited, adapted from illustrations by James A. Hopson and Claire Vanderslice

The fossil record helps scientists learn about the evolution of mammals from early synapsids. These illustrations, which are based on a number of fossils, show changes in the skull structure of synapsids. The jaws of early synapsids, such as *Dimetrodon,* had seven bones. The dentary bone, shaded red, became larger in intermediate synapsids and evolved into the single-boned jaw of mammals. Intermediate synapsids also evolved different types of teeth, such as molars and canines. These changes were accompanied by the development of larger, stronger jaw muscles, suggesting that these animals could chew food more thoroughly than early synapsids. This chewing ability is characteristic of mammals.

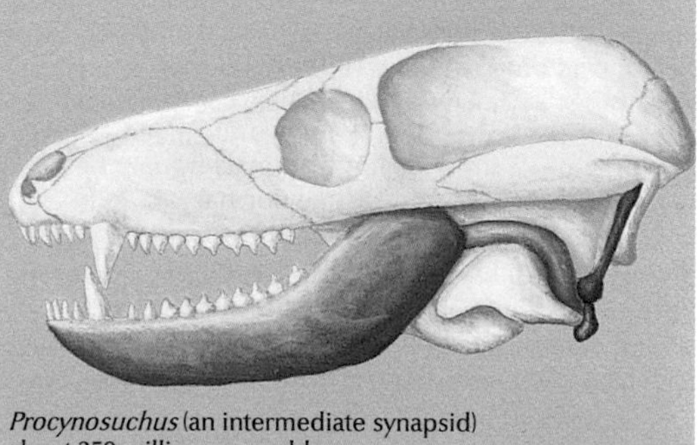

Procynosuchus (an intermediate synapsid) about 250 million years old

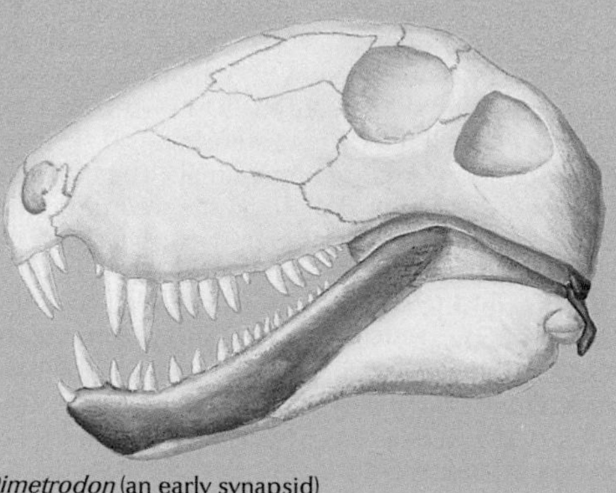

Dimetrodon (an early synapsid) about 280 million years old

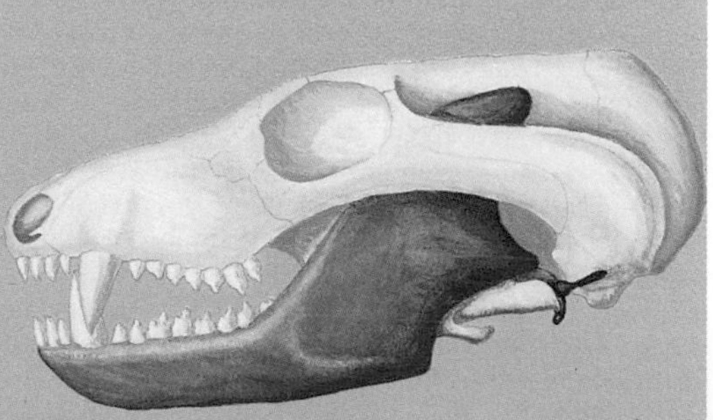

Probainognathus (a late synapsid) about 235 million years old

of one species will not respond to the male courtship of other species. If mating does occur between species, such matings may produce offspring that cannot survive or reproduce. A mule, for example, is the offspring of a female horse and a male donkey, and it is sterile.

Many species remain distinct even though they can interbreed and produce fertile offspring. In northwestern California, the Western sword fern has adapted to moist, shady habitats, while the narrowleaf sword fern has adapted to sites with drier soil and higher levels of light. Ferns reproduce by means of tiny cells called *spores,* which can blow in the wind for long distances. These California sword fern species live close enough to each other to interbreed and produce hybrids. Although the hybrids are fertile, they do not successfully reproduce in the Western sword fern's habitat or in the narrowleaf sword fern's habitat. Thus, natural selection favors keeping only one type of fern in each habitat, preserving the distinctiveness of each species.

Many biologists believe *speciation,* or the evolution of a new species, often begins when a species is separated into two or more geographically isolated groups. The geographic isolation of land species may result from the movement of continents over millions of years or from the division of habitats by glaciers, rivers, and other features. The rise of land bridges, such as the Isthmus of Panama, may separate marine species.

Over time, isolated populations evolve in different ways because their environments differ and because genetic drift and different mutations occur in each population. If geographic isolation lasts long enough, the populations may grow so dissimilar that each becomes adapted to a completely different environment, or the populations develop reproductive isolating factors and lose the ability to breed with each other. In either case, the populations have thus become distinct species.

Speciation sometimes takes millions of years, but it often occurs more rapidly. Rapid speciation is especially likely after a species settles in a new habitat, such as an unpopulated island. The founding population often experiences genetic drift and becomes subject to strong new forces of natural selection, such as a different climate or food supply. Occasionally, a major increase in the number of chromosomes, called *polyploidy,* can give rise to a new species. One form of polyploidy called *allopolyploidy* commonly occurs in plants and can give rise to new species within two generations.

Evidence of evolution

Evidence of evolution comes from observations of sources that document or indicate the occurrence of evolution. These sources include the fossil record, the geographic distribution of species, embryology, vestigial organs, and comparative anatomy. Evidence of evolution also comes from directly observing evolving populations and from artificial selection.

The fossil record provides some of the strongest evidence of evolution. Most organisms preserved as fossils were buried under layers of mud or sand that later turned into rock. Scientists determine the age of fossils by means of *potassium-argon dating, uranium-series dating,* and other dating methods. In such methods, researchers estimate how old the fossils are by measuring the amounts of certain *radioactive isotopes* (unstable forms of chemical elements) that they contain.

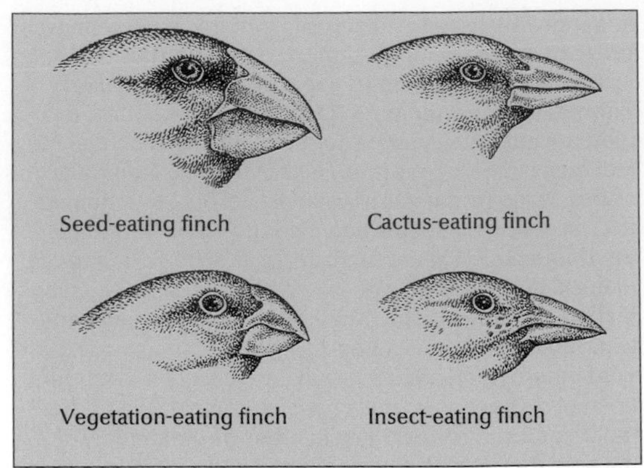

WORLD BOOK illustrations by Patricia J. Wynne; adapted from *Darwin's Finches* by David Lack, used with permission of Cambridge University Press

Specialized adaptations in finches on the Galapagos Islands resulted from competition for limited food. Different groups of finches developed beaks adapted to various kinds of food. After many generations, these groups evolved into separate species.

The fossil record has many gaps because relatively few species were preserved. Nevertheless, *paleontologists* (scientists who study prehistoric life) have found enough fossils to form a fairly complete record that documents much of the history of life on Earth.

The fossil record shows a progression from the earliest types of one-celled life to the first simple, multicelled organisms, and from these organisms to the many simple and complex organisms living today. Fossils found in ancient layers of rock include the simplest forms of life. They differ greatly from many organisms that exist today. Fossils in recently formed layers of rock include complex as well as simple forms of life and are more similar to living plants and animals. Thus, the fossil record shows that many species became extinct, and that the species alive today have not always lived on Earth.

The fossil record also documents many examples of continuous evolutionary change and speciation. A famous example is the evolution of mammals from early *synapsids.* Certain synapsids were the ancestors of mammals, and they had some mammalian characteristics. However, in other respects they somewhat resembled reptiles. Synapsids first appeared about 300 million years ago, but the first mammals did not appear until about 200 million years ago. Between these two periods, scientists have found many remains of *transitional forms,* animals with characteristics of both mammals and early synapsids. The skeletons of the first synapsids show few mammalian characteristics. Later synapsid skeletons are nearly identical to those of mammals. The transition from early synapsids to mammals is so gradual that scientists cannot fix an exact point when synapsids gave rise to true mammals.

Geographic distribution of species, also known as *biogeography,* provides important evidence for the theory of evolution. Certain island groups, called *oceanic islands,* arose from the sea floor and have never been connected to continents. The species found on oceanic islands are those that can travel easily, particularly over large stretches of water. These islands are rich in flying insects, bats, birds, and certain types of plants that floated to the islands as seeds. But oceanic islands lack many major types of animals and plants that live on continents. For example, the Galapagos Islands have no native amphibians or land mammals. These animals cannot easily migrate from continents to islands.

In addition, the majority of species found on oceanic islands are most similar to those on the nearest mainland, even if the environment and climate are different. The Galapagos Islands, for instance, lie off the coast of mainland Ecuador in South America. The islands are much drier and rockier than the coast, which has a humid climate and lush tropical forests. But the plants and birds on the Galapagos Islands more closely resemble those of the wet, tropical coast than they do the plants and birds of other arid islands. This suggests that the first species to inhabit the Galapagos Islands came from South America rather than originating on the islands.

Oceanic islands contain a far smaller variety of species than do continents, and some island species are found nowhere else. The Galapagos Islands, for example, have 21 native species of land birds. Of these, 13 species are finches—a much higher proportion of finches than exists on any continent. The finches developed as different species partially because they ate different foods. They thus evolved specialized beaks and other adaptations for their different eating habits. These finch species live only on the Galapagos Islands. Therefore, the distribution of species supports the idea that a limited number of species came to the islands from the nearest mainland and then evolved into new species.

Embryology is the study of the way organisms develop during the earliest stages of life. The embryonic development of many organisms includes peculiar events that can be explained by the evolution of the organism from another species. For example, a mammal embryo forms three different pairs of kidneys in succession during its development. The first two pairs of kidneys perform no function and break down and disappear shortly after they form. The third kidney pair then takes shape and develops into the mature, functioning kidneys of the mammal. In an embryo of a fish, amphibian, or reptile, however, one of the first two types of kidney pairs becomes the animal's mature kidneys. These events suggest that mammals have retained some developmental features of their evolutionary ancestors. Scientists call this phenomenon *recapitulation.*

Vestigial organs are the useless remains of organs that were once useful in an evolutionary ancestor. For example, many species of animals that live in caves are blind but still have eyes. Some species have nearly complete eyes but lack an optic nerve, while others have tiny, malformed eyes. Some cave-dwelling crayfish have eyestalks but no eyes. They evolved from ancestors with functioning eyes. Because eyes are useless in a dark habitat, and may indeed be harmful if they are injured, mutations that damaged the vision of these species did not decrease their fitness. Thus these species lost their sight over time.

Comparative anatomy is the comparison of anatomical structures in different organisms. Such comparisons often indicate how evolution occurred. For example, the forelimbs of amphibians, reptiles, birds, and mammals all have a similar bone structure. This similarity suggests that these animals evolved from a common ancestor.

Direct observation of evolution is commonplace because much evolutionary change occurs rapidly. Scientists have observed both *anagenesis* (evolution within species over time) and speciation.

An important example of observed anagenesis involves the virus HIV-1. The virus gradually weakens the immune system in most infected individuals, eventually leading to AIDS, the final, life-threatening stage of HIV infection. The virus uses a protein to bind to human proteins and infect human cells. Two major types of the protein exist, called the *nonsyncytium inducing* (NSI) form and the *syncytium inducing* (SI) form. The SI form, which is more lethal to the cells it infects, can evolve from the NSI form through two simple mutations. Almost all new HIV-1 infections start with the NSI form, which is better adapted to healthy human immune systems. As the virus gradually weakens the patient's immune system, however, natural selection favors the SI form. Once the SI form has become common in an infected patient, the person usually dies from an illness that takes advantage of the body's weakened immune system. This frightening example of anagenetic change has occurred millions of times in AIDS patients.

Scientists have also directly observed speciation in

New species may evolve rapidly. The anomalous sunflower, *far right,* probably developed from a cross of the common sunflower, *below left,* and the prairie sunflower, *below right,* after only a few generations. An anomalous sunflower shares traits of both ancestral species. For example, the leaf bracts under its petals have the longer shape of the prairie sunflower's bracts and the hairiness of the common sunflower's.

David R. Frazier Photolibrary

Artificial selection has caused dramatic changes in species. Plant breeders used artificial selection to produce broccoli, cabbage, cauliflower, and kohlrabi, *shown,* from a single species.

the laboratory. One important study involved the anomalous sunflower, which grows in the southwestern United States. Researchers found that this species evolved from hybrids of two other sunflower species, the common sunflower and the prairie sunflower, after only a few generations. By crossbreeding the common and prairie sunflowers in the laboratory, researchers produced, on several different attempts, hybrid species genetically similar to the anomalous sunflower.

Artificial selection. Animal and plant breeders use a method similar to natural selection to produce new varieties. Breeders commonly breed only the individuals in a species that show desired characteristics. This process, called *artificial selection,* eventually leads to large changes in a species. For example, the various breeds of dogs differ widely in size, appearance, and behavior. They probably descended, however, from one dog species and were bred to develop various traits. Many of these traits helped the dog perform a specific job, such as hunting badgers or herding sheep.

Plant breeders developed most food crops from wild ancestors by the same process. For example, cabbage, broccoli, kohlrabi, cauliflower, and Brussels sprouts all belong to a single species that was selectively bred to evolve different characteristics.

Artificial selection differs from natural selection only because human beings—instead of the natural environment—determine which characteristics give individuals an advantage in reproduction. The ability of artificial selection to cause dramatic changes in a short time leaves little doubt that natural selection could cause larger changes over the vast spans of earth's history.

History of the theory of evolution

Early theories. Two French naturalists, Comte de Buffon and Baron Cuvier, conducted some of the first scientific investigations of evolution in the 1700's. They concluded from their studies of fossils and living animals that life on earth had undergone a series of changes. But neither Buffon nor Cuvier had any idea how long ago these changes had occurred.

In 1809, the French naturalist Chevalier de Lamarck formulated the first comprehensive theory of evolution. He observed that an animal's body parts could change during its lifetime, depending on the extent to which it used them. Organs and muscles that were often used became larger and stronger, but those that were rarely used tended to shrink. According to Lamarck, such acquired traits became hereditary. His theory of the inheritance of acquired characteristics influenced many scientists. Later discoveries in genetics disproved his theory.

Darwin's theory. In 1858, Charles R. Darwin introduced a theory of evolution that, in modified form, is accepted by almost every scientist today. It states that all species evolved from a few common ancestors by means of natural selection. Darwin further elaborated the theory in his book, *The Origin of Species* (1859), which became a best-seller. Alfred R. Wallace, another British naturalist, devised an identical theory that was introduced along with Darwin's. However, Darwin developed his theory much more thoroughly, and his work has become better known. The British zoologist Thomas Henry Huxley and others helped advance Darwin's work.

Darwin used three principal sources in developing his theory. These were (1) his personal observations, (2) the geological theory of the British scientist Sir Charles Lyell, and (3) the population theory of the British economist Thomas Robert Malthus. Darwin made many of his observations as a member of a scientific expedition aboard the H.M.S. *Beagle* from 1831 to 1836. The ship made stops along the coast of South America, and Darwin collected many specimens of plants and animals and wrote detailed notes.

Darwin was particularly impressed by the variety of species on the Galapagos Islands. He found striking differences not only between species on the islands and those on the mainland, but also among those on each island. Darwin's findings led him to reject the idea that all living things were created as they currently existed. He then searched for another explanation for the origin of species.

The theories of Lyell and Malthus influenced Darwin's ideas about the earth's history and the relationship between living things and their environment. Lyell's *Principles of Geology,* published in the early 1830's, stated that the earth had been formed by natural processes over long periods. Darwin wondered whether life on earth had also developed gradually as a result of natural processes. In 1798, Malthus wrote that the growth of the human population would someday exceed the food supply unless checked by such factors as war and disease. Darwin assumed that environmental factors also regulated the population of all other living things. He concluded that only the individuals most fit in their environment would tend to survive and pass on their characteristics to their offspring.

The synthetic theory was formulated during the 1930's and 1940's by a number of scientists, including four American biologists—Sewall Wright, George G. Simpson, Russian-born Theodosius Dobzhansky, and German-born Ernst W. Mayr—and two British geneticists, Ronald A. Fisher and J. B. S. Haldane. Their theory *synthesizes* (combines) Darwin's theory of natural selection with the principles of genetics and other sciences. Darwin had observed that the characteristics of organisms may change during the process of being passed on to offspring. However, he could not explain how or why these changes took place because the principles of genetics were not yet known.

The genetic principles of variation and mutation filled this gap in Darwin's theory. Gregor Mendel, an Austrian monk, had discovered the principles of genetics in the 1860's. Mendel's findings remained unnoticed until the early 1900's, when the science of genetics was established. About 1910, the American biologist Thomas Hunt Morgan discovered that chromosomes carry genes. Morgan also described the process of recombination, in which chromosomes exchange genes among one another, producing new combinations of hereditary traits.

The creation of the synthetic theory did not lead to universal agreement on all details of evolution. For example, some scientists emphasized the importance of both genetic drift and natural selection in shaping adaptive evolution. But others felt that genetic drift did not play a meaningful role in adaptation. This and other controversies still exist within the synthetic theory.

Contributions from other scientific fields. Discoveries in other fields have enabled biologists to study evolutionary processes in far greater detail. Some of the major contributions have come from *molecular biology,* which deals with the genetic processes that underlie all evolution. In the 1940's, molecular biologists identified DNA as the substance in chromosomes that carries hereditary information. In the 1950's and 1960's, studies of DNA revealed much about its structure and its role in evolutionary changes. These studies have led scientists to believe that, at the molecular level, evolution occurs through changes in the DNA.

In the 1960's and 1970's, molecular biologists developed methods to determine partial sequences of DNA molecules. These genetic surveys revealed that virtually all species have much genetic variation in their *gene pools,* the genes collectively shared by the entire species or population. Scientists thus learned that genetic variation, the raw material of all evolutionary change, occurred in abundance.

At the same time, molecular biologists developed techniques to compare genes in different species. Such comparisons enabled biologists to determine the evolutionary histories of species more precisely. For example, zoologists did not know whether the giant panda was more closely related to raccoons or to bears. But DNA analysis has led scientists to classify giant pandas as bears.

In the 1990's, molecular biologists developed techniques for recovering small amounts of DNA from some fossils. These techniques have enabled scientists to directly examine prehistoric genes in the laboratory. Because of such advances, biologists can more accurately test their ideas about specific aspects of evolution. For example, scientists compared DNA from fossils of early human beings called Neandertals (also spelled Neanderthals) with modern human DNA. They found that, on average, the differences between Neandertal DNA and modern human DNA were considerably greater than the differences between the DNA of any two populations of modern human beings. Such research shows how closely all modern human beings are related to one another genetically.

Developmental biology, the science of how a fertilized egg develops into an individual organism, has also contributed to evolution. Starting in the 1990's, developmental biologists found that a common set of genes controls basic aspects of development in different plants and animals. These aspects include the formation of body segments in animals as diverse as worms and human beings. Such findings imply that the abovementioned genes were present long ago in the common ancestors of most species, and have remained unchanged even while being used to construct diverse body plans.

Finally, the area of *paleontology* (the study of the fossil record) continues to contribute to our knowledge of evolution. During the 1900's, paleontologists discovered fossils that indicated life on Earth was about 3 ½ billion years old, far older than previously believed. Paleontologists also used fossil evidence to show that Earth's evolutionary history included several mass extinctions. For example, many scholars now believe that a collision with an asteroid led to a mass extinction that killed off the dinosaurs. This major extinction enabled mammals to become the world's dominant large-bodied animals.

Acceptance of evolution

Today, the theory of evolution is considered the most important fundamental concept in the biological sciences. Nearly all scientists accept it. However, large numbers of people opposed the theory when it was introduced. Many people still do not accept it today.

In Darwin's time, the theory of evolution was attacked by many scientists, religious leaders, and other groups. Biologists argued that the evolutionary concept of hereditary variations within species contradicted the theory of blending inheritance. According to this theory, which was popular during the 1800's, hereditary characteristics became mixed and diluted as the blood carried them from one generation to another.

By the early 1900's, discoveries in genetics and other fields had resolved virtually all the original scientific objections to evolution. But other philosophical or religious objections remained. Some Christian leaders denounced the idea of evolution because it conflicted with their interpretation of the Biblical account of the Creation and suggested that human beings had evolved from apelike ancestors.

In the United States, much controversy centered on whether evolution should be taught in schools. In the 1920's, some states passed laws banning such teaching in public schools. In 1925, John T. Scopes, a Tennessee high-school teacher, was convicted in the famous "monkey trial" of teaching Darwin's theory (see **Scopes trial**). Scopes's conviction was later overturned because of a legal error, but few public schools included evolution in the biology curriculum for many years after the trial.

In 1968, the Supreme Court of the United States ruled that laws banning the teaching of evolution were unconstitutional. The ruling stated that such laws made religious considerations part of the curriculum and thus violated the First Amendment to the Constitution. During the 1970's and 1980's, many religious groups proposed legislation that would require evolution to be taught along with an opposing view called *creationism.* Creationists believe that each species has remained relatively unchanged since the Creation and that no species has evolved from any other. *Strict creationists* accept the Bible's account of the Creation as literal truth. They believe Earth is only thousands of years old. They also hold that all species were created simultaneously and that much of early life was destroyed by a global flood.

In 1981, Arkansas became the first state to enact a law requiring public schools to teach creationism whenever evolution is taught. However, a federal court declared this law unconstitutional before it went into effect. The court ruled that creationism constituted a religious and not a scientific explanation of life. Therefore, the court held that the Arkansas law violated the separation of church and state guaranteed by the First Amendment.

Because of these rulings, opponents of evolution have largely abandoned their efforts to obtain laws banning its teaching. But such opponents have turned their attentions toward influencing local school boards to reduce or eliminate the teaching of evolution in biology classes.

A number of people have tried to combine aspects of evolutionary theory and creationism. One of the most prominent such theories is the *intelligent design theory.* It states that Earth is in fact billions of years old, rejecting a literal interpretation of the Bible. But it also argues that an "intelligent designer," similar or equal to the Biblical God, must have played a role in the origin of life.

Many people—including some Christians, Muslims, and Orthodox Jews—still do not accept the theory of evolution because it conflicts with their religious beliefs. Many others, however, accept the basic principles of evolution within the framework of their religion. For example, some people interpret the story of the Creation as a symbolic and not a literal account of the origin of life. They find this symbolic interpretation compatible with evolutionary biology. For many, the idea that human beings evolved from other forms of life does not diminish the uniqueness of human capabilities and the achievements of human civilization. Alan R. Templeton

Related articles in *World Book* include:

Animal (The origin and development of animals)
Biogenesis
Creationism
Darwin, Charles R.
Evolutionary psychology
Fiske, John
Fossil
Genetics (Population genetics)
Gould, Stephen J.
Haeckel, Ernst H.
Hamilton, William Donald
Heredity (Heredity and natural selection)
Huxley, Thomas H.
Intelligent design
Lamarck, Chevalier de
Lyell, Sir Charles
Malthus, Thomas Robert
Mutation
Natural selection
Prehistoric animal
Prehistoric people
Races, Human (Evolutionary theory)
Spencer, Herbert
Teilhard de Chardin, Pierre
Wallace, Alfred R.
Weismann, August

Outline

I. Main ideas of evolutionary theory
II. Causes of evolutionary change
A. Mutation
B. Natural selection
C. Genetic drift
III. Evolution of new species
IV. Evidence of evolution
A. The fossil record
B. Geographic distribution of species
C. Embryology
D. Vestigial organs
E. Comparative anatomy
F. Direct observation of evolution
G. Artificial selection
V. History of the theory of evolution
A. Early theories
B. Darwin's theory
C. The synthetic theory
D. Contributions from other scientific fields
VI. Acceptance of evolution

Questions

What evidence of evolution do fossils provide?
What are reproductive isolating factors? How are they important to the evolution of new species?
How does natural selection affect the characteristics of species?
What are some of the forms of natural selection?
How does mutation introduce new inherited characteristics?
What is genetic drift?
What three main sources did Charles Darwin use in formulating his theory of evolution?
How have studies of DNA advanced the theory of evolution?
What is an example of a vestigial organ?
What is recapitulation?

Additional resources

Larson, Edward J. *Evolution: The Remarkable History of a Scientific Theory.* Modern Lib., 2004.
Mayr, Ernst. *What Evolution Is.* 2001. Reprint. Basic Bks., 2002.
Pagel, Mark D., ed. *Encyclopedia of Evolution.* 2 vols. Oxford, 2002.
Sloan, Christopher. *The Human Story: Our Evolution from Prehistoric Ancestors to Today.* National Geographic Soc., 2004. Younger readers.

Evolutionary psychology is the study of how evolution has shaped the way people think, feel, and act. For example, an evolutionary psychologist may wonder why people like sweet flavors. He or she might reason that the preference evolved because people who liked sweets would have been better fed, and more likely to survive, in a world where food was hard to get.

This simple example illustrates that preferences that were adaptive in the past are not always so today. Human beings evolved in a world where all food came from wild plants and game. Today, however, food is widely cultivated and generally abundant, and many people are overweight. The example also shows how biology and culture work together. For example, human babies must be taught what to eat. Their learning, however, is guided by innate flavor preferences that evolved over the course of human prehistory.

Evolutionary psychologists attempt to explain many aspects of human nature, some obvious, some not. For example, they examine why people are more likely to do favors for relatives than strangers, why men are more physically aggressive than women, why people are interested in gossip, and even why people fear snakes more than automobiles. Some aspects of human nature are desirable, such as being generous, while others, such as cheating and aggression, are not. The fact that some human behaviors are the result of evolution does not necessarily mean that they are desirable today. Evolutionary psychologists believe that people can work to change undesirable behaviors once they understand how they evolved. Elizabeth Cashdan

See also **Adaptation; Evolution; Natural selection; Psychology.**

Ewe. See **Sheep.**

Ewell, *YOO uhl,* **Richard Stoddert** (1817-1872), was a Confederate general in the American Civil War. He led a division under General Stonewall Jackson in the Shenandoah Valley campaign of 1862, distinguishing himself in battles at Winchester, Strasburg, and Cross Keys. Also in 1862, he aided Jackson in the defense of Richmond, Virginia, and fought in the Battle of the Seven Days. Ewell participated in the Battle of Cedar Mountain and in the

Second Bull Run campaign (also called Manassas).

At Groveton, Virginia, on Aug. 28, 1862, Ewell was wounded and lost a leg. Ewell returned to duty as a lieutenant general in May 1863, though he had to be lifted to his horse and strapped in the saddle.

Ewell then commanded the Second Corps, formerly led by Jackson. He took the corps through the Pennsylvania campaign and played a controversial role in the battle of Gettysburg, Pennsylvania, in July 1863. Several of Ewell's subordinates thought he should occupy Cemetery Ridge. Ewell, apparently taking literally General Robert E. Lee's orders to occupy Gettysburg, refused to seize Culp's Hill (near Cemetery Ridge) on the first day. As a result, Union troops took the hill and used it to anchor their line. Ewell finally tried to capture Culp's Hill but failed.

In 1864, Ewell led his corps in the battles of the Wilderness and Spotsylvania Court House. Later that year, he commanded the Richmond defenses. After Lee gave up the defense of Petersburg, Virginia, and Richmond in 1865, Ewell took charge of the remnant of a corps. That year, during the retreat toward Appomattox, Virginia, Ewell's corps was captured at Sayler's Creek, Virginia.

Ewell was born on Feb. 8, 1817, in Washington, D.C., of Virginia parents. He graduated from the United States Military Academy and fought in the Mexican War (1846-1848). Although Ewell favored the Union, he went with the South when Virginia withdrew from the United States in 1861. He died on Jan. 5, 1872.

Steven E. Woodworth

Ewing, Patrick (1962-), ranks among the leading centers in college and professional basketball history. He became known for his all-around game. Ewing played most of his professional career with the New York Knicks of the National Basketball Association (NBA). He holds the team's career records for scoring, rebounding, blocked shots, and steals.

Patrick Aloysius Ewing was born on Aug. 5, 1962, in Kingston, Jamaica. His family moved to the United States in 1975. He attended Georgetown University from 1981 to 1985, leading his team to the national collegiate championship in the 1983-1984 season. He was named collegiate Player of the Year in 1984-1985.

The Knicks selected Ewing as the first player taken in the 1985 NBA draft. He was the league's Rookie of the Year for 1985-1986. Ewing won gold medals in the Summer Olympic Games as a member of the United States basketball team in 1984, as a college player, and in 1992, as a professional. In 2000, Ewing was traded to the Seattle SuperSonics. Ewing joined the Orlando Magic in 2001.

Ewing retired as a player in 2002 and became an assistant coach with the Washington Wizards of the NBA. Ewing was an assistant coach with the Houston Rockets from 2003 to 2006. He joined the Orlando Magic as an assistant coach in 2007.

Ewing was elected to the Naismith Memorial Basketball Hall of Fame in 2008. Ewing's son, Patrick Ewing, Jr., played college basketball at Indiana University and Georgetown University. Neil Milbert

Ex parte Milligan, *ehks PAHR tee,* was a legal case in which the Supreme Court of the United States ruled that civilians cannot be tried by military courts if civil courts are available. The ruling, one of the most important in the history of American civil liberties, defined the limits of military power over civilians in wartime.

Bridgeman Art Library

A knight returns Excalibur, the legendary sword of King Arthur, to the mysterious Lady of the Lake upon Arthur's death. The story is shown here in a French illustration from the 1300's.

During the American Civil War (1861-1865), a military court in Indiana convicted Lambdin Milligan of cooperating with the Confederates. Milligan appealed to the Supreme Court to decide if he was being justly imprisoned. In 1866, the Supreme Court ruled unanimously that the military court, authorized by the president, was illegal because civil courts were open nearby. Milligan was freed from prison. The Supreme Court also ruled that if civil courts are open, not even Congress can create military courts to try civilians. Stanley I. Kutler

Ex post facto is a Latin term meaning *from what is done afterwards.* An *ex post facto* law is one that not only will make a particular act a crime from the time it is passed, but will also punish any person who has already committed the act. In many countries, legislators have had the power to pass such laws. Today, ex post facto laws are almost universally condemned. The Constitution of the United States and state constitutions prohibit such laws. Paul C. Giannelli

Excalibur, *ehk SKAL uh buhr,* was the sword of King Arthur, a legendary British ruler of medieval times. There are two versions of how Arthur got the sword. In one version, which probably originated in the French poet Robert de Boron's *Merlin* (about 1200), Excalibur was embedded in a block of stone or in an anvil. Only the rightful heir to the throne of England could pull it out. Only Arthur succeeded, proving his right to be king.

Another version of the legend is found in the *Suite du Merlin* (about 1230). In it, Arthur received the sword and its valuable scabbard, which protected the bearer from injury, from the mysterious Lady of the Lake. She lived in a castle at the bottom of a magic lake. Just before Arthur died, he commanded a knight to throw Excalibur into the lake. When the knight did so, a hand rose from the water and pulled it down. The two versions of the legend are combined in Sir Thomas Malory's *Morte Darthur* (1470). Edmund Reiss

Exchange rate is the price of one nation's currency expressed in terms of another country's currency. An

American who buys a product from a company in the United Kingdom might have to pay for it in British pounds. The American would exchange dollars for pounds at the current exchange rate. For example, if the rate were $1.25 to the pound, the American would pay $25 for a British sweater that cost 20 pounds. If Americans bought more British products, the demand for pounds would increase and the pound would rise in price against the dollar. Thus, if the pound rose to $1.50, the American would have to pay $30 for the sweater.

From the late 1800's to the early 1900's, most major trading nations had their own fixed exchange rates under a system called the *international gold standard.* The governments of nations on the gold standard guaranteed to redeem their currency for a specified amount of gold. In the early 1900's, for example, the dollar was valued at about 26 grains (1.7 grams) of gold, and the pound at about 126 grains (8.2 grams). The exchange rate of the pound was thus fixed at about $4.85.

Most nations abandoned the gold standard during the 1930's and adopted a system called *pegging* after World War II ended in 1945. Under this system, a government bought and sold enough U.S. dollars in exchange for its own money to keep the exchange rate steady. If the Japanese yen fell, the Japanese government used its reserves of U.S. dollars or other international money to buy yen. The resulting increase in demand for yen caused the price to climb again, keeping the exchange rate pegged at the desired level.

Since the early 1970's, the major trading countries have had *floating exchange rates.* With such rates, the price of a nation's currency rises and falls in relation to world demand for that currency. Actually, however, most governments intervene if the exchange rate for their currency rises or falls too far. For this reason, the system is often called *managed floating.*

People buy and sell foreign currency through banks and special brokerage firms. The current price of a currency is called the *spot rate.* Banks and brokers also buy and sell contracts for the future delivery of currency at a price called the *forward rate.* Robert M. Stern

Related articles in ***World Book*** include:

Balance of payments
Convertibility
Devaluation
Economics (The world economy)
Gold (Money)
Gold standard
Money (Money and international finance)

Excise is a tax on the manufacture, sale, or use of goods or services levied by local, state, or national governments. It is usually levied on one or a few products. But the taxed party usually adds the amount of the tax to the price of the goods or services, making the buyer the real taxpayer. Many cities and states place a general tax called a *sales tax* on the sale of all products (see **Sales tax**). Excise taxes also include fees paid for business licenses. Most excise tax revenue comes from the sale of tobacco, alcohol, and gasoline. Vito Tanzi

Exclamation point. See **Punctuation.**

Excommunication is the most severe penalty a religious body can impose on a member. It is used only for the most serious violations of the religion's rules. The penalty varies with the religion. In some religions, an excommunicated person is barred from any of the religion's ceremonies. A religion may also prohibit other members from associating with the excommunicated individual. The procedure for excommunication differs according to the religious body and the nature of the offense. Some excommunications take the form of a declaration by a congregation, minister, or bishop. Others result automatically when the individual breaks certain rules of the religion. For example, Roman Catholics are automatically excommunicated if they physically attack the pope or become a heretic. Jill Raitt

Excretion. See **Elimination.**

Execution, in civil law, see **Debt**. In criminal law, see **Capital punishment**.

Executive, *ehg ZEHK yuh tihv,* is the branch of government that enforces the laws. The United States Constitution divides the work of government into three parts, *legislative, executive,* and *judicial.* Congress has the duty of legislation, or passing laws; the courts have the duty of judging; and the United States president is the chief executive, who carries out the laws. The individual states divide the work of government in a similar way, with the governor as executive. In a monarchy, a king or queen today typically serves as a symbolic head of state. The true executive is usually a prime minister who serves as head of government. Kenneth Janda

See also **Cabinet; Governor general; President.**

Executive order, in United States law, is an official direction, proclamation, or statement issued by the president. Executive orders carry the force of law, even though they do not require congressional approval. The president's power to issue executive orders is an *implied power*—that is, it is not specifically mentioned in the Constitution. However, it is considered necessary for effective government. Although the term *executive order* is mainly used in the United States, leaders of many other constitutional democracies have similar powers.

President George Washington issued the first executive order in the United States in 1789. It instructed the heads of government departments to make a "clear account" of matters in their departments. One of the most famous executive orders was the Emancipation Proclamation, issued by Abraham Lincoln in 1863. It declared freedom for all slaves in the areas then under Confederate control. In 2001, President George W. Bush issued a series of executive orders aimed at eliminating terrorist organizations in the United States and abroad.

Executive orders can be controversial, because they allow the president to make policy changes while bypassing legislative processes set forth by the Constitution. Some executive orders have been challenged or overturned by Congress or in court. Michael A. Genovese

Executor, *ehg ZEHK yuh tuhr,* is a person who is named in a will to carry out the provisions of the will. Some people die without leaving a will, or without naming an executor if they do leave a will. In such cases, a probate court appoints an *administrator* in place of an executor. An administrator's duties are the same as those of an executor.

An executor's chief duty is to handle and dispose of the *estate* (money and other property left by the dead person). A probate court supervises the executor's handling of the estate. The executor must offer the will for *probate.* Probate is a court process in which probate court judges determine whether a will is legally valid.

The executor pays all taxes and claims against the estate. Then the executor pays the *legacies* (inheritances) provided for in the will.

Executors file a report on their management of an estate with the probate court. Executors may take the cost of their expenses and the fee for their services out of the money in the estate. They are paid at rates that are set by law. They usually make a money pledge called a *bond,* in which they agree to perform their duties honestly.

Any adult who is sound in mind and of good reputation may be an executor. Many executors are members of the family of the deceased person, and they often serve without compensation. Banks serve as the executors of numerous wills. The executor typically hires an attorney to assist in administering the deceased person's estate.

An individual may refuse to act as executor. But a person who accepts the job and later wishes to give it up must get a court's permission to do so.

William M. McGovern

See also **Administrator; Estate; Probate; Will.**

Exercise. See **Physical fitness.**

Exercise stress test. See **Stress test.**

Exile, *EHG zyl,* is banishment from one's own land. A person who has been punished by being exiled is called an *exile.* Exile was a common form of punishment for crimes and political offenses in ancient Palestine, Greece, and Rome. Civil wars often resulted in exile for leaders of the losing side.

In modern times, many countries have sent criminals and political offenders to distant parts of their realms. Thus, the United Kingdom sent convicts to the American Colonies and Australia to provide a source of labor to develop the new lands. In the mid-1900's in the Soviet Union, criminals and political offenders were sent in great numbers to work in Siberia. Most exiles of the present day are people who fled from their own countries because they were threatened by the tyrannical governments there. The Constitution of the United States prohibits the exile of a U.S. citizen. However, a noncitizen can be deported from the United States back to his or her country of origin.

The homesickness of the exile is a favorite theme of literature. In the Bible, Cain, sent to wander over the face of the earth, cries out that his punishment is more than he can bear. Anthony D'Amato

Existentialism, *EHG zihs TEHN shuh lihz uhm,* is a philosophical movement that developed in continental Europe in the 1800's and 1900's. It is called Existentialism because most of its members are primarily interested in the nature of *existence* or *being,* by which they usually mean *human existence.* Although the philosophers generally considered to be Existentialists often disagree with each other and sometimes even resent being classified together, they have been grouped together because they share many problems, interests, and ideas.

Existentialism grew out of the work of two thinkers of the 1800's: Søren Kierkegaard, a Danish philosopher and Protestant theologian, who is generally considered the movement's founder, and Friedrich Nietzsche, a German philosopher. Edmund Husserl, a German philosopher not usually considered an Existentialist but the founder of his own movement, *phenomenology,* was nevertheless one of the greatest influences on Existentialism.

The most prominent Existentialist thinkers of the 1900's include the French writers Albert Camus, Jean-Paul Sartre, and Gabriel Marcel; the German philosophers Karl Jaspers and Martin Heidegger; the Russian religious and political thinker Nicolas Berdyaev; and the Jewish philosopher Martin Buber.

What is Existentialism?

Existentialism is largely a revolt against traditional European philosophy, which reached its climax during the late 1700's and early 1800's in the impressive systems of the German philosophers Immanuel Kant and Georg Wilhelm Friedrich Hegel. Traditional philosophers tended to consider philosophy as a science. They tried to produce principles of knowledge that would be objective, universally true, and certain. The Existentialists reject the methods and ideals of science as being improper for philosophy. They argue that objective, universal, and certain knowledge is an unattainable ideal. They also believe this ideal has blinded philosophers to the basic features of human existence. The Existentialists do not make the traditional attempt to grasp the ultimate nature of the world in abstract systems of thought. Instead, they investigate what it is like to be an *individual* human being living in the world.

The Existentialists stress the fact that every individual, even the philosopher or scientist seeking absolute knowledge, is only a limited human being. Thus, every person must face important and difficult decisions with only limited knowledge and time in which to make these decisions.

For the Existentialists, this predicament lies at the heart of the human condition. They see human life as being a series of decisions that must be made with no way of knowing conclusively what the correct choices are. The individual must continually decide what is true and what is false; what is right and what is wrong; which beliefs to accept and which ones to reject; what to do and what not to do. Yet, there are no objective standards or rules to which a person can turn for answers to problems of choice because different standards supply conflicting advice. The individual therefore must decide which standards to accept and which ones to reject.

The Existentialists conclude, therefore, that human choice is *subjective,* because individuals finally must make their own choices without help from such external standards as laws, ethical rules, or traditions. Because individuals make their own choices, they are *free;* but because they freely choose, they are completely *responsible* for their choices. The Existentialists emphasize that freedom is necessarily accompanied by responsibility. Furthermore, since individuals are forced to choose for themselves, they have their freedom—and therefore their responsibility—thrust upon them. They are "condemned to be free."

For Existentialism, responsibility is the dark side of freedom. When individuals realize that they are completely responsible for their decisions, actions, and beliefs, they are overcome by *anxiety.* They try to escape from this anxiety by ignoring or denying their freedom and their responsibility. But because this amounts to ignoring or denying their actual situation, they succeed only in deceiving themselves. The Existentialists criticize this flight from freedom and responsibility into *self-*

deception. They insist that individuals must accept full responsibility for their behavior, no matter how difficult. If an individual is to live meaningfully and *authentically,* he or she must become fully aware of the true character of the human situation and bravely accept it.

The Existentialists believe that people learn about themselves best by examining the most extreme forms of human experience. They write about such topics as death and the shadow it casts on life; the difficulty, if not the impossibility, of maintaining satisfactory relationships with other people; the ultimate futility and absurdity of life; the terrifying possibility of suicide; the alienation of the individual from society, nature, and other individuals; and the inescapable presence of anxiety and dread. This concentration upon the most extreme and emotional aspects of experience contrasts sharply with the main emphasis of contemporary philosophy in England and the United States. This philosophy focuses upon more commonplace situations, and upon the nature of language rather than experience.

The influence of Existentialism

Several leading Existentialists have expressed their ideas in novels, poems, short stories, and plays. The Existentialists feel that philosophy should not be divorced from art. They believe philosophy is more like art and less like science than most other philosophers have believed. Moreover, the Existentialists have involved themselves in social and political disputes. They believe that it is the responsibility of all persons to *engage* in these disputes and *commit* themselves to a side.

Existential theologians do not try to base religion on rational demonstration. They argue that the problem of religious belief is not a problem involving proof or disproof, but a decision, which, like other human decisions, must be made separately by each individual in the absence of conclusive evidence. The Existentialist's interest in religion is primarily an interest in human religious experience. Ivan Soll

Related articles in *World Book* include:

Beauvoir, Simone de	Jaspers, Karl
Berdyaev, Nicolas	Kierkegaard, Søren A.
Camus, Albert	Nietzsche, Friedrich
Heidegger, Martin	Sartre, Jean-Paul

Exodus is the second book of the Bible. The preceding book, Genesis, introduces the story of the Israelite people. But the actual history of Israel as a nation begins in Exodus. The book presents the idea of a God who brings freedom to the downtrodden and forms a lasting relationship with them. Although God and the Israelites are central to Exodus, the Israelite leader Moses is the main character in the book. Moses serves as a link between God and Israel, and he dominates the events in the book.

The word *exodus* comes from an ancient Greek term that means *going out.* The book's first 19 chapters describe the Exodus, in which the Israelites departed from Egypt, where they had been slaves. The Israelites traveled to Mount Sinai and entered into a *covenant* (agreement) with God. At Mount Sinai, God gave Moses the Ten Commandments (20:2-17) and a set of laws known as the Book of the Covenant (20:22 through 23:33). The last section of the book (chapters 25-40) deals with the construction of the Tabernacle (sanctuary) built by Moses and the Israelites.

The narrative of the Exodus includes two hymns in verse, the Song of Moses (15:1-18), and the Song of Miriam (15:21). The songs may date back to the time of the historical Exodus event, which probably took place in the early 1200's B.C. Carol L. Meyers

See also **Bible; Moses; Tabernacle; Ten Commandments.**

Exorcism, *EHK sawr sihz uhm,* is the act of driving away the Devil or other evil spirits that possess, influence, or control a person. Exorcism is practiced throughout the world and presupposes the existence of evil forces in the lives of human beings.

Many cultures believe that evil spirits and the Devil can tempt a person to do something wrong, for example, tell a lie or commit a crime. They can even dominate an individual by temporarily taking control of the person's body.

When an evil spirit takes control of an individual or of an individual's actions, the person is said to be *possessed.* A possessed person may go into convulsions, acquire extraordinary strength, or shout curses—with no apparent explanation. Sometimes the evil spirit affects objects near the possessed person. For example, the evil spirit might cause objects to fly through the air. It also could take control of a room or of an entire building.

Possession is difficult to verify because the phenomenon could result from causes other than evil spirits. For example, a supposedly possessed person might really be suffering a mental or physical illness.

Some Christian denominations and other religions have ceremonies for driving out devils and evil spirits. The New Testament tells that Jesus Christ exorcised devils. Jesus also gave his apostles the power to drive out devils. In the Roman Catholic Church, an exorcism is a ceremony that consists of a series of prayers recited over the possessed person.

In many cultures, religious specialists, such as *shamans,* are skilled at exorcisms. The Roman Catholic Church allows some priests to perform exorcisms. The church's sacrament of baptism and the blessing of holy oil and holy water include prayers that ask God for protection from attacks by devils. Sarah M. Pike

Expansion is an increase in the size of a body without the addition of material to the body. Most substances expand when they are heated and contract when they are cooled. Gases naturally expand to fill their containers. But gases also expand when heated and contract when cooled. If a gas is heated in a container that prevents expansion, the pressure of the gas increases (see **Gas** [How gases behave; Gas laws]).

Expansion results from a change in energy. An object's temperature is related to its *internal energy.* This energy is contained within the vibrations of an object's atoms and molecules. Raising the temperature increases these vibrations. In a gas, raising the temperature also increases the speed at which the atoms or molecules move about. The increased movement forces the atoms or molecules farther apart, resulting in expansion.

Different materials expand by different amounts in response to the same increase in temperature. For example, aluminum expands twice as much as iron under the same temperature increase. D. Keith Hollingsworth

See also **Heat** (Changes in size).

Expansionism. See **Imperialism.**

Explorers throughout history have traveled for adventure and to learn about unknown parts of the world. In 1911, two teams of explorers raced across Antarctica to become the first to reach the South Pole. Roald Amundsen of Norway and his team were the first to that goal. In this tinted black-and-white photograph, Amundsen, *left,* uses a sextant to determine his precise position at the pole.

Exploration

Exploration is the act of people traveling to and investigating places unknown to them. People have explored the world since modern human beings—members of our own species, *Homo sapiens*—originated more than 100,000 years ago. But we have only a limited understanding of the earliest human exploration. Knowledge of human exploration improves after about 1500 B.C., when people began using written language to record their travels.

People undertook exploration for different purposes. Some explorers traveled for adventure or sought to learn more about an unknown part of the world. Others hoped to gain fame or wealth for themselves or to expand their country's trade or territory. Still others set out on expeditions to faraway lands for religious reasons.

In many cases, as explorers came upon places that were new to them, they encountered people who had been living in these areas for centuries. What was unknown to explorers was often well known to the people living there. For this reason, scholars use such terms as *exploration* and *discovery* carefully. These terms apply only to travelers and their observations of the regions they visit. When Europeans arrived in the Americas in the late 1400's, for example, they found both continents inhabited by Native Americans. Columbus's voyage to America was a discovery for the people of Europe. But it was not a discovery to the millions of people already living there.

Native peoples often understood their environments much better than explorers. They sometimes helped explorers by acting as interpreters and providing information about geography and sources of food and water. At other times, explorers ran into conflict with local people who resisted explorers' efforts to study them, use their labor, or colonize their lands.

The first explorers

Scholars believe that the earliest humans originated in southern and eastern Africa. These early people traveled far from their original homelands. They settled Africa and spread across Asia and Europe. During the last ice age, from about 100,000 to 11,500 years ago, sea levels were lower than they are today. Land joined some areas now separated by water. For example, New Guinea and Australia formed a single continent. As early as 50,000 years ago, prehistoric seafaring explorers sailed from Southeast Asia to colonize Australia. Somewhat later, people from northeast Asia entered Alaska. They trav-

Outline

I. The first explorers
II. Ancient exploration
A. The Phoenicians
B. The Greeks
C. The Chinese
D. The Romans
E. The Tuniit
III. Medieval exploration
A. Viking exploration
B. Muslim exploration
C. Chinese exploration
D. Inuit exploration
E. Medieval European exploration
IV. The age of European exploration
A. Reaching the tip of Africa
B. Columbus reaches America
C. The voyage around Africa
D. Exploring the New World
E. Magellan's globe-circling expedition
F. Spain's conquests in the New World
G. The search for a northern passage
V. Linking the globe
A. The French and English in North America
B. Crossing North America
C. The Russians in Siberia
D. Exploring the Pacific
E. Exploring Australia's interior
F. The exploration of Africa
G. Arctic exploration
H. The North Pole
I. The exploration of Antarctica
VI. The new frontiers
A. Deep-sea exploration
B. Space exploration

eled across a land bridge that connected North America and Asia. A waterway called the Bering Strait separates the two continents today. Asian explorers may also have traveled by boat along the coasts of Asia and North America. Scholars disagree on when humans first arrived in the Americas. But by 10,000 years ago, people inhabited nearly all parts of North and South America.

At least 3,000 years ago, the Lapita people from the islands of Southeast Asia set out on the first of many voyages on the Pacific Ocean. These seafarers sailed over long stretches of water in large double-hulled canoes. They lacked navigational instruments but used the stars for navigation. They eventually settled Fiji, Hawaii, New Zealand, Samoa, Tahiti, Tonga, and other Pacific Islands. A few scholars believe that these early sailors discovered new islands by accident. But many others think that these early Pacific seafarers planned their voyages of exploration and colonization.

Ancient exploration

Within the era of written history, ancient peoples in the Middle East and along the shores of the Mediterranean Sea explored parts of Europe, Africa, and Asia. In the 1400's B.C., Queen Hatshepsut *(hat SHEHP soot)* of Egypt sent an expedition by way of the Red Sea to the Land of Punt. The exact location of Punt is not known. It may have been in southwest Arabia or on the Somali coast of Africa.

Ancient and medieval exploration

The map at the right shows how much of the world's lands (yellow) and seas (blue) were known to Europeans by the A.D. 1300's. The enlargement below shows the routes of some ancient and medieval expeditions, beginning with the Egyptian exploration of the 1400's B.C.—one of the first ever recorded.

Egyptians 1400's B.C.
Phoenicians 1100's B.C.
Carthaginians 400's B.C.
Alexander the Great 334-323 B.C.
Pytheas 300's B.C.
Zhang Qian 128-126 B.C.
Vikings 800's - 1000's
Marco Polo 1271-1274
Ibn Batuta 1330-1332, 1352-1353
Zheng He 1431-1433

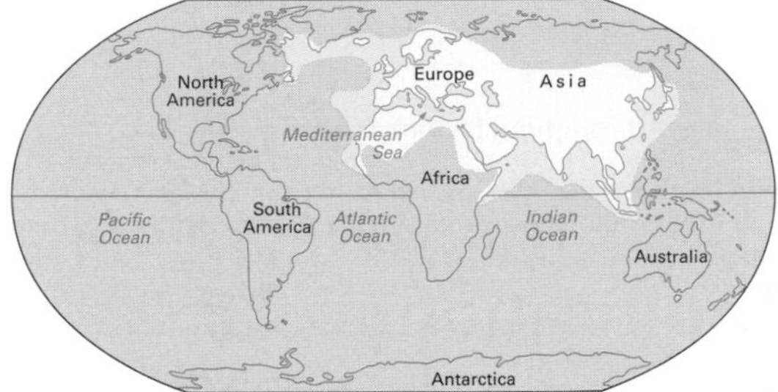

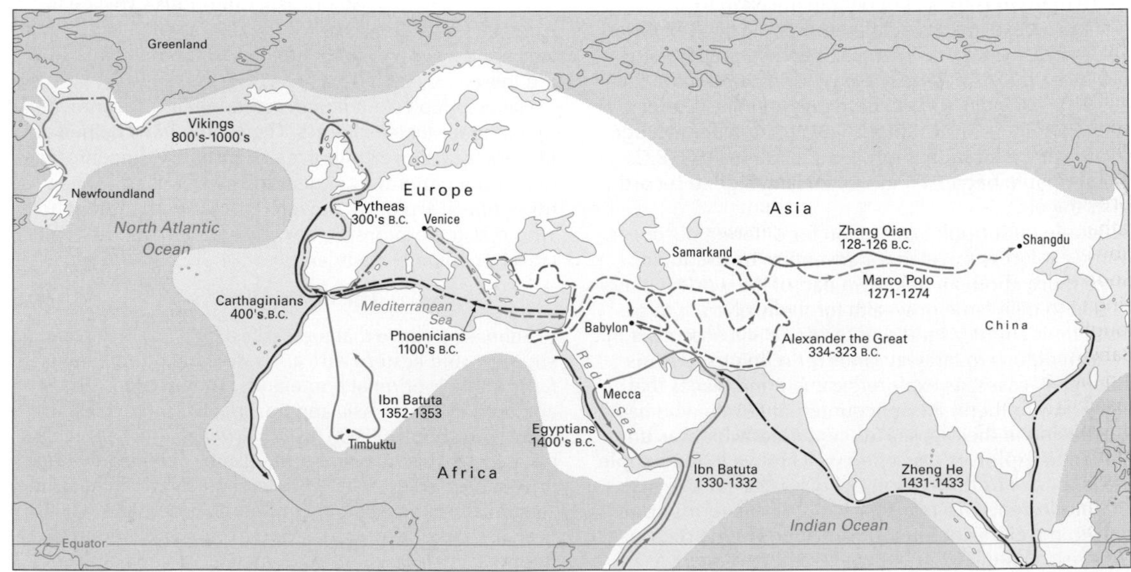

WORLD BOOK maps

© Craig Ellenwood, Alamy Images

The Lapita people explored the Pacific Ocean about 3,000 years ago. An ancient rock drawing from Hawaii, *shown here,* depicts one of their large seafaring canoes equipped with a sail.

The Phoenicians, whose civilization developed on the coast of the Mediterranean Sea, were sailors, navigators, and traders. They sailed far into the Mediterranean to trade and establish colonies. About 500 B.C., the Carthaginian statesman and navigator Hanno set out with 60 vessels. Hanno's expedition took him down the west coast of Africa. He traveled perhaps as far as Sierra Leone or the Gulf of Guinea.

The Greeks expanded geographical knowledge by founding colonies. There were Greek colonies in Turkey, Italy, and southern France, and along the coast of the Black Sea. The Greeks were also the first people to write about exploration and to describe the world as they knew it. Herodotus *(hih RAHD uh tuhs),* a Greek historian of the 400's B.C., included much geographical information in his books.

One of the most important Greek explorers was Pytheas *(PIHTH ee uhs).* During the 300's B.C., he sailed up the coasts of Spain and France and around the islands of Great Britain and Ireland. He then probably entered the North Sea. Pytheas mentioned a land called Thule *(THOO lee),* which may have been Norway. For many years, Mediterranean people considered Thule to be the farthest inhabited part of the world to the northwest.

Also in the 300's B.C., Alexander the Great launched a military campaign that greatly expanded the world known to the Greeks. Alexander was the son of King Philip II of Macedonia, a country north of Greece. Philip had defeated the Greeks and formed a union between Greece and Macedonia. After Alexander succeeded his father, he set out to expand Macedonian and Greek power. In 334 B.C., Alexander led his army into Turkey. Soon after, he defeated the Persian army. The young king then marched south to conquer Egypt. Next, he fought his way across western Asia. He conquered Babylonia, Persia, and much of Afghanistan. After crossing the Indus River in Pakistan, Alexander's soldiers refused to go any farther. He and his men then sailed down the Indus to the Indian Ocean. Alexander and part of his army returned to the Middle East by land. But Nearchus *(nee AHR kuhs),* one of his officers, sailed from the mouth of the Indus to the Persian Gulf.

The Chinese. An explorer named Zhang Qian *(jahng chee ehn),* also spelled Chang Ch'ien, carried out the most significant Chinese expeditions in ancient times. From 138 to 109 B.C., Zhang traveled in the service of the Emperor Wudi (Wu-ti). The emperor wished to develop diplomatic relations with people in western Asia. Zhang traveled as far as a river called the Amu Darya in Uzbekistan. Zhang's reports expanded Chinese ideas of the world. They also laid the foundation for later trade between China and the Roman Empire, especially in silk.

The Romans. The Roman Empire reached its greatest extent about A.D. 100. It stretched from Britain through much of Europe and the Middle East, and across Egypt and the rest of northern Africa. The Romans did not engage in much exploration. Through trade, however, they acquired information about areas beyond their empire, such as the east coast of Africa and the Indian Ocean. The writings of Ptolemy *(TAHL uh mee)* preserved much of what was known about the world in ancient times. Ptolemy was a geographer and astronomer who lived in Egypt during the 100's.

The Tuniit. In Northeast Asia, the Tuniit *(TOO neet)* people began a series of migrations across the Bering Strait into Arctic North America. *Tuniit* is the Inuit name for these people, who inhabited the Arctic before the Inuit arrived. Archaeologists refer to the Tuniit as the Dorset culture. The Tuniit hunted seals, walruses, and narwhals. They spread across Canada to Greenland by about 500 B.C. By about 900 A.D., the Tuniit had settlements in Greenland, Baffin Island, and Labrador. But they disappeared soon after the Inuit arrived.

Medieval exploration

After the collapse of the western Roman Empire in the late 400's, Europe was divided into small kingdoms and other states. For about the next 600 to 800 years, most Europeans had neither the means nor the desire to engage in exploration.

© Chris Hellier, Alamy Images

Zheng He was the most famous medieval explorer in Chinese history. He commanded seven naval expeditions from 1405 to 1433, exploring lands along the coasts of Asia and Africa.

The period of history from about the A.D. 400's through the 1400's is called the Middle Ages. During this period, Muslims—that is, followers of the religion of Islam—established a huge empire. The Islamic Empire eventually extended throughout the Middle East and across northern Africa. Many Muslims became expert navigators. Muslim merchant ships with *lateen* (triangular) sails ranged throughout the Indian Ocean, going as far as eastern Africa and Southeast Asia.

By about the 1200's, the Chinese and Europeans had a renewed interest in exploration. By that time, explorers could find their direction more easily because of the development of the magnetic compass. Some scholars believe that the Chinese were the first to use the compass for navigation about 1100. Muslims and northern Europeans quickly adopted the device. Other scholars believe that Muslims and northern Europeans independently developed the compass for ship navigation.

Viking exploration. The most important European explorers during the Middle Ages were the Vikings, also called the Norse. The Vikings originally came from Scandinavia. About 800, they settled the Shetlands, the Faroes, and other islands in the North Atlantic Ocean. About 860, a storm drove a Viking ship to a large island that was later named Iceland. The Norse began to settle Iceland about 870, and it became the base for later voyages. About 900, Gunnbjörn Ulfsson *(GOON byawrn OOLF suhn)*, a Viking leader, sighted Greenland. About 982, Erik the Red began exploring the coast of this huge island. Erik and other Vikings later established colonies there. About 986, another Viking leader, Bjarni Herjolfsson *(BYAHR nee hehr YOHLF suhn)*, was driven off course while sailing from Iceland to Greenland. Herjolfsson sighted a coastline to the west—probably North America—but he did not land there. Instead, he went on to Greenland.

About 1000, Leif Eriksson led an exploring party to the land Herjolfsson had sighted. Leif was the son of Erik the Red. Leif set up a base at a place he called Vinland. Most experts believe that Vinland was the Canadian island of Newfoundland. The Vikings made several other voyages to Vinland and established a colony there. But conflicts with the native peoples and other problems led the Vikings to abandon the colony about 1014.

Muslim exploration. Muslims studied the writings of ancient authorities and produced outstanding geographies and maps. During the 1100's, for example, al-Idrīsī *(uhl ih DREE see)* traveled widely through the Middle East. After moving to the court of King Roger II of Sicily, al-Idrīsī prepared an important geographical treatise, often called *The Book of Roger*. Completed in 1154, it surveyed all the countries of the world known to Europeans and Muslims of that time. The most celebrated Muslim explorer was Ibn Battūta *(IHB uhn bat TOO tah)*, who was born in Morocco. From 1325 to 1354, he traveled as far as India and China. He also visited the Mali Empire in western Africa south of the Sahara. His account of his travels is often called *Rihla (Journey)*.

Chinese exploration. During the Middle Ages, Chinese explorers made long journeys throughout Asia and the Middle East. Until about the 1200's, most of these travels were religious *pilgrimages* (journeys to sacred places). For example, the Buddhist monk Xuanzang *(shyoo an zahng)* set out in 629 for India, the birthplace of Buddhism. Xuanzang, often spelled Hsuan-tsang, visited many Buddhist holy places over a 16-year period. He also gathered much information about the history and geography of the region. The largest Chinese expeditions took place during the early 1400's. From 1405 to 1433, Zheng He *(juhng huh)* commanded seven expeditions, each involving more than 100 wooden ships. Zheng, also spelled Cheng, sailed from the East China Sea to the Indian Ocean and to the east African coast.

Granger Collection

The astrolabe was one of the most important navigational instruments on voyages of discovery. The astrolabe, along with the quadrant, enabled sailors to determine latitude more accurately.

Inuit exploration. By 1000, the Inuit of northeastern Asia began to migrate into Arctic North America. They gradually displaced the Tuniit people, who had originally inhabited the region. The Inuit established settlements across the Arctic, from Alaska to eastern Greenland and south to Labrador and Hudson Bay. Although the Inuit did not record their travels in writing, they passed down stories of their travels through generations. They used wooden carvings as maps of the coastlines they visited. The Inuit developed technology, such as sleds, kayaks, and igloos, that was well-suited for Arctic travel. In the 1800's and 1900's, non-Inuit explorers of the Arctic adopted most of these technologies.

Medieval European exploration. During the mid-1200's, Europeans came into more direct contact with central and eastern Asia than ever before. At that time, the Mongols ruled most of Asia. European leaders hoped to convert the Mongols to Christianity and persuade them to become allies against the Muslims in the Middle East and northern Africa. In the 1240's and 1250's, several Franciscan friars, including John of Plano Carpini and William of Rubruck, visited the *khan* (Mongol leader) at Karakorum in Mongolia. The friars failed to convert the khan to Christianity, but they brought back much information about eastern Asia.

The most famous European traveler in Asia in the 1200's was Marco Polo, a native of Venice. In 1271, when Marco was 17, he accompanied his father and his uncle to China. The two older men were merchants who had visited China in the 1260's. Kublai Khan, the Mongol emperor of China, treated them well. Marco made such a favorable impression on Kublai Khan that the Mongol ruler sent him on official missions throughout the kingdom. After returning to Venice in 1295, the Genoese took Marco prisoner during a conflict between Venice and Genoa. While in captivity, he dictated an account of his travels. His book, called *Description of the World* (1298), became widely popular. It was the first to provide Europeans with detailed and accurate information about China's impressive civilization.

The age of European exploration

By the 1400's, many Europeans wanted to buy products from Asia. The most desired products included jewels, silk, and such spices as cinnamon, cloves, and pepper.

Turkish Muslims controlled much of the main overland route between Europe and Asia. Muslims also controlled the sea routes from Asia to the Middle East. The Italian city of Venice held a monopoly on trade in spices and eastern luxury goods between the Muslim ports and the rest of Europe. As a result, other Europeans became eager to bypass the old routes and find a direct ocean route to the eastern part of Asia. Europeans then called that region "the Indies." Europeans also hoped to make converts to Christianity and so strike a blow against the Muslims.

Portugal and Spain took the lead in seeking a direct ocean route to the Indies. By 1500, a new kind of ship known as the *caravel* made long voyages possible. The caravel combined square sails with the triangular lateen sails used by Muslims. The invention of new navigation instruments also aided exploration by sea. The most important devices were the *astrolabe* and *quadrant,* which enabled sailors to determine latitude more accurately. The expeditions of Portugal and Spain opened an active period of exploration. Their voyages of exploration eventually led to the European colonization of America.

Reaching the tip of Africa. During the early 1400's, Portuguese explorers concentrated their attention on the west coast of Africa. Prince Henry, a son of King John I of Portugal, became known as Henry the Navigator. He never went on a voyage of exploration himself. But he encouraged and sponsored many expeditions. Henry wanted to increase Portugal's trade along the African coast. He wished to discover the source of the gold that Muslim traders had carried north from central Africa for centuries. He also hoped to find the legendary Christian kingdom of Prester John. For hundreds of years, travelers had claimed that a man known as Prester John ruled a vast kingdom in Asia. Explorers traveling to Asia found

The age of European exploration

European knowledge of the world greatly expanded during the 1400's and 1500's, as shown by the yellow and blue areas on this map. European explorers of the time sailed around Africa to Asia and began to map the Americas.

WORLD BOOK map

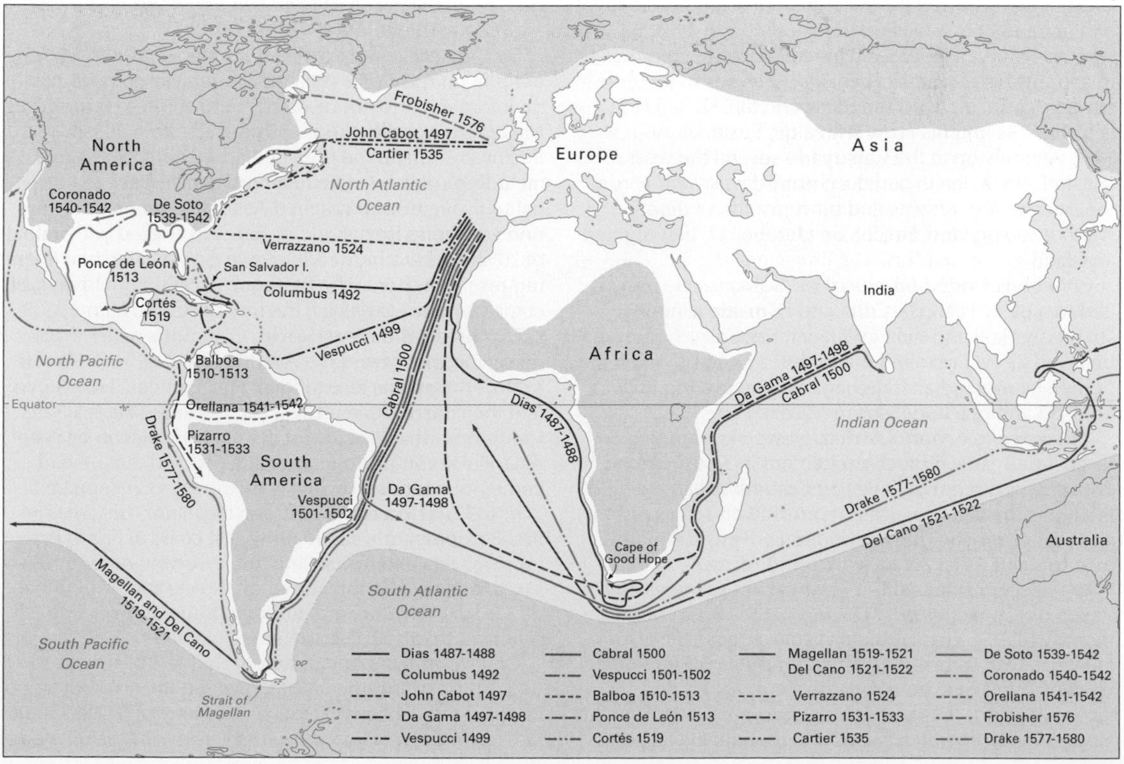

no evidence of this kingdom, so later reports placed his empire somewhere in Africa.

Henry's crews sailed farther and farther south along the African coast. By the time Henry died in 1460, they had traced the coast as far south as Sierra Leone. During these voyages, the Portuguese collected gold dust and African captives who were sold into slavery. After 1500, when the settlement of the Americas created a demand for slaves, other Europeans began to sail to the west African coast to join in the slave trade.

During the late 1400's, the Portuguese became increasingly hopeful of reaching the southern end of Africa. They believed that such a discovery would reveal a way of sailing to India. In 1487, the Portuguese explorer Bartolomeu Dias *(BAHR tul uh MEH oo DEE uhs)* set out to find a route around Africa. As Dias sailed along the continent's southwestern coast, a violent storm blew his ships south of the tip of the continent. He then turned east and sailed into the Indian Ocean in early 1488 without sighting the tip of Africa. After turning north again, Dias reached the east coast of Africa. His crew, however, then forced him to return to Portugal. On the return voyage, he saw a point of land jutting from the continent's southern tip. The Portuguese named it the Cape of Good Hope because its discovery indicated hope that a sea route to India had been found.

Columbus reaches America. As the Portuguese searched for an eastward sea route to Asia, Christopher Columbus looked west. Columbus, a sea captain from Genoa, Italy, developed a plan to reach Asia by sailing across the Atlantic Ocean. He was convinced that his plan would work. However, he underestimated the distance between western Europe and Japan—and he did not know that a large land mass lay in the way.

Columbus could not persuade the Portuguese to give him command of a westward expedition. In 1485, he went to Spain. He eventually persuaded Queen Isabella to support his plan. The Spanish queen gave him three small vessels: the *Niña,* the *Pinta,* and the *Santa María.*

Columbus and his crew left Palos, Spain, on Aug. 3, 1492. After a stop at the Canary Islands, off the west coast of Africa, the expedition headed westward across the Atlantic. The crew sailed for more than a month without seeing land. Finally, on October 12, they sighted an island.

Columbus landed on one of the Bahamas. He also visited two other islands—Cuba and Hispaniola (now shared by Haiti and the Dominican Republic). Columbus believed he had reached the Indies, and so he called the people he met Indians. He began his return trip in January 1493 and reached Palos in March.

The voyage around Africa. News of Columbus's discoveries caused much excitement in Spain. But the Portuguese did not believe that Columbus had reached the Indies because he did not return with spices or other Asian products. They remained convinced that the best route to Asia was to sail around Africa.

In 1497, King Manuel I of Portugal chose the navigator Vasco da Gama *(VAHSH koo duh GAHM uh)* to sail all the way to Asia. On July 8, da Gama set out from Lisbon, Portugal, with four ships. Instead of sailing close to the west African coast, he swung out into the Atlantic to find favorable winds. He rounded the Cape of Good Hope on November 22 and then sailed into the Indian Ocean. At Malindi, in Kenya, he found an experienced Arab pilot, Ahmad ibn Mājid *(AHM ahd IHB uhn MAH jihd),* who agreed to show the way to India.

Granger Collection

The caravel was used by Spanish and Portuguese sailors for ocean exploration and trade during the 1500's and 1600's. Caravels combined square sails with triangular *lateen* sails.

Da Gama reached Kozhikode on the southwest coast of India on May 20, 1498. Kozhikode's Hindu ruler had no interest in the goods da Gama brought to trade. The Muslim merchants there considered him a possible business rival. But he obtained some gems and spices, including pepper and cinnamon, to take back to Portugal to prove he had reached Asia. Da Gama made a second voyage to Kozhikode in 1502. He arrived with a fleet of 20 ships, bombarded the town, and established Portuguese rule there. The Portuguese called the town Calicut, a variation of Kalikat, the town's Arabic name.

Exploring the New World. Columbus made three more voyages across the Atlantic from 1493 to 1504. He explored Jamaica, Puerto Rico, and Trinidad. He also visited the coasts of Venezuela and Central America. Columbus always believed that he had been in or near Asia. However, people gradually realized that he had come upon lands previously unknown to Europeans.

In 1497, John Cabot, an Italian navigator, became the first European to visit the northeast coast of North America since the Vikings. Sailing in the service of King Henry VII of England, Cabot landed on the east coast of Canada. Cabot's voyage helped lay the foundation of English claims to North America.

Other explorers began to visit South America. In 1500, two explorers independently reached the area where Portugal would later establish its colony of Brazil. One of the explorers was Vicente Yáñez Pinzón *(bee THEHN tay*

YAH nyehth peen THAWN). Pinzón was a Spaniard who had commanded the *Niña* on Columbus's first voyage. Pinzón explored the mouth of the Amazon River. The other explorer to reach Brazil was Pedro Álvares Cabral *(PAY throo AHL vuh reesh kuh BRAHL),* a Portuguese captain. Cabral was sailing west in the Atlantic on his way to India.

Amerigo Vespucci *(uh MEHR uh goh veh SPOO chee),* a merchant and navigator born in Italy, also traveled to the Americas. He sailed along the eastern coast of South America from 1499 to 1502. He was the first person to refer to the lands he had visited as a "New World." In 1507, a German geographer placed a Latin version of Vespucci's first name—that is, America—on a map of the newly found southern continent. This name was later applied to North America as well.

In 1513, the Spanish explorer Vasco Núñez de Balboa *(VAHS koh NOO nyayth day bal BOH uh)* led an expedition across Panama. Balboa traveled from Panama's Atlantic coast to its Pacific coast. He became the first European to see the eastern shore of the Pacific Ocean. His finding helped prove that the New World was indeed a huge land mass between Europe and Asia.

Magellan's globe-circling expedition. Confirmation that America was a vast new continent came in 1517. In that year, Ferdinand Magellan *(muh JEHL uhn),* a Portuguese navigator, sailed to Asia by way of South America. King Charles I of Spain agreed to sponsor Magellan's expedition because the Portuguese now controlled the route to Asia around Africa. If Magellan succeeded, Spain would have its own route to Asia. At the time, Magellan did not know how large South America was.

Magellan sailed from Spain on Sept. 20, 1519, with five ships. After reaching the northeast coast of Brazil, he sailed southward. He arrived at Puerto San Julián, Argentina. He spent the winter there and farther south at Puerto Santa Cruz, Argentina.

Magellan set sail from Puerto Santa Cruz on Oct. 18, 1520. Three days later, the ships entered a passage now known as the Strait of Magellan at the southern tip of South America. On November 28, three of the five ships sailed out of the strait into the Pacific Ocean. One of the other two ships had been wrecked in a storm, and one had turned back to Spain.

In the Pacific, the explorers sailed for more than three months without sighting any land except two uninhabited islands. Food ran out, and the sailors ate oxhides and rats to stay alive. In March 1521, Magellan reached the island of Guam, where he was able to gather supplies. He then sailed to the Philippine Islands. There, he became involved in a conflict among the native people. Magellan was killed in a battle on April 27, 1521.

After Magellan's death, the expedition abandoned another ship. The remaining two vessels sailed to the Spice Islands (now part of Indonesia). One ship, the *Victoria,* then sailed west. Magellan's lieutenant, Juan Sebastián del Cano *(hwahn say BAHS TYAHN dehl KAHN oh),* commanded the ship. The *Victoria* crossed the Indian Ocean and sailed around the Cape of Good Hope. Badly damaged, the ship reached Spain on Sept. 6, 1522. It had completed the first trip around the world.

Spain's conquests in the New World. During the early 1500's, Spanish explorers pushed across most of Central and South America. They carried with them smallpox and other diseases that were unknown in the Americas. Native Americans had no resistance to these diseases. As a result, thousands sickened and died. The Spanish explorers established colonies in the new lands. Royal officials, Roman Catholic priests, and settlers arrived soon after the explorers. The Spaniards typically forced the Indians to work for them. The Spaniards brought sugar cane, wheat, and other new plants to the Americas. In addition, they introduced cattle, horses, sheep, and other domestic animals. They took back to Europe many plants that were unknown there, such as corn and potatoes.

Hernán Cortés *(kawr TEHZ)* commanded one of the most important Spanish expeditions in the New World. Cortés left Cuba in 1519 with more than 600 men. He sailed to the Mexican state of Yucatán, which was a center of Maya civilization. Cortés moved along the coast of Mexico and then inland to Tenochtitlan (now Mexico City), the capital of the Aztec Empire. Along the way, he met an Indian woman named Malinche, whom the Spaniards called Doña Marina. Malinche, who knew both the Maya and the Aztec languages, served as an interpreter for Cortés.

By 1521, Cortés had subdued the Aztec and taken control of their empire. Mexico then became a base for Spanish exploration of Central and North America.

Other Spanish expeditions explored and conquered much of South America. From 1527 to 1529, Sebastian Cabot, a son of John Cabot, explored the continent. He sailed up the Rio de la Plata and the Paraná and Paraguay rivers in Argentina and Paraguay. Cabot was looking for a "white king" who was supposedly rich in silver. Other explorers searched for a fabulous golden kingdom in South America, especially in Colombia and Venezuela. This kingdom was usually called El Dorado, which means "the gilded."

In 1532 and 1533, the Spanish explorer Francisco Pizarro *(frahn THEES koh pee THAHR roh)* conquered the Inca. From their home in Peru, the Inca ruled a huge empire. It included parts of Argentina, Bolivia, Chile, Colombia, and Ecuador. From 1535 to 1537, Diego de Almagro *(DYAY goh deh ahl MAHG roh),* a member of Pizarro's party, explored South America. He traveled through parts of Bolivia and Argentina and crossed the Andes Mountains into Chile. Francisco de Orellana *(frahn THEES koh day oh ray YAH nah),* another veteran of Pizarro's expedition, also explored the continent. In 1541 and 1542, he sailed from the Andes Mountains down the mighty Amazon River to its mouth on the Atlantic Ocean in Brazil.

During the 1500's, Spaniards explored much territory that became part of the United States. In 1513, Juan Ponce de León *(hwahn PAWN say day lay AWN)* sailed from Puerto Rico and landed on the east coast of Florida. He then sailed around the southern tip of Florida and into the Gulf of Mexico. He next explored the southwest coast of Florida before returning to Puerto Rico.

In 1539, Hernando de Soto *(dih SOH toh)* led an expedition of more than 600 people. De Soto sailed from Cuba to the west coast of Florida. In search of gold, he traveled through the southern United States, including Georgia, Alabama, Mississippi, and Arkansas. The explorers found no gold, but they became the first Europeans to reach the Mississippi River. After de Soto died of fever in 1542, the survivors sailed down the Mississippi. They eventually reached Mexico by way of the Gulf of Mexico.

In 1540, Francisco Vásquez de Coronado *(frahn THEES koh BAHS kayth day kawr uh NAHTH oh)* set out from Campostela near the west coast of Mexico. He hoped to find the legendary Seven Cities of Cíbola. These supposedly rich and flourishing cities were thought to lie north of Mexico City. Coronado traveled through Arizona, New Mexico, Texas, Oklahoma, and Kansas. He found no important cities. But Coronado's and de Soto's expeditions gave Europeans a good idea of the width of North America.

The search for a northern passage. During the 1500's, the known sea routes to Asia were long, and they were controlled by Spain and Portugal. As a result, other European nations tried to find alternate, shorter routes. Some explorers looked for a Northwest Passage—that is, a waterway that would allow ships to sail through or north of North America to reach Asia. Others looked for a Northeast Passage north of Europe. However, none of the explorers found a Northwest or Northeast passage. The search continued for centuries.

In 1524, King Francis I of France sent Giovanni da Verrazzano *(joh VAHN ee dah VEHR uh ZAH noh)* to North America to find a passage to Asia. Verrazzano, an Italian navigator, explored the east coast. He sailed from about Cape Fear in North Carolina to Newfoundland. But he did not find a passage.

Jacques Cartier *(zhahk kahr TYAY)*, a French explorer, also failed to find a passage on two voyages from 1534 to 1536. However, he became the first European to see the St. Lawrence River in Canada. His voyages helped establish French claims to the region.

Several English explorers searched unsuccessfully for a Northwest Passage in North America. From 1576 to 1578, Martin Frobisher made three voyages. He reached what is now called Frobisher Bay in northeastern Canada. In 1585, John Davis, another English navigator, discovered and explored Davis Strait between Greenland and Canada. He also found Cumberland Sound in northeastern Canada. English merchants sent three expeditions in search of a Northeast Passage from 1553 to 1580. However, these expeditions got only as far as the Kara Sea north of Russia before they turned back. Willem Barents *(WIHL uhm BAR uhnts)*, a Dutch navigator, looked for the Northeast Passage during the 1590's. He sailed farther north than any other European had in a recorded voyage. Barents explored Spitsbergen and other islands in the Arctic Ocean.

Linking the globe

By 1600, the Spanish had explored Central and South America and parts of North America. Spain had established numerous colonies there. Spain tried to claim all of North America. But the French and English set up their own colonies and explored much of the continent themselves. Meanwhile, Russians moved east to explore Siberia and Alaska.

During the European Enlightenment, a historical period from the late 1600's to the late 1700's, the goals of exploration began to change. Expeditions of the 1500's and 1600's focused on trade, religious missions, and colonization. By the 1700's and into the 1800's, exploration focused increasingly on science. However, European rulers did not support scientific expeditions simply to increase knowledge. Science offered the promise of more accurate maps, the discovery of new and valuable resources, and international prestige.

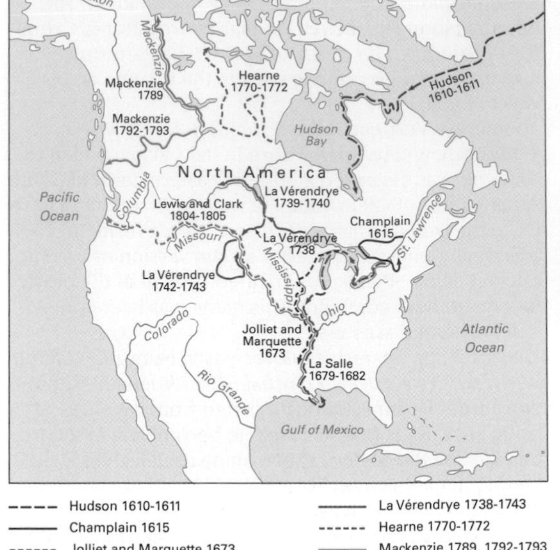

The exploration of North America by Europeans in the 1600's and 1700's revealed the continent's shape and much of the interior. American explorers pushed westward in the early 1800's.

European explorers gradually filled in the outlines of the areas unknown to them. They mapped the Pacific Ocean, worked their way through the interiors of Australia and Africa, and reached the Arctic and Antarctic. Finally, in the 1900's, they raced to reach the North and South poles.

The French and English in North America. During the 1600's, the French and English founded colonies in Canada and the United States. The French and English, like the Spanish before them, unknowingly introduced smallpox and other new diseases into the areas. As before, many Indians died from these diseases. The French and English also traded with the Indians for furs, such as beaver and fox. Traders learned much about the land from the Indians, who acted as interpreters and guides.

Samuel de Champlain *(sham PLAYN)*, a French explorer and geographer, charted the Atlantic coast. He mapped it from Cape Breton Island in Canada to Martha's Vineyard in Massachusetts. In 1608, he founded the city of Quebec as a fur-trading post. Over the next eight years, he traveled extensively and explored the rivers and lakes of the region. In 1609, Champlain became the first European to reach Lake Champlain, the lake in New York, Vermont, and Quebec that now bears his name.

The French also explored the Mississippi River. In 1673, Louis Jolliet *(lwee JOH lee eht)*, a fur trader, and

Jacques Marquette *(zhahk mahr KEHT),* a Roman Catholic priest, reached the river. Starting near Prairie du Chien, Wisconsin, they paddled canoes south to where the Mississippi meets the Arkansas River. In 1682, René-Robert Cavelier, Sieur de La Salle *(ruh NAY raw BEHR kah vehl YAY syoor duh luh SAL),* led an expedition down the Illinois River. He began near Peoria, Illinois, and traveled down the Mississippi to its mouth at the Gulf of Mexico. La Salle claimed the entire region drained by the Mississippi for France. He named it Louisiana in honor of King Louis XIV.

Colonists founded the first permanent English settlement in North America at Jamestown, Virginia, in 1607. By the end of 1670, English settlements existed in 12 of the 13 original colonies.

England also claimed much of eastern Canada. England based this claim in part on a voyage of the English navigator Henry Hudson. Hudson was looking for a Northwest Passage. In 1610, he sailed through a strait in northeastern Canada into a large body of water he thought was the Pacific Ocean. It was really the huge bay now known as Hudson Bay.

Crossing North America. During the 1700's, French and British explorers pushed westward across the northern parts of North America. They also discovered the northern limits of the continent.

In 1738 and 1739, the French-Canadian fur trader Pierre Gaultier de Varennes, Sieur de La Vérendrye *(pyehr goh TYAY duh vah REHN syoor duh lah vay rahn DREE)* and his sons explored Manitoba and North Dakota. In 1742 and 1743, two of the sons, Louis-Joseph and François, traveled as far as Montana and Wyoming.

From 1770 to 1772, the British explorer Samuel Hearne explored the land north of Churchill, Manitoba. Hearne went as far north as the Coppermine River, which flows into the Arctic Ocean.

Alexander Mackenzie, an agent of a fur-trading company called the North West Company, further explored northern North America. In 1789, he traveled north from the western tip of Lake Athabasca in Alberta to the mouth of the river now named after him. In 1792 and 1793, he journeyed from Lake Athabasca across the Rocky Mountains to the Pacific Ocean.

Two U.S. Army officers, Meriwether Lewis and William Clark, began an important expedition to the Pacific Northwest in 1804. In May of that year, they set out from St. Louis and traveled up the Missouri River. They spent the winter with Mandan Indians near Bismarck, North Dakota. There, they met Sacagawea *(sah KAH guh WEE uh),* a Shoshone woman who agreed to be their interpreter. The following spring, the expedition continued up the Missouri and crossed the Rockies. Once past the mountains, the explorers pushed to the Columbia River. They followed the river to the Pacific Ocean, reaching it in November 1805. Lewis and Clark returned to St. Louis in 1806. They brought back valuable information about the land, plant and animal life, and peoples they encountered on their journey.

Although their expedition was successful, it had little impact on Americans back home. Lewis and Clark's journals remained unpublished for many years, and the materials they collected became lost. Only in the 1900's did Americans rediscover and begin to appreciate the importance of this expedition.

The Russians in Siberia. The exploration of Siberia—the vast region in northern Asia between the Ural Mountains and the Pacific Ocean—began in 1581. That year, Yermak Timofeyevich *(yur MAHK tyihm uh FYAY uh vyich),* a Russian military leader, conquered the ruler of a territory called Sibir just east of the Ural Mountains. The name Siberia was then applied to the entire region.

During the early 1600's, Russians moved eastward across Siberia. They came upon Lake Baikal in 1643. By 1650, Russians had reached the Sea of Okhotsk in the northern Pacific and had rounded the Chukchi Peninsula in northeastern Asia. In the late 1690's, a Russian soldier named Vladimir V. Atlasov *(AT luh sawf)* conquered the peoples of the Kamchatka Peninsula on the Pacific coast of eastern Russia.

In 1728, Vitus Bering *(VEE tus BAIR ihng),* a Danish seaman in the service of Russia, led an expedition that sailed from Kamchatka north through the strait now named after him. But he did not see North America because of dense fog. In 1741, Bering headed a larger expedition. He and his chief lieutenant, Aleksei I. Chirikov *(CHIHR yuh kuhf),* sailed on different ships. Both men saw the coast of Alaska. Bering also sighted Mount St. Elias and landed briefly on Kayak Island. As a result of Bering's voyages, Russia claimed Alaska. In 1784, the Russians established the first European colony there, on Kodiak Island.

Exploring the Pacific. The Pacific Ocean was still largely unknown to Europeans in 1600. In the 1600's and 1700's, Dutch, English, and French navigators sailed throughout the Pacific. They discovered many islands. European voyagers also hoped to find the mysterious Terra Australis Incognita (Unknown Southern Continent). The Europeans of the time believed this legendary large and fertile continent lay in the South Pacific to balance the northern continents of Europe and Asia.

After 1750, two developments made long Pacific voyages safer than they had been. First, sailors began to realize that fresh food would prevent scurvy. This disease, which results from a lack of vitamin C, had caused many illnesses and deaths on earlier voyages. Captains now tried to have supplies of fresh foods on hand for their crews. Second, in the late 1700's, navigators began to use the *chronometer,* a precise timepiece that enabled them to determine longitude more accurately. As a result, they could pinpoint their position at sea and establish the exact location of newly found islands.

In the early 1600's, the Dutch began to establish control over Indonesia. This area became the starting point for Dutch voyages of exploration in the Pacific. From 1606 to 1636, Willem Jansz *(WIHL uhm YAHNS)* and other Dutch navigators reached the coast of Australia. But they did not establish colonies there. In 1642 and 1643, the Dutch navigator Abel Janszoon Tasman *(AH buhl YAHN sohn TAZ muhn)* reached the island now called Tasmania, which is named after him. From there, he sighted New Zealand. In 1644, he sailed along and explored Australia's northern and western coasts.

During the second half of the 1700's, the French and the British took the lead in exploring the Pacific. In 1766, Louis-Antoine de Bougainville *(lwee ahn TWAHN duh boo gahn VEEL)* began what would be the first French voyage around the world. In January 1768, Bougainville entered the Pacific by way of the Strait of Magellan. In

April, he reached the island of Tahiti. Samuel Wallis, a British explorer, had visited Tahiti the year before. Bougainville's later account of the island's people and climate made Tahiti seem like an earthly paradise to many Europeans.

Bougainville was the first European to see several islands in the Pacific, including one in the Solomon group now named after him. Among Bougainville's crew was probably the first woman to sail around the world. This young Frenchwoman, named Jeanne Baret *(zhahn bah RAY)*, disguised herself as a male servant to one of the scientists on the expedition. The ship's company did not detect her gender until the expedition reached Tahiti. The Tahitians quickly realized that she was a woman.

The most influential explorer of the Pacific was James Cook. Cook, a British naval officer, made three long voyages from 1768 to 1779. These voyages provided much scientific information about the waters and islands of the Pacific. The information contributed to European colonization of Australia and other territories. Cook's first voyage was mainly a scientific expedition. Cook also had orders from the British Navy to look for the Unknown Southern Continent. He did not find it. But he did explore New Zealand and the eastern coast of Australia.

Cook searched for the Unknown Southern Continent during his second voyage as well. In 1773 and 1774, he crossed the Antarctic Circle and went farther south than any other explorer up to that time. But he could not find an Unknown Southern Continent. During his third voyage, Cook set out to look for an outlet of the Northwest Passage in the northern Pacific. In 1778, he sailed north through the Bering Strait until ice blocked his way. He found no outlet. The following year, Cook was killed in a dispute with natives on the island of Hawaii.

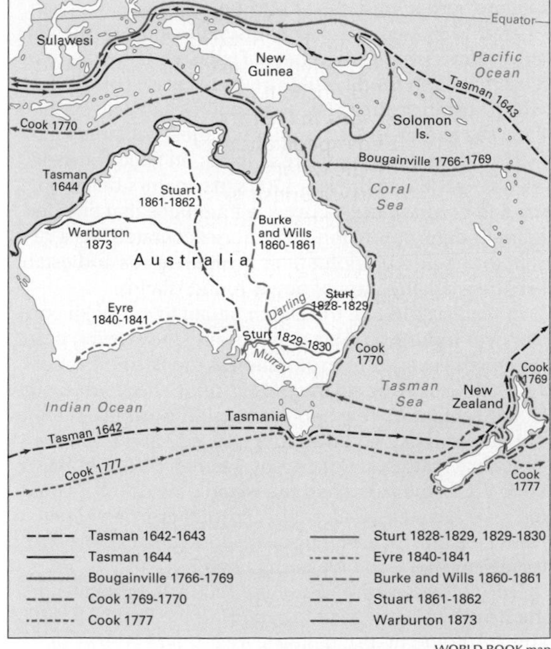

The European exploration of Australia began with sea voyages that reached the area during the 1600's and 1700's. Explorers crossed the interior of the continent in the 1800's.

Exploring Australia's interior. The exploration of Australia began soon after the British established a colony for convicts near Sydney in 1788. The British often fought with the original inhabitants, known as Aborigines. In addition, thousands of Aborigines died from diseases introduced by the Europeans. However, some Aborigines acted as guides and pointed out sources of food and water to explorers.

At first, exploration centered on the Sydney area. In 1829, an expedition led by Charles Sturt, a British Army officer, reached the Darling River. In 1829 and 1830, Sturt led a second expedition that sailed down the Murrumbidgee and Murray rivers to the sea near Adelaide.

Exploration of the interior of Australia was difficult and dangerous because much of it is desert. The British explorer Edward John Eyre (pronounced *air)* became the first European to make an overland journey across Australia from east to west. His expedition in 1840 and 1841 closely followed the southern coast of Australia. The first European party to cross Australia from south to north was led by Robert O'Hara Burke, an Irish-born explorer; and William John Wills, a British-born explorer. Burke and Wills left Melbourne in 1860. They reached the Gulf of Carpentaria in 1861. The two explorers starved to death on the return trip. Meanwhile, John McDouall Stuart, a Scottish-born explorer, also tried to cross Australia. Stuart made several unsuccessful attempts before making a round trip between the southern and northern coasts in 1861 and 1862.

The exploration of Africa. By the late 1700's, Europeans had grown familiar with the coasts of Africa. The interior of the continent, however, remained a mystery. Exploration of the interior was difficult because of harsh terrain and the presence of deadly diseases, such as malaria and dysentery. Despite these obstacles, Europeans explored most of Africa south of the Sahara during the late 1700's and the 1800's. During the late 1800's, Europeans combined exploration with conquest and colonized most of the African continent.

During the late 1700's and early 1800's, European explorers tried to solve a mystery that had puzzled geographers for centuries. Ancient writers told of an important African river called the Niger. But they did not know where it began, in what direction it flowed, and where it ended. In 1796, Mungo Park, a Scottish explorer, reached the Niger near Ségou, in Mali. He found that the river flows from west to east. In 1830, the British explorer Richard Lemon Lander sailed down the Niger to its mouth in the Gulf of Guinea. During the 1820's, Alexander Gordon Laing, a Scottish explorer, and René Caillié *(ruh NAY cah YAY)*, a Frenchman, separately visited Timbuktu, a great city near the Niger in Mali.

By the late 1700's, Europeans were familiar with the lower Nile. The lower Nile is formed by the meeting of two rivers called the Blue Nile and the White Nile at Khartoum, in Sudan. But the source of the rivers remained a mystery. In 1770, James Bruce, a Scottish explorer, reached the source of the Blue Nile in the mountains of Ethiopia.

In 1857, the British explorers Richard Francis Burton and John Hanning Speke began to search for the source of the White Nile. In 1858, they reached Lake Tanganyika, which is bordered by Burundi and Tanzania in the east and Congo (Kinshasa) and Zambia in the west. Arabs

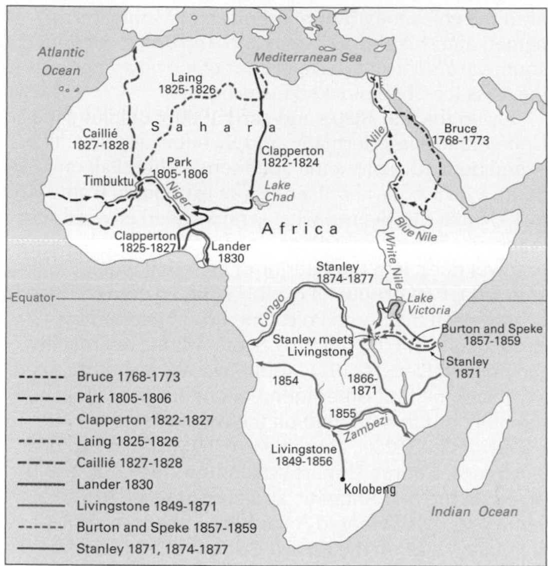

WORLD BOOK map

Exploring the interior of Africa. During the 1700's and 1800's, European expeditions explored the regions of the great rivers of Africa—the Congo, Niger, Nile, and Zambezi. Explorers also crisscrossed the western and southern parts of the continent.

Granger Collection

"Dr. Livingstone, I presume?" With those words, reporter Henry Morton Stanley, *left,* greeted explorer David Livingstone, *right,* at their famous meeting in 1871. Stanley went to Africa to find Livingstone, who had not been heard from for several years.

in the region told Burton and Speke about another large lake nearby. Speke went alone to find the lake and became convinced that it was the source of the Nile. He named it Lake Victoria in honor of Queen Victoria of the United Kingdom. This lake, known as Victoria Nyanza in Africa, lies partly in Kenya, Tanzania, and Uganda.

Speke returned to Lake Victoria in 1862. He identified the source of the Nile as a large waterfall at the lake's northern end. This waterfall is now submerged by the Nalubaale Dam. Burton and others believed that Speke was wrong, but later explorers proved him right.

In the early 1860's, a British explorer named Samuel White Baker explored many rivers of eastern Africa. He traveled with a companion, Florence, who later became his wife. In 1864, they became the first Europeans to reach Lake Albert (Albert Nyanza) and Murchison Falls.

The most famous European explorer in Africa was David Livingstone, a Scottish missionary. From 1853 to 1856, he became the first European to cross Africa. In 1855, he became the first European to see the Victoria Falls on the Zambezi River. He followed the Zambezi during part of his journey from Angola to Mozambique. In 1859, during a later expedition in southeast Africa, he reached Lake Nyasa, also known as Lake Malawi. From 1866 until his death in 1873, Livingstone explored the lakes and rivers of central Africa.

In 1869, the *New York Herald* assigned its reporter Henry Morton Stanley to go to Africa to find Livingstone. Livingstone had not been heard from in several years. The story of how Stanley found Livingstone near Lake Tanganyika in 1871 captured the imagination of people around the world (see **Stanley and Livingstone**). Stanley became an important explorer himself. From 1874 to 1877, he crossed central Africa from east to west. He also explored the Congo River. His explorations during the 1880's helped answer questions about the Congo and Nile rivers.

Arctic exploration. By 1800, the discoveries of early explorers had revealed much about the Arctic. However, no one had found either the Northwest or the Northeast passage. European governments realized that these northern passages, if they could be found, would be too hazardous for commercial shipping. Nevertheless, they continued to search for the Northwest and Northeast passages as a way to demonstrate the bravery of their explorers and the advanced technology of their ships.

The Arctic passages. In the early 1800's, the British Navy began to send expeditions to try to find a Northwest Passage in Arctic waters north of Canada. In 1819, William Edward Parry, a British naval officer, almost succeeded. He found an entrance to the Northwest Passage. He sailed through Lancaster Sound more than halfway to the Pacific, as far west as Melville Island.

In 1845, Sir John Franklin left England with two ships and 128 men to search for the passage. By 1848, nothing had been heard from Franklin and his men. The remains of the expedition were found in 1859. Franklin and his crew had died after their ships became jammed in sea ice. From 1850 to 1854, Robert McClure, a commander of one of the search ships, traveled from the Bering Strait to the Atlantic. He claimed that he had found the Northwest Passage. But he had sailed on several ships and had gone part of the way over ice on sleds. As a result, it was not clear whether a single ship could travel through the passage. This feat was finally accomplished from 1903 to 1906 by Roald Amundsen *(ROH ahl AH muhn suhn).* Amundsen, a Norwegian explorer, sailed from the Atlantic Ocean to the Bering Strait.

Meanwhile, Nils Adolf Erik Nordenskjöld *(nihls AH dawlf AY rihk NOOR duhn SHOOLD),* a Swedish explorer, completed the Northeast Passage from Europe to Asia. In July 1878, he sailed east from Tromsø, Norway, and reached the Pacific Ocean a year later.

The North Pole. During the 1800's, European explorers turned their attention to the North Pole. Reaching the pole was a symbolic quest that had little practical value. The cold and ice of the Arctic made exploration extremely dangerous. Ships could get trapped in sea ice or destroyed by it. Food was scarce, and starvation was a real danger if explorers used up their supplies.

During the late 1800's, many people believed that there was open water in the Arctic Ocean and that the North Pole might be reached by ship. But it soon became clear that the Arctic Ocean has a permanent cover of ice that explorers would have to cross by sled to reach the pole.

From 1898 to 1905, Robert E. Peary, an American explorer, led expeditions to try to reach the North Pole. He began his final expedition in 1908. It headed north to the pole from Ellesmere Island in the Canadian Arctic in early 1909. Peary claimed to have reached the North Pole on April 6, 1909. His party included his chief assistant, Matthew A. Henson, and four Inuit men: Ootah, Egigingwah, Seegloo, and Ooqueah. Upon returning to the United States, Peary learned that another American explorer, Frederick A. Cook, claimed to have reached the pole a year before Peary, on April 21, 1908. By 1910, most experts decided that Peary's story was more believable than Cook's. But the dispute has never been definitely settled. Neither man offered convincing proof that he had reached the North Pole.

The invention of the airplane and other technological advances in the 1900's brought new methods of polar exploration. In 1926, Richard E. Byrd, an American naval officer, and Floyd Bennett, an American pilot, claimed they flew from Svalbard to the North Pole and back. Some scholars today dispute that claim. Also in 1926, a team of explorers flew from Svalbard to Alaska by way of the North Pole in an airship called the *Norge.* The explorers included Umberto Nobile *(um BER taw NOH bee lay),* an Italian Air Force officer, who piloted the craft; Lincoln Ellsworth, an American civil engineer; and Roald Amundsen, who had earlier sailed through the Northwest Passage. In 1958, the U.S. nuclear-powered submarine *Nautilus* passed underneath Arctic ice to the position of the North Pole.

The exploration of Antarctica. By the early 1800's, Antarctica remained the only continent still unknown to the world. This uninhabited frigid continent was difficult to reach and explore. Stormy, ice-filled waters surround it, and a thick layer of ice covers it.

Nobody knows who first saw the Antarctic continent. But many historians divide the credit among three individuals known to have sighted Antarctica on separate voyages in 1820. These three are Edward Bransfield, a British naval officer; Nathaniel Brown Palmer, an American sea captain; and Fabian von Bellingshausen, of the Russian Imperial Navy.

Several countries sent expeditions to Antarctica to carry out scientific research. In 1840, an American naval officer named Charles Wilkes led an expedition that charted part of the coast. From 1839 to 1843, James Clark Ross, a British naval officer, commanded an expedition that sailed into what is now the Ross Sea. Ross discovered the volcanoes Mount Erebus and Mount Terror, named after his ships, *Erebus* and *Terror.* He continued southward until a massive barrier of ice now known as the Ross Ice Shelf blocked his progress.

During the late 1890's and early 1900's, Belgium, the United Kingdom, Germany, and Sweden sent scientific expeditions to explore the continent. Robert Falcon Scott, a British naval officer, led an expedition from 1901 to 1904 that discovered what is now called Edward VII Peninsula. Scott's expedition used sleds pulled by dogs to travel deep into the interior of the continent.

In 1911, two groups of explorers raced across Antarctica to reach the South Pole. One group was led by Amundsen, and the other by Scott. Amundsen reached the pole on Dec. 14, 1911, about five weeks before Scott. Scott and the four other members of his group reached the pole, but they all died on the return trip.

During the 1920's, aircraft were first used to explore Antarctica. George Hubert Wilkins, an Australian explorer, made the first Antarctic airplane flight in 1928. The same year, Byrd went to Antarctica with three airplanes. He built a base on the Ross Ice Shelf called Little America. On Nov. 28 and 29, 1929, he led the first flight, piloted by Bernt Balchen, over the South Pole.

During the 1950's, many nations built bases on Antarctica from which to conduct scientific research. In 1957 and 1958, an expedition led by Vivian Fuchs *(fyooks),* a British geologist, accomplished the first overland crossing of Antarctica. The explorers used snow tractors and dog teams to make the crossing. Their journey covered 2,158 miles (3,473 kilometers) and took 99 days.

In 1989 and 1990, Will Steger of the United States led a team from six nations across Antarctica. The expedition traveled by dog sled and ski. It was the first to cross the continent without motorized vehicles.

Antarctic ice trapped the *Endurance,* the ship carrying the British explorer Ernest Shackleton and his crew in 1915. Ice crushed the ship, but the crew escaped and were rescued.

The new frontiers

Throughout history, the unknown has attracted explorers to Earth's farthest and most isolated places. Today, this same urge continues to draw men and women toward new frontiers of exploration: the ocean depths and outer space.

Deep-sea exploration. Early explorers and geographers were curious about the seas and the life in them. They often measured the depth of the oceans. They also tried to determine deep-sea temperatures and used dredges to haul marine life up to the surface.

The United Kingdom's Royal Navy and the Royal Society, a British scientific association, organized the first expedition devoted entirely to the study of the sea. A naval vessel called the *Challenger* was specially equipped for

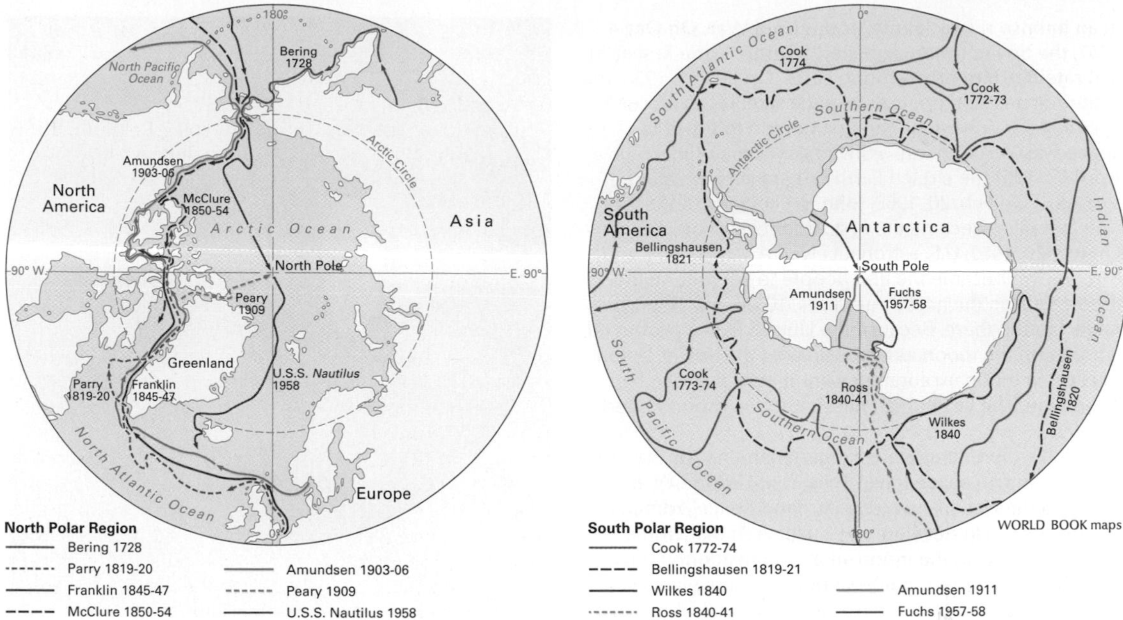

Exploration of the frigid polar regions began during the 1700's. However, explorers did not reach the North Pole until 1908 or 1909 and did not arrive at the South Pole until 1911.

the expedition in 1872. Captain George S. Nares commanded. Charles Wyville Thomson, a Scottish naturalist, headed a team of scientists. The *Challenger* spent more than three years at sea and traveled nearly 70,000 miles (113,000 kilometers). The expedition made hundreds of measurements, gathered much information about the ocean floor, and discovered many marine organisms.

In the mid-1900's, explorers and scientists began to get firsthand views of the underwater world. In 1943, Jacques-Yves Cousteau *(zhahk eev koo STOH)*, a French naval officer, and Émile Gagnan *(ay MEEL GAHN yahn)*, a French engineer, invented the aqualung. This device allowed divers to breathe air from canisters on their backs and to move freely underwater.

In the late 1900's, divers penetrated deep into the ocean with the help of improved suits and breathing apparatus. In 1979, Sylvia A. Earle, an American marine biologist, made a record-breaking dive. She descended 1,250 feet (381 meters) to the ocean floor off Hawaii wearing a kind of diving suit called a *Jim suit.* The suit is named for the British diver Jim Jarrett, who made the first dives with it in the 1920's.

Explorers also used deep-sea vessels known as *submersibles* to study the oceans. In 1934, William Beebe, an American naturalist, and Otis Barton, an American engineer, descended 3,028 feet (923 meters) into waters off Bermuda in a vehicle called a *bathysphere.*

The Swiss physicist Auguste Piccard *(oh GOOST pee KAHR)* made a major contribution to ocean exploration during the 1940's. He invented a diving vehicle known as a *bathyscaph.* It could descend farther than any craft of its day. In 1960, Piccard's son Jacques and Donald Walsh of the U.S. Navy used a bathyscaph to dive into the Mariana Trench, a valley in the Pacific Ocean floor that is the lowest known place in the world. They reached the bottom at 35,800 feet (10,911 meters) beneath the surface.

By the late 1900's, the marine geologist Robert D. Ballard and other scientists had developed new types of equipment to explore the sea. Their equipment included remotely operated diving vessels and robots. In the late 1970's, Ballard and a team of explorers discovered strange worms and other life forms at the bottom of the Pacific Ocean. For more information on deep-sea exploration, see **Ocean** (Exploring the ocean).

Space exploration. Long before the invention of rockets, humans explored Earth's atmosphere in lighter-than-air craft. In 1783, two Frenchmen made the first human free flight in a hot air balloon. The two—Jean-François Pilâtre de Rozier, a scientist, and François Laurent, Marquis d'Arlandes, a nobleman—drifted over Paris for about 25 minutes. For the next century, explorers used lighter-than-air craft, such as balloons and dirigibles, to learn more about the regions above Earth.

The first rockets used for space exploration were developed for warfare during World War II (1939-1945). Germany developed a rocket called the V-2. The United States captured some of these rockets and used them to launch exploratory instruments into the atmosphere after the war.

After World War II ended, the United States and the Soviet Union engaged

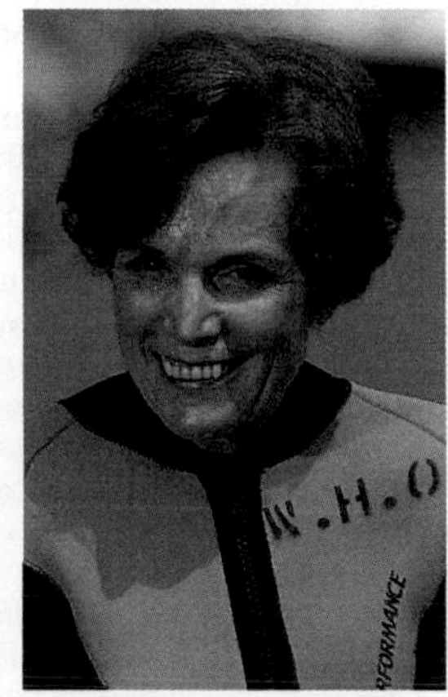

© Seth Resnick

Sylvia A. Earle of the United States made a record-breaking ocean dive near Hawaii in 1979.

in an intense rivalry known as the Cold War. On Oct. 4, 1957, the Soviet Union launched Sputnik 1, the first artificial satellite, into orbit around Earth. On Jan. 31, 1958, the United States sent up its first space satellite, Explorer 1.

Human space travel. The first person to travel in space was Yuri Gagarin, a Soviet Air Force officer. On April 12, 1961, he circled Earth in a spacecraft called Vostok 1. On Feb. 20, 1962, John H. Glenn, Jr., a U.S. Marine test pilot, became the first American to orbit Earth. On July 20, 1969, U.S. astronauts Neil A. Armstrong and Buzz Aldrin became the first people to set foot on the moon. During the next three years, 10 other U.S. astronauts landed there. Because the United States portrayed landing on the moon as a race against the Soviet Union, interest in moon exploration waned after the race had been won. The last human mission to the moon ended in 1972.

In 2003, the United States began planning for the next stage in human space travel. President George W. Bush directed the National Aeronautics and Space Administration (NASA) to develop new spacecraft that would return astronauts to the moon. In 2010, President Barack Obama revised these goals. Under Obama's plan, astronauts would by-pass the moon and travel to other destinations in the solar system instead. The plan called for sending the first humans to visit an asteroid by 2025. By the 2030's, Obama said, "I believe we can send humans to orbit Mars and return them safely to Earth. And landing on Mars will follow."

Robotic spacecraft have conducted more space exploration than human space travelers have. Starting in the late 1950's, robotic craft flew to the moon and to other planets in the solar system to gather information. In 1977, the United States launched Voyager 1 and Voyager 2. The Voyagers were two identical spacecraft with powerful telescopic cameras. From 1979 to 1981, both spacecraft flew near Jupiter and Saturn. Voyager 2 passed Uranus in 1986 and Neptune in 1989. Both spacecraft sent back data and photographs that greatly enriched scientists' knowledge of these planets. The United States launched the Hubble Space Telescope in 1990. This orbiting telescope provided the sharpest pictures of heavenly bodies taken up to that time.

Today, space exploration by robotic probes continues. NASA launched the Mars Exploration Rover Mission in 2003 and 2004. The mission studied water and geology on Mars. Cassini, a spacecraft sent to study Saturn, launched in 1997. In 2005, Cassini dropped a probe, called Huygens, onto Saturn's moon Titan. The Huygens probe landed on Titan and briefly sent back images of the moon's surface. Its landing ranked as the most distant landing ever achieved by a human-built craft.

Meanwhile, the two Voyager probes have traveled to the edge of our solar system. Between 2030 and 2040, they will enter interstellar space. Their flights rank as the most distant journey of human-made spacecraft yet achieved. Michael F. Robinson

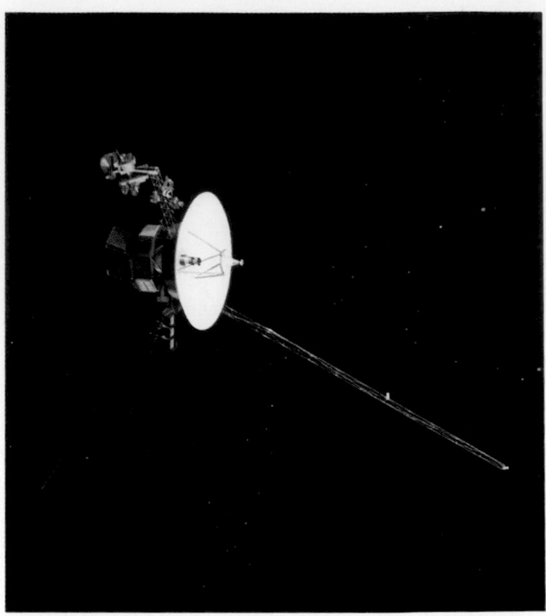

NASA/JPL

The Voyager 1 spacecraft, launched in 1977, has traveled farther than any other explorer from Earth. It has explored the outer planets and will leave the solar system sometime after 2030.

Related articles. For biographies of space explorers, see the *Related articles* listed in the **Astronaut** article. See also:

American explorers

Andrews, Roy Chapman
Ballard, Robert Duane
Bartlett, Robert Abram
Beebe, William
Bonneville, Benjamin de
Bridger, Jim
Byrd, Richard Evelyn
Clark, William
Colter, John
Cook, Frederick Albert
Earle, Sylvia Alice
Eielson, Carl Ben
Ellsworth, Lincoln
Frémont, John Charles
Gray, Robert
Henson, Matthew Alexander
Lewis, Meriwether
Long, Stephen Harriman
MacMillan, Donald Baxter
Muir, John
Peary, Robert Edwin
Pike, Zebulon Montgomery
Powell, John Wesley
Roosevelt, Theodore, Jr.
Smith, Jedediah Strong
Stephens, John Lloyd
Wilkes, Charles

Canadian explorers

Bernier, Joseph Elzéar
Fraser, Simon
Mackenzie, Sir Alexander
McKay, Alexander
Thompson, David

English explorers

Baffin, William
Burton, Sir Richard Francis
Cook, James
Dampier, William
Davis, John
Drake, Sir Francis
Franklin, Sir John
Frobisher, Sir Martin
Fuchs, Sir Vivian Ernest
Gilbert, Sir Humphrey
Hearne, Samuel
Henday, Anthony
Hudson, Henry
Kingsley, Mary Henrietta
Newport, Christopher
Parry, Sir William Edward
Puget, Peter
Raleigh, Sir Walter
Ross, Sir James Clark
Scott, Robert Falcon
Vancouver, George
Wallace, Alfred Russell

French explorers

Brulé, Etienne
Cartier, Jacques
Champlain, Samuel de
Cousteau, Jacques-Yves
Du Gua, Pierre, Sieur de Monts
Groseilliers, Médard Chouart, Sieur des
Jolliet, Louis
La Salle, René-Robert Cavelier, Sieur de
La Vérendrye, Pierre Gaultier de Varennes, Sieur de
Le Moyne, Jean Baptiste, Sieur de Bienville
Le Moyne, Pierre, Sieur d'Iberville

Marquette, Jacques	Roberval, Jean François de La Roque, Sieur de
Nicolet, Jean	Tonty, Henri de
Radisson, Pierre Esprit	

Italian explorers

Cabot, John	Polo, Marco
Cabot, Sebastian	Verrazzano, Giovanni da
Columbus, Christopher	Vespucci, Amerigo
Kino, Eusebio Francisco	

Norwegian explorers

Amundsen, Roald	Leif Eriksson
Erik the Red	Nansen, Fridtjof

Portuguese explorers

Cabral, Pedro Álvares	Henry the Navigator
Da Gama, Vasco	Magellan, Ferdinand
Dias, Bartolomeu	

Spanish explorers

Ayllón, Lucas Vásquez de	Jiménez de Quesada, Gonzalo
Balboa, Vasco Núñez de	Menéndez de Avilés, Pedro
Cabeza de Vaca, Álvar Núñez	Narváez, Pánfilo de
Cabrillo, Juan Rodríguez	Oñate, Juan de
Coronado, Francisco Vásquez de	Orellana, Francisco de
Cortés, Hernán	Pizarro, Francisco
De Soto, Hernando	Ponce de León, Juan
	Torres, Luis Vaez de

Other explorers

Alexander the Great
Barents, Willem
Bering, Vitus
Bruce, James
Emin Pasha
Estevanico
Hennepin, Louis
Hillary, Sir Edmund Percival
Ibn Battūta
McClure, Sir Robert John Le Mesurier
Nordenskjöld, Nils Adolf Erik
Park, Mungo
Piccard, Auguste
Piccard, Jacques
Piccard, Jean
Pytheas
Shackleton, Sir Ernest Henry
Stanley and Livingstone
Tasman, Abel Janszoon
Wilkins, Sir Hubert

Other related articles

Africa (History)	Latin America (History)
Antarctica (Exploration)	Lewis and Clark expedition
Arctic (Arctic exploration)	Map (History)
Astronaut	Northwest Passage
Australia (History)	Ocean (Exploring the ocean)
Balloon (History)	Ptolemy
Caravel	Ship (History)
Cíbola, Seven Cities of	Space exploration
Colonialism	Trade route
Deep sea (Exploration)	Vikings
El Dorado	Vinland
Fur trade	
Geography	

Additional resources

Level I

Aronson, Marc, and Glenn, J. W. *The World Made New: Why the Age of Exploration Happened and How It Changed the World.* National Geographic Children's Bks., 2007.

Freedman, Russell. *Who Was First? Discovering the Americas.* Clarion, 2007.

Gifford, Clive. *10 Explorers Who Changed the World.* Kingfisher, 2008.

Ross, Stewart. *Into the Unknown: How Great Explorers Found Their Way by Land, Sea, and Air.* Candlewick Pr., 2011.

Level II

Buisseret, David, ed. *The Oxford Companion to World Exploration.* 2 vols. Oxford, 2007.

Hanbury-Tenison, Robin, ed. *The Great Explorers.* Thames & Hudson, 2010.

Howgego, Raymond J. *The Encyclopedia of Exploration.* 4 vols. Hordern Hse., 2003-2008.

MacLeod, Alasdair. *Explorers.* DK Pub., 2010.

Explosive is a material that produces a rapid, violent reaction when heated or struck. The reaction gives off large amounts of gases. The expanding gases produce extreme pressure, giving explosives their destructive power.

Explosives serve many different purposes. Construction workers use explosives to blast away rocks and to tunnel through mountains. Miners use explosives to break up rock deep underground to extract minerals and petroleum. In war, explosives are widely used to destroy buildings, bridges, vehicles, ships, and airplanes and to harm enemy troops. Terrorists also use explosives, taking advantage of their dramatic and frightening power.

Explosives may be solids, liquids, or gases. Most explosives consist of a fuel and an *oxidizer*—a substance that supplies the oxygen needed to burn the fuel.

Explosive power varies with the rate of the chemical reaction. Conventional explosives are often grouped into two categories: *high explosives* and *low explosives.* The most powerful explosives involve nuclear reactions rather than chemical reactions. For a detailed discussion of nuclear explosions, see **Nuclear weapon.**

High explosives explode in reactions called *detonations.* In detonation, the chemical reaction takes place at an extremely high rate. The reaction spreads through the explosive material faster than sound can travel through it. The supersonic reaction creates extremely powerful shock waves that can shatter metal and stone.

The most common modern high explosive is *emulsion explosive.* It is often used in mining and construction blasting. Other common types of high explosives include nitroglycerin, RDX, TNT, PETN, and pentolite, a combination of TNT and PETN. Artillery shells, bombs, grenades, and guided missiles contain high explosives.

Plastic explosives combine high explosives with a moldable material, such as oil or wax. They can be formed into various shapes. C4 is a common plastic explosive. Most plastic explosives contain chemical *taggants* (tracers), making it easy for authorities to detect them.

Low explosives are those that *deflagrate* (burn rapidly) rather than detonate. In deflagration, the reaction spreads slower than the speed of sound. But deflagration still produces hot, high-pressure gases. The most common type of low explosive is gunpowder. It serves as a *propellant* to shoot projectiles from guns and other weapons. Fireworks also make use of low explosives.

Explosive sensitivity. Explosives also vary in their *sensitivity*—that is, how easy they are to set off. They are often divided into three categories by sensitivity: *primary explosives, secondary explosives,* and *blasting agents.*

Primary explosives are the most sensitive, or the easiest to explode. A small amount of heat—even a spark of static electricity—can set off a primary explosive. Common primary explosives include lead azide, lead styphnate, and mercury fulminate.

Secondary explosives are less sensitive—but generally more powerful—than primary explosives. Secondary explosives are designed so that they can be stored, transported, and handled safely. They usually form the bulk of high explosive devices. Blasting agents are the least sensitive explosives. Secondary explosives and blasting agents are typically triggered by using primary explosives. Paul Worsey

Related articles in *World Book* include:

Ammunition	Fuse	Mine warfare
Bomb	Guncotton	Nitroglycerin
Depth charge	Gunpowder	PETN
DuPont Company	Improvised explosive device	Plastic explosive
Dynamite		RDX
Fireworks	Maxim, Hudson	TNT

Exports and imports are the articles shipped from and into a country. The term *export* comes from Latin words meaning *to carry out. Import* comes from Latin words that mean *to carry in.*

The pattern of exports and imports

Reasons for exports and imports. A country exports goods chiefly under the following conditions: (1) if the country is one of the world's few suppliers of a certain product; (2) if the country produces the merchandise at a lower cost than other countries can; or (3) if the country's goods are in demand because of their superior quality.

Some imports consist of goods that are not produced domestically. For example, the climate of the mainland United States is not suitable for growing coffee. For this reason, the United States imports coffee beans from countries in Latin America and Africa. But most imports purchased by large countries consist of goods that are similar to locally produced goods but different in price or quality. For example, the United States imports inexpensive Hyundai automobiles from South Korea and luxury BMW and Mercedes-Benz cars from Germany, even though automakers in the United States produce many other cars.

Reasons for change. A nation's pattern of exports and imports tends to change over the years. This change may be due to technological developments. For example, the discovery of synthetic substitutes for such natural products as silk and rubber reduced the need to import these natural products. The development of new products often creates new trade patterns because people in all countries want these conveniences wherever they are produced. Foreign investment, such as building factories in other countries, may enable countries to export products that they previously imported.

Government policies may affect the exports and imports of a country. For example, lowering tariffs allows greater imports of products from abroad. In the same way, lowering of trade barriers by other countries opens markets for exports.

Attitudes toward exports and imports

Popular opinion within a country usually favors national exports over imports. Many people, particularly local producers and workers, believe exports create jobs. They resent imported products—especially ones that compete with similar products made in their own country. Many people think that imports lower living standards by decreasing job opportunities at home and by causing money to be spent outside the country.

Economists, in contrast with the public, believe that exports and imports are equally important. To the economist, it is more efficient and economical for a nation to import from abroad goods that are either cheaper or of better quality. The nation can then use its resources, work force, and equipment to specialize in goods that it produces better than other countries—and to export those goods. Further, most economists believe that imports act as a spur for domestic manufacturers to improve their products and cut their costs.

Government policies

Export promotion. Some governments artificially promote their nation's exports by giving exporters a cash grant called a *subsidy.* For example, the European Union (EU), an economic and political association of European countries, guarantees its member nations a minimum price for exporting wheat and butter. When the world market price for wheat or butter falls below that price, the EU pays the member a subsidy to cover the difference between the lower market price and the higher guaranteed price.

Another artificial arrangement to promote exports consists of special tax incentives. A government may exempt export industries from corporate taxes that other businesses must pay. A government may also increase exports by reducing the value of its currency in relation to other countries' currencies. Such a reduction makes the exporting country's goods cheaper for importers—and consumers—in other countries.

Import restrictions. A common restrictive device is the import *tariff,* a tax on imports. The United States limits its imports chiefly by imposing tariffs. Many other countries restrict trade with an *import quota,* which sets an absolute limit on imports. Efficient producers may be able to lower their prices enough to absorb a tariff and still export their goods. But no degree of efficiency can help producers when they face a rigid limit on the number of items a country may import.

Developing countries, such as Brazil and India, often use regulations called *foreign exchange controls* to restrict imports. Such controls limit the payments importers may make to foreign suppliers for certain goods.

Unexpected costs and delays at the customs office are still another type of import restriction. For example, a customs officer may place an arbitrarily high value on certain imports. When tariff duties are based on such valuations, an arbitrarily high valuation imposes unexpected costs on importers. Strict health or safety requirements may also present a barrier to trade.

Government policy toward imports varies with a nation's degree of industrial development. The economically most advanced nations, such as the United States, Japan, and the nations of Western Europe, tend to favor lowering import restrictions. They want to widen world markets for their exports and to promote economic growth and productive efficiency. Their advanced industries rely on product research and skilled management for competitiveness in world markets. Some of the more advanced developing nations, such as Chile, Mexico,

South Korea, Thailand, and some Eastern European nations, reduced import barriers in the 1980's.

Many of the less developed countries in Africa, Asia, and Latin America still rely on import restrictions. They feel that such protection is necessary for the growth of their infant industries. They point to the importance of restrictions in the past industrial growth of economically advanced nations. Gary Hufbauer

Related articles. See the sections on *Trade* in various country articles. See also the following articles:

Balance of payments	International trade
Free trade	Reciprocal trade agreement
General Agreement on Tariffs and Trade	Tariff
	Trade

Exposition. See Fair.

Expressionism was an art movement that flourished in the early 1900's. Art critics invented the term to describe a style of painting which developed from, and in reaction to, the kind of painting called Impressionism. Impressionist painters were mainly concerned with how the surface of objects appeared to the eye at a particular moment. Expressionists tried to give form to their strong inner feelings. They tried to portray life as modified and distorted by their personal interpretation of reality. To them, truth or beauty was in the mind and the soul, not in the eye. See **Impressionism; Postimpressionism.**

The emotional range of Expressionist art encompasses both intense joy and deep despair. Expressionist imagery accordingly may be either bright and ecstatic or dark and painful. Vincent van Gogh's *The Starry Night* (1889) is a good example of a joyful Expressionist work. Van Gogh deliberately distorted the size and appearance of the heavenly bodies, using vivid colors and energetic, swirling brushstrokes. The painting is an expression of van Gogh's highly personal experience of the star-filled night sky, rather than a record of how such a sky appears to the observant eye. The rapturous excitement of the painting is primarily the product of van Gogh's mind and emotions. Edvard Munch's painting *The Scream* (1893), with its image of intense anxiety and alienation, represents the darker side of Expressionism. *The Scream* is reproduced in the **Munch, Edvard** article.

Expressionist painting. Elements of Expressionism can be traced at least as far back as the Spanish painter El Greco in the early 1600's. The Expressionist movement itself began in the late 1800's. Its leading figures were van Gogh of the Netherlands, Munch of Norway, Paul Gauguin of France, and James Ensor of Belgium.

The first group organized to promote the Expressionist idea was called *Die Brücke* (The Bridge). It flourished in Germany from 1905 to 1913. Emil Nolde and Ernst Ludwig Kirchner were two of its best-known members. A later and more influential group was called *Der Blaue Reiter* (The Blue Rider). It included Wassily Kandinsky of Russia, Paul Klee of Switzerland, and Franz Marc of Germany. Through its paintings and writings, *Der Blaue Reiter* influenced the work of many artists, especially Georges Rouault of France, Marc Chagall of Russia, Max Beckmann and George Grosz of Germany, and Oskar Kokoschka of Austria.

Paintings by Gauguin, Kandinsky, and Kokoschka appear in the *Expressionism* section of the **Painting** article.

Expressionist writing, especially drama, flourished in the early 1900's. Expressionist playwrights were influenced by the dramatic forms and stage techniques made popular by August Strindberg of Sweden. Expressionist drama first developed as a movement in Germany. Its influence spread, reaching its height after World War I (1914-1918) in the plays of Ernst Toller, Frank Wedekind, Georg Kaiser, and Josef and Karel Čapek. In the United States, the plays of Elmer Rice, Eugene O'Neill, and others show the influence of Expressionism.

Characters in Expressionist drama tend to be one-sided, standing for single ideas and attitudes. They are placed in situations in which the objects of the outer world are distorted to reveal the tortured minds of the characters or the dramatist. Playwrights achieved these effects with symbolic settings, bizarre lighting, and non-realistic acting. See **Drama** (Modern drama: Ibsen to World War II; picture).

Expressionist drama often showed the influence of modern psychology by reflecting the inner frustrations of the dramatist. Many plays showed characters in the grip of fear and other violent emotions. Some playwrights, influenced by the philosophy of Karl Marx, criticized the evils they saw in society.

The influence of Expressionism can also be seen in the fiction of the German-Czech author Franz Kafka and in some German poetry of the early 1900's. Although Expressionism is no longer a specific movement, its aims and methods may still be found in much contemporary drama and art. David Cateforis

Related articles in *World Book* include:

Abstract Expressionism	Beckmann, Max
Barlach, Ernst Heinrich	Čapek, Karel

Friedrichstrasse, Berlin (1914), a pastel by Ernst Ludwig Kirchner; Staatsgalerie, Stuttgart, Germany

An Expressionist painting shows how artists use distortion and bright colors to create an intense emotional impact.

Ensor, James
Gauguin, Paul
German literature (Expressionism)
Greco, El
Grosz, George
Kafka, Franz
Kaiser, Georg
Kandinsky, Wassily
Klee, Paul
Kokoschka, Oskar
Motion picture (Filmmaking in Europe)
O'Neill, Eugene
Opera (The search for new forms)
Rice, Elmer
Schiele, Egon
Strindberg, August
Van Gogh, Vincent

Extinction occurs when every member of a *species* (kind) of living thing has died. All types of life may suffer extinction, including animals, plants, fungi, and bacteria. In fact, most biologists think that more than 99 percent of the species that have ever lived are now extinct.

Extinction plays an important part in *evolution* (the development of living things over time). According to evolutionary theory, the members of a species with traits best suited to the environment leave more offspring. If the environment changes, different traits may become favorable. Individuals with those traits will leave more descendants, changing the overall character of the species. In this way, a species can adapt to its environment. If a species cannot adapt, it may become extinct. The extinction of a species may provide opportunities for new species to evolve. See **Natural selection.**

Species vary greatly in their potential for extinction. Some species live in a small area or rely on a single food source. Relatively small disruptions may cause such species to become extinct. Other species are widespread and can survive in a variety of conditions. These species are more resistant to extinction.

Generally, species live for 1 million to 10 million years. However, some species have lived much longer. For example, the gray whale has lived for about 30 million years. Some species of plants have lived for more than 100 million years, since the time of the dinosaurs. The horseshoe crab has existed for about 445 million years.

Background extinction. Gradual extinctions occur all the time through the ordinary mechanisms of evolution. They are known as *background extinctions.*

Changes in the environment cause many background extinctions. For example, if less rain begins to fall in a forest, the area may become grassland. Species that depend on the forest may become extinct if they cannot move to other forests or adapt to the new environment.

Species also become extinct when they are unable to compete for limited resources. For example, a species may appear in an area and compete with an existing species for food. If the new species is better able to collect the food, the original species may become extinct.

Mass extinction. Several times in Earth's history, vast numbers of species have died out suddenly. These catastrophic episodes are known as *mass extinctions.* There have been five mass extinctions that wiped out at least 50 percent of species living at the time. Such extinctions may allow for the rise of new groups. For example, the extinction of dinosaurs enabled mammals to flourish.

Scientists divide Earth's history into *periods* (see **Earth** [table: Outline of Earth's history]). A mass extinction may mark the boundary between two periods. For example, the largest mass extinction occurred between the Permian and the Triassic periods. It can be called the Permian-Triassic extinction. A mass extinction may also be identified by the period it ended. Thus, the Permian-Triassic extinction may also be called the Permian extinction.

Mass extinctions may result from severe volcanic eruptions, the impact of large asteroids, shifts in sea level, loss of oxygen in the oceans, or other catastrophic changes. Scientists cannot always agree on the causes of a particular mass extinction.

The Ordovician extinction occurred about 444 million years ago, when relatively little life had spread to land. Many species in the oceans died. The mass extinction was caused largely by global cooling and an *ice age,* a period when glaciers covered much of Earth. Shifts in sea level and oxygen levels also played a role.

The Devonian extinction occurred about 359 million years ago. It mainly affected ocean life, especially coral reefs. The mass extinction likely had several causes, some of them related to the spread of root-bearing plants on land. These plants may have caused more nutrients to wash into the oceans, reducing oxygen levels. The plants also may have contributed to climate change.

The Permian extinction occurred about 251 million years ago. It was by far the worst mass extinction. About 95 percent of species became extinct, including most life in the oceans. Most scientists believe that the Permian extinction was caused in large part by tremendous volcanic eruptions in what is now Siberia. Gases released by the eruptions caused rapid climate change and acid rain, and reduced oxygen levels in the oceans.

The Triassic extinction occurred about 200 million years ago. It may have been caused by volcanic eruptions, changes in sea level, changes in ocean chemistry, or a combination of these events. The Triassic extinction enabled dinosaurs to become the major land animals.

The Cretaceous extinction occurred about 65 million years ago. At this time, nearly all large animals became extinct, including the dinosaurs. Most scientists believe the mass extinction was caused by an asteroid impact. This impact could have thrown large amounts of dust and debris into the atmosphere. These materials would have blocked sunlight and caused a long winter, killing much plant life. The impact also may have caused global warming, acid rain, and wildfires. There also were giant volcanic eruptions in India at this time.

Modern extinction. Many hundreds of species have become extinct in the last 500 years. Famous examples include the dodo, the Tasmanian tiger, and the passenger pigeon. In addition, many unknown species have likely become extinct in modern times. Scientists believe that extinctions are occurring so rapidly that many spe-

The mammoth is an extinct relative of modern elephants. The mammoth thrived for millions of years, during a time of frequent ice ages. It became extinct about 4,000 years ago. Most scientists believe climate change and overhunting by human beings drove the mammoth to extinction.

WORLD BOOK illustration by Alex Ebel

cies disappear before they can be identified.

Human beings cause many modern extinctions. The most important cause of these extinctions is habitat destruction. For example, clearing forests can cause many extinctions. People have hunted some species to extinction. People also spread species to new environments, where they may harm native life. Environmental pollution threatens many species. Scientists also worry that *global warming,* an increase in the average temperature at Earth's surface, could cause many species to become extinct (see **Global warming**).

Scientists estimate that extinctions are now occurring at a rate about 50 to 1,000 times greater than that of normal background extinction. Some scientists worry about a "sixth mass extinction," this one caused by humans.

Many people are trying to preserve living things from extinction. For example, it is illegal in many countries to hunt or otherwise harm endangered species. Governments have established wildlife sanctuaries to protect natural habitats. Scientists breed endangered animals and plants. Several species have become extinct in the wild but survive in zoos or research centers. Some of these species have been successfully reintroduced into the wild. David P. G. Bond

See also **Endangered species; Prehistoric animal.**

Extortion is the attempt to obtain money or property by threatening to physically harm a person, injure a person's property or reputation, or accuse a person of a crime. The payment, or bribe, is often called *hush money.* The meaning of the term *extortion* was originally limited to the collection of illegal fees by a public official. Today, such a crime is called *bribery.* If a private person does it, it is called *blackmail.* Both crimes are considered kinds of extortion, and they are punishable by a prison term or fine, or both. See also **Blackmail; Bribery; Racketeering.** Charles F. Wellford

Extract is a concentrated preparation of certain substances obtained from plants, herbs, flowers, or animal tissues. Extracts are widely used as flavorings in cooking. Popular flavoring extracts include almond, lemon, mint, and vanilla extracts. Extracts are also used in cosmetics, medicines, and perfumes.

Several methods are used to prepare extracts. For example, orange extract is obtained by pressing or squeezing orange rinds, which contain flavorful oils. Vanilla extract is made by soaking crushed vanilla beans in a mixture of alcohol and water. Meat extracts are produced by boiling meat in liquid and then reducing the cooking liquid to a paste by evaporation.

Many drugs are extracted from plants. For example, morphine, a painkiller, comes from the opium poppy. Cosmetic extracts, called *essences,* are used in perfume, soap, toothpaste, and shampoo. They include ambergris, balsam, benzoin, castor, and musk.

Jane Ann Raymond Bowers

See also **Meat extract; Perfume.**

Extradition, *EHKS truh DIHSH uhn,* is the handing over by one state or country to another of people accused of crimes. The word *extradition* comes from two Latin words meaning *out of* and *delivering up.*

In early times, people who committed crimes were able to escape punishment by fleeing to another country. But in the late 1700's, nations began to arrange extradition treaties among themselves. Such treaties provide that proper authorities must return people accused of certain crimes to the country in which they committed the crimes at the demand of that country.

Ordinarily, people cannot be extradited for political crimes. Many countries refuse to extradite a person if the country objects to a penalty the demanding country may impose. The United States has extradition treaties with many countries. The U.S. Constitution provides that any state, on demand of another state, shall extradite a person accused of a crime. Michael J. Bushbaum

Extrasensory perception, abbreviated ESP, describes a way of communicating or of being aware of something without using the known senses. An awareness of another person's thoughts without the use of sight, hearing, taste, touch, or smell would be an example of ESP. The study of extrasensory perception is part of the field of psychology called *parapsychology.*

What parapsychologists study. Extrasensory perception is commonly divided into three kinds of phenomena: (1) telepathy, (2) clairvoyance, and (3) precognition. Telepathy is the sensing of a person's thoughts or feelings in some unknown way. Clairvoyance is an awareness of objects, events, or people without the use of the known senses. Precognition is knowledge of a future event by unknown means. Some parapsychologists also study phenomena related to ESP, such as *psychokinesis.* Psychokinesis is the mental control of physical objects, such as influencing the fall of dice.

Early ESP research. Classic ESP experiments, developed and used mainly between the 1930's and the 1960's, involved card guessing. Researchers often used a deck of 25 special ESP cards (also called Zener cards, named for the American psychologist Karl E. Zener). Each Zener card had one of five symbols on it, such as a circle or a plus sign. In a simple test of telepathy, a person called the *sender* would randomly draw a card from a shuffled deck and concentrate on its symbol. A second person, called the *receiver,* usually sat in another room and would try to name the symbol that the sender was thinking of. In an experiment on clairvoyance, the sender would take cards from the deck one at a time but would not look at the symbols, and the receiver would try to name them. In a test for precognition, the cards would be selected after the receiver made a guess.

Modern ESP research. ESP researchers improved their experiments in many ways by the 1970's and 1980's. Senders now usually view photographs or short scenes from a movie instead of Zener cards. The receiver is then told that the sender is looking at a photograph or movie scene and is asked to describe it, without being given any other information. Experimenters take many precautions so that all known ordinary explanations for successful guessing can be ruled out.

Modern ESP experimenters analyze their results using statistical methods. These methods compare the actual results to what would be expected if the receiver were just guessing and not using ESP. In the most basic method of analysis, the actual target photograph and three additional "decoy photographs" are shown to the receiver. The receiver is asked which one he or she thinks the sender was trying to send. By chance, receivers should pick the correct photograph about one-fourth of the time. However, many ESP studies have found that receivers do so about one-third of the time.

Since the 1970's, laboratories have conducted thousands of scientific ESP experiments. The success rate of about one-third has remained consistent. To some, this rate provides strong statistical evidence that the results are not due to chance. However, many scientists are reluctant to accept that these experiments provide evidence for extrasensory perception. Many believe that the existence of ESP would require a change in thinking about the fundamental laws of physics. Current theories in physics do not provide an explanation for how ESP can exist. The existence of ESP will remain controversial until a scientific explanation is found for how it works.

Possible misunderstandings. Some scientists point out that the evidence for ESP is controversial because many personal experiences that appear to be the result of ESP can be explained by psychological processes of which most people are not aware. People often do not know how events around them set off their thoughts. Two people who know each other well may both experience a similar chain of thoughts when exposed to a common stimulus. For example, a husband and wife may be reading together and not paying much attention to music on a radio. Then certain music triggers in each of them the memory of a person they met several years ago but have not encountered since. Just as one of them is about to bring up the person's name, the other one mentions it. These similar thoughts may seem to be an instance of extrasensory perception. Neither person may realize that the music actually set off both of their thoughts. Other experiences that seem to involve ESP may, in fact, be simple coincidences. Everyone will likely experience improbable events that seem to be ESP on occasion—just by chance. Jessica Utts

See also **Clairvoyance; Parapsychology; Psychical research; Telepathy.**

Extraterrestrial intelligence, *EHKS truh tuh REHS tree uhl,* is life originating beyond Earth that has such abilities as thinking and learning. Space probes have discovered no life—let alone intelligent life—on the other planets or the moons of our solar system. However, many scientists think that intelligent life could exist on worlds around other stars. Beings that originate beyond Earth are frequently referred to as *extraterrestrials* or simply *aliens.*

Scientists think that intelligent life may exist on other worlds because the universe contains a vast number of stars and planets. Our own galaxy, the Milky Way, has hundreds of billions of stars. Many scientists think that from 10 percent to more than 50 percent of these stars may have planets, and so our galaxy alone could contain more than a trillion planets. Furthermore, the universe has more than 100 billion galaxies. Scientists expect that many planets do not have the conditions—such as liquid water—necessary to support life as we know it. But if even a tiny fraction of planets have the right conditions, the Milky Way still might contain millions of worlds with life, and perhaps some with intelligent life.

One effort to find extraterrestrial intelligence is called SETI, which stands for Search for Extraterrestrial Intelligence. SETI research involves looking in the vicinity of other stars for signals sent by extraterrestrials in the form of light or radio waves. In 1960, the American astronomer Frank Drake conducted the first SETI experiment. He used a radio telescope to try to detect signals coming from around two relatively nearby stars. During the 1990's and early 2000's, scientists used radio telescopes to hunt for signals coming from many hundreds of stars. Also in the 2000's, researchers began building the Allen Telescope Array in California, which was designed to conduct SETI studies of about 1 million stars.

In the late 1990's, astronomers also began searching for signals in the form of brief, bright flashes of visible light. Scientists think that an extraterrestrial intelligence might produce such flashes with powerful lasers. The flashes could briefly outshine the star near which they originate, but might last only billionths of a second or less. Natural sources are not known to produce such flashes. Astronomers have used visible-light telescopes and electronic equipment to try to detect such events.

Many people wonder whether intelligent extraterrestrial life could have come to Earth. Each year, thousands of people report seeing unidentified flying objects (UFO's). Some people believe that such objects could be spacecraft from other worlds. But scientists who study UFO reports have found that most sightings can be explained as ordinary things, such as airplanes or balloons, or as natural astronomical objects, such as meteors or bright stars. Scientists have no evidence that Earth has ever been visited by extraterrestrials. Seth Shostak

See also **Astrobiology; Life** (The search for life on other worlds); **SETI Institute; Unidentified flying object.**

Extreme unction. See **Anointing of the sick.**

Extremophile is an organism that grows best in environments that, because of one or more extremely difficult conditions, cannot easily support other life. These conditions may be divided into two basic types. *Physical extremes* include harsh temperatures and high water pressure or radiation levels. *Chemical extremes* include high levels of salt or acid chemicals. Most extremophiles belong to the *archaea* or *bacteria* group of microscopic, one-celled organisms. Scientists often divide extremophiles into several other categories, based on the conditions in which the organisms thrive. Individual *species* (kinds) may belong to more than one of these groups.

Extremophiles that live in physical extremes include *thermophiles,* which grow best in temperatures of 113 °F (45 °C) or above. *Psychrophiles* prefer colder habitats. They cannot survive temperatures higher than 68 °F (20 °C). Many *barophiles,* or *piezophiles,* thrive in the deep sea or other places with high water pressure. *Xerophiles* live in such dry places as deserts or the insides of dried fruit. *Radioresistants* can grow in areas with high levels of radiation. One species, *Deinococcus radiodurans,* can survive radiation levels hundreds of times greater than levels that would kill a human being.

Extremophiles that live in chemical extremes include *halophiles,* which grow best in areas with high amounts of salt. Another group, the *acidophiles,* prefer habitats with high levels of acid chemicals. Chemical extremes may occur in mining sites, hot springs, or salty water.

Many extremophiles have proved useful to people. Antibiotics and other pharmaceutical products are derived from these organisms. Extremophiles also provide ingredients for detergents, food supplements, and other products. In addition, scientists believe radioresistants and other extremophiles may help clean up areas damaged by radiation or harmful chemicals. Kesen Ma

See also **Archaea; Bacteria; Hydrothermal vent.**

Extrovert, when used nontechnically, means a sociable person who makes friends easily. In psychiatry, the word has a somewhat different meaning. The Swiss psychiatrist Carl G. Jung defined *extroversion* as turning the interests and energies of the mind toward events, people, and things of the outer world. As a result, extroverts are more interested in what is going on around them than in their own thoughts and feelings. In normal people, extroversion is counterbalanced by introversion, and a wholesome balance is maintained between the two tendencies (see **Introvert**). Paula J. Clayton

Extrusion is the process of shaping a piece of solid material, such as aluminum, by forcing it through a smaller opening. A large press is used to force the material through a shaped hole called a *die.* Extrusion produces many shapes, including bars, tubes, and wires. Metals, plastics, and rubber can be extruded.

The direct process (also called forward process) is the most widely used method of extrusion. In this process, a *ram* (plunger) pushes against a *billet* (short piece of metal or plastic) from one end of an enclosed chamber. The ram forces metal or plastic material through a die opening at the other end of the chamber. Such great force is used that the material flows out of the die like toothpaste out of a tube.

Aluminum beverage cans are made with a specialized extrusion process known as *impact extrusion.* In impact extrusion, the material is forced into a hollow cylinder or tube shape.

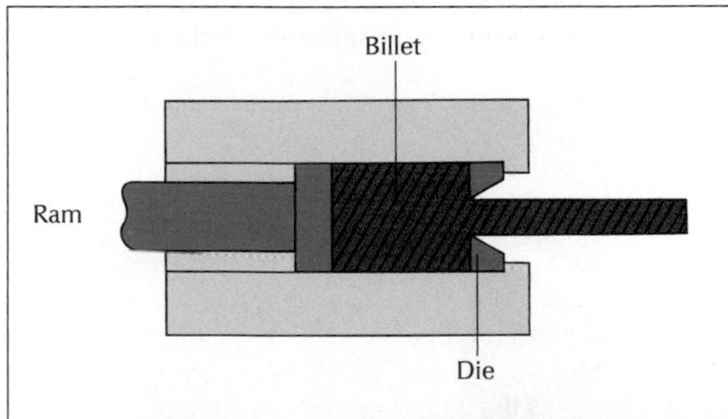

WORLD BOOK diagram by Arthur Grebetz

In extrusion, a solid material such as metal is shaped by forcing it through the opening in a die. The ram at one end of a cylinder pushes against a short piece of metal called a *billet.* The billet flows out of the other end of the cylinder.

Extrusion for metals can be done with either room temperature or heated material. The hot extrusion process is used most often because heat improves the material's ability to be shaped. Heat also reduces the force required for shaping. Before extrusion, metal billets can be heated to temperatures ranging from 400 °F (204 °C) to more than 2000 °F (1093 °C), depending on the type of metal that is extruded.

During plastic extrusion, plastic pellets are heated and mixed with additives in a chamber called an extruder. The soft plastic mass is forced through the extrusion die and cooled as it exits. Extruding plastics can produce such shapes as pipe for homes and fine threads for clothing. Rose M. Torielli and Robert C. Voigt

See also **Plastics** (Extrusion); **Rubber** (Shaping).

Exxon Mobil Corporation is a large petroleum company. It was formed in 1999 when the two largest oil companies in the United States, the Exxon and Mobil corporations, merged. The company is also known as ExxonMobil.

Both Exxon and Mobil began as part of the Standard Oil Trust established by John D. Rockefeller in 1882. In 1911, an antitrust ruling by the Supreme Court of the United States forced the trust to dissolve. The trust was broken up into 34 companies, including the Standard Oil Company of New Jersey and the Standard Oil Company of New York. The New Jersey company changed its name to Exxon Corporation in 1972. The Standard Oil Company of New York became Mobil Oil Corporation in 1966. In 1976, Mobil Oil became a subsidiary of a newly formed Mobil Corporation.

ExxonMobil's principal activities include every phase of the oil and natural gas industry. It owns thousands of oil wells and natural gas wells and about 40 refineries, which can produce a total of more than 6 million barrels per day. It owns or shares ownership in thousands of miles of pipeline and operates one of the world's largest tanker fleets. More than 30,000 service stations worldwide sell the company's products. It also takes part in the research and development of such energy sources as coal, hydrogen, and solar power. In addition, the company manufactures *petrochemicals* (chemicals made from petroleum or natural gas) and has mining interests. ExxonMobil's headquarters are in Irving, Texas.

Before the merger with Mobil, Exxon was involved in one of the largest oil spills in U.S. history. In 1989, the tanker *Exxon Valdez* struck a reef off southeastern Alaska, spilling nearly 11 million gallons (42 million liters) of crude oil. Exxon paid over $3.5 billion for cleanup, compensation, and environmental restoration. See also **Alaska** (Recent developments); **Exxon Valdez oil spill.**

Critically reviewed by Exxon Mobil Corporation

Exxon Valdez oil spill was one of the worst environmental disasters in United States history. In March 1989, the oil tanker *Exxon Valdez* struck a reef off southeastern Alaska. The tanker spilled nearly 11 million gallons (42 million liters) of crude oil into Prince William Sound, part of the Gulf of Alaska. The oil polluted beaches and fishing waters and caused great harm to wildlife.

On the night of March 23, the *Exxon Valdez* left Valdez, Alaska, with 53 million gallons (200 million liters) of crude oil. The Exxon Corporation—a petroleum company now known as ExxonMobil—owned the ship, and Captain Joseph J. Hazelwood commanded it. About two hours after leaving the dock, Hazelwood set the *Valdez* on autopilot and left a junior officer in charge. Early on March 24, the *Valdez* ran aground on Bligh Reef. Several of the ship's cargo tanks ruptured, and millions of gallons of oil poured into Prince William Sound. The spill contaminated about 1,300 miles (2,100 kilometers) of coastline and killed many thousands of animals.

The disaster brought worldwide attention to issues of oil tanker safety. In March 1990, an Alaska court found Captain Hazelwood guilty of "negligent discharge of oil." He was fined and sentenced to community service. In September 1991, Exxon pleaded guilty to several violations related to the spill. The company paid hundreds of millions of dollars in fines. Kenneth J. Shenkman

Eyck, Jan Van. See Van Eyck, Jan.

Eye

Eye is the organ of sight. It is our most important organ for finding out about the world around us. We use our eyes in almost everything we do—reading, working, recognizing faces, watching movies and television, playing games, and countless other activities. Sight is our most precious sense, and many people fear blindness more than any other disability.

The human eyeball measures only about 1 inch (25 millimeters) in diameter. Yet the eye can see objects as far away as a star and as tiny as a grain of sand. The eye can quickly adjust its focus between a distant point and a near one. It can be accurately directed toward an object even while the head is moving.

The eye does not actually see objects. Instead, it sees the light they reflect or give off. The eye can see in bright light and in dim light, but it cannot see in no light at all. Light rays enter the eye through transparent tissues. The eye changes the rays into electrical signals. The signals are then sent to the brain, which interprets them as visual images.

This article deals mainly with the human eye. It discusses the parts of the eye, how we see, defects and diseases of the eye, and care of the eye. The last section of the article describes some of the differences in the eyes of various kinds of animals.

Parts of the eye

Each eyeball is set in a protective cone-shaped cavity in the skull. This cavity is called the *orbit* or *socket*. Its ridges form the brow and the cheekbone. Fatty tissue inside the orbit nearly surrounds the eyeball and cushions it. The soft tissue also enables the eye to turn easily in the orbit. Six muscles move the eyeball in much the same way that strings move the parts of a puppet.

Around the eye are the *eyelids,* the *conjunctiva,* the *lacrimal glands,* and the *lacrimal sac.* Three layers of tissue form the wall of the eyeball: (1) the sclera and the cornea, (2) the uveal tract, and (3) the retina. Inside the eyeball is a clear, jellylike substance called the *vitreous humor.* This substance occupies about 80 percent of the eyeball. It helps maintain the shape of the eye and the pressure within the eyeball.

The outer parts. The front of the eyeball is protected by the eyelids. Eyelashes on the lids screen out some of the dust and other particles that might otherwise enter the eye. Any sudden movement in front of the eye—or anything that touches the eyelashes—causes the lids to blink in a protective reflex action.

The conjunctiva is a membrane that lines the inside of the eyelids and extends over the front of the white part of the eye. It produces *mucus,* a clear, slimy fluid that lubricates the inside of the eyelid and the outside of the eyeball. The conjunctiva also produces some tears, which help keep the eye moist and clean. However, most tears are made by the lacrimal glands. A lacrimal gland lies at the upper outer corner of each orbit. Every time a person blinks, the eyelids spread a smooth layer of mucus and tears over the eye. These fluids then flow into tiny canals in the lids. The canals lead to the lacrimal sac, a pouch at the lower inner corner of each orbit. From the lacrimal sac, the mucus and tears drain through a passage into the nose. After crying, a person may have to blow the nose to clear this drainage system of the excess tears.

The sclera and the cornea consist of tough tissues that make up the outer layer of the eyeball and give it strength. The sclera covers about five-sixths of the eyeball, and the cornea about one-sixth. The sclera is the white part of the eye. It has the strength and feel of soft leather. Although the sclera appears to have many blood vessels on its surface, most of these vessels are part of the conjunctiva. The cornea has no blood vessels at all and has relatively little internal moisture. As a result, it is transparent. The cornea lies in front of the colored part of the eye and resembles the crystal of a wrist watch. The cornea enables light rays to enter the eyeball.

The uveal tract is the middle layer of the wall of the eyeball. It has three parts. They are, from front to back: (1) the iris, (2) the ciliary body, and (3) the choroid.

The iris is the colored disk behind the cornea. The color of the iris comes from a brownish-black substance called *melanin.* The more melanin there is and the closer it is to the surface of the tissue, the darker the color of the iris. For example, there is more melanin in brown eyes—and the melanin is closer to the surface—than in

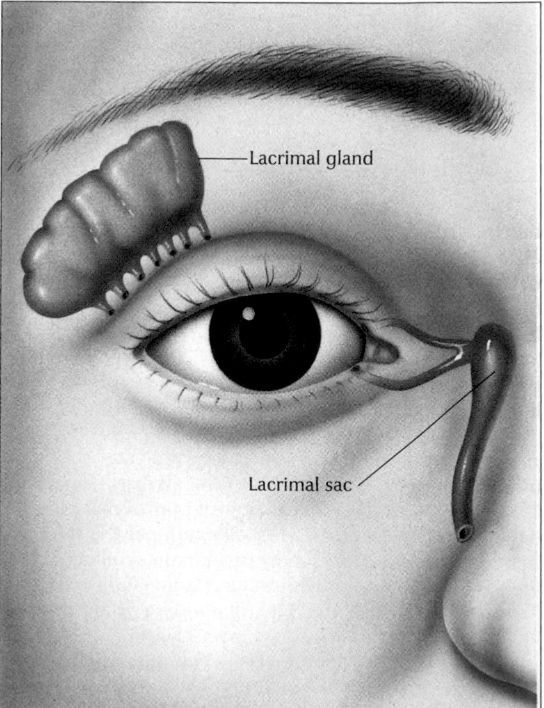

WORLD BOOK illustration by Charles Wellek

The human eyes produce tears by means of the *lacrimal glands,* one of which lies above each eyeball. The tears wash the surface of the eye and then flow into canals leading to the *lacrimal sac.* From here, the tears drain into the nose.

Morton F. Goldberg, the contributor of this article, is the Joseph Green Professor of Ophthalmology and former Chairman of the Department of Ophthalmology at the Wilmer Eye Institute of the Johns Hopkins School of Medicine in Baltimore.

Parts of the eye The visible parts of the eyeball are the white *sclera* and the colored *iris.* A clear membrane called the *conjunctiva* covers the sclera. The transparent *cornea* lies in front of the iris. The *lens* is connected to the *ciliary body.* Inside the eyeball is a clear substance called *vitreous humor.* The *retina,* which underlies the *choroid,* changes light rays into electrical signals. The *optic nerve* carries the signals to the brain. The *fovea centralis,* a pit in the *macula lutea,* is the area of sharpest vision.

WORLD BOOK illustrations by Charles Wellek

Eye
muscles
Optic
nerve
Vitreous humor
Cornea
Iris
Lens
Macula
lutea
Fovea
centralis
Ciliary body
Sclera
Choroid
Conjunctiva
Retina

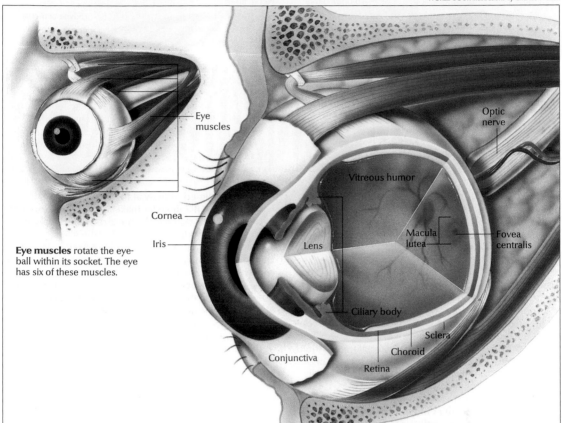

Eye muscles rotate the eyeball within its socket. The eye has six of these muscles.

blue eyes. In addition to giving the iris color, melanin absorbs strong light that might otherwise dazzle the eye or cause blurred vision. Melanin is the same substance found in freckles and that gives skin and hair their color. People called *albinos* have little or no melanin. *True* (complete) albinos have milky-white skin, white hair, and blue or translucent irises. Poor vision and sensitivity to light is common in all types of albinos. See **Albino**.

At the center of the iris is a round opening called the *pupil,* which looks like a black circle. The size of the pupil determines the amount of light that enters the eye. Two muscles in the iris automatically adjust the size of the pupil to the level of light. In dim light, the *dilator muscle* enlarges the pupil. As much light as possible can then enter the eye. In bright light, the *sphincter muscle* makes the pupil smaller, which prevents too much light from entering the eye. The pupil also becomes smaller when the eye looks at a nearby object, thus bringing the image into sharp focus.

The ciliary body encircles the iris. It is connected by strong fibers to the *crystalline lens,* which lies directly behind the iris. The lens is a flexible structure about the size and shape of an aspirin tablet. Like the cornea, the lens is transparent because it has no blood vessels and

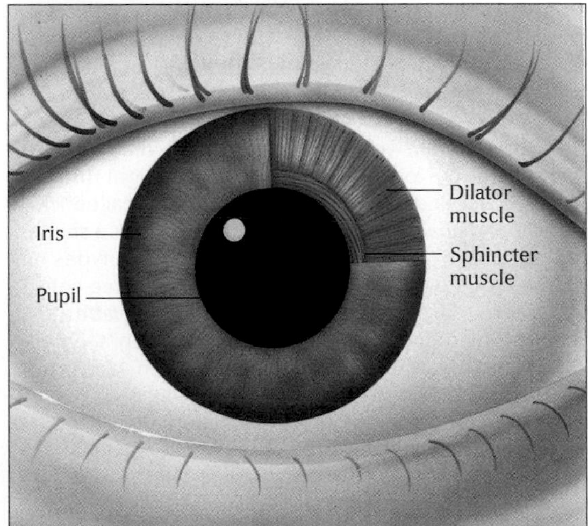

WORLD BOOK illustration by Charles Wellek

The iris has a round opening called the *pupil,* which regulates the amount of light that enters the eye. In dim light, the *dilator muscle* pulls the pupil open wider. In bright light, the *sphincter muscle* tightens around the pupil and makes it smaller.

Structure of the retina

The retina has cells called *rods* and *cones,* which absorb light rays and change them into electrical signals. The cones are concentrated in the *macula.* Light rays from objects are focused by the eye to come together at the *fovea centralis,* a tiny pit in the center of the macula. Nerve fibers attached to the rods and cones form the optic nerve.

WORLD BOOK diagram by Charles Wellek

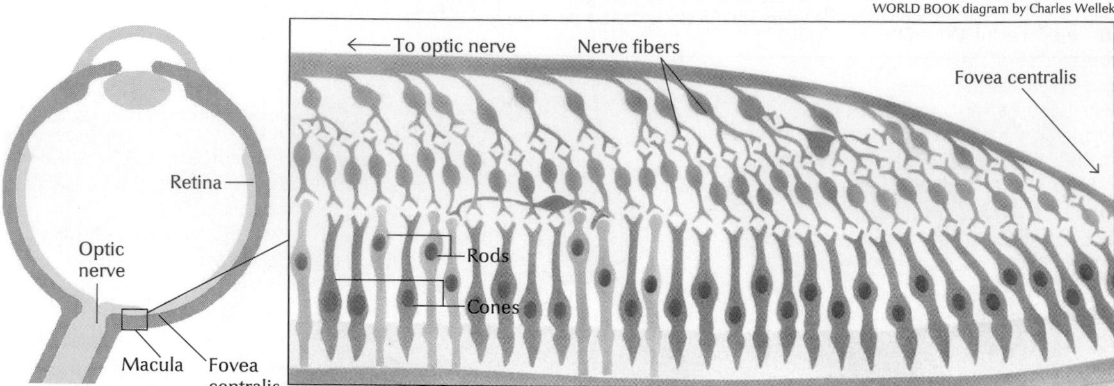

is relatively dehydrated. The muscles of the ciliary body make constant adjustments in the shape of the lens. These adjustments produce a sharp visual image at all times as the eye shifts focus between nearby and distant objects. The ciliary body also produces a clear, watery fluid called *aqueous humor.* This fluid nourishes and lubricates the cornea and the lens, and it fills the area between them. The ciliary body produces aqueous humor continuously. The old fluid flows into a drainage system at a spongy, circular groove where the cornea and the sclera meet. It then travels through the veins of the conjunctiva into the veins of the neck.

The choroid forms the back of the uveal tract. It looks and feels like a blotter soaked with black ink. The choroid has many blood vessels. Blood from the choroid nourishes the outer part of the retina.

The retina makes up the innermost layer of the wall of the eyeball. It is about as fragile as a piece of wet tissue paper. Light-sensitive cells in the retina absorb light rays and change them into electrical signals. There are two types of these cells—*rods* and *cones.* The cells are named for their shape. The retina has about 120 million rods and about 6 million cones. Other cells in the retina, called *intrinsically photosensitive retinal ganglion cells* (ipRGC's), detect light and help identify images.

Bits of *pigment* (colored material) in the rods and cones absorb even the smallest particle of light that strikes the retina. The pigment in the rods is called *rhodopsin* or *visual purple.* It enables the eye to see shades of gray and to see in dim light. There are three types of pigment in the cones. They enable the eye to see colors and to see sharp images in bright light. *Cyanolabe* absorbs blue light. *Chlorolabe* absorbs green light. *Erythrolabe* absorbs red light. These pigments enable us to distinguish more than 200 colors.

Near the center of the retina is a round area called the *macula lutea* or *macula.* The macula consists chiefly of cones. It produces a sharp image of scenes at which the eyes are directly aimed, especially in bright light. The rest of the retina provides *peripheral vision*—that is, it enables the eyes to see objects to the side while looking straight ahead. Most of the rods lie in this part of the retina. Because rods are more sensitive in the dark than cones, faint objects often can be seen more clearly if the eyes are not aimed directly at them. For example, looking to the side of a dim star makes its image fall on the part of the retina that has the most rods and provides the best vision in dim light.

Nerve fibers attached to the rods and cones join at the center of the retina and form the *optic nerve.* This nerve consists of about a million fibers. It serves as a flexible cable that connects the eyeball to the brain. In fact, the optic nerve and the retina are actually extensions of the brain. The optic nerve carries the electrical signals produced in the retina to the brain, which interprets them as visual images.

The point where the optic nerve enters the eye is known as the *blind spot.* It has no rods or cones and therefore cannot respond to light. Normally, a person does not notice the blind spot because it covers such a small area and the eyes make so many quick movements. In addition, anything the blind spot of one eye cannot see is seen by the other eye. See **Blind spot.**

How we see

Focusing. Light rays that enter the eye must come to a point on the retina for a clear visual image to form. However, the light rays that objects reflect or give off do not naturally move toward one another. Instead, they either spread out or travel almost parallel. The focusing parts of the eye—the cornea and the lens—bend the rays toward one another. The cornea provides most of the *refracting* (bending) power of the eye. After light rays pass through the cornea, they travel through the aqueous humor and the pupil to the lens. The lens bends the rays even closer together before they go through the vitreous humor and strike the retina. Light rays from objects at which the eyes are aimed come together at the *fovea centralis,* a tiny pit in the center of the macula. It is the area of sharpest vision. Light rays from objects to the sides strike more peripheral areas of the retina.

The refracting power of the lens changes constantly as the eye shifts focus between nearby objects and distant ones. Light rays from nearby objects spread out, and those from distant objects travel nearly parallel. Therefore, the lens must provide greater bending power to make the light rays from nearby objects come together. This additional power is produced by a process called *accommodation.* In this process, one of the muscles of the ciliary body contracts, thereby relaxing the fibers that connect the ciliary body to the lens. As a result, the lens becomes rounder and thicker and thus more powerful. When the eye looks at distant objects, the muscle of the ciliary body relaxes. This action tightens the fibers that are connected to the lens, and the lens becomes flatter. For this reason, the eye cannot form a sharp image of a nearby object and a distant one at the same time.

Depth perception is the ability to judge distance and to tell the thickness of objects. The lens system of the eye, like the lens of a camera, reverses images. Thus, the images that form on the retina are much like those produced on film in a camera. The images are upside down and reversed left to right. They are also flat, as in a photograph. However, the brain interprets the images as they really are. The ability of the brain to interpret retinal images right-side up, unreversed, and in depth comes from experience that begins at a person's birth.

The optic nerves from the two eyes meet at the base of the brain at a point called the *optic chiasm.* At the optic chiasm, half the nerve fibers from each eye cross over and join the fibers from the other eye. Each side of the brain receives visual messages from both eyes. The nerve fibers from the right half of each eye enter the right side of the brain. These fibers carry visual messages from objects that are to a person's left. The

How the eye focuses

Distance vision

Distant objects reflect or give off light rays that are nearly parallel as they enter the eye. The cornea and the lens bend the rays toward one another, which makes them come together on the retina and form a clear visual image.

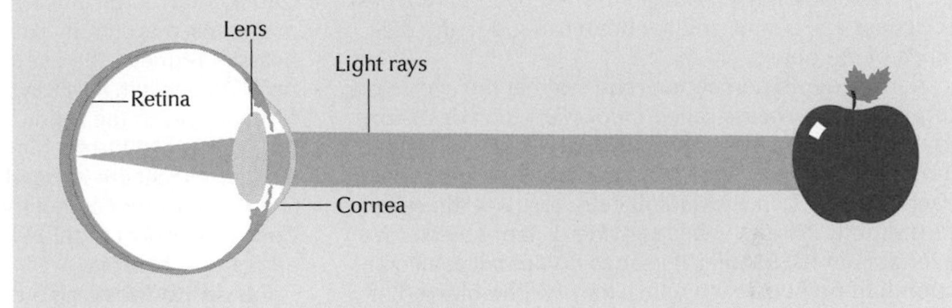

Near vision

Nearby objects reflect or give off light rays that are spreading out as they enter the eye. Greater bending power is thus needed to bring these rays together. The lens provides this power by becoming rounder and thicker in a process called *accommodation.*

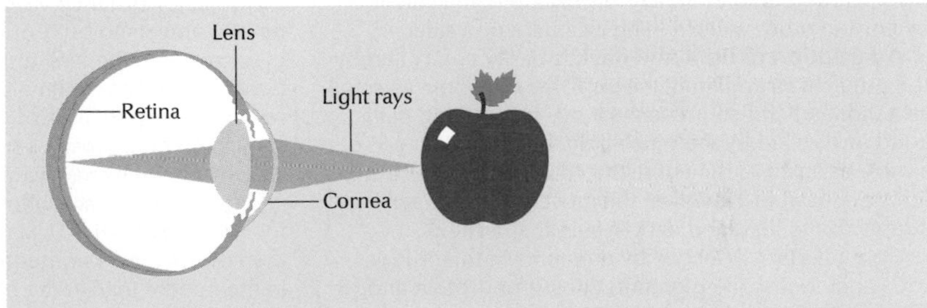

WORLD BOOK diagrams by Linda Kinnaman

How we see in depth

Depth perception is the ability to judge distance and to tell the thickness of objects. Because the eyes are set slightly apart, each one sees objects from a slightly different angle. As a result, each eye sends a slightly different message to the brain. Some of the nerve fibers from each eye cross over at the *optic chiasm.* Each side of the brain thus receives visual messages from both eyes. The brain puts the images together and so provides depth perception.

WORLD BOOK diagram

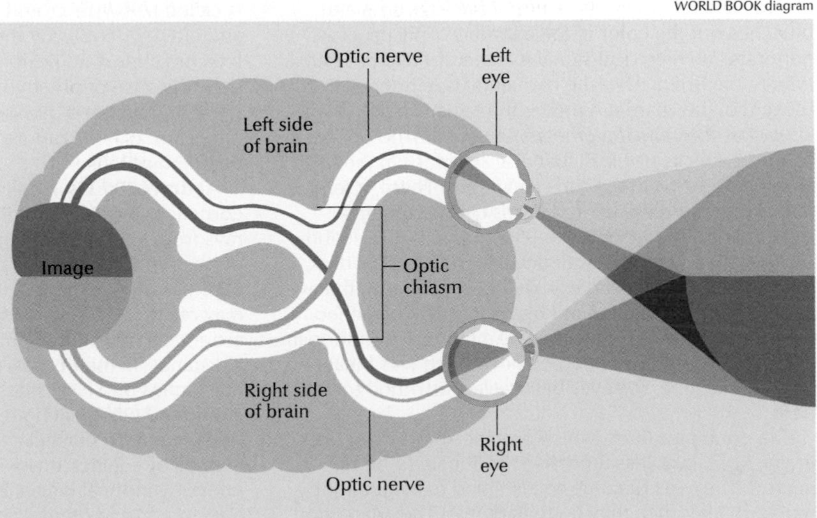

nerve fibers from the left half of each eye enter the left side of the brain. These fibers carry visual messages from objects that are to a person's right. Thus, if one side of the brain becomes damaged, the opposite side of a person's field of vision may be reduced. Such damage may occur as a result of a stroke, injury, or tumor.

The eyes are about 2 ½ inches (6.4 centimeters) apart from center to center. For this reason, each eye sees things from a slightly different angle and sends slightly different messages to the brain. The difference can be demonstrated by focusing on a nearby object first with one eye closed and then with the other eye closed. The image seen with each eye is slightly different. The brain puts the images together and thus provides depth perception, also called *stereoscopic vision* or *three-dimensional vision.* The image formed by the brain has thickness and shape, and the brain can judge the distance of the object.

Normal depth perception requires that the eyes work together in a process called *binocular vision* or *fusion.* In this process, the eye muscles move the eyes so that light rays from an object fall at a corresponding point on each retina. When viewing objects close up, the eyes turn slightly inward. When viewing distant objects, the eyes are almost parallel. If images do not fall at a corresponding point on each retina, they will be blurred or be seen as double, or the brain will ignore one of them.

In most people, visual messages are stronger in one eye and on one side of the brain than the other. Most people are "right-eyed" or "left-eyed," just as they are right-handed or left-handed. For example, they favor one eye or the other when aiming a camera or a rifle.

Adaptation to light and dark is partly controlled by the pupil. In strong light, the pupil may become as small as a pinhead and so prevent the eye from being damaged or dazzled by too much light. In the dark, it can get almost as large as the entire iris, thus letting in as much light as possible. However, the most important part of adaptation to light and dark occurs in the retina.

Light rays are absorbed by pigments in the retina's rods and cones. The pigments consist of protein and vitamin A. Vitamin A helps give the pigments their color. The color enables the pigments to absorb light. Light changes the chemical structure of the vitamin A and bleaches out the color in the pigments. This process generates an electrical signal that the optic nerve transmits to the brain. After the pigments have been bleached, the vitamin A moves into a part of the retina known as the *retinal pigmented epithelium* (RPE). The vitamin regains its original chemical structure in the RPE and then returns to the rods and cones. There, it joins with protein molecules and forms fresh pigments.

The renewal of rhodopsin—the pigment that enables the eye to see in dim light—occurs largely in the dark. Immediately after being exposed to bright light, the eyes cannot see well in dim light because of the bleached rhodopsin. It takes about 10 to 30 minutes for rhodopsin to be renewed, depending on how much was bleached. During this time, the eyes become accustomed to the dark.

The cone pigments, which provide sharp vision in bright light, take less time than rhodopsin to be renewed. The eyes become accustomed to bright light much quicker than they do to darkness. The adaptation from darkness to light depends largely on changes in the retina's nerve cells.

Defects of the eye

Defects of the eye are among the most common of all physical disorders. Certain defects cannot be cured, but vision can be improved by means of eyeglasses, contact lenses, or surgery. The most common defects of the eye include (1) nearsightedness, (2) farsightedness, (3) astigmatism, (4) strabismus, and (5) color blindness. A type of surgery called *LASIK (la*ser in *si*tu *k*eratomileusis) can correct nearsightedness, farsightedness, and astigmatism. In this surgery, a laser is used to reshape the cornea.

Nearsightedness, also called *myopia,* is characterized by blurred distance vision, though near vision remains sharp except in extreme cases. In most cases of nearsightedness, the eyeball is too long from front to back. As a result, light rays from distant objects meet before they reach the retina. When the light rays do strike the retina, they form a blurred image. Eyeglasses or contact lenses that are *concave* bring the light rays together at the retina and correct most cases of nearsightedness. Concave lenses are thinner in the middle than at the edges. See **Myopia.**

Farsightedness, also called *hyperopia,* occurs in most cases because the eyeball is too short from front to back. Unless the lens accommodates, light rays from distant objects reach the retina before they meet, causing a blurred image. The lens of a normal eye remains relatively flat for distance vision and becomes thicker for nearby objects to be brought into focus. In a farsighted eye, however, the lens must also thicken for sharp distance vision. The retina of the farsighted eye therefore receives sharp images of distant objects. But the constant use of the muscles of the ciliary body to adjust the shape of the lens may cause eyestrain and headaches. In addition, the lens sometimes may not thicken enough for sharp near vision. Glasses or contact lenses that are *convex* correct farsightedness. Convex lenses are thicker in the middle than at the edges. See **Farsightedness.**

Between the ages of 40 to 50, a person's lens begins to harden and to lose its ability to thicken. This condition is called *presbyopia,* and it affects nearly all middle-aged and elderly people. By the time a person is about 60, the lens has almost no flexibility and can barely accommodate. Because of presbyopia, most middle-aged and elderly people need glasses for reading and close work. If they wore glasses before, they may need new glasses with bifocal lenses.

Astigmatism is usually caused by a misshapen cornea. As a result of the abnormal shape, all the light rays from an object do not come together at one point on the retina. Some rays may focus on the retina. But others may meet before they reach the retina, or they may reach the retina before they meet. Most cases of astigmatism produce blurred vision both nearby and at a distance. In mild cases, there may be eyestrain and headaches but fairly sharp vision. Astigmatism may be combined with nearsightedness, farsightedness, or presbyopia. To correct astigmatism, doctors prescribe glasses or contact lenses that have *cylindrical components.* Cylindrical lenses have greater bending power in one axis than in others. See **Astigmatism.**

Defects of the eye

Eye defects are among the most common physical disorders. They include (1) nearsightedness, (2) farsightedness, and (3) astigmatism. These defects cannot usually be cured, but vision can be made normal in most cases by means of eyeglasses or contact lenses, or, occasionally, by surgery.

WORLD BOOK photos

WORLD BOOK diagrams by Linda Kinnaman

Nearsightedness occurs if light rays from distant objects meet before they reach the retina. In most cases, distance vision is blurred, but near vision is sharp. Glasses or contacts that have *concave lenses* bring the rays together at the retina and correct nearsightedness.

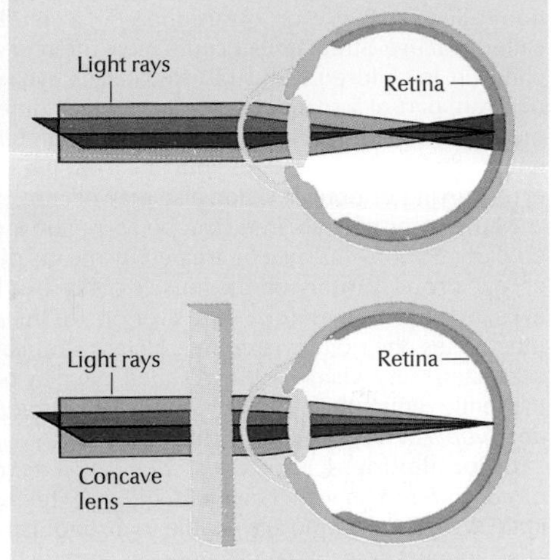

Farsightedness occurs if light rays from distant objects reach the retina before they meet. In many cases, the lens can accommodate enough for sharp distance vision but not sharp near vision. Glasses or contacts that have *convex lenses* correct farsightedness.

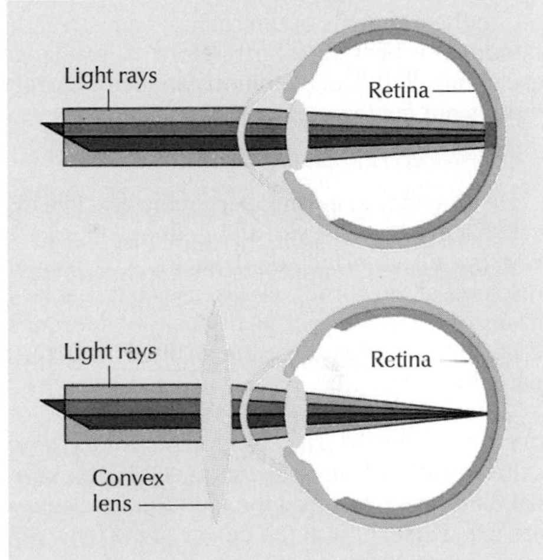

Astigmatism results if all the light rays from an object do not come together at one point in the eye. Most cases of astigmatism produce blurred vision both nearby and at a distance. Eyeglasses or contact lenses that have *cylindrical lenses* correct the defect.

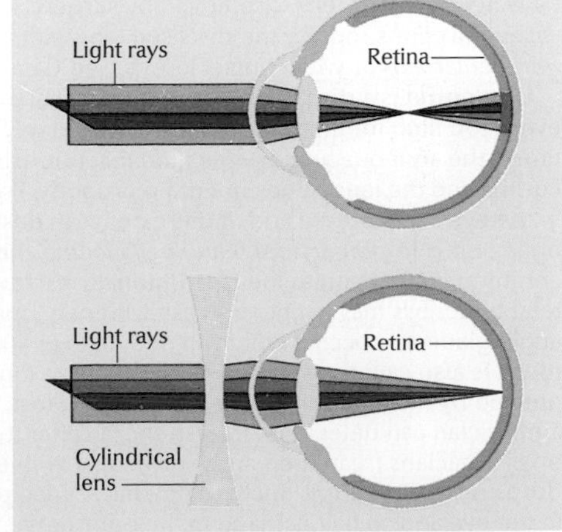

Strabismus is a defect in which the eyes are not used together. One of the eyes is *deviated* (turned too far in one direction) all or part of the time. In most cases, the deviated eye is turned either toward the nose, a condition called *cross-eye,* or toward the side, a condition called *walleye.* Strabismus occurs most often in young children. In children with strabismus, each eye sees a different part of a scene and sends a greatly different message to the brain. In most cases, the brain tends to ignore the weaker message—the one from the deviated eye. Blurring or double vision also may occur.

Many cases of strabismus can be corrected if detected early. Strabismus may be treated by means of glasses, eye drops, surgery on the muscles of one or both eyes, or a patch worn for a time over one of the eyes—in most cases, the nondeviated one. Unless strabismus is corrected early, vision in the deviated eye may be permanently reduced. This condition is called *strabismic amblyopia* or *lazy eye.* See **Strabismus.**

Color blindness, also called *color vision deficiency* or *color-defective vision,* refers to difficulty telling colors apart. Very few people are unable to distinguish colors at all. In most cases of color blindness, certain colors are confused with others. For example, a green object may appear brown. Color blindness is caused by abnormalities in the pigments of the retina's cones. Nearly all color blindness is present at birth. More males than females are color blind. The condition cannot be corrected, but it does not get worse. See **Color blindness.**

Diseases of the eye

Disease may affect any part of the eye. Eye diseases cause a great majority of all blindness. Injuries cause the rest. Eye diseases include (1) cataract, (2) glaucoma, (3) diseases of the cornea, (4) diseases of the sclera, (5) diseases of the uveal tract, (6) diseases of the retina, (7) diseases of the optic nerve, and (8) diseases of the outer parts of the eye.

Cataract is a condition in which part or all of the lens becomes clouded. The clouded part of the lens is also called a cataract. Severely reduced vision—or even partial blindness—results if the cloudiness covers a large area, is dense, or is at the center of the lens. However, some cataracts cause little or no loss of vision. Most cataracts result from aging. If a cataract causes enough loss of vision that it interferes greatly with a person's daily activities, the lens is removed by surgery. In most cases, surgeons replace the diseased lens with a plastic *intraocular lens* or with contact lenses. See **Cataract.**

Glaucoma is a disease in which the pressure in the eye is too high for the health of the optic nerve. Sometimes, the aqueous humor—the fluid that nourishes the cornea and the lens—does not drain properly. Pressure in the eye can increase and, if untreated, can destroy the optic nerve. In *primary open-angle glaucoma,* the most common type, vision to the side gradually narrows, and total blindness may eventually result. Primary open-angle glaucoma occurs chiefly in people over 40 years old. It is also called *chronic simple glaucoma.* It goes unnoticed by most people until some vision is lost, though a physician can detect the disease shortly after it develops. Physicians treat open-angle glaucoma with eye drops or laser therapy. Such treatments reduce pressure in the eye and so halt damage to the optic nerve. Most patients must use the eye drops throughout life and some will require periodic laser treatments. If these therapies are not effective, a new drainage channel for the aqueous humor is surgically made or the old channels are surgically reopened.

A type of glaucoma called *primary narrow-angle glaucoma* or *acute glaucoma* may occur suddenly at any age. Its symptoms include pain in the eyes or forehead and seeing halos or rainbows around lights. Immediate surgery or laser treatment may be necessary to prevent blindness. See **Glaucoma.**

Diseases of the cornea are among the most common eye disorders. The cornea has less protection than any other part of the eyeball. It may be accidentally scratched by an overworn contact lens, a fingernail, or a particle that flies into the eye, and a painful infection can result. Inflammation of the cornea may be caused by the *herpes simplex virus,* the same virus that causes cold sores. Physicians treat infections of the cornea with antibiotics, often in the form of drops or ointments.

A disease called *keratoconus* leads to a deformed cornea. As the disease progresses, the cornea becomes cone-shaped. In the early stages, keratoconus can be treated with glasses or contact lenses. In severe cases, the cornea may be removed by surgery and replaced with a cornea from a person who recently died. The replacement comes from an agency called an *eye bank* (see **Eye bank**). This operation is known as a *corneal transplant* or *corneal graft* and is used to treat many disorders that cause diseased corneas.

Diseases of the sclera, the white part of the eye, are relatively uncommon. Inflammation of the sclera is called *scleritis.* It is often caused by an infection or an allergy, but may also be associated with arthritis. Physicians usually treat scleritis with eye drops or pills.

Disorders of the eye's outer parts

These illustrations show four eye disorders. A *sty* resembles a pimple on the eyelid. A *chalazion* may form a lump under the eyelid. *Conjunctivitis* is an inflammation of the conjunctiva. A *subconjunctival hemorrhage* is a broken blood vessel in the conjunctiva. It is harmless and should clear up in a week or two.

WORLD BOOK illustrations by Charles Wellek

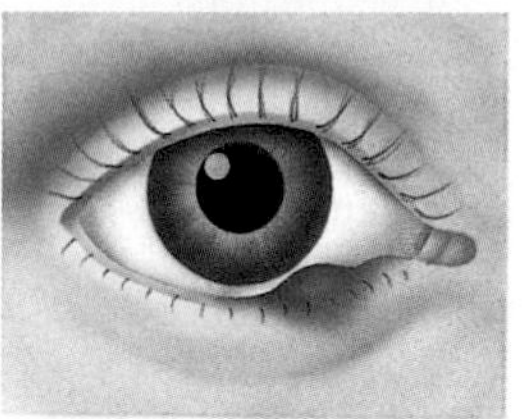

Sty

Chalazion

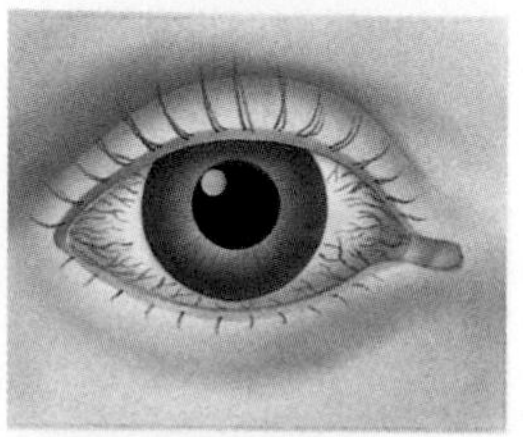

Conjunctivitis

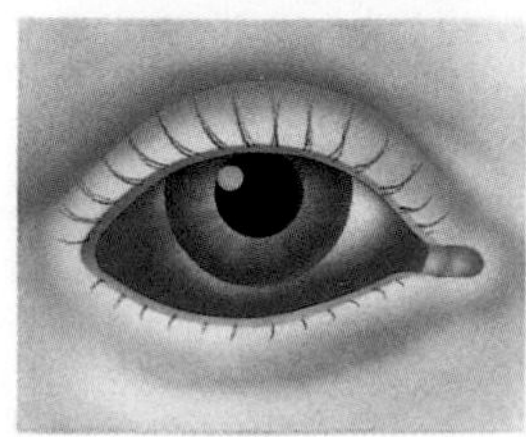

Subconjunctival hemorrhage

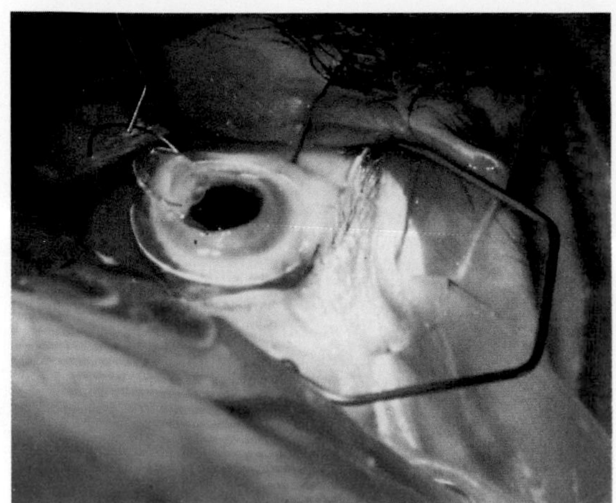

© Chet Szymecki, Phototake

A plastic intraocular lens can restore normal vision in a patient following removal of a cataract. A cataract clouds the eye's lens, causing progressive vision loss. This intraocular lens is being placed in a surgically created incision at the edge of the cornea.

Diseases of the uveal tract. An inflammation of the uveal tract is called *uveitis.* Such diseases include *iritis,* inflammation of the iris; *cyclitis,* inflammation of the ciliary body; and *choroiditis,* inflammation of the choroid. In many instances, the cause of these diseases cannot be determined. Physicians treat such cases by prescribing medications that reduce the inflammation. The uveal tract may also be attacked by a cancerous tumor called a *melanoma.* Physicians may remove the tumor or the entire eye, or they may use other techniques, such as radiation treatments, to prevent the cancer from spreading.

Diseases of the retina. A number of diseases can damage the retina. One of the most common causes of blindness among adults is *diabetic retinopathy,* which strikes some people who have chronic diabetes. After many years of diabetes, the blood vessels of the retina may leak, close up, or begin to grow. These conditions may cause blood to enter the vitreous humor, the clear, jellylike fluid inside the eyeball. The blood makes the vitreous *opaque* (nontransparent), causing blindness. In some cases, a major surgical procedure called a *vitrectomy* can remove the blood and restore vision. In another procedure, a narrow beam of light from a laser destroys the abnormal vessels of the retina before blood enters the vitreous.

Diabetic retinopathy—and many other disorders of the eye—can also result in a *detached retina.* In this condition, the retina pulls away from the choroid. A detached retina can be corrected surgically by indenting the wall of the eyeball so that the choroid meets the retina. If this procedure is successful, the retina then remains attached to the choroid. Vitrectomy can also be used to reattach the retina.

One of a group of diseases called *macular degeneration* may affect the macula, the part of the retina responsible for sharp central vision. The patient loses the ability to see objects at which the eyes are directly aimed, though vision to the side remains. Some cases of macular degeneration are inherited. The most common form, called *age-related macular degeneration* (AMD), appears in old age. Special magnifying devices enable some patients to see well enough to read. There are two major types of macular degeneration. *Dry macular degeneration,* in which the macular tissue wastes away with age, can be treated with specific vitamins, antioxidants, and minerals. *Wet macular degeneration,* in which abnormal and leaky blood vessels grow in the macula, can be treated with lasers and through the regular injection of certain medications directly into the vitreous jelly. These medications act by interfering with the growth of blood vessels in the macula.

A group of diseases called *retinitis pigmentosa* chiefly affects the rods and cones of the retina. One of the first symptoms is *night blindness,* in which a person sees poorly or not at all in dim light or at night. Many patients lose vision to the side and are left with only *tunnel vision.* Some gradually become blind. Retinitis pigmentosa is inherited. Vitamin A, taken in high doses under medical supervision, has been shown to slow the progression of some aspects of this group of diseases.

Cancer of the retina is called *retinoblastoma.* In many cases, it is inherited, and a tumor forms in the retina in early childhood. Doctors treat the disease with drugs or, in some cases, X rays. Some patients must have the eye removed.

A blood disease called *sickle cell anemia* damages many parts of the body and may eventually result in death. The disease can cause a condition known as *sickle cell retinopathy.* In this condition, the blood vessels of the retina may clot and then may begin to grow and bleed. Blindness may result. Some cases of sickle cell retinopathy can be treated successfully by means of a laser or by eye surgery. See **Sickle cell anemia.**

A condition called *retinopathy of prematurity* can occur in some premature infants. Immediately after birth, premature infants are sometimes placed in incubators, which provide warmth and a high level of oxygen. How-

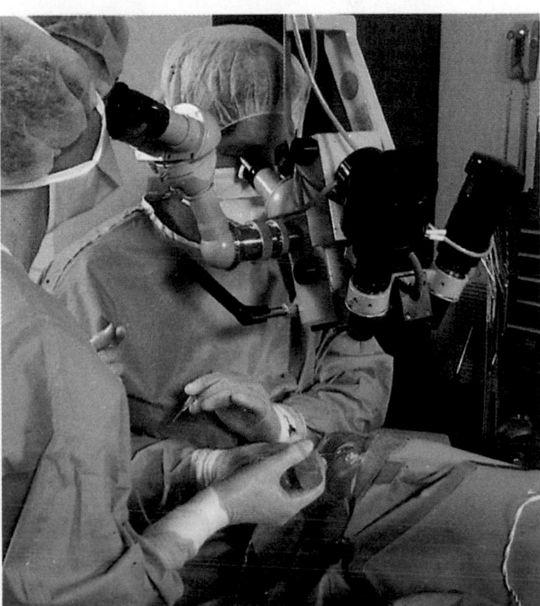

© Bob Hahn, Taurus

Eye surgery is often performed with the aid of a microscope to magnify the small, delicate structures of the eye.

When to consult an eye doctor

Doctors recommend that everyone have an eye examination shortly after birth and at least every few years until the age of 40. Thereafter, the eyes should be examined about once a year or every two years. In addition, the eyes should be examined any time one of the following conditions persists:

1. Blurred vision.
2. Constant rubbing of the eyes.
3. Cross-eye or walleye.
4. Difficulty seeing either nearby objects or distant ones.
5. Double vision.
6. A drooping eyelid.
7. Excessive tearing by the eyes.
8. The feeling of having a particle in one eye or both eyes.
9. Pain in an eye or brow.
10. Poorer vision in one eye than the other.
11. Redness of the eyes.
12. Seeing flashes of light or spots in front of the eyes.
13. Seeing halos or rainbows around lights.
14. Sensitivity of the eyes to light.
15. Squinting.
16. A white or yellow appearance to the pupil.
17. Inequality in the size of the two pupils.

ever, the incubator's high oxygen level may contribute to abnormal development of the blood vessels of the retina in some infants. This condition can lead to permanently reduced vision or even blindness. Physicians may use laser treatments or a surgical technique called *cryotherapy* to treat retinopathy of prematurity. Cryotherapy involves freezing part of the eye in order to stop or slow the growth of abnormal tissue in the retina.

Diseases of the optic nerve. The optic nerve can be damaged by *optic neuritis* (inflammation of the optic nerve), tumors, infection, and other diseases. Not all diseases of the optic nerve can be treated.

Diseases of the outer parts. Various diseases can affect the outer parts of the eye. A *sty* is an infection of one of the sacs from which the eyelashes grow. A sty looks like a pimple on the edge of the eyelid. Sties may be treated by applying a moist, warm cloth and with prescribed antibiotics. In some cases, pus from a sty may have to be drained by minor surgery. See **Sty**.

A *chalazion* is a blocked gland along the inside of the eyelid. If the gland becomes infected, a lump may form under the lid. The infected gland is treated the same way as a sty. After the infection clears up, the chalazion may be removed by minor surgery.

Conjunctivitis is an inflammation of the conjunctiva, the membrane that lines the eyelids and covers the surface of the eyeball. Some types of conjunctivitis are called *pinkeye.* The disease may be caused by an infection, by an allergy, or by such substances as smoke or smog. The eyes become red and watery, and pus may form. Many types of conjunctivitis are contagious. They are often spread when someone uses the same towel or swims in the same swimming pool as a person who has the disease. Doctors often treat conjunctivitis with eye drops. They also may advise patients to take precautions so as to avoid infecting others. See **Conjunctivitis.**

Some animal eyes Most animals have organs of some kind that sense light. In some animals, these organs can only tell light from dark. The eyes of certain other animals can see objects clearly even in dim light.

WORLD BOOK illustrations by John Dawson

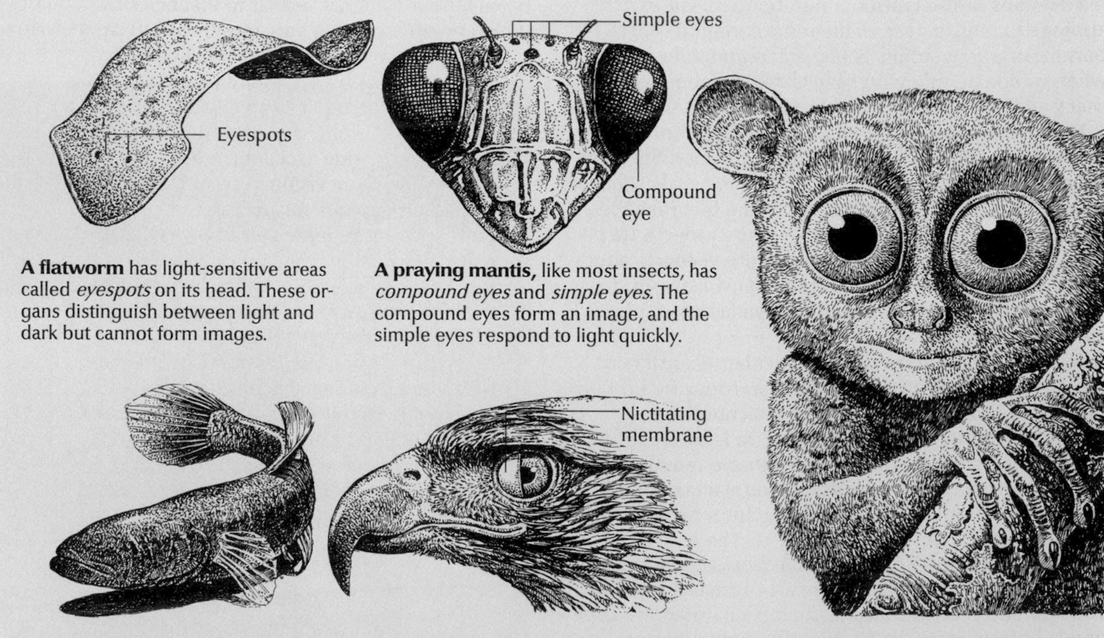

A flatworm has light-sensitive areas called *eyespots* on its head. These organs distinguish between light and dark but cannot form images.

A praying mantis, like most insects, has *compound eyes* and *simple eyes.* The compound eyes form an image, and the simple eyes respond to light quickly.

A cavefish swims in the dark waters of caves and has sightless eyes. Many animals that live in darkness have eyes that can see little or nothing.

A red-tailed hawk, like most other birds, has a third eyelid called a *nictitating membrane.* Birds close the membrane to blink and the other lids to sleep.

A tarsier, a small mammal of Southeast Asia, has exceptionally large eyes. The eyes provide these animals with excellent vision in dim light.

A severe form of conjunctivitis called *trachoma* is caused by a microscopic organism. The disease is treated with drugs or surgery or both. Trachoma is a rare disease in the industrialized world, but it is a leading cause of blindness in many less developed countries. See **Trachoma.**

Care of the eye

Preventing eye damage. The most common eye injuries are caused by blows to the eye, by particles that enter the eye, and by chemical burns, explosions, and firearms. Many such injuries can be prevented. For example, safety glasses or goggles protect the eyes from particles that may be thrown from electric saws, grinding wheels, and other power tools. Some athletes also wear safety glasses to prevent eye injuries caused by balls, rackets, hockey pucks, and other sports equipment. In most cases, specks of dust or other particles that enter the eye can be removed by blinking gently or by flushing the eye with water. If the particle does not come out, it should be removed by a physician. A fragment of glass, metal, or wood—or any particle stuck on the cornea—also should be removed by a physician. If chemicals enter the eye, they should be washed out immediately with large amounts of water, and a physician should be consulted at once.

The eyes can also be damaged through improper use of contact lenses, eye makeup, and sun lamps. Infection may develop if contact lenses are not clean before they are inserted in the eyes. The hands also should be clean, and saliva should never be used to moisten the lenses before inserting them. People should not wear contact lenses longer than the time prescribed by the eye doctor. Eye infections also may result from sharing eye makeup or from moistening the cosmetics with saliva to apply them. The light of a sun lamp can cause painful burns of the cornea. Special goggles should be worn when using a sun lamp. No one should ever look directly at the sun, even during an eclipse.

Receiving regular eye examinations. Doctors recommend that everyone have an eye examination shortly after birth and every few years until the age of 40. Thereafter, eyes should be examined once a year or every two years. Eye examinations may be given by an optometrist or an ophthalmologist. Optometrists are licensed professionals who test vision and prescribe glasses and contact lenses. Ophthalmologists, also called oculists, are medical doctors who specialize in the eye. They test vision, prescribe glasses and contact lenses, and treat eye diseases by medication, lasers, and surgery. Opticians make and sell glasses and contact lenses prescribed by optometrists and ophthalmologists.

One of the most familiar parts of an eye examination tests *visual acuity* (sharpness of vision) at a distance. This test involves reading letters from a chart a certain distance away—usually 20 feet (6 meters). The letters of each line are smaller than those in the line above. A person who can read all the lines that a normal eye can see from 20 feet (6 meters) has normal visual acuity. This vision is expressed as 20/20 (6/6 in the metric system). A higher denominator indicates a visual defect. For example, a person with 20/40 (6/12) vision must be 20 feet (6 meters) from the chart to read all the lines that a normal eye can see from 40 feet (12 meters). Each eye is tested individually, and one eye may have better vision than the other. Optometrists and ophthalmologists also test near vision and side vision.

Ophthalmologists and optometrists also examine the inside of the eye for any sign of disease. By looking through the pupil with various instruments, these specialists can examine the blood vessels of the retina, the fibers of the optic nerve, and the health of the macula. The condition of these structures may indicate not only an eye disease but also the advance of such diseases as diabetes, high blood pressure, or macular degeneration. For this reason, physicians also look into the eye as part of a routine physical examination.

Eyes of animals

Most animals have organs of some kind that sense light. The most elementary of these organs are called *eyespots.* Eyespots are light-sensitive areas on the bodies of flatworms, starfish, and certain other *invertebrates* (animals without a backbone). The organs can distinguish between light and dark but cannot form images.

Other invertebrates have true eyes. Most kinds of insects have two large *compound eyes.* These eyes consist of many tiny lenses. Each lens admits light rays from one direction—one bit of the total scene that the insect sees. All the bits combine and form an image. Many adult insects also have three *simple eyes* set in a triangle between the compound eyes. Each simple eye has one lens. The simple eyes do not form images, but they respond to light quickly. Most *crustaceans,* such as lobsters, have two compound eyes, and many species also have a simple eye. *Arachnids,* insectlike animals that include spiders and scorpions, have only simple eyes.

The eyes of most *vertebrates* (animals with a backbone) have a structure similar to that of the human eye. However, the eyes may vary greatly in certain details. For example, many vertebrates that live in total darkness, such as in deep caves, have tiny eyes that can see little or nothing. On the other hand, owls and some other animals that hunt at night have extremely large eyes and pupils, which provide excellent vision in dim light. Cats also have good night vision. A mirrorlike structure in the eye called the *tapetum lucidum* reflects light onto the retina. The structure makes a cat's eyes appear to glow at night when light is reflected off them.

Most birds have three eyelids—an upper lid, a lower lid, and a *nictitating membrane,* which moves sideways. The animals use the nictitating membrane to blink, and they close the upper and lower lids when sleeping. Birds have the best visual acuity of all animals, including human beings. For example, a vulture can see a dead animal on the ground from a height of up to 2 ½ miles (4 kilometers). Morton F. Goldberg

Related articles in *World Book* include:

Disorders of the eye

Astigmatism
Blindness
Cataract
Color blindness
Conjunctivitis
Farsightedness
Glaucoma
Iritis
Macular degeneration
Myopia
Nystagmus
Ophthalmia
Snow blindness
Strabismus
Sty
Trachoma

Other related articles

Artificial eye
Blind spot

Color (How we see color)
Compound eye
Contact lens
Eye bank
Glasses
Laser (Heating)
LASIK surgery
Lighting
Ophthalmology
Ophthalmoscope
Optical illusion
Optometry
Tears

Outline

I. Parts of the eye
- A. The outer parts
- B. The sclera and the cornea
- C. The uveal tract
- D. The retina

II. How we see
- A. Focusing
- B. Depth perception
- C. Adaptation to light and dark

III. Defects of the eye
- A. Nearsightedness
- B. Farsightedness
- C. Astigmatism
- D. Strabismus
- E. Color blindness

IV. Diseases of the eye
- A. Cataract
- B. Glaucoma
- C. Diseases of the cornea
- D. Diseases of the sclera
- E. Diseases of the uveal tract
- F. Diseases of the retina
- G. Diseases of the optic nerve
- H. Diseases of the outer parts

V. Care of the eye
- A. Preventing eye damage
- B. Receiving regular eye examinations

VI. Eyes of animals

Questions

Which parts of the eye focus light rays on the retina?
How do the pigments of the rods and cones differ in their response to light?
What are compound eyes? Simple eyes?
What does the optic nerve do?
What makes the cornea transparent?
What is strabismus? A cataract? Glaucoma?
What part of the eyeball regulates the amount of light that enters the eye?
Why do most middle-aged and elderly people need glasses for reading and close work?
What is diabetic retinopathy?
Why is it impossible for the human eye to form a sharp image of a nearby object and a distant one at the same time?

Additional resources

Level I

Cobb, Vicki. *Open Your Eyes: Discover Your Sense of Sight.* Millbrook, 2002.
Dossenbach, Monika and Hans D. *Eye Openers! All About Animal Vision.* Blackbirch Pr., 1998.
Silverstein, Alvin, and others. *Seeing.* 21st Century Bks., 2001.

Level II

Grierson, Ian. *The Eye Book: Eyes and Eye Problems Explained.* Liverpool Univ. Pr., 2000.
Oyster, Clyde W. *The Human Eye.* Sinauer, 1999.
Sutton, Amy L., ed. *Eye Care Sourcebook: Basic Consumer Health Information About Eye Care and Eye Disorders.* 2nd ed. Omnigraphics, 2003.

Eye bank is a nonprofit agency through which eyes removed shortly after death are distributed to specially trained surgeons. These surgeons perform an operation called a *corneal transplant* on people who are blind from diseases that cause scarring of the *cornea.* The cornea is the transparent outer layer through which light enters the eye (see **Eye** [Diseases of the cornea]). The operation consists of replacing the central portion of the scarred cornea with clear corneal tissue.

An eye remains suitable for surgery for only a short time after removal from the body. A surgeon must remove the donor's eyes within three hours after death and pack them in special containers just above freezing temperature. The container is rushed to an eye bank, where the eyes are carefully examined and tested to determine if they are suitable for surgery. An eye surgeon who has patients waiting for surgery is notified that an eye is available. The surgeon sends a patient to the hospital, and the operation is performed immediately after arrival of the eye.

The first eye bank was formed in 1944 in New York City. Many eye banks have since developed in other cities and countries. People who wish to donate their eyes should register with an eye bank. Prospective donors can then sign legal documents to donate their eyes upon death. If a person has not signed such documents, the nearest relative must give legal permission for removal of the eyes after death. Some donated eyes may be unsuitable for corneal transplantation. But such eyes can be used for study and research. David E. Eifrig

Eyeglasses. See Glasses.

Eyre, Lake. See Lake Eyre.

Ezekiel, Book of, is a book of the Bible named for a Jewish prophet. Ezekiel's ministry lasted from 593 to 572 or 571 B.C. With the prophets Jeremiah and Isaiah, he was one of the major interpreters of the Babylonian Exile. The exile was a period that followed the Babylonian conquest of the kingdom of Judah and its capital of Jerusalem in 587 or 586 B.C.

Chapters 1-24 of the book present Ezekiel's prophecies that calamities will strike the people of Jerusalem and Judah as God's punishment for their sins. Chapters 25-32 consist of Ezekiel's prophecies against neighboring nations for defying God's will and rejoicing over the misfortunes of the Israelites. In chapters 33-48, Ezekiel prophesies Israel's restoration and salvation.

Ezekiel was a priest as well as a prophet. He stressed the importance of following religious law and strictly obeying religious forms and ceremonies. In the book, Ezekiel describes many strange visions. For example, chapter 1 includes a vision of God's dazzling throne chariot in the sky. In chapter 37, Ezekiel describes the valley of dry bones. In this vision, the prophet portrays the exiled Israelites as bones coming to life and being transported back to Judah. Eric M. Meyers

See also **Bible** (The Prophets).

Ezra, Book of, is a book of the Bible. Jewish editions of the Bible combine Ezra with the Book of Nehemiah in a collection of books called the Writings. Ezra is a separate book in Christian Bibles placed in a group called the Historical Books.

The Book of Ezra was written about 400 B.C. It recounts the story of the Jews' return from their exile in Babylonia, which had begun with the Babylonian conquest of the Jews in 587 or 586 B.C. The book also describes the rebuilding of the Temple in Jerusalem after the Babylonians had destroyed the original Temple.

Ezra was a priest and scribe who led a group of exiles back to Jerusalem, probably in 458 B.C., but no later than 397 B.C. He was responsible for a number of religious and social reforms. These reforms included the cancellation of marriages between Jews and non-Jews. Ezra 7:27 to 9:15 is known as Ezra's memoirs, because the passage is written in a form similar to a diary. Ezra 7-10 summarizes his achievements. Eric M. Meyers

See also **Bible** (The Hebrew Bible).